W9-BYL-568

A DICTIONARY OF
CATCH
PHRASES

The first edition of *A Dictionary of Catch Phrases* made the front page of *The New York Times*. It was Eric Partridge's last major work before his death. But even before it appeared in print, Partridge was already at work on revision, augmenting and correcting what had been the first edition's weaker aspect, the treatment of *American* catch phrases.

Partridge had almost completed his notes toward this second edition when increasing frailty forced him to hand them on to Paul Beale to edit. Beale was already fully engaged in preparing the eighth edition of the *Dictionary of Slang and Unconventional English* for publication, so it was not until several years later that he could begin to tackle the present work. With all of the additions noted by Partridge, this second edition is half as large again as the first. It is also more informative about the origins of many of the catch phrases included in the first edition.

Eric Partridge is acknowledged to be the Samuel Johnson of the twentieth century. His editor, **Paul Beale**, first met Mr. Partridge in 1974 and began working closely with him in 1978.

OTHER WORKS BY ERIC PARTRIDGE

Chamber of Horrors: Officialese, British and American
A Classical Dictionary of the Vulgar Tongue by Francis Grose, ed.
Comic Alphabets: A Light-Hearted History
A Dictionary of Clichés
A Dictionary of Forces' Slang (with Wilfred Granville and Frank Roberts)
A Dictionary of Historical Slang
A Dictionary of Slang and Unconventional English
A Dictionary of the Underworld
Eighteenth-Century English Romantic Poetry
English: A Course for Human Beings
The French Romantics' Knowledge of English Literature
Glimpses
Journey to the Edge of Morning
Lexicography: A Personal Memoir
The Long Trail (with John Brophy)
Name into Word
Name this Child: A Dictionary of Christian or Given Names
A New Testament Word Book
Origins: An Etymological Dictionary of Modern English
Shakespeare's Bawdy: An Essay and A Glossary
Slang Today and Yesterday
A Smaller Slang Dictionary
Swift's 'Polite Conversation': A Commentary Edition
Usage and Abusage: A Guide to Good English
And Seven Volumes of Essays on Language (General) and Words (Particular)

A DICTIONARY OF
CATCH
PHRASES

**American and British,
from the Sixteenth Century to the Present Day**

**Revised and Updated Edition
Edited by Paul Beale**

ERIC PARTRIDGE

Scarborough House

While fully acknowledging the help and encouragement given to me by my publishers, I dedicate this second edition of A *Dictionary of Catch Phrases,* with profound gratitude, to

The entire staff of St. Luke's Ward and its associated clinics: cleaners; auxiliaries; nurses; doctors; consultants; surgeons; and others in the background—all who were on duty at the Leicester Royal Infirmary, 1–13 April and 30 October–3 November 1982, and in the clinics ever since.

Without their skill and care I would have been denied the privilege and delight of editing this book.

P.B.

SCARBOROUGH HOUSE
Lanham, Maryland 20706

FIRST TRADE PAPERBACK EDITION 1992

Revised hardcover edition first published in the United States of America in 1986
by Stein and Day/*Publishers*
First edition published in the United States of America
by Stein and Day/*Publishers* in 1977
Second printing 1978
Paperback edition 1979
Copyright © 1977, 1985 by the estate of Eric Partridge
Preface to the revised edition and other new material, selection of entries,
copyright © 1985 by Paul Beale
All rights reserved
Printed in the United States of America

Library of Congress Cataloging-in-Publication Data

Partridge, Eric, 1894.
   A dictionary of catch phrases, American and British, from the sixteenth century
to the present day.

   Enl. ed. of: A dictionary of catch phrases, British and American, from the
sixteenth century to the present day. 1977.
   1. English language—Terms and phrases. 2. English
language—Slang—Dictionaries. 3. Americanisms.
I. Beale, Paul. II. Partridge, Eric, 1894–1979.
Dictionary of catch phrases, British and American, from the sixteenth century to
the present day.
III. Title.
PE1689.P297   1986   423'.1   85-40997

ISBN 0-8128-8536-8

Contents

Preface to the First Edition

After a longish period of *ad hoc* reading and note-making (with, since, a continual 'spare-time' reading) I began to write, not merely compile, this dictionary in September 1973 and completed the writing almost exactly two years later.

I have been deeply interested in catch phrases ever since during the First World War when, a private in the Australian infantry, I heard so many; in both *Slang Today and Yesterday* and, 1937 onwards, *A Dictionary of Slang and Unconventional English*, I have paid them considerable – and increasing – attention. Moreover, as I have always read rather widely in American fiction and humour, I did not start from scratch in that vast field.

But I could not have adequately treated either the catch phrases of the United States or those of the British Commonwealth of Nations without the constant, faithful, extraordinarily generous assistance of friends and acquaintances and pen-friends. In the list of acknowledgments, I have named all the more copious and helpful – at least, I like to think that I've done so. Probably there are a few unforgivable omissions; I can but ask forgiveness.

There are, however, three acknowledgments, in a different order of things, to be made right here. I have to thank *Newsweek* for permission to quote a long passage from an article by the late John – son of Ring – Lardner; and Mr Edward Albee for his unqualified permission to quote freely from his perturbing and remarkable plays, so sensitive to the nuances of colloquial usage. In yet another order, I owe a very special debt to Mr Norman Franklin, who has, a score of times, saved me from making an ass of myself and, several score of times, supplied much-needed information.

The Introduction is intentionally very brief: I don't pretend to an ability to define the indefinable: I have merely attempted to indicate what a catch phrase is, there being many varieties of this elusive phenomenon; a phenomenon at once linguistic and literary – one that furnishes numerous *marginalia* to social history and to the thought-patterns of civilization.

Finally, a caution. I have, although very seldom, written an entry in such a way as to allow the reader to see just how it grew from a vague idea into a certainty or, at least, a virtual certainty.

Late 1976   E.P.

Introduction to the First Edition

Man is a creature who lives not by bread alone, but principally by catchwords.
R. L. Stevenson, *Virginibus Puerisque* (Part II), 1881

Friends – and others – have often asked me, 'What the devil *is* a catch phrase?' I don't know. But I do know that my sympathy lies with the lexicographers.

Consult the standard dictionaries, the best and the greatest: you will notice that they tacitly admit the impossibility of precise definition. Perhaps cravenly, I hope that the following brief 'wafflings' will be reinforced by the willingness of readers to allow that 'example is better than precept' and thus enable me to 'get away with it'. A pen-friend, who has, for thirty years or more, copiously contributed both slang terms, on the one hand, and catch phrases (not, of course, necessarily slangy) on the other, tells me that the best definition he has seen is this: 'A catch phrase is a phrase that has caught on, and pleases the populace.' I'll go along with that, provided these substitutions be accepted: 'saying' for 'phrase'; and 'public' for the tendentious 'populace'.

Frequently, catch phrases are not, in the grammarians' sense, phrases at all, but sentences. Catch phrases, like the closely linked proverbial sayings, are self-contained, as, obviously, clichés are too. Catch phrases are usually more pointed and 'human' than clichés, although the former sometimes arise from, and often they generate, the latter. Occasionally, catch phrases stem from *too* famous quotations. Catch phrases often supply – indeed they are – conversational gambits; often, too, they add a pithy, perhaps earthy, comment. Apart from the unavoidable 'he-she' and 'we-you-they' conveniences, they are immutable. You will have perceived that the categories Catch Phrase, Proverbial Saying, Famous Quotations, Cliché, may co-exist: they are not snobbishly exclusive, any one of any other. All depends on the context, the nuance, the tone.

Precepts mystify: examples clarify. Here, in roughly chronological order, are a few catch phrases.

The proverbial *no one can say black is my eye* developed, probably late in the sixteenth century, into the catch phrase, *black is* – later, *black's* – *your eye*, you're at fault, you're guilty, whence *black's the white of my eye*, a nautical protestation of innocence. Nor is this catch phrase entirely extinct.

I'll have your guts for garters, a threat originally serious, but in late nineteenth to twentieth century usually humorous, has likewise had an astonishingly long history. In Robert Greene's *James the Fourth*, 1598, we find, 'I'll make garters of thy guts, thou villain'; and in an early seventeenth-century parish register, my formidably erudite friend, Dr Jack Lindsay, discovered the prototype: *I'll have your guts for garter points.* In the twentieth century, the modern form has been mostly a Cockney, and often a racecourse, semi-humorous threat.

Another catch phrase with an historical background is *hay is for horses*, which duly acquired the variant *'ay is for 'orses.* In Swift's *Polite Conversation* (the most fertile and valuable single literary source of them all), 1738, we read:

NEVEROUT: Hay, Madam, did you call me?

MISS: Hay! Why; hay is for horses.

Nowadays, the catch phrase is usually addressed to someone who has used either *hey* (as in 'Hey there, you!') or *eh?* for 'I beg your pardon.' This refreshing domesticity – compare, for instance, *'she' is a cat's mother* – became, inevitably in its colloquial form, *'ay is for 'orses*, incorporated in the Comic Phonetic Alphabet. You know the sort of thing: *'B is for honey'* – *'C is for fish'* – and the rest of it. Perhaps, however, I should add that, in Swift, *hay* is a mere phonetic variant of the exclamatory *hey* and is therefore associated with *eh*, whence the entirely natural *'ay is....*

A characteristically nineteenth-century catch phrase is *Lushington is his master*, he's a drunkard, which has derived from the synonymous eighteenth to nineteenth-century *Alderman Lushington is concerned.* Clearly there is both a pun on *lush*, an old low-slang term for strong liquor, and on that convivial society or club known as *the City of Lushington* (recorded by the indispensable *Oxford English Dictionary*).

Originating early in the present century, *hullo, baby! – how's nurse?* was an urban and civilian jocularity before the licentious soldiery blithely adopted and popularized it during those extraordinarily formative years, 1914–18. It was spoken to any girl pushing a perambulator. So far as I'm aware, it had, in the army and the air force at least, fallen into disuse by the time the Second World War arrived; it does, however, exemplify the wit and the humour that mark so many catch phrases.

A WW2 phrase that has impressed me with its wit (and its realism) is the mock-Latin *illegitimis non carborundum*, which, after the war, spread to civilians throughout the British Commonwealth, even to those who had no Latin. Meaning 'Don't let the bastards grind' – idiomatically 'wear' and colloquially 'get' – 'you down', it is generally supposed to have been coined by Military Intelligence. *To coin a phrase – that figures.* (Two other post-WW2 catch phrases.)

But *illegitimis non carborundum* does not stand alone in its gravity. I'll cite only two other, at first intensely serious, catch phrases: the First World War's *hanging on the old barbed wire*; and the socially and sociologically, racially and historically, far-reaching and important creation of the (probably early) 1930s, a catch phrase remaining predominantly grave – to wit, *some of my best friends are Jews*, to which I shall attempt to do justice.

Watch how you go!   Eric Partridge

Modifications of the Original Introduction

I should like to modify – perhaps rather to amend – what I have written about the 'immutability' of catch phrases by quoting from two letters, for I should hate to sound dogmatic on a subject that precludes dogma.

The earlier (1977) comes from Mr Robert Claiborne of New York City and Truro, Mass.:

> While sharing your inability to define rigorously a catch phrase, I must cavil at your dictum 'they are immutable'. See (among many examples) *be good...*, *before you came...*, and *better than a dig in the eye*.... Indeed, the catch phrase, to the extent it is a form of folk wit, *must*, like folk songs, proverbs and the like vary both in time and in space. Thus their 'immutability' is relative. I would guess that the longer the life, and the greater the geographical distribution, of a c.p., the greater the variation. Granted, with the rise of broadcast communications, many c.pp. will be invented, spread and disappear without change – but others will, I think, still follow the traditional (and therefore variable) pattern.

This proposed modification has been urged both by several amicable reviewers and by knowledgeable, alert and intelligent friends, notably Prof. John W. Clark and Mr Vernon Noble. The latter wrote to me in 1978:

> As an addition to your introductory note..., I would define a catch phrase thus: An observation or remark – often witty or philosophical, but not necessarily either – that has 'caught on' among a substantial number of people and has been repeated for a long period. It has tickled the imagination and has been accepted as a truism or as an apt commentary on current affairs, fashions or attitudes.
>
> If one accepts this definition, it is often difficult to decide which quotation from the field of entertainment is justified for inclusion. There is no problem with radio and television, because knowledge of these media is widespread; but the theatre and the music-hall present difficulties, because the audience – taking the country as a whole – was [and is] restricted. In general, only those theatre and music-hall catch phrases which were snapped-up by the sophisticated (that is, those who were [and are] able to attend places of entertainment and spread [the phrases] in conversation), and those repeated in newspapers, [other] periodicals and in books, can be given the distinction: so many had a comparatively small circulation and a short life.
>
> I really don't think [that, for instance] Robey's 'I meanter say' or Weldon's 'sno use' can be regarded as [eligible]; partly because of the [reasons mentioned]

above; partly because they were not original; nor had they any relevance outside the theatrical [and music-hall] audiences.... They have long been lost, and they were not current long enough to merit inclusion.

E.P., 1978

Acknowledgments to the First Edition

I have not counted the number of entries; it can hardly be less than 3,000 – a figure that will, I hope, be increased both by my own further research and by further contributions from my loyal helpers, as well as from all those reviewers and general readers who will have noticed omissions and defects.

To generous friends and acquaintances and pen-friends I owe much: and of these, perhaps the most helpful have been the following (an asterisk* indicates a very considerable indebtedness):

*Mr Laurie Atkinson, who has contributed so much to the later editions of *DSUE* – and so much to this book.

The late Mr Sidney J. Baker, author of *The Australian Language*.

*Mr Paul Beale of Loughborough.

British Library, the: the staff for courteous assistance.

Rear-Admiral P. W. Brock, CB, DSO.

*Mr W. J. Burke, for many years the head of *Look*'s research department.

*Professor Emeritus John W. Clark, University of Minnesota, invaluably and from the beginning.

The late Mr Norris M. Davidson of Gwynedd, Pennsylvania.

Professor Ralph W. V. Elliott of University House, Canberra.

Professor John T. Fain, University of Florida.

*Mr Norman Franklin, the Chairman of Messrs Routledge & Kegan Paul. As if he hadn't already more than enough 'on his plate'!

*The late Julian Franklyn, heraldist and an authority on Cockney custom and speech.

Mr Christopher Fry, welcomely 'out of the blue' on several occasions.

*The late Wilfred Granville – like Mr Franklyn, an indefatigable helper – who died on 23 March 1974.

Mr Ben Grauer, the well known interviewer (etc.) on American radio and TV – like most extremely busy men, this dynamo has always been courteous, patient, helpful.

Mr Arthur Gray of Auckland, New Zealand.

Dr Edward Hodnett, American scholar.

*Dr Douglas Leechman, an authority on Canadiana.

Mr Y. Mindel of Kfar Tabor, Lower Galilee.

*Colonel Albert Moe, United States Marine Corps, ret.; over a long period.

Professor Emeritus S. H. Monk of the University of Minnesota.

Mrs Patricia Newnham of Hampstead.

*Mr (formerly Squadron Leader) Vernon Noble, journalist, author, BBC man (ret.)

Mr John O'Riordan, Librarian of Southgate Library, North London, for keeping me supplied with contemporary fiction.

Professor Emeritus Ashley Cooper Partridge, University of the Witwatersrand.

Mr Fernley O. Pascoe of Camborne, Cornwall.

Mrs Shirley M. Pearce of West Wickham, Kent.

Mr Ronald Pearsall, authority on Victorian and Edwardian themes.

*Mr Albert B. Petch of Bournemouth, Hampshire; a good and fruitful friend for many, many years.

*Mr Barry Prentice of Sydney, Australia; copiously and perspicaciously.

Professor Emeritus F. E. L. Priestley, University of Toronto.

Mrs Camilla Raab of Routledge & Kegan Paul.

*Mr Peter Sanders of Godalming, Surrey.

Professor Harold Shapiro, University of North Carolina.

*The late Frank Shaw, authority on 'Scouse' – the speech of the Merseyside. (See the note at *do the other* in the dictionary.)

*Dr Joseph T. Shipley of New York; patiently and most helpfully.

Miss Patricia Sigl, an American resident in London; authority on the eighteenth-century theatre.

Mr Lawrence Smith of Totley, Sheffield.

*Mr Ramsay Spencer (bless him too) of Camberley, Surrey.

Mr Oliver Stonor of Morebath, Devonshire; several valuable reminders.

Mrs Margaret Thomson of Bray-on-Thames.

Mr Cyril Whelan of St Brelade, Jersey, CI; contributions of much distinction.

The late Colonel Archie White, VC, author of *The Story of Army Education.*

Miss Eileen Wood of Routledge & Kegan Paul.

Mr and Mrs Arthur Wrigglesworth, the friends with whom I lived surrounded by comfort and considerateness: he for unwittingly supplying me with indirect evidence; she for her exceptional knowledge of music, whether classical or popular (not 'pop'), including songs.

Preface to the Second Edition

Although this compilation bears the title *A Dictionary of Catch Phrases*, and that seems the neatest possible summation for such a rag-bag, I agree with many reviewers, critics and correspondents in rejecting the idea that all the entries herein are catch phrases. I take a catch phrase to be a phrase having – at least to begin with – a recognized source. That source may be an individual, most often an entertainer; or a group, by which I mean a show of any sort: music-hall, play, film, but notably radio or television comedy. A really good catch phrase is a piece of free-standing nonsense; it hardly needs a context.

A fair number of the entries do fall into my 'genuine' catch phrase class, but the book includes as well many examples from the following randomly-ordered and by no means exhaustive list: greetings; toasts; exclamations; exhortations; threats; invitations; jokes and puns (many fossilized); colourful clichés; popularly accepted misquotations; modern proverbs, adages and maxims (and adaptations of old ones); euphemisms; well-worn, and also currently bright new, similes and hyperbole; and some that are no more than vulgar idiom, vivid expressions that took Eric Partridge's fancy. As he himself wrote (at **you can say that again**, on p. 261 of the first edition):

> There is no such thing as an inviolable and immutable classification of permanent inter-distinction between any one and any other of the three groups: catchphrases, proverbial sayings, clichés. What's more, the almost infinite number – hence also the variety – of contexts for familiar phrases (a very useful 'umbrella' term) means that a phrase can exist simultaneously in any two of these groups. Language, by its very nature, is insusceptible of being straitjacketed.

Quite right! How do we – should we even try to – distinguish the category (?categories) into which we can place, for example, *she hasn't got a ha'penny to jingle on a tombstone* and *he was so poor even his brother was made in Hong Kong*? Which leads me to another point borne more strongly upon me with each successive reading of the Dictionary: so many of the phrases are actually jibes and insults; how much verbal cruelty seems to amuse us! I haven't added them up, but it feels as though over half the entries are in this class.

But *who's counting?*, and *never mind the quality, feel the width*: here are a few *ball-park figures*. E.P. thought (see Acknowledgments to the first edition) that he had written some 3,000 entries. He undersold himself; there were over 4,000. Of these, some 2,500 remain in their original state, while nearly 1,200 have been significantly, and in many cases greatly, augmented or otherwise amended. A few of the most doubtfully eligible originals have been omitted, and the remaining entries in the first edition have been so radically re-written as to be virtually new. These last, together with the new additions, total almost 1,800 entries.

I am only too aware that the coverage of the US field is far from comprehensive (see my remarks at REGIONAL CATCHPHRASES in the main text), and I can't help feeling that – despite the magnificently generous efforts of his American helpers – E.P. was being rather ambitious in trying to cover that area at all. Coverage of British phrases is more complete, as befits a book that is, I suggest, aimed mainly at British readers. Let it be treated as a chance for those readers to appreciate a selection of picturesque Americanisms, while displaying for Americans as much of our goods as we can get on show. The same limitations apply of course to the countries of the British Commonwealth, from which striking examples have been equally generously supplied.

As well as the 1,500 or so new entries transcribed from E.P.'s notes (handed on to me only two months before his death on 1 June 1979) there is a small scattering for which I am responsible. These latter, and those entries that have been completely re-written, bear my initials: '(P.B.)'. All else is E.P.'s own. For economy's sake, to compress the original so as to make room for the new material, I have made much greater use of abbreviation; exact dates of private letters, now no longer accessible, have been reduced to year only; and the names of the most copious contributors to bare initials. Private sources are always cited in parentheses; a printed source, if forming the last element of an entry, stands free.

The greatest difference between this and the first edition is the inclusion of an index. The idea was suggested by one of E.P.'s non-anglophone contributors, Mr J.B. Mindel of Lower Galilee, and the more I worked on the book the more necessary an index became. I did not want to tamper any more than I could help with E.P.'s last major work, but at the same time I was, and am, dissatisfied with an alphabetical order which uses non-significant words as leaders (*he's, it'd, she'll, that, this*, etc.): such an arrangement can only obscure the keywords for all readers except those who know each catchphrase, and all its variants, by heart. And indeed, when I had compiled the index to keywords, I found that it threw up quite a noticeable amount of previously unremarked duplication which I was then able to remove; it would be unfair to say that the index thus almost made room for itself – but it sometimes seemed like it. The index will also enable those readers who think they know of an omission to be absolutely sure before informing me of it, as I hope they will, for this, like the *Dictionary of Slang and Unconventional English*, is a book that should continue to move with the times. For ease of reference the index has been integrated with the main text, and index entries are as short as they can be; while apparently cryptic, each will lead the reader to one particular phrase.

The phrases in the Dictionary are a form of verbal shorthand, and it is curious to note what words (= ideas) predominate: by far the most outstanding, with almost 80 entries (and I leave it to readers to ponder for themselves the implications of this), is *shit*. Fourth comes *mother*, with 45 – but poor old *father* lags way behind with only

15; *dogs*, 36, outnumber *cats*, 28, while the foreign country uppermost in our minds is *China*, with 18 mentions: clearly it must epitomize all that is most exotic to the English-speaking world.

The book stands in its own right, but it is intended also as a companion volume to Partridge's *Dictionary of Slang*. Some critics have, to put it mildly, questioned the latter's claim to be a serious reference work; I am inclined to agree with them, and certainly I would not arrogate the title for this present compilation. It may in the future come to be regarded as a serious source for studies of 'how they lived in those days', as some of E.P.'s earlier sources already are (Grose, Jon Bee, etc.); I can only regret that it lies beyond my capabilities to provide an accompanying sound-recording so that future listeners could hear just what accents and intonations were so vital to the catch phrases.

Meanwhile, for our present generation, may I suggest that this book be regarded – despite the fact that by no means *all* the entries are indelicate – rather as a happy browsing area, an amusement arcade for those not ashamed to admit sympathy with a certain coarse strain in our common humanity, a cheerful earthy thread that links us to the very earliest phrases in the book, and back, through Dan Chaucer, to Rome, Greece and further still. I strongly suspect E.P. himself of producing the unrepentantly vulgar parody: 'a dirty mind is a joy for ever.'

June 1984

Paul Beale

Acknowledgments to the Second Edition

Paul Beale writes:
Every work of this kind is necessarily a co-operative effort; even the great Dr Johnson had a crew of paid helpers. During the editing of this Dictionary I have had the extraordinary good fortune to enjoy the best of all lexicographical worlds: autonomy in the right to my own decisions, without pressure or hustle, *and* the generous, kindly and entirely voluntary help of a like-minded band of enthusiasts, on both sides of the North Atlantic, and further afield. It would be invidious to rank them other than as E.P. did: in alphabetical order. I thank on his behalf those whose material I have transcribed from his notes, and especially those who have continued to supply me with new suggestions and comments since his death on 1 June 1979.

There is, however, one person who deserves my special thanks: Mr Nigel Rees. I owe him particular gratitude for freely-granted permission to plunder his compilation of showbiz catch phrases, *Very Interesting... but Stupid!*, published as an Unwin Paperback, 1980. Even a casual glance will reveal how greatly Mr Rees's research has enriched this present work.

I list below the other main contributors to the second edition and, following precedent, an asterisk marks those whose names appear most often as sources; a † denotes those who are also acknowledged in the first edition (details above). No private source lacks acknowledgment in the main text.
* Professor Leonard R.N. Ashley, City University of New York.
*† Mr Laurie Atkinson, first thanked by E.P. in the 3rd edn of *DSUE*, 1948.
*† Rear-Admiral P.W. Brock, CB, DSO.
* Professor Anthony Brown, Western Carolina University.
*† Mr W.J. Burke.
* Mr Robert Claiborne of New York.
*† Professor Emeritus John W. Clark.
Mr P. Daniel.
Mr S.G. Dixon of North Harrow.
*† Professor Emeritus John T. Fain.
Mr Michael Goldman of Sydenham.
Mr Harry Griffiths, Australia.
Mr P.V. Harris of Southampton.
M. Paul Janssen of Tilff, Belgium.
Dr George A. Krzymowski of New Orleans.

Dr Robin Leech of Edmonton, Alberta.
Mr Simon Levene of London.
*[†] Colonel Albert F. Moe, USMC, ret.
*[†] Mr Vernon Noble.
Cdr C. Parsons, RN, ret.
* Lt Cdr F.L. Peppitt, RNR.
*[†] The late Albert B. Petch who had helped E.P. so long and so faithfully; he, like L.A., was first thanked in the 3rd edn of *DSUE*, 1948. He died on 23 March 1981.
* Sir Edward W. Playfair.
[†] Mr Barry Prentice.
Mr Hugh Quetton of Montreal.
Mrs Ursula Roberts of Hongkong.
*[†] Mr Peter Sanders.
[†] Professor Harold Shapiro.
*[†] Dr Joseph T. Shipley.
Mr David Short.
* Mr John Skehan, Radio Telefís Éireann, Dublin.
Mr Jack Slater of Oldham, Lancashire.
Mr John B. Smith, Bath University of Technology.
*[†] Mr Ramsey Spencer.
* Mr Eric Townley, musicologist.
* Miss B.G. Trew, Great Doddington, Northants.
* Mr Maurice Wedgewood, Deputy Editor of the *Northern Echo*.

Abbreviations

A.B.	Prof. Anthony Brown.
abbr.	abbreviate(d), -ing
Adams	Franklin P. Adams (1881–1960), *Baseball's Sad Lexicon*, 1936 (?)
Am	John Russell Bartlett, *Americanisms*, 1848; 2nd edn, 1859; 4th ed., 1877.
anon.	anonymous
Apperson	G. L. Apperson, *English Proverbs and Proverbial Phrases*, 1929.
approx.	approximate(ly).
AS	Sidney J. Baker, *Australia Speaks*, 1953
Ashley	Prof. Leonard N. R. Ashley
Aus.	Australia(n)
Baker	Sidney J. Baker, *Australian Slang*, 1942; 3rd edn, 1943; revised ed., 1959
Bartlett	John Russell Bartlett, *Bartlett's Familiar Quotations*, 14th edn, 1968
Baumann	Heinrich Baumann, *Londonismen*, 1887
BE	B. E., Gent, *Dictionary of the Canting Crew*, 1698–9
Benham	Gurney Benham, *Dictionary of Quotations*, 1907, revised ed., 1948
Berrey	Lester V. Berrey and Melvin Van Den Bark, *The American Thesaurus of Slang*, 1942
B. G. T.	Miss Betty G. Trew
B & L	A. Barrère and C. G. Leland, *Dictionary*, 2 vols, 1889–90
Bowen	F. Bowen, *Sea Slang*, 1929
B & P	John Brophy and Eric Partridge, *Songs and Slang of the British Soldier: 1914–18*, 1930; 3rd edn, 1931; republished as *The Long Trail*, 1965
B. P.	Barry Prentice
Brit.	British
BQ	Burton Stevenson, *Book of Quotations*, 5th edn, 1946
Brewer	E. C. Brewer, *Dictionary of Phrase and Fable*, revised and enlarged edn, 1952
Brophy	John Brophy, *English Prose*, 1932
C	century
c.	*circa* (about the year –)
Can.	Canada; Canadian
cf	compare

Clarke	John Clarke, *Paroemiologia*, 1639. Sometimes noted as *P*
CM	Clarence Major, *Black Slang: A Dictionary of Afro-American Talk*, 1970 (US), 1971 (UK)
Cobb	Irvin S. Cobb, *Eating in Two or Three Languages*, 1919
Cohen	J.M. and M.J. Cohen, *Penguin Dictionary of Quotations*, 1960
coll.	colloquial(ly)
Collinson	W.E. Collinson, *Contemporary English: A Personal Speech Record*, 1927
c.p.	catch phrase; pl., c.pp.
DAE	W.L. Craigie and R.J. Hulbert, *A Dictionary of American English*, 1938–44
D.Am.	M. M. Mathews, *A Dictionary of Americanisms*, 1950
DCCU	Helen Dahlskog, *A Dictionary of Contemporary and Colloquial Usage*, 1971
DD	Oliver Herford, *The Deb's Dictionary*, 1931
Dict. Aus. Coll.	See Wilkes
DNWP	Anne Baker, *A Dictionary of Northamptonshire Words and Phrases*, 1854
DSUE	Eric Partridge, *A Dictionary of Slang*, 1937; edn quoted is usu. 8th edn, 1984, ed. Paul Beale
ed	edited; ed.; edition (in body of text)
EDD	Joseph Wright, ed, *The English Dialect Dictionary*, 1896–1905
e.g.	for example
Egan	edition of Grose (q.v.), 1823
EJ	Edward B. Jenkinson, *People, Words and Dictionaries*, 1972
elab.	elaborated, elaboration
E.P.	Eric Partridge
esp.	especial(ly)
Fain	Prof. John T. Fain
Farb	Peter Farb, *Word Play*, 1973 (US), 1974 (UK)
Farmer	John S. Farmer, *Americanisms – Old and New*, 1889
F & G	E. Fraser and J. Gibbons, *Soldier and Sailor Words and Phrases*, 1925
F & H	John S. Farmer and W.E. Henley, *Slang and Its Analogues*, 1890–1904
fig.	figurative(ly)
Folb	Edith A. Folb, *A Comparative Study of Urban Black Argot*, 1972
Foster	Brian Foster, *The Changing English Language*, 1968
Fr.	French
Fuller	Thomas ('Proverbs') Fuller, *Proverbs*, 1732
G	Thomas Fuller, *Gnomologia: Adagies and Proverbs*, 1732
gen.	general(ly)
Ger.	German
Gr.	Greek

Granville	Wilfred Granville, *Dictionary of Theatrical Terms*, 1952
Greig	J. Y. T. Greig, *Breaking Priscian's Head; or English as She Will be Wrote and Spoke*, 1928
Grose	Francis Grose, *A Classical Dictionary of the Vulgar Tongue*, 1785; 2nd edn, 1788; 3rd edn, 1796; Pierce Egan edn, 1823
Heywood	John Heywood, *Proverbs*, 1546
HLM	H. L. Mencken, *The American Language*, 1921; 2nd edn, 1922; 4th edn, 1936; Supp. 1 = Supplement One, 1945; Supp. 2 = Supplement Two, 1948
Holt	Alfred A. Holt, *Phrase Origins*, 1936
H & P	J. L. Hunt and A. G. Pringle, *Service. Slang*, 1943
Hotten	John Camden Hotten, *The Slang Dictionary*, 1859; 2nd edn, 1860; 3rd edn, 1864; 4th edn, 1870; 5th edn, 1874
Howell	James Howell, *Proverbs*, 1659
ibid.	*ibidem*, in the same authority or book
Irwin	Godfrey Irwin, *American Tramp and Underworld Songs and Slang*, 1931
It.	Italian
Jamieson	John Jamieson, *An Etymological Dictionary of the Scottish Language*, 1808
Janssen	Paul Janssen
JB	'Jon Bee', *Dictionary*, 1823
joc.	jocular(ly)
J.W.C.	Prof. John W. Clark
Kelly	James Kelly, *Collection of Scottish Proverbs*, 1721
L.	Latin
L. A.	Laurie Atkinson
LB	*The Lexicon Ballatronicum*, 1811; repub'd 1971, 1981
l.c.	in or at the passage or book cited
lit.	literal(ly)
Lyell	T. Lyell, *Slang, Phrase and Idiom in Colloquial English*, 1931
M	James Maitland, *The American Slang Dictionary*, 1891
Mackay	Charles Mackay's essay 'Popular Follies of Great Cities', in *Memoirs of Extraordinary Popular Delusions*, 1841. Available in reprint
McKnight	G. H. McKnight, *English Words and Their Background*, 1923
Manchon	J. Manchon, *Le Slang*, 1923
Matsell	George Matsell, *Vocabulum*, 1859
MN	Merchant Navy
Moe	Col. Albert F. Moe
Moncrieff	W. T. Moncrieff, *Tom and Jerry, or Life in London* (a comedy), 1821
Noble	Vernon Noble
NZ	New Zealand

NZS	Sidney J. Baker, *New Zealand Slang*, 1941
ob.	obsolescent
occ.	occasional(ly)
ODEP	*The Oxford Dictionary of English Proverbs*, 3rd edn, 1970
ODQ	*The Oxford Dictionary of Quotations*
OED	*The Oxford Dictionary*; *OED* Supp.: Supplement, 1933
orig.	origin; original; originate(d); originating
P	See Clarke
P.B.	Paul Beale
Peppitt	Lt Cdr F. L. Peppitt
Petch	Albert B. Petch
PG	Francis Grose, *A Proverbial Glossary*, 1787
PGR	E. Partridge, W. Granville and F. Roberts, *A Dictionary of Forces' Slang: 1939–45*, 1948
pl.	plural
prec.	preceding (see prec. = see the preceding entry)
prod.	produced
pub'd	published
quot'n	quotation
RAF	Royal Air Force
Ray	John ('Proverbial') Ray, *English Proverbs*, 1670; 2nd edn, 1678; enlarged edn, 1813
R. C.	Robert Claiborne
RCAF	Royal Canadian Air Force
Regt.	Regiment
RN	Royal Navy
RS	Ramsey Spencer
S	Jonathan Swift, *Polite Conversation*, 1738, in E.P.'s edn, 1963
Safire	William Safire, *The New Language of Politics*, 1968
Sailors' Slang	Wilfred Granville, *A Dictionary of Sailors' Slang*, 1962
Sanders	Peter Sanders
sc.	L: *scilicet*, namely
SE	Standard English
Shaw	Frank Shaw
Shipley	Prof. Joseph T. Shipley
Skehan	John Skehan
SS	Wilfred Granville, *Sea Slang of the Twentieth Century*, 1945
Stevenson	Burton Stevenson, *Dictionary of Quotations*, 5th edn, 1946
STY	Eric Partridge, *Slang Today and Yesterday*, 1933
synon.	synonym; synonymous with
Thornton	R. H. Thornton, *American Glossary*, 1912
U	Eric Partridge, *A Dictionary of the Underworld*, 2nd edn, 1961; *U3* = 3rd edn supplement, 1968
UK	United Kingdom; also as adjective; British

US	United States of America; also as adjective, American
usu.	usual(ly)
V	Schele de Vere, *Americanisms,* 1871; 2nd edn, 1872
var.	variant; variation
Vaux	John Hardy Vaux, 'Glossary of Cant', in *Memoirs*, written *c.* 1812, pub'd 1818
VIBS	Nigel Rees, *Very Interesting... But Stupid: Catchphrases from the World of Entertainment*, 1980
Ware	J. Redding Ware, *Passing English,* 1909
Webster	Noah Webster (1758–1843). *The Living Webster Encyclopedia of the English Language; American Dictionary of the English Language*, 1828; *Webster's New International Dictionary*, 1909, 2nd edn, 1934; *Webster's Third New International Dictionary*, 3rd edn
Wedgewood	Maurice Wedgewood
Weekley	Ernest Weekley, *An Etymological Dictionary of Modern English,* 1921
W & F	H. Wentworth and S. B. Flexner, *A Dictionary of American Slang*, 1960; 2nd Supplemented edn, 1975
Wilkes	G. A. Wilkes, *Dictionary of Australian Colloquialisms*, 1978
W-J	C. H. Ward-Jackson, *It's a Piece of Cake, or RAF Slang Made Easy,* 1943
W. J. B.	Mr W. J. Burke
WW1	First World War (1914–18)
WW2	Second World War (1939–45)
YB	Henry Yule and A. C. Burnell, *Hobson-Jobson*, 1886: edn by W. Crooke, 1903
[...]	signifies that the entry so enclosed, although doubtfully eligible, is yet worthy of comment
(–he)	signifies that the key phrase is frequently preceded by *he* (or whatever word appears in parentheses)
†	obsolete

A

A. See: what does 'A'.

A.C.A.B. 'In *New Society*, mid-1977, there was an article by a Newcastle journalist, who had been arrested at an industrial-dispute "demo". He spent the night in cells and was fascinated by the graffito *A.C.A.B.* all over the walls. A fellow inmate, more used to the situation, explained, "All coppers are bastards". This has now appeared on walls near the Loughborough police station. Another written c.p., like "—rule(s) O.K."' (P.B., 1977). By a 'written c.p.' is meant a catchphrase customarily written rather than spoken; yet only marginally so. And the date of *A.C.A.B.*? In this form, the phrase hardly precedes 1970, but, spoken in full, it existed as least as early as the 1920s. Basically, however, **all coppers are bastards**, q.v., is a mere var. of '[All those in authority] are bastards': an age-old expression of resentment against the restrainers, the keepers of law and order, no matter how inoffensive, how innocent the latter may be.

à d'autres! Tell that to the Marines! It occurs in Shadwell, *The Sullen Lovers*, 1668, Act IV: 'Ninny. Pshaw, pshaw, ad'autre, ad'autre, I can't abide you should put your tricks upon me' – glossed thus by George Saintsbury in his edn of four Shadwell plays: 'I.e. "à d'autres" ("tell someone else that"). It was a specially fashionable French catchword among English coxcombs and coquettes of the time. See Dryden's *Marriage à la Mode*, 1673. In short, fashionable in the fashionable London of *c.* 1660–80.

Abbott. See: hey, A.

abbrev. See: excuse my a.

abdabs. See: don't come the old.

abdomen. See: officers have.

aboard. See: welcome.

Abos. See: give it back.

about. See: you're all a.

about as high as three penn'orth (or **pennyworth**) **of coppers.** C.p. applied to very short persons: *c.* 1870–1950. As *sixpenn'orth* it had occurred in Robert Surtees, *Jorrocks's Jaunts and Jollities*, 1838, as R.C. reminds me.

about as much use as two men gone sick, with prec. *he's* either stated or understood, is a British Army c.p., dating from either during or very soon after WW2. (P.B., 1974.) See also **headache**...

absolutely, Mr Gallagher?—Positively, Mr Sheean! had 'some vogue in US from 1920s, from the vaudeville team of Gallagher and Sheean. Virtually extinct by 1950s' (R.C., 1977). It spread to Aus., where I heard it in 1920s, and presumably also to Can. and the UK.

Abyssinia! belongs to ONE-WORD CATCH PHRASES. It means 'I'll be seein(g) you' and dates from the Abyssinian War, 1935–6. P.B.: but might it not have arisen from the earlier, British, campaign of 1899, against the 'Mad Mullah', or even Gen. Napier's expedition of 1868? J.W.C. remarks, 1977, 'In US, much older than the Abyssinian War; I remember it

clearly from my high-school classmates in the early '20s'. Very much in the line of schoolboy puns of the *Alaska* = I'll ask her; *Jamaica* = Did you make her?; and *dip your Turkey in Greece* [grease] type.

accident. See: since Auntie: what would happen.

accidentally on purpose. Only apparently accidental, but really – and often maliciously – on purpose: since *c.* 1880 in Brit. and since *c.* 1885 in US, according to W & F, who add that, in the latter, it was 'in popular student use *c.* 1940'.

accidents will happen in the best regulated families. See **it happens.** ...

according to plan was, in WW1 *communiqués*, a distressingly frequent excuse for failure, e.g. an enforced retreat; it soon became used ironically for anything, however trivial, that did *not* go according to plan. 'Oh, nonsense, old man! All according to plan, don't you know?' (The Germans, in their *communiqués*, used an equivalent: *planmässig*.) In WW2, there was the similar phrase, *withdrawing to a prepared position*. In the US, precisely the same process took place – but during the latter half of WW2 and after (R.C., 1977). Occ. satirised in the absurdity of *a strategic advance to the rear* (A.B., 1978). Cf. **advancing....**

account. See: that accounts.

acid. See: don't come the a.

acknowledge. See: I acknowledge.

acorns. See: you'll come.

acres. See: three acres; wider.

acrobats. See: may all your kids.

act. See: everybody wants; get into; get your act.

act of Parliament, ladies and gentlemen! See **time, gentlemen, please!**

act to follow – a hard or **a tough.** (Usu. prec. by *he's* or *that's.*) 'Originally, and probably before 1920, referring to an outstandingly successful vaudeville act which might well cast a shade over the following act, but since at least 1930, applied to any outstanding performance or especially able person. Often carries the implication, "I'll try to equal his success, but don't blame me if I fail."' (R.C., 1978). P.B.: some use in UK since *c.* 1975.

act your age! Act naturally – not as if you were much younger than, in fact, you are: adopted, *c.* 1920, from US, where it had an alternative – **be your age!**, likewise adopted. (*DSUE*; Berrey.) 'The Australian senses for both include "don't be gullible" "don't be naïve"' (Neil Lovett, 1978), See also **be your age!** and **grow up!**

action. See: sharp's; slice; that's where the a.; this is where.

actor. See: born a gentleman.

actress. See: as the actress.

Ada. See: up a shade.

Adam. See: ever since.

add. See: it adds.

admiral. See: tap the a.

Admiralty. See: even the A.; and:
Admiralty could not be more arch – the. 'The *Guardian*, 2 Dec. 1977, in a notice of a new London revue that apparently opened rather coyly, has "The Admiralty, as they used to say, could not be more arch"' (P.B.). This distinctively London c.p. of very approx. 1925–60 was clearly based on the adj. *arch* – teasingly, or affectedly, playful – and the Admiralty Arch, one of London's architectural landmarks. Among c.pp., such deft witticisms are regrettably scarce.
admit. See: I acknowledge.
advancing in an easterly direction. (Often prec. by *again*.) This var. of **according to plan**, q.v., was 'used all too often in the [N. African] desert [in 1940–3], the enemy being, of course, to the west of us – we hoped. The ultimate in cynicism was "we shall fight to the last man and the last round of ammunition and then withdraw to previously prepared positions". The Germans were even worse, making official bombast out of private humour' (Peter Sanders, 1978; he served there).
advice. See: Punch's.
aeroplane. See: Percival.
afflicted. See: don't mock.
afford. See: don't touch.
afloat. See: he that is; my back.
afraid. See: 'tis only I; who's afraid.
after his end (– he's). This is a C20 workmen's c.p., applied to a man 'chasing' a woman, *end* connoting 'tail', as the var. *after his hole* makes clear.
after the Lord Mayor's show; or, in full, **after the Lord Mayor's show comes the shit-cart.** Orig. (late C19) a Cockney c.p. applied to the cleaning-up (esp. of horse-dung) necessary after the Lord Mayor of London's annual procession and soon extended to any comparable situation; hence in WW1 it was, mostly on the Western Front, addressed to a man returning from leave, esp. if he were just in time for a 'show' – as 'the troops', with a rueful jocularity, described an attack. Among civilians, it is extant, although not in cultured or highly educated circles.
after you, Claude – no, after you, Cecil! Characterizing an old-world, old-time, courtesy, this exchange of civilities occurred in an 'ITMA' show, produced by the BBC in (I seem to remember) 1940. Although it was already, in 1946, slightly ob., yet it is still, in the latish 1970s, far from being†.
The Can. version, as Dr Douglas Leechman informed me in 1959, is **after you, my dear Alphonse – no, after you, Gaston**, with var. **after you, Alphonse** (Leechman, 1969, 'In derision of French bowing and scraping') – and was, by 1960, slightly ob., and by 1970, very; current also in US, where, however, it often look the form, **you first, my dear Alphonse** (or **Alfonso**). Note that all of them were spoken in an ingratiating manner.
The latter form, US and derivatively also Can., has attracted much nostalgic attention, mostly from the US. Four days after this book's appearance in the UK, W.J.B. wrote: 'The characters Alphonse and Gaston were created by the US cartoonist Frederick Burr Opper [1857–1937] for his comic strip "Alphonse and Gaston". Readers of this strip [its heyday was 1902–4, with occ. appearances for a year or two later] often made deep bows to a friend and said "After you, my dear Alphonse" and the person addressed would reply "After you, my dear Gaston".' J.W.C. soon commented that 'it had a very long life, till *c.* 1925, and I'm not sure that it is yet quite extinct.' And then Shipley referred to both Coulton Waugh, who, in *The Comics*, 1947, noted that these two elegant Frenchmen had become 'national figures'; and to Jerry Robinson, who, in *The Comics: an Illustrated History of Comic Strip Art*, 1974, regards this as the first of innumerable phrases and words that were to contribute to the American idiom. It was, said Waugh, a comic illustration of 'the inefficiency of over-politeness'. As a sidelight, Mr Eric Townley has told me that *after you, Alphonse* 'was quite wittily used for the title of a jazz record made in 1957, in which the instrumentation was two trumpets, two trombones, two tenor saxes, plus rhythm section. First the two trumpet players alternate with each other in 12-bar solos, each taking three such solos, then the two trombones, and so on. A musical *Alphonse and Gaston*!'
And R.C. has noted that a metaphorical *Alphonse and Gaston* often. implied 'mere buck-passing'. In general, however, Alphonse and Gaston 'are immortalised in the American idiom... as a universally understood symbol of excessive politeness.'
P.B.: it would appear, then, that the Claude and Cecil of 'Itma' were derived, consciously or not, from Opper's memorable originals.
after you I come first is a US var. [P.B.: ? perversion] of the prec. (Berrey.) Cf:
after you is manners implies the speaker's consciousness, usu. joc. and ironic, of inferiority: since late C17; by 1900, ob. – and by 1940, virtually †. As so often happens, the earliest printed record occurs in S, 1738 (Dialogue II): 'Oh! madam: after you is good manners.' Elliptical for: 'For me to come after you – to make way for you – is only right.'
after you, miss, with the two two's and the two b's. See **two white...**
after you, my dear Alphonse (or **Alfonso**). See **after you, Claude.**
after you with the po, Jane! A joc. elab. of 'After you with (this or that)!' 'From mockery of bedroom usage of phrase of bygone days of outdoor privies. Early C20, perhaps late C19' (L.A., 1976). I'd date it as *c.* 1880–1920 in literal use, and in burlesque allusion for a few years more.
after you with the push! A street – esp. London – c.p. addressed no less politely than ironically to one who has rudely pushed his way past the speaker: *c.* 1900–14. Ware.
after you with the trough! Addressed to someone who has belched and implying not only that he has eaten too fast but also that he has the manners, or the lack of manners, expectable of a pig: orig., *c.* 1930 or a little earlier, in the N. Country and still, in 1970 anyway, used mostly there.
again. See: off again; phantom; pick him; play it; Richard's; sold again; spray it; that boy; you can say.
against my religion – it's or **that's** (or some specified activity). A joc. excuse, as in e.g. 'It's against my religion to partake of alcohol before the noon gun sounds, but since you're twisting my arm...', or 'No, it's against my religion to subscribe to raffles, but seeing as it's *you* selling the tickets...'; perhaps orig. 'Services', but anyway heavy bar-side humour: since mid C20.
In the same gen. field is the c.p. used to parry an invitation to do something risky, for which *against my religion* might well be used instead: (*Sorry, but*) *I'm a devout coward.* (P.B.)
age. See: act your age; and:
age before beauty is mostly a girl's mock courtesy addressed to an old – or, at best, an elderly – man: late C19–20, but rarely heard after (say) 1960.
On entering a room, two people would joke:
'Age before beauty!'
'No, dust before the broom.'
(With thanks to Mrs Shirley M. Pearce, 1975.)
P.B.: this entry in the 1st ed. provoked a number of responses, the first being my own, while proof-reading the work, that usage had, by 1940, come to be extended, esp. as a jocularity between almost any pair of people. E.P.'s further notes continue: Peter Sanders, 1978, writes 'Also (one girl to another) "age before innocence", a bitchy c.p. to which the counter is "pearls before swine"'; and Prof. Harold Shapiro reminds me that this counter originated as a characteristic retort by Dorothy Parker (1893–1967). The phrase is still current in Aus. (Neil Lovett, in *The National Times*, 23–28 Jan. 1978) [as it is in UK: P.B.]. A further 1978 commentary on its U.S. usage comes from Mr George A. Krzymowski of New Orleans: 'In his *A Treasury of American Folklore*, 1944,

its editor, drawing on Clifton Johnson's *What They Say in New England*, 1896, has this: – When two boys in school go for a drink to the water pail at the same time, number one hands the glass to number two and says "Age before beauty". Number two takes it, and says, "Men before monkeys". Number one finishes the dialogue and keeps up his end by responding, "The dirt before the broom"'.

But, for Brit. usage, the most illuminating comment I have received is this from the Dowager Lady Gainford, 1979: 'I am now 78 and I have never heard the phrase used in the sense [above].... I have always heard it used by an older woman to a younger who stands aside to let her go first. It is a pretty and graceful way of acknowledging the courtesy – and of accepting it – instead of the two standing outside a doorway saying "After you" – "No, after you" and so on. My aunts and other older women used this phrase to me when I was a girl and young woman, and I still use it to women younger than myself. I can't ever remember anyone using it in the rather ugly, faintly malicious way suggested by your entry. Where can it have come from ? The elderly man might well say it to the pretty young thing: but surely not the other way round?'

age of miracles is past – the was contentiously used by free-thinkers during C18, challengingly by agnostics during C19 and by all cynics and most sceptics in C20. By (say) 1918, it had become a cliché; by 1945 or 1946, it was so often employed, both derisively and in such varied applications, that since then it has been also a c.p. A manifest miracle, yet I've never seen it posed, is recorded in the penultimate paragraph of **some of my best friends are Jews.**

P.B.: I suggested to E.P. that just as frequent in later C20 is the delighted and surprised exclam. **the age of miracles is NOT past**, on the sometimes minor, but nevertheless gratifying, occasions when this is discovered. He agreed, as did Michael Goldman, who, in 1978, supplied the var. *the time of miracles is not past.*

agents. See: I have my a.

Agnest. See: I don't know whether.

agony. See: ee, it was.

agree. See: I couldn't agree.

ah! que je can be bête! What a fool – or, how stupid – I am! This c.p. of *c.* 1899–1912 is, by Redding Ware, classified as 'half-society', by which he presumably means 'the fashionable section of the *demi-monde*'. Macaronic: Fr. *que*, how, and *je*, I, and *bête*, stupid.

ah there! 'What can be more revolting than phrases like *Whoa, Emma; Ah there!; Get there Eli; Go it, Susan. I'll hold your bonnet; Everybody's doing it; Good night, Irene; O you kid!* in vogue' – that is, in the US – 'not long ago.' Thus McKnight. Cf:

ah there, my size, I'll steal you. In a footnote on p. 566 of the 4th edn, 1936, HLM includes this phrase among half a dozen of which he says that when the 'logical content' of the phrase is sheer silliness the populace quickly tires of it: 'Thus "Ah there, my size, I'll steal you". "Where did you get that hat?" [q.v.] ... and their congeners were all short-lived.' Obviously it's US, but, so far, I've been unable to determine, even approximately, how long it did last – or precisely when. Cf. **that's my size.**

aha, me proud beauty! 'Roughly, "Now I've got you [a woman] where I want you!" Orig. (late C19?) quoted from, or at least epitomising the sexual ethos of, some old-time theatrical villain but, since 1920s or earlier, often used only for comic effect. Often accompanied by a moustache-twirling gesture. Certainly US, prob. also Brit. Now all but extinct? (R.C., 1978), Yes; Surrey-side, or Transpontine, Melodrama since *c.* 1890 or perhaps even 1880;† by 1945.

ahead. See: if you want to get.

aid. See: what's this in aid of.

ail. See: good for what.

aim. See: not ambition; we aim.

'ain't' ain't grammar is a humorous phrase, elicited by

someone's use of *ain't*, as e.g. in 'That ain't funny': since *c.* 1920. On its usage in US, R.C. wrote, 1977, 'A much more elaborate version was current in my schooldays (late 1920s): "Ain't ain't a good word to use, that's why it ain't in the dictionary, that's why I ain't gonna use ain't any more".' But whether so long a version can be classified as a c.p. is debatable.

ain't coming on that tab, usu. prec. by **I.** (I) don't agree to that, or with it: orig. Harlem jive talk, very rapidly spread to popular music, thence to the US world of entertainment: *c.* 1938–50. (*The New Cab Calloway's Hepsters Dictionary*, 1944, which adds: 'Usually abbreviated to "I ain't coming"'.)

ain't it a fact? and **ain't it the truth?** are US phrases dating *c.* 1910 – or earlier – and recorded in Berrey; the latter is also recorded by McKnight. Both are exclamatory rather than interrogative. R.C., 1977: 'Usually [it has] a certain rueful overtone – one wishes it were *not* a fact. Now ob.'

ain't it a shame, eh? ain't it a shame? 'Another ITMA phrase, spoken by Carleton Hobbs as the nameless man who told banal tales ("I waited for hours in the fish queue ... and a man took my plaice") and always prefaced and concluded them with "ain't it a shame?"' (*VIBS*).

ain't it grand to be blooming well dead! – current in the 1930s, but naturally WW2 killed it – comes from a Leslie Sarony song of the period. (Noble, 1976.) Clearly a pun on 'Ain't it grand (just) to be alive!'

ain't love grand! expresses pleasure, orig. at being in love, derivatively in other situations; and often either ironically or derisively. US at first (and still so), it became, *c.* 1930, also Brit.; I heard it, 1919 or 1920, in Aus. Cf:

ain't Nature grand (? or !) is a 'c.p. apposite to anything from illegitimate offspring to tripping over a muddy path' (L.A., 1974): late C19–20.

ain't nobody (or **no one**) **here but us chickens!** prec. by **there,** 'is applied to an occasion when unexpectedly few persons are present, but may also be used with the implication "and everybody else had better stay away!"' (P.B., 1976): adopted in UK *c.* 1950, from the US, where it had existed prob. since late or latish C19 and was based on a story about a chicken-thief surprised by the owner, who calls 'Anybody there?' and is greeted by this resourceful reply. Of the story itself, several variations inevitably exist, and the line became, *c.* 1950, the chorus of a popular song. That the c.p. is extant appears from this allusion in Frank Ross, *Sleeping Dogs*, 1978: 'And no heroics, O.K.? If anyone comes knocking, there ain't no one here but us termites.'

ain't sayin(g) nothin(g) is an American Negro 'phrase referring to a matter or person of little merit, respect or value. Synonym: *'tain't no big thang,* q.v. Recorded in *The Third Ear*, 1971, Apparently since *c.* 1950, perhaps a decade earlier. (With thanks to M. Paul Janssen.)

ain't that a laugh? Well, that really is a joke: US: C20. (Moe, 1975.)

ain't that it? This confirms the truth of a statement; in short, telling it 'like it is' – Cf **tell it like it is,** and the Brit. equivalent **well, this is it!,** qq.v. American Negro: since(?) mid-C20. Recorded in *The Third Ear*, 1971.

ain't that nothin'! implies a usu. irritated displeasure, is characteristically US, dates from *c.* 1920, and derives from – and forms – the opposite of the next. R.C., 1977, 'the phrase is dead and buried, and unlamented'.

ain't that something – or, in rural dialect, **somepin'!** Indicative of considerable pleasure, this pleasantly terse US c.p. dates from *c.* 1918. (Berrey.) J.W.C., 1977, glosses 'Admiration rather than pleasure generally'. Cf. *isn't that something.*

ain't that the limit? Can you beat that?: US: C20. (Moe, 1975.)

ain't that the truth? Emphatic var. of **ain't it a fact?:** id.: ibid.

ain't we got fun (? or !) This late C19–20 US c.p. roughly answers to the Brit. *We don't get* (or *haven't got) much money, but we do see life!* (Moe, 1975.) It 'owes its arrival to a popular song of that title' (Benny Green, in *Spectator*, 10 Sep. 1977); Fain, 1977, cites the relevant lines: 'In the morning, in the evening, ain't we got fun!/Not much money but, oh honey, ain't we got fun!', and adds that the words and music were by Richard A. Whiting, in a revue, *Satires of 1920*, prod. by Arthur West. The title recurred in a couple of motion-picture musicals of the 1950s. Prof. Fain cites *American Popular Songs*, ed. David Ewen, 1966. R.C., also 1977, declared it to be 'moribund, at least'.

ain't you got no couf? Have you no manners, no *savoir-faire*, no dress-sense, etc.?: army: early 1970s. Since *couf* represents the † *couth* of *uncouth*, cf the formation of *ain't ain't grammar*, a deliberate illiteracy. (P.B., 1974.)

ain't you got no homes to go to? see **time, gentlemen, please.**

ain't you right! This US c.p. was 'circulating in the year 1920' (McKnight), esp. among students; it seems to have died out by 1930.

ain't you the one though! is a UK 'deflationary exclamation', orig. and mostly Cockney: late C19–20. (A reminder from R.C., 1977.) P.B.: contrast the usu. admiring 'Ooh, you are a one!', of someone mildly daring.

ain't you (or **yer**) **wild you** (or **ye'**) **can't get at it?** was, *c.* 1910–30, loudly and jeeringly intoned, at young girls passing, by Cockney adolescent youths, as Julian Franklyn told me in 1968. From the louts, who usu. added *yer muvver's sewn yer draws up*, it ascended, *c.* 1920, to Cockney children as a 'taunting call, especially by children able to keep some desired object to themselves' (L.A., also 1968).

air. See: come up for; give it air; that sure; you'll have no.

air force. See: they can make.

Airedale. See: don't be an A.

airship. See: you'll have no.

aisles. See: I had 'em.

Akeybo. See: beats Akeybo.

Al. See: you know me.

Alamo. See: remember the A.

alas, my poor brother! A generalisation of a famous Bovril (beef extract) advertisement, which can be dated late C19–earlyish 20, to judge by this courteous clarification from 'The Bovril Bureau. News, views and recipes', Messrs Suson Deacon, in a letter, 1977, from Miss Judy Regis: ' "Alas, My Poor Brother" is the most famous of the early Bovril advertisements: it was designed by W.H. Caffyn and first appeared as a poster in 1896'. It showed a fine-looking bull mourning the brother quintessenced in a tin of Bovril. (The phrase was recorded in 1927 by the late Prof. W.E. Collinson in his valuable book; I remember seeing it in the *Strand Magazine*, where so many famous advertisements appeared – and not a few c.pp. originated). Cf. **prevents that sinking feeling**, q.v.

alcohol. See: protocol.

Alderman Lushington is concerned and **Lushington is his master**, respectively 'Well, he *drinks*, you know' and 'He's a hopeless drunkard' – indeed *Lushington* (or *lushington*) soon came to mean 'drunkard'. The former belongs to *c.* 1780–1900, the latter to *c.* 1825–90. Perhaps a pun on the low-slang *lush*, strong liquor, and *Lushington*, the brewer; with influence from *the City of Lushington*, a convivial society that, flourishing *c.* 1750–1895, is recorded by *OED*. This use of *concerned* occurs in several C18–19 c.pp.

'alf (orig. spelt **'arf**) **a mo, Kaiser!** belongs to the years 1915–18: it was, in fact, a 1915–16 recruiting poster thus captioned, the picture showing 'a "Tommy" lighting a cigarette prior to unslinging his rifle and going into action. The catch phrase was widely adopted in England' (F & G). Cf. **Kitchener wants you.** The phrase survived, in civilian use, until the late 1930s, and not only in UK.

Alice. See: knock three times: up Alice's.

Alice Springs. See: from arsehole.

Alice, where art thou? 'was the title of a Victorian song by Alfred ("I dreamt I dwelt in marble halls") Bunn ... It was simply [this] title that became a sort of catch phrase' (Christopher Fry, 1978). A true c.p.: I have known it since *c.* 1908, but it had been one for 70 or more years before that.

By 1950 it was ob.; yet even by 1978, not †. A famous theatrical manager, Alfred Bunn (? 1796–1860) was known as 'poet Bunn'; he wrote and translated libretti, and produced the operas of M.W. Balfe, including *The Bohemian Girl*, which, 1843, contained the song 'I dreamt ...' *Alice, where art thou?* is enshrined in *ODQ*.

alive and well and living in ... See **God is alive and well ...**

alive-o. See: catch 'em all; still a.; two brothers.

all. See: that's all; you're all.

all about. See: you're all a.; like shit.

all alive and kissing. See **still alive and kissing.**

all alone (or **all by** (one)**self**) **like a country dunny** is an Aus. c.p., expressive of loneliness or solitude: since *c.* 1930, or more prob. since *c.* 1910. (Baker, *Australia Speaks*, 1953; Wilkes, 1978.) *Dunny* shortens *dunnaken*, lit, 'shithouse'; the word came to England with the Gypsies and was at first an underworld, and at best a low, term.

all ashore as is (or **that's**) **going ashore!** 'Used, outside of the original context, by e.g., the driver of a car hastening his passengers – or rather the passengers' friends – taking over long to say good-bye' (J.W.C., 1968). Although Prof. Clark is reporting a US usage, this was most prob. orig. Brit., and perhaps esp. Cockney, dating back to the days of scheduled passenger liners.

all behind in Melbourne, confined to Western Aus., is applied to persons very broad-beamed; it prob. dates from the late 1940s. (Jim Ramsay, *Cop It Sweet*, 1977.) Clearly it was prompted by the next group, than which it is far less well known.

all behind, like a (or **the**) **cow's tail**, or **like a fat woman**, or **like Barney's bull.** All are phrases applied to one who is extremely late, or much delayed, in arriving or in getting something finished ('Here I am again, all behind like ... '). The first is clearly of rural orig., is prob. the prototype, and may go back to, at a guess, *c.* 1870, and perhaps much earlier, as B.G.T., Northants, suggests. This form, with var. *a donkey's tail*, is recorded as an American usage also, prob. approx. contemporaneous with the Brit. (Berrey, 1942). The *fat woman* version is often used lit., in Aus., 'having a very large bottom', and may then be shortened to *all behind*; cf **all bum**, and the prec. Apparently commoner in Aus. is the *all behind* var., from which the *all behind* may be omitted; it too is a Brit. ruralism that has emigrated; but see also **like Barney's bull.** Further on the *fat woman* var., Mr Maurice Wedgwood of *The Northern Echo* comments, 'I would guess, late C19–20; familiar [to me] from my earliest years, the 1920s, in a working-class family reflecting C19 folk culture.'

Fain, 1977, notes that *you're the cow's tail* is, in US, addressed to one who is late, esp. the latest, in arriving at a party: since the 1930s.

all betty! (or **it's all betty!**) It's all up – the 'caper' is over, the game lost – we've completely failed: an underworld c.p. of *c.* 1870–1920; the opposite of **it's all bob** or **Bob's your uncle**, this sort of pun (*Bob – Betty*) being not rare in cant; but also deriving from **all my eye and Betty Martin.** (Recorded by B & L.)

all bitter and twisted. See **crazy mixed-up ...**

all bum! was, *c.* 1860–1900, a street – esp. a London street – cry directed at a woman wearing a bustle; therefore cf **all behind, like a fat woman.** For *all bum and bustle*, see **all tits and teeth.**

all chiefs and no Indians. Since *c.* 1950, at latest, has been applied in UK to any concern or establishment that seems to be 'all bosses and no workers', 'all presidents (or chairmen) and no, or too few, minor executives', and similar nuances; cf. John Braine's var. in *The Pious Agent*, 1975. ' "Well, we're a merchant bank, after all. More officers than privates, so to speak." ' It most prob. orig. in US, where, as R.C. remarks, 'it has certainly been current for many years'; in US it has the occ. var. *too many chiefs and not enough Indians*, as A.B., 1978, notes. An Aus. elab. arising early in WW2 was ... *like the University Regiment*, but this did not long survive the peace. The phrase is unrecorded by Berrey and *D. Am.*, and so, at least for US usage, I would hazard the guess for date: throughout C20.

all clever stuff. See **it's all clever stuff.**

all come out in the wash. See **it'll all come out ...**

all contributions gratefully received, with *however small* orig. and still often added. Used lit. it is does not, of course, qualify; used allusively or in very different circumstances, it has, since *c.* 1925, been a c.p., as in ' "Dying for a smoke! Anyone give me a cigarette?" A long silence. Then "All I have left is half a cigarette – the one behind my ear. Welcome to that, if you want it." No silence. "All contributions gratefully received. Ta." ' (From a novel published in 1969, Catherine Aird's *The Complete Steel.*) See also **small contributions ...**

all coppers are is a 'truncated version of the c.p. "All coppers are bastards", current since, at latest, 1945. This itself is only the last line of the chanted jingle, "I'll sing you a song, it's not very long: all coppers .... etc." Obviously one would choose one's company with care before letting this dangerously abusive statement loose, even in jest' (P.B., 1974). I heard it first in the late 1920s, and I suspect that it has existed throughout C20 and, among professional criminals and crooks, for at least a generation longer. It is a slanderous misstatement at the expense of an, in the majority, fine body of men, grossly underpaid ever since it was founded. Cf, semantically, 'once a policeman, always a policeman', which is not a c.p., for it follows the pattern of 'once a schoolteacher, always a schoolteacher', a much-exaggerated piece of dogma. Every profession, trade, occupation, has its black sheep. See also **A.C.A.B.**

all day! is a children's and young people's rejoinder to the query 'What's the date – is it the *X*th?' If the question is simply 'What's the date?' the answer is 'The *X*th – *all day.*' Arising *c.* 1890 – if not a decade or two earlier – it was, by 1960, very slightly ob., yet it doesn't, even now, look at all moribund.

all done by kindness! This ironic late C19–20 phrase occurs in that unjustly forgotten novel, W.L. George's *The Making of an Englishman*, 1914. It is often used in joc. explanatory response to, e.g., 'How on earth did you manage to do *that*?'; also as in 'Not at all! All done by kindness, I assure you' – 'a nonchalant c.p. of dismissal of thanks for an action that is done to someone else's advantage' (Granville, letter, 1969). It seems, as Prof. T. B.W. Reid has (1974) reminded me, to have orig. with performing animals and the assurances of their trainers. Cf and contrast **all done with mirrors.**

all done up like a dog's dinner. See **all dressed up ...**

all done with (occ. by) **mirrors** (– **it's**). A phrase uttered when something very clever or extremely ingenious has been done. Wedgwood, 1977, tells me: 'Late C19–20, from widening popular knowledge – a "knowing" awareness – of stage conjuring-devices formerly accepted with awe. C19 illusionists used mirrors in celebrated acts such as Pepper's Ghost.' In Noël Coward's *Private Lives*, performed and pub'd in 1933, occurs (Act II) this illuminating example:

AMANDA [*wistfully clutching his hand*]: That's serious enough, isn't it?

ELYOT: No, no, it isn't. Death's very laughable, such a cunning little mystery. All done with mirrors.

The occ. var. *all done with pieces of string* is prob. a derivative influenced by the splendid contraptions designed by W. Heath Robinson. A US var. is *all done with a simple twist of the wrist*: 'also probably referring to a conjuror's explanation of his legerdemain' (R.C., 1977). A.B., 1978, has usefully added that the *mirrors*, the predominant version, is sometimes prec. by *it must be* or *it must have been.*

all dressed up and no place (US) (or **nowhere**) **to go** orig. *c.* 1915, in a 'song by Raymond Hitchcock, an American comedian' (Collinson): by 1937 it was ob. – as it still is, yet, like **all day!** above, very far from †.

all dressed up for a poppy show. An occ. var., Brit. rural, of the following collection:

all dressed up like a Christmas-tree or **in Christmas-tree order;** ... **like a dog's dinner;** ... **like a ham bone;** ... **like a pox-doctor's clerk;** and the US **like Mrs Astor's horse;** *all* occ. omitted in all of them. *All done up ...* or *all got up ...* are fairly frequent variants, and, in later C20, *all tarted up ...* would be understood as synon.

The *like a Christmas-tree* version, late C19–20 but almost † by 1970, may be the earliest of the group; it had the WW1 British soldiers' offshoot *all dressed up in Christmas-tree order*, which, however, meant specifically in full service marching order.

... like a dog's dinner is the best known: dating since *c.* 1925 in the Services, esp. the Army, it attained considerable popularity there during WW2 and, *c.* 1955, spread rapidly among civilians. In Can. it has, since *c.* 1910, had a var., *all dolled up like a barber's cat*, defined by Leechman as 'resplendently dressed'. (The former: PGR, 1948; the latter: *DSUE.*) P.B.: influences on these phrases may have been *dog-robbers*, a C20, orig. RN, officers' term for a tweed civilian suit; and *like the barber's cat: all wind and piss!*

... like a ham bone, dating since *c.* 1850 but ob. by 1970, is a very English, esp. a Midlands, c.p. of the domestic kind. B.G.T., 1978, glosses it thus: 'It referred probably to the paper frill round the joint when it was brought to table.'

... like a pox-doctor's clerk, i.e. flashily: current since, very approx., *c.* 1870, was in fairly gen. use until the 1960s. I heard it first in the 1920s, but not since WW2. [P.B.: it continued in widespread services' use at least until the mid–1970s.] Wilkes, 1978, defines it as 'dressed nattily, but in bad taste', claims it as Aus., implies that, as such, it is extant; but I'm reasonably sure that it went to Australia from England. But *a pox-doctor's clerk*, and its var. *a horse-doctor's clerk* (without *like*) had, in UK, a different usage: 'These were, in my younger days [1920s–40s] a way of explaining one's occupation if some impertinent person asked what you did for a living' (Anon., letter, 1978). See also the quot'n at **if you can't fight ...**

... like Mrs Astor's horse, the horse often qualified as *pet* (Ashley) or *plush* (R.C.): Claiborne adds 'The Mrs Astor in question was the doyenne of New York society *c.* 1890; hence presumably dating from that era'; he cites Stanley Walker, *Mrs Astor's Horse*, *c.* 1935, and implies that the phrase was ob. by *c.* 1940. Ashley writes, 1979, 'I think the Mrs Astor is one of the two wives (Ava Lowe Willing or Madeleine Talmadge Force) of the US industrialist who died in 1912.'

all duck or no dinner, 'The final fling which may lead to either triumph or disaster' (Skehan, 1984): Anglo-Irish: C20. Cf. synon. **shit or bust** and **Sydney or the bush.**

all fine ladies are witches: C18. In S, Dialogue II, we find:

LADY SM.: You have hit it; I believe you are a Witch.

MISS: O, Madam, the Gentlemen say. all fine Ladies are Witches; but I pretend to no such Thing.

An allusion to women's intuition?

all gas and gaiters is the shortened – the c.p. – form of 'All is gas and gaiters' in Dickens's *Nicholas Nickleby*, 1838–9. In civilian life, the c.p. is often applied to bishops and archbishops: a ref. to the gaiters they wear and to the facile eloquence beloved by so many of them: indeed *gas and gaiters* has come to mean 'mere verbiage'. But the c.p. was not much used after *c.* 1950, until it was notably revived in, and by, the television-to-radio transfer programme 'All Gas and Gaiters' (or, as Noble has described it, 'fun with the clergy'), which started on 30 Jan. 1967 and ended on 17 June 1971, as Barry Took, author of the delightful *Laughter in the Air*, 1976, has informed me. See also **attitude is the art of gunnery ...**

all good clean fun. See **it's all good ...**

all hands and the cook, lit. 'a phrase used in an emergency when every hand is called to guard the herd, when the cattle are unusually restless or there is imminent danger of a stampede' (Ramon F. Adams, *Western Words*, 2nd ed., 1968), it spread, in the American West, far beyond the cowboys as a general alert – and was occ. used facetiously. Recorded also by Berrey, 1942.

all hands on deck! See **man the pumps!**

all honey or all turd with them (– **it's**). They are either close friends or bitter enemies – they fly from one extreme to the other. The phrase occurs in Pepys, *Diary*, 13 Dec. 1663 (R.S.), and is recorded in Grose, 3rd ed., 1796; it may have lasted until the end of C19, among the less mealy-mouthed, for it seems to have prompted a military var.: B.G.T., 1978, reports an ex-soldier as saying, 'Oh, them, they're either all shit or all shine.'

all human life is there (occ. **here**)! The 'there' version is orig. 'A News of the World advertising slogan which took on a certain life of its own in the rest of the world' (*VIBS*).

all I know is what I read in the papers, which we owe to Will Rogers, the so-called 'cowboy philosopher', is the c.p. form of the words beginning his 'letter' of 21 May 1926: '*Dear Mr Coolidge*: Well all I know is just what I read in the papers' (Will Rogers, *The Letters of a Self-Made Diplomat to His President*, 1927): by which he meant that all he knew of events in the US was what he could glean from the English newspapers. A particular and topical ref. became, as is the way in the genesis of c.pp., gen. and enduring: and this one has 'worn very well', esp. in US, where, very properly, it has always been far more popular than in UK, not that it's in the least rare even in Britain. W.J.B. has, 1975, told me that, in the US, it continues to be very widely used.

The interpretation made above is very British, however natural it may sound. An old friend, Dr. Joseph T. Shipley, wrote thus to me, 1974:

I showed [your 'item']…a publisher. He said: 'This misses the point. Wherever Will Rogers was, the expression means: "*I'm just an ordinary citizen*. I don't read the highbrow journals, the magazines that tell you the news isn't so; I'm not a professor: I don't go to listen to men that call themselves experts: all I know is what I read in the papers – and that makes me as good a citizen as the next man."

'The sentence also implies: "I don't trust them pernickety persuaders always telling you they know what isn't so. I get my facts from the papers, and that's good enough for me."'

Then, on his own account, Dr Shipley adds:

(Note the naïve implication: 'All I *know*….' If it's in the papers, it's true. A man may try to lie to me; print doesn't lie!) The catch phrase 'All I know is what I read in the papers' is an implied assertion that all *you* (i.e., anyone) can know is what you read in the papers; and my opinion is therefore as good as the next man's, and that's the way it is and should be in this democracy. That's what Will Rogers felt, and that's the spirit underlying his humor and a main source of his popularity.

A long discussion for a short sentence! But it does mean more than it says. And I think the final implication above (that the simple man is as qualified a citizen as the self-styled expert) deserves mention.

Yes, indeed!

Sanders, 1978, makes the point, re-inforcing the Brit. interpretation: 'Also "it must be true, I read it in the papers" – a c.p. used with particular point when talking to journalists and meaning that they'd written more nonsense than usual. Probably later than 1945.'

By W.J.B. I have been able to conclude the matter of the phrase's origin: he writes, 1979, 'Almost every expert attributes this saying to comedian Will Rogers. I am at present reading a current biography of Herbert Bayard Swope by Alfred Aldan Lewis entitled *Man of the World*, 1978.

'On p. 108…is the following: "Will Rogers once asked

Swope how he had acquired his prodigious store of information, and he modestly replied 'I only know what I read in the newspapers'. The remark so impressed Rogers that he used it as part of his monologue in several editions of the *Ziegfeld Follies*."

'I believe this to be a true account. Rogers was a frequent visitor at Swope's summer home at Sands Point, Long Island, N.Y., and it is agreed that Swope was one of the best conversationalists in America. An executive editor of the old New York *World*, he made it a practice to read daily every newspaper of importance published in the U.S., and [of] the English-speaking world, for that matter. That is where he got most of his information, and his remark to Rogers was an honest one, a natural one.'

That, I'd say, settles the origin.

all I want is the facts, ma'am. See **all we want…**

all in my eye. See **all my eye…**

all in the mind. See **it's all in the mind…**

all in the seven; all in the twelve. See **it's all in the seven**, and **…twelve.**

all is bob. See **and Bob's your uncle.**

all is forgiven. See **come back…** and **come home…**

all is rug. See **all's rug.**

all jam and Jerusalem is a slightly derogatory c.p. directed at Women's Institutes since *c.* 1925. Whereas *jam* arises from the jam-making contests, *Jerusalem* refers to Blake's 'Jerusalem' being sung at every meeting – less in piety than as a signature. A very English phrase concerning a very English institution.

Wedgwood agrees, 1977, that it may be 'slightly derogatory', but adds that it is 'interesting to note that the Women's Institutes have used it (or approved its use) as the title of a 1977 history of the movement, *Jam and Jerusalem*, by Simon Goodenough…: a bold humour that is to the credit of the W.I.'s.'

all join hands and panic! Joc. var. of **when in danger…**; see also **if in danger…**

all Lombard Street to a Brummagem six pence is a c.p., a joc. var. of **all Lombard Street to a China orange.** Meaning 'heavy odds', the original and originating … *China orange* (a piece of chinaware) has the further variants … *to ninepence* and … *to an egg-shell*; all three variants arose in C19, and all, as c. pp., are †. The ref. is to the wealth of this famous London street. The idea has a US equivalent, (*it is* or *I'll lay*) *dollars to doughnuts*, recorded by *D. Am.* for 1904 in the form *it is*…, but ob. by c. 1970, as R.C. tells me, 1977. Note, however, that *ODEP* treats *all Lombard Street to a china orange* as a proverbial saying, which, therefore, it prob. was, at least in origin, and records it for 1832; *ODEP* also records an apparently short-lived *I'll lay all Lombard Street to an egg-shell*, with date 1752. P.B.: was this last a pun, perhaps?

all mouth and trousers. 'Noisy and worthless stuff: "He's all mouth and trousers" ' (David Powis, *Signs of Crime*, 1977): the underworld and its fringes: since (?) mid-C20. Cf, **all wind and piss.** (P.B.) L.A., 1964, had noted the phrase's use on radio and TV, and E.P. that it is a euph. for *all prick and breeches*, addressed, as *you're all …*, or applied, *he's all …*, to a loud-mouthed, blustering fellow: since *c.* 1920.

all my eye (and Betty Martin), often prec. by **it's** or **that's.** 'That is utter nonsense.' The shorter form seems to have been the earlier, Goldsmith using it in 1768; yet Francis Grose, in his dictionary, shows the var. *that's my eye, Betty Martin* to have been already familiar in 1785. Grose's form became † before 1900, as did such variants as all *my eye, Betty* (Thomas Moore, 1819) and *all my eye and Tommy* (John Poole's *Hamlet Travestied*, 1811), this mysterious *Tommy* recurring, as Ernest Weekley long ago pointed out, in the phrases *like Hell and Tommy* and the earlier *play Hell and Tommy.* The predominant short form is (*that's*) *all my eye*, which recurs in, e.g., R.S. Surtees, *Hillingdon Hall; or, The Cockney Squire*, 1845; there, in chapter XVI, we read, '"The land's worked out!" says another, slopin' off in the night without payin' his rent. "That's all my eye!" exclaimed Mr Jorrocks.' Surtees uses it again in *Hawbuck Grange*, 1847.

I think that the orig. form was *all my eye!*, which later acquired the var. *my eye!:* perhaps cf. the slangy and synon. Fr. *mon oeil!* which could, indeed, have generated *all my eye*, if, in fact, the Fr. phrase preceded the English, although prob. each arose independently of the other and was created by that 'spontaneous combustion' which would account for so much that is otherwise unaccountable in English. The full *all my eye and Betty Martin* is less used in the 1970s than it was in the 1870s, but 'there's life in the old girl yet'.

Inevitably the *and Betty Martin* part of the complete phrase has caused much trouble and even more hot air: who *was* she? I suspect that she was a 'character' of the lusty London of the 1770s and that no record of her exists other than in this c.p. In *The Disagreeable Surprise: A Musical Farce*,? 1828. George Daniel makes Billy Bombast say, 'My first literary attempt was a flaming advertisement ... My next was a Satirical Poem ... I then composed the whole art and mystery of Blacking or Every Man his own Polisher; which turned out all Betty Martin ... ' and thus offers us yet another var.; and in the Earl of Glengall's *The Irish Tutor; or, New Lights: A Comic Piece*, performed in 1823 and pub'd *c*. 1830, the spurious Dr O'Toole says to his tutor, 'Hark ye, sirrah, hem – [*Aside to him*] It's all Betty Martin. I have demanded myself by brushing your coat, to *tache* you modesty.' 'Jon Bee' in his dictionary, 1823, propounded a theory silently adopted a generation later by William Camden Hotten, that *Betty Martin* derives from, and corrupts, the. L. *o(h), mihi, beate Martine* (St Martin of Tours), which, they said, occurs in a prayer that apparently doesn't exist. Slightly more probable is the theory advanced by Dr L.A. Waddell in his highly speculative book, *The Phoenician Origin of Britons, Scots, and Anglo-Saxons*, 1914; to the effect that *all my eye and Betty Martin* derives, entire, from L. *O mihi, Britomartis*, 'Oh, (bring help) to me, Britomartis', who, we are told, was the tutelary goddess of Crete and whose cult was either identical or, at the least, associated with the sun-cult of the Phoenicians – who traded with Britons for Cornish tin. Such etymologies lose sight of a basic problem: how did – how *could* – the Cockneys, among whom the phrase originated, ever come to even encounter either of these two religious and erudite L. phrases? The relationship appears wildly improbable.

Such energetic ingenuity is supererogatory, these erudite imaginings being inherently much less convincing than the theory of simple English origin. To me, anyway, *all my eye and Betty Martin!* no more than elaborates *all my eye!*; and as for Betty Martin, well! the English language, in its less formal aspects, affords many examples of mysterious characters appearing in a phrase and recorded nowhere else. In this instance, however, there was, in the (?) latter part of C18, 'an abandoned woman' named Grace, an actress, who induced a Mr Martin to marry her. She became notorious as Betty Martin: and favourite expressions of hers were *my eye!* and *all my eye*, as Charles Lee Lewis tells us in his *Memoirs*, 1805. Even that immensely erudite poet, Southey, remarked, in *The Doctor*, 1834–7, that he was 'puzzled by this expression'. (And Mr Ronald Pearsall, of Landscove, Devon, imparts *his* erudition to me, 1975.)

In South Africa, *Betsy*. (Prof. A.C. Partridge.)

E.P. later noted that in *Blackwood's Magazine*, Mar. 1824 (No. 86, p. 307) 'Bill Truck', in his entertaining naval lowerdeck serial *The Man-o'-War's Man*, has a senior petty officer shout at the seamen attending church parade, 'Can't you recollect ... that you are going to prayers? – Come, heave ahead, forward there, – D – n the fellows, they ought to walk one after another as mim and as sulky as old Betty Martin at a funeral.' Here, *mim* is a widely spread dial. term for 'primly silent, demure', while *sulky* bears the archaic sense, 'solemn'. There's a poss. semantic equation with (*as*)

demure as a whore at a christening. (This I owe to Col. Moe.) P.B.: it may be of interest that in the collected ed. of the serial, pub'd 1843 by Blackwoods, the phrase has been altered to 'as mim and orderly as old Betty Martin ... ' 'Bill Truck' (pseud., i.e. David Stewart, d. 1850) makes considerable use of the phrases *all in my eye; all in my eye and Betty; and all in my eye and Betty Martin*. The story, to which the 1843 ed. carries a foreword dated Oct. 1821, concerns lowerdeck life from the naval mutiny of 1797 to the Anglo-US War of 1812, and appears to be an authentic, thinly-fictionalised, eye-witness account. Cf the next two entries.

all my eye and my elbow! and **all my eye and my grandmother!** are London variants of **all my eye and Betty Martin**: strictly, the *grandmother* version stems from the *elbow* version. The latter is recorded by Ware for 1882, and seems to have fallen into disuse by 1920; the former is recorded in Baumann, 1887, and was ob. by 1937, † by 1970. Note also *so's your grandfather!*, which, expressing incredulity, has been current since late C19 – is still very much alive, although, by 1970, mildly ob., and has been gen. throughout England.

all my eye and Peggy Martin (– *that's*). A C20 (and earlier?) North Country var. of **all my eye and Betty Martin**. Noble, 1974, glosses it: 'Romantic nonsense, not to be believed. Long common in the north of England. There probably was a romancer named Peggy Martin.'

all my (or **me**) **own work** is a c.p. only when used figuratively – chiefly when the tone is either joc. or ironic, esp. if ironically self-deprecatory. Dating from *c*. 1920, it orig., I believe, in the drawings and paintings displayed by pavement artists. Cf **alone I did it**, which is not, of course, synon.

all night in, with the inside out is a ruefully ironic, yet humorous, Trinity House Lighthouse c.p., applied to the four-hour watch beginning at midnight. Peppitt cites J.M. Lewis, *Ceaseless Vigil*, 1970.

all on top. That's untrue!: a.c.p. of the Brit. underworld; dating from *c*. 1920. The evidence is all – but *only* – on top; in short, superficial.

all over bar (occ. **but**) **the shouting** (– *it's*). Orig. – the earliest record apparently occurs in C.J. Apperley's *The Life of a Sportsman*, 1842 – both the Brit. and the US form was (*it's*) *all over but the shouting*, but in late C19 – 20 it has predominantly been ... *bar the shouting*. As c.pp. they developed, late in C19, from the proverbial or semi-proverbial *all is over but shouting* (Apperley's version); the *bar* form occurs in Adam Lindsay Gordon's poem, *How We Beat the Favourite*, 1869, as 'The race is all over, bar shouting'. In Henry Arthur Jones, *The Manoeuvres of Jane*, 1898, near end of Act IV, there is a rare var.:

STEPHEN: Well, George, how goes it?

SIR G: All over, I think, except the shouting.

This is a particularly interesting example, for it is sometimes a genuine proverbial saying and sometimes a genuine c.p.; in C20, almost entirely a c.p.

The US form, I've been very firmly told, has always been *all over but the shouting*. Yet A.B., 1978, modifies this by stating that Americans occ. use *except*.

all over the place like a mad woman's shit. Used in Aus. to describe a state of complete untidiness or confusion. (C. Raab.) P.B.: *knitting* is sometimes politely substituted for *shit*, and I have also heard the var. *custard*: all, later C20.

all part of life's rich pattern! (– *it's* or, less often, **heigh ho!**). This is an ironically resigned, yet far from submissive, reflection upon the vicissitudes of life. 'I've heard this from more and more unlikely people over the past, say, five years' (P.B.).

Also as 'tapestry', and – perhaps the orig. quoted by Nigel Rees in BBC Radio 4 'Quote, Unquote', 18 July 1983, Arthur Marshall in his persona as games mistress, in 1930s – ... *part of life's rich pageant*. Given later impetus by Peter Sellers as Inspector Clouseau, in a film *c*. 1960.

all part of the service – it's. See **just part of** ....

all parts bearing an equal strain. All is well – 'no complaints': RN: since *c.* 1930. Derivatively, since *c.* 1945, it is also applied to oneself, or to another, lying down comfortably.

all piss and wind, with no ref. to the cat, is the Aus. version of **all wind and piss like a barber's cat,** q.v. (Neil Lovett, 1978.)

all pissed-up and nothing to show (sc. *for it*) is a working-class phrase addressed – or used in ref. to one who has spent all his wages or all his winnings on drink: since *c.* 1920. On the analogy – indeed, moulded to the shape – of **all dressed up and nowhere to go.**

all present and correct! All correct; all in order, as in Ronald Knox, *Still Dead*, 1934, ' "Is that all present and correct?" "Couldn't be better." ' It comes from the sergeant-major's phrase, used in reporting on a parade to the officer in charge.

all profit! is a C20 barbers' c.p., spoken usu. to the customer himself, when no 'dressing' is required on the hair.

all promise and no performance 'is applied to female flirts' (Petch, 1969): since *c.* 1920; by the late 1970s, ob. Cf **all show ...**

all quiet on the Potomac; all quiet in the Shipka Pass and **all quiet on the Western Front.** The first is the earliest, although decidedly not the model for the other two. It is, obviously, US: and it naturally arose during the Civil War (1861–5) from its frequent application – either by Secretary of War Cameron or by General McClellan or, as is probable, by both – to a comparatively quiet period in 1861–2 on that sector. It enraged a public that wanted action and soon caught on, esp. in joc. and often somewhat derisive irony; it remained a very gen. c.p. for the whole of a generation and even for some forty years; Berrey adjudges it to have become † by 1910. (For fuller information. see notably *D. Am.*)

In the US, *all's quiet* – but usu. *all quiet* – *on the Western Front* derives 'from the standard official phrase as issued daily by the War Department during relatively calm ... periods during ... WW1' (Berrey), but as a c.p. it was, of course, applied to periods or situations devoid of fighting or quarrelling or mere bickering, precisely as in Britain 'at home and abroad'; indeed, the US official phrase was adopted from the War Office's *communiqués*, which, even during the latter half of that war, roused the derision and ribaldry of the men fighting it instead of writing about it – it was *they* who originated the c.p., which persisted right up to WW2 and is still used. Erich Maria Remarque's *Im Westen Nichts Neues* (Berlin. 1929), admirably translated by A.H. Wheen as *All Quiet on the Western Front* and pub'd by Putnam in 1929, reinforced the popularity and still further widened the use of the phrase. In 1969, J.W.C. wrote to tell me that it was 'a real c.p., at least in this country [US], in that it is indiscriminately used, without ref. to WW1'. W.J.B. has rightly suggested, 1978, that I add a ref. to the song *All Quiet Along the Potomac Tonight*, pub'd 1864, with words by Lamar Fontaine and music by John Hill Hewett. (Source: Edward B. Marks, *They All Had Glamour*.) [P.B.: this song, made known to hearers in UK by the records, mid-C20, of the US folk-singer Burl Ives, brings out the irony of the 'all quiet': all may indeed be 'quiet' on the frontline as a whole, but still individual men are being killed by snipers or by desultory shelling.]

The c.p. *all quiet on the Western Front* owes nothing to the US *all quiet on the Potomac*: it was suggested by *all quiet in the Shipka Pass*, which, current in 1915–16, refers to – or, rather, was prompted by – Vasily Vereshchagin's bitter cartoons of a Russian soldier being gradually, ineluctably, buried in falling snow during the Russo-Turkish War of 1877–8; this is a pass through the Balkan Mountains and was the scene of exceptionally bloody fighting; and Vereshchagin's paintings acquired a just fame far beyond Russia. That fame led to a revival of interest in Vereshchagin's war paintings and cartoons, an interest culminating in the journalistic, hence also a brief military, c.p., *all quiet in the Shipka Pass*. (I myself never heard it during WW1, either on Gallipoli or in Egypt or on the Western Front.)

all right. See: fuck you, Jack; sex is; she's all; this is a bit; this is all; what's the matter with father; and:

all right, already! 'Enough!, shut up!, stop!: Jewish' (Ashley): US; and Brit., where often used joc. by non-Jews, with a mock-Jewish accent: later C20.

all right, all right, as in Dorothy L. Sayers, *Murder Must Advertise*, 1933, ' "She's a smart jane, all right, all right" ', is an intensive tag that may have come to UK from Can., for it appears in John Sandilands, *Western Canadian Dictionary and Phrase-Book*, 2nd ed., 1913, as in, e.g., 'I think I can hold down this job all right, all right.' How long it had existed in Can. (not only in the West, I surmise), I don't profess to know; perhaps as early as *c.* 1880.

all right! Don't pipe it! 'Addressed to a man who speaks too loud, in the manner of a Tannoy [public-address system], for all to hear when *not* all should hear' (Granville, 1970): RN lowerdeck: since *c.* 1930.

all right for some! (– *it's*). 'Some people have all the luck. A c.p. of disgruntlement by one of the luckless' (Granville, 1969): C20, P.B.: but the disgruntlement thus expressed is quite often joc. Cf:

all right for you is ironically addressed to those who are worse off than oneself: the fighting Services': since *c.* 1940. J.W.C., 1977, adds this modification: 'In US, used only – and paradoxically – as an expression of resentment of a slight or refused favor or an unfair advantage taken; it often carries the subaudition of "We aren't friends any more" or "I'll get even with you"; mainly children's; older than my memory [say, 1908], and still current (among children seriously, among adults humorously).' This interpretation is confirmed by R.C. P.B.: in Brit. usage it may be simply a more personalised version of the prec., as in 'It's all right for *you* [sc. to laugh, etc.]'

all right, it's all wrong. 'Heard on and off' (Petch, 1969): Brit.: since *c.* 1955. But the US form has *but all right!* added: and it is glossed thus by A.B., 1978: 'It indicates frustration ... when one has to accept something he doesn't altogether like, but which he sees as acceptable in a practical, or a political way to carry out some plan or project. Hughes Rudd, CBS Morning News Show, often used it' – WW2 onwards – and he has had a very distinguished career as a newsman.

all right on the night (that is, on the first night – the opening night), an actors' c.p., applied to a bad – esp. a very bad – dress rehearsal, dates from *c.* 1870, as its occurrence in Kipling's *Stalky & Co.*, pub'd 1899 but referring to his own schooldays, virtually proves (R.C.; R.S.; Granville). It has, since *c.* 1920, gained a wider acceptance – an application, in the larger world, to small things going wrong, but optimistically hoped to go right – to judge by its extension and allusiveness in Nichol Fleming's *Hush*, 1971, 'I've always found the soft sell almost irresistible .... "It'll be all right on the night," I said.' This, perhaps the most famous of all theatrical c.pp., shortens *it will all come right on the night*, which has a var. *it will be all right on the night*.

all right up to now. All is well – so far: 1878 – *c.* 1915: orig., and always, mostly feminine. 'Used by Herbert Campbell ... in Covent Garden Theatre Pantomime, 1878', as Ware, himself a writer of light comedies, tells us; he adds that it derives from '*enceinte* women making this remark as to their condition'; the phrase became used also in other circumstances.

all right – you did hear a seal bark indicates a resigned, long-suffering, vocal agreement (and mental disagreement) with someone who insists that something odd is indeed happening: US: since *c.* 1950. It was occasioned by James Thurber's famous caption and sketch (of a seal leaning over the headboard of a bed and barking as it looks down at a married couple, the woman insistent and the man sceptical), appearing orig. in the *New Yorker* and reprinted in one of his inimitable collections of sketches. R.C. comments, 1977, 'Never common, I think, and now dead.' P.B.: the collection was titled *The Seal in the Bedroom*, and the caption in full ran 'All Right, Have

It Your Way – You Heard a Seal Bark'. I'm pretty sure that this was always used as a quot'n from a recognised source, rather than qualifying as a c.p.

all round my hat! was a derisive, orig. and always predominantly Cockney, retort, connoting 'What nonsense you're talking': approx. *c.* 1834–90. Perhaps from the broadside ballad, 'All Round my Hat I Wears a Green Willow'. A derivative sense appears in *spicy as all round my hat*, a slangy expression meaning 'sensational' and occurring in *Punch*, 1882.

That comic song, written by John Hansett, with music by John Valentine, was – according to the British Museum Library's *Modern Music Catalogue* – first sung in 1834; it was included in *The Franklin Square Song Collection*, 8 parts, 1881–91, pub'd in New York.

Mackay noted the c.p. in his long essay. The phrase and the song became so popular that George Dibdin Pitt's 'domestic drama', *Susan Hopley; or, The Vicissitudes of a Servant Girl*, 1841, III, ii, ends with the stage directions: '*Music . . . Dicky sings "All Round My Hat" and leads the Donkey off.*' And in R.S. Surtees, *Handley Cross*, 1854, vol. II, the chapter titled 'The Stud Sale', we find:

'Well done!' exclaimed Mr Jorrocks, patting the orator's back.

'Keep the tambourine a rowlin'!' growled Pigg, turning his quid, and patting the horse's head.

'All round my' at!' squeaked Benjamin in the crowd.

Cf. **queer as Dick's hatband**, q.v.

all round St Paul's, not forgetting the trunkmaker's daughter was a book-world c.p. used in late C18–early 19 and applied to unsalable books. The *OED* quoted *The Globe* of 1 July 1890: 'By the trunkmaker was understood . . . the depository for unsalable books.' At that period – and, indeed, until 'the London blitz' of 1940–1 – the district around St Paul's was famous for its bookshops and its book-publishers.

all serene!, short for *it's all serene* (quiet, safe, favourable), is enshrined in Dickens's comment, 1853: 'An audience will sit in a theatre and listen to a string of brilliant witticisms, with perfect immobility; but let some fellow . . . roar out "It's all serene", or "Catch 'em alive, oh!" (this last is sure to take), pit, boxes, and gallery roar with laughter.' M. has the entry: '**Serene** (Eng.). "all serene", all right; a phrase taken from a comic song and used, when first introduced, on all occasions. Now it is seldom heard.' That sharp observer of current speech, R.S. Surtees, in *Plain or Ringlets*, 1860, chapter LV, writes, 'On this auspicious day, however, it was "all serene" as old Saddlebags said.' It was, in England, still being used right up to WW2.

all shit and biscuits, like the bottom of a baby's pram. Very messy and untidy: domestic. (Edwin Haines to P.B., 1962, with var. *like a crow's nest, all shit and twigs.*) Cf *all crumbs* at **all wind . . .**

all shit or all shine with them. See **all honey . . .**

all show and no go (– **he's** or **she's**). This C20 US c.p. is 'said of someone who puts on airs with promise of "great expectations" but who fails entirely or falls woefully short of the goal. [It is] usually a sexual reference to one who *teases* but not *pleases*, or to a racehorse that looks good but performs badly' (A.B., 1978). Cf **all promise . . .**

all singing, all dancing has, since *c.* 1970, been 'applied to machines, systems, etc., meaning that they have every possible elaboration attached. Common in computer circles'. Complementary is *bells and whistles*, those elaborations, additions, modifications, which make the systems and machines, e.g. computers, go all singing and dancing. (Playfair, 1977.) P.B.: *Listener*, 22 Feb. 1979, applied the term to a new battle tank.

[all Sir Garnet! and **all Sirgarneo!** All right! Everything is correct and in good order: since *c.* 1885, the former; since *c.* 1895, the latter, on the analogy of such locutions as *all aliveo*; both slightly ob. by 1915, very much so by 1935, and † by 1940. From *c.* 1890 there existed the Cockney var. *all Sir Garny*, as in Edwin Pugh, *Harry the Cockney*, 1912. From the military fame of Sir Garnet (later Viscount) Wolseley (1833–1923) – almost as famous in his day as Lord Roberts ('Bobs') was in his – who served both actively and brilliantly from 1852–85. He did much

to improve the lot of the Other Ranks, who often debased *Sir Garnet* to *Sirgarneo*, whence *Sigarneo*, whence *Sigarno*. In the debased forms it was quite common among Commonwealth troops. (B & P.) But I'd say that none of them is a true c.p.]

all smoke, gammon and spinach (occ. **pickles**). All nonsense: *c.* 1870–1900. An elab. of the slangy *gammon and spinach* (used by, e.g., Dickens in 1849), nonsense, humbug, itself an elab. of *gammon*, nonsense.

all systems go, 'literally the statement of readiness for launching manned and unmanned rocket systems for space exploration from Cape Canaveral, esp. for the moon landings in the late 1960s and early 1970s was popularized through worldwide television coverage. The words were taken up in Britain [*c.* 1970] and America [*c.* 1969] as a c.p. for preparedness for any endeavour, often used humorously' (Noble, 1974). *DCCU*, independently in 1971 after appearing, 1970, in some editions of Webster, with this example, 'It's *all systems go* here, so let's take off'.

[all talk and no cider. 'That's a great deal of talk and no results' (Berrey, 1942): US: C20; by 1970, ob., and by 1975 †, as Col. Moe tells me, 1975. Later, however, he adds that the phrase is 'of long standing, but still heard occasionally', and quotes from *Salmagundi*, I, 7 (4 April 1807) – where Washington Irving, in 'Letter from Mustapha Rub-a-dub Keli Khan', has this passage:

Now after all it is an even chance that the subject of this prodigious arguing, quarrelling and talking is an affair of no importance and ends entirely in smoke. May it not then be said, the whole nation have been talking to no purpose? The people, in fact, seem to be somewhat conscious of this propensity to talk, by which they are characterized, and have a favourite proverb on the subject, viz. 'all talk and no cider'.

In short, all talk and no cider should perhaps be classified, not as c.p. but as a proverbial saying, apparently from late, maybe mid, C18. To me it sounds like a mislaid aphorism coined by that master of aphorism, Benjamin Franklin (1706–90) – as in his *Poor Richard's Almanack*, 1732–57. Clearly reminiscent is Artemus Ward's 'What we want is more cider and less talk'. Nevertheless, I have included the phrase in deference to several US friends whose opinion is never to be ignored.]

[all talk and no pussy makes Jack a dull boy puns on the old Brit. and US proverb *all work and no play makes Jack a dull boy*, and is a potential c.p. that has not, I think, quite 'made the grade'. It occurs in John Dos Passos, *Chosen Country*, 1951. Here *pussy* is used in the slang sense, the outward appearance, esp. the pubic hair, of the female genitals, hence woman as sex object, hence copulation.]

all that meat and no potatoes is a US, derivatively a Can., c.p., certainly current since the 1940s. 'As a rude teenager, I would have applied this to any flabby, eunuch-like fatty . . . ; since then, I've heard it applied to ineffective, overweight politicians, with an intellectual, rather than a sexual, insult intended' (Hugh Quetton, 1978). It has a 'meaning far from precise, but approximately "too much of a good thing"—as an all-meat meal would indeed be: US, from? 1920s, fortified by a popular song of the 1940s with that title and refrain. Extinct, I would say, for nigh on 20 years' (R.C., 1978). 'I encountered it first many years ago, used by a black jazz musician to express admiration for a rather impressive *décolletage*. I have not noticed it attaining any wide use in Canada' (Priestley, 1978).

all that the name implies is a 'c.p., which originated in a chance expression used during the *cause célèbre* of the Rev. Henry Ward Beecher' (Farmer): US: *c.* 1875–90. The trial took place in 1875; Beecher died in 1889.

all that's between me and prostitution (occ. **the streets**, with or without introductory **that's**). A 'rueful cry on [one's] finding practically nothing in one's purse or pocket': later C20. 'I've heard it only from males' (P.B., 1976); and I've heard it only from females. Which, once again, goes to show how careful one should be to eschew dogmatism. Cf **that's all I have . . .**

9

all the better for seeing you! is the cheerfully courteous answer to 'How *are* you?': late C19–20. Contrast **none the better** . . .

all the jails must be empty tonight or, less often, **today**. 'Apropos at seeing a large, rather diversified group of people with whom one is closely or relatively familiar. Rather a club-type expression, I suppose, and usually a friendly one. I can't say that I've ever seen it written down. It may have arisen during early Prohibition days, 1919–33, in relation to an exceptionally large gathering at a "speakeasy" [illicit tavern]—or at several "speakeasies" on any given night' (A.B., 1978): US.

all the same in a hundred years. See **it'll all be the same** . . .

all the traffic will bear (– that's). Lit., it relates to fares and freights; only fig. is it a c.p., meaning that the situation, whether financial or other, precludes anything more. Orig. – ? *c.* 1945 – US, it was adopted *c.* 1948 in Can. and *c.* 1955 in UK. It is, Leechman tells me, said to derive from a US magnate's cynicism. R.C., 1977, comments that in its lit. meaning, it was not, of course, a c.p.; it seems to have become one in or very soon after 1906, when certain railroad abuses were abolished in USA.

all there and a ha'p'orth over was, *c.* 1870–1914, the superlative of *all there* used as a term of approval. M.

all there but the most of you! was a low, raffish c.p. applied (as if you hadn't guessed!) to copulation: mid C19–20 – but by *c.* 1950, †.

all things (occ. **everything**) **to all men, and nothing to one man** is aimed at prostitutes or at 'enthusiastic amateurs' or at promiscuous girls or women in general. I first heard it in 1940 – and rather think it didn't much precede that date.

all tits and teeth. (Of a woman) having protrusive breasts and large teeth: a low c.p. of C20. Hence, a still low but predominantly Cockney c.p., dating from *c.* 1910 and applied to a woman wearing an insincere smile and exhibiting a notable skill in displaying the amplitude of her bosom (*il y a du monde au balcon*). An alert and erudite friend, writing to me in 1967, recalled that he had sometimes heard this phrase elab. to ' " . . . like a third-row chorus girl", i.e. one who can neither sing nor dance, and depends upon the display of her exceptional physique to keep her on the stage'. P.B.: cf. *all bum and bustle*, which epitomises equally well another type of woman: the middle-aged or elderly bustling and bossy sort.

all together like Brown's (or **Browne's**) **cows** (– we're). We're alone: an Anglo-Irish c.p. of late C19–20. This fellow Brown – a creature merely of anecdotal tradition, not a character in history–possessed only one cow. Clearly of rural, prob. of rustic, origin. (Owed to the late Frank Shaw, the authority on Scouse.)

all together: one at a time! A RN Petty Officers' 'exasperated exhortation to a puffing boat's crew unable to keep stroke' (Peppitt, 1977): from 1920 at latest, and prob. since late C19.

all up. A US railroadmen's c.p. of C20; used by 'a train crew that has completed its work before quitting time' (Ramon F. Adams, *The Language of the Railroader*, 1977, an engaging work pub'd by the University of Oklahoma Press, by whose generous permission I quote the eight c.pp. I've there encountered).

all up in here. Synon. with *where it's at*: American Negro: since 1960 at latest. *The Third Ear*, 1971.

all very large and fine! indicates either ironic approval or incredulity or even derision: 1886, from 'the refrain of a song sung by Mr Herbert Campbell' (Ware) and much in vogue for a couple of years; by 1935, slightly ob., and by 1950 †, its place having been taken by *all very fine and large*, usu. prec, by *it's* or *that's*.

all we want is the facts, ma'am (, **just the facts**)! 'Jack Webb as Joe Friday, the fast-talking [monotonous-voiced] cop in the American TV series *Dragnet* (1951–8, 1967–9)' (*VIBS*). Occ. rendered as *just give me the facts, ma'am; all I wants is the facts.*

all white and spiteful. See **white and spiteful.**

all wind and piss like a barber's cat is contemptuous of a man given to much talk, esp. to much boasting, and little, if any, performance: prob. since *c.* 1800, for it clearly derives from the semi-proverbial C18–19 *like the barber's cat, all wind and piss.* Cf also the C20 slang phrase, *pissing like the barber's cat*, applied to prolific output – which I owe (1975) to Mr C. A. Worth. The phrase has naturally generated a var. or two, and at least one shortening; as in *like a barber's cat, all wind and no water*, current in the C20 MN and cited in *Seamen and the Sea*, ed. R. Hope, 1965, and as in *all wind and no piss*, current in both RN and MN, meaning 'all talk, no action' – current since the late 1940s, if not earlier (Peppitt, 1977). And then there's the domestic *all wind and piss like the bottom of a baby's pram*, which itself has the var., *all crumbs and piss . . .* , both dating from early C20 (Eric Townley, 1978). P.B.: but the last is a different sense: it means messily untidy; see also **all shit** . . . With *all wind . . .* Cf **all mouth . . .** , q.v.; J.B. Smith, Bath, draws attention to the Cumbrian dial. *all wind and woo like a burnywind's* [=smith's] *bellows* (*EDD*, at *wind*).

all wrapped up and tied with (or **in**) **blue ribbon** means that everything has been neatly and cosily settled: US: since *c.* 1965, or perhaps a decade earlier. In Michael Wolfe's novel, *Man on a String*, 1973, thus: 'Anyway it was his problem. So there it was, all wrapped up and tied in blue ribbon' (Moe, 1976). P.B.: there was, late 1940s, a popular song with the refrain 'Put (or wrap?) it in a box, tie it with a ribbon, and throw it in the deep blue sea', with may have derived from– or perhaps started – this phrase.

all's rug (or **all rug** or **it's all rug**). 'It's all Rug, c. [i.e., cant]. The Game is secured' (B.E., Gent, 1698) – all is safe: late C17–mid 19. Cf both the proverbial *snug as a bug in a rug* and:

all's snug! All is safe: an underworld c.p. of C18–mid 19. A var. of prec. See *U* for a more detailed treatment.

alley. See: right up; set 'em up.

alley-marble. See: just my a.

alligator. See: see you later.

almond. See: parrot.

aloft. See: come aloft.

alone. See: I want to be; let him a.; let me a.; we are not a.; and:

alone I did it is both Brit. and US. My only early record of this latish C19–20 c.p. occurs in Act I of Alfred Sutro's *The Fascinating Mr Vanderbildt*, performed and pub'd in 1906:

VANDERBILDT: Your doing, of course?

CLARICE: Alone I did it.

As Anthony Burgess pointed out in *TLS*, 26 Aug. 1977, *alone I did it* had a prototype: 'It was Coriolanus who first said *Alone I did it* (V, v, 114).' That passage did not, at that time, create a c.p.; yet a latish C19 revival of the Shakespearian tragedy so titled prob. started it on its c.p. course. By 1940 ob.; by 1970 almost †, but not yet, 1978, entirely so. P.B.: there is also the deliberately illiterate var. *alone I done it.* Cf. the rather different **all my own work.**

along. See: get along.

Alphonse. See: after you.

already. See: all right; it's a living.

[although (or **though**) **I say it who** (occ, **that**) **shouldn't,** with orig. illiterate, but soon deliberately joc., var. **(al)though I says it as shouldn't.** A borderline case, which, after much thought, I adjudge to be not a c.p. but a hackneyed quot'n, going at least as far back, as *though I say it that should not say it* (often, in C19–20, . . . *that shouldn't*) in Beaumont and Fletcher's *Wit at Several Weapons*, II, ii.]

always be nice to people on your way up: you may meet them (**again**) **on your way down**; but perhaps more often without *always*. I did not become conscious of this as a c.p. – for several years I had regarded it as merely a cynical epigram – until mid-1975: and then, within a month, I read John Braine's exemplarily intelligent, witty, genuinely exciting novel of espionage, *The Pious Agent*, 1975. There, a senior official of the KGB said to an up-and-coming young agent, 'And, as the saying goes, always be nice to people on your way up. You may meet them again on your way down.' Cf this from 'Number Ten' in John Osborne's *The Entertainer* (prod. and pub'd in 1957), where Billy, the old-timer, says: 'Well, Eddie's still up there all right. He's still up there. (To Jean.) I always used to say to him, we all used to say: "Eddie, always be good" ', etc. Occ. either *good* or *kind* has been substituted for *nice*.

It seems, however, that it was orig. US: Bartlett attributes it (with a cautionary 'also attributed to Jimmy Durante', who was born in 1893) to Wilson Mizner, in the form *be nice to people on your way up because you'll meet 'em on your way* down. Ashley, 1982, supplies the US var. *don't be nasty to people*... See also **as you go up...**

always in trouble, like a Drury Lane whore is a late C19–20 phrase reprehending one who wallows in self-pity, also one who deplores a series of personal misfortunes. Prostitutes frequenting this area have always tended to dramatize their troubles – or so the legend goes.

always merry and bright! 'Alfred Lester, music-hall star – who was always lugubrious, needless to say' (*VIBS*). P.B.: earlier C20; but Lester was quoting: see **cheer up, cully...**

always read the small print!, with emphasis on both *always* and *small*. In business and legal matters, make damn' sure you know what you're letting yourself in for: since *c.* 1955. This print is so small that you endanger your eyesight if you do read it carefully; if you don't read it, you merely risk bankruptcy.

am I boring you? See **excuse my wart!**

am I burned up! Am I angry! – or irritated! – or resentful! A US c.p. dating since *c.* 1920. (Berrey.) Cf:

am I hurting you? See **you're kneeling...**

am I insulated! and **am I irrigated!** Am I insulted – am I irritated! Both of these US c.pp., recorded by Berrey, were shortlived: say 1930–45. Clearly intentional puns, not malapropisms. But the first lingered: A.B. writes, 1978, 'I've heard it, mid 1950s, thus: "I represent that remark – it insulates me"; I *think* the American comedian Jimmy Durante used it on occasion.' Cf **I resemble that remark.**

am I is or am I ain't?, am I or am I not?; **are we is or are we ain't?**, are we or aren't we? The former is a derivative of **is you is or is you ain't?**, q.v.

amazed. See: **I was a.**

ambition. See: **no ambition.**

ambulance. See: **get the a.**

American. See: **great American; speak all.**

AMERICAN BORDERLINERS: HISTORICAL. Of the various candidates, three stand out from the rest:
1. **damn the torpedoes – full steam ahead!;**
2. **don't fire till you see the whites of their eyes;**
3. **you may fire when you are ready, Gridley.**

The first is listed in, e.g., Burton Stevenson's *Book of Quotations* as **damn the torpedoes!** and attributed to David Glasgow Farragut, at the Battle of Mobile Bay on 5 Aug. 1864. As a c.p., from *c.* 1880, it = damn it all, we'll take the risk! R.C. charitably reminds me that, 'to give more point to this quotation, one should be aware that the "torpedoes" ...were what we now call "mines".'

The second was the command issued by the US commander at the Battle of Bunker Hill on 17 June 1775. Being the only one of the three to have attained British currency, this has been accorded an individual entry.

The third is, in *BQ*, attributed to Admiral George Dewey as having been said to the Captain of his flagship at the Battle of Manila on 1 May 1898. (It occurs in Dewey's *Autobiography* at p. 214.)

Of the trio, J.W.C., 1968, says that he thinks they qualify as c.pp. 'When they are used, they are almost always used *without* reference to the original situation. But I will agree that, if there is a clear and valuable distinction between famous quotation, cliché, and catch phrase, they may be the

first or the second rather than the third.' I'd say that *damn the torpedoes* and *you may fire when you are ready, Gridley* are both famous quot'n and cliché and that *don't fire till you see the whites of their eyes* is both quot'n and c.p., but in C20 predominantly the latter.

AMERICAN POLITICAL SLOGANS JUST FAILING TO MAKE THE GRADE Dr Joseph T. Shipley, in a letter, 1974, writes thus pertinently and convincingly:

remember the Alamo: after the garrison was wiped out, became the battle cry of General Houston in Mexico, 1836, when Texas was annexed to the US.

remember the Maine: after the battleship was attacked in Havana Harbor in 1896, the battle cry for the war against Spain.

remember Pearl Harbor: after the airplane strike of 7 December 1941, the battle-cry rallying our country against Japan.

All of these seem to me to be propaganda slogans, rather than catch phrases.

I agree, but include them, nonetheless.

AMERICAN BORDERLINES: THE WEST

In Ramon F. Adams, *Western Words: A Dictionary*, 1944, rev. ed. 1968, I notice in the introduction such phrases as *a heart in his brisket as big as a saddle blanket, so drunk he couldn't hit the ground with his hat in three throws, raised hell and put a chunk under it, he'd fight you till hell freezes over and then skate with you on the ice.* The solid core of the last, the orig. c.p., is clearly **till hell freezes over**, q.v.; likewise, the third is a fanciful elab. of the coll. **raise hell.** Genuine c. pp. from this delightful book (which I quote with the very generous permission of the University of Oklahoma Press) will be found elsewhere in these pages.

AMERICAN RESPONSES TO STUPID QUESTIONS

Examples of such phrases inevitably occur elsewhere in the dictionary. But the ensuing contribution from a young American deserves to be quoted. 'In response to what is considered a stupid question I've often heard nonsense retorts such as the following from people throughout the country:

do chickens have lips?

can snakes do push-ups?

do frogs have water-tight ass-holes?

is the Pope Catholic?

does a bear shit in the woods?

These last two phrases are frequently used together in the variant *is a bear Catholic—does the Pope shit in the woods?*" (George A. Krzymowski, a medical student, New Orleans, 1978). I had heard *is the Pope Catholic?*, which has had some currency in UK since *c.* 1950 at latest. The others sound not only very American, but characteristically undergraduate. Nevertheless, Simon Levene, 1979, vouches for the adoption in UK of *is the Pope Catholic?* and *does a bear shit in the woods?*

ammunition, See: **praise.**

amuse yourself: don't mind me! Meaning 'Have your fun!' it was orig. US, mostly teenagers' and students' of the early 1920s, as recorded by McKnight; adopted in UK *c.* 1924, but by 1960 virtually †. R.C. notes, 1977, 'the curtailed version, *don't mind me*, clearly implies "you're making a nuisance of yourself!" P.B.: but in Brit., I think, it is the sarcastic fling of a youngster expressing hurt at being left out of some game or enterprise.

amused. See: **we are not a.**

and a double helping too. See **double helping.**

and a merry Christmas to you too! An ironic c.p., dating since *c.* 1930, and virtually synon. with 'The same to you – with knobs on!' (Petch, 1969.) P.B.: but it is also sometimes used in the sense of 'Thank you for nothing!', i.e. you haven't helped me one bit by what you have just done.

and all like that. A var, of **and like that.**

and all that (i.e., and all such things) was SE until 1929, when Robert Graves changed all that in his very distinguished war book, *Goodbye to All That*. [E.P. la‌er reconsidered thus:] I have come to think that, since WW2, the phrase has been gradually reverting to its status as an ordinary free-and-easy example of good coll. Eng., and that it had completed the cycle by 1970. The influence of Robert Graves's title had been reinforced by that of W.C. Sellar & R.J. Yeatman's skit on English history, *1066 and All That*, which appeared in 1930. Cf. **ten sixty-six** ...

and all that jazz. And all that sort of thing; 'and all the rest concerning the subject under discussion, as in "Sex and all that jazz". 1960 plus' (Granville, in a letter 1969). Adopted in UK from the US, perhaps via Can.; by W & F recorded in a quot'n from a newspaper article of 16 Feb. 1958, but already current a year or two earlier. In US, it bore – as indeed it came, in UK, to bear – the further sense 'and all that nonsense'.

[**and away we go!** This has been claimed as a US c.p. Yet the general concensus of opinion is that it isn't a genuine c.p. at all. I have gone to considerable trouble to find out. It formed an exit line of 'the American vaudeville, nightclub, radio, movie and TV comic Jackie Gleason [in] his first comedy-variety series on television in the early 1950s' – as that esteemed critic, Maurice Dolbier, wrote to me in 1978. Cf. **how sweet it is**, q.v. P.B.: with the accent heavily on *way*, the phrase has had some currency in UK.]

and Bob's your uncle! And all will be well; all will be perfect: since c. 1890. 'You go and ask for the job – and he remembers your name – and Bob's your uncle.' Aus. as well as Brit., a fairly late example occurring in Michael Gilbert's 'Modus Operandi', a story in the collection entitled *Stay of Execution*, 1971, and an earlier in John Arden's *When Is a Door Not a Door?*, prod. 1958, pub'd 1967. The origin remains a mystery; just poss. it was prompted by the cant (then low-slang) phrase, *all is bob*, 'all is safe'. Folk-etymologically, the origin is said to lie in the open and unashamed nepotism practised by some British premier or other famous politician, as the late Frank Shaw reminded me late in 1968. An occ. C20 elab. is to add *and Mary Cook's your aunt*, to which L.A. adds, 1976, the var. *and Fanny's your aunt*, which, he says, was made simply because of an association with *fanny*, the female pudend, esp. among raffish adolescent males.

P.B.: in 1979, Mrs Ursula Roberts wrote from Hong Kong, drawing my attention to the following in P. Brendon, *Eminent Edwardians*, 1979: 'When, in 1887, Balfour was unexpectedly promoted to the vital frontline post of Chief Secretary for Ireland by his uncle Robert, Lord Salisbury (a stroke of nepotism that inspired the catch-phrase "Bob's your uncle"), Parnell's supporters desired him as "the scented popinjay" ...

and call it 'it', Let's say the job is done, as in 'I'll just take the duster round the room, and call it "it" ' (Granville, 1969): mostly domestic: since c. 1950.

and did he marry poor blind Nell? An Aus. c.p. dating from c. 1910 or perhaps a little earlier. I cannot – nor should I try to – do better than to quote my pen-friend Barry Prentice:
A rhetorical question asked about anything improbable. Also as a euphemism for *like fucking hell*. Ex the saga of *Poor Blind Nell*. (Cf *Ballocky Bill the Sailor*, *The Bastard from the Bush*, etc.) As in 'and did he marry ... ?' – 'He did! – (*softly*) Like fuckin(g) hell!' *Poor Blind Nell* itself is used to describe any simple girl who is over-trusting where men are concerned.

and don't you forget it! – *and* being often omitted. A c.p. orig. (– 1888) US; adopted c. 1890. After being admonitory, it became an almost pointless intensive. The expression so infuriated John Farmer that, in 1889, he inveighed thus: 'One of the popular catch-phrases which every now and then seize hold of the popular taste (or want of taste) and run their course like wildfire through all the large centres of population. They convey no special idea, rational or irrational, and can only be described as utterly senseless and vulgar.' Vulgar

they often are: only rarely are they senseless, for although the meaning is often imprecise, the general purport is usually very clear indeed. Berrey, 1942, classifies it as a c.p. of affirmation. R.C. adds, 1977, 'generally implies that "it" is an unpleasant but unforgettable fact – e.g., "*I'm* the boss around here, and don't you forget it!" ' In UK, *either* is often tacked on; in the US, *too* (A.B., 1978).

and God help those who are caught helping themselves! A witty Aus. comment on the cliché-proverb 'God helps those who help themselves'. I first heard it c. 1913, and it was already common usage.

and he didn't! is a tailors' c.p., referring to – or implying – a discreditable action: c. 1870 – 1920.

and her mother came too. In his *Popular Music of the 20's*, 1976, Ronald Pearsall writes, 'A to Z, at the Prince of Wales [in London] starred Gertrude Lawrence and Jack Buchanan, produced a first-rate song in "And her mother came too" with music by Ivor Novello, and ran for 433 performances' in the early 1920s. It caught on as a c.p., which itself ran on until c. 1939 and then lingered for a decade.

and his name is mud! An exclamatory c.p., commenting on a foolish speech in the House of Commons or on one who has been heavily defeated or disgraced: since c. 1815. In C20 the meaning is weaker: merely 'he has been discredited; he is out of favour with, e.g., a woman'. Also *my name is mud* and *is my name mud*, with *is* emphasised, 'mostly because of some blunder' (A.B., 1978). Moreover, in some parts of the US, it means 'He faces ruin or even death'. The association with the Dr Mudd who set W.J. Booth's leg after that assassin of Lincoln had escaped from Ford's Theatre, and who was unfairly tried as an accessory after the fact, is folk-etymology. Cf the folk-etym. recorded at **break a leg**. (J.W.C., 1978.)

and how! indicates intensive emphasis of what one has just said or intensive agreement with what someone else has just said: orig. US (Berrey), dating from c. 1925 and prob. translating the *e come!* of the very large Italian population; adopted in UK by 1935 at latest: Frank Shaw, 1969, says that it came from early US 'talkies' and had very much of a vogue in the UK during the 1930s, the vogue, by the way, lasting until at least 1945 and the usage still (1975) fairly active; it was moreover, recorded by EP in *A Dictionary of Clichés*, 1940. In Gelett Burgess, *Two O'Clock Courage*, 1934: 'I said: "But I'm afraid you're ill!" – "*And how!*" she said dreamily. "Ain't I got a right to be if I want to, mister?" Her eyes didn't even open.'
Clarence B. Kelland, *Speak Easily*, c. 1935:
'Is a drinking-song essential?' I asked.
'And how!' said Mr Greb.
The phrase recurs in Kelland's *Dreamland*, 1938. An early English example occurs in Maurice Lincoln's witty novel, *Oh! Definitely*, 1933; and in Alec Waugh's *Wheels within Wheels*, 1933, a young American exclaims: 'Oh boy, if you could see the look in my mother's face at times! She thinks she's living in a fairy tale. And as for that girl, oh boy and how! You should just see her!' Cf:

and I don't mean maybe! (or occ. ... **perhaps!**) – with *and* often omitted. Berrey, 1942, records both as Americanisms: and Americanisms they remained. They seem to have arisen c. 1920. Benny Green states that the phrase 'was established by the popular song of 1922, "Yes, Sir, That's My Baby", second line, "No sir, don't mean maybe".' And Fain gives the composers of the song as Walter Donaldson and Gus Kahn.

and like it! 'A naval expression anticipating a grouse and added to any instruction for an awkward and unwanted job' (H & P); it prob. arose during WW1. P.B.: by mid–C20 it had spread beyond the RN to the other Services; I recall my ex Gunner officer father saying, e.g. 'So they don't want to fix it? Well, they can jolly well get on with it – and like it!' Cf **away you go, laughing!**

and like that. 'The summarized continuation, or indication of a continued series, has long been a staple of kids' talk. *Etcetera etcetera* was followed by *blah-blah-blah*, and more recently by *and all that stuff* or *and like that*' (Willian Safire, 'Y'know What I'm Saying?' in *The New York Times Magazine*, 23 July 1978): since *c.* 1976(?) P.B.: *and all like that* is another version. I have also heard, *c.* 1980, *and and and*, and among Brit. Army signallers, the vocalised morse *dee-dah dee-dah dee-dah*. Cf **and all that jazz.**

and little Audrey laughed and laughed and laughed. See **little Audrey…**

and no error! See **and no mistake!**

and no flies. And no doubt about it all: a c.p. tag of the lower and lower-middle classes of *c.* 1835–70. (Mayhew, 1851.) No flies are allowed to settle on it and thus obscure the patent truth. See also **no flies…**

and no kidding! I mean it. An extension of **no kidding!**, q.v. Berrey.

and no mistake, dating from *c.* 1810 (*(OED* records it for 1818) and meaning 'undoubtedly', has generated the much later, rather less used, *and no error* (recorded by Baumann): very gen. until *c.* 1920, but not yet (1976) †. Both of these phrases were adopted in the US: M records them in 1891 and illuminatingly adds, ' "Don't you make no error" is the ungrammatical method of asserting that what has been said is a fact.' Berrey notes *and no mistake* as an 'expression of affirmation'.

and no mogue? A tailors' c.p., implying slight incredulity, 'That's true?': since *c.* 1880. Something of a mystery, *mogue* perhaps derives from Fr. *moquerie* but more prob. derives from gypsies' and Ger. underworld *mogeln*, to cheat, reaching into England by way of Yiddish.

and no whistle is another tailors' c.p., implying that the speaker is, in the, fact, although not in appearance, referring to himself: *c.* 1860–1900.

and not a bone in the truck imputes time-wasting during hours of work, as in 'Ten o'clock – and not a bone in the truck' (loading hasn't even been started): mostly in factories and mostly Aus.: C20. Cf **eleven o'clock…**, q.v.

and now for something completely different. 'Originated with the BBC TV show *Monty Python's Flying Circus*, and satirised the news programme introducers' habit of using the phrase to link two dissimilar news (or magazine programme) items. Now so well known that no radio man can possibly use it' (Derek Parker, 1977). The *Monty Python* series was first broadcast in 1969.

and once more, for the gods! 'Addressed to someone who sneezes (or, more rarely, breaks wind) several times. The allusion I take to be theatrical' (Keith Sayers, 1984). P.B.: but cf the aversion of bad luck in the similar use of **bless you!**, supposed to refer back to the days when a sneeze was a symptom of the onset of the plague. (P.B.)

and one for the road. See **one for the road.**

[**and so he died** and **and then she died** are Restoration-drama tags verging on c. pp.; but only verging. See Dryden's plays in Montague Summers's edn at p. 419]

and so she prayed me to tell ye (with slight variations) is an almost meaningless c.p. originating in Restoration comedy – for instance, in Duffet's burlesque, *The Mock Tempest*, 1675.

and so to bed! is both a famous quot'n from Pepys's *Diary* (1659 onwards) and a c.p. since 1926, when James Bernard Fagan (1873–1933) had his very successful comedy, *And So to Bed*, played on the London stage; when pub'd in 1927, it bore the sub-title 'An Adventure with Pepys'.

But, as Vernon Noble has kindly reminded me, 1974, it had been becoming a c.p. for perhaps seventy years before the play established it as one: '*The Diary of Samuel Pepys* became familiar to the public with Lord Braybrooke's text, especially his fourth edition of 1854. Revisions in the latter part of the century extended the Diary's popularity.'

and so we say farewell. Usu. said in a mock-American accent, it is a burlesque'd quot'n become c.p., from the fade-out to B-grade film travelogues. The great comedian and magnificent mimic, Peter Sellers, epitomised them all in his superb skit which ends 'and so we say "farewell" to Bal-ham, gateway to the South!', the record of which helped so much to popularise the phrase in the late 1950s. (P.B.)

and so what? An early occ. var. of **so what?**

and that ain't hay! is recorded by W & F as occurring always after the mention of a specific sum and as meaning 'that's a lot of money', e.g. in 'He makes $30,000 a year, and that ain't hay'. They neither assign nor hazard a date, but the *OED*'s 2nd Sup. has it in a quot'n from Raymond Chandler, *The Lady in the Lake*, 1944. The late John Lardner, brilliant son of famous father, Ring Lardner, writes in the 'Minstrel Memories' article forming part of *Strong Cigars and Lovely Women*, a selection pub'd in 1951, of pieces appearing in *Newsweek*, 1949–51:

If Louie Ambers
Should come our way,
He brings the title,
And that ain't hay.

an extension showing how very familiar the phrase must have been by (say) 1950.

and that goes. That's final – there's no more to be said. US: since *c.* 1925, perhaps much earlier, but I lack a record earlier than Berrey. R.C., 1977, writes that the phrase was 'dead and buried by 1970'. Cf:

and that goes double! The same to you!: US: since *c.* 1930. Berrey.

and that is that. See **and that's that!**

and that's flat! – *and* occ. omitted. Of *that's flat*, Berrey, 1942, says that it is 'used to emphasize or conclude a preceding remark'. I'd guess that it has been in US use since late C19. In Brit. use it has been so long established – it occurs as early as Shakespeare – that it cannot be rated as a c.p. at all.

and that's no lie, a c.p. of emphasis, implies that the speaker isn't too sure that he'll be believed: since *c.* 1920.

and that's that! – *and* occ. omitted; emphatic var. of:

and that is that; also **well, that's that!** The first is both Brit. and US, Berrey explaining it as 'that is the end of the matter, so much for that'; so too the second; the third, connoting a rueful resignation, occurs in Terence Rattigan's *While the Sun Shines*, performed on Christmas Eve, 1943, at the Globe Theatre, London, and pub'd in 1944:

MABEL: … When I read you were getting married I thought, well, that's that. He'll just fade quietly away and I won't ever see him again.

I cannot remember having heard the phrase before I came to England in 1921; certainly not during WW1, although I strongly suspect that the phrase (*and*) *that's that!* arose precisely then.

The apparently formal, but really the emphatic, *and that is that* occurs in Edward Albee's *Who's Afraid of Virginia Woolf?*, prod. and pub'd in 1962:

GEORGE TO WIFE MARTHA: I'll hold your hand when it's dark and you're afraid of the bogey man … but I will not light your cigarette. And that, as they say, is that.

and that's your lot! That's all you're going to receive, so don't expect any more: since *c.* 1920. Often used by wives to their husbands, or by women to their lovers. See also **aye, aye, that's yer lot!**

and the band played on. 'Things went on as usual – or even more vague in meaning [than **then the band began to play,** q.v.]' (Leechman, 1969, on the Can. usage). Philip M. Arnold of Oklahoma provides the source of this c.p., 1978: 'In 1895 a song titled "The Band Played on", with words by John F. Palmer, was published in New York. This is the refrain, which is still remembered in the United States by older people:

"Casey would waltz with a strawberry blonde,
And the band played on.
He'd glide across the floor with the girl he ador'd,
And the band played on.

13

But his brain was so loaded it nearly exploded,
The poor girl would shake with alarm.
He'd ne'er leave the girl with the strawberry curl,
And the band played on." '

and the best of British (luck). See **best of British luck to you.**

and the next object is ... ! 'Phrase used by the Mystery Voice in the radio quiz *Twenty Questions* – raised to catchphrase level by Norman Hackforth's deep, fruity rendering of such gems as: "And the next object is ... the odour in the larder" ' (*VIBS*).

and the rest! has, since *c*. 1860, sarcastically and trenchantly implied that something important or, at the least, essential has been omitted – or that reticence has been carried too far.

and then some! This Americanism goes back to *c*. 1910 and – on the evidence of *OED* – was anglicized in or *c*. 1913. The thoroughness of its adoption by Britain is proved in an odd way: Prof. J. W. Mackail in his *Aeneid*, 1930, finds a parallel in Book VIII, line 487, *tormenti genus*.

The US phrase seems to have arisen as a mere elab. of the Scots *and some* ('and much more so'), as in Ross's pastoral poem *Helemore*, 1768, and, perhaps more significantly, in lexicographer Jamieson's exemplification, 'She's as bonny as you, and some'; and again in *EDD. And then some!* was current in Western Canada by early C20: witness John Sandilands, *Western Canadian Dictionary*, 2nd ed., 1913, ' ... an afterthought to suggest that there is any amount of excellence expected or held in reserve.'

and then the band began to play. See **then the band began to play.**

and there's more where that came from is one of the many and various c.pp. we owe to 'The Goon Show', which, beginning as 'The Crazy People', ran from 28 May 1951 until 28 Jan. 1960. It had excellent producers and script writers (esp. Eric Sykes); its three best actors were Spike Milligan, original, provocative, in the best sense anarchistic; Peter Sellers, with his superb flair for characterisation and his brilliant mimicry; and Harry Secombe, central figure, rock-like personality holding them all together, 'the catalyst'. They were ably and selflessly assisted by others. (See Barry Took, *Laughter in the Air*, 1976, which I paraphrase.)

There have been three collections of 'Goon Show' programmes [in book form]. There has also been Harry Secombe's *Goon for Lunch*, 1975. P.B., 1977, has excerpted for me the following passage, with comments: 'When the Show comes to an end ... , the [studio] audience leaves – some of them bewildered, the *aficionados* gleefully repeating the Bluebottle – Eccles exchanges, or the familiar catch phrase: "And there's more where that came from".'

'This', says P.B., 'really did catch on, sometimes with an emphatic [var.] "And there's plenty more where ... ", and is still to be heard occasionally, even from speakers who quite probably are unaware of the origin.'

P.B.: sadly, perhaps I should add that when I asked E.P. if he used to listen to 'The Goon Show', he admitted that he had never heard it; he 'seldom had time to listen to the radio'. The show seems to be as popular as ever: the BBC are now, Summer 1982, running a repeat series of the pick of the programmes.

and to prove it, I'm here! See **I've arrived ...**

and very nice too! See **very nice too!**

and what's the matter with Hannah? is 'a slangy c.p., generally tailed on to a statement or remark without the slightest sense of congruity' (Farmer): US: ? *c*. 1875–1900. P.B.: poor old Hannah seems to 'cop it' in c. pp.: Cf **Sister Hannah ... ,** and **that's the man as married Hannah!**

and when she bumps she bounces. See **when she bumps ....**

and who am I to contradict him? See **Who am I ...**

and whose little girl are you? And who may *you* be?: a male c.p., dating from *c*. 1905. Perhaps it orig. in the film world, where, at parties, the stars sometimes took their children. On the cover of the *Sunday Times* Magazine of 11 June 1972 appeared the face of a lovely girl and her famous and lovely film actress mother, the caption being 'And whose little girl

are you?' – with the explanatory sub-title, 'The stars and their daughters'. A.B., 1978, 'Sometimes, if a man were in quest of sexual intimacy, he might add "tonight".'

and you too!, occ. shortened to **and you!** A C20 c.p. addressed to someone suspect of unexpressed insult or recrimination. In the Armed Forces, it has, since 1914 or 1915, presupposed an unvoiced *fuck you!*, as, e.g., from a soldier awarded detention, with the officer saying or, more usu. thinking, *and you (too)!*. P.B.: to judge from Bob Newhart's splendid monologue, 'The Driving Instructor', the US equivalent is *and you, fella!* Cf **so are you!**

angel(s). See: be an a.; house devil; roll on, death.

anger, See: 'fuck me!'; more in anger.

angle of dangle is inversely proportional to the heat of the meat – the. This was a c.p. among better-educated National Servicemen of the 1950s, axiomatic for the degree of male sexual excitement. E.P. slightly misconstrued a note I sent him about it, 1974, but commented in his entry for this 2nd ed., 'it might be compared to Senior Common Room wit in its mellower moments – well, almost.' (P.B.)

angry. See: I'm not mad; if you are angry.

Angus. See: I don't know whether.

animal See: there ain't no sech.

Ann, Anna, Anne, Annie. See: how old; I'm Anne; san fairy; Sister Anna; up in Annie's; and:

Anna Maria Jeanetta Sophia Aronia Bonia Lovell-Frye-Giles. A chant, perhaps from a music-hall song, used by my grandmothers to delight and mystify their children, early C20. (P.B.)

[**anniversary of the siege of Gibraltar – the.** 'Since the great siege lasted from 1779 to 1783, this could be unofficially celebrated whenever desired' (Rear-Adm P.W. Brock, 1969): toast; late (?middle) C19–20.]

another. See: ask another; if it isn't; tell me a.; that's another; there's another; you are a.; you have another.

another clean shirt oughta (ought to) see ya (or you) out. You look as if you might die at any moment: NZ since *c*. 1930 or a little earlier. It occurs in, e.g, Gordon Slatter, *A Gun in My Hand*, 1959. Clumsily humorous rather than callously hard-boiled.

another county heard from! 'A c.p. used when one of a company breaks wind or interjects something' (Leechman): Can.: since *c*. 1935. From 'the receiving of election results from various counties. In the US, however, although of the same electoral orig. and arising much earlier, this c.p. means that a 'previously unknown and often unexpected and despised opinion has been expressed' (J.W.C., 1977).

another day, another dollar. 'Said thankfully at the end of a hardworking day. I have often used this myself and have heard many others use it' (Mrs Shirley M. Pearce, 1975). Since the late 1940s and presumably adopted from the US, where it has been current since. *c*. 1910: 'We meet someone and inquire: "How goes it?" or "How's tricks?" or "How you doing?" and more often than not our friend answers, "Another day, another dollar", meaning he is "keeping his head above water", holding on, not getting rich, but still working .... I have heard the expression most of my adult life' (W.J.B. 1975). In his *The Kidnap Kid*, 1975, Tony Kendrick employs is allusively. Anthony Burgess in his review of the 1st ed. of this Dictionary, *TLS*, 26 Aug. 1977, noted that the dovetail answer is *a million days, a million dollars*.

'This was a saying that a [London] docker had when it had been a bad day and they looked forward to earning another "dollar" the next day. This was usually followed by saying that "you can't make a good day out of a bad one" ' (Ash).

Meanwhile, back in the USA, that superb master of the unconventional rhyme, Ogden Nash (1902–71), could end his 1960s verse, 'A Man Can Complain, Can't He' (A Lament for Those Who Think Old):

I'm old too soon, yet young too long;
Could Swift himself have planned it droller?

Timor vitae conturbat me;
Another day, another dolor.

another fellow's is applied to something not new – not by its possessor but by some wag: *c.* 1880–1910. B & L.

another fine mess you've gotten (US) or **got** (UK) **me into!** This c.p. of the 1930s and 1940s, taken from the Laurel and Hardy films 'has come back into general use due to the re-run of their old films on TV' (John Skehan, 1977). Hardy's injured look as he says this to his partner has an irresistable tragicomic poignancy. Often prec. by *here's*. Little Stan Laurel (1890–1965) and fat Oliver Hardy (1892–1957) made a wonderful pair; the phrase was Hardy's standing reproach to his – on the screen – duller-witted partner; in the fact, Laurel was the more intelligent of the two – and the better actor. (Much indebted to Maurice Wedgewood, 1978.)

another good man gone! A men's ruefully regretful remark passed on a man either engaged to be married or, esp., very recently married: late C19–20. Petch remarks that, since *c.* 1920, it has had a var.: *another good man gone wrong!*

another little drink won't do us any harm: since *c.* 1920. From the refrain of a very popular song.

another nail in my coffin. In 1974, Vernon Noble sent me this note: 'Long before medical science officially condemned cigarettes as a hazard to health there was a catch phrase "Another nail in my coffin" as a person lighted a cigarette. This was an ironical answer to those who rebuked a cigarette-smoker who coughed: usually to an anxious wife. I have known this phrase in the North of England for something like 50 years': and I have known it used by Australians si .ce *c.* 1910 and in the South of England since 1921. Dr. J.T. Shipley reminds me, 1977, of the poss. relevance of the old couplet: It's not the cough that carries him off, But the coffin they carry him off in.

another one for the van! Someone else has had to be taken to the lunatic asylum: Cockneys': since *c.* 1920. P.B.: more prob. a not very subtle way of saying 'You're mad!' Cf **send for the green van!**

another push and you'd have been a Chink (or **a nigger**). A brutal c.p. employed by workmen in a slanging match, or by youths bullying boys in a factory: C20, but, for *nigger*, esp. since *c.* 1950. This insult imputes a colour-no-objection promiscuity in the addressee's mother.

another Redskin bit (occ. and loosely, **hit**) **the dust.** A boys' and youths' c.p.: late C19–early 20. From boys' books, written mostly by American authors, but read very widely in Britain too. (L.A., 1977.)

another voice from the peanut gallery is often addressed to an irrelevant or insignificant interrupter, whether from the cheapest seats at a theatre or a music-hall, or at Speakers' Corner, Hyde Park, London: C20 Brit., although supplied by a true American conversant with the speech-ways of England, viz. A.B., 1978.

answer. See: ask a silly; don't answer; I decline; if you have to; knows all; there's no answer.

answer is a lemon – the; also **the answer's a lemon.** A derisive reply to a query – or a request – needing a 'yes' or a 'no' but hoping for 'yes'; a 'sarcastic remark – acidic in its conclusion', as Noble aptly calls it; orig. (*c.* 1910) US – cf the US slang *lemon*, used since *c.* 1900, for 'a sharp verbal thrust, criticism, or retort' (W & F); adopted in England *c.* 1919. Its origin lies either in a lemon's sourness or, according to legend, in an improper, indeed an exceedingly smutty, story circulating during the 1920s. In Maurice Lincoln's novel, *Oh! Definitely*, 1933, occurs this illuminating dialogue:

'Written by some fellow with long hair who lives in Bloomsbury, I expect,' said Horace.
'Why?' said Peter.
'Why what?'
'Well, why would he have long hair like that and live where you said?'
'The answer's a lemon,' said Horace.

In the US, the thought is expressed a little differently. In 1974, my loyal old friend W.J.B. wrote to me thus:

In the US we have a phrase *I drew a lemon* or *It turned out to be a lemon*, etc. If we buy a new car which has 'bugs' in it, isn't working properly, we say, *It's a lemon.*

For years we have had slot machines in gambling joints. You put in a coin, pull a lever, and a row of the conventional objects appear on the face of the machine, bells, plums, etc. If you get a whole row of the same objects, all balls, say, you win, and out drops a handful of coins. If you hit the 'jackpot', as they say, you win big. You probably know all about this. But the point I want to make is that you may draw a whole row of yellow *lemons*, and *you get nothing*. Lemons mean a bust, a disappointment. Hence, when someone says *I drew a lemon*, the slot machine connotation is well understood.

But Shipley, 1977, suggests that it prob. derives from a very popular song, *c.* 1905, with its last lines of the chorus:

'But I picked a lemon in the garden of love,
Where they say only peaches grow.'

answer is (or **answer's**) **in the infirmary** (– **my** or **the**). My answer is Yes: late C19–early 20; ob. by 1937, virtually † by 1945. A pun on *in the affirmative.* Hence, 'My answer's unfavourable' or 'The news in bad': since *c.* 1910 and, immediately after, much more gen. than the earlier sense, but itself † by 1950.

answer is in the plural, and they bounce – the. 'A polite (?) way of saying 'Balls!' [nonsense]. *The Penguin Dictionary of Modern Quotations*, 1971, credits it to Sir Edward Lutyens (1869–1944), 'before a Royal Commission'. My guess is that it was already an established c.p. when he used it' (Sanders, 1978). My opinion too. By 1978, slightly ob. P.B.: cf the ambiguous comment scrawled, e.g. in the margin of a report with which the reader disagrees: 'Round objects'.

Antonio. See: oh, oh.

any B.F. (or **b.f.** or **bloody fool**) **can be uncomfortable.** 'Alleged to be a Guards' maxim. It certainly expressed the attitude of the Guards Armoured Division when I had dealings with them in Schleswig-Holstein in 1946. Wonderful chaps!' (Rear-Adm. P.W. Brock, CB, DSO, 1969): whether maxim or not, certainly a c.p. and, later, enjoying a much wider currency. Sanders, 1978, writes 'Heard as early as 1939 from a WW1 "dug-out" ... It is, I suspect, as old as warfare.' It sounds, like *any fool can be* or *can make himself uncomfortable*, like a Napoleonic Wars (1796–1815) sarcasm: I'll go even further and say that this C20 c.p. is prob. based on some famous general's comment on the discomforts of a long campaign – and who more likely than Wellington? Several very knowledgeable friends (and *their* friends) agree that it does sound characteristic of Wellington.

any colour you like, so long as it's black. Henry Ford (1863–1947) instituted the Ford Motor Company in 1903 and was its president from then until 1919 and again in 1943–45. In the interval, his son Edsel (1893–1943) was the president. These words formed Henry Ford's offer of the Model T to American buyers; and during the later 1940s this witty slogan began to catch on with the Brit. public; by 1950, it had become well established as a c.p., with the dry, humorous connotation, 'That's your limited choice, so take it or leave it, but I advise you to take it'. (Based on a note from John Skehan, 1977.)

any complaints? 'is still used by ex-Servicemen as a way of opening a conversation where there's nothing else to say. [and] *stand by your beds!* is still flippanthy said by them when somebody comes into a room' (an anon. correspondent, 1978). The references are to WW2 and after. Orig. the former was asked by the Orderly Officer doing his meal-time rounds of the Other Ranks' dining-hall; the latter was the command usu. given by the NCO in charge of a barrack-room when an inspecting officer entered. Cf the RAF's scurrilous couplet:

Stand by your beds! Here comes the Air Chief Marshal;
Four great rings upon his arm – and still he wants your arsehole.

See also the entry at **stand by your beds!** (P.B.)

any day you'ave the money, I 'ave the time. A prostitutes' or, derivatively, an enthusiastic amateurs' or near-amateurs' c.p., dating since *c.* 1910 and used mostly by Londoners. See Charles Drummond, *Death at the Furlong Post*, 1967, where the c.p. is employed allusively: 'The Inspector ... laid down seven pound notes. "Fair and square?" – "Yes, love, any day you 'ave the money, I 'ave the time." Ag. laughed.' Also US. 'I think there was a song in the 1930s or 1940s entitled "If you've got the money, honey, I've got the time" ' (A.B., 1978). P.B.: the phrase has led, in UK, to the c.p. response to the innocent query, 'Have you (*or* has anybody) got the time?' (i.e. what o'clock is it?): *I've got the time if you've got the money.* Another unhelpful answer is *if you've got the inclination.* See also **I've got the time ...** and **yes, but not ...**

any fool can be uncomfortable. See **any B.F. ...**

any joy? Any luck?: orig. US, since *c.* 1930, according to E.P., but very widely used indeed, in the Brit. Services, esp. in RAF after (and perhaps during) WW2. It had become, by early 1950s, jargon: when a fighter, airborne, failed to find his target aircraft, he would report to ground control 'No joy', and continue to report thus until he either found the target, or was forced to return to base. (P.B.)

any more for any more? Does anyone want a second helping?: military mess-orderlies' c.p. of WW1 – and, fig., later; by 1939, slightly ob. – yet still far from †. In WW1, 'also used by the man running a Crown and Anchor board or a House outfit, asking others to join in before the game commenced' (B & P).

any more for the Skylark? A joc. c.p. of C20. The invitation of seaside pleasure-boat owners, so many of these boats so named, became a generalized invitation.

any more, Mrs Moore? – is there or **have you.** Merely an elab. of *any more*: C20. (P.B.)

any of these men here? Dating from *c.* 1910, this is a military Other Ranks' c.p. A wag, imitating a sergeant-major at a kit inspection, would ask, 'Knife, fork, spoon' and sometimes a reply would come, 'Yes, *he* is'; either the wag or a third party would obligingly ask, '*Who* is?' and would receive the obliging reply, 'Arseholes'.

any publicity, good or bad, is better than none, provided they spell the name right. This politicians' c.p. dates from the mid-1930s: the UK and the Commonwealth. (A reminder, 1978, from my old Australian friend Archie – A.E., – Pearse.)

anyone for tennis? See **tennis, anyone?**

anyone here seen Kelley? See **has anybody here ...**

anyone who goes to a psychoanalyst ... See **you need your head examined.**

[**anyone who hates children and (small) dogs can't be all bad** is a cultured and literate American c.p., sometimes wrongly attributed to W.C. Fields (1879–1946). It formed part of a short ad-libbed speech made by Leo Rosten at a Masquers' Club banquet held, in Hollywood, on 17 Feb. 1939, in honour of Fields's 25th year in show business. It remains a famous quot'n; it has not quite become a c.p.]

anyone's bet – it's or **that's.** 'Who can say?' or 'Nobody can say for certain'; since early 1970s.

anything. See: bring anything; can you do; don't do a.; he'd fuck a.; I'll try; if you want; never does; they can make.

[**anything for a laugh**, often prec. by *he'll* or *he'd do*, is applied lit. and then is a cliché; but when the implication is that he'll go too far to achieve that laudable purpose when laughter is inappropriate, it tends to be regarded as a c.p.: since *c.* 1945. (Petch, 1969.)]

anything for a quiet wife is a c.p. var – less vaguely, 'a jocular perversion' (Petch) – of *anything for a quiet life*; itself a proverbial saying; the former dates from *c.* 1968; the latter prob. from late C17 (see *ODEP*). Cf **deft and dumb.**

anything goes! Anything is permissible; 'do exactly as you please': dates from *c.* 1930 in the US and was popularised, 1934, by a Cole Porter song and a musical comedy so titled;

the c.p. soon reached the UK. (Wedgewood, 1977.) In short, that American musical comedy (which is still revived) adopted its title from an already existing c.p., as J.W.C. has pointed out: a splendid example of the fact that certain titles of plays, films and songs have not originated but merely reinforced, rendered still more popular, phrases already firmly, or perhaps not very firmly, established.

Cf **Miss Otis regrets.**

anything I (really) like ... See **anything you like ...**

anything like that you can enjoy! In his delightful and kindly autobiography, *Shop Boy*, written *c.* 1922 but not pub'd until 1983, John Birch Thomas remembers London's old Crystal Palace in the early 1880s: 'Only the centre part was illuminated. The side courts where the statues were seemed quite dark, but they were the most crowded ... Many couples were sitting in dark corners, and passers-by made remarks to tease them. "I'll tell your Mother, Maudie," and "Anything like that you *can* enjoy," but nobody took offence. Everybody was enjoying themselves and all was jolly.' Thomas's memory was remarkably vivid in its detail, and these phrases have the true ring of ephemeral c. pp. (P.B.)

anything! so help me! God help me!: orig. euph. and almost proletarian: *c.* 1918–39. Manchon.

anything that *can* go wrong *will* go wrong. 'This c.p. is known as Murphy's law' (B.P., 1975). It is known in UK and Aus. as well as in US, where it prob. started, *c.* 1950, in the form *if anything can go wrong, it will.* In UK it has, since *c.* 1970, been known less politely as **Sod's law**, q.v. Orig. scientist-engineer jargon, but becoming gen. with the post-Sputnik awareness of science. I suspect that Murphy is the archetypal (and stereotyped) Irish immigrant under whose ministrations things were guaranteed to go wrong. Murphy's law is, of course, merely a scientific formulation of a much earlier recognised aspect of human affairs, the Buttered Side Principle, first set down by James Payn (1830–98) who, in 1884, wrote:

I never had a piece of toast
Particularly long and wide
But fell upon the sandy floor
And always on the buttered side.

P.B: Payn was merely, and rather simplifyingly, echoing Tom Hood the Younger (1834–74), who had earlier parodied the famous quatrain beginning 'I never nursed a dear gazelle', in Thomas Moore's *Lalla Rookh*, 1817. Hood's version ran:

'I never nursed a dear gazelle,
To glad me with its dappled hide,
But when it came to know me well
It fell upon its buttered side.'

Much has now been written, seriously and in fun, about Murphy and his law. The even more pessimistic, like myself, often add the corollary *and if it can't go wrong, it might.* Those interested in further treatment of the subject are referred to Paul Dickson, *The Official Rules*, 1978 (US), 1980 (UK), an excellent compendium of related material, and a pregnant source of many a potential c.p.

anything you *like* is (either) illegal, immoral, or fattening. ' "Sorry, Chum, nothing. Not allowed." – "Always the same. Anything you like is illegal, immoral or fattening," he giggled, "That's a chestnut for you." Brand sighed. "I've heard it – often." Thus Margaret Hinxman in a novel pub'd in 1977. It goes back, I think, to *c.* 1940, although I don't recall having heard it until *c.* 1960. 'I have heard it, and variants, and used it, for, I suppose, 20–25 years' (Peter Cochrane, 1977).

It derives from Alexander Woollcott (1887–1943), who, in *The Knock at the Stage Door*, wrote: 'All the things I really like to do are either immoral, illegal or fattening.' (Yehuda Mindel, 1977). The altered form is Brit. and it did not truly 'catch on' in UK until the late 1940s or very early 1950s. Woollcott's orig. appeared in *Readers' Digest*, Dec. 1933. It is, however, worth noting, as J.W.C. points out, 1977, that in the US the c.p. form is always *everything* (*I like*)..

anyway, it's winning the war. See **it's winning...**

anywhere. See: **we're not going.**

anywhere down there! A c.p. uttered by tailors when something is dropped on the floor: *c.* 1860–1910.

[apa changkul dua malam. 'An example of "mangled Malay" from the 1950s. Literally the whole was meant to translate "What-ho to-night?" Intelligence Corps people during the Malayan Emergency (late 1940s–early 1950s)'. (P.B., 1975). The spelling *changkul* is as amended by Anthony Burgess, in *TLS*, 26 Aug. 1977. Cf **satu empat jalan.**]

apologise. See: **never explain.**

appeal. See: **let's appeal; no heart.**

applaud. See: **don't applaud.**

apple. See: **you haven't got; you've picked.**

Appleby. See: **how lies.**

apples. See: **how do you like; how we.**

apples – it's or she's; or she'll be apples. [P.B.: occ., more fully: *she'll be right, mate – she'll be apples.*] 'Everything is, or will be, all right'; 'it will prosper or succeed': Aus.: since *c.* 1950. The form *she'll be apples* was noted in a witty review by Philip Howard in *The Times*, 24 Mar. 1977, of the late Grahame Johnston's *Oxford Pocket Dictionary of Australian English*. [P.B.: this form was current among Australian Servicemen a decade earlier.] Cf **she'll be jake**, q.v. It's just poss. that the phrase was prompted by the archaic **how we apples swim**, q.v. But G.A. Wilkes, *Dictionary of Australian Colloquialisms*, 1978, prefers *everything's apples*, with earliest printed ref. in 1952, and an orig. either in *apple-pie order* or in rhyming slang *apples and spice*, nice – Aus., the Brit. being *apples and rice.*

apples a pound pears derides barrow boys, who often use strange or even nonsensical cries, deemed by some customers to be misleading: since *c.* 1925. Although L.A., 1976, declared that, since *c.* 1945, the phrase has been no more than a 'Cockney street-market fruit-stall jocular shout', and although another correspondent declared it to be 'plain daft', yet it should be noted that this c.p. may have been influenced by the famous Cockney rhyming-slang *apples and pears* (stairs): see that entry in Julian Franklyn's dependable and entertaining *Rhyming Slang.*

apply. See: **no Irish.**

appointment. See: **couldn't see.**

appray (or appree) la guerre, often written *gare*; **après la guerre.** 'Sometime – or perhaps never'; or, simply, 'never'; a British army, esp. a Tommy, c.p. of 1915–18. Often *appray la gare finee*, being the Fr. *après la guerre finie*, after the end of the war. 'A hopeless soldier would often be heard to say, for instance: "When shall I see my happy home again?" or "When shall I get my back pay? Appree la Gare" – i.e., Never' (F & G). '*Après la guerre* carried two connotations for the soldier. It was used jokingly for the indefinite and remote future, e.g. "When will you marry me? – oh, après la guerre" .... And, secondly, the phrase was a depository of secret sentiment. The two usages are clearly seen in the ribald ditty composed by some unknown warrior – "Après la guerre finie" [sung to the tune of 'Sous les ponts de Paris']' (B & P, who failed to note the third connotation: 'Never').

apprehend. See; I apprehend.

[après nous le déluge, both a UK and a US contender during C20 among the educated for the status of c.p., is reputed to have been said in 1757, by Jeanne, Marquise de la Pompadour, to Frederick the Great, as the invaluable 'Bartlett' tells us, means 'after us the flood' and connotes 'What do we care what happens after we die?' but – perhaps more often in US than in UK – it has sometimes been changed to *après moi* ... , 'What do I care?' (Proposed by John T. Fain). P.B.: but in later C20 has it not rather the sense 'We are (or may well be) the last generation to enjoy civilisation as we know it – how appallingly sad!']

apron. See: **he's had; weaving.**

Aquascutum. See: **it's awfully.**

Arbroath. See: ONE WORD.

arch: See: **Admiralty.**

Archer up! he – or it – is certain to win: a London c.p. of 1881–6. From the very famous, very great, jockey, Fred Archer, who, having achieved fame in 1881, died in 1886. Another 'jockey' c.p. is **come on, Steve!**

Archibald, certainly not! A c.p. satirizing a prim and prudish feminine refusal of sexual intimacy: *c.* 1911–20 for its heyday; by 1940, virtually †. From the title and refrain of a music-hall song written by John L. St John – a well-known song-writer usu. known as Lee St John; the song owed most of its popularity to George Robey. The c.p. was noted by Collinson.

P.B.: there is a possible connection between this c.p. and the WW1 slang *archie* = anti-aircraft gunfire: see *Archibald* in *DSUE.*

are there any more at home like you? A C20 c.p. addressed to a (very) pretty girl; by 1940, ob.; by 1970, † – except among those with long memories. From the very popular musical comedy *Floradora*, which, performed first in 1900, contained the song, 'Tell me, pretty maiden, are there any more at home like you?'

are we downhearted? Political in origin (*c.* 1906) it did not achieve the status of a true c.p. until WW1 and was not, I believe, at all – if at all – gen. before late 1915. In B & P, John Brophy, at p. 194, wrote:

The original –
Are we downhearted? No!
soon became the vehement –
Are we downhearted? – Yes!

But this was intended as humorous comment. Sometimes it would be expanded, and declaimed by alternate voices, thus:

Are we downhearted?
No!
Then you damn (or bloody) soon will be!

are we is or are we ain't? See **is you** *is* **or is you ain't?**

are yer courtin'? 'One of the questions Wilfred Pickles would use nudgingly in his long-running radio quiz *Have A Go*, chatting up spinster contestants of any age from nineteen to ninety' (*VIBS*). In his broadest Yorkshire accent, of course.

are yew werkin'? is Liverpool c.p. of 'the hungry Twenties and in frequent use until *c.* 1940 – and in occ. use for some ten years longer. (Shaw, 1968.)

are you a man or a mouse? Orig. and predominantly US, Berrey glossing it thus: 'disparagingly of a timorous person'. Adopted in England *c.* 1945 and there used joc., esp. by female to male. 'Catch phrases tend to breed ripostes, which in their turn breed others, and it is hard to know where to stop. Thus *are you a man or* [a] *mouse?* is regularly followed by *a mouse: my wife's frightened of mice*' (Anthony Burgess, in *TLS*, 26 Aug. 1977). P.B.: equally common, among the honest, is the frank riposte *squeak, squeak!*

are you anywhere? Do you possess – or have on you – any drugs? A US negroes' c.p., since *c.* 1950. CM.

are you asking me or (are you) telling me?, with *to do something* understood. A well-mannered reproof to someone who, without justification, expects something to be done; 'Are you ordering me or asking with a *please?*' I first heard it during the 1920s, but surmise that it goes back to more courteous Edwardian days.

are you casting nasturtiums? Are you making aspersions?: joc., deliberate malapropism: mostly lower-middle class: C20; by 1965, ob. (P.B., 1976.) cf **answer is in the infirmary.**

are you financial? Have you enough – or plenty of – money readily available?: Aus.: since mid-1940s. (Camilla Raab, 1977.)

[are you for real?, like **it's for real:** not catch, but ordinary colloquial, phrases.]

are you getting too proud to speak to anyone now? – with *are* often omitted – is addressed to one who has failed to notice the speaker when passing: C20.

are you going to walk about, or pay for a room? is 'an impatient whore's question after a client has dithered too long' (a correspondent, in 1969): C20.

are you happy in the Service? and are you happy in your work? See **happy in the Service?**

are you in my way? is 'a c.p. reminder of egotistical obliviousness' (L.A.): since *c.* 1925. Also US; Berrey solemnly explains it as 'am I in your way?', although R.C., 1978, writes 'never very common in US, and certainly ob., if not extinct, today.' P.B. glosses it somewhat differently: 'Jocular phrase used as "Excuse me, may I come (*or* reach) past you" or to forestall another's having to ask one to make room.'

are you is or are you ain't? A var. of **is you *is* or is you *ain't*?**

are you keeping it for the worms? A Can. c.p., dating from *c.* 1940, and addressed to a female rejecting sexual advances. (Here, 'it' is the hymen.) Accidentally reminiscent of Shakespeare's famous attack on the value of virginity as such. E.P. later noted: The Shakespeare influence is valid, but Prof. D.J. Enright, in *Encounter*, Dec. 1977, is, of course, right in attributing the more immediate, more pertinent, source to Andrew Marvell (1621–78) in *To His Coy Mistress*, thus: 'Much more reminiscent of Marvell's playful play, "Worms shall try/That long preserved Virginity".'

are you kidding? Are you joking? But also an ironically derisive exclam. = Surely you're not serious? Dating since *c.* 1945, it was prob. suggested by the US c.p., *no kidding?* and in its turn, it prob. occasioned the Brit. *you must be joking!*

In Act I, Scene i, of Terence Rattigan's *Variation on a Theme*, both performed and pub'd in 1958:

RON: You'll get a good settlement, I hope. [On remarrying.]

ROSE: Are you kidding? I'm settling for half the Ruhr.

P.B., 1982: in 1976 I mentioned to E.P. that there had been, in the Army at least, and since *c.* 1960, the dovetail retort *no, it's just the way me* (or *my*) *coat hangs*. Only recently I have heard the American var. ..... *sweater hangs*.

are you looking at *me?* 'It's no good looking at me like that – I'm not the culprit, *or* I didn't do it, *or* I am not going to offer to do it.' One of those domestic or semi-domestic phrases it's impossible to date with any accuracy: prob. since late C19; my own memory of it doesn't precede 1910.

are you nervous in the Service? During WW2, this formed the US version of the Brit. **are you happy in the Service?** (J.W.C., 1977.)

are you pulling the right string? Are you going the right way about it? or, occ., are you correct? A cabinet-makers' c.p., dating from 1863, says Ware; apparently † by 1940. Ware derives it from small measurements made with the aid of lengths of string, but, as B.G.T. pertinently remarks: 'Could not this refer to marionettes? One hardly "pulls" string to make measurements' – which of course makes Ware's supposition incongruous. And R.C., 1977, adds 'I propose that it is at least suggested by the concept of "pulling (political) strings".'

are you sitting comfortably? (Then I'll begin) comes 'from the children's radio programme, "Listen with Mother" ', and on 5 Sep. 1977 was noted, as omission from the 1st ed. of this Dictionary, by Dr Robert Burchfield, CBE, in the BBC programme 'Kaleidoscope'. These words formed the constant introductory line; the series began in Jan. 1950. A c.p. of the 1950s–60s. [P.B.: still heard in the early 1980s.] (With the kind permission of the BBC, via Rosemary Hart, the producer of 'Kaleidoscope'.) 'Julia Lang is credited with introducing the phrase' (*VIBS*).

are you talking to me or chewing a brick? (With *are you* often omitted). 'One of the long list of questions or remarks imputing idiocy in the person addressed' (Brian W. Aldiss, 1978): since *c.* 1950.

are you there with your bears? There you are again! – esp. with a connotation of 'so soon': *c.* 1570–1840. It occurs in Lyly,

1592–James Howel, 1642–Richardson (the novelist), 1740–Scott, 1820. (Apperson.) From the itinerant bear-leaders' regular visits to certain districts.

are you trying to tell me something? 'Modern US, probably UK now, though not widely: response to a less than clear hint' (Wedgwood, 1977). In the US not, so far as I have noticed, before *c.* 1955. In UK, yes: since *c.* 1965, but whether as emergent cliché or as a potential c.p., I should not yet (1977) care to say.

are you up? is a US journalistic c.p., meaning 'are you free of the work you were doing?' (Berrey, 1942). Perhaps throughout C20; but prob., since *c.* 1950, no more than a journalistic colloquialism.

are you winning? 'A rhetorical greeting: since *c.* 1960' (P.B., 1975). It has another connotation, that of 'another way of saying something when there is nothing to say' (an anon. correspondent, 1978, who dates it back a decade earlier). Prob. prompted by **we're winning**, q.v.

are you with me? Do you understand? Its var. *are you with me still?* implies 'Do you still follow me *or* the argument?' Since *c.* 1920. (Prof. James R. Sutherland, 1977.) P.B.: in later C20 often shortened to *with me?*; the person following the argument may interject *with you!*, to show that he does.

are your boots laced? Do you understand what I'm saying *or* what I'm talking about?: US Negroes'. Eric Townley, 1978, draws attention to 'Get Your Books Laced, Papa', a title recorded on 18 Apr. 1940 by Woody Herman and his orchestra. In his valuable *Tell Your Story: A Dictionary of Jazz and Blues Recordings, 1917–50*, 1976, E.T. explains the title of the record as 'Become aware and informed of the latest trends; get knowledgeable and up-to-date about the situation.'

are your hands clean? (Pause.) **Would you mind turning my balls over?** 'A low expression used among [the numerous] workingmen who think that they are not "men" if they can use a dozen words without including some filth' (Petch, 1969): since *c.* 1920.

aren't we all? – often prec. by *but*. But surely we're all alike in *that*? Since *c.* 1918 or perhaps ten or even twenty years earlier. In Frederick Lonsdale's comedy, *Aren't We All*, 1924, occurs this passage:

VICAR: Grenham, you called me a bloody old fool.

LORD GRENHAM: But aren't we all, old friend?

Berrey, in 1942, records it as US – which it had become by adoption. J.W.C. noted, 1977, after the appearance of this Dictionary's 1st ed.: ' "Don't we all?" is widely current in US, perhaps specially applied to copulation. Also widely used is "Doesn't everyone?" – almost always applied to a very rich woman saying, e.g., "*Of course* we have two yachts".' The Brit. and US versions are contemporaneous.

P.B.: One of Britain's best known newspaper strip-cartoon characters of the mid-C20 appeared in the *Daily Mirror, c.* 1938–51; created by Bernard Graddon, he was Captain A.R.P. Reilly-Ffoull, of Arntwee Hall, Much Cackling, Gertshire. (The A.R.P. is a pun too: it stood 'in real life' for Air Raid Precautions, hence, those who organised, supervised, and effected these precautions.)

aren't you the one! expresses admiration whether complete or quizzical or rueful: US: since *c.* 1942; not much used since *c.* 1972. (Mr Ben Grauer, in conversation, 1973.) It is a counterpart of the Brit. **you are a one!** P.B.: but *aren't you the one!* also, e.g. *isn't she the one!* have had some use in UK, later C20. Often suffixed by *then!*, when nuance is quizzical or rueful.

arf a mo, Kaiser! See: **'alf a mo** ...

argue. See: **don't argue.**

argument. See: **typical.**

Arizona. See: **happy as ducks.**

'ark at 'er! See: **hark at her!**

arm(s). See: **bit tight; chance your a.; flings; having a good; hit me now; I have a bone; I'll first; I'll pull; I'll tear; it's what; shoot it; throws his; you could twist.**

arm and a leg – an. This US c.p. occurs in two forms: *they charge you* – or *you've got to pay – an arm and a leg*; 'The price is exorbitant': 'general US for at least 30 years, though by now somewhat hackneyed' (R.C., 1978). The Brit. equivalents, *it costs the earth* or *they charge (you) the earth* are not c.pp. but ordinary hyperboles. P.B.: I first heard *it costs an arm and a leg* from Miss Stella Keenan in 1975 soon after her return to UK from US; that the phrase has become at least partially anglicised is shown by an allusive cartoon on the cover of *Time Out*, in the Spring of 1982, showing a would be traveller on the London Underground, where the fares had just been raised enormously, offering his sawn-off arm and leg at the ticket window; and the Poppy Day Appeal poster for 1983 showed two maimed ex-Servicemen, one without an arm, the other with only one leg. Cf **if it takes a leg,** the prob. orig.

Armenians. See: clever chaps; remember the starving.

army. See: it's a way; in an old a.; join the a.; thank God; there's the right; they can make; they tame; you, and who; your mother wears.

army corps. See: if you call.

army left! and **army, right!** is an army drill instructors' c.p. addressed to a recruit turning, or wheeling, in the wrong direction and dating, I think, since WW1. PGR.

around the world for a zack, an Aus. c.p. dating since *c.* 1950, is applied to any cheap and potent wine. A *zack* is the old sixpence, the new 5 cents. Jim Ramsay, *Cop It Sweet*, 1977.

arrive. See: I've arrived.

arse. See: close as God's; couldn't hit; cover your ass; 'dab!'; doesn't know; don't get your a.; don't let your mouth; don't tear the; flies; for a musical; get your ass; give your arse; hasn't got a ha'penny; here's me; I don't let; if I stick; in a pig's; it fits him; it's a poor a.; it's bad manners; kiss my a.; lend his; lights; living on the bone; lose his a.; more arse; much use as my; my arse; my ears; no heart; scratch his; shake the lead; she had; she walks; so is my; thimble; thinks the sun; tight as; took his; up a; wet arse; why don't you just; yes, my a.; you can ax; you can smell; you couldn't see; you want to know; you'd forget; you're full; your arse; your ass.

arsehole. See: buggered about; doesn't know; eh? to me; from arsehole; telegram; your ass-hole; and:

arsehole of the world, and Shaiba's halfway up it – (you know the old saying,) the Persian Gulf's the. This, an Army and RAF deprecatory c.p., dates from the early 1920s. 'At Shaiba – properly Sha'aiba – there was for many years, a transit camp' (L.A.). [P.B.: say, approx. 1920–55. The RAF also commemorated the appalling place with a dirge, still current among older airmen in the 1950s, 'Those Shaiba Blues'.]

But this unwelcome distinction has, since the middle 1920s, been claimed by the RAF for such other unpopular, hell-hole, stations as Aden, Basra, Freetown, and Suez.

Australians often refer to a place as **the arsehole of the world** if they think it to be inferior in, e.g., climate and amenities to their own city or town.

P.B.: a later refinement of this topographical denigration is the allusive *if the world had to have an enema*, (e.g. *Aden)'s the place they'd shove it*, (or grammatical variants of the same).

art. See: I don't know much.

art mistress. See: as the actress.

art of gunnery. See: attitude.

art thou there (? or !). Oh! so the penny has dropped – you understand at last – you've tumbled to it: *c.* 1660–1730. Thomas Shadwell, *The Scowrers*, Act III, opening scene:

CLAR[A]: Oh, Sister, the Sight of this Man has ruin'd me: I never shall recover it.

EUG[ENIA]: Ah! Art thou there, 'faith, recover it! Why, who would put a Stop to Love? Give Reins to it, and let it run away with thee.

Arthur or Martha. See I don't know whether...

article. See: that's the a.

article one, paragraph one. In the RN, 'A reply to any complaint' (John Laffin, *Jack Tar*, 1969): C20. There is no such article.

as...as... The similes formed on this pattern are to be found under the relevant adj., e.g. **good a scholar as my horse Ball,** etc., or at **much... as...,** e.g. **much chance as....**

[**as ever is** is not a c.p., but a cliché tag connoting emphasis, as in 'this next winter as ever is' (Edward Lear, *c.* 1873).]

as I am a gentleman and a soldier belongs apparently to the approx. period 1570–1640, as an asseveration or occ. a remonstration, and for its meaning should be compared with the C19–20 stock phrase, yet hardly a c.p., *an officer and a gentleman*. Ben Jonson, in his *Every Man in His Humour*, staged in 1598 and pub'd in 1601, has Cob the water-bearer say of Captain Bobadil: 'O, I have a guest [a lodger] – he teaches me – he swears the legiblest of any man christened: "By St George! – the foot of Pharaoh! – the body of me! – as I am gentleman and a soldier!" – such dainty oaths' (I, iii). At I, iv, Bobadil himself says, 'I protest to you, as I am a gentleman and a soldier, I ne'er changed words with his like.'

The shortened form, *as I am a gentleman*, occurs frequently in the comedies of *c.* 1580–1640, e.g. John Fletcher's *The Pilgrim*, IV, ii, where Pedro exclaims:

Murdering a man, ye Rascals?
Ye inhumane slaves, off, off, and leave this cruelty,
Or as I am a Gentleman: do ye brave me?

Beaumont and Fletcher, *Love's Cure*, written not later than 1616, in III, ii, has:

BOB: You'll come, Sir?
PIO: As I am a Gentleman.
BOB: A man o' the Sword should never break his word.

Cf **you are a gentleman....**

as I am a person. This c.p. of emphasis, apparently current *c.* 1660–1750, comes, for instance, in Congreve's *The Way of the World*, staged and pub'd in 1700, at IV, ii, where Lady Wishfort says: 'Well, Sir Rowland, you have the way – you are no novice in the labyrinth of love – you have the clue. But, as I am a person, Sir Rowland, you must not attribute my yielding to any sinister appetite, or indigestion of widowhood....' Later (V, ii) she declares, 'As I am a person 'tis true; – she was never suffered to play with a male child, though but in coats; nay, her very babies [i.e. dolls] were of the feminine gender.' Cf **as I live,** and

as I am a sinner – and I certainly *am*! This asseveration dates *c.* 1650–1750. *SOD* cites, for 1682, 'As I am sinner, my eager stomach crokes and calls for Dinner'. (Thanks to Simon Levene.)

as I am honest (i.e. honourable) and **truly as I live** are c.pps. of asseveration, reassurance, or mere emphasis: late C16–17. In Beaumont and Fletcher's *The Chances* (prob. by Fletcher alone), written not later than 1625 and pub'd in 1639, at II, ii, John, a lusty young Spanish gentleman designing to pay ardent court to a lovely woman, says woefully:

Now may I hang myself, this commendation
Has broke the neck of all my hopes: for now
Must I cry, no forsooth, and I [i.e. ay] forsooth, and surely,
And truly as I live, and as I am honest. He
Has done these things for 'nonce too; for he knows
Like a most envious Rascal as he is,
I am not honest, nor desire to be,
Especially this way.

The latter phrase elaborates *truly*, honestly, certainly, and connotes 'as certain as the fact that I am alive'. Cf **as I am a gentleman.**

as I have breath and **as I have life.** The former, a var. of

as I live and breathe, is more often as **as I've breath**; it occurs in Mark Lemon's *Hearts Are Trumps*, performed and pub'd in 1849, thus at I, ii:

GOAD: One morning a silver spoon was missing, and the next day you were ditto.

JOE: But I didn't steal it! As I've breath, I didn't, master!

The latter, also a var. of **as I live**, occurs in R.B. Sheridan's *The Duenna*, staged and pub'd in 1775:

ISAAC: Good lack, with what eyes a father sees! As I have life, she is the very reverse of all this.

And again in Sheridan's *The School for Scandal*, performed in 1777, pub'd 1779, at V, iii.

'Perhaps,' as A.B. suggests, 1978, 'picked up in the US from the motto of the State of South Carolina: *Dum spiro, spero*, "While I breathe, I hope".' South Carolina ratified the Federal Union in 1788.

as I hope to be saved is a c.p. of (orig., solemn) asseveration: *c.* 1650–1850; and then it gradually lost currency until, by 1920 at latest, it had entirely disappeared. In *The Sullen Lovers*, staged and pub'd in 1668, Thomas Shadwell writes in II, iii:

NINNY: But I'll tell you; there are not above ten or twelve thousand lines in all the poems; and, as I hope to be saved, I asked him but twelve pence a line, one line with another.

Sly, in Act IV of Colley Cibber's *Love's Last Shift* (or, as a Frenchman gleefully translated it, *La Dernière chemise de l'amour*), performed in 1694 and pub'd the next year, says: 'Bless me! O Lord! Dear Madam, I beg your pardon: as I hope to be sav'd, Madam, 'tis a mistake: I took him for Mr – .'

In 1720, Charles Shadwell (son of Thomas) uses it in *The Plotting Lovers; or The Dismal Squire*: Samuel Foote's *The Minor*, 1760, in Act I, in the scene between Sir William Wealthy and Samuel Shift, the latter says:

Would you believe it, as I hope to be saved, we dined, supped, and wetted five-and-thirty guineas... in order to settle the terms; and, after all, the scoundrel would not lend us a stiver.

It can also be found in Foote's *The Maid of Bath*, 1778, and Thomas Shadwell uses it again in *The Woman Captain*, 1680.

In 1816, in Samuel James Arnold's *Free and Easy. A Musical Farce*, I, ii, Mr and Mrs Courtly discuss an unexpected and cavalier guest:

COU: Did you ever see such an original?
MRS C: Very amusing, indeed!
COU: Vastly pleasant!
MRS C: Familiar – free and easy.
COU: And d-d disagreeable, as I hope to be saved.

There are variants, dating from Chaucer and even earlier; but this particular form is the only one to have become a c.p. – and it probably arose among pious Nonconformists.

as I hope to live likewise asseverates, during the very approximate period 1650–1820. Thomas Shadwell, *The Sullen Lovers*, 1668, at III, i, has: 'Not I, sir, as I hope to live.'

In 1784, in Hannah Cowley's *A Bold Stroke for a Husband*, at II, ii, Don Caesar exclaims: 'Beginning! as I hope to live; aye I see 'tis in vain.'

In George Colman the Younger's *Ways and Means; or a Trip to Dover*, 1788, the whimsical Sir David Dunder, apropos of a man cramped into the corner of a coach, exclaims: 'Took him for dead, as I hope to live.'

as I live and breathe – rarely *if* – often shortened to **as I live**, which, however, sometimes appears to be the more emphatic form. Indicating confidence or assurance, it arose, very approx., *c.* 1645. Of the numerous examples, these will perhaps serve:

Thomas Killigrew, *The Parson's Wedding*, 1664, II, i at end, Lady Love-all, 'an old Stallion Hunting Widow', being ardently pressed by the lively Mr Jolly, exclaims: 'Hang me, I'll call aloud; why, *Nan!* you may force me; But, as I live, I'll do nothing' – yet does.

In Thomas Shadwell's *Epsom Wells*, performed in Dec. 1672 and pub'd in 1673,at IV, i (lines 210–12 of D.M. Walmsley's edn), Mrs Jilt soliloquizes thus: 'Miserable Woman, how unlucky am I? but I am resolv'd never to *give* over 'till I get a Husband, if I live and breath [*sic*].' Cf also IV, i (lines 651–62), Fribble speaking: 'Oh monstrous impudence! the Woman's possess'd, as I hope to breathe.'

John Crowne, in Act II of *The Country Wit*, performed in 1675, pub'd 1693, makes Ramble exclaim: 'Oh dull rogue that I am! I have staid till she's gone: gone as I live!'

In Colley Cibber's *Woman's Wit; or, The Lady in Fashion*, 1697, in the first scene of Act V, Leonora exclaims: 'Ha! muffled in a cloak! O! for a glimpse of him! – My Lord Livermore, as I live!'

In William Burnaby's *Love Betray'd* (an adaptation of Shakespeare's *Twelfth Night*), performed and pub'd in 1703, I, i (p. 354, lines 6–7 of F.E. Budd's edn of Burnaby's plays), Emilia exclaims to Villaretta: 'Cousin *Frances* drunk, as I live!'

Arthur Murphy, *The Apprentice*, 1756, at II, i: Charlotte speaks: 'Dear Heart, don't let us stand fooling here; as I live and breathe, we shall both be taken, for heaven's sake, let us make our escape.'

Samuel Foote, *The Author*, 1757, Act I, Sprightly to Cape: 'Cape, to your post; here they are, i' faith, a coachful! Mr and Mrs Cadwallader, and your flame, the sister, as I live!'

In George Colman's *The Deuce Is In Him*, 1763, in II, i, Tamper exclaims: 'Belford's Belleisle lady, as I live!' where *as I live* = well, I'm damned!

George Colman and David Garrick, *The Clandestine Marriage*, 1766, III, i ('Scene Changes to another Apartment'); Miss Sterling remarks: 'As I live, Madam, yonder comes Sir John.' Garrick employs it twice in another play of the same year, *Neck or Nothing*. George Colman uses *as I live* again in *The English Merchant*, 1767, Act V.

In 1784, John O'Keeffe, *The Young Master*, employs it very effectually in IV, i.

In 1787, Elizabeth Inchbald, *The Midnight Hour* (a translation from the Fr.), has the shorter form.

In 1792, Thomas Holcroft, *The Road to Ruin*, at III, i. also has the shorter form.

Arthur Murphy, *The Way to Keep Him*, 1794, III, i:

MRS BELL[MOUR]: I really think you would make an admirable Vauxhall poet.

LOVE[MORE]: Nay, now you flatter me.

MRS BELL: No, as I live, it is very pretty.

Frederick Reynolds, an extremely popular light dramatist, in *The Delinquent; or, Seeing Company*, 1805, has Old Doric soliloquize thus: 'I'm safe at home at last – [*Looking round*] and, as I live – our villa is a pretty partnership concern – so snug – so tasty!'

In J.V. Millingen's *The Bee-Hive: A Musical Farce*, 1811, at I, ii, Cicely exclaims: 'As I live, the very uniform!'

W.C. Oulton's *The Sleep-Walker; or, Which Is the Lady? A Farce*, 1812, in I, i, causes Squire Rattlepate to burble, 'As I live, here is Mr Jorum, the landlord of the George.'

In 1820, Theodore Hook, in his very popular comedy, *Exchange No Robbery*, employs the shorter form, which had, by 1790 at latest, become the predominant form.

In 1829, George Colman the Younger uses it in *X.Y.Z.: A Farce*, at II, i; in 1830, both J.B. Buckstone, *Snakes in the Grass*, another farce, at I, i, and Caroline Boaden, *The First of April; A Farce*, at I, iii, also use it; all three, in the short form.

In 1845, to go to a novelist for a change, R.S. Surtees, *Hillingdon Hall; or The Cockney Squire*, beginning chapter III with the heading:

'Ecce iterum Crispinus,'

Here's old Jorrocks again, as we live! – *Free Translation*. A late example occurs in Thomas Morton the Elder, *'Methinks I See My Father!' or, 'Who's My Father?'*, ? 1850, I, i, 'Why, as I live, here he comes.' The phrase had always occurred frequently in connection with someone's arrival on the scene.

The phase, even in its shorter form, began to become slightly ob. *c.* 1900; yet it is extant; it appears as late as in Terence Rattigan's comedy, *French without Tears*, performed on 6 Nov. 1936 and pub'd in 1937. In Act I:

(Enter Marianne, the maid, with a plate of scrambled eggs and bacon, placing them in front of Brian.)
BRIAN: Ah, mes œufs, as I live.

I find it again, this time in Anglo-Irish, in Peter Driscoll, *In Connection with Kilshaw*, 1974: ' "Kilshaw's handwriting? Are you sure?" – "As I live, Harry." '

And the full phrase appears in May Mackintosh, *The Double Dealers*, 1975, ' "You're in love with him!" he said accusingly. "As I live and breathe, love at first sight, no less." '

Moreover, *as I live and breathe* had US currency from I don't know when until at least 1942, when it was recorded by Berrey.

as I live by bread exemplifies how very easy it is to 'slip up' with c.pp.: I had some record of it and then mislaid it! But, if I remember correctly, it belongs to mid C17 – mid 18. It may have been prompted by the long-† oath, *God's bread*, lit. the sacramental bread.

as I roved out. See **it's 'as I roved...'**

as I used to was is a joc. var. of 'as I used to be': C20; by 1950, ob., and by 1970, †. Somerset Maugham, *Cakes and Ale*, 1930, ' "I'm not so young as I used to was." '
P.B.: still, c. 1980, heard occ. in the parody, 'The old grey mare ain't what she used to was'.

as if I cared! 'Sam Fairfechan (played by Hugh Morton) in *ITMA*. He would say [in a strong Welsh Accent], "Good morning, how are you today?" and immediately follow with "As if I cared" ' (*VIBS*). See TOMMY HANDLEY.

as if I'm ever likely to forget the bloody place! – the place being Belgium. *Remember Belgium!*, orig. a recruiting slogan-become-c.p., 'was heard with ironic and bitter intonations in the muddy wastes of the Salient. And some literal-minded, painstaking individual, anxious that the point be rubbed well in, would be tempted to add: "As if I'm ever likely to forget the bloody place!" ' (John Brophy at p. 194 of the first edn [1930] of B & P, reprinted, after a generation, as *The Long Trail*).

as long as I can buy milk... See **why buy a book...**

as Moss caught his mare napping: c. 1500–1870; in mid C18–early 19, often *Morse*; in C19, mainly dial. Refers to catching someone asleep, hence by surprise. 'The allusions to this saying and song in C16–17 are very numerous,' says G.L. Apperson in his pioneering and excellent book. Moss – ? a mythical farmer – appears to have caught his elusive mare by feeding her through a hurdle, as in a cited quot'n dated 1597.

as much chance... See **much chance...**

as the actress said to the bishop – and vice versa. An innuendo scabrously added to an entirely innocent remark, as in 'It's too stiff for me to manage it – as the actress said to the bishop' or, conversely, 'I can't see what I'm doing – as the bishop said to the actress'. Certainly in RAF use c. 1944–7, but prob. going back to Edwardian days; only very slightly ob. by 1975, it is likely to outlive most of us.

A good example occurs in John Osborne's *A Sense of Detachment*, prod. on 3 Dec. 1972 and pub'd 1973, in Act I:
INTERRUPTER: You're trying to have it all ways, aren't you?
GIRL: As the actress said to the bishop.
Another excellent example occurs in Len Deighton's remarkable WW2 novel *Bomber*, 1970:

'He worked out the position of the short circuit on paper, but it was enough to make a strong man weep, watching him trying to fix it: gentleman's fingers.'

'As the actress said to the bishop,' said Digby.
Another in Martin Russell's novel, *Double Hit*, 1973:

Alongside a turntable in an alcove stood an open record-case... The player was a stereo job in moulded mahogany...

'Admiring my equipment?' Adrian re-emerged with a sandwich on a plate. 'As the actress said to the bishop. You get a terrific tone... at least, so the man assured me as he installed it all: I've never yet managed to do exactly what he did, as the bishop said to the actress.'

'As the bishop said to the actress = *Not having jokes of its own, spoken English turns ordinary statements into jokes by adding this phrase afterwards*' (*Punch*, 10 Oct. 1973). (Cf **bit of how's-your-father**.)
Either form tends to attract the other to cap it. P.B.: it may even be reduced to *as the A said to the B*. Nigel Rees, in *VIBS*, notes the var. *as the art mistress said to the gardener*, and comments 'this originated during Beryl Reid's stint as Monica in *Educating Archie* [BBC radio comedy series, late 1940s]. (I have always used it in preference to the original.)'
Cf the next, and **as the Windmill girl said...**

as the girl said to the sailor (less often **the soldier**) – and vice versa. An end-c.p., to soften a double, esp. if sexual, meaning: like the prec. phrase, it seems to have arisen in Edwardian times. Based – or so I've been told – upon a prototype about someone coming into money. Cf the C20 *as the monkey said*, a tag to a smoking-room story. Example: ' "We didn't come here just to look at the scenery," as the soldier said to the girl in the park.' Cf **what the soldier said...**, and **that's gone...**

as the Governor of North Carolina said to the Governor of South Carolina: it's a long time between drinks; either part is often used separately, the former allusively and with a significant pause, the latter either lit. or fig.: a famous quot'n that, c. 1880, became a c.p., almost entirely US, although known to – and used by – Americanophiles since c. 1920 – witness, e.g., Alec Waugh, *So Lovers Dream*, 1931:
'I suppose we've all got a barmaid side to us,' said Gordon [an Englishman].
'I know I've got a barman side to me,' said Gregory [an American].
'As the Governor of North Carolina said to the Governor of South Carolina,' said Francis [another American].
In the inestimable, rather than merely estimable, Bartlett, the *quotation* is given as 'Do you know what the Governor of South Carolina said to the Governor of North Carolina? It's a long time between drinks, observed that powerful thinker.' In *BQ* (5th edn, 1946), the formidable editor states that *it's a long time between drinks* 'is undoubtedly an invention' and adds that 'the expression antedates the Civil War'. See also **it's a long time between drinks.**

as the man in the play says occurs frequently in the comedies and farces of c. 1780–1840; it lends humorous authority to a perhaps frivolous statement. A felicitous example comes in Andrew Cherry's extremely popular and enviably durable comedy, *The Soldier's Daughter*, 1804, IV, i, where the drily humorous Timothy, to Frank Heartall's 'Tim! Timothy! – Where are you hurrying, my old boy?' replies:
Hey sir! Did you speak to me? Lord, I ask pardon, sir! – As the man in the play says, 'My grief was blind, and did not see you.' Heigho!
P.B.: a mid- and later C20 equivalent is the radio comedian's *it says here*, i.e. 'in my script', esp. as an excuse for a feeble joke. Cf:

as the man said was, c, 1969, imported from US ('Heard in the last year or two' (Petch, 1974); in the fact, a little earlier), where current since c. 1950. It lends authority – occ., a humorous warning – to what *has* been said.

as the monkey said. 'In English vulgar speech the monkey is often made to figure as a witty, pragmatically wise, ribald simulacrum of unrestrained mankind. Of the numerous instances, "You must draw the line somewhere, as the monkey said when peeing across the carpet" is typical. The phrase " ... as the monkey said" is invariable in the context' (L.A., 1969): since (?) c. 1870.
Also US, as Fain hastened to point out: 'Note the American *as the monkey said when he sat down on the lawnmower*, a rejoinder when someone says "balls!" College talk of the 1920s'. But in England, and in US (A.B.), the main use of 'monkey/lawnmower' is as an elab. of *they're off,*' cried (or *shrieked*) *the monkey*, a proletarian c.p. (late C19–20) applied to a race, notably a horserace just started, hence to

something that has come loose. A further var. of '*they're off!*' is *as the monkey cried when he slid down the razorblade*, and, without the monkey, there is the shorter, punning *they're off, Mr Cutts*. A.B., 1979, adds the (? mainly US) '*I'm getting a little behind in my work*', *said the butcher as he backed into the meat-grinder*.

Other monkey 'sayings', all couched in semi-proverbial form, are '*A little goes a long way*', *as the monkey said when he pee'd over the cliff* (or, locally, *over Beachy Head*); '*all is not gold that glitters*', *as the monkey said when he pee'd in the sunshine*; and the perhaps mainly Can. (? since *c.* 1930) '*that remains to be seen*', *as the monkey said when he shat in the sugar-bowl*. This latter selection – there are no doubt many others in folk-memory – are all humorous elaborations, each of a cliché, a truism that must have so irritated some wit that he vented his exasperation in scatology.

The archetype of the genre is prob. **every little helps ...** , q.v. See also the five prec. entries, and the next one. (E.P.; P.B.)

as the Windmill girl said to the stockbroker, dating since *c.* 1940, follows the pattern of **as the actress said ...** ; its vogue has lingered. The Windmill Theatre, London, justly prided itself on staying open throughout WW2. (R.S., 1977.)

as we say in France, apparently current *c.* 1820–1900, was mainly a Londoners' c.p. It occurs in, e.g., R.S. Surtees, *Handley Cross*, 1854, Vol. II, in the chapter entitled 'The Cut-'Em-Down Quads':

'I vish we may!' exclaimed Mr Jorrocks, brightening up; 'Somehow the day feels softer; but the hair [i.e. air] generally is after a fall. Howsomever, *nous verrons*, as we say in France: it'll be a long time before we can 'unt, though – 'edges will be full o' snow.'

as wears a head is a tag c.p., current *c.* 1660–1730 and meaning 'as a human being can be'. In Thomas Shadwell's *The Scowrers: A Comedy*, 1691, at III, i, we read:

BLUST[ER]: I am glad to hear you say so: Your Worship's as wise a Man – –

WHACK[UM]: As wears a Head in the City.

DING[BOY]: As wears a Pair of Horns there. [*Aside.*]

The phrase occurs often in Shadwell and other – and later – writers of comedies.

as you are stout, be merciful! A middle- and upper-class c.p. of C18. S (Dialogue I), 1738:

COL[ONEL]: Have you spoke with all your Friends?

NEV[EROUT]: Colonel, as you are stout, be merciful.

LORD SP[ARKISH]: Come, agree, agree, the Law's costly.

It had been recorded in 1721 by Kelly.

Here, *stout* does not mean 'obese, corpulent' but 'strong' or 'brave', as a gallant soldier is brave and fearless – and needs to be strong.

In C19 *stout* gave way to *strong* (*ODEP*, 3rd edn, 1970). But this proverb-c.p. did not, I think, long survive WW1.

[**as you go up, be kind to those coming down: you may meet them (coming up again) as you go down**. In *Something of Myself*, pub'd 1937 (the year after his death), Rudyard Kipling wrote, 'One met men going up and down the ladder in every shape of misery and success', which I think alludes to a c.p. I've been hearing since *c.* 1925, but been unable to nail down. [P.B.: E.P. *had* nailed it down: see **always be nice ...** , which appeared in the 1st ed. of this Dictionary. I include this doublet from his subsequent notes for this present ed. because of the classical sources following.] It possesses the quality of the more sophisticated sort of proverb; this longer version sounds more like an aphorism than a c.p., but it has a shorter form [**always be nice ...**], which neatly epitomises the vicissitudes of 'the rat race' and of the struggle for power. Ultimately it follows the thought pattern instituted by the Biblical 'That which was first has turned, and now is last' (*Isaiah*, 48, 12); cf 'Many that are first shall be last; and the last shall be first', which comes from Euripides, *Hippolytus*, l. 982. 'It also suggests all those phrases stemming from the concept of the wheel of fortune'

(W.J.B., 1978 – to whom I owe the Biblical and Euripidean quot'ns). The several versions have had some currency in the US, apparently since *c.* 1960, as Col. Moe has ascertained for me.]

as you were! 'Used ... to one who is going too fast in his assertions' (Hotten, 1864): mid C19 – early C20. But since *c.* 1915, it has signified 'Sorry! *My* mistake'. The origin of the latter sense (and, of course, of the former) is made clear by F & G: 'The ordinary military word of command, used colloquially by way of acknowledging a mistake in anything said, e.g. "I saw Smith – as you were – I mean Brown." ' Much used in WW2: 'The [military] phrase spread to ordinary conversation. "See you at Groppi's [in Cairo] at 9.30 – as you were, 10 o'clock" ' (PGR).

ash. See: one flash.

ashore. See: all ashore; come ashore.

ask. See: don't ask; don't say No; granted; I ask; I didn't ask; I only asked; I took; I'll 'ave; if you have to; knock three; nobody asked; thought; to make a fool; we asked; who asked; you asked.

ask a silly question and you'll get a silly answer (in US **ask a stupid ...**); also **ask silly questions and you'll get silly answers**: both versions often shortened, to elliptical **ask a silly question!** and **ask silly questions**. This is, in late (? mid) C19–20, the c.p. evolved from an old proverb, *ask no questions and you'll be told no lies*.

ask another!; also **ask me another!** Don't be silly!: mostly Cockneys': late C19–20, orig. addressed to someone asking a stale riddle. Ware records *ask another!* for 1896. In 1942 Berrey records *ask me another!*, which, orig. Eng., prob. goes back to the 1890s. An early example occurs in 'Taffrail' (Cdr H. Taprell Dorling), *Pincher Martin, O.D.* [Ordinary Duty Seaman], [1916]: ' "Silly blighter!" said the first lieutenant unsympathetically. "What the dooce did he want to get in the way for?" – "Ask me another," laughed Tickle.'

ask cheeks near Cunnyborough! A low London – female only – c.p. of mid C18 – mid C19. Lit. 'Ask my arse!' (Grose, 1785.) *Cunnyborough* = the borough, hence area, of *cunny* = *cunt*. Cf the male **ask mine**, or **my, arse!**

ask me! was common among US students at the beginning of the 1920s. Recorded by McKnight.

ask me another! See **ask another!**

ask mine (later **my**) **arse!** Orig. nautical, always low, c.p. of evasive reply to a question: mid C18–20. (Grose, 1788.) Cf **ask cheeks near Cunnyborough** and also **so is mine** – later **my – arse**.

[**ask no questions and you'll hear** (or **be told**) **no lies** is not a c.p. but a proverb.]

ask silly questions and you'll get silly answers! See **ask a silly question ....**

ask the man in charge! See **don't ask me**.

ask yourself! Be reasonable – be sensible: Aus.: since *c.* 1925. (Sidney J. Baker, *Australian Slang*, 1942.) Prob. elliptical for *Well, just ask yourself!* See also **I ask myself**.

asking. See: are you asking; I'm only a.; none the better; not you by; now you're a.; that's asking.

ass. See; arse; only asses.

ass in a sling – have, or **get**, (one's). Prec. by any pronoun (*I, you, he*, etc.) in any number or in any tense, as, e.g., 'he has (*or* he's got) his ass in a sling', it has been glossed by R.C., 1978, thus: 'To be in deep and (usually) painful difficulties. Literally, to have a kick in the ass so powerful as to necessitate the sort of sling used to support an injured arm. General US, since WW2 at latest, and probably working class use even earlier. By 1950s so widely known that our famous political cartoonist, Herblock, could play on it without words. [In 1954] the US Senate was finally compelled to move against Senator Joseph McCarthy [1908–57] ... As hearings on the motion to formally censure him began, he injured (or claimed to have injured) his arm, and appeared at the hearings with it supported by a sling. When censure was finally voted, [the political cartoonist] Herblock depicted

McCarthy emerging grimly from the Senate chambers, his arm in one sling, his fundament in another. No caption was given – or needed.'

Hence, of course, *don't get your ass in a sling*: 'Don't do or say anything you can't get out of or remedy' (Fain, 1977): since the 1930s.

astern. See: remember your; sailing ship.

astonish. See: you astonish; and:

astonish me! An educated, cultured, intelligent c.p., dating from early 1960s. In Derek Robinson, *Rotten with Honour*, 1973:

'...There is still a good chance.'

Hale waited. 'Go on,' he muttered. 'Astonish me.'

'I think I might.'

Kingsley Amis, in *Observer*, 4 Sep. 1977, says that it 'must be straight from "Etonne-moi, Jean", Diaghilev to Cocteau'. The ambience of the Eng. c.p. being congruent, I think that Mr Amis is prob. right. Sergei Diaghilev (1872–1929) was, of course, the great Russian ballet producer; and Jean Cocteau (1889–1963), the French poet, playwright, novelist, who rather specialised in the art of *étonner les bourgeois*. If this orig. be correct, it comes from an Eng. translation of a book about either Diaghilev or Cocteau.

P.B.: or it may be simply a 'cultured' var. of the more common **surprise me!** q.v.

at a church with a chimney in it. S. 1738, Dialogue I (p. 103, my edn):

LADY ANSW[ERALL]: Why, Colonel; I was at Church.

COL[ONEL]: Nay, then I will be hang'd, and my Horse too.

NEV[EROUT]: I believe her Ladyship was at a Church, with a Chimney in it [i.e. at a private house; but also applicable to an inn].

This c.p. has been current throughout C18–20, although little since *c*. 1920 and, by *c*. 1970, virtually †.

'at done it! 'That's done it' – 'That *caps* it'. See **if you can't fight ...** In Cockney, *'at* can be either *hat* or *that*, so there's a neat, thoroughly intentional, pun.

at least she won't die wondering. See She will die wondering.

at this moment in time was being used to a nauseating extent in 1974 – as, indeed, it is still [1977] – and Noble, 1974, remarks:

As you know, it's become a cliché. But I now find that its use is considered so ridiculous by the more sensitive kind of people that it is coming into their conversation sarcastically as a catch phrase. It is one of those American importations that had at first a use for emphasis but has outstayed its welcome.

J.W.C. has noted that the cliché *at that point in time* was very frequently used during the Watergate hearings.

To Vernon Noble's just comment, Mr S.C. Dixon, 1978, subjoins this well-deserved acerbity: 'To which I add "In this day and age" and any reference to "at the grass roots". (At our grass roots are worms.)'

atap. See: up, Guards.

atta boy! is how Edward Albee writes the next, in Act III of *Who's Afraid of Virginia Woolf?*, 1962.

attaboy! is only apparently a 'one-word c.p.', for, via *'at's the boy!*, it stands for *that's the boy!*, an expression of warm approval, either for something exceptionally well done or for especially good behaviour; exclamatory approbation: since *c*. 1910 in US (W & F); adopted in Britain in the last year (1918) of WW1 – recorded by F & G, 1925, and see, e.g., Dorothy L. Sayers, *Murder Must Advertise*, 1933, ' "Picture of nice girl bending down to put the cushion in the corner of the [railway] carriage. And the headline [of the advertisement]? *'Don't let them pinch your seat.*' " "Attaboy!" said Mr Bredon [Lord Peter Wimsey].'

Much less common were *attababy!* (Berrey) and *attagirl!* (W & F, 1960 – although in use long before that date). See also **thatta boy.**

A.B. adds, 1978, 'I've heard a similar expression, used by coaches to inspire a successful athlete: *way to go* (*fellow*):

US: since *c*. 1950. [It means] "That's how to do it!" Revitalised on American television, especially in "Rowan and Martin's Laugh-in", 1960s.'

attention must be paid. 'Last week, on a theater program, I saw a few reminiscences. Among them was the remark: "Arthur Miller's *Death of a Salesman*" [it opened in New York, 10 Feb. 1949] "gave us a catch phrase, Mildred Dunnock's line: 'Attention must be paid'." The sentence has had some general use, but was, I think, rather a vogue expression than one making any lasting stay in the language' (Shipley, 1975). R.C., 1977, 'It retained enough (limited) currency in 1975 to figure as the peroration of an attorney's summation.'

attitude is the art of gunnery and whiskers make the man. This c.p. has – by the rest of the Royal Navy – been applied to gunnery officers, who were also said to be 'all gas and gaiters': 'the gas being their exaggerated emphasis on the word of command, and the gaiters being worn by officers and men at gun drill and on the parade ground' (Rear-Adm. P. W. Brock, CB, DSO, 1969): since *c*. 1885. Naval gunnery became much more important when John Arbuthnot Fisher (1841–1920) was appointed the captain in charge of the gunnery school in the late 1880s; he and his disciples vastly improved both the standard of gunnery and the status of gunnery officers and men.

The lower-deck version is *h'attitude is the h'art of gunnery and whiskers make the man*, recorded by Granville.

au reservoir! '*Au revoir!*' According to Frank Shaw – I'm not doubting his word – this c.p. valediction was occasioned by *Punch* when, in 1899, 'two engineering experts went to Egypt to survey the Nile water resources': the phrase apparently caught on almost immediately; by 1940, ob. and by 1950 †. The slangy truncation, *au rev!*, however, did not rise to the pinnacle or status of c.p. Cf **olive oil**, q.v.

au revoir. See: say au r.

Audley. See: John Orderly.

aunt. See: I wouldn't call; if my aunt; oh, my giddy; still running.

Aunt Fanny. See: cor! chase; like A.; my Aunt F.

Aunt Hattie. See: mad as.

Aunt Mitty. See: your Aunt M.

Aunt Susie. See: so's your A.

auntie. See: eat up; I haven't laughed; once round; since auntie.

Austin Reed. See: just part.

Australian as a meat-pie (– **as**). Thoroughly, emphatically, obviously Australian: since (apparently) the late 1960s. 'From the prominency of meat pie in the Australian diet' (G.A. Wilkes, *Dict. Aus. Coll.*, 1978 – an exemplar of what such a book should be).

'ave a piece of gat(t)oo is a Cockney c.p. that, dating from *c*. 1929, forms a good-tempered yet derisive 'take-off' uttered lacking the (supposed) gentility of a knowledge of French, at the expense of those who air a tiny knowledge of that elegant language. (Based on a note from L.A., 1976.)

average. See: smarter.

aw, forget it! A US c.p. current at least as early as 1911. ('The Function and Use of Slang' in *The Pedagogical Seminary*, Mar. 1912.) It became **forget it**, q.v.

aw, gee, you don't really love me, baby! was [during the latter part of WW2 and after] said to be the G.I.s' approach to a girl for favours' (an anon. correspondent, 1978).

'aw, shit, lootenant!'; an' the lootenant shat. 'Borrowed from the US army; a scornful c.p. used by the other ranks to describe ineffective and easily browbeaten subalterns. Often, to utter the first half of the phrase is enough' (P.B., 1974): US, since *c*. 1942; also Brit. by the latish 1950s.

aw shucks! 'The conventional US and Canadian expression of yokel embarrassment. "Aw shucks! I couldn't say that to a lady!" ' (Leechman): since *c*. 1910 and, as used by others than yokels, often joc. and always a c.p. It occurs, with a ref. to Huckleberry Finn, in John D. MacDonald's *The Girl, the Gold Watch and Everything*, 1962. Cf next. R.C., 1977, suggests, 'almost certainly a euphemism (albeit unconscious) for "aw shit!" ' P.B.: cf the use of synon. *Oh, sugar!* in Brit. Eng.

aw, shucks, Ma, I can't dance is a US c.p. that 'used to indicate the futility of [trying to do] something beyond one's ability, but sometimes because of something beyond one's control' (Moe, 1976): apparently ob. by *c.* 1950 and † by *c.* 1960. 'In the past (the 1920s) it was frequently given more fully as "Aw shucks, Ma, I can't dance, 'cause when I dance I sweat, and when I sweat I stink, and when I stink the boys won't dance with me. Aw shucks, Ma, I can't dance." ' Clearly rural in origin, and then employed much more widely, it is one of several bucolicisms that became mock rustic, P.B.: cf the Brit. mock rustic 'Don't make I laugh, 'cause when I laughs, I pees myself, and when I pees myself that runs all down my leg.' A Can. version, noted in the 1st edn. of this book as used 'just for something to say', was *shit, mother, I can't dance.*

aw, your fadder's (occ. **father's**) **mustache!** An elab. of **your fadder's mustache!**, q.v.

away. See: have it a.; leg over; mugs; one that got; take it a.; up, up, and.

away, the lads! 'North of England regional, but known all over [Britain]. Its use sanctified by President Carter recently ... It is, I think, a Geordie cry of encouragement for any group engaged in any activity. Chanted at soccer matches, especially when teams like Newcastle are engaged' (Skehan, 1978). P.B.: sometimes rendered in print as 'Ho-waaay the laads!' It can also be used in the singular, '... the lad!'

away with the mixer! Either 'Let's go ahead!' or derivatively 'Now we're going ahead': since *c.* 1946. A concrete-mixer or a cocktail-mixer?

away you go, laughing! A 'c.p. of jocular dismissal, especially in the Services, after missing, e.g., a day's leave or the issue of an item of one's kit. "Nothing to be done about it" – "Make the best of it" – " Grin and bear it". WW2' (L.A., 1976). Cf **and like it!**, q.v.

awful. See: now you'll; you are awful; you're awful.

axe. See: where the chicken; you can axe.

axe-handle. See: out in the woodshed.

axle. See: here we come.

'ay is for 'orses. See **hay is for horses.**

ay thang yew! I thank you! Since the mid-1930s, when comedian Arthur Askey constantly used it on radio – notably in 'Band Wagon' – and elsewhere, but, from *c.* 1955, less and less general. That great comedian reputedly 'borrowed it from the London bus conductors' (*Radio Times*, 28 June–4 July 1975). Cf **thanking you!**

aye, aye, don't bust yer corsets! Don't get excited all about nothing! 'A deliberate cod [i.e., hoaxing] catch phrase used by Lance Percival on a radio show years ago. A send-up of catch phrases' (John Sparry, 1977). Parodies seldom last long: nor did this one, 'Invented by me for Lance Percival, but I can't remember for which show!': thus Barry Took, author of the delightful *Laughter in the Air*, 1976.

aye, aye, that's yer lot! 'Jimmy Wheeler (1910–73) was a cockney [music-hall and radio] comedian with a fruity voice redolent of beer, jellied eels and winkles. He would appear in a bookmaker's suit, complete with spiv moustache and hat, and play the violin. At the end of his fiddle piece he would break off his act and intone this catchphrase' (*VIBS*). The c.p. was converted by the public to a much wider application: post-WW2. See also **and that's your lot!**

aye, aye, we've got a right one 'ere! See **We've got a right one 'ere!**

aye, So is Christmas! See **coming?** ...

B

B.E.F. will all go home. In one boat – the. 'In 1917 old expressions such as "a bon time" and "trays beans" were not much heard; another had arisen, "The B.E.F. will all go home – in one boat"' (Edmund Blunden, *Undertones of War*, 1928). More officers' than men's: 1917–18 only. The BEF was, of course, the British Expeditionary Force in France. Cf **it'll be over by Christmas.**

B.F.N. See **good-bye for now!**

baboon. See: **you are a thief.**

baby. See: believe me, b.; burn, baby; hang in; hello, baby; I don't know nothin'; I got eyes; if you're going; keep the faith; kill that b.; no poes; oh, baby; okay, baby; swing it, b.; they can make; this won't; wait for b.; who loves; you've come.

baby in every bottle – (there's) a. 'About 15 years ago a colleague of mine, Edwin Hill, then in Nottingham, used to say this of well-known brands of stout. I got the impression it was Services' slang' (J.B.S., 1979). P.B.: a version of the (?folk-lore) 'Guinness and oysters' recipe for human fertility.

baby wants a pair of shoes; also, in Aus., **... a new pair ...** ; and, in US, **baby needs shoes.** A dicing gamblers' c.p. of C20: orig. underworld, esp. in prisons; by 1940, also fairly gen. See also **this won't buy baby a frock.**

bacca. See: beer, bum.

bachelor. See: then the town.

back. See: don't get your b.; face would; get off my b.; give it b.; go back; got calluses; guess who's; her clothes; here's the b.; hold me b.; home and dried; it's got a b.; join the b.; living high; mind your backs; more hair; no back; oh, my achin'; oh, well! back; put a galley; round the b.; sir, I see; strong b.; take it off; that'll put your; that's what gets; there and; wake up at; what he doesn't; why don't you go; you're on the pig's.

back at the ranch. See **meanwhile, back ...**

back in the old routine! 'Here we go again!' applied to an anecdote, a lecture, and the like, but also, more commonly – and lit. – to resumption of work after a holiday or break: since late 1940s. Prob. from 'showbiz'. (P.B.)

back in your kennel! See **get back into your box!**

back o' (occ. of) Bourke. 'In the remote and uncivilised regions generally' (Wilkes): a famous Aus. c.p., dating from *c.*1890. Lit., 'beyond the most remote town in north-west N.S.W.' Cf *back of the black stump*, q.v. at **black stump.**

back o' me hand to ye! See **Here's the back ...**

back pedal! Steady – that can hardly be true; in short, tell that to the marines: *c.* 1910–35. From cycling. Collinson.

back teeth. See **my back teeth ...**

back to square one, sometimes shortened to **square one!**; in full, **let's go back ....** Let's start again – by going back to the point of starting – often through reluctant necessity. 'The BBC's old method of dividing the [soccer] pitch for commen-

tary purposes [before the age of TV] was the origin (in January 1927) of the phrase' (John Peel, 'Squaring up for the Cup', caption to accompany illustration/diagram, in *The Times*, 22 May 1982; the article further mentions 'the numbers [up to 8] ... correspond with those in squares superimposed on a map of the Wembley pitch printed in the *Radio Times*'); but the commentators themselves took it from such games as Snakes and Ladders, where an unlucky fall of the dice took one from the top to the bottom line. In *The Deadly Joker*, 1963, 'Nicholas Blake' (Cecil Day Lewis) uses it in this short form. But it has also been suggested that the phrase derives from the game of hopscotch. 'The grid from which football commentators worked did indeed resemble a hopscotch pitch' (R.S., 1974). Petch, 1974, notifies me that 'the latest form used' is *back to square one – and the one before that* – with the var. *back to square nought* ('a square worse than when it started': Richard Miers, *Shoot to Kill*, 1959), as P.B. tells me. Well, that's the Brit. story (and we're stuck with it!), but J.W.C., noting in 1978 that the phrase has been current in US since *c.* 1960 at latest, glosses and comments: 'We're right back where we started – we've made no net progress. Originally and literally, landing one's counter (in a table game) – according to the throw of the dice – on the unluckiest of sequential "squares", reacting "back to square one", i.e. move your counter back to the beginning' – thus reinforcing the ref. to the snakes-and-ladders and ludo type of game, which is the picture in most later C20 hearers' minds anyway.

back to the cactus! An Australian navy's c.p., dating from the 1930s and meaning 'back to duty – after leave'. The ref. is to the prickly pear that forms a feature of the Aus. rural scene, esp. in the outback. Dal Stivens, for instance, uses it in a story written in 1944 and pub'd 1946, in *The Courtship of Uncle Henry*. Cf **back to the war!**

back to the drawing-board! (occ ... *old drawing-board*), prob. orig. with 'a famous Peter Arno (*The New Yorker*) drawing of the war years, black humour, [an] aircraft exploding into the ground, designers on the field remarking "Ah well, back to the old drawing-board"' (Wedgewood, 1977). Confirmed by William Hewison in *The Cartoon Connection: The Art of Pictorial Humour*, 1977, although in the form *well, back to the drawing-board*, with an allusion to cartoon captions that have got into the language and with the remark, ' ... spoken by a quite unworried man with a roll of technical drawings under his arm as he watched an aeroplane disintegrate on the ground'. (The inimitable Peter Arno's real name was Curtis Arnoux Peters; born in 1904, he died in 1968. He was a Yale graduate and nobody's fool.) As a c.p., it came to denote 'the comprehensive reappraisal required when a lengthy, complicated and expensive project has produced a fiasco' (R.C., 1977). P.B.: in UK, where it is widely known, the phrase is often loosely used for no more than simply 'Let's get back to work', in the sense 'Oh well, back to the old grindstone!'

back to the jute mill! is a solely US var. of the next but one: 'I first heard it ... in 1938 by military personnel serving in the Far East' (Moe, 1975). See also **back to the salt mines**.

back to the kennel! is a US c.p. of contemptuous disparagement: *c.* 1925–50. (Berrey.) Speaking to a person as if to a dog. Cf **get back into your box!**

back to the salt mines! – *salt* being often omitted and *well* often prec. I first heard it early in the 1950s, but its Brit. use prob. goes back to *c.* 1945. It was imported from the US and, there, may have orig. late in C19. Col. Moe thinks *back to the mines!* is the earliest form and attributes it to a play of the 1890s, *Siberia*, with its dramatic poster of a party of Russians proceeding to Siberia 'under the lashes of the Cossacks'. He cites Henry Collins Brown, *In the Golden Nineties*, 1928, chapter III, 'The Theatre. (Old Time Posters)'. In Irving S. Cobb, *Murder Day by Day*, 1933: ' "That would be Terence," he said. "Well, Gilly, it's back to the mines for me, and this day I'll need to have my brain grinding in two – three different places at once." '

From the Western idea – not so far wrong at that! – that, in both imperial and in communist Russia, political prisoners were sent to do hard labour in the salt mines of Siberia. Berrey records the addition of *ye slaves*.

There are two variants quite well known in the US but unknown in Britain: **back to the jute mill!** and *back to the chain gang*, the former noted by Moe (1975) and the latter by Berrey (1942). A.B., 1978, writes 'I've heard *back to the (old) grist mill!* and *back to the (old) boiler factory!* Both US, [respectively] north and mid-western. Tentative dating: mid C19–mid 20'. Of the *salt mines* form, R.C., 1978, commented, 'Now obsolescent in the US'. In the UK also.

back to the war! This WW1 c.p. was used by Tommies returning to the Line after a leave or, esp., after a tour of duty in back areas.

back up! A US c.p., dating *c.* 1919–40. George Ade, in Act I of *The College Widow* ('A Pictorial Comedy in Four Acts'), 1924: 'She wanted me to come back and board with her mother this year. (One of the [college] boys says, "Back up?" Another chuckles – another whistles ....)' Here, *back up* prob. = 'to corroborate, to prove', rather than 'to explain in detail'.

back wheel. See: your wheel's.

backbiters. See: your bosom.

backbone. See: I was doing it; I'm so empty.

backside. See: sparrows.

backwards. See: where the crows; and:

backwards, the way Mollie went to church, or with *backwards* omitted. She *didn't* go; hence, 'reverse what has just been said!': Anglo-Irish wit: C20.

backyard. See: stay in; you can't play.

bacon. See: crackling; good voice; if only.

bad. See: can't be bad; go on with; that's just too; that's too bad; you've picked.

bad luck to him! See **luck to him ...**

bad manners to speak when your arse is full. See **it's bad manners ...**

bad tenant. See: better an empty.

bag(s). See: couldn't knock; get a bag; go and bag; it's in the bag; looks like a bag; over the top; rough as; they're all the same; what's in.

Bagshaw. See: baw-haw.

bail him out! See LIVERPOOL.

baker. See: not today.

balderdash, poppycock and piffle! That's nonsense: Aus. educated and cultured, or merely cultured, c.p., dating from the early 1960s. A euph. for the low slang *balls!*

But apparently the Aus. phrase adapts the English *balderdash, piffle and poppycock*, used by Harcourt Williams on the West End stage as early as 1946, as Mr Norman Franklin tells me (1974).

ball. See: good a scholar; it's your b.; so you want; that's the way; that's the whole; you play b.

ball and chain. See: if I stick.

ball-game. See: different ball-g.; not my b.; that's the old b.

ball park. See: in the same.

ballocks. See: has his; more bollocks; it's like a nigger; stands out.

Ballocky Bill the Sailor (orig. **BB the S**) **just returned from the sea**; less correctly but very frequently spelt *bollicky*. This mythical character has been commemorated in a low ballad of late C19–20 and he becomes the subject of a c.p. when either the short or the long version was, by way of evasion, used by British soldiers in WW1. Ballocky Bill was – and is – reputed to have been most generously genital'd: cf the vulgar *ballocks*, testicles; but at least partly operative is the dialectal *ballocky*, left-handed, hence clumsy. 'As "Barnacle Bill the Sailor" he became respectable enough to be recorded as a song between the wars' (Sanders, 1978), P.B.: it was a little, half-sized record, and I played it over and over, scratchily on a wind-up gramophone: 'It's only me, from over the sea, says ...'

balloon. See: like the man who fell; went down; what time; and:

[**balloon?** All right?: an underworld one-word c.p., current in the 1930s. James Curtis, *You're in the Racket Too*, 1937.]

balls. See: are your hands; bigger the b.; cold enough; don't get your arse; eh? to me; I wouldn't give; I'll have your b.; if my aunt; my arse is.

balls, bees and buggery!; also **balls, picnics and parties!** The former, a c.p. of late C19–20, seems to have occasioned the latter, a c.p. dating from *c.* 1925. They are punning and stylized amplifications and elaborations of the exclam. *balls!*, nonsense.

[**'balls!' cried the King: the Queen laughed because she wanted to** and **'balls!' cried the Queen: the King laughed because he wanted to (two).** Separately or together. J.W.C. roundly declares that this US pair of phrases 'not only never were, but could not have become, catch phrases, because they don't and can't apply to a situation' (1975). Col. Moe, on the other hand, thinks that they have two applications: (1) 'referring to nonsense or foolishness: "It's ridiculous" – "That's a laugh" – "Don't be an Airedale" ...'; and (2) 'expletive of profanity, cursing, or oath: "Go to hell!" – etc.'. Both of these gentlemen place it as far back as the 1930s (JWC) or the 1920s (AM), and one adjudges it to have been, orig., current among students; both, moreover, say that it is extant.

Ashley, 1983, provides a more 'rational' version: *'balls!' said the Queen. 'If I had to* [two], *I'd be king,'* P.B.: perhaps not c.pp., but certainly 'mini-monologues', with which cf, e.g., *'hell!' said the duchess ...*]

ball's in your court. See **it's your ball**.

balls on him like a scoutmaster, usu. prec. by **he has**. A low NZ and Can. c.p. dating from *c.* 1925 and based upon the scurrilous idea, formerly – and still? – current among the ignorant, that many scoutmasters are active homosexuals.

balls to that lark! There's nothing doing *or* I don't think much of that idea: NZ (and elsewhere): since *c.* 1910. A c.p. extension of *balls to that*, common in Britain late C19–20. P.B.: in later C20 Britain, (?) esp. in the Forces, there are the variants *fuck* (or *sod this* or) *that for a lark!*

balls to you, love! is a C20 var. – an elab. – of the rather older *balls to you* itself, of course, also a c.p., low and masculine. It reflects both the workman's contempt for the white-collar worker and his own ignorance of lawn tennis, the precise ref. being to the game of mixed doubles at the suburban lawn tennis club level. P.B.: in 1976, I mentioned to E.P. the var. ..., *ducky!* (instead of *love*); his comment was, 'True; but it came somewhat later and at, I think, a slightly lower social level.'

Banagher. See: bangs B.

banana(s). See: have a b.; yes, we have.

banana boat. See: came over.

banana skin. See: you've got one foot.

band. See: and the band; beats the band; then the band.

bandicoot. See: like a b.

bandit. See: make out.

bang, bang, you're dead! – often written **bang! bang! you're dead.** In UK, it is mostly a children's c.p., dating from *c.* 1960 and resulting from an excessive televiewing of 'Westerns'. [P.B.: I would put it back to *c.* 1940, if not earlier, and the influence of 'Western' films – and WW2.] Orig. it was US: indeed, in US slang, a *bang-bang* is a 'Western' (a cowboy movie) – 'from the high incidence of gunshots in such films' (W & F); as a US c.p., *bang-bang! = drop dead!*, q.v., and antedates 1960. It is perhaps worth recalling that, in 1929, the brilliant, witty, entertaining George Ade published a collection of narratives first appearing in the late 1890s and called them *Bang! Bang!*

In the Winter, 1966, issue of *Film Quarterly*, Richard Whitehall, in 'The Heroes Are Tired', writes 'The violence which had for so long been stylized into "Bang, bang, you're dead!" had [in 'Westerns', by mid-1950s] become more brutal and punishing.' And in Jack D. Hunter's 'thriller', *Spies Inc.*, 1969, occurs this significant use of the c.p.: 'I could not visualize Carl strolling into the motel office and saying, Hey, pal .... I could, though, visualize Carl strolling into the motel office and saying, Bang, bang – you're dead.'

In 1973, June Drummond, an English novelist, named one of her books *Bang! Bang! You're Dead!*

The var. *boom! boom! you're dead!*, based on US soldiers WW2 *boom-boom*, a small calibre rifle or a pistol, is used by Donald MacKenzie (Canadian-born) in his novel, *The Kyle Contract*, 1970.

bang, crash, sausage and mash! 'A childish c.p., celebrating any joyful noise, such as two saucepan lids being clashed together. Formerly, say before WW2, sausage and mash was a cheap, nourishing and filling meal for labourers and children. Probably dates from WW1 and is still current with my grandson' (Sanders, 1978).

bang goes sixpence! In *Punch*, 5 Dec. 1868, p. 235, appeared a cartoon by Charles Keene showing two Scotsmen conversing; the caption, entitled 'Thrift', is:

'*Peebles Body* (*to Townsman who was supposed to be in London on a visit*), "E-eh, Mac! Ye're sune hame again!"

Mac. "E-eh, it's just a ruinous place, that! Mun, A had na' been the-erre abune Twa Hoours when – *Bang* – went *saxpence!!!*"'

The c.p. *bang goes sixpence!* was popularised by Sir Harry Lauder, and in the form *bang went sixpence*, is joc. applied to any small expense incurred, esp. for entertainment and with a light heart, although it has also, in C20, been increasingly addressed to someone exceedingly careful about small expenses. Weekley shrewdly suggested that *bang* suggests abruptness.

According to *The English Comic Album*, by Leonard Russell and Nicholas Bentley, 1948, '*bang goes saxpence* was overheard on a Glasgow street corner by Sir John Gilbert [1817–97, artist], told to Birket Foster [1825–99, another artist], retold to Foster's friends and eventually sent to Keene [Charles Samuel Keene, 1823–91, comic artist on *Punch*].'

bang on! was a bomber crews' c.p. of WW2 and it meant that everything was all right; in the nuances 'dead accurate' and 'strikingly apposite', it was adopted by civilians in 1945, a notable early example occurring in Nicholas Blake's *Head of a Traveller*, 1948. cf **right on!**, q.v.

bang to rights! 'A fair cop' – a justifiable arrest for an obvious crime: underworld, since before 1930. Hence, a police and London's East End c.p. by 1935 at latest, and a fairly gen. slangy c.p. since *c.* 1950. Note Frank Norman's engaging criminal reminiscences, *Bang to Rights*, 1958. For the *bang* part of the phrase, cf **bang on!**; *to rights* = rightfully. Esp. in *catch* (or *caught*) *bang to rights*, 'catch (or caught) red-

handed', which is recorded in David Powis, *The Signs of Crime*, 1977, as still actively current.

bangs Banagher and Banagher bangs the world – that or **this.** The mainly Anglo-Irish *bang*, to defeat, to surpass, supplies the key, as also does the var., *that* (or *this*) *beats Banagher and Banagher beats the world*. The orig. and predominant Anglo-Irish proverbial saying is *this bangs ...* ; it dates from not later than 1850, and it seems to have become a c.p. within a decade. It occurs in, e.g., Rolf Boldrewood, *My Run Home*, 1897, in a passage concerning a period *c.* 1860. See P.W. Joyce, *English as We Speak It in Ireland*, 1910, and note that *Banagher*, a village in King's County, Ireland (now Co. Offaly), as Weekley, neatly aligning [to] *beat creation*, once noted, was perhaps chosen because of its echoic similarity to *bang*.

In 1891, M records the composite var., *that bangs Banagher, and Banagher beats the devil*, and adds, 'An Irish expression [equivalent] to "that beats the Dutch" ' – by which, clearly, it has been influenced: cf. therefore, that **beats the Dutch**. Subsidiarily cf **that beats the band**. P.B.: N.W. Bancroft, *From Recruit to Staff Sergeant*, 1885, has, from *c.* 1840, *... and Banagher banged the devil!*, spoken by an Irishman in the Bengal Artillery. Cf also **beats Akeybo ...**

bangs like a shithouse rat, with *she* expressed or understood. She copulates vigorously, noisily, and almost ferociously: Aus.: since *c.* 1930. Here, *shithouse* denotes an outdoor earth-closet. P.B.: has var. *... shithouse door*.

bank. See: been robbing; cry all the way; it's like money.

bankers' hours. 'A comment on someone leaving work early. American banks normally close their doors – though not their offices – at 3 p.m., in contrast to the 5–6 p.m. of other commercial enterprises. Current from 1930s, now ob. or †' (R.C., 1977).

banner. See: carry the b.; Sister Anna.

banns. See: married.

bar. See: belly up; I wouldn't know him; if I need you.

bar the shouting. See **all over bar ...**

bar's open – the. This US c.p. is spoken by a host to a guest, e.g. a friendly visitor, perhaps esp. if the cocktails are a little slow in appearing: prob. since the mid 1930s: from the language of barmen. (J.W.C., 1977.)

barbed wire. See: hanging.

barber. See: every barber; she couldn't; that's the b.

barber's cat. See: all dressed; all wind.

bare. See: so bare.

barefoot. See: caught cold; keep'em; must have been lying; you must have been.

Barker. See: steady, B.

barking. See: dogs are barking it; my dogs.

Barking Creek. See: like the ladies.

Barkis is willin' indicates to a girl that a man is willing and ready to marry her: a famous quot'n become, *c.* 1870, a c.p. Later (C20) extended loosely to indicate willingness to do anything short of risking life or limb, money or position. In Dickens, *David Copperfield* (chapter V), 1849, Barkis sends this message to Peggotty.

barmaid's (*or* – **man's**) **apron.** See: he's had.

barmy. See: Ginger; let me out!

barn. See: couldn't hit; let her go; were you.

barn door. See: built like; couldn't hit.

barn door is open. See **keep him in ...**

Barney. See: all behind; give him the money; like Barney's.

barracks. See: cheer up, there's: into bed.

barrel. See: I'll shoot; more fun; noise like; shooting; that's better beer.

barrow. See: get off me; mind the b.

bash it up to you! Run away and stop bothering me: Aus.: esp. in WW2, among Servicemen, but apparently surviving until *c*, 1960. AS.

bashful. See: you tell 'em, kid.

basinful. See: I'll have a b.

bastard(s). See: A.C.A.B.; dear mother, it's a bastard; die, you; happy as a b.; here's a belly; it's a b.; like a b.; spit on; they used; who called.

bastard from the bush – the. An Aus. c.p., dating from the late 1880s: Wilkes's quot'ns range from Henry Lawson, 1892, to 1975; he defines it as an uncivilized interloper who imposes himself on the society [the company] he enters.' He adds that the most famous quot'n is not by Lawson, though in the latter's style: ' "Have a cigarette, mate?" said the Captain of the Push [the gang's leader]. "I'll have the flaming packet!" said the Bastard from the Bush.'

Bates. See: been to see.

Bath. See: go to B.; I knew it.

bathe. See: silent.

Battersea Dogs'-Home here! 'A facetious answer to a telephone call: Army, 1950s, and poss. extant' (P.B., 1975). For the non-UK, esp. the non-London reader: Battersea is a well-known district of the Capital, and this is a famous home for lost dogs. Cf **city morgue...**, q.v.

battle. See: gradually; how goes the b.; how's battle.

battleship(s). See: do you want to buy; it rots.

[**baw-haw, quoth Bagshaw.** You're a liar!: half a proverbial saying, half a c.p.: c. 1550–1700. F & H cite Levins and Nashe. It seems that *baw-haw* may be a var. of *baw-haw*, an echoic term of derision or contempt, and that the surname *Bagshaw* was chosen solely because it rhymed.]

be a devil! or, in full, **oh, come on: be a devil** (or even **a real devil**) is an ironically merry invitation to someone to be, for once, generous or audacious, as in 'Oh, come on, Billy, be a devil and buy yourself a beer' or in 'Be a real devil, Joe, and buy her a whisky': since c. 1945. This c.p. belongs to the thought-pattern connoted by Lilian Jackson Braun, when, in *The Cat Who Could Read Backwards*, 1966, she wrote: '"Come on, have another tomato juice," Ron invited. "Live it up." ' Contrast **be an angel!**

be a good girl and have a good time! A predominantly Can. c.p., addressed to someone – not necessarily female – setting off for a party or a dance: since c. 1930. Inevitably it invited the comment, 'Well, make up your mind!' – which itself, c. 1935, became a c.p.

be an angel! 'Please do me a favour', as in 'Be an angel: just pop upstairs and fetch my handbag': mainly middle-class feminine usage – from anyone else, esp. male, definitely affected: since c. 1930, poss. much earlier. Cf and contrast **be a devil!** (P.B.)

be content, take two! is a domesticity of the Brit. upper-middle class and affectionately ironic: since c. 1935. (Playfair.)

be good! is a c.p. substitute, both US and Brit., for *au revoir!* It dates from 1907, when, in the USA, lyricist Harrington and composer Tate produced the song, *Be Good! If You Can't Be Good, Be Careful!* – introduced by actress Alice Lloyd, as Edward B. Marks, who sometimes omitted first names, tells us in *They All Sang*, 1934. (By courtesy of W. J. B.) It somewhat facetiously exhorts the departer to behave well. In B & P, 1930, John Brophy noted that, during WW1, it was used mostly by officers, sometimes extended to *be good – and if you can't be good, be careful* – perhaps adopted from the pre-1914 musical, *The Girl in a Taxi*, as Mr Ronald Pearsall suggests. But, in 1975, a correspondent (Mr G. Maytum of Strood, Kent) tells me: 'I have a humorous postcard dated 16 September 1908 and depicting a couple on a couch; the caption reads "Be good, and if you can't be good, be careful, and if you can't be careful, get married." ' Col. Moe, 1975, notes a US var. for ... *get married* – and that is *be sanitary*. It had, orig., a sexual meaning that soon disappeared in the simple form. An excellent example occurs in Terence Rattigan's *Who Is Sylvia?* (played in 1950, pub'd in 1951), where Williams the manservant, going off for the evening, says to the two mannequins visiting his lordship: 'Well, goodnight, ladies. Be good!' (he knowing that that's the last thing they're expected to be, or intend to be.) Since the middle 1930s, the longer form has often become still longer by the addition of *and if you can't be careful, buy a pram*, which, among Americans, becomes ... *name it after me*. Its US use is recorded by Berrey, 1942, and occurs in, e.g., E.V. Cunningham, *Phyllis*, 1962, 'He was proud of his Americanisms, that man Gorschov. "Be good," he said to me.' Certainly it caught on in US. Mr Derrick Kay records, as current in 1934: 'Be good! If you can't be good, be careful. If you can't be careful, name the first child after me.' Alan Brien, in the *Sunday Times* of 12 Jan. 1975, recalls that during his schooldays in the 1930s, the c.p. ran: 'Be good! And if you can't be good, be careful! And if you can't be careful, remember the dates.'

On 19 Jan. 1975, Mr F. G. Cowley of Swansea, gleefully writing to the *Sunday Times*, pointed out that 'Salimbere, the Franciscan chronicler writing in the thirteenth century, reports that the phrase (*sinon caste, tamen caute*) was frequently used by Italian priests and attributed by them to St Paul .... I have failed to trace the catch phrase in the Epistles of St Paul.' The L. may be rendered, 'If not chastely, yet cautiously' (or prudently), and it affords an excellent example of the medieval monastic fondness for alliteration. But surely Mr Cowley doesn't believe that a thoroughly English c.p., as *if you can't be good, be careful* certainly is, could have been orig. by anything so remote as the L. Here is a neat example of the inevitable recurrence of a thought-pattern, such as we find also in **does your mother know you're out?**, q.v. There are naturally other variants: A.B., 1978, notes the US *if you can't be good, have fun*, and *be good, or have fun and name it after me*.

be kind or **nice to people ...** See **always be nice ...**

be like dad: keep mum!, a punning WW2 slogan, became, for a short period ending c. 1955, something of a c.p., esp. among Service and ex-Service men and women. Neat; for the slogan means, be like father – keep mum, i.e maintain mother, but also keep quiet, refrain from loose talk. In Catherine Aird, *A Late Phoenix*, 1970:

'Walls have ears,' murmured Dr Dabbe, getting into his surgical gown.

'Be like Dad, keep Mum,' Sloan was surprised to hear himself responding.

Moreover, 'this was the subject of an official illustrated notice in WW2' (Brock). The allusive shortening *be like dad!* has, since c. 1950, been used by the underworld and its fringes as a warning: 'Keep quiet!' (David Powis, *The Signs of Crime*, 1977). Then there's the occ. humorous *mum, be like dad*, but this may be merely a virtual nonce-use or, as the erudite used to say and textual critics still do, a *hapax legomenon*.

be like that! Often prefaced with a polite or palliative *Oh, all right* or *OK, then* or *Well*, or the half-resigned *Oh, well*; and sometimes with *then, see if I care!* tacked on afterwards: addressed to someone disagreeing or refusing, esp. in a matter of personal importance; orig., c. 1971, at Oxford; soon, more gen. and widespread. P.B.: but see also **don't be like that!**

be lucky! is, orig., an underworld, esp. ex-convicts', c.p., synon. with *au revoir!* or *cheerio!*: since c. 1930; by c. 1950, gen. Cockney. P.B. Yuill, *Hazell Plays Solomon*, 1974, two Cockneys parting:

'I'll let you know, Tel.'

'Be lucky.'

Lucky, in one's criminal activities. P.B.: perhaps from East End Jewish: cf its almost exact opposite. *I* (*we, she*, etc.) *should be so lucky!*-'I (etc.) am most unlikely ever to be so fortunate [in the way someone else has just suggested].'

be my Georgie Best! is an Association Football world var. – in Britain – of the next: since 1970. From Georgie Best, the wayward 'soccer' star; always far commoner among spectators and other 'fans' than among players and managements. The fact that this var. is rhyming slang serves to heighten the importance of **be my guest** by showing how firmly it was embedded in colloquial usage at all levels: otherwise the meaning wouldn't have been obvious. P.B.: by 1980, †.

be my guest! is said to someone wishing to borrow something not valuable, nor otherwise important, enough to be worth returning, or wishing to do something trivial; often equivalent to 'You're welcome!: since *c.* 1950. It was current in Aus. before 1967, the date of Frank 'Hardy's *Billy Borker Yarns Again*. A pleasant English example occurs in Dick Francis's novel, *Forfeit*, 1968, where wife and husband, after making love, say:

'Goodnight, Ty.'
'Goodnight, honey.'
'Thanks for everything.'
'Be my guest.'

The c.p. is also US (the earliest example I've noticed being in Ellery Queen, *Death Spins the Platter*, 1962, at the end of chapter XIV) – as in Hugh Pentecost's novel, *The Gilded Nightmare*, 1968:

'I am now ... in search of a surface fact.'
'Be my guest.'
'Do you know what time the Countless Zetterstrom is supposed to arrive today?'

There are many examples of this phrase in Brit. and US fiction, as well as two in John Mortimer's witty play, *Collaborators*, prod. in 1970 and pub'd in 1971: e.g. in Hillary Waugh, *Finish Me Off*, 1970: Ellery Queen, *A Fine and Private Place*, 1971; Frederic Mullally, *The Malta Conspiracy*, 1972 (' "Be my guest, as they say." '); Mickey Spillane, *The Erection Set*, 1972, but already in 1966 (*The By-Pass Control*). By 1972, indeed, the phrase had become so much a part of everyday speech that several big horse-races 'over the sticks' were won by a horse named Be My Guest. That so agreeable a c.p. should so thoroughly have established itself is a fact worth recording.

be nice to people on your way up .... See **always be nice ....**

be seeing you! – in US, often **be seein' yuh!** – is short for *I'll be seeing you* and is itself often shortened to *seeing you!* or *see you!*: a very common non-final valediction since the middle 1940s, 'especially among the young and the vulgar' (J.W.C., 1975), it has even been punningly modified as *Abyssinia* (q.v.). Terence Rattigan, *Who Is Sylvia?*, played in 1950 and pub'd in 1951, causes a 'gentleman's gentleman' to end a telephone conversation with: 'O.K. Be seeing you.'

It also had, in the US, in the legal profession, a short-lived var.: *I'll be suing you* (Berrey, 1942).

be your age! Stop being childish! Act like a grown-up and use your intelligence! Adopted, *c.* 1934, from the US. Gelett Burgess, US wit, provides an early example in *Two O' Clock Courage*, 1934, thus:

'I don't know,' I said. 'I don't believe I did.'
'You don't know? How come? See here, be your age. You can tell me, you know.' Then she sat back in her chair silently studying me.

An early English example occurs in Denis Mackail, *Back Again*, 1936, ' "And now go to bed, will you, and be your age." ' In 1942, Berrey glosses it as = don't be ridiculous!; he adduces the synonym, *act your age!*, q.v.

Since the middle 1940s, current in Aus. witness, e.g., the story 'The Unluckiest Man in the World' in *Billy Borker Yarns Again*, 1967.

Cf **get wise to yourself!; grow up!; hurry up and get born!; why don't you get wise to yourself?**

be yourself! Pull yourself together! – i.e., be your *better* self! Adopted *c.* 1934 – cf the prec. entry – from US. (It was, as a Brit. phrase, recorded in the Supplement of the 3rd edn of *COD*.) Berrey glosses it as = don't be ridiculous! 'Modern US: *be you!*' (A.B., 1978). P.B.: cf the slogan of that Tom Wolfe has called 'The Me Generation', i.e. the one in which duty to one's fellow men takes second place to the duty of pleasuring oneself: 'I gotta be me!'

beads. See: Where Maggie.

beam. See: fork.

bean(s). See: every little b.; how many beans; it's a whole new can.

beanfeast. See: what a b.

bear(s). See: AMERICAN RESPONSES; are you there; clumsy as a cub; go carry; go stick your nose; have you any more; if it were a b.; like Jack; long-tailed; quick and nimble; smarter; yes, I also.

beast. See; come up, I say.

beastly. See: don't let's be.

beat. See: can you beat; I'll tear; if you can't b.; that beats; you can't b.; and:

beat it while the going is good! was orig. a US young students' c.p. from before 1912; it had become gen. US by 1915 at latest and adopted in UK by *c.* 1919. R.C., 1978, recalls that during the 1930s – 40s it had a humorous, punning var.: *go find a drum and beat it!* – which reminds P.B. of a Can. synon. of the late 1950s, *why don't you make like an ice-hockey team and puck off!*

beats a kick in the head. See **better than a dig in the eye.**

beats Akeybo, and Akeybo beats the devil (– it or that) arose before 1874 and fell into disuse during the late 1930s. (Hotten. 5th edn.) *Akeybo* remains, I believe, a mystery; there is, just possibly, a link with Welsh Gypsy *ake tu!*, a toast, lit. 'Here thou art!' – cf **here's to you!**

But Michael Coplin, of Ballymahoo, Co. Longford, Eire, writes, 1978: 'I used to hear my father and uncles using this phrase in the 1960s and early 1970s, whilst playing three-card brag [a poker-style card game] in Stepney, London. *Akeybo*, pronounced *a-key-boo*, was Ace, King, Queen, a run, i.e. *ay-kay-queue*. The only run which beats akeybo is A – 2 – 3'. For form, cf **bangs Bangher ...**

beats cock-fighting – **it** or **that.** It (or that) *is* remarkable, superior, or startling: a c.p. since early C19, though foreshadowed in Gauden's *Tears of the Church*, 1659. A good example, meaning 'Well, that is most extraordinary' occurs in 'Bill Truck', 'The Man-o'-War's-Man' ... Man', 'serialised in *Blackwood's Magazine*, Sep. 1821, p. 165:, [The] Lieutenant, with the affected calmness of a victorious soothsayer, ... exclaimed, "D—n me, that beats cock-fighting!"' (Moe). Cf:

beats creation – **it** or **that.** That's remarkable, even if only in effrontery: mid C19 – early 20. It had, *c.* 1905 – 40, some currency in UK. Weekley.

beats me (sometimes, but not always, prec. by *it* or *that*). 'I've never heard' (Brit.) or 'I never heard' (US) 'the like of it'; 'It baffles me': late C19 – 20, although not until *c.* 1920 in Brit. 'Widely current in both senses' (J.W.C., 1977); P.B.: in Brit. the latter sense is the commoner.

beats the band – **it** (or **that**). That beats everything; that's excessive or remarkable; since *c.* 1880 in UK, and soon going to the Commonwealth and to the USA, where usu. *don't that beat the band*, often prec. by *now*, and, as in UK, rare after *c.* 1940.

beats the Dutch .... See **that beats the Dutch.**

beats the hell out of me – **it.** A US elab. of **beats me**: since *c.* 1930. (George A. Przymowski, 1978.)

beats working (with *it* or *that* rarely prec., yet always understood). 'Jocular comment on a job, implying that, whatever its other merits, it requires very little exertion' (R.C., 1978): US: from late 1940s.

beautiful but dumb, orig. (? late 1920s) US, became Can. in late 1930s; foisted on far too many 'dizzy blondes' less stupid than they seemed to be. In WW2 a Services' slogan-poster was captioned 'She's not so dumb; careless talk costs lives.

beautiful(ly). See: black is b.; hello, beautiful; oh, you b.; preparing; yes, but b.

beautiful downtown Burbank! 'Rowan and Martin in their *Laugh-In* coined this ironic compliment to the place in Los Angeles where NBC TV studios are situated. A quintessential late 1960s sound was that of the announcer, Gray Owens, intoning 'This is beautiful downtown Burbank'. *Laugh-In* was broadcast from 1967 – 72 and briefly revived in 1977' (*VIBS*, the very title of which is taken from *Laugh-In*).

beautiful pair of brown eyes – a. 'A fine pair of breasts. Sometimes with a slight pause between the *br*.- and the *-own* of *brown*, i.e. a mock-recovery from a slip of the tongue. It could refer to nipples, I suppose, but I have also heard *blue eyes*; neither expression was very common: 1950s' (P.B., 1976 – who adds, six years later: a spot of what we have now learnt to call male chauvinist piggery), Occ., more weakly, *a nice pair* . . .

beauty. See: age before; aha, me proud; you beaut!

beaver. See: there goes beef.

becalmed. See: I am b.

because I cannot be had is a ? C16 also an early C17 rhyming reply to the question, *why are ye so sad?* as in Nicholas Udall's comedy, *Ralph Roister Doister*, 1544, III, iii (lines 11 – 13 in F.S. Boas's edn, *Five Pre-Shakespearean Comedies*):

> MERRYGREEK: . . . But speak ye so faintly? or why are ye so sad?
>
> ROISTER DOISTER: Thou knowest the proverb – because I cannot be had.

Such a question with such an answer can hardly form a proverb: and the lack of sense in itself indicates that the status is: c.p.

because it's there! The famous mountaineer George Leigh Mallory (1886 – 1924), when asked why he wanted to climb Mount Everest, replied, 'Because it's there!' Mallory failed to reach the top, and vanished in the attempt. Edmund (later Sir Edmund) Hillary became, in 1953, the first man to succeed, and when asked why he had wanted to try, also replied, 'Because it was there!' It could be argued that it was Hillary who re-popularised the phrase and promoted it from famous saying to c.p. (It is illuminating to compare the various dictionaries of quotations: and salutary to conclude that to dogmatise is to risk a 'final verdict'.) But it only really became a c.p. when it was humorously or wryly advanced as 'a foolish reason for a foolish act', mostly among those who were conscious of the origin.

because the higher the fewer is a mainly Cockney c.p. answer to the mainly Cockney question *what does a mouse do when it spins?* or, perhaps more often, to *why is a mouse when it spins?* Hardly before 1900. (With thanks, both to the late Julian Franklyn and to R.S.) For other examples of the same kind of deliberate *non sequitur*, cf **do they have ponies down a pit? – what was the name of the engine-driver? – which would you rather, or go fishing?**

See also **why is a mouse . . .**

bed. See: and so to bed; caught cold; fetch; have you shit; I should have stood; I wouldn't kick; into bed; it's nice; pay the woman; reds; so crooked; stand by your; up with the lark; you know what thought.

bee. See: pretend.

Beecham's pills. See: time and tide.

beef. See: more beef; there goes b.; Tom Tit; what's b.; where's the b.

beef-skid. See: first.

beef to the heels. 'A derisive [and unkind] description of a girl's thick ankles, which run from calf to heel in one sad, straight line' (Leechman). Can.: since *c.* 1910. Cf the synon. *Mullingar heifer* (in *DSUE*).

been a long day, hasn't it? 'Almost meaningless – fills a conversational pause' (Shaw, 1969): since *c.* 1950. P.B.: but not a c.p. when used of a day that has been a weary, difficult while in pass, 'Lord, it's been a long day!' Cf the title of the Beatles' film, 'A Long Day's Night'.

been and gone (or **gorn**) **and done it,** prec. by **I've** or **you've** or **he's** or **she's**, etc. A joc., occ. rueful, emphatic form of *been and done it,* itself tautologically emphatic for *done it,* as in 'Well, I've been and gone and done it' = I've got married: late C19 – 20. An early example comes in one of P.G. Wodehouse's school stories, his earliest form of humour: *Tales of St Austin's,* 1903, 'Captain Kettle had, in the expressive language of the man in the street, been and gone and done

it.' Mr Adam J. Apt notes that a much earlier occurrence is in one of *The Bab Ballads* of W.S. Gilbert, 1869, 1873. And R.C., that it 'has a variant, *now you've [been and] gone and done it!'*

been around the horn. A US c.p., applied to 'a truck with a high mileage on the speedometer [? rather the odometer]', as Berrey, 1942, records. Prob. refers to Cape Horn, the southernmost tip of South America: in short, 'a hell of a long way'.

been robbing a bank? is addressed to someone who, clearly in funds, is rather throwing his money about: C20.

been to see Captain Bates? is a greeting to one recently released from prison: late C19 – early 20. 'Captain Bates was a well-known prison-governor' (Ware).

beer. See: bricks; I'm only here; if only; it's the beer; laugh?; never mind buying; that's better b.; what do you want?; what's a man.

beer, bum and bacca (tobacco). The reputed, almost legendary, pleasures of a sailor's life; since *c.* 1870. Since *c.* 1910, there has existed the var. *rum, bum and bacca.* In C20, usu. *baccy,* in both versions. It has, since *c.* 1950, occasioned the var. *salt pork, sodomy and the lash,* clearly applicable only to 'the bad old days'. In 1977, *beer, bum and baccy,* as a title, raised no public outcry, for it was used humorously (Sanders, 1978).

beer is best, a brewers' slogan, became, *c.* 1930, a c.p. – and by 1970, slightly ob. John G. Brandon, *The Pawn Shop Murder,* 1936, 'Sterling blokes these, all of whom agreed . . . with Mr Pennington that, in moments of relaxation, Beer is Best.'

P.B.: did the slogan come from G.K. Chesterton's rousing poem *The Secret People,* in which the idea of ale forms a refrain, or vice versa?: 'It may be we are meant to mark with our riot and our rest/God's scorn for all men governing. It may be beer is best.' G.K.C. died in 1936, and the poem appears to be post-Russian Revolution.

beer soup. See: sex and.

beer today, gone tomorrow is a c.p. punning parody of *here today* (and) *gone tomorrow,* connoting brevity: *c.* 1941 – 60.

[**bee's knees – that's the** suggests the very peak of perfection or the ultimate in beauty, attractiveness, desirability: *c.* 1930 – 40, in UK. In 1936 I overheard a girl described as 'a screamer, a smasher, a – oh! the bee's knees'. Orig. (*c.* 1925) US – as was *the cat's meow,* which, arising in 1926 (W & F), hardly survived the great economic depression and did not, so far as I know, reach UK. Neither of these is strictly a c.p. at all, and nor are the *cat's pajamas* (US) or *pyjamas* (UK), and *the cat's whiskers.*]

bees. See: balls, bees.

beeswax. See: none of your.

before. See: I been; I've heard; mixture.

before you bought your shovel – which should be compared with the next – is a tailors' c.p., implying that something has been either done or thought of before, and it hardly antedates the C20: before you were even old enough to use a toy shovel.

before you came (or, illiterately yet gen., **come**) **up,** either 'before you came up to the front line' or 'before you joined up' (esp. to a bumptious young soldier), suggests to the man addressed a vast ignorance and inexperience of warfare; army Other Ranks': WW1, but obviously not before late 1915. Variants were *'fore you 'listed; before you had a regimental number* or the much commoner *before your number was dry* (on your kit bag) or *up* or *your number's still wet,* never very gen. – and current only in 1917 – 18 – or *before you knew what a button-stick was* (a button-stick being a gadget that protected one's uniform from polish overflowing from buttons being polished); *before you was breeched* (wore trousers) or *before you nipped* (went to school); *before your ballocks dropped* or *before you lost the cradle-marks off your arse; when your mother was (still) cutting bread on you; while you were clapping your hands at Charlie* (Chaplin, of course); *when you were off to school* (with several tags); *I was cutting barbed wire while you was* – or *were* – *cutting your milk teeth.*

(All these were recorded by B & P.) And P.V. Harris, 1978, remembers from his WW1 service *before your arse was as big as a shirt button* as another 'old soldiers' sneer at recruits'.

The prototype was the proverbial saying, *your mamma's milk is scarce out of your nose yet*, recorded by 'proverbial' Fuller in 1732. There exists, moreover, a Shakespearean adumbration; occurring in *Troilus and Cressida*: 'Whose wit was mouldy ere your grandsires had nails on their toes.'

By far the most used form was *before you come* (or *came*) *up*: 'the classic crushing retort of the private soldier. The unanswerable argument from experience and seniority' (John Brophy in B & P). It survived into WW2, when 'the reply of one who was asked to believe something that did not seem credible was: "Do you think I came up yesterday?"' (PGR).

[**before your very eyes,** Arthur Askey's gag (1930s and after), is at best a borderliner.]

beg. See: he can make.

begin. See: Wogs.

begonias. See: you'll bust.

behind. See: all behind; if you are angry; there's shit; you're getting TV.

behind the eight-ball (– he's). He's in trouble or at a disadvantage: US: since *c.* 1930. 'The only black ball on the pool table and hence bad luck' (Fain, 1977).

being fattened for the slaughter. See **fattened** ...

Belgian(s). See: give it to; it's an old B.

Belgium. See: if it's Tuesday; remember B.

believe. See: can't believe; I believe; I can't believe; I wouldn't b.; imbars; oh, I believe; would you b.; you better b.; you have hit.

believe it or not! Miss Monica Baldwin, who was a nun from 1914 until 1941, found herself puzzled and often bewildered by all the new words and phrases, as by all the new features of life, when she emerged to a new Britain. She was 'equally bewildered when friends said, "It's your funeral" or "Believe it or not"' (Foster) – as she attested in her autobiographical *I Leap over the Wall*, 1949.

Shipley amplifies: 'The phrase was popularized here [USA], at least, by Ripley's long-running column of strange facts; used widely, preparatory to a seemingly incredible statement' – also in Britain, to which the column was syndicated. One does, however, need to remember that Ripley had adopted a cliché already current. All the same, the change in status occurred very soon after Robert Leroy Ripley (1893–1949) 'began his cartoon [series] on December 19, 1918, with a rough drawing of a man who ran 100 yards backwards in 14 seconds. From a woman with a beard trailing the ground to a two-headed rooster, he ran his "authenticated" cartoons from a million-dollar estate on Long Island Sound ... his cartoons have been collected in at least 4 books. [The first appeared in 1928.] According to the *Dictionary of American Biography*, Supplement Four, 50 years after he began (and 19 after his death), his *Believe It or Not* phenomena were still appearing in 17 languages, in 330 newspapers, in 32 countries' (Shipley, 1977). There's glory for you! And, as a minor bonus, he inaugurated and sustained one of the half-dozen best-established c.pp. of the English-speaking world; one that has already endured since 1919.

To this I need only add that R.C. writes, 1978, 'I have now traced this to Joyce's *Exiles* (1918) where it is used conversationally, evidently as ellipsis for "whether you believe it or not". Sense then, as always, "It may sound improbable, but is nonetheless true".'

believe me! seems to have, as a c.p., orig. among young US students *c.* 1910 or 1911: A.H. Melville, 'An Investigation of the Function and Use of Slang' – in *The Pedagogical Seminary*, March 1912. Also in Berrey, 1942.

believe me, baby! is a US c.p., 'circulating in the year 1920', esp. among students, as McKnight remarks; † by 1930, at latest.

believe you me! A vaguely emphatic, somewhat conventional c.p. of C20. In PGR, Granville notes that 'this is the [naval] Gunnery Instructor's emphasis to any statement. "Believe you me, that is the only way to do the job."' A more recent example occurs in Lynton Lamb's urbane 'thriller', *Return Frame*, 1972: '"Well, mister, we was soon out to Renters Hard. Lot going on, believe you me."' Also in Berrey. Cf **believe me!** and **you better believe it!**

bell(s). See: does that ring; it's got bells; pull the other; ring Mahony's; saved by; there's a blow; who boiled; with bells.

bell-boy. See: don't ask me.

bellows. See: fresh hand.

bells and whistles. See **all-singing, all-dancing.**

bells of hell go ting-a-ling-a-ling, for you but not for me – the. 'From being a mere parody, to a popular tune, of a revivalist hymn, it became, *c.* 1910, a c.p. of smug self-congratulation when one other, or others, got into trouble' (L.A., 1977). P.B.: Eric Hiscock, who took *The Bells of Hell Go Ting-a-Ling-a-Ling* as the title of his 'Autobiographical Fragment without maps', 1976, covering his experiences in WW1, prefaced the book with the song and added '(Soldiers' marching song, World War I)'. The song appeared, to good effect, in Brendan Behan's play *The Hostage*, 1959.

belly. See: better than a dig; bless your little b.; here's a b.; how's your b.; I could take; it's a poor b.; keystone; lower than; officers have; what? have you pigs.

belly button. See: I'm so empty; my belly.

belly up! belly up to the bar, boys! Drinks on the house, boys!: Can.: C20. Cf the US underworld, mostly pickpockets', c.p., *belly up*?, Have a drink! – *c.* 1930–50. Prompted by the English-speaking world's toast, *bottoms up*!

bending. See: don't let me; my word if I catch.

Bengal. See: Madras.

Benjamin Brown. See: my name is B.

Benson. See: when I was with.

bent. See: on pleasure.

Bentley. See: gently.

Beowulf to Virginia Woolf. See **from Beowulf** ...

Bergami. See: O begga.

Berlin by Christmas! and **Berlin or bust!** The former is British, referring to Christmas 1914; the latter is US, partially adopted by British soldiers; and both are blush-making. For both, see B & P: for the latter, note esp. Ring W. Lardner, *Treat 'Em Rough* (Letters from Jack the Kaiser Killer), 1918. Of this 1917–18 c.p., used by the US army even before the users reached Europe, Lardner says little in Jack's first letter (23 Sep.); but of the attitude, he implies much – by noting the patriotic hyperboles affected by the vain, gabby, boastful ex-'busher' named Jack Keefe, and apparently that attitude offended him as much as it did John Brophy.

berries. See: it's the b.

Bessie. See: not a word to.

best. See: don't shoot; who was the b.; your best.

best by (taste) test was a US c.p. of *c.* 1945–7. It arose as Royal Crown Cola's slogan for a soft-drink: *best by (taste) test.* W & F remark that it became 'generalized in meaning to have some ... fad use' – the sense being 'I like it' and the application being to almost anything likable.

best dressed. See: first up.

best of (British) luck (to you)! – (and) the. 'Frankie Howerd claims to have given this phrase immortality: 'It came about when I introduced into radio *Variety Bandbox* those appallingly badly sung mock operas, starring the show's bandleader Billy Ternent (tenor), Madame Vere-Roper (soprano) and Frankie Howerd (bass – "the lowest of the low"). Vera while singing would pause for breath before a high C and as she mustered herself for this musical Everest I would mutter, "And the best of luck!" Later it became: "And the best of British luck!" The phrase is so common now that I frequently surprise people when I tell them it was my catchphrase on *Variety Bandbox*' (VIBS).

That is one version. In the 1st ed. of this Dictionary, E.P.

had: A c.p., dating since *c.* 1943 or 1944, and meaning exactly the opposite, the intonation being ironic – or even sardonic. Orig. an army phrase: in 1942–early 1944.[When Frankie Howerd was in the Royal Artillery; the phrase may have lingered subconsciously in his mind until his very effective use of it on the radio], things weren't going any too well for the British, and the phrase was characteristically British in its ironic implications; by 1950, fairly – and by 1955, quite – gen. It perhaps owes something to **over the top and the best of luck!**, q.v. It was, by the late Frank Shaw (of Scouse fame), described as that 'amazing modern phrase in mock-hearty tone'; he also remarked that it is used 'in false "old boy" tone. "You'll lose – but – good luck, friend" – sardonic. Emphatic "British" mocking of such phrases in old patriotic plays.' Petch, 1974, adds that, since *c.* 1960, the phrase is often shortened to (*and*) *the best of British!* P.B.: I have heard it, mostly *c.* 1960, parodied yet further as *and the breast of duck!*

best thing since sliced bread – the forms a Brit. var., since *c.* 1950, of the US (**it's**) **the greatest thing…**, q.v. 'Primary use is in appreciation of a pretty girl…. It appeared in *Guardian*, 13 Sep. 1977, p. 13, as a headline to an article on the bread strike. Interesting example of the journalistic trick of the reverse c.p., where a known c.p. is taken and referred back to its literal meaning' (Playfair, 1977).

[**best things in life are free** – the. This lies between cliché and c.p.: both US and Brit.: since 1956. (This reminder comes from my namesake, Prof. A.C. Partridge, 1978; the following gloss a few months later from Eric Townley.) In 1927, the song thus titled formed part of the Broadway musical *Good News*; that song was composed by Ray Henderson and the words were written by Lew Brown and Buddy De Sylva; a recording appeared in the same year. But *the best things in life are free* remained a cliché until 1956, when a film, also so titled, based on the careers of De Sylva, Brown and Henderson, consolidated the saying and converted it into a c.p.; the main parts were played by Dan Dailey, Gordon McRae, Ernest Borgnine. 'There were some recordings of the song around this time, but I think that it must have been the film itself' which ensured the popularity of the saying.]

bet. See: anyone's bet; I bet; I wouldn't bet; like to bet; that's your bet; want to bet; you bet; you can bet.

[**bet you a million to a bit of dirt!** – **bet a pound to a pinch of shit!** – **bet your boots!** – **bet your bottom dollar!** – **bet your life!** These 'bets' are asseverative exclamations at the colloquial level. They are not true c.pp.]

bets (or **betting**) **like the Watsons.** To bet very heavily, as at the races: Aus.: apparently since the 1920s.

better. See: every day; far better; none the b.; old enough; one squint; 'tis better; two heads, you better; you make a b.; you'd be far; you're a b.; your cough.

better an empty house than a bad tenant is the late C19–20 c.p. form of the C18–19 proverb, … *than an ill tenant*, recorded by *ODEP*. With var. *better out than in*, the c.p. is uttered, usu. by the perpetrator, concerning a loud fart. The shorter and pithier form has, since *c.* 1970 [P.B.: I'd say, since *c.* 1950 at latest] been the commoner; the older and wittier version seems to have been kept alive mainly by undergraduates. (A blend of reminders by Playfair and Levene 1977.) L.A., 1974, dates the shorter from *c.* 1920: it may often be prec. by *that's*. Playfair adds: 'Normally without the *that's* in my experience; almost an exclamation. Applies also to burps and baby's wind'. A.B., 1979, notes that 'it applies to both farting and belching. I've heard, from the mid-western US, *there's more room out there than in here*, with the appropriate finger-gestures'. Cf **it's the beer speaking.**

better for your asking. See **none the better…**

better fuckers (or, euph., **pickers**) **than fighters**, often prec. by **they're.** Applied to those soldiers in WW1 who frequented Fr. or Belgian brothels whenever they had the money: WW1.

better in health than good condition (– **he's** or **she's**): C18. S (1738), first dialogue:

LADY SM[ART]: How has your Lordship done this long Time?

COL[ONEL]: Faith, Madam, he's better in Health than good Condition.

Better, that is, than he looks – perhaps a shade too fat, but healthy.

better 'ole. See: if you know of.

better out than in! See **better an empty house…**

better Red than dead. 'It is better to live [even] under communist rule than to die. This c.p. is probably not of folk origin' (B.P., 1975): in Aus., and elsewhere: prob. since the late 1940s. Prof. D.J. Enright, in *Encounter*, Dec. 1977, writes, 'Solzhenitsen (and John R. Silber, *Encounter*, Feb. 1977) credit, or discredit Bertrand Russell [1872–1970] with the saying.' The US version, during the 1950s among conservative groups, was *better dead than red* (R.C., 1977). Sometimes in question form: see **would you rather be Red…**

better since you licked them. See **how's your poor feet?**

better than a dig in the eye with a blunt stick or, more gen., … **than a poke in the eye with a sharp** (Aus., or **burnt**) **stick** (often prec. with a stoical *I suppose it is…*: Wilkes); … **than a kick in the pants** or **up the arse**, the Can. version being **…than a kick in the ass with a frozen boot**; US, **it beats a kick in the head**; … **than a slap in** (or **across**) **the belly** (or **kisser**) **with a wet fish** (or **lettuce**); … **than sleeping with a dead policeman.** Better than nothing or, since *c.* 1920, very much better than nothing. Most seem to have orig. late in C19. Cf Grose, 1788: *this is better than a thump on the back with a stone*, said on 'giving anyone a drink of good liquor on a cold morning', and contrast:

better than a drowned policeman. Of a person: attractive; very pleasant; expert: *c.* 1900–15. In e.g., J.B. Priestley, *Faraway*, 1932. Contrast the prec.

better than dog-running from Blockhouse, not as good as a run ashore in Istambul. Occurring in that excellent naval novelist John Winton's *The Fighting Temeraire*, 1971, it means 'fair to middling' and has been used by the RN throughout C20. Lt Cdr F.L. Peppitt, RNR, explained it thus to me in 1972: 'Fort Blockhouse = H.M.S. *Dolphin*, the submarine shore base in Portsmouth; dog-running = sail in the morning, drive to exercise with surface ships, back to base at night; Istambul – the mystic East to submariners (probably from their Dardanelles and Black Sea patrols in WW1).'

better you than me. See **rather you than me.**

betty. See: all betty.

Betty Martin. See: all my eye.

between a rock and a hard place. 'Between Scylla and Charybdis [whereby perhaps prompted]. Originally naval…, since 1950s or earlier, but now fairly general [in US] and indeed, somewhat hackneyed' (R.C., 1978).

between a shit and a sweat (– **he's**). 'Nervous enough to be sweating but not (quite) to the point of losing control of one's bowels: low US: from 1930s or earlier, now ob.' (R.C., 1978).

[**between you and me and the bed-** or **gate-post,** 'confidentially': lying between proverb and cliché and c.p., but nearest to the first and farthest from the third. See esp. *ODEP*.]

Beulah, peel me a grape. See **peel me a grape.**

beware your latter end. See **remember your next astern.**

bibful. See: you sure slobbered.

Bible. See: I wouldn't believe.

bicycle. See: sex and.

big. See: if, (and); if I was as big; if it's too big; if they're big; in the big; large m.; last of the big; me and my; pay up; think big; this town; what's the big; yea big; you have grown; you're a big girl (lad); you're getting a big; you've got a big; your eyes.

big as life. See **large as life….**

Big Brother is watching you! This joc., often emphasized finger-waggingly, monitory, indeed minatory, c.p., became one within a few weeks after George Orwell's prophetic novel, *Nineteen Eighty-Four*, salutarily shocked the British public in 1949; at first, only in literary and cultured circles, then very soon, among the educated, and by *c.* 1955, among the remainder of the at least moderately intelligent, esp. those who take some interest in political and sociological history; then it gradually spread by sheer force of hearsay until, by *c.* 1960, it had gained fairly wide currency, those users who had never read Orwell tending to burlesque the somewhat sinister undertone into a painfully obvious overtone.

The ref. occurs in Book 1, chapter I. 'Before that, "Big Brother" was used in the sense of someone being protective – as in a family. But Orwell changed all that, with his tale of a TV set in every home and officialdom watching', as Noble remarked 1975; he appended a quot'n from his *Nicknames Past and Present*, 1976: 'Big Brother: watchful officialdom, dictatorial in its powers, from the sinister omnipotent leader of a subservient country in George Orwell's [book].'

Of its US usage, Col. Moe remarked, 1975: 'It has appeared here in cartoons criticizing governmental surveillance and supervision over private affairs with a lessening of personal freedom. It had frequent usage when the Internal Revenue Service began using computers to check the personal income tax returns.' It has been applied to any sort of "thought control".' And later, J.W.C. wrote: 'It has been widely current – increasingly so, since Watergate and especially the current scandal about the CIA and more recently about the FBI – ever since the book was published. It may not be common among the uneducated, but it certainly is among the educated, or at least the "socially aware" educated.'

I also have to thank Col. Moe for this revealing ref. in *Washington Star* of 16 Aug. 1975, in a letter to the editor:

FBI Director Clarence Kelley's appearance before the American Bar Association in Montreal is another reason why Congress should drastically overhaul and reorganize the FBI so that it cannot further infringe upon the civil liberties and democratic freedoms of the American people. Kelley's Big-Brother-is-watching-you philosophy, in the name of 'national security', smacks of police-state dictatorship rationale. Shades of Beria!

big conk: big cock; complementarily, **big conk: big cunt.** This earthy c.p. implies that a big nose implies a large penis or a large vulva: late C19–20, perhaps since *c.* 1800. 'According to *American Notes and Queries*, Sep. 1967, Erasmus included in his *Adagia* the aphorism *bene nasati, bene menticulati*' (D.J. Barr, 1970): '(men) big-nosed: (men) well-penis'd.' Cf **big man...; long nose...; large mouth...;** and **weak eyes....**

big deal! has, say W & F, 1960, been very widely used by US students and that its employment as a c.p., deflating the addressee's pretensions or enthusiasm or eagerness of attitude or of proposal or proposition, is (in, of course, 1960) 'fast supplanting the earlier uses' (*non*-c.pp.); they add that it was 'popularized by comedian Arnold Stang... *c.* 1946, and [again, on a different radio programme] *c.* 1950'. The c.p. rapidly 'caught on' in both Can., *c.* 1947, and Aus., *c.* 1950, perhaps a few years earlier than in UK, where, Shaw opined in 1969, it appeared in the early 1950s. R.C. added, 1976, 'The US sense is rather "much ado about nothing!"'

[**big hand for the visiting fireman – a.** Not a c.p. but a conventionalism, perhaps even a cliché.]

big man, big prick; small man, all prick. Lit., this vulgar yet vigorous expression extols virility; but fig. – and only thus does it become a c.p. – it is satirical, 'apostrophizing dolts, dupes, or dunderheads', as one of my wittiest correspondents puts it: C20. R.C. comments, 1977, 'The "small man" part, I think, rather refers to the exaggerated aggressiveness of some small men (over-compensation, of course) which may indeed lead them to behave like "pricks", or very objectionable fellows.' Cf **big conk**, q.v.

big production; no story. 'Capsule description of a person or situation in whom (or which) promise far outruns performance.... Obviously borrowed from Hollywood's description

of an elaborately produced but insubstantial opus – and how many there were and are! Current in the 1950s and 60s. Now obsolescent' (R.C., 1977). Cf **don't make a production of it!**

big ship. See: roll on, big.

big shot? big shit! A c.p. derisive of someone who has just been called 'a big shot'; often shortened to *big shit*. Since *c.* 1910, but less and less used since *c.* 1950.

bigger the balls, the better the man – the. An army instructors' c.p. of 1948 – witness Edmund Ions. *A Call to Arms*, 1972 – and prob. for some years earlier. Another of those myths which are so common among men addicted to preferring quantity to quality. P.B.: cf the use of the term 'balls', since the late 1970s, to mean 'courage, bravado, go-getting aggressiveness', sometimes paradoxically applied even to women: 'Lisa's got balls'.

bigger the fire, the bigger the fool – the. An Aus., orig. (late 1890s) – and with deadly literalness – bushwalkers' c.p. that had, by *c.* 1900, been generalized to mean 'the more noise a man makes, the less sense he speaks' – esp. applicable to politicians.

bigger they are, the harder they fall – the; the taller they are the further (or **farther**) **they fall.** This indicates a fearless defiance of one's superiors: late C19–20; used also in US; very common in the army of WW1. Prob. it orig. in the boxing-booths; its popularity has been attributed to Bob Fitzsimmons on the eve of his match with James J. Jeffries, a much bigger man.

biggest fuck-up since Dunkirk or **since Mons – the.** The former refers to WW2, the latter to WW1. Neither was ever used by 'the troops' during the wars, so far as I remember (and, having served in both, I'm unlikely to forget), or indeed since. Oddly, they have been employed by the underworld since the late 1940s; witness David Powis, *The Signs of Crime*, 1977. Why two such remarkable achievements, such gallantry, such – for Dunkirk – brilliant improvisation, have been singled out for 'snide' derision, can derive only from crass ignorance and stupidity. (Here *fuck-up* means 'disaster'.) P.B.: but, *pace* E.P.'s spirited defence of his old comrades-in-arms, and viewed more objectively, neither retreat, however gallant, was anything other than a disastrous defeat; brilliant improvisation there was indeed but lamentably little planning, except in hindsight.

biggest liar this side of the black stump – the. A special derivative from **black stump.**

bike. See: don't get off; mind my; on your; went for.

bilberry. See: he'll make.

bill. See: strike or; that, Bill.

Bill Bailey. See: won't you come home.

Bill's mother's. See: black over.

Billy Paterson. See: who struck Billy.

binding. See: to make the cheese.

bingo. See: by the great.

bip bam, thank you, ma'am! (I'd have expected *bim bam...*) and **wham, bam, thank you** (or **ye**), **ma'am!** The former is a negro c.p. – a 'descriptive phrase expressing gratitude to a woman after love-making, from a popular song' (CM) – which adapted it from the latter phrase, which, lit., has, since *c.* 1895, afforded an either cynical or jocularly brutal comment on sexual intercourse. The *wham bam* part of the phrase is, as you might expect, the slangy US adjective and adverb, *wham-bam*, 'rapid(ly) and roughly' – hence 'displaying more energy and enthusiasm than finesse' (W & F), hence, in love-making, without tenderness or considerateness. A.B., 1978, 'I've heard it [in USA] *biff bam*'.

bippy. See: you bet your sweet.

bird(s). See: he's done; it's your ball; only birds; open season; that's for the; watch the; what do you mean; you can't fly.

bird is flown – the, is an underworld c.p. of *c.* 1810–60; it signifies that a prisoner has escaped from jail or that a criminal has left his hiding-place. (JB.) It is just possible that here is a ref. to 'Charles I in pursuit of Pym, Hampden & Co.', as Mr Norman Franklin has proposed.

bird never flew on one wing, See **you can't fly...**

biscuits. See: **all shit.**

biscuits hang high. 'A hobo's message to fellow hobos that there is a scarcity of food handouts in the vicinity' (Ramon F. Adams, *The Language of the Railroader*, 1977): hobo(e)s' (late C19–20), whence US railwaymen's. Contrast **everything is lovely...**, q.v.

bishop. See: **as the actress; what! a b.**

bishop! (rarely) is short for **oh, bishop!** and it greets, derisively, the announcement of (very) stale news: on the *Conway* training ship during the 1890s. Attested by John Masefield, the English poet and laureate, who served on her.

bishop hath blessed it – the, was a C16 c.p., applied 'when a thing speedeth not well' (Tyndale, 1528).

bishop's sister's son – he is the, is another C16 c.p., this time ecclesiastical, yet again authorized by Tyndale in 1528; it implies that 'he' has influence in high places – nepotism, in fact.

bit. See: **have you bit; how's your belly; tavern bitch; what's bit; where the pig.**

bit of all right. See **this is a bit of all right.**

[**bit of how's-your-father – a,** and **a bit of the other.** 'A bit of the other, something on the side, a bit of how's-your-father, slap and tickle, etc. = "An expression of tenderness for a member of the other sex." (Spoken English is very rich in these poetic romantic phrases)': *Punch*, 10 Oct. 1973, 'Complete Vocabulary of Spoken English', anonymously but wittily, satirically, ironically written by Miles Kington, the literary editor: since *c.* 1950. Strictly, these two phrases are sited on the no-man's-land that lies between cliché and c.p. See also **how's your father?**]

bit of string with a hole in it – I've (or **I've got**) **a...** See **I've got a...**

[**bit of the other – a.** See **bit of how's-your-father – a.**]

bit of what you fancy does you good – a. This is a frequent misquotation of **little of what you fancy...**, q.v.

bit tight under the arms – a. A C20 joc., for it refers to a pair of trousers much too large for the wearer.

bit you? – what's. See **what's bit you?**

bitch. See: **in and out; or your b.; tavern bitch.**

bitched, buggered and bewildered. See **stewed, screwed...**

bite. See: **I wouldn't have; I'll bite; it's staring; kick; bollock; look on; where the dogs.**

bite in the collar or the cod-piece? (– **do they**): a piscatorial c.p. of *c.* 1750–1830. Captain Francis Grose, who was himself something of a wag, and a wit, described this as 'water wit to anglers'. Hence, prob. 'a veiled insult – in effect, "Do you have lice?"' (R.C.). Ultimately there may, as Shipley has suggested, be a ref. to a very ancient riddle proposed by Hesiod. A returning fisherman remarks:

What I caught, I left behind;
What I brought, I could'nt find.

Answer: fleas. A more modern instance: by a fisherman returning with an empty creel, the answer to 'Any bites?' is 'Mosquito bites'.

biting you? – what's. See **what's bit you?**

bitter and twisted – all. See **crazy mixed-up...**

black. See: **any colour; could sell; give it back; hey, Johnny; nobody can; shut mouth.**

black cat and a tin of Vaseline – a. 'Proverbially the last resort in cases of sexual frustration' (a correspondent, 1973): fairly common in the Fighting Services during WW2; also civilian, both before and after that war.

black friars! or **Blackfriars!** Beware! Look out!: underworld: *c.* 1830–1914. Perhaps *black* because it's an ominous colour and *friars* used in a hostile way; or *Blackfriars* because it was once a very shady district indeed.

black is beautiful has, since *c.* 1950, been a slogan of US negroes, and as such it is clearly ineligible, but when it is jocularly misused by 'Whitey' it *is* a c.p. – white men's only, of course – dating from *c.* 1960.

black is (later, often **black's**) **your eye!** These c.p. forms

of the proverbial *no one* – occ. *you* or *he*, etc. – *can say black is* – or *black's* – *my eye*, no one can justly accuse me of wrongdoing, no one can justifiably find fault with me; the c.p., therefore, means 'you are at fault' or 'you are guilty'. The proverbial forms date C15–19 and C17–20; *black's your eye*, although increasingly ob. since *c.* 1910, is not yet entirely†; the c.p. forms, prob. from C16 and C18. Formal documentation is given by the admirable 3rd edn (ed. by F.P. Wilson and, later, his wife) of the *ODEP*. Less formal evidences are these:

The comparable and apparently derivative *black's the white of my eye* is 'an old-time sea protestation of innocence' (Bowen); Beaumont and Fletcher, *Love's Cure*, or *The Martial Maid*, written not later than 1616, III, i, in which Alguazier, a corrupt constable, says to a whore:

Go to, I know you, and I have contrived;
Y'are a delinquent....
....

I can say, black's your eye, though it be grey.

In James Shirley's, *The Bird in a Cage*, performed in 1632 and pub'd a year later, II, i (p. 397 of the Dyce edn), Bonamico says, 'If you have a mind to rail at them, or kick some of their loose flesh out, they shall not say *black's your eye*, nor with all their lynxes' eyes discover you' — where 'them' = the importunate or the troublesome or the hostile; and in Thomas Shadwell, *The Amorous Bigot: With the Second Part of Tegue O Diodly. A Comedy*, 1690, at II, i:

TEG[UE]: Out and avoyd my Presence; I will lose my Reputation, if I will be after speaking vid dee in de Street indeed.

GRE[MIA]: I defy any one to say Black's my Eye; I beseech your Reverence, come into my House.

See also **nobody can say black's my eye.**

black over Bill's mother's – it's (usu. **a bit**). A weather c.p. applied to dark clouds looming – in no matter what quarters of the sky. The phrase is very common, later C20, in the East Midlands, but is by no means limited to that region, for I have heard it also from a Scotsman in Sussex, where also I heard the var. *it's a bit brighter over...* (P.B.)

black stump – back, or **this side, of the.** Whereas *back of,* beyond, denotes 'in the bush' or remote country, arose *c.* 1920, has been archaic since *c.* 1970, and prob. derives 'from the bushman's habit of giving such directions' (B.P.), *this side of,* as Jim Ramsay pointed out in 1977, connotes superlative quality, as in 'the biggest dog, the biggest liar, this side of the black stump', arose *c.* 1950 or a little earlier, and may have orig. in the idea of great distance (*beyond,* or *back of, the black stump,* 'darkest Australia').

Wilkes, properly sceptical of this or that black stump, defines *the black stump* as 'an imaginary last post of civilization'; his examples cover only the years 1954–70, but it must have arisen some years earlier, and it has been very active during the 1970s. Now a part of Australian folklore.

The subject merits a serious examination: and there exist half a dozen scholars capable of treating it more than adequately. (Note written 11 Aug. 1978.)

P.B.: *Beyond the Black Stump* is the title of a novel by Nevil Shute, pub'd 1956.

blackbird. See: **mind your worm.**

blacking brush. See: **after you, miss.**

Blackpool appears in at least two regional c.pp.: *do you come from Blackpool?*, a North Country equivalent of **were you born in a barn?**; the orig. being that 'Blackpool was supposed to have swing doors'. And *Blackpool's a fool to it,* 'spoken of any bright lights or any garish sight' (Mr Jack Eva, 1978): since the 1920s.

blacksmith. See: **I bet your.**

blades. See: **how are you fixed.**

blame. See: **it's the poor what.**

blanket. See: **gone for a Burton; sticks like; thin as.**

bleed. See: **don't open; my heart; your lips; your nose.**

bless. See: **God bless.**

bless you! Until the later 1970s, this was usu. only a stock response to someone's sneezing (cf the Ger. *Gesundheit!*), but then suddenly it became a pleasant, all-purpose benediction, thanks, or farewell, that gained epidemic c.p. status, and has not yet (1982) much diminished in popularity. (P.B.)

bless your little belly! This lower-middle class c.p. was certainly current *c.* 1910, and prob. goes back to *c.* 1890; by 1940, archaic, 'Addressed to a child zestfully eating a lot of food' (L.A., 1974). Cf:

bless your little cotton socks! Thank you!: a middle-class c.p. dating from *c.* 1905 and becoming, by 1960, archaic. The elab. *bless your little heart and cotton socks!*, arose *c.* 1910 and disappeared *c.* 1918. Although the two phrases are always benevolent, they never exceed affection. P.B.: since mid-C20, and often said of others, e.g. *bless his* or *her little...*, a joc, benediction/thanks, as in 'Oh, bless their little cotton socks – they've left everything ready for us'; or simply in admiration of a baby, child, even a pet animal.

blessing. See: you missed.

Blighty. See: roll on, B.

blimey, Charlie (or **Charley**)! A NZ and Aus. c.p. used as a safety-valve for pent-up emotions: C20. Aus. offers a synonym: *blimey, Teddy*. But why *Charley* or, for that matter, *Teddy*, I don't know, yet have the temerity to suggest that they are friendly and companionable diminutives. P.B.: cf the Brit. var. *Cor blimey O'Riley!*

blind. See: go up with; have among; I don't care if I do go b.; I see; if you blind; steal; wouldn't give; you're blind.

blind Freddie could see that, often prec. by *even*. 'Any fool could see that': Aus.: since the 1930s. Wilkes glosses Blind Freddie as 'an imaginary figure representing the highest degree of disability or incompetence and so used as a standard of comparison' and mentions that Sidney J. Baker had credibly derived the c.p. from a blind hawker in the Sydney of the 1930s. Occ. in the form *even blind Freddie wouldn't miss it*.

blinded with science is an Aus. and NZ c.p. celebrating the victory of intelligence over mere physical strength: late C19–20. From boxing: 'it arose when the scientific boxer began, *c.* 1880, to defeat the old bruisers' (Julian Franklyn), perhaps with Jim Corbett's defeat of John L. Sullivan. Cf the WW2's clearly derivative army *blind with science*, to explain away – e.g., to a commanding officer – an offence, esp. by talking busily and technically.

blinds. See: get inside; pull down.

bliss. See: ignorance.

bloater. See: or my prick.

block. See: I'm speaking.

block goes on – the. An underworld c.p., dating from *c.* 1920 and meaning 'an illegal practice has been forestalled or circumvented by Law' or that 'something desirable comes to an end' (Frank Norman's immensely readable *Bang to Rights*, 1958).

Blockhouse. See: better than dog.

bloke. See: pick a b.

blondes. See: gentlemen.

blood. See: every hair; too rich; yer blood's.

blood for breakfast (– there's). An RN c.p. indicating (late C19–20) that the admiral's or the captain's temper is very bad this morning. In WW2, it had spread to the other two fighting Services, but predominantly as *there'll be blood for breakfast, let alone tea* (last three words often omitted) and notably as a warning from NCOs, either to other NCOs or to privates or their equivalents; moreover, by *c.* 1943, it had spread to civilians.

The navy has, throughout C20, had its own var., strictly an intensive: *there'll be blood and fur for breakfast*, a hint – from e.g. the Commander's messenger – that 'a Hate is brewing' (John Laffin, *Jack Tar*, 1969). And B.G.T., 1978, mentions the offshoot *there'll be blood for supper*, 'There will be an unpleasant reckoning at the end of the day'.

blood's worth bottling. See yer blood's...

bloody flag is out. See flag of defiance.

bloody oath! See my bloody oath!

blow. See: dry up; for show; I didn't blow; look what; she would take; strike a b.; there she; there's a b.; what's this blown; when did you.

blow a dog off a chain. See it'd blow a dog...

blow, Gabriel, blow! is a US negro c.p., imputing credulity and simplemindedness in 'Whitey': (?) since *c.* 1920. CM explains it as springing from a US folk-tale. Among US musicians, *Gabriel* is a (usu. professional) trumpet player. Perhaps, for those who don't read The Bible, it is cautionary to add that 'the original reference is to the Archangel Gabriel and his Last Trump' (R.C.).

blow in the bell. See there's a blow...

blow it out! This low US c.p. expresses either anger or incredulity at another's lies or exaggerations or excessive optimism: Armed Forces': WW2 and after. Elliptical for *blow it out [of] your ass-hole* (W. & F.).

blown in! – look (or **see**) **what the wind has.** See look what the wind...

blue. See: since Pontius.

blue eyes. See: beautiful pair.

blue mud. See: you're full.

blue pencil. See: not blue.

blue ribbon. See: all wrapped.

blue shirt at the masthead – a, usu. prec. by **there's.** There is a call for assistance in an emergency: nautical: late C19–20. From the blue flag shown on the occasion.

blue-stockinged, white-topped, slotted jobs was, during WW2, a RN officers' allusion to the WRNS ('the Wrens'). Cf *happiness is Wren-shaped*, a (young) officers' car sticker, an example of that general fad which, in a minor way, forms one of the *marginalia* of the social history of Britain in the 1970s. (Based on a comment from Lt Cdr F.L. Peppitt, 1977.)

bluey. See: dogs are pissing.

blunt stick. See: better than a dig.

blurt, master constable! In his edn of *The Works of Thomas Middleton* (3 vols. 1885–6), A.H. Bullen says of the title of Middleton's earliest extant play, *Blurt, Master Constable,* pub'd in 1602: '"Blurt" was a contemptuous interjection; and "Blurt! Master Constable!" appears to have been a proverbial expression'; but 'catch phrase' would be an apter description and classification. Howell says, 'Blurt, Mr Constable, spoken in derision'. The phrase is recorded by Apperson but excluded by *ODEP*. Cf the early sense of *blurt*, 'to puff scornfully', but also note that, in C19–20, *blurt* has been euph. for 'to fart'; cf. further, the theatrical and music-hall 'raspberry'. Apparently *blurt, master constable* was current *c.* 1570–1700. Middleton's titular use indicates that the general intent of this lively play should be apprehended before the play even begins; in other words, the phrase indicates the widespread and well-established character of the saying.

Cf Thomas Dekker, *The Honest Whore*, Pt I (1604), I, v:
FLUELLO: Will you not pledge me then?
CANDIDO: Yes, but not in that: Great love is shown in little.
FLUELLO: Blurt on your sentences! [Wise sayings.]

Dyce's comment on *blurt* is, 'An exclamation of contempt, equivalent to "a fig for".'

blushes. See: spare my.

board the monkey fucked the duck on – the. A nonsense c.p. popular among Other Ranks, esp. National Servicemen, in the early 1950s, it was akin to some of the chants, monologues and taunts of their grandfathers, recorded in B&P. This one was evoked by any mention of a board, whether duck-board (perhaps the orig. influence), notice-board, or War Office Selection Board which screened potential officers. Cf its 'twin', *the tin that Rin-Tin-Tin shit in*. (P.B.)

boarders. See: stand by to.

boarding-house. See: thin as.

boat. See: B.E.F.; don't rock; eyes in; I didn't come up; I didn't just; I'd like to get; I'm in the b.; just got; one drink; roll on, big; ship; sit down, you're.

Boat Race night. See: up and down.

boat sails on Tuesday – the. A 'stock remark by London managers when an American act fails upon its first performance' (Berrey): theatrical and music-hall: since c. 1920, but little used since c. 1950. Contrast:

boat's left – the. This RN c.p., dating since c. 1910, means 'you're too late' – 'you've "had it" '. The boat referred to is that which takes men ashore on short leave. A.B., 1978: 'I've also heard [in US] "the boat sank" and "the (or your) boat is sunk"; but not in a long time.'

bob. See: get you!; go along, Bob!

bob down! you're spotted! Your argument – reason – excuse – etc. – is so feeble that you needn't continue: since c. 1920.

Bob's your uncle! See and Bob's your uncle.

bobbin. See: that's the end.

body. See: bring on the b.; how does your b.; how's the body; where's the body; you too.

boggle. See: mind boggles.

boil. See: go and boil; who boiled.

boiler factory. See: back to the salt mines.

boils. See: heads on 'em.

bollard. See: pull up a b.

boloney. See: it's boloney.

bomb. See: it went; we bombed.

bomb-hole. See: cor! chase.

bone(s). See: and not a bone; I have a bone; living on the b.; pick the bone; throw your.

bonnet. See: go it, Susan; this won't buy.

boo hoo! Cry on – I'm not at all sorry for you!: US: since c. 1930. A mocking, taunting c.p., based on boo hoo! as a conventionally indicative imitation of young children's crying. W & F.

book(s). See: he's in the book; one for the b.; read any; talks like; three on; what a turn-up; why buy; you can kiss; you.

'book!' (or 'book! book!') he says, and can't (even) read a paper yet. This c.p., dating c. 1890 – 1914, is addressed to one who has broken wind 'on a short note' not merely emphatically but explosively. Leechman, 1976, further states that it is of East Anglian origin. But why book? Because, as R.S. convincingly proposes, 1977, 'book is an inspired onomatopoeic for a curt, crepitant fart. The reference emphasizes the ignorant grossness of one who so erupts in company. (Just think of some newspapers, and he can't read even them!)'

booked any good Reds lately? See read any good books lately?

books won't freeze – the. 'A common byword in the northwest cattle country during the boom days when eastern and foreign capital was so eager to buy cattle interests' when things looked bad – as, for instance, during a long severe blizzard; the ref. being to the sale of a herd by a ranch-records count. Credited to a saloon keeper who, during such a blizzard, said to cattle owners gathered in his place, 'Cheer up, boys; whatever happens, the books won't freeze' (whatever happens to the cattle). The remark caught on, and thus 'created a saying that has survived through the years'. But Ramon F. Adams does not indicate when the c.p. arose: at a guess, the 1880s.

Booligal. See: Hay, Hell.

boom. See: top your.

boom, boom! (Pron. with the oo short, as in North Country bum, and usu. said very quickly as a suffix to a last sentence, as) 'Verbal underlining to the punch line of a gag. [The comedian] Ernie Wise suggests that it is like the drum thud or trumpet sting used, particularly by Americans, to point a joke. Music-hall star Billy Bennett (who died in 1942) may have been the first to use this device to emphasise his comic couplets. Morecambe and Wise, Basil Brush and many others have taken it up' (VIBS). It was, I think, its use by the fox puppet 'Basil Brush', or rather, his manipulator, who did more than anyone to spread the c.p., via children captivated by TV, in the early 1970s. (P.B.)

boom! boom! you're dead! See bang! bang! you're dead!

boomerangs. See: could sell.

[**boomps-a-daisy** is hardly a c.p. – but rather a nursery and general domestic formula of comfort addressed to a child that has knocked its head or, more commonly, fallen down: late (?mid) C19–20. Clearly modelled on ups-a-daisy! – which nobody, I hope, would classify as a c.p. P.B.: the latter is occ. parodied as oops or whoops a bloody buttercup! Boomps-a-daisy may, pace E.P., have qualified as a c.p. in the late 1930s, due to the popularity of the urban folk-dance with the chorus Hands (touch hands) – Knees (touch knees) – and boomps-a-daisy (turn and collide bottoms)!]

boot(s). See: chewy; dig in; got your boot; half-crown; in your boot; it didn't go; not in these; them wot's; there's shit; when Paddy; your mother wears.

boots laced. See: are your boots.

bored. See: doesn't know; ought to be b.

boring. See: excuse my wart.

born. See: hurry up; I wasn't; it took; just in time; there's one; we are all; were you; you haven't got; you were born.

born a gentleman: died an actor is a theatrical c.p. of late C19 – 20; by 1960, slowly dying – yet by 1973, far from dead. Apparently recorded first in Granville, 1952.

born dead – he was. He lacks energy: US: since c. 1920. (Fain, 1977.)

born in a barn? See: were you born in a barn?

born near the plantain root is a Jamaican c.p., meaning 'born in a rural district and coming to live and work in a town': since c, 1930. (F.G. Cassidy & R.B. Page, Dictionary of Jamaican English, 1980; a ref. owed to Neil Lovett, of Adelaide.) Here, plantain = banana.

born with a pack of cards in one hand, a bottle of booze in the other, and a fag in his (or her) mouth refers to one who is born to the raffish manner: since c. 1950.

born with the horn. A coarse c.p., applied to a womanizer: late C19 – 20. This is the slang horn, an erection.

Borough Hill. See: it's gone.

borrow. See: do you want to b.

bosom friends. See: your bosom.

both. See: God bless you both; there are two; this town; you and me; you tell me and.

bother. See: don't bother; go away; shoo.

bots. See: how are the bots.

bottle. See: baby in every; like a fort; stab.

bottling. See: yer blood's.

bottom. See: don't tear the; so dumb.

[**bottoms up!**, like **no heeltaps!**, could, I suppose, be called a drinking c.p.; but then drinking phrases, unless they are otherwise used, are excluded as ordinary slang.]

bought. See: I nearly.

bounce. See: answer is in the plural; that's the way the ball; when she bumps.

Bourke. See: back o' Bourke.

Bourke Street. See: doesn't know.

bow. See: take a bow.

bow-wow. See: daddy wouldn't; wow-wow!

bowels. See: don't get your arse; keep your b.

bowl of cherries. See: life is just.

box. See: couldn't knock; get back; it didn't strike; no hide; open the box; they're all in.

box open (pause) box shut! was a soldiers' c.p. of WW1. It implied that the donor, although glad to be generous, had, in company, to curb his generosity: he possessed only a few cigarettes. (B. & P.) Cf canteen open . . . .

boy(s). See: getting a big; go away, boy; holding; I believe you, my boy; I didn't raise; if you can't; jobs for; lovely bit; match me; Miles's; not on your life; oh, boy; separate the men; shit me; stand to; that boy; that's my boy; thatta; there, boys; who's a pretty; you silly; you're getting a big.

boy! is the shortened form, as **boy! oh boy** is the elab., of **oh boy!**

Boy Jones. See: that Boy Jones.

Boyle. See: vote for B.

boys call 'meal' after her. 'You could eat her!': *c.* 1950–75: perhaps mostly Liverpudlian. (Shaw, 1969.)

boys scout: girls guide, a pun on 'Boy Scouts and Girl Guides'; meaning *boys scout* on the look-out for girls, and *girls guide* the boys to the desired spot; current among the older members of the complementary movements: certainly during the 1920s and 1930s and perhaps both before and since. Neil Lovett recalls hearing, *c.* 1946, the Aus. var, *the boy scouts and the girl guides.*

bra is a girl's best friend – a, occ. prec. by *square shape* or *pear shape*, is an Aus. feminine c.p., dating from *c.* 1950. It presents her outline to the best advantage.

brace up! warns the person addressed that what is to follow, whether in speech or in writing, will probably come as a shock; for instance, in telling the recipient that he has been rebuffed or snubbed: since *c.* 1940. (Royston Lambert, *The Hothouse Society*, 1968.) The c.p. shape of the coll. *brace yourself!*

braces. See: don't let your braces; let your b.

brains. See: bullshit; hang crape; he's got his; how do you like your eggs; if you had; more ballocks; sit down and rest; wrong side; you don't have the b.; you haven't.

brains. In *if* (*they,* etc.) *had any brains* (*they'd,* etc.) *be dangerous:* an insult of the early 1980s. Mrs Joyce Hughes told me she'd heard it used of 'the clerks at the Social' (the Dept. of Social Security offices) at Liverpool; and Mrs Rachel Bacon the *if you had*... version, in Loughborough, Leics; both: early 1984. Cf **hang crape on your nose** ... (P.B.)

Bramah knows, I don't is a euph. (*c.* 1880–1910) for 'God knows – I don't!' Better spelt *Brahma*.

brandy. See: round the back.

brandy is Latin for (a) goose; and tace is Latin for a candle (or, much later, **fish**); also in shorter form, **brandy is Latin for goose** (or **fish**), the former dating from late C16, the latter from *c.* 1850. Brewer has neatly posed the pun: '*What is the Latin for goose?* (Answer) *Brandy.* The pun is on the word *answer. Anser* is Latin for goose, which brandy follows as surely and quickly as an answer follows a question.' Then why *fish?* Mayhew tells us that the richer kinds of fish produce queasiness, the stomach's stability being restored best by a drink of good brandy.

And what of the appendage, 'and *tace* is Latin for a candle'? It occurs as early as 1676, and also in S, 1738; *tace* = Latin *tace!* (be, or keep, silent) and therefore the appendage forms a warning against indiscreet speech. The precise connection with a candle remains disputable – indeed, mysterious.

Both parts of the whole, whether in combination or separately, are, among the classically educated, extant (although only just). L. used to be the requisite, and the badge of a gentleman: since WW2, it seems to be unrequired of even a scholar.

brandy is Latin for pig and goose is, according to Halliwell, 1847, 'an apology for drinking a dram after either': a perhaps mainly rural var. of the first part of the prec. c.p.: C19 – early C20.

brass fittings. See: same to you; with knobs.

brass knocker on a shithouse door – a. A N. Country c.p. applied to 'a cheap and gaudy ornament in an incongruous setting' (Edwin Haines, 1978): C20, and prob. earlier.

brass monkey. See: cold enough.

brass tacks. See: let's get down to b.

brasses cleaned by candlelight ... See **on my shit-list.**

brawn. See: brinded.

brayvo, Hicks! and **brayvo, Rouse!** The former covers the approx. period 1850–1910; the latter, prob. prompted by the former, *c.* 1900–14; mean 'splendid!' or 'well done!'; the former belongs to music-halls and theatres, the latter to East London in general; the former was, late C19 – early 20, used esp. in South London. Of the former, J. Redding Ware, who

was always very good in the entire field of entertainment, writes, 'In approbation of muscular demonstration .... From Hicks, a celebrated ... actor ... more esp. "upon the Surrey side ... ", e.g. "Brayvo Hicks – into 'er again".' Of the latter phrase, Ware remarks that it derives from 'the name of an enterprising proprietor of "The Eagle" ...; a theatre ... in the City Road' A very successful, though unauthorized, presenter of French light opera, notably 'all the best of Auber's work'.

Brazen Nose College. See: you were bred.

Brazil. See: there's an awful; where the nuts.

bread. See: as I live by b.; best thing since; cant a slug; I'm so hungry; it's the greatest.

break. See: you break; you may have.

break a leg! A US actors' c.p., meaning 'Good luck!' and anecdotally dated since mid-April 1865. It has been said (by whom originally, I don't profess to know) to have orig. in that incident in which John Wilkes Booth, little-known but fanatical actor, who, on 14 April 1865, assassinated Abraham Lincoln at Ford's Theatre, Washington. D.C., and broke his leg when, immediately after, he jumped on to the stage. I owe this anecdotal origin to Edward C. Lawless, MD, of San Francisco; he added: 'The phrase was more popular in the 30's and 40's [than it is now: 1975]. It was used among actors just before one of them [was due to go] before an audience for the first time.'

But the consensus of opinion among scholars and theatrical people dismisses that origin, mainly because the phrase does not appear to have arisen before C20.

Moe, 1975, cites Sherman Louis Sergel, editor of *The Language of Show Biz,* Chicago, 1973. Mr Sergel, after quoting the phrase as *break a leg* or *go break a leg,* writes:

What you are supposed to tell someone just before he goes onstage on opening night. Also used, though more rarely, for any performance. It is a way of wishing him well without breaking the superstitious injunction against saying the words, 'good luck'. This is to avoid tempting the gods. It seems to be a widespread custom in the theatre. In Germany you are invited to suffer a *Hals und beinbruch,* or neck and bonebreak. Sometimes this is accompanied by the application of the well-wisher's knee in the rump, just to get things started .... (Note: no one seems to know the [place of] origin or the history of the phrase, though a number of our editors suspect it to be English in origin.)

Col. Moe adds: 'An offshoot of the theatre usage seems to be to a person about to embark on a voyage – in the nature of "Bon Voyage" or "Have a nice trip".'

To take a risk ('Partridge is always game', my best friend, who died in action in the autumn of 1918, mendaciously punned in the summer of 1916 on the Somme): I gravely doubt the currency of the phrase before WW1; like Col. Moe, I propose its origin in 'a variant translation from the German'.

R.S., a fine German scholar, compares the perhaps WW1 and certainly the WW2 (and prob. since 1936 when the Luftwaffe was reconstituted) *Hals- und Beinbruch,* 'Break your neck and leg!' = 'Happy landings!' He thinks that the aviation c.p. *may* have existed since the earliest days of flying. In short, the Ger. pilots' phrase could well have been adopted by the Ger. theatre, whence, in translation, it passed – just possibly via the Brit. theatre – to the US as early as the 1920s. R.S. adds the note that Ger. *bein* means both 'bone' and 'leg'; in C20, more usu. 'leg'. 'The Luftwaffe use is almost certainly punning.' Paul Janssen, 1981, notes the comparable Fr. theatrical *bonne merde!*

In the US theatre, J.W.C. wrote, 1975, 'the c.p. may also be spoken by a director or a producer or a stage manager or a property man or a dresser or a costumes mistress or a stage hand'; he noted that 'any or all of these deplore and despise its use by a "layman".'

Concerning i.s Can. currency, Leechman, 1975, sent me this comment: 'Theatre, radio, etc. Do your best! Go in and win! A facetious cry of encouragement, heard on radio, 29 December 1974. The speaker implied that it was frequently used.'

Cf **fall through the trap door!**

But there is a second US usage, prob. quite independent: 'a sarcastic refusal to comply with a request', recorded in *American Speech*, April 1947, by Jane W. Arnold, 'The Language of Delinquent Boys'. (Owed to Moe.)

break it down! Stop talking like that! Also, change the subject!: Aus.: since *c*. 1920. It occurs in, e.g., Lawson Glassop's fine war novel, *We Were the Rats* [the 'Desert Rats'], 1944. 'Additional meanings are "don't exaggerate" and "don't expect me to believe that". I suggest that the latter is the original meaning, which would support the etymology: break it (that strong drink) down (with water); I can't swallow (believe) it as it is' (Neil Lovett, 1978). Agreed!

break it up! Disperse! Hence, get moving and keep moving! A Can. official c.p., adopted, *c*. 1930, from US; adopted by UK *c*. 1935. Hence, a couple embracing may be exhorted, 'Break it up!': since the late 1930s, and as much Brit. as Can. or US.

breakfast. See: blood; buggered about; call me anything; doesn't know; from arsehole; half-crown; I could do it; I've eaten; I've had more; where the bull; you can see.

breath. See: as I have; colder than; don't hold; good trumpeter; if I have b.; it's a poor soldier; lend us your b.

breathing. See: no, but I'm b.

bred. See: you were bred.

breech. See: scratch my b.

breeches. See: lot of water; all mouth.

breed. See: mixing.

breeze. See: it's a breeze.

Brer Rabbit, he lay low. An intimation that silence, in speech or action, would be wise: US: C20; since *c*, 1945, ob. except among the educated. From Joel Chandler Harris's *The Tar Baby* (1904) and *Uncle Remus and Brer Rabbit*, 1906. (Enlarged from a note by A.B., 1978.) P.B.: E.P.'s dates refer to collected editions of the stories; in fact the 'Tar Baby' first appeared in 1880.

brewery. See: couldn't organize.

brick. See: are you talking; 'eave; London; what do you expect; yeah, you; you've got a swinging.

brick shithouse. See: built like; floats.

bricks, muck, and beer: last things first. (Here, *muck* is mortar.) 'A very common saying among bricklayers' (Mr Jack Stearn, 1978): C20.

bride. See: here comes; off like; up and down; you make a muckhill.

bride's nightie. See: off like a b.

bridge. See: our 'Arbour; pull in; water.

bridges, bridges!, a printers' c.p. of *c*, 1890 – 1930, is 'a cry to arrest a long-winded story', says Ware, who, perhaps correctly, proposes as origin the Fr. *abrégeons*, let us shorten it.

bridle. See: weaving.

bright. See: clean, bright; see you b.

bright-eyed (or bright eyes) and bushy tailed, meaning 'alertly active – and ready for anything,' may have been US – Moe vouches for its use in 1933 – before it became Can. Leechman remembers hearing it in 1956 and in 1959 tells me that it was 'incorporated in a current popular song'. From the usual aspect of squirrels and other such quadrupeds. The phrase 'is particularly associated with the "Wrens" during and after WW2 … A long, pompous screed about the morals of female personnel came from … the Admiralty to a shore establishment, where it was succinctly translated by the Senior Naval Officer as "Wrens will be bright-eyed and bushy-tailed at all times". A Wren's was the only uniform that did anything for a girl' (Sanders, 1978).

Brighton. See: we're all going.

brim. See: wider.

brinded pig will make a good brawn to breed upon – a. This c.p. of *c*. 1670 – 1760 is recorded in Ray's *Proverbs* with the comment, 'A red-headed man will make a good stallion.'

bring anything with you? – the laconic abridgement of **did you bring anything with you?** – is a Can. drug addicts' c.p. of *c*. 1950 – 60 – and means 'have you any narcotics on you?'

bring on the body! A US film-industry c.p.: since *c*. 1930. Berrey clarifies thus: 'request that actor come into camera range'.

bring on the dancing girls! Let's watch – or do – something more entertaining or exciting, for *this* is a crashing bore. It was recorded in 1920, by P.G. Wodehouse in *Bring on the Girls*: '… the stock impresario's cliché during Broadway musical rehearsals during Wodehouse's time as a lyricist between 1916 and 1923' (Benny Green, 1977); evidently *bring on the dancing girls* had become a 'showbiz' c.p. a little before 1920; thence gen. American, whence – early in the 1920s – Brit. P.B.: in later C20, when still in occ. use, perhaps more often thought of as being from the pleasant practice of Oriental potentates: when bored with their guests, they order the dancers to appear. Mr P.V. Harris, of Southampton, adds, 1979: '[the phrase] always used to be followed by "Let joy be unconfined",' which perhaps re-inforces the 'oriental' image.

bring the house down. See **don't clap so hard …**

[**bring us back a parrot?** Addressed, in late C19 – 20, but ob. by 1940, to someone leaving for a hot country, this is a 'borderliner': c.p. or cliché? The latter, I think.]

bringing on the pains again 'is commonly used by ex-Servicemen [of WW2] when something is mentioned that brings back memories of the days of official repression' (Anon., 1978).

British. See: three hearty.

British luck. See: best of.

Britons never shall be slaves (or wage slaves) (pause) not willingly. These c.p. adaptations of 'Britons never, never shall be slaves' date from the early 1920s.

Broadway. See: give my regards.

broke. See: let's go for; you may have.

broken. See: gall.

broom. See: if I stick; she carries.

broth. See: sup Simon.

brothel. See: couldn't organize.

brother. See: alas, my poor; Big B.; if I am; just the job for; no, I'm Reddy's; not me, Sare; oh, brother; two brothers.

brow. See: fan.

Brown, brown. See: do it up; get your knees; he'll spit; hello, my old; his nose; I need a piss; my name is Ben; speak up; tail of my; that wouldn't; you're so full.

brown boots and no breakfast. See **half-crown millionaires …**

brown eyes. See: beautiful pair.

Brown's cows. See: all together.

bruise. See: no thanks, I.

bruise easily, but I heal quick – I. (Or var. *he bruises easy, but he heals quick*.) This US c.p., dating since the 1920s, is applied to one who recovers quickly from accident or illness, a shock or a set-back; one who is emotionally or otherwise resilient. Prob. orig. in a comic strip. (J.W.C., 1977.)

Brummagem sixpence. See: all Lombard.

brush-up. See: wash.

Brussels. See: mind the B.

brutal. See: it's brutal.

brutal and licentious soldiery. Dating from 1891, when Kipling used it in *Life's Handicap*, where Private Mulvaney ironically satirizes a Victorian civilian attitude to the Regular Army, an attitude not yet extinct; common among army officers, wryly joc. Kipling's phrase seems to have been an unconscious merging of two late C18 phrases: *a rapacious and licentious soldiery*, occurring in Burke's *Speech on Fox's East India Bill*, 1738; and *the uncontrolled licentiousness of a brutal and insolent soldiery*, in Thomas, Baron Erskine's *Defence of William Stone*, 1796; both of these two phrases are cited in *ODQ*. P.B.: by mid-C20 always joc., and often shortened to *the brutal and licentious*.

brute. See: feed the brute.

brute force and ignorance. P.B. wrote, 1974:

Usually in connection with things mechanical, to make them work, or to repair them, by 'shit or bust' methods. To force anything, e.g. a lock. 'So she won't ackle [work, act, perform], eh? All right, then, we'll just have to use brute force and ignorance on the bastard.'

Brian W. Aldiss, 1978, qualified it further: 'Very often it took the form *brute force and bloody ignorance*', which certainly scans better.

bubbles. See: she would take.

buck. See: it's all a bit; Powder River.

buck stops here – the. As Alfred Steinberg tells us in *The Man from Missouri*, 1962, this was 'a sign on Truman's desk as president'. Harry S. Truman (1884–1972) became President of the United States at the death of F.D. Roosevelt in April 1945 and, because he had exhibited an ability with which few had credited him, again 1948–53, this time on a Fair Deal platform. At exactly which stage of presidency (presumably the earlier) the famous 'ultimatum' (= the evasion of responsibility ends at this point) appeared, it is hard to say. Cf **if you can't stand the heat ...** and, marginally, **I'm from Missouri.**

bucket. See: go and soak; I didn't come up; squeeze him; well, well.

bucketful. See: cough it up.

Buckingham. See: off with.

buckle. See: if you are angry.

Buckley. See: who struck B.; and:

Buckley's (chance); you've got Buckley's (chance), and **you haven't,** or **he hasn't,** (occ. a) **Buckley's (chance); (there are just) two chances: Buckley's and none** (very emphatic), and the commoner **mine,** or **yours, and Buckley's;** and, for *chance*, either *hope* or *show* is occ. substituted. *Buckley's* and *Buckley's chance,* i.e. 'no chance at all or, at best, only a very slim one', are the two forms most frequently used; and they prob. date from the 1870s or very early 1880s. The late Sidney J. Baker says, 'Perhaps commemorating a convict named Buckley who escaped to the bush from the Port Philip Convict settlement in 1803 and lived with the Aborigines for thirty-two years; he then gave himself up; died in 1856.' The c.p. *could,* therefore, have arisen in that year. Marcus Clarke's article 'Buckley, the Escaped Convict' appeared in his posthumous *Stories of Australia in the Eafly Days*, 1897, and thus reinforced what had, by then, already become a legend: a part of Aus. folklore. In his admirable *Dict. Coll. Aus.,* Wilkes accords it a valuable entry; and adds, 'Another suggested derivation is a pun on the Melbourne firm of Buckley and Nunn': entertaining, but merest folk etymology, which, it is only fair to mention, Wilkes implicitly dismisses by carefully saying nothing about its eligibility. Some day, I hope, an Australian scholar will write a long article on the subject.

buckshee(s). See: long time; R.C.s.

[**buddy, can you spare a dime.** 'Not a catch phrase – title of post-Depression popular song *c.* 1932, sung by Harry Richman ... recounting tear-jerk saga of a rich man reduced to street begging'. Ben Grauer on Christmas Day 1975. P.B.: the song, lyrics by Harburg, music by Gorney, was actually 'Brother, can you spare a dime?', but the *buddy* version is the one that has survived, and so, as a popular misquotation, deserves almost to qualify as a c.p.]

budgerigar. See: perched.

buffalo. See: squeezes.

Buffs. See: steady, the B.

bug. See: sleep tight; what's eating.

bugger(s). See: dear Mother, it's a bugger; it's a bugger; let's not play.

bugger this: I've got a train (or **a plane) to catch!** Or, more politely, 'Excuse me, but ... ' 'An excuse to escape a bore or a boring situation': since *c.* 1950. (Jack Slater, 1978.)

buggered about from arse-(h)ole(s) to breakfast time. As *he* or

they buggered me or *us about ...; I was* or *we were buggered ...* In *Observer,* 5 Sep. 1977, Kingsley Amis commented: 'Vivid, yet mysterious in chronology'. It prob. dates back to late C19; I first heard it during WW1, used by a Cockney – and almost certainly it is of Cockney origin.

buggery. See: balls, bees.

buggy-ride. See: thanks for the b.

built for comfort, (but) not for speed. More commonly in US than in UK, it is 'applied to a lady of very substantial charms, not necessarily in derogation (some like 'em that way). From 1930s; now obsolescent' (R.C., 1978).

built like a brick shithouse. To his brief note in the 1st ed., that this is a C20 low Can. phrase, applied to 'a very well-made fellow', E.P. later added the following:

It has a much wider application and distribution that I had supposed; it has even, in Brit., prompted the var. *built like a barn door*, said of, e.g., a Rugby forward. In Brit., as elsewhere, it is usu. used of a female: author Brian Aldiss remarks that *she's built like* – or *she's like a brick-built shithouse* is 'a term of decided admiration for what is at once solid and female'; he thinks that the c.p. 'must date from at least early C20, when such buildings had scarcity value'. It migrated to Aus., where it was extant in 1978 (Neil Lovett). Widely known also in US which, for a woman, has the var. *stacked ...* (R.C., 1977). Fain, 1978, notes that *built ...* 'became prevalent in the US at a time when most outdoor shithouses were made of wood, and a brick shithouse was really something to write home about'; he dates it from *c.* 1900 or a decade earlier. A.B. commented, 'sometimes, in the Southern US, is added "with hot and cold folding doors and running water" – obviously sexual'. Another American gloss, this from Richard Wilbur, of Cummington, Mass., 1978, cannot be omitted: having noted that it has always applied to a 'well, fully and sexily constructed' female, he says, 'I suppose that *brick* implies not only bulk, but expensiveness, luxury: the usual American jakes being wooden and rickety'. Cf **floats like ...**

bull. See: cow calves; charge like; couldn't hit; fit as; flies; full of fuck; it's not the b.; like Barney's; then the town; thimble; tight as; where the b.

bullet. See: I wouldn't have; and:

bullet with my name on it – there's a, refers to a fear, a belief, that one will be killed – or, at the least, severely wounded – in action: WW1, certainly, but I suspect that it may have arisen twenty to twenty-five years earlier. A. W. Bacon, *Adventures in Kitchener's Army* has, ' ... and every soldier believed that unless the bullet with your name on came your way, no other one would hit you' (a quot'n I owe to Col. Archie White, VC). Cf **when yer name's on it ...**

bullshit. See: I feel like; imbars; little b.

bullshit baffles brains is an army officers' c.p. of WW2. The bullshit comes from others, the brains from the speaker. P.B.: this military adage persisted, and not only among officers, well into the 1970s – and is, no doubt, still relevant, even if ob. (which I don't suppose it is)! Cf *excrementum vincit cerebellum.*

bully. See: don't bully; and:

bully for you! Capital! Splendid! Fine! Well done! In 1864–1866, it had a tremendous vogue in the US and lingered on well into C20; it reached England *c.* 1870 and lasted until *c.* 1920. Then, among the middle-class young, it has had a vogue, but only as used mockingly during the early 1970s, and Neil Lovett adds, 1978, 'This is still used ironically by young and old in South Australia.' P.B.: it may also be used of a third person. There is a Gerald du Maurier cartoon in a late 1880s *Punch* of which the caption ends 'Bully for little Timpkins!'

bum. See: all bum; beer, bum; go stick your nose; how's your old; mum, me; she has legs; with thumb.

bump. See: give your head; tell that to a one-; when she; and:

bumps! – now she and **what ho! she bumps!** Well, that's splendid or excellent!: esp., *c.* 1895–1910 and since *c.* 1899 'about the time of the South African War' (Collinson): at first, Londoners' and then, by *c.* 1914, gen.; the latter is satirically applied to 'any display of vigour – especially feminine' (Ware). See also **who ho ...**

bun. See: penny; there's a bun.

bundle. See: cold enough.

bunk. See: under the.

bunny. See: does your b.; I'll be the b.

Burbank. See: beautiful downtown.

Burlington Bertie from Bow, I am – I'm. Based on Ella Shields's music-hall song, it promptly became a c.p., ob. by *c.* 1920, except among the ancient. '*I'm Burlington Bertie from Bow* was the classic transvestite ditty' (Ronald Pearsall, *Edwardian Popular Music*, 1975).

burn. See: when are they.

burn, baby, burn! In the beginning, *c.* 1964, it was a mainly negro c.p.; popularised by that effervescent Negro disc jockey, Magnificent Montague, it became a battle cry among Black revolutionaries. In 1971, *The Third Ear* commented that it 'was a form of encouragement shouted at singers, musicians, and orators long before the urban disturbances of the long hot summers, at which time it became a pun.' At some point the great fire in the Watts district of Los Angeles on 13 Aug. 1965 intervened and gave the cry a special connotation. (Based on information from Paul Janssen.)

burned up. See: am I burned up.

burner. See: now you're cooking; put it on.

burning. See: that man; when it's smoking.

Burton. See: gone for a B.

bury. See: carry me out; we are all.

bus. See: face would; women are.

bush. See: bastard from the b.; push in the b.; rag on; Sydney; takes the rag; that's strictly b.

Bush Week. See: what do you think this is: Bush.

bushy-tailed. See: bright-eyed.

business. See: good business; we're in b.; wrong business; and:

business as usual (with 'despite difficulty and danger' understood) was a c.p. of WW1; during the 1930s, it was used, in the main, ironically; during WW2 – if used at all – (mostly) literally; since then, it has been derisively condemnatory of a blind complacency. Its post-WW2 history is lucidly and wittily treated in Safire.

bust. See: either the cow; I must or; Pike's Peak; you'll bust.

busy. See: now we're; and:

busy as a dog building a nest in high grass. 'Apropos someone very intent on a chore – or whatever purpose. Also *busy as a jockey's whip on a long shot coming down the stretch*' (A.B., 1978): US: since late C19. The former bears also the sense 'all worked-up, especially about some trivial matter' (A.B. again, who dates the latter as current during the later 1940s.

busy as (or **busier than**) **a one-armed paperhanger** (– as), exceedingly busy, is a US c.p., dating since *c.* 1910. The *busier* version is recorded by Berrey in 1942, with the optional addition of *with the itch* or *with a broken suspender button* (suspender being, in American usage, braces to keep up one's trousers). The prototype, the orig., may have been O. Henry (1862–1910), 'The Ethics of Pig', in *The Gentle Grafter*, 1908, 'Busy as a one-armed man with the nettle rash pasting on wall-paper' (J.W.C., 1977), See also 'TAD' DORGAN. P.B.: the version used in the British Army, and also, I think, among Australian Servicemen, since *c.* 1960, is *busy as a one-armed paperhanger with crabs* (i.e., afflicted with body lice).

but I'm all right *now*! Hattie Jacques as Sophie Tuckshop, a food-obsessed schoolgirl in ITMA, q.v., always cramming herself; she would recite a list of disparate foods, liable to turn anyone queasy, and then proclaim triumphantly this c.p.

but that's a mere detail. See: detail...

but that's another story. In his *Rudyard Kipling*, 1940, Edward B. Shanks states that 'Kipling had a maddening talent for the invention of phrases and he set all England saying, "But that's another story"' – not only England, but also the entire

Empire (as it was then) and they are still saying it. It occurs in 'Three and an Extra' in *Plain Tales from the Hills*, 1888. But the prototype could have been Sterne's 'That's another story, replied my father' (*Tristram Shandy*, 1760–67, at II, 17). The c.p. became so popular, so widespread, that, by 1930 at latest, it was a cliché.

but there's good tobacco in between. See **fool at one end...**

but yes indeed! was, in 1923, recorded by McKnight as being regarded by youthful US students as 'old fogeys'': late (?mid) C19–20. Cf the homely US *yes indeed!*, which is, in part, dialectal. As Fain suggests, 'Probably from [Fr.] *mais oui*'.

butcher. See: I'm speaking; like the butcher's; that must.

butt. See: butts; dumb.

butter. See: 'dab!'; guns before; smear.

butter-box. See: lines like.

buttercup. See: upsy-daisy.

button. See: don't push the; panic stations.

butts on you, ducks! was, in the 1940s, a US army request for a partially smoked cigarette. (Berrey.) Apparently *ducks* is used merely because it approximates to a rhyme.

buy. See: cheaper; daddy wouldn't; dear Mother, it's a bugger; do you want to buy; doesn't buy; don't act; don't applaud; don't buy; don't let your mouth; eye it; going to buy; I'll bite; if only; if you vant; if you're going; money can't; never mind buying; oh, mummy; remember the girl; stop me; this won't; two pence; why buy; would you buy.

buy a bewk (i.e., book)! See LIVERPOOL CATCH PHRASES.

buy a prop! Buy some stock!: stockbrokers': *c.* 1885–1940. The market needs to be supported.

buy me and stop one. A common written c.p. of the 1970s, frequently found scrawled on contraceptive-vending devices in public conveniences: a witty reversal of the slogan coined by a well known icecream manufacturer, pre-WW2, for use on the bicycles of peddling/pedalling salesmen. See **stop me and...** (P.B.)

buy me one of those, daddy. A var. of **oh, mummy...**

buzz. See: pretend.

buzz-saw. See: don't monkey.

by Christchurch, houya? A NZ juvenile c.p. of C20. A euph. and 'Maorified' shape of *by crikey, who are you?*

by Jove, I needed that! (A drink understood). A 'gag' popularized by Ken Dodd, who presumably 'thought it up'; he used it as an 'opener', after playing 'a quick burst on me banjo'. It also occurs as a 'line' in the Goon Show. (P.B., 1975.) The US version is *thanks, I needed that*, from the world of entertainment, esp. Johnny Carson on the *Tonight* show and D. Adams on the *Get Smart* show, both on TV (A.B., 1978).

by guess and by God. 'Thoughtlessly (by guesswork rather than by ratiocination), hence unlikely to succeed except by Divine intervention': US: C20. In, e.g., Dashiell Hammett, *Maltese Falcon*, 1930' (R.C., 1979). P.B.: known also in Brit.: I remember hearing it applied to student navigators in the RAF, early 1950s.

by the grace of God and a few Marines 'has been used to indicate the accomplishment of some difficult task even though only one Marine may have been involved.... It received extensive coverage and publicity in WW2 when General MacArthur waded ashore on his "return" to the Philippines. The Marines that preceded him and were already there erected a sign on the beach to greet him with "By the grace of God and a few Marines, MacArthur returned to the Philippines": which shows that the implication is that God needed a title help from the Marine Corps' (Col. Albert Moe, USMC, ret., 1975). Its use preceded WW2, perhaps by a generation, and clearly it is a Marine Corps c.p.

Later, Col. Moe noted that an occ. var. appears as WW1 book titled by a USMC general, Albertus Wright Catlin, *With the Help of God and a Few Marines* (1919). Walter A. Dyer in the Introduction, p. xvi, [writes]: 'With the help of God and a few Marines is a phrase that has been attributed to nearly every naval hero from John Paul Jones to Admiral Dewey, and it fits, It... somehow expresses the very spirit of the Corps'.... I am inclined to doubt... that the phrase was used by either John Paul Jones or Admiral Dewey.

by the great god Bingo. A c.p. asseveration – and of satire on the popularity of – indeed, the craze for – that game: since *c.* 1962. P.B.: perhaps more ephemeral pun than genuine c.p.

by you, you're an expert; by me, you're an expert; but, by experts, are you an expert? 'A polite expression of doubt as to the capacities of the person addressed. Often with some specific form of expertise (engineer, musician, etc.) substituted for "expert". American, from 1960s, although probably never common. As [the] syntax suggests, almost literally translated from Yiddish, in which "expert" would be *maven*, lit. wise man, scholar' (R.C., 1977).

'bye for now! See **good-bye for now.**

C

C.O.D. 'A blessing on an outgoing, a comment on an incoming, shell' (B & P): British Other Ranks': WW1. Lit. 'cash on delivery'.

cabbage leaves. See: who's smoking.

cabbage-looking. See: not so green.

cable. See: nothing to c.

cackle. See: cut the c.

cactus. See: back to the c.

cads. See: play the game.

cage. See: that really rattled.

cake(s). See: cut yourself; hurry up the; if I knew; it's a piece; that takes the c.; there's a bun; they want their; vy!

cake is getting thin – the. One's money is running short: Cockneys': C20. In Cockney slang of C20 (ob. by 1950), *a cake* is a pile of currency or bank notes. The US version: *the cake has gotten thin*.

Calais. See: Wogs.

calamity. See: oh, calamity.

calf. See: it's not the bull; that must; you are a c.

California, here I come! I'm on my way to success: US: C20. Orig. in ref. to the film industry, as J.W.C. tells me, 1968. In Jean Pott's novel, *The Little Lie*, of that same year, a man says, 'Nineteen years since I took off in that good old jalopy. California, here I come. Only I never made it' yet he had indeed intended to go to California and he *was* using the c.p. deliberately and allusively. I seem to have a vague memory – *can* one be vaguer than that? – of Al Jolson singing a very popular song either thus or similarly titled; also an equally vague impression that it was this song which 'sparked off' the c.p. itself. Well, for once, an impression was – in the main – correct. In 1923, Al Jolson interpolated this song, the words by himself and Buddy de Sylva and the music by Joseph Meyer, into a musical comedy, *Bombo*, first mounted in 1921. But I was lucky, for three friends at the Savile Club, Dallas Bower and the late Luthar Mendes and John Foster White, whose aggregate knowledge of the film industry's history is encyclopedic, came to my aid in 1973 and thus spared me the blushes proper to ignorance exposed.

The phrase has exercised at least some small influence in Britain: a clear allusion occurs in Robert Crawford's 'thriller', *Kiss the Boss Goodbye*, 1970:

'We can't afford to wait,' he said ...

'Thrumbleton,' I said, 'here I come.'

And the *New Yorker*, on 6 Aug. 1973, heads a review of books about the state thus: 'California, Here I Come'.

'Surely adumbrated, at least, by the 1849–50 Gold Rush slogans like "California or bust" ' (R.C., 1977). Certainly! What's more, the phrase 'can hardly have arisen from the song, whose second line is "Right back where I started from"' (Jack Eva, 1978). True; yet the title may have had something to do with the popularity of the c.p.

call. See: daft; don't call; duty calls; if you c.; many are called; run up; you take.

call it eight bells! (– **let's**). This nautical, mostly RN, c.p. dates, so far as I've been able to ascertain, from *c*. 1890: and it serves as a convenient and most acceptable excuse for drinking before noon, before which time it has long been held unseemly to take strong liquor. (Ware, 1909.) See also *Sailor Slang*.

call me (or **you can call me**) **anything** (or **what**) **you like, so** (or **as**) **long as you don't call me late for breakfast.** This mostly Aus. c.p., belonging to late C19 – 20, is used by one who has been addressed by the wrong name – or by a hesitant or embarrassed no-naming. A.B., 1978, recalls, 'I've heard it [in England] "call me anything but late" – obviously a truncated version'. Cf **say** *something*, **even if it's only 'goodbye'.**

call me cut. In Nathaniel Field's *A Woman Is a Weathercock*, 1612, at IV, ii:

PENDANT: ... For profit, this marriage (God speed it!) marries you to it; and for pleasure, if I help you not to that as cheap as any man in England, call me cut.

In the Mermaid Series, A Wilson Verity's footnote runs thus: 'A proverbial phrase, and a term of reproach, "cut" being commonly used to designate a horse with a cut tail'; rather, I'd say, an asseveration – 'call me a liar!' – than a reproach, and a c.p. rather than a proverbial phrase, apparently of the very approx period, 1570 – 1650.

calluses. See: got calluses.

calves. See: his calves; real.

calves' heads are best hot is jeeringly spoken by a third party in apology for someone so ill-mannered as to sit down to eat with his hat on: C19 – 20, but ob. by 1940. (I've lost the authorizing ref.: in *DSUE*, 1937, it appears without one.)

came over with the banana boat. A var., perhaps even more derogatory, of the next, and applied mainly to the dark-skinned races.

came over with the onion boat! is a C20 c.p. – rare before 1920 – spoken with the well-known British insularity and contempt for foreigners; orig. in ref. to the Breton onion-vendors, who still (late 1975) contribute to the saving of the London scene from drabness. Sometimes it occurs in the form, 'You don't think that I came over in the onion boat, do you?' Occ. 'cattle boat' is used, at first in ref. to cargo boats from Ger. ports; or of Italians it is often said, 'Came over with an icecream barrow'. Two rarer phrases – both used joc. – are 'came over with the Mormons' or 'came over with the morons', the latter not before 1930. (The last two are owed to an old contributor, Mr Albert B. Petch, 1946.) These phrases. and the *banana* version, are to be compared with the prob. earlier *do you think I came over the tater* (potato) *boat, then?*: 'Do you think I'm that simple?' – 'connected with simple Irish immigrants or seasonal farm workers' (B.G.T., 1978). The connection is doubtless correct and prob. the latter c.p. has been current since *c.* 1920. P.B.: but Irish immigrants were arriving in great numbers for nearly a century before then.

came the dawn! At last you understand, or he understands. 'Originally (1920s) almost certainly a sub-title from [silent] motion pictures [and] indicating merely the passage of time, but with the coming of "talkies" [it] became a metaphor for the [slow] dawning of understanding: American; now ob.' (R.C., 1978). But there soon emerged a further c.p., meaning then came *disappointment* or *disillusionment* (Berrey, 1942); the roseate, liquor-generated dreams of 'the night before' have disappeared by the morning.

came up smelling like roses. See **could fall in the shit...**

came up with the rations; in full, **it**–or **they**–**came up....** A soldiers' c.p. of both WW1 and WW2, when it was either derisively or bitterly applied to medals easily won or haphazardly apportioned because a (say) brigade was due for at least some sort of metallic recognition. (PGR.) This is not to say that the recipients had not deserved *some*thing: merely that a 'mentioned in despatches' would normally have sufficed. The most trenchant of all adverse criticisms of a certain type – or, rather, types – of medal-acquirers occurs in a brilliant story by C. E. Montague. I once remarked to my friend the late Col. Archie White, VC. that nobody could say anything nasty about *his* award; he replied, 'All the *truly* brave men were dead before WW1 ended.'

camels. See: **if the camels.**

camera. See: **things you.**

camp as a row of tents (as). Spectacularly histrionic and affected in gesture and speech, as also in manner and movement; lit., of a blatantly homosexual male – or, in the sophisticated slang of the 1960s and 1970s. 'a roaring queer'. The pun, manifestly, is on the noun *camp* (or encampment) and the slang adjective *camp*, lit. 'homosexual' or 'Lesbian', hence 'excessively affected or theatrical in speech or manner'. I didn't see this c.p. in print until I read John Gardner's amusing essay on that recognized sport which was formerly known as *épater les bourgeois.*

can a duck swim? or **can a fish swim?** See **duck swim.**

can a moose crochet? This is the title of an American recording made in 1967, and composed by Johnny Hodges. The sleeve note on this L.P. by Stanley Dance says of the title: 'The peculiar humour of this folk phrase, used as an emphatic negative, – "Well, hardly" or "No, that's impossible" – appealed to Johnny when he heard it out West. (Eric Townley, 1978.)

can do? and **can do!** 'Can you do it?' and 'Yes, I can do it': orig. and still pidgin (mid C19–20); hence in RN, hence also in army, use for 'All right?' and 'Yes, all right!' Used lit., it occurs, 1914, in 'Bartimeus', *Naval Occasions*, where it is put into the mouth of a Chinese messman employed on one of HM ships 'on the China Station'; as Col. Archie White, VC, told me in 1968, 'The Chinese store-keeper's OK in any part of Asia. "Have you got Navy Cut medium?" – "Can do!"'' The negative reply is *no can do!*–so general that, in the navy, it is often 'abridged' to *NCD* (PGR and *Sailors' Slang.*) *Can do* and *no can do* were very common among Servicemen in WW2. P.B.: and US: 'Two [British] infantry battalions ... were detached [from Shanghai] to garrison Tientsin, which they reached at a moment of crisis [1926] ... and were soon followed by United States Marines ... With proper pride in their achievement, the Americans displayed, in brass letters attached to their lapels, the bold motto "Can Do", to which the British ... responded with the bald assertion (cut out of gold paper and sewn to their tunics) – "Have Done"!' (Charles Drage, *General of Fortune*, 1963).

can I do you now, sir? In his book *Itma, 1939–1948*, pub'd in Dec. 1948, Frank Worsley, the producer of the show and, along with Ted Kavanagh, the brilliant script-writer, and Tommy Handley, who presented and, indeed, 'made' Mr 'ITMA' himself, having written about the period Sep.

1939–July 1940, comes to the renewal of the radio programme 'ITMA' with these words:

It will be noticed that up to now there has been no mention of one of our most popular characters, the beloved Cockney Charlady, *Mrs Mopp* (played by Dorothy Summers). This famous personage did not make her first appearance through the equally famous ITMA door until 10th October 1940, when, with a clatter of bucket and brush, she burst into the Mayor's Parlour and that delightful hoarse voice was heard to ask – CAN I DO FOR YOU NOW, SIR?

Surely there is something wrong with this picture? There is indeed. 'Can I do *for* you now, sir?' – one word too many for the nation-wide slogan [*sic*] that swept the whole country, indeed the entire English-speaking globe, in a few months. Yet those were her very first words. Later – by a sheer accident – they became 'Can I *do* you *now*, sir?' and that's how they remained.

The immortal words were spoken by Mrs Mopp to Tommy Handley. And, inevitably Ted Kavanagh also, in his rushed, yet very readable, biography of Tommy Handley – it appeared in 1949, within a few months of Handley's death – refers to the phrase. For an account of the phrases themselves, Frank Worsley's is by far the better book.

Note, however, that this justly famous c.p. had what seems to have been its forerunner, certainly its adumbration: Frank Worsley had, earlier in his book, recorded that within six weeks of 13 Sep. 1939, when the show began, at least three phrases had become established as c.pp.: *Funf speaking – I always do my best for all my gentlemen* – and *I wish I had as many shillings.* (Cf the separate entries for the first and third.) Worsley had remarked that among the early characters playing in 'ITMA' was '*Mrs Tickle*, the office charlady (played in the pantomime tradition by a man – Maurice Denham). Lola Tickle, it may be remembered, kept asserting that she "always did her best for all her gentlemen", particularly her favourite, MR ITMA.' Yet it is doubtful whether this admirable sentiment prevailed for even a week after *can I do you now, sir?* hit Britain like a tornado.

'The extraordinary thing is that such phrases [as Mrs Mopp's 'Can I do you now, sir?' – 'I go, I come back' – etc., from 'ITMA'] are still used by people who were not born when Tommy Handley flourished' (Vernon Noble, for many years associated with the BBC in Manchester, in a letter, 1973).

As R.C. has acutely and correctly remarked, 1977: 'The transition from "Can I do for you now?" to the shorter version probably did not come about by "sheer accident" – since "do you" has a sexual innuendo that "do for" lacks.' Which explains why working women, especially in munitions factories, habitually greeted the 'gag' with screeches of ribald laughter.

can I have a ball and chain? See **if I stick a broom...**

can I help you with that? I'd like to have some of that: *c.* 1895–1940. Ware remarks, 'When said to the fairer sex the import is different': in Shakespearean phrase, ' "Let us exchange flesh." '

can I speak to you? 'The commonest euphemism for "Are you willing to listen to a corrupt proposal I am about to put to you?" The phrase is used with intensity and a "knowing" glance' (David Powis, *The Signs of Crime*, 1977): underworld and fringes: prob. since the late 1940s.

The US comedienne Joan Rivers has made a c.p. of *can we talk...*, and that has been used as the title of her record, issued late 1983 (*Time Out*).

can of worms – it's a. 'It's an extremely complex problem.' Very common, since *c.* 1974, in the US, but current there since the 1950s, W. & F. glossing it, 1960, as 'not common'; adopted in the UK, mid-1977. (J.W.C., 1977.) See also **that's another can of worms; let's not open...** and **you've got a smile...**

can put her (or his) shoes under my bed. See **he can put...**

can read and write, with prec. *I* understood. 'Sometimes used in a self deprecatory way of referring to one's own abilities, to raise a slight laugh' (Anon., 1978): since *c.* 1950.

can snakes do push-ups? See AMERICAN RESPONSES.

can the comedy! Cut out the funny stuff: US, mostly students': 1920s. (McKnight; Berrey.) 'Var., *cut the (crude) comedy*' (R.C., 1977). See also **lay off...**

can we talk? See **can I speak...**

can you beat it? (or, more specifically, **that?**) This coll. c.p. is both Brit., recorded in e.g. *DSUE*, 1937, and US, recorded in e.g. Berrey, 1942; the preponderance of evidence suggests that the phrase was adopted by UK from US. The gen. sense is 'Can you better that – for impudence or excellence or unexpectedness?' and it seems to have been current throughout the C20. A fairly recent example occurs in Noël Coward's *Nude with Violin*, produced and pub'd in 1956:

CLINTON: Why did she never divorce him?

SEBASTIEN: She is a woman of the highest principles, and a Catholic.

CLINTON: Can you beat that?

Clinton, it should be added, is a US journalist. Cf the following from his *Pretty Polly Barlow* (Section 3), in *Pretty Polly Barlow and other stories*, 1964:

'She died about half an hour ago in the hospital.'

'Can you beat that?' Lorelei's fluent English had recently been idiomatically enriched by the visit to Singapore of an American aircraft carrier.

can you do anything with your ears? Uttered in a tone of mild, polite curiosity, in order to embarrass someone who has been particularly maladroit, it is one of those c.pp. that E.P. labelled 'ephemeral parochialisms', in that it was shared by a few members of a certain Army unit, *c.* 1960. It stems from the story of two strangers forced to share a restaurant table: one peppers his soup; this causes him to sneeze, whereupon his spectacles fall into the soup. Blindly, he scratches his head, and his toupee falls to the floor; blushing, he bends to pick it up, and, in doing so, farts loudly. This last evokes the query from the other man, who has been sitting quietly amazed at these antics (which may, of course, be embellished further). (P.B., with thanks to P.J. Emrys Jones.) Cf **what do you do for an encore?**

can you 'ear (or hear) me, Mother? (Usu. pron. with a North Country accent.) The c.p., one of the first to catch on among all those that have emanated from radio, was orig. an *ad lib* by the comedian Sandy Powell, who recalls, in *VIBS*:

'I was doing an hour's show on the radio, live, from Broadcasting House in London, 1932 – 3, and doing a sketch called "Sandy at the North Pole". I was supposed to be broadcasting home and wanting to speak to my mother. When I got to the line, "Can you hear me, mother?" I dropped my script on the studio floor. While I was picking up the sheets all I could do was repeat the phrase over and over. Well, that was on a Saturday night. The following week I was appearing at the Hippodrome, Coventry, and the manager came to me at the band rehearsal with a request: "You'll say that tonight, won't you?" I said, "What?" He said, "Can you hear me, mother? Everybody's saying it. Say it and see," So I did and the whole audience joined in and I've been stuck with it ever since.'

In the *Guardian*, 12 Mar. 1975, Stephen Dixon, in a nostalgic, witty article, 'Haul of Fame', a set of memories of music-hall and radio comedians, writes:

'Can you hear me, mother?' Another great music hall comedian ripe for revival is Sandy Powell, now 75 .... His fraudulent, harassed ventriloquist and inept conjurer acts ... [In these] Powell's routines have been polished to perfection ... the routines are a master humorist's brilliant evocation of all that was seedy and third-rate in variety.

Moreover, Harry Stanley's appreciation, *Can You Hear Me, Mother?* – subtitled *Sandy Powell's Lifetime in Music*, appeared later in 1975.

Can you 'ear me, Mother? is most appositely and delightfully burlesqued in John Osborne's play *Look Back in Anger* (prod. 1956, pub'd 1957), at I, i, where Jimmy, well launched in a rousingly eloquent tirade against his upper-class mother-in-law, says: 'She's as rough as a night in a Bombay brothel, and as tough as a matelot's arm. She's probably in that bloody cistern, taking down every word we say. (*Kicks cistern.*) Can you 'ear me, mother?'

can you feature that? Lit. 'Can you understand that?' but, in slangy usage, it indicates astonishment: US students': in 1920 and for a few more years. McKnight; Berrey.

can you hear me, Mother? See **can you 'ear me, Mother?**

can you say uncle to that? is a dustmen's c.p. of *c.* 1900 – 14. Clearly, *say uncle* means 'reply'. Ware notes that the c.p. answer to the question is *Yes – I can;* the emphasis on *can* in both the question and the answer rather suggests that there is a pun on dust*bins.*

can you see him coming, Sister Anne? A 'woman's mock-stagy whisper to any other female on look-out for caller or visitor' (L. A., 1974): late C19–20; ob. by 1970. An allusion to the Bluebeard fairy-tale.

can you tell which is the white goose, or the grey goose the gander? occurs in S (Second Conversation), 1739, where young Neverout asks Miss Notable this 'trick' question – the sort that admits of no answer, like *which would you rather, or go fishing?* Miss neatly replies, 'They say, a Fool will ask more Questions, than twenty wise men can answer.' I doubt whether this 'trick' long outlived its century.

can you tie that? is a US c.p., expressive of amazement or profound admiration–or both; recorded by Berrey in 1942, but existing from much earlier. Cf:

can you top that? A rather later var., also US, of the prec. It is closely related to *top that (one)!*, try to better, or outdo, that – itself perhaps a c.p., recorded by Berrey, 1942, but arising at least a decade earlier. Cf *can you beat it?*

canary. See: kill another; my mother would; sings more; you're as much.

Candid Camera. See: smile, you're on.

candles. See: come on tally; hands off your; tace.

candy. See: don't buy; steal.

canoe. See: paddle.

cant a slug into your bread room! was a nautical c.p. of mid C18 – early C19; it meant 'Drink a dram' and was recorded by Grose, 1788.

can't be bad! is a 'cliché response, which I heard in the latter half of 1973, as a term of approbation or congratulation, e.g. "Hey! I've just got an Income Tax rebate of ninety quid." – "Can't be bad!" Fairly loosely used in army circles. From a Beatles' song, at the height of their fame, " ... she loves you, yeah, yeah, and you know it can't be bad ..."' (P.B., 1974). A.B., 1978, suggests, 'Probably from the cliché "It can't be as bad as all that" – humorous response to a complainer.' Cf semantically **is that good?**

can't be did! (or, in full, **it can't be did!**) This jocularity, arising *c.* 1890, was by 1937 (*DSUE*) 'very ob.' and by 1970 fatally moribund; yet even in late 1973 I heard it – from, odd though this may seem, a teenager. These deliberate mispronunciations were tiresomely common during the approx period, 1890–1914; one of the few salutary effects of WW1 was to kill off most of 'em.

can't believe a word he says, even when he's whistling (– you), is a West Country c.p. of self-evident meaning, current in later C20. (Mr Bob Patten, via J.B. Smith, 1979.)

can't claim a halfpenny (or **ha'penny**) indicates that one has 'a complete alibi which is carefully concocted when one is about to face a charge' (H & P). It dated from *c.* 1930, was mostly army, and, by *c.* 1970, virtually †. Understand: 'They cannot claim even a ha'penny from me, chum!'

can't complain! and **no complaints!** I have nothing to *really* complain about: Brit. (perhaps rather the former) and US (perhaps rather the latter): C19–20, for the former, since *c.* 1920 the latter. A US example occurs in, e.g., Jean Potts, *An Affair of the Heart*, 1970, 'Hilda had sounded exactly the same way she always did .... Had said the things she always said: "How's tricks?" and "Can't complain" and "Bye now".' A much earlier English example occurs in R.S. Surtees, *Hawbuck Grange; or, The Sporting Adventures of Thomas Scott. Esq.*, 1847, in Chapter I:

'It was the fifteenth season of my hunting the country, and now I'm in my thirty-eighth – *time flies.*'

'It passes lightly over you, Sir, though,' observed Tom. 'Middling,' replied he, cheerfully. 'Middling–can't complain ...'

In C20, a frequent var. is *can't grumble*, as in *Punch*, 1 Oct. 1973, 'Complete Vocabulary of Spoken English': 'Can't grumble = "*I am about to give you a long list of my complaints.*" '

R/Adml Brock, 1977, noted the RN var. *mustn't complain*, current throughout C20, as has been the gen. use of *mustn't grumble*.

can't fly a kite! Applied to an inferior pilot: mostly US: since *c.* 1917. (Berrey, 1942.) P.B.: the Brit. version would be *(he) couldn't fly ...* ; cf the entries at **couldn't ...**

can't get the wood. See **you can't get the wood.**

can't have my telly! and **the old man must be working overtime** are references, the former by the victim and the latter by others, to a woman with many (young) children; the former since *c.* 1950, the latter of late C19–20. (Mr Frederick Leech, 1972.)

can't help it – he (or **she**), is used joc. when someone is seen acting, or heard talking, eccentrically or oddly: C20. (Petch.)

can't see it is a lower-middle-class and lower-class c.p. of *c.* 1890–1914 and it means 'I don't see why I should – *esp.*, do it' (Ware).

can't sleep here, Jack: Town Hall steps. 'When I was active (1957–59) in the Royal Navy, and possibly thereafter... an occasional phrase was "Can't sleep here, Jack: Town Hall steps", really intended for a drunken sailor who had collapsed on the way back, with an implication that [the speaker] would help him reach his destination. By extension it could be used by any sailor found "skiving" (semi-legitimately avoiding duty or superior attention) – and if it was a good "skive" then implicitly you could go [and] join him' (Keith Sayer, Perth, WA, 1984).

can't tell shit from Shinola, usu. prec. by **he**. 'Originally (before 1930) US Armed Forces, in which Shinola was the "issue" boot polish; later, gen.; now ob.' (R.C., 1977), See also **doesn't know ...**

can't you feel the shrimps? was a Cockney c.p. of *c.* 1870–1914 and it meant 'Don't you smell the sea?' (Ware.)

canteen open, Mind your fingers! Canteen closed. A RN lowerdeck c.p., dating from *c.* 1920 and spoken by a seaman offering, rather summarily, a packet of cigarettes to a group of messmates. (*Sailors' Slang.*) Cf **box open ....**

cap-tallies. See: **different ships.**

captain. See: **fucking; lieutenants; this is your c.; we are lost.**

Captain Bates. See **been to see ....**

captain is at home (or **is come**) – **the.** She is having her period: mid C18–19. A pun on *catamenia*, menstruation. (Grose, 1796.) Cf **(the) Cardinal is come.**

captured a sugar-boat, usu. prec. by **they** – occ. **we – must have.** A NZ c.p., current during WW1 and serving to explain the issue of an unusually liberal ration of sugar.

car. See: **pass along; would you buy.**

carborundum. See: **illegitimis.**

card(s). See: **give him a c.; that's a sure; you play the cards.**

Cardinal is come – the. She is having her period: mid C18–mid C19. (Grose, 1796.) By a pun on *red*, the colour held to characterize a Cardinal of the Catholic Church. Cf **captain is at home.**

care. See: **as if I cared; doesn't care; have a care; I could; I couldn't; I didn't know you cared; I don't care; Jack doesn't; oh, I say, I rather; sailors don't; take care.**

care whether the cow calves or the bull breaks its bloody neck – not to, with *I* or any other pronoun, in any number or

in any tense. Not give a damn: apparently from *c.* 1890. The best example I have encountered occurs in Robert Graves, *Good-Bye to All That*, 1929: 'In an inferior battalion the men would prefer a wound to bronchitis.... In a bad battalion they did not care "Whether", in the trench phrase, "the cow calved or the bull broke its bloody neck".' But the Army had taken it from civilians. (Petch.) The phrase is extant, although slightly ob. (Note made 1978.) A NZ version, later C20, is *I couldn't care less if the cow calves or breaks its leg*: cf **couldn't care less**, and **either the cow ....**

careful. See: **be good.**

careful! you're speaking of the whore I love! See **sir, you are speaking ....**

Carl the caretaker's in charge. The front line – on the Western Front only – is quiet: a soldiers' c.p. of WW1, esp. during 1917–18 and, in the latter year, among US as well as British troops. Quite a saga arose about this quiet, methodical, mythical old man,

whom the Kaiser left in charge while the troops were elsewhere... sometimes he was credited with a family, a 'Missus' and 'three little nippers'. Sometimes he was 'Hans the Grenadier', owing to an occasional fancy for a night bombing party. Sometimes he was called 'Minnie's husband' [a Minnie being the Ger. *Minenwerfer* or trench mortar] (F&G, who were so very good at this sort of thing).

carpenter. See: **jack-knife; never be rude; there is the door.**

carpet. See: **married on.**

carrot. See: **take a c.**

Carruthers. See: **natives are.**

carry. See: **what you can't.**

carry a big stick. See **speak softly ...**

carry guts to a bear. See **go carry guts ....**

carry me out and bury me decent! (or **decently!**) indicated the speaker's incredulity – occ. his displeasure – at something he has just seen or just heard: *c.* 1770–1930; during the period *c.* 1870–1930, usu. shortened to **carry me out!** Post-1850 variants included *carry me out and leave me in the gutter – carry me upstairs – carry me home – * and *whoa, carry me out.* (Ware.) Cf **good night!** and **let me die!** A US equivalent was, *c.* 1870–1910, *you can have my hat*, as M remarked in 1891.

carry on, Jeeves, stiff upper lip! Be courageous in this adversity: both Brit. and US, since soon after 1924, when the first 'Bertie Wooster and his valet Jeeves' novels by P.G. Wodehouse appeared. Far too many reviewers, critics, academics have failed to perceive that Wodehouse wrote a pellucid, easy, unpedantic prose.

carry on, London! This public-spirited c.p. was frequently heard during the period from mid-June to early Sep. 1944, when London suffered from the Ger. V1 (flying bomb) blitz, and then from early Sep. of that year until Mar. 1945, when it suffered from the V2 (rocket) blitz. It derived from the 'sign-off' of a BBC radio weekly magazine programme 'In Town Tonight', which ran for many years. The c.p. lasted beyond Mar. 1945, but in a more joc. spirit and in even the most trivial circumstances. P.B.: Nigel Rees, in *VIBS*, notes that 'In Town Tonight' started its long run just before WW2; and that the first person to say the phrase was Freddie Grisewood.

carry on, Sergeant-Major! 'Go ahead! – oh, yes, do that! – I've finished, so *you* do as you like': military (mostly 'Other Ranks'): ever since early 1915. It orig. in the company commander's order to his SM, but was also used by any officer inspecting a parade; in the latter instance, it signified that the officer had completed his inspection of the parade and that the paraded troops were now the SM's responsibility: now and then, it was spoken by a lazy or an incompetent officer 'passing the buck'.

carry on smokin(g)! 'Sub-Lieutenant Eric 'Heartthrob' Barker in the navy version of the radio show *Merry Go Round*, which ran from 1943 to 1948' (*VIBS*). 'A flippant way of ending a conversation; imitating the supposed manner of the officer and gentleman' (Anon., 1979): among the Other Ranks of the British Army during the latter half of WW2 – and among civilians since. P.B.: of course, the phrase was often used in all seriousness by officers when, e.g. they wished to address a body of men quite informally, to leave the men at their ease.

carry the banner, you've got the biggest navel. 'The answer to the question "What shall *I* do?" from a completely useless person. Said to have originated with the Salvation Army, which seems most improbable. From *c.* 1920' (Sanders, 1978). But cf **Sister Anna shall carry the banner!**, q.v.

carrying all before her is a raffishly joc. or facetious c.p., dating from *c.* 1920 and indicating that the woman or girl to whom it is applied either has a liberally developed bust or is rather prominently pregnant.

carrying the news to Mary. 'Said of a horse that is running off with a saddle on his back' (Adams): implying speed and apparent haste: Western US: late C19–20. P.B.: but also, surely, the news that the rider – Mary's husband or lover – will not be coming back?

cartload of monkeys and the wheel won't turn – a. A children's c.p., 'shouted after a crowd of people cycling, or riding, slowly past, or sitting in a bus, or a coach, awaiting departure' (Peter Ibbotson, 1963): since *c.* 1890; by 1960, slightly ob., but not yet, 1977, †.

Casbah. See: come with me.

case. See: don't get on; don't make a Federal; get off my c.; let's case; let's get down to brass; nothing to do.

case of the tail wagging the dog – a. An example of *post hoc, ergo propter hoc:* Brit. and US: C20. P.B.: more often said of instances in which the rank and file of an organisation becomes powerful enough to force the hand of its leaders, so as to affect the latter's decisions in a perhaps adverse way.

case the joint. See **let's case ...**

Casey. See: hurrah.

cash. See: I don't let.

cast me. See: Gaw.

casting nasturtiums. See: are you c.

cat. See: black cat; enough to make; get the cat; give the cat; has the cat; he'll spit; I wouldn't trust; I'm skinning; kill another; like a snob's; like something; long and; more hair; no further; no more chance; pay over; raining; 'she' is a cat's; silence; smear; spit on; what a tail; who ate; who shot; yes, a cat; you can't have more; you kill my; you're in mourning.

cat laugh – enough to (or **it would**) **make a.** (It is) very funny or ludicrous since *c.* 1820. Apperson cites Planché, 1851, and Stanley Weyman, 1898.

cat-shit. See: common.

catbird seat. See: in the cat.

catch. See: don't let me; first catch; is that a c.; my word, if I c. [**catch?** is a US one-word c.p., meaning 'Do you understand me, or see the joke?' and current since *c,* 1910. (J.W.C., 1977.) Elliptical for 'do you catch my meaning *or* drift?']

catch a cold. See **do not catch a cold.**

catch 'em all alive-o! Orig. – *c.* 1850 – a fishermen's c.p., it had, by 1853 or a year or two earlier, gained a tremendous general vogue; yet by 1880, or very soon after, it fell into disuse.

catch 'em young, treat 'em rough, tell 'em nothing – with the second and third injunctions sometimes reversed – has, since *c.* 1920, been popular as a male jocularity, occ. more serious than joc.; not much heard since *c.* 1960 – which is perhaps just as well, as a masculine attitude offending more sensitive minds.

catch me at it! – often, and in C20 always, shortened to **catch me!**, with a complementary **catch you (at it)!** It dates from *c.* 1770. The former occurs in, e.g., Mrs Hannah Cowley (1743–1809), dramatist, and in Scottish novelist, John Galt (1779–1839); the latter in Dickens, in an allusive form: ' "Catch you at forgetting anything!" exclaimed Carker.'

catching. See: is it c.

cats have nine lives, and (or **but**) **women ten cats' lives** is obviously an elab. of the proverb, *cats have nine lives*, in ref. to their exceptional powers of survival; the c.p. belongs to the very approx period, 1750–1850 and it appears in Grose.

cat's meow – the. See **bee's knees – that's the.**

cat's mother – the. 'Sometimes a reply to "Who are you?"' (Petch, 1969). It dates from early C20, and was prob. prompted by **'she' is a cat's mother**, q.v.

cats of nine tails of all prices – he has is a low and callous c.p. of *c.* 1770–1840: it is applied to the public hangman. Grose, 1796, at **cart.**

catstails all hot. 'It is perilous to say "he's a poet" to a Cockney lest he "come out with" the time-honoured riposte "but he doesn't know it", and one runs a grave risk in saying "what?" forcibly of being assailed with "Catstails all hot" ' (W. Matthews, *Cockney Past and Present*, 1938). Cf **that's a rhyme ...**

cattle. See: hurry no.

catty. See: chatty.

caught. See: thou shalt.

caught cold by lying in bed barefoot – he (or **she**). Grose, 2nd edn, 1788, records this mid C18–mid C19 c.p. and explains that it was applied both to outright valetudinarians and to persons merely fussy, not neurotic, about their health. Cf **must have been drinking...**, **have been lying...**

caution. See: you ain't 'alf.

cavalry. See: form; and.

cavalry are coming (or **are here**) – **the.** Help is coming or has arrived: late C19–20, but after *c.* 1940 always ironic. From the literal military sense. Cf the US **the marines have landed.**

cavalry subalterns. See: thick as.

Cazaly. See: up there.

cease. See: this practice.

Cecil. See: after you.

ceiling. See: have a good look.

cement. See: Tom Mix.

central casting. See: that's straight.

cents. See: two cents.

certain. See: must be hurtin'.

certainly not. See: Archibald.

c'est la guerre! is a military c.p., offered as an apology or excuse for – or as an explanation of – any shortage or shortcoming. Cf Anon., *C'est la Guerre: Fragments from a War Diary*, 1930. From the continual, the constant, Fr. apology for any deficiency or failure whatsoever, adopted in 1915 by the British soldier and in late 1917 by the US. In Clarence B. Kelland's war novel, *The Little Moment of Happiness*, 1919, occurs this passage:

> She shrugged her shoulders and said, with that calm resignation which is so much to be met with, '*C'est la guerre ...*. It is the war.' That is a phrase which explains everything, excuses everything in France today [1918]. '*C'est la guerre.*' One offers it to explain the lateness of trains, the price of cheese, poverty. The lack of sugar, morale, everything great or small. '*C'est la guerre*' is the countersign of the epoch. It embraces everything.

chain. See: it'd blow; pull the c.; what's the time by; who pulled.

chain gang. See: back to the salt mines.

chair(s). See: has all; knob; someone must have died.

chalk it up! Just look at that!: *c.* 1920–40. Recorded in Manchon: *regarde-moi ça!* Worthy of at least ephemeral admiration or astonishment. Neil Lovett remarks, 1978, 'This is used in Australia ... when a person scores a victory (usually verbal) over one who is usually the victor. Also *chalk that up!*' P.B.: in Britain, at least, sometimes accompanied by the gesture of wetting the forefinger and drawing the mark on an imaginary blackboard; a var. is to make the imaginary mark on one's own chest or arm. Often the gesture alone is enough. Contrast **challik it oop!**

chalk it up to experience! 'There's nothing to be done about it (a mistake or a mishap) except learn from it: US and Brit.: C20 and prob. earlier. The direct source of the metaphor is presumably the tavern slate' (R.C., 1978). Cf:

challik it oop! Esp. in a tavern, 'Put it to my credit!': a theatrical c.p. presumably introduced by some comedian, not necessarily a professional 'funny man', who deliberately perverted *chalk*; phonetically, *challik* is a vocalization of the S.E word. Recorded in 1909 by Ware, it seems to have arisen in the 1890s; by 1930, ob. Dialectal *challik* is of course, *chalk*: notations of credit were – although less after *c.* 1960 – chalked up on a board at the back of the bar. See also **chalk it up!**

chance(s). See: Buckley's; from Tinker; hasn't got a Chinaman's; how's chances; much chance; no chance; no more c.

[**chance is** (or, less commonly, **would be**) **a fine thing**, where *chance* is misused for *opportunity* and where, in the *would be* form, *opportunity* sometimes displaces *chance*, was orig. and still predominantly is, a c.p., but it has, I should have thought, become a proverb; yet it figures neither in the dictionaries of proverbs nor in (at least most of) those of quotations. Its gen. sense is either 'I only wish I had the opportunity!' or, more often, 'You don't know what you'd do if you got the chance or had the opportunity'; it is said esp. to a girl or, come to that, a woman, with an implication of sexual opportunity – and then 'madam' is usually appended as in ' "I wouldn't have anything to do with him, no matter how much I wanted a man." – "Chance is a fine thing, madam." ' It is also a stock reply by a married woman to a spinster declaring that she doesn't want to marry. It must go back a long way, perhaps as far as Restoration times; I have to admit that the earliest example I've found in literature occurs in William Stanley Houghton's rightly famous play, *Hindle Wakes*, 1912. The sexual sense appears to have been the orig. sense, for clearly the c.p. owes much to the C16–17 proverb, *opportunity is whoredom's bawd* (see notably *ODEP*).

Jeremy Seabrook, *Speech of the Underprivileged*, 1967, sub-titled 'A Hundred Years of Family Life and Tradition in a Working-class Street' (in Northampton), affords a splendid commentary: 'Of a woman who disapproved of other people's sexual success, they would say, "It's easy enough to hold down the latch when nobody's trying to get in".' Compare, for picturesque shrewdness, ' "It's a sign of a hard winter when the hay starts to run after the horse" – referring to a girl who reverses the conventional process of courtship by openly and shamelessly setting her cap at the man.']

chance your arm! is the c.p. shape of *chance it!*, in the nuances 'have a go, anyway' – 'give it a try, you never know your luck': since *c.* 1870. It orig. among tailors, but before the turn of the century it had become, and it remained, predominantly a soldiers' saying, as it was a soldiers', esp. Other Ranks', attitude: 'Take a risk in the hope of achieving your purpose, esp. as it's a worthwhile purpose, even though you may lose your stripes.' Yet 'arm' suggests an origin, not in tailoring but in boxing. The var. *chance your mitt* belongs to C20; in comparison, however, it is so little used – at least a c.p. – that it hardly ranks as a c.p.

change. See: it's the c.; keep the c.; ninety-nine, a; take your c.; wind changes; wind of c.; you can hear; you'll get no.

change the record! See: **put another record on!**

channel. See: storm; this channel.

chant. See: don't chant.

chaos. See: if there's; Mudros.

chapel. See: that will stop.

chapel hat-pegs. See: stands out.

chaplain. See: go see.

charge like the Light Brigade or **a wounded bull**, usu. prec. by *they*. Their prices or charges are very high: the former is both UK and Aus.; the latter, Aus. only (in, e.g. Ruth Park's *Guide to Sydney*; since *c.* 1950 and 1955 resp. (Jack Slater, 1978.)

charge of the Nanny Goat Lancers – the. 'A saying we kids had, in the 1920s, when youngsters were running about helterskelter' (Anon., 1978): Brit. juvenile; by 1940, †.

Charley,-ie. See: blimey; chase me, C.; clap hands; gi'us a kiss; good old C.; hold my C.; kiss my arse; vas you dere.

Charley's Aunt. See: still running.

Charlie Brown. See: you're a good man.

Charlie Chan. See: what's your song.

Charley's dead is current among schoolgirls 'to indicate that one's slip or petticoat is showing below the hem of her skirt; cf "it's snowing" or a reference to "next week's washing" ' (P.B., 1974): since *c.* 1945. B.G.T., 1978, notes the synon. *you love your mother better than your father* – or the other way round: *c.* 1925–60; and J.B. Smith, of Bath, writes, 1979, 'About 25 years ago in Stoke-on-Trent children would use the expression *S.O.S.* (= "slip on show") to indicate to a lady that she was improperly dressed. I've not heard it since.' Cf also **your washing...**

charming. See: very funny.

chase. See: go and chase; oh, chase.

chase me Aunt Fanny... See: **cor! chase me...**

chase me, Charley (or **Charlie**) is recorded by Brophy, who says, 'We should not' – we Britons – 'pharisaically (stifling all memories of our sinful past, such as "Chase me, Charlie!" and "Keep your hair on!") talk and think as if American slang consisted only of "Says you!" and "Oh, yeah!" and "big boy" '; belongs esp. to the years *c.* 1890–1914, and prob., as Noble tells me, either springs from, or owes much to, a music-hall song. It clearly survived until after WW2, to judge by the fact that the RN, in 1940–5, applied *chase-me-Charley* to a radio-controlled glider bomb used by the Germans; and may well owe something to the next.

Benny Green, reviewing the 1st ed. of this dictionary in *Spectator*, 10 Sep. 1977, observed that the phrase owes it survival after WW2 'less to Royal Navy radio messages than to a Noël Coward revue called *Ace of Clubs* which included the song "Chase Me Charlie".

chase me, girls!, an Edwardian c.p., going back to *c.* 1895 and forward to 3 Aug. 1914, indicates high male spirits and a gloriously assured optimism. Contrast **chase yourself!**

chase me, Jimmy! See **oh, chase me!**

chase me, winger... See **cor! chase me...**

chase yourself! Oh, run away – or, at the least, *go away!*: Aus.: *c.* 1910–20. In, e.g., C. J. Dennis's 'classic' of Australian, mostly Sydneysiders', sentiment and slang, *The Songs of a Sentimental Bloke*, 1915. Also US, usu. in the form *go chase yourself!*: 'still prevalent' (Fain, 1977). Also *oh, go chase yourself!* and *why don't you go chase yourself?*, as A.B. tells me. In Aus., 'This is now often *go* (*and*) *chase yourself*, the [shorter form] perhaps suggesting that it's been to the US and back since 1920' (Neil Lovett, 1978). See also **go and chase yourself!**

chat. See: let me c.

chatty, catty and scatty. 'Used in jocular disparagement of that type of female who is all tongue and no brains [and no sense]' (Petch, 1969): since *c.* 1950. *Scatty* = scatter-brained.

cheap. See: crutches; it's as c.; straw's.

cheap and cheerful. 'Should not this be included?' asks Michael Goldman, 1978. Yes, indeed. 'It is contemporary middleclass and in fairly common use. It is used deprecatingly, e.g. of a carpet one has bought for a week-end cottage and wouldn't have at home; or critically of someone else's choice of decoration or clothing' (M.G.). He adds that he has heard it since *c.* 1968 but has been assured that it is much older: since, I'd hazard, *c.* 1950, on Britain's return to comparative security and modest affluence. It seems to apply esp. to women's clothes and accessories. In *The Sunday Times*, 9 July 1978, Michael Roberts, in a fashion note: 'The scarf? It's very cheap and cheerful.' P.B.: perhaps in deliberate contrast to the next entry. Simon Hoggart, in *New Society*, 10 Mar. 1983, notes the var. *cheap but cheerful* in use among middle-class young women in South London bed-sitters.

cheap and nasty, like Short's in the Strand was recorded in the *Athenaeum* of 29 Oct. 1864, in ref. to the ordinary phrase *cheap and nasty*, 'or, in a local form, "cheap and nasty, like Short's in the Strand", a proverb [not, of course, a proverb at all] applied to the founder of cheap dinners', a gibe applicable certainly no later than WW1: Londoners': *c.* 1860 – 1940.

cheap at half the price, often prec. by **it's** or **it would be.** That's a very reasonable price: a c.p. applied when one is well satisfied with a price either asked or charged, and dating from at least as early as 1920 – I suspect as far back as *c.* 1890. The implication is: 'At half the price you're asking, it would be cheap; yet the article is so good that one can hardly object to the charge' – sometimes with the nuance 'It's cheap – since you're asking only half the price that is being asked in some shops.' This is one of those intensely idiomatic phrases which, in their general ostensible meaning, are taken for granted, yet which, on examination, prove to be hard to explain.

I owe a brilliant comment, and a salutary objection, to Mr Kingsley Amis (*Observer*, 4 Sep. 1977): 'I think it's an ironical inversion of the salesman's claim, "cheap at double the price", and means what it says, it would be cheap at half the price, i.e. it's bloody expensive.' In US, always ironical; and ob. since *c.* 1940 (J.W.C.). P.B.: Christiana Dunhill, however, writing to a newspaper (I have only her printed letter, no ref., except to K.A.'s repeating himself on 27 Nov. 1977), maintains, ' "Cheap at half the price" means "bloody cheap" – or "good value" as Partridge more modestly explains. (My experience of this expression comes from the rag trade).' It seems that we must, in the words of the (genuine) old Chinese expression, 'settle the matter by leaving it unsettled'.

cheaper to grow skin than to buy it (– **it's**) is a western US phrase 'said by one who does not wear gloves' (Berrey): C20.

Cheat 'em. See: Starve 'em.

cheated the starter (– **they**) is applied to a married couple whose first child arrives before it is conventionally expectable: C20.

[**cheats never prosper.** 'This', writes B.P. in 1975, 'may be a proverb, but it is not in *ODEP*. I myself have never heard it in UK; I did hear it, more than once, in Aus., 1908 – early 1915 and 1919 – 21. Yet, as I am told, 1975, it has been used by English children since *c.* 1955 at latest. Prob. it *is* to be classified as a proverb. Semantically cf the parallel *crime doesn't pay*, which, clearly, is a cliché. P.B.: in Iona & Peter Opie, *The Lore and Language of Schoolchildren*, 1959, p. 182: 'Amongst London boys a cheat is generally referred to as a "wog", sometimes a "clot". The girls cry out "Cheats never prosper" or just "cheater".' And to take this piece of wishful thinking back further, B.G.T. notes, 1978, 'This was a very common phrase on the playgrounds of English schools in the 1920s.' *The Concise Oxford Dict. of Proverbs*, 1982, has made good the omission noted by B.P., with adumbrations from 1805, and a quot'n using exactly these words, from one of Richmal Crompton's William books, 1935.

cheek. See: more arse.

cheeks. See: ask cheeks.

cheeky monkey! A gag of Al Read's, since the late 1950s. (E.P.) Amplified by Maurice Wedgewood (b. 1917) in 1977, thus: 'More than a gag of Read's: his appeal indeed lay in his acute ear for demotic Northern speech forms. Familiar to me all my life... Could be "cheeky little monkey" – usually, anyway, applied by [? to] boys or young adults.' See also **right, monkey!**

cheer up: the first seven years are the worst. See **first seven years.** . . . Cf:

cheer up: the worst is yet to come is a US c.p. of ironic encouragement: since (?) *c.* 1918. Berrey.

cheer up, cully, you'll soon be dead! A C20 Brit. c.p. either orig. in, or occurring in and thus being popularised by, the song 'I've got a motter: "Always be merry and bright"', from Monckton & Talbot's *The Arcadians*, 1909, a musical show that, Noble noted in 1978, became a favourite production of amateur entertainment societies, and is still in the repertoire. Julian Franklyn wrote, 1968, that the song was always rendered 'in a painfully miserable tone'; it was orig. sung by Alfred Lester, playing the role of a jockey (adds Derek Parker, 1977). In this form the c.p. occurs in *Mid-Watch Musings*, 1912, a series of RN sketches by 'Guns, Q.C.' & 'Phil Theeluker'; slightly altered, it re-appears a few years later in H.V. Esmond's *The Law Divine*, first performed on 29 Aug. 1918 although not pub'd until 1922, where in Act III, referring to a Ger. air raid of 1918, is this piece of dialogue:

JACK: . . . Where's cook?

NELLIE: She's sitting on the stairs, sir, for the moment.

BILL: Let's have her in.

TED (*calls*): Cheer up, cooky – you'll soon be dead.

The song, 'I've got a motter', was scripted by Arthur Wimperis (1874 – 1953), a very gifted and successful songwriter. (Thanks are due also to Maurice Wedgewood.)

cheer up: there's a barracks in Nenagh is an ironic Anglo-Irish c.p. dating from roughly 1970, or a year or two earlier. (D.B. Gardner, quoting the RTE 'Sunday Miscellany' programme of 18 Sep. 1978.) Nenagh is a small town in County Tipperary, in southern Eire.

cheerful. See: cheap and c.

cheers. See: three hearty.

cheers are running up my legs – the. 'Used to deflate (esp. senior to junior) importance of local "buzz" [rumour; commendatory report in newspaper; 'and all that']. Sarcasm cannot come more scathing than this' (L.A., 1975): since *c.* 1950. The reverberations of the cheering are so loud that they set up vibrations affecting one's legs.

cheers for now! 'Goodbye and good luck!' By itself hardly a c.p., but in conjunction with the dovetail reply, (*and*) *screams for later*, it is one: since *c.* 1950. (Cyril Whelan, 1975.)

cheese. See: hard cheese; that's the c.; to make the c.

cheese it, the (or **de** or **duh**) **cops!** A C20 c.p., 'Originally a delinquent juveniles' warning cry, but later [it had] some general use, in which "the cops" became a metaphor for the approach of authority or retribution. Now dead, except as a conscious archaism' (R.C. 1978). But it went to the US from the UK, where, as *cheese it!*, it had been a common underworld term. Despite some wild guesses, *cheese* prob. disguises *cease* (*it*). See *Underworld*. P.B.: but, among schoolboys of the 1940s, *oh* (or *aw*), *cheese it!* meant rather 'What rotten luck!', an exclam, of disappointment, as well as, in other contexts, 'Stop!' (esp. of teasing or ragging).

cheese won't choke her! is partly a proverbial saying and partly – predominantly, I'd say – a c.p. It occurs in, e.g., S in the First Conversation, where the company is discussing a rakish toast of the town and Lady Answerall says, 'She looks as if Butter would not melt in her Mouth; but I warrant Cheese won't choak her' – where the latter statement implies that she is physically intimate with men. *Cheese*, as used here, is familiar English for what is physiologically and medically known as smegma.

cherries. See: life is just a bowl.

chest. See: that'll grow.

chew gum. See: so stupid.

chew it finer! A request to someone to use simpler words: Western US: late C19 – 20. Ramon F. Adams, 1968 ed.

chewie. See **chewy . . .**

chewing a brick. See: are you talking.

chews nails and spits rust, with prec. *he* either expressed or understood. This predominantly Anglo-Irish expression is, in C20, applied to someone 'rough and tough' or wishing to appear so. (Skehan, 1977.)

chewy on your boot! is current in Aus. Football and is directed at an opponent player about to shoot at goal: since *c.*1950. *Chewy*, chewing-gum, on the boot will, obviously, prevent the ball from travelling far. (Jim Ramsey, *Cop It Sweet*, 1977.) In full: *hope you have chewie*, or *chewy, on your boot!* Wilkes.

chickens. See: ain't nobody; choke, chicken; keep your thanks; there'll be a c.; what's the difference; where c.; your pigeon.

chief. See: not me, C.

chief steward. See: fight.

Chiefie. See: don't take it.

chiefs. See: all chiefs.

child. See: eleven o'clock; fireman; hit me now; my long-lost; not for this; steal.

children. See: anyone who hates; not in front; remember the starving; rich; some people; women in.

chimney. See: at a church; married at.

chin. See: dimple in c.; wipe your.

chin-cough. See: tail will catch.

chin-strap. See: get off your; lean on.

China. See: I'd like to get; oil; remember the starving; sailing for; she is so; what's that got; what's that? the population.

Chinaman. See: hasn't got a C.; how high is a; I must have killed; six knots.

Chinese. See: clever chaps; in the words; R.C.s; what they; you're out.

Chink. See: another push.

Chios. See: Mudros.

chips are down – the. This is final – the situation is both grave and urgent; this could mean 'the end', be disastrous; anything you now do could be irrevocable. The English-Language Institute of America's *DCCU* 1971 (earlier – 1970 – in some editions of Webster), glosses it as 'The time has come when we can no longer avoid making a fateful decision'. Of this US c.p., the earliest quot'n in W & F is of 1949, 'When the chips are down, a man shows what he really is'; but the c.p. goes back, I believe, to well before WW1. The 'chips' concerned are the counters used in poker and other games of chance.

chips with everything has, since c. 1960, been applied to that sort of British tourist abroad which remains hopelessly insular. Potato chips with every meat dish. (Skehan, 1977.) This c.p. formed the title of a play, about Other Ranks in the RAF, by Arnold Wesker, pub'd 1967.

chirruping like a three-badge budgie [= budgerigar]. 'Fussing around to no useful purpose': WRNS (the Wrens): 1950s. The three badges are Long Service and Good Conduct stripes, (Peppitt.) P.B.: the RN seems to 'have a thing' about budgerigars: cf the use of *paraffin budgie* for a helicopter.

chocks away! 'Get on with the job!': RAF: since c. 1920. In their timely little Fighting Services' glossary, H & P explain that the literal meaning is 'Remove the wooden chocks and let the 'planes get off the ground'; *chocks away!*, therefore, is short for *pull the chocks away!* Hence applied to '*any* first run of anything mechanical' (Lawrence Smith, 1975).

chocolate. See: I'm not out.

choice. See: you pays.

choke. See: cheese won't; I'll push; and:

choke away: the churchyard's near! A callously joc. admonition to any one coughing badly: mid C17–early C19. It is recorded by, e.g. Ray in 1678 and Grose in 1796. Cf the slang *churchyard cough*, a severe one. Cf:

choke, chicken: more are hatching is a synon. c.p.: C18–early C19, then mostly dialectal. It occurs in S and also Grose, 1796. The phrase has survived in the latish C19–20 domestic *choke up, chicken*, said by a mother to a small child choking over its food; 'a consolatory cliché rather than a catch phrase' (Playfair, 1977). *Choke up, chicken* derives from the full original. Even in 1978, domestically and mostly femininely, far from † (B.G.T.).

choke you? – didn't that and **it's a wonder that didn't choke you!** C19–20 comments, mostly good-natured, on a thundering great, or a truly notable, lie. Prob. prompted by the C17–18 semi-proverbial 'If a lie could have choked him, that would have done it' (Ray, 1678).

chooks. See: hope your.

[**choose, proud fool; I did but ask you** comes towards the end of the First Conversation in S, and looks rather like a c.p., but I can't feel sure about it:

MISS: Every fool can do as they're bid... do it yourself.

NEV[EROUT]: Chuse, proud Fool; I did but ask you.]

chop. See: if it moves; pork chop.

chopped hay. See: you are sick.

Christchurch. See: by Christchurch.

christening. See: demure; hopping; like a moll.

Christian. See: gentleman.

Christian born, donkey-rigged, and throws a tread like a cabby's whip has, esp. in the Bethnal Green area of London, been throughout C20 and prob. also in latish C19, applied to a 'stout fellow', generously-genital'd, and strong. (Mr. C.A. Worth, who in a letter, 1975, says he first heard it, as a young man, in 1938.) Cf the low-slang *chuck a tread* (of the male), to coit.

Christian Herald. See: dear Mother, please.

Christians, awake! Salute this happy deck! A RN wakey-wakey call, apparently of c. 1900–14, and prob. localised to a few ships, perhaps to one only. (Peppitt, 1977.) P.B.: a parody on the first line of a much loved Christmas carol, substituting *deck* for 'morn'.

Christmas. See: and a merry; Berlin by; coming?; doesn't know; it'll be over; join? when; never mind, it'll; no hide; what else did you; you have grown; and:

'**Christmas comes but once a year': Thank God!** is a c.p. dating from c. 1945 and is spoken by those who hate to see what the profiteers have made of Christmas. The quot'n part of the c.p. is a cliché, uttered by those who feel that the celebration of Christmas justifies any expense or excess.

Christmas tree. See: all dressed; I didn't come up; I've seen better.

Christmas turkey. See: you're full.

chuckle. See: you wouldn't c.

chums. See: what would you.

chunk. See: 'til who laid.

church. See: at a church; backwards; Hunt's like a bastard; see you in c.; standing; that will stop; you're in the wrong.

churchyard. See: choke away.

churl. See: I won't put.

cigar. See: close, but; love and.

cinch. See: his cinch; and:

cinch – it's, or **that's, a.** It's a certainty; hence, that's dead easy: since c. 1890: US, orig. south-western but by 1900 at the latest, gen. throughout the US. In his celebrated essay 'The Function of Slang' (*Harper's Magazine*, July 1893), the even more celebrated Brander Mathews, university professor and dean, wrote thus: 'From the Southwest came "cinch" [a certainty], from the tightening of the girths of the pack-mules, and so by extension indicating a grasp of anything so firm that it cannot get away'; W & F add, 'From the cinch of a saddle, which secures it' – but it has to be a *strong* girth. There exists a very common var., *it's a lead-pipe cinch*, which has been current throughout most, perhaps all, of C20. 'I suppose it refers to the softness of lead, as opposed to copper or brass, making it easy for the plumber to get a good grip with his wrench' (J.W.C., 1977). The orig. phrase soon travelled to western Canada: Sandilands, 1913, glosses it: 'That's *a cinch*, that's a certainty, or that's easy'. P.B.: and, by late 1930s at latest, also Brit., esp. among schoolboys.

cinders. See: go and eat; yours to a c.

circles. See: when in danger.

circular saw. See: like being.

City Hall. See: you can't fight.

city morgue: duty corpse speaking is a telephone c.p.: army, mostly in the orderly rooms and among other headquarters personnel: 1950s–60s. 'American influence obvious here' (P.B., 1974). To which A.B. adds, from USA, 'I've heard some interesting variations: "city pool-hall: eight-ball speaking"; "county jail: which inmate do you want?"; "This is the Devil speaking: who in hell do you want to talk to?" ': they date from perhaps as early as the 1930s. Cf **Battersea Dogs' Home . . .**

clank! clank! A derisive cry, used against Australians: C20. A friend of mine writes: 'I learned this from an Aussie!' He also writes: 'From the sound of convicts' chains' – an allusion to the days when Australia was utilized as a dumping-ground for Britain's criminals. Contrast:

clank, clank, I'm a tank. 'A taunt directed at any member of RAC or RTR whose mental ability is not up to the speaker's; usually delivered in a stupid, ponderous voice' (P.B., 1974): since *c.* 1950. Royal Armoured Corps and Royal Tank Regiment.

clap. See: don't clap; and:

clap hands, here comes Charlie! was the main refrain (' ... here comes Charlie now') of the signature tune of Charlie Kunz (pron. *coons*), a very popular light pianist in the earlier days of broadcasting by the BBC. His *clap hands* ... continues to be embedded in the language of c.p.and (usu.) pointless remarks to this day. (P.B., 1984.)

clap your hands! is a 'silly witticism [addressed] to person carrying something like large tray (in bar); and, if he drops it or anything breakable, *don't bother to pick it up!*' (Shaw, 1969): since *c.* 1940. Often, *now, clap* ... Cf **they go better loaded!**

Clark Gable. See: who do you think you are?

class. See: go to the top; join the back.

class will tell. Quality or, esp., ability is what counts the most; for instance, the best man – or the best horse – usually wins: C20. In 1968, in my orig. entry for this c.p., I wrote, 'This c.p. may easily become a proverb of the more colloquial kind': it hasn't yet (1976) done so, but it's still a possibility.

Claude. See: after you.

clean. See: he washes; it's all good c.; it's good c.; keep it c.; keep your nose; knackers; only a little; yours? or c.

clean and polish! we're winning the war! This military c.p. of 1915 – 18 was scathingly applied by the Other Ranks, notably in or near the front line, to the 'spit and polish' attitude adopted by a number of antediluvian officers. Note that, for *clean*, *spit* was often substituted and that, if additional irony were felt to be desirable, *no wonder* was inserted before 'we're winning ...'.

'If one wished to pretend a justification of someone else's routine order, especially of an exasperating triviality, one exclaimed: "Well, I suppose it's winning" – or "helping to win" – "the war" ' (B & P). Cf:

clean, bright and slightly oiled. This WW1 advice to the infantryman on the condition in which his rifle should be kept was already, by 1917, an officers' joc. c.p., with a pun on the slang *oiled*, tipsy, and it is extant, although, by *c.* 1960, slightly ob. A post-WW2 example: 'We find the guns .... Everything is clean, bright and, where necessary, slightly oiled' (Jack Ripley, *Davis Doesn't Live Here Any More*, 1971): clearly reminiscent of and allusive to the old army phrase and prob. of Gerald Kersh's volume of short stories, *Clean, Bright and Slightly Oiled* (1946) – its own title richly allusive.

clean shirt. See: another clean.

cleaners. See: leave it for.

clear as mud (– as) is a joc. or, rather, a joc. ironic c.p., mud being anything but clear: *as clear as muddy water*: obscure: since *c.* 1820 or perhaps a generation earlier. It occurs in, e.g., Barham's *Ingoldsby Legends*, 1842, 'That's clear as mud' (*OED*). Contrast the late C19 – early C20 school slang *as sure as mud*, utterly sure.

Normally such similes do not rank as c.pp., but because of its ironic character, as in the exchange 'Is that quite clear to you now?' – 'Yes, as clear as mud!', this one, I think, does.

clever. See: if you had; it's a c.

clever chaps (often **devils**) **these Chinese!**; also occ. **damned clever** (or **dead clever**) **chaps these Chinese!** This RN c.p., which came to be heard in the other two Services and became, in the later 1940s, fairly gen. among ('U' rather than 'non-U') civilians, did not, so far as I've been able to discover, antedate the C20, is used as a quizzical, or an ironical, comment upon an explanation of some device or process, esp. if it hasn't been fully understood. It's a

some-what back-handed compliment to Chinese inventiveness and ingenuity. There must be much earlier examples in print, but I'm ashamed to admit that the earliest I have noted occurs at p. 154 of John Winton's *We Saw the Sun*, 1960. Since *c.* 1945, *Chinese* has been now and then displaced by *Japs*.

The phrase seems to have some currency in the US, to judge by this quot'n from Patrick Buchanan, *A Requiem of Sharks*, 1973:

'May you live in interesting times,' she said.
'What's that?'
'An ancient Chinese curse.'
'Very clever, those Chinese,' I said.

And R.C., 1977, notes that, 'as *damned clever, these Chinese*, [it has been] current in US, from at least the 1930s; now ob.'

climbing trees to get away from it. See **getting any?**

clinch. See: hard in.

cling. See: sticks like.

clock. See: face would; got a clock; many faces; see you under; upside; Victoria; you lie.

clock tower. See: cor! chase.

clockwork orange. See: queer as a.

clog. See: he'll clog; sup it.

close. See: if you're close; on that.

close as God's curse to a whore's arse, or **close as shirt and shitten arse,** both often prec. by **as,** stands in the No-Man's-Land between c.p. and proverbial saying and is characteristic of its earthy, outspoken, too often brutal, period, mid C18 – early 19. Grose, 1785.

close, but no cigar (– *it was*) is a US c.p., used mostly in sporting contests: since *c.* 1930. Prob. from a cigar often being presented to the winner of some minor competition. Cf the Brit. **give the gentleman a coconut.**

close counts in horse-shoes and in hand-grenades, but not in this game. A US equivalent of **close as God's curse ... :** since *c.* 1950. (A.B., 1978.)

close hangar (or **the hangar**) **doors!;** var., **hangar doors closed!** An RAF c.p., signifying 'Stop talking shop!' and dating from *c.* 1935. (Recorded H & P: *close hangar doors!* And by C.H. Ward-Jackson, *It's a Piece of Cake,* same year: *close the hangar doors.* And EP, *A Dictionary of RAF Slang,* 1945: *hangar doors closed.*) Granville, in a letter, 1969, has glossed *close the hangar doors* thus, 'Catch phrase addressed to anyone in the RAF or ex-RAF who is fond of indulging in reminiscences or shop when in mixed or civilian company.' By 1974, slightly ob. even among the most conservative ex-RAF 'types'.

close your eyes and guess what God has sent (sometimes **brought**) **you!** is a playful, or even a joc., c.p. of C20 and often accompanies the gesture of a girl placing her hands over your (masculine) eyes. P.B.: Cf *shut your eyes and open your hands,* a c.p. used when presenting a surprise gift – or, ironically, when giving something quite useless: C20.

close your eyes and think of England! is a late C19–20 c.p., employed by Britons living in distant countries (and esp. if in difficult conditions) when life has become particularly hard or distressing. B.P., 1975, says:

If it is not used in Australia [that is, by Australians] I have heard it on British television programs. In her *Journal* of 1912, Lady Hillingdon wrote, 'I am happy now that Charles calls on my bedchamber less frequently than of old. As it is, I endure but two calls a week and when I hear his steps outside my door I lie down on my bed, close my eyes, open my legs and think of England.' I do not know whether the *Journal* was published in full, but this passage is frequently quoted.

Used as title of an article in the *Economist,* 12 Apr. 1975; and in Nov. 1977 a farce opened at the Apollo Theatre, London, with the title *Shut Your Eyes and Think of England.* L.A., 1974, back-dates it: 'It is generally rumoured to have been said to Queen Victoria on her wedding night by her lady-in-waiting or 'some close relative.' Playfair regards the Lady Hillingdon source as most improbable (she didn't die until 1940); and he is almost certainly right in so doing. He proposes the view that the phrase began, among Britons living abroad, as a serious, literal c.p., 'which provided an excellent origin for a jocular sexual c.p.' He adds that he has always supposed it to be 'an invented joke ... in a jocular misuse of something once said by or about an exile ... I think I first heard it in the 1930s' (1977), to which Sanders adds, 1978, '[It] is now entirely jocular; the advice a with-it mother gives to her daughter on her wedding-day – when the "happy couple" have been living together for years. Sir Osbert Lancaster's pocket cartoon in the *Daily Express* of 15 Aug. 1976 depicted a scared and be-sandal'd male holding a newspaper with the headline BIRTH RATE DOWN AGAIN [and] being embraced by a be-trousered, bare-footed female saying "Come on, Cyril – just shut your eyes and think of England!" '

closer. See: get away; stand closer.

closet. See: come out of the.

closing in. See: hills.

clot. See: clumsy clot.

cloth. See: nice bit.

cloth-ears – he has (or **has got** or **he's got**) is a Cockney c.p. of C20 and is applied to one who, not wishing to hear, pretends that he doesn't. From caps with heavy ear-flaps.

clothes. See: her clothes; I'd rather sleep.

clothes-pin. See: that's the sort.

cloud. See: every silver; get off my c.; I'm off in a c.; upside; wait till.

cloud Nine – he's or **she's**, or **was, on** is a US c.p., dating since c. 1965, and meaning 'blissfully happy' or 'very happily placed, or supposing he or she is so'; *DCCU* exemplifies it thus: 'She was on cloud nine after he proposed'. Perhaps from the slangy *be over the moon*, to be ecstatically happy. P.B.: or an advance on the earlier *cloud lucky seven*?

club. See: join the c.; join? when; she's joined; there's at least; welcome to the c.

cluck. See: couldn't drive.

clumsy as a cub bear handling his prick (– **as**). A low Can. c.p. applied to an extremely clumsy person: C20.

clumsy clot! An expression of exasperation at someone's incompetence, made into a c.p. by 'Jimmy Edwards in *Take It From Here* – a hangover from RAF wartime slang' (*VIBS*). This popular BBC radio comedy series was broadcast late 1940s – early 1950s.

coach. See: who's robbing.

coaches won't run over him – the. A c.p. of, I'd guess, mid C18 – mid 19, for it first appears, 1813, in an enlarged edn of Ray. It means 'He's in gaol'. Semantically, it is comparable with **where the flies won't get it.**

coalyard. See: don't act.

coat. See: I won't take; I'll hold your c.

cobblers. See: that's a load.

cock(s). See: big cock; come on, let's; hands' off your; wotcher; you never get; your ass-hole.

cock-fighting. See: beats cock-f.

cock-stand. See: this will.

cocking-handle. See: woppity.

cock's tooth. See: I live at.

coco. See: I should c.

cocoa. See: roll on, c.

coconut. See: every one; give the gentleman; that accounts.

cod. See: stands out.

cod-piece. See: bite.

Cod War. See: like a mercenary.

coffee. See: there's an awful; wake up; and:

coffee, 5 cents; coffee (aber coffee), 10 cents. 'It originated among (esp. New York) Jews, in self-mockery. The "aber" is specifically Yiddish rather than generally Ger. [lit. "but"]. A paraphrase would be something like this: "The price of 'coffee' in this lunch room is five cents; oh, of course, if you want *real* coffee, it's ten cents" '(J.W.C., 1975): since mid-C20.

coffee, tea, or me? A c.p. 'mocking airline stewardess's helpfulness' (Ashley, 1984): later C20.

coffin. See: another nail; shut mouth; you want portholes.

coin. See: to coin.

coke. See: go and eat.

colander. See: like a fart.

cold. See: dice; do not catch; first term; I've been left; is it cold; it'll be a cold; no worse; not so cold; out into the c.; too old; you will catch.

cold as a witch's tit – it's (as). 'The temperature of the ambient atmosphere is extremely low. Since witches were traditionally rather hot-blooded, this may reflect a confusion between "witch" and the obsolescent "litch", a bundle, a handful, of, e.g. tangled straw (*Webster's Second International*, 1934). US proletarian, from 1930s or earlier, now obsolescent' (R.C., 1978). Also, of course, intensified: *colder than a witch's tit*, applied to unfriendliness in Can. usage, as Robin Leech notes, 1979.

cold day in hell. See: **it'll be a cold day ...**

cold enough to freeze the balls off a brass monkey (– **it's**, or *it's so cold it would freeze ...*). Exceedingly cold: very common throughout the English-speaking world. Euphemisms and variants are expectably common; for instance, the TV comedy 'The Two Ronnies' (very late 1973 or very early 1974) offered *cold enough to freeze the brass buttons off a flunkey*, but it didn't, so far as I know, 'catch on'; then there was the euph. once printed in 'a Manchester University *Rag Bag*: "The cold in Moscow was so intense that the brass monkeys on top of the Kremlin were heard to utter a high falsetto shriek"' – which also, more subtly, alludes to that other testicular c.p., **too late! too late!** 'In US, current from at least the 1930s, but *nuts* not balls' (R.C., 1977), and A.B., also American, writes, 1978, 'I've heard a rather humorous variant, *cold enough to freeze the brass off a bald monkey*, said to a more prudish person, but with the "reminder" intact.' In polite company, *ears* may be substituted, and Berrey, 1942, notes *tail*. The Army, c. 1900 – 40, had the var. *cold enough to make a Jew drop his bundle*.

'*Brass-monkey weather* has become a perfectly respectable phrase,' wrote Sanders in 1978, and added, 'Shortly before WW2, The Crazy Gang at the Palladium played a sketch wearing fur coats, hats, gloves, etc. When the brass balls fell from a pawnbroker's sign, one of them exclaimed, "Blimey, I didn't know it was *that* cold!" ' Ashley, 1984, from US, writes that *cold enough...* is sometimes elab. there into *I wouldn't want to be a pawnbroker's sign on a night like this.*

P.B.: E.P., in his supplementary notes, wrote, 'Because the weather's so bitterly cold that it would freeze not only an ordinary living monkey's testicles off, but even a metal one's.' And that is, I think, how the majority of the phrase's users apprehend it, despite the naval historians' perhaps correct claim that it dates back to the days when cannon-balls were stacked on a brass tray known as a monkey; intense cold would cause the metal to contract, and the pile would roll apart – but that's not very convincing against E.P.'s commonsense approach, is it? Especially when one remembers the very popular statuette group of 'the three wise monkeys' ('Hear no evil', etc.) to be found in so many early C20 households, and often made of brass.

colder than a step-mother's breath. Extremely cold: US: since c. 1920. (J.W.C., 1978.) Cf **cold as a witch's ...**

Colin Bell. See: tell 'em.

Coliseum. See: shag.

collapse of stout party has, since c. 1880, been applied to Victorian humour. See esp. Ronald Pearsall, *Collapse of Stout Party*, 1976, a history and study of the subject. P.B.: the orig. lies in the finale of a number of mid-C19 *Punch's* verbosely and over-explanatorily captioned cartoons.

collar. See: bite in the c.; she thinks.

Colney Hatch for you! You're crazy! This topographical

imputation belongs to *c*. 1890 – 1914 and might be compared to the WW1 army's *stone Win(n)ick*, insane; Colney Hatch belongs to London, Winnick to Lancashire.

colour. See: any colour; horse of another; let's see; up she.

column A. See: one from.

comb. See: there's more in.

come. See: don't come; how are they coming; I didn't c.; I go; I've seen 'em c.; it's all coming; let 'em all; marry; some day; then comes; this is where we; we are coming; when I c.; where's he coming; who was the best; women are; won't you; wouldn't come; you have another; you'll come; you've come.

come again (! or, more often, ?). Repeat that, please! or Please explain! As a question, *come again?*, What do you mean? Current in the British Empire, later Commonwealth of Nations, since *c*. 1919; Noël Coward uses it in *Relative Values*, 1951 (at II, ii) and Terence Rattigan a little earlier in *While the Sun Shines*, 1943 (II); although by *c*. 1960 less used than before, it is still far from being even ob. prob. because it is at once terse and picturesque; I read it as recently as 1972 in Philip Cleife's speech-alert and speech-sensitive novel, *The Slick and the Dead*, and as Paul Janssen tells me, in, e.g. *Time*, 29 May 1978: ' " ... you know, Billy's a pussycat, really." – "Come again, Burton?" – "A pussycat with chutzpah." ' (*Chutzpah* = impudence; adopted from Yiddish.)

W & F, oddly enough, cite no US example earlier than 1952, although it must, I think, have been current there since *c*. 1910; and CM notes it as having been popular among US negroes of the 1940s.

come aloft! is a c.p. of *c*. 1670 – 1700 or prob. for much longer. Meaning – approx. – 'Let's enjoy ourselves', perhaps with ref. to, or an undertone of, *'high* with wine', it was prob., at first, naval. It occurs in Thomas Shadwell, *The Virtuoso*, performed and pub'd in 1676, at I, i, where Sir Samuel Hearty ('one that, by the Help of humorous, nonsensical By-words, takes himself to be a great Wit') speaks: 'We were on the high Ropes, i' faith. Hey poop – troll – come aloft, Boys, ha, ha. Ah Rogues, that you had been with us, i' faith. Ha, ha, ha.'

And very early in Act II, the same foolish coxcomb exclaims, ' ... if any man manages an Intrigue better than I, I will never hope for a Masquerade more, or expect to Dance my self again into any Lady's Affection, and about that Business [i.e., and set about the business of making love]. Come aloft, Sir *Samuel*, I say – .'

come along, Bob! See **go along, Bob!**

come and get it! Come and eat! Dinner *or* lunch *or* tea *or* supper is ready: orig., in the army, the cooks' or the orderlies' cry, deriving from the British army's bugle-call, 'Come to the cook house door, boys, come to the cookhouse door'; from the British army it passed to the US and to the Dominions armies: latish C19 – 20. Adopted in camps of all sorts everywhere; Berrey, for instance, noting it as a dinner call in the US West. It was naturally taken up by cowboys, drovers, sheepshearers, lumbermen, labour – esp. construction – camps. Then finally – say about 1950 – it became also a sort of c.p.: 'Mother facetiously calls to meals, from cowboy films' (Shaw, 1968). In James Hadley Chases's US novel, *You're Dead without Money*, 1972, occurs this passage, which shows it very clearly indeed as a c.p.:

He turned off the T.V. as Judy came out of the bathroom.

He got to his feet and grinned at her.

'Come and get it,' she said and going to the bed, she lay down, swung up her long legs and beckoned to him.

'Universal and frequent. A real c.p., I think': thus J.W.C., 1975, of its US usage, to which R.C. adds, 1977, 'In US, sometimes followed by *or I'll throw it away*. P.B.: often as a chant, with emphasis on a long-drawn-out *get.*

come and have a pickle was, in 1878 – *c*. 1914, English Society, 'an invitation to a quick unceremonious meal' that rapidly became a c.p. Cf:

come and have one or **come and see your pa** or **come and wash your neck**: invitations to come and have a drink: respectively

gen., dating from *c*. 1880; gen., of *c*. 1870 – 1910; nautical, of *c*. 1860 – 1914. Ware records the first and the third.

come ashore, Jack! as a c.p. addressed by civilians to sailors, antedates WW2 and perhaps WW1. It is a 'warning to a sailor who is fond of telling salty stories [*sea* stories, not ribald or obscene stories as such] or indulging too freely in NAVALESE' (*Sailors' Slang*).

come back (with or without **Fred**), **all is forgiven.** A 'humorously despairing c.p., sometimes used of someone who has left a certain post or organization on posting, transfer, demob, etc., in which his know-how would now be helpful' (P.B., 1974): army: since *c*. 1950.

Come back, all is forgiven is itself a c.p., of much wider application and clearly the source of the army's specialized c.p: 'From the Personal Column of the *Daily Mail* 4 May 1896 (the first number and therefore a faked entry), "Uncle Jim, come back at once, all is forgiven. Bring the pawn ticket with you" ' (Mr S.C. Dixon, 1978). Despite what a couple of irritated reviewers said of the 1st ed. of this Dictionary, I still feel that it is better to keep this c.p. separate from the similar **come home, all is forgiven,** q.v.

come down from the flies! A C20 theatrical c.p.: 'Corresponds to "come off it" and is addressed to an actor or actress with a tendency to self-inflation over a minor success' (Granville).

come down in the last shower – I didn't. See: **didn't come down ...**

come from Wigan. See **comes from Wigan.**

come home, all is forgiven is a late C19 – 20 c.p., dedriving from a frequent pre-1914 advertisement in 'the agony column' of *The Times*. I've even, on a 1973 in-lieu-of-a-Christmas-card 'spoof' map, enlivened with comic directions, seen it burlesqued as 'Go back – all is forgiven.'

A rather pleasant example occurs in Ted Allbeury's novel, *A Choice of Enemies*, 1973: ' " ... They've got a message for you from Joe Steiner." Bill grinned. "Joe said 'Come home all is forgiven'." And oddly enough that rather weak joke made me feel I was back in the club again.' Also well worth noting is 'the *graffito* in the Cambridge Union lavatory: "Come home, Oedipus – all is forgiven. Love, Mother," which is usually followed by "Over my dead body, Father" ' (an anon. correspondent, 1977). See **come back ...**

come home with your knickers torn and say you found the money!, prec. by an understood *you* (or *you have*). Do you expect me to believe *that*?: C20. Based upon a perhaps true story of an irate, prob. lower-middle-class, mother addressing her errant, usu. teenage, daughter. It is, indeed, indicative (as a friend of mine has remarked) of 'extreme scepticism'. Cf **you'll be telling me ....**

come hup, I say, you hugly beast! See **come up, I say ....**

come in and see how the poor live! As a c.p., a joc. 'Come in!' – 'but often to deprecate relatively straitened circumstances. (Early 1900s [; but still] used by surviving Victorians [and Edwardians])' (L.A., 1975). In the US, a common var. of *the poor* is *the other half* (J.W.C., 1977) – as it is also in UK, and still current (P.B., 1982).

come in: don't knock! is addressed ironically to someone entering a room, an office, without permission and without even knocking: C20. Occ. both ironic and ungracious.

come in if you be fat appears in S, 1738: to someone knocking at the door, Lady Smart calls, 'Who's there? You're on the wrong Side of the Door; come in if you be fat'; current throughout most of C18 – 19, except that in C19 the form is usu. ... *if you're fat*. Either because fat people are commonly supposed to be jolly and therefore good company, or because thin ones may be more expensive to entertain. R.S., 1971, has pertinently asked, 'May not Swift have had in mind Shakespeare's *Julius Caesar*, "Let me have men about me that are fat;/Sleek-headed men and such as sleep o'nights;/Yond Cassius hath a lean and hungry look;/He thinks too much; such men are dangerous"?'

come in, Number (e.g. **six**), **your time is up.** 'Used originally by hirers of [pleasure rowing-]boats, but subsequently applied generally to anyone who has had his innings' – a 'good run', a long career: since c. 1950. (Skehan, 1977.)

come inside! 'implies that the person addressed is mad to be doing what he *is* doing': since c. 1930; by 1975 ob., but far from †. 'From a *Punch* cartoon, depicting a lunatic gazing, from over the wall, at a fisherman, who has been there, fruitlessly, for six hours' (Simon Levine, 1977).

come into my parlo(u)r, said the spider to the fly is a Brit. c.p., dating from the 1880s. Prob. a slight adaptation of the song, *Will You Walk into My Parlor, Said the Spider to the Fly*, pub'd at that time and sung by Kate Castleton. (W. J. B.) See **will you walk** ....

come off! Elliptical for the next, it arose, c. 1910, in US and was adopted in UK c. 1919 and fell into disuse c. 1935. It occurs, c. 1917, in S.R. Strait's 'Straight Talk' in the *Boston Globe*.

come off it! See:

come off the grass! Orig. US, it was, c. 1890, adopted in UK where, since c. 1910, it has predominated in its shortened form, *come off it* which, since c. 1918, is also US (W & F). Its senses waver between 'don't show off!' and 'don't exaggerate, don't tell lies!' From the signboard in parks and gardens, 'Keep off the grass!' 'The commonest US current sense of "come off it" is "Stop talking nonsense" '(J.W.C., 1977).

come off the roof! Don't be so superior! Don't be so high and mighty: lower-middle and lower class c.p.: c. 1880 – 1940, but ob. by 1930. It occurs in, e.g., W. Pett Ridge, *Minor Dialogues*, 1895. Cf:

come off your perch (or horse). Don't act so superior! Come down to earth! Don't be so high-falutin'! US, esp. students' in the early 1920s (McKnight), but also gen. US (witness, e.g., Berrey, 1942, and W & F, 1960); note, however, that *come off your horse!* derives from 'to *come off one's high horse'*, which clearly is not a c.p.

come on! See **oh, come on!**

come on board! 'Join in the fun!'; or simply a general welcome to a staff or a group: US: C20. Not necessarily of naval origin; more prob. from train conductors' 'All aboard!' – shouted just before a train is due to start. (J.W.C., 1968; W.J.B., 1977.) See also **welcome aboard!**

come on in out of the war! is a WW2 c.p., used by civilians during bombing raids and clearly meaning 'Take shelter!' and no less clearly burlesquing 'Come on in out of the rain!'

come on in, the water's fine (or really warm). A seaside cliché, which when 'applied to *any* hesitant individual (not merely in a seaside context), [is] surely a legitimate c.p.' (R.C., 1977). Agreed.

come on, it's not a disco was, at Loughborough Grammar School (and at other schools?), used as a rebuke for doing something out of context: 'Don't make a fool of yourself' (D. & R. McPheely, 1978).

come on, let's be having you! Let go of yer (or your) cocks and put on yer (or your) socks! A reveille call, or rather the lower-deck p.p. version of it: RN: late C19–20. P.B.: not unknown in the Army and the RAF. And R.C. notes, 1977, 'The US Armed Forces' version is *drop your cocks and grab your socks*'. Shorter, but no sweeter.

come on, my lucky lads; also **come on: you don't want to live for ever!**; sometimes the latter was added to the former. During WW1 these two c.pp. were addressed by company, or by regimental, sergeant-majors to their men in the moment before the jump-off (mostly it was a scrambling from the trenches) for an attack; occ. a rallying-cry; and in neither moment possessing always the inspiriting quality they were, by these heroic fellows, deemed to possess. For a notable example, see Hugh Kimber's arresting and remarkable novel, *Prelude to Calvary*, 1933. Perhaps the injunction had been used ever since early in the Napoleonic Wars. The US version (*come on, you sons of bitches, do you want to live for ever?*) was immortalized by Carl Sandburg in his poem, 'Losers'. Of the US form, Col. Moe writes, 1975: 'It finds usage to encourage someone to "get on with it" and not to slacken or stop in an effort .... It may be classed as of

"limited usage". I have never heard it used in the singular, ... even though a single individual may be the target of the phrase.'

In 1977, Ramsey Spencer, military historian and excellent German (and French) scholar, convincingly proposed an earlier origin for the longer version and thus relegated *come (on)*, *my lucky lads* to derivation from, and subordination to, the other form. 'Frederick the Great [1712–86, King of Prussia from 1740 until his death] was the author of this, and we had English troops fighting in Germany (e.g. Battle of Minden, 1759) in the Seven Years' War [1756–63], so they could well have picked it up then, although, so far as I know, none of 'em fought in *his* wars. On the other hand, George III recruited the King's German Legion to serve in the British Army – they later formed a valuable part of Wellington's Army; and Frederick was admired enough by other German tribes for his sayings to be appreciated by non-Prussian professional soldiers, so there is another possible link.

According to *The Oxford Dictionary of Quotations* and to *Bartlett's Familiar Quotations*, Frederick's words, shouted when the Guards hesitated at Kolin, 18 June 1757, were *Ihr Racker, Wallt ihr ewig leben? Rascals, would you live forever?*'

Cf **now then, me lucky lads!**

come on, pay up ... See **pay up and look ...**

come on, Steve! Get a move on! Hurry up!: mostly Cockney: c. 1923–40. From the fame of Steve Donohue, the jockey.

come on, stew, get back in the pot! 'Said to a drunkard' (Berrey, 1942): US: ? c. 1920–40. A pun on US slang *stew*, a drunkard.

come on tally plonk (or, carrying the process of 'Hobson-Jobson' a stage further) **come on taller** [tallow] **candle!** How are you?: British army on the Western Front during WW1. A masterly attempt by the Tommy to adapt the Fr. *comment allez-vous?* to his own need and measure.

come out and fight dacent! is an Anglo-Irish c.p. of late C19–20; it is also the older version of the lit. – and fig. – C20 *come outside and say that!*, which, when fig., almost qualifies as a c.p.

come out in the wash. See **it'll all come out ...**

come out of it! Cheer up!: US: since c. 1930 (Berrey, 1942); 'now dead and, I think, never common' (R.C., 1977). Lit., 'Come out of your fit of despondency!', and akin to *come off it!*

come out of that hat: I can't see your feet! was a (mostly boys') street cry to a man wearing a 'topper' or top hat: c. 1875–1900. It soon acquired the variants '*at* and *come out from underneath that* (h)*at*. Cf *crawl out of that hat*, at **pull down your vest!**

come out of the closet! Orig. – c. 1970, perhaps a couple of years earlier – addressed to a crypto-homosexual, it became 'so common that, since c. 1974, it has been used comically at publicly proclaiming any secret practice, however innocent, thought by some to be mildly discreditable; such as reading thrillers' (J.W.C., 1977).

come the raw prawn. See **don't come the raw prawn ...**

come to cues! This theatrical c.p. is 'directed at anyone fond of long-winded narrative, or garrulously explanatory. "Come to cues, old boy, I'm busy"' – 'Get on with the story!' It arose, c. 1880 or earlier, from 'rehearsal practice of giving a hesitant actor the cue line only' (WG, 1948).

come to Hecuba! See **cut to Hecuba!**

come to papa! A US dicing gamblers' exclamation as they throw dice – 'an entreaty for a winning throw' (Berrey): C20. Of domestic origin: a father's blandishment addressed to his (very) young daughter.

come to the Russian war! In Charles Drage's biography of Generalissimo Chiang Kai Shek's bodyguard, General Morris Cohen, *Two-Gun Cohen*, 1954, the latter reminisces, of his boyhood in the East End of London, 1890s: 'Down the stone stairs I went with Yutke trailing after me yelling

"Come to the Russian war, boys! Come to the Russian war!" (I know this was forty years after the Crimean campaign but we stuck to old slogans in Stepney and this was still our battlecry.)' (P.B.)

come up and see me sometime! Orig. (1934) US – a 'gag' of the famous Mae West – it prob. became a widely used US c.p.: in 1942, Berrey, in a synonymy for a 'flirtatious glance', includes the 'come-up-and-see-me-some-time look'. Moreover, this humorously euphemistic sexual invitation very soon crossed the Atlantic; in Dodie Smith's comedy, *Call It a Day*, performed in 1935 and pub'd in 1936, occurs, at II, iii, this passage:

BEATRICE: Why not bring all the papers up to my flat this evening?

ROGER: Am I being invited to come up and see you some time?

BEATRICE (*a moment's pause and then she looks straight at him*): Yes.

In a letter, 1969, Prof. Samuel H. Monk tells me that this was Miss West's famous line in the play *Diamond Lil*, first performed on 9 April 1928 and having a long run (it didn't reach London until early in 1948); her own adaptation, *Come On Up – Ring Twice*, appeared in 1952; but it was prob. the film version, *She Done Him Wrong*, he says, which, first shown in 1933, brought a world-wide currency to an invitation already well known: 'her rendering of the invitation with postures became immediately famous. I've even seen a young child in the '30s perform the act. I feel confident that it moved from the streets as a sentence, to art via Miss West, to American students and the world at large'. But Nigel Rees (*VIBS*), points out that 'Mae West does not quite say these words in … *She Done Him Wrong*. What she does say (to a very young Cary Grant) is: "You know I always did like a man in uniform. And that one fits you grand. Why don't you *come up some time and see me?*" The easier to articulate version is said to Mae West by W.C. Fields in *My Little Chickadee* (1939).'

The phrase has for some years, in the US, been employed freely, as a question, usu. prec. by *whyncha*, illiterate 'for 'why don't you' (J.W.C., 1977). Moreover, 'the Yale Puppeteers, who performed around the country in the 1940s, had a puppet Mae West, who said: "You don't have to come up and see me any more; I'm living on the ground floor now"' (Shipley, 1977). Cf **me Tarzan …**

For the male counterpart, see:

come up and see my etchings was, perhaps, orig. a US students' c.p. that rapidly gained a much wider currency: throughout the US, thence in Can. and UK and, prob. indicative of US influence in 1943–5, Aus. Formerly I suspected that it was prompted by **come up and see me some time!**; yet it could well have been the other way about. In his letter (see prec.), Prof. S.H. Monk writes:

I am certain that I knew this sentence by the midtwenties. Actually I knew no one who had a collection of etchings or who was suave enough to seduce a young thing in this manner. But the phrase certainly floated in and out of cartoons and jokes. To me, it has an 1890-ish or Edwardian tone, and I suspect that it existed in 'sophisticated' urban society before it ever reached me. I think that this can still sometimes be heard, but it is definitely 'corny'.

Perhaps confirmatory of Prof. Monk's shrewd remarks is the fact that in Susannah Centlivre's comedy, *The Man's Bewitched* (1710), Act III, where Belinda, Maria, Constant and Lovely are in the study, and Lovely exclaims, 'Interrogating! Nay, then 'tis proper to be alone; there is a very pretty Collection of Prints in the next Room, Madam, will you give me leave to explain them to you?' Maria answers, 'Any Thing that may divert your Love – Subject.'

It should, however, be noted that this c.p. perhaps derives from Surreyside melodrama – the villain enticing the innocent maiden.

come up for air! Rest a while!: Aus.: since late 1940s. Perhaps from pearl-diving, but prompted by 'End the kissing for a while, I need air': Can.: since *c.* 1930. But J.W.C., 1977, points out that in US it bears a different connotation, 'Stop talking for a minute', addressed to an inveterate monologuist.

come up (but correctly hup), I say, you hugly beast! '*Handley Cross* was not a success when it was first published. It was only later in the [19th] century that Jorrocks and his *bons mots* ("Come hup, I say, you hugly beast") became household words' (J. F. C. Harrison, *The Early Victorians* (1832–51), pub'd in 1971). Except among hunting people, this c.p. has been little heard since *c.* 1940.

come up smelling of … and **come up with a gold watch** (or **a new suit**). See **could fall in the shit …**

come with me to the Casbah! Often pron. in a mock French accent, and always said with a suggestive leer, or a snigger. Usu. attributed to the actor Charles Boyer, but in Guy Rais's obituary of him in *Daily Telegraph*, 28 Aug. 1978, we read that 'He insisted that he never said the line in the film [*Algiers*, 1938] that was often attributed to him – "Come wiz me to the Casbar " … " The line was entirely the creation of a press agent, and it has plagued me ever since I can remember", he said.' I, for one, take Boyer's word for it: and I can guess what that word would have been.

The Casbah was orig. the citadel and palace of an Arab state, hence the surrounding native quarter of any North African city, e.g. Algiers or Cairo, and supposed to be a scene of romance, but usually disappointing and dangerous.

Cf **me Tarzan …**

comedy. See: can the c.

comes and goes. See **he comes and goes.**

comes from Wigan, with or without *he* (rarely *she*) prec., means that he's thoroughly or hopelessly provincial, a real 'hayseed': as a c.p., it dates from *c.* 1920; but derogatory references to Wigan – in the fact, a rather attractive Lancashire town – go back to *c.* 1890; cf its use in George Orwell's *The Road to Wigan Pier*, 1937. P.B.: in Norman Nicholson's poem 'At the Musical Festival', in *Sea to the West*, 1981, he uses the phrase *give it Wigan* for to have 'a damned good try': the poem ends 'God grant me guts to die Giving it Wigan'. Cf **that went better in Wigan.**

comes on like gangbusters. See **gangbusters.**

comfort. See: built for; money can't.

comfortable. See: make yourself c.

comfortably. See: are you sitting.

comforting. See: grateful.

comic song. See: fuck that for a c.

coming? Ay, so is Christmas! is a C18–20 c.p. addressed to one who, saying 'Coming!' (in a minute), takes an inordinately long time to arrive. S, 1738 (First Conversation) has:

LADY SM[ART]: Did you call *Betty?*

FOOTMAN: She's coming, Madam.

LADY SM: Coming? Ay so is *Christmas.*

By *c.* 1850, the *ay* was often omitted; but in R.S. Surtees, *Plain or Ringlets*, 1860, chapter LXVIII, we still find:

'His Grace *is* coming, and the Earl too,' replied Mr Haggish …

'Coming! aye, so is Christmas,' sneered Mr Ellenger.

Neil Lovett, 1976: 'This is still very popular in Australia – without the *ay*, of course.' In C20 usu. reduced to *so is*, or *so's*, *Christmas*, the *coming* having been already mentioned.

coming, Mother! has been described by W & F in 1960 as a 'synthetic fad expression' – i.e., a c.p. that achieved a vogue. J.W.C. amplified in 1977: 'This was the invariable second line of each episode of a radio serial called "The Aldrich Family", spoken by the adolescent son of the family, in response to the invariable first line, spoken by his mother, "*Henry! Henry Aldrich!*" It belonged to the 1930s, before TV. … it hardly ever got into point.'

'It was used in [the US] in the 1940s as part of the opening routine of [a] radio program:

MOTHER (peremptorily): Henry? Henry Aldrich!

HENRY (squeaky voice, resigned): Coming, mother!

The c.p. was used for years with Henry's inflection by speakers jocularly seeking sympathy for being ordered about. One still hears it occasionally from Americans over forty' (Dr Donald L. Martin of the Richard Bland College, 1977).

This was a weekly program, every Saturday night, and it generated a group of motion pictures: and this movie series strongly reinforced the influence of the radio series. (Mr. C.W. Williams and, independently, Mr Arthur M. Shapiro, both 1977.) 'The phrase may have its origin in the opening lines of Mark Twain's classic, *The Adventures of Tom Sawyer* (1876): "Tom – you Tom"' (A.B., 1978).

For the UK, Mr Keith Sayer of Perth, W. Aus. but born in Leeds, recalls (1984) a similar introduction to the BBC's late 1940s radio broadcasts of a 'series of children's programmes based on the 'Just William' books of Richmal Crompton. They were introduced by:

A portion of signature tune.

BBC ANNOUNCER: We present 'Just –

LOUD MATRIARCHAL VOICE: Will-YUM! [Second syllable pitched higher].

BOY'S HURRIED REPLY: Coming, Mother!

Resumption of signature tune.

P.B.: was this conscious plagiarism by the BBC, or an entirely independent coinage?

coming up on a lorry (– **it's**) is a joc. c.p., dating from *c.* 1910 and referring to something small – a letter, a packet – that has failed to arrive when it was expected. B.G.T., 1978, notes the occ., rather short-lived var.: *coming up by Pickford's van*. P.B.: Messrs Pickford's large blue pantechnicons have been a familiar sight for many decades.

command. See: don't go over.

commence. See: gradely.

comment. See: no comment.

commercial. See: right old.

committee. See: on behalf.

common. See: they're both.

common as cat-shit and twice as nasty! (– **as**).

This Cockney c.p. dates from *c.* 1920 – if not from twenty years earlier – and it is applied either to a person one regards as beneath oneself or, less often, to an inferior article. (Julian Franklyn, 1968.) More frequent is *common as dirt ...*, prob. going back to mid C19. The N. Country form is *... mucky ...* which itself possesses a var., dating from 1973: *common as muck! – no!* commoner, used by, e.g., Frankie Howerd in 'Up Pompeii', a TV comedy series. Cf **soft as shit and twice as nasty**, and **mean as pig-shit**, qq.v.

company. See: I like your c.; I prefer.

complain. See: can't complain; you going.

complaints. See: any complaints.

complexion. See: that schoolgirl.

compliment paid and no expense. A middle and upper-middle class c.p. uttered 'when someone does not accept an invitation' (Playfair, 1977).

compree. See: no compree.

concerned. See: Alderman; Nash; Palmer; quodding; slanging; wedding; York Street.

condition. See: better in health; I'm in c.

confess. See: I acknowledge; and:

confess and be hanged! is a late C16 – 18 semi-proverbial c.p.: 'You lie!' Lit., be shriven and be hanged! (Apperson.) Cf the proverbial 'Tell the truth and shame the Devil!'

Confucius he say. This is an introductory gag to words of homely wisdom – homespun philosophy that is often cynical in an engagingly ingenious way; it is couched in a supposedly Chinese grammar and style. Although heard earlier, it did not, I think, achieve full status until *c.* 1920: certainly it had, by 1960, become slightly ob. In Colin Dexter's *Last Bus to Woodstock*, 1975:

Tomsett drained his glass. ' ... I've always been a bit dubious about this rape business.'

'Confucius, he say girl with skirt up, she run faster than man with trousers down, eh?'

The two older [dons] smiled politely at the tired old joke, but Melhuish wished he hadn't repeated it; off-key, over-familiar.

It may also be applied by auditor to a speaker's sage generalization. A tribute to the fame of the ancient Chinese moralist and philosopher.

Reviewing the 1st ed. of this Dictionary, in *Observer*, 4 Sep. 1977, Kingsley Amis wrote that it also introduces 'phrase satirising homely wisdom by impropriety, often mild ... , sometimes involving word-play (*girl who sit on jockey's lap soon get hot tip*).'

J.W.C., 1977, observed that 'the almost universal US form omitted the "he"', while Ashley, 1979, for US, lists it as 'Confucius says'.

Cf the educated US and Brit. *thus spake Zarathustra* (*c.* 1890 – 1930), 'used ironically when a pompous remark is made' (Fain, 1977). The phrase did linger on. From Nietzsche's *Also Sprach Zarathustra*, 1883 ff, which inaugurated that Germanic conception of the Superman which, discernible during WW1, reached its peak during the 1930s in the thin disguise of Aryan man.

P.B.: in the *Analects of Confucius*, the sage's sayings are usu. introduced by the classical Chinese *Kong zi yue*, lit. 'Master Kong said'. *Kong* is pron. *koong*, and the *zi* is the contracted form of *fuzi* (an honorific for a teacher), whence came the latinised - *fucius*.

conk. See: big conk; you've got a big.

Connaught. See: go to Hell or.

Connolly. See: luck of Eric.

conscience. See: standing.

consider all propositions carefully, like the nice girl of Portsmouth. A C20 saying, common among gypsies, it was recorded by the late D. Reeve in *No Place Like Home*, 1960.

constable. See: I apprehend.

[consult your friendly neighbourhood, or (occ., and only in UK) **local,** whoever's in your mind as the expert in the trade, profession, sport, or what not. This isn't a c.p., for the operative final word is variable. It is a cliché pattern; cf the syntactical pattern of, e.g., *came the dawn*, hence the show-down, the crunch, or whatever.]

contemplating infinity or (one's) **navel** 'is one way of describing how some people do nothing' (an anon. correspondent, 1978): since *c.* 1950, at latest.

contradict. See: who am I.

contributions. See: all c.; small c.

control. See: everything is under.

cook. See: all hands; how do you like; I'll leave it all; now you're cooking; only a fool; put a stone; ruffin; she couldn't c.; what's cooking; when it's smoking; who called; yes, but beautifully.

cook-girl. See: please, I want.

cook-shop. See: you couldn't be served.

cookie. See: that's the way the c.

Cook's. See: follow the man.

cool. See: don't lose; warm; and:

cool it: Simmer down! Calm down! Relax!: US: since *c.* 1955 (W & F); it became, by the late 1960s. common also in UK – and in the rest of the Commonwealth. A natural development from SE *cool*, unafraid, unflustered. In the US, mostly a teenagers', and negroes', phrase; in a Philadelphia newspaper of late May or early June 1970, Sidney J. Harris, in a witty poem entitled 'This Cat Doesn't Dig All that Groovy Talk', declares:

If I were king, I'd promptly rule it

Out of bonds [sic] to murmur, 'cool it'.

An elab., mostly negro and beatnik and hippie and jazz, arose almost immediately: *cool it, man!*

cop(s). See: cheese it; it's a fair.

cop it sweet! 'Be a good loser!' – 'Grin and bear it!': Aus.: since late 1940s. This phrase forms the title of Jim Ramsay's entertaining little 'dictionary of Australian slang and common usage'; he notes the nuance, 'Take the blame, even when it's unjust!'

cop that lot! This Aus. c.p., dating since *c.* 1930 and alluded to by Nino Culotta in his book, *Cop This Lot*, 1960, means 'Just look at those people or that incident or scene or display!' and implies either astonishment or admiration – or, on the other hand, derision or contempt. Cf:

cop this! An Aus. 'expression drawing attention to something or someone' (Jim Ramsay, 1977: see **cop it ...**) since *c.* 1945. Take note, or notice, of this, *cop* having the basic and predominant sense, 'to take, to receive'. Cf the WW1 Tommies' phrase *cop a packet*, to be fatally wounded.

cop this, young 'Arry! This was, in the late 1940s, a 'gag' uttered by Roy Rene in the *McCackie Mansions* sketches, just before he clipped the lad on the ear. It caught on as a playful Aus. c.p., e.g. 'by someone passing a cup of tea' (Wilkes), or in more boisterous horse-play, throwing things about (B.P.). This, however, is the c.p. form of the gag itself, which ran *Young Harry, cop this!* (Harry Griffiths, the original Young Harry, 1978; he has shown me a script dated 21 Oct. 1947). Cf the US **sock it to me**, and **one of my mob**.

copacetic (or phonetically **copasetic,** *-ce-*or-*se-* pron. *see*) – **it's** or **it is**; var. **everything's copacetic**, often extended to ... *with me, him,* etc. 'Everything's fine'. First dictionaried, so far as I've discovered, by *Webster's Second International*, 1934, where it is defined as 'capital; snappy; prime'; classified as slang, no origin proposed. *Webster's Third*, 1961, defines it as 'very satisfactory; fine and dandy ('everything is copacetic with me this morning'), and adds 'origin unknown'. Berrey, 1942, gives the occ. var. *copasetec*: defines it as 'safe as houses', and also as 'a signal that the coast is clear, no policemen are in sight'. W & F, 1960, provide a date, 1926, spelt *kopasetee*, and say 'From the Yiddish': an acceptable theory.

Now for that Yiddish origin. Shipley writes, 1979: 'Four scholars in the field agree that *copacetic* is Hebrew, via Yiddish. Hebrew (ha) *kol b' ts dik:* lit. "everything is in justice" – i.e. all is as it should be; OK!; excellent, copacetic. The last syllable shifts easily to the English adjectival ending *-ic*, Latin *-icus*. Two men in their early 60s, whom I asked, said they had *never* heard the word. It is virtually obsolete, though it did have a lively vogue some years ago.' He adds, 'I haven't heard *copacetic* in some ten years.' The heyday of the c.p. seems to have been *c.* 1920 – 45.

It is, however, fair to mention that several other scholars (notably Col. Moe, 1979) prefer an origin 'in the Negro slang of Harlem in New York City' and cite, from the glossary 'Negro Words and Phrases' to Carl Van Vechten's *Nigger Heaven* (Harlem itself), 1926: '*kopasetee*: an approbatory epithet somewhat stronger than *all right*'. Unfortunately these supporters of a Negro etymology omit to mention the Negro, or perhaps rather the African Negro, word (or phrase) from which it derives.

I myself lean towards the Yiddish etym. proposed by Dr Shipley: yet I shouldn't care to become dogmatic and finally rule out the Negro derivation. (1979.) One reason why I decline to 'go out on a limb' and plump for the Yiddish origin is that (as Col. Moe tells me) 'Bill "Bojangles" Robinson (Negro tap-dancer, singer, actor) is often looked upon as the coiner of the word. I disagree. I believe that he acquired it in Harlem prior to 1900 and popularized it.' Robinson was proud of the fame that 'his' word had attained; he had early used it to indicate his pleasure and satisfaction with the world in which he performed. A sidelight: 'Bojangles' often extended or elaborated his tag-line thus: 'Everything is copacetic, everything is rosy, the goose hangs high'.

My inquiries into the phrase were instituted by W.J.B., 1978, who remarked that he found no mention of *it's copacetic* [in the 1st ed. of this Dictionary] and added, 'If everything is fine and dandy, O.K., cosy and special, we say *It's copacetic.*'

coppers. See: A.C.A.B.; Davy; even the Admiralty; steal; streets; when Adam.

cor! chase me Aunt Fanny round the clock tower and **cor! chase me, winger, round the wash-house!** Both of these c.pp. are used by RN ratings to express either astonishment or incredulity: but whereas the former belongs to Chatham, where the clock tower forms a very prominent feature of the landscape, and has been current for most, if not all, of C20, the latter was a fairly gen. c.p. of the approx. period 1947 – 57. A *winger* is naval for a chum, a pal. P.B.: but from my WW2 childhood, and later, say *c.* 1940 onwards, I recall children using the variants, *cor, chase me* (or *my*) *Aunt Fanny round the gasworks* (or, while the war was on, *the bomb-(h)ole)!*

corn(s). See: hell hath; I acknowledge; that horse.

corncob. See: she walks.

corner. See: it's your c.; round the c.; with the c.

corpse. See: city morgue.

corruption. See: shit and c.

corsets. See: aye, aye, don't.

corvette would roll on wet grass – a. A Royal Navy's and very soon also the other English-speaking navies' c.p. of WW2. In the *Sunday Times* Weekly Review of 9 Aug. 1970, Nicholas Montsarrat records it and glosses it thus: 'Corvettes were abominable ships to live in, in any kind of weather; ... they pitched and rolled and swung with a brutal persistence as long as any breeze blew.'

cost. See high cost.

cost an arm and a leg. See **arm and a leg.**

cost yer!, lit. 'You may have it – providing you're prepared to pay for it' and used thus in prisons since the 1920s, has come, among friends there, hence among ex-convicts, hence also among their relatives and among their friends and acquaintances, to be used jokingly, e.g. in affectionate irony. P.B.: by the early 1970s, and usu. in the form *it'll cost yer!*, an extremely popular gen. c.p., perhaps esp. among comprehensive-school children, as my wife, teaching them at the time, attests. The phrase's vogue waned, but it may still be heard occ., 1982.

cotton socks. See: bless your little c.

cough. See: do you spit; I'd hate; you've a bad; your cough's.

cough it up, to expectorate, qualifies as a c.p. in its elaborations *cough it up: it could be a gold watch* and *cough it up; (even) if it's only a bucketful, it will ease you*, which date from early C20. (S.C. Dixon, 1978.)

cough lozenge. See: that's a c.

coughing better (or **well**) **tonight, eh?** It is 'a quip from the Edwardian variety theatre which came into common parlance to accompany a cough; the creation of Lancashire comedian George Formby (Senior), who, as it were, made a virtue of necessity. In *Vaudeville Days*, 1935, W.H. Board-man explains: "He [G.F.] was another of those game fellows of the halls who wouldn't let physical illness prevent his going on the stage and delighting his public. His side remarks to the leader of the orchestra became a joke in itself. He would come on the stage in a burlesque of the athlete who is always boasting about his prowess ... He usually began his patter with an irritating cough: the music would be halted, and he would smile pathetically at the leader and say, 'Coughin' better tonight, Ernest, eh?' Very few in the audience knew that the cough was not feigned: poor George's lungs had been affected"' (Noble, 1976). *VIBS* notes further that George Formby, who died 'of a tubercular condition' in 1921, was known as 'the Wigan Nightingale'.

could eat me without salt. See **I could eat that ...**

could eat the hind leg off a donkey; often prec. by *I*, occ. by *he*. I'm (etc.) extremely hungry: late C19 – 20. 'This has obviously been formed on the analogy of the ordinary colloquial phrase, *talk the hind leg off a donkey*, i.e. excessively' (Playfair, 1977). The Can. shape (*teste* Leechman) is *I could* *eat a horse, if you took his shoes off*, with which cf the even more voracious version quoted (from a long-distance lorry-driver) in *New Society*, 28 May 1981: *I could eat a scabby horse between bedrags.*

could fall into (the) shit (or, Can., **shitcart) and come up smelling of** (usu. **violets**, sometimes **roses**); Cockney var., **could fall into a cart** (or **dump** or **heap** or **load** or **pile) of shit and come out with a gold watch** (or **with a new suit on**). [Any of these variants is usu. prec. by *he*, but why should we be sexist? Let the ladies share whatever good fortune is going! P.B.] All may be prec. by *he* (or *she*) *is so lucky that he* (or *she*) . . . , as in the more polite version, *(he's) so lucky that if (he) fell in* (or *into) the river (he'd) only get dusty.* All may be applied either to an exceptionally, or an habitually lucky person or to someone extraordinarily lucky upon a specific occasion..

Skehan, 1977, notes that the allusive *he came up* (or *you come out*, etc.) *smelling like roses* is applied to someone emerging untarnished from a 'sticky' situation C20. R.C. confirms this phrase's use in US since 1930s at latest. And A.B., 1978, adds that *wade* is, in US, often substituted for *fall* in the relevant versions; while the US form of the 'river' version is *(he) could fall on (his) face and not hurt it.* Jack Slater writes from Lancashire, 1978, that Oldham and Rochdale employ an amusing var.: *if he fell off the Co-op (roof), he'd land in the Divvy* (Cash Dividend).

could I have that in writing? – to which *please* is courteously but not very often added. Addressed to one who has spoken very flatteringly or, at the least, complimentarily of the speaker's abilities or character: since *c.* 1945. Cf **thank you for those few kind words** – of which it forms, in essence, a synonym or, at worst, an approx. equivalent.

could sell ice-boxes to (the) Eskimos – **he**. He's a wonderful salesman: US: since *c.* 1955. (R.C., 1977.) The Aus. version is, naturally, *he could sell boomerangs to the blacks* (Wilkes, *Dict. Aus. Coll.*, quot'n dated 1974). P.B.: in UK, . . . *refrigerators* . . . Contrast **couldn't organize . . .**

couldn't agree more. See **I couldn't agree . . .**

couldn't care fewer. See **I couldn't care fewer.**

couldn't care less. See **I couldn't care less.**

couldn't do it in the time. See **you couldn't do it . . .**

couldn't drive nails in a snowbank and **couldn't teach a settin' hen to cluck** are, among US cowboys, applied to 'an ignorant person': C20, and prob. since latish C19.

couldn't give a monkey's (orig., . . . **a monkey's fuck** or **toss**). Applied to anyone who acts without care or consideration for the consequences or for other people: since *c.* 1970, in the fuller versions, but soon shortened. Perhaps not a true c.p., being only the latest in a long line – a very long line – of *couldn't* (or *doesn't*) *give a* care, e.g. *a fouter, a damn, a cuss* (see *DSUE* at *not care* . . .), but used very widely since mid-1970s, at least in demotic speech. A *Punch* cartoon of *c.* 1977 showed an armoured van bearing the slogan (genuine) 'Securicor cares'; hurtling across its bows is another armoured van, with two masked men in the cab and, on the side, the words 'Burglars don't give a monkey's'. (P.B.)

couldn't hit the inside of a barn (polite) or . . . **a bull in the arse with a scoop-shovel**; either version is, naturally, often prec. by *you*. A C20 Can. c.p. addressed to a very poor marksman.

But of course this isn't only Can.: J.W.C. adds, 1977, 'The common US variant is "couldn't hit the side of a barn door" – clearly a thoughtless conflation of " . . . hit a barn door" and "hit the side of a barn"'. Of the latter, Edward Hodnett writes, 1975, 'Origin obscure, but rural. Main lease of life in baseball: the opposing pitcher is so wild *he couldn't*, etc. (and so can't get the ball over the plate)'. A.B., also from US, 1979: 'Even more ridiculing is *you couldn't hit the right side of a barn with a scatter-shot* or *a shotgun*. It includes more than marksmanship: it applies to such games as darts, baseball, golf – and many others'. The US form(s) may have prec. the Can. and may go back to late C19 or even a half-century earlier.

P.B.: these US versions are well known in UK also, where there is also, e.g. *couldn't hit a haystack at five yards*—but I do not propose this as a c.p. (?are the others), since in my own case it is almost the literal truth.

couldn't knock the skin off a rice-pudding (–**he** or **you**) expresses extreme contempt of (usu.) a weakling, or of a coward: C20, but particularly common in the Forces during WW1. A US – and Brit. – var. is *he* (or *you) couldn't fight* or *punch his* (or *your) way out of a paper bag*: since *c.* 1910 (Moe). P.B.: cf the contempt for a poor boxer in the punning Brit. disparagement *box? Him, box? He couldn't box bloody kippers!* Other sneers at a man boasting of his strength or of his abilities at fisticuffs are: *(you) couldn't blow the froth off a pint* or *couldn't knock a pint back*. A predominantly Aus. version of the *paper bag* idea is *couldn't fight a bag of shit*. A var. on the theme is *he took* (or *it took him) three rounds to lick a stamp*, and *(you) couldn't do it in the time.*

couldn't organize a fuck in a brothel; or **piss-up** – i.e., a drinking bout – **in a brewery**; or **sell ice-water in hell** (elliptical for *he* or *you* . . .). The first two belong to the Other Ranks (or the ratings) in the British fighting Services, hence also among civilians, date from ? 1920s or 1930s, are as low as they're picturesque, and are derisively directed at grossly inefficient superiors. The third is US, dates prob. from the early 1920s (? during the torrid days of Prohibition), and is 'said of an incompetent salesman' (Berrey).; cf. **could sell . . .** P.B.: since *c.* 1950, the *piss-up in a brewery* version has, I think, been by far the more common of the first two.

couldn't pull a settin' hen off the nest is – or was – applied to 'an old-fashioned locomotive whose pulling power is weak' (Ramon F. Adams, *Language of the Railroader*, 1977): US train crews': late C19 – mid 20. Cf **couldn't drive nails . . .**

couldn't punch his way . . . See **couldn't knock . . .**

couldn't ride nothin' wilder'n a wheelchair is 'a cowboy's phrase for a man with no riding ability' (Adams): US: C20.

couldn't see a joke except by appointment: and he'd probably be late for that has, since *c.* 1955, been applied to a very, very 'dim' or slow-witted person. (Granville, 1968.)

couldn't speak a threepenny bit (–**I**, **he**, etc.). I (etc.) just couldn't speak at all: London streets': *c.* 1890 – 1914. (Ware.) P.B.: the silver threepenny piece was for several decades the smallest coin of the realm.

couldn't teach . . . See **couldn't drive nails . . .**

couldn't throw your hat over the workhouse wall. See **you couldn't throw . . .**

count. See: Mexicans; stand up and; start; who's counting.

counter. See: if you're going.

countersunk. See: doesn't know.

country. See: it's a freak; you could piss.

country cousin is here – **my** (or **her**). A US feminine euph. for 'I am having my monthly period': C20. Cf (the) **curse is upon me**, and note the allusion to *country matters*, that pun on *cunt* which figures in Shakespeare (*Hamlet*, III, ii). Manchon lists the Brit. var. *her country cousins* (or *her relations) have come*: *c.* 1850 – 1940.

country dunny. See: all alone.

county. See: another county.

county jail. See: city morgue.

courage. See: fresh kiss.

course(s). See: horses for; that's about.

court. See: see you in c.; silence.

courting. See: are yer.

cousin. See: country cousin; marry.

cover your ass! 'Make sure *you're* not vulnerable' or 'you are not blamed' – with overtones of *I'm all right, Jack*: US, orig. in Vietnam during the 1960s and then gen. in the 1970s. (R.C., 1978.)

cow(s). See: his calves; I need that; Malley's; more lip; that's the tune; there was; three acres; 'tis not; who's milking; why buy.

cow calves. See: care whether.

coward. See: against my religion.

cowboy. See: ride 'em.

cow's tail. See: all behind.

crabs. See: busy as a one.

crack. See: don't crack; fair go; must have been lying; not what it's; you must have been lying.

'cracked in the right place', as the girl said, often prec. by *yes! but*, is the low c.p. reply to an insinuation or an imputation or an allegation of insanity or extreme eccentricity or foolhardy rashness. 'You really must be *cracked!*' I first heard it in 1922, but it's a good deal older than that: it rather sounds as if it orig. among raffish Edwardians.
    Cf *you must have been sleeping near a crack*, q.v. at **must have been lying**...

crackling is not what it was or **what it used to be.** This sadly wistful, or a wryly nostalgic, male c.p. voices the feeling, states the conviction, of one's later years that, 'whatever the crackling, the savour of the bite is not as it was in one's former years' (L.A., 1974); since c. 1920 or perhaps a decade earlier. Here, *crackling* = girls regarded as sexual pleasure; *crackling* is bar-room slang for the female pudenda. P.B.: cf the radio comedy series 'The Goon Show' (1950s) occ. 'filler', *What happened to the streaky bacon we used to get before the war?*

crap. See: went for.

crape. See: hang crape.

crawl. See: what would shock; what's bit; and:

crawl out of that hat! A US c.p. of c. 1870–80. See quot'n at **pull down your vest!**, and cf **come out of that hat!**

crazy. See: I may be; and:

crazy as a two-bob watch, etc. See **silly as a two-bob watch.**

crazy like a fox (–he's). 'Apparently crazy, but with far more method than madness. Said, e.g., of someone engaged in seemingly hare-brained speculations that turn out very profitably. American, from 1930s and probably earlier' (R.C., 1978). Recorded by Berrey, 1942, and used by the American humorist S. J. Perelman as the title of a book, 1945.

crazy mixed-up kid – a (or **just a**) was orig. and still is a US c.p.; in the late 1940s, it was adopted in UK. It applies to a youth confusingly troubled with psychological problems (aren't most of us?), esp. if he is, or if he pretends to be, unable to distinguish between the good and the bad, an inability that tends to disappear when the failure operates to his disadvantage as opposed to his advantage. P.B.: cf the phrase used in the Forces, 1950s–60s, to describe someone badly warped by life's mishaps, of, e.g., a man psychologically scarred by wartime experiences, (*he's*) *all bitter and twisted.* Sometimes said compassionately, but more often unthinkingly and insensitively.

creation. See: that beats c.

creator. See: worships.

creek. See: up Shit.

creeps out like the shadow – he. As musician, singer, dancer, he performs wonderfully, in a smooth, sophisticated manner: Harlem jive, then US entertainment in general. (Cab Calloway, 1940.) Contrast **gangbusters.**

cricket. See: not cricket.

cried all the way... See **cry all the way to the bank.**

cripples. See: go it, you.

crochet. See: can a moose.

crock. See: that's a real c.

crocodile. See: see you later.

crooked. See: so crooked; straight; Y is.

crooked straight-edge. See: go and fetch.

crops. See: how's crops.

Crosby. See: where there's life.

cross. See: it's not so; keep your fingers; put a cross; wouldn't be seen.

cross, I win; pile, you lose, synon. with **heads, I win; tails, you lose,** was current, so far as I've been able to determine, in C17–18. It occurs in Butler's *Hudibras*, 1678,

thus:
    That you as sure, may Pick and Choose,
    As Cross I win, and Pile you lose. (Apperson.)
The *cross* is the 'face', the *pile* the reverse, of a coin.

cross my heart! is a c.p. of declaration that one is telling the truth: mid C19–20. Orig., a solemn religious guarantee. It is short for (*I*) *cross my heart and may I die,* itself prob. elliptical for *cross my heart and may I die, if I so much as tell a lie.* 'Schoolgirls' c.p. protestation of honesty. "Is this true, Janet?" – "Cross my heart!"' (Granville, 1968).
    Among children in C20, in US as in UK, it is more usual to elab. *Cross my heart and hope to die!* (J.W.C., 1977; P.B.) – The shorter form is recorded by the *OED*, 2nd Supp., 1908; and I have reason to think that it has existed since late C19. P.B.: cf the later C20 appeal for veracious certainty, *can you really say, hand on heart, that...?*

cross my palm with silver (– first,)! A 'joc. request for a "small consideration", a bribe where none is needed, where the transaction is perfectly legal' (P.B., 1976). Since, if I remember correctly, at least as early as the 1930s. From the gypsy fortune-teller's centuried request to a prospective client. L.A., 1976, remarked that it also half-seriously intimates that a tip would not come amiss.

cross the T's. See **go back and cross...**

crow(s). See: don't crow; I wouldn't know him; where the crows.

crowd. See: it'll pass.

crumble. See: that's the way the cookie.

crusher. See: fear.

crutch(es). See: funny as a c.; go it, you; and:

crutches are cheap is a jocularly ironic comment upon very strenuous, esp. if violent, physical effort, notably in athletics: mid C19–20; by 1935, slightly ob., but still far from †. It has the var. *wooden legs are cheap.* Mr S.G. Dixon records, 1978, that his father, earlyish C20, had a saying, '(It) runs in the family–like wooden legs'. Cf **go it, you cripples!**

crutches for meddlers and legs for lame ducks seems to be a var. of **lareovers for meddlers.** (Brought to my notice, 1975, by Mr B. Bass of Marshfield, Avon.) 'Sticking my neck out' I hazard the guess that it arose c. 1870.

cry. See: let her cry; what am I; and:

cry all the way to the bank, either as *I'll cry*... or as *He cried*.... A US c.p. dating from c. 1960 and adopted in UK in the late 1960s is ironically used by someone, or of someone, whose work is adversely criticized on literary or artistic or musical grounds – that is, by such criteria – but who has had the temerity to make a fortune by it. R.C. amplifies, 1978: 'I am informed by a friend that this originated with Liberace, who replied to one of his most outspoken critics (and there were plenty) with the telegram, *I cried all the way to the bank;* it made the front page of, though was not headlined on, *Variety,* the American newspaper of "show-bizz".' The extremely colourful pianist Liberace (pron. *Libberrarchy*), who affected a very sentimental style of performance, flourished in the late 1950s and the 1960s and, though less in the 1970s. Occ., straight-forwardly, *laugh all the way...*

cry mapsticks! I cry you mercy: lower-class c.p. of late C17 – mid C18. It occurs in Swift (*OED*) and appears to be a perversion, joc. not illiterate, of SE *cry mercy* and *mopsticks.*

cry 'uncle'. See **say 'uncle'.**

cucumber sandwiches. See: going home.

cues. See: come to cues.

cully. See: cheer up, c.

Cunnyborough. See: ask cheeks.

cunt. See: big conk; for king; he's a cunt; I will not; large mouth; my name is 'Unt; old soldier; standing; take yer 'at; who called.

cunt like a horse-collar – a, often prec. **she has** or **she's got.** Whereas the shorter form is rural imagery in a slang phrase, the longer is a rural, esp. a farmers', c.p. – and prob. goes back to late C19. Granville, 1974, applied it to 'a much-used "lay".'

cup. See: no cups.

cup of tea. See just my alley-marble.

cuppa tea, a Bex and a good lie-down – a. 'The Australian remedy for most problems' (Camilla Raab): since the 1950s. A Bex is an Aspro.

curate. See: good in parts.

curb your hilarity! See desist! ...

curdles (one's) **milk** (usu. intro. by *it*) is directed at – not necessarily addressed to – one whose behaviour sours 'the milk of human kindness': since *c.* 1925. (One of the many c.pp. I owe to the alertness and kindness of Mr Laurie Atkinson.)

curse. See: work is the curse.

curse is upon me – the. A female's notification, humorously formal and deliberately archaic, that she is having her period: a domestic c.p.: probably ?mid C19 – 20; certainly throughout C20. Often laconically shortened to *the curse; the curse* is itself elliptical for *the curse of Eve.*

It is poss., as R.S. has suggested, 1977, that the c.p. arose among the female readers of Tennyson's poem, *The Lady of Shalott*, pub'd 1852: ' "The curse has come upon me," cried the Lady of Shalott'. Because of Tennyson's popularity – he had been made Poet Laureate in 1850 – this origination can hardly be dismissed as utterly improbable. It evokes from J.W.C., 1977, the pleasant reminiscence: 'Some fifty years ago, when Harvard professors were still repeating their lectures to girls at Barnard [College], the girls always awaited the moment when J.L.L., teaching Victorian poetry, thundered forth this line. He didn't know what it connoted to them.' This was John Livingston Lowes (1867 – 1945), who 'professed' at Harvard from 1918 onwards and who wrote *The Road to Xanadu*, 1927, a luminous interpretation of the sources of Coleridge's famous poem; his book became almost as well known in Britain as in the USA.

curse you, Red Baron! From Charles M. Schulz's world-famous comic strip *Peanuts:* the beagle Snoopy in his persona of WW1 fighter ace always falling victim to the tactics of the unseen (but genuine) German ace Baron Manfred von Richthofen, who fought in a red-painted plane. (P.B.)

curtains. See: more curtains; and:

curtains for you! is explained by Berrey in 1942 as 'the end for you, enough from you' – that's enough argument or talk from you; but orig. this US c.p. implied 'the end of life', whether lit. by death or fig. by imprisonment or a totally disabling accident or disease: since *c.* 1920. In *c.* 1944, it was adopted in UK from US Servicemen on leave (or, indeed, duty). Orig. from the curtain that is dropped upon – and therefore conceals – the stage upon which a play has just ended. Often shortened to *curtains!*

curve. See: you threw.

cussedness of the universe tends to a maximum – the. It was current among Brit. physicists between the Wars, and was employed allusively as 'The Fourth General Law'. A mock-serious use of 'the universe' for 'this earth'. Cf sod's law.

custard. See: happy in the Service; that cuts.

custom. See: it's an old Belgian; your custom.

[**customer is always right – the**, teeters on the tightrope with c.p. at one end and cliché at the other. Commercial: C20. An American correspondent has, 1978, told me that he once saw 'a sign in a brothel – written with humorous intent, but also with some clarity: "The customer always comes first".']

cut. See: call me cut; hard in; I cut; I'll strike; my stomach; that cut; that doesn't; we'll cut; you'll have your; you're so sharp.

cut a long story short. See to cut...

cut bait. See: fish, or.

cut me a little slack! 'Give me a break, a chance': American Negro usage: since (?) *c.* 1955. *The Third Ear*, 1971, adds that it is 'sometimes used as a greeting'. Norris M. Davidson, 1971, however, glosses *he cut me some slack* as 'he did me a favour', and attributes it to US teenagers, with a vogue for a brief period, *c.* 1968–72.

cut off my legs and call me Shorty! A US c.p., dating from before 1945 and bearing no very precise meaning. (Sanders, 1975.) But Harold Shapiro writes, 1975:

A jocular exclamation of surprise, verging on wonderment if not disbelief.... It's the sort of exclamation ordinarily introduced by 'Well'.... There is also a conflation of this c.p. with another exclamation of surprise, *Well, shut my mouth,* producing *Well, shut my mouth and call me Shorty.* This last was popularized, I think, if not invented by Phil Harris in the early 1940s. Harris was a radio personality, bandleader and comedian, who presented himself as a mock whiskey-guzzling Southerner. 'There was a recording of this, made by Louis Armstrong, on May 11, 1940, and the composer is given as Raye' (Eric Townley, 1978: see his *Tell Your Story*, 1976). In the same song, occurs 'Cut off my hair and call me Baldy' (Jack Eva, 1978).

cut the cackle and come to the 'orses! Let's get down to business! late C19–20. (*OED* 2nd Supp.; 1889, Vol I of Barrère & Leland.) Either from horse-dealing or from horse-racing. Occ, *'osses;* and R.C., 1977, notes the US var...*and get to the 'orses* or *'osses.*

cut the (crude) comedy! See can the comedy!

cut to Hecuba (or **come to Hecuba**) is a 'relic from Shakespeare and was an artifice employed by many old producers to shorten matinées by cutting out long speeches' (Michael Warwick, 'Theatrical Jargon of the Old Days' in *Stage*, 3 Oct. 1968): theatrical: *c.* 1880–1940. The ref. is to

What's Hecuba to him or he to Hecuba
That he should weep for her?

in Act II, Scene ii, of *Hamlet.*

cut your kiddin'! was a US students' and teenagers' c.p. of the early 1920s. McKnight, a scholarly, very readable, attractive book.

cut yourself a piece of cake! is recorded, as an English c.p., in Supplement 2 (p. 65, fn. 1), 1948, of HLM, along with *how's your poor feet?, does your mother know you're out?, keep your hair on!.* I myself have never heard it; I hazard the guess that it belonged to the extremely approx period *c.* 1890–1940. Noble, 1978, referring to his journalistic days, wrote, 'I'm reminded that whenever I entered Gracie Fields's dressing-room for an interview in the 1930s, she used to greet me with "Come in, lad, and cut thisen a piece o'cake"; another was.., "Sit thisen down and make thiself look a bit less".'

cutlery. See: hold yer 'ush.

cuts no ice. See that cuts no ice.

Cyril. See: nice one.

D

'dab!' quoth Dawkins when he hit his wife on the arse with a pound of butter was applied, mid C18–mid 19, to any noisy impact; it appears in Grose, 1785; to *dab* is 'to pat, to give with a pat' – and it was presumably a witticism prompted by a *dab*, or pat, of butter. Cf:

dab, says Daniel was a nautical c.p. of *c.* 1790–1860: applied to 'lying bread and butter fashion' in bed or bunk. It occurs in 'A Real Paddy', *Real Life in Ireland*, 1822.

dad. See: be like dad; go to the pub; he never had; here we come; I'll 'ave to ask; real nervous.

daddy. See: don't go down; I'll be a ding-dong; what did you do; what do you think this is; and:

daddy, buy me one of those. See oh, mummy!..., of which this is a var.

daddy wouldn't buy me a bow-wow is mostly 'used in a seemingly petulant manner as a complaint that the speaker's request for something (probably trivial...) has been denied. As you suspected, it was the title of a song and appeared in the refrain. TABRAR, Joseph, "Daddy Wouldn't Buy Me a Bow-Wow" (1892). It has been referred to as "delightful bit of nonsense, whose comedy lay in the infallible trick of having a grown person talk like a child". The "comic success" was one of the major hits of the decade' (Moe, 1975). Sung by Vesta Victoria, it is memorialized in Edward B. Marks, *They All Sang*, 1934, as W.J.B. tells me.

daddy's yacht. See: what do you think this is.

daft. See: don't act; how daft; not so d.; och man.

daft, I call it! A juvenile c.p. of the early 1940s, popularised by the cartoons of Huge McNeill (1910–79) in the children's comic *The Knockout*. *The Times*, H,M.'s obituary, 6 Nov. 1979.

dagger. See: take a d.

dam of that was a whisker – the. This was a coll. and dialectal c.p. of *c.* 1660–1810 and was applied to a great lie. (Ray, 1678 – cited by Apperson.) Could *whisker* have been a pun on whisper? That it wasn't a misprint is virtually proved by the existence of the almost synon. the mother of that was a whisker.

damage. See: what's the d.

dame. See: that dame.

damn a horse if I do! A strong – almost a violent – refusal or rejection: *c.* 1810–60. 'Jon Bee', in his dictionary of slang and cant, 1823, shrewdly postulates an origin in *damn me for a horse if I do* (any such thing).

damn the torpedoes: full stream ahead! See AMERICAN HISTORICAL BORDERLINERS – and cf the Irvin S. Cobb quot'n at where do we go from here?

damn' white of you – that's. Lit., 'That's decent of you' – that's very kind or obliging of you – it was a cliché, but since early C20 it has usu. been heavily ironic: by *c.* 1970, at latest, ob. (R.C., 1978.) A var. of mighty white..., q.v.

damned. See: you're damned.

dance. See: aw, shucks, Ma; may he d.; nothing to make; Punch has done; save the last; shall we; stop that; Tenth; when you d.; and:

dance at your funeral – I'll (but occ. he'll or she'll). 'An old slanging-match catch phrase' (Albert B. Petch, who has helped me for well over thirty years): since *c.* 1880 – pure guesswork, this; almost certainly current at least as early as 1900. In essence, this is a taunt and, by the speaker, regarded as a 'finalizer'.

dancer. See: you must be a good.

dancing girls. See: bring on the d.

dandruff. See: how's your d.

dandy. See: isn't that just d.

danger. See: if in d.; when in d.

dangerous. See: I'm a ball.

dangle. See: angle; I shall see; let your braces.

Daniel. See: dab, says.

dark. See: hush; I feel like; I wouldn't like; it is as good; keep it d.; only way; result; tall, dark; when it gets.

darken. See: never darken.

darlings. See: hello, my darlings.

darn' clever these Armenians! (or Chinese!) is the US version of damned clever these Chinese, q.v. at clever chaps these Chinese! Berrey, 1942, has it – and notes what was presumably the earlier form, darn' clever these Chinese!

dashboard. See: keep your head.

date. See: you date.

daughter. See: don't laugh; have you heard the news; like the butcher's; would you like your.

David. See: send it down.

Davy putting on the coppers for the parson (or parsons) is a nautical c.p. comment on an approaching storm at sea: since *c.* 1830; by 1945, virtually extinct. The sailors' belief that there is an arch-devil of the sea is clearly implied.

dawn. See: came the dawn; oh, to be; you'll be shot.

Dawkins. See: 'dab!'.

day. See: all day; another day; any day; been a long; every day; fine day; full rich day; golden eagle; happy days; have a good; he never had; hurry no; I like work; I wish my; it will last; it's just one of those d.; lie of the d.; like a winter's; little man; made my; may you live; my mother told; one of these fine; one of these wet; one of those; punch a Pom; rooster; shit a day; some day; ten days; that will be; this is my; this is not my; 'tis not; 'twill; what a gay.

day the omelette hit the fan – the. 'The day when everything went wrong', is a not very common var. of when shit hits the fan and was adopted, *c.* 1966, from the US.

day war broke out – the. (Usu. in a rather ponderous Northern accent.) A catchphrase created for radio by [the comedian] Robb Wilton (1881–1957). "The day war broke out, my missus looked at me and said, 'Eh! What good are you?'"

When circumstances changed, amended to "the day *peace* broke out"' (*VIBS*). WW2, of course.

days to do're getting fewer is a jingle (*do're – fewer*) c.p. 'I was in Cyprus at the end of the 1950s and of national servicemen – who were, naturally, greatly preoccupied with questions of time: done and time to do. Catch Phrases like "Days to do're getting fewer" and question and answer rituals like "Days to do?" "Very few" were common' (P.B., 1974).

Deacon. See: let her go.

dead. See: ain't it grand; bang, bang; better red; born dead; Charley's dead; cheer up, cully; drop dead; Givum's; go stick your nose; hang crape; I wish I may; I wouldn't be caught *or* found; it's dead; it's staring; Nelson's; not yet; once a knight; one of these fine mornings; say nothing; trumpeter; who's dead; whose dog; would you rather be; wouldn't be seen; you'll be a; you'll be in; you'll wake; and:

dead! and she never called me 'mother', with *she* often omitted; also with the fairly frequent var., **dead, dead, and she...** This c.p., dating from the 1880s to 1890s, is used satirically to melodrama, esp. of the Surreyside, or 'Transpontine', Drama, which flourished at that period, although it survived, heartily enough, until WW1, and from which, of course, it came; thence it was transferred to similar or reminiscent situations. It occurs in, e.g., Christopher Bush, *The Case of the April Fool*, 1933.

The wording is based upon – for the words of the c.p. do not occur in – T.A. Palmer's dramatized version, 1874, of Mrs Henry Wood's *East Lynne*. (See *ODQ*; and cf the entry in Granville.)

I heard it often, as a soldiers' derisive chant, during WW1; much less often during WW2.

My good friend, Mr Albert B. Petch, writing in 1974, recalls 'an old morality picture that my mother had in her parlour: it showed a poor ragged woman peering through the window of a mansion at a little coffin, and the caption read, "Dead – and never called me Mother!"'

dead but he won't lie down (– he's), current since *c.* 1910, does not, as one might suppose, imply great courage: what it implies is great stupidity – a complete lack of common sense. It was, on ITV, used in a series called 'Sam', showing mining life in Yorkshire about WW1 period (Petch, 1974).

dead clever these Chinese! See **clever chaps these Chinese.**

deaf. See: speak a little.

deal. See: big deal; he who; it's a d.; you play the cards.

deal of glass about – (there's) a. Mostly it was applied to a flashy person or a showy thing, but it did almost mean 'first-class' or 'the thing, the ticket': *c.* 1880–1940, for the secondary meaning; the first is extant, although slightly ob. Prob. from large show-windows or show-cases. P.B.: or does the phrase refer rather to paste, or stage, jewellery?

deal of weather about – a, mostly prefaced by there's. There's a storm approaching – we're in for bad weather: nautical: mid C19–20. Ware.

dear Mother (or Mum), I am sending you ten shillings: but not this week is a lower- and lower-middle-class – hence a WW1 army (Other Ranks')–c.p. of C20; less common among soldiers in WW2 than it had been in 1914–18, when it served as a kind of self-mockingly humorous, jocularly cynical, chant. (B & P.) Cf:

dear Mother, it's a bastard!, with the 'dovetail' – **dear Son, so are you** – is later than, and was perhaps generated by, the next. Not, I think, before *c.* 1920. (P.B., 1975).

dear Mother, it's a bugger! Sell the pig and buy me out. This is another army (Other Ranks') c.p., dating since *c.* 1910 and expressing disgust with Service life and at the loss of home comforts. P.B.: this lingered until c. 1970 at least, with the dovetail *dear Son, pig dead. Soldier on!* B & P, 1931, has the more euphonious *dear Son, pig's gone...* In a duplicate entry in the first ed., E.P. wrote that the orig. phrase was an RN Lowerdeck c.p. dating back poss. to late C19. Cf **who wouldn't sell a farm...**

dear Mother, respectful – or **dear Mum,** affectionate, **Please send me one pound and 'The Christian Herald'. P.S. Don't bother with 'The Christian Herald'. Your loving son,—** This c.p. belongs to WW2 and was common among Servicemen – other ranks, naturally; not among officers.

dear Mother, sell the pig and buy me out! Cf **dear Mother, it's a bugger...**

dear old pals! 'A derisive chanted cat-call or song when boxers funk action or are in a clinch' (Petch): boxing spectators': C20. It no less neatly than humorously derives from the song 'Dear Old Pals, Jolly Old Pals' – very popular on festive occasions.

dear sir (spelt 'C-U-R') and **dear sir or madman.** Facetious c.pp. occasioned by someone's proposing to write a formal letter, said either by the writer or by one standing by: since mid-C20 at latest. Cf **'sir' to you.** (P.B.)

dear son, so are you! See **dear Mother, it's a bastard!**

death. See: don't open; fate; it's the change; kiss of d.; may he dance; roll on, d.; 'til death; you will die; you'll be the d.

death adders in your pocket? – (have you) got. 'Don't be so bloody mean!' This Aus. c.p., dating from *c.* 1935, implies that one is afraid to put hand in pocket to pay for, e.g., a drink. (Jim Ramsay, *Cop It Sweet*, 1977.) Cf **snake in your pocket?**

death-warrant is out – his (or, occ., **my** or **your**). This police c.p. dates from late C19. In his *London Side-Lights*, 1908, Clarence Rook informs us that 'when a constable is transferred against his will from one division to another, the process is alluded to in the phrase, "His death-warrant is out". For this is a form of punishment for offences which do not demand dismissal.' W.J.B., 1977, notes that, in US this takes the form *he is signing his death-warrant.*

debts. See: first turn.

decent. See: that's decent.

deception. See: where the d.

decisions, decisions (often prec. by an anguished *oh,*)! 'Used in the most trivial of circumstances, e.g. "What shall we have for supper?" – "shall we phone now or leave it?" – "which of these sweets do you want?" All may call forth this response from the one being questioned' (P.B., 1976): since *c.* 1955, and still going strong, early 1980s.

deck. See: keep it on; leave the d.; man the; playing with; some deck; spit on.

declare. See: well, I d.

deep. See: it's getting.

defiance. See: flag.

definitely. See: oh, definitely.

deft and dumb is a c.p. that, obviously parodying *deaf and dumb*, arose *c.* 1940; it indicates the speaker's idea of an ideal wife or mistress. Cf **anything for a quiet wife.**

deliver de letter, de sooner de better is an Aus. 'message to the postman that is put on the back of envelopes, in the same way as SWALK [sealed with a loving kiss], etc.' (B.P.): since *c.* 1950, if not a little earlier. But whereas SWALK and its variants are non-cultured conventionalisms, *deliver de letter...* is a deliberate travesty or 'guying' or 'send-up' of 'New Australians'' illiteracies.

Not unknown [P.B.:? orig.] in US, then in UK. 'At the end of the song *Please, Mister Postman*, issued on the Beatles' 2nd LP (Nov. 1963), John Lennon sings this phrase. In the US, initially recorded very early in the 1960s by a group called "The Marvilettes" and described as "once an American chart-stopper"' (Paul Janssen, 1977). P.B.: the phrase feels older than E.P. allow: I'm pretty sure it was around in my 1940s childhood.

Dempsey. See: if I was as big.

demure as a whore (notably **an old whore) at a christening** (– as) is picturesquely and earthily synon. with 'extremely demure': C18–20. Grose records it in 1788, but it appears, in the shorter form, in Captain Alexander Smith's *The Life of Jonathan Wild*, 1726; and I've seen it in one or two C18 comedies. Cf **you shape...**

Denmark. See: something is.
department. See: that's not my d.
depend. See: it all depends.
depending on what school you went to. 'A c.p. used by cowards who give two pronunciations of a rare, or a foreign, word' (B.P.): Aus.: since *c.* 1950. Not unheard – although not yet, I believe, a c.p. – elsewhere; I've encountered it in England – in the grammatical var. *depending on which school you went to.*
depends on what you mean by... See **it all depends...**
derision. See: shit and corruption.
desist! curb your hilarity! 'And there were the George Robey quips which became, for a period, catch phrases – "Desist! Curb your hilarity" was one, I think: there were several, all ephemeral, but common talk in their time' (Noble, 1973). Nigel Rees, in *VIBS*, adds the quotations, '"Desist! I am surprised at you, Agnes!" (pronounced "Ag-er-ness"). Also... "Go *out!*", "Get *out!*" or simply "*Out!*"' Cf:
desist, refrain, and cease – cf the prec. – was a Robey 'gag' that, current in June 1911–14 and then heard decreasingly did not die until *c.* 1960; and even then it lingered in the memory of many. The Coronation (of George V) number of *Punch*, 7 June 1911, 'paraded caricatures of eminent men named George. These included George Robey, with the couplet
   To all who would invade your Royal peace
   Three words have I – "Desist", "Refrain", and "Cease".'
(Thus Vernon Noble, 1975.)
destiny. See: fucked by.
Destry rides again! See **rides again.**
detail! – but that's a mere; *but* is occ. omitted, and the shortened form, *a mere detail!*, has always, in C20 been fairly frequent. It dates from the 1890s, when the complete phrase was used humorously to make light of something either very difficult or rather important – in short, a meiosis entirely characteristic of British, perhaps most notably of English, *mores.*
   It need not, I hope, be added that, used lit., the phrase does not qualify as a c.p.; for some, unfortunately, it does so need.
details. See: spare me.
detective. See: I'm Hawkshaw.
devil. See: be a devil; beats Akeybo; dimple in chin; God's good; house devil; if the d.; ruffin; shore; Sunday saints; that devil; there's a pair; where it was; and:
devil a bit, says Punch – the. This joc. yet decidedly firm negative belongs to the very approx. period 1850–1910. It elaborates a merely coll., gen., non-c.p., *the devil a bit*, current since *c.* 1700 – if not a decade or so earlier.
[**Devil is alive and well and living at** — (locality variable) – **the.** Prob. the orig. of **God is alive and well** ..., q.v.]
Devil is beating his wife – the. See **it's a monkey's wedding.**
devil's own luck and my own (too) – the, provides a c.p. var. of the *the devil's own luck,* very bad luck: late C19–20.
devout. See: against my religion.
diamonds. See: do it again.
dice. See: no dice; and:
dice or cold – the, and **the dice are hot.** Few gamblers are winning – or, many are winning: dicing gamblers': C20.
dick. See: had the Richard; too short.
Dick's hatband. See: queer as D.
did. See: can't be did; and:
did it drop (occ. *fall*) **off a lorry?** In the shady fringes of crime – e.g., in shady public-houses – and esp. among transport men, this is a graceful, delicate way of asking 'Was it stolen?' or even 'And you stole it, I suppose': since *c.* 1950 (Petch, 1974). Used as a synon. of the once very much more gen. euph., 'found before it was lost'.
   P.B.: in the 1970s and early 80s, *fall* is much the more common, and in other tenses, e.g. 'It fell off the back of a lorry, I suppose?' 'The back of' seems now to be an integral part of the phrase, and *dropped off* (*the back of*) *a lorry* arose very soon after – or did it precede? – the question. In *Graffiti*

4, 1982, Nigel Rees lists *This is the lorry it fell off* as seen written in the dust on (of course) the back of a lorry. David Powis, in *The Signs of Crime*, 1977, glosses *fell off a lorry* thus: 'Ironic explanation, given more humorously than seriously, when asked to account for the possession of valuable property, obviously stolen'. And a useful example occurs in John Wainwright, *Cause for a Killing*, 1974, where a shady character, standing at a window and looking down at a busy London street, says:
   They are not thieves. [*This is bitterly ironical.*] They use a phrase. 'It fell off the back of a lorry.' That's the expression, friend. It covers everything from transistors to three-piece suites. From fountain pens to fur coats. They all 'fall off the back of a lorry'. And those mugs down there buy them at give-away prices. And don't ask awkward questions.
B.P., 1975, notes that in Aus. it's a *truck*, and the same is true for the US.
did it hurt? This C20 c.p. 'is heard in joc. use in several ways, as "Did it hurt?" when a chap has said that he had been thinking' (Petch, 1966). Ironic? Often. Unkindly? Rarely. A.B. notes, 1978, that in the US it is sometimes intensified by adding *real good.*
did she fall or was she pushed? was orig. – that is, in the raffish 1890s – as still, applied to a girl deprived of her virginity; then to a person stumbling; in C20, occ. shouted (not, of course in the most respectable theatres) at an old style actress. In 1936 it appeared in the much-lamented witty and wildly humorous Thorne Smith's novel of the punning title, *Did She Fall?*, which reinforced the phrase's applicability to murder cases. But the phrase is of English origin, perhaps as early as 1908, in a (true) murder case – that of Violet Charlesworth, found dead at the foot of a cliff near Beachy Head.
did they forget to feed the dingoes? is a 'jocular greeting to an unexpected arrival' (Wilkes, *Dict.*, 1977): Aus. Wilkes's sole quot'n is for 1968; I suspect a rural origin going further back by at least 20 years.
did you bring anything with you? See **bring anything...**
did you enjoy your trip? often shortened to **enjoy your trip?** 'I'll tell you a catch-phrase which used to delight me when I was very small. It used to be said by my grandmother's maid when I was playing about in the kitchen. If I got too obstreperous and shuffled up one of the mats on the floor, she always said "Mind my Brussels!" [i.e., Brussels carpet]. I found it marvellously witty at the time. A later version, often heard in the 1930s, was "Did you enjoy your trip?" or simply "Enjoy your trip?" when anyone caught a toe on anything' (Christopher Fry, 1974).
   I don't think *mind my Brussels!* did truly become a c.p. The other certainly did and has, I believe, been current from *c.* 1920; also it contained a neat pun on *trip*, a short voyage or journey, and *trip*, a near-fall.
   And then, a little later, CF wrote to inform me that Mrs Robert Gittings (the biographer Jo Manton) had, a day or so before, heard one workman say to another on a scaffolding, apropos a luckily non-fatal stumble, 'Enjoy your trip?' So the phrase has lingered on: and it deserves its longevity.
   'About 1950, the following story was going the rounds. A technician fell over a cable while a BBC team was photographing the Royal Family in Buckingham Palace. The King [George VI, who reigned 1937–52], helping him up, asked "Have a good trip?" It has the ring of truth, from that most human of kings' (Sanders, 1978). P.B.: and, in fact, *have a good trip?* or! is the usual form of this c.p. in later C20. The Aus. version is *have a nice trip?* (B.P.).
did you ever?, indicating surprise or astonishment or admiration, is elliptical for 'Did you ever see or hear (or hear of) the like?'; arose *c.* 1875 and was orig. US. In *Doc Horne*, 1899, George Ade wrote:
   'I could see the train coming along through the woods, and I made a final spurt.'

'Did you ever!' observed Mrs Milbury, with an upward roll of the eyes.

By 1900 at latest, it was also Brit. P.B.: cf the earlier C20 children's chant, 'Well, I never! Did you ever/See a monkey dressed in leather?'

did you ever see a dream walking? 'In a Kipling story you may read that "the houses" – the audiences of the music-halls – "used to coo" over Nellie Farren. Only for Vesta Tilley have I heard houses coo. A later [than 1900] song asked, "Did you ever see a dream walking?" I saw Vesta Tilley walk' (Harold Brighouse in *What I Have Had: Chapters in Autobiography*, 1953). Enlarging upon this, Eric Townley writes, 1978, 'The song was composed by Harrey Revel and Mack Gordon and featured in the 1934 musical film *Sitting Pretty*, starring Jack Oakie and Ginger Rogers. The song became quite popular and was played by British dance bands in 1934 – 5. I remember that the phrase was used quite a lot whenever a pretty girl was cited, at least up to WW2. This [song] must have popularised [the c.p.], even if the song was taken from an earlier c.p.' – which it was! P.B.: the phrase is still remembered, early 1980s, but may now be ironically applied rather to any abstracted, head-in-the-air, not-with-this-world youth of either sex.

did you get the rent? Did you find a customer? This – or had you guessed? – is a prostitutes' c.p., dating, apparently, from late C19. (*U.*)

did you hear anything knock? See do you hear . . . ?

did you now! and **do you now!** Of the former, Granville said that it is a 'sarcastic c.p. addressed to one who boasts of bringing off a coup or achieving something of which he was not thought capable'; of the latter, 'Much the same as [did you now!]; 1960's; via TV' (letter, 1969). The former is the commoner and the earlier – it goes back at least as far as 1930 and has (I think) been used throughout the century; nor would it surprise me if I were to discover it in a publication issued in the 1890s or even the 1880s.

did you say something? and **did you speak?** are addressed to someone who has just broken wind: late C19 – 20. They belong to the raffishly polite conversation of the public bar.

did you shoot it yourself? 'Commonly said in my experience to a lady wearing an expensive (-looking) coat made of animal skins' (John B. Smith, Bath, 1979). Besides being an oblique plea for the cause of conservation, perhaps also a sly dig at the feminine boast, 'and I knitted it myself'. (P.B.)

diddled by the dangling dong . . . See fucked by the fickle finger . . .

didn't come down in the last shower – I, he, etc. 'I'm more experienced and shrewd than you think': Aus.: late C19 – 20. With occ. *rain* for *shower*. (Wilkes, 1977.) Cf **I didn't come . . .**

didn't even get to first base. See first base . . .

didn't have a pot to pee (or **piss**) **in. See pot to pee . . .**

didn't have a tail feather left. 'Said of a cowboy cleaned out at the gambling table or otherwise completely broke' (Adams): Western US: very approx. 1870 – 1930.

didn't he (or **she, we, they,** etc.) **do well!** 'During 1973 Bruce Forsyth in "The Generation Game" on BBC 1 on Saturday evenings had the catch phrase "Didn't they do well!" after competitive games in the studio for which prizes were given. You now hear it in pub conversation, with attempts to imitate his chuckling voice' (Noble, 1974). 'It is said to have arisen . . . with what a studio attendant used to shout from the lighting grid during rehearsals' (*VIBS*). Forsyth's 'they' applied, as Wedgwood explains, 1977, to 'ordinary family pairs (father-daughter, mother-son, or whatever) in the contests', and was soon adapted. In the *Evening News*, 24 Jan. 1975, a full-page advertisement issued by Messrs Tate and Lyle was headed 'Didn't he do well!'; the 'he' refers to their advertisement 'little man', Mr Cube. And in March 1975 I noticed that the London Co-operative Society's milk bottles bore, printed on them, 'Didn't we do well!' – where 'we' referred to careful housewives.

didn't know . . . See doesn't know . . .

didn't win any (illiterately *no*) **medals**, mostly thus tersely; sometimes prec. by *he*, rarely by *she* or *you*. He made no profit or gained no advantage: a Cockney c.p., dating from late 1918.

A.B., 1978: 'In the US, *cigars* for medals'. Cf **close, but no cigar.**

didn't you sink the *Emden*? – expressing a profound contempt either of arrogance or of a colossal conceit induced by an excessively laudatory 'Press' – was frequently heard in the Australian army, 1915 – 18. The Australian cruiser *Sydney* had, at the Cocos Islands in 1914, destroyed the roving Ger. cruiser *Emden*. Recorded both by F & G and by B & P.

die. See: I wish I may; I'm going to; if I die; if the camels; laugh?; let me be hanged; let me die; may I die; never say; no, no; old soldiers; root; she will die; there'll be pie; what a wonderful; what did your; you are a mouth; you will die; you'll die; and:

die, you bastard! A callous c.p., addressed to anyone, including oneself, who is coughing violently or painfully: army: later C20. (P.B., 1976.)

died. See: has the cat d.; I haven't laughed; ole man; someone must have; that's the true; who died; you'd have d.; and:

died of wounds, recorded by F & G and B & P as current in the British Army throughout WW1, is synon. with other such expressions as *hanging on the* (*old*) *barbed wire* and *up in Annie's room*; they were the standardized replies to queries about an absent man's whereabouts. P.B.: the phrase lingered into WW2.

diesel. See: tiger.

Dieu et mon droit (pron. *dright*): **fuck you, Jack, I'm all right** was, notably in 1914 – 15, a var. of **fuck you, Jack, I'm all right**, the Fr. phrase being dragged in to form a jingle but itself acquiring independent status and surviving until 1970 at least, although not much heard after *c.* 1960. Julian Franklyn.

difference. See: it's the same d.; no difference; vive la d.; what's the d.

different. See: and now for; how different; that's a d.

different ball game – it's or **that's a.** ' "Different rules apply." An American c.p. which is common in Australia' (B.P., 1975) and in NZ (Mrs Margaret Davies, for earlier 1970s): as US, since the 1930s (? earlier); as Aus., since the mid-1940s and prob. occasioned by US servicemen. Lit., 'not *base* ball, but, e.g. basketball or handball', i.e. another subject, an entirely different matter.

But in 1977 E.P. noted, of *it's a different*, or *a whole new*, *ball game*: the situation has entirely changed: US, whence also Brit.: the *whole new* form since *c.* 1970. It was 'used by the Secretary of the Environment when addressing Local Government officials, [some time in] June 1975' (R.S., 1977). But the *ball game* itself, in senses 'condition; situation; centre of activity or interest or concern; a competition', had not, by March 1977, migrated from the US to the UK. However, Playfair wrote, only 6 months later, 'Now, with many variants, common in the UK, particularly, I think, among business people'.

different drummer. See it's a different . . .

different ships, different cap-tallies (RN) or **long-splices** (MN). Different countries, different customs: nautical: the latter, C19 – 20, is recorded by Bowen; the former belongs to C20 only. A cap tally is a cap ribbon bearing the name of a man's ship.

It is alleged to have been an adage of the notorious crimp, Paddy West, who operated in Liverpool *c.* 1870. See esp. Stan Hugill, *Sailortown*, 1967.

different strokes for different folks. Each to his own taste: orig., US Negro; but by *c.* 1970, in gen. use. At first, the 'strokes were perhaps sexual' (R.C., 1977). The Brit. version has *blokes* for folks: witness George Sims, *Rex Mundi*, 1978.

difficult. See: why be.

difficult we do at once; the impossible will take a little longer – the. 'He quoted [this] from a saying in frequent use in Fourteenth Army, and added with a grin, "For miracles we like a month's notice!" "You're lucky," I answered, "you've got two!"' (FM The Viscount Slim, *Defeat into Victory*, 1956, on the difficulties of crossing the Chindwin River, Burma, 1944). The *COD of Proverbs* quotes an adumbration found in Trollope, *Phineas Redux* II, 1873. Since WW2 this saying has been taken one stage further, to *the impossible we do at once; miracles take a little longer.* (P.B.)

difficulty. See: with difficulty.

dig. See: I really dig; steal; where did they; and:

dig in and fill your boots; often *and* is omitted. Eat hearty!: fill not only your belly but, if you wish, your boots as well: RN: C20. (PGR, 1948.) Cf **eat up...** and **muck in...**

dig in the eye. See **better than a dig...**

dig you later! was a negro 'expression of farewell' current during the 1930s and decreasingly so in the 1940s. Cf **see you later!**

digging a grave (or **digging for worms**) (in full, **he is** or **they are...**) is a C20 cricketers' c.p. applied to a batsman, or batsmen, doing a bit of 'gardening', i.e. patting the pitch and picking up loose pieces of turf, often a deliberate ploy in the art of gamesmanship.

digit. See: extract.

dim as a Toc-H lamp (, as). Imputes dim- or dull-wittedness: dates from WW1. A couple of reviewers [of the 1st ed. of this Dictionary] reminded me of this in Sep. 1977 and mentioned that, although ob., it lingered on, nostalgically. The c.p. refers to Talbot House, Poperinghe, set up by the Rev. 'Tubby' Clayton as a social centre for British Army Other Ranks on the Western Front, WW1. There still exists a Toc–H organisation. The phrase passed to the RAF of WW2 and survived until past 1960. On 17 Oct. 1977, someone on a radio programme declared that he 'used it all the time'. P.B.: but it's obsolescence was emphasised by the fact that the BBC's (presumably young) typist transcribing the programme (actually 'Stop the Week' conducted by Robert Robinson) spelt the phrase 'dim as a tockage lamp'. An anon. correspondent adds, 1978, that it was occ. varied in WW2 by (*as*) *dim as a NAAFI* (or *Naffy*) *candle.*

dimple in chin, devil within was partly a potential proverb, but predominantly a c.p., 'jingle used as a challenge to a girl, in the hope of learning more of the devil within:? C19–1930, at least' (L.A., 1970). It's one of those sayings that, like **I'll have your guts for garters**, turn out to be a century or two earlier than even a wild surmise. Cf the proverbial *cold hands, warm heart.*

din-din. See: eat your d.

dine. See; get off that; some days.

dined. See: dogs have.

ding-dong. See I'll be a d.

dingoes. See: did they forget.

dinner. See: all duck; done like; done up like a dog's; half an hour; I've had more; there were four; they don't pipe.

dipped into my pockets – it (or that) has. That has occasioned me a great deal of expense: c. 1875–1914. Recorded in that rare book, Baumann.

dipper. See in your d.

dirt. See: get some d.; it's good clean; more dirt; only a little clean; what's the d.

dirt before the broom. See **age before beauty.**

dirty. See: he washes; how's your d.; hungry; like a winter's; marry; quick and d.; rough as; where the d.; you dirty; you don't have; you're a d.

dirty face. See: who're you calling.

dirty mind is a constant joy, or **a joy for ever** – a. Punning 'a thing of beauty is a joy for ever' (Keats, *Endymion*, 1818), this c.p. has been current since Edwardian days, What gay dogs they were! Or was it simply *l'homme moyen sensuel?*

dirty work at the crossroads! Sexual intercourse, but also minor amorous intimacies; in joc. innuendo: C20. Hence also applied to anything 'fishy'. From the lit. sense, 'foul play', which so often takes – or used to take – place at cross-roads.

A ref. to, a comment upon, a love affair or a piece of love-making occurs in the play, *The Law Divine,* performed on 29 Aug. 1918, pub. in 1922, and written by H.V. Esmond: 'TED (*slowly*): I believe Pop's a bit of knut.' Then, a few lines later, 'Hot work at the cross-roads – eh, my lad?'

Throughout WW1, the phrase was continually being used as a jocularity, rendered the more trenchant because cross-roads were invariably a target for the Ger. guns. Cf **one of these dark nights.**

disco. See: come on, it's.

disorder. See: order.

disremember. See: if I d.

ditch. See: let me be hanged.

ditto here was a US c.p. – attested by Berrey – of c. 1925–50. Gen meaning is 'The same goes for me' – 'I think so too' – 'So do I.' Cf **that makes two of us.**

ditty box. See: there I was.

diver. See: don't forget.

diving. See: ticker.

Dixie. See: you ain't just.

do. See: can do; can I do; everybody's doing; fair do's; how am I; how to do; I don't care; I'll do; it won't do; it's not done; man's gotta; monkey see; no can do; nothing doing; well, yer do; what can I; what does it matter; what shall; what would you; what's that got; you can't do; you know what.

do as Garrick did. The ref. being to the famous David Garrick (1717–79), greatest English actor of C18, the c.p. is naturally theatrical – current among actors (and actresses) – and this, Granville tells us, is 'the advice given to a disgruntled star who is upset by an adverse press notice. The great David Garrick is said' – erroneously – 'to have written his own notices'.

do as I do was, c. 1860–1914, a c.p. used – not only in public-houses – as an invitation to someone to have a drink; current on both sides of the Atlantic. Farmer.

do as my shirt does! is, so far as the nature of the invitation allows, a polite var. of **'Kiss my arse!'**: C18–20, but, except among the literary, † by 1940. Whether Tom Durfey (1653–1723), using it towards the end of his life, coined it or was, as I suspect, popularizing it, I don't know.

do chickens have lips? and **do frogs have watertight assholes?** See AMERICAN RESPONSES.

do I ducks! is a Cockney c.p. of C20 and less a euph. than a humorously polite var. (an exercise of wit) of the somewhat abrupt 'I do not!' Perhaps via 'Do I hell!' – itself standing for the robust, vigorous, earthy 'Do I *fuck!*' The *s* of *ducks* is a 'confuser' of *duck,* itself a rhyme.

do I have to (or **must I) draw a diagram** or **spell it out?** See **spell it out.**

do I have to stand on my head? See **what do you expect...**

do I not! is a c.p. asseverative of 'I certainly do': Heard on and off' (Petch, 1974); it has, I'd say, existed throughout C20.

do I owe you anything? or **what do I owe you?** is. late C19–20, an indirect, yet remarkably effectual, remark addressed to someone who has been staring either persistently or without reason at oneself.

Cf **do you think you'll know me...**

do it! was a US negro c.p. of the 1920s and 1930s. In effect, it unnecessarily encouraged 'one who was already demonstrating any sort of cultural refinement or artistic skill' (CM).

...do it... Not so much a c.p. as a 'catch formula' (very popular late 1970s – early '80s) in which the notoriously ambiguous verb *do* is coupled with some aspect of a profession or occupation to produce a *double entendre,* and the resulting slogan is used as an office-wall motto, car-sticker, etc. I was reminded of it by seeing a muddy Landrover carrying on its windscreen the legend 'Young Farmers do it in their wellies' [i.e. wellington boots]; I can add that librarians do it by the book – and lexicographers do it by harmless drudgery. (P.B.)

do it again, Ikey: I saw diamonds! Please say it again, because it sounds a bit too good to be true: a proletarian c.p. of *c.* 1890–1914. It occurs in W. L. George's novel, *The Making of an Englishman*, which, historically, is all the more important because of its year of publication: 1914.

do it now! orig. as a business slogan, but clearly, by lending itself to joc., even to semi-irrelevant, misuse, it became a c.p., at first in the world of business, yet very soon also socially: it prec. 1910 but, as a c.p., it fell, in UK, into disuse slightly before, rather than because of, WW2; but in Aus. was still common in 1965 – and presumably later. (Recorded in 1927 in the late Prof. W.E. Collinson's invaluable book; at a time, that is, before the study of spoken or other familiar English became almost *dē rigueur.)*

do it, or else! If you don't do it, you can expect trouble: a reasonably polite and almost reasonable threat: US: since *c.* 1925. Berrey.

do it the hard way! is a Can. c.p., dating from *c.* 1910 and often prec. by *that's right!* and often either elab. or rounded off with *standing up in a hammock* (copulation insinuated): derisively shouted at a (very) awkward workman struggling, somewhat unsuccessfully, to do his job. (Leechman.)

do it up, Brown! Do your job well! US: since *c*, 1930. 'It must refer to John Brown's raid on Harper's Ferry, Virginia, 1859, which instigated our Civil War' (A.B., 1978).

do me a favour! Sometimes with **look!** prec., and with **will you?** as an emphatic suffix; also, occ., illiterate, or mock-illiterate, **do us a favour!** Run away!; Stop talking!; what an absurd suggestion!: since the late 1940s. Basically equivalent to 'Please!', but it has several nuances – esp. minatory or expostulatory or derisive, as in Arnold Wesker's play *Chicken Soup with Barley*, 1958:

MONTY: Ten thousand bloody sightseers! Do me a favour, it wasn't a bank holiday [but a 'demo' and a clash with the police].

or in Ngaio Marsh, *Clutch of Constables*, 1968:

'But your wife– –'

'Wife? Do me a favour! She's my mum!'

Cf Jack Ripley. *Davis Doesn't Live Here Any More*. 1971. '"Do me a favour." I snap. "Keep your nose out of my affairs."' And there are many examples in later novels.

It derives from and modifies and extends the sense and application of an underworld c.p. that, dating from the early 1940s. conveys a warning: *do yourself a favour.*

Cf **do you mind?**

do not, or **don't, catch a cold!** 'Primarily a business c.p., meaning "Don't suffer a loss", it occurred in the *Observer*, 4 Sep. 1977 (p. 14), as a headline, "Do Not Catch a Cold with Gold": since *c.* 1955' (Playfair, 1977). Note that US has a var. *you can,* or *might, catch a cold doing that,* i.e. get into trouble, of which A.B. remarks, 1979: 'I recall this from films of the 1940s–50s'.

do one for me! is a predominantly male joc. addressed to someone going into a public convenience, esp. in bitterly cold weather: C20. (Granville, 1969.) P.B.: I have occ. heard the helpful response: *All right! Which side do you shake it?* Cf **have one for me.**

do others before they do you! is a post-1918 c.p., a joc. cynical adaptaton of *do unto others as you would be done by.* Often it implies 'Get them before they get *you!*'

do tell! You don't say so! Used lit., it obviously isn't a c.p.; used either ironically or sarcastically or with a deceptive incredulity, it *is* one. As a Can. c.p., it dates from *c.* 1945. But the Can. c.p. is simply an adoption of the US, mostly New England. M recorded it in 1891; and in 1889 Farmer called it: a senseless catch-phrase, lugged in everywhere, in season and out of season. . . . It forms a very useful non-committal interjection for listeners who feel that some remark is expected of them; it is thus equivalent to the 'really?' 'indeed?' of English people. A similar phrase in the South is . . . 'You don't say so?' which a Yankee will vary by 'I want to know!' 'Do tell' is also used as a decoy.

V confirmed it as having orig. among, and been confined to, New Englanders.

But the phrase long antedates 1889. In 1848 *D.Am.* described it as 'a vulgar exclamation common in New England, and synonymous with really! indeed! is it possible!'

A year later, the famour British geologist Sir Charles Lyell, in *A Second Visit to the United States in the Years 1845–6*, 2 vols, revealingly says:

Among the most common singularities of expression are the following: 'I should admire to see him' for 'I should like to see him', 'I want to know' and 'Do tell', both exclamations of surprise, answering to our 'Dear me' These last, however, are rarely heard in society above the middling class [vol. I. p. 163, Oct. 1845].

To date it as at least as early as 1820 seems reasonable, for it occurs in John Neal's *The Down-Easters*, 2 vols, 1833, at chapter 1, p. 61, thus:

Why that are [= that there] chap you was with below, said the Down Easter.

George Middleton, hey? – do tell! – is that his name?

And it was still common at least as late as 1920, when Clarence Budington Kelland, in his novel, *Catty Atkins*, writes:

'It would be runnin' away. We've been runnin' away right along.'

'Do tell,' says I. 'From what?'

Oddly enough, Kelland had already in 1919 written this passage:

'I'm no Sunday-school boy –' said Dick O'Meara.

'Do tell,' gibed Eldredge.

And in 1838, T.C. Haliburton in *The Clockmaker; or, The Sayings and Doings of Samuel Slick, of Slicksville*, 2nd Series (p. 118), has Sam Slick of Connecticut saying, 'Why, he'll only larf at it [a painting] – he larfs at everything that ain't Yankee. Larf! said I, now do tell: I guess I'd be very sorry to do such an ungenteel thing to any one – much less, miss, to a young lady like you.'

Prob. some US scholar has written an article on *do tell!* If not, the oversight should promptly be remedied, for this is one of the most persistent, perhaps the *most* persistent, of all US c.pp.: and – intentionally, of course – I've merely scratched a square foot of the surface.

'Now merely rustic or mock-rustic in US' (J.W.C., 1977).

do the other! is a c.p. retort to 'I don't like it'; has the var. *well, lump it;* and belongs to C20. (One of the many sent to me – this, in 1969 – by the late Frank Shaw, the authority on Scouse, the dialect of the Merseyside. He had long been an Excise Officer before he became a writer and a radio man. His knowledge of popular speech, of general colloquialism, of the language of music-hall and theatre was immense: and he was immensely generous with that knowledge.)

do they have ponies down a pit? is one of the better-known Cockney c.pp. used derisively and by way of provocative interrogation; two others are *what was the name of the engine driver?* and *why is a mouse when it spins?* These C20 phrases either express the deepest boredom or are designed to start a violent argument or even a quarrel.

do what comes naturally dates from *c.* 1920 and is a c.p. of advice to a young man doubtful how he should treat a girl he's fond of, yet perhaps excessively respects; a generalization – not a euph. for – the less polite (and less brutal than it sounds) frequently proffered 'I should screw the girl if I were you'. Common among lusty young males and also among maturer, would-be helpful males.

Shipley writes, 1977: 'Ethel Merman, as Annie Oakley in the musical comedy, "Annie, Get Your Gun" (1946), had a delightfully humorous song, "Doing What Comes Naturally" – which undoubtedly helped keep the phrase alive.'

do you...? See also entries at **d'you...?**

do you come as friend or as enema? This c.p., obviously punning on *enemy*, reflects the anxiety felt by patients in a hospital ward: since *c.* 1940. (L.A., 1976) If *that's* all they have to worry about, they're lucky!

do you come from Blackpool? See **Blackpool**. The West Sussex version names the village of Yapton, to mean *were you born in a barn?*, notes John B. Smith, Bath, 1979.

do you come here often? 'Stemming from tongue-tied advance [to the girls] of the boys of the dance-hall era [of the 1920s–30s and again of the late 1940s–50s]. This conventionalism is still used in a jokey way' (Skehan, 1977). Only in this jokey way, dating from *c.* 1950, does it qualify as a c.p. P.B.: and no doubt instrumental was its use in the BBC radio-comedy series 'The Goon Show', where it was given the dove-tail answer *only in the mating season.* 'Goon Show' c.pp. were predominant in the 1950s.

do you feel like that? was, *c.* 1880–1940, a satirical c.p. addressed by workmen, and by others of the working class, either to anyone engaged in unusual work or to a lazy person doing any work at all. Ware.

do you have time for a small one? US var. of **is there room for a small one?**

do (or **did**) **you hear anything knock?** was a cant c.p. of *c.* 1810–70 and it meant either 'Do – or Did – you understand this?' or 'Do – or Did – you take the hint?' (See *U,* at *hear anything knocking.*)

do you hear the news? A nautical c.p., almost a formula, 'used in turning out the relief watch' (Bowen): mid C19–20.

[**do you know?** may have been a c.p. in 1883–*c.* 1890, after its adoption in 1884 by Beerbohm Tree in *The Private Secretary,* as Ware tells us; but it is one of those almost meaningless tags which should, I think, be classified as clichés rather than as c.pp.]

do you know any other funny stories? dates from *c.* 1935 and either signifies 'Do you think I'm green *or* a fool?' or implies 'You're a great leg-puller *or* kidder!' or even, very discreetly, 'You're a liar!' The sting resides in 'other'. Cf **have you any more...**

do you know something? is partly a tag, introducing gently what might otherwise come abruptly or unkindly, and partly a c.p., 'heard on and off' (Petch, 1974), of quietly humorous intent, as when a fellow says to a girl, 'Do you know something? I rather *like* you.' Cf:

do you know what? is a mainly US var. of *you know what?*, q.v. It occurs in e.g. Damon Runyon's 'Brooklyn Is All Right', the second story in his *My Wife Ethel,* 1939:

Dear Sir the other night my wife Ethel was reading the paper and she says Joe do you know what? I ses here Ethel why do you always start to say something by asking me a question?...Ethel ses why Joe that is not a question at all. That is just to get you to notice me so I can tell you something.

Who could have put it more neatly than that?

'In South Australia [since *c.* 1930], the invariable reply of a young school child [has been]: *you're mad and I'm not*' (Neil Lovett, 1976).

do you know where I'm coming from? Do you understand what I'm saying? :US: since *c.* 1969. (Norris M. Davidson, 1971.)

do you mind (? or !–or both). 'Very common a few years ago, now dying out but not fast enough' (Sanders, 1968), and still (1977) not ob., let alone †: dating from since the early 1950s. In 1969 Granville glossed the expression thus: 'Addressed to an intruder into conversation or into any circle where the addressee is not wanted or is otherwise unwelcome'; later in 1969, R.S. mentioned that it is 'spoken emphatically and on a descending scale; a sarcastic and barely courteous form of "Mind your own business"'; and in 1975, P. B. described it as 'a very common [expression] of reproach or expostulation, perhaps used more by girls and women than by men. Usually uttered in a rather whining tone.' Cf. L. A., 1974: 'A woman's facetiously affected indignation at imputation of unladylike behaviour'. A good example is '"You wouldn't much like it if *you* went mad." – "*Do* you mind?"' In the *New Yorker* of 26 May 1973, there is a drawing of a 'snooty'

couple examining the pieces in an *avant garde* exhibition, and the woman says to her husband. 'Do you mind? I'm forming an opinion.' The phrase seems to have reached the US *c.* 1970.

An equally, though differently, effective example comes in John Mortimer's percipient comedy, *Collect Your Hand Luggage,* prod. in 1961:

OFFICIAL: Have you checked your luggage, sir?

CRISPIN *(embracing both girls)*: This is all the luggage I possess.

SUSAN *(wriggling away from him):* Do you mind?

Note that in the collection of stories, *Pretty Polly Barlow,* 1964, in the one titled 'Me and the Girls', Noël Coward makes one of his characters say, 'She's got this "thing" about me not really being queer but only having caught it like a bad habit. Would you mind!' In itself a never very gen. c.p. of the 1950s–60s, *would you mind?* is important only because it so obviously varies *do you mind?* An illuminating example of the parent c.p. occurs in Martin Russell's novel, *Deadline,* 1971:

'Does that mean [that] at present you're bogged down [in your investigations]?'

'Do you mind?' The superintendent raised a pained hand. 'Police are active pursuing a number of theories...that'll do till we hit on something promising.'

Like **do yourself a favour,** q.v., this c.p. reminds me of a line in some melodramatic novel of the Edwardian period: 'Under the innocent exterior there lurks a veiled menace' (where a self-respecting writer would have preferred 'innocuous' to 'innocent'). Clearly it possesses a trenchant terseness that has attracted the susceptible minds of its multitudinous users.

do you need a knife and fork? See **sort 'em out!**

do you now? See **did you now?**

do you see any green in my eye? You must take me for a fool! *or* What do you take me for – an inexperienced idiot?: since *c.* 1840. Noted both by Benham and by Collinson. Cf the Fr. *je la connais* (understood: *cette histoire-là*). In late C19–20, although very rarely since *c* 1940, *do you see any green stuff in my eye? –* cf **not so green as I'm cabbage-looking;** *green* has for centuries implied either inexperience or credulity – or both. Cf also **see anything green?**

do you see what I see? A c.p. serving 'to express astonishment at unexpected "vision" of former fellow members of army or RAF unit turning up again *en route* to another posting, or home to Blighty; hence in similar general use. 1942–6 [in the Armed Förces]. I still use it' (L.A., 1975).

do you spit much with that cough? was, *c.* 1910–30, a Can. c.p. addressed to one who has just broken wind.

do you take? – short for *do you take my meaning? –* was an English c.p. of *c.* 1780–1930. George Colman the Younger, in his comedy, *The Poor Gentleman,* pub'd in 1802, has in I, ii:

OLL [APOD]...He he! – Do you take, good sir? do you take?

SIR C[HARLES]: Take! – Oh, nobody can miss.

Then in II, i, we find this:

OLL: Right – the name's nothing; merit's all. Rhubarb's rhubarb, call it what you will. Do you take, corporal, do you take?

FOSS: I never took any in all my life an' please your honour.

OLL: That's very well – very well indeed! Thank you, corporal; I own you one. [Cf **I owe you one.**]

Foss, a corporal, newly returned from long years of campaigning abroad, would not know the civilian c.pp. of the day.

do you think I came over with the tater boat? See **came over with the onion boat.**

do you think I came up yesterday? See **before you came up,** final paragraph.

do you think (or, if addressed to a third person, **does he think**)

I can shit miracles! This mainly Londoners' c.p. dates from *c.* 1920, for certain; but prob. from a decade or two earlier.

did you think I'm made of money? See **you must think I'm made of money.**

do you think I've just been dug up? is often shortened to *think I've just been dug up?* Do you think I'm a fool? Dating since *c.* 1915, it is to be related to **do you see any green in my eye?**, the implication being that a plant 'just dug up' is – naturally – green.

do you think you'll know me again? (or **you'll know me again, won't you?**) is addressed to someone staring at the speaker, esp. if the addressee does not, in soberest fact, know him: C20. The former is polite; the latter aggressive and pointed.
     Cf **do I owe ...** and **next time you see me ...**

do you think you're on your daddy's yacht? See **what do you think this is?**

do you think your father was a glazier? See **glazier.**

do you wanna buy a duck? Orig. form of **wanna buy a duck,** q.v. See also **how's the mommah?**

do you want a knife and fork? See **sort 'em out!**

do you want to bet on it? See **want to bet on it?**

do you want to borrow something? is a late C19–20 c.p. addressed to a flatterer.

do you want to buy a battleship? (or, abruptly, **want to buy a battleship?**) often slovened to *wanna buy ...* This RAF c.p., dating from 1940, means 'Do you want to make water?' and is addressed to a fellow Serviceman whom one has, with exquisite humour, awakened with the express purpose of asking him this infuriating question. An elab. of 'to pump ship', to urinate, and a (somewhat veiled) ironic allusion to flag days.

do you want to know the lay of the land? That's her. Current in US since *c.* 1930; by mid-1970s ob. (J.W.C., 1974.) It contains the double pun: 'the *lie* of the land' and 'a good *lay*', a girl sexually available and adept. Cf **lay of the last minstrel.**

do you want to make a Federal case of it? See **don't make a Federal ...**

do you want to start something? See **just start something!**

do your own thing! a US hippies' c.p., dating from the late 1950s, is ambiguous, for it can mean either 'Do your own (esp., dirty) work!' or 'Mind your own business!' or, as usually, 'Follow your own bent!' J.W.C. noted, 1977, that it was by then, in US [as in UK: P.B.], *only* 'Follow your own bent!' By 1980, it had a dated ring to it.

do your own time! Work out your sentence quietly and uncomplainingly – don't foist your woes upon others!: US underworld, since *c.* 1919. Occurring in Lewis E. Lawes's, *20,000 Years in Sing-Sing,* 1932, thus, 'You mustn't let anyone else do your bit. Do your own time. Be careful of the wolves in the institution.' It forms the little of Don Castle's *Do Your Own Time,* 1938.

do yourself a favour!, dating from *c.* 1945, introduces a warning, as in 'Do yourself a favour! Watch out for that fellow – he's an informer'. The meaning current in 1976 is, rather, 'go away!'; 'Buzz off!'; 'Scram!' (Norman Franklin). See also **do me a favour!**

doan't tha thee-tha me! Thee-tha thasen an' see 'ow tha likes it! A 'jocular assumption of dignity from one Yorkshireman to another; protesting need of the dignified distance and respect of "you"' (L.A., 1974): mostly Yorkshire since the 1920s.

Doc. See: **what's up, Doc.**

dockyard clock. See: **you lie.**

doctor. See: **he's a doctor; is there a d.; just what; my son; shit a day; yes, teacher; you're the d.**

Doctor Livingstone, I presume is both a very famous quot'n and a remarkably persistent c.p.; the words were spoken in 1871 by H.M., later Sir Henry, Stanley (1841–1904), when he, a journalist, at last came up with David Livingstone (1813–73) in Central Africa. Livingstone, physician,

missionary, explorer, was thought to be lost; the well-known proprietor of the *New York Herald,* James Gordon Bennett, financed a search party; Stanley, as hard-working as he was alert to the main chance, 'cashed in' by publishing, the very next year, *How I Discovered Livingstone* – and later became even more famous with *In Darkest Africa.*

As a c.p., it arose, *c.* 1885, as a skit upon Englishmen's traditional punctiliousness in no matter what circumstances, even to dressing for dinner at night, but it was almost immediately extended to almost any fortuitous, or any unexpected, meeting, whether between strangers or even between friends. In Anthony Hope's *Father Stafford.* 1891. occurs this passage:

> As they went in, they met Eugene, hands in pockets and pipe in mouth, looking immensely bored. 'Dr Livingstone. I presume?' said he. 'Excuse the mode of address, but I've not seen a soul all the morning and thought I must have dropped down somewhere in Africa.'

The quot'n – or perhaps rather the c.p. – has become so embedded in the structure of English that it can be alluded to in a US 'thriller', Thomas Patrick McMahon's *The Issue of the Bishop's Blood,* 1972, in this way:

> His tailoring had changed. Either he had bought a boat, or he was made up for a party. He was wearing a blue brass-buttoned yachting jacket, improbably white pants and spotless, white, rubber-soled shoes.
>
> 'Sir Thomas Lipton. I presume.' I said sourly.
>
> He raised his bushy eyebrows. 'Still the same nasty bastard, aren't you? Sit down, long time no see.'

For those unfamiliar with yachting history, Sir Thomas Lipton (1850–1931) was equally famous for the brands of tea he sold and for his five gallant attempts ('the world's best loser'), from 1899 to 1930, to win the America's Cup with his various yachts, all named *Shamrock.*

A strange and pleasant footnote to the history of the phrase is the apparent foreshadowing that occurs early in Act V, Scene i, of Sheridan's celebrated comedy *The School for Scandal,* performed in 1777 (but unpub'd until 1799); Joseph Surface, having just entered, says: 'Sir, I beg you ten thousand pardons for keeping you a moment waiting – Mr Stanley, I presume.'

Rather odd, isn't it? Now, if it could be proved that H. M. Stanley had seen a performance of the play, or merely read it, not long before he set out for Africa ...

doddle. See: **it's a doddle.**

Dodge. See: **who wouldn't.**

does a bear shit in the woods? See AMERICAN RESPONSES.

does he think I can shit miracles? A var. of **do you think I can ...?**

does it? A sarcastic retort: *c.* 1870–1940.

does it hurt? See **did it hurt?**

does it ring a bell? See **does that ring ...**

does Macy's tell Gimbel's? is 'applied to any competition, especially one involving a surprising and sometimes mysterious victory': US: since late 1940s. From the names of two of the largest department stores in New York City; 'neither informs the other of an advantageous [trade secret]' (J.W.C., 1977). 'This is one of the more popular phrases in the US.' These stores have branches all over the USA. 'They are highly competitive and spend millions in advertising. When someone seeks to obtain valuable information from another person, with the purpose of profiting by it, the cautious reply is often: "Would Macy's tell Gimbel's?" No one misses the meaning' (W.J.B., 1978). R.C., 1979, amplifies, '[this phrase refers] to the long-time rivalry between these two large department stores, located only a block apart on Herald Square, nationally publicised (perhaps along with the phrase itself) by the (1950s) motion picture, *Miracle on 34th Street* (Herald Square is at 34th and 6th Ave.). Somewhat ob. now, since the growing pre-eminence of Macy's has made the rivalry "no contest". Certainly well enough known nationally to be played on in various popular novels of the late '50s and 60s.'

does that, or **it**, **ring a bell** or **any bells (with you)?** 'Does that suggest anything (further)?' – 'Can you supply further information?' – 'Does what I have said evoke any (useful) associations in your mind?': in US, since *c*. 1950, but in the UK since *c*. 1915. Whence, inevitably and immediately, the positive form *that*, or *it*, *rings a bell*, 'that sounds familiar', or 'that vaguely reminds me of something relevant'. In UK, the c.p. has acquired the shorter, and allusive, positive var., as Petch noted, 1969, *ding-dong!* Perhaps from the ringing of a telephone or door bell or, less prob., the striking of a clock. (Not to be confused with the orig. US *ring the bell*, to succeed – from one or other of several fairground devices.)

does your bunny like carrots? '[Heard in] 1915–16 and no doubt existing earlier. Street boys to girls, jocular familiarity, with sexual symbolism' (L.A., 1969): mostly London: prob. late C19–20. With *bunny*, cf. the slang *pussy*, female pudend.

does your head ache? See **get your hair cut!**

does your mother know you're out? This c.p., sometimes joc., sometimes sarcastic, but esp. addressed derisively to someone displaying either an exceptional simplicity or a youthful conceit or presumption, is, all in all, perhaps the most remarkable – certainly one of the three of four most remarkable – of all British c.pp. It dates, according to the admirably dependable Benham, from 1838; it recurs in *Punch*, 1841; and heaven knows how often since! The *OED* pin-points the 1838 ref. by quoting *Bentley's Miscellany*: ' "How's your mother? Does she know that you are out?" ' Baumann cites the variants *what will your mother say?* and *did you tell your mother?* neither of which I have ever heard: they presumably flourished only briefly. There has, however, been, since *c*. 1900, a c.p. reply, used mainly by Cockneys and virtually † by 1950: *yes, she gave me a farthing to buy a monkey with – are you for sale?*, recorded in Manchon's valuable little dictionary. Frank Shaw, 1968, noted that this national c.p. was 'addressed to jolly girls', but that, in Liverpool, from *c*. 1920 onward, it was 'very sarcastic, like *we had* [one or other expletive] *dozens of these*'.

A very early critical commentary on this remarkably and continuously popular phrase occurs in Mackay:

The next phrase [after *flare up!*] that enjoyed the favour of the million was less concise and seems to have been originally aimed against precocious youths who gave themselves the airs of manhood before their time. '*Does your mother know you're out?*' was the provoking query addressed to young men of more than reasonable swagger, who smoked cigars in the streets, and wore false whiskers to look irresistible. We have seen many a conceited fellow who could not suffer a woman to pass him without staring her out of countenance, reduced at once into his natural insignificance by the mere utterance of this phrase.... What rendered it so provoking was the doubt it implied as to the capability of self-guidance possessed by the person to whom it was addressed. '*Does your mother know you're out?*' was a query of mock concern and solicitude, implying regret and concern that one so young and inexperienced in the ways of a great city should be allowed to ander about without the guidance of a parent.

This agrees entirely with the impression created by the earliest US ref. I've found.

Twice in vol. I of the Robert Surtees novel *Handley Cross; or Mr Jorrocks's Hunt*, 1854, the phrase occurs; in the chapter 'Another Sporting Lector' it is mentioned as 'a familiar inquiry that may safely be hazarded to a bumptious boy in a jacket'; and in an early chapter ('Belinda's Beau') it figures more topically in a scene where a couple of 'real swells' (Mr Jorrocks and a handsome young fellow), visiting a bulldog fight, are greeted with ribald cries:

'Make way for the real swells wot pay!' roared a stentorian voice from the rafters.

'Crikey, it's the Lord Mayor!' responded a shrill one from below.

'Does your mother know you're out?' inquired a squeaking voice just behind.

'There's a brace of plummy ones!' exclaimed another, as Bowker and Jorrocks stood up together.

It had also occurred notably in R.H. Barham's *The Ingoldsby Legends*, 2nd Series, 1842, concerning a 'poor old Buffer' victimized by a clever swindler ('Misadventures at Margate'):

I went and told the Constable my property to track;
He asked if 'I did not wish that I might get it back?'
I answered, 'To be sure I do! – It's what I've come about.'
He smiled and said, 'Sir, does your mother know that you are out?'

Note that this c.p. was also US, 'very popular *c*. 1900, but long obsolete' (W.J.B., 1968); and popular long before 1900, witness T.C. Haliburton, *The Clockmaker*, 3rd Series, 1840; a dancing girl, backstage at a New York theatre, and a country lad, having been taken there, proceed thus: 'Comin' up and tappin' me on the shoulder with her fan, to wake me up like, said she, Pray, my good feller "Does your mother know you're out?" – The whole room burst out a-larfin' at me.'

Moe reinforces Haliburton's point by citing the *Boston Daily Evening Transcript* of 18 Sep. 1838: 'These mysterious words were found posted on the corners of the streets in New York, some weeks since. The inscription was probably a labor of love, and intended to remind frolic-loving damsels of the danger they incurred by being out at improper hours, and on not very proper business. The phrase soon passed into a byword, and was as soon caught at as an attractive title for a new piece, which has been played with success at New York, and will be produced ... at the Tremont this evening.'

In *The Life of the Party*, 1919, Irvin S. Cobb – that genuinely US humorist – describes how a group of young people 'rag a fancy-clothes-party reveller thus: ' "Algernon, does your mother know you're out?" "Three cheers for Algy, the walkin' comic valentine." "Algy, Algy – oh, you cutey Algy!" These jolly Greenwich Villagers were going to make a song of his name.'

In 1942, Berrey merely lists the phrase as US.

A modern sidelight is furnished by Moe's quot'n of the opening lines of the song 'Cecilia', *c*. 1957: 'Does your mother know you're out, Cecilia?/Does she know that I'm about, Cecilia?' But, as Shipley warns, 1978, 'Perhaps mention the (serious) obverse of this. For at least seven years the nightly news broadcast (on CBS TV) has begun, "It's 10 o' clock; do you know where your children are?" '

But there is yet another noteworthy aspect of this phrase; has it ancient prototypes? In 1971, my old and dauntingly learned friend Jack Lindsay, after 'doing a Macaulay' ('As every schoolboy knows'), tells me that 'this question occurs in the Memnonia. (Ancient Thebes, Egypt, Valley of the Kings – J. Baillet, *Descriptions grecques et latines des tombeaux des rois ou syringes*, 1926, Nos 1922 and 1926. See my *Gods on the Roman Nile*, p. 338.) The fact that it occurs twice shows that it was not a chance invention but a Gr. slang phrase.'

Independently, Dr Brian Cook, of New York, had, 1969, written to me about these two examples, the Gr. words being ἡ πού σὲ μήτηρ 'εκτὸς οτ 'επίσταται, first published, with appropriate comment, by M.N. Tod in *Journal of Egyptian Archaeology*, XI, 1952, p. 256; where it is also related that a famous Classical scholar, John Conington, was, while a schoolboy at Rugby (1838–43), challenged by a friend,

'You're a swell at Greek verses, Conington: turn this into an iambic– "Does your mother know you're out?" '

Promptly came the reply, 'Μων ὀι μήτηρ, τεκνον, ὡζ θυραινζ ἐι?'

This prototype does not, of course, justify a justification for deriving the English c.p. from an ancient *graffito*: such coincidences arise from the fact that, throughout the ages and in all countries, certain *thought-patterns* are discernible: and in the sphere of informal and unconventional speech, they almost inevitably occur. Cf **be good–and if you can't be good, be careful; Kilroy was here**; and the quot'n at **who's your hatter?**

does your mother like a monkey? is a C20 school taunt c.p., from one boy to another. (Granville, 1968.)

does your mother take in washing? belongs to *c.* 1900–30, although it continued to be heard, now and then, for a decade or more after that. A vague phrase, with (I think) no specific insult implied but with a mild imputation of poverty. It occurs in Howard Spring's novel, *My Son, My Son*, 1918.

The full form, as Christopher Fry reminds me, adds *if she doesn't, she ought to*, the whole c.p. being usu. chanted. Origin? I confess that I don't know; but I do remember having heard it during the 1920s and 1930s and I suspect that it may date from the late C19.

does your mother want a rabbit? is a c.p. of *c.* 1890–1914. It derives from the stock question (addressed to a child) of the itinerant rabbit-vendors and is therefore not scabrous in origin – whatever may have happened to it in its c.p. stage. (B & P.) As a children's chant, it went on … *Sell her one for ninepence*! (P.B.)

does your nose swell (or itch)? – often completed, as logic would demand, by **at this or at that**. Are you angry (usu… swell) or annoyed (usu. …itch)?: C20. Cf **my nose itches.**

doesn't buy groceries, often prec. by **it**. A US c.p., implying that such or such an act or activity brings in no money: since *c.* 1920 (Berrey). Cf the Brit. **this won't buy Baby a frock.**

doesn't care much when he (or she) spends when he (or she) has no money (–he or **she)**. This c.p. hits very effectively at one who, penniless, talks as if 'rolling in the stuff': since *c.* 1952. I've heard it very seldom since *c.* 1950.

doesn't do *that* on gin and kippers! A man (or woman or dog) needs a proper and sensible diet, neither haphazard feeding nor fanciful titbits: since *c.* 1930. (L.A., 1976.)

doesn't everyone? See **aren't we all?**

doesn't have a pot to piss (later, also **pee**) **in.** See **pot to pee in.**

doesn't it make you want to spit?! That is, in disgust: since the late 1930s. An Arthur Askey 'gag' in 'Band Wagon', 1st Series (?late) 1937, 2nd Series 1938, 3rd Series soon after WW2 started. (*Radio Times*, 28 June–4 July 1975, in notice of AA's autobiography.)

VIBS adds 'Arthur Askey admits he was rapped over the knuckles for introducing this "unpleasant" expression on *Band Waggon*. "[Lord] Reith thought it a bit vulgar but I was in the driving seat – the show was so popular – so he couldn't fire me. I suppose I said it all the more!" '

doesn't know … Many and varied are the phrases beginning **he** (much less often **she**) **doesn't know**, to denote ignorance or stupidity of one sort or another. A representative – but far from complete – selection is given here. Perhaps one of the most earthily picturesque to be applied to someone who is, in the speaker's contemptuous opinion, a complete fool, is *he doesn't know if his arsehole is bored or punched*, which prob. orig. in engineering workshops *c.* 1910. It was soon elab., and is vividly exemplified in T.E. Lawrence, *The Mint*, which, not pub'd until 1955, was written in the 1920s about his life as an aircraftman in the RAF: on p. 117, 'The silly twat didn't know if his arse-hole was bored, punched, drilled or countersunk', where the allusive use proves how well known the c.p. had become. L.A., 1976, noted that the c.p. may have a minatory use, as in 'If I have to come over to you, you won't know if …', but the basic form remains as in T.E.L. Among Can. Army officers during WW2, and in the Brit. Services since then, in an anglicized version, there has been the further elab. *that guy don't know if his ass-hole was drilled, dug, seamed* (or *reamed*), *bored or (just) naturally evaginated*. Neil Lovett supplies, 1978, an Aus. later C20 version that includes the fearsome finale … *or eaten out by white ants*. A US version, along slightly different lines, but

with the same import, is supplied, 1975, by Moe: *he doesn't know his ass* (or, politely, *ear*) *from a hole in the ground* or a *hot rock* or (R.C., 1977) *from third base* or (W.J.B., 1977) the earlier *from a slingshot* (i.e. a round pebble or a bullet fired from a sling or catapult). UK usage prefers *he doesn't know his arse from his elbow*, or, in later C20, the 'cleaned-up' but still recognisable var. attributed to the famous conductor Sir Henry Wood, … *his brass from his oboe*. US again, esp. military in WW2, is … *shit from Shinola* (a kind of polish).

He doesn't know enough to pee down the wind is a mostly Can. phrase: since *c.* 1920 (Leechman). To describe someone in a dilemma there is the C20 US *he doesn't know whether to shit or go blind* (Fain, 1977); the Brit., mainly nautical, … *if* (or *whether*) *he wants a shit or a haircut*; and Paul Theroux, witty and urbane, mentioned as one of his 'favourites' that he found missing when reviewing the 1st ed. of this book, 'so confused that he *doesn't* (or *didn't*) *know whether to scratch his watch or wind his ass*', which he glossed 'US Army: *c.* 1860–1900'. For one who ignores – or is ignorant of – the golden mean, there is the low Can. *he doesn't know the difference between shitting and tearing his arse*: since the 1920s; with this last cf **don't tear the arse …**

For someone in a muddle, confused or stupid, we have the simple *he doesn't know if* (or *whether*) *it's Christmas or Easter*, or *whether it's Pancake Tuesday or half-past breakfast time* (a conflation used on Brit. TV in 1968); Aus. versions are (in Sydney) *whether it's Pitt Street or Christmas* or, alliteratively, *Palm Sunday*, and (in Victoria) *whether it's Tuesday or Bourke Street*: these are from mid-C20, and are listed in Wilkes. In this same general 'family' comes also *he doesn't know where he lives* or, orig. an illiteracy, but soon intentional and joc., *'e don't know where 'e lives* or *where 'e's at*. Slightly different in tone is *he doesn't* (or *don't*) *know he's born* (Petch, 1974): this goes back to *c.* 1870, if not a generation or two earlier; it has two nuances: either, he is very stupid or innocent, or, he doesn't know how lucky he is. And of someone 'who sets about a job or embroils himself in argument without knowledge or understanding or with wrong-headed idea' (L.A., 1974): *he doesn't know which way he's playing*: since *c.* 1920.

Many of the above (and I repeat, the list is in no way to be taken as exhaustive: please see also the collection at KNOW, in the Appendix to *DSUE*, 8th ed.) may of course be used in the accusatory form *you don't know …*! (P.B.) Cf:

doesn't know where his arse hangs is applied to a 'man, especially a young man, who is thought not to have come to grips with himself as he is, instead of the would-be "hero" figure of boyhood. I have never heard it said of a woman' (L.A., 1976) – nor have I. It dates from at least as early as 1920 and prob. from late C19. P.B.: Robert Barltop and Jim Wolveridge, however, in their penetrating study of Cockneys and Cockney life, *The Muvver Tongue*, 1980, write, p. 45: 'For the man who has got on in the world and become greedy in the process: "Since he's come into money he doesn't know where his arse hangs".' There exists also the form *he* (or *I*) *doesn't* (or *don't*) *know which side his* or (*my*) *arse hangs*, implying that the poor fellow is either hopelessly bewildered or in a state of complete indecision.

dog(s). See: anyone who hates; busy as a dog; case of the tail; done up like; don't sell; fucking; he's a whole; hungry dog; Hunt's dog; I have to see; I might as well; I'm a true; if I am; if I had; it'd blow; it's a dog's; let the dog; like Tom; my dogs; raining; see a dog; see a man; shouldn't happen; stands out; straight; such a dawg; that wouldn't; there's life; they gotta; top mate; try it; wanted; where the dogs; who shot; whose dog; you kill my; and:

dog at everyone's heels – a. A sophisticated 'c.p. for [male] homosexuality: recognition of the ambivalence of sex' (L.A., 1976): since *c.* 1960.

dog-fight. See: I wouldn't wear.

dog-running. See: better than dog.

dog-watch. See: you haven't been.

dogs are barking it in the street – the. This Aus. c.p., dating since c. 1920, is applied to something that, supposed to be a secret, is in fact very widely known – in short, an open secret. Neil Lovett adds, 1978, that, among those who bet on horses, it is often shortened to *the dogs are barking it*, applied to a horse expected to win.

dogs are pissing on your bluey (swag) – **the.** As exhortation, 'Wake up!' More gen., 'something unpleasant is happening to your little world': in the glossary to Alexander Buzo's *Three Plays*, 1973. The former sense recurs in his *The Roy Murphy Show*, performed in 1971. Aus.

dog's dinner. See: all dressed; done up like.

dogs have not dined – the. Recorded by Grose in 1785, this mid C18–early C19 c.p. is addressed to one whose shirt is hanging out at the back and therefore inviting the attention of any playful dog.

doll. See: living doll; making dolls'; oh, you beautiful.

dollar(s). See: another day; look like a million; you have to spend.

dollars to doughnuts. See **all Lombard Street ...**

dolled up. See: all dressed.

donah. See: never introduce.

done. See: honest, I; that's as well.

done like a dinner. Completely worsted or 'done for': Aus.: since c. 1830 and still (1978) current. Lit., 'roasted' or 'done to a turn'. Admirably documented by Wilkes.

done, or **dressed, up like a dog's dinner.** The *done* form derived, c. 1945' from the *dressed*, which, originating c. 1925 in the British Army, spread rapidly in the other Services during WW2, in the sense 'wearing one's best – strictly, better – uniform'. (P.G.R.) Thence among civilians. See also **all dressed up like ...**

done up like a sore toe or **finger.** 'Dressed up, and looking uncomfortable' (Wilkes): Aus.: since very early C20. Whence, since the 1950s, 'looking conspicuous'.

donkey. See: could eat; hurry no; penny more; there's no point; what's knocked; when Adam; who stole the d.

don't act so daft or I'll buy you a coalyard is a joc. c.p., dating since c. 1956. (Franklyn.) Why a coalyard? 'Your guess is as good as mine'; even so, I'll hazard the conjecture that then the addressee could blacken his face as much and as often as he liked, and act like a 'black and white' comedian.

don't all rush at once! A later C20 var. of the next, which may, however, be said by someone knowing that there will be a rush. (P.B.)

don't all speak at once! is used by someone who, having made an offer or a suggestion, is greeted with a conspicuous lack of enthusiasm: since c. 1880, if not considerably earlier; both Brit. and US. Walter Woods, US playwright, in *Billy the Kid*, produced in 1907, has this passage in Act II:

MOLLY: [*Enters from dance hall.*] Who wants to dance? Well – don't all speak at once.

don't answer that! There's no need to make any comment, much less to answer the question! *or* Well, no – perhaps you'd better *not* answer that!: as a genuine c.p., only since c. 1960. (Lit., it goes – expectably – back as far as modern English does.) A good example occurs in David Craig's novel, *Contact Lost*, 1970: ' "Why am I doing all the talking? Don't answer that!" '

don't applaud: (just) throw money! A c.p. used by street singers and other street performers: C20. Perhaps of humorous Jewish orig. Esp. in the form *no, don't applaud, just throw money* it became, c. 1930, gen, 'in response for a favour' (P.B.). In the programme for his one-man show 'Aspects of Max Wall' in 1975, Max Wall wrote, 'If you enjoy my show – please don't applaud, just leave jewellery at the stage door – no paste, please' (Simon Levene). S.L. also notes the comparable *don't thank me: buy me something!*: mostly feminine; occ., masculine mock-feminine: since c. 1955.

don't argue (, Hutton's is best). 'Rugby football fans around the world know the straight-arm fend-off as a "Don't argue" and its origins go back to the turn of the century' (*Australian*, 14 Apr. 1977). Wilkes explains how it generated the slogan, itself *Don't argue, Hutton's is best*, of the J.B. Hutton Pty Ltd; that slogan became an Aus. c.p.

don't ask! A c.p. used by someone in an awkward predicament, to fend off questions as to how he or she got into that unpleasant situation – it would take too long to explain, and could be embarrassing as well: US: since c. 1965. (P.B.)

don't ask *me*, I only live here or **work here**; var. **don't ask *me*, ask the man in charge** or **I don't make the rules, I just work here.** But poss. the commonest form is **I only work here** q.v., usu. prec. by *I don't*, or *wouldn't*, *know*, orig., c. 1925, US, but adopted in UK by 1945. It is 'a usually impudent response by a subordinate to an outsider's inquiry. The "subordinate" – e.g. an overworked housewife – may resent [his or her] subordination. Perhaps ob., but not†' (J.W.C., 1977). P.B.: an ephemeral version, current among Leicestershire schoolboys in 1977, was *don't ask* me, *I'm only ze bell-boy*, passed on to me by the brothers McPheely with the comment that it should be said in a mock-German accent, 'like Adolf Hitler imitating Groncho Marx'. It must have had a source somewhere, but I confess my ignorance of it.

don't be an Airedale! Don't be such a bitch!: US: early 1920s. (Moe; W & F.) Unfair to this breed of dog.

don't be filthy! Don't be foul-mouthed *or* bawdy *or* suggestive!: since the late 1930s; not much heard since c. 1960. A 'gag' by Arthur Askey in 'Band Wagon', c. 1937–40. (*Radio Times*, 28 June – 4 July 1975; AA's autobiography *Before Your Very Eyes*.)

don't be fright! 'Sirdani, the radio magician (sic), *circa* 1944' (*VIBS*).

don't be funny! Don't be ridiculous – I'd never dream of doing such a thing: Can.: since c. 1930, perhaps five or ten years earlier. (Leechman.) Perhaps of US orig.: Berrey, 1942, records it. Certainly well known among English children in the later 1940s (P.B.), and still in common use in Aus., 1978 (Neil Lovett). Perhaps influential in forming the series to be found at **you're joking!**

don't be like that! and **don't be that way!** These US c.pp. date from the late 1920s; Berrey records the former; in *DSUE* I've noted its adoption, c. 1948, into UK. The gen. sense is 'Don't behave in that objectionable – or in that unreasonable and ludicrous – way.'
Cf **be like that!**

don't bet on it! See **I wouldn't bet on it!**

don't bother me now, my hands are wet. This British soldiers' c.p. of 1914–18 – it seems to have disappeared before WW2 – arises from 'the weary impatience of harassed mothers' repelling the attention-claiming of young children. B&P.

don't bother to pick it up! See **clap your hands!**

don't bully the troops! is another WW1 soldiers' c.p., this one being addressed to a noisy or aggressive or excessive talker. (B.&.P.) P.B.: a later C20 version was *don't harass the troops!*, with *harass* pron. the US way, accent on the second syllable. Also *quit harassing the troops!*, obviously from the US.

don't bust yer corsets! See **aye, aye, don't ...**

don't buy your candy where you buy your groceries is a milder version of **never shit where you eat,** q.v. 'A semi-proverbial injunction against carrying on sexual intercourse at one's place of employment' (R.C., 1978): US: since c. 1940 – or a decade earlier.

don't call us, we'll call you. Thank you for coming to be interviewed – we'll let you know *or* We have your letter – esp. letter of application for a job or an interview – and we'll let you know our decision: either a businessman's polite brush-off or a gentle intimation of probable rejection or a selection board's (or committee's) final remark to a candidate whose interview has, in effect, ended: since c. 1945; orig. US, arising either in the film or in the theatrical world, with the one reinforcing the other, and the c.p. becoming gen. in the early 1950s and then very soon becoming Brit. as well. (W. J. B., former head of *Look*'s research department, in a letter, 1968.)

In Bill Turner's novel, *Circle of Squares*, 1969, a man, having been shadowed by detectives instead of by crooks (as he had suspected them of being), goes into a police station to complain and finds himself being greeted by one of his shadowers, 'Don't call us, we'll call you.'

Then in Peter Townsend's novel *Out of Focus*, 1971, occurs this passage:

'Be in the bar of the Reina Cristina in Algeciras at nine o'clock to-morrow evening.'

Konrad laughed. 'Don't call us, we'll call you.'

In the same year, a well-known novelist described the slight var. *don't call me – I'll call you* as 'a threadbare joke' – and indeed the joke had begun to lose its pristine charm.

'It is generally understood that this is mere prevarication, and the result will turn out unfavourable. "How d'you get on?" – "Oh, you know; Don't call us, *etcetera*"' (P.B., 1975).

The pertinence and popularity of the phrase had rendered it virtually inevitable that the predominant form should generate a var. or two. It did, by late 1970: *don't ring us – we'll ring you*. Moreover, on 12 Oct. 1970, the *Guardian* could head an article 'Don't Tell Us – We'll Tell You' in the justifiable expectation of being not merely understood but even appreciated.

don't chant the poker! and **don't sing it!** Don't exaggerate!: a proletarian c.p. of *c.* 1870 – 1914 (B & L, vol. I, 1889). Here, *chant* is 'to advertise, as with a street cry'; but as for *poker* – well, I don't know precisely why, but clearly *chant the poker* was at the barrow-boy, or the Petticoat Lane, level.

don't clap so hard: you'll bring the house down. (It's a very old house!) An ironic call to the audience by a comedian greeted with resounding silence at one of his best jokes: music-hall: since the 1870s or 1880s; by 1960, ob.; now (1975) a nostalgic survival. John Osborne uses it two or three times in *The Entertainer*, 1957; I had heard it, 1925 or 1926, at either the Victoria Palace or the old Holborn Empire. Simon Levene, 1978, adds the var. *don't clap too hard: we're all in a very old building.*

don't come it: you never used to! is a 'protest at putting on "side" or pretence. (The rider seems to me to be a music-hall elaboration, or embellishment, and undercurrent)' (L.A., 1968): since *c.* 1910; by 1970, slightly ob. Cf **come off it!**

don't come the acid with me! 'Don't be insolent!' Also 'Don't be nasty *or* unpleasant *or* sarcastic!' Also 'Don't throw your weight about!' and 'Don't be officious!': Services': C20, but little used after *c.* 1970. *Don't come the old acid*, in the last pair of senses, is partly a fringe-of-the-under-world c.p. (Based on *DSUE*; R.C., 1977; and David Powis, *Signs of Crime*, 1977.) Cf the next two entries.

don't come (or **give me**) **the old abdabs!** Don't tell me the tale – don't try to fool me or throw dust in my eyes: C20, but esp. in 1939 – 45. By itself, *abdabs* was, during WW2, occ. used for 'afters' (a second course of a meal): so perhaps the phrase basically means 'Don't elaborate!' It may have been influenced by 'the screaming abdabs', an attack of *delirium tremens.*

don't come the (old) tin soldier with me! 'Don't be so presumptuously impertinent!' and 'Don't try your old-soldier tricks on *me*!' and 'Don't be obstructive!' A fringe-of-the-underworld derivative of the old military, whence the post-WW1 civilian, slang *come the old soldier*. (DSUE; Powis, 1977.) P.B.: to Mrs Dorothy Birkett I owe report of the fearsome Glaswegian threat *don't come the little tin soldier with* me, *laddie, or I'll melt ye!*

don't come the raw prawn! 'Don't try to put one over me!' – 'Don't try to impose on me!' This c.p. arose, during WW2, in the Australian Army; Wilkes's earliest printed date is 1942; in 1946 Rohan Rivett, *Behind Bamboo* (a prisoner-

of-war story) writes, '*Raw prawn* something far-fetched, difficult to swallow, absurd'. Apparently first dictionaried by the late Grahame Johnston, in *The Australian Pocket Oxford Dictionary*, 1976. A raw prawn is less edible than a cooked one. P.B.: if in fact to do with cooking, then perhaps orig. a ref. to the Japanese delicacy. I have also heard the phrase used to mean 'Don't pretend to be the naive innocent!'

don't confuse me with the facts. See **I've made up my mind …**

don't crack the steward down the middle. 'Don't overwork – don't be unpleasant to – the steward': RN lowerdeck: since the 1950s. Here, *crack* puns on the proverbial effeminacy of stewards. (Peppitt, 1977.)

don't crow so loud, rooster: you might lay an egg! Oh! Do stop boasting or bragging: a US c.p., dating from *c.* 1920; recorded by Berrey in 1942; slightly out of date by 1950, but still used by – or, at the least, familiar to – old-timers as late as 1970; and never adopted in UK despite its homely picturesqueness.

don't do anything I wouldn't do! is an Eng. – and an Aus. and, by adoption, US – c.p., dating from *c.* 1910 or from a lustrum or even a decade earlier, and intended as merely joc. advice. (Cf **be good – and if you can't be good, be careful!**) During WW2, in the Services, it served as a 'c.p. addressed to anyone going on leave, especially if suspected of going on a "dirty week-end"' (Granville, 1969).

Examples later than WW2 abound, as, for instance, in Anne Morice, *Death in the Grand Manor*, 1970:

' 'Bye, 'bye,' Mary called after us. 'And don't do anything I wouldn't do.'

'I wonder what there is that Mary wouldn't do?' I said. Although less frequent than before WW2, this c.p. is still very far from being †.

Usu. there is a sexual connotation as in Owen Sela, *The Kiriov Tapes*, 1973, 'Paul … threw open the door with a flourish. "There, lovelies," he cried, "it's all yours. And don't do anything I wouldn't do."'

'I have an idea,' writes Sanders, 1968, 'this comes from *Punch*. The counter is "That gives me plenty of scope".'

Since *c.* 1918, also US. In Ring W. Lardner ('The Facts' – in *How to Write Short Stories*, 1926): 'I will let you know how I come out that is if you answer this letter. In the mean wile girlie au reservoir and don't do nothing I would not do.' Berrey records it.

don't do anything: just stand there! (Cf **don't just stand there … !**) In *Observer*, 4 Sep. 1977, Kingsley Amis remarked on the former: 'Said in rehearsal to an actor who tries to hog the audience's attention during another's important speech', and added that it 'is probably better in the form I have come across – *don't just do something – stand there*'.

don't do anything you couldn't eat! is an Aus. c.p., dating from *c.* 1930 and meaning 'Don't take on anything you can't do' – 'Don't start something you can't finish.' (Baker.) By 1960, rather old-fashioned.

It was prompted by *to bite off more than one can chew*; and perhaps it forms a deliberate elab. of that phrase.

don't do me any (illiterately, **no**) **favors!** 'What you are proposing is no favor to me: US: from 1930s' (R.C., 1977). Cf **do me a favour.**

don't *do* that (or) **you'll give me a dickey strawberry!** Don't do that – it'll give me (cause me to develop or have) a weak heart; since *c.* 1960 – perhaps a decade or even a generation earlier. (Mrs Ronald Pearsall, 1978.) *Dickey* is old-established slang for 'in a dangerous, or a weak, condition', as in 'His health is very dickey'; and, here, *strawberry* is elliptical rhyming slang, *strawberry* tart – heart.

don't dynamite! Don't be angry!: 1883 – *c.* 1900: a non-cultured, non-aristocratic phrase, 'result of the Irish pranks in Great Britain with this explosive' (Ware). Cf:

don't excite! Keep cool! Elliptical for 'Don't excite yourself!': *c.* 1895 – 1939. Recorded by *The Concise Oxford Dictionary*, in the Supplement of 1934, it occurs as early as in E. H.

Hornung's once extremely popular *Raffles*, 1899: ' "All right, guv'nor," drawled Raffles: "don't excite. It's a fair cop." '

don't fall back in it! See **don't shit in your mess-kit!**

don't fear! See **don't you fear!**

don't fire until (or, loosely, **till**) **you see the whites of their eyes.** At the Battle of Bunker Hill, 1775, the US General Israel Pitman or, according to other authorities, General Joseph Warren or Colonel William Prescott – such being the stuff of which history is made and such the evidence from which so much of it has been written – issued this order to his troops: 'Men, you are all marksmen – don't one of you fire until you see the whites of their eyes.'

This famous US quot'n became, at some point early in C20, also a c.p.: a c.p. when used, as since *c.* 1940 it has been used, without ref. to the orig. situation; in this respect it should be aligned with the two other US historical c.pp. noted at AMERICAN HISTORICAL BORDERLINERS. J.W.C. has, 1975, pointed out that, as a c.p., it is used 'always with reference to a comparable situation (metaphorically comparable, never literal; never, that is, of an armed conflict, but only of a debate or dispute or the like)'.

By 1945 at latest, *don't fire* .... was also a Brit. c.p. and, as such, it has often been employed allusively, as in this passage in John Welcome's *Hard to Handle*, 1964, where the second speaker is a girl:

'I won't be more than a few minutes. If you see anyone taking an undue interest in the car ... watch him until I come back.'

'I won't shoot until I see the whites of his eyes.'

Here, *shoot* represents an occ. var. *but* only in UK.

don't force it, Phoebe! 'Don't try so hard *or* too hard': in the *Daily Mirror*, 19 Nov. 1976, the comedian Charlie Chester wrote, 'I created it for one of my radio shows [the post-WW2 *Stand Easy*]. Catch phrases had to be the gimmick in those days' and added, as examples, *I can hear you* and *I say, what a smasher!*, q.v. He is quoted, in *VIBS*, as saying, 'I had a vision of this nurse putting a needle in the arm. She says to me, "Do you dance?" I said "No", so she says, "You will in a minute. The needle's very blunt!" And I thought – "Well ... don't force it, Phoebe!" I found that it not only fitted there, it fitted everywhere else.'

don't forget the diver! During the short run of six 'ITMA' broadcasts, in the summer of 1940, while the relevant departments of the BBC were at Bangor,

the Diver [played by Horace Percival] made the first of his lugubrious entrances and his even more doleful exits [with the words] 'Don't forget the Diver!' ... His few words very soon became part of the country's vocabulary ... and it was not long before 'Don't forget the Diver' was heard on all sides, in bars, in buses, on stations, even from disembodied voices in the blackout, and practically no lift descended without someone saying, in those weak tones, 'I'm going down now. sir!'

So tells us the producer himself, Frank Worsley, in his *Itma*, (December) 1948. Referring to latish 1948, Worsley says 'Even now I sometimes hear someone mutter "Don't forget the Diver!" ' He might have added that 'going down now, sir' was, as a c.p., often the preferred form. But Anthony Burgess, 1977, notes that rather than 'preferred form', *going down now, sir*, or, in full, *I'm going down now, sir* is its pendant.

The late Stephen Potter, in *The Sense of Humour*, 1954, wrote concerning the landlord of a certain public house:

Every now and then he utters some of the accepted comic phrases of our age, quite isolated, quite without reference, 'Mind my bike' he will say. Then a little later: 'Time I gave it the old one-two.' Gave what he does not say ... Then 'Don't forget the diver' is perhaps the next phrase which happens to come to the surface.

VIBS records that 'It was taken from Tommy Handley's [the star of 'ITMA'] memories of a man who used to dive off New Brighton pier on the Wirral around 1920. "Don't forget

the diver, sir, don't forget the diver," he would say, collecting money in a fishing net. An eyewitness of the actual diver recalls: "he was not so young, only had one leg, and used to dive from a great height as passengers left the ferry boat from Liverpool. ... [he] was, I think, a casualty of the First World War." '

See also **give it the old one-two.**

don't fret! See **don't you fret!**

don't get mad, get even! 'Don't get angry – get even!' or 'Revenge is ultimately more satisfying than mere demonstrative rage.' Perhaps as much a popular proverb as a c.p.: gen. US: since *c.* 1965. (R.C., 1978.)

don't get off your bike! 'Don't get upset'; 'Don't lose control of yourself': Aus.: since the 1930s. (Wilkes.) Contrast **on your bike!**

don't get on my case! 'Don't intrude on my most private life, nor on my inner self': US Negroes': since *c.* 1960. *The Third Ear*, 1971, defines this sense of *case* as 'an imaginary region of the mind in which [are] centered one's vulnerable points, eccentricities, and sensitivities'. (Paul Janssen.) Cf **get off my case!**

don't get smart! 'Don't try to be clever *or* smart *or* "Smart Alec"!': US: since *c.* 1925. (Berrey.) A.B., 1978, writes, 'I've heard it extended to "don't be a smart ass [Brit.: *arse*]" or "don't get so (*or* too) smart-assed".'

don't get your arse (occ. **balls** or **bowels**) **in an uproar** and **don't get your shit hot** and **don't get your knickers in a twist** (or **twisted**). Don't get so excited or, esp., angrily excited: all are low; none, I think, precedes C20; the second is Can.: but whereas the first and second are addressed by men to men, the third (i.e. the last) is addressed, by either sex, to male or female – or, as L.A. puts it, 'a reproof to (over-)indignant man by treating him as a flustered woman'. The US version is *don't get your bowels in an uproar*, which carries no social taboo; but, as R.C. points out, even in the US, *balls* is commoner than *bowels*.

Don't get your knickers in a twist has the occ. var., *no need to get* ... , 'Don't become cantankerous or touchy. [Whence the positive – *not* ranking as a c.p.] "You've got your knickers in a twist": facts, ideas, wrong or confused' (L.A., 1976). Cf the slang phrase *get* (one's) *knitting twisted*, get one's ideas and facts confused. Note also: 'Basil Brush [see **boom! boom!**] ought to have got a mention ... , if only as the populariser of the c.p. for the younger generation' (Prof. D.J. Enright, in *Encounter*, Dec. 1977). Aus. has a very popular alliterative var., *don't get your knickers in a knot* (Neil Lovett, 1978).

don't get your ass in a sling. See **ass in a sling.**

don't get your back up! 'There is, of course, little that is distinctively American in the idea of putting one's back up when inclined to be angry; but as a street catch phrase, one time very popular, it claims a place' (Farmer): *c.* 1880–90. Extant in Aus. (Neil Lovett, in *The National Times*, 23–28 Jan. 1978).

don't get your knickers in a twist! See **don't get your arse in an uproar!**

don't give me that! Tell that to the Marines!: since *c.* 1920. The implication is, 'Don't take me for a fool when you talk like that!' In Terence Rattigan's *Love in Idleness*, first performed on 20 Dec. 1944 and pub'd in 1945, in the opening speech, Olivia Brown on the telephone says:

'Treasury? Hullo, Dicky? Olivia. Is there a chance of a word with the Chancellor?. ... Don't give me that. If I know him he's in the middle of a nice game of battleships with you at this moment.'

It became also Can. and US, Berrey recording it in 1942 in the forms *don't give me* – or *us* – *that!* and, less commonly, *don't give me* – or *us* – *one of those!* A US elab. is *don't give me that jive*, noted by HLM in Supp. 2 and by W & F, 1960; it was adopted in UK, esp. among jazz addicts, as early as 1950. A.B., 1978: 'American version, *don't give me that shit!* – often preceded by *aw*: since late 1940s.'; some Brit.

use, later C20, also (P.B.). It has been current in Aus. since *c.* 1955 (Neil Lovett, 1978). *Don't give me that jazz!* superseded ... *jive c.* 1950; both the *jazz* and the *jive* forms came to UK from US (James R. Sutherland, 1977). Cf: **don't give me that toffee!** Don't give me that wrapped-up, glib explanation!: this c.p. is exceptional in having a very limited currency – among RAF airmen in Malta since *c.* 1950; by 1970, slightly old-fashioned; but worthy of inclusion for its value in comparison with the prec. c.p. and **don't give me the old abdabs**, q.v. at **don't come.** ... (L.A., 1967.)

don't give up the ship!, noted by Berrey as a c.p., is one of those which began their chequered careers as famous quotations. The full words, spoken, as his final order, by Captain James Lawrence, commanding the US frigate *Chesapeake* on 1 June 1813, as he was carried below fatally wounded, before the capture of his ship by the British frigate *Shannon*, were: 'Tell the men to fire faster and not to give up the ship; fight her till she sinks', which, strictly, form the famous quotation, whereas *don't give up the ship!* forms the c.p. (with thanks to Bartlett) – a conflated abridgement of a kind familiar to all historians.

Don't give up the ship! has, since *c.* 1870, if not far earlier, been a US c.p. of encouragement; nor has it, in C20, been entirely unknown in Britain and the Commonwealth.

In Bert Leston Taylor and W.C. Gibson's *Extra Dry*, 1906, 'Hennessy Martel's farewell words, as he breathed his last sober breath in Gottlieb Kirschenwasser's arms, were: "Don't give up the ship!"' is a mock-heroic allusion. Contrast, at **where do we go from here, boys?**, Irvin S. Cobb's mention in his patriotic *The Glory of the Coming*, 1919.

don't go down the mine, daddy! comes from a famous old tear-jerking song that, in WW1, formed a soldiers' chant and very soon after it – say in 1920 – became a c.p.; not much heard since WW2 and very little heard since 1970.

don't go hog-wild! is 'an American saying, used to restrain someone's mad behaviour or mad pursuit of something' (W.J.B., 1977): since the 1920s, but by *c.* 1970, slightly ob. *Hog-wild* is defined by Berrey, 1942, as 'angry, excited'; by W & F, 1960, as 'wildly excited'.

don't go out of your way! An ironic admonition, both Brit. and US, to one who, being asked to do something entirely reasonable, is clearly reluctant to comply: since *c.* 1930 or a little earlier. (W.J.B. 1977.)

don't go over my head when you're under my command is a US 'Services' warning': C20. (Ashley, 1983.)

don't hold your breath! is elliptical for 'Don't hold your breath in expectation or excitement' and has the special sense 'Don't count on it': orig.? during WW2 – and predominantly US, as in Anne Blaisdell, *Practice to Deceive*, 1971:

'That air conditioning! You suppose they'll ever get around to us?'

'Don't hold your breath,' said Rodriguez.

The implication is that, even if it did happen, they would have to wait some considerable time.

An English example occurs in Donald MacKenzie's novel of suspense, *The Spreewald Collection*, 1975:

'Up yours,' grunted the warder. 'I know your kind. You'll be back for a certainty!'

Hamilton closed his right eye. 'Don't hold your breath. And take good care of those ulcers!'

Neil Lovett writes, 'I've often heard "I wouldn't hold my breath (if I were you)"'; he further cites an allusive example in *The Advertiser* (Australia), 21 Sep. 1978: '... Victorian racing administrators, while expressing some interest in a recently mooted $2–3 m. race for Flemington [a famous racecourse] are not holding their breaths waiting for it to happen.'

don't hurry, Hopkins! was, *c.* 1865–1900, a US c.p., addressed to (very) slow persons; Farmer remarks that it is 'used ironically in the West in speaking to persons who are very slow in their work, or tardy in meeting an obligation'. It derived from the C17–18 English proverbial or semi-

proverbial *as well come* – or *as hasty* – *as Hopkins, that came to jail overnight and was hanged the next morning*, which clearly implied 'Don't be too hasty!'

don't I know it!, expressing, somewhat ruefully, 'How well I know it!' – is both US (recorded by, e.g., Berrey) and Brit. – and arose *c.* 1880, if not considerably earlier.

don't it beat the band! Current in US in C20; recorded in, e.g., the *Boston Globe* of *c.* 1970. A var. of **that beats the band.**

don't just stand there: do something! orig., very naturally, as a literal exhortation. But it has been so frequently employed that, *c.* 1940, it became a c.p., both Brit. and US, with a connotation either humorous or allusive or, indeed, both, as in the title of the US Charles Williams's exciting and delightful novel, *Don't Just Stand There*, 1966. It was, I suppose, inevitable that some wit should reverse it to *don't do anything – just stand there!* R.C., 1977, adds 'Perhaps the best-known reversal is from Father Philip Bonigan, epitomising passive resistance: "Don't just do something–stand there!"' And perhaps the most amusing is Bob Hope's saying to the strip-tease dancer Gipsy Rose Lee: 'Don't just stand there – undo something,? in the 1940s. (Thanks to David F. Nicol, 1978.) Cf **don't do anything ...**, q.v.

don't keep a good woman waiting! 'Advice in a social context, with sexual innuendo' (L.A., 1969): humorous rather than euph.: late C19–20.

don't knock it! 'It may not be exactly what you, or we, wanted, but it's by no means worthless.' 'It could be a lot worse than it is.' US: since late 1930s. An elab. appeared in the 1960s: *don't knock it if you haven't tried it*, i.e. 'don't criticise it if ...', a response by a practitioner of some more or less unconventional activity to a critic of it, when many such activities burgeoned among youths and some others. (R.C., 1978).

don't knock the rock! was orig. (1957) the title of the main song in the Columbia film so titled and featuring Bill Haley and the Comets. A year earlier, Bill Haley and his Comets had appeared in *Rock Around the Clock*, which contained a valedictory c.p. that became famous: *see you later, alligator*. (Ronald Pearsall, 1975.) It promptly migrated to UK, where it tended to be used to express resentment at criticism of Rock-and-Roll. An illuminating commentary has, also in 1975, been sent to me by Mr Cyril Whelan:

[It] can be placed more or less precisely at 1957 [that is, as a c.p.]. Small-town America, pre-Vietnam ... fresh-faced youth worries only about acne, high-school grades, Peggy-Sue next door, and the new Rock 'n' Roll developing from jazz and black rhythm and blues into a white mainstream of music exclusively for the newly *post*-pubescent. ... *The Rock* was Rock 'n' Roll. Hence *don't knock the rock* = Mummy and Daddy, don't chastise the new music, it symbolizes once and for all [the belief] that Generation is private property (the myth of every generation?). The phrase was extremely powerful until the late 1950s, when 'the Rock' became increasingly *passé* – until it was embarrassingly outmoded by the new popular music developments.

But Mr Ben Grauer has, much later in 1975, assured me that it lives again, and means 'Don't ignore the strength and reliability of *X* – person, institution, custom – with ultimate ref. to the Rock of Gibraltar.

don't know ... See **doesn't know ...**; **know from a bar of soap**; and: **don't know from nothing.** See **I don't know ...**

don't know who's which from when's what (– I). I know nothing whatever about it: lower classes' c.p., according to Ware: 1897–*c.* 1905.

don't laugh, lady: your daughter may be inside! was, during the Aus. 1950s, painted on old cars driven by young people, but was also used by young people in general in ref. to such cars. 'Young people rarely own old cars in this more affluent era' (B.P., 1975). 'Also, and probably earlier, US' (R.C., 1977).

don't let anyone sell you a wooden nutmeg!, later shortened to **don't take any wooden nutmegs!**, 'stems from Colonial days when sharpers or itinerant peddlers in Connecticut sold imitation nutmegs carved out of wood [and] was a common admonition to the unwary' (W.J.B., 1975; he adds that 'Connecticut is sometimes called "The Nutmeg State"'). T.C. Haliburton, in *The Clockmaker; or, The Sayings and Doings of Sam Slick, of Slicksville*, 1837, mentions 'the facture of wooden nutmegs, ... a real Yankee patent invention' (Olives Stonor, 1977). See also **don't take any wooden nickels!**

don't let me catch you bending! was, *c.* 1890–1960, a joc. c.p., implying 'Don't let me catch you at a disadvantage.' (P.G. Wodehouse, *Psmith in the City*, 1910; Lyell.) A person bending invites a kick. Cf **my word, if I catch ...**

don't let your braces dangle in the shit! is a workmen's, by adoption a Servicemen's, c.p. of late C19–20, but I never heard it in the WW2 army or RAF. In the army of 1914–18 it was sometimes chanted. P.B.: but a version lingers on, in the chorus of a bawdy, uproarious song about a man who put a lobster in his wife's chamber-pot: 'Row-tiddly-oh, shit or bust! Never let your goolies [testicles] dangle in the dust!'

don't let your mouth overload your ass – less commonly, **don't let your mouth buy what your ass can't pay for** – least commonly, **don't let your mouth write a check your ass can't cash** all mean 'Don't talk too much' and esp. 'Don't boast': 'argot elicited from Black male youths living in the South central Los Angeles ghetto' (Folb): since *c.* 1960, at a guess. Extremely localized, but because of its pungent earthiness and vividness, worth recording. (In localization, cf **don't give me that toffee!**)

don't let's be beastly to the poor Germans was current from the middle 1920s to the very early 1930s, and then rapidly less up to WW2, and was very popular among those inhabitants of Great Britain, particularly the 'intellectuals', who hadn't suffered much during WW1; especially perhaps among the women writers and artists and musicians.

Then, in WW2, a shortened form – *don't let's be beastly to the Germans*, arose: Noël Coward dignified the original by that omission of *poor*, to retain which would have been farcical. The long lyric was sung by Coward in his inimitably conversational 'throw-away' manner, so much more effectual than an emphatically jingoistic treatment could ever have been. He both created and, in a sense, revived this c.p.

don't let's play games! is 'used when a person tries to evade the issue by quibbling or prevaricating' (Petch, 1974), the sense being 'Don't waste time by fooling about'. I first heard it *c.* 1960, but I think it arose very soon after the end (1945) of WW2.

P.B.: an earlyish occurrence is in Patrick Campbell, *Life in Thin Slices*, a 1951 reprint of collected magazine pieces: '"Girls," I said, "let's not play about. Let's exercise our *minds*."'

don't look down! You'd soon find the hole (or, allusively, **you'd find it soon enough) if there was hair round it!** is an army drill-sergeant's admonition to recruits as they fumble to fix bayonets – when practised, they don't need to look: late C19–20. Ribald and pertinent. B & P.

don't look now, but I think we'e being followed (or **but I think someone's following us**) became, *c.* 1933, a c.p., joc. allusive to timorous women's mostly imaginary fear; by 1960, †, the fear remaining, but mostly of *not* being followed. P.B.: the shortened form, *don't look now, but*, may now, 1982, be ob. but is by no means extinct; it is used to another person or small group, joc., when drawing attention to, or commenting upon, e.g. someone else who has just entered a restaurant. The speaker knows full well that his hearers are likely at once to swing round to look.

don't lose your cool! Don't lose your temper: 'common in the 1960s, but seems to be dying out' (Sanders, 1978). Adopted from US.

don't make a Federal case of it! (Often prec. by *all right* or *OK* or some other protestation, and occ. *let's not* instead of *don't*.) W&F, 1960, define *make a ...* as 'to overemphasize

the importance of something; especially, to exaggerate someone's mistake or bad judgement when criticizing or reprimanding him.' R.C., 1976, 'Most likely, I think, originally cant [the language of the underworld], from the fact that criminal cases in Federal courts are more difficult to "fix" than others' (i.e., in State or municipal courts). US, since late 1940s; by 1964, current in Aus. (Jack Slater, 1978), and occ. heard also in UK (P.B.).

don't make a Judy (Fitzsimmons) of yourself! Don't make a fool of yourself *or* Don't be a fool!: perhaps orig. Anglo-Irish: since earlyish C19. Harold Shapiro, 1977, notes that Ruskin wrote in a letter dated 1845, 'We shall make such Judy Fitzsimmons of ourselves as never were'. John Brougham, in the final scene of *Po-Ca-Hon-Tas, or The Gentle Savage* (a play full of puns, mostly outrageous), performed in 1855, allows himself this absurdity:

SMITH: *Judas!* You haven't yet sub*dued* John Smith!
KING: Don't make a *Judy* of yourself!

But who was the original Judy Fitzsimmons?

don't make a meal of it! (– **all right,**). 'Sometimes said to a person who is making a long story of nothing much' (Petch, 1968); also, 'You're going on too long about the matter' or You're making far too much fuss about it' or even 'Oh! Stop moaning!' since *c.* 1950. Cf:

don't make a production of it! (– **all right!**) dates from the late 1930s and is addressed to one who makes a simple matter seem difficult and very important; very common among Servicemen during WW2; ob. by 1970, but still far from †. It derives from film (moving picture)-makers' productions; cf Royal Navy's slang phrase, *make an evolution*, to do something with maximum fuss.

don't make I laugh, it makes I pee I's drawers! '(Mock-yokel, mock-feminine, used by boys and men). Indicates "protest" at being overcome by fooling and jocularity, and thus keeps jollity going' (L.A., 1974). These are variants of this theme: cf:

don't make me laugh: I've got a split lip! (or **I've cut my lip!**) This C20 c.p., moribund by 1940, yet not, in its shorter form, dead by 1976, occurs in, e.g., Leonard Merrick's *Peggy Harper*, 1911, in the form ... *I've got a split lip* and in Collinson, as ... *I've cut my lip*; since *c.* 1920, mostly shortened to *don't make me laugh*, whence, since *c.* 1925, *don't make me smile*, which has, since *c.* 1930, had a humorous var. *don't make I smile* (mercifully a short-lived var.). An excellent example of the shortened form comes in John Mortimer's *Gloucester Road*, one of the four short plays comprising John Mortimer's *Come As You are*, all prod. at the New Theatre, London, on 27 Jan. 1970 and pub'd in 1971:

BUNNY: [*To Mike, her husband.*] You're jealous!
MIKE: Jealous! Of that (*Lost for words*)... four letter man. That wet handshake with his co-respondent's shoes and a bit of Brillo pad stuck under his nose. ... Jealous ... of Toby Delgado! Don't make me laugh!

Don't make me laugh! was adopted by the US, apparently *c.* 1918 or 1919, Berrey recording also the predominantly US var. *don't make me laugh – I've got a cracked lip.* The earliest printed record of the US use of *don't make me laugh* I happen to have noted occurs in Leonard Hastings Nason, *A Corporal Once*, 1930; and I owe that to Col. Moe.

Cf **you make me laugh.**

don't make waves! See **sit down, you're rocking the boat!**

don't mensh! was a lower-middle-class c.p. of *c.* 1900–39, WW2 apparently and creditably killing it off. Obviously it derives from the polite formula, *don't mention it!*, itself prob. elliptical for ... (*for*) *it's a trifle.* Cf:

don't mention that! was current only *c.* 1882–4; arising topically from a notorious libel case, as Ware tells us, it naturally disappeared soon after the case lost its attraction for the public. In form, it deliberately varies the *don't mention it* of the prec. entry.

don't mind if I do. See **I don't mind ...**

don't mind me! Go ahead – don't mind me!: usu. ironic, with an undertone of resentment: late C19–20. Cf **are you in my way?**

don't mock the afflicted! 'which we used to say at Dulwich [College] when someone made an earnest balls-up of a job' (Simon Levene, 1977), is included to exemplify the admittedly rather obvious point that there exist, all over the world, what we might call parochial or 'in' c.pp. unknown to the rest of us.

don't monkey with the buzz-saw! 'Don't interfere, or involve yourself, with the person or situation under discussion, or you might get hurt: gen. US, C20 or earlier, now certainly ob. and perhaps†' (R.C., 1977).

don't open your eyes: (or) you'll bleed to death. This 'heartless morning greeting to one with a hangover' was current among RN officers in the 1950s and '60s, and perhaps later. (Cdr C. Parsons, 1977.) I heard this in the 1960s among Army NCOs (P.B.). Cf **eyes like piss-holes** ...

don't pee in your pants! 'Said to a fidgety, impatient fellow: American: since c. 1930 (?). Fidgetiness is, among children, a sign that they need to pass water; among adults, more usually of impatience' (George A. Krzymowski, 1978).

don't pick me up before I fall, applied to a premature correction or criticism, prob. goes back to late C18: cf Bill Truck, 'The Man-of-War's Man' in *Blackwood's Edinburgh Magazine*, Jan. 1822, 'O ho! my smart fellows, don't you be after picking me up before I fall.'

don't pipe it! See **all right! Don't** ...

don't play silly buggers. See **let's not play** ...

don't push the panic button! Don't panic!; esp., Whatever you do, don't panic unnecessarily: 'nuclear age' (as Fain describes it) – but, as a c.p., only since c. 1950. The ref. is to a button that, once pressed, will cause a nuclear warhead to be released.

Cf **panic stations**, q.v.

don't push your pulheems! This c.p., current in a smallish part of the British Army later 1960s, affords an excellent example of those c.pp. so specialist and so tending to be ephemeral that they may fairly be excluded from a general dictionary, yet are so apt that one excludes them with regret. P.B., 1974, described it as a var. of **don't push** (or **crowd**) **your luck!**, i.e. do not presume too much upon your present state of reasonably good fortune to demand further beneficence. 'PULHEEMS is an acronym for the points checked in judging a serviceman's fitness: *p*hysical capacity; *u*pper limbs; *l*ocomotion; *h*earing; *ee*: left and right *e*yes; *m*ental capacity; *s*tability, mental and physical'.

don't ring us: we'll ring you, an occ. var. of **don't call us** ..., q.v., occurs in, e.g., John Mortimer, *Collaborators*, 1973 – in Act II, allusively.

don't rock the boat! Don't disturb the *status quo!* Everything's going nicely – don't start spoiling things: since c. 1950, at least as an established c.p., as in Philip Purser, *The Holy Father's Navy*, 1971:

'Maybe we don't want to rock the boat.'

'Don't rock the boat! – It could be the BBC call-sign these days.'

See also **sit down: you're rocking the boat!** Note also the 'usage in politics and the City to prevent a maverick from going his own way' (Norman Franklin, 1976).

don't say I told you! is an Anglo-Irish c.p. of late C19–20. Cf the more usual, and expressive, **mind you, I've said nothing**, q.v.

don't say No until (usu. **till**) **you are** (usu. **you're**) **asked!** Addressed to one who has declined an offer or an invitation before it has been made: C18–20. Orig., *don't you say no* ..... as in Dialogue I of S. In C19–20 *before* is occ. substituted for *until*, and *invited* for *asked*. Also, mid C19–20: *it's manners to wait until you are* – or *till you're* – *asked*. Cf **I wouldn't say No!**

don't see it! See **I don't see it!**

don't sell me a dog! Don't deceive, don't cheat, me!: society: c.

1860–80. (Ware.) Cf the slangy *to sell someone a pup*, to swindle him.

don't shit in your (or **the**) **mess-kit!** and **don't fall back in it!** Don't foul your own nest: US: since c. 1942. (A.B., 1978.)

don't shit the troops! See **you wouldn't shit me**.

don't shoot the pianist! (or, as orig., **do not** ...) **he's doing his best** was adopted, c. 1918, from the US, where current, at first as a saloon notice in the Wild West, since c. 1860. A US var. was *don't shoot the piano-player: he's doing the best he can*. According to Stevenson, the correct form was *please do not shoot the pianist – he is doing his best*, and Stevenson's gloss is: 'Oscar Wilde, telling of a notice seen by him in a Western bar-room during his American tour, in a lecture delivered in 1883.' An occ. var. is **don't shoot the engine-driver** ...

don't shoot until you see the whites of their eyes. See **don't fire** ... .

don't sing it! See **don't chant the poker!**

don't some mothers 'ave 'em! See **some mothers do** ...

don't spare the horses. See the third paragraph of **home, James** ... .

don't spend it all at once! or ... **all in one place!** See **here's a ha'penny** ...

don't spit: remember the Johnstown Flood orig. in – and prob. began to be used very soon after – the great flood on 31 May 1889 and was 'killed' either by the disaster of Pearl Harbor on 10 Dec. 1941, as I used to think, or by Prohibition, as Dr Joseph T. Shipley expounded the matter in a letter to me, 1974:

In the saloons* that abounded before Prohibition [1919–33] some had sawdust strewn on the floor (even in the big cities like New York) for readier absorption of spilled beer and expectorations, for easier sweeping. And of course they all had NO SPITTING signs. I remember signs with comic turns – used in the saloons, but also on sale in the stores that specialize in party novelties, signs, and practical jokes: NO SPITTING ALOUD: DON'T SPIT: REMEMBER THE JOHNSTOWN FLOOD.

During Prohibition, the speakeasies had a different make-up, with emphasis on quiet drinking, mainly of hard liquors. And after repeal, in 1933, the law required every place that sold liquor to sell food – hence a different structure, with a front bar where usually both men and women congregated, and no longer any promiscuous spitting – no spittoon.

In 1912 – I remember the date because it was my Senior year at college – I saw a burlesque act. Two bums see a pretty girl, sitting on a park bench. They plot to 'make' her. The dominant one tells the other to go by and insult her; then he will come along, chase him away, comfort the girl – and win her. They start; when the second drives the first away, and she turns to her rescuer, she cries on his shoulder – and he says: DON'T CRY: REMEMBER THE JOHNSTOWN FLOOD. The audience howled at the turn of the known expression.

* His footnote: 'Saloons were open to men only. Spittoons everywhere!'

In *The American Language*, HLM wrote thus (on p. 424 of the 2nd edn. 1921): 'It would be difficult to match, in any other folk-literature, such examples [of extravagant and pungent humour] as "I'd rather have them say 'There he goes', than 'Here he lies'"' or "Don't spit: remember the Johnstown Flood".'

don't step back ... See **there's shit not far behind**.

don't strain yourself! 'C.p. sarcasm at slow, as if indifferent, co-operation' (L.A., 1974): C20, perhaps earlier. I first heard it, c. 1913, in Aus., and R.C., 1977, vouches for its use in the US over the same period.

don't sweat it! Take it easy – above all, don't worry!: US: since c. 1960. Recorded by *DCCU*. P.B.: in later C20 UK, shortened to *no sweat!*

don't take any wooden nickels! is described by W & F as 'a c.

1920 fad phrase' and glossed as 'Take care of yourself; protect yourself' (a wooden nickel having, of course, no legal value): but this US c.p. lasted right up to WW2 and dates, I suspect, since *c.* 1900. It was adopted by Canadians; Leechman, 1959, remarking in a letter to me, 'A c.p. of the last fifty years, and still heard occasionally'. And note that in Ring W. Lardner's *The Real Dope*, 1919, it occurs in Jack Keefe's letter of 16 May 1918, thus: 'In the mean wile' – until we meet again – 'don't take no wood nickles and don't get impatient and be a good girlie and save up your loving for me.' Cf **don't let anyone sell you a wooden nutmeg!**

don't take it out, Chiefie. I'll walk off. This RN c.p., dating since *c.* 1930 (? a decade earlier), is a seaman's conciliatory joke to the Chief Petty Officer after a reprimand.

don't take me up until I fall. See **don't pick me up ...** This var. in P.W. Joyce, *English in Ireland*, 1910.

don't tear it, lady! '[I] suggest a witticism, meaning – originally, at any rate – "Don't unfold and investigate the goods so actively", don't pull things around' (Wedgewood, 1977, commenting on E.P.'s orig. idea that the phrase perhaps started among London's street-markets). But the derivative sense, the true sense of the c.p., was explained by Anthony Burgess in *The TLS*, 26 Aug. 1977, thus: '[It] should properly be followed by *I'll take the piece* ... [and] it refers to a woman breaking wind'. And in *Books and Bookmen*, Oct. 1977, Oliver Stonor, also, reminds me of the dovetail and adds that the c.p. occurs in A.M. Binstead, *Gal's Gossip* (very early 1900s.) Cf:

don't (or, occ., **let's not**) **tear the arse out of it!** All right, there's no need to exaggerate! *or* you are putting too much, and unnecessary, effort into what you are doing: Army: since mid-C20. A var. is *don't* (or *let's not*) *kick the bottom out of it!* (P.B.)

don't tell me! and **never tell me!** Don't tell me that – it's too silly (or too preposterous or too incredible) to believe: respectively mid C18 – 20 and, by 1935 slightly ob.; and C17 – 20 and, by 1935, extremely ob. and, by 1970, †. The *OED* quotes Shakespeare in *Othello* and Foote (*don't ... !*).

don't tell *me*: I'll tell *you!* is either repressive or merely anticipatory – of someone clearly about to impart a piece of news or scandal already known to the speaker: since the latter half of WW2 (Shaw, 1968.) It soon came (*c.* 1950) to acquire the nuance 'I already know the answer, perhaps better than you do'. In 1969, a well-known diagnostician told me about one of his clients, a man self-confident and something of a know-all, who visits him several times a year and always initiates the encounter by saying 'Don't tell me – I'll tell you'. Contrast:

don't tell me: let me guess! This humorous anticipatory c.p. dates from *c.* 1940 and, in its early period, was often prec. by **no!** and occ. by **now**. Also in the early days, the predominant form was ... *I'll guess*. R.C., 1978, adds that 'In the US, the implication is "You don't need to tell me, I know it already."'

don't tell me your troubles. I suggested to E.P. in 1976 that the more usu. Brit. form of **you have your troubles**, q.v., is *don't tell me your troubles, I* ['ve] *got troubles of my own*, which I think was a song title. (P.B.)

don't tell more than six. A joc. roundabout way of saying 'Don't tell anyone!': Londoners': June 1937 – Aug. 1939. (I can no longer remember why, in *DSUE*, I could be so precise; there once existed an excellent reason.)

don't thank me: buy me something! See **don't applaud ...**

don't thou thee-thou me! See **doan't tha ...**

[**don't throw the baby out with the bath-water**, which appeared in the 1st ed. of this Dict., is more proverb than c.p., and is treated accordingly in the *Concise Oxford Dictionary of Proverbs*, 1982. P.B.]

don't touch what you can't afford. 'I was at the local builder's recently, buying some cement. One assistant reached behind his colleague to get a bill and caressed the latter's back with mock affection. This was the response' (John B. Smith,

Bath, 1979). The innuendo is clear, but for the form, cf **if you vant to buy a vatch**, q.v.

don't turn that side to London. This commercial c.p., condemning either goods or persons, implies that in London only the best is wanted. Ware records it in 1909 and I'd guess that its approx. life began *c.* 1890 and ended in 1914.

don't wake him up! is enshrined in HLM, 1921. 'Poor fellow! He lives in the past – or in a pleasant day dream – or in a state of euphoria; and it'd be a pity to wake him.' Contrast:

don't wake it (later, more usu. **that**) **up!** Don't talk about it, it's better to drop and forget the subject. In short, let sleeping dogs lie. Aus.: since *c.* 1920. Orig. entry corrected by Neil Lovett, in *The National Times*, 23 – 28 Jan. 1978.

don't want to know! In British jails of C20 this is a prisoners' plea of ignorance. It amounts to 'I don't know and I don't want to know – safer *not* to'. P.B.: in later C20 this plea, or statement, has had a much wider usage than E.P. allows here, in the sense 'Don't tell me [your reasons, excuses, etc.]!' Also transferable, as in 'How did you get on? Did you manage to convince them?' – 'No chance! They just didn't want to know.'

don't we all? See **aren't we all?**

don't wear it: eat it! a US c.p. of very approx. 1930 – 45, was addressed to 'a sloppy eater' (Berrey).

don't worry: it may never happen is intended as salutary advice to the worried-looking or, still more joc., to the merely thoughtful-looking: since *c.* 1916. Current during WW1, but chiefly among civilians, was an elongated version, 'thought up' by one of the intellectuals of the day. Cf **don't you fret!**

don't worry: use Sunlight! was current during the first thirty years of C20 and was adopted from a famous advertisement for Sunlight Soap. (Collinson.) The late Alexander McQueen, that very erudite Englishman who migrated to the US, vouched, in a letter, 1953, for its use by, or slightly before, 1905.

don't you fear! (or **don't fear!**) has two nuances: 'Take my word for it' and 'Certainly not!': since *c.* 1870; by 1940, rather old-fashioned; by 1970, virtually †. Cf **never fear!**

don't you forget it! See **and don't you forget it!**

don't you fret! (or **don't fret!**) You have no cause to worry – addressed sarcastically to someone worrying needlessly: late C19 – 20; by 1950, the former was decidedly old-fashioned, and by 1970, the latter was falling into disuse. Somewhat more crudely expressed is the synon. *don't* (*you*) *worry your fat!*, from earlier C20. Cf. **don't worry: it may never happen** and **I should worry**.

don't you know there's a war on? See **remember there's a war on!**

don't you wish you knew! Wouldn't you like to know? *or* I won't tell you: US: since *c.* 1920; by 1970, slightly ob. Berrey.

don't you wish you may get it! was a c.p. of *c.* 1830 – 60; it means 'I don't think much of your chance of getting it' and therefore 'I'll bet you don't get it!' It occurs in R.H. Barham, *The Ingoldsby Legends*, Second Series, 1842 (see the quot'n at **does your mother know you're out?**), and in a couple of the very early issues of *Punch*, i.e. in the early 1840s.

doom and gloom, gloom and doom. A recurrent phrase of the leprechaun, played by Tommie Steele, in the film 'Finian's Rainbow', 1968. The phrase prob. did not orig. with the film; rather, the film gave focus to an expression engendered by anti-nuclear anxiety: *gloom-and-doom* has continued in use, often as an adj., until the early 1980s. Cf next. (P.B.)

doomed! We be all doomed! – we be. C.p. uttered by Spasm, butler to Lady Counterblast, in the radio-comedy series 'Round the Horne' (1965 – 67): '"Get thee away from this doomed pile" croaks the old loony. "We be doomed – we all be doomed"' (*Round the Horne*, by Barry Took & Marty Feldman, 1974, p. 11). Spasm was played by Kenneth Williams. The phrase was often rendered loosely, by would-be imitators, as *doomed, doomed, we're all doomed!,* and people were still, in the earlier 1970s, saying 'Oh, doom!' at any slight – or not so slight – mishap. (P.B.)

door(s). See: bangs like; brass knocker; fall through; goodbye, and; leaves his fiddle; lost the key; near the; never darken; next way; open the d.; please, mother; shut that; there is the d.; wrong side; you make a better.

doorstep. See: never shit; you don't shit.

Dorgan. See: 'TAD'· DORGAN.

double. See: and that goes; makes you see; men over.

double-breasted. See: where men.

double helping too – and a. 'Said of a very attractive girl. She's got twice as much as most. Post-WW2' (Sanders, 1978).

doubt. See: no possible; there's no d.; when in danger; when in doubt.

dough. See: let's see.

doughnut. See: take a running; that accounts.

Dover waggoner. See: put this.

down. See: don't look down; I'm down; iron's down; it's a good flat; left hand; put her d.; send her d.; that's what; trap is; what goes up; what's going; you can't keep.

down, Fido! and the synon. **down, Rover!** are feminine commands to desist from intimate approaches: 'Simmer down!' or 'Cool down!'; but also 'Get off your high horse' – 'Don't be "stuffy" [stiff or haughty]': US: C20. (W. J. B., 1977.) Cf **down, Upsey!**

down in the forest something stirred; burlesqued as **down in the forest something's turd.** This domestic c.p., referring sometimes to incipient sexual desire in either partner or esp. in both, and sometimes to a consummated coition, dates from 1915, when Sir Landon Ronald's very popular song was pub'd. A few years later (1920 at latest) the irrepressible Cockney parodied that c.p. by applying it to a bird's, mostly a pigeon's, droppings landed on someone, the remark being uttered by onlooker or, wryly, by victim.

down on his knees and it! A male 'facetious exclamation at [the sight of] a man kneeling down to do a job of work' (L.A., 1974); hence, a joc. ref. to a man performing a marital duty: since the 1920s.

down (or up) the Swanee (– going). On the slippery slope, or already gone, to perdition, bankruptcy and ruin: I first heard the *down* version in 1980, 'There's several textile firms already down the Swanee, and now Courtaulds look likely to follow' (Ian Pearsall, Barrow-in-Furness), the synon. *up* form appeared a couple of years later. But why this echo of Stephen Foster's famous song. *The Old Folks at Home?* (P.B.)

down to Larkin (– it's). It's costing nothing, as in '"Who is paying for this round?" – "Shush! It's down to Larkin"' (Powis, *Signs of Crime*, 1977). This is an underworld and near-underworld c.p., dating since *c.* 1950. I've been unable to trace precisely who *Larkin* was: the best I can do is to guess that he was either a generous landlord or 'one of the last of the big-time spenders'. (Note made 1978.)

down, Upsey! 'Joan Harben as a fast-talking character in *ITMA*, to her dog' (*VIBS*). See TOMMY HANDLEY. There may have been a *double entendre* in the show itself – the phrase was always an interruption to the main gist of Joan Harben's monologue – but I, as a child, was unaware of it. It soon, however, came to be used in the same way as **down, Fido!**, above. (P.B.)

down went McGinty was a US c.p. of 1889 – *c.* 1914. This was a song, words by Joe Flynn, who sang it with Sheridan in 1899 and thus fathered the c.p. (W.J.B.) Cf **up goes McGinty's goat.** J.W.C. notes, 1979, that while it was current, it was nearly always followed by *to the bottom of the sea.*

downhearted. See: are we d.

dozens. See: we had d.

drag. See: like something; my arse is; what you can't.

drag! – it's a and **what a drag!** It's a bore, a tremendous nuisance, What a bore *or* nuisance!: since the early 1950s, when it came to England from the US; by 1980, somewhat ob.

dragged screaming from the tart shop is an Aus. c.p., 'applied to politicians who have come reluctantly to face an election', and first used by Alfred Deakin in 1904. (Wilkes, 1978.) The tart shop is a confectioner's, not a brothel.

draw. See: long may.

drawers. See: don't make I laugh; give him Maggie's; it's all over now; red hat; up and down; up with petticoats; winter drawers.

drawing-board. See: back to the d.

dream. See: did you ever see; I dreamt; I'm dreaming.

dress. See: this won't buy.

dressed-up. See: all dressed; horses that are; mutton.

drift. See: get the d.; snow again.

drill. See: doesn't know; what's the d.

drink. See: another little; from drinking; give it a drink; he pisses; he'd drink; I never d.; I'll drink; it's a long time; must have been drinking; one drink; too thick.

drinking classes. See: work is.

drip. See: what a d.

dripping. See: good for your mother; like the butcher's.

drop. See: good to; has the penny; I nearly; not a bad; penny has; tune in; when you dance; you've dropped.

drop dead! and its var., **why don't you drop dead!**, are US in origin and, in US, date from the late 1930s (W&F's earliest recording is for 1951, but the longer phrase appears in Berrey, 1942). Only the terse, more telling, form migrated to UK *c.* 1949, to become almost a status symbol of teenagers, probably via Can., where well-established by *c.* 1946. It is only fair to the US and Can. to add that there, too, it was used mainly by teenagers; although, in all three countries rather old-fashioned by 1965, it was still being employed by Brit. teenagers as late as 1974; not unnaturally, this particular callousness, being so vigorous and effective, was fostered by the film companies. An illuminating late Brit. example occurs in Paul Geddes's novel, *A November Wind*, 1970:

'I don't have to worry,' said Wetherton. 'You do.'
The man smiled briefly. 'Do you mind if I ask you a favour? Drop dead.' It wasn't fresh, but he said it well, even with panache.

Cf also this example from John Osborne's *Look Back in Anger* (prod. 1956 and pub'd 1957), at III, i:

JIMMY: ... Let's have that paper, stupid!
CLIFF: Why don't you drop dead!

drop dead twice! intensifies the c.p. preceding this one: US: since early 1960s. Recorded by *DCCU*. Often 'initialled' *D.D.T.*

drop off! 'Desist!' or 'Depart!' – according to circumstances: Aus., mostly among teenagers: late 1960s – mid 1970s. (Neil Lovett, 1978.) Prob. set going by **drop dead!**, q.v., itself long current in Aus., until ousted by this version.

drop the gun, Louis! An 'impressionist's phrase that appears to have been invented rather that quoted [cf **I want to be alone**]. What Humphrey Bogart says to Claude Rains in [the film] *Casablanca* [1942] is no more than "Not so fast, Louis!"' (*VIBS*).

drop your cocks ... See **come on, let's be having you!**

drop the other shoe! 'Well, go ahead and say the next obvious thing!' Both Brit. and US, but much commoner in the former, it covers most of C20, although rarely heard since the 1930s. It arose from a story about a lodging-house.

drop your traces and rest awhile, addressed to a coach- or a buggy-driver; **fall off and cool your saddle**, variants **get off and rest your hat** and **light and rest your saddle**, addressed to a horse-rider: Western US c.pp. of late C19–20, but rare even in the wildest and woolliest West, by 1945. Berrey.

dropped right in it, with prec. I stated or, at least, understood. I really fell in the shit!; occ. 'I really did put my foot in it' – but mostly, 'I truly got into serious, or very awkward, trouble': since *c.* 1910; 'still heard on and off' (Petch, 1971).

drown. See: I'll shoot; not waving; she'll never; take a dagger.

drowned policeman. See: better than a dig.

drums. See: natives are.

drummer. See: it's a different.

dry. See: I have no pain; I work; it all rubs; it dries; laugh?; not a dry; sent; tap run; your pump.

dry up and blow away! Go away – don't bother me!: teenagers', esp. the coffee-bar set: c. 1957–9. A blend, prob. inconscient, of the slang *dry up!* ('Stop talking!') and *blow!* ('Go away! Depart!'). Inherently artificial, this witticism soon perished. Recorded by Michael Gilderdale in his article, 'A Glossary of Our Times' in the *News Chronicle*, 22 May 1958.

dry your eyes! A response to one who has been indulging in self-pity: Aus.: since the late 1940s. (Mrs Camilla Raab, 1977.)

Duchess. See: 'fuck me!'; 'hell!', said; ring up; you're a long time coming.

duck(s). See: all duck; board the monkey; crutches; do I ducks; fine day; get your ducks; go fuck; happy as ducks; I forgot to duck; it fits him; nice weather; tight as; wanna buy; weaving; what's the difference; you can't quack.

duck swim? – can or **could a**; or, less often, **does a duck swim?** In answer to a question, it expresses 'Well, of course' or 'Obviously'. It has been common to both the UK since latish C19 and to the US since c. 1900. (R.C.) It could be regarded as the c.p. form of the proverbial *will a duck swim?*: cf *ODEP*, 3rd ed., p. 207. Cf also James Joyce, *Ulysses*, 1922 (p. 405 of the standard ed.): ' "Could you make a hole in another pint?" – "Could a duck swim?" says I' (reminder from Simon Levene). A var. is *will a fish swim?* Cf AMERICAN RESPONSES.

duckhouse. See: that's one up.

ducky. See: isn't that just too.

dug up. See: do you think I've.

duke. See: give my regards to the duke; gradely; when the Duke; who dealt; you going; you're a long.

Duke of Argyll. See: God bless.

dull. See: never a dull.

dumb. See: beautiful but; deft; molasses in; of all the d.; so dumb.

dump. See: what a d.

dun is (but usu. **dun's**) **the mouse** is both a c.p. and a quibble, made when someone says 'done'; when spoken urgently, it implies 'Keep still and quiet!' It was current c. 1580–1640. A mouse is dun coloured and therefore, if still, hard to see. A later form (C17) is *dun as a mouse*, which seems to have arisen from a confusion of *dun's*: 'dun is', and *duns*: 'dun as'. Apperson.

Dunkirk. See: biggest fuck-up; that's the old D.

dunny. See: all alone; hope your; if it was raining.

duration. See: roll on, big.

Durban. See: off to D.

dust. See: another Redskin; could fall; don't let your braces; excuse my dust; fall out and; I'm off in a cloud; watch my; where the crows; you couldn't see.

dustbin. See: like the man who fought.

Dutch. See: that beats; and:

Dutch are in Holland – the. A WW1 children's catch, prec. by, e.g. 'Heard the latest?' or 'D'you know what's happened?', although prob. it goes back a long way before 1914, for *the Dutch have taken Holland* was a C17 – early 18 form of *Queen Anne's dead.* (P.B., with thanks to my mother-in-law, Mrs Phyllis Hughes, 1983.)

Dutchman. See: I cut; I'm a D.; wind enough.

duty calls! 'Excuse me, I must go to the Gents' (little used by women for the Ladies'): since c. 1916, at latest, as an Army officers' c.p., and among civilians since c. 1919. It occurred in ITV's 'Coronation Street', episode broadcast 21 Dec. 1966 (Petch).

dying. See: high cost.

dynamite. See: don't dynamite; what's the d.

d'you... See also entries at **do you...**

d'you know something? was adopted, c. 1945, from the US, where it had existed since c. 1930. It could, orig. have been prompted by the Ger. *Weisst du 'was* (short for *etwas*), 'Do you know what?' – and have come into US speech via the Ger. immigrants, as Foster suggests.

d'you mind? is the more coll. form of **do you mind?**

d'you need (or **want**) **a knife and fork?** See **sort 'em out!**

d'you (occ. **d'ye**) **want jam on both sides?** is a British Army c.p., essentially of WW1, although it lingered on, among the older men, into WW2; it was addressed to someone making an unreasonable request. (B & P.)

But the more usual – and gen. – form was *d'you want jam on it?*, Haven't you had enough? Aren't you satisfied? This seems to have been the earlier, perhaps an elab., of *jam on it*, a most agreeable surplus – and common to all three Services – and lasting rather longer.

It was not unknown in the US, where however, the paired **d'you want egg in your beer?** or **do you want beer with egg in it?** are much commoner. J.W.C. adds, 1977, 'As a matter of fact, not a bad combination': which, after all, forms the whole point of the question.

See also **what do you want? Eggs...** , and **what do you want? Jam...**

E

'e. For *'e don't know where 'e lives* see **doesn't know...**, and for *'e never 'ad no mother* see **he never...**

'e be arf (or 'alf) sharp, 'e be. 'Dialect, e.g. Sussex dialect, or mock dialect, said of one who lacks understanding of his, or the, circumstances' (L.A., 1977). Elliptical for *...only 'arf sharp*: C20; but as a c.p., prob. not earlier than *c.* 1930 and apparently ob, by *c.* 1970.

'e dunno where 'e are! was a c.p., predominantly Cockney, of the 1890s; it was applied to a half-wit or, at best, a moron or, rather, to someone acting in such a way; and esp. to one who has lost his sense of reality. Julian Franklyn, who knew so much of and about the music-halls, once told me that this c.p. arose in a music-hall song: 'Since Jack Jones come into a 'arf a'nounce o' snuff, 'e dunno where 'e are. 'E's got the cheek and impudence to call 'ee's muvver Ma.' The song was sung by Gus Elen (1863–1940) during the Edwardian period. (See, e.g. Ronald Pearsall, *Edwardian Popular Music*, 1975.) Shaw, 1969, adduces a var. *she dunno where she are*, and thinks that this was a joke from *Punch*. Cf **doesn't know...**, para. 3.

'e's lovely, Mrs Hoskins, 'e's lovely! 'From Ted Ray and Kitty Bluett in radio comedy series "Ray's a Laugh" late 1940s and 1950s' (Noble, 1975). Uttered in a Northern-accented, high-pitched voice, and always *à propos* 'Young Doctor 'Ardcastle' (P.B.). Cf **ee, it was agony, Ivy!**

eagle. See: golden.

ear(s). See: can you do; cloth-ears; eyes and ears; get your ears; I didn't ask; I got ears; let's play it; my ears; pull in; pull your ear; shake your; speak a little; that'll pin; Walls; will she; word in your.

early. See: first term; vote early.

earn. See: you have to spend.

earwig! earwig! (often shortened to **earwig!**). 'Be quiet – there's someone listening': Brit. underworld: *c.* 1830–1914 and perhaps later. It occurs in the invaluable *Sessions Papers* (which, incidentally, I was the first scholar to examine linguistically and systematically), 10 Apr. 1849, thus: 'He said "earwig, earwig"... they were then silent.' A pun both on the lit. sense of *earwig* and on ear; cf the US underworld pun in (*Lake*) *Erie*, *'eary*.

Easter. See: doesn't know.

easterly direction. See: advancing.

easy. See: go easy; make it e.; she rapes; shit me; there must be.

easy as shaking drops off your John (, it's as). It's dead easy: essentially masculine: since *c.* 1945 – if not ten, twenty, thirty years earlier. (*John = John Thomas*, now a rather outmoded euph.)

easy as you know how or, in full, it's as easy.... It is simplicity itself – if you know how; in the RAF slang of WW2, 'It's a piece of cake'. It orig. either in 1940 or, at the latest, in early 1941; by 1950, slightly ob., and by 1970, virtually†. (Granville, 1968.)

easy does it! Do it gently, take your time!: since *c.* 1840. Cf **softly, softly...**.

easy over the pimples or the stones! Go more slowly! Be a bit more careful! R.S., 1977, explains the phrase thus: 'It was a witness at the June 1733 London Sessions who used *pimple stones* for the pebbles found on a very drunken sea-cook who came ashore to shoot up the streets of London with a pistol, just for the hell of it. Having just been engaged in shovelling ballast on board, he filled his pockets with *pimple stones* to save money on lead shot'. Which would put the phrase to the earlyish 1730s and presuppose a long subterranean life, as prob. many more such phrases have had, and enjoyed, far beyond the printed records – cf **I'll have your guts for garters**.

eat. See: don't do anything you; don't wear; formerly; go and eat; he hath eaten; hokey-pokey; I can't believe; I could eat; I'll eat; I'll go out; I've done; I've eaten; it must have been; never shit; only eating; she looks; they're eating; we won't; what's eating; who ate; you are sick; you look; and:

eat more fruit! was a c.p. of *c.* 1926–34. (Collinson.) From the famous trade slogan.

eat one! and eat shit! 'You're crazy – go away and bother someone else': US schoolboys': very approx. late 1940s–1960s (A.B., 1978.)

eat up: you're at your auntie's is a Scottish c.p. invitation to 'eat hearty': late C19–20. (Mrs M. C. Thomson of Bray-on-Thames, 1975.) Aunts being notably generous to their nephews and nieces. Cf **dig in...**.

eat your din-din. Uttered in imitation of Bette Davis, a line she says to Joan Crawford in the film *What Ever Happened to Baby Jane?*, 1962. 'Nasty', comments Ashley, 1979.

eat your heart out (, fella)! 'Doesn't *that* make you jealous or envious?: since mid-1960s; but, even by 1978, neither very widespread nor gen. in UK, whither it migrated from US. Neil Lovett notes, 1978, that in Aus. it has been current, without *fella*, since *c.* 1965, to mean 'Grow thin, fall ill, with envy or worry or grief, and see if *I* care'; the phrase was prob. popularised in Aus. by the TV programme 'Laugh-In', of American origin. 'But, I note in Sep. 1978, it has gained ground in Brit.: in Bryan Forbes's *International Velvet*, 1978, I find it employed allusively: 'He took the manuscript [a story written by a schoolgirl] from her... "Harold Robbins, eat your heart out!"' (H.R. being, of course, one of the world's half-dozen best-selling novelists during the middle and late 1970s).

eaten the rump, See **he hath eaten the rump**.

'eave 'arf a brick at 'im! Current from the mid-1850s to 1914, and still quoted in later C20, this phrase reflects the prejudiced, illiterate British lower-class attitude towards foreigners. It was inspired by a Leech cartoon in *Punch*, 25 Feb. 1854, p. 82, showing two miners regarding a gentleman, or toff, walking past; entitled 'Further Illustration of the

Mining Districts', the caption runs:
First Polite Native. "Who's 'im, Bill?"
Second ditto. "A stranger!"
First ditto. "'Eave 'arf a brick at 'im!"
(A reminder from Simon Levene.) Cf **Wogs begin at Calais,** q.v.

Eccles. See: shut up, E.

ecky thump! 'In *The Real Coronation Street*, by Ken Irwin, 1970, he has "One of the most popular figures who ever walked down the Street was Angela Crow... 'Ecky thump!' – her usual throwaway remark for any occasion, sad or amusing – became something of a National Catch-phrase"': thus Petch, who added H.V. Kershaw, *Coronation Street: Early Days*, 1976, '"Ecky thump," said Elsie, "you're taking up enough room, aren't you?"' P.B.: cf the lower middle-class exclam *flippin' 'eck*, and the N. Country expression of disbelieve or denial *does* (e.g. *he*) *'eck as like!*

edge. See: thin edge.

education has been sadly neglected, mostly – and, as c.p., always – introduced by *your*. This is usu. joc. but occ. said in friendly seriousness, dating from c. 1905; and applied mostly to matters of quite unremarkable unimportance.

ee, if ever a man soofered [= suffered]! One of the c.pp. used in the act featuring Mr Lovejoy, Enoch and Ramsbottom, on 'Happidrome', the BBC music-hall programme that did much to cheer Saturday nights on the Home Front during WW2. Mr Lovejoy (Harry Korris) would hold forth, only to be interrupted by Enoch (Robbie Vincent), whose c.p. was a bleated *Let me tell you...!*; at the conclusion of Enoch's 'say', the impatient Lovejoy would exclaim *Take him away, Ramsbottom!*, and conclude *ee, if ever...* There was, of course – judge by the names! – a strong North Country flavour to their turn, which always ended with them singing, 'We three in Happidrome...' (David Bartlett; Mrs Camilla Raab, 1982.)

ee, it was agony, Ivy! 'A popular c.p. from the radio show, 'Ray's a Laugh', late 1940s. It was uttered falsetto by a character addressed by "Ivy" as "Mrs 'Oskins"' (P.B., 1975). Noble, on the other hand, remembers it as having never really 'caught on'. (1976.)

ee, mum, me bum's numb. See me bum's numb...

ee, what a to-do! – by 1965, seldom heard and, by 1976,† – enjoyed a brief popularity; it had orig. in a gag of Robb Wilton's. (Noble, 1976.) See **day war broke out.**

eels. See: noise like.

effort, St Swithin's! 'An urging, rallying cry, used by, I think, Joyce Grenfell in one of her games-mistress roles. It achieved a certain popularity at the time, late 1940s' (P.B., 1975). *St Swithin's*, as used here, particularizes 'English girls' Public Schools'. Wedgwood, 1977, confirms that it was Joyce Grenfell, in the film 'The Happiest Days of Our Life', 1949. Cf **jolly hockey sticks.**

egg(s). See: don't crow; golden; good in parts; how do you like; if only I had; putting your; what do you want?; what's that got; wipe the egg; you must come; and:

egg on (one's) **face** – **get** or (**have**) **got,** as in 'You've got ... ', is applied to someone who has made, whether socially, politically or commercially, a fool of himself or has committed a (usu. considerable) *gaffe*: adopted, c. 1973, in the UK, from the US, where widely current since c. 1970. Mr (later Sir) Freddie Laker was quoted by the BBC in May 1974, on his challenge to British Airways that he could run Concorde aircraft at a profit, 'Some people are going to end up with a lot of egg on their faces over this one'. Ob. by 1983.

egg-shell. See: all Lombard.

eggs are cooked – **the.** That's done it! *or* 'His number is up': NZ: since c. 1910.

Egyptian medal. See: you're showing.

eh? to me! – strictly **'eh?' to me** – (why,) **you'll be saying 'arseholes' to the C.O. next!** 'A c.p. of jocularly dignified reproof (L.A.): RAF: since c. 1930. P.B.: by the mid-1950s

the var. *you'll be saying 'balls!' to the Queen* (or *'balls to the Queen!'*) *next* was applied, in the Army, to any man having a good grouse.

eight. See: take eight; we want e.

eight-ball. See: behind; city morgue.

eight bells. See: call it.

eight eyes. See: I will knock out.

Eisenhower. See: over-paid.

either piss (or **shit**) **or get off the pot!** See **shit, or get off the pot!**

either the cow calves or she busts. 'Either the chance will come off or there will be a disaster. The situation when club-hauling off a lee shore. Used in the Merchant Navy, 1920s' (Peppitt, 1975) – and, I think, before and since. It prob. derives from a rural proverb, or proverbial saying. Cf **care whether the cow...**

elastic. See: you should use.

elastic band. See: this is an orchestra.

elbow(s). See: doesn't know; going in; grandmother and; long and; more power; my elbow; scratch my; up and down; who is at.

elbow in the hawser – an, with introductory **there's** either stated or understood: a nautical c.p., applied to a ship that, with two anchors down, swings twice the wrong way, causing the cables to take half a turn round one another. (Bowen.) Since c. 1810 or perhaps 1800. It occurs in W. N. Glascock, *Sketch-Book I*, 1825.

election. See: sweating.

elementary, my dear Watson! – occ. distorted as **obvious, my dear Watson** – is an educated c.p. current throughout C20. 'I notice that the revival of interest in Sherlock Holmes – a play, books and a TV programme – has reintroduced "Elementary, my dear Watson". This must be one of the most persistent of literary catch phrases since Conan Doyle coined it' (Noble, 1974). It is not a literal quot'n, for it rationalizes Arthur Conan Doyle's, '"Excellent!" I [Dr Watson] cried. "Elementary," said he [Sherlock Holmes]' in *The Memoirs of Sherlock Holmes*, 1893, in the story titled 'The Crooked Man', where also occurs 'You know my methods, Watson' [q.v.]. These two quotations and the resultant two c.pp. have generated the further c.p., **Sherlock Holmes!,** q.v.

A good supporting quot'n is this, from Harold Brighouse's *What's Bred in the Bone*, performed in 1927 and pub'd in 1928:

JOAN: ... I knew from the moment we came in to-night that you couldn't intend to go on living here.
ETHEL: Tell me, Sherlock. My name is Watson.
JOAN: Your dress, my child. Your dress and this room. They don't match.

Ashley, 1979, notes that in US '*elementary, my dear Watson* is often the joking answer to "What school did you go to?", elementary schools here being equivalent to the UK infants' or junior schools.' And so they used to be known in UK, so perhaps the joke started there after all (P.B.).

elephant. See: who are you shoving.

eleven o'clock and no poes emptied. 'Factory wit of mock dismay at being behind with work' (L. A., 1969): late C19 – 20. But, in the form *no poes emptied, no babies scraped*, it is a man's jibe at woman's dismay at delay in her work, no beds made, no potatoes peeled. The *poes* are of course '*pots* de chambre' (chamber pots).

Skehan, 1984, adds the var. **... and not a child in the house washed,** 'quite often used by Terry Wogan on his [BBC] radio show, but stemming from his Dublin sojourn'. Cf **and not a bone...**

Eliza. See: outside.

Eliza smiles is a Brit., esp. an English, underworld c.p., dating from c. 1870–1910 and applied to a planned robbery that looks like being very successful. Eliza prob. represents the generic servant girl – a class eminently serviceable to fore-sighted burglars. (*U*.)

else. See: that's a different; what else; you, and who.

Emden. See: didn't you sink.

Emma. See: whoa, Emma.

empty. See: better an empty; I'm so e.

emu. See: hope your.

encore. See: what do you do.

end. See: after his end; fed at both ends; fool; full stop; how's it all; I'll tear; it's not my end; it's not the end; like a rope; that's the end; that's the living; this is the end; trying; well?; with a hook; you could piss; and:

end is (or **end's**) **a-wagging – the.** The end of the job is in sight: naval: mid C19–20. According to the late Wilfred Granville, 'From sailing days when, after much "pulley-hauley", the end of a rope was in sight.'

end of story. See **full stop** ...

end of the bobbin. See **that's the end of the bobbin!**

endearment. See: term of e.

enema. See: do you come as.

enemies. See: even paranoids; how goes the e.; public; shouldn't happen; we have met; with friends.

engine-driver. See: don't shoot; I'm speaking; what was the name.

England. See: close your eyes; good evening, E.; good old E.; things I do for E.; wake up, E.

English. See: no speak; veddy.

English as she is spoke. The broken English spoken by many foreigners; hence, as a c.p., the English spoken by the illiterate, the semi-literate – and the abominably careless: C20. With a pun on *broke* for *broken*, as we see from the shortlived var. (never a c.p.), *English as she is broke.* J.M. & M.J. Cohen, in their *Penguin Dictionary of Modern Quotations*, 1971, attribute it to the title of a book by A.W. Tuer (1838–1910): *A Portuguese-English Conversational Guide.*

enjoy. See: anything like that; lie back.

enjoy your trip? See **did you enjoy your trip?**

enjoy yourself and have a go! Drive, so as to scatter the head (presumably the cluster of bowls or 'woods' at the Jack end): S. African c.p. employed by players in the game of bowls: C20. (Prof A. C. Partridge, 1968.) Cf **it's in your eye!, you're not here!** and **have a go, Joe.**

enough. See: fair enough; getting any; near enough; not enough; old enough; once is e.; this town; wind enough; you can't get high; you couldn't pay; you look.

enough said! is a c.p. of hearty agreement, both Brit. (late C19–20) and derivatively US (C20), recorded by Berrey. Cf **nuff said!**

enough to give you a fit on the mat. Very amusing or laughable: non-cultured, non-aristocratic, non-upper-middle class: *c.* 1890–1920, then rapidly fading to complete obsoleteness by 1930. (W. L. George's novel *The Making of an Englishman*, 1914.) Cf the next, which is, in fact, its prob. prompter.

enough to (or **it would**) **make a cat laugh.** It is extremely funny, very droll, ludicrous: C19–20. The US form – *teste* Berrey – tends to be *that's enough* .... Recorded by Apperson, it verges on the proverbial.

enough to make my gran turn in her urn is applied to acts and attitudes that would have shocked grandma: since *c.* 1960 ('heard on and off, these permissive days': Petch, 1974); notably lower-and lower-middle-class in origin and predominantly so in practice. A var. on the cliché *turn in her grave.*

enough to make you weep (– **it's**) is applied, whether in wry comment or as rueful exclam., to a ludicrous and exasperating situation or result: current since at least as early as the 1930s. (Eric Townley, 1978.)

enough to piss off the Pope (– **it's**), lit., '"enough to anger, outrage, disgust, the Pope", it expresses any such emotion and implies "It's hard to make me angry [etc.], but you've succeeded." Current' (A.B., 1978): US: prob. since C20. Deriving from the much commoner *pissed off*, angry, disgusted, etc., borrowed during WW2 from British troops by American.

enough to put whiskers on you (– **it's**). 'It's enough to age you

or one': *c.* 1890–1970. (Brian Aldiss, 1978.) Cf *whiskers on it*, applied to a joke, a pun, a story; esp. 'That's got whiskers on it' – to which is often added 'I fell, *or* nearly fell, out of my high chair when I first heard it.'

entitled. See: you're entitled.

Epps's cocoa. See: grateful.

equal strain. See: all parts.

'ere! what's all this? Sometimes **'ere! 'ere! what's all this?** See **you can't do that there 'ere!**

Eric Connolly. See: luck of.

Eric or Little by Little (or **little by little**) is a c.p. addressed to, or directed at, very shy, esp. sexually slow, youths; since *c.* 1860; by 1950, ob., and by 1970, †. It derives from the phenomenal popularity of Dean F. W. Farrar's novel of Public School life, *Eric; or Little by Little*, 1858, the antithesis of the sunny *St Winifred's; or The World of School*, 1862: *Eric* tells the story of a boy going slowly to the bad and ending tragically.

Erie. See: on the E.

Errol. See: in like Flynn.

errors. See: no hits.

Eskimos. See: could sell.

etchings. See: come up and see my.

even. See: don't get mad.

even blind Freddie wouldn't miss it. See **blind Freddie** ...

even break. See: never give.

even paranoids have real enemies. 'A retort to accusations that the speaker is being "paranoid" – i.e., seeing imaginary dangers. From late 1960s, and now with greater point than ever, since revelations of illegal activities by, e. g. the C.I.A. and F.B.I., which many people were "paranoid" about, have shown that the enemies are real enough' (R.C., 1978): US. P.B.: the phrase has crossed the Atlantic in the version *just because you're paranoid, it doesn't mean to say they aren't all out to get you.*

even the Admiralty can't boil you in the coppers or put you in the family way. Well, things might be worse *or* When things go badly, always remember this: RN: C20. (R/Adml P. W. Brock, 1968.) An apt comparison is afforded by **they can make you do anything** ...

even when he's whistling. See **can't believe him** ...

even your best friend(s) won't tell you. See **your best friend(s)** ...

ever. See: did you ever; and:

[**ever**, in *am I* or *is he ever*; *did I* or *he ever*; etc. Half-way between a humorous locution and a c.p., this Can. expression 'corresponds to the British intensive **not half!** [q.v.] "Did you get wet?" – "Did I ever!"' Certainly post-WW2 and prob. since *c.* 1960. (Hugh E. Quetton, of Montreal, 1978.) P.B.: but I found this usage also in great vogue among Australian servicemen in Hong Kong, 1960s, which perhaps suggests a common orig. in US.]

ever since Adam was an oakum boy. 'A colloquial Navy phrase to indicate that something goes back to ancient history' (F & G): mid C19–20; by 1950, ob. Cf **since Pontius was a pilot**, q.v., and E.P.'s remarks at **when Adam** ...

Evers. See: from Tinker.

every barber knows that. That's common gossip: US: C20. (Berrey.) Implying that barbers are commonly the repository of gossip and rumour, whether at the strictly local or, preferably, at the national – or even international – level.

every day and in every way, to which, in the orig. form, is added **I am getting better and better.** This, the slogan enunciated by Dr Coué, almost immediately became a fashionable c.p. of 1923–6; the c.p. accompanied the fad's meteoric decline, which began very soon indeed after his death in 1926.

Emile Coué, born in 1857, was, in brief, the Fr. originator of a psychotherapeutic system of autosuggestion called, for short, Couéism. In 1910 he established, at Nancy, a clinic where his system might be practised; his patients were instructed to repeat as frequently as possible his formula, which his enemies slightly misrepresented as a slogan, 'Day by day, in every way, I am getting better and better.' He lectured in both England and the US. His teachings are summarized in the book translated as *Self-Mastery through Conscious Autosuggestion*, pub'd on both sides of the Atlantic in 1922. In its wake came such expositions and popularizations as Frank Bennett's *M. Coué and His Gospel of Health* and Cyrus Brooks's *The Practice of Autosuggestion by the Method of Emile Coué*, with a foreword by Coué himself, both pub'd in 1922; and during the next three or four years several other writers 'jumped on the band wagon'. While I attended the University of Oxford in 1921–3, a vast battery of wit and witticism was, in 1922 onwards, turned on the numerous disciples: and the formula-become-c.p. had what it would be cowardly to describe as other than a furore, for it amounted to far more than a mere vogue.

'Up like a rocket and down like a stick': Coué's claims were falsified by sadly inadequate results in physical betterment.

every dog ... See **foxes ...**

every hair a rope yarn; every finger a marline-spike; every drop of blood, Stockholm tar is 'an old nautical phrase [or, rather, a trio of linked phrases] descriptive of the real dyed-in-the-wool sailor of the windjammer era' (*Sailors' Slang*): only very approx. *c*. 1850–1910. But Peppitt, 1977, notes that as *every thumb a fid, every finger a marline spike*, he 'first heard it in 1946, from men who joined the Royal Navy in the 1920s, and since in both Merchant and Royal Navy, to describe a seaman in his finger-tips, capable of splicing with his bare hands.'

every home should have one, orig. an advertising slogan, has, both in Brit. and in US, been applied – since, I think, the 1920s – to all sorts of things, ranging from common objects to babies to non-material things, as in Ivor Drummond, *The Power of the Bug*, 1974:

'With a new car we are clean. We go a little further away, get a new car, and make a plan.'

'Yeah, we want one of those,' said Colly. 'Every home should have one.'

every little bean should be heard as well as seen. 'According to my uncle, who was in the First World War, this used to be a common thing to say ... when breaking wind. Compare the German *Jedes Böhnchen hat sein tönchen*' (J. B. Smith, Bath, 1979). i.e. 'every little bean has its little tune'; cf the slang *musical fruit* for vegetables, esp. beans, that have a markedly flatulent effect. (P.B.)

every little helps, as the old woman said when she pissed in the sea is a c.p. uttered when one urinates into sea or stream, hence to any tiny contribution to a cause, esp. a subscription or a street, or other, collection of funds: mid C19–20. R.C., 1977: 'The American version is simply *every little bit helps*', while Shipley queries, 'Shouldn't this be labelled a Wellerism?' From the constant use of such similes by Samuel Weller in *The Pickwick Papers* (1836–7): e.g., Out with it, as the man said when his little boy swallowed a farthing. There are constantly new ones, as mine in *In Praise of English* [1977] ... I'm thirsty myself, as the old lady said when the baby fell into the fishpond.' P.B.: it may be that this later version using 'the old woman' makes a c.p. out of a proverb, but I doubt it. The proverbial form is, as recorded in the *Concise Oxford Dict. of Proverbs*, 1982, **... as the wren said, when she pissed in the sea**, which dates back at least as far as *c*. 1600 – and a French version, using an *ant*, goes back even further. Cf **as the monkey said**.

every night about this time is an Aus. c.p., dating from *c*. 1955 and orig. in radio announcements and referring to habitual sexual intercourse.

every one a coconut! derives from a fairground barker's cry, uttered to induce the crowd to join in the coconut shy, where the prize awarded for success was a coconut. In the late C19 and right through (although decreasingly) to this day, the 'event' or competition has existed: and very soon, it became

a c.p., by being applied in other ways and acquiring the general sense of 'You've gained a success every time you try', as, for instance, a famous novelist with successive novels; I heard it, as a c.p., used by an educated and highly reputed professional man, as late as 1974. Cf **every player ...** , and **give the gentleman ...**

every picture tells a story. This, the exact wording that accompanied 'the distressing pictures of human suffering amenable to treatment by Doane's Backache Kidney Pills, supplies us with the useful Every picture tells a story – often used derisively of anecdotal paintings' (Collinson) and of anyone clutching his lumbago-afflicted back: C20; ob. by 1935 and, excepting among those of fifty or over, † by 1960. These advertisements appeared regularly in such magazines as *The Strand*, above all, and *The Windsor*. The picture showed a person bent over with pain. The c.p. had an occ. var., **oh, my aching back!** – which was resuscitated, with a new bearing, during the latter half of WW2 (so see **oh, my achin' back!**).

every player wins a prize 'is a phrase common among Australian side-show barkers (sometimes called *spielers*) at district shows (fairs) and the Royal Shows held in the capital cities – except Brisbane, which has its Exhibition – each year. It has since become a general exhortation to the reluctant [and is] especially loved by paradoxically unceremonious fellows called Masters of Ceremonies at balls, socials and similar tribal gatherings' (Neil Lovett, 1978): Aus.: since the late 1940s, if not a decade or two earlier. Cf **every one a coconut!**

every silver lining has its cloud. The old proverb, used by Milton, 1634 (*COD of Proverbs*, 1982) was thus pessimistically reversed by Noël Coward in his marvellously melancholy song of the late 1930s. 'There are bad times just around the corner'. The gloomy view so succinctly expressed has all the makings of an early 1980s c.p. (P.B., with thanks to Mrs Margaret Davies, Lesotho, 1983.)

every thumb a fid ... See **every hair a rope yarn ...**

every time he opens his mouth he puts his foot in it. Both Brit. and US (Berrey), this c.p. dates from *c*. 1920 (I first heard it in the early 1920s) or perhaps a decade earlier. By a pun on *put one's foot in it*, to make a social mistake. Shipley notes that it was of Sir Boyle Roche, a Dublin politician, that it was first said.

everybody. See: **in everybody's**; **is everybody**.

everybody out! (with emphasis on *ev*). 'Miriam Karlin in her best flame-thrower voice, as Paddy, the Cockney shop-stewardess in *The Rag Trade*. This programme had the unusual distinction of running on BBC TV from 1961 to 1965, then being revived by London Weekend Television from 1977' (*VIBS*). P.B.: now firmly connected in many people's minds with strikers of all sorts.

everybody say 'aah!' 'A commiserative sound, the *aah* being uttered on a long-drawn-out falling tone. It is used to greet, and to lessen the impact of, any tale of woe ... It seems to be the verbal equivalent of the old Army gesture of scraping a violin to indicate mock sorrow at a hard luck tale' (P.B., 1977): 1970s.

everybody wants to get into the act was promptly adopted from a frequent 'line' of Jimmy 'Schnozzle' Durante, the late American comedian, 1930s–50s, and still very active in the 1970s. 'Protest at "having one's thunder stolen", or, more loosely, where too many cooks are stirring the broth' (Wedgewood, 1978). Often, loosely, ... *in on the act*.

everybody works but father, orig. an English song, pub'd in the 1890s, was, in US, revived by Jean Hayes and sung by Lew Dockstader. Edward B. Marks, *They All Sang*, 1934. (W.J.B.) The phrase is, in the song, followed by 'But father works all day' – which alters the *prima facie* meaning of those first four words.

everybody's doing it, doing it, doing it characterizes the years 1912–14 at least, up to 4 Aug.; it comes from a wildly popular song, the ref. being to the ragtime dance known as the Turkey trot, 'the rage' in 1912–13 – and is recorded in, e.g., Robert Keable's wildly popular novel, *Simon Called Peter*, 1921. Ragtime, precursor of jazz, arrived *c.* 1910: and this particular dance was extremely popular during the war years 1914–18, esp. among naval and army officers.

The words come from Irving Berlin's song, *Everybody's Doing It Now*, copyrighted in New York in 1912. The chorus runs: 'Everybody's doin' it, doin' it, everybody's doin' it now'; and the song ends: 'Everybody's doin' it now'.

'A veiled sexual innuendo, even in 1912, which became much more explicit in Cole Porter's (*c.* 1928) "Let's Do It"' (R.C., 1977). 'Let's do it: let's fall in love', along with Porter's 'What Is This Thing Called Love?', adorned the musical titled *Wake Up and Dream*.

Nasty little boys in the 1940s, and prob. before and since, added a next line, '…picking their nose and chewing it, chewing it' (P.B.).

everybody's (or **everything's**) **pulling, but nothing's moving.** 'Intense activity has, so far, yielded no results': since late 1930s; little heard since *c.* 1970. It occurs in, e.g., Margery Allingham's novels. (R.C., 1978.)

everything. See: for the man; I'm like; now I've heard; she has e.; you can't have e.

everything but the kitchen sink. Virtually everything: both US, throughout C20, and Brit., although common only since *c.* 1945. The nuances differ in the two countries: US, 'often (and, I think, originally) "She showed everything but the kitchen sink"' (J.W.C., 1977); UK and the Commonwealth, as in 'He threw everything at me but the kitchen sink'. Occ., later C20, for emphasis and allusively, *everything, including the kitchen sink.* Cf **you've forgotten the piano.**

everything I like is either immoral… is a frequent var. of **anything you like…**

everything in the garden's lovely! All goes well: C20; slightly ob. by 1935, yet, among people aged (say) fifty or more, still far from † in 1974; for instance I heard a real Cockney' cleaner on the British Museum staff use it, in the portico, on 28 Feb. 1974. It was prompted by **everything is nice in your garden,** q.v. below, and a fairly early Commonwealth example occurs in G.B. Lancaster's *Jim of the Ranges*, 1910. Cf **everything is lovely and the goose hangs high,** and:

everything in the garden's lovely, except the gardener 'refers to Dad, who often looks like a scarecrow when he is gardening' (Petch, 1974): suburban witticism, at almost any social level below that of the upper-middle class, and manifesting an affectionate malice: since *c.* 1945. Obviously an elab. of the prec.

everything in the shop window, nothing in the shop. All shadow and no substance – all promise and no (or very poor) performance: since *c.* 1920. It is applied to, e.g. those girls who do their damnedest to catch a man, get him, but lack the qualities to keep him, for, having displayed all their wares, they have exhausted their repertoire and lack the permanent, retentive graces.

everything is apples. See **apples.**

everything is (or **everything's**) **coming up roses.** Things are going unusually – or very – well: since *c.* 1950. (Skehan, who, in 1977, remarked upon the preponderance of roses among flowers in c.pp. Violets come second.)

everything is George. All goes well, esp. for me: a beatnik c.p. of *c.* 1959–70. Why George and not Tom or Bill or John, I don't know. An origin as topical and fortuitous as this one is usually impossible to ascertain – unless one's exceptionally lucky. Ashley notes that it goes with **copacetic,** q.v. Cf **that's real George.**

everything is lovely and the goose hangs high. All goes well: US rural: since *c.* 1860; ob. by 1940, but not yet † in 1976. Farmer glosses it, '… all is going swimmingly; all is serene'; *D.Am.* cites the shortened phrase, *the goose hangs high,* as meaning 'prospects are bright; things look encouraging' – and adds that no satisfactory origin has been found. The ref. seems to be 'ɔ a plucked goose hanging high and well out of a

fox's reach. R.C. writes, 1977, 'Another suggested (and to me plausible) etymology is as a distortion of "the goose honks high" – meaning that the weather is fine and the migrating geese are operating at height.'

everything is marvellous for you. See **you have it made.**

everything is nice in your garden, orig. in society and passing well beyond it, was, in 1896–*c.* 1910 'a gentle protest against self-laudation', as Ware, who supplies an anecdotal origin, put it in 1909; he also developed the link with **everything in the garden's lovely.** Note that whereas *everything is nice… is* always used ironically, the later c.p. is rarely so used.

everything is peaches down in Georgia. A C20 equivalent of **everything is lovely….** 'As every American knows, Georgia peaches are delicious… The popular song with this title came out in 1918, but whether the song generated the c.p. or the c.p. was used for the song, I don't know' (Eric Townley, 1978). J.W.C. added the necessary corrective: 'It is now and then heard as a c.p., but ironically: everything is [or may be] peaches in Georgia – but not here': he refers to recent usage, say the 1970s.

everything is (or **everything's**) **under control;** also **everything under control.** A Services' c.p., dating from *c.* 1930 and applicable to any situation where things are 'ticking over nicely'. (Recorded by H & P.) Noël Coward, in *Peace in Our Time,* performed and pub'd 1947, has, in I, iv, this piece of dialogue:

FRED (*brokenly*): Stevie… How did you get here? It's all too much to believe – all in a minute…

STEVIE: It's all right, Dad – everything's under control.

everything on top and nothing handy. See **just like a midshipman's chest…**

everywhere. See: my spies.

evidence. See: it'll all be put; what the soldier.

examined. See: you need your head.

excellent. See: spirit.

excite. See: don't excite.

excrementum cerebellum vincit. A humorously erudite WW2 army officers' 'translation' into L. of **bullshit baffles brains.** Cf **illegitimis non carborundum.**

excuse. See: you should e.

excuse me! I beg to differ: S. African: since *c.* 1930. (Prof. A.C. Partridge, 1974.) For its US use, Ashley, 1979, notes that, pron, 'excuuuuse *me*!' it 'is the c.p. of currently "wild and crazy guy" US comedian Steve Martin. It has really caught on.'

excuse me for living! See **pardon me for living!**

excuse me, I have to see a man about a god is an irreverent c.p., derisively dismissive of 'famous last words', whether used as cliché or as c.p.: *c.* 1955–75. (Petch, 1974.) Obviously a pun on the c.p. **I have to see a man about a dog.**

excuse me, I've got a train (or **a plane**) **to catch.** See **bugger this, I've got…**

excuse me reaching! A lower-middle-class c.p. that has, in C20, been uttered when one reaches for something at the mealtime table; by 1935, slightly ob. – and by 1950 †. With a pun on *retching.*

excuse my abbrev (pronounced *abbreve*), **it's a hab.** A c.p. either addressed to or, at mildest, directed at someone addicted to trivial and constant abridgement; lit., 'Excuse my *habit of abbreviating.*' It belongs to a very brief period indeed: *c.* 1910–12. Such abbreviations were much commoner *c.* 1890–1912 than before – or since.

excuse my dust! Excuse me, please; I'm sorry: US, orig. Western: C20. From the inconvenience caused by a vehicle to the occupants of the one immediately following it along a dusty road. My friend J.W.C. comments, 1968: '"I'm 'way ahead of you, and you're not very bright". Possibly antedates the automobile, but I doubt it. At any rate, common for at least 50 years, [that is, since *c.* 1920] and even now, when few roads are dusty.' It became the title of a film, 1951, starring Red Skelton and an assortment of antique automotive machines; and, as Harold Shapiro noted, 1977, it was helped along by the fact that Dorothy Parker (1893–1967) proposed it as her epitaph.

excuse my (or the) French! See: **pardon my French!**

excuse my pig: he's a friend! 'A c.p. used when a companion disgraces one by, e.g., breaking wind while drinking at the bar' (P.B., 1974): since *c.* 1950. By joc. inversion of *friend* and *pig*. Cf **is he with you?** and **you can't take him anywhere.**

excuse my wart! These words represent a 'gag' that, in the 1940s, became a full-blooded c.p. only when they were uttered by a person shaking hands with his middle finger crooked into the palm. (P.B., 1977.) A good example of the fairly rare gestural c.p. P.B.: thus E.P.'s paraphrase of one of my notes to him. Cf **am I boring you?**, uttered while the speaker jabs a stiff awl-like forefinger into his victim's back; and **walk this way, please!** – in imitation of a floor-walker's invitation – said while adopted some grotesque gait. See also **guess who's back**, and **I feel an awful heel.**

exercise. See: that is the; this is the way.

expect. See: I'll expect; what can you e.; what do you e.

expectation. See: 'fuck me!'

expense. See: compliment.

experience. See: chalk it up to.

expert. See: by you; you're the e.

explain. See: never explain; that accounts.

expression. See: you should excuse.

exterminate! exterminate! 'The BBC's science-fiction series [ostensibly for children] *Dr Who* has given rise to numerous beasties but none so successful as the Daleks – mobile pepper-pots with antennae whose metallic voices bark out 'exterminate! exterminate!' as they set about doing so with ray guns. Much imitated by children' (*VIBS*): 1970s.

extra two inches you're supposed to get after you're forty – the. This Armed Forces' c.p. of 1939–45 referred to an entirely imaginary phallic compensation for the years that have gone before and perhaps been wasted or, at the least, misused. One of the numerous myths that sex, whether male or female, has evoked.

extract the manual digit! 'Get a move on!' This is a deliberate, mock-euph., ironic synon. of *get your finger out!*, q.v. at **take your finger out!** (Camilla Raab, 1977.) P.B.: the *manual* is sometimes omitted, and there is a mock-Latin var. *extractum digitum.*

eyadon, yauden, yaydon, negidicrop dibombit! 'Jon Pertwee as Svenson, the Norwegian stoker, in Navy *Merry Go Round* [BBC radio comedy series, late 1940s], whose cod Norwegian (based on close scrutiny of wartime news broadcasts) always ended up with these words' (*VIBS*). Much imitated at the time.

eye(s). See: beautiful pair; better than a dig; black is your; bright-eyed; close your eyes; do you see any green; don't fire; don't open; dry your; get your eye; I could shit; I could take; I got eyes; I need a piss; I was doing it; I will knock; I'll push; in a pig's; it's in your eye; keep your eye; making dolls'; mind your eye; my elbow; nobody can; now you see; pay over; rise and; steal; talk a glass; there he goes; through; two upon; weak eyes; where the crows; you need eyes; you still; you were just; you're blind; you're so full; you've dropped; you've got eyes; your eyes.

eye! eye! In his popular and very readable *The Underworld,* 1953, Jim Phelan, who knew what he was talking about, writes, 'Every time Alf said "Eye-eye", it was a call for vigilance'. Dating since *c.* 1920, this Brit underworld c.p. derives from – in the sense that it stands for – 'Keep your *eye*, yes your *eye*, on' somebody or something.

eye it, try it, buy it! is a US trade slogan (for Chevrolet automobiles, to be precise) that, W & F tell us in 1960, 'finds some generalized use [for] looking at, trying, or sampling anything': since the early 1950s, but, as R.C. points out, 1977, 'I doubt whether this ever had any considerable currency. Certainly dead before 1970'.

eyebrows. See: toast.

eyeful. See: got your e.

eyes and ears of the world – the. An Aus. c.p. dating since *c.* 1950 and ironically addressed to – or aimed at – someone who speaks as if he has all the latest information. It comes from the motto of Gaumont British News. (B.P.)

eyes are bigger than your stomach. See: your eyes...

eyes in the boat! Keep your eyes on the job: nautical: late C19–20. Watch your oars – not that pretty girl over there. Playfair adds, 1977, that, in origin, it was 'not nautical in the usual sense, but relates to rowing as a sport; shouted by the coach from the bank'.

eyes like piss-holes in the snow (usu. prec. by *he has* or *he's got*). 'One of the most graphic phrases that is applied to the aspect of someone suffering "the morning after the night before": *he's got eyes like....*' (Brian W. Aldiss, 1978): since *c.* 1920. Cf **don't open your eyes...**

eyesight. See: it'll do.

f.h.o. and **f.t.i.** See **family: hands off!**

f.u.b.a.r. See **fubar.**

face(s). See: egg; give your f.; go and fry; I never remember; I'll push; I'm not just; is my f.; it's staring; let's face; many faces; pay over; same old f.; wipe the egg; wipe the shit; yes, my arse; you are a thief; and:

face that only a mother could love, and she died laughing – a. Perhaps the ultimate in wry, pitying, semi-joc., derision of ugliness. Cf:

face would stop a clock – her, or **she's got a face that would stop a clock,** may be applied unkindly and derisively to the battle-axe or rear-end-of-a-bus sort of face: since c. 1890; 'still-heard' in 1974, Mr A.B. Petch assures me and as I have, myself, noticed. P.B.: earlier than *the back of a bus* came *like the back end of a tram.*

fact(s). See: ain't it a f.; all we want is the f.; I have made.

fade away. See: old soldiers.

fag. See: how's the fag.

fag-paper. See: stand on a f.

fail. See: if all else; may your prick; words.

faint. See: she will go.

fair. See: it's like a nigger; it's not right; like a fart; plays as f.; you have made; and:

fair cop! See **it's a fair cop.**

fair do's, mostly written **fair doo's.** At first, it was written *fair dues,* as in C. T. Clarkson and J. Hall Richardson, *Police,* 1889, 'Now then, fair dues; let everybody be searched. I have no money about me' – so it must have gone back to 1880 or earlier. After c. 1930, the orig. two-worder became a four-worder: *fair doo's all round.*

fair enough! is elliptical for 'Well, *that's* fair enough' – 'that sounds plausible', *or* 'I'll accept that statement or offer', but also used as a question (common among instructors), 'Satisfied?' *or* 'Convinced?' *or* 'Is that agreeable to you?' It dates from the 1920s, and until c. 1946 it remained a predominantly Services', esp. RAF, c.p., which, c. 1940, spread to Aus. and NZ. Its continuing Aus. currency is attested by Jim Ramsay, *Cop It Sweet!,* 1977.

P.B.: so well known was the phrase in the immediate post-WW2 period that there was even an appalling pun: 'I am a fairy. My name is Nuff. I'm the....'

fair, fat and forty goes back much earlier that I should have thought: recorded in anon., *The New Swell's Night Guide,* 1846, it may safely be orig. in the raffish 1820s (Egan, Moncrieff, *et al.*). A vulgar parody, current – although not very widely so – during the 1940s but mercifully killed by WW2, was *fair, fat and farty,* which, perhaps earthily true, fell rather short of being *très galant.* Playfair tells me, 1977, that it has generated a mnemonic among medical students, *fair, fat, forty, fecund and flatulent,* descriptive of the sort of woman likely to suffer from cholecystitis. The shorter version perhaps distorts John O'Keefe's 'fat, fair and forty'

in the play *Irish Minnie.* O'Keefe (1747–1833) wrote some fifty comedies, some of them musical.

The ribald version exemplifies a variation of the linguistic process I call 'spontaneous combustion'; it sprang from and flourished in the rich soil of those British Isles dialects which pronounce *forty* as *farty.*

fair go! 'Be fair!' or 'Be reasonable!' An orig. and predominantly Aus. var. of **fair enough!** (*APOD,* 1976.) It comes from the gambling game of two-up, 'the call... indicating that all the rules have been satisfied... at the same time enjoining that there be no hindrance'. Hence, 'the elementary fair treatment to which anyone must be entitled' (Wilkes, *Dict. Aus. Coll.,* 1978). *Not* a c.p.; merely an ordinary Aus. coll. The same stricture applies to the synon. *fair crack of the whip.* Yet it can perhaps be adjudged to be a c.p. when used as an exclam., whether protest or plea or humorous disclaimer. Wilkes's earliest quot'n is for 1938, yet it had been used at least as early as 1908 within my own recollection.

fair to middling. A joc. reply to 'How are you?' or 'How's it, or things, going?' the jocularity taking the form of a pun, 'fair' and 'middling' being synon. Its c.p. usage clearly derives from the normal coll. usage, which goes back to early C20: orig. in UK, it prob. went c. 1920 to US, and thence c. 1945 to Aus. (Shapiro; Fain, 1977.) It has, in UK later C20, the occ. var. *fair to muddling* (P.B., 1976), and B.G.T. reminded me, 1978, that in England *mustn't grumble* has, since the late 1920s, often been added as an amelioration.

faith. See: keep the f.

fake. See: no, but you hum.

fall. See: did she; he's fallen; I didn't come up; like the man who fell.

fall into a cart and **fall into the shit.** See **could fall....**

fall off and cool your saddle. See **drop your traces....**

fall off the roof is a c.p. only in *I've* or *she's (just) fallen off the roof,* a US feminine expression meaning 'I've (just) started my period' and part-euph. said to a friend or a husband: late, perhaps mid-, C19–20, but by c. 1960 no longer used. (A.B., 1978.)

fall out and dust your medals! 'A derisive dismissive sometimes used to end an argument among Army contemporaries, who may not in fact have any medals to dust' (P.B., 1974): post WW2, Cf:

fall out, the officers! 'Still used derisively by those who, during WW2, had the brains to qualify for promotion to officer' (an anon. correspondent, 1978). From the parade-ground command.

fall through the trap door! is an occ. var., likewise US and dating not earlier than 1904, not later than 1916, of **break a leg!** 'I have heard [it]. Sothern once tried for the first 15 minutes of a play to whisper to Julia Marlowe that the trap on that stage was faulty; she thought he was trying to

85

"upstage" her and kept shying away' (Shipley, 1975). Edward Hugh Sothern (1859–1936), born in New Orleans, the son of English actor Edward Sothern (1826–81), 'led', in Shakespearean drama, with Julia Marlowe (retired 1924) at the Lyceum Theater in New York during the periods 1904–7 and 1909–16. Cf **break a leg!**

fallen away from a horse-load to a cart-load dates c. 1650–1850, is recorded by Grose (1796) and earlier by S, and by Ray, and somewhat ironically means 'grown suddenly fatter – and very fat'.

false as my knife (– **as**). 'My knife and my life are as likely to cut me as anyone else': a bitter, mainly rural, middle-class c.p.: C20. *The Countryman Cottage Life Book,* ed. F. Archer, 1974. Since the urban exodus to the country became 'the thing to do'.

false teeth. See: somebody's.

fame at last! This is a c.p. only when it is used ironically, as when uttered by one who has just seen his name in Company Orders for, e.g. fire picket, guard duty, or similar nuisance; usu. prec. by *ah! or aha!* or such like interjection; army (Other Ranks'): since c. 1946. (P.B., 1974.) But also, of course, in other occupational and social contexts.

families. See: it happens; like a bastard.

family, hands off! or **family, hold off,** but – for obvious reasons – customarily abbr. to *f.h.o.,* is a domestic c.p. employed by the middle class as a warning that a certain dish is not to be eaten by members of the family when guests are present, there being insufficient for all: mid C19–20. The var. *family, hold back,* abbr. to *f.h.b.,* was very usual before WW2, and was also the main US version. Corollaries were *m.i.k.* (more in kitchen) and *f.t.i.* (family, tuck in!); My friend Mr Basil Page, FRCS, to whom I owe the latter, tells me that he remembers it as used by his parents during the 1920s.

family way. See: even the Admiralty; more kid; Sister Anna.

famous last words! 'A catch-phrase rejoinder to such fatuous statements as "Flak's not really dangerous"' (PGR): RAF, thence to the other two Services: since 1939 and, 1945 onwards, among civilians. A joc., when not a jeering, ref. to the 'famous last words' of History, e.g. 'It can't – or it could never – happpen here' or, notably, 'in this country', whichever country the speaker or writer belongs to; see the separate entry at **it can't happen here.**

Famous last words orig. as 'a satirical comment on the kind of feature once popular in such magazines as *Great Thoughts* and *Titbits* and was directed especially at such daring statements as could easily be refuted with proof often tragic' (Shaw; 1969).

A neat example occurs in Terence Rattigan's comedy, *Variation on a Theme,* 1958, at I, ii:

ROSE: No, it's red, impair and my age tonight. At chemmy it's bancos. The banks won't run.

MONA: Famous last words.

The phrase was adopted by the US, as in Hartley Howard, *Million Dollar Snapshot,* 1971:

'If you had any sense you'd ask me to stick around until you whistled up some reinforcements.'

'No need for that. Sergeant Goslin will be back soon.'

'Famous Last Words,' I said.

This c.p. has become so embedded in colloquial English that the words can be employed allusively, as in Karen Campbell's *Suddenly in the Air,* 1969: 'I smiled. "We're doing remarkably well." These were famous last words.'

In short, one of the most memorable and trenchant of all c.pp.

fan. See: day the omelette; lie down; when shit.

fan my brow! Expresses astonishment or even amazement: US: C. 1920–40. (Fain, 1977.)

fancy. See: just fancy; little of what; none of your f.

Fanny. See: and Bob's; cor! chase; off yer; only pretty.

far better off in a home. See **you'd be far better off...**

farce. See: for a musical.

farewell. See: and so we say; sailor's f.; soldier's f.

farewell and a thousand, with a comma or a dash after *farewell.* A thousand times farewell! *or* Farewell – and a thousand thanks! *or* Farewell – and the best of luck! Belonging, so far as I've been able to discover, to the very approx. period c. 1550–1640. It occurs in, e.g., George Peele's play, *The Old Wives' Tale,* 1595 (lines 248–9 in A.H. Bullen's edn):

ERESTUS: ...Neighbour, farewell.

LAMPRISCUS: Farewell, and a thousand.

Alexander Dyce compares Thomas Middleton's 'Let me hug thee: farewell, and a thousand' in *A Trick to Catch an Old One,* 1608. Semantically, cf the slangy C20 *thanks a million!* (times, not dollars).

farm. See: sold the f.; who wouldn't.

fart. See: much chance as a f.; that will stop; and:

fart in a colander. See **like a fart...**

fart's the cry of an imprisoned turd – a. Dating from c. 1930 (or a little earlier), this c.p., as essentially poetical as it is superficially coarse, either satirizes – pungently yet benevolently – the condition of one who, having just broken wind, might properly go to the water-closet or unrepentingly apologizes for having broken it. Clearly an allusion to the cry of a bird imprisoned in a cage.

farted. See: 'gip'.

farther. See: I can't go.

farther down the street (or **block**) **you go, the tougher they get: and I live in the last house – the.** A US urban boast, 'Current, mainly juvenile, in the 1920s, but thereafter used as conscious and comic hyperbole; now virtually extinct' (R.C., 1978).

fashion. See: spends.

fast. See: so fast; you can't: they.

faster. See: I can't go.

fat. See: come in if; don't you fret; fair, fat; he'd skin; short, fat.

fate. See: fucked by.

fate worse than death – a, the rape of a female, or even a genteel seduction (prob. since mid C18), became, in the raffish period, 1880–1910, a callously joc., then, 1910 onwards, a merely humorous, often derisive, c.p. applied to girls willing enough, and finally, c. 1915, applied by girls themselves – or, come to that, women – to intercourse between the unmarried or between a married and an unmarried person. Sanders adds, 1978, 'The "liberated" woman is alleged to refer to marriage as "the fate that is worse than the fate worse than death"'.

When used seriously, it is a cliché.

father. See: Charley's dead; everybody works; glazier; go to father; Hamlet, I; how's your f.; I bet you f.; I cannot; I haven't laughed; I was doing; what's the matter with f.; when father; you were just; your fadder's; your mother.

father keeps on doing it! comes from a popular song, dates from c. 1920, refers to a man with a repetitiously large family.

Father Abraham. See: we are coming.

father, dear father, come home to me now, The clock in the steeple strikes one, with the second part usu. omitted. 'This American c.p. is still used mockingly to someone who has had a few too many; even though it arose in the 1890s, from a sentimental ballad; the plea of a young girl to her father to leave the tavern' (J.W.C., 1977). P.B.: the authorship of the ballad is unknown, according to the compilers of *American Ballads, Naughty, Ribald and Classic,* 1952.

father's backbone. See: I was doing it when.

Father's Day. See: happy as a bastard.

fattened for the slaughter (– **being**) refers to a 'rest' period, i.e. one – a week, ten days, a fortnight – spent out of the line; esp. for the very lucky, at a rest camp: joc. among infantrymen, mostly on the Western Front in 1917–18.

fattening. See: anything you like.

favour(s). See: do me a f.; do yourself; don't do me; I could do that; I could do you.

fear. See: don't you f.; never fear; and:

fear God and tip the crusher! is a RN lower-deck motto of C20. A *crusher* is slang for a Regulating Petty Officer, a Warrant Officer, in the RN police. PGR.

feather(s). See: didn't have a; got a feather; ruffin; she walks.

feather duster. See: rooster.

features. See: hello, features.

fed at both ends, as they say – in full, **she should get a bit fatter, fed** .... – is a low c.p., applied to a slim bride and dating from before 1958, when I first heard it. Contrast **feed the brute!**

fed-up. See: fucked and.

Federal case. See: don't make a F.

feed. See: did they forget; I was there; where the bull.

feed the brute!, introduced by one or other of these: 'Always remember' or 'All you have to do is ....', or 'The secret is ...' or 'The great, or main thing, is to ...', none of which, obviously, can be part of the c.p. itself, far the commonest form being simply *feed the brute!* This feminine c.p. is used either by mothers to daughters about to marry or by wives, esp. if young. Often there's the overt meaning 'That'll keep him amiable, content, happy – and you too'. The covert implication is that a well-fed man is the more readily amorous and the more capable of attending to his wife vigorously and frequently. In the US, however, it is 'regularly taken to mean, in order to keep him in a good temper rather than amorous' (J.W.C., 1977).
    This, one of the best-known and widest-spread of all c.pp., arose in *Punch*, 1886 (vol. LXXXIX, p. 206), where, to a young wife complaining of her husband's absences from home and of his neglect of her, a widow speaks these fateful words. But it is no longer apprehended as a famous quot'n.

feeding time at the zoo – it's. 'An undisciplined assault on food and drink': since the late 1940s; hence, since *c.* 1960, 'a disorderly but excited scene'. Definitions from Wilkes, *Dict. Aus. Coll.*; my datings.

feel. See: do you feel; find; have a feel; I feel; if it feels; let's feel; never mind the quality; wreck.

feel free! Elliptical for 'Feel free to do whatever you asked to do'. Almost synon. with, although less common than, **be my guest!** US: since the early 1950s. (R.C., 1977). P.B. had, 1976, confirmed its Brit. currency, but thought that it didn't reach UK until the 1960s.

feeling no pain 'is still, I suspect, an approved American reply to "How are you" enquiries; it signifies that one is drunk, and fully intending to become incapable' (Russell Davies, in *New Statesman*, 9 Sep. 1977). Christopher Morley uses it in *The Ironing Board*, 1947, as W&F inform us. It may have been prompted by 'I feel no pain, dear, mother, now', q.v. at **I have no pain ...**

feel. See: do you feel; find; have a feel; I feel; if it feels; let's feel; never mind the quality; wreck.

feel free! Elliptical for 'Feel free to do whatever you asked to do'. Almost synon. with, although less common than, **be my guest!** US: since the early 1950s. (R.C., 1977). P.B. had, 1976, confirmed its Brit. currency, but thought that it didn't reach UK until the 1960s.

feeling no pain 'is still, I suspect, an approved American reply to "How are you" enquiries; it signifies that one is drunk, and fully intending to become incapable' (Russell Davies, in *New Statesman*, 9 Sep. 1977). Christopher Morley uses it in *The Ironing Board*, 1947, as W&F inform us. It may have been prompted by 'I feel no pain, dear, mother, now q.v. at **I have no pain ...**

feet. See: come out of that; get your f.; how's your poor; my feet; oh, my poor; patter; so fast; take a load; you'd have been; your feet.

Felix keeps on walking. In Collinson we read of 'the popular phrase "Felix keeps on walking" from Felix's loping walk in the picture-house' – the ref. being, of course, to Felix the Cat. This c.p. belongs to the 1920s and has a var. *Felix kept on walking*, which Benham gives as orig. in 1923.
    Mr Eric Fearon, of Southgate, London, recalled Felix's

signature tune:
> Felix keeps on walking,
> Keeps on walking still.
> With his hands behind him,
> You will always find him.

> When a sudden strong wind blew,
> Right into the air he flew;
> He just murmured "Toodle–oo",
> And he kept on walking still.

fell in. See: get fell.

fell off (the back of) a lorry. See **did it fall ...**

fellow(s). See: I say, you f.; stick around; two other; you wouldn't fool.

Fenackerpan. See **Finackerpan.**

fence. See: she wants; there's a nigger.

fetch. See: go and fetch.

fetch your bed and we'll keep you! is a C20 c.p. addressed either to an over-frequent visitor or 'sometimes among working-men to one who is always hungry and who can eat up any spare bait that is going around' (Petch, 1946).

few. See: there are only; you win.

fewer. See: because the higher; couldn't care fewer; days to do.

fickle finger of fate. See **fucked by the fickle ...**

fid. See: every hair.

fiddle. See: leaves his.

fiddler. See: going in; in and out; up and down.

Fido. See: down, Fido.

field(s). See: good field; little fields; put them; were you; wouldn't be seen; you're all about; you're way out.

fiendish clever, these Chinese results from a 'Goon Show' var. on **clever chaps, these Chinese.**

fie upon pride when geese go bare-legged! A proverbial c.p. retort made to a lowly person showing undue pride: late C17–18, BE.

fifty cents. See: would you for.

fifty million Frenchmen can't be wrong. 'The last line (and, I think, title) of a popular song of WW1, extolling the supreme virtue of copulation, though in veiled terms. No longer extant, but for a few years a c.p.' (J.W.C., 1977).

fight. See: come out and; if you can't f.; Jack doesn't; put them; step outside; you can't f.

fight between a fox and a chief steward – a. A Merchant Navy synon. for 'a very devious operation': C20. (Peppitt.) But then, a chief steward *needs* to be very, very shrewd.

fighter(s). See: better fuckers; I'm a lover.

fighting. See: that's fighting; them's fighting; what's yer f.

figure. See: you figure.

figures can't lie, but liars can figure. A c.p. rejoinder to the cliché, *figures can't* (or *don't*) *lie*: US since the 1920s (R.C., 1977), whence Aus. since *c.* 1960 (B.P., 1975).

fill. See: once before.

fill your boots! See **dig in ...**

filthy. See: don't be f.

Finackerpan or **Fenackerpan.** 'A catch phrase expression [cf ONE-WORD CATCH PHRASES] I heard on and off, years ago, in the North of England ... it was sung in "The Good Old Days" TV programme, 12 Jan. 1968' (Petch, 1969): so, very approx., *c.* 1905–35. Rather vague in meaning, it seems to have connoted 'Nonsense' or 'I don't believe that'. Improbably, yet not impossibly, it may have been suggested by 'You *finagle, man*'.
    In John Harris's WW1 novel, *Covenant with Death*, 1961 (p. 339) we read, 'He grinned slyly and announced a ditty entitled *Fred Fenackerpan, or the Hero who Made Victoria Cross* ... a bawdy ballad'. A pun on Victoria Cross, the decoration, and pseudonym of a popular sexy female novelist of early C20.

financial. See: are you.

find. See: don't look down; dumb; lost a pound; speak as; trying; and:

find another man to bring the money home. See **go and find ...**

find, feel, fuck, and forget is the navy's mainly lower-deck sexual motto, dating from *c.* 1890 and often, in C20, alluded to as *the four F method*. R.C., 1977, adds, 'In US "find *'em* [etc.]". "The 4-F method": punned on the 4-F draft classification (WW2), meaning unfit for military service. In the Services, it was a widely held belief that the 4-F's ... were all too fit for other, civilian duties, which they performed *vice* the absent conscripts'. A.B., 1978, notes the var. 5-F method: *find 'em, feel 'em, frig 'em, fuck 'em and foget 'em*, which he dates as common in the 1950s, in US.

find out. See: that's for me.

fine and large. See **all very large and fine.**

fine day for (the young) ducks – a, and **fine weather for ducks** and **great weather for ducks.** A joc. way of referring to an extremely wet day: respectively mid C19–20, but † by 1920; late C19–20; and since *c.* 1820. The second is the commonest; Dickens used the third in 1840. (Apperson.) There are, in C20, also the variants **lovely** or **nice weather for ducks**, q.v.

fine day for quacks – a. This humorous var. of the prec. refers to quack doctors and their like; but not confined to fair grounds, it can refer to 'phoneys' everywhere: since *c.* 1950 in its gen. application.

fine day for travelling – it's a. Aus., orig. and mostly rural: since *c.* 1920, Ernestine Hill, *The Territory*, 1951, ' "It's a fine day for travelling," they told him – the time-honoured phrase that all over the outback is notice to quit' (Wilkes, *Dict. Aus. Coll.*).

fine mess. See: another fine.

fine morning to catch herrings on Newmarket Heath – a, is the mid C17–mid C18 equivalent of **fine weather for ducks** above. Apperson.

fine night to run away with another man's wife – a. An elab. way of saying 'It's a fine night': late C16–early 19. Apperson cites Florio, Rowley, S (in the var. *a delicate night. ...*).

fine weather for ducks. See **fine day ...**

finess. See: one squint.

finger. See: done up like a sore; every hair; fucked by; I lift; if you don't want; keep your f.; mind your f.; pain in his; smell; sucked; take your f.; two upon.

finger-lickin' good – it's. Orig. and still (1978) applied to food, it does occ. appear with other applications, Described by Prof. Ralph W.V. Elliott, 1977, as 'that singularly unappetizing commercial catch phrase', it derives from the posters advertising Kentucky Fried Chicken. During 1975–77 one saw it on bill boards everywhere.

finger of suspicion points at you! – the. This cliché of the old-style (say *c.* 1870–1940) crime story has, since *c.* 1925, become a humorous c.p., often employed in the most trivial circumstances. (P.B., 1975.)

finger out! and **fingers!** See **take your finger out.**

fingers crossed – keep (Brit.) or **get** (US) **your.** See **keep your fingers ...**

fings ain't wot they used ter (or **t'**) **be.** Things aren't what they used to be (as if they ever had been!): this Cockney form of a very general impression and conviction going back perhaps centuries became a c.p. only in 1960 when Frank Norman's play, *Fings Ain't Wot They Used t' Be*, with lyrics by Lionel Bart, achieved a considerable success.

To quote only one novel, Karen Campbell's *Suddenly in the Air*, 1969, offers this:

'Then I've a few dollars I managed to hang on to. But even they aren't worth what they used to be.' I hummed 'Fings ain't what they used to be' under my breath.

finish. See: him all; I've started; job and; nice guys.

finished. See: have you quite; he finished.

Finnegan. See: off again.

fire. See: bigger the f.; don't fire; fool at one end and a f.; hip; I wouldn't piss; keeping the; where's the f.; who looks; worried.

fire's gone out – the, lit. 'An engine has stopped', was a Fleet Air Arm saying that, in that Arm, became a c.p.; the phrase prob. arose during the 1930s, but it didn't rank as a c.p. until during WW2 and didn't last for many years after it. An example of characteristically British *sang-froid* and manly meiosis. PGR.

fire drill in a Chinese insane asylum. See **I've seen more order ...**

fire-poker. See: take that f.

fireman, save my child! 'I've often heard this derisive cry but am not sure whether in England or in Canada' (Leechman, 1968); both, I suspect: C20. Prob. from the Surreyside melodramas of late C19–20. I've not heard it since the 1920s, but think that it was prob. current up to WW2.

Anthony Burgess, reviewing the first ed. of this Dict. in *TLS*, 26 Aug. 1977, commented, 'That very foul catchphrase dialogue beginning *Fireman, save my child* is practically a whole black-out sketch'. But is a 'catch-phrase dialogue' strictly a c.p.? Such dialogues are better described as 'chants': see esp. John Brophy's and my *The Long Trail*, 1965, an amalgamation of the three editions, 1930–2, of *Songs and Slang of the British Soldier, 1914–1918*.

firm. See: so firm.

first. See: there's a f.; to make a fool; women and.

first base – he (we, etc.) never (even) got to indicates that someone had no success at all; is US, obviously from baseball; is applied to any appropriate situation; and dates from the 1920s at latest. (J.W.C., 1978.) P.B.: there is a var. **... past first base.** Cf **five-yard line.**

first catch your hare is the c.p. counterpart of that sage and salutary proverb which runs *don't count your chickens before they are hatched*, which B.P., 1975, in ref. to Aus. usage, interprets as 'Make sure that you have the raw materials before starting' an enterprise. As a c.p., it goes back to well before 1900 and is the very usual misquotation of a piece of culinary advice given to house-wives by 'A Lady' (Mrs Hannah Glasse) in her book, *The Art of Cookery*, 1747: 'Take your hare when it is cased' or skinned; but who was the first person effectually to misquote, we do not know.

The phrase had, in C19–early 20, a very close US counterpart: *first catch the rabbit.* 'It results from old recipes, such as this one in the *Daily Citizen*, Vicksburg, Miss., of 2 July 1863: "The way to cook a rabbit is "first catch the rabbit." Since the phrase is in "quotes", it is evident that it was already an old saying. In late C19–20, it has been used to convey either the principle "First things first" or the precaution "Don't act prematurely" ' (W.J.B., 1977). 'In the US, often used sarcastically of someone who's on the wrong track' (Shipley, 1977).

first hundred years are the hardest (US) or **worst** (Brit.) – **(the),** belongs to the C20. Berrey glosses it thus: 'the first difficulties are the greatest'; perhaps rather 'the earliest-encountered difficulties seem to be the worst'; R.C., 1977, writes, 'This and its correlatives have [in the US at least] the connotation, "You may not believe it now, but one gets used to it in time"'. Cf this predominantly civilian c.p. with the next entry and also with **the first seven years are the worst** and **it'll all be the same in a hundred years.** See also TAD DORGAN'S ... P.B.: but elsewhere in the first ed. E.P. had noted that *they say the first hundred years are the hardest* was a favourite, in 1917–18, among US soldiers on the Western Front, citing HLM, 1922.

first million is the hardest – the. The first million dollars are the hardest to make or, as Berrey puts it, 'the first earnings are the most difficult': since *c.* 1920.

first on the top-sail and last on the beef-skid was, in the Royal Navy of *c.* 1860–1920, applied to an able-bodied seaman; it meant that he was first-class, 'first on the job and last at the mess table'. Ware.

first seven years are the worst – the – often introduced by **cheer up!** – was a British Army c.p. of late 1915–18. Glossed thus by John Brophy in B & P: 'Ironic with a jocular despair. ... Usually either Job's comfort to a grouser or a whimsical encouragement to oneself; it was rarely heard before that 1916–17 winter which drove the iron fairly into men's hearts and souls.'

P.B., 1975, says: 'A rueful c.p. concerning, for example, the 2-year National Service [in Britain for some years, after WW2]; "Oh, well, never mind, they say the first two years are the worst". The time-measure is, of course, variable.'

For a much less bitter, much more generalized, reaction to one aspect of *la condition humaine*, see **first hundred years...** above.

first term too early, second term too cold, third term too late is an Aus., esp. a Sydney, undergraduates' c.p., dating from *c.* 1925. Supplied by B.P., who has also supplied the comparable *freshers work first term, nobody works second term, everybody works third term*, which orig. at about the same time. (I never heard either when, 1914 and 1919–21, I was a Queensland undergraduate.) P.B., 1976, 'I heard this, again, fairly recently, applied to UK universities, with *term* changed to *year*' (this refers to the second version).

first turn of the screw cancels all debts – the. A 'catch phrase used when someone is worried about his dues ashore. A cheer-up from a messmate' (Granville, letter, 1962): RN: since the late 1940s. The screw mentioned is, naturally, the ship's: and the sentiment is so optimistic as to verge upon the mythical.

first up, best dressed is an Aus. domestic c.p.: C20. Employed 'where members of a family use each other's [or one another's] clothes' (B.P., 1975). Wedgewood adds, 1976, 'I have also heard this as an Irish joke (told by Val Doonican); but, of course, showbiz borrows as it sees fit'.

firty-free fevvers on a frush's froat, sometimes prec. by **free fahsend free 'undred and**, dates apparently from the 1920s and is, in L.A.'s compact language, 'the two-way dialect speech class chaffing formula of and by Cockneys'. An analysis of this c.p., both semantically and phonetically, would either cause any self-respecting phonetician *un véritable frisson d'horreur* or afford him a saturnalia of sensual recognition. Cf **ee, mum ...**

fish and find out! is an evasive reply to a question one doesn't wish to answer: since *c.* 1890; by 1940, becoming ob. yet, by 1975, not quite †. At once pert and pointed.

fish. See: or would you; peddle; shooting; tomorrow; wet arse; what's that got; ye gods.

fish, or cut bait! Please finish what you're trying to do, or else stop, so that someone else can try or get the chance to do it: US: 'since *c.* 1876; archaic and dial [ectal]' (W & F, who, 1960, compare **shit or get off the pot**).

[**fishin'** ... 'Two deaf acquaintances, seated on opposite banks of a stream: "Fishin'?" – "No! Fishin'!" – "Oh, I thought you was fishin'." This exchange formed, in the middle 1920s, a chant, even a sort of password, in Britain' (Dr Lindsay Verrier, 1976).]

fishing. See: what shall we do.

fit. See: it fits.

fit as a Malley bull on Sunday(s). Extremely fit – bursting with the *rudest* health – randy and rarin' to go: Aus.: since *c.* 1960. (B.P.; P.B. in 1976.) Wilkes, *Dict. Aus. Coll.*, lists the shorter *fit as a mallee bull*, defines *mallee* as 'the scrub', and quotes Jim McNeil, 1974: 'a beast toughened by spartan living conditions', Cf **Malley's cow.**

fit for Ruffians Hall. See **he is only fit ...**

fit on the mat. See: enough to give.

fit where they touch; fits where it touches; fits him like a duck's ass. See **it fits ...**

Fitzsimmons. See: don't make a Judy.

five eggs, and four of them rotten. See **putting your two penn'orth in.**

five. See: slap.

five will get you ten (dollars) forms the US equivalent of the Brit. **I'll lay you six to four.** It occurs neither in Berrey, 1942, nor in W&F, 1960, 1975, yet I have often see it in US novels

since the 1930s and it has passed into gen. usage for 'I'm reasonably sure'.

five-yard line. See: I got 'em.

fiver. See: here's a fiver.

fix. See: I'll do you; you've fixed.

fizz. See: it didn't f.

flag of defiance is out – the; also the bloody flag is out. He has a red face caused by drink; also, he is drunk: nautical: late C17–early C19, BE; Grose.

flag officers. See: midshipmen.

flagpole. See: run it up.

flames. See: I don't care if you burst; what do you expect.

flare up! This c.p. of *c.* 1832–45, and then, for perhaps twenty years prob. a nostalgic survival, was a cry of joy or triumph or jubilation or, indeed, of joyous defiance to the world in general or to a particular situation: 'Let 'em all come!' Mackay says, 'It took its rise in the time of the Reform riots, when Bristol was nearly half burned by the infuriated populace. The flames were said to have *flared up* in the devoted city.' (Mackay's long passage on the phrase is well worth reading.) In the c.p., the sense is sometimes that of the verb *flare up* and sometimes that of the noun *flare-up.*

flash. See: one flash; quarter.

flatter only to deceive. See **horses that ...**

flattery will get you nowhere. Don't go to the trouble of trying to persuade by flattering me: esp. from women to men, and perhaps commoner in US than in UK and the Commonwealth ('This is a very common c.p.': B.P.);' un-heard by me before 1950, but probably going back to *c.* 1945' (J.W.C., 1968). In Ellery Queen's *A Fine and Private Place*, 1971, I note:

'You're a clever adversary indeed. One of the cleverest in my experience.'

'Flattery will get you nowhere, Queen,' the murderer said, 'Gallop along on your fairy tale.'

The phrase has become so much a part of the Brit. coll. composite that it occurs thus in a sports page title of an article – 'Flattery Will Get You Nowhere' – in the *Evening Standard* of 29 March 1974. There is even a humorous var. *flattery will get you everywhere* – not very common.

R.C., 1978, concerning its later US usage: 'Now sometimes ironic, in response to an uncomplimentary remark' – as also, occ., in Brit. (P.B.)

fleas. See: sleep tight; so bare; who are you shoving; wild, woolly.

Fleet's lit up! – the. What Nigel Rees, in *VIBS*, calls 'the most famous broadcasting boob of all time'. From *Ariel*, the BBC's staff magazine, 7 July 1977, I quote, with their generous permission: 'the toss of a coin gave...the nation a new catch phrase, following the Spithead Naval Review in 1937...It was...Lieutenant Commander Tommy Woodrooffe who caused a sensation when he came to describe the fleet illuminations.' He had been celebrating with some old shipmates and 'when the time came for him to go on the air, he could produce just one comment, "The fleet is all lit up," which he repeated five times...But Britain had a new catch phrase which became a popular music-hall song and Woodrooffe went on to enjoy a distinguished career with the BBC as a commentator.' That toss of a coin occurred when Commander Desmond Stride and Lieutenant Commander Thomas Woodrooffe tossed up to decide which of them should do the afternoon, and which the evening, commentary; it fell to Woodrooffe to deliver the latter. The exact date of the broadcast was 20 May 1937.

The orig. words may have been 'The Fleet (*or* fleet) is all lit up', but the predominant form of the c.p. omits 'all'; at least, that is how I remember it – and so do several well-informed persons I asked about it. Absolute historical accuracy in such topical c.pp. is extraordinarily difficult to attain, as a comparison of the *Ariel* piece and on ensuing letter, with the Letters Editor's footnote, in the *Radio Times* for 23–29 July 1977, will show. The letter proved that

Woodrooffe was already very well known for his part in the commentary on the Coronation Procession; and the Letters Editor's footnote made it very clear that his 'The Fleet's lit up' broadcast 'was not the end of his radio career; in 1938 and 1939 he was the BBC's only commentator at the F.A. Cup Final, and the Grand National and the Derby. When war broke out he returned to the Navy, and did little broadcasting after 1939'.

But the matter doesn't end there. In 1977, Mr Maurice Wedgewood, Deputy Editor of the *Northern Echo*, supplied the following information. Woodrooffe, at the time, was Deputy Director of Outside Broadcasting for the BBC. 'From the deck of HMS Nelson he was describing the illumination of the Fleet following its Coronation Review by King George VI. Listeners heard a somewhat incoherent commentary in which "The Fleet's lit up – it's all lit up" was repeated several times, to which was added the alarming and mystifying intelligence, "It's gone – the Fleet has disappeared". After four minutes the scheduled 15-minute broadcast was faded out [by Harman Grisewood, the duty announcer] and replaced by dance music.' Wedgewood enriched his comments with the tail-piece: 'Establishing the new c.p. publicly, so to speak, an unknown reveller a couple of nights later briefly interrupted a programme of dance music to announce, "We're all lit up". In the following year "a musical frolic" at the London Hippodrome was entitled "The Fleet's Lit Up" and in 1943 a song in the show *Strike a New Note* was "I'm gonna get lit up when the lights go up in° London".' That 'musical frolic' was Jack Hylton's new revue, which 'ran for a very long time' (Derek Parker, 1977, who, concerning Woodrooffe's *gaffe*, noted that 'Reith didn't dismiss him, though he was suspended from duty for a while').

Mr Parker, in the same letter, told me that '"The Fleet's lit up" was not the *only* phrase spoken on the celebrated occasion... [Woodrooffe] started his [piece] with the quoted words, went on into a long and rambling commentary... The first few words of his commentary were: "At the present moment, the whole fleet's liddup – an' when I say liddup, I mean liddup by fairy lamps"', with confusion increasing in incoherence and general mangling.'

Someone is bound to ask, 'But why not simply go to the authoritative history of the BBC from its inception in 1922 until the Independent Television Act of 1954, when the BBC's monopoly ended: Asa Briggs's 3-volumed work, *The History of Broadcasting in Great Britain*, 1961–74?' Well, I have done so. On p.98 of Volume II comes this passage: 'The broadcasting of the unforgettable remarks of Lieut. Commander Woodrooffe at the Spithead Review of May 1937, beginning with the phrase "The Fleet is all lit up"...'; and on p. 621, '...the only problem at the Cup Final between Preston North End and Huddersfield Town [in 1938] was that after he had unhesitatingly predicted the wrong result (a Preston defeat) Thomas Woodrooffe, the commentator, had to eat his hat'.

So much for historical exactitude! One can understand the basis of Henry Ford's mythical 'History is bunk', He later explained: 'I did not say it [history] *was* bunk. It was bunk to *me*...I did not need it very bad' (*The Penguin Book of Modern Quotations*).

flesh. See: press the f.

flies. See: and no f.; come down from; no flies; where do f.; where the f.; wild, woolly; you've dropped.

flies around a bull's arse – like. Applied to a group of impressionally young males, or females, around an exceptionally attractive female, or male, respectively: N, Country: since late C 19. (Eddie Haines, 1978) P.B.: cf the synon. Malay *ada gula, ada sumut*, 'where there's sugar, there are the ants'.

flings (or **throws**) (**his**) **money around like a man with no arms** (– **he**). Refers to a man exceptionally close-fisted: Brit. and Aus.: since *c.* 1930. For dry, biting humour, cf the synon.

(have you) got death-adders in your pocket? (L.A., and Baker, 1959.)

flippin' kids. 'The "catchphrase of the year" in 1951, according to [the ventriloquist] Peter Brough, in whose [radio comedy] series *Educating Archie* it was spoken by Tony Hancock as yet another of the dummy's ['Archie Andrews'] long line of tutors. For a while, "the lad 'imself" was billed as "Tony (Flippin' Kids) Hancock" before moving on to his own shows [notably, 'Hancock's Half Hour'], which more or less eschewed catchphrases' (*VIBS*).

floating. See: I need a piss.

floats like a brick-built shithouse, with *she* understood, is the Merchant Navy's ironic description of a vessel that is very slow because so heavily built: since *c.* 1950. (Peppitt.) Cf **built like...**, the prob. source fo this MN use.

flog. See: so bare.

floor. See: if I stick.

flop. See: that's the way the cookie.

flowers. See: no flowers; say it with.

flu. See: if he had.

fluff. See: here's fluff.

fly. See: I'd love; I'm Anne; May bees; only birds; rushing; shoo; straighten; where the crows; you can't fly; and:

fly a kite. See: can't fly; go fly.

fly! All is discovered! See **hist! We are observed.**

fly-time. See: tight as.

flying low without a licence. Having one's fly-buttons (or zip) undone: schoolchildren's: later C20. (James Williamson, 1978.) A pun on *flying* in general and, in particular, a man's trouser *flies*. Cf **you're showing...**

Flynn. See: in like F.

fog. See: stands out; storm; what do you think that.

folk(s). See different strokes; hallo, folks; there's nowt.

follow. See: act to f.; don't look now; tinkle.

follow that! 'Beat, cap, or better *that!*', applied to action, remark, witticism, pun. 'Modern, US, familiar in UK. Extended as necessary, *Now follow that*; *Let's see you follow that*; etc....Fairly loose application – possibly echo of stage usage and the difficulty of one act or turn following a brilliant act or turn immediately preceding' (Wedgwood, 1977). I have heard it; but not before *c.* 1970. It prob. goes back to the 1950s. Cf **act to follow.**

follow the man from Cook's! 'Come along, follow me; etc. All my life!' says Leechman, in early 1969, thus placing it as Brit., C20, and Can., since *c.* 1908. The ref. is, obviously, to Cook's celebrated tours.

follow your nose! – often supplemented with **and you can't go wrong** or **you are sure to go straight** – is a non-cultured c.p. addressed to someone asking the way: since before 1854. Other forms, e.g....*and you will be there directly* (C17) are earlier; moreover, the phrase was clearly adumbrated in C14. (Apperson.) B.E. glosses *follow your nose!* thus: 'Said in a jeer to those that know not the way, and are bid to smell it out.' Contrast:

follow your own way: you'll live the longer occurs in S, Dialogue I, and seems to be a c.p. of *c.* 1700–60.

follower. See: leader.

Foo was here was, in 1914–5, the Aus. equivalent of **Kilroy was here.** In the Royal Australian Air Force, Foo was a favourite gremlin whose name may have come from a very popular US cartoon strip, 'Smokey Stover', where the titular character used *foo* as a stop-gap name for anything of which he couldn't be bothered to remember the correct name.

fool(s). See: bigger the fire; choose, proud; I may be; I'm like; like all fools; much wit; oh, I say, I am; only a f.; only birds; so fools; to make a f.; when I want; you could have fooled; you may go; you wouldn't fool; and:

fool at one end and a fire at the other – a. 'This refers to a cigarette smoker – according to non-smokers. The counter is "but there's good tobacco in between". By Scouts between the wars?' (Sanders, 1978). That would make its currency 1919–38. P.B.: but it occurred as a line in the satirical song

'Cigarettes, and Whiskey, and wild, wild women', recorded by the American group, Spike Jones and His City Slickers, c. 1950. Patterned on:

fool at one end and a maggot at the other – a; and **a fool at the end of a stick** are mid C18–early C20 'gibes on an angler' (Grose, 1788). It has another var., *worm* substituted for *maggot*, attributed to Dr Johnson; cf the proverb, *a fishing-rod has a fool at one end and a fish at the other*, and, for the attitude expressed, **come inside!**

foolish. See: quarter.

fools seldom differ. See **great minds think alike.**

foot. See: every time; I cut; I'll go hopping; kiss my f.; more like; put (one's) f.; when the Duke; dealt; you've got one; your ass-hole.

for a musical farce/ You must waggle (or wriggle) your arse,/If you want the production to go (or succeed). 'A musical show verity' of *c.* 1890–1935, (L.A. 1976.) Prob. from a parody of a music-hall popular song (a 'prompt' from Dr David Bridgeman-Sutton, 1978).

for God's sake, sing! I used to hear this fairly often *c.* 1912–30, but never since *c*, 1940, in the gen. sense, *'Please do something that pleasures me, so that I don't have to look at your face!'* It had been prompted by an anecdote of a man recently married to a woman gifted with a wonderful voice, but cursed with an extremely ugly face.

for half a farthing I'd do it. I'd need very little encouragement to be persuaded to do it: *c.* 1860–1914. Baumann.

for kicks. See **I only do it for kicks.**

for king and cunt is a Services' reply to the question. 'What are *you* fighting for?': earlier half of C20. With an obvious pun on 'for king and country'. P.B.: prob. simply a quot'n from the old Services' ribald song that includes the lines, 'To piss, to piss–Two pistols in my hand,/to fight for my cunt (*bis*)–to fight for my count-er-ee!'

for my next trick, followed by a significant pause. Uttered by someone, whether the culprit or one of his 'audience', who has just made a mess of things: since the early 1930s, for certain, but prob. since *c.* 1900. 'From the patter of stage magicians, who traditionally and blasphemously attribute the *gaffe* to Jesus Christ' (Shaw, 1968). As Mr Shaw phrased it a little later, 'Comic apology after a minor mishap. From music-hall acrobat or juggler or magician. World of entertainment. Hence in more general use for *any* minor mishap.'

for obvious reasons. When used lit., clearly does not qualify, but used when the reasons are *not* obvious, as bafflement or mere padding, or in parody of its sometimes patronising tone, is it near enough a border-liner: since mid 1970s (P.B.)

for show and not for blow. This Aus. c.p., meaning 'for display rather than for use', was orig. applied to a neatly folded handkerchief in the breast pocket and, when used lit., was not, of course, a c.p. at all; only when, *c.* 1950 onwards, it was applied to comparable things, did it achieve the dignified status of a genuine c.p.

for the birds. See **that's for the birds.**

for the hell of it and its elaborations, **just for the hell of it** (US, hence also Brit.) and **for the sheer hell of it** (Brit. only). Simply – or merely – or just – for the pleasure of doing it, experiencing it, seeing it, etc.; to express a reckless independence: orig. – ?*c.* 1910 – US, hence also – ?early 1940s – Brit.; of the elaborations, the former since *c.* 1930 in the US and since *c.* 1945 in UK, and the later (*...sheer...*) since *c.* 1950. (Based, for US usage, on a letter, 1975, from Harold Shapiro.)

The best Brit. example I happen to have encountered of *just for the hell of it* occurs in Norman F. Simpson's *The Hole*, performed in 1958. Early in this diabolically clever surrealist play Lorna remarks, referring to boxer Spider, 'I know people who claim to have seen him hold his opponent off with the ace of diamonds just long enough to reload his dice, and then perhaps he'd huff him two or three times just for the hell of it, and then you'd see it! Then you'd see the real *coup de grace*...

for the man who has everything. 'Seriously and literally used (since 1950?) in advertisements of gifts, especially Christmas, conspicuously useless and conspicuously costly; common as a c.p. used in mockery, mostly of an object [sometimes] the former, but usually the latter. [The c.p. is] not much later than the commercial [usage]' (J.W.C., 1977). Trepidantly, I suggest – feel, not know – that it did not become a c.p. earlier than the latish 1950s. Although not unknown in the UK among those who possess American friends or who read the *New Yorker* and often see *The New York Times*, it has not (1978) become a Brit. c.p. P.B.: but Brit. advertisers have used the slogan too.

for the widows and orphans – it's; or, in full, **all the money I take goes to the widows and orphans.** A cheapjacks' and market grafters' cynical c.p., dating from late C19 or very early C20; by 1960, slightly outmoded and by 1970, virtually †. (Petch, 1966.)

for this relief, much thanks! is the c.p. form, applied in late C19–20 to a much-needed urination, of the quot'n from Shakespeare's *Hamlet*, I, lines 8–9:

For this relief much thanks; 'tis bitter cold,
And I am sick at heart.

The relief of a military guard.

for those few kind words, many (occ. **my best) thanks.** (Only the *many* form is strictly a c.p.) A joc., often 'hammed up' but, no less often, ironic, exclam. of gratitude, esp. from one who is or has very recently been, suffering much misfortune. P.B.: in later C20 more usu. **thank you for those few kind words,** q.v.

for what we are about to receive. Of this mid C18–20 RN c.p., C. S. Forester, in *The Happy Return,* 1937, has written, '"For what we are about to receive –," said Bush, repeating the hackneyed blasphemy quoted in every ship awaiting a broadside.'

From the Grace said before meals. 'For what we are about to receive, the Lord make us truly thankful'.

for you the war is over was, 1940–5. used by British prisoners of war in Italy, where they were thus addressed, on their arrival, by the It. authorities. It was used joc. P.B.: in 1946, Martin Jordan pub'd his apparently sole novel, thus titled, about life in the Italian PoW camps. The phrase crops up again, as a joke, in McGowan & Hands, *Don't Cry For Me...*, 1983, about the Falklands War.

for your information is a sarcastic reply to an impertinent question asked by a nosy busybody: since *c.* 1955. (Petch, 1974.) With ironic allusion to the legitimate queries of commerce – and bureaucracy. P.B.: this is usu. the prefix to the reply.

forbid. See: perish.

force. See: brute force; don't force; may the Force.

fore you listed. Before you enlisted: a var. of **before you came** – or **come–up.**

foreman. See: near the.

forest. See: down in; worried.

forget. See: and don't you f.; as if I'm ever likely; aw, forget it; don't forget; find; I forget; I'll forget; you were born; you'd forget; you've forgotten.

forget it! – a var. of **and don't you forget!** – occurs in S.R. Strait's 'Straight Talk' in the *Boston Globe* in *c.* 1917. But it also, since the 1930s in the US (Berrey, 1942) and derivatively since *c.* 1950 in UK and the Commonwealth, has a different sense, 'It's not worth worrying, or even thinking, about'. Among US negroes, it 'implies that the listener has not properly understood what is in question or being explained; *example*, "If you think this dictionary was easy to put together, *forget it!*"' (CM). P.B.: I question E.P.'s linking *forget it!* with *and don't you forget it!* He has also omitted the use of *forget it!* in exasperation at someone's inability to grasp what the speaker is trying to explain or direct.

forgive. See: Gawd.

forgive me for swearing! See S, Dialogue I: 'MISS: [*stooping for* *a Pin.*] I have heard 'em say, a Pin a-Day, is a Groat a Year. Well, as I hope to be marryed (forgive me for Swearing) I vow it is a Needle.' This C18 c.p. means no more than 'if I may mention it'. Contrast rather than cf **pardon my French!**

fork. See: tinkle; white man.

fork in the beam! is a late C19–20 RN c.p. – and a firm order from the sub-lieutenant for all junior midshipmen to retire from the gunroom, which they thereupon did to remain outside until recalled. *'Fork in the beam* was merely an intimation that there was too much noise being made, and the banishment a hint for them to keep quiet in the future' (*Sailors' Slang*). Granville explains that there was an old gunroom – i.e., midshipmen's mess – 'custom of placing a fork in a deck beam above the sub-lieutenant's head, which was a sign that he wanted privacy'.

form. See: how's your dirty; what's the drill; what's the f.

form square to receive cavalry! This old military order has, throughout C20, been used, first by the Army and then, to a limited extent traditionally and humorously, 'as a warning when unpleasant or unwelcome company is sighted. Much the same as the Navy's "Stand by to receive boarders"' (Sanders, 1978). P.B.: the RN version is frequently civilianised as 'stand by to *repel* boarders!'

formerly I could eat all, but now I leave nothing. S. Dialogue II, has:

> LADY ANSW[ERALL]: God bless you, Colonel, you have a good Stroak with you. [That is, you're a notable trencher-man.]
>
> COL: O Madam, formerly I could eat all, but now I leave nothing; I eat but one Meal a-Day.
>
> MISS: What? I suppose, Colonel, that's from Morning till Night.

The precise meaning: 'My appetite remains excellent,' Tone: waggish. Date: C18–19.

fornicate. See: only birds.

fortnight. See: I'd rather keep.

forty. See: extra two inches; fair, fat; life begins; men over; once a knight; too old.

forty acres. See: three acres; wouldn't be seen.

forty-foot pole – would't touch it with a. See **wouldn't touch it . . . .**

forty pounds of steam behind him; occ. prec. by **with**. This RN c.p., dating from *c.* 1900, is applied to someone receiving an order to go immediately on draft, and derives from the fact that, at one time in the Navy's history, safety valves 'went off at a pressure of forty pounds.' *Sailors' Slang.*

forum. See: funny thing.

fought. See: like the man who f.

fought the battle of Paris – he. A US witticism of the 1920s and '30s: 'said of one who was stationed in Paris during the First World War' (Berrey).

found out. See: thou shalt.

four exits from jail is a US convicts' c.p. of C20. 'Spindrift' – an English ex-member of a gang – has, in *Yankee Slang*, 1932, explained it as 'Pay out, run out, work out (serve the term), and die out – meaning to die in [jail]'.

four F's. See: find, feel.

four-inch plank. See: thick as.

four minutes. See: I've only got.

fourpence. See: going round; good evening, Mrs. Wood.

four-speed walking stick. See: queer as.

fours and fives. See: none of your fancy.

fourteen hundred (new fives). There's stranger in the Exchange: a Stock Exchange warning cry, dating from *c.* 1870. For a very long time, the Stock Exchange had only 1,399 members; by 1930, the cry was ob. Why 'five'? Perhaps because one of its slang senses was 'a hand' (four fingers plus thumb).

fox. See: crazy like a fox; fight; they've shot; worried.

foxes always smell their own hole first. A c.p., dating *c.*1890–1914 and uttered by the culprit trying to shift the blame of a wind-breaking on to the first person complaining.

The US version is *every dog smells his own fart:* late C19–20 (Fain, 1977).

France. See: as we say; somewhere; when you dance.

frayed. See: his cinch.

freckle. See: two hairs.

Fred. See: come back.

Fred Barnes. See: where men.

Freddie. See: blind Freddie.

free. See: best things; feel free; it's a freak; standing; and:

free as shit from a goose – I'm (as). 'I'm completely uninvolved' in some misdoing: US: since at least as early as *c.* 1930; not much heard now, and never very common. (J.W.C., 1977.)

free, gracious and for nothing is a c.p. var., would-be witty, of the coll. *free, gratis and for nothing,* and lasting only *c.* 1885–1900.

free trade or protection? A raffish c.p., applied since *c.* 1905 to women's knickers or panties loose and open or tight-fitting and closed. By the early 1940s, at latest, ob.

freeze. See: books won't; 'til hell.

French. See: pardon my.

Frenchmen. See: fifty.

fresh. See: you're too f.

fresh hand at the bellows – a; often **there's a . . . .** A sailing-ship c.p. of mid C19–early C20; said when, esp. after a lull, the wind freshened.

fresh kiss, fresh courage. In *Yours Unfaithfully,* written by Miles Malleson and pub'd in 1933, a writer speaks thus in Act III:

> STEPHEN . . . Damn it! No, Alan! I'm not going to have 'special treatment' as a writer! Temperament, and all that. There's a proverb [*it isn't one*] among 'business' men in the 'city' – have you ever heard it? – 'Fresh Kiss, Fresh Courage'. Business men! They aren't supposed to deal in temperaments. 'Fresh Kiss, Fresh Courage.'

Apparently *c.* 1925–39.

freshers work first term. See **first term.**

fret. See: don't you f.; I should f.

friar. See: where it was.

Friday. See: ghost; golden; have a feel; he finished; it's Friday; t.G.i.F.; tomorrow will; and:

Friday! 'Another ITMA one and, probably, the most infuriatingly senseless of the lot' (Simon Levene, 1977). I had forgotten it – not a c.p. that carried much impact. Cf TOMMY HANDLEY . . . , q.v. P.B.: *VIBS* explains, 'Any remark ending with the word [Friday] – or one sounding like it – would bring the response, "Friday?" and the counter-response, "Friday!"'.

friend(s). See: do you come as; excuse my pig; good evening, friends; how to win; I'll tell nobody; I'm going to do; Les; shake hands; some of my; we're just; who's your f.; who's your lady; with a little; with friends; you're not my f.; your best f.; your bosom; and:

friend has come – my (little), and **I have friends to stay** are female euph. c.pp., announcing that the menstrual period has started: C19–20; by 1935, ob., and by 1950 †. A var., dating since *c.* 1830 and † by 1950, was *I have my auntie (or grandmother) to stay.* Cf (the) *captain is at home,* and **country cousin . . .**

frock. See: this won't.

frog. See: when he says.

froggish. See: if you feel.

from arse(h)ole to breakfast-time, as in, e.g. *(we were) buggered about from . . . ,* meaning harassed and upset from start to finish, and chased all over the place, is a vulgar C20 expression coming somewhere between a c.p. and a slang idiom. It has the euph. var., 'to describe something lengthy and tedious' (B.G.T. 1978), *it lasted from ear-'ole to breakfast-time,* and in Aus., *from Alice Springs to breakfast-time,* 'from one end of the country to the other, everywhere' (from Alice Springs, 'the isolated chief town of Central Australia'): the quot'n coming from the glossary to Alexander Buzo's *Three Plays,* 1973; it occurs in *Norm and Ahmed,* performed in 1968. It is just possible that, in this context, *breakfast-time* may orig. have been a ref. to breast-feeding. (P.B.)

from Beowulf to Virginia Woolf. An academic c.p., applied to a comprehensive course in English literature; its heyday was *c.* 1945–75. Virginia Woolf died in 1941 and we have begun to recognize writers prominent since her time, remarked Prof. Ralph W. Elliott in 1977, when he called this a 'familiar literary portmanteau catch phrase'.

from drinking out of damp glasses has, prob. throughout C20, been ironically applied to one who is speaking hoarsely (a 'gin-fogged voice'), as if from a cold thereby incurred. In R.H. Mottram's excellent *The Spanish Farm Trilogy*, 1927, we read: 'He did not blink...but suggested, in his voice, hoarse...from drinking out of damp glasses'. It remains current, although perhaps less commonly used than during *c.* 1910–60: its quiet wit and dry humour may ensure it a very long life.

P.B.: elsewhere in his notes, E.P. wrote, of *must have been drinking out of a damp glass* (or *mug* or *pot*), that it is a joc. c.p. either addressed or in ref. to someone who has caught a cold or is afflicted with rheumatism. A.B., 1978, pertinently points out, of its US currency, 'The person was drinking *draft* beer! The joke being that if you sit in a *draft* [Brit. *draught*] you may catch a cold. 1930s–40s.'
Cf **must have been lying in bed barefoot.**

from Greenland's icy waters to India's coral strand/Our good old NATO forces are getting out of hand is 'a riposte to a **snafu**: within NATO during exercises. John Winton, *The Fighting Temeraire*, 1971' (Peppitt). Prob. since *c.* 1965. An irreverent parody, with 'waters' for 'mountains', of the first four lines of Bishop Reginald Heber's famous hymn, *From Greenland's Icy Mountains*. Heber was Bishop of Calcutta 1822–26, and died in the latter year.

from marbles to manslaughter. A raffish London c.p. of *c.* 1830–70. In *An Autobiography*, 1860, Renton Nicholson wrote: 'About the year 1831 or 1832, play [i.e., gambling] first became common. Harding Ackland...an inveterate and spirited player at anything, "from marbles to manslaughter", as the saying is, opened the first shilling hell in the metropolis.'

from the sublime to the gorblimey. General, as an occ. var. of the cliché *from the sublime to the ridiculous.* (P.B., 1975.) Rachel Ferguson, *Evenfield*, 1942, writing of the 1920s: 'as the comedian put it, to descend from the sublime to the gorblimey' (p. 73). Petch, 1969, observes that the 'deep' Cockney form is *from the serblime...*, as in J.D. Strange, *The Price of Victory* (in WW1), 1930. There may even have been a midway stage, *from the sorblimey...*, influenced by the Anglo-Irish *sor* for *sir*.

from Tinker to Evers to Chance – but usu. **from** is omitted – was a US baseball c.p. referring to a clever 'play' concerted by three players, the names deriving from the trio that had devised and perfected it. For a while, it became so widespread that the following allusion in 'The Score in the Stand', part of Robert Benchley's *Love Conquers All*, 1923, must have been clear to many readers:

SEVENTH INNING: Libby called 'Everybody up!' as if he had just originated the idea and seemed proudly pleased when every one stood up. Taussig threw money to the boy for a bag of peanuts who tossed the bag to Levy who kept it. Taussig to boy to Levy.

Apparently it has been current since *c.* 1920; and in 1968, J.W.C. comments thus, 'Certainly is used generally of any triumph achieved by adroit and quick-witted co-ordination of two or more persons.... Everybody understands its origin in baseball.'

In Franklin P. Adams occur the touching lines:
These are the saddest of possible words:
'Tinker to Evers to Chance'
....
....
Words that are heavy with nothing but trouble:

'Tinker to Evers to Chance'.
He adds a gloss:
Joe Tinker, Johnny Evers and Frank Chance were members of the Chicago Cubs, the first at shortstop, the second at second base, and the third at first base. With a runner at first base, Tinker would stop a ground hit, toss the ball to Evers, and Evers would whip the ball to first before the man who hit the ball could get there, making a double play which was frequently repeated. [Cited in *BQ*.]

In *Guns*, 1976, Ed McBain neatly applies it to a cleverly concerted hold-up, and in a way that shows he assumed it to be readily understandable by his American readers.

from who laid the chunk implies either superior quality or quick decisive action. 'A common description of great speed is "He burned the breeze" – rode very fast – "from who laid the chunk"' (Adams): Western US, esp. among cowboys: (?) *c.* 1880–1940. Semantic origin, obscure.

front. See: not in f.; you're starring.

frozen over, and in September, too! 'From a road production of *Uncle Tom's Cabin* [i.e., the play from Harriet Beecher Stowe's 1852 novel; the novel was sub-titled *Life Among the Lowly*] in the last century: the escaping slave was supposed to jump from a cliff into the Mississippi and swim to freedom, but when the mattress behind the set was forgotten one night, he hit the stage floor with a tremendous thud, reappeared from behind the scenery, and, with this ad lib explanation, ran off across the stage "river" for his exit. Now used as a c.p. supplying or mocking the need for a ready if implausible explanation. I first heard this from that brilliant expert on the drama of the last century, Prof. Alan Downer of Princeton, but have heard it since the late Prof. Downer's time, largely in theatrical circles and often from people who have no idea of the origin of the phrase' (Ashley, 1982).

fruit. See: eat more.

fruitcake. See: nutty.

fry. See: go and fry.

fubar. There exists yet another WW2 var. on the **snafu** (q.v.) theme: *F. U. B. A. R.*, solidified as *fubar*: fucked up beyond all recognition, which Arthur M. Shapiro, 1977, ranks as 'better known than IMFU'.

fuck. See: couldn't organize; find; full of f.; go fuck; he'd fuck; take a running; you play like; you wouldn't f.

fuck a day keeps the doctor away – a. See **shit a day ....**

fuck 'em all! expresses a (usu. cheerful) defiance to the world in general or to this or that circumstance or situation in particular: since *c.* 1919. In the famous old army song *Bless 'Em All*, the orig. words were *fuck 'em all.* Cf:

fuck 'em all, bar six; and they can be the pall-bearers. 'I first heard this expansive expletive or c.p. in 1960' (P.B., 1974). It arose *c.* 1944 and was adopted from the US Army. Mr Beale tells me that James Crumley's novel about the US Army, *One to Count Cadence* (1969), 'carried as a prologue what the author labelled an "old Army prayer"':

Fuck 'em all bar nine –
Six for pall-bearers,
Two for road-guards,
And one to count cadence.

Skehan, 1977, supplies a perhaps earlier var.: *fuck 'em all, bar Nelson – and fuck him too!*

fuck 'em and leave 'em is 'proverbially the correct way to treat women. Very commonly used' (an anon. correspondent, 1973): late (? mid) C19 – 20. Sanders, 1978, adds, 'The motto of the British Cavalry, according to the rest of the army, was "love 'em and ride on", which, on mechanisation, became "screw and bolt". The first cavalry regiment was mechanised in 1928, so "screw and bolt" could date from then'. P.B.: with P.S.'s pun, cf the joke headline for the story of the madman who raped several laundresses and then vanished: 'Nut screws washers and bolts'. This *fuck 'em ...* version is perhaps a coarsening and vulgarization of the orig. **I must love you and leave you,** q.v.

fuck 'em, give 'em stew! Army cooks' contemptuous attitude to the rest of the troops: post-WW2; now used widely outside the Army. (Jack Slater, 1978.) An attitude that, however, was possible only in isolated surroundings and towards small detached sections – or in chaotic circumstances of active service. P.B.: in 21 years of Army service I never heard this slander on the Army Catering Corps – which is not to say that there were not plenty of other, mostly joc., jibes at that Corps' expense.

fuck me, I'll never smile again! An odd US 'expression of despair': 1950s–60s. (A.B., 1978.)

'fuck me!' said the Duchess, more in hope than anger, current since *c.* 1910, is a var. of the much more frequent **'hell!' said the Duchess,** q.v. Russell Davies in *New Statesman,* 1 Sep. 1977, stated that the follow-up, in his experience, is 'stirring her tea with the other hand'. Oddly, *I've* never heard *stirring her tea* related to the Duchess, only to the Princess: see **some day my Prince will come.** 'Anon.', 1978, reminds me that there's another follow-up: *and the Duke did so and drew her on like a pair of gloves,* existing at least as early as *c.* 1930. P.B.: by 1950 at latest the 'gloves' had been replaced by *a sweaty old sea-boot,* and the Duchess spoke *more in hope than expectation* – justifiably, because the Duke replied, wearily, 'What, again?', before stubbing his cigar on the mantel-piece, and drawing her on in this indelicate fashion. The whole thing is hardly to be classed as a c.p., since it is more of an oft-repeated and, in the Forces at any rate, well known short monologue.

fuck on the group – there's (or, usu. in narrative, **there was).** 'All hell has broken loose', it was pandemonium, panic, rush and bustle: Army: 1950s–60s, perhaps WW2. 'They hadn't done just as the brigadier ordered, and he found out, and there was *fuck* on the group!' Superseded by synon. *the shit hit the fan.* (P.B.)

fuck that for a comic song! (or a **top hat!**) I emphatically disagree; I strongly disapprove: sporting world and raffish world: C20. (Shaw, 1969.)

Lit., *that's* no comic song or *that's* not a real top hat. Brian W. Aldiss, 1978, notes the WW2 var. *fuck that for a game of darts.* Cf:

fuck that (or **this**) **for a lark!** 'Expression of dissatisfaction and disgust at some uncongenial task or situation' (P.B., 1974): C20. 'There is also a military var.: *fuck this* [or *that*] *for a game of soldiers!*' (ibid.): since the late 1940s. See also **balls to that lark!**

fuck-up. See: biggest fuck-up.

fuck you, buddy, I'm shipping out is a US version of the next. Recorded by *DCCU,* 1971.

fuck you, Jack, I'm all right.

Among invented sayings . . . one was general and typified concisely the implied and the often explicit arrogance of many senior officers towards the ranks. This was (the first word is a polite synonym for the one actually used) [in those days, *fuck* could not be printed] –

Curse you, Jack, I'm all right!

Thus John Brophy in Appendix A, Chants and Sayings, of B & P, pub'd in 1930 – and over thirty years later, 'consolidated' and revised as *The Long Trail.* In the 2nd edn, Brophy adds: 'The original form, i.e. in 1914, was:

Dieu et mon droit.

F – you, Jack, I'm all right.

pronounced with a strong Cockney accent, *droit* rhyming with *right.* By 1916, the original saying had been almost completely forgotten.' But this longer form was, I'm pretty sure, an elab. of the at first nautical *fuck you, Jack, I'm all right,* which seems to have arisen *c.* 1880.

The spread of that phrase to the army caused the unbeatable and ever-ingenious Royal Navy to coin a new c.p. of its own: *fuck you, Jack, I'm inboard* or, 'in other words, "Pull the ladder up, Jack, I'm all right"' (PGR).

Not to be outdone, the RAF, having adopted *fuck you, Jack, I'm all right,* decided to invent its own c.p. This they did – *fuck you, Jack, I'm fire-proof,* i.e. invulnerable; an

officers' pun on this: *per ardua asbestos.* [P.B.: this latter was not only officers': witness *The Mint,* T.E. Lawrence's account of life as a recruit in the RAF in 1922.]

The original phrase has, since WW2, experienced many euphemisms, allusions, translations, absorptions, mostly as the result of its own virility and trenchancy, but, in part, also as a result of the tremendous success of the film, *I'm All Right, Jack,* starring Peter Sellers and Ian Carmichael, 1960. A good example of euph. appears in Terence Rattigan, *Variation on a Theme,* 1958, near the end of Act I, where Ron says, 'But that's how I was told when I was a kid – in this world, Ron boy, they said, you've got to work it so it's "F.U., Jack, I'm all right", or you go under.'

An illuminating allusion-*cum*-absorption occurs in Laurence Meynell's excitingly entertaining novel, *Virgin Luck,* 1963: 'I could afford to have no ill feelings. I had made the bus; she hadn't. She was Jack; I was all right.'

'The bowdlerized variant "I'm all right, Jack" is much commoner in this mealy-mouthed country' – or so an extremely well informed American informed me in 1977. See also **I'm fire-proof.**

fucked and far from home, feeling utterly miserable, mentally and physically: an army c.p. of WW1, but believed to have had a civilian existence since *c.* 1905 or a little earlier: orig., it was supposed to represent the despair of a girl seduced and abandoned – and stranded. The earliest form of the phrase, recorded in 1899, seems to have been *fucked-up and far from home.* P.B.: since *c.* 1950 at latest, usu. *fed-up, fucked-up and far from home.*

fucked by the fickle finger of fate. Down on one's luck; blighted by an unexpected stroke of misfortune; done for: current in US and Can. since *c.* 1930, often in the shortened or allusive form *the fickle finger of fate. VIBS* notes that the latter was the name given to a mock talent show segment of the US TV comedy series, Rowan and Martin's 'Laugh-In', '("Who knows when the Fickle Finger of Fate may beckon *you* to stardom?")'. Its usage shows clearly in '"Check off Phase I," Marty said cryptically. "The fickle finger of fate has struck"' (Hank Searls, *Pentagon,* 1971, p. 21). Moe, 1977, noted an elab. var., *diddled by the dangling dong of destiny,* which seems not to have caught on, in spite of its imitative alliteration; and R.C., later in 1977, cited the occ. var. *five fickle fingers . . . ,* adding 'expression of annoyance at a bit of bad luck'. Adopted in UK by 1960 at latest in its (*fucked by*) *the fickle finger of fate* version.

fuckers. See: better fuckers.

fucking the Captain's dog, whether expletive or interrogative. 'Currying favor with authority': US Regular Army: latish C19–20. 'Someone gets a special favor. Another asks, "What have you been doing (to get that)? Fucking the Captain's dog?"' (A.B., 1978).

full. See: poke full; shoot it; wish in; woods; wouldn't say; yes sir; you're full.

full march. See: Scotch Greys.

full of fuck and half-starved, often prec. – but occ. followed – by **like a straw-yard bull,** was, *c.* 1870–1940, a low but friendly reply to 'How goes it?'

full of larceny, often ushered-in by **it's,** is a US theatrical c.p., 'said of an act which has stolen its "gags"' (Berrey, 1942): apparently dating from the 1920s.

full rich day – a, usu. prec. by *have you had* or *I've had.* The latter is 'spoken satirically and ruefully of "one of those days" [when everything goes wrong]' (J.W.C., 1977): US: since (?) *c.* 1955. Cf **one of those days,** q.v. I suspect that it derides the cliché *a full rich day* (non-ironic, of course).

full stop, end of story; sometimes merely *full stop!;* indeed the full form may be an elab. of *full stop!* itself. The short form indicates 'end of incident, matter, statement' – as in 'I'm no kitten on the keys; or, more precisely, I'm no kitten, full stop!' (L.A., 1976). Since the late 1950s. Cf **period!**

The full form denotes 'That's the perhaps unexpected end of the story' and seems to have arisen early in the 1960s. P.B.

wrote, 1974, '[I] first heard it in a cavalry regiment in Hong Kong, 1970; e.g., "So he applied to marry this bar-girl, and the next thing, he was kit-packed and on the plane (shipped out). Full stop, end of story! Tough!"' But gen., not specifically Services'; perhaps – or, rather, prob. – journalistic at first.

fun. See: ain't we got; having fun; it's all good clean; more fun.

funeral. See: dance at; late for; too slow; your funeral.

Funf speaking! or, orig. and better, **this is Funf speaking!** At the second programme – 26 Sep. 1939 – of 'It's That Man Again', later to be known as 'ITMA'; 'the supreme telephone character of them all – the notorious FUNF ... the embodiment of all the nation's spy-neuroses, a product of the times ... an ineffective, comic spy' arrived, to become immediately famous. 'Those blood-curdling tones, so soon to be heard being reproduced all over the country, were actually obtained by Jack Train speaking into a tumbler.' The name *Funf*, pronounced *foonf*, derives from the Ger. for 'five': the producer, Francis Worsley, had overheard his small son counting in Ger. and decided that this was precisely what he needed.

In his book, *Itma*, 1948, Worsley continues:

Although his first series was a comparatively short one, finishing in February, 1940, it was really the FUNF SERIES, for very soon after his introduction he became a nationwide craze. Children everywhere began playing Funf, just as they do now with Dick Barton, and no person with a family reputation for wit would dream of prefacing a telephone conversation with any other words than 'This is FUNF SPEAKING!' ... Everywhere one went, Funf kept cropping up. In the black-out two people would collide. 'Sorry. Who's that?' one would say, and like a flash would come the answer 'Funf!' Perhaps a workman would accidentally drop a brick down near a mate below. ''Ere, who threw that?' and from somewhere up in the scaffolding a raucous voice would bellow 'Funf!'

The heyday of this c.p. was brief: late 1939 – all 1940. But throughout the rest of the war, it continued to be one; and it would occ. be heard at least as late as 1950.

See also TOMMY HANDLEY ...

funny. See: don't be f.; it ain't f.; now, there's; once is f.; see you in the f.; very funny; what a f.; and:

funny as a crutch (– as). 'Not funny at all. Current [in US] from 1930s' (R.C., 1977). This 'sick' joke has the var. (*as*) *funny as a rubber crutch* as a palliative; the Morrises, William and Mary, mentioned it at least once in their 'Words, Wit and Wisdom' column, and in 1978 at least two correspondents independently recalled it.

funny as a piece of string, with or without prec. *as* or occ. 'yes', as in 'Don't you think that funny?' – 'Yes, as funny as a piece of string!' A NZ c.p., dating since *c*. 1930. (Harold Griffiths, 1970.) But it's ironic usage is less common than the straight, genuinely funny sense. Moreover, the phrase can be employed freely, as in 'It was as funny ... '

funny peculiar or funny ha-ha? is the c.p. comment upon the frequent statement that 'Something funny happened today': since *c*. 1924. One of the earliest dependable examples of the c.p. occurs in Act III of Ian Hay Beith's *Housemaster*, 1938. An Aus. example occurs in Alexander Buzo's *Rooted*, at I, iii. Prompted by the dual-sense *funny* – causing amusement, and the derivative *funny* – odd, strange, peculiar, puzzling, with the '*funny* bone' probably intervening. Cf **ha! ha! ha!**

It is inevitable that there should be variations, as in Nichol Fleming, *Czech Point*, 1970:

She planted a kiss on my cheek. The car almost ran off the road.

'You are a funny creature.'

'Funny ha-ha or funny peculiar?' I asked.

'A bit of both.' We both laughed.

funny stories. See: do you know any; have you any.

funny thing happened (to me) on the way to the theatre (tonight) – **a.** 'Traditional comedian's lead-in to joke. Origin not known' (*VIBS*). As Playfair notes, 1977, 'the c.p. element [of the phrase] consists in substituting other words, such as "Forum", for "theatre"', where he alludes to the title of a play that, starring Zero Mostel (d. 1977), appeared at the Alvin Theatre, New York, on 8 May 1962. The film of 'A Funny Thing Happened on My Way to the Forum' was first shown in 1966. Of variations on the theme, Michael Goldman, 1978, instances the use of 'studio' for 'theatre' by radio comedians; and J. W. C., 1977, writes that the phrase was 'ruefully adapted by Adlai Stevenson [1900–65] in a speech just after his loss of the presidential election of 1952 (or *perhaps* on the identical occasion in 1956, but I don't think so) as "A funny thing happened on my way to the White House" ... The allusion was universally understood'.

fur coat, no knickers. See **red hat ...**

further. See: I'll see you f.

fury. See: hell hath.

Fusilier. See: you're a F.

fustest. See: git there.

future. See: no future.

G

Gabriel. See: blow, G.

Gad, sir, when I was in Poona. 'A c.p. common among adults and older children or adolescents alike as [up to c. 1940, then only occ., and now only ironically or mock-nostalgically]: "Gad, sir, when I was in Poona ..." spoken in mimicry or mockery of the red-faced Anglo-Indian colonel who was also the club bore, the latter being in civil or military guise, a stock property of humorous writing of the time. The phrase was, of course, significant beyond this of impatience among youth with those venerable military or ex-military figures who, before WW1, had inspired a more reverent attitude' (Mr P. Daniel, 1978). It was only after WW1 (1914–18) that the expression became a c.p. Cf **two other fellows from Poona**, and **when I was in Patagonia**, qq.v. P.B.: as one who as a child was familiar with the phrase c. 1940, I know that we found the very name of Poona hilarious long before any awareness of its significance as a major military headquarters.

gaiters. See: all gas; guns, gas.

gal. See: I'll have your gal.

gall. See: of all the nerve; you've got your nerve; and;

gall not yet broken or, in full, **his gall is not yet broken.** A Brit. underworld c.p. that, used in mid C18–mid C19, was applied ironically to a clearly dispirited, even despairing, prisoner, either by the warders or by his fellow-prisoners. (Recorded by Grose, 1785.) A pun on the long-obsolete *galls*, or *gall*, courage.

Gallagher. See: absolutely, Mr G.; hi, ho! let her go; let her go.

gallery. See: no remarks.

gallop. See: if I stick.

galloper. See: his means.

gamble on that!; orig. **you can**, or **may, gamble on that** A c.p. synonym of 'assuredly!' or 'certainly!': adopted c. 1870 from the US, where used since before 1866, when humorist Artemus Ward used it; in Britain, † by 1960 and ob. by 1940; in US apparently † by 1940, ob. by 1920.

game. See: high, low; I do not like; I'm a true; if I have the name; it's a g.; it's an old army; it's only a g.; it's the only g.; name of; play the g.; plays a g.; talks a good; that's the name; there's a one-eyed; what a g.; and:

Game as Ned Kelly (– as). It is recorded in Wilkes, *Dict. Aus. Coll.*, 1978, where the earliest printed ref. is dated 1945, but it has been current for very much longer, the bank-robber so named having been hanged in 1880; his last words – so myth, perhaps fact, has it – were 'Such is life'; now a part of Aus. folk-history. P.B.: Wilkes also lists the variants *game as a pebble* (later C19–early 20), and ... *a piss-ant* (mid-C20), but E.P.'s notes make no mention of these equally picturesque similes.

game of darts. See: fuck that for a comic.

game of soldiers. See: fuck that for a lark.

games. See: don't let's play.

gammon and spinach. See: all smoke.

Gamp is my name and Gamp my natur' is, lit., a familiar quot'n from Dickens, but if another surname is substituted, the quot'n, no longer such, becomes a c.p., educated and, indeed, cultured, of late C19–20 (cited by Collinson) but rather less used after, than before, 1940.

gang. See: hail.

gangbusters occurs in two US c.pp.: (e.g., he) *comes on like gangbusters* and (e.g., it's) *going like gangbusters*. The first means that he plays or sings or dances exceptionally, esp. in a spectacular way: perhaps orig. Harlem jive, hence US entertainment in gen., and noted by Cat Calloway, 1944. Often shortened to *he really comes on*: contrast **creeps on like a shadow**. The *going like* ... is applied to something moving, or selling, very rapidly, and is contemporary with *comes on* ... R.C., who sends a quot'n from *The Boston Globe* of 14. July 1978, explains: '"Gangbusters" was a popular radio program of the 1940s; the ref. is either to the success of the program itself or (more likely) to the vigorous and successful pursuit of gangsters by its police protagonists'. Ashley, however, recalls, 1982, that the programme always began with a hullaballoo of fast car noises, police sirens, shrieking tyres, etc., and that it was this well-conveyed urgency that prompted the phrases.

gangway for a naval officer!: or, occ., **gangway! make way for** ... The latter is the English, the former the Aus. and NZ, WW1 c.p. F&G give the longer form only and gloss it thus: 'An expression, heard sometimes among New Zealand Army men, anywhere and on any occasion, meaning "Get out of the way", "Stand back", "Clear a passage"' – but chiefly the third. '"Gangway!" is ordinarily a common warning call on board ship' for bystanders to make way for someone, or a party, engaged on the ship's business. In B&P, John Brophy writes, 'GANGWAY FOR A NAVAL OFFICER! – A facetious method of asking for a passage through a group of soldiers, or of announcing *sotto voce* the approach of some self-important officer or NCO.' P.B.: the shorter form was still current among older soldiers in the 1960s.

In WW2 the corresponding, yet independent, c.p. among US servicemen was *make way for a* (or *the*) *lady with a baby* or *with a* (or *the*) *pram*, q.v.

gaol. See: see you in court; worse in.

garbage. See: leave the g.

garbage in, garbage out! 'The computermen's c.p. *par excellence.* Now so well known as to have the recognized abbr. GIGO (pron. with a long *i*). It means simply that if one feeds into the machines, for processing, material that is rubbish, then rubbish will be churned out in return. From US and current since the widespread use of data-processing machines' (P.B., 1975). The *Concise Oxford Dict. of Proverbs*, 1982, gives an early source in print at 1964.

garden. See: everything in the g.; everything is nice; I'll go out.

gardener. See: as the actress; everything in the garden.

Garrick. See: do as G.

garters. See: half past kissing; I'll have your guts.

gas. See: all gas; guns, gas; it's a g.; now you're cooking; or out; and:

gas is out – my or his or your, etc. I've run out of, or I'm short of, money: Brit. underworld since *c*. 1950, and gen. low slang since *c*. 1960. (Robert Roberts, *Imprisoned Tongues*, 1968.) Here, *gas* implies the wherewithal to keep warm.

gassed at Mons (and **on the wire at Mons**). See **hanging on the wire** and **Mons** ....

Gaston. See: after you.

gasworks. See: cor! chase; once round.

gate(s). See: little fields; saw; you're swinging; and:

gate's shut, short for **my gate's shut**, means 'I'll say no more'; 'I have no more to say': Aus.: since *c*. 1920. See D'Arcy Niland, *Call Me When the Cross Turns Over*, 1958:
  'No,' she insisted. 'I want to know.'
  'No good prodding me. My gate's shut.'
Of rural origin.

gateau. See: 'ave a piece.

Gath. See: tell it not.

gaudy. See: neat.

Gaw, or **Gawd**, **cast me**, **don't ask me!** A horse-racing c.p., dating from the late 1940s. In the *Sunday Telegraph*, 7 May 1967, in an anon. article its author says, 'An expression by a racing chap, such as "Gaw-cast-me-don't-ask-me" means blood-pressure soaring. It usually denotes that a fancied horse has fell over or something – says Danny' (who, on the inside, is telling the reporter, who, relatively, is on the outside). A sort of rhyming slang: indeed *cast* prob. rhymes on the illiterate *ast*, ask.

Gawd forgive him the prayers he said! He did curse and swear! This, according to Ware in 1909, is an evasive Cockney comment: *c*. 1880–1930.

gay. See: that's all gay; what a gay.

gee, look it! This Can. children's c.p. of astonishment, or of excited interest, was adopted, *c*. 1950, from the US, where current since the middle 1940s. Leechman, writing in 1959, adds, 'I recently read the next step: "Oh, lookit at that!"' By itself *lookit*, means 'look here' and presumably slovens *look at it*. P.B.: and Charles M. Schulz in his 'Peanuts' Cartoon strip,? *c*. 1970, had his hero Charlie Brown, much pestered with requests by his younger sister to 'Lookit! Lookit!', reply testily, 'I *am* lookiting!'

geese go bare-legged. See: fie ...

geese flying out of (one's) **backside.** See **Sparrows** ...

gelt gait zu gelt. ' "Money makes money" (Yiddish saying common in the underworld of commercial fraud)' (David Powis, *The Signs of Crime*, 1977): since *c*. 1950 at latest. Strictly *gelt geht zu gelt*, lit. 'money goes to money'. In the underworld, *gelt*, from German *geld* (*via* Yiddish, of course), is 'money'.

gentleman. See: as I am a g.; born a g.; give the g.; I won't put; officers and g.; time, g.

[**gentleman (and) a scholar and a fine judge of whiskey** – a. When, a few years ago, I first heard this, I regarded it as a neat, familiar quot'n. Well, there exists Robert Burns's 'gentleman and scholar' (1786), but I've found no record of the full phrase; perhaps wrongly, I surmise that the latter part – *and a fine judge of whiskey* – was added by some Dublin wit; I merely hazard the guess that the whole has been a virtual c.p., educated and urbane, since early C20. Mr Jack Slater, of Oldham, Lancashire, tells me, 1978, that he heard the first part in Australia's Northern Teritory during the period 1957–61, and the addition from an American doctor in Bokhara, Uzbekistan, in 1969; he mentions that *he is*, or *he's*, often prefaces the statement. Playfair writes, 1977, that, if the spelling *whiskey* is correct, my 'Dublin surmise must be right' and adds that 'at the beginning of C19, no one would have regarded being a judge of whisk(e)y as anything to boast about'; he implies that he wouldn't

disagree to my theory that the full phrase orig. *c*. 1890. I think that *c*. 1890–1950 it verged on becoming a c.p., but that it never fully qualified. P.B.: I had never heard the *fine judge* ... part, but recall that in British Army messes in Germany, *c*. 1960, the phrase *Sir, you are a Christian, a scholar and a gentleman* was often used as joc. fulsome, though quite genuine, thanks for a favour rendered.]

gentlemen prefer blondes has been a US c.p. since 1925 and a Brit. since 1926: in the former year, Anita Loos pub'd a book so titled, with dramatization the following year. She herself realized that this 'Illuminating Diary of a Professional Lady, a novel that satirized two naïve, yet impudent and successful, sirens of the jazz age' (James D. Hart), has a title conveying less than the truth, for three years later, she brought out the rather less popular *But Gentlemen Marry Brunettes*, itself no more veracious than a self-respecting epigram needs to be. Although still alive, it has, since *c*. 1943, been steadily losing its vogue; yet I shouldn't care to predict how much longer it will last.

Anita Loos will perhaps best be remembered for 'Kissing your hand may make you feel very, very good, but a diamond and sapphire bracelet lasts for ever' (*Gentlemen Prefer Blondes*, ch. 4). Nevertheless, her two most famous book-titles combined to form the c.p. *gentlemen prefer blondes but marry brunettes*, which became † by *c*. 1960, as J.W.C. reminded me, 1977. (This entry written 13 Sep. 1978, 'just to keep the record straight'.)

gentlemen present, ladies (– there are or **there're**) is a joc., yet also satirical and slightly censorious, var., dating from 1945, of the like (*there are*) *ladies present, gentlemen*, so please mind your language.

gently, Bentley! 'Jimmy Edwards used to growl this euphonious coinage at Dick Bentley in *Take It From Here*' (*VIBS*), whenever the latter became excited, in the radio comedy series so popular in the later 1940s – early 50s. The c.p. was seized upon by the public at large and used whenever needed for 'Take it easy!' or 'Gently does it'. It survived the demise of the series by a decade or more. (P.B.)

George. See: everything is G.; let George; that's real.

George! – **let's join,** and **where's George?** were a pair of linked c.pp. that orig. in 1935, in advertisements set forth by Messrs Joseph Lyons, who, in elucidating the mystery, state that George is *at Lyonch* and that George has *gone to Lyonch* or lunch at a 'Joe Lyons's'. This *George* may be regarded as typical of any middle- (though not upper-middle) class householder, esp. if he is married; it had earlier been, as it still is, a conventionalized, rather plebeian, English form of address to a stranger: cf the US *Mac*.

Both of these phrases lasted only for the years 1935–6; and *where's George?* – consecrated in Benham – almost immediately came to be applied to any male person noticed as being unexpectedly absent. Messrs Lyons's advertisement-pictures showed a pathetically vacant stool or chair.

George Dandin. See: tu l'as voulu.

George, don't do that! 'Not a proper catchphrase but a quotation from Joyce Grenfell's Nursery School sketches. Part of its charm lay in our never knowing *what* it was that George was doing' (*VIBS*). I entirely agree with Nigel Rees that the phrase deserves an entry in any work of this sort, if only to commemorate one aspect of Joyce Grenfell's (1910–79) brilliantly evocative monologues that were so ideally suited to radio. Another 'difficult' child in this imaginary class was Sidney, who, when teacher suggested that each should choose the flower he or she would like to be, evoked the disapproving 'No, Sidney, you *can't* be a holly leaf!' (P.B.)

Georgia. See: everything is peaches.

Georgie Best. See: be my G.

geritol. See: protocol.

Germans. See: don't let's be.

get a bag! is a cricket spectators' cry to a fielder missing an easy catch, mostly in Aus. and NZ: late C19–20. The implication is twofold: that he should be the team's twelfth man, who carries the bag, but also and predominantly that, if he were to hold out an open and empty bag instead of his bare hands, he'd stand a much better chance of making the catch.

get a grip of your knickers! This is a c.p. elab. of the simple *get a grip!* itself elliptical for 'come along, get a grip of yourself (*or* -selves)!', meaning 'pull yourself together: act smartly, sharply and sensibly'. *Get a grip!* (often pron. *gerragrip*) was a favourite exhortation among Service, esp. Army, NCOs around mid C20, and the *knickers* elab. may have arisen under the influence of **get your knickers untwisted!** (P.B.)

get a horse! According to Mr Norris M. Davidson, a retired radio commentator on music, including opera, and very widely read, who was born *c.* 1908, this

was a common American phrase in my childhood, when the motor car or automobile, as we called it, was a novelty. The roads not being paved were full of mud holes; tires were apt to burst, engines conked out and publications like *Life, Puck* and *Judge* were filled with illustrations about stranded motorists. Many showed the car being towed ignominiously by a horse. Urchins would shout 'Get a horse!' at every daring motorist. *Punch* used to be filled with similar illustrations, but I'm not sure whether the English lads used this phrase. One would think they would have. 'Get a horse!' is sometimes heard even to-day. [Letter of 1968].

The c.p. has a fairly common var., *hire a horse!* In 1968 W.J.B. wrote, 'Obsolete. Phrase used in disparagement of early automobiles. Cf **get out and get under!**, and contrast **I've got an 'orse!**

get a load of that! or **... of this!** Just look at that!; just listen to this!: both were orig. US (a US record titled 'Get a Load of This' appeared in 1926: Eric Townley, 1978), and both phrases bore both senses: adopted in UK *c.* 1943.

get a number! See **get some service in!**

get a saddle! 'One logger's admonishment to another logger not to "ride the saw" ... neglect his end of the job' (Adams): among lumberjacks in NW US: C20.

get along with you! and **go along with you!** Be quiet and stop talking nonsense! Stop flattering me – stop fooling me!: used playfully and joc. or, at the very least, good humouredly. The former, used by Dickens in 1837 (*OED*), arose *c.* 1830; the latter, *c.* 1850. Cf **get out!**

get (one's) ass in a sling. See **don't get your ass....**

get away closer! is, as Ware coyly puts it, 'an invitation to yet more pronounced devotion': late C19–20; ob. by 1935 and virtually † by 1945. At first a costers', it very soon became a gen. Cockneys', c.p. Cf **stop it, I like it!**

get back in the pot! See **come on, stew....**

get back into your box! We've heard enough from you, be quiet: orig. (1880s) US, it was anglicized by *c.* 1900. Apparently it comes from the stables. Neil Lovett, 1978, notes that the Aus. form has *in* for *into*. Cf *get back to your kennel!*,q.v. at **back to the kennel.**

get down to the nitty-gritty. See **let's get down....**

get fell in! Fall in: among NCOs, it amounted to a c.p. – grammatically interesting, because, from being a mere illiteracy, it became consecrated; orig. and always army, it spread to the other Services. PGR.

get hep! 'Get wise to yourself!'; 'Act your age!'; 'Grow up and be alert!': US: late 1950s–1960s, 'By 1977, dead' (Fain). Cf **be your age!**

get in, knob, you're posted! An RAF c.p., uttered when one has heard of an imminent posting to another camp or district and is gaily determined to have a last fling, usu. sexual: 1939–45. Then mostly historical (*knob* being slang for the *glans penis*). Cf the low c.p., **get in, knob, it's your birthday!**, in joyous exclam. at the sight of intimate female flesh: army: C20. Also cf **you wouldn't knob it!**

get in there! 'Give it all you have!' – really go to work on it: Harlem jive, then US entertainment as a whole, finally gen.: since *c.* 1938. (Cab Calloway, 1944.) It derives from:

get in there and pitch! 'Instead of dreaming and endlessly talking, take an active physical part in the effort, the attempt the struggle' – or, more gen., 'Stop talking and work or act!' A US c.p. of C20, from the game of baseball.

get in there, Moreton! See **Oh, get in there....**

get in there, Murdoch! 'was a catch phrase in my younger days; and I believe it had something to do with a poplar footballer' (Noble 1974): *c.* 1920–35.

get inside and pull the blinds down! Get out of the public view and hide in shame!: a Cockney c.p. that, *c.* 1860–1940, was addressed to a poor horseman. (Recorded both by Ware and in Benham.)

get into the act! 'Said to anyone not doing his share of the common task': US: since *c.* 1930. Orig. addressed to a vaudeville actor not over-exerting himself. (J.W.C., 1978.) Occ. *let's get into the act!* See also **everybody wants to get....**

get it! is 'a cry of encouragement to one engaged in doing something positive and exciting' (CM): US negroes': 1920s–50s. Make sure you get what you want *or* Do what you intend.

get it all together! and **get it together!** See **get your act together!**

get lost! Oh run away and stop bothering me! Adopted from the US, *c.* 1944 in Aus. from US Servicemen, and *c.* 1949 in UK. For an English example see Dominic Devine, *Dead Trouble*, 1971:

Sarah kept pace with her. 'I need you help, Betty,' she said.

'Get lost.'

Also Can., with var. *go and get lost:* 'of long standing' (Leechman, 1969).

P.B.: E.P.'s reason for including this, while apparently rejecting the equally common (in both senses) *get knotted*, or *nicked*, or *stuffed*, and so many others of the same import, is not clear to me.

get Maggie's drawers! See **give him Maggie's drawers!**

get me, Steve? See **got me, Steve?**

get off and milk it! 'Shouted by schoolboys at passing cycling-club riders (1950s),' says Mrs Shirley M. Pearce (1975), who continues:

up, up, up! was a similar cry, but was also uttered by groups of sports cyclists when passing members of the more sedate CTC (Cyclists' Touring Club). 1950s.

King of the Road! was an advertising slogan of, I believe, Lucas cycle lamps and dynamos. This would be shouted at lone racing or sports cyclists or at the leader of a bunch of touring cyclists. The same slogan [the first of the three] was used to embarrass large-breasted lady cyclists, as the connection between the shape of the Lucas dynamo lamp and the breasts of the lady in question was supposed to be obvious. 1950s.

P.B.: I was amused, only a week or two before reaching this entry for the 2nd edition late in 1982, to hear *get off and milk it!* chanted as I cycled past a group of 12-year olds on their way to school, in Loughborough, Leicestershire.

get off me barrer! is purely Cockney; a comic ending 'to fit any number of music-hall songs... On chromatic scale, very roughly goes CBCED. I'd date its origin with *good evening, friends* at 1880s; and its currency stretches to the present. Both are a pleasant self-parody of fairly simplistic group melody-making' (Cyril Whelan, 1975). But it more prob. dates from late 1940s or early 1950s, when used by a radio comedian – ?Arthur English.

get off my back! 'Stop nagging (at) me!'; 'Stop being a nuisance! Leave me alone!': often in the form 'Look, get off my back, will you!': Aus. and Brit., perhaps adopted from US: since *c*, 1940. (*AS*; Neil Lovett, 1978.)

get off my case! 'Let – and *leave* me alone!' Much used by US Negroes in the late 1960s and 1970s. (Landy, *Underground*.) Cf **don't get on ...**

get off my cloud! 'Stop bothering me!' Paul Janssen has reminded me, 1978, that this 'was the title of a very popular record: The Rolling Stones, 1965. The phrase had some vogue in the late 1960s among young people'.

get off my neck! 'Stop trying to bluff *or* fool me!': mostly English military: from *c.* 1915. It derives from the synon. *oh, Gertie, get off my neck!*, a predominantly Cockney c.p. of *c.* 1905 – 15.

get off that dime! 'Addressed to a couple dancing in extremely close contact (i.e., close enough that they could both stand on the same dime) and presumably deriving sexual satisfaction [therefrom]. From 1930s or earlier, but now extinct with decline of "touch" dancing. Also, couples seeking sexual excitement are [nowadays] more likely to go to bed than dancing ... Also some general current use in the sense "get moving"' (R.C., 1978), P.B.: with the later sense, cf the Brit. *get your finger out!*, q.v. at **take ...**

get off your knees! is a Services', but esp. RAF, c.p., which, when directed by a NCO to an airman, signifies that the latter's job seems too much for him or that he is just plain lazy, but which, when spoken by a friend, was an encouraging 'shout to a comrade coming in tired from a march, or showing similar signs of distress' (PGR): since *c.* 1920. Behind the impatience lies the encouragement of 'You're *not* beaten by your knees'. The RAF occ. employed the var. **get off your chin-strap!**, with which cf **lean on your chin-straps.**

get on! See **get out!**

get on line! 'Literally, from the queues; figuratively, and as a c.p., Join the long queue of people with similar problems, feelings, opinions, etc., e.g. "I'd like to slug that son of a bitch!" (i.e., "Wouldn't we all!") Perhaps orig. New York City, where "get *on* line" is the standard proletarian version of "get *in* line" (R.C., 1977). I prefer the c.p. to be dated from the 1950s. P.B.: cf the Brit. **join the club!**

get out! Stop flattering me! Tell that to the Marines: the former sense, used predominantly by females, the latter by males: since *c.* 1830. Dickens was one of the earliest to honour it in print. And as J. W. C. notes, 1977, *get out!* and *get on!* are both Brit. and US for 'Stop fooling' or 'Stop lying': late C19 – 20. P.B.: to the same 'family' belong the idiomatic *get away!* and the Northern dialect *give over!* the latter 'given widespread appeal by [the comedian] Al Read' (*VIBS*), Cf **get along ...**

get out and get under! was 'heard by my father in the Sheffield Empire *c.* 1895 – 1900, when the motor car began to appear' (Lawrence Smith, 1976). Apparently it survived up to WW1 and after; for Smith recounts that he heard it, during the late 1940s, in Aus., where, after being lit. applied to the need to get under a car or a truck and see, then if necessary repair what was wrong, it 'caught on' as a c.p. and, perhaps independently, also in Yorkshire at least. But it wasn't only a Yorkshire and Aus. c.p., as R. S. makes clear in this excerpt from some notes, 1976: 'An elaboration of *get out!* especially in the Cockney form, *git out an' git under!* From a briefly popular song, *Get Out and Get Under the Moon, c.* 1910.' Noble, 1976, writes, 'The date I have for the song is 1913. ... The song tells of a man taking his girl for a ride, and the car breaking down. ...

"He'd have to get under, get out and get under" [it]. It was a very popular music-hall song, and **get out and get under** was a catch phrase right into the First World War.' The date 1913 is supported by James Laver's *Edwardian Promenade*, 1958. It looks, therefore, as if the two songs reinforced each other, as frequently happens.

Ronald Pearsall, *Edwardian Popular Music*, 1975: 'Typical of quintessential ragtime ... [it was] sung in the [London] Hippodrome revue *Hello Tango*. In many ways it is the American equivalent of the London music-hall narrative song, but, unlike most of the British numbers, it was contemporary.' An accompanying reproduction of the sheet-music cover has 'He'd have to get under – get out and get under. (To fix up his automobile.) Written by Grant Clarke and Edgar Leslie. Composed by Maurice Abrahams...

Sung with immense popularity by Gerald Kirby.'

get out and walk! See **pick the bones out of that!**

get some dirt on your tapes! Get some experience as an NCO – esp., before you start throwing your weight about: Services': since *c.* 1920.

get some sea-time in! (– you want to) A Merchant Navy taunt, of the 1950s – 60s, to ratings in the RN: in short, the emphasis lies on *sea*. (Peppitt.) But P. Daniel, 1978, glosses the longer version as an RN (lowerdeck) c.p. expressing scorn of the addressee's (much) shorter service. Perhaps the orig. of: **get some service in!** and **get some time in!**, often shortened to **get some in!**; and **get a number!**, the last being the most insulting: Services': c.pp., dating from *c.* 1920 – although the last may date from *c.* 1917. P.B.: get some in! was still being used, *ad nauseam* and mostly joc., among National Servicemen in the late 1950s.

get stuck in! 'A form of exhortation used by NZ Rugby supporters in addressing the players, means "Play much harder". Used also in other games, and in general contexts, e.g., when a job is being done. The idea seems to be that adhesiveness connotes vigour and enthusiasm. In common use since about 1920' (Arthur Gray, in a list of NZ c.pp. he sent me in 1969). Still current in Aus., this c.p. has migrated to UK.

get (often **git**) **the ambulance!** An urban c.p. addressed to a drunk person: 1897 – *c.* 1940. Ware.

get the cat to lick it off! and **try a piece of sandpaper!** Unkind advice to youths with down on their cheeks or their upper lip: C20; but little heard since WW2. Cf **smear it with butter ...**

get the drift? Do you understand what I'm saying?: US: since the late 1920s. (W & F.) From 'the (general) *drift* of the conversation'. Cf **got me, Steve?**

get the hook! This US c.p., derives 'from the days, up to *c.* 1930, of amateur vandeville contests; it was said that the managers kept a long hook in the wings to drag off incompetent but stubbornly persistent performers. Not, of course, a c.p. in those circumstances, but it is one when some guest is not succeeding in entertaining the company; sometimes extended to losing a job' (J. W. C., 1978).

get the lead out of your pants! is the US 'pop' musicians', but also a gen. US, slangy c.p., synon. with **get stuck in!**: since *c.* 1930. (Berrey.)

The phrase soon became reduced to *get the lead out*, of which J. W. C. writes, 1975: 'Universal; though always humorous; recognized as vulgar, but used by educated people – to each other only, however – as a kind of *healthy* vulgarism. ... [It means] Get up and get busy. It originated (I *think*) in the language of sergeants (perhaps especially drill sergeants] in Hitler's war'.

A.B. adds, 1978, that it has the variants *get the lead out of your britches* or *ass* or *butt*. Cf **shake the lead out of your ass!**

get the shilling ready! Prepare to subscribe!: 1897 – 8, esp. with ref. to the *Daily Telegraph's* shilling fund for the London hospitals, one of the charities characterizing the sixtieth year of Queen Victoria's reign. Ware.

get the shovel! 'Said when a lot of bullshit is being spread around' (Fain, 1977): US: since *c.* 1960 or a little earlier.

get them off you! 'A mindless greeting sometimes addressed to unknown girls': Anglo-Irish: since *c.* 1960. (Skehan, 1977.) Here, 'them' clearly signifies 'panties' and 'mindless' refers to mindless young toughs. P.B.: cf the even simpler 'get'em down' howled, chanted, roared by 'manly' Englishmen at professional strippers; does the insult sound any less offensive in an Irish accent?

get up, Joe! is the c.p. involved in 'asking a fellow "viper" to accept a mariyuana cigarette' (the US Senate Hearings, *Illicit Drug Traffic*, 1955). R.C., 1977, comments: 'As evanescent as most drug terms. Now long dead – as is "viper" itself'. These drug c. pp. are hardly worthy of inclusion, yet one can hardly ignore them completely.

get up them stairs! A Services', perhaps esp. RAF, c.p. addressed by his comrades to a man (mostly if married) about to go on leave: since *c.* 1940. Before the phrase achieved widespread use and radio renown, i.e. in 1942, **Blossom** – generic for a woman – either prec. or followed the rest.

A valuable sidelight on the vitality of this c.p. occurs in Margaret Powell, *The Treasure Upstairs*, 1970: 'So, I told her a thing or two I'd seen going on on the backstairs between the men of the house and the housemaids and parlour-maids. It wasn't romantic love I told her about, it was plain, straight-forward "Get up them stairs!"' And P.B., 1974, remarks that it 'has lasted well'.

See also **remember I'm your mother**, which puts it back to WW1.

get wise to yourself! Don't be ridiculous – grow up! This US c.p. goes back to *c.* 1910, if not earlier. (Berrey.) But, as Neil Lovett comments, 1978, it has become, if it hasn't always been, almost as much a cliché as a c.p. Cf **why don't you get wise ...**

get with it! Be alert to – or conversant with – or understanding of and sympathetic to – the current state of affairs or condition or information: US: since *c.* 1950; adopted by UK as well as the Commonwealth, *c.* 1960. To *get with it* is to make oneself, to be, familiar with life as it is lived right now.

get you! (emphasis on *you*) and **he's got ten bob each way on himself** are female teenagers' 'deflaters' addressed to conceited young men: *c.* 1957–9. R.C., 1977, notes that, in US, it is not specifically a teenagers' c.p.; and B.G.T., 1978, notes that '"He's got a bob on himself" is a phrase well known in Northamptonshire for many years, well before 1957' – in short, since early C20. P.B.: was *get you!*, or *get your* (e.g. nose out of it)!, the orig. of the Cockneys' derisive *gertcha!*? A *bob* is pre-decimal-currency slang for a shilling, now known as 'five pee'.

get your act together!; **get it (all) together!** 'Get yourself, or yourselves, organized, aware – your ideas and plans and feelings clarified!' A US, mostly youthful, exhortation, dating since mid–? early–1960s. In, e.g., the excellent *DCCU*.

The orig. form seems to have been the former and from 'showbiz'. Orig. US, it passed, *c.* 1970, to Can., the UK, Aus. and elsewhere. P.B.: in Brit. English, *get it together!* could trace legitimate descent from drill sergeants' efforts to instil uniformity into awkward squads' evolutions.

get your ass in gear! '"Get moving!" or "Start working!"' General US from 1960s or earlier; probably originally Services? "Your ass" as a figure for "yourself", as in many other expressions (e.g. "Get your ass out of here!" [see next]); "in gear" from the obvious fact that a motor vehicle will not move until put in gear' (R.C., 1978). A.B. also comments, 1978, on the fact that this phrase and *get your shit together* [see **get your ducks ...**] are 'probably more common (on the street) now' than the cliché *put your thinking cap on.*

get your (dead or **fat** or **tired) ass out of** (or **outa) here!** 'Go away, please!': US: 1950s and since. (A.B., 1978.)

get (or **go and get) your brains examined!** See **you need your head examined.**

get your ducks in a row! Be prepared: US: C20. It has the 1960s–70s vulgar synon. *get your shit together!* (A.B., 1978.)

get your ears dropped! A facetious Can. c.p., dating since *c.* 1955 and addressed to one whose hair is so long that it hides the ears. (Leechman.)

get your ears pinned back or **down!** 'Consider yourself put in your place: US, 1920s–and still' (Fain, 1977).

get your ears put back! Get your hair cut! – or, rather, keep your hair closely trimmed: the army in WW1. Cf **get your hair cut!**

get your eye in a sling! – a proletarian c.p. of *c.* 1890–1930 – was, in effect, 'a warning that you may receive a sudden and early black eye, calling for a bandage – the sling in question' (Ware). For a US counterpart, cf **ass in a sling.**

get your feet wet! was 'originally said to a timid bather.

Universally understood and used, as a c.p., and as an imperative, usually addressed to someone faced with a task he is fearful of' (J.W.C., 1968): US: C20.

get your finger out! A very common var. of **take ...**

get your hair cut! was a 'non-U' c.p. of *c.* 1882–1912; Leechman judges its heyday to have been *c.* 1900. (B&P; Benham.) It has the var. *go and get your hair cut*, as in Collinson, who adds, 'From a song, I think'; Benham prefers an origin in the London streets; it could be both. My friend Jerry Burke (W.J.B.) directs me to two passages in A.A. Milne's *Autobiography*, where, at pp. 27 and 85 of the US edn, 1939, the author, referring to the period 1882–93, has some interesting things to say about this c.p.; including a suggestion that he himself and his middle-class exact contemporaries may have inspired the music-hall song. Vernon Noble tells me that it comes from a song with that title sung by George Beauchamp, a famous comedian of the late Victorian music-hall.

This entry reminded Peter Sanders, 1978, of the elaborate, standard sarcasms of recruit-training NCOs to servicemen during WW2, and afterwards, in the years of National Service, e.g. 'Am I hurting you?' or 'Does your head ache?' to be followed on denial by 'Well, I should be *or* It bleedin' well should – I'm standing on your fuckin' hair!' The joke, for the recruit, wore horribly thin after his third visit to the barber in a week (P.B., with feeling).

get your head cut in! 'Get wise!': US railroaders' (railwaymen's): C20. Also *he has his head cut in*, 'Sensible; said of a man who is as much under control as a train with its air brakes cut in' (Ramon F. Adams, *Language of the Railroader*, 1977).

get your knee brown! 'Men with Overseas Service to their credit tell Home Service chaps to do this' (H & P): since *c.* 1925. P.B.: this taunt was immensely popular among those National Servicemen in stations where it was possible to boast to new arrivals, notably the Middle and Far East, i.e. during the period esp. later 1940s–1960; but doubtless still alive among Regulars yet, 1980s.

get your knickers untwisted! – often prec. by **you want** (i.e., need) **to** – is a male c.p., dating from *c.* 1950, and it means, in general. 'You should clarify your ideas', and, in particular, to do this in order to extricate yourself from a troublesome impasse. P.B.: but, pace E.P., this is not so much a c.p. as a logical extension of the observation 'You've got your knickers in a twist'. Also frequently heard as *Don't get your knickers ...* By early 1980s, slightly ob.

get your steel helmets! (or **tin hats!**) is the army's counterpart (1940–5) to the RAF's *line!*, 'That's a piece of line-shooting'; 'often accompanied,' as John Bebbington, librarian, tells me, 'by the gesture of handle-turning, like that of a street organist, to the tune of da-di-di-da'. P.B.: by early 1950s, often, more urgently, *grab your ...* , if someone showed signs of launching into a 'wory' (elliptical for 'war story'). See also **swing that lamp, Jack!**

getting a big boy now, i.e. of age, is 'applied satirically to strong lusty young fellows' since the 1880s, Ware tells us, and that it comes from the 'leading phrase of the refrain of a song made popular by Herbert Campbell'. But it is also used defensively by a man made to feel that he is being excessively mothered and patronized. See also **you're getting a big boy now.**

getting a big girl now. See **you're getting. ...**

getting any (or **any lately**) or **enough?** is an Aus. male c.p., dating from *c.* 1930 and used mostly by manual workers, esp. on one meeting another; it implies, 'Have you "made" any girls lately?' Sidney J. Baker, 1959, lists these 'formulas of reply': *climbing trees to get away from it – got to swim under water to dodge it –* and *so busy I've had to put a man on (to help me)*: all of which sound like 'line-shoots' to end all 'line-shoots'. Neil Lovett, 1978, adds *got to beat 'em off with a big stick*, and Eric Fearon, 1984, *have to fight them off at the traffic lights.*

It has migrated to the UK, as Wedgewood implies when,

1977, he commented, 'Interesting, and typical of the time, that, in the mid 1970s, this is being "played on", tongue in saucy cheek, by display advertisements: e.g., milk'. In 1977, Jim Ramsay, in *Cop It Sweet!*, noted the wider [Aus.] meaning, 'a customary greeting to which only a facetious reply is needed'. Cf the US *getting much?*, with *pussy* understood: from before 1920, still actively current in the 1940s, but now ob. (R.C., 1977). P.B.: but A.H. Lewis, 1975, notes the use of the elliptical 'Lately?' as greeting on Merseyside in the 1930s, and in this form it was still common among the Other Ranks in the Forces, 1950s onwards.

ghastly. See: what a g.

ghost walks on Friday – the; the ghost does not walk; when will the ghost walk?; has the ghost walked yet? There is – or is not – any money for salaries and wages; when will there be – has there been – such money? These are theatrical c.pp., dating from the 1840s; the first printed recording was in *Household Words*, 1853. The origin: Shakespeare's *Hamlet*, I,i. R.C.'s suggestion, 1977, 'Could it be that, given the last cast of that play, the company business manager often "doubled" as the ghost?' may be right.

Friday is the traditional pay-day in the theatre. The related **what time's Treasury?** is clearly derivative; it dates from *c.* 1870. And cf the Forces' **golden eagle shits.**

gi' us a kiss and call me Charlie! is applied to 'one who sets about a job or embroils himself in argument without knowledge or understanding or with wrong-headed ideas' (L.A., 1974): since *c.* 1920.

gi' us y' hand! Among men, a joc. reply to solicitous 'How do you feel (, Jock)?': imitation Scottish: 1941–5, mostly in the Armed Forces. (L.A., 1974.)

Gibraltar. See: anniversary.

giddy. See: oh, my g.

giddy little kipper (or whelk) is a Cockney c.p., dating from the 1880s and addressed to another or to oneself in approbation of the clothes one is wearing, esp. on a festive occasion; it became † by 1940 at latest.

gift. See: it's a gift.

gift of the grab – (he) has the. He is successfully 'on the make'; he is making easy money: since the late 1940s. An easy pun on *the gift of the gab*. (Petch, 1974.)

giggles nest. See: have you found.

Gilbert. See: 'gip'.

gild the lily – I have to or **I'm going to** or **I must.** I must urinate: US male: since *c.* 1930, but 'rarely heard today ... primarily used by beer-drinkers' (Moe, 1978). A particular use of the common conflation of Shakespeare's line in *King John*, IV, ii: 'To gild refinèd gold, to paint the lily'.

Gimbel's. See: does Macy's.

gimlet. See: Hamlet.

gimme! gimme! gimme! Lit. 'Give me – give me – give me', it characterizes the attitude of the taker, not the giver: since *c.* 1960. Orig. US, it was duly adopted in UK where the attitude is equally common. (Mrs M.C. Thomson of Bray-on-Thames, 1975.)

gin. See: doesn't do; hopping.

Ginger. See: speak up.

Ginger, you're barmy! is a good-humoured streets' and, in general, non-aristocratic c.p. of C20's first decade; Noble, 1976, thinks that it orig. in a music-hall song. *Barmy* = mentally deficient, crazy. A 1940s–50s schoolchildren's cry addressed to any red-headed male was ... – *you ought to join the army*.

'gip', quoth Gilbert when his mare farted was a C17–18 c.p. addressed to one who is 'pertish and forward'. It occurs in Howell's collection of proverbs, 1659, and it had the var. noted by Ray in 1678: '*gib with an ill rubbing' – quoth Badger when his mare kicked*. (Apperson.)

Gipper – get (or, often, **win**) **one for the;** whence **that's one for the Gipper.** 'Do your best for the team!': Notre Dame, then almost Statewide, footballers': *c.* 1928–40. From George Gipp (1895–1931) who, after playing (1917–20), became the

N.D. coach; brilliant player and brilliant coach. (A.B., 1978.)

girdle. See: ne'er an M.

girl(s). See: and whose; as the girl said; be a good g.; bra is; bring on the dancing; chase me, girls; consider; cracked; I bet you; I'm not that kind; if you can't get; it's been a very; it's like a nigger; once aboard; remember the g.; stand always; that's gone; there's life; what can; what they; what's a nice; when a girl; why girls; women are; you have grown; you'll be telling; you're a big g.

girls are hauling on the tow-rope – the, is 'an old navy expression applied to a ship coming home to pay off' (F & G): *c.* 1870–1914.

girls are like buses. See **women are like buses.**

gissa job (= give us [i.e., me] a job)! 'Yosser Hughes, burly Scouser [Liverpudlian] ..., pleads, "Gissa job. I kin do that. I kin do anything." He's desperate for A Job, and all that goes with it' (*The Sunday Times Mag.*, 9 Jan. 1983, article about 'Alan Bleasdale's saga of hard times in the Liverpool of the 1980s, *Boys from the Black Stuff*', a BBC TV series of 5 plays, almost at once repeated).

My thanks to Bill Loach for alerting me to this, perhaps the first real c.p. of our new unemployment age; I soon heard it for myself, and saw it as graffito, early 1983. *Loughborough & Coalville Trader*, 23 Feb. 1983, had a frontpage headline '220th time lucky for "Gizzajob" man' (Mike had at last found a post). (P.B.)

git the ambulance! See **get the ambulance!**

git there fustest with the mostest! is a 'semi-proverbial recipe for military success, with occasional application in anything that requires speed and concentration of forces: US since *c.* 1870, but obsolete, except in historical context. A sort of "familiar misquotation" ascribed to General Nathan Bedford Forrest, leader of a very effective Confederate cavalry force in the eastern Mississippi Valley during the American Civil War (1861–65). Historians aver that Forrest would never have expressed himself in such sub-literate terms, so that the "quotation", if such it be, is presumably either a paraphrase of Forrest by one of his troopers, or a "Yankee" imitation of what Confederates "ought" to talk like' (R.C., 1978).

give. See: don't give; I wouldn't g.; I'll give; what gives; wouldn't give.

give 'em that old razzle-dazzle! 'Keep the show, the entertainment, bright and lively!' A US 'showbiz' c.p. that prob. arose during the 1920s. In the *Christian Science Monitor*, 16 Sep. 1977, p. 13, there occurs a piece captioned ' "Chicago" sparkles with "that old razzle-dazzle" ', written by Thor Eckert, Jr., and dealing with the Broadway show, *Chicago*, (W.J.B.)

give her twopence! was an Aus. c.p. of the late 1945–7 (the cost then rose) – 'used on sighting a beautiful female child, i.e. Give her twopence to ring you when she is sixteen' (the age of consent). (B.P.)

give him a card! Just hark at him boasting!: RN: since *c.* 1940. Legend has it that, in eastern Mediterranean waters, early in WW2, it was customary to pass to anyone boasting of his exploits a card bearing the comforting words. 'I don't believe you, but do carry on! I'm a bit of a bull-shitter myself.' By 1970, ob.

give him a rolling for his all-over! A Cockney c.p., punning on and synon. with 'Give him a *Roland* for his *Oliver*'. i.e. tit for tat: *c.* 1890–1914. Ware.

give him Maggie's drawers! Perhaps more frequently **get Maggie's drawers!** A US army (and then also Marine Corps) c.p.: C20.

Originally it referred to the use of a red flag which was waved in front of the target to indicate a miss. At one time, it had a limited usage away from the rifle range to convey the idea that the teller of a tale had failed to make a point and was hooted down in derision; [or] that the listener to a tale had failed to understand or get the point being made; that someone had made a mistake, or that someone had failed to achieve his objective. [Moe, 1975.]

P.B.: Was there a connection with the old ribald song that has the chorus: 'They were tattered, they were torn, round the arsehole they were worn: the old red flannel drawers that Maggie wore'?

give him the money, Barney. In a letter, 1974, Noble writes: This was for a long time after the war [WW2] a phrase introduced by Wilfred Pickles in the very long-running 'Have a Go' radio broadcasts and repeated by millions of people. The 'Barney' referred to was Barney Colehan, producer of the show in BBC North Region, where it originated, and the man who handed out the money prizes to contestants in the simple general knowledge contests. Nigel Rees, in *VIBS*, adds, 'Later, [Pickles's wife] Mabel supervised the prizes, hence the alternative "Give him the money, Mabel" and the references to "Mabel at the table"', P.B.: as a c.p. it was always said in imitation of Pickles's strong Yorkshire accent. Russell Davies, in *New Statesman*, 9 Sep. 1977, remembers the latter phrase as *what's on the table, Mabel?*, and notes that it caught on just as widely as *give him the money, Barney*.

give it a drink! 'A cat-call of disapproval directed at a bad singer or actor' by the audience: C20. (Granville.)

give it a name! See **name yours!**

give it a rest! For heaven's sake, stop talking – or, indeed, making a noise of any kind!: C20. From **give us a rest,** q.v.

give it a whirl! ' "Try it – you may be lucky; it is worth the effort." The var. *it's worth a whirl* I have heard (BBC, *The Archers*) as recently as 5 Dec. 1977, although I feel it is at least twenty years earlier' (R.S., 1978). It goes back to 1950 at least and, I believe, dates from the 1930s. P.B.: according to *DSUE* the Can. *take a whirl at* (something) has been current since *c.* 1925; and in Aus. *birl* or *burl* substitutes in these phrases, e.g. *let's give it a birl.*

give it air! Stop talking nonsense! A US c.p., mostly in student use, of the early 1920s. McKnight.

give it back to the abos or **the blacks!** The former is recorded for 1951, the latter for 1946; but clearly they date from much earlier. Wilkes classifies it as an Aus. 'expression of disgust at any inhospitable feature of Australia'; he thinks – rightly, I'd say – that it may have been patterned on the US *hand it back to the Indians!*, similarly applied.

give it the old college try (often prec. by **let's** or **we'll**). 'Do one's utmost, though success is uncertain. Gen. US from *c.* 1960. Paraphrased, if not actually quoted, from one or more of the innumerable "rah rah" college football films of the 1930s and 40s, the burden of which was that you can win if you try, no matter the odds. Hence often with a certain ironic twist, sometimes becoming equivalent to "Go through the motions," even if little or nothing is accomplished' (R.C., 1980).

give it the old one-two (sometimes prec. by **let's**)! is applied to any vigorous action (esp. one in two parts) in any context, or, perhaps more commonly, speech in a dispute: US: since *c.* 1920; partially adopted in UK by *c.* 1940. It comes from boxing: a blow to the belly followed, with the other hand, by one to the chin: enough to knock anyone out. (J.W.C., 1978.) See also **don't forget the diver,** the quot'n from Stephen Potter.

give it to the Belgians! was, among NZ soldiers serving in WW1 – more precisely in the latter half of that war, the humorous advice offered to a comrade either complaining about the food or his clothes or enquiring what the hell he was expected to do with some unwanted equipment. Cf **remember Belgium!**

give me some skin! Shake hands – esp. with one person's flat palm brushing the other's flat palm: US jive c.p. of *c.* 1935; it caught on and acquired a rhyme: *give me some skin, Flynn!* Cf *slip me five!*, which, current since WW1, prompted the *skin* phrase. (W & F.) CM regards it as a distinctly Negro c.p. Cf **slap me five!**

give me strength (short for the lit. *God give me strength* to bear it) is, as B.P. (1975) neatly puts it, 'a secular prayer. Used when one hears of some new misfortune or of an example of imbecility.' Orig. Aus., since *c.* 1920. But also current in UK.

The lit. *God give me strength* was prob. the earlier as a c.p., the shortened being a weakened form; and, based on a ribald myth, it expresses exasperation at the folly or stupidity or clumsiness of others, or at interruptions by others. Since *c.* 1950, it has gradually become, not ob., but less and less used, as L.A. has reminded me, 1974.

give my regards to Broadway! is a US c.p. of *c.* 1904–50, initiated by George M. Cohan's song, so titled, in *Little Johnny Jones.* (W.J.B.)

give my regards to the duke! (usu. prec. by **please**). A compliment to a man on his sexual prowess: Brit. and US: 1917 or 18, and then reminiscently until *c.* 1930. From a several-versioned story of an English duchess visiting wounded soldiers and eliciting a reply from one man that he had been hit by shrapnel in his genitals, and her rejoinder. (A reminder from Fain, 1977.) A shortish life – but a ribald one.

give order: thank you please! 'Colin Crompton's injunction to the members of [ITV] Granada's *Wheeltappers and Shunters Social Club* (1974–7), of which he was the deadpan concert chairman. ... "Like most successful catchphrases it wasn't manufactured," says Colin. "It has been used by club concert chairmen for years – and still is. I suppose it was the exaggerated accent and facial expression which helped it 'catch on' " ' (*VIBS*). Peter Dacre, in the *Sunday Express*, 23 Oct. 1977, writes that the 'commanding cry "Give Order" has become a national catch phrase'.

give the cat another goldfish! 'Let's be devils – damn the expense!' I've heard it since the latish 1940s, but did not consciously remember it until I read in John Wainwright's *Pool of Tears*, 1977, ' "What do you think, Lenny ... a hundred [copies of a photograph]?" – "Two hundred," said Lennox. "Let's go wild – give the cat another goldfish ..." ' See also **kill another canary ...,** and **never mind, it'll soon ...**

give the gentleman a coconut! Addressed to anyone making a successful effort, as in 'Right first time – give the gentleman a coconut!': C20. Orig. a fair-ground stall-holder's congratulation to a successful competitor at a coconut-shy booth: with a ball he has knocked a coconut off its perch. (Granville, 1968.) R.C., 1977: 'In US, a *cigar*, with same provenance. By 1977, almost †, cigar-smoking having much declined. Cf *close, but no cigar* [q.v.].' See also **every one a coconut!**

give us ... See gi' us and gissa.

give us a little of the old McGoo! is, Berrey tells us in 1942, a US film director's 'way of asking a star to display some sex appeal, as with exposed limbs'; † by 1945, W&F in 1960 curtly dismissing it as 'Sex appeal. *Some c. 1930 use. Obs[olete].*' Who McGoo was, I don't know; there seems to be some reference to the US slang, *goo*, a sticky mess, itself perhaps from *glue.*

give the little lady a great big hand is a 'master of ceremonies' request for applause for an artiste, now often used mockingly' (Ashley, 1984): US.

give us a rest!, writes James Maitland in 1891, was 'a slang phrase of recent introduction used when a tedious story is being told. Equivalent to *you make me tired*': US: *c.* 1885–1910. A.B., 1978, adds, 'I've heard, too, "Why don't you just hang it up?" – Quit whatever you're doing! 1960s and current.' Cf **give it a rest.**

give your arse a chance!, often prec. by **shut up** (or **stop talking) and,** is a low C20 use. It was particularly common in the Australian Forces, 1914–18. The politer *give your ears a chance!* arose *c.* 1920; 'sometimes said to one who never stops talking' (Petch, 1974). The var. *shut up and ...* has prompted Brian W. Aldiss to write to me, 1978: 'For symmetry and wit, this does not rival the phrase as I heard and used it *c.* 1939–48 in Public School and Army, viz.: *shut your arse and give your mouth a chance.* In this form, the phrase can be seen to relate to the equally insulting *you're talking through your arse.*'

Give your arse a chance reappears in Powis, *The Signs of Crime*, 1977, as an underworld and near-underworld c.p., without a dating, but prob. since *c.* 1920. Powis also mentions the *ears* var.

Note also that the c.p. became equally common in the US.

give your face a joy-ride! is a cheery admonition, addressed to someone looking mournful: since *c.* 1930, but heard decreasingly little after *c.* 1950, and by 1970, †.

give your head a bump! 'Pull yourself together. Wake up. Bestir yourself' (F&G): army: *c.* 1900–20, esp. during WW1. As a means of sharp arousing; perhaps also an allusion to phrenological bumps. P.B.: in the Army, early 1970s, we used to talk of *bump-starting the mind*, an allusion to the shunting method of starting motor vehicles too cold to be self-started.

give yourself a bit of an overhauling! Go and have a wash and a general clean-up!: *c.* 1912–40. Prob. from cleaning a motor car.

given away with a pound of tea is 'a Cockney c.p. of joc. disparagement, as in "Mum's new hat looks as if it was given away with a pound o' tea" and "Jack says his new bike was *not* given away with a pound o' tea"' (Julian Franklyn): since *c.* 1880, but much less gen. since *c.* 1914 than before that date; and by 1940 ob., by 1960 †. From the pre-WW1 grocers' practice of making a free gift with every pound of tea or with any fair-sized order.

In F. Anstey's *Mr Punch's Model Music-Hall Songs and Dramas*, 1892, No. 3, 'A Democratic Ditty' entitled 'Given Away with a Pound of Tea' begins thus:

Some Grocers have taken to keeping a stock
Of ornaments – such as a vase, or a clock –
With a ticket on each where the words you may see:
'To be given away – with a Pound of Tea!'

In a later 'Vice-Versa' Anstey book, *Salted Almonds*, 1906, the story 'At a Moment's Notice' contains the passage: 'I had heard Monty discuss the Reggie Ballimore that was [the narrator] and give him away with a pound of tea, so to speak – and I hadn't turned a hair.'

But much the earliest record appears to occur towards the end of Act I of Arthur Wing Pinero's comedy, *The Rocket*, performed in 1883 (although not pub'd until 1905):

WALK[INSHAW]: ... Go, sir, fetch my child.
JOSLYN: Do I understand then, Sir, that you consent?
WALK: The daughter of the Chevalier Walkinshaw and the son of a tea dealer. The arms of the Walkinshaws crossed with a pair of scales and a pig-tailed Chinaman. Motto, 'Given away with a pound of tea.' Go, sir, fetch my child, my heart is broken.

(The old hypocrite!)

It has a pleasant coda: 'In WW2 an officer or NCO who had been promoted was liable to be asked, "Have you just bought a pound of tea?" – by those less fortunate, of course' (Sanders, 1978). This links with the occ. var. *they give them away with a pound of tea*, which, still current in the 1970s, recurs in, e.g., David Powis's *The Signs of Crime*, 1977.

Givum's dead and Lendum's very bad (dangerously ill). In *Punch*, 16 Oct. 1869, occurs the greengrocer woman's answer to the small girl asking, "Mother says, will you give her a lettuce?" – "Give! Tell yer mother Givum's dead, and Lendum's very bad. Nothink for nothink 'ere, and precious little for sixpence!!" So G.B. Shaw was plagiarizing when he altered it to "tuppence": see **nothing for nothing** ... (P.B.)

glad. See: so glad; what's the good word.

Gladstone. See: what did G.; what's yer fighting.

glance. See: I'm Hawkshaw.

glass. See: deal of g.; from drinking.

glass eye. See: talk a g.

glasses. See: get your glasses; only asses.

glazier? – is (occ. **was**) **your father a.** Addressed to one who blocks the light. orig. that from a window, but soon also that

from a lamp, a candle, a fire: C18–20, but little used since *c.* 1950. In S (Dialogue I), occur the words, 'I believe your father was no glazier'; and in Grose, 1788, we find the gloss: 'If it is answered in the negative, the rejoinder is – I wish he was, that he might make a window through your body to enable us to see the fire or light.' In late C19–20 Aus., ... *glassmaker* (B.P.); and the US has the variants, *your father didn't make windows!* and *your father wasn't a glassmaker!* both current since at least as early as 1930, and prob. dating from late C19. In US sometimes prec. by *do you think* (your father was, e.g. a glazier)? (A.B.) Cf **were you born in a barn?**

gleam. See: I was doing it; you were just.

glimpses of the obvious dates either from the very late C19 or from the very early C20; heyday, *c.* 1920–40; partially eclipsed during the next fifteen years or so; partially revived since the middle 1950s. It can, obviously, be employed as a headline, but its more important usage is that of a usu. smiling interposition into, or comment upon, a truism or a cliché. P.B.: occ., even more sarcastically, as *blinding glimpses* ...

gloom. See: doom and g.

gloves. See: 'fuck me!'; what? a bishop's.

glow. See: horses sweat.

glue. See: you have your g.; and:

glue did not hold – the. You were baulked: you missed your aim. (Ray, enlarged edn, 1813.) *c.* 1780–1860. Perhaps orig. a proverbial saying, but prob. always a true c.p. Apperson glosses it as 'Your plan(s) or wish(es) went, or have gone, wrong', i.e. they came unstuck.

glue-pot has come unstuck – the. His body emits the odour of a genital sweat or, strictly, of a seminal emission: a low c.p., dating from *c.* 1880 but † – or, at the least, ob. – by 1940. I first heard it used by a rather coarse lower-middle-class woman in 1913.

go. See: enjoy yourself; fair go; growl; have a go; here we go; how are you going; how do we go; I could go; I'll go; I've seen 'em come; it's a go; it's all go; mind how; must you stay; no go; orft we; pore ole thing; rarin'; sell in May; still going; there he goes; there you go; watch how; we don't want; what a wonderful; what goes; what you say; when a girl; when you gotta; when you've got; where did that; where do we; while I'm; and:

go along, Bob! and **come along, Bob!**, current *c.* 1800–30 and recorded by JB, are obscure in meaning and, apparently, dubious in taste.

go along with you! See **get along with you!**

go and ... See also entries where *go* is followed directly by a verb, e.g. **go stick your nose ...**

go and bag your head! Oh, shut up and run away!: an Aus. c.p., dating from *c.* 1920. Neil Lovett, 1978, notes that it has become, through US influence, *go bag your head!* Cf many of the **go and ...** entries below, and the prec. entry.

go and boil your head! Oh! don't be silly: a proletarian injunction: C20; little used since *c.* 1945. It occurs in, e.g., Compton Mackenzie, *Water on the Brain*, 1933. Of the Cockney var. *garn, boil yer 'ead!*, Leechman has remarked, 'Heard in England before 1904.' Cf the prec. and the next two.

go and chase yourself! 'Oh, run away and stop bothering me!': US: arising *c.* 1910 or even a decade earlier, it was recorded by S. R. Strait in the *Boston Globe* of *c.* 1917. (W. J. B.) But more often as **go chase yourself!** – the form cited by Strait. See also **chase yourself!**

go and eat coke! This c.p. of the London slums indicates a lively and impatient contempt: *c.* 1870–1940. It is used rather often in the school novels and short stories by 'Frank Richards' (i.e. Charles Hamilton). F & H cite the coarse var. *go and shit cinders!* – not a schoolboy phrase. P.B.: the two phrases were occ. linked thus: *go and eat coke and then you'll shit* (or *you can shit*) *cinders!*; still to be heard (*and* among schoolboys) in 1950s.

go and fetch the crooked straight-edge! (or **rubber hammer** or **wall-stretcher!**) is an 'April Fool catch': mid C19–20; one or other of them may go back considerably earlier. To discriminate: carpenters tend to prefer the first: engineers' shops, the second; and warehousemen, the third. There exists the occ. var. with *left-handed screwdriver.*

P.B.: not restricted to 'April fool' jests, these catches were and are traditionally used to try the wit of apprentices to the various trades. Others are *rubber hammer for glass nails; a tin of red, white and blue paint*, or, as B.G.T. notes, 1978, *of striped paint*; and the US var. *a left-handed monkey-wrench.* Berrey, 1942, records *send for the overweights* as a (US) 'joke on a green stable hand', which seems to belong with these other examples. See also FOOLS' ERRANDS in the Appendix to *DSUE*, 8th ed.

go and find another man to bring the money home! is addressed by husband to nagging wife: C20. It is reputed to be a certain stopper of a domestic difference or even a quarrel. A certain dry humour makes it memorable.

go and fry your face! – belonging to the approx. period, 1870–1905 – is hardly an educated c.p. It expresses either incredulity or derision or contempt; cf the † Suffolk *fry your feet!*, don't talk nonsense (*EDD*). In US, the *and* is omitted; R.C. cites Raymond Chandler, *The Long Goodbye*, 1954.

go and get lost! See **get lost!**

go and get your brains examined! See **get your brains examined!**

go and get your mother to take your nappies off! (or **go and get your nappies changed!**) is a working-class girls' retort to callow youths' **does your mother know you're out?** (q.v.): C20. (Julian Franklyn.)

go and have a ride! – the first two words being sometimes omitted. Run away and stop bothering me! *or* Go to hell!: since *c.* 1920; ob. by 1970. Like *go and take a running jump* (*at yourself*) it is occ. a euph. for *fuck off!* – with allusions to the slangy *jump* and *ride*, (of the male), to copulate with.

go! And never darken my doors again. See **never darken ...**

go and play in the traffic! is a Can. var. ('very recent': Leechman, 1969) of **get lost!** But it seems to have gone to Canada from Scotland, to judge by the *Blackwood's Magazine* review of this book, Sep. 1977: 'Exasperated Glasgow mothers have been giving this facetious advice to their children since the 1950s'.

go and play trains! See **run away and play trains!**

go and see a taxidermist! was, in 1943–5, an RAF var. on the theme of 'Go and get *stuffed!*' P.B.: but similar allusions continue to be made in civilian life, and in Aus., well into later C20.

go and shit cinders! See **go and eat coke!**

go and soak your head in a bucket! 'Said by an annoyed person to someone who is in an ill-tempered mood and lets the speaker know it verbally. Variants: *go* (*and*) *take a cold shower!* and *go* (*and*) *stick your head in a toilet!* [Mostly] 1930s–1950s; not in general use now' (A.B., 1978).

go away, boy, you're bothering me, a US c.p., dates from early in C20; not much used since WW2. R.C., 1977, suggests that its prob. orig. lies in 'the *sotto voce* remark of a street "pitchman" to an intrusive small boy whose questions or comments are interfering with his patter. Certainly used by W.C. Fields [1880–1946: famous American entertainer], but hardly original with him'. 'Sideshow barker talk,' agrees Ashley, 1982, adding '"Step right up, ladies and gentlemen, for ten cents, the tenth part of a dollar ..."' is part of the spiel.' See *it's an old army game*, and cf *shoo, fly, don't bother me.*

go back and cross the T's! This RN c.p. has, since *c.* 1920, been ironically directed at any helmsman, but usu. a learner coxswain, who has 'written his name' in the ship's wake by steering an erratic course. (*Sailors' Slang*, 1962; recorded earlier in PGR, 1948.)

P.B.: G.E. Evans, in *The Days We Have Seen*, 1975, quotes a North Sea drifterman recalling his first attempt at steering, *c.* 1920: 'The old man [skipper] he come from below

once, and he says: "I don't mind you writing your name, but for God's sake don't go back and rub it out!"'

go break a leg! See **break a leg!**

go carry guts to a bear! occurs in a commonplace book kept, 1874–75, by a gentleman (identity unknown) living in Philadelphia, thus: 'Where is the spirit of 1776? Degraded Americans of the North, *go carry guts to a bear.*'As its possessor remarks, 'It had to be an expression well known in 1875 in the United States, and a real red-blooded one, to boot.' Apparently it means 'Be brave and resolute and prepared to take a considerable risk' (W. J. B., 1977). It is not recorded in *D.Am.*, not in Berrey, 1942, nor in 'Bartlett', 1968 ed. Moe, 1977, thinks that it might possibly be connected with the derogatory *not fit to carry guts to a bear.* The two interpretations are not contradictory but complementary: a rallying cry; an appeal, through shame, to courage; an insult firing men to show that they *are* men.

go chase yourself! See **go and chase ...**

go do me something (often prec. by *so,*). '"There's nothing *I* can do about it." Orig. Jewish-American, from 1930s. Elliptically, "Do anything you like to me – *that* won't change the situation"'(R.C., 1978.)

[**go easy, Mabel!** 'Take it easy! Don't get excited! Cool it! Let up on me!' Based on a popular song 1909, it may have achieved a brief period of c.p. success; W. J. B. doubts its eligibility, but cf the later, and very similar **don't force it, Phoebe!**]

go'er on! An exclamatory c.p. made when a broker or a jobber wishes to continue buying or selling the same shares: Stock Exchange: C20, but less used since WW2. A sort of financial *attaboy!*.

go find a drum, and beat it! See **beat it while the going's good.**

go fly a kite! 'Go away; don't bother me; go and do something else': Can.: 'fairly recent, in my experience' (Leechman, 1977). Cf **shoo fly** ... Adopted from US: see Berrey, 1942.

go fuck a duck! '"Get lost!" "Beat it!" Current, 1920s [, in US], now virtually dead. Rhyming variant of "Go fuck yourself!"' (R.C., 1977). The latter was itself proposed, by A.B. in 1978, as a C20 c.p. and glossed 'Get out of here; go away; bother someone else!' P.B.: the expression *Cor!* (or *Gawd!*, etc.) *Fuck a duck!* was a fairly common exclam. of irritation, dismay, surprise, etc., in the British Army, 1960s–70s.

go have your hair bobbed (occ. prec. by **aw,**) Shut up!: US: 1920, Robert Benchley uses it in *Love Conquers All*, 1923 – See the quot'n at **oh, is that so?**

go home and tell your mother she wants you. 'To get rid of a troublesome child' (Wilkes, 1979): Aus.: since *c.* 1930(?).

go it, Ned! is a naval c.p. of encouragement: *c.* 1810–50. It occurs in W.N. Glascock's lively *Sailors and Saints*, 1829.

go it, Susan, I'll hold your bonnet. 'What can be more revolting than phrases like *Whoa, Emma; Ah, there!; Get there, Eli; Go it, Susan, I'll hold your bonnet; Everybody's doing it; Good night, Irene; Oh you kid!* in vogue not long ago' (McKnight): *c.* 1919–29.

go it, you cripples! (occ. **cripple!**) An ironic, often senseless, adjuration, orig. to the crippled or disabled, but soon to anyone, esp. in sports and games, to move sharply, to 'get a move on': C19–20; by 1940, slightly ob., Often added: **wooden, or crutches, legs are cheap**, seldom heard after WW1. It occurs in Thackeray, 1840. Its senseless usage or aspect is very clearly seen in Robert Surtees, *Mr Sponge's Sporting Tour*, 1853 (in vol. II, Chapter L, 'Farmer Peastraw's Diné-Matinée'):

'...Who the Dickens are you?'

'Who the Dickens are you?' replied I.

'Bravo!' shouted Sir Harry.

'Capital!' exclaimed Seedybuck.

'Go it, you cripples! Newgate's on fire!' shouted Captain Quod.

Surtees uses it again in *Mr Pacey Romford's Hounds*, 1865 (he had died in 1862): or rather, he uses *go it, you cripples!*

Newgate's on fire! – which leads one to suspect that the double adjuration was the orig. form: it at least makes sense.

Mr Lance Tonkin of Dunedin, NZ has, 1974, sent me two useful pieces of information: a newspaper pub'd 1845, in Hobart, Van Diemen's Land (later, Tasmania), reported that a group of women, presumably convicts, fighting in the streets, used this c.p.; and that, in his NZ schooldays, *c.* 1908, he and his companions 'used this... as an encouraging phrase'. I suspect that it didn't in Brit., Aus., NZ (and perhaps elsewhere) fall into disuse until between WW1 and WW2. P.B.: I think later still, having certainly heard it post–WW2 at, e.g., 'friendly' football matches.

go jump in the lake! 'A rebuke to pride, with the notion of "get out"' (*The Pedagogical Seminary*, v. XIX, 1912) provides the earliest example. (Mrs Ursula Roberts, Hong Kong.)

go, man, go! is an extension of the slang *go!*, an 'exhortation to dig, get with it, swing' (the *Daily Colonist*, Victoria, BC, 16 Apr. 1959). This US jazz c.p., dating from *c.* 1946, rapidly became also Can. and in or *c.* 1948, English. (The *locus classicus* is Norman D. Hinton's article in the American Dialect Society's periodical, Nov. 1958.) A Negro Jazz-players' coinage. P.B.: the expression became closely associated, in the public mind, with the 'fast' life of hippies, drug addicts and hill's-angles. One of the best of Alan Hunter's gripping series of crime novels, featuring the policeman Gently, is *Gently Go Man*, 1961.

go off. See: you can go.

go on! See get out!

go on with your bad self! A US Blacks' 'expression said to someone who is doing something he does not ordinarily do or exaggerating something he normally does, A positive, encouraging statement' (Paul Janssen, glossing Landy's *Underground*, a work that exhibits wide reading and much personal experience): 1960s and 70s.

go peddle your papers! 'Get about your business – and out of mine!': US: since 1920s, or earlier. 'Now ob., or †, with the extinction of the newsboy who literally peddled papers on the street' (R.C., 1977). Cf **peddle your own fish!**

go see the chaplain! – with **go** often omitted. 'The meaning = shut up, quit bitching, stop complaining, e.g. "Stop telling me your troubles and woes – I'm not interested – but go tell them to the chaplain and he will issue you a crying towel." [US] armed forces usage' (Moe, 1975). And J.W.C. writes: 'Certainly very common, and as a c.p., in the US Army 30 years ago. Now seldom heard (at least among civilians) except among ex-Servicemen'; he adds, 'often with the subaudition, "Your complaint is trivial, or commonplace, or both".'

go shoe the goose! A derisive–or an utterly incredulous–retort: late C16–18. (Recorded by, e.g., BE) Cf **go to hell and pump thunder! for sense; of rural origin.**

P.B.: but K.J.Bonser in his detailed study, *The Drovers*, 1970, while acknowledging the devision, nonetheless records that geese that were driven long distances, for instance from Wales to the London markets, were first made to walk through a compound of tar, sawdust and sand two or three times. This gave them a kind of additional sole that would eventually peel off clean.

go sit on a tack! is a slangy US c.p. meaning 'Run away and don't bother me!' (cf **shoo, fly**) and dating from *c.* 1930. R.C. adds that it was † by 1977. Cf **run up a tack...**

go stick your head in the toilet! See **go and soak...**

go stick your nose up a dead bear's bum! The journalist René Cutforth (1909–84) mentioned, in a TV programme mid-1973, that he had, during the Korean war (1950-3), been directed to do this by a pre-occupied Australian infantryman he was trying to interview. This picturesque phrase was seized upon and used to death in the British Army Unit I was serving with at the time. (P.B.)

go to Bath (and get your head shaved)! In the 2nd Supp. to the *OED*, *Bath* is described as 'a place of consignment for a person one does not wish to see again; in the phrase *to go to Bath*, chiefly used imperatively'; quot'ns from Barham, 1837, and Thackeray, 1858. The longer and later *...and get your head shaved* is there recorded for 1908. Both forms were, I think, † by 1930 at latest.

go to father! Go to hell!: earlier C20. B.G.T., 1982, recalls a friend 40 years ago, but harking back to the first decade or so of this century, reciting the explanation:

'Go to father,' she said, when I asked her to wed,
But she knew that I knew that her father was dead,
And she knew that I knew what a life he had led,
So she knew that I knew what she meant when she said:
'Go to father!'

go to grass! is, said Hotten in 1859, 'a common answer to a troublesome or inquisitive person': ob. by 1880 and † by 1900 in UK, it lingered in US until *c.* 1920 (J.W.C., 1977), and in Aus. so late as the 1940s (Neil Lovett, 1978). Said to have been orig. US. Perhaps from putting an old horse out to grass.

go to hell and pump thunder! indicates either derision or unmitigated incredulity: late C19. Cf the much earlier **go shoe the goose!** P.B.: the phrase lingered into earlier C20 (Mrs Gwynneth Reed, 1980), and, as (*well*,) *I'll go to hell...*, was also used to express surprise. With this latter, cf **I'll go hopping...**

go to Hell or Connaught! In 1909, Ware, having said 'historical', wrote thus: 'Be off. From the time of Cromwell, but still heard, especially in Protestant Ireland. Means utter repudiation of the person addressed. The Parliament (1653–54) passed a law, driving away all the people of Ireland who owned any land, out of Ulster, Munster, and Leinster.' More precisely, the meaning is, 'Go where you like but don't bother me with where you're going'; and Connaught was one of the ancient kingdoms – later, provinces – of Ireland.

go to the back of the class! See **join the back of the queue!**

go to the pub, Dad! 'This expression I have overheard (in my occupation as a photographer) from teenagers...mostly Maori; used in the situation where a poor type has said or suggested a course of action that is "square" or out of type for the spokesman or -woman' (Colin Keith, 1974): NZ: since *c.* 1970.

go to the top of the class! is a remark one makes to somebody who has answered quickly and accurately: since *c.* 1948. 'Far older in US than 1948 – by perhaps a century; and "head" is commoner [there] than "top"' (J.W.C., 1977). Cf:

go up one! Excellent! Good for you!: late C19–20. From a schoolteacher's promotion of a bright and successful pupil. Cf the prec. entry–and contrast **go 'way back.**

go up with the blind 'was what you were supposed to do in the morning after a night with a woman in bed; an indication of the enervating effects of copulation. It implied that you couldn't hold the [window-] blind down. I heard this in the mid-1930s' (an anon. correspondent, 1978): mostly army: since *c.* 1910: † by 1950.

go 'way back and sit down! A US students' c.p. of the 1920s (McKnight); it survived, in gen. usage, until WW2 at least, although, as R.C., 1977, writes: 'it can hardly have been at all common, since I never heard it in 1930s (as a student)–or any other time'.

go West, young man, go West is a mainly Brit. elab. of *go West, young man*, often credited to Horace Greeley (1811–72), who indeed popularized it; but the man originating it was John Barsone Lane Soule (1815–91), who in 1851, used it in an article pub'd in the *Express* at Terre Haute, Indiana, as Bartlett informs us. 'At first meaning exactly what it says, the expression at length became a mere catch-phrase, and was used in season and out of season' (Farmer) – a most revealing early comment upon its transition from famous quot'n to equally famous c.p., with an astonishingly long life. No less significant is the fact that, in George Ade, *The Slim Princess*, 1908 we find this allusion:

'Strange,' she murmured. 'You are the second person I have met to-day who advises me to go away to the west.'

'That's the tip!' he exclaimed with fervor. 'Go west and when you start, keep on going.'

The two characters being an Oriental princess and a rich young American. It had, slightly modified, appeared in James J. McClosky's *Across the Continent; Or. Scenes from New York Life and the Pacific Railroad*, performed in 1870, although 'the version here reproduced is largely the work of...Oliver Doud Bryson'; not pub'd until 1940. In Act II:

JOE: [Interrupts.] I trust that our paths may lie in different directions, but if in our walk through life we should ever meet, fear will never cause me to turn aside from avenging a wrong.

AND [ERLY]: Nor me from avenging an insult.

JOHN: Oh, go West, young fellow, and shoot snipe.

But when *go West, young man* was adopted in UK, it is difficult to say: my own impression is that it did so *c.* 1950 and that the Laurel and Hardy film had something to do with its British popularization.

goat. See: more kid; that gets; up goes; you get my.

God(s). See: by guess; by the grace; Christmas; close as God's; close your eyes; fear God; for God's sake; God's good; if you see; pity the poor; take yer 'at; who died; ye gods; you don't have the brains; you haven't got; and:

God bless the Duke of Argyll! is, according to Hotten, a Scottish c.p., addressed to one who shrugs his shoulders or scratches himself as if he were troubled with life: C19–20. An allusion to certain posts erected in Glasgow by his Grace's authority–or so Southern report has it! Mr Andrew Haggard, 1947, tells me these posts were erected on certain large tracts of land belonging to [his Grace] where there were no trees or boulders and where sheep, in consequence of having nothing to rub against, were always getting 'cast'. The shepherds, who were not uncommonly verminous, used these posts to scratch their backs against and, when doing so, blessed the Duke. Contrast:

God bless you! Addressed to one who sneezes: C18–20. Fuller (1732) says, 'He's a friend at a sneeze: the most you can get out of him is a *God bless you.*' R.S., 1977 comments, 'I have for long understood that this phrase related to the incidence of bubonic plague in this country [UK] or at least to the Great Plague of 1665. It seems that sneezing was taken as one of the early symptoms of this murderous infection, so what more natural than to invoke a blessing upon a possible victim? The end of the children's traditional game "Ring-a-ring-o'-roses" is: "Tishoo! Tishoo! All fall down!"–which summarizes the mighmare very neatly. *Si non e vero...*; but I'm not the inventor [of the theory]!' P.B.: cf the synon. German use of *Gesundheit!*, (good) health!

God bless you both! is 'the ironic aside (*sotto voce*) when a "thin" laugh greets a comedian's best gag' (Granville): theatrical and music-hall: C20. Cf **it must be the land-lady.**

God give me strength! See **give me strength!**

God have mercy (but usu. **Godamercy**) **horse!** 'An almost meaningless proverbial exclamation' (Apperson) that was, *c.* 1530–1730, also a c.p. In Tarlton's *Jests*, 1611, it is mentioned as 'a by word thorow London'. P.B.: *horse* was perhaps a corruption of 'on us'?

God help the poor sailors on a night like this! See **pity the poor sailor...**

God help those... See **and God help...**

[God is alive and well and living in—(locality variable) has, by Mr D.R. Bartlett, MA, FLA, to whom I owe it, been glossed as a 'parody of a religious slogan of some kind, popularized recently on lavatory walls' (1975). I had never heard it or, come to that, seen it. The slogan was itself, I suspect, drawn from the frequent reply in any such dialogue as this:

'I haven't seen X for ages. Is he dead, d'you know?'

'Oh, no! He's alive and well and living in Manchester' [or any other place or area].

Moreover, I think that *God* is a deliberate var. of the ecclesiastical c.p., *the Devil is alive and well and living at*–, which may go back to early in C20, although I must admit that I had never heard of it until 4 April 1975 (from P.B.). Frankly, I doubt whether either saying is a true c.p.

These alternatives have set going a sentence-pattern, a syntactical pattern, if you prefer that description. As P.B. has pointed out, the following passage from a review (*The Times Literary Supplement*, 4 April 1975) of Constantine Fitzgibbon's *The Golden Age* exemplifies the fact: 'Orpheus then makes a pact with Mephistopheles and thereby recovers his memory in full. The Monster is alive and well, and living in the New Bodleian in the guise of a gently retiring Byzantine emperor.' This kind of thing had begun to happen at least as early as the 1920s, as we see in the progeny–e.g., 'came the crunch'–engendered by the films' *came the dawn.*

The phrase was at its height during the late 1960s–early 70s, as Mr Malcolm G. Taggart, the Library, University of East Anglia, has reminded me; and Paul Janssen has mentioned, 1977, that the celebrated Belgian-born French chansonnier, Jacques Brel, by going underground and then surfacing, caused the Brit. and US saying to be translated as *Jacques Brel est bel et bien vivant à Paris*; on 15 Nov. 1977 came his first long-playing record since 1966. (The genesis of the c.p. may have been: thought-pattern; c.p.; cliché.) His vast popularity was such that *Playboy* pub'd in Jan. 1970 an article, 'Brel: Going Strong', which began, 'With no end in sight, *Jacques Brel is alive and well and living in Paris* went through its 700th performance this past October'. Note, however, that R.C., 1977, comments, 'Its immediate origin (1960s) was rather a reply to the common cliché of that period, "God is dead"'.]

God (or God only) knows, I don't and God knows, and He won't split! The former c.p. of emphatic reply to a question belongs to C19–20; it is the modern shape of the mid C16–18 *God himself tell you, I cannot*, recorded in Florio's dictionary, 1598. The irreverent *He won't split!* var. belongs to C20; I first heard it in 1912 in Australia, but it isn't either specifically or predominantly Aus. Leechman recalls that, during WW1, it was, in the form GOK, a 'cryptic medical annotation for any undiagnosed complaint'. It is also, of course, US: C20 (Berrey, 1942). In Aus., since *c.* 1955. *tell* has largely displaced *split* (Neil Lovett, 1978).

God pays and the synon. **if I don't pay you, God Almighty will.** The former, current in late C16–18, appears thus in Ben Jonson's *Epigrams*, 1612:

To every cause he meets, this voice he brays,
His only answer is to all, God pays.

The latter belongs to C19–20. Used esp. by discharged naval seamen and by soldiers, who assumed a right to public charity.

God will get you for that! 'From *Maude*, a TV series starring Bea Arthur: response to insult or annoyance (usu. directed towards husband)' (Ashley, 1984): US.

Godamercy, horse! See **God mercy, horse!**

God's good, and the Devil's not a bad 'un! I first heard this as part of a short monologue in the language of Liverpool, included in a BBC Radio 4 'You and Yours' programme (23 May 1984) about regional slang. It was 'translated' by Brain Jacques, of BBC Radio Merseyside, as 'All things are in the lap of Allah'. Within a week my wife, working at the time in an old people's home, mentioned that she had heard it muttered by an elderly woman resident from Yorkshire. It feels like a cross between c.p. and placatory proverb. (P.B.)

goes around with thumb in bum... See **with thumb...**

goes for my money–usu. **he** occ. **she.** He's the man (or woman) for me–the person I favour: *c.* 1540–1660. (See esp. the *OED.*) Cf the Standard English *he's the man for my money*, which isn't a c.p., because the form can be varied according to persons and the saying can be applied also to quadrupeds or even to inanimate objects.

goffer. See: I'll draw.

going. See: vice going; that's going; and:

going down now, sir. See **don't forget the diver,** at end of the opening paragraph.

going home to eat cucumber sandwiches on the lawn? is one of those envious c.pp. still applied by a non-existent lower class to a non-existent upper class; more specifically by one who has a regional accent to one who speaks Standard English with a pure accent. As if the eating, by a 'gracious liver', of cucumber sandwiches on the lawn were somehow offensive to one who eats whelks in a kitchen 'fug'.

going in and out like a fiddler's elbow is an 'Anglo-Irish description of anyone jumpy or unsettled' (Skehan, 1977).

going is good. See: beat it.

going like gangbusters. See **gangbusters.**

going round the world for fourpence. Applied to someone becoming merrily drunk 'on the cheap': Aus.: very approx. c. 1930–60.

going through 'L' is applied to learner drivers, who have to stand a lot from instructors and the police' (Petch): since c. 1950; but little used since 1970. Obviously a pun on *going through hell*, having a thoroughly bad time, and on the '*L* for learner' sign hung on the back of cars.

going to buy anything? was, in 1896–c. 1930, an urban c.p.: an 'evasive request for a drink' (Ware, who elaborates).

going to hell in a hand-basket–he's or **she's** or **the world's.** 'Current [in US] for "Nothing's all right any more" or "we're sinking fast, boys!" Since the 1920s, I'd guess' (A.B., 1978).

going–until c. 1940. often **going out–to see a man about a dog.** See **see a man about a dog...**

gold. See: there's gold.

gold watch. See: cough it up; could fall; what's the time by.

golden eagle shits on Friday–the; also **the eagle shits on pay day; and the golden eagle lays its eggs.** The first is the British army and the RAF version, dating since 1941, of the second, which is the US army's c.p., dating since before WW2 and meaning 'Pay-day is on Friday'; the third is Brit and it means 'It's pay-day'. In the Services, the normal weekly pay-day is a Friday; the eagle concerned is that which figures on the US dollar.

P.B.: I'm sure that many of us in the RAF in the early 1950s connected the 'golden eagle' with the RAF's own emblem that we wore as our shoulder-flashes. Forces' pay-day was later moved to Thursday before being, for many, superseded by payment direct to one's bank account.

On pay-day itself, a US var. was *this is the day the eagle shits* (Fain, 1977).

golden rivet. See: watch out.

goldfish. See: give the cat.

goldmine. See: she's sitting.

Gomorrah to you! Good morning to you: a raffish c.p. of c. 1900–14. (Ware.) Punning on *good morrow!*, archaic for 'good morning!', and on '*sod* you!'–*Sodom and Gomorrah.*

gone. See: that's gone.

Gone and done it. See: been and gone.

gone for a Burton and gone for a shit with a rug round him, usu. prec. by **he's.** He's 'had it'–bought it'–'been killed', e.g. in an air raid over Germany: RAF: since 1939–or at least I've found no earlier record. Hence, 1941 and onwards, loosely 'He's absent' or 'He's not to be found'–'He's missing'. It remains an open question whether the phrase refers to a glass of Burton ale [P.B.: i.e., *heavy* ale] or, as I think, a suit made by Messrs Montague Burton, as the longer phrase seems to indicate, esp. as it too seems to have arisen in 1939. This longer phrase refers to a general practice in Service hospitals and, as a c.p., predominantly means 'He's been a long time absent'. Often **blanket** for **rug.**

The idea of going into Burton's for a ready-made suit is most probably connected with the folk-saying that someone has got a wooden suit–that is, a coffin' (Noble, 1977). Cf the *wooden surtout* entries in *DSUE* and *Underworld.*

Here I interpose a theory worth mention, for it has been propounded by David Garnett, who dates it back to WW1. He says that, 'on watching an aircraft crash in flames, onlookers would exclaim, "He's gone for a burnt 'on"'. He adds, 'This was politely slurred, and Burton either substi-

tuted or misheard'. The *Burton* would then have referred to Burton ale, not the tailors, which Paul Theroux and D.G. think did not exist at that period. (I am grateful to Mr Paul Theroux, who has kindly passed to me Mr Garnett's letter to *him.*) Well, I myself never heard either *gone for a burnt 'un* or *gone for a Burton* used on the Western Front, nor have I seen it in any book dealing with WW1–and, heaven knows, I've read hundreds of them. [And he wrote one: see *Three Personal Records of the War,* R.H. Mottram, John Easton, E.P., 1929: P.B.] By this, I do not mean that I doubt Mr Garnett's word; I merely doubt the use of the expression as a c.p. before WW2.

The old controversy continues–if anything, with increasing acrimony. I still prefer the tailoring orig., but now think that the trivial sense preceded the tragic. In 1978, Peter Sanders wrote: 'My wife, who was in the WAAF during WW2, tells me that the RAF took over some billiard halls above the Montague Burton shops as medical centres and consequently the excuse "he (or she) has gone for a Burton" originally meant no more than absence for a medical inspection, inoculation, etc.'

P.B.: similarly, *gone for a shit...* may have started with the more trivial idea of simply being in hospital. This phrase, too, has been dated back to WW1, by Mr P.V. Harris, 1979. Cf the next few, synop, entries.

gone for a posh shit was, during WW2, an Army equivalent of the prec. (Brian W. Aldiss, 1978.) P.B.: perhaps simply a var. of *gone for a shit with a rug wrapped round him.* Cf **went for a crap ...**

gone north about. See **he's gone north about.**

gone to lift his lying (or **lying-on**) **time** is an Anglo-Irish c.p. of C20. It occurs in, e.g., Patrick MacGill and is applied to a labourer recently dead.

gone to lynch. See **George–let's join.**

good. See: be good; beat it; finger-lickin'; good evening, Mrs Wood; good gracious, it's; Guinness; have you any g.; I'm like; if it ain't g.; if it feels; is that g.; it is as g.; it's all g.; it's good; keep yourself; like all fools; little of what; looks good; near enough; never had it; no good; oh, bloody; read any; sex and; she's good; that's a g.; they came; what's the g.; you can put it where; you can't keep; you look; you make as; you're a g.; your guess; your pump; and:

good a scholar as my horse Ball (–as). No scholar at all–indeed, these words may have formed the second half of the saying. Used by John Clarke in 1639, it seems to have been current c. 1620–70.

good business! That's good! *or* I'm glad to hear *that*!: since c. 1880. Arthur Wing Pinero, in the opening scene of *Playgoers,* 1913, has:

THE MISTRESS ... Darling, I am convinced that at last our miseries are ended and that we are in for a run of luck.
THE MASTER: (*lighting a cigarette*) Good business, if that's the case!

Earlier, Pinero's great rival, Henry Arthur Jones, in *The Lackey's Carnival,* 1900, writes in Act IV:

SIR G: And, Bertie, you might bring your men round from the Compasses.
BERTIE: What? Good business!

good-bye or **goodbye.** See: say au revoir; say something; and:

good-bye, and bolt the door, bugger you!, with the last two words omitted when the c.p. is uttered in polite company: 'a parting without a blessing' is how Frank Shaw described it, 1969: lower and lower-middle class: C20.

good-by-ee! This was, c. 1915–20, the c.p. form of *good-bye!* (Collinson.) It occurred in several popular songs of the period. P.B.: but the main one, of four humorous verses and chorus, was the one so titled, written and composed by R.P. Weston and Bert Lee, copyright date 1917. of interest to those who may think that *bird* is a modern term for a girl or sweet heart is the line attributed to 'Brother Bertie', a lieutenant: 'Remember me to all the "Birds"!' I quote the whole chorus for its splendid period flavour:

Good-bye-ee! good-bye-ee! Wipe the tear, baby dear,
from your eye-ee.
Tho' it's hard to part, I know, I'll be tickled to death to go.
Don't cry-ee! don't sigh-ee! There's a silver lining in the
sky-ee.
Bon soir, old thing! cheer-i-o! chin-chin! Nah-poo!
Toodle-oo!
Good-bye-ee! Good-bye-ee!

good-bye for now! has been very frequent, esp. over the telephone, since *c.* 1960, and it should be compared with **ta-ta for now**, q.v. at TOMMY HANDLEY CATCH PHRASES. It was soon used also in the shorter from *'bye for now*, itself further shortened to *BFN*.

good-bye to all that! is a regretful, often nostalgic, c.p., dating from 1929, when Rovert Graves's autobiography *Good-bye to All That* appeared, to invest an old cliché with a much wider currency and a much wider application, as, e.g., in James Leasor's *Passport to Peril*, 1966.

good evening. See: hello, good; and:

[**good evening, England! (This is Gillie Potter speaking to you in English)**–and very precise and well-spoken English it was, too. I am not proposing this as a popular c.p., it was too personal for that, but there *was* some enthusiastic imitation of Potter's *good evening England! VIBS*, to which I am indebted for the reminder, has 'Potter's radio talks [usu. monologues, given as one turn of many in a variety show] delivered with an assumed pedagogic and superior air, recounted the doings of the Marshmallow family of Hogsnorton Towers–a delight from the 1940s and early 1950s now alas, absent from the air'. (P.B.)]

good evening, friends! is, like **get off me barrer**, a comic ending 'to fit any number of music-hall songs. ... On the chromatic scale goes (e.g.) ABAC, played very slowly ... originated as a convenient end sequence for part-singing like Barber's-shop quartets. Cf **get off me barrer**.' (Cyril Whelan, 1975.)

good evening, Mrs Wood, is fourpence any good? lasted from *c.* 1910 to *c.* 1950; that it lasted so long was due to its rhyme–and its implication. P.B.: it became (? orig. as) the first line of a ribald poem still recited by naughty schoolboys in the mid-1950s.

good field, no hit. (Lit., a good fielder, but a poor hitter, i.e. batter.) W.J.B. writes, 1975:

A baseball catch phrase which caught on and is still current is 'Good field no hit'. ... In the spring of 1924 the Brooklyn 'Dodgers' were training at Clearwater, Florida. One of the 'Dodger' players was Moe Berg, who later became America's No. 1 atomic spy. Miguel Gonzales, a coach for the St Louis 'Cardinals', was also in Clearwater at that time. Mike Kelley of Minneapolis wanted to buy Berg for his team and wired Gonzales for his opinion of Berg's potentialities. Gonzales wired back the four-word message 'Good field, no hit'. The expression ... has been used ever since as a description of anyone good in one field and inept in another. My authority is ... *Moe Berg Athlete, Scholar, Spy*, by Louis Kaufman, Barbara Fitzgerald and Tom Sewell, 1974, pp. 137–8. The authors wrote: 'It is ironic that the suave and polished Berg should have been the subject of baseball's most illiterate message.' Berg wrote and spoke several languages, including Japanese and Chinese. It was touch and go whether German scientists in WWII would produce an atomic bomb before the US did. With such a weapon the Germans could have won the war. Berg was sent to Switzerland to spy on visiting German scientists known to be working on the bomb. Berg spied on Professor Werner Heisenberg, the leading scientist working for the Germans.

good for what ails you. 'C.p. used when offering drink, food, etc.' (Ashley, 1979): US: later C20. P.B.: cf the ambiguous Brit. synon. *it's good for the parts*.

good goods! is 'addressed to one who has donned a new suit; said with Jewish intonation and an industrious feeling of the quality of the cloth' (Leechman): Can.: since *c.* 150. R.C., 1977, notes that it was also current in the US: 'now extinct'.

American usage has a humorously witty equivalent: *shoot him in the pants, the coat belongs to me*, characterizing business acumen and dating, prob., since the 1930s (Fain, 1977). Cf **never mind the quality ...**

[**good grief!** This has been proposed by an eminent scholar; but all such mere euphemisms for *good God!* are ineligible. On the other hand, *'good grief, it's granny!* seems to have been a Southern US c.p. for "The gig's [i.e. game's] up–we're caught!"–said when someone, not necessarily Grandmother, makes an unexpected, yet not *always* unpleasing, appearance. [Since] 1940s, I'd guess' (A.B., 1978). Perhaps orig. juvenile and, I'd say, slightly ob. by the late 1970s. P.B.: but E.P. was apparently unaware of the immense, worldwide popularity of Charles M. Schulz's strip cartoon 'Peanuts', which has surely raised *good grief!* to the status of c.p., and with which it is, in later C20, always associated. The third (US) collection of these cartoons, after *Peanuts* and *More Peanuts* was, inevitably, *Good Grief, More Peanuts!*]

good (or sweet) herbs! (or **'erbs!**) Excellent or excellently: a mostly postmen's c.p. of *c.* 1910–30. (Manchon.) From a street vendors' cry.

good hunting! This, at first a sportsmen's c.p., dates from the 1890s–and means, without elab. or deviousness, 'Good luck!' The phrase was popularized, perhaps even started on its career as a c.p., by Kipling's *The Jungle Book*, 1894, 2nd edn in 1895. In his *Shadow Play*, pub'd in 1936. Noël Coward uses it thus:

YOUNG MAN: Will you excuse me–I have to dance with Lady Dukes.

VICKY: Certainly.

YOUNG MAN: Good hunting.

And in the final scene of *Blithe Spirit*, both played and pub'd in 1941, he has Madame Arcati, who is addicted to the fashionable slang of the 1920s, saying, 'Don't trouble–I can find my way. Cheerio once more and good hunting!' Cf **good hunting!**

good idea (pause), **son** (emphatic)! This was a Max Bygraves 'gag' of (?) the late 1950s–early 1960s. 'I think that he eventually made it the chorus punch line of a song' (P.B., 1975). The radio comedy series in which M.B. started this c.p. was 'Educating Archie', 'starring' Archie Andrews, the dummy of ventriloquist Peter Brough. (*VIBS.*)

good in parts, like the curate's egg. It was Prof. W.E. Collinson who, in 1927, noticed it as a c.p.–and so it has remained ever since. During WW1 and for a few years afterwards, it justified H.W. Fowler's condemnation, 'a battered ornament'; during the first decade, it was, rather, a cultured allusion.

From an illustrated joke by Gerald Du Maurier in *Punch*, 1895 (vol. CIX, p. 222). A curate is taking breakfast in his Bishop's home:

'I'm afraid you've got a bad egg, Mr Jones.'

'Oh no, my Lord, I assure you! Parts of it are excellent.'

The same sort of 'rationalization'–or, if you prefer that angle, of conflation–occurs in **elementary, my dear Watson!** J.W.C., 1977, notes, 'In US, *like the curates' egg* usually stands by itself. It is limited to, and usually understood only by, the sophisticated, partly because most Americans don't know what a curate is'.

good look round–have a. See **have a good look round....good luck to him!** See **luck to him....**

good men are scarce: not many of us left. 'With the cliché-maker, this follows **look after yourself!**' (Shaw) as a pendant: since at least as early as 1920. By itself, *good men*–occ. *folk(s)–are scarce* is a cliché: the c.p. elaborates it.

good morning. See: Napoleon's; and:

good morning, have you used Pears soap? In his witty review of the reprint of the famous *Pears Cyclopaedia* as first pub'd in 1877–'Next to cleanliness' in *TLS*, 6 Jan. 1978–Maurice Richardson rightly stated that 'There has never been advertising like that for Pears Soap. It created an image that lasted for into the twentieth century. It seemed to transcend the boundaries of commerce ... The genius behind Pears advertising was Thomas J. Barratt, born in 1841. In 1865 ... he picked up the eldest Miss Pears, married her and joined the firm ... His was the slogan, "Good morning, have you used Pears Soap?" He inspired the famous posters: the *Punch* tramp saying "Two years ago I used your Soap. Since when I have used no other!" [a cartoon by Harry Furniss that appeared in *Punch*, 26 Apr. 1884; 'Pears, with permission from *Punch*, added the firm's name to the cartoon and issued it as one of thousands of handbills distributed in the 1880s and 1890s' (Nigel Rees, *Slogans*, 1982)], which was a skit on Lillie Langtry's testimonial; the muscular squalling baby reaching out from his bath, captioned "He won't be happy till he gets it"; and, of course, Millais's little monster "Bubbles".' (With the reviewer's and the TLS's generous permission.) As a c.p. it was ob. by 1930, † by 1950. See also **since when I have used no other**, and **preparing to be a beautiful lady.**

good morning, sir! Was there something? was Sam Costa's weekly entry line in the BBC's 'Much Binding in the Marsh' (?1944–5 and after), as P.B. reminds me, 1971. The 'gag' caught on. The second member of the line is, of course, elliptical for 'Was there something you needed?' Like so many radio c.pp., its intonation was all-important.

good night. See: it's good night; thank you and; and:

good night! This c.p. retort vigorously expresses the height of incredulity or the depth of comic despair or undiluted delight; it arose *c.* 1880; by 1935 it was ob., by 1976–virtually †, yet still heard occ. and not only among the old.

In the late C19 it acquired the nuance 'That's *done* it'–cf **that's torn it**: since *c.* 1920, indeed, the predominant sense of *good night!* has been 'That's finished it'–'That's the end', or, as Ware has it, 'This is too much–I think I must be going'.

A notable adumbration occurs in Shakespeare's I *Henry IV*, I, iii, lines 191 ff.:

WORCESTER: As full of peril and adventurous spirit
As to o'er-walk a current roaring loud
On the unsteadfast footing of a spear.
HOTSPUR: If he fall in, good night!

Inevitably, the phrase was, apparently *c.* 1910., adopted in the US: and in 1960, W&F remarked that it expressed 'surprise, disgust or anger' and that it served also as a euph. for *good God!* Unfortunately they supply no date, no other information no comment. It is therefore worth recording that, in the essay titled 'Lesson Number One' in *Of All Things*, 1922, Robert Benchley wrote: 'As he cranked it again, George said ... that he could take a joke as well as the next man, but that, good night! what was the use of being an ass?' At about the same time, H.L. Mencken noted the phrase in *The American Language*: and what finer consecration could a phrase receive than this dual mention? An earlier example occurs in S.R. Strait's 'Straight Talk' in the *Boston Globe* of *c.* 1917. (W.J.B.) Cf the next three entries.

good night, Gracie. 'Said with resignation, as by George Burns of Burns & [Gracie] Allen, the comedy duo: now a c.p. expressing frustration with a stupid remark' (Ashley) – i.e., the sort of remark that was Gracie's speciality in the act: US: since mid C20.

good night, Irene! (Pron. *Ire.*) 'Common in my Alabama world *c.* 1910–14 to express surprise or even mild dismay. It had its currency about then, and I am sure that I used it. It *may* be a phrase from the title of, or the principal song, in a musical comedy' (Prof. S.H. Monk, 1968). It was also current among US students of the second decade, as McKnight declares.

'Rene Cutforth, *Order to View*, 1969, Ch. XI, reporting the war in Korea: "The Korean War was fought all that winter [1950–1] to the strains of 'Goodnight, Irene'. In tents and foxholes and ruined mud-houses and on the snowy tops of mountains, when you tuned in the wireless, that was what you got, take it or leave it, Nearly everybody took it ... It was the hummed accompaniment of every activity. There

was nothing gay about, or even sad ..." Forgive the long quotation, but I think it explains how the old c.p. was given a new lease of life' (P.B., 1976).

'Immediate sources the (? folk) song "Irene, good night", from *c.* 1900, or earlier, which, much later, became the theme song of the late great Negro folk and blues singer, Heddie ("Leadbelly") Ledbetter' (R.C., 1977).

P.B.: one verse of the *c.* 1950 song ran:
Last Saturday night I got married; me and my wife settled
down.
Now me and my wife are parted, I'm gonna take another
stroll down town.

'Good night, Irene' formed the only words of the chorus, which droned on for three lines before ending 'I'll see you in my dreams'. Almost as dirge-like to wage a war to as the contemporary 'Dear John', which also dwelt on a lover's unfaithfulness.

good night, McGuinness! A NZ version of **good night, nurse!**: *c.* 1910–35. I've no idea who this briefly famous McGuinness may have been.

good night, Mrs Calabash! The great American comedian, Jimmy 'Schnozzle' Durante, 'took a break from performing only once – to care for his first wife Jeanne Olsen, when she was slowly dying in the 1940s. Though he later married again, he would invoke Jeanne's nickname at the end of his TV appearances: for a few seconds, [he] would turn uncharacteristically somber and then bow off with the line, "Good night, Mrs Calabash, wherever you are"' (*Time* obituary of J.D., 1893–1980, 11 Feb. 1980). A.B., 1978, wrote, 'I have heard others using it as a parting gambit, on leaving a party or something of the sort'.

good night, nurse!, although it prob. dates from *c.* 1910, became popular during – and largely because of – WW1, with particular ref. to the naval and military hospitals for Other Ranks. It is synon. with and clearly prompted by the simple, the basic, **good night!** Cf **good night, Irene!** and such other phrases as **carry me out! – let me die! – that's torn it!**

good night, sweet repose, followed either by *half the bed and all the clothes* or by *slam the door in the doctor's nose*; in both versions they perform two functions: nursery rhyme and childish c.p. They belong to mid (? late) C19 and mid C20, although the former lingers on. (Sanders, 1978.) Cf **sleep tight!** ...

good night, Vienna comes from the title of a romantic operetta, 1932, book and lyrics by Eric Maschwitz, music by George Posford, the whole serving as a vehicle for Richard Tauber. 'Its main song was "Good night, Vienna" (you city of a million melodies)' (Ronald Pearsall, 1975). As a c.p. it has been described by Cyril Whelan, 1975, as 'a pen-knife phrase, in that it can be put to a variety of different uses – often apparently contradictory. "If the officer catches us up to this, it's Good Night, Vienna, for the lot of us." – "So I met the girl. We had a few drinks. Back to her place, and Good Night, Vienna".' Its appeal and currency are due only to the fact that it's mildly pleasing to the tongue in a racy sort of way and bounces quite happily on the ear of the listener.

good old Charlie-ee! 'Richard Murdoch's interjection from *Much Binding In The Marsh*' (VIBS). *Much Binding*, starring R.M., Kenneth Horne and Sam Costa, started during WW2 as the RAF's contribution to radio comedy, and continued with undiminished popularity into the late 1940s. This c.p., already a regular feature of the show, was used to enormously good effect when Murdoch and Horne took part in the Royal Command Variety Show of 1948, very soon after the birth of Prince Charles. It was always uttered as a chant. (P.B.)

good old England! and **good old terra firma!** are railwaymen's ironic c.pp., applied since *c.* 1920, to 'off the railroad, at trap points'.

good place to be from – a (– *it's*). 'A veiled animadversion to someone's saying that he is from such-and-such a place, i.e., a good place to get away from: US: current 1950s; now ob.' (R.C., 1977). Cf **nice place to live out of.**

good question. Michael Innes, in the *The Mysterious Commission*, 1974, has:

'Do particular gangs going after this sort of thing have their regular and identifiable techniques?'

'Good question.' It was to be presumed that Detective Superintendent Keybird was in the habit of conducting seminars at police colleges.

See also **that's a good question** and **very good question.**

good shit would do you more good – a. This is a low c.p. addressed to one who says 'I could do with a woman': late C19–20, but by 1970 slightly ob. 'The current US variant is *there's nothing like a good shit'* (J.W.C., 1977). P.B.: all of which is vulgarly reminiscent of Kipling's line, in his verse 'The Betrothed', c. 1885, 'And a woman is only a woman, but a good cigar is a smoke'.

good soldier never looks behind him – a, is an orig. – 1914 or 1915 – military c.p., become by 1918 common enough among civilians, but I've not heard it for many years. Meaning 'You have no right to criticize the heels of my boots or shoes', it is an ingenuously ironic misapplication of an old army adage.

good thinking!, often introduced by **that's.** That's a sound – an excellent – idea; What a wonderful suggestion!: heard from c. 1960 onwards, but not a genuine Brit. c.p. until c. 1969. Orig. a serious comment; but as c.p., joc. In the *Daily Telegraph* colour supplement, 27 Oct. 1972, I noticed this advertisement:

'I've brought you a glass of BLUE NUN, sir ...'

'Good thinking, Cranston – just hold it there while I land this killer pike.'

And on the evening before, a Congregational minister had used it to an intelligent member of the congregation at a church meeting.

In 1974, Marshall Pugh, in *A Dream of Treason*, uses it thus:

'Arab terrorists,' Max said. 'How would you set about it?'

'Well, I'd keep a sharp eye out for sandals,' Middlemass said. . . . .

'Good thinking,' Max said.

The phrase came from the US, where it had arisen, c. 1950, among the advertising and publicity agencies of New York's Madison Avenue and had, by the middle or late 1950s, become a US c.p. – not unassisted by the 'Good thinking, Batman' of the Batman 'comic' strips.

good time coming – there's a is a cliché that often evokes the c.p. riposte, **yes, but it's a (damn') long time coming**, ironical, sometimes cynical, occ. bitter; dating since c. 1942. (Owed to Mr A.B. Petch, who has an almost uncanny ear for the catch phrases of the street and the pub, the bus and the train, and the domestic, and a very keen eye for the more popular newspapers. My note of 17 Sep. 1978.)

good time was had by all – a. In 1937, the late Miss Stevie Smith's book of verse, *A Good Time Was Had by All* appeared: and within five years in UK and by 1950 at latest in the US, the words of the title had become a c.p. – so thoroughly that it is employed allusively in Clarence Budington Kelland's *Counterfeit Gentleman*, 1956: ' "One night at dinner we had a justice of the Supreme Court, the president of a university, a truck driver who did card tricks and an Aleutian Islander with a trained seal. A good time was had by all." '

It had not, by 1974, attained a general currency [E.P. later changed his mind on this dating, when M. Paul Janssen drew his attention to the Beatles' album *Sergeant Pepper's Lonely Hearts Club Band*, released 1 June 1967. In the song 'Being for the Benefit of Mr Kite' is the line 'A splendid time is guaranteed for all'. However,] it has remained a predominantly literary and cultured phrase. But it has become so integrated in the speech of cultured Britons and Americans that it can occur with devastating naturalness, as in Amanda Cross's US novel, *Poetic Justice*, 1970, thus: 'How they got

through the subsequent two hours ... Kate never properly knew. But such a good time was had by all that they quite happily voted Mr Cornford a distinction.' And in May Mackintosh's British novel, *Appointment in Andalusia*, 1972: 'Once the Spanish police start getting suspicious they are liable to clap you in gaol and then start thinking the matter over. It's their policy not to rush their thinking, so I assure you a good time is not had by all.'

Perhaps six months before Stevie Smith's death, I wrote to her and asked whether she had coined the phrase or adopted and popularized it. Her explanation was startlingly simple: she took it from parish magazines, where a church picnic or outing or social evening or other sociable occasion, almost inevitably generated the comment, 'A good time was had by all.'

She herself asked, 'Are you the Eric Partridge of the Slang dictionary. But no! he must by now be dead.' I assured her that I, at any rate, suffered from the delusion – and lived within the illusion – that I was still alive and busy and *compos*. Then she died rather unexpectedly: but then, don't we all live under the dispensation of a *D.V.*?

good to the last drop. 'Maxwell House's coffee slogan – "good to the last drop" – has seen some generalized use – "thoroughly or completely good or enjoyable" ' (W&F, p. 604). Berrey, 2nd edn, 1952, had included it in the synonymy for 'excellent'. J.W.C., 1968, wrote: 'Disused (I think) by then, because people were always saying, "What's wrong with the last drop?" But still a c.p., used of other things than beverages – speeches, e.g.'

This US c.p. was, c. 1960, adopted in UK. Nigel Rees, in *Slogans*, 1982, dates its US use as the Maxwell House slogan from c. 1907.

good trumpeter. In (usu. *he) would make a good trumpeter, for he smells strong*, with the second part omitted increasingly often: mid C18–mid C19. In Grose, 1788, the latter part of the c.p. is **for he has a strong breath.** It means 'He has fetid breath'; and it plays on *strong breath*, bad breath, but good lungs.

good voice to beg bacon – a, was, c. 1680–1770, a c.p. derisive of a poor, or even a thoroughly bad, voice. BE.

good young man – a, was, 1910–c. 1914, a trenchant proletarian c.p. applied to a hypocrite. Orig., Ware tells us, by Arthur Roberts in a song.

good yunting! 'Employed jocularly by costermongers as a means of wishing the next-stall neighbour (and some regular, understanding customers) a Merry Christmas, a Happy New Year, a pleasant Easter, and so on' (Franklyn, 1968): since c. 1918. Influenced by **good hunting!** in sense and, as Ashley (New York) points out, 1979, it puns on or parodies the Yiddish for "happy holiday", *gut yontif*, or, as Levene (London), 1983, prefers, *'good yomtov ... pronounced (for ease) yontoff*; the word itself means "good day" – i.e. festival day'.

goodness. See: my goodness.

goodness gracious, it's good! 'From an advertisement for Martha White Brand Flour ... A motto, really, but it is applied to many things: 1930s–1940s – [the] present' (A.B., 1978).

goodness gracious me! 'The key phrase in Peter Sellers's Indian doctor impersonation ... It first occurred in a song recorded by Sellers and Sophia Loren based on their parts in the film of [G.B.] Shaw's *The Millionairess'(VIBS)*.

goodness me, it's number 3 is of the consecrated c.pp. in the game of bingo; brevity and a rhyme being the prime essentials: since the early 1950s. P.B.: but this is only one of many; for a long list of housey-housey, tombola, or bingo calls, see the Appendix to *DSUE*, 8th ed.

good night. See **good night.**

goods. See: good goods; if you don't want.

goolies. See: don't let your braces.

GOON SHOW CATCH PHRASES. ' ... from the Goon Show it is odd [of E.P.] to have picked "have a gorilla" and "Time for your

O.B.E., Neddy" as favourites, when "Shut up, Eccles" and Little Jim's "He's fallen in the wah-tah", among others, were better and more widely adapted for use in life's silly situations' (Russell Davies in *New Statesman*, 9 Sep. 1977, reviewing the first ed. of this book). Cf the entry **no, I'm trying to give them up.** [P.B.: but the truth is, as E.P. told me, he had never listened to the 'Goon Show', was too busy 'beavering away' at his reading and writing; and so all his 'Goon Show' entries were hearsay, from correspondents who would have assumed that he *had* heard at least some of the series.]

'The Goon Show' ran from mid-1951 to 28 Jan. 1961: and it has been neatly and justly summarized by Barry Took, in *Laughter in the Air: an Informal History of British Radio Comedy*, 1976: '[It] was a stupendous achievement in broadcasting; it became a hit mainly because it echoed the mood of disenchantment that was then current, and stood the supposedly real world its head. Thanks to the team work of its producers, writers and stars it was brave and adventurous and fast-paced, and nothing captured the imagination in quite the same way until the emergence of "Monty Python's Flying Circus" on television in the late 'sixties.'

goose. See: free as; go shoe; loose; shit off; such a reason; weaving; who stole the **g**.; you don't have the brains.

gorblimey. See: from the sublime.

gorilla. See: have a g.

got a clock (– he's). He's carrying a bag with a time-bomb in it: a Londoners' c.p. of 1883, in ref. to the activities of the dynamitards. *Plus ça change*...

got a feather in your trousers? is addressed to a boy giggling suddenly and, it seems, inexplicably, as in 'What's the matter, son? Got...?' C20. cf synon. **have you found a giggle's nest?**

got a snake in your pocket? See **snake in...?**

got all the moves – esp. he's. 'He's extremely skilful – i.e., he knows exactly where to move (lit. or fig.) and when. Orig. (?1960s) applied to basketball players, according to the *New York Times* Sports Department; later applied to players in other sports, and within the last six years to any expert operator' (R.C. cites a cartoon in *The New Yorker*, 22 May 1978: 'That's E. W. Feesley. He's got all the moves').

got any hard? This was *c.* 1920–40, a c.p. addressed, in Southampton (England) bars to a stranger and implying that he may have been to sea and therefore may, just possibly, have some hard tobacco, i.e. tobacco in blocks, to spare. It was more of a joke than a serious question.

got calluses from pattin' his own back – he's. A cowboy's description of a braggart: the American West. (Adams, 1968.)

got 'em on the five-yard line. See **five-yard line.**

got in just under the wire (– , e.g. he). 'He arrived in the nick of time – barely made it' (A.B., 1979): date uncertain: C20. Neither Berrey nor W & F have it.

got it in one! You've guessed the answer, or grasped the point, at the first attempt: US: since *c.* 1930. R.C. cites A. Winward, *Fives Wild*, 1976.

got it off or **got it all off** – or **got it all off pat**, prec. by **I** or **you** or **he** (or **she**), means that the lesson has been thoroughly learnt: schoolchildren's: since *c.* 1920. P.B.: *pat* in this sense, for all its coll. sound, is Standard English, and goes back to C17: *SOD* cites Pepys.

got (or **get**) **me, Steve?** Do you understand? This US c.p., dating from very early in C20, was anglicized by 1910. As *got me, Steve?*, it was recorded as early as 1914 by W. L. George in his striking novel, *The Making of an Englishman*; and as *got me?* or *got me, Steve?*, it was, in 1925, glossed thus by F & G: '... A phrase current in the War from an American film drama in which the "hero" kept producing a revolver to stress his points.' Agatha Christie in *Why Didn't They Ask Evans?*, 1934: '"I get you, Steve"... and... the queer phrase represented sympathy and understanding.' The posi-

tive form is either *I get you, Steve* or *I've got you, Steve*.

The simple *got me?* was noted by A. H. Melville in 'An Investigation of the Function and Use of Slang', a long article published in *The Pedagogical Seminary* of March 1912 and based on a school test made in 1911. *I get you, Steve* is the form in which it was recorded by Berrey in 1942. J. W. C., 1977, notes that now, 'In US, "got you" is very common: "I understand you" – even without preceding "Get me?" "Steve" now (though not formerly) almost always omitted [both] in question and in "Got you"'.

got to swim under water to dodge it! See **getting any?**

got up. See: all dressed.

got your boot on! You're well-informed and alert, 'you know what it is all about' (Cab Calloway, 1944): Harlem jive, then New York and finally the US world of entertainment: *c.* 1938–50. Basic sense: prepared.

got your eyeful? Have you had a good look?: raffish: since *c.* 1910 or a little earlier. Cf *take an eyeful*, to look long or carefully, slang current in late C19–early 20.

got your glasses on! You're being snooty, superior: orig. Harlem jive, then gen. US entertainment: *c.* 1938–50. Cab Calloway, 1944.

gotcha! or **got you!** I understand you: US: from the 1930s or earlier. Cf **got me, Steve**, q.v. On the other hand, R.C., 1977, adjudged it to have been † since the 1930s. Evidently, it rather depends on which part of the US you've mostly lived in. Contrast **get you!**

gotta. See: when you g.

Gozo. See: just the job for; not me, Sare.

grab(s). See: gift; how does that; that grabs; up for.

grab your steel helmets! See **swing that lamp, Jack!**

grace. See: Patience.

Gracie. See: good night, G.

gracious. See: free, gracious; goodness gracious.

['**gradely lads,**' said the Duke [of Wellington], '**Let battle commence!**' Simply 'Let's begin!' From Stanley Holloway's monologue of the late 1930s, 'Sam! Sam, pick up tha musket!' (P.B., 1976.) Although not since *c.* 1970, I've heard the elliptical *let battle commence!* Certainly it was a potential c.p. The adjective *gradely* is N. Country dialect, meaning 'handsome, good, honest, true, etc.' 'Gradely lads' might now be rendered, by a Duke, as 'Splendid chaps'.]

[GRAFFITI. 'Worth mentioning? Some of the most frequent formulae creep into the spoken and written language' (Playfair, 1977). Point taken! But they are *very* few! Cf **A. C. A. B.** and **rule(s) OK**. P.B.: anyone who disagrees with E.P. is referred to the delights of Nigel Rees's collections, *Graffiti Lives, OK* and the subsequent *Graffiti 2, 3* and *4*, with, I hope, more to follow.]

grammar. See: 'ain't' ain't.

grandmother. See: all my eye and my elbow; enough to make my gran; I haven't laughed; and:

grandmother and mine had four elbows – her (or his). In S, Dialogue I, we read:

LORD SP: Pray, my Lady *Smart*, what kin are you to Lord *Pozz*?

LADY SM: Why, his Grandmother and mine had four Elbows.

We are both human beings – there's no closer relationship than that.

Apparently a c.p. of late C17 – mid 18.

grandmother is with me. See **friend has come.**

granny. See: good grief; muck in; my Aunt; steal; you've shot.

granted as soon as asked is a lower-middle-class c.p. of C20. 'Rudyard Kipling in "Wireless" [*Traffics and Discoveries*, 1902; cf **grateful and comforting**] puts the phrase into the mouth of a pompous young man to whom no apology had in fact been offered – only an explanation' (R.S., 1977). Kipling possessed a very shrewd observation and perception of character. And in Noël Coward's sketch, 'Cat's Cradle' (written in 1928), we come upon this:

MISS M: False modesty's one thing, Miss Tassel, and loose thinking's another.

MISS T: I beg your pardon.

MISS M: Granted as soon as asked.

Sometimes extended to *granted as soon as asked, I'm sure*, or shortened to *granted, I'm sure*. P.B.: occ. used in mockery of this type of genteelness.

grape(s). See: I'm not out; in the grip; peel me.

grass. See: come off the g.; corvette; go to grass; keep off; tall weed; your ass is g.; and:

grass is getting short – the. 'In mining, an expression meaning that operations are endangered because of diminishing funds' (Adams): Western US: C20.

[**grass is greener on the other side of the fence – the.** C20 version of a proverb adumbrated by Erasmus: English translation of 1545 (*Concise Oxford Dict. of Proverbs*, 1982).]

grateful. See: they don't yell.

grateful and comforting, like Epps's cocoa. Often with the last three words omitted, as in Collinson. It was taken from a famous advertisement issued by Epps's Cocoa. The c.p. arose in the very late C19 and was, apparently, still flourishing during the 1920s.

In I, ii, of Noël Coward's perturbing play, *Peace in Our Time*, 1947, George Bourne remarks that 'One quick brandy, like Epps's cocoa, would be both grateful and comforting' and when Ger. Albrecht asks 'Who is Epps?' George replies, 'Epps's Cocoa – it's an advertisement that I remember when I was a little boy – "Epps's Cocoa – Both grateful and comforting"'.

P.B.: In Kipling's collection of short stories, *Traffics and Discoveries*, 1904, in 'Wireless' (written two years earlier), the consumptive Northern chemist, handed a strong concoction by the narrator, says "Twon't make me drunk, will it? I'm almost a teetotaller. My word! That's grateful and comforting.' And as Mr John Shearman, Hon. Secretary of the Kipling Society, pointed out to me in 1978, 'The phrase occurs in at least one other Kipling story ... ; this is "A Flight of Fact", collected in *Land and Sea Tales* [,1923]: "What's betel-nut like, Jerry?" – "Grateful and comfortin'. Warms you all through and makes you spit pink. It's non-intoxicating ..."' It occurs also earlier still, in George Du Maurier's *Peter Ibbetson*, 1891; was it by then already a slogan, or was it 'floating loose' in the language?

gratuitous untruth. See: unbounded.

grave. See: digging; you would not be; you've got one.

graveyard. See: if I hit.

grease. See: no grease; noise like.

great. See: it's a great; pissed on from; shit on from.

[**great American dream – the**; and **the great American novel**, tempting although it be to treat them as c.pp., orig. and predominantly US, are fundamentally clichés, employed mostly by journalists, publicists, satirists.]

great minds think alike does not appear in the dictionaries of quotations, nor in those of proverbs. It seems to have arisen *c.* 1890, perhaps a decade earlier, as a c.p., and a c.p. it has remained: any remark, esp. about a trivial matter, that could be answered by 'I happen to think the same' or by 'We agree entirely on that point' can be capped by *great minds think alike*, a phrase that has become so embedded in ordinary, everyday English that, on 7 Oct. 1973, one of London's 'nationals' had an article headed 'Great Minds Think Unalike'.

Prof. D. J. Enright, in *Encounter*, Dec. 1977, fittingly chides me for having failed to notice that it occurs in *Everyman's Dict. of Quotations and Proverbs*. P.B.: and now, 1982, the *Concise Oxford Dict. of Proverbs* has traced the idea, if not the exact words, back to 1618. Unimpressed listeners to the 'great minds' are sometimes apt to remark, 'and fools seldom differ': C20. Cf **two minds ...**

Great War. See: what did you do.

great weather for ducks. See **fine day ...**

greatest. See: I am the g.; it's the greatest thing.

greedy. See: not greedy.

[**Greeks had a word for it – the.** Occurs in Zoë Akins's play, *The Greeks Had a Word for It*, 1929; and in a letter to Burton Stevenson, the author of two famous dictionaries of quotations, she explains that, in Stevenson's words, 'the phrase is original and grew out of the dialogue'. It 'caught on' with a notable celerity: by 1930, it was common both in the US and, by virtually instantaneous adoption, in UK (whence, by 1931, in the Commonwealth). Had Zoë Akins's words appeared in the text – they had done so, orig., but were cut out – this would indisputably have ranked as a famous quot'n; as they did not, but were preserved only in the title, I'm tempted to classify it as a c.p.]

green. See: do you see any; little green; not so g.; see anything; send for the g.; tell a g.; what's in.

green lime, please! is a C20 theatrical c.p., 'sometimes murmured today when a line savours of melodrama', as Granville told us. He explained its origin thus: 'A melodrama villain indicated his diabolical intentions in the light of a green lime. At rehearsals when mouthing his lines he used to remind the stage manager that he would require the green limelight in that speech, "on the night".'

greener the other side ... See **grass is greener ...**

Greenland. See: from Greenland's

greeting. See: Napoleon's.

[**greetings!** 'This one-word c.p. was extremely popular in US during WW2 [more precisely, 1942–5] and somewhat after, until the US Armed Services draft system was abandoned. It was the first word, a salutation, on a draft notice, which came by mail, 1940s–60s' (A. B., 1978). Obviously, not when used lit. P.B.: did the United States Armed Forces take the word from the King's Commission: 'To Our Trusty and Well-Beloved ... , Greetings,'?]

gremlins have got into it – the. See the Vernon Noble quot'n at **press on, regardless.**

grief. See: good grief.

grindstone. See: oh, well! back.

grip. See: get a grip; in the grip.

grist mill. See: back to the salt mines.

groceries. See: doesn't buy; don't buy.

ground. See: I told Wilbur; it doesn't stand; it's not off; you don't piss; your feet.

ground and bolted. See: I've been through.

group. See: fuck on.

grow. See: I grow; I've seen 'em g.; legs grew; roses; that'll grow; they don't g.; you can't g.; you have grown; and:

grow on trees – it doesn't or, of currency and bank-notes, **they don't ... .**; and **you seem to think money grows on trees.** These are c.pp. addressed to – or directed at – those who think that money just happens to be always and immediately available or is, at worst, very easily obtained; an exasperated reply to an unanswerable request for money: late C19–20. 'The mass of men lead lives of quiet desperation' (Thoreau). Cf **you must think I'm made of money.**

grow up! and **why don't you grow up?** are synon. with **be your age!:** since the late 1930s in UK. Perhaps orig. US: Berrey records it. The gen. sense is 'Don't be ridiculous!'. Cf **act your age!** A.B., 1978, remarks of US usage, 'C20, and prob. of C19 origin'.

growl you may, but go you must! A nautical c.p. uttered 'when the watch below have to turn out of their bunks to shorten sail in bad weather' (Bowen): *c.* 1870–1910.

grub. See: lovely grub.

grunt. See: what can you expect.

guard. See: on guard.

Guards. See: up, Guards.

Guardsmen. See: rarest

guerre. See: appray la guerre; c'est la guerre.

guess. See: by guess; close your eyes; don't tell me, let; I guess; no, don't tell; no prizes; you guessed; you have another; your guess; and:

guess who's back! is an Aus. c.p. 'uttered with one hand on hearer's back' (B.P.): it antedates 1945 (Neil Lovett, in *The National Times*, 23–28 Jan. 1978). A pun on *whose back*. Cf **excuse my wart**, q.v. Influenced by:

[**guess who's here!** 'You'll (*or* You'd) never guess who has arrived *or* is here!' It lies in the no-man's land between c.p. and cliché: C20.]

guest. See: be my g.

guilty. See: not guilty.

guinea. See: worth a g.

Guinness is good for you, as a c.p. deriving from a famous advertisement for Guinness stout, dates from the late 1920s. It occurs in fiction at least as early as 1930, the year when Dorothy L. Sayers's 'deteccer', *Strong Poison*, appeared.

In Act I of H. M. Harwood's *The Man in Possession*, pub'd in the same year, Raymond asks his draper father, 'Why shouldn't you advertise, too? Think of it! Worthington's Beer woven into one leg and Eno's Fruit Salt into the other. "Guinness is good for you", on the back of every tie. You couldn't miss it – you'd see it every day.'

I recorded it in the first edn, 1933, of *STY*.

Gulliver. See: send for G.

gum tree. See: possum.

gun. See: drop the gun; have gun; I'm a true; it's wonderful; things you see.

Gundy. See: no good to G.

Gunga Din. See: you're a better man.

gunnery. See: attitude is the art.

gunpowder. See: there's a smell.

[**guns before butter.** 'It's the shortening of a pronouncement made by [the German Nazi leader] Goering in 1936' (Kingsley Amis, 1977). Almost a c.p., when used facetiously.]

guns, gas and gaiters. This C20 c.p. of the RN was 'applied to the gunnery officers, who were the first to introduce the polished gaiters for work in the mud at Whale Island' (Bowen, 1929). Since *c.* 1940, also ecclesiastical. Cf both **all gas and gaiters** and **attitude is the art of gunnery** ....

guts. See: go carry; I'll have your g.; if you had; midshipmen; more guts; my guts.

guy(s). See: nice guys; who are these; you sure know; and:

guy could get hurt that way – **a** was in WW2, and before and after it, applied by Americans ('stunt men' – Servicemen – and others) to any particularly hazardous enterprise. (Arthur Wrigglesworth, 1975.) Cf **you sure know how to hurt a guy.**

gypsy. See: it's the gypsy; take your washing.

gyros have toppled – **his** or **your**. Applied to someone staggering drunkenly: Fleet Air Arm: since *c.* 1940. 'From behaviour of aircraft instruments' gyroscopes after certain violent manoeuvres' (Cdr C. Parsons, RN, 1973; his service covered the years 1937–60).

H

ha-ha. See: funny peculiar.

ha, ha, bloody ha! is 'a sarcastic c.p. that greets any stupid question' (Granville, 1969); or 'Exposing feebleness of a sarcastic or apt rejoinder' (L.A., 1969): since *c.* 1950. It had, by later C20, naturally been shortened to *ha bloody ha!*, as in Dick Francis's 'thriller', *Risk*, 1977: 'If I hadn't gone suddenly blind (and it didn't feel like it), I was lying somewhere where no light penetrated. Brilliant deduction. Most constructive. Ha bloody ha.' P.B.: also, in less 'polite' circles, *Oh, ha fucking ha!* From, of course, the written representation of the sound of laughter; cf **that's a good question**, and contrast:

ha! ha! ha! 'This mocking pretence to be amused, [with] last *ha* emphasized, I believe to come from [Frank] Richards [proper name, Charles Hamilton]. But it was often in the old "comics". Still used' (Shaw, 1968); and still occ. in 1977. Cf both the prec., and **funny peculiar or funny ha-ha?**

[had it – I've (or you've or he's, etc.). Not a true c.p. See esp. **have had it** and **had it in a big way**, both in the *DSUE* and in PGR at *had it*. P.B.: but the frequent use, in later C20, of (e.g., I've) **had it up to here**, accompanied by a gesture of the flat hand held horizontally at neck level, or even higher, perhaps does qualify. Cf **had the Richard.**]

had one but (occ. and) the wheel came off, mostly prec. by **we**. A lower- and lower-middle-class, hence also a military (Other Ranks') c.p. directed at an unintelligible speaker or speech, often a *gamin* comment on words, or even a single word, not understood; but also expressive of a feigned helpfulness, or a droll regret, or a *gamin* comment: since *c.* 1890; a little less frequent since WW2. Perhaps slightly commoner in Liverpool than elsewhere in England; but very widely used – in, e.g. Aus. Occ., in UK, simply *had one, but it went off* (Eric Fearon, 1984).

had the Richard or the dick, usu. prec. by *it's* or *that's*, is Aus., dating from *c.* 1950 and referring to something that has outworn its usefulness or broken down beyond repair, esp. a motorcar or other machinery, or even furniture or crockery. (Heard by Jack Slater, 1965–9, in New South Wales, as he told me in 1978.) P.B.: perhaps local – it is not recorded by Wilkes – and poss. connected with that *dick* which is a slang term for the penis.

had your penn'orth or do you want a ha'penny change? is, notably among Londoners, addressed to someone staring at the speaker: since *c.* 1920. (L.A., 1967.)

A good example of Cockney sarcasm at its humorously trenchant best.

had your time. See **you've had your time.**

haf you any rrrelatifs in Chermany? See **ve haf vays and means.**

haha! heehee! 'Briefly *c.* 1920 … was used as a greeting – without any counter' (R.S., 1975): *c.* 1921–4. Cf **pip-pip!** and **tootle-oo!**

hail, hail, the gang's all here! was orig. and popularized by a

1917 song so titled, words by Estrom, music by Morse, sung by Sullivan, as one learns from Edward B. Marks, *They All Sang*, 1934, and as I learned from my friend, W.J.B. Ed. McBain uses it as c.p. title for one of his detective novels.

Haines. See: my name is H.

hair(s). See: don't look down; every hair; get your h.; his hair; I washed; keep your h.; more hair; shall I put; she had; that'll grow; there's hair; two hairs; you can't grow.

half. See: he's a cunt; no, half; not half; you ain't 'alf; you don't know the h.; and:

half an hour is soon lost at dinner. In S, Dialogue II, Lord Smart says, 'Pray edge a little to make more room for Sir *John*. Sir *John*, fall to, you know half an Hour is soon lost at Dinner', which is the only record I have of this c.p., joc. ironic and reminiscent of very long sessions: prob. *c.* 1690–1760.

half an hour past hanging time, mostly prec. by **it's**. Also in S is this c.p. reply to 'What's the time?':

NEV[EROUT]: [to Lady Answerall] Pray, Madam, do you tell me, for I let my Watch run down.

LADY ANSW: Why, 'tis half an Hour past Hanging Time.

Common in C18–19, but now rare; displaced by **half past …** A further var. was *an hour past …*

half-crown millionaires: all bay window and no pantry is applied to people occupying newly-built 'desirable residences' and unwisely considering themselves 'a cut above the rest': provincial England: *c.* 1925–40 and then rapidly becoming †. (B.G.T., 1978.) P.B.: half-a-crown became 12½ pence on decimalization of currency in 1971, but used of course to buy considerably more than 12½p does now. Cf the synon. *brown boots and no breakfast*, recalled from the same date and milieu, on a 'phone-in' programme in which I took part for BBC Radio Leicester, 20 June 1984.

half left. See **no, half left!**

half past kissing time and time to kiss again, or simply **it's kissing time.** These c.pp. belonged mostly to London and flourished *c.* 1880–1930, although they have lingered on. Orig. usu. a low c.p. reply to a woman asking a man the time; the longer phrase is recorded by B & L in 1889. It comes from a popular song by one G. Anthony:

It's half-past kissing-time, and time to kiss again.
For time is always on the move, an ne'er will still remain;
No matter what the hour is, you may rely on this:
It's always half-past kissing-time, and always time to kiss.

The longer form has also, like the shorter, been, in C20, addressed to children continually asking one the time, as HLM records in 1922. A.B., 1978, notes for the US: 'I've also heard, when someone asked the time of day, the flippant reply, "Half past my elbow and a quarter to my thumb." Meaning that the replies did not have a watch or did not

114

know what time it was. Also: "Half past my ass and a quarter to my bum!" The latter prompted by the former: *thumb – bum* [and the false rhyme *past – ass*]: 1950s, maybe earlier'.

Mrs Barbara Huston recalls her Westmoreland-born mother using a var. 'put-down' reply in 1950s, though surely N. Country traditional: 'half past three quarters, and if you want to be hanged I'll lend you me [my] garters'. With this last, cf the prec. entry.

half-starved. See: full of fuck.

half-struck. See: like one o'clock.

half the bed and all the clothes. See **good night, sweet repose.**

half the world are squirrels. See TAD DORGAN.

half your luck! I wish I had even a half of your good luck: Aus.: since *c.* 1915. (Baker, 1942) Spoken with a semi-humorous ruefulness.

hallo. See: hello, ...

[**halt the –, steady the –, and let the –** go by, where 'the first two dashes represent the speaker's unit, the third the squad or battalion encountered', exemplified the fact that in WW1, 'on the line of march, greetings were usually exchanged by meeting regiments' or battalions or other units (B & P, 1931). But this was a chant rather than a c.p. The same remark applies to *Gorblimey! here comes –* or *come – the –* and to **here they come – mooching along, all of a bloody heap.** Cf **steady, the Buffs!**]

halter. See: 'nay, nay!'; you break.

ham. See: if only.

ham bone. See: all dressed.

ham? Haven't had ham since (e.g. **Tuesday**). (The *h*'s may be dropped.) A contemplative remark made on picking one's teeth: earlier C20. I have no idea how widely used; my father, from whom I heard it in the 1940s, attributed it to some long-forgotten stage sketch involving tramps. (P.B.)

Hamlet, I am the father's gimlet is a punning theatrical c.p., based on the ghost of Hamlet's father: very approx. *c.* 1880–1925. (Shaw, 1968.)

Hamlet in its eternity. 'An actors' jocular phrase descriptive of a performance of Shakespeare's *Hamlet* in its *entirety*. It goes on for ever' (Granville): C20. As *Macbeth* is the shortest of the tragedies, so is *Hamlet* the longest of all Shakespeare's plays.

hammer. See: go and fetch; hay, lass; how are they hanging; I see; it ain't the 'untin'; that's the h.

hand(s). See: all hands; are your h.; clap; don't bother me; dumb; family; fresh hand; from Greenland's; gi' us y'hand; here's the back; hold my h.; I have to hand; I'll hand; if I am; if not pleased; it come off; keep your h.; left hand; let me shake; look, no; man the; more like; my pocket; ninety-nine, a; now you see; one hand; push in the bush; put (one's) foot; shake hands; some day; they sat; took his; what's the matter with your; when my wife; who dealt; wish in; with a five.

hand-basket. See: going to hell.

hand-grenades. See: close counts.

hand it back to the Indians. See **give it back to the abos.**

hand on heart. See **cross my heart.**

hands off, buster! A girl to a venturesome male or, derivatively, to someone 'attempting to talk her into, or out of, something: 1930s–40s From motion pictures, I think. Akin to "Cool it, kiddo!" and others like' (A.B., 1978).

hands off your cocks and pull up your socks! A British Army, esp. an orderly corporals', reveille call to men in barracks: C20 and perhaps going back a further twenty-or-so years. A late example occurs as the opening speech of Act II of Arnold Wesker's *Chips with Everything*, pub'd in 1962. Peter F. Reynolds, 1979, adds, 'should be supplemented: *Hands off candles – on to sandals* (thought to be appropriate for ladies)': mid C20.

hands up! Oh, for heaven's sake, stop talking!: orig. a lower-class c.p.: *c.* 1885–1914. From the police command to surrender. Recorded in a history of the police pub'd in 1888.

handsome. See: tall, dark; this is not only; and:

[**handsome husband and a thousand** (or **ten thousand**) [**pounds**]

a year – a. A common domestic saying among women when a sandwich, small cake or other morsel is left over on the plate. (P.B., 1978.) Halfway between folklore, or semi-proverbial saying, and a c.p.: mid C19–20. The sum of money naturally tended to increase with inflation.]

handwriting. See: just my h.; that's just my.

hang. See: doesn't know where; everything is lovely; hop and; how are they hanging; how ya; I work; if I had; it's nice to have; let it all; more guts; something to h.; that's where the big; whose dog; your washing.

hang (or **put**) **crape on your nose: your brains are dead!** Wake up!; stop talking nonsense!: US. An early example in print occurs in Olive Dent, *V.A.D. in France*, 1917: 'Just now among the patients we have a Russian, a member of the Canadian Army ... His language is a most amusing jumble of English, French, and American ... his despondency was not deep enough to prevent him admonishing a youth ... in choicest Russo-Americanese: "Hang crep on yar nose. Yar brain's deat"' (with thanks to Mrs Barbara Huston). HLM notes that a serious Brit. periodical (*English*, 1919) recorded its impact upon London in 1918–19; despite its vividness and picturesqueness, that impact was very brief. P.B.: brief perhaps *because* of its striking impact: the more vividly contrived a phrase, the more quickly it gets 'used to death'.

hang in there, baby! – with **baby** soon discarded and with **in** emphasized: US: 'It means "Stick with it" and is addressed to someone doing a good job in difficult circumstances; it's a word of encouragement' and has been current 'for possibly as long as five years' (Miss Mary Priebe, of Seattle, *via* P.B., 1975). In fact, it is recorded in *DCCU*, 1971. W.J.B., 1975, amplified M.P.'s note:

A common expression, an everyday one. It is simply an admonition to keep fighting when the odds are against you, probably an expression around the prize ring to begin with, then applied to other sports. [It] is addressed pleadingly or encouragingly both to individual participant and to the team as a whole, and is often heard at football games, baseball games, etc. Its application to non-athletic endeavours, such as telling your friend to 'buck up' when he is 'down' or 'blue' or 'licked' was an easy transition from your *playing fields of Eton* to the common situations of downheartedness. 'Hang in there' goes back a long ways, predating our 'Hippie' era.

The Hippies, however, adopted it early in the 1960s; 'lately taken up by sports and politics, to advocate fortitude' (Ben Grauer, 25 Dec. 1975).

In the *New York Post*, 20 Feb. 1976, Max Lerner noted the 'bid' being made by the phrase and added. 'But will it hang in there?' R.C., 1977, remarked, 'The "baby" marks it as almost certainly of Negro origin, but now general – though becoming rare'.

hang loose! 'Take it easy – relax!' Lit., 'Don't go all tense!': US: dating since middle or latish 1950s (W&F, 1960), and extremely common since *c.* 1970. Often in the naunce 'Shed all your inhibitions!', as in Cyra McFadden, *The Serial: A Year in the Life of Martin County*, 1977. Cf **how ya hangin**'?

hang saving! In S, Dialogue II, see:

COL[ONEL]: Faith, my Lord ... I wish we had a Bit of your Lordship's *Oxfordshire* Cheese.

LORD SM[ART]: Come, hang saving, bring us a halfporth of Cheese.

This is a joc. c.p. rather than a proverb and has been used over a very long period: C17–20, although little before 1650 and very little since *c.* 1940. Phonetically, *halfporth* is a clumsy contraction of *halfpennyworth*: *ha'p'orth* is both scripturally and phonetically perfect. It has been displaced by *hang the expense!*: mid C19–20. Cf. **give the cat another goldfish.**

hang the Kaiser!, often **oh, hang....**, was a humorous c.p. current among soldiers during the latter half of WW1, when the men had become unutterably bored by the newspaper talk about him. It was not, in the c.p., meant lit., although, inevitably, the phrase implied a ref., still humorous and tolerant, to that possibility.

hang your number out to dry! A post-1918 var. of **before you came up**: Services'. H&P.

hangar. See: if I stack; lost the key.

hangar doors closed! See **close hangar doors!**

hanged. See: confess; half past kissing; I'll be h.; let me be h.; noose; stay and; then I; who boiled.

hanging on the (usu. **the old**) **barbed wire**, with the topical var. **hanging on the barbed wire at**, e.g. Loos, both versions being often shortened to **on the barbed wire**, was an army (mostly among the Other Ranks) reply to the query 'Where is So-and-So?': late 1915–18. The ref. is to men left dead on the enemy wire entanglements after an attack.

The gloss in B&P (3rd edn) is worth quoting: 'These [other replies] referred only to a person whose whereabouts was unknown – or not to be disclosed:

Died of wounds. –
Hanging on the (barbed) wire. –
On the wire at Mons. –
Gassed at Mons.

There was, of course, no wire at the Retreat from Mons and gas was unknown at that time.' This retreat began on 24 Aug. 1914 and was halted at Le Cateau, where the Anglo-French forces repulsed the enemy; and the Battle of Loos took place thirteen months later.

hanging-time. See: half an hour past.

hangs up his fiddle when he comes home. See **leaves his fiddle...**

Hannah. See: and what's the matter; Sister Anna; so help me; that's the man.

Hanover. See: well, I'll go.

Hans the Grenadier is in charge. See **Carl the caretaker's in charge.**

ha'penny (or halfpenny). See: can't claim; had your penn'orth; hasn't got a h.; here's a h.; keep your hand; they want their.

ha'porth. See: all there and.

happen. See: don't worry; it can't h.; it couldn't h.; it happens; it's all happening; nothing h.; shouldn't happen; swoppin'; what would h.; what's happening; worse things.

happiness. See: money can't.

happiness is Wren-shaped. See **blue-stockinged...**, and cf **bright-eyed...**

happy. See: are you h.; I'm keeping; is everybody; sit down; still h.; what's the odds; you're happy; and:

happy (sometimes, **lucky**) **as a bastard on Father's Day** (–**as**). Very unhappy or unlucky – or both: an Aus. sardonic felicity, dating since c. 1950. Wilkes's two earliest examples are from Frank Hardy, 1958 (*lucky*) and 1967 (*happy*). Cf **like a bastard....**

happy as a dead pig in mud – (e.g. **I'm**) **just as.** Western US, esp. cowboys', version of the next. The *Cape Cod Times*, 27 Aug. 1977, reports Roy Rogers, 65-year-old 'King of the Cowboys' saying this on a festive occasion. (W.J.B.)

happy as a pig in shit (–**as**). Blissfully happy or contented: C19–20. 'A pig wallowing in mud – presumably admixed with shit – is presumed to be at the acme of contentment. (There is no implication that the person referred to is necessarily piggish.) An obviously rural metaphor, which surprisingly remains current, if somewhat ob., in the 1970s' (R.C., 1978). P.B.: I assume that R.C. is writing of US usage, but the phrase was extremely popular and common in the Brit. Armed Forces at least as late as 1975. Ashley, 1984, calls it 'the Southern [US] idea of bliss'.

happy as ducks i Arizona (–**as**) is a Westerners', e.g. cowboys', phrase that means 'anything but happy, *very* unhappy': C20. (Berrey, 1942.) Arizona has a notoriously dry climate, decidedly not a ducks' paradise.

happy days are here again was orig. a US song, words by Agar and music by Yellen; sung and pub'd in 1929. 'Incidentally, this song became Franklin D. Roosevelt's political theme song' (W.J.B., 1975). It also became a US c.p. and, at the end of WW2 in Europe, an immensely popular Brit.

sentimental song.

happy horseshit! 'Ironic for "Well, so what?" or "no shit, Sherlock": 1950s and onwards. (A.B., 1978.)

happy in the Service? or, in full, **are you happy...?** is the RN's, hence also the RAF's, version of the Army's **are you happy in your work?**: phrases that, arising in 1940 or perhaps in late 1939, are addressed to someone who is engaged in work either dirty or difficult or downright dangerous. PGR's comment is, 'Cheery greeting to someone who obviously isn't'; irony in moments of harassment'. P.B.: it is always used in parody of a typical senior inspecting officer's stereotyped question as he stops to speak to every, e.g. 10th, man drawn up on parade. Another, later (1960s), version was 'Everything all right, eh? No lumps in the custard?'; and there was the even more cynical parody of the unheeding nature of such questioning: 'Married, are you? No? Good! Children all right?' Both these were always spoken in imitation of senior officer's rather 'fruity' accent.

Cf **are you nervous...**

happy right. See **you're happy right.**

harass. See: don't bully.

harbour. See: our 'Arbour.

harbourmaster. See: no further.

hard. See: got any; it's a hard; no, but I'm; you don't piss; you're only.

hard act to follow. See **act to follow.**

[**hard cheese!** 'Bad luck!' 'My theory of its origin is that gourmets prefer soft cheeses, which have a short storage life, and that a request for their preference is often answered, "Sorry! Only hard cheese", (Sanders, 1978). The expression has existed since the late C19, but has been used decreasingly since *c.* 1940. But it is not a fully qualified c.p. P.B.: I think that E.P. is being inconsistent, since he allows full c.p. status for the synon. **tough shit!** and **tough titty!**; but surely mere coarseness and vulgarity are insufficient qualifications? And while Mr Sanders's theory is plausible, I prefer a connection with that 'cheese' so popular with the mid-Victorians for 'the best; the done thing', apparently deriving from Persian and Hindi *chiz*, 'thing'.]

hard in a clinch, and no knife to cut the seizing is a nautical c.p. of *c.* 1860–1910, refers to cordage, and means 'in an extremely difficult situation, with apparently no way out'. P.B.: cf the WW2 RN phrase *run out to a clinch*, glossed by 'Giraldus' (Gerald O'Driscoll) in *Sailors Have a Word for It*, 1943; 'A state of acute bankruptcy. A ship is run out to a clinch when she cannot pay out any more cable'.

hard on the setting sun was, *c.* 1895–1914, a journalistic c.p., expressive of contempt for the Red Indian; the *People*, on 13 June 1897, referred to it as 'a characteristic by-word'. Ware, 1909.

hard or soft? is a US c.p., current early C20 but 'less and less common since *c*, 1930, although not yet obsolete. A rejoinder – with perhaps a faint air of rebuke for using foul language – to [the exclam.] *shit!*' (J.W.C., 1977). Cf the two entries at **yours or...**

hard place. See: between a rock.

hard titty! See **tough titty!**

harder than pulling a soldier off your sister, prec. mostly by **it's** but sometimes by **that's.** This low, mostly RN, c.p. dates from *c.* 1939 and applies to circumstances in which compliance would be disagreeable or repugnant.

hardships. See: ships?

Hardly. See: kiss me, H.

have. See: first catch.

hark (but usu. **'ark**) **at her**, more often **'er!** A derisive C20 c.p., directed at a woman, 'uttering supposedly well-meaning of high-sounding sentiments' (L.A.). Evocative of back-street disputes in which one woman derides another.

harm. See: I don't wish; no harm; and:

harm can come to a young lad that way; alternatively **a young lad can come to harm in that way**: Can be applied to all sorts of situations, usu. physical with a sexual implication. I was reminded of it by a conversation about mixing with lesbians, in one of Alan Hunter's excellent crime stories (all notable for his fine ear for modern idiom), *Gently with the Ladies*, 1965. An ironic use of the warning doled out by the stern father-figures of an earlier day.

harp. See: I took my h.

harpers. See: have among you.

harry. See: cop this; you tell 'em, kid.

Harwell. See: no return ticket.

Harwich. See: they're all up.

has all his (or her) chairs at home – he or **she.** 'This is a specifically Lancashire expression, dating probably from about the turn of the century. A fuller version is "She has her feet on the ground and all her chains at home"' (Jack Eva, 1978). P.B.: cf, e.g. *he's got all his buttons*, 'he is a bright fellow, no-one can fool *him*'; but very often it is the absence of these commodities, whether chairs, buttons, onions, etc., that calls forth comment.

has anybody here seen Kelly? was orig., 1909, an English song, words by Murphy and music by Letters, and the c.p.followed immediately; now (1976) seldom heard. In US, Nora Bayes popularized the song, in McKenna's American version as it appeared in *Jolly Bachelors*. (W.J.B.)

has his ballocks in the right place (– he) expresses warm approval of a man well set-up and level-headed: C20.

has more money than I (or **you**) **could poke a stick at,** with **has** often omitted; often, too, prec. by **he** or **she.** He's (she's) very rich: Aus.: since *c.* 1920. See, in Frank Hardy, *Billy Booker Yarns Again*, 1967, 'The Parrot...tells Hot Horse: "Your tips have cost me more money than I could poke a stick at."' Perhaps it would be more precise to say that the c.p. is *more money*....The 'US version – whose semantics are equally obscure – is...*shake a stick at.* From C19; ob. by 1940s; now † (R.C., 1977). P.B.: perhaps so much as to be even beyond envy?

has Mr Sharp come in yet? is a monitory c.p. addressed by one shopkeeper or other trader to another 'to signify that a customer of suspected honesty is about' (Hotten, 1864): *c.* 1850–1940. Cf **two upon ten.**

has the cat died? 'Asked among onlookers when a man appears with his trousers "at half-mast"; that is, he is wearing braces that have so hitched up his trousers that quite a length of ankle shows below the bottoms. Sounds like "orig. schoolchildren's"' (P.B., 1979), Date? Perhaps since *c.* 1920. Flags at half-mast signify national mourning.

has the cat got your tongue? Often, as in John Mortimer's *The Judge*, 1967, at I, v, shortened to **cat got your tongue?** A mid C19–20 c.p., Brit. and US, meaning 'Have you lost your tongue? Can't you speak?' It forms one of the small group of domestic phrases; often used in speaking to a child that, after some mischief, refuses to speak or to answer questions. A late example occurs in Janet Green's novel, *My Turn Now*, 1971: 'Taken totally by surprise. I couldn't speak. I just stood there...literally gaping. He laughed. "What's the matter? Cat got your tongue?"'

A still later example occurs in E.V. Cunningham, *Millie*, 1973 (Brit. edn, 1974):

'Peace,' I replied, and...sat and started at Millie.

'Cat got your tongue?'

Cf the analogous French idiom, *je jette (ou donne) ma langue au chat*, 'I give up; I can't guess (the riddle or conundrum); I have nothing to say'. (R.S.)

has the ghost walked yet? See **ghost walks on Friday.**

has the penny dropped (, at last)? 'Do you *now* understand what was meant, or needs to be done?': since the early 1930s. From coin-operated devices such as telephones, the machines in an amusement arcade – or the latches in public conveniences. See also **penny has dropped.**

has your mother sold her mangle? An urban, chiefly Londoners', c.p. of no precise application: rather low: since the 1830s. There is apparently some ref. to a woman taking in washing – or no longer doing so.

Mackay, immediately after having dealt with **there he goes with his eye out!**, writes:

Another very odd phrase came into repute in a brief space afterwards, in the form of the impertinent and not universally apposite query, *'Has you mother sold her mangle?'* But its popularity was not of that boisterous and cordial kind which ensures a long continuance of favour. What tended to impede its progress was, that it could not well be applied to the older portions of society [because it hadn't long been invented? P.B.: or because they were considered too old to have mangle-vending mothers around?]

It consequently ran but a brief career, and then sank into oblivion.

hasn't got a Chinaman's chance (– he). He has no chance at all: US: since 1849 or 1850. It orig., W&F tell us, in the California Gold Rush, when Chinese, in the hope – it could hardly have been expectation – of finding gold, worked streams and old claims abandoned by white prospectors; an orig. to which was added the contributory factor of 'the hard life and times' of Chinese immigrants living in a virtual enclave of society.

The phrase was taken to Australia by those optimists who had joined, somewhat late, in the Rush of 1849 onwards. When, many years later, I first (in 1908) heard the phrase, it was always in the form *he hasn't-* or *hasn't got – a China-man's chance in hell.*

The form commonest in UK is...*a snowflake's chance*...C20.

Cf **much chance as a snowball**...and **no more chance**....

hasn't got a ha'penny to jingle on a tombstone (– usu. he) is synon. with **(he) hasn't got (or a) sixpence to scratch his arse with;** the meaning of both is seld-evident; both are low, and date mid C19–mid 20 – and perhaps illustrate the rise in the cost of living. The 'ha'penny' version, with *sou* substituted in the mouth of a French girl using racy English slang, *c.* 1900, occurs in Rachel Ferguson, *Evenfield*, 1942 (p. 79).

hasn't had it so long. See **she hasn't had it so long.**

hasn't sucked that out of his fingers. See **sucked**....

hasty as a sheep: as soon as the tail is up, the turd is out. A low, mostly rural c.p.: mid C19–mid 20.

hat. See: all round my h.; come out of that; here's yer hat; hold onto; I'll eat; I'll have your h.; if you can't fight; if you see; if you want to get; in your hat; is my hat; it's old hat; keep that under; lost his hat; may I pee; past your; shoot that; six hat; take yer 'at; that's him; what a shocking; when Adam; where did you get that h.; who stole the donkey; you couldn't throw.

Hatch. See: match!

hatched. See: he never had.

hate. See: I'd hate; you must h.; you'll hate; and:

hate, hate, he killed your mate! Screamed by instructors at recruits on bayonet practice, to urge them to greater ferocity. Quoted, with justifiable loathing, by Peregrine Worsthorne, discussing his WW2 experience, in *The World of the Public School*, 1977. (Mr Allan Chapman, FLA.)

hatter. See: who's your h.

h'attitude is the h'art of gunnery is the lower-deck version of **attitude is the art of gunnery.** q.v.

have. See: is that a catch; let's have; nice place you; or what; thanks for having; what has she; will you h.; yes, we h.; you can h.; you too; you've had; and:

have a banana! was, *c.* 1900–39, low – or, rather, a lower-class – c.p. expression of contempt; by association with the popular music-hall song, 'I had a banana/With Lady Diana', a sexual implication accrued. Not unknown in the British Army during WW1. Cf **yes, we have no bananas today,** and **take a carrot!**

have a care or there'll be havoc here is a comic threat: C20; ob. by 1950, † by 1970. (Mr S.G. Dixon, 1978. Dating: E.P.) P.B.: a horrid pun!

have a feel till Friday. 'Until pay-day, enjoy what is offered. A feel instead of a fuck, and pay on Friday. Cockney girls' (a correspondent, 1969): C20.

have a go! See **enjoy yourself!**

have a go, Joe, your mother will (or **mother'll**) **never know,** often shortened to **have a go, Joe!** A c.p. of encouragement addressed to a very shy, or a reluctant, man: Cockneys' and Armed Forces': since c. 1935. 'Have a Go' became the title of the Wilfred Pickles radio quiz-show (see **give him the money**), and was incorporated into the show's signature tune, 'Have a go, Joe, come and have a go...'

[**have a good** (or **fine** or **nice**) **day** and **have yourself a good** (or **fine**) **day today and a better one tomorrow.** Both farewells occur in Jethro K. Lieberman & Neil S. Rhodes, *The Complete CB Handbook*, 1976: common among US truckers (long-distance lorry-drivers): since c. 1950; hence, in gen. use. The former has existed as a cliché since the 1920s, and it was from its excessive use that, since the late 1960s, it has become almost derisive and often ironic – in short, a c.p. (Prompted by C.P. Snow, Lord Snow of Leicester, on 22 Sep. 1977, referring to British currency.) Fain, 1977, remarked that the shorter version has been 'monotonously prevalent' in the US since the early 1970s; and indeed Max Lerner, writing of its vogue use, in the *New York Post* of 20 Feb. 1976, titled his article 'Have a Good Phrase'. It very soon made its way to Can. and UK. Sometimes with **take care!**, q.v.]

have a good look round – or, in full, **have a good look round, for you won't see anything but the ceiling for a day or two.** This military c.p. of WW1 – and, although perhaps less generally, WW2 – was applied to the ardour of soldiers on leave towards their wives (whether fully legal or common-law). Cf the slangy **lie feet uppermost**, of women receiving a man sexually.

have a good trip? See **did you enjoy...**

have a gorilla? (sometimes prec. by **here–**) was Neddy Seagoon's (Harry Secombe's offer of a cigarette in the BBC 'Goon Show' of the 1950s. The standard reply was 'No thanks, I only smoke baboons'; later, the invitation was declined in the undying words, **no, I'm trying to give them up.** See **GOON SHOW...** P.B.: the phrase was perhaps suggested by the word *cigarillo*, a small, thin cigar. A further, var. 'dovetail' was *no, have a monkey, they're milder*, and a var. of the orig. was *have a portrait of Queen Victoria.*

have a heart! Don't be so hard-hearted! Steady! Go easy! Current since c. 1880, it has been a little less common after c. 1940 than before. Common also in US: H.L. Mencken recorded it in *The American Language* in a list of c.pp once very popular, but soon become threadbare and void of either piquancy or any precise meaning; and Berrey in 1942. Its American heyday was c. 1910–18; cited as **now**...by S.R. Strait in the *Boston Globe* in c. 1917 (W.J.B.).

have a nice trip? See **did you enjoy...**

have a scratch! has two meanings, both of which I owe to friends as loyal and helpful as they are – or were – intelligent and well-informed. Apparently the slightly earlier is a 'c.p. of satirical encouragement to someone at a loss for answer or information' (L.A.): C20. 'A suggestion that the puzzled one should scratch his head [for the answer, or for inspiration]' (Leechman).

The second, orig. and predominantly Cockney, dating from c. 1910, is a c.p. of contemptuous dismissal, as in 'Oi, go orn! 'Op it! Go and 'ave a scratch!' (the late Julian Franklyn). From advice given to someone flea-ridden.

have a snort! See **oh, bloody good....**

have among (or **at**) **ye** (later **you**), **my blind harpers!** – with **my** very frequently omitted. Look out for your heads! Look out for yourselves!: this c.p. was, C16–early C19, 'used in throwing or shooting at random among a crowd' (Grose). It lay on the borderline between c.p. and proverbial saying; as early as 1546, Heywood adjudged it to be the latter; but by (say) 1660, at latest, it had, I believe, become the former.

Perhaps from coppers thrown to several blind beggars.

This is so notable and expressive a phrase that it merits exemplification. In John Day's comedy, *Humour out of Breath*, in 1609, we read, at IV, iii:

PAGE: Lord, what scambling [i.e. scrambling] shift has he made for a kiss, and cannot get it neither; a little higher, so so; are you blind, my lord?

HORTENSIO: As a parblind poet: have amongst you, blind harpers.

John Dryden, *The Wild Gallant*, 1662, at IV, i, has:

[*They Dance a round Dance, and Sing the Tune.*]
Enter Isabella *and* Constance.

ISA: Are you at that Sport, i' faith? Have among you, blind Harpers.

[*She falls into the Dance.*]

There the sense has become, 'Here goes!'

In *The London Cuckolds*, performed in 1681 and pub'd in 1682, Edward Ravenscroft, at III, ii, has Drodle firing a musket into a cellar where he thinks some thieves to be and he announces the action with the words *have amongst you, blind harpers.*

George Farquhar in *The Constant Couple*, performed 1699 and pub'd in 1700, at V, i, employs an occ. var.:

FOOTMAN: Sir, we must do as our young mistress commands us.

SIR HARRY: Nay, then have among ye, dogs, [*Throws money among them; they scramble, and take it up.*]

In *The Relapse; or, Virtue in Danger*, 1696, Sir John Vanbrugh uses a common derivative var. at IV, v:

SIR TUN: [*Within*] Fire [the blunderbuss], porter.

PORTER: [*Fires.*] Have among ye, my masters.

Much later, David Garrick, in his comedy, *The Male Coquette*, 1757, in II, 'Scene, the Club-Room', uses a very frequent C18 form, thus:

DAF [FODIL]: There, then, have among you. [*Throws the letter upon the table.*]

That is to quote a very few among very many examples occurring in C17–18 literature, principally in comedies.

Cf the WW1 use of **share that among you!**

have among ye (or **you**), **my masters.** See prec., the quot'n from Vanbrugh.

have at the plum-tree! is a late C17–19 c.p., either semi-proverbial or, more likely, in allusion to some popular bawdy song, for there is clearly a ref. to *plum-tree*, the female pudenda. It occurs several times in the plays of Thomas Middleton, e.g. *The Widow*, performed c. 1614.

have at thee (or **ye** or **you**). 'Take this!' – whatever 'this' may be – uttered in defiance or offer or challenge; sometimes, Look out for yourself! *or* yourselves! *also*, Here's good luck or good health to you!: frequently in the literature, mostly the comedies, of c. 1540–1750 and even later. Among playwrights using it are Shakespeare (in *Love's Labour's Lost*, at V, iii: 'Have at you, then, affection's men-at-arms!'), John Fletcher, Beaumont and Fletcher, Thomas Shadwell, Colley Cibber, John Till Allingham, George Macfarren.

Clearly owing much to **have among ye, blind harpers,** this ubiquitous c.p. may be amusingly exemplified by Shadwell's *The Amorous Bigot*, 1690; in I, i, Elvira, having made up her face, exclaims, 'Ha, my dear unknown Love, have at thee!' (Look out for yourself!) – and by Allingham's *Mrs Wiggins: A Comic Piece*, 1803, in I, ii ('A Tavern'), where Old Wiggins, a mighty trencherman, exclaims over 'a Basin of Turtle': 'Ah! The smell is delicious – (*Tucks the napkin under his chin*) – the taste must be exquisite – come, have at you!'

In its C18 – early C19 period very often, and occ. earlier, the phrase was used playfully or joc., with a light ironic touch.

have gun, will travel is taken from the personal advertisement column ('the agony column') of *The Times*, where, of course, it was entirely serious; something comic about it ensured its promotion to the status of a c.p., dating, I suspect, since c. 1900, certainly from as early as c. 1920, although I have to admit that I didn't often hear it before WW2. Perhaps it also owed something to 'the thick-ear' novel of the Bulldog Drummond type, for, as a c.p., it bears an undertone of 'I'm ready, or game, for anything'. Something of a vogue phrase, it generated such frivolities as *have pen, will write*. The phrase became so engrained in the language that in the *Daily Mail* of 21 Oct. 1969, in the 'Showpiece' section, Harold Wale titles his notice of the film *Hard Contract*, 'Have bed, will travel'.

The 'surge of usage in 1960s followed US television Western series, *Paladin*, 1957–61, starring Richard Boone, and shown in UK, under the title "Have Gun – Will Travel"' (Wedgewood, 1977). Yet it certainly was a c.p. – and common enough during the inter-war years; certainly also, it went underground throughout WW2 [P.B.: because so *many* people then had guns and were travelling?] and until the Boone revival. And it is still travelling; on 6 Feb. 1978 *Time* (Europe), on p. 60, remarked, 'She [Catherine Denevue] plays a Bogart-like private eye, who has gun–will travel' (thanks to Paul Janssen).

have I got news for you! (with *have* and *news* emphasized, and occ. prec. by *oh, boy*). 'I have information that you (in particular) will find startling or unwelcome: from 1950s (?). Prob. TV origin' (R.C., 1977). Mainly US, with some Brit. imitation. P.B.: merely a more emphatic version of **I've got news...**, q.v. As Ashley, 1979, remarks, it implies 'You don't know the half of it!'

have it away: bap! A virtually meaningless c.p. evolved among the Other Ranks of an Army Signals unit in Cyprus, late 1950s; it was what E.P. termed 'an ephemeral parochialism', but it did its bit towards maintaining morale when such boosts were badly needed. Cf **it's all a bit of buck**. (P.B.)

have one for me. Have a drink for me, as I've no time to go into the pub, or remain in the club, for one: C20. (Granville, 1969.) Cf **do one for me**, of which it is often a var.: which sense came first? Prob. the one of this entry (P.B.).

have you a licence? was a mid C18 – early C19 c.p., addressed to someone clearing his throat noisily. Grose, 1785, refers to the Act against hawkers and pedlars – and there's an obvious pun on the double sense of *hawking*. P.B.: and in mid–later C20 *have you got a licence for that (thing)?* is sometimes facetiously addressed to someone smoking a particularly foul and offensive pipe, coping inadequately with some gadget, e.g. a typewriter, or to someone with a new baby – the refs here being not, of course, to hawking, but to driving and dog licences.

have you any good in your heart? Lit., 'Are you a kind person?' what Petch, 1969, described as 'the "ear-biter's" standard lead-off', or standard approach by persistent borrowers: since the 1920s, but little heard since *c.* 1970. Another version was *have you any kind thoughts in your mind?*

have you any more funny stories? and **now tell me the one about the three bears.** Tell me another! These are c.pp. of polite scepticism, or of polite boredom: mostly in Brit. and Aus.: since the late 1920s or the early 1930s.

Cf synon. **do you know any other...**, and **yes, I also know the one...**

have you bit your nose? You look both surprised and distressed: mostly lower and lower-middle class: very approx, *c.* 1860–90. D.B. Gardner, 1977, cites William H.G. Kingston's stories for boys, *Peter the Whaler*, 1851.

have you death adders in your pocket? See **death adders...**

have you ever been tickled, missis? Cf Vernon Noble's comment at **can you 'ear me, Mother?** In a letter, 1973, Noble mentions that this 'Ken Dodds phrase usually begins as an "intro" to his act. "I was tickled to death. Have *you* ever been tickled, missis?"'

have you found a giggles nest? is a lower-class C19 c.p. addressed to someone giggling or tittering or to someone laughing senselessly or excessively. By a pun on an imaginary *giggle's nest* and on '(a fit of the) giggles'. If there's a *laughing*

jackass (the kookaburra), why not a *giggle* bird? Cf **got a feather in your trousers?**

P.B.: it lasted longer than E.P. allows: I was asked this by a Sussex farmer in the early 1940s.

have you got the weight? have you 'caught on'? – do you understand?: RN: since *c.* 1930. Semantically cf 'the *onus* of the proof'.

have you had a full, rich day? See **full rich day.**

have you heard any good stories lately? exemplifies the use of c.pp. as social gambits and dates from (if I remember rightly) *c.* 1930. Noël Coward's *Relative Values*, performed in 1951 and pub'd in 1952, II, i, ends with precisely this gambit. It sometimes varies to *heard any good ones lately?* (A.B., 1978).

In the 1920s, another such gambit used to be, 'Have you been to – *or* seen – any good plays lately?': but it didn't so take the public fancy as to have 'made the grade'.

have you heard the latest? – to which the reply, with or without a pause to enable one's interlocutor or audience the opportunity to say, 'No! Tell me' – is *It's not out yet*. A joc. c.p., employed predominantly, in fact almost exclusively, among men: C20. (Petch, 1974, reminds me of this one; I first heard it, *c.* 1920, in Aus.)

have you heard the news? The squire (or the squire's daughter) has been foully (or most foully) murdered. This c.p., very common *c.* 1905–30, satirizes the late Victorian and early Edwardian melodrama. It was much used by the British soldier in WW1, as B&P testify. It occurs in Philip MacDonald's 'thriller', *Rope to Spare*, 1932; and in a letter, 1946, Petch remarks, 'Jokers still come on with it.'

have you pigs in your belly? See **what? have you pigs...?**

have you quite finished? – for instance, talking in general or complaining or adversely criticizing or merely rambling pointlessly on and on: 'since the 1920's (? earlier). Very genteelly "sarky"' (Shaw). P.B.: an equally pained and heavily sarcastic version is *when you've quite finished* ['we can then get on' being understood]; perhaps mostly feminine usage.

have you read any good books lately? See **read any...**

have you seen a dream walking? is a var. of **did you ever see a dream walking?**, q.v.

have you seen the Shah? This c.p., current mostly among Londoners but derivatively heard often enough among provincials, arose from a visit of the Shah of Persia, in 1873, to Queen Victoria. A very popular, but short-lived song commemorated the event (Ronald Pearsall, *Victorian Popular Music*, 1973).

have you shat? is, among workmen and in the Services, either caustically or joc., said to someone who has broken wind rather noisily: since *c.* 1920. (L.A., 1976.) P.B: not so much a c.p. as a stock accusation.

have you shit the bed? A low late C19–20 c.p., addressed to one who has got out of bed rather earlier than usual. As pointed out, it is earthy.

have you shook? was a late C18 – mid C19 underworld c.p., explained thus by J.H. Vaux in the glossary written in 1812 and included in his *Memoirs*, pub'd in 1818: 'Have you *shook?*...did you succeed in getting any thing? When two persons rob in company, it is generally the province, or part, of one to *shake* (that is, obtain the *swagg*), and the other to carry, that is, bear it to a place of safety.'

have yourself a fine day. See **have a good day.**

haven't his best friends told him? See **your best friend...**

haversacks. See: I'll be laughing.

having a good arm? A C20, esp. a WW1, military c.p. applied to a soldier wearing numerous badges on his sleeve – e.g., 'farrier' or 'Lewis gunner' or 'marksman'. Perhaps influenced by *having a good war*, a successful or very lucky war.

[**having a wonderful time; wish you were here**, a favourite cliché, usu. scrawled on a postcard from a friend on holiday, and prob. dating from the 1870s or 1880s, has, by its exacerbating frequency, naturally been good-humouredly derided – and therefore become almost a c.p. It was not unknown among soldiers serving in the grim, wet, bitterly cold trenches on the Western Front. 1914–18.

Later, the *a* was sometimes omitted: *Having Wonderful Time* was 'the title of a musical comedy by Arthur Kober, prod. at the Lyceum Theatre, New York, on Feb, 20, 1937; he followed it with *Wish You Were Here* (with Joshua Logan and Harold Rome) at the Majestic, June 26, 1952. The movie of *Having Wonderful Time* won the Roi Cooper Megrue Prize in 1938' (Shipley, 1977). And, in US, there seems to have been some influence by a George Kaufman & Moss Hart comedy of the 1930s, as R.C. tells me.] See also **wish you were here.**

having fun? is an ironical c.p., dating since *c.* 1950 and addressed to someone obviously having difficulties or in trouble. Cf **are you happy in the Service** or **in your work?**

'In US, more often addressed to someone annoying; with the implied "*You* may be having fun, but *we* are not amused"' (R.C., 1977).

havoc. See: have a care.

Hawkshaw. See: I'm H.

hawser. See: elbow.

hay. See: and that ain't h.; you are sick.

Hay, Hell and Booligal. An Aus. c.p., adopted from the title of a poem by A.B. 'Banjo' Paterson, who, moreover, in *Rio Grande's Last Race*, 1902, wrote, 'Oh, send us to our just reward/In Hay or Hell, but, gracious Lord,/Deliver us from Booligal!' Booligal is a town in western New South Wales; Hay, too, belongs to NSW and was earlier called Lang's Crossing 'because it was a ford on the Murrumbidgee River for cattle bound for Victoria' (A.W. Reed, *Place Names of Australia*, 1973). I owe the c.p. to Prof. G.A. Wilkes; but a very pertinent gloss must be added: the saying was based on the English proverbial *from Hell, Hull and Halifax, Good Lord deliver us*, dating from C16, as the *ODEP* informs us, but offers no citation later than C17, even though it is still (1978) unforgotten.

hay is for horses or, in the Comic Phonetic Alphabet and as a c.p. reminiscent of the CPA, **'ay is for 'orses**, the latter perhaps prompted by the conversion of the exclamatory *hey* to *eh*. This is a c.p. addressed to someone who says *hey!* or *eh?* for 'I beg your pardon': C18–20. It is one of the longest-lived of all c.pp. (**black is your eye!** having flourished notably longer), and was recorded in S, towards the end of Dialogue I:

NEV [EROUT]: Hay, Madam, did you call me?
MISS: Hay! Why; Hay is for Horses.

For a fuller treatment of this refreshing domestic c.p., see my *Comic Alphabets*, 1961, and cf my commentary edn (1963) of S's witty book. Cf **straw's cheaper.**

hay (or **Hey lass, let's be hammered for life on Sunday!** A lower classes', perhaps orig. a metal-workers', c.p. of late C19–early C20. Ware, however, plausibly advances the theory that the phrase came from 'the work of the blacksmith at Gretna Green. It was said of him jocularly that he hammered couples together rather than married them': an attractive guess, and prob. accurate.

haystack. See: couldn't hit.

he broke his pick is, the US, said of a man discharged from a job: *c.* 1920–60. (Berrey.) Without a pick, a certain type of manual labourer is obviously useless. Also *I broke my pick*, 'a miner's saying, meaning that he is discouraged' (Adams): California: mid C19–mid 20.

he can make it sit up and beg indicates that a man has become exceptionally skilful in working some material. esp. a metal: orig. among metal workers; since *c.* 1930 or maybe a decade earlier. Perhaps it derives from the late C19–20 low c.p., *it sits up and begs* or *it is sitting up and begging*, where *it* is clearly the male organ and the allusion is to making a dog sit up and beg for, e.g., a piece of meat.

he can pick the bones out of that! See **pick the bones!**

he can put his shoes under my bed any time he likes. He's

sexually acceptable to *me*: feminine, mostly in Aus.: since *c.* 1920 (B.P., 1974).

he comes and goes is 'an occasional usage' – *not* a very frequent c.p. – 'for a man of the *Love 'em and leave 'em* type, with emphasis on the *come*' (Petch, 1976): not only public-house humour: since *c.* 1950, or perhaps a decade or two earlier.

he could eat me without salt. See **I could eat ...**

he finished up Friday, usu. said on a Saturday or a Monday. 'When the reply comes, "Who?", the answer is "Robinson Crusoe",' An Aus. c.p. dating from *c.* 1950. (Jack Slater, 1978.) The insidious factor and influence of alliteration in popular speech.

he has gone to visit his uncle was a mid C18–19 c.p., applied to 'one who leaves his wife soon after marriage' (Grose, 1785).

he hath been at shrift! This C16 ecclesiastical c.p. was applied to a man betrayed he knows not how. (Tyndale, *The Obedience of a Christian Man*, 1528.) The implication is that, contrary to almost inviolable practice, he has been betrayed by the priest to whom he confessed.

he hath eaten the rump is partly a proverbial saying and partly a c.p. of *c.* 1660–1800; said of one who is constantly talking.

'Pepys (*Diary*, 11 Feb. 1660) describes the public rejoicing and excitement when General [George Monck or] Monk ... compelled the Rump [Parliament] to admit the Excluded Members of the Long Parliament, thus clearing the way for the Restoration. Public roasting and eating of rumps in the streets of London was general, accompanied by copious healths. This would explain the given date 1660; the phrase *may* have been applied orig. to Puritan converts to Royalism talking hard so as to make their sudden conversion convincing' (R.S., 1977).

Presumably this c.p. did not last much longer than that year, although it would be remembered for some time.

he is ... See also **he's**

he is none of John Whoball's children. He's not easy to fool: late C16–17. Cf **whoa-ball**, a milkmaid, itself prob. a compound of *whoa!* and *Ball*, a common name for a cow; i.e., he is not your allegedly typical country bumpkin.

he is only fit for Ruffians (or **Ruffins**) **Hall** is a mid C17–early C19 Londoners' c.p., applied to an overdressed apprentice. Ruffians Hall was that part of Smithfield 'where Trials of Skill were played by ordinary Ruffianly people with Sword and Buckler' (Blount's dictionary, 1674). The c.p. was recorded in C17 and again in *PG*.

he knows, you know, with emphasis on *he* and *knows*. He's an authority on a specific subject; he's an exceptionally knowledgeable fellow in general: since mid-1940s. In 1977 Mr Barry Took (author of *Laughter in the Air*) used it of an acquaintance of his, when he amiably replied to several questions of mine. Contrast rather than compare **she knows, you know.**

he never had no mother: he (or **he just**) **hatched out when his dad pissed against a wall one hot day** is a low military c.p. of C20. (I regret to admit that never did I hear it in either WW1 or WW2: and I spent most of my time in the ranks.) P.B.: in other words, 'He's a right bastard!', and the object of everyone's loathing. I heard the phrase a number of times during my Army service, 1953–74, and suspect that it continues even yet. I doubt very much that it would ever be *she never ...*, but E.P. included as a separate insult in the first ed. of this book *you weren't born: you were pissed up against the wall and hatched in the sun.*

he pisses more than he drinks was a semi-proverbial c.p., prec. by **vainglorious man** and directed at a braggart: late C17–early 19. (BE; Grose.) P.B.: cf the use, in later C20, of *piss-artist*, in its sense not of 'drunkard', but applied to one who 'flannels and bullshits' his way through life, promising much and producing little.

he squats to pee. 'He's effeminate', with occ. imputation of the homosexually passive role: mostly US: late C19–20. (W.J.B., 1977.)

he that is at a low ebb at Newgate may soon be afloat at Tyburn was *c.* 1660–1810, a.c.p. implying that he who was condemned at Newgate might end by being hanged – his heels afloat, i.e. dangling in the air – at Tyburn. 'Proverbs' Fuller, *PG.*

he thinks it's just to pee through is applied to an unsophisticated youth: C20.

he was wrapped in the tail of his mother's smock. See **wrapped up.** ...

he washes clean and dries dirty. 'The classic excuse for a slovenly rating who disgraced his Division on an important occasion by appearing unshaven and unwashed: now a part of naval folklore, and applied to any "scruffy" rating' (*Sailors' Slang*); so far as I know, first recorded in *SS* in 1949, but going back, I think, to *c.* 1920. But for B.G.T., 1978, the phrase recalls the [prob. older, and domestic] Warwickshire [? more gen.] *a clean wash and a dirty wipe,* said 'when a child wets or soaps his face, and then, without rinsing, wipes the dirt onto the towel when drying'.

he who smelt it dealt it. Juvenile answer to anyone sniffing suspiciously and saying 'Who was that?'; another riposte was *he who denied it supplied it,* rather less gen. An Etonian accusation was *J'accuse.* The first two have, since *c.* 1960, had a fairly wide currency. (Simon Levene 1977.)

he will ... See **he will**...

he won't be happy till he gets it. See **good morning have you used** ...

he wouldn't say 'shit'... See **wouldn't say 'shit'**...

he would ... See **he'd** ...

he'd drink the stuff if he had to strain it through a shitty cloth! A low Can. c.p. that, dating from *c.* 1920, means that he's a hopeless drunkard. Skehan, 1977, notes the Anglo-Irish synon. *he'd drink off a sore leg:* since *c.* 1930.

he'd fuck a snake if he could get it to hold still or **get someone to hold it.** 'He is spectacularly horny (implicitly from deprivation). Certainly from 1960s, but prob. much earlier' (R.C., 1977). It prob. arose in 'The Wild West', very early in C20. Cf:

he'd fuck (or **shag**) **anything on two legs** (or **anything with a hole in it**) is an admiring, mostly Services c.p. that pays tribute to a reputedly spectacular sexual urge and potency, but not necessarily implying satyriasis. A late C19–20 gen. synon. applying to an inveterate womanizer, is **he will** (or **he'll**) **shag anything from seventeen to seventy.** A.B., 1978, supplies a US var.: **... anything that can walk.**

he'd skin a louse for the fat is a phrase applied in UK to an extremely parsimonious man: late C19–20. (B.G.T., 1978.) Cf 'I've known *he'd skin a turd for a tanner* since *c.* 1950, and latterby I have met it among the employees of Fords, Dagenham, [Essex], the bearers of a great wealth of (? uncharted) English' (David Short, 1978). The shorter *he'd skin a turd* has been low Can. since late C19.

he'll clog ageean. C20: Noble, 1974, says:
He'll live long enough to wear out another clog sole. Still current in the West Riding, although far fewer clogs are worn to need repairing. (Similarly: 'He'll mucky another clean collar.') The West Riding [of Yorkshire] is rich in 'sayings', some, like this one, becoming catch-phrases with wider connotations than the original meaning. Cf **another clean shirt** ...

he'll do to ride the river with is 'the highest compliment that can be paid to a cowman. It originated back in the old trial days when brave men had to swim herds across swollen, treacherous rivers' (Adams): cowboys': *c.* 1860–1940.

he'll leap over your head was a hunting c.p. of *c.* 1830–1900. In R.S. Surtees, *Handley Cross,* 1854, vol. I, in the chapter headed 'Another Sporting Lector' (lecture by Mr Jorrocks), occurs this passage, 'If a chap axes if your neg will jump timber, say, "He'll leap over your 'ead".'

he'll make nineteen bits (or **bites**) **of a bilberry** is a pejorative c.p. of *c.* 1640–1700. He'll make a meal of what's only a mouthful. Ray.

he'll shag anything from seventeen to seventy. See **he'd fuck anything on two legs.**

he'll spit brown and call the cat a ring-tailed bustard. An 'ironic c.p. directed against a young naval rating who is seen to be acting "stroppy" ' – i.e., bloody-minded – 'after a short time in the Service. A potential "skate" or Queen's hard bargain' (Granville, 1968): since the late 1940s. Cf **spit on the deck** ...

he'll take off any minute now. He's in a 'flap' – exceedingly excited; also, He's very angry indeed – likely to 'hit the ceiling': RAF: since 1938. From aeroplanes taking off in departure.

he's a cunt and a half is applied to any extremely objectionable fellow; as a c.p., dates from the middle or late 1950s; and derives from the low slang *cunt,* anybody one intensely dislikes. (See esp. *DSUE* supplement.)

he's a doctor. He's a cunnilingist or, slangily, a '*m*uff *d*iver', from *muff,* female public hair: *m.d.* becomes *M.D.,* a Doctor of medicine: US college wit: attested for 1956, but current since the late 1940s; less commonly used after than before 1970. (An anon. American scholar, 1977.)

he's a fine fellow but his muck (or **shit**) **stinks.** He *is* a fine fellow, but, after all, he's only human: proletarian: C20. Cf **they think their shit doesn't stink.**

he's a Mr Nonesuch. See **Nonesuch.**

he's a poet ... See **that's a rhyme.**

he's a regular Indian and **he's on the Indian list.** These Can. c.pp., dating since *c.* 1925, are applied to an habitual drunkard, esp. to one to whom it is illegal to sell liquor. It is illegal to sell liquor to Indians coming from any of their Settlements or reserves. (Prof. F.E.L. Priestley.)

he's a whole team and a horse to spare, often elab. by the addition of **and a (big) dog under the wagon** – and even more often shortened to **he's** – or come to that, **she's** – **a whole team.** He's a very fine and capable fellow, or she's a very fine woman: US, orig. and chiefly New England. Farmer records the shortest form and the longest. The predominant form occurs in T.C. Haliburton, *The Clockmaker,* in all three Series (1837, 1838, 1840) and in its sequel, *The Attaché,* 1843–4, e.g. in Series II, vol. 1, p. 8, thus: ' ... It does one good to look at her. She is a whole team and a horse to spare, that gal. – that's a fact.' Apparently, this c.p. was current during the approx. period *c.* 1830–1900.

he's been looking in your paybook! is an Armed Forces' c.p. of 1939–45 in ref. to a third person's imputation of illegitimacy or other sexual irregularity, a Serviceman's paybook recording many intimate details: and therefore it should be compared with the Australian soldiers' c.p. of 1914–18: **you've been reading my letters.**

he's been to Whitehall. He's looking very cheerful: an army officers' c.p. of *c.* 1860–1905. From an extension of leave obtained from the War Office. Ware.

he's done so much bird is an underworld, esp. a convicts' c.p. dating from *c.* 1945. It occurs in Tony Parker and Robert Allerton, *The Courage of His Convictions,* 1962. A pun on the twittering of a bird and on cant *bird,* imprisonment, which is short for the rhyming slang *bird-line,* time (in prison).

he's fallen in the water! 'Spoken by Little Jim (Spike Milligan) in *The Goon Show.* "Oh, dear children – look what's happened to Uncle Harry!" Little Jim (helpfully, in simple sing-song voice): "He's fallen in the wa-ter!" ' (*VIBS*). One of those c.pp. in which the correct intonation is essential and accounts so much for their popularity, See also GOON SHOW ...

he's gone north about. A nautical c.p. that, dating *c.* 1860–1900, refers to a sailor that has died by other than drowning. B&L.

he's got a wild hair in his crotch or **up his arse.** See **she had a hair** ...

he's got (or **carries**) **his brains between his legs.** 'More balls than brains', i.e. obsessed with sex: raffish: C20. (George Forwood, 1962.)

he's got it up there. See **here's where you want it.**

he's got ten bob each way on himself. See **get you!**

he's had a smell (occ. a sniff) of the barman's apron. This c.p. refers to one who very easily gets drunk: since *c.* 1910. P.B.: in later C20, more usu. in the form *one sniff at* (or *of*) *the barmaid's apron and he's away.* Cf the Aus. synon. (*he's*) *a two-pot screamer.*

he's in the book all right, but doesn't know what page he's on. He has only a vague idea of what he's doing; he's right, but has no idea how or why: Aus.: since *c.* 1925. Baker, 1942.

he's in the catbird seat. See **in the catbird seat.**

he's living on the bone... See **living on the bone of his arse.**

he's lovely, Mrs Hoskins... See **'e's lovely...**

he's making his will. See **making his will.**

he's not so well since he fell off the organ. This joc. c.p. – often a communal jest – has, throughout the C20, been addressed, not always unkindly, to a member of the company. The allusion is to an organ-grinder's monkey.

he's not tight, but he's taken up a lot of slack is a Can. c.p. – 'recent', says Leechman, 1969, and meaning 'He's not tight-fisted, but he *is* very careful with his money.' But contrast **I'm not tight...**

he's one of us. This imputation of homosexuality may orig. have been euph., was prompted by the certainly euph. *one of those*, a homosexual, dates from *c.* 1910, and is a homosexual c.p. Contrast **one of my mob,** q.v.

he's playing hell with himself applies to a man conspicuously grumbling and muttering to himself: since *c.* 1950 or a few years earlier.

he's saving them all for Liza has, since before 1909, been applied by the lower and lower-middle classes to 'a good young man who will not use oaths or strike blows' (Ware). It derives from that mythical youth who wouldn't give a beggar a penny because he was saving all his money for his girl.

he's saying something! See **talk to me!**

he's so tight he squeaks. See **tight as....**

he's the whole show. He's the important man – or thinks he is – in the matter concerned: since *c.* 1912. Orig. from 'showbiz', it is US and cited in 'Straight Talk', by S. R. Strait, in the *Boston Globe* of *c.* 1917. By *c.* 1945, †. (W.J.B.) Cf *in the big league,* and **he's a whole team.**

head. See: as wears; don't go over; get your h.; give your h.; go and bag; go and soak; go to Bath; he'll leap; heavy – ; here's me; hip; his hair; hold up; I need that; I wish my; I'll tear; I'm going to get; if it was raining; if your h.; keep your h.; like a sheep's; never louse; off with; pull your h.; riding out; sex rears; swim out; tavern; there's more; they're all the same; two heads; you got rocks; you need; you'd forget; you've got eyes.

headache. See: I live at.

head cut in. See **get your head...**

headache – as much use as a; no more use than a headache. Useless: C20. The former occurs in, e.g. Dorothy L. Sayers, *Unnatural Death,* 1927, but may be merely a shortening of the more usu. (*about*) *as much use as a sick headache,* that Richard Blaker, in *Medal Without Bar,* 1930, puts into the mouth of a Regular Army sergeant, 1915, as 'just about as much use as a sick eddick'. Cf **about as much use...**

heads I win, tails you lose. This is a mock wager; 'I cannot fail!': since *c.* 1830. It was anticipated by Thomas Shadwell, *Epsom Wells,* 1672, thus: 'Worse than *Cross I win, Pile you lose*'. (Apperson.)

It became also US before – prob. well before – the end of C19. J.W.C. says, 1975, 'Certainly common here'.

heads on 'em like boils is an Aus. two-up players' c.p., referring to coins that have yielded a long run of heads: since *c.* 1910. For a wonderful account of a two-up game, Lawson Glassop's gambling story, *Lucky Palmer,* 1948, could hardly be bettered. Cf Aus. card-players' c.p., **heads on 'em like mice,** indicating a very strong hand.

heads will roll is the c.p. form of a proposition, whether assertive or interrogative, so common that it might be

regarded as a cliché, yet so pointed that it doesn't run this risk. 'Many important people, primarily in Government and secondarily in large institutions or corporations, will, as the result of this pompous *gaffe* or that swindle, lose their jobs.' As a c.p., it dates from the mid 1940s. Based on a communication from Playfair, 1977.

heal. See **bruise easily.**

health. See: better in h.; Madras; wear it in h.; what, me?

heap. See: here they come.

hear. See: can you 'ear; do you h.; every little bean; have you heard; I hear; I say, I say; I've heard; let's have you; now I've heard; roll on, my; stop me; they can hear; this I must; what do you h.; you ain't heard; you can h.; you hear me; you heard.

hear my tale or kiss my tail! – orig. and often prec. by **either.** At line 120 of George Peele's *The Old Wives' Tale,* 1595, in A.H. Bullen's ed. of Greene's and Peele's plays and poems, Madge, the blacksmith's wife, telling an old wives' tale, is interrupted by Frolic; she promptly exclaims 'Nay, either hear my tale or kiss my tail', i.e. Don't interrupt my story. In 1595, *tail* meant either 'posterior' or 'penis'; in general, *kiss my tail* was an early equivalent of *kiss my arse.* There is, I think, little doubt that (*either*) *hear my tale or kiss my tail* is a homely c.p. of Elizabethan and Jacobean and prob. Caroline and perhaps even Restoration times.

heard the news? See **have you heard the news?**

heart. See: cross my h.; eat your h.; have a h.; have you any good; keep your 'earts; my heart; no heart; past your; you have a h.; you may have; you're all h.

heart-strings. See: playing it.

hearth. See: keystone.

heat. See: if you can't stand; it must be the h.

heaven. See: I hope we; parson would.

heavy. See: shit weighs; steal; and:

heavy-heavy hangs over your head was, very approx. *c.* 1910–50, a warning 'to duck something overhead' (Berrey); not, one would have thought, an urgent warning – it's far too wordy.

Hector. See: since H.

Hecuba. See: cut to H.

hedge. See: wrong side.

heel(s). See: beef to the h.; dog; I feel an awful; not a h.; she has round; your heels.

heigh-ho! See **all part of life's rich pattern.**

height. See: pissed on from; on from.

hell. See: beats the h.; bells of h.; couldn't organize; for the h.; go to h.; going to h.; Hay, hell; he's playing; I'll go hopping; I'll see you in h.; it'll be a cold day; it's hell; like hell; much chance as a snow; no more chance; retreat?; that's a h.; 'til hell; and:

hell hath (or holds) no fury like a woman's corns. This joc. punning c.p., apparently not antedating the C20, obviously burlesques the famous quot'n from William Congreve's *The Mourning Bride,* 1697:

Heaven has no rage like love to hatred turn'd,
Nor hell a fury like a woman scorn'd.

hell in a hand-basket. See **going to hell...**

hell in there. Esp. as in *Gad, it must be* (or *must have been*) *hell in there!* uttered in a 'superior officer', is yet another of the very popular c.pp. to have orig. in the GOON SHOW, q.v. (P.B.)

hell! said the Duchess when she caught her teats in the mangle, often shortened, allusively, to the opening four words. Dating from *c.* 1895, it was frequently used in WW1, although seldom in the ranks; after WW1, the shorter form has predominated, often with no ref. whatsoever to the orig.: cf Michael Arlen's novel, *Hell! Said the Duchess,* 1934. So well established by that time was the phrase that, on 11 Jan. 1936, *The Times Literary Supplement* could wittily caption a review of Daniel George's *A Peck of Troubles,* with the words, 'Said the Duchess'. On 20 March 1937, in the same newspaper supplement, the reviewer of *DSUE* remarked that 'The saga of the Duchess, "who had taken no part in the conversation", was on men's lips at least forty years ago'.

A C20 var. is *hell! said the Duke, pulling the Duchess on like a jack-boot;* another C20 var., but Can., is *hell! cried the Duchess and flung down her cigar.*

See also **'fuck me!', said the Duchess ...**, and cf two others of the same genre, **'balls!' said the Queen ...**, and **'shit!', said the King ...**

hell's a-poppin', occ. with loose added. 'Said of one on a spree' (Berrey); but also = 'Things are really swinging': US: *c.* 1930–60. The phrase was greatly popularized, and spread to UK, by being used as the title of a crazy, surrealist-humoured play, of which a film, starring Abbott and Costello, was later made. The play had a zany, spectacular lobby (Brit. 'foyer') accompaniment, and was performed in the late 1930s. I saw the film, of which the title was spelt *Helzapoppin*. (Thanks to Shipley and R.C.)

hello, and if you see Susie. See **say hey!**

hello, baby! How's nurse? was a civilian c.p., dating from early in C20, before it was adopted by the licentious soldiery for use in WW1; (so far as I know) by the time WW2 began. It was 'addressed to any girl pushing a perambulator' (B&P, 1931).

hello, beautiful! A male 'getting-off' gambit addressed to a pretty girl and current since *c.* 1935; by *c.* 1970, virtually †. The corresponding girl-to-boy gambit is *hullo, handsome!,* current since *c.* 1940 and not yet (1975) †.

hello, features! A satirical and quizzical, yet friendly, form of address: *c.* 1900–14. (Ware, who classifies it as proletarian.) 'According to my Aussie mates in Hong Kong [early 1960s], it was short for "penis-features" or "fuck-features" – depending on how much you didn't like the bloke addressed' (P.B., 1976). And Lovett, also Aus. adduces in 1978 *hello, shit-features* and *hello, cunt-features.*

hello, folks! 'When Arthur Askey used this expression in the first *Band Waggon* broadcast in 1938 he received a call from Tommy Handley telling him to lay off, as Handley considered it to be *his* catchphrase. Askey coined "hello, playmates!" [q.v.] instead and Handley continued to use "hello, folks!" throughout *ITMA*, after which the Goons took up the cry and gave it a strangled delivery. Harry Secombe extended this to "hello, folks, and what about the workers?", and Eric Morecambe gave it an almost sexual connotation by referring to "a touch of hello folks and what about the workers!"' (*VIBS*). P.B.: the Secombe-style *hello, folks!* was the one preferred and very common in later C20.

hello, good evening, and welcome! 'David Frost's greeting, which contrives to say three things where only one is needed. Now an essential part of the Frost-impersonator's kit' (*VIBS*). It has in the 1970s, been adopted by many people as a greeting' (Ms Jane Gilman, in the *Oxford Mail*, 8 Sep. 1977).

hello, handsome! See **hello, beautiful!**

hello, hello, hello! The tradtional, British policeman's monitory comment upon an untoward incident or situation – becomes a c.p. when it's employed allusively, as it has been since *c.* 1960 at the latest and prob. since *c.* 1945 or 1946, and as in the story of that young police officer who, on returning home unexpectedly early, finds his wife in bed with three men, mildly exclaims, 'Hullo, hullo, hullo!', thus causing her to burst into tears and sobbingly reproach the clumsy inadvertent fellow with the classic words, 'Darling, you didn't say hullo to *me!*'

R.C., 1977, correctly compares it with the Cockney *nah, then, wot's all this?*, and adds that, when used in a gen. sense, 'It perhaps qualifies as a c.p.' He's right. P.B.: the *h*'s are often dropped.

hello, honky-tonks! 'Clarence, the camp gentleman played by Dick Emery' (*VIBS*): particularly popular *c.* 1970.

hello, Jim! (pron. *Jee-heem* and/or 'sung'). 'Spike Milligan's Jim Spriggs in *The Goon Show*' (*VIBS*). P.B.: a very popular

c.p. at the height of the Goon cult and still, early 1980s, heard occ.; esp. of course, to people called Jim, for whom it must have worn very threadbare. See GOON SHOW.

hello, my darlings! uttered in a fluted, affected voice, was coined by the well-known comedian Charlie Drake, late 1960s(?), who later made it the "chorus" of a song' (P.B., 1977).

hello! (or **what cheer!**, pron. *whatcher!*) **my** (or **me**) **old brown son, how are you** (or **'ow are yer?**) was a well-known WW1 (soldiers') greeting, promptly taken into civilian life. The 'brown' refers to the khaki uniform. (Julian Franklyn; L.A.; inter-confirmatory information.)

hello, playmates! is 'Arthur Askey's cheerful greeting introduced (and long used) in his record-running pre-Second World War radio entertainment "Band Waggon", described by Gale Pedrick in BBC Year Book 1948 as "grandfather of all BBC series", continued through the war and after' (Noble, 1975). It would be safe to say that it had become a very widely used gen. c.p. by 1945 at the latest. See also **hello, folks!**

hello, sailor! Although originating earlier, it apparently became an indubitable c.p. in 1975. In 1976, P.B., who had been reading the proofs of the first ed. of this book (pub'd 5 Sep. 1977) told me that he had been telling a colleague about it, and that this colleague's young daughters had immediately exclaimed, 'Ooh, has it got *hello, sailor?*' [It hadn't – so thank you, Katie and Joan]. Also, P.B. continued, 'The advertisers of Captain Morgan rum are running a new series of gigantic posters: one of the first two I've seen is "You don't say 'Hello, Sailor' to a Captain Morgan drinker".' Often addressed by a heterosexual to a homosexual male, the allusion being to the ambivalent sexuality of some sailors.

P.B.: in his *Goon for Lunch*, 1975, Sir Harry Secombe, writing of the early or mid 1950s, recalls a studio scene: '"Sing us the news, Wal [Wallace Greenslade, the Goon Show's announcer]." Spike Milligan has decided to stand on his head. Wally replies with a good-natured Naval phrase. "Hello, Sailor" lisps Peter [Sellers], looking up archly from under the piano, where he has retired for a short kip.'

[**hello, sucker!** is a sort of c.p. greeting by a night-club proprietor or manager to a prospective customer: US: *c.* 1930–50. (Berrey.) Ashley, 1982, attributes it to the speakeasy proprietress Texas Guinan.]

hello yourself (or **your own self**) **and see how you like it!** was a proletarian c.p. of *c.* 1910. It occurs in W. Pett Ridge, *Minor Dialogues*, 1895. But, as David Francis pointed out to me, 1977, it appears earlier, in Mark Twain's *Adventures of Tom Sawyer*, 1876, chapter 6. The words are spoken by Huckleberry Finn.

help. See: can I h.; can't help; every little h.; it's the poor; not if I can; with a little; you don't have to be mad.

help! sharks! See **too late! too late!**

help yourself! Please *do!*; Please yourself!; Just as you please!: since *c.* 1917. It occurs in, e.g., Richard Blaker, *Enter, a Messenger*, 1926. 'Often said in reply to "Can – or may – I use your 'phone?"' (Petch, 1967).

It passed to the US *c.* 1918. Irvin S. Cobb, *Murder Day by Day*, 1933, writes,

He asked ... if he might be permitted to take a last look at the deceased.

'Help yourself,' said the widow. 'He's laid out upstairs in the front room. Just you walk up, Mr McKenna.'

Other enlightening examples are these:
June Drummond, *The Saboteurs*, 1967:
'I'm looking for Joe Riddle.'
'Next door,' said the man. 'Help yourself.'
Nichol Fleming, *Counter Paradise*, 1968:
'I'd like to check that car of yours.'
'Help yourself.'
Hartley Howard, *Million Dollar Snapshot*, 1971:
'Before you ask your questions, is it all right for me to ask one of mine?'

Terrel shrugged and said, 'Help yourself. I'm in no hurry.' Cf **be my guest!**

helping. See: **double.**

hemp is growing for the villain – the; also **hemp is grown for you.** Applied to a rogue 'born to be hanged' with a hempen rope: late C18–19. JB; Ware.

hen. See: **couldn't drive; couldn't pull; when hens.**

hence the pyramids. This c.p. is either applied to an unintentional *non sequitur* or deliberately said as an ironically joc. *non sequitur:* late C19–20, but not much used since WW2. It derives from a passage in the very rude, very droll recitation known to the earthy as *The Showman* and recorded in B & P, 1931. Cf **that accounts for the milk ...**, q.v.

Henry's made a lady out of Lizzie was current in the US, during the late 1920s, 'when production of the famous Ford car, Model T, affectionately nicknamed [*Tin*] *Lizzie* came to an end and Model A was introduced to the public. Henry Ford had great hopes for this more sophisticated car, but his son Edsel was more cautious. "But Henry's name was enough to bring in 400,000 orders within two weeks, and the country had a new catch phrase to bandy around": James Brough, *The Ford Dynasty,* 1978' (Noble, 1978).

her clothes sit on her like a saddle on a sow's back. Applied to an ill-dressed woman, this c.p. – recorded by BE – belongs to the very approx. period 1660–1750.

her knitting's out is a RN c.p. that, in WW2, was applied to a minesweeper that has her gear over the side. PGR.

hers. See: **good herbs.**

here am I, slaving over a hot stove all day (sc. *while all* you *do is* (e.g.) *sit at a desk*). Used lit., i.e. seriously and aggrievedly, it is manifestly not a c.p. But, as P.B.: points out, 1975, it is often employed joc.: and then it is incipiently one: '*The* [utterance] of the hard-pressed housewife'. R.C., 1977, adds, 'The *locus classicus* is the title of a drawing, *c.* 1912 (?), by the great caricaturist Art Young (1866–1943): "Here am I, standin' over a hot stove all day, and you workin' in a nice, cool sewer!"'

here come de judge. 'Was much used in the late 1960s on *Rowan and Martin's Laugh-In* [a US TV comedy series]. It originated with a Negro vaudeville veteran, Dewey 'Pigmeat' Markham, to introduce a series of blackout sketches:

JUDGE: Have you ever been up before me?
DEFENDANT: I don't know – What time do you get up?

Pigmeat himself appeared on *Laugh-In*' (*VIBS*).
P.B.: for Brit. audiences the phrase would carry reminders of **silence in court**, q.v., and its elaborations. A.B., 1978, notes that, in the TV show, it was usu. prec. by **order in de** (or *the*) **court**, and R.C. adds that he remembers it as *heah come ...*

here comes the bride! is a joc. c.p. used – in the girl's presence – when an engagement is announced: since *c.* 1920. P.B.: in UK, at any rate, the phrase recalls the naughty boys' parody of the wedding march:

Here comes the bride,
All fat and wide!
See how she wobbles from side to side!

here endeth the first lesson is a Protestant c.p., employed by the bored after a long speech or lecture or gratuitous exposition: since *c.* 1870; by 1960, slightly ob. A dependable criterion of a bore is that he explains, at length, something nobody has asked him to explain.

here goes! See **here we go!**

here they come, mooching along, all of a bloody heap. B & P say: 'If one saw one's own or preferably another unit arriving in billets after a long march, one shouted:

Here they come
Mooching along
All of a bloody heap.'

A WW1 British army chanting c.p. Note *mooching* instead of *marching.* Cf **halt the ...**

here they come smoking their pipes! This c.p. of the Billingsgate fish-buyers was shouted when, at auctions, the bids were

rapid and high: *c.* 1870–1940. Ware remarks that the c.p. prob. signified 'independence and determination' – and he's prob. right.

here we are again! At first (*c.* 1880) a form of greeting, it has, in C20 been very much a c.p. It was prob. orig. by Harry Paine, that clown, who in the 1870s and 1880s, at Drury Lane, began the Boxing Night harlequinade with a somersault and a cheerful 'Here we are again!' The late Frank Shaw writing to me, 1968, remarked that it was 'still used, by e.g., seaside pierrots' – a statement reinforced by Noble's comment in a letter, 1973: 'Joey the Clown in the old Harlequinade – forerunner and for many years an essential ingredient of pantomime – introduced the c.p. "Here we are again!" – which people are still saying without knowing how it originated.' Nigel Rees, in *VIBS*, notes that the orig. 'Joey the Clown' was Joseph Grimaldi (1779–1837).

The phrase had been revitalized by the WW1 soldiers' song:

We're here because we're here.
Because we're here, because we're here.
Oh, here we are, oh, here we are.
Oh, here we are again –

recorded in Benham, 1948, and there glossed as 'Soldiers' Song. *c.* 1916'. But that song merges

We're here
Because we're here;
We're here
Because we're here,
Because we're here

with

Here we are,
Here we are,
Here we are again –

repeated *ad nauseam.* And even that combined version gave way to a music-hall 'prettying', which began with

Here we are, here we are,
Here we are again!

and ended with the lines

Hullo! Hullo!
Here we are again!

(See B & P, 1931, or that reconstruction, which, planned by EP and edited by John Brophy, appeared in 1965 as *The Long Trail*: What the Soldier Said and Sang in 1914–1918.)

Allan Monkhouse's *The Ray*, 1928, has, in Act III, this passage:

BRANSOME: How d'y' do? (*He bows to Robert.*)
ROBERT: This is unexpected, Mr Bransome.
BRANSOME: Yes, here we are again.

Bransome is a businessman of the theatre; the phrase has, for him, a reminiscence of the old song.

Harold Shapiro comments, 1977, 'With the variant *here we are, all right!* it was the clown's traditional shout on his entrance, but it's older than Harry Paine in origin. It appears, for example, in *Sketches by Boz* (see "Astley's") and is already used as a c.p. by 1845, when Ruskin writes to his father, "I took four hours before breakfast ... and here we are all right – as the clown says," (See my *Ruskin in Italy,* 1972, p. 178).'

here we come, mum, dad's on the axle was a schoolboys' c.p., dating since *c.* 1910 and expressing satisfaction and delight at speed on bicycle or scooter, hence, among young men, at the happy or successful completion of some other activity.

here we go! (or, implying repetition, **here we go again**) arose, I think, *c.* 1850 or 1860, but I lack any early printed record; I remember it from *c.* 1902. Cf the longer-lived **here goes!**, used by J. H. Newman in a letter dated 1829, as the *OED* tells us, and approximately meaning. 'There's not much chance, but I'll *try*' or, often, 'Now for it!'

But, as R.C. points out, 1977, 'In the form *here we go again*, the US usage more usually implies that "we're in for a repetition of an experience that was none too enjoyable the last time"'. P.B.: true also by Brit. usage of the phrase, since *c.* 1950 at latest: usu. prec. by 'Oh, Lor'!' – or something more emphatic, and uttered in a tone of despair, ironic, woeful, or resigned.

here you are then! 'A quip at the time of the First World War, 1914–18, with indelicacy in the innuendo and embellished in a drone: "You can have it all/Up against the wall!" and developed into scabrous verse' (L.A., 1975). Cf **it's only human nature, after all.**

here's a belly never reared a bastard. This Anglo-Irish c.p. of mid C19 – early C20 designates a boaster, whether female or, derivatively, who has 'suited action to the words. Obsolete' (Shaw, 1968).

here's a couple of matchsticks. A mostly workman's jocularity addressed to someone sleepy early in the day and accompanied by a gesture of handing him two so that he may prop his eyes open: late C19–20.

here's a fiver (or **a five-pound note**) **for you** is addressed to one who has received mail consisting wholly or mainly of bills and perhaps circulars: C20.

here's a ha'penny (or **a penny**): **don't spend it all at one shop** (or **all at once**) is a jocularity accompanying the munificent gift to a (young) child: late C19–20; by 1960, ob.; by 1970, virtually †.. R.C., 1977, cites M. Page, *Fast Company*, *c.* 1936, for the ob. US var. *don't spend it all in one place.* P.B.: and *don't spend it all at once!* is still a joc. accompaniment in UK to the handing over of a very small sum, usu. in change.

[**here's fluff in your latch-key!** could, I suppose, be called 'a drinking c.p.' – current during WW2 among RAF officers and occurring in, e.g., Terence Rattigan's *Flare Path*, 1942, and enduring for several years after the war. But, predominantly a toast and nothing more, it is ineligible.]

[**here's hair on your chest!** and **here's how!**, being toasts, are not genuine c.pp.]

here's how!, by itself, is ineligible, for it's a mere drinking conventionalism. It has, however, prompted the elab.:

here's how! I don't mean 'how'; I mean 'when'. I know how. A correspondent from Highworth, Wiltshire, mentions having heard it in 1944. And A.B., from the US, 1978, adds '"I know how – *who* is the problem": since *c.* 1950s.'

here's incident! In *The Dramatist*, 1793, Frederick Reynolds causes his unsuccessful playwright, Vapid, who extols the virtues of theatrical incident, to use it several times; for instance, early in Act II, Vapid, realizing that he has just made a tremendous *faux pas* with Lady Waitfor't, exclaims, 'Mercy on me: – here's incident!' In a University of London MA thesis, Miss Madge Collins, writing about Reynolds, mentions that *here's incident!* became a c.p.

In the same scene, when the irate Lady, in departing, declares, 'Oh! I'll be revenged, I'm determined', Vapid *solus* remarks, 'What a great exit! very well! – I've got an incident, however.' A little later, Marianne bids him hide behind a sofa; he comments, 'Behind this sopha! here's an incident!' And in Act V:

MARIANNE: Did you really love me, Mr Vapid?
VAPID: Hey day! recovered! – here's incident!
MARIANNE: But did you really love me, Mr Vapid?
VAPID: Yes I did – here's stage effect!

With thanks to Miss Patricia Sigl.

here's looking at you, kid! 'Humphrey Bogart to Ingrid Bergman in the film *Casablanca*. A quotation turned into a catchphrase by Bogart impersonators' (*VIBS*). P.B.: but *here's looking at you*, and *I looks towards you* are merely drinking conventionalisms; see **here's fluff**, etc. The raffish *here's looking up your kilt* (, *squire*), however picturesque, should prob. also be included in the latter category: examples in point occur, passim, in the *Guardian*, in the strips of that admirable cartoonist Posy Simmonds.

here's me head: me arse is comin'! (or **here's my head: my arse is coming!**) A workmen's c.p., dating since *c.* 1895, but not much used since *c.* 1940, the female type having become much less frequent. It refers to a girl, or woman, wearing

high heels and walking with head and shoulders well forward and with posterior, esp. shapely or buxom, well behind. It derives from the mostly Midlands description of a forward-sloping person, as in 'Oh, he's all *here's me head, me arse is comin'* (which I owe to Mr Richard Merry).

[**here's mud in your eye!** is a very famous army officers' toast of WW1, *not* a c.p.]

here's Peter the Painter, a joc. c.p. of *c.* 1910–20, derives from the legendary figure supposed to have taken a leading part in 'the battle of Sidney Street' (London) in 1910.

here's the back of my hand to you! At the end of Dialogue I in S, Miss Notable says, 'Well, Mr *Neverout*; here's the Back of my Hand to you' – which is a flippant and probably challenging goodbye of late C17 – mid C18.

P.B.: but elsewhere in the 1st ed. of this book, E.P. included *the back o' me hand to ye!*, which he glossed as 'an Anglo-Irish retort: late C19–20. Prob. lit. "a slap", but perhaps euph.' To this R.C. later added that this version is also heard in US: 'A mild, mock-Irish, mock-threat. (The back of the hand consists of knuckles.) Current from 1920s and prob. much earlier, from the days of the "stage Irishman" (*fl.* 1870)'.

[**here's to crime!**, being a toast, however common, is ineligible.]

here's where you want it! – accompanied by the speaker's touching or clearly indicating his own head, e.g. by a tap on his own forehead, means 'You must use your intelligence': since *c.* 1890. Cf the very closely related C20 c.p., **he's got it up there** – he's very intelligent indeed.

here's yer back! See LIVERPOOL CATCH PHRASES.

here's yer hat! what's yer 'urry? and **here's your hat! what's your hurry?** The late Frank Shaw, in a letter, 1968, thought that this was the orig. Brit. should have known. He described it as a 'graceless farewell to visitor. North Country.' He dated it as 'since *c.* 1920', but intimated that it had perhaps arisen ten or even twenty years earlier.

W. J. B., 1968, informed me that the US version is *here's your hat* – don't rush! On the other hand, Col. Moe, 1975, unequivocally and unquestioningly presents *here's your hat – what's your hurry?* as the US form.

I'd hate to be compelled to decide the priority: and, anyway, I lack the evidence to do so.

hero. See: my hero.

herring-barrel. See: I wouldn't walk.

herrings. See: fine morning.

Hesperus. See: wreck.

hey, Abbott! is recorded in W & F's list of seven 'Synthetic Fad Expressions' – without explanation or date.

R.C., 1977, explains: 'Undoubtedly borrowed from the [film] comedy team of [Bud] Abbott and [Lou] Costello (*fl.* 1935–55) – but only very marginally a c.p. Now extinct'; and Dr Donald L. Martin, 1977, expands, 'It was used by the young ... to mean "Help! Get me out of this!" but I haven't heard it used since the early 1950s'. D.L.M. adds that the last syllable was stressed and extended.

[**hey, damme!** (See the Gifford quot'n at **what's to pay?**) Although a comic actor's 'gag' in a well-known, minor late C18 play, it cannot, any more than any other 'oathy' exclamation, be called a c.p.]

hey, Johnny! You like my sister? She outside, all black; inside, all cherry-red, just like Queen Victoria: bloody good bloke! 'A soldier's parody of the sales talk of any Oriental pimp' (P.B., 1974): since the middle 1940s.

hey, lass, let's be .... See **hay, lass ....**

hey, mudder, give my brudder the udder under! 'This Canadian c.p., used almost as a tongue-twister and clearly [originating] from one, has been current since *c.* 1930, although never – for rather obvious reasons – very general' (*DSUE* Supplement). This kind of brutally and brutishly callous insensitivity is particularly repellent and probably issues from an almost animal rebellion against the restraints of decent society.

hi, ho! Let her go, Gallagher! is a US c.p., dating from 1887, the years of William Delaney's song thus titled. (W. J. B.) See also **let her go, Deacon.**

hi ho, Silver! (Or *hey ho, heighho, hi-yo*, etc.) Listed by W. & F as one of seven 'Synthetic Fad Expressions' (1960 ed., p. 655), it is explained by Prof. Harold Shapiro, 1975, thus:

One of the most popular radio serials of the 1930s and 1940s was 'The Lone Ranger'. Some Lone Ranger movie serials were also made. The Long Ranger was a sort of cowboy Robin Hood, who wore a mask, used silver bullets (sparingly), rode a white horse named Silver, and had an Indian sidekick named Tonto, who in turn rode a horse named Scout (to urge his horse on, he said: 'Gettum up, Scout!'). Every week for a half-hour, 'the masked rider of the Plains, with his great horse Silver, and his faithful Indian companion Tonto,' righted wrongs. – to the accompaniment, at the beginning and end of the program, of the anapaestic melody of the William Tell Overture. Well, at the beginning and end of the program the Lone Ranger urged his horse on with a great call of 'Hi ho, Silver, awa-a-ay!' In the middle of the program he merely said 'Hi ho, Silver!' As a c.p., *Hi Ho, Silver* could be used in an endless variety of (jocular) ways (e.g., 'Let's go!' or to signify something grand, as in 'Who does he think he is, Hi Ho, Silver?'); but, however used, it always referred to that radio serial.

And Ashley, 1984, adds *who was that masked man?*, 'as the Lone Ranger rides off into the sunset – meaning: that person did us some favor'.

As an example of the c.p.'s endurance and widespread popularity, there is this, from McGowan & Hands, *Don't Cry for Me* ... , 1983, (an account of the Falklands War 'from the sharp end'):

'The [raft] graunched up against the beach, and with [British] Marines shouting, "' Hiyo, Silver," the [armoured vehicles] lurched off through the icy water and onto dry land.'

Hicks. See: brayvo.

hide. See: more arse; no hide.

hide-and-seek. See: plays a game.

hiding. See: on a hiding.

high. See: about as h.; biscuits hang; everything is lovely; his pockets; how high; how is that; living high; yea big; you can only; you can't get h.; and:

high cost of dying – the, orig. and still US, was adopted in UK *c.* 1942, but confined to the middle and higher reaches of society. Clearly it puns that constant topic of conversation, *the high cost of living*.

high, low, jack and the game (where Jack is the knave in a pack of cards): US, either entirely or predominantly: J. W. C., 1968, says:

Announcement by the decisive complete winner of a card game .... As a c.p., spoken by, or of, the unquestioned winner of any contest .... Mark Twain uses the term, though I don't remember where. Probably no longer universally or even commonly understood, but it certainly was in the latter half of the 19th century.

It derives from the card game known as All Fours or Seven Up or Old-Sledge or High-Low-Jack. 'As a c.p., now obsolete,' writes J.W.C., 1975, 'except, like Euchre, in rural hinterlands, but it was certainly common in my childhood (oh, say, *c.* 1910–20).' He adds: 'Literally, the announcement of the highest possible heard; as a c.p., the crowing proclamation of complete victory in any contest.' To which he subjoins '[My wife] remembers a variant, "High, low, Jack, and win" – which I have never heard.'

Jack Slater, 1978, adds, 'This phrase is used in [Lancashire] engineering workshops and working men's clubs to describe the Last Rites given by a Catholic priest to a dying man, as in "They gave him the high-low-Jack (– game)", i.e. the sign of the cross'.

higher the fever. See: because the h.

hike. See: mix me.

hills. See: take to; there's gold.

hills are closing in on him – the. He's become very odd-beginning to go mad: among the United Nations troops in Korea: *c.* 1953–5. From the forbidding hills and mountains of Korea. (Anon., 'Slanguage', in *Iddiwah*, the New Zealand soldiers' periodical of 1953–4.) P.B.: Cf the terms used among Allied prisoners-of-war in WW2 to describe the same unhappy state: *wire-happy*, and *the wire's closing in.*

him all bugger-up finish. Orig., in Papua New Guinea pidgin, it meant 'dead'; it has been 'adapted in Australia to anything that has finally failed, e.g. a car or a university career' (Camilla Raab, 1977): since *c.* 1950. It is amazing what the various pidgins can do with a very small vocabulary.

hinge. See: tongue; twinges.

hint. See: I can take; and:

hint! hint! 'A c.p. accompaniment to any hint that's about as subtle as a jab in the ribs. In a bookshop: "This looks a fascinating book. Hey, it's my birthday next week – hint, hint!"' (P.B., 1976). I didn't hear it until *c.* 1965, but it goes back, I think, to *c.* 1955.

hip. See: lower than.

hip, Michael, your head's on fire! A street c.p. addressed to a red-haired man: mid C18 – mid C19. (Grose, 1785.) P.B.: *Michael* because he was likely to be Irish?

hire a horse! See **get a horse!**

his calves don't suck the right cows. 'A cowboys' reference to a rustler [cattle thief]' (Adams): Western US: C20. Cf:

his cinch is getting frayed is 'said of one who has worn out his welcome' (Adams): late C19 – mid 20, in Western US, esp. among cowboys.

his hair grows through his head. He is on the road to ruin: mid C16 – early C18. Apperson cites Skelton. Deloney, Motteux. Hair instead of brains.

His horse's head is swollen so big that he cannot come out of his stables. He owes a great deal of money to the ostler: C17.

his master's voice comes from that famous picture advertisement in which the faithful dog listens wistfully to a record of his dead master's beloved voice; these words capitalized form the trade name of HMV records and record-players. The c.p. arose early in C20 and is extant, although rather less used after than before WW2. In *The Curious Crime of Miss Julia Blossom*, 1970, by Laurence Meynell, a novelist exceptionally sensitive to dialogue, we read:

'If you don't realize that [the end of the affair between her husband and his secretary], Miss Vavasour, I am sure my husband will when he and I have talked together. Good night.'

'His Master's Voice,' Selina had said ... It hadn't been much of a retort but it was the best she could think of.

The term is also in use among railwaymen, as a nickname for a deputy foreman, as Frank McKenna notes in his *The Railway Workers, 1840–1970*, 1980.

Every record issued by HMV bears a trademark reproducing the advertisement, and, by the way, 'the little terrier's name was Nipper' (Leechman).

his means are two pops and a galloper is an underworld c.p. of *c.* 1740–1830; it means that he's a highwayman, his two main needs being a brace of pistols and a fast horse; and it appears in the 2nd edn. of Grose.

his mother never raised a squib. He's a very brave fellow: Aus.: C20. (Baker, 1959.) In Aus. slang, a *squib* is a faintheart, one who tends to back out of an undertaking.

his nose is always brown. 'He's a sycophant of the lowest order' – and so is the c.p.: C20.

his pockets are high is, in the US, said of a very tall man: since *c.* 1930. (Fain, 1977.)

his stockings are of (later **belong to**) **two parishes.** He is wearing stockings that don't match: *c.* 1770–1850. Grose, 1796.

hist! we are observed is a joc. ironic C20 c.p., burlesqued by Hilaire Belloc in his 'spy' novel, *But Soft – We Are Observed*,

1928, and † by 1940. It satirizes the language of spy melodramas.

An odd adumbration occurs in Thomas Morton's famous comedy, *Speed the Plough*, 1796. In I, i, Gerald says 'Hush! Conceal yourself; we are observed; [come] this way.'

'More likely', writes R.C., 1977, 'satirizing Victorian sentimental drama, in which a couple is "observed in compromising circumstances"'. P.B.: cf the even more melodramatic *fly! All is discovered*, prob. also from the source suggested by R.C., and of which somebody – was it 'Saki'? – wrote that the arrival of a telegram bearing these words was guaranteed to make even a bishop think twice. Cf **we are not alone**.

hit(s). See: good field; if I hit; no hits; pretend; when shit; you have hit.

hit me now with the child in my (or **me**) **arms**. 'Pretended fear of imminent assault. Dublin provenance, I think, used extensively up to about the 1940s' (Skehan, 1984).

hit the road, Jack! 'A command to someone to leave' (CM). Paul Janssen writes, 'It was partly popularized by a hit song (early 1960s) which went "Hit the road, Jack, and don't you come back no more, no more ... " (Ray Charles)'. The phrase itself goes back, among hoboes, to early C20 or latish C19 and is therefore not predominantly Negro as I had at first thought because of my source for it. Cf such books as Godfrey Irwin's *American Tramp and Underworld Songs and Slang*, 1931 [pub'd by Scholartis, E.P.'s own firm], Jack London's *The Road*, 1907, or even Josiah Flynt's *Tramping with Tramps*, 1899, and *The Little Brother*, 1902.

hockey-sticks. See: jolly h.

hog. See: living high: root; useless.

hog-law's got 'em is a US railwaymen's c.p., 'said of [a] crew which has been on duty their full sixteen hours' (Berrey, 1942): hardly for long after *c.* 1950. *Hog-law* = the law regulating the working day. Var., *monkey got 'em*, 'caught on the road after sixteen hours' (Ramon F. Adams, *The Railroader*, 1977).

hog-wild. See: don't go hog.

hoist. See: who's hoisting.

hokey-pokey, penny a lump: the more you eat, the more you pump 'is often chanted derisively at children who have some ice cream, bought in the streets, by those who have none' (Petch, 1946): working-class children's: since *c.* 1902.

It may have been adopted and adapted from the US, where, however, it was applied to grated ice, with various-coloured syrups (to one's choice) poured over it; Shipley, 1977, recalls a chant sung by children, *c.* 1900, the same as the Brit. version, but with *jump* for the more indelicate *pump*.

hold. See: don't hold; glue; he'd fuck a snake; I'll hold; I'm skinning; Knocked-knees; miraculous; that'll hold; thinks he; yes, but who; you're holding; and:

hold 'em and squeeze 'em, a C20 US c.p., derives from the instructors' advice on the rifle range: after sighting and aligning one's rifle on the target, to squeeze the trigger gently: all literal and technical. Its derivative, c.p. sense was 'Do it carefully, patiently, thoroughly!' Col. Moe thought, 1975, that the phrase was ob. or even †, by then.

hold everything! See **hold your horses!**

hold her, Newt! She's a rarin'. W.J.B., 1969, writes:

Goes back to the early '20's or earlier than that: I suspect it started in a comic strip or an early movie. A country bumpkin, presumably named Newt [for Newton], trying to hold a fractious horse or mare as she rears and stands on her hind feet, is the picture I conjure up, but the phrase itself can mean any number of things.

McKnight records it as being used by US university students in 1920.

Note that in gen. US slang, *newt* is 'a stupid person. *Some use since c.* 1925' (W & F) – perhaps from *neuter*, as in 'a neuter cat'.

It was adopted, *c.* 1948, in Can. 'pseudo-rural, with a

touch of contempt for the rustics' (Leechman).

R.C., 1977, disputes the W & F etymology and rates the 'stupid person' sense as irrelevant.

hold me back! 'Mock fury. Implication that if you don't hold me back, I may hit someone' (Skehan, 1978): C20. I remember hearing it, 1915, in Egypt, among the AIF. P.B.: sometimes elab. by addition of mock plea, *well, go on, hold me!*, implying 'in case he sees me coming and hits me first'. Cf *wanna fight? I'll hold your coat!*

hold my hand and call me Charlie! goes back to *c.* 1930, but was, by 1960, ob. and by 1970†. Mostly derisive; addressed by youth to girl. Cf **chase me, Charlie!** and **chase me, girls**, qq.v.

hold onto your hat! 'We are about to embark on an exciting and possibly dangerous course of action. Originally from speeding in an open car and/or riding a roller coaster' (R.C., 1978). Both Brit. and US: C20; but, in the UK at least, ob. by 1970.

hold up your head: there's money bid for you. Don't be so modest: people think well of you: a semi-proverbial c.p. of mid C17–mid C19. Apperson cites S, who uses the full saying, and Marryat, who uses the shorter, i.e. *there's money bid for you*. Perhaps from slave markets.

hold yer 'ush and watch thi cutlery! Shut up – and watch your property, especially your household goods!: North Country: since *c.* 1920 (? a decade earlier). 'First heard in Sheffield at a dinner in October 1938. Very dialect[al], this one!' (Lawrence Smith, 1975).

hold your horses! 'Now just wait a minute: you're going too fast, you're assuming too much' (J.W.C., 1977): US: the *OED New Supp.* cites a passage from the *Picayune* (New Orleans), 1844, and an Aus. employment from J.S. Robb, *Streaks of a Squatter Life*, 1847. It has long been used in UK in this sense, but also as 'Hold up the job until further orders!': since *c.* 1890; orig., the Royal Artillery, but since *c.* 1930 heard frequently in also the RAF and even in the RN.

(H & P.) The RAF used, from 1940, a var., *hold everything!*, which, however, had, by 1944, become jargon or, if you prefer, a virtually official order. P.B.: a joc. var. since *c.* 1950, if not earlier, among Servicemen has been *hold your water!*

holding the line with a man and a boy. 'The silence and inertia in the German trenches were a puzzle, and the old remark about "holding the line with a man and a boy" was passed round among us' (Edmund Blunden. *Undertones of War*, 1928): among British soldiers during WW1; applied to any thinly held line or trench and prob. going back to *c.* 1895.

hole. See: don't look down; foxes; he'd fuck anything; I need that; I've got a bit; if you know; put the wood; she would sell.

[**holiday at Peckham** (or, derivatively, **holiday with him**) – **it is all**. It is all over with him: late C18–early C20. There is a pun on *peck*, food, and *peckish*, hungary. Perhaps, rather, a proverbial saying.]

Holland. See: Dutch.

holocaust. See: unrelieved.

holocausts and holy causes neatly encapsulates 'Man's history' (Petch, 1978): since the latish 1940s.

holy. See: more holy.

[**holy moley!** See **Shazam!** Ineligible because merely a mild oath: by assimilation, to *holy*, *Moses* has become *Moley* or *moley*; or perhaps *holy Mary* has become so assimilated. But this is to exambulate into the illimitable vastitude of approximate and penumbral conjecture. Or, to adopt the Grecian mode, '...polysyllabic hypothesis'. P.B.: E.P. may have had a classical education, but he was unaware, apparently, that the orig. 'Captain Marvel' and 'Batman' oaths, *holy* (something harmless), were in turn spoofed in later C20 by whatever seemed relevant to the situation: Nigel Rees, in *VIBS*, instances *holy flypaper!, holy cow!, holy felony!, holy geography!, holy schizophrenia!, holy haberdashery!*, etc., and adds, 'The prefix 'holy' to any exclamation was particularly the province of Batman and [his boy

127

assistant] Robin, characters created by Bob Kane and featured in best-selling comic books for over thirty years before they were portrayed by Adam West and Burt Ward in the TV film series.']

holy water. See: when hens.

home. See: are there more; B.E.F.; captain is at; come home; every home; father dear; fucked and; go and find; go home; going home; has all; Jack's come; leaves his fiddle; let's go h.; man wasn't; nothing to cable; papa's; time, gentlemen; what is that; why curls; why girls; won't you; you'd be far.

home and dried on the pig's back. Cf **home on the pig's back** than which it is perhaps commoner, certainly more widely distributed. This longer form occurs, in Australia, in, e.g. Vance Palmer, *The Passage*, 1930. The predominantly UK and Anglo-Irish elab. is *home and dried with the blanket on*, which 'stems from horse-racing, but [it] is used for any mission accomplished' (Skehan, 1977).

But note that Australians use *home and dried* (the commonest) or the punning *home and fried* (the earliest recorded in print) or *home and hosed* or *home with a rug on* (the least common). *Home and dried* was adopted by Australian soldiers from the British soldiers during WW1. See esp. Wilkes, *Dict. Aus. Coll.*

home, James, and don't spare the horses! dates from *c.* 1870 – if not earlier; orig. addressed, esp. by a man about town, a clubman, to his private coachman, and then, when the motor car gained the ascendancy, to his chauffeur. Until *c.* 1925, the full wording was gen.; after that date – and increasingly – it has often been shortened to *home, James!*; since *c.* 1945, often spoken to a friend giving one a lift home by car.

Always good-tempered and humorous, this c.p. has become so thoroughly and intimately incorporated into the language that it can be employed as allusively, and even subtly, as this: '"Yes, sir; no, sir; three bags full, sir." Which just about summed it up. Bags full, and home, John. And don't spare Alitalia' (Manning O'Brine's espionage 'thriller', *Mills*, 1969, chapter 39). On the other hand, Catherine Aird's police 'thriller' of the same year, *The Complete Steel,* has this passage:

Detective Constable Crosby turned the police car....

'Home James, and don't spare the horses,' commanded Sloan, climbing in.

'Beg pardon, sir?'

Sloan sighed. 'Headquarters, Crosby, please.'

But then, the constable *was* a rather dull fellow.

Adopted in US. but no one seems to know, even roughly, when. My old friend (much younger than I), John W. Clark, writes, 1975, 'Less common than it once was'; he also notes that, in US, the two members of the phrase – that is, *home James*, and *don't spare the horses* – have long become discrete and that the former is 'even more hackneyed than' the latter.

'This was the title of a popular song *c.* 1934, which I remember hearing on the radio frequently and was particularly associated with Ambrose and his orchestra, and was sung by Elsie Carlisle. From that time on I remember hearing and using this catch phrase frequently, but not before, so probably that song gave the c.p. a popular boost' (Eric Townley, 1978).

home on the pig's back is used either adjectively or adverbially: 'very successful!' – 'easily and thoroughly': mostly in NZ and Aus.; since *c.* 1910; perhaps prompted by such idiomatic phrase as *to save one's bacon* and *bring home the bacon*. But see **home and dried**.

home was never like this! expresses deep satisfaction and content at pleasure and comfort experienced in a home other than one's own. I never heard it before WW2, when, indeed, it may well have arisen.

It can, however, be – and often is – 'employed when one finds oneself in a very difficult or dangerous situation, ranging from filthy lodgings to a battle' (Skehan, 1977) – with which cf **how different...**, q.v. but it orig. in the US: John

H. Flynn's vaudeville song *Yip-I-Addy-I-ay*, 1908, 'about a girl (Sally from Spring Valley) who went to New York, fell in love with a 'cellist and never returned to the rural scene. The last four lines of the thrice-repeated chorus went like this:

My heart wants to holler "hurray!"

Song of joy, song of bliss.

Home was never like this.

Yip-I-Addy-I-Ay!

In this context, the contrast is perhaps rather between home-town dullness and big-city excitement' (Richard Wilbur, Cummington, Mass., 1978).

honest, I never done it. 'The supposed plea of a villain when taken into the nick, is commonly used to express innocence' (anon., 1978): prob. first among the police and then much more widely. P.B.: the *honest* may be transferred to the end, as in, e.g., 'I never touched it, honest!' Neither is really a c.p.

honest Injun (occ. **Indian**)! 'Honour bright!', you can take my word for it: orig., early 1880s, US; in Brit. use by *c.* 1895, mostly owing to the popularity of Mark Twain's books; ob. by mid C20. Cf **scout's honour.**

honest. See: as I am h.

honey. See: all honey; it ain't all.

honky-tonks. See: hello, honky.

honour. See: scout's.

hook. See: get the hook; three on; with a hook.

Hooky Walker! – often shortened to **Hooky!** or to **Walker!** This phrase signifies either that something is not true or that it will not occur: C19–20, but little heard since WW2. (*LB* – in effect, the 4th edn of Grose).

Also, 'Be off!': since *c.* 1830. Soon *Walker!*, as in Dickens's *Christmas Carol*, 1843:

'Buy it,' said Scrooge.

'Walker!' said the boy.

According to JB, the phrase orig. in one John Walker, a prevaricating, hook-nosed spy – which is perhaps true, but is probably a felicitous piece of folk-etymology – an elab. of *Walker!*, Walk off, Oh, run away.

As so often with c.pp. of the 1820s and 1830s, the *locus classicus* occurs in Mackay:

Hookey Walker, derived from the chorus of a popular ballad, was also [like *what a shocking bad hat!*] high in favour at one time, and served, like its predecessor *Quoz*, to answer all questions. In the course of time the latter word [i.e. (*Hooky*) *Walker!*] alone became the favourite, and was uttered with a peculiar drawl upon the first syllable, a sharp turn upon the last. If a lively servant girl was importuned for a kiss by a fellow she did not care about, she cocked her little nose, and cried '*Walker!*' If a dustman asked his friend for the loan of a shilling, and his friend was either unable or unwilling to accommodate him, the probable answer he would receive was '*Walker!*' If a drunken man was reeling about the streets, and a boy pulled his coat-tails, or a man knocked his hat over his eyes to make fun of him, the joke was always accompanied by the same exclamation. This lasted for two or three months, and '*Walker!*' walked off the stage, never more to be revived. This may have been partly, yet certainly was far from being wholly, true. It recurred both in Dickens, as above, and in the Surtees novel *Hillingdon Hall*, 1845, chapter XXXVIII:

'Mrs Flather won't hear of it unless they are agreeable.'

'Ookey Walker!' grunted Mr Jorrocks [a true Cockney].

A C20 var., ob. by 1950, was *that's a Walker!*, that's untrue. P.B.: the phrase lingered also, until mid-C20,' in the 'inevitable' nickname *Hooky* given to any Serviceman surnamed Walker.

hoot him! This derisively contemptuous Aus. Juvenile c.p. of *c.* 1910–40 means either 'Look at him!' or 'Hark at him!' according to the circumstances. It occurs frequently in Norman Lindsay's novel about boys, *Saturdee*, 1933.

hop along, Sister Mary, hop along! 'When the yobbos ogled the girls in the local "monkey run" [at York. *c.* 1919] and the girls passed by, the yobs used to sing, or call, after them, "Hop along, Sister Mary, hop along". I do not know the origin'

Noble, 1977 explains: 'It was contained in, or arose from, an extremely popular music-hall song, "Sister Mary Walked Like That" – written by Gus Levaine and sung by John Nash. It was uproariously encored whenever Nash sang it, in late Victorian times, because he made it into a "performance", imitating, with exaggeration, the mincing gait of a young girl. It was published as sheet music and had a vogue as a comic song right into Edwardian times'.

hop and hang all summer on the white spruce is a Can. lumbermen's c.p. and prob. dates since late C19. It occurs in e.g., the novels of John Beames.

hope(s). See: 'fuck me!'; I hope; parson would; some hopes; what a h.; while there's life.

hope I don't intrude or **I'm not interrupting...** See I hope...

hope (or I hope) it keeps fine for you. A military c.p., often ironic or derisive, of WW1, than which it was also both a little earlier and later. (Ernest Raymond, *The Jesting Army*, 1930.) It was, orig. a parting phrase; but it is often a passing comment upon a project – e.g., an important journey – mentioned by the second party. Granville, 1969, pointed out to me that sometimes it is 'directed against one who is seen to take risks, whether in drink or in any other hazardous indulgence. "I think I'll have another gin." "O.K., but I hope it keeps fine for you!"'

A fairly frequent var. is *hope you have a fine day for it*. This c.p., in its predominant form, has become so imbedded in coll. usage that it can be employed allusively, as in Adam Hall, *The Tango Briefing*, 1973: 'Of course he'd go straight into signals with London and ten minutes from now they'd have an emergency meeting at the Bureau and I hoped it'd keep fine for them.'

hope to be saved. See **as I hope to...**

hope to die. See **cross heart...**

hope (or I hope) your rabbit dies! A joc. imprecation current, throughout C20. It occurs in, e.g., Dorothy L. Sayers's 'thriller', *Have His Carcase*, 1932. It orig. as a curse, 'I hope you lose virility!' – cf the eroticism of **pop goes the weasel!** Well, that's one theory; my own is that it orig. as one child's threat to another.

'As a malediction, Australians use *I hope your fowls* (or *chooks) die!*, and I've heard an extreme variant, *I hope your chooks turn to emus and kick your dunny down!*' (Lovett, 1978): since *c.* 1950. Wilkes cites this as *may your chooks* [chickens]... A *dunny* = an outdoor privy. Contrast **may your rabbits flourish!**

hope you've got! – what a (also **some hope!** (or **hopes!**) and **what a hope!** (or **what hopes!**) All these forms bear only one meaning: that of a discouraging c.p. reply, or remark, to one who is confident of obtaining some privilege or other. Current throughout C20 (and prob. from *c.* 1890) in the lower reaches of Society but esp. widespread during WW1 and WW2, notably among the soldiery in the former and in all three Services in the latter. Cf the later C20 even more pessimistic *no chance!*

Hopkins. See: don't hurry.

hopping. See: I'll go h.

hopping around like a gin at a christening. This Aus. c.p., dating since early C20, did not become gen. until *c.* 1930. Used by an Australian in the *Radio Times*, 9 Feb. 1967, as Petch noticed. A *gin* is a female Aboriginal. Clearly prompted by the C18–20 UK (*as*) *demure as a whore at a christening*. Gen. sense: 'ill at ease; embarrassed'. It has Aus. variants, *moll* and *streetgirl* (Wilkes, *Dict. Aus. Coll.*).

Horace. See: stop it, H.; what did H.

horn. See: been around; born with the h.; ought to be.

horse(s). See: could eat; cut the cackle; damn a horse; get a horse; God have; good a scholar; hay is for; he's a whole; his horse's; hold your; home, James; hunting; I work; I'm so hungry; I've got an 'orse; it ain't the 'untin'; keystone; King's

horse; riding his; that must; then I; there's an 'oss; they that ride; yes, but who; you will die; and:

horse, a horse, my kingdom for a horse! – a. In *The Life and Times of Shakespeare*, 1968, by Maria Pia Rosignolo, occurs this statement: 'Richard III's cry of "A horse, a horse, my kingdom for a horse" immediately became a popular expression' – that is, a c.p. – still current today, esp. among actors and even, one hears, among disappointed punters at the race-courses. The phrase is in *King Richard III*, at V, iv, 7.

horse-back. See: who put.

horse-collar. See: cunt.

horse-doctor's clerk. Var. of *pox-doctor's clerk* in **all dressed up like...**

horse-load. See: fallen away.

Horse-Marines. See: tell that to the H.

horse of another (or **a different) colour** (US **color) – a.** Usu. prec. by (*but) that's*. That's quite another matter: orig. (1790s) US; anglicized *c.* 1840 by Barham's *Ingoldsby Legends*. Very prob. suggested by Shakespeare's 'My purpose is indeed a horse of that colour' (*Twelfth Night*, II,iii, 181). The phrase is sometimes intensified by the addition of *quite* or *very*. OED and Supp.

horse-shit. See: happy horse; try some; what a load.

horse-shoes. See: close counts.

horses for courses orig., not unnaturally, in horse-racing circles perhaps as early as 1860, and then, *c.* 1890, became an upper-middle-class and upper-class c.p., applied to suitable marriages as opposed to *mésalliances*, but since *c.* 1945 applied mostly – and throughout a wider social range – to the potentialities of all kinds of competitions, and by later C20 even simply to what is appropriate in given circumstances. By a rudimentary process of rhyming.

horse's head is swollen so big.... See **his horse's head....**

horses sweat, men perspire, (and) ladies only glow is directed, in mild and often humorous reproof, at a man saying that he sweats and esp. at a man saying that a woman does: C20; by 1960, slightly ob.; since that date, many women have preferred to *sweat*. P.B.: this form has been the basis of many puns and variants; I have heard it used ironically of privates, NCOs, and officcers. See also **midshipmen have guts...**

horses that are all dressed up but (have) nowhere to go and **horses who,** or **which, flatter only to deceive** are common among the sporting, esp. the racing, crowd, including the commentators; applied to horses that look fitter and more handsome than their performance will show them to be: since *c.* 1950(?). Both were mentioned in the BBC Radio 4 programme 'Stop the Week', 11 Oct. 1977. (With the BBC's kind permission.) P.B.: both are, of course, common phrases here given special application, and the latter is, perhaps, an echo of Emerson's observation, 1844: 'We love flattery, even though we are not deceived by it, because it shows that we are of importance enough to be courted'.

hose. See: they hosed.

hostile. See: natives were.

hot. See: calves'; catsails; dice; don't get your arse; I've had more; it came; some like; steal; that's a bit h.; worried.

hot and strong – I like my (or **he likes his) women.** This Aus. c.p., dating from *c.* 1945. derives from 'I like my coffee – and my women – hot and strong' or some var. thereof and has prob. been influenced by the prescription 'Coffee should be as *hot* as hell, as *sweet* as love and as *black* as night.' Cf **hot, sweet...**

hot as a dimestore pistol – he's or **she's.** 'Lucky, as in a poker game, or (sometimes temporarily) extremely proficient at something' (J.W.C., 1977): US: *c.* 1920–40. R.C., 1978, offers the var. *hot as*, or *hotter than, a two-dollar pistol*: 'A cheap pistol that heats up rapidly when fired'.

hot as a female fox. See **worried as a pregnant fox...**

hot dinners – have had more (anything) than... See **I've had more women...**

hotel. See:there goes his.

hotter than... See the **hot as...** phrases.

[**hot, sweet and filthy** was, among prisoners of war in the Far East, 1943–5, a canteen name – not a c.p. – for, an allusion to coffee.]

hot time in the old town tonight – a, often – indeed predominantly – prec. by **there'll be.** The shorter form, the earlier version, formed the title of an American song, words by Metz and music by Hayden, published in 1896. 'This was the song sung in Cuba during the Spanish American War [1898] and has become a part of our language. Popular with college students after a football victory' (W.J.B., 1975.) Current also in and the Commonwealth since early in C20. Less heard since WW2.

hour. See: I like your company .

hóur past hanging time. See **half an hour past...**

house. See: better an empty; don't clap; farther down; is there a doctor; make yourself at; not a dry; ours is a nice; take yer 'at; well, I'll go; and:

house broke up is a military (Other Rank's) c.p., indicating utter despair: *c.* 1870–1940. Ware.

house devil, sheet angel describes a man authoritative and aggressive in the home but meek and unobtrusive outside it: C20. (Daniel Farson, 1977.)

[**housey housey!** The traditional cry that summons players of House: mostly military: C20. On the borderline of c.p., yet never quite achieving that status.]

how. See: here's how.

how about a repeat performance? See *how did it go?*

how about that, with emphasis on '*bout*, is a US c.p. that, dating from the 1930s, became, early in the 1960s, very gen. indeed. 'Not a question, but an expression of surprise at what one has [just] heard' (Shipley, 1975). Noted by Prof S.I. Hayakawa in an American newspaper article, 'Language Changes. Slang is Imaginative, Picturesque', appearing late in 1973. Equivalent to **what do you know?** and adopted in UK in the late 1950s, often with the addition of *then*, and since *c.* 1960, in the var. *how's about that, then* (to which Jimmy Savile, OBE, adds also 'guys and gals').

See the following in Mickey Spillane, *The Erection Set*, 1972:

'There were incidents in New York, there were incidents here.... All checked with the police,' Lagen said. 'The handiwork of an expert?'
'How about that?'

how am I doin'? What do you think of that?: US: since *c.* 1935. (Berrey) Ashley, of its later C20 usage, notes, 1983, 'c.p. at least in New York City where Mayor Edward Koch has often used the expression (there's more boasting than insincerity in it)'.

how are the bots biting? How are you?: a NZ medical c.p., since *c.* 1929; by 1970, rather outmoded. Here, *bots* is short for *bot flies*, which afflict horses.

how are the troops treating you? is an Aus. (not, one suspects, entirely respectable, nor obsessively virtuous) women's c.p. of 1939–45, then merely allusive, finally historical.

how are they coming? addressed to a man, 'One of the peculiar ways of asking how you are doing or how are you getting along' (Sandilands, 1913): Western Can.: late C19 – mid-20. Here, 'they' ranges from jobs to opportunities. Perhaps orig. from angling. P.B.: or from horses? Cf *are you winning?* used in the same way.

how are they hanging?, with *are* often omitted. Also *how's your hammer hanging?* How's your sex life?' Both are US, the former ref. the testicles, the latter to the penis; both are low, the latter is proletarian; the former is ob., the latter long †. They date from the 1920s. (R.C., 1977) P.B.: cf the Brit. joc. *how's your old parts?*, i.e. private parts, in brief use in the Army, early 1960s.

how are we? A joc. c.p. greeting: C20. May be followed by *then*, or *today*. Often part of a doctor's or a parson's repertoire.

how are you fixed for blades? 'King C. Gillette founded the [Gillette] company in Boston, Mass., in 1901. He [had] designed the first "safety razor" in the summer of 1895'. A.B. thus implies that *how...blades* was current as a US c.p. for a while:? *c.* 1905–15.

how are you going? An Aus. c.p. of greeting; since *c.* 1920. How are you faring? How *are you? (B.P.)* Cf '**ow you going, mate?** and **how's it goin'?**

how are you off for soap? was, *c.* 1830–1920, an urban c.p. It means no more than 'How are you doing?' – 'How are you?' and occurs in Frederick Marryat, *Peter Simple*, 1834, 'Well, Reefer, how are you off for soap?' (*OED.*) The late Frank Shaw, 1969, cites the *Comic Calendar* of 1841: 'If it has any meaning, [that meaning would be] "If you're not well off, off!"' If you're not rich, run away!

how are you popping (up)? or **how yer poppin'?** How are you?: Aus.: *c.* 1885–1955. It occurs in Henry Lawson, 1894, and in Norman Lindsay, 1933, and in Sarah Campion, 1942. Recorded by Wilkes, with his customary excellent documentation.

how can you? is elliptical for 'How can you be so foolish *or* stupid?' or 'How can you behave so?', or esp. 'How *can* you bear to make such a feeble pun or joke?': since at least as early as *c.* 1910. P.B.: but hardly a c.p. Rather a mere specialised use of idiom, for tense and pronoun can both change, and implications can differ: e.g. 'How *could* they [have been so insensitive]?'; 'How *could* she [contemplate marrying such a man]?'; etc.

how can you just be so? was an ephemeral (*c.* 1919–22) US university students' var. of **how did you get that way?** McKnight.

how daft can we (or **they**) **get?** 'Used in reference to the way we – or they – allow ourselves to be humbugged by advertisers and politicians' (Petch, 1974): since *c.* 1950. 'Commoner than either is *how daft can you* (i.e., one) *get?*; its usage is far more widely spread, and it goes back to *c.* 1930: a general comment in all sorts of contexts' (Wedgwood, 1977). Cf **daft, I call it!** P.B.: but see E.P.'s dismissal of **how stupid...**

how did it go? or **how's it go again?** or **how about a repeat performance?** 'Uttered when anyone makes an odd noise, e.g. chokes over his soup [or] gives a strangled shriek of pain or surprise: an onlooker/listener may facetiously say, "That was good! *how* did it go?"' (P.B., 1976). I don't remember hearing it before 1955. Cf **can you do anything...**

how did (occ. **how do**) **you get that way?** How did you come to get into that condition? – whatever the condition implied: US: from before 1922; anglicized by 1930. (*OED* Supp.)

It was recorded in HLM, and in the definitive edn of 1936, on p. 566, occurs a valuable footnote; McKnight mentions it in 1923, and, in the same year, Robert Benchley uses it in *Love Conquers All*; Berrey includes it in a group of expressions glossed as 'Don't be ridiculous!'

Cf **don't be that way!** (its origin?) and **oh, is that so?** Its popularity and its longevity probably result from its forcible and apposite sense and wording.

how *did* you guess? See **you have hit it.**

how different, how very different, is the home life of our own dear Queen? 'The *ODQ* tells how, at the end of Sarah Bernhardt's impassioned, almost hysterical, rendering of Cleopatra's reaction to the news of Mark Anthony's defeat at Actium, "a middle-aged British matron was heard to say to her neighbour: 'How different, how very different is the home life of our own dear Queen!' (Victoria.)' It has been a potential c.p. since the very early 1880s, when the great actress toured Britain; at first jocular; later, half-serious, especially after the Watergate and Lockheed scandals [earlier 1970s]' (Sanders, 1978). P.B.: it prob. now qualifies, early 1980s, since I have heard misquoted variants, e.g. *so unlike the home life* and *how unlike the home life...* Cf **home was never like this!**

how do we go? What chance is there 'of obtaining something unspecified yet known to the person questioned'? (B & P):

an army c.p. of 1915–18, then rather more gen.; ob. by 1937 and † by 1940. Prob. elliptical for 'How do we go about getting it?'

how do you do, Mister Brown? In his enchanting book, *A Time of Gifts*, 1977, Patrick Leigh-Fermor, walking through Germany, mentioned a young girl who, in Jan. 1934, 'daringly said [to him] "How do you do, Mister Brown?" (This was the only line of an idiotic and now mercifully forgotten song, repeated *ad infinitum*; it had swept the world two years before [i.e., *c.* 1932–33].) The line of the song was almost the only English they knew [the other girl being the daring one's friend].'

how do you get that way? See **how did you...?**

how do you like them apples? What do you think of *that*? – equivalent to **how am I doin'?**:since (early?) 1930s. (Berrey.) In *The American Dream*, prod. and pub'd in 1961, Edward Albee writes:

GRANDMA: They wanted satisfaction; they wanted their money back. That's what they wanted.

MRS BARKER: My, my, my.

GRANDMA: How do you like *them* apples?

MRS BARKER: My, my, my.

R.C., 1977, adds, 'Usually said with a certain air of defiance, implying that the apples in question may not be very tasty to the person addressed'.

how do you like your eggs cooked or **done?** An Aus. c.p., dating from *c.* 1908, very common among the soldiery of 1914–18, and not yet †, it is usu. a malicious comment upon another's misfortune. By 1915, a c.p. reply had been evolved: **scrambled, like your brains, you** (or **yer**) **bastard!**

This may have been prompted by the prob. mid-C19–20 half-sung 'How do like your murphies done? Boil 'em with their jackets on!' – where 'murphies' is slang for potatoes, (B.G.T., 1978, in ref. to her grandfather.)

how do you sell your string? Do you take me for a fool? I see through your planned swindle, hoax, etc.: underworld c.p.: C19. It occurs in H.D. Miles, *Dick Turpin*, 1841. Prob. suggested by the underworld *get* (someone) *into a line*, to set him up for a swindle or to engage his attention while a robbery is being effected nearby.

how do you work? is another underworld c.p.: How do you make a living now?: *c.* 1770–1840. (George Parker, *Life's Painter*, 1789.) Cf the modern police sense of *modus operandi* or manner of committing a crime.

how does that grab you? What do you think of that? Does that interest, or very much interest, you? Does that excite you?: it occurs in *Playboy*, Sep. 1967 (p. 210); in *The New Yorker*, 21 Feb, 1970, cited by Barnhart, 1973, but earlier dictionaried by *DCCU*, 1971, and had been popularized by Nancy Sinatra in her song, 'How Does That Grab You, Darling?', released in late 1966 or early 1967. (Owed entirely to Paul Janssen, 1977.) It quickly spread from US to UK, to Can., and to Aus., where it prompted the var. *how does that affect you*? (Mrs Camilla Raab). P.B.: the *you* is usu. pron. *ya* or *yer*, and the phrase was ob. by 1980. One of its difficulties, at least in UK, was that it never produced a really satisfactory response, but merely the rather tame *it grabs me very nicely* or *well*, or *it doesn't grab me at all*. But see also **that grabs me...**

how does your body politic? In S. Dialogue I, Lord Sparkish says to the maid, 'Mrs *Betty*, how does your Body politick?' – which prompts the gallant Colonel to remonstrate, '*Fye*, my Lord, you'll make Mrs *Betty* blush.' Apparently this was a rude c.p. of *c.* 1700–60, prob. with a pun on a now long †sense of *body*: belly. Perhaps cf the C20 c.p., **how's your belly off for spots?**

how fares your old trunk? is a jeer at a large-nosed man: *c.* 1680–1850. (BE; Grose.) The ref. is to an elephant's trunk.

how goes the battle? is a Can. greeting, usu. joc.: since *c.* 1945. (Donald J. Barr, 1976, who adds, 'I found an example in R.E. Knowles, *Undertow*, 1976.) but see also **how's battle?**

how goes (or **What says**) **the enemy?** What's the time?: this orig.

as a quot'n, from Frederick Reynolds, *The Dramatist*, prod. 1789, pub'd 1793. In Act I, 'Ennui the Timekiller – whose business in life is to murder the hour' soliloquizes thus:

I've an idea I don't like the Lady Waitfor't – she wishes to trick me out of my match with Miss Courtney, and if I could trick her in return – (*takes out his watch*). How goes the enemy – only one o'clock! I thought it had been that an hour ago.

When he finds that it is, in fact, past two o'clock Lord Scratch asks, 'And you're delighted because it's an hour', and he replies, 'To be sure I am – my dear friend to be sure I am, the enemy has lost a limb.' In III he again asks, 'How goes the enemy? more than half the day over! – tol de roll lol! [*humming a tune*] – I'm as happy as if I was at a fire, or a general riot.'

It almost immediately became a – usu. somewhat facetious – c.p. and it has remained one, although it hasn't been much employed since 1939. I used to hear it occ. from my father (1863–1952), from childhood into early manhood: and I suspect that he no more thought of it as being a c.p. than, at the age of (say) six, I did: which rather tends to show how a quot'n held worthy of record by Benham, Stevenson, the *ODQ*, can also have become engrained in the very texture of coll. English.

how high is a Chinaman? A reply to, or a comment in kind, to a question either stupid or unanswerable: 'attributed to the late Will Hay, music-hall star; with a pun on *How Hi*, fancy name for a Chinaman' (Oliver Stonor, 1976). Prob. since *c.* 1930. Will Hay excelled in schoolroom 'sketches', and, adds P.B., this is a schoolboys' 'catch' par excellence. Perhaps suggested by the equally unanswerable *how long is a piece of string*? Cf:

how high is up? A retort to an unanswerable question: US: since *c.* 1920. (Edward Hodnett, 1975.) Cf **how old is Ann(e)?** and **which would you rather – or go fishing?** and **why is a mouse when it spins?**

how is... See **how's...**

how is (or **how's**) **that for high?** 'An enquiry often made a few years ago on all occasions, but now out of date. Meaning, it has none' (M): US. But a few pages later, Maitland glosses the c.p. thus, 'An enquiry often made nowadays in regard to practically any happening': so perhaps we had better assign it to the very approx. period 1876–95; its Brit. currency to *c.* 1885–1900. Of its Brit. usage, Derek Roberts commented, 1972, 'Calling attention to audacity or outrageous cheek'; he implies that it achieved popularity among cyclists – cycling was, *c.* 1895–99, 'all the rage' in Society.

Two years earlier than Maitland, Farmer, in 1889, had dealt with it rather more spaciously:

A modern slang expression, which has to a large extent taken the place of *bully* [excellent]...borrowed from a low game, known as Old Sledge, where the high depends, not on the card itself, but on the adversary's hand. Hence, the phrase means, 'What kind of attempt is that at a great achievement?' It is of Western origin, having made its appearance in some of the Northwestern journals, but has spread, as words do, rapidly all over the Union [Schele de Vere, 1871] and has found its way to England also. A familiar nursery-rhyme has been altered to 'suit the times':

Mary had a little lamb.

It jumped up to the sky,

And when it landed on its feet,

Cried, '*How is that for high?*'

It appears also in Bartlett, 4th edn, 1877, and is there glossed, 'What do you think of it?'

how lies the land? and **who has any land(s) in Appleby?** Grose, 1785, has this entry: LAND, as, how lies the land, how stands the reckoning; who has any land in Appleby, a question asked the man at whose door the glass stands long, or who does not circulate it in due time' – an amplification of the entry in BE '"Who has any lands in Appleby?" a question askt the man at whose door the glass stands long.' Current *c.*

1670–1830. The English place-name *Appleby*, the county town of Westmorland, may orig. have referred to cider (made from *apples*) – by a pun, for that country is not particularly noted for its fruit.

how long have you been in this regiment, chum? How long have *you* been in the Navy?: RN lower-deck: C20. (Granville.)

how long is a piece of string (when it's wet)? (and sometimes with *and if so, why?* added). A trick question to which there is no possible answer: since *c.* 1920 or even earlier. It evokes several ripostes. Cf **how high is up?** and **long as a piece…**

[**how many beans make five?** securely occupies an indeterminate point on the no-man's-land between 'catch' question and c.p. I first heard it as a schoolboy (say 1900–10), but it prob. goes back to the ludicrously – and unashamedly – palmiest days of Victorian wit and humour, approx. 1870–95. The answer, supplied by Mrs C. Raab is, all in one breath: *two-beans-two-half-beans-one-and-a-half-beans-and-half-a-bean.* Barlthop and Wolveridge, however, in *The Muvver Tongue*, provide the much more practical *six if you're a buyer, four if you're a seller.*]

how many times? 'I heard this on and off during the First World War. When a Tommy had got married while on leave, his chums would generally pull his leg and ask "How many times?" when he got back. They meant how many times had he made love to his bride on the first night' (Petch): 1914–18.

'This goes back [in the US] at least to the 1890s… Obviously the question must be common to the entire English-speaking world and therefore not a c.p. at all' (Shipley, who attributes its popularity in the US to Chauncey Mitchell Depew (1834–1928), a famous lawyer, senator, wit).

how much? What did you say? What do you mean?: since *c.* 1845; slightly ob. by 1914, but not yet †. In 1852, F. Smedley employed it thus:

Then my answer must…depend on the…'

'On the how much?' inquired Frere, considerably mystified.

how much to get out? 'A facetious remark to one taking the entry fee at the door for a jumble sale or a charity function' (Petch, 1974): since *c.* 1930.

how nice and what a lot! This facetious c.p., dating since *c.* 1930 but ob. by *c.* 1960, expresses a profound gratification. Applied to, e.g., a very generous helping of cream.

how old is Ann(e)? is a US c.p. that had a vogue in (?) late C19 – early C20 and nostalgically lingers on, as Col. tells me, 1975. A trick, almost meaningless question; poss. prompted by '*anno* domini' in its coll. sense '(old) age'. J.W.C., 1975, writes:

I have heard it all my life (though *very* rarely since [the early 1920s]. It is – or rather was – a mocking sequel to some utterly unanswerable question, or at least a question abstruse or unintelligible to the user of the phrase, e.g. 'Do you suppose it will be raining like this a year from today?' (unanswerable by anybody) and 'Are Bolyai's and Lobachevski's geometries both hyperbolic, or is one of them elliptic or spherical like Riesmann's?' (hopelessly beyond the scope of the user of the phrase). It is (was) *always* a sequel to someone else's question – never an introductory utterance. It commonly had an undertone of derision (of a silly question) or inverted snobbery (of an abstruse one).

And Shipley, 1976, adds, 'William McKinley, successful candidate for the Presidency, said in his 1896 election campaign, that his opponent William Jennings's free-silver policy was "a perfect enigma like Anne's age".' The c.p. orig. as a specific conundrum, but cf **how high is up?** and its cross-refs.

how right you are!, late C19–20, almost certainly occasioned **I couldn't agree with you more**, which, in its turn, prompted **I couldn't care less.**

how strong are you? How are you off for money?: US tramps': C20. In *The Milk and Honey Route*, 1931, 'Dean Stiff'

remarks, 'If you have a *pile* you answer, "So strong, I stink."'

[**how stupid can you get?** is merely one of a number of such questions, e.g. *how mean can you get? how low…? or how 'square'…?* But R.C., 1977, comments, ref. *how stupid* or *silly…*, 'The person under discussion is near the absolute limit of human stupidity, (*You* = impersonal 'one'): US, from at least 1950s [I'd say 1940s]; still current.' Cf **how daft can we get?**]

[**how sweet it is!** – however enthusiastically proposed by a couple of correspondents – does not qualify as a true c.p., for, however well known it was (and it was, for perhaps a decade, very well known), it was always closely associated with Jackie Gleason 'as his opening line and trademark in every TV show of his': it was an allusion, I should now say the same thing about **hey, Abbott.** (Note made 1978, with a heavy debt to J.W.C.)

Maurice Dolbier wrote to me, 1978, thus: '[It] is an affirmation of life, often in reference to the beauties of the dancing girls around him [Jackie Gleason]: this and **and away we go!** [q.v.] gained wide currency with his first comedy series in the early 1950s.

Moreover, 'There's unanimous agreement among those I've consulted that Jackie Gleason's *how sweet it is!* does not qualify as a c.p. It's an exclamation *he* used (up to some five years ago), but it does not seem to have caught on for general use' (Shipley, 1978).

For the general issue raised – that of eligibility – compare Vernon Noble's animadversions in my MODIFICATIONS OF THE ORIGINAL INTRODUCTION at the beginning of this book.]

[**how the other half lives** is not a c.p. but, by its very nature, a cliché – and it is not, as a c.p. must be, autonomous.]

how to do it and not get it – occ. with the addition,

by one who did it and got it. An Aus. c.p. that, dating since *c.* 1950, refers to books that purport to be guides to marriage. 'Those who can, do; those who can't, talk about it.'

how to win (loosely, **make**) **friends and influence people**, orig. a business *quasi*-slogan, had, by *c.* 1935, at latest, in US and by *c.* 1945 in UK, become a c.p. – often ironic and derisive. It has, since *c.* 1960, been so incorporated into both US and Brit. English that it can be employed allusively and flexibly, as in Alistair MacLean's novel, *Ice Station Zebra*, 1963 (at p. 189):

'In this line of business I never tell anyone anything unless I think he can help me by having that knowledge.'

'You must win an awful lot of friends and influence an awful lot of people.' Swanson said dryly.

'It gets embarrassing.'

Cf also Desmond Bagley, *Landslide*, 1967, a novel with a Canadian 'hero' and setting:

He was another of those cracker-barrel characters who think they've got the franchise on wisecracks – small towns are full of them. I was in no mood for making friends, although I would have to try to influence people pretty soon.

Then, in 1970, we find Val Gielgud, in his adult 'thriller', *The Candle-Holders*, presenting us with a hypothetical play and a witty title, thus: 'When I told her that a play called, *How to Make Beds and Influence People* was bound to fail…'

It became established by the book, so titled, written by Dale Carnegie (1885–1955) and pub'd in 1936, but the c.p. had arisen two or three years earlier: Dale Carnegie had, after all – for many years before 1936 – run a school for public speaking, toast-making, personal relationships in business. (With thanks to W.J.B.)

how too too! See **too too.**

how we apples swim! How we enjoy ourselves – what a good time we have!: C16–20, but ob. by 1920, and by 1970 virtually †. Often enlarged by **quoth the horse-turd,** which occurs in Ray, 1670; the longer form is prob. the orig., for it shows that there is a precise application to a *parvenu*, a pretender, a person socially out of his depth. In his *Works*, vol. III, William Hogarth writes, 'He assumes a consequential air ... and strutting among the historical artists cries, how we apples swim.' As horse-turds floating down a stream pretend to be apples, so ...: cf that other proverbial c.p. of *c.* 1650–1800: **'a bumble-bee in a cow-turd thinks himself a king'** (likewise listed by the admirable Apperson). Apperson cites such other authorities as Clark, 1639, and Edward Fitz-Gerald, 1852.

[**how will** or (**how'll**) **you have it?**, an invitation to drink, lies between cliché and c.p.: and is, I believe, the former rather than the latter.]

how would ... See **how'd ...**

how would you be? is an Aus. c.p. form of the greeting 'How do you do?' and differs from it by requiring an answer: since early 1950s. Its secondary sense is synon. with **how's your dirty rotten form?** (B.P., 1975). P.B.: often pron. *'ow'd yer be?* Cf **how you going, mate?**

how ya hangin'? Loose, I hope. 'Very common in the US underground: *c.* mid-1960s–early 1970s' (Paul Janssen, 1977). Here *loose*–'relaxed'. Cf **hang loose!**

how yer poppin'? See **how are you popping?**

[**how you doing?** is a coll. US greeting and obviously elliptical for *how are you doing?* No less obviously, however, it cannot justifiably be classified as a c.p. And cf the entry at **another day, another dollar!**]

[**how you going, mate?** An even more Aus. form of **how are you going?**, q.v.; a 'deeper' form yet is the phrase uttered almost as one word, *owyergoinmay – torrite?*, which presupposes that the 'mate' *is* all right. It has, since *c.* 1955, carried a dovetail or response: *very how* (Mrs C. Raab, 1977).]

how'd you like to be the ice-man? was an ephemeral US c.p. included by HLM, 1936, in a group of phrases that he has attacked for 'sheer silliness' (p. 566, footnote 1). On the subject of c.pp., Mencken tended to speak *de haut en bas* and occ. missed the point, as when he called this one silly. 'Before the days of refrigerators, the iceman was as familiar a figure of US households as the milkman still is in England; he daily delivered the blocks of ice which "fuelled" the primitive ice-chests of those days. By reputation he also assuaged the sexual needs of many a lonely or frustrated housewife – to say nothing of his own. Hence the [comparatively] short-lived c.p.' (R.S., 1977). To which I merely add that in the Eugene O'Neill (1888–1953) play, *The Iceman Cometh*, 1946, 'the pattern changes because Hickey's traditional joke about his wife and the iceman is not forthcoming'; Hickey himself is the 'Iceman of Death' (James D. Hart, *The Oxford Companion to American Literature*, 4th ed., 1965).

however hard you shake it ... See **when you dance in France ...**

how's about ... See **how about ...**

how's battle? (or, less general, **how's the battle?**) was, in 1934–6, a greeting current among the cultured. Elliptical for *the battle of life* and ref. the mid-1930s Crisis. See also **how goes the battle?**

how's biz? How is business?: Aus. since *c.* 1945. (B.P.)

how's chances? What are the opportunities – for, e.g., doing business?: US: since *c.* 1930. Berrey.

how's crops? A US, orig. and mainly Western, c.p. of greeting: C20. (Berrey.) Of entirely natural origin in agricultural areas.

how's it? How are you?: S. African: since *c.* 1920 (A.C. Partridge, 1974). Either short for 'how's it with *you*?' or short for 'how's it going?' or, less prob., influenced by Ger. *wie geht's?* how goes it?

how's it all going to end? A joc. c.p. that, current *c.* 1906–10 arose from a popular song of *c.* 1906: 'Little Winston, little friend,' with the refrain, 'How's it all going to end?'

how's it goin'? (US) (or ... **going?**) (Brit.) is an 'extremely common greeting' (J.W.C., 1968): certainly since 1920 and prob. ever since late C19. Related to **how's things?**

how's pickin's? How are you doing? – How are you? – Howdy?: US underworld: C20. In a letter to me, 1938. Godfrey Irwin wrote, 'Without any definite indication that

stealing is on'. Cf Shakespeare's Autolycus, picker-up of unconsidered trifles.

how's that? See **owsat** (or **owzat**).

how's that for high? See **how is that for high?**

how's that, umpire? What have you to say about that? How about that? What price – ?: since *c.* 1880: very English, as one would expect from its origin in cricket, but, as Lovett notes, 1978, still common in Aus.

how's the body? How do you feel? Mostly, How are you?: Anglo-Irish: late C19–20. In. e.g., Brendan Behan, *Borstal Boy*, 1958.

how's the fag trade? A polite request for a cigarette: esp. in Suffolk: since *c.* 1910. *Fag*, a cigarette.

how's the mommah? In his *Vaudeville Days*, 1953, Joe Laurie, Jr, wrote: 'Harry Cooper did a Hebe [i.e., Jewish] comic, no make-up except for an oversized derby' which he kept dipping through the act to imaginary women in the audience, saying "How's the Mommah?" which became one of the catch lines in vaude years before "Do you wanna buy a duck?" and "Wass you dare, Sharlie?"' W.J.B., 1977, adds, 'US: early – C20. It had a vogue. Today there are many references to the "Jewish Momma" or "Jewish Mama" in books and on TV'.

See also **vas you dere ...**

how's the weather up there? 'An almost obsolete hackneyed "how do you do?" (introductory, not daily) to a very tall person' (J.W.C., 1975): US: C20. Cf **is it cold ...?**

how's the world treating (or **been treating**) **you?** A very popular form of greeting, esp. to one not seen for a long time: C20.

how's things? An extremely popular c.p., current throughout C20.

how's tricks? How are things going? How are you?: a US friendly greeting: C20; by 1920, also Brit. (From card games.) Prob. from nautical *trick*, a turn at the wheel. In, e.g.: George Ade, *True Bills*, 1904; Maurice Lincoln, *I, Said the Sparrow*, 1925 (US speaker); H.M. Harwood, *So Far and No Father*, 1932; Michael Harrison, 1935; Terence Rattigan. *The Deep Blue Sea*, 1952; Jean Potts, *An Affair of the Heart*, 1970.

how's your belly (off) for spots? How are you faring? How are you?: a proletarian c.p. of *c.* 1900–25. Cf **how does your body politic?** and:

how's your belly where the pig bit you? A facetious greeting: very approx. since the 1930s. (Paul Theroux, 'Word Game', in *Guardian*, 8 Sep. 1977.) Cf prec.

how's your dandruff? A vulgar, mostly lower-middle-class greeting: since *c.* 1950; by 1965, ob.; by 1975, †.

how's your dirty rotten form?; sometimes *dirty* is omitted; often shortened to **how's your form?** 'This c.p. is not really a question, but is used when someone wins a lottery, passes an exam or gets a promotion. It is sometimes elaborated to ... *dirty, rotten, stinking form?*' (B.P.): Aus.: since the early 1950s.

how's your father? John Brophy, in the 'Chants and Sayings' section of B&P, says:

When the War [WW1] broke out, the new armies subsisted for a time on what catch phrases the music-halls produced. 'How's your father?' was one of the most popular, turned to all sorts of ribald, ridiculous and heroic uses. This was the last utterance of at least one dandified but efficient subaltern, dying of stomach wounds.

See also Stuart Cloete's *How Young They Died* (a novel about WW1), 1969:

Jim went to the Empire .... Vaudeville, Variety, Dancers, trick cyclists, Harry Lauder, Marie Lloyd. Stars. Harry Tate, with his 'How's your father?' gag. Chorus girls in uniform, drilling. Spangles, tights and music with emphasis on the brass. War songs ...

That the c.p. survived, even if only as an historical and perhaps nostalgic memory, until well after WW2, appears from the fact that in 1967, Ruth Rendell, in *Wolf to the Slaughter,* could write: '"How's your father?" he said and when he said it he realized it was a foolish catch-phrase', and that on the front page of the *Daily Mail*, 23 April 1969, Miss Bernadette Devlin was reported as saying after her maiden speech in the House of Commons: 'It is the ritual which gets you over being nervous. All this stand up, sit down, kneel and hows-your-father was so funny', where *hows-your-father* means nonsense. Frank Shaw wrote, 1965, 'Cockney uses [it] for "thingummy" – often rather vulgarly. "He's been getting his 'ow's-yer-father off her". Other usages.'

It figures in the excellent representation of c.pp. in Benham, 1948 – its first appearance in a famous (and first-class) work of reference.

Concerning the nostalgic, although only partial, revival, Mr G.W. Williams wrote, 1978, to tell me that, shortly after he had heard the phrase given new life in the translation of *The Lady from Maxim's*, he heard it again 'at the Young Vic, just a short distance from the National Theatre. It appeared in some of the free-for-all ad-lib dialogue of the "Scapin" that the Young Vic has in repertory. It seemed ... that the Young Vic was deliberately echoing the successful production at the National. A nice touch.'

P.B.: in later C20 the sexual innuendo mentioned by Frank Shaw is often expressed as *a bit*, or *a spot, of the old how's-your-father*: see also **bit of how's ...**

how's your hammer hanging? See **how are they hanging?**

how's your love life? dates *c.* 1960; **how's your sex life?** from *c.* 1960. A 'catch-phrase question addressed to a girl or girls by youth(s) wanting to "get off"' (Granville, 1969). Current also in US, with var. *how's it treatin' ya?*: since *c.* 1960. (A.B., 1978.)

how's your mother off for dripping? (– *wotcher, cock*). 'Used orig. by a BBC comedian, *c.* 1940–50, and taken up by the [vulgar] populace' (Jace Slater, 1978).

how's your old bum? A c.p. greeting in certain Army Signals units, *c.* 1955–65. It usu. evoked the answer 'Oh, shut up!', to which the further response was 'So's mine – must be the weather!' (P.B.)

how's your old parts? See **how are they hanging?**

how's your poor (often **pore**) **feet?** was a c.p. 'rampant' in 1862, very popular until 1870, revived *c.* 1889, but ob. again by *c.* 1895 – and † by 1910. It occurs in G.A. Sala's *Breakfast in Bed*, 1863.

It arose from some social occasion: and there are two or three anecdotes to support this, two of them referring to the presence of Royalty. Benham 1948, proposes an earlier date: 'This is alleged to have been a jocular saying in allusion to the fatigue resulting from visiting the Great Exhibition of 1851. (A retort, which also came into vogue, was, "Better since you licked them".)'

Clearly, the Great Exhibition version would rule out the presence of Royalty. No less clearly, the exact social occasion originating the phrase was soon forgotten and the phrase became senseless: HLM selected it as one of the stupider c.pp. This one seems to have reached the US.

'Rude boys used to call after soldiers in the street "How's your pore feet?" – an allusion to the fact that so many of our troops were frostbitten in the Crimea due to inadequate boots. [J. Rodway, historian] added that this was a catch phrase already current' (Mr M.J. Lansdown, 1978). The Crimea War was fought 1853–56.

Cf **oh, my poor feet!**

how's your sex life? See **how's your love life?**

how's your sister? is a rather pointless c.p., dating from *c.* 1910, but by 1970 rarely heard. A friend writes, 'I believe this to be based on an anecdote. A punter, colliding with a barge, complained: "See what you've done? Broke one of my oars." "Did I, lovey? Speakin' of oars, how's your broke your sister?" This may be in [Robert Graves's] *Lars Porsena*, 1927.' *Si non è vero ...*

There is a French vulgar riposte – 'Et ta soeur!' – which I heard before WW2 and may now be obsolescent (Camilla Raab, 1976). It goes back to before WW1. Paul Janssen adds to this: ' "Et ta soeur!" is far from being obsolescent, even

among the younger generation, I assure you! ... The *Petit Robert* (newly enlarged, updated ed., 1978) has 'Se dit ironiquement pour inviter quelqu'un à se mêler de ce qui le regarde, ou pour couper court à des propos insupportables ou invraisemblables.'

Hoyt's. See: **man outside.**

[hubba! hubba! was, in the 1940s (?also the 1950s), 'an expression of approval' (CM) among US Negroes and occ. among whites. But also an Aus. cry of approval, dating since *c.* 1930 and used either by teenagers in ref. – or addressed – to a pretty girl, or domestically and conventionally, as, for instance, when a young husband admires his wife's new gown, as B.P. tells me; the Aus. expression could, just possibly, be related to the Cornish *hubba*, a fishing cry. But mere animal noises – cf the approbatory *yum-yum* – hardly qualify as true c.pp.

E.P. later noted that it was not of Cornish, but rather of Erse orig., to be aligned with *hubbub*, said to have derived from an Irish cry. (*OED.*) Of its US usage, J.W.C., 1977, says, 'In the US armed forces in WW2, a (usually NCO's) exhortation to hurry up. Very common and still lingers among ex-servicemen'. P.B.: an acquaintance of mine who had served in Korea, alongside US troops, used the elab. *hubba-hubba! ding-ding!* See also **woo-woo ...**]

Hughie. See: **send her down.**

hullo ... See **hello ...**

hum. See: **no, but you hum.**

human. See: **all human; to-er.**

humble-bee in a cow-turd thinks himself a king – a. See **how we apples swim!**

hundred. See: **first hundred; it'll all be the same; ninety-nine.**

hungry. See: **I'm so h.; and:**

hungry dog will eat a dirty pudding – a. This c.p. borders on the proverbial saying, deprecates fastidiousness and dates from *c.* 1850. L.A., to whom I owe it, compares that other virtual proverbial saying, *you don't look at the mantelpiece while you're poking the fire*, which, belonging to late C19–20, has a sexual connotation.

Hunt. See: **my name is 'Unt; so bare.**

Hunt's dog, (which) will neither go to church nor stay at home – like. A semi-proverbial c.p., applied to a most unreasonably discontented person: mid C17–20. (Apperson.) Grose explains it anecdotally by ref. to a certain labourer's mastiff. Attributed to – or claimed by – various English counties.

hunting. See: **good hunting.**

hunting a horse was – and is, though now ob. – used as 'a common excuse for a presence or [an] absence not easily explained; also a common alibi for being on another cattleman's range' (Adams): since *c.* 1880(?).

hurrah for Casey! That's excellent – splendid – fine!: Aus.: C20. (Baker.) From a famous political election.

hurry. See: don't hurry; here's yer hat.

hurry no man's cattle: you may keep a donkey yourself some day was a C19 hunting c.p., quoted thus by R.S. Surtees, *Handley Cross: or, Mr Jorrock's Hunt*, 1854, vol. I, in the chapter titled 'Another Sporting Lector' (Lecture): ' "Hurry no man's cattle! you may keep ..." is the answer to the last' – i.e., to 'Over you go; the longer you look the less you'll like it.'

hurry up and get born! Wake up – you're years behind the times! Be your age!: US: since *c.* 1910. 'Our American visitors', said an English writer at the end of the war [in *English*, March 1919] 'are startling London with vivid phrases. Some of them are well known by now, "Hurry up and get born" is one of them'; so wrote HLM, 1922. Berrey lists it in a synonymy for 'Don't be ridiculous!' Not much heard since *c.* 1960.

hurry up and wait! A 'summary of "the Army way": orders must be executed "on the double" – regardless of actual emergency' (R.C., 1978): US: late 1940s or early 1950s. *The Third Ear*, 1971.

hurry up the cakes! Farmer, 1889, writes: 'Look sharp! Be quick! Buckwheat and other hot cakes form a staple dish at many American tables, and the phrase is one often heard in this connection. It has now become pure slang – an injunction to expedite movement': as a c.p., it dates since *c.* 1830–1910.

An early recording is that in *Am.* Bartlett says that the phrase 'originated in the common New York eating-houses, where it is the custom for the waiters to bawl out the name of each dish as fast as ordered, that the person who serves up may get it ready without delay'.

hurt. See: did it h.; guy; I'm not mad; if this keeps on; more dirt; must be hurtin'; nobody hurt; this hurts; you sure know.

husband. See: handsome; woman and.

hush, keep it dark. 'Commander High-Price (Jon Pertwee) in Navy *Merry Go Round*, subsequently *Waterlogged Spa*' (*VIBS*): mid-1940s. These were radio comedy series, and the c.p. enjoyed great popularity, perhaps esp. among schoolboys, at the time; one of those c.pp. in which intonation is so important: the *hush-sh-sh* was always well drawn-out. (P.B.) See also **keep it dark.**

hustlers don't call showdowns is a US, esp. Negroes', c.p., almost equivalent to 'beggars can't be choosers". A *hustler* is one who earns a living 'shadily' or even by petty crime. A *showdown* is here a disclosure of evidence, or a test of superiority. It dates from *c.* 1950. (Paul Janssen.)

Hutton's. See: don't argue.

I

I acknowledge (or **admit** or **confess**) **the corn** is a c.p. deriving from *acknowledge the corn*, to plead guilty to a minor charge in order to avoid being charged for a much graver offence. 'I know the story but not the dates. A man was accused of stealing four horses and the corn that fed them; he said, "I acknowledge the corn". The original, the true, c.p. went out of use, I suppose, with the decline of the Wild West and [the abolition of] summary hanging for horse thieves' (Shipley, 1977). Perhaps, therefore, c. 1835–1900. The earlier limit has been established by *DAm* and *OED*, esp. its second Supp.

I ain't coming. See **ain't coming on that tab**.

I always do my best for all my gentlemen, sir?, third paragraph. See **can I do you now, sir?**, third paragraph.

I am becalmed, the sail sticks to the mast. 'My shirt sticks to my back' – says Grose, 1785; he adds, 'a piece of sea wit sported in hot weather'; a nautical c.p. of mid C18–late C19.

I am here to tell you! I tell you emphatically: a c.p. of affirmation: since c. 1945; by 1975, slightly ob. In his *Pretty Polly Barlow*, 1964, Noël Coward, at the story titled 'Me and the Girls', writes: 'George Banks [the narrator] and his six Bombshells I am here to tell you began their merry career by opening a brand new night spot in Montevideo.'

I am (or **I'm**) **not here.** I don't feel inclined to work; or, I wish to be left alone: tailors': since c. 1870. (B&L.) Cf **I want to be alone**.

I am the greatest or, depending on the mood, **the prettiest**, 'Muhammad Ali (formerly Cassius Clay) admits that he acquired his "I am the greatest ... I am the prettiest" routine from the wrestler, Gorgeous George, whom he saw in Las Vegas. "I noticed they all paid to get in – and I said, 'This is a good idea!'" On occasion, Ali admitted to a group of school children: "I'm not really the greatest. I only say I'm the greatest because it sells tickets"' (*VIBS*): adopted in UK as a c.p., or perhaps rather as allusive quot'n, c. 1970.

I *am* the vicar! is 'used when someone mistakes one's name or position. From the well-known children's dialogue game which starts with a man pursuing a girl, and goes on to such exchanges as "My mother wouldn't like it!" – "Your mother's not going to get it!" [or "Nonsense, she loved it!" (P.B.)] and concludes: "I'll tell the vicar!" – "I *am* the vicar!"' (Derek Parker, in *The Times*, 9 Sep. 1977). This adult c.p. dates from very approx. the mid 1920s or the early 1930s. See also **to the woods!**

I apprehend you without a constable. Recorded in the Dialogue I of S, this smart c.p. of c. 1700–60, signifying 'I take your meaning', contains a pun on *apprehend* – to seize, hence to arrest – and *apprehend* – to understand.

I ask myself. A politician's rhetorical cliché, become c.p. in the early 1980s when used for humorous effect: e.g. 'Why is he such a Charlie, I ask myself', or the speaker may pluralise the phrase, 'Where do we go from here, we ask ourselves'. Cf

and contrast **ask yourself!**, q.v., and see also **orft we jolly well go.** (P.B.)

I ask you! – often prec. by **well**. It is an intensive of the statement to which it is appended. It is characteristically C20, but may have arisen in the late 1880s; there seems to be an allusion in F. Anstey's *Voces Populi*, 1890 – a collection of 'sketches' that had appeared in *Punch*, in the piece entitled 'Sunday Afternoon in Hyde Park', where a well-educated, well-dressed demagogue harangues the crowd: 'But, I ask you – (*he drops all playfulness and becomes sinister*) if we – the down-trodden slaves of the aristocracy – were to go to them.' The tone of voice is usually derisive. It implies 'That's ridiculous, don't you think?' In *Letter to a Dead Girl*, 1971, Selwyn Jepson provides an excellent example:

'How can my finances be involved because I met Mrs Kinnon once in my life for a couple of minutes? I ask you!' Harry begged not to be asked.

Cf this from Anne Morice's *Death of a Gay Dog*, 1971: 'My dear, you must be joking! When did you ever see anything so pretentious? ... I ask you! Just look at the way he's tarted it up!'

It occurs, as one would expect, in comedies of the 1920s and 1930s (and after). Miles Malleson, in *The Fanatics*, 1924, has an opening scene with parents talking about their son:

MRS FREEMAN: He came home.
MR FREEMAN: Eh? What excuse did he give?
MRS FREEMAN: I only heard him upstairs in his attic ... playing the piano.
MR FREEMAN: *Playing the piano*!!! I ask you ... a grown man ... what is 'e? Twenty-six.

And in H.M. Harwood's *The Old Folks at Home*, played 1933, pub'd 1934, the opening scene contains the lines:

LIZA: You needn't have bothered with lizards, darling.
JANE: (warningly) Now, Liza!
LIZA: Well, I ask you. He's been simply living with these lizards for months, and all he's found out is that males can behave like females. I could have shown him that in half an hour, anywhere in London.

Somewhere about 1930, the phrase was established in the US; Berrey includes it in a synonymy for 'I don't believe it!'.

The phrase seems to have derived from French and could well have arisen during the mid 1850s. In 1851 appeared *Le Dictionnaire des Dictionnaires*, which records: "Peut-on tolérer cela? Je vous le démande"; and the C20 *Robert*, noting the var. *je vous le démande un peu*, says that this familiar or highly coll. expression 'marque l'étonnement, la réprobation' and '= certainement pas'. (Paul Janssen, 1977.)

I asked for that! and got it! Since c. 1930. Cited in the *Daily Mail* book page on 15 May 1975.

I been there before. Yes, I know all about that – 'I've had some': US. It prob. became a c.p. very soon after Mark Twain (1835–1910) reached the height of his literary powers in the mid 1880s, after *Tom Sawyer*, 1876, *Life on the Mississippi*, 1883, and *Huckleberry Finn*, 1884. The third of these three masterpieces ended with the unforgettable words, 'I been there before'. Rarely has a famous, only in small part because easily remembered, quot'n achieved an enduring fame as a c.p. It must rank as one of the half-dozen most celebrated in the English language. It was so long ago I read *Huckleberry Finn* that I had forgotten reading its memorable conclusion. (It was R.C. who jogged my memory.) A demotic version of *et ego in Arcadia vixi*.

I believe yer, my boy. See **I believe you, my boy.**

I believe you. See **I believe you** (or **yer**), **my boy**, and **oh, I believe you . . . .**, with which cf:

I believe you, (but) thousands wouldn't (in which the I is heavily emphasised) is a late C19–20 c.p. indicative either of friendship victorious over incredulity or tactfully implying that the addressee is a liar. There is a var., as in R.H. Mottram, *The Spanish Farm* (a WW1 novel), 1927:
> 'I did twelve months in the line as a platoon commander. How long did you do that?'
> 'Twelve months about!'
> 'I believe you where thousands wouldn't . . .'

In *Billy Borker Yarns Again*, 1967, Frank Hardy uses the predominant form. Perhaps an elab. of the next. In the US, *thousands* occ. becomes *millions* and the phrase often becomes *there are thousands* (occ. *millions*) *who wouldn't* (A.B., 1978. And French has 'Je vous crois! Je pense ainsi, je pense comme vous; et aussi: c'est évident!' (Paul Janssen cites *Robert*).

I believe you (or **yer**), **my boy**. Of this c.p., which fell a victim to WW2, *The Referee*, on 18 Oct. 1885, wrote, ' 'Tis forty years since Buckstone's drama, *The Green Bushes*, was first played at the Adelphi, and since Paul Bedford's [that most popular actor's] "I believe yer, my boy!" found its way on to tongues of the multitude.' [P.B.: Albert Smith, in *The Natural History of the Gent*, 1847, amplifies: 'Possibly the next [imitation] will be [of] Mr. Paul Bedford, when he rolls his *r* and says, "Come along, my r-r-r-r-rummy cove; come along comealong comealong! how are you? how d'ye do? here we are! I'm a looking at you like bricksy-wicksy wicksies – I believe you my boy-y-y-y-y!"']

Clearly, however, the theatrical ref. was forgotten by myriads ignorant of the play: with the result that *my boy* soon came to be omitted.

Perhaps even more clearly, a reading of C19 plays reveals that the satirical *I believe you* had existed before John Buckstone's play was prod. in 1845. George Dibdin Pitt's *Susan Hopley; or, the Vicissitudes of a Servant Girl: A Domestic Drama*, performed 1841, III, ii, contains a passage between ladies' maid Gimp and Dicky Dean the Cockney. Gimp says, 'What a fascinating fellow! Does he dance too?' and Dicky replies, 'I believe you; cuts capers, and goes through his steps. . . . All the managers run after him.' ('Him' is a donkey and Dicky is teasing the girl.)

A rather more serious ref. occurs in Dion Boucicault's play, *Mercy Dodd; or, Presumptive Evidence*, performed in London, 1869, and in Philadelphia, 1874; it is cited as evidence of the early use of the simple *I believe you!* – not the literal but the ironic – thus, in I, i, where, in reply to Mercy Dodd's 'Do you mean that you have ever been confined in prison?' Will Coveney says, 'Portland Bill. Off and on all my life!' and, at her further query, 'What for?', exclaims, 'Trespass! As I grow'd up I found the world belonged to other people, and I'd no business anywhere in it. Prison! I believe you! What d'ye call living outside in the streets of London?'

And an example from a better playwright: Henry Arthur Jones, in *An Old Master*, performed 1880, has this passage:
> MATT[HEW]: . . . Is she kind and good-natured?
> SIMP[KIN]: Well, between you and me, she's a fire-eating old cat.
> MATT: Is she though? What, proud and ill-tempered?

SIMP: I believe you.

Conclusion: Buckstone's *I believe yer, my boy* – often misquoted as *I believe you . . .* – sprang from the generic irony, *I believe you*: and *I believe you*, although less used after WW2 than before it, was, as late as 1976, still far from moribund.

I bet! and **I'll bet!** are elliptical for 'I bet you did *or* do *or* will!' and have been current since *c.* 1870 at latest. A good example of the *I'll bet!* form occurs in Terence Rattigan, *After the Dance*, performed and pub'd in 1939; in III, i, we find one character saying, 'I've been reading Gibbon', and his interlocutor derisively exclaiming, 'I'll bet you have.'

I bet you say that to all the girls, orig. and still frequently a feminine defensive conventionalism, has been also used, since the mid 1930s (if not earlier), as a derisive counterattack: and when thus used, it is a c.p.

I bet your father was a blacksmith! 'A Londoner in 1943 said to me "I bet your father was a blacksmith", meaning "You've hit the nail on the head"' (B. G.T., 1978), i.e. 'You've spoken the exact truth – you've gone straight to the nub of the matter': it prob. dates from *c.* 1850; by late 1970s, slightly ob. Cf **I think you are a witch.**

I broke my pick. See **he broke . . .**

I brought this for you, sir! 'Mrs Mopp (Dorothy Summers) giving her customary present to Tommy Handley in *ITMA*' (*VIBS*). P.B.: always uttered in a rather plaintively ingratiating tone; T. H.'s usual response was 'Oh, how nice! What *is* it?' See **TOMMY HANDLEY . . .**

I can always open me legs and make a bit (can't I?) has, I'm told, been a prostitutes' self-consolatory c.p. dating since *c.* 1930. It has, however, become *c.* 1940, rather more widely used.

I can hardly wait! See **I can't wait!**

I can hear you. See **don't fore it . . .**

I can take a hint (– **all right,**) is an 'ironic comment on a command or [an] unvarnished request to do something. American and British from 1960s or earlier' (R.C., 1978). In Brit., rather since the 1930s.

I cannot tell a lie (– **Father,**). A US c.p., often heard also in UK, 'mocking Parson Weems's story of [the boy] George Washington and the [felled] cherry tree' (Ashley, 1979).

I can't believe I ate the whole thing. 'From TV advert for Alka-Seltzer, now used jokingly' (Ashley, 1984): US.

I can't do a thing with it. See **I washed my hair . . .**

I can't go faster than my legs will carry me. This C18 – mid C19 c.p. occurs in S, in the opening dialogue:
> LADY SM[ART]: Come, get ready my Things, where has the Wench been these three Hours?
> BETTY [A MAID]: Madam, I can't go faster than my legs will carry me.

The saying would seem to have belonged to the lower-middle class.

'I've also heard "I can't go (*or* walk) farther than my legs will carry me"' (A.B., 1978, who dates it as late or latish C19.)

I can't see it. See **I don't see it.**

I can't *think*! is uttered in a tone of disgust or amazement; is elliptical for 'I can't think, or imagine, what you mean *or* suppose you're doing' – and then the speaker almost always proceeds to tell the addressee his or, more often, her unfavourable opinion; is lower and lower-middle class; and is certainly at least late C19–20, but prob. goes back to (say) 1800 – cf **you can't think**, which, I'd say, prototyped it.

I can't wait (or **I can hardly wait** – the former Brit. the latter both Brit. and US) is an ironic c.p., applied to an imminent and undesired encounter or other occurrence: since *c.* 1930. In *Present Laughter*, pub'd in 1943, Noël Coward, in Act II writes:
> FRED: . . . She's coming to the station to-morrow morning to see us off, you don't mind, do you?
> GARRY: I can't wait.

It recurs in *South Sea Bubble*, performed and pub'd in

1956, at II, i, and in *Nude with Violin*, likewise prod. and pub'd in 1956, at III, ii.

In Norman F. Simpson's truly remarkable *One Way Pendulum: A Farce in a New Dimension*, prod. in 1959 and pub'd in 1960, we read:

MRS G.: (*off*) It's only until he gets them all trained, Sylvia.
SYLVIA: ... Gets them trained! I can't wait!

In *The Allingham Case-Book*, 1969, Margery Allingham, who had died in 1966, wrote:

'She'll be delighted to see you, Campion.'
'I can hardly wait.'
'You'll have to,' said Oates grimly.

Ross Macdonald, in *The Goodbye Look*, 1969, has:

'Dr Smitherham ... will introduce you to the parents when it's convenient.'
'I can hardly wait,' Maclennan said under his breath.

In 1971, the same novelist, in *The Underground Man:*

'Have you ever been arrested?' I said.
'No. I can hardly wait.'
'It isn't funny. If the authorities wanted to throw the book at you, they could be rough ... '

Frank Norman, in *Much Ado about Nuffink*, 1974, also uses it:

'And what's so special about you?'
'I might tell you one of these fine days,' I winked at her. 'That is, if you play your cards right.'
'I can hardly wait,' she parried.

I could care less is, in the US, 'becoming more common among the vulgar (only, so far)' for **I couldn't care less**, q.v., as J.W.C. notes, 1978. P.B.: perhaps influenced by the shape of *I should smile* or *I should worry*.

I could do it (or that) **before breakfast.** That's easy: C20: perhaps orig. and mainly Aus. In the US, 'sometimes varied to "I could do it (*or* that) in a minute": since *c.* 1940' (A.B., 1978).

I could do that (occ., more politely, **her**) **a (real) favour** is 'a tribute to the charms of an attractive girl, or a picture of one' (L.A.): since *c.* 1945. Contrast:

I could do you a favour. As from one man to another, it menacingly intimates a show of physical strength; it is either joc. in a healthy way or implicative of a contemptuous claim for animal superiority: since *c.* 1930. (L.A., 1969.)

I could eat that without salt. A would-be smart youths' c.p. applicable to a pretty girl happening to pass by: not in polite society: since *c.* 1945. Often *without salt* is omitted: cf its opposite, *I couldn't eat that*, applicable to a very unattractive girl. Pamela Branch. *The Wooden Overcoat*, 1951, 'I couldn't eat the last one' (a lodger).

The complementary girls' c.p. is *he could eat me without salt*, he loves me madly; I suspect that this c.p. may go back to C18.

R.C. compares Kipling's *The Gadsbys*, 1889, where a woman confides that 'Being kissed by a man without a moustache is like eating an egg without salt'.

Cf **she looks as if she could eat me without salt** – two centuries older.

I could eat a horse and chase the rider! See **I'm so hungry ...**

I could go for you in a big way, if used among men, imputes effeminacy or softness: since *c.* 1942. If by men to women, it implies male desire manifested in the usual way.

I could shit through the eye of a needle is a low c.p. uttered 'on the morning after:' C20.

P.B.: this unpleasant manifestation is not necessarily, since mid C20, the result of a hangover, but may result from food-poisoning, or any other illness. For extra emphasis, *without touching the sides* may be added.

I could take up the slack of my belly and wipe my eyes with it. I'm damned hungry! A nautical c.p., common on ships inadequately victualled: late C19–20. Cf **I'm so empty ...** , and **my stomach thinks ...**

I couldn't agree with you more (usu. shortened to **I couldn't agree more**) is the prompter of **I couldn't care less**; it dates

since *c.* 1936, was at first a Society c.p. that, by 1940, was very common among Service officers, and is still heard often enough, even though it has never been nearly so popular as its junior; on the other hand, it has always remained a civilised, urbane, cultured – or, at the least, an educated – c.p. So very English, it yet became, by the late 1950s, also US, as in Edward Albee, *Who's Afraid of Virginia Woolf?*, 1962, in Act I:

NICK: I was going to say ... why give it up until you have to?
MARTHA: I couldn't agree with you more. (*They both smile, and there is a rapport established.*) I couldn't agree with you more.

And as in Amanda Cross, *The James Joyce Murder*, 1967.

'That woman again? It seems scarcely believable.'
'I couldn't agree more.'

Although less gen. in the 1970s than in the 1930s and 1940s, it is only a little less so: and a pleasant example occurs in Laurence Meynell, *The Curious Crime*, 1970:

'What's the use of being paid good money if you don't spend it?'
'I couldn't agree more,' Colin said gratefully.

There is also a very good one in Michael Innes's contribution to *Winter's Crimes*, edited by George Hardinge, 1972:

'Then the trustees ought to have done that job themselves.'
'I couldn't agree more. But they're lazy bastards.'

Very naturally, this c.p. appears in comedy, for instance Noël Coward's *Present Laughter*, 1943, Act II in which Joanna says: ' ... It's an adult point of view and I salute it. I couldn't agree with you more.'

In Coward's *Relative Values*, performed 1951, at I, ii, the following occurs:

FELICITY: There's nothing inferior about her, social or otherwise.
PETER: All right, all right – I couldn't agree with you more.

His *South Sea Bubble*, 1956, has, at III, i:

BOFFIN: Perhaps she didn't drive very well. Or perhaps she was drunk – what do you think?
SANDRA: I couldn't agree with you more.

P.B.: so common was the phrase in the late 1940s that the occ. var. *I couldn't A with you M* had some vogue.

I couldn't care fewer was, *c.* 1959 – 62, an occ. var. of the next. Such inanity couldn't last very long; it did last longer than it deserved to do.

I couldn't care less. I'm entirely indifferent – it really doesn't matter either way: prompted by **I couldn't agree (with you) more**: arose *c.* 1940, orig. among the upper-middle class, but by 1945 fairly gen. socially and extremely popular among those who did use it; by the late 1940s, almost everybody was doing so. Since *c.* 1945, also Aus., as in Alexander Buzo's *Rooted* (performed in 1969 and pub'd in 1973), I, iii. In 1952, Sydney Moseley, *God Help America!*, could write, 'Ordinary citizens "couldn't have cared less!" – to use a cant post-war phrase current in England'; clearly he couldn't have heard it before 1945, but that misfortune doesn't invalidate the main point of his statement.

The phrase migrated to the US and, well before 1970, it had become so thoroughly naturalized there that it could be employed allusively, as in Stanley Ellin, *The Man from Nowhere*, 1970:

'How did she react? .... Did it seem to hit a nerve?'

Elinor shook her head. 'She couldn't have cared less.

Cf John D. Macdonald, *Dress Her in Indigo*, 1969, '"I haven't any idea where Rocko went, and I couldn't care less."' And Helen Nielsen, *Shot on Location*, 1971,

'Koumaris won't like it.'
'I couldn't care less.'

Leechman, 1969, writes of its Can. currency, 'Perhaps 25 years old, in my experience'. See this entry in *DSUE*, 8th ed., and cf the WW1 **care whether the cow ...**

P.B.: I think that E.P. here does less than justice to a

certain type of reckless gallantry, or rather a shining courage that refuses to be baulked by any consideration of the risks, that is to be found, for example, in Anthony Phelps's story of the Air Transport Auxiliary (ATA, Civilian ferry pilots) work in WW2. This informal history, pub'd 1946, was titled – *I Couldn't Care Less.*

I cut my foot on a Dutchman's razor means 'I stepped in a cow-pile' (Brit. 'cow-pat') or 'on a horse (*or* dog) turd': US: heydaying *c.* 1915–30, but still heard occ. (Fain, 1979.) A humorous excuse, esp. among boys.

I decline to answer, on the usual grounds has, since soon after the Fifth Amendment to the Constitution of the United States came into force in 1952, been a US c.p., 'a jocular refusal to answer an embarrassing or personal question. The usual grounds … are "on the ground that the answer might tend to incriminate me" … Many Communists and alleged Communists, under investigation by Congressional bodies, were forced to "take the Fifth" … in most cases, less to avoid incriminating themselves than to avoid being made (under threat of jail) to incriminate others' (R.C., 1977). P.B.: versions such as 'I plead the Fifth Amendment' and 'I refuse to answer, on the grounds of the Fifth Amendment' have also, in later C20, been heard in UK.

I didn't ask what keeps your ears apart. This low, very witty c.p., dating since *c.* 1949, is the devastating counter to the low comment, or rejoinder, *balls!* or *ballocks!*, nonsense! Prob. suggested by to *have more brawn* (or *balls*) than brains.

I didn't blow it out of my nose. A Can. c.p., dating from the late 1950s, meaning 'I didn't do it off hand or easily'. Leechman, 1967, wrote to me: 'Ex a French c.p., I believe. Heard in the last few years.'

I didn't come down in the last shower See **didn't come down** …

I didn't come up in the last bucket (or **with the last boat**); **I didn't fall off a Christmas tree.** The first, C20, is RN; the second and third are more recent, arising in the middle 1940s and commoner in the Services than among civilians. All three mean 'I know my way about–I'm not to be fooled'. (The first: Granville; the other two, L.A., 1967.) Cf **I didn't just** …

I didn't get a sausage (or **so much as a tickle**). I got nothing for my pains, esp. I got no money: since *c.* 1945. P.B.: hardly a c.p., since it can be used of other persons, e.g. *she didn't* … , *they won't get* …

I didn't just get off the boat, y'know! 'Used in the US – it refers to immigration to the US, an *ignorant*, though not *stupid*, newcomer to these shores. It originated in late C19, I should think, or very early C20' (A.B., 1978). Cf **didn't come down** … and **I didn't come up** …

I didn't know that. In 1974, my late friend Norris M. Davidson, of Gwynedd, Pennsylvania, wrote:

We have a new Catch Phrase over here. It is 'I didn't know that!' About a year ago, the Ford Motor Company introduced a series of radio and TV commercials in which their 'salesman' extolled some of the superior points of the new Ford car – or truck [lorry]. His prospective customer then said: 'I didn't know that!' The phrase is now being echoed by comedians, radio announcers, and the like – upon the slightest provocation. The phrase is stated in 3 descending notes on the first 3 words – and 'that', the 4th word, is accented and returns to the original note used on 'I'. Silly, isn't it? But there you are!

I didn't know (or **know that**) **you cared.** See **this is so sudden**, near beginning and near end. Note that it is usu. spoken gushingly and simperingly, in ref. to a gift made, not to the speaker but to a third person. Current in Brit. and Aus., and prob. elsewhere, since *c.* 1945. R.C., 1977, confirms: 'It has been current also in the US; and everywhere it has often borne an ironic note: that is, as a response to some critical or unpleasant remark'. P.B.: a frequent var. is (*there, and*) *I never knew you cared!*

I didn't raise my boy to be a soldier was *c.* 1914–19, a US c.p.,

generated by the song so titled, with words by Bryan, **music** by Piantadosi, rendition by Ed Morton. (W.J.B.)

I didn't think that was sun-tan on your nose is a C20 – and esp. Suffolk – c.p., implying that the addressee is a 'creeper', a toady.

I do not like this game! 'Peter Sellers [in his idiot adolescent persona] as Bluebottle in *The Goon Show.*

SEAGOON: Now, Bluebottle, take this stick of dynamite.
BLUEBOTTLE: No, I do not like this game!'

Thus *VIBS*, P.B. adds: Sellers had a characteristically snickering whimper to go with this c.p., and in this role would always address Neddie Seagoon (Harry Secombe) as 'my captain'. Another typical example occurs in Spike Milligan, *The Goon Cartoons*, 1982, an illustrated version of orig. scripts:

BLUEBOTTLE: Heu, Hen Hu – what was that, my captain?
SEAGOON: A man-eating tiger!
BLUEBOTTLE: I do not like this game. I'm going home – I just remembered, it's my turn in the barrel.

I don't care if I do! and **I don't mind if I do!** I am disposed, I should rather like, to do something. Yes, please!: the former since *c.* 1700, the latter since *c.* 1910. The latter became 'the rage' and by 1946 almost a public nuisance; but then, it had been a Tommy Handley 'gag' in the famous WW2 'ITMA' show. (EP, 'Those Radio Catch Phrases', in the *Radio Times*, 6 Dec. 1946.) It occurs, for instance, in Aus.: Frank Hardy's *Billy Borker Yarns Again*, 1967. [P.B.: not surprisingly, and perhaps not from 'ITMA', to judge by this observation in Cyril Pearl's biography, *Morrison of Peking*, 1967: 'At the end of his … diary [for 1903] Morrison made a few random notes on the Australian scene … The commonest phrase in Australia was "Well, I don't mind if I do",'] The former, on the other hand, had, by far, the greater impact in the US, where it has been recorded over a long span of time, for instance in T. C. Haliburton's *The Clockmaker*, 2nd Series, 1838, 'Won't you join us? Well, said I, I don't care if I do.' Also in Farmer, 1889, and in Berrey, 1942. But the US usage was anticipated by, e.g., Henry Carey in *The Contrivances*, 1715:

ARG[US]: … But wouldn't drink, honest friend?
ROB[IN]: I don't care an [= if] I do, a bit or so; for to say truth, I'm mortal dry.

Cf Joseph Elsworth, *The Rival Valets: A Farce*, performed in 1825; in I, i, the housekeeper says to valet Frank, 'Will you come in and have a little refreshment', to which he replies, 'Why, I don't care if I do.'

The later phrase appeared in print very soon after it began to be used in 'ITMA' and, by 1948, it had become so embedded in everyday speech that it could be employed in an allusive pun: on the back of Frank Worsley's *Itma*, published in 1948, was an advertisement for Croid Glue, with the letterpress: '"A tube of CROID, Colonel?" – "I don't mind if I GLUE, Sir!"' Colonel Chinstrap, played by Jack Train, first appeared in 'ITMA' during the autumn of 1940, the famous words being, on the very first occasion, in a rather different form:

VOICE: Father's a fool, by Gad, and if he'd been in my regiment in India, I'd have had him drummed out.
TOM: Didn't I meet you in Rumbellipoor, sir?
VOICE: You did not, sir. I was never there.
TOM: Then you must have a double.
VOICE: Thanks, I will.

[P.B.: 'Chinstrap' affected a fruity, but rather elderly and quavery, military drinker's voice, which those using the c.p. would often try to imitate, and he often added 'Sir' to the acceptance].

The c.p., *I don't mind if I do*, had its adumbrations; and my own impression – no more than an impression – is that it arose, *c.* 1860, among the upper-middle class. If so, it gradually achieved a much wider currency; and, thanks to 'ITMA', by the end of 1940, a classless currency. I noticed that 'Taffrail' – Henry Taprell Dorling – in *Pincher Martin*,

O.D., 1915, mentions a shy youth using the joc. var., **I don't mind if I does**. In John Boland's novel, *Kidnap*, 1970, in a lower-middle-class setting:

'Another cake, Mrs Thomson?' ...

'Thanks, love, I don't mind if I do.'

The phrase was inevitably taken up by the theatre. Noël Coward's *Peace in Our Time*, 1947, II, iv (a public house) has the following dialogue:

PHYLLIS: Anyone want another drop before closing?

There's still some left in the bottle.

ALMA: You have it, Phyllis.

PHYLLIS: I don't mind if I do. (*She pours the remains of the champagne*.) Here's how!

Coward uses it again in *Relative Values*, prod. in 1951, at the end, and yet again in *South Sea Bubble*, 1956.

In short, *I don't mind if I do* could almost be said to belong to the social structure of Britain. Yet it has, I suspect, established its predominance in the US too. In *The American Dream*, 1961, Edward Albee uses it thus:

MOMMY: ... Won't you come in?

MRS BARKER: ... I don't mind if I do.

Its social acceptability in Britain is questioned in Michael Innes's *The Mysterious Commission*, 1974:

'May I offer you a glass of sherry?' he asked. 'It seems a reasonable hour for something of the sort.'

'I don't mind if I do,' Mr Peach (although back with another wholly inadmissible locution) made a small gesture which was entirely a gentleman's.

Nigel Rees, in *VIBS*, recalls that 'the phrase had been in existence long before [its ITMA popularity]. *Punch* carried a cartoon in 1880 with the following caption:

PORTER: Virginia Water!

BIBULOUS OLD GENTLEMAN (seated in a railway carriage): Gin and water! I don't mind if I do!'

I don't care if I do go blind. A defiant rejection of the once gen. statement that masturbation, whether frequent or even occasional, caused blindness: late C19 – mid 20. Brian W. Aldiss, 1978, adds: 'Ideally accompanied by a brisk slapping of the back of the neck. Words and action generally provoked by a (probably inaccessible) woman'. Cf **I don't want to be a sergeant-pilot**. Ashley, 1979, remarks: 'On the warning that masturbation makes you go blind: "I'm only going to do it until I have to wear glasses"'.

I don't care if you burst into flame (s)! An unsympathetic response to the polite query 'Do you mind if I smoke?': gen. c.p.: since WW2, at latest. Perhaps cf **what do you expect me to do** ... for an orig. (P.B.)

I don't fink! See **I don't think!**

I don't go much on it. I don't much care for it; usu. I dislike it: since *c.* 1925.

I don't have to! was, *c.* 1920–5, current among US university students.

I don't know! – often spoken in a tone of exasperation and, late C19–20, belonging to those strata of society which once would have been classified as lower class and lower-middle class. On Saturday, 3 July 1971, I overheard in Holborn, London, a woman exclaim to her husband, less helpful than he might have been with their over-tired fretful two-year-old child, 'Reely, Bill! *I* don't know!' Elliptical for 'I don't know what to say' (or 'think').

I don't know from nothing. 'I know absolutely nothing about it': US: C20. (Berrey.) Orig. an illiteracy, it very soon, except among the cultured and a few of the educated, passed into gen. usage, prob. because of its vigour. P.B.: but may also be used of persons other than *I*.

[**I don't know much about Art, but I know what I like** ranks as No. 1 in Gelett Burgess's list of 'bromides' (i.e., boring and too often repeated remarks) on pp. 24–32 of his witty monograph, *Are You a Bromide?*, 1906. It lies on the border between c.p. and cliché: both Brit. and US, and dating, I'd say, since the middle or later 1890s: still with us, but, as R.C. remarks, 1977, 'In recent years, not infrequently switched to

"... but I know what I *don't* like"'.]

I don't know nothin' about birthin' babies, Miss Scarlett. 'Rejection of any responsibility: delivered in the voice of Butterfly McQueen in the film *Gone With the Wind*, 1939, a high, black, flibbertygibbet voice' (Ashley, 1984).

I don't know whether I'm Angus or Agnes is a 'Men Only' c.p., 'used in very cold weather or after swimming in cold water.... "I'm so cold I don't know...."' (Leechman): Can.: since *c.* 1930. P.B.: cf the physiological observation, almost a c.p., made in the same circumstances, 'Usually seven inches and one wrinkle; now it's seven wrinkles and an inch'. Cf **more wrinkles** ... , and:

I don't know whether I'm Arthur or Martha. Expression used by men or women about themselves or another, meaning 'coming or going' or a general state of muddle – no overt sexual overtones. In general use in Aus. since at least the 1950s. (Camilla Raab.) But Ashley, writing of US usage, 1979, says, '*Arthur and Martha* is a *gay* expression still very current among *Sadie and Maisie* (sado-masochistic homosexuals)'.

I don't let my mouth write checks my ass can't cash. 'Virtually unknown in New York. Los Angeles (Hollywood) was, for a time, proud to show its vulgarity' (Shipley, 1977).

I don't lie, I sit. S, Dialogue I, has:

COL[ONEL]: Indeed, Madam, that's Lye.

LADY ANSW[ERALL]: Well, 'tie better I should lye, than you should lose your Manners. Besides, I don't lye, I sit.

Whether this punning retort ever became a full c.p., I lack the evidence to decide.]

I don't like this game. See **I do not like** ...

I don't like yours and **I don't think much of yours** (or **the one you're getting**). 'This should be included as a c.p. used referring to two girls approaching, especially when one is less attractive than the other' (Michael Goldman, 1978). In both, *yours*, and in the latter, *you're*, is heavily emphasised. Of the second version, Simon Levene writes, 1978, that it has a certain appeal because of its 'uncompromisingly masculine offensiveness' and because it sums up very neatly an adolescent way of life in roughish urban areas. It has delicious undertones of rogue males in amiably competitive kerb-crawling'. P.B.: I first heard it, in the Services, in the very early 1950s; it was always joc. A further var. is *I don't reckon much to* ...

I don't make the rules, I just live (or **work**) **here**, the second half very often standing by itself and therefore recorded separately. 'Don't ask *me* – ask the boss!': US: since *c.* 1955. (J.W.C., 1977.) See **don't ask me** ...

I don't mean maybe! See **and I don't mean maybe!**

I don't mind being shit on, but to hell with having it rubbed in! 'I can take so much, but there *is* a limit': N. Country; C20. (Eddie Haines, 1978.)

I don't mind if I do! See **I don't care if I do!**

I don't see it – often shortened to **don't see it!** The 4th edn of *DAm* has both forms: 'A very common expression, equivalent to dissent': since *c.* 1860 or perhaps a decade earlier. Adopted in UK *c.* 1890. R.C., 1977, 'Often with *can't* instead of *don't*'.

I don't see the Joe Miller of it. I don't see the joke; I don't see any fun in doing this: *c.* 1810–95. Here, a *Joe Miller* is a jest, from the sense 'a jest book', orig. a specific jest book that, pub'd 1739, was identified with, although not written by, the famous comedian, Joseph Miller (1684–1738).

I *don't* think! reverses the ironical statement it follows: mainly proletarian: since *c.* 1880 (Cf the slangy *not half!*, most decidedly so!) The *OED* adduces this effective example from Dickens, 1837: '"Amiably disposed ... , I don't think," resumed Mr Weller, in a tone of moral reproof.' In the late C19–20, it often elicits the retort, *you don't look as if you do* or *I didn't suppose you did*, and in C20 – at least up to *c.* 1950 – one often, Cockney fashion, substitutes *fink* for *think*.

In 1927, Collinson wrote:

The frivolous use of the vulgar I don't think or fink in

emphatic refutation of a foregoing statement. Thus [H. G. Wells, *Christina Albert's Father*, 1925] has 'as for bringing a contrite heart ... I don't fink'. This expression was much used in the early years of the century, but always with an awareness of its vulgar origin.

Since *c.* 1960, mostly *I don't think!*

A few years earlier, Noël Coward had, in his (I think) first pub'd although not first written, play, *'I'll Leave it to You.' A Light Comedy in Three Acts*, performed on 21 July 1920 at the New Theatre, London, and pub'd two or three months later, in Act I, soon after Uncle Daniel arrives:

DANIEL: Don't leave me all alone. I'm a timid creature.
SYLVIA: *(turns)* After all that broncho busting! I don't think!

Miles Malleson had forestalled Coward when, late in 1914, he wrote *'D' Company*, pub'd in 1916, only to see all copies soon destroyed by public prosecution; there:

ALF: You're a liar. An' I tell yer why .... We're goin' ter Africa.
TILLEY: Africa, I don't fink.

This play was reprinted in 1925. A year earlier, Malleson in *The Fanatics*, Act II, has a chorus girl remarking: 'That man gave her another ring yesterday ... must of cost *hundreds*. She says there is nothing in it ... I *don't* think.'

The phrase travelled to the US. In HLM, 1922: '*Shoo-fly* afflicted the American people for at least two years, and "I *don't* think" ... quite as long.' In the definitive edn, 1936, Mencken altered 'two years' to 'four or five years' and said that *I don't think* was 'scarcely less long-lived'.

I don't think much of yours (or **... of the one you're getting**). See **I don't like yours.**

I don't want to be a sergeant-pilot, anyway was, *c.* 1935–55, a joc. RAF c.p., alluding to masturbation, which has so long been reputed to impair one's mental and physical powers. Cf **I don't care if I do go blind.**

I don't want to play in your yard (or **backyard**). A mock-childish US c.p. of *c.* 1894–1929; adopted in UK *c.* 1895, and in the Commonwealth *c.* 1896. Occasioned by the song so titled, pub'd in 1894, words by Philip Wingate, music by H. W. Petrie, sung by the Lynon sisters. Edward B. Marks, *They All Sang*, 1934.

I don't wish him (or **you**) **any harm, but I hope he** (or **you**) **break(s) his** (or **your**) **neck!** Both a servicemen's and a (mostly proletarian) civilian c.p.: C20. (Mr P. Daniel, 1978.) P.B.: the threat may be varied, so perhaps only the first half of the expression is really the c.p.

I don't wish to know that. See **I say, I say ...**

I dood it, i.e. **I doed** or **do'd it**, I did it, is a US c.p. – W & F call it a 'fad expression' – of *c.* 1945–55. Either mock-puerile or mock-illiterate. They attribute it to some popular comedian. Donald L. Martin, 1977, illuminates: 'Comes from radio, specifically from the character of "The Mean Widdle Kid" created by Red Skelton during the period you indicate. Whenever the Kid contemplated some devilment, he went through the routine: "KID: Do I dood it? ... If I dood it, I get a lickin? ... (the triumph of mischief over fear) I DOOD IT!" This was used as a c.p. in the sense of the rather trivial "full steam ahead and damn the torpedoes" state of mind, but I haven't heard it in ten years'. For *damn the torpedoes*, SEE AMERICAN HISTORICAL BORDERLINERS.

I dreamt I met you — unfortunately! A humorous greeting: C20. 'An often used c.p., and still' (Shaw, 1968).

I drew a lemon. See **answer is a lemon —** latter half of entry.

I feel an awful heel is spoken to the accompaniment of a hand placed upon the addressee's back or shoulder: Aus. juvenile: since *c.* 1930 (B.P.) See also **excuse my wart!**

I feel for you but I can't reach you! is a US c.p. of sympathy: *c.* 1930–50. (Berrey) Moe, 1977, 'said to a person who relates a hard-luck story and who expects an expression of sympathy'.

I feel like a mushroom: everyone keeps me in the dark and is always feeding me bullshit. A US witticism of the 1970s.

(George A. Krzymowski, New Orleans, 1978.) P.B.: I saw this slogan on a T-shirt in England, 1979, and a version of it was current during the Falklands War, 1982, as Gareth Parry reported in the *Guardian*, 2 July 1982: 'The [Royal Fleet Auxiliary crews] considered themselves "mushrooms" – they were kept in the dark about almost everything'. Cf **I'm always out of the picture ...**

I feel like Barney's bull. See **all behind, like Barney's bull.**

I forgot the question! A repetition phrase from Goldie Hawn, at one time the resident blonde dum-dum of [the US TV comedy series, Rowan & Martin's] *Laugh-In*. In the middle of a quick exchange she would giggle and then miaow "I forgot the question!" At first her fluffs were a case of misreading cue cards, then they became part of her act' (*VIBS*): late 1960s.

I forgot to duck. 'Response if someone asks where you got the black eye. It comes from an old music-hall comedy sketch. One of the comics describes how he beat Jack Sharkey around the ring for 14 rounds. The dénouement comes in the 15th round, when he forgot to duck' (Skehan, 1984). P.B.: of the Lithuanian sailor John Cocoskey, whose ring-name was Jack Sharkey, Denzil Batchelor writes in *Big Fight*, 1955, that he 'became perhaps the least impressive heavyweight champion of the world in the history of glove-fighting'.

I get you, Steve! I understand: US: C20; by 1915, also Aus.; and known in UK, prob. since early C20. This is the version cited by S.R. Strait in 'Straight Talk', published by the *Boston Globe* in *c.* 1917. (W.J.B.) Cf and see **got me, Steve?**

I give up! is both Brit. and US (in, e.g., Berrey) and its dates since *c.* 1890 in Brit. and perhaps a little later in US. It expresses a comic or rueful sense of futility or even despair.

I go, I come back. This WW2 c.p. began with 'ITMA' as produced at Bangor in mid-1940. Frank Worsley, in *Itma*, 1948, writes: 'During this series [of six shows, ending on 24 July 1940] many of the famous crop of ITMA characters made their first bow, the first one to do so being *Ali Oop.* the saucy postcard-vendor (played by Horace Percival).' Later in the book, as he reviews ITMA's run of over three hundred performances, he says. 'People still remember *Ali Oop*, with his hoarse whisper, "I go, I come back"'; but by 1950 it had, except reminiscently, become ob. – and by 1960, virtually†. Cf the entry at TOMMY HANDLEY CATCH PHRASES.

I got ears for what you're saying. Now you're really talking sensibly – or very. pertinently indeed: US Negroes': since *c.* 1940, although esp. in the 1940s. CM remarks that it 'sometimes implies approval of what is being heard'. Cf **I got eyes ....**

I got (or **had**) **'em** (or esp. **her**) **one the five-yard line** is applied when something untoward and frustrating has occurred: US: since *c.* 1930. It comes from US football. A US correspondent says, in 1968:

When the attacking team gets as near to the goal as five yards (the field being 100 yards long), it is very likely to make a touch-down. As a catch phrase, used, e.g. by an almost but not quite successful seducer: 'I had her on the five-yard line – and just then the God-damned doorbell rung!'.

I got eyes for you, baby! 'I am interested in you, my dear': US: since *c.* 1930. (A.B., 1978.)

I got mine, how are you making out? – with *I* and *you* emphasized. A rather cynical, utterly self-centred American Navy c.p., dating from at least as early as 1930. Col. A.F. Moe, USMC, ret., compares it with the USMC's c.p. usage of *semper fi*, short for *semper fidelis*, always faithful, and R.C., 1977, adds to that: 'My late friend Blake Ehrlich, journalist and sometime member of the USMC, claimed that the "wird for word" translation of *semper fi* was "Fuck you, Johnny, I got mine!" So cf the Brit. version **fuck you, Jack, I'm all right!** and its many variants: for semantic synonymity see pp. 40, 301, 302 of Anton Myrer's *The Big War* (WW2), 1957.

Moe also notes that *semper fi* has been employed as a c.p.

since not later than 1920 and that it is not merely cynical but often callous.

I got news for you. See **I've got news for you.**

I got your number. US: since *c.* 1912. Cited by S.R. Strait in his merry verses ('Straight Talk') in the *Boston Globe* in *c.* 1917, it means 'I see what you mean – or are up to' and was, by 1960, almost†. But J.W.C. reported, 1977, that 'up to' nuance was then still current.

I gotta million of 'em was, orig., the property of Jimmy 'Schnozzle' Durante (middle and late 1940s and the 1950s): and, by its popularity, the tag became a c.p., often used with no very precise application or meaning (W.J.B.) It was adopted in Britain as **I've got a million of them,** q.v.

I grow while I'm standing is, in Aus., a C20 c.p. used in declining a proffered seat. (B.P., 1974.) It seems to have evolved from the UK *stand and grow good*, 'the version I've always known' (B.G.T., 1978), which prob. dates from mid C19 and was ob. by 1970.

I guess you're tyring to tell me something. From being a cliché, this has, since *c.* 1965, become, when heavily ironic, a c.p., as when a young man says it to a girl telling him to *drop dead* and he is implying 'You've made your point very clear': gen. US, since *c.* 1955. (Paraphrase of R.C., 1978 note.)

I had a shit, shave, shower.... See **I've had a shit....**

I had 'em (or **her**) **on the five-yard line.** See **I got 'em....**

I had 'em rolling in the aisles; *rolling* often omitted. Spoken by a comedian successful in making his audience laugh uproariously: music-hall and theatre: since *c.* 1920. Granville cites the shorter form and glosses it thus: 'A comedian's boast that his gags so reduced the audience to helplessness through laughter that the people at the end seats fell into the aisles.' Cf **not a dry seat in the house.** R.C., 1978, notes that 'another US version is *laid 'em in the aisles*'.

I have... See also **I've...**

I have a bone in my leg, C18–20, not much used after *c.* 1940; **...in my arm,** C17–18; **...in my throat,** the predominant form of C16. A humorous excuse for a feigned inability to walk S, Dialogue III, has:

NEV[EROUT]: Miss come be kind for once, and order me a Dish of Coffee.

MISS: Pray, go yourself; let us wear out the oldest first. Besides, I can't go, for I have a Bone in my Leg.

I have (or **I've**) **a picture of Lord Roberts (in full dress).** 'A c.p. rejoinder to someone asking for something' (L.A.): mostly army and RAF: since *c.* 1918, by which time it would no longer have much 'trading' value. P.B.: usu. prec. by *no, but....*; ob. by 1950. See also **sorry, no....**

I have a visitor (or **visitors**). A Victorian and Edwardian euph. c.p., 'I.have a flea – or fleas – on me or in my bed or...'; during WW1, *I have visitors* meant 'I have body lice.'

I have friends to stay. See **friend has come....**

I have (or **I've**) **had my moments.** 'My achievements (e.g., sexual) may not be conspicuous but are substantial. Often with implication that they are at least as substantial as those of others, who choose to recount their "moments" more explicitly. Educated US use since 1940(?), but the understatement suggests UK origin' (R.C., 1977). Right, on all counts! The c.p. has, since *c.* 1965, acquired far wider meaning, e.g. exciting experiences, successes, and so forth. (Playfair, 1977.) And A.B., 1978, tells me that, in its sexual connotation it is, in US and by both sexes, occ. altered to *I've had my ups and downs.* P.B.: in UK, often mock illiterate, *Oh, I've 'ad me moments, y'know!* See also **we all have our moments.**

I have influence in the right quarter. See **influence....**

I have (or **I've**) **made up my mind. Don't confuse me with the facts.** 'A US Admiral quite recently. Seems to be gaining currency in the Royal Navy' (RA P.W. Brock, 1969). 'Also *my mind's made up....* Certainly [in US, from] before 1960' (R.C., 1977).

I have my agents. I'm well informed in the matter, I have private sources of information: among army and air force officers and NCOs: since 1939. (Rohan D. Rivett, *Behind Bamboo*, 1946, concerning prisoners-of-war in Japan.) In joc allusion to 'secret agents'. 'In US, almost always followed by "everywhere"' (J.W.C., 1977), and 'Often a jocular reply to "How on earth did you know that?"' (R.C., 1977). Since *c.* 1970, mostly among civilians, also *I have my spies*, which has predominated (Paul Janssen cites *The Third Ear*, 1971). See also **my spies....**

I have news for you. See **I've got news....**

I have no pain, dear Mother, now,/But oh! I am so dry, is a famous quot'n from a poem by Edward Farmer (1809–76), *The Collier's Dying Child.* In a shanty parody, this became 'I feel no pain, dear Mother, now,/But oh! I am so dry' – with the ribald addition, 'Please lead me to a brewery/And leave me there to die' (the invaluable Cohen). S.G. Dixon, 1978, adds the var. '...Connect me with the brewery and lay me down to die'.

L.A., 1974, justly remarked that the first two lines were 'often quoted with dramatic emphasis when the speaker had nothing better to say.' (Early 1900s – mid C20.) To which I should, I fear, add the precautionary gloss, 'That's a pun on a speaker, or an actor, *drying up*'.

I have to hand it to you! 'I must say – you're very good at it indeed.' 'I recognize your superiority.': US: C20. (Berrey.) R.C., 1977, explains, '"It" being a figurative prize. But often ironic – that is, the prize being for stupidity rather than [intelligence or] skill'. P.B.: also heard in other tenses and persons, as in, e.g. 'You had to hand it to him – he was a really smooth operator!' Cf **I'll hand it....**

I have (or **I've got**) **to see a man about a dog** is often offered as an explanation of – a reply to – someone's awkward question about one's destination; more often, simply 'Excuse me – I must leave you now': Brit. and US: late C19–20. Also, in C20, a casual remark that one has to go to the lavatory. In the US of *c.* 1920, it meant particularly 'I must go out and buy some liquor' (W & F).

A humorous var. that never became very gen.: *I have to see a dog about a man.*

I haven't a thing to wear. Of specifically feminine c.pp., this is the most commonly used; even more widely used than **you know what men are.** It dates from at least as early as 1890 – and prob. goes further back by a generation.

What she means is, 'For this very special occasion. I haven't a dress, a gown, a robe, that I haven't already worn at least once': and men should, ostensibly, sympathize, for, after all, it's a damnably awkward situation.

I haven't laughed so much (or **so hard**) **since my mother** (or **since grandma** or **auntie**) **caught her** (**left**) **tit** (or **her tits**) **in the mangle.** I haven't laughed so much for a long time: low and raffish: C20. A 'sick joke' current many years before 'sick' humour became a fashion. In *The Cruel Sea*, 1951, Nicholas Monsarrat has *...since Ma caught her tits...* (R.S.). Also Can., and prob. wider spread still.

Cf the Eng. c.p. *I haven't laughed so much since father died*, described by Granville, 1969, as 'a light-hearted comment on hearing about a mishap to someone who is unpopular': which sets things in a rather clearer light.

See also **since Auntie...**

I hear (or **note**) **what you say.** '"I don't accept or agree with what you have just said," Quite common: I have heard both forms from different people within a week recently' (Playfair, 1977). Cf:

I hear you is a Scottish c.p., dating since *c.* 1905. Early in Aug. 1970, the late Lord Reith was interviewed by Mr Malcolm Muggeridge; in the course of the interview, the following bit of dialogue occurred:

REITH: I hear you.

MUGGERIDGE: Going back –

REITH: Did you get what I said just now?

MUGGERIDGE: You said *I hear you.*

REITH: That's a Scots expression.

MUGGERIDGE: What does it signify?

REITH: I hear you – that the remark is not worth answering or that the remark you made was untrue.
Contrast **you heard!**
US usage began *c.* 1960, as Fain declared, 1977, in the sense of 'I understand'. In that very intelligent 'send-up', Cyra McFadden's *The Serial*, 1977, occurs: '"I hear you," Ginger said, sighing. "Really, I hear you."' R.C., 1978, thinks that, in the US, it orig. among the Negroes, with the var. *I hear you talking*. Then there's the elab. in the prec. entlry., and as *I hear what you are saying*, both US and Can., as Hugh Quetton reminded me, 1978. In short, the Brit. use of the phrase was very prob. the earlier; yet the US use may have been independent.

P.B.: *c.* 1977–8 there was also a vogue, in e.g. committees, boardrooms, etc., for 'I hear you say...', where what was 'heard' was the underlying implication of what the original speaker had said – interpreted by the hearer; not so much a disagreement, as an attempted clarification. I even heard a non-conformist minister exclaim in despair, 'I can't hear what I'm saying!' This was not the same minister as the one who, in a sermon, declaimed – in non-vogue English – the corrective, 'I think what Jesus was *trying* to say was...'

I heard the voice of Moses say. See **roll on, my bloody twelve!**

I hope I don't intrude and **I hope I'm not interrupting anything** (! or ?). The latter 'is often heard on TV when anybody enters a room and finds a couple kissing or embracing' (Petch, 1976): since the 1920s. The former is much older and began with John Poole's very successful farce, *Paul Pry*, 1825, although when it became a c.p. is a date impossible to pin-point. (Thanks to Oliver Stonor.)

I hope it keeps fine for you. See **hope it....**

I hope to tell you! A US c.p. of affirmation: since *c.* 1925; by 1960, virtually†. (Berrey.)

I hope we shall meet in heaven. S, opens in St James's Park with the following:

COLONEL: Well met, by Lord.

LORD SP[ARKISH]: Thank you, Colonel; a Parson would have said, I hope we shall meet in Heaven.

This orig. as a pious ecclesiastical convention of C17–20; it soon gained a much wider currency, as the quot'n shows.

I hope you have chewy on your boot. See *Chewy....*

I hope your rabbit dies! See **hope your....**

I kid you not. 'No kidding' – I mean it, I'm being serious: since the middle 1950s; by 1970, slightly ob. In Francis Clifford, *The Hunting-Ground*, 1964, an English journalist uses it on several occasions: and I suspect that it was orig. and that it remained predominantly – journalistic. Note that in the *Sunday Times*, 5 Nov. 1972, Alan Brien writes,

Argued last night at a *Time* magazine party with Kingsley Amis....

'I kid you not,' said Kingsley.

'By the way, does he [a character in a Kingsley Amis novel] say "I kid you not"?' 'No! But then neither do I.'

'Popularized by the film [1954] of Herman Wouk's The *"Caine" Mutiny* [1951], a novel in which it was the deposed Captain Queeg's "trademark". It lingers still in some people's speech' (P.B., 1975). By *c.* 1960, also Aus.: it occurs in Alexander Buzo's *The Roy Murphy Show*, performed in 1971.

On the analogy of the archaic Standard Eng. *I like you not, I love you not*, etc.

I knew it in the bath is a theatrical c.p. of C20: 'an actor's jocular lament when he dries up at rehearsals. Like so many stage catch-phrases, it is probably true' (Granville).

I know and you know, but it (or **the thing**) **doesn't know**, where *it* or *the thing* is usually a machine or a mechanical device: mainly Aus.: since the late 1940s. Used esp. by workmen to justify, or partly justify, some malpractice. (B.P.)

I know one thing and that ain't (occ. **isn't**) **two**. I know this certainly and emphatically, as in 'But one thing I do know, and that ain't two; he used to be very dirty' – which occurs in one of the novels, and collections of stories, written, *c.*

1895–1925, by Edwin Pugh: predominantly Cockney: since *c.* 1880.

R.C. aptly recalls 'the Classical Greek proverb "the fox knows many things, but the hedgehog knows one big thing". Perhaps better, "many tricks... one great trick" (Archilochus, *c.* 700 BC).'

I left you in this position. P.B. wrote, 1974:

Army c.p. from the manual of Drill Instruction, chapter 2 onwards. After the introduction, every subsequent lesson begins thus, and as all senior NCOs have to teach a drill lesson as part of their promotion qualifying course, all are familiar with the phrase. As you can imagine, it lays itself open to all sorts of parody and abuse.

Since, at least, 1945. Cf the navy's **it should not be possible.**

I lift up my finger and I say tweet tweet, hush hush, but now, come come enjoyed a brief popularity as a c.p. in the 1930s. From the lyric of a Leslie Sarony song of the period. (Noble, 1976.)

I like Ike, which began as a political campaign slogan for Dwight (popularly Ike) Eisenhower, came to mean '"I don't know why but I just like it", referring to anything from apple pie to Zen Buddhism' (W&F, in the Introduction to the Appendix); but by 1970, it was, as a c.p., virtually†.

Main factors in the popularity of the phrase were Eisenhower's own vast popularity and the effectiveness of the long *i* used thrice, the rhyme *like – Ike*, the three successive mono-syllables, as Farb points out.

I like it, with *like* quietly or, at worst, not raucously emphasized. Perhaps it was, at first, a Services' c.p. of approbation, as P.B. supposed when, in 1974, he wrote, 'I first heard it in the later 1950s, when I saw a major running up and down the touchlines at a regimental football match, shouting, "I *like* it, Signals. I *like* it!" at intervals. It is still current.' It has, in the fact, been widely used by middle and upper class civilians since *c.* 1960, esp. among the educated and cultured. What's more, it reflects the understatement characteristic of all such Britons and esp. Englishmen. It has quietly become so gen. that by 1978 at latest it was often shortened to a laconic '*like* it', as my son-in-law David Mann remarked then.

I like it but it doesn't like me. This semi-joc., ruefully serious, c.p. of C19–20, refers to food or drink, or even work, that one likes but that disagrees with one. This is, in fact, the modern form of a c.p. that goes back to *c.* 1700 or perhaps a little earlier, *I love it...*, as in Dialogue I of S:

LADY SM[ART]: Madam, do you love Bohea tea?

LADY ANSW[ERALL]: Why really, Madam, I must confess, I do love it; but it does not love me.

I like me: who do you like? 'Report called forth by anyone displaying an unseemly high opinion of himself. General' (P.B., 1975): since *c.* 1950.

I like my women hot and strong. See **hot and strong....**

I like that! See well, I like that!

I like work: I could watch it all day. Suggested as an Aus. c.p. since *c.* 1950 (B.P.) this is actually, as my very old friend, the immensely well-read Oliver Stonor points out, a quot'n from Jerome K. Jerome, *Three Men in a Boat*, 1889.

P.B.: the actual passage, in Ch. XV, arises when it is suggested that the book's narrator should take his turn at sculling: he demurs, 'It is not that I object to the work, mind you; I like work; it fascinates me. I can sit and look at it for hours. I love to keep it by me; the idea of getting rid of it nearly breaks my heart' – and there is a whole page (244, in my now sadly disintegrating first edn copy) in similar delightful vein.

I like your company, but your hours don't suit. A parting phrase: late C19–20. (Russell Davies, reviewing this book in *New Statesman*, 9 Sep. 1977.) P.B.: cf an earlier version, a reversal of the polite form, that was (? invented, and) used by C.J. Vaughan (1816–97) to break up, e.g. tutorials: 'Can't you go? Must you stay?'

I like your nerve! See **of the nerve!**

I live at the sign of the cock's tooth and headache was, in late C18–early 19, a tart reply to an impertinent and inquisitive 'Where do you live?' Grose, 1796.

I live in the last house. See farther down the street...

I look like the last of pee-time. 'I look like the wrath of God' (cliché) – awful, terrible: Indiana, Tennessee, and the States between: only among intimates, and mostly feminine: C20. (J.W.C., 1977.) Cf:

I look like the wreck of the *Hesperus*. See wreck of the Hesperus.

[**I looks towards you** and its response, **I catches your eye**, are drinking conventions rather than true c.pp. Both of them occur in Nevil Shute's novel, *Pastoral*, 1944, as Peter Sanders has reminded me, as he has reminded me of so much else. They are prob. Cockney in orig., and may go back as far as 1850 or even earlier.]

I love it but it doesn't love me. See I like it....

I love my jest an the ship were sinking, where *an* was already archaic for 'if' or, better, 'even if': apparently *c.* 1660–1720; at first and always predominantly a nautical c.p. In *Love for Love* (at III, iii), 1795, William Congreve has Ben ('half home-bred and half sea-bred') exclaim, 'Handsome! he! me! he! nay, forsooth, an you be for joking, I'll joke with you; for I love my jest, an the Ship were sinking, as we say'n at sea.'

I love my life, but oh, you kid! was a US c.p. of *c.* 1916–40. The 'kid', it seems, was the usual sexy little bit of 'sucker bait'. Recorded in HLM, second edn, at p.424. R.C. comments, 1978, 'Moribund but not yet dead – witness the play, *I Love My Wife*, recently opened on Broadway. Now more commonly a jocular "pass" directed at the "kid" in question – or perhaps a general comment on marital fidelity: I am happily married, but not yet blind'.

See also **oh, you kid!**

I love you too. 'Ironic response to an approbrious remark – one unpleasant enough to demand a reply, but not worth picking a fight over. In one sense, a way of saying "Fuck you too" politely: US: since [*c.* 1960]' (R.C., 1978). P.B.: not unknown in UK, prob. adopted via TV. Cf earlier **and you!**, q.v.

I married him for better or for worse, but not for lunch is an Aus. 'c.p. used by a woman whose husband has retired, works at home or comes home for his midday meal' (B.P., 1975): since the 1940s. A pun on the words in the Anglican marriage service. Playfair notes, 1977, that it has been familiar also to Britons since at least as early as the latish 1960s.

I may be crazy but I ain't no fool dates from 1904, and, although not much used since *c.* 1950, is not yet (1976) †. US, it became almost immediately a c.p. when Bert Williams introduced it by singing, in the 1904 song thus titled, words by Rogers and music by Williams. (W.J.B. cites Edward B. Marks's *They All Sang*, 1934.)

[**I meanter say**, popularized by George Robey, could, I suppose, be called a c.p. Robey (1869–1954) was at the height of his music-hall fame for an exceptionally long time, esp. *c.* 1900–30. But he was making fun of the very widely used cliché 'I mean to say', a stop-gap apology by those who are not very good at explaining things. P.B.: cf the later C20 'Y'know what I mean'; and see **well, this is it...**]

I might as well plough with dogs! All this is most ineffectual: C17–20; that, by *c.* 1700, had become semi-proverbial and was, by *c.* 1860, used only in dialect. Apperson.

I must have killed a Chinaman is, in Aus. applied to a run of bad luck: C20. It derives from a widespread belief held there. I remember hearing it among 'the Aussies' of WW1.

I must have notice of that question. I don't wish to reply, or to answer; you're being difficult or awkward: since the early 1950s. 'From parliamentary procedure' (Shaw). Often spoken with a smile.

I must (or I really must) have one of those was an ephemeral c.p. of the early 1880–*c.* 1880–3, to be delusorily precise – deriving from a comic song and therefore, not at all surprisingly, non-aristocratic. Ware.

I must love and leave you – but, rather more usu., **I must love you and leave you** dates from *c.* 1880 – perhaps from a decade earlier – and prob. comes from dialect; apparently the Cheshire dialect – see Dr Bridges's *Cheshire Proverbs*, 1917. Outside of dialect, *I must love you...* is, I think, not proverbial but a genuine c.p., as its occurrence in H.V. Esmond's *The Law Divine*, performed on 29 Aug. 1918 (and pub'd in 1922) makes clear in Act II:

> EDIE: (*going to door*) Well, after this little social intercourse, I must love you and leave you.

In short, when used, lit., it is semi-proverbial; but when, as in that quot'n it means no more than 'Very sorry, but I *must* go', it is a c.p.

This shortening has become more gen. than the full, the livelier, the instantly comprehensible form ..., *as sailors do their wives*. Either form is often a both joc. and polite way of saying *au revoir* to, e.g., one's neighbours. (Based on a note from L.A., 1976, who adds that the c.p. is used 'especially between women at the end of a chat when taking leave'.) There is a var. *I'll love you and leave you.* P.B.: all forms are usu., as in the quot'n, prefaced by an introductory *well*, ... cf **fuck'em and leave'em.**

I must or I'll bust. 'I simply must go to the w.c.' – the toilet – the loo – the john – or whatever the predominant term may be: a mainly Aus. c.p.: since *c.* 1925.

I must ring up the Duchess. See Duchess....

I nearly dropped my cork leg! Because of amazement or agitation: late C19–20 (Miss Christime Gray, 1978). P.B.: a version heard in later C20, usu. explained by 'I was so surprised *or* took aback *or* flabbergasted, etc. that' *I nearly bought my own beer!* cf **laugh?...**

I need (or want) a piss so bad, my back teeth are floating (or **awash**) or ...**I can taste it; I need a shit so bad my eyes are brown.** These are Can. – need I say, decidedly low Can. – c.pp. of C20. R.C. notes, 1978, that the *floating* version 'has been current in US from at least the 1930s', and Lovett, 1978, supplied the var. *awash* from Aus. cf *I must or I'll bust.*

I need that like I need a hole in the (or my) **head!** I don't need it at all – indeed, it would be hateful, or disastrous, or ludicrous: adopted in Brit. *c.* 1950, from US, where it was extremely popular *c.* 1948. W & F, 1960, remark that it was 'popularized by comedians', and Leo Rosten, in his delightful *The Joys of Yiddish*, 1968, has aligned it with, e.g. *get lost!* and *I should have such luck*, as a Yiddishism; he gives it in the form *I need it like a hole in the head.* The Yiddish for 'a hole in the head' is *loch in Kop* – cf Ger. *loch im Kopf* (= *Loch in dem Kopf*).

Fain, 1978, writes: 'I've heard it slightly altered [in US], "I need that like I need *another* hole in the head", and sometimes the pronoun possessive comes after, as in "She needs that like another hole in her head"'. He notes an occ. var. *I need that like a cow does two tails.*

I needed that! See **by Jove...**

I never drink (pause) **wine.** 'From Bela Lugosi as Dracula (in his Hungarian accent)' (Ashley, 1984): US: from the film, *Dracula*, 1931.

I never liked it, anyway! 'Of something broken, lost, mock-resignedly; can be sour grapes meant to amuse, show you're a philosophical type' (Shaw, 1969); 'If a housewife breaks something, she tends to declare, "I never liked it, anyway", often in a resigned tone of voice' (Shaw, later in same year). The late Frank Shaw dated it as arising in the late 1940s.

Contrast **it come off in me 'and, mum** (or **ma'am**).

I never remember a name and (or but) **I always forget a face** is 'c.p. when people are discussing their inability to remember names and faces' (B.P.): Aus.: since the late 1940s. Prompted by the cliché, 'I never remember a name but I always remember' – or 'I never forget' – 'a face.'

Relevant is Groucho Marx's wisecrack, 'I never forget a face, but in your case I'll make an exception'. (With thanks to Maurice Wedgewood, 1977.)

I note what you say. See **I hear what you say.**

I only asked. 'A bigger vogue than either [**I won't take me coat off** or **she knows, yer know**] was another comedy call sign Partridge has passed over, Bernard Bresslaw's "I only asked", from *the Army Game*: still used, in hurt tones, when someone has addressed you snappishly (whether you have "asked" a question or not)' (Russell Davies, reviewing the first ed. of this book, in *New Statesman*, 9 Sep. 1977). I stand reproved.

Nigel Rees, in *VIBS*, says, 'Quite the most popular catchphrase of the late 1950s, Bernard Bresslaw played a large, gormless private – "Popeye" Popplewell – in Granada TV's Army Game (1957–62) and this was his response whenever someone put him down.' Cf **I'm only asking.**

I only do it for (occ. **for the**) **kicks.** I shouldn't do it at all if I didn't get a thrill out of it: since the 1950s. (Fernley O. Pascoe, 1975) Adopted from US, where it arose during the 1920s (Fain, 1977). P.B.: in later C20, prob. as often of other persons, e.g. *she only...*; cf **I'm only here for the beer.**

I only work here (emphasis on *work*). I am not responsible for my employer's policy or methods: since the late 1940s. (B.P.) 'In my experience this is usually preceded by one of two phrases: *don't mind me*, which gives the whole c.p. an air of martyrdom, and *don't blame me*, which may have directly prompted *I only work here*. All three can be used alone, the complete versions being so familiar that the auditor will draw the correct inference' (Lovett, 1978). See **don't ask me...**

I owe you one 'means that I will retaliate for some advantage which another has obtained, or for an injury done' (*Am*, 1877): US: only very approx. *c.* 1840–1900. The expression seems to have migrated from England, for George Colman the Younger, in *The Poor Gentleman: A Comedy*, pub'd 1802, in I, ii, uses it to mean 'I am very much obliged to you' – esp. for a witticism, a jest, a pun:

OLL: I am now Cornet Ollapod...at your service.
SIR C: I wish you joy of your appointment. You may now distil water for the shop from the laurels you gather in the field.
OLL: Water for – Oh! laurel-water. He! he! Come, that's very well, indeed! Thank you, good sir – I owe you one!

Perhaps elliptical for 'I owe you a drink for that', because in II, i, Ollapod says, 'Come, that's very well! very well indeed, for a bumpkin! Thank you, good Stephen, I owe you half a one.'

I prefer your room to your company is a middle-middle-class hint, containing a middling pun and prob. dating from *c.* 1880.

I rather care for that! See **oh, I, I say, I rather...**

I read (or, in UK, **I've read**) **about people like you, but I've never met one before.** A US c.p.: since *c.* 1945; partially adopted in the UK during the early 1950s. (Mr S. Daniel, 1978.)

I read you. I understand you: US: since *c.* 1960. (Fain, 1977.) Synon. with **I hear you.** P.B.: perhaps prompted by radio/telephony procedure: cf *I read you loud and clear*, q.v. at **message received.**

I really dig it! I understand it thoroughly and enjoy it immensely: US: since *c.* 1960; and among young Britons since *c.* 1962. A specializing of the generic *dig it*, to understand, hence to understand and enjoy something.

I'd exile on the farthest frigate
Those who claim they 'really dig it' –

says Sydney J. Harris, in *This Cat Doesn't Dig All That Groovy Talk* (see **right on!**).

P.B.: Fain, 1977, suggests, 'Much earlier – probably comes from the Spanish Civil War period [1936–9] *diga me*, tell me', which may be so, but, in UK at least, the phrase is inseparably associated with the invasion by the Hippie influence from the USA.

I really must have one of those. See **I must have...**

I refer you to Smith! imputes a lie or a boast: 1897 – *c.* 1889. As Ware tells us, it comes 'from a character named Smith with

an affliction of lying in *The Prodigal Father* (Strand Theatre, 1897)'. Redding Ware had an enviable knowledge of the theatre, to which he had contributed several light comedies of some merit; he was also a close observer of the vogues and eccentricities of everyday colloquial English.

I resemble that remark; with *remark* often ommitted. A waggish c.p. retort to any joc. insult: since the 1920s. Orig. a juvenile pun on 'I *resent* that remark'; I first heard it in *c.* 1930 and last heard it on 22 Nov. 1974.

'Often followed by "It insulates me" (insults). I first heard this in 1952, in Tennessee' (A.B., 1978). P.B.: this is the same kind of humour as in the use of deliberate malaprop-isms like 'Are you casting nasturtiums?' (aspersions), and 'Serpently!' for 'Certainly!' Cf **am I insulated?**

I saw diamonds. See **do it again, Ikey.**

[**I say!** Whether as a means of obtaining attention or in admiration or astonishment, it cannot, strictly, be called a c.p. Both US, as in *Am*, 1877, land Brit., as in Ware. Contrast:]

I say, I am a fool! See **oh, I, I say, I am a fool!**

I say, I say, I say! In 1968, the late Wilfred Granville wrote to me as follows about this c.p. and about **I do not wish to know that** and **kindly leave the stage:**

Kindly Leave the Stage is the title of a recent TV programme that is said to contain the corniest gag in the history of the music-hall. . . . This programme was on BBC1 this autumn. Some of the old-timers were roped in to give the authentic touch.

A character, mid-stage, is interrupted by a 'comic' rushing up to him yelling 'I say, I say, I say'. First character shushes him off with 'Kindly leave the stage'; intruder persists with some fatuous question, such as 'Why do chickens lay eggs?' First gent irritably, 'Why *do* chickens lay eggs?' Intruder, 'Because they can't lay bricks.' That sort of feeble stuff! Years old in the music-halls, e.g. the Metropolitan, Edgware Road, in the 1890s, or the old Bedford, Camden Town, and such like houses in that era of entertainment. Sometimes a number of so-called 'comics' would come on the stage in succession to harass the lone lead with the bloody 'I say, I say, I say' thing until it became irritating.

For some years after it had died in the music-halls, 'comics' used it in touring musicals (known as 'E-flat Revues') or in concert parties at the seaside. A lull followed this in the 1929–1939 period until, with the formation of ENSA, during WW2, when many 'comics' who had not had a job for many years reintroduced this 'I say...' business with the fatuous question thing. But it used to be a feature in the old times when variety bills catered for unsophisticated audiences upon whom subtler comedy would have been wasted. So you could fairly say the 1890s, as a date for the period [of its heyday].

He goes on to say: '"I don't wish to know that" is a brush-off when the "I say, I say" fellow tries to interrupt the lead's patter. I asked my wife if, in her young days, she had personally heard this "I say..." business; she remembers it clearly in a concert party while she was on holiday. It was usually a "second comic's" technique.'

Support comes from Fredrick Lonsdale's *The High Road*, performed in 1927, and rewritten as an acting edn. and copyrighted, in 1928, near the end of Act II:

LORD TRENCH: (*turning to* LADY TRENCH) Let me catch you in your bath, that's all!
HILARY: (*...jovially*) I say! I say! I say!

Hilary, by the way, is a good, rather vulgar, little man.

I don't wish to know that, however, has now (later C20) the further meaning, as Camilla Raab points out, 1977: 'I dare say, but, in my opinion, it is utterly irrelevant', e.g. a comment on 'But, Mum, *all* the *other* girls are wearing them!'

Nigel Rees, in *VIBS*, concerning the synon. US *I don't want to hear about it*, writes, 'A repetition line from Dan

Rowan and Dick Martin's routine in [the late 1960s TV comedy series] *Laugh-In*. Martin is endlessly on the look-out for "action" while Rowan can hardly keep his partner's mind off sex:

ROWAN (fretting about Martin's frail appearance): For your own good, you should pick up some weight.

MARTIN: Shoulda been with me last night. I picked up 118 pounds.

ROWAN: I don't want to hear about it.'

I say, what a smasher! dates from late 1945 and comes from the BBC radio programme, 'Stand Easy' – a post-war version or reshaping of 'Merry-Go-Round'. Perhaps first written *about* by myself in 'Those Radio Phrases', printed in the *Radio Times* of 6 Dec. 1946 – an article I was invited to contribute but could not have written without the material generously supplied by Mr Campbell Nairne, who, at the time Deputy Editor, became Editor.

Mrs Shirley M. Pearce, 1975, in ref. to the years 1939–50, when she was a child and then a young girl, supplied the following 'From a well-known toothpaste advertisement of WW2':

On seeing a good-looking girl, [one would say]:

'I say, what a smasher–
Two fried eggs and a bacon rasher!'

On seeing a plain girl:

'Spotlight on charm!' (Sarcastically.)

Cf **don't force it, Phoebe!**

I say, you fellows! is a schoolboys' c.p., dating since *c.* 1940 but, by 1970, somewhat less popular in those discriminating circles. In Frank Richards's Greyfriars School stories, the long-famous character, Billy Bunter, is constantly using these hallowed words. The author's real name was Charles Hamilton.

The phrase was given new life when the Billy Bunter stories were broadcast on TV in the 1950s and, as noted in *VIBs*, was 'given a memorably metallic ring in Gerald Campion's brilliant characterisation [of Bunter]'.

I see, said the blind man. An elab. and humorous way of saying 'I understand', but implying, of course, that although one understands, one doesn't fully do so – as indeed, the dovetail (which R.S., 1977, remembers hearing as a schoolboy in 1915) *when he couldn't see at all*, makes clear. B.G.T., 1978, confirms this and adds that it has been esp. common among schoolchildren. In the US, it is much earlier: 'it was common in my parent's speech, and probably in their parents' (J.W.C., 1977): which would take it back to *c.* 1860. And Ashley, 1983, also from US, supplies the punning *'I see', said the blind man, as he picked up his hammer and saw*.

I shall fall into the ragman's hands. See **my rents....**

I shall return! See **like MacArthur...**

I shall see you dangle in the sheriff's picture-fame. 'I shall see you hanging on the gallows' (Grose, 1785): underworld: *c.* 1750–1830.

I shan't play! I don't like it at all; I'm annoyed: Aus.: since *c.* 1885; ob. by 1935; by 1965, virtually †. Neil Lovett, in *The National Times*, 23–28 Jan. 1978, notes that it became more commonly *I won't play!* From the peevish childishness expectable in children; half-joc., in orig. at least. P.B.: but, at any rate in the 1940s, it was recognised as a c.p. among children in UK, with var. *I'm not playing* (, *so there*), or shortened to *shan't play!*

I should be so lucky! More or less synon. with **what a hope...!**, q.v.: orig. US of Yiddish orig., since *c.* 1930. It has, since *c.* 1960, been 'very widely used in Britain' (Michael Goldman, 1978). Other pronouns may be substituted for *I*, and whereas the *I* form connotes a dry, deprecatory cheerful acceptance of improbability, the *you* form is derisive.

I should coco! 'I should say so!' – indicating emphatic agreement: 'Bare agreement (like *I should shay so*); almost in code; sly doubt, caustic comment being held in reserve, but implied': Cockney: C20. (L.A., 1974.) *Coco* = imperfect rhyming slang for *I should say* or *think so*.

I should fret! *I* should worry! – It's no business of mine: US: C20. (Berrey.) 'Never common, now dead. In US, *fret* has gradually lost the sense "worry"' (R.C., 1978).

I should have (better, **of**) **stood in bed!** is US and it implies that one has had so unhappy or frustrating or unsuccessful a day that one might just as well have *stayed* in bed: since *c.* 1935 (W & F). A.B., 1978, notes, 'I've heard this one most frequently stated when Friday falls on the 13th day of a month'.

In *Strong Cigars and Lovely Women*, 1951, John Lardner, that talented son of a talented father who died untimely, as charming as he was able (I had an hour's chat with him while he was *en route* to report the Olympic Games about to be held, 1952, in Melbourne), wrote:

It may well be that Mr [Joe] Jacobs is the first fight manager in history to be tapped for [Bartlett's] *Familiar Quotations*...No quotation book that calls itself a quotation book can look you in the eye these days unless it includes 'I should of stood in bed'.

This department notes that the book has been further enlarged to accommodate the second of Joe's great coinages: 'We wuz robbed!' The phrase is attributed by some scholars to Anon. and by others to Ibid., but it was work of Jacobs. It was uttered after that Schmeling and Mr Jacobs had licked the stuffing out of Jack Sharkey, only to hear the verdict go against them. [In Bartlett, given as 'we *was* robbed'.]

According to the poet [Uncle Daniel] Parker [the New York *Daily Mirror* poet]...the origin of 'I should of stood in bed' is wrongly described in the book. It seems there is a nonsensical footnote to the effect that Jacobs gave birth to the words after losing a bet on the World Series of 1934. As it happens, the great man coined them 2 feet from your correspondent. It was the only time I heard a famous quotation in the making... On this occasion – 1935, it was – he was seeing his first and last ball game. Mr Jacobs had the seat behind me in the press box at Detroit for the opening game of the World Series, though Lonnie Warneke was pitching very nifty ball for the Cubs, Mr Jacobs did not like it. An icy wind was curdling his blood, along with everyone else's. It was the coldest ball game I can remember.

A neighbour asked Joe what he thought of baseball, and Joe to him, these deathless words did speak: 'I should of stood in bed'...So now Joe, in the heavenly meadows, has a piece of Bartlett's *Familiar Quotations*. It is a nice break for both sides.

The edn of Bartlett must have been that of 1948, where, incidentally, the date is *not* given as 1934, but correctly as 1935.

(With thanks to *Newsweek*, for the International Editorial service, for their generous and valued permission to quote this passage.)

I should live so long! I'll be very lucky indeed to be still alive at the period – *or* that – you've just mentioned: US; esp., US Jews, this being an entirely Yiddish idiom: since *c.* 1920, if not much earlier. The great authority on Yiddish, Leo Rosten, firmly holds (9 June 1975) that it is neither c.p. nor cliché and notes that *'you* should live so long' also is very common. But R.C., 1978, protests: 'Pace Rosten, I'd say it is definitely a c.p. since normal use is figurative, not literal. That is, "I'd like to live long enough for that to happen – but I won't". In other words, "It would be nice if it did, but it won't."' I agree with Robert Claiborne.

I should murmur. See **I should smile.**

I should of stood in bed. See **I should have stood in bed.**

I should say! "Hearty enthusiasm in youth finds an expression such as *yes, indeed*, a dead form of the language. *I should say* soon proves inadequate, and the conditional future changes to the active future, *I'll say*. The process once started runs to the limit, *I'll tell the world*'(McKnight): US university students': *c.* 1920–2. It occurs earlier in Western Can. Cf.

I should smile! I shall – with pleasure! The *OED* gives the earliest Brit. example as at 1891. It came from the US. Charles H. Hoyt (1859–99), in *A Bunch of Keys; or, The Hotel*, performed in 1883, wrote in Act III,

SNAG: ...Do you require a room?

P.F.: You bet.

SNAG: Well, I should smile.

John Kendrick Bangs, famous for his *Houseboat on the Styx*, wrote *Katharine: A Travesty*, 1888, and in it occurs the passage:

TRANIO: Well, sirrah, what news is't thou has brought? Is the wedding finished? Are the cuckoos caught?

GREMIO: Well, I should smile. That wedding was unique.

In *The Pedagogical Seminary*, March 1912, A.H. Melville, in an article titled 'An Investigation of the Function and Use of Slang', based upon a test paper answered by boys and girls of four grades, presumably in 1911, classed *I should smile* as 'temporary' and, concerning this and seven or eight others current at this particular seat of learning, wrote: 'Most of these expressions drop out of usage as soon as the time or occurrence which recalls or represents them is forgotten.' But this particular c.p. had already been in use almost thirty years at least: even such so-called ephemeralities tend to be far more widely distributed and longer-lived than the user or even the recorder tends to think.

Clearly Mr Melville had failed to consult M, who says: *I should smile* or *snicker* or *murmur*, vulgarisms much in use to signify acquiescence with a statement made. 'Are you going to the picnic?' 'Well, I should smile.' A little of this goes a long way, but scores of expressions of this character are in use, so some reference to them is necessary.

The variants *snicker* and *murmur* were not adopted in UK and did not, I believe, last very long in US.

I should smile is recorded, 1942, by Berrey: but this fact does not necessarily mean that it was still, at that date, extant in the US. It occurs early in Western Can. Sandilands, 1930, glosses it thus: 'I should say so. Sometimes it is varied in the words *I should say*. (Another importation from the States.)'

In England, I heard it occ. during the period 1921–39. Cf the later sense of **you wouldn't knob it**, and:

I should worry! I'm certainly not worrying about that!: since *c.* 1910 in Britain and the Commonwealth. A modern example occurs in Jack Ripley, *Davis Doesn't Live Here Any More*, 1971, '"I should worry! I have already broken so many rules, an extra breakage will go unnoticed."' It is sometimes linked with a following **it'll all be the same in a hundred years**.

It was borrowed from the US. Mencken states that *I should worry* ('probably borrowed, in turn, from the Yiddish' – 'From the Yiddish' unequivocally, says Shipley, 1975) was, by Britons, 'absurdly changed... into *I should not worry*': presumably he had heard it so misused or, more likely, taken a correspondent's word for it that they did: but I myself never heard the misuse. Berrey lists it as a synonym of 'It's not my concern'. W & F includes it – and regards it as a synonym of 'I don't care' or 'I have no reason for alarm or concern'. Its US currency seems not to have prec. the C20; my earliest record rather indicates 'since *c.* 1910', the phrase being memorialized in S.R. Strait's 'Straight Talk', published in the *Boston Globe*, in *c.* 1917.

W.J.B., 1978, recalls that 'in the US of the 1920s, young people used to chant" I should worry, I should care,/I should marry a millionaire" – probably from a song'.

I stepped over a snake. 'I had a stroke of good luck': US rural: C20, but ob. since *c.* 1965. Fain, 1978, has referred to it as 'an old farmers' c.p.' of 50 years ago'.

I thank you! See **ay thang yew!**

I think it's going to rain. Let's depart: US: ? middle and late 1960s. Cliquey, originating among Frank Sinatra's 'clan' and perhaps orig. by him; used esp. as an 'in' phrase at a party threatening to become dull or boring. (Paul Janssen, 1978.)

I think you are a witch. Thomas Heywood, in Act I of 'The Second Part' (1631) of *The Fair Maid of the West*, causes Toota, Queen of Fesse, to say to Clem, the Clown:

Now, sir, you are of England?

CLEM: And I think you are a witch.

QUEEN: How, sirrah?

CLEM: A foolish proverb we use in our country, which to give you in other words, is as much as to say, You have hit the nail on the head.

At a rough guess, it was current *c.* 1605–55; and prob. it lent itself to irony. Cf **you have hit it...**, and **I bet your father...**

I think your policemen are wonderful has, by newspapermen, been credibly attributed to celebrities, not unnaturally female, visiting Britain: since the 1930s. From being a visitors' cliché it rapidly became a Brit. c.p., usu. joc. and occ. ironic. P.B.: tenuously relevant may be simpering Bobbies being told by their inspector, 'And now, boys, before Miss Poppy Spotlight presents the cup to the tug-o'-war team she wishes me to mention that she simply adores policemen.'"

I thought I had seen everything. A var. of **now I've seen everything**, q.v. at **now I've heard...**

I thought I should die laughing. See **laugh? I thought...**

I thought you'd never ask or **...you were never going to ask.** See **thought you'd...**

I told Wilbur, I told Orville, and I'm telling you: the damn thing will never leave the ground. 'As advice to the Wright Brothers, not very serious objection to the feasibility of a proposed project: used in the RCAF in the 1950s, probably of cartoon punch-line origin' (Ashley, 1982).

I took my harp to the party, but no one (or nobody) asked me to play. 'This must be a catch phrase – you can tell by the way people join in on the second half' (Russell Davies, reviewing the first ed. of this book, in *New Statesman*, 9 Sep. 1977). Neatly allusive is this: 'Although people still give musical evenings... it was now very much a declining habit... The girl who took her harp to the party would rarely have been asked to play' (Ronald Pearsall, *Popular Music of the 20's*, 1976). It prob. arose during the late 1920s.

I undercumstumble the laws of crackology. 'A phrase to mock one who has a liking for jaw-breaking words' (L.A., 1976): latish C19 – early 20. The bogus *crackology* puns *cracked* in the head, crazy [P.B.: or 'crack-jaw words']; and *undercumstumble* blends *understand* + *comprehend* +slang *tumble* to something, i.e. suddenly realise. Influenced by the dialect *undercumstand*. P.B.: and cf the early C18 – early 19 *your humble condumble*, 'your humble servant', as in S., 1738.

I used to be in the family way, now I'm in every bastard's way. See **Sister Hannah, you'll carry the banner.**

I used your soap two years ago. See **good morning, have you used...**

I want a piss so bad... See **I need a...**

I want it yesterday. 'Immediately, if not sooner. Current in US from 1940s. Probably originally Hollywood, notorious for its devotion to **hurry up and wait**, q.v.' (R.C., 1978).

I want three volunteers: you, you and you! This is 'the NCO's answer to the old [i.e. experienced] soldier's determination never to volunteer for anything' (Skehan, 1977): and how right that old soldier is! The number varies, but 'three' predominates and is integral to the c.p., which had orig. in the British Army, perhaps as far back as the Crimean War or even the Napoleonic Wars; certainly it was very common during WW1.

I want to be alone is reputed to have been a plea made frequently by Greta Garbo at the height of her fame. Certainly she either originated it, or popularized it, as a c.p. – cf the US slang, *do a Garbo*, to evade publicity. (Berrey; W&F.) No less certainly, Greta Garbo was not a solitary: she merely insisted on privacy. With her friends at Hollywood, as the late Lothar Mendes once told me, she was warm-hearted and delightful. It became also British and was, as late as 22 April 1974, used in the ITV 'Coronation Street' series (as Mr A.B. Petch has reminded me).

P.B.: will this one ever be satisfactorily cleared up? In *Observer*, Supp., Oct. 1979: 'It was to Porter that Garbo imparted the revelation that she had never said "I want to be alone." She explained to him, "I only said I want to be *let* alone." It was perhaps this article that prompted Prof. Hayashi Shuseki, of Mukogawa Women's University, Japan, to write to E.P. in 1979: 'Garbo, in a film called *Grand Hotel* (from the play [orig. a novel] by Vicki Baum), played the part of a famous ballerina. In one scene, when her lover had deserted her, a friend tried to console her, and she said, "I want to be alone." That's all. It was just a line in a play.'

Ashley, 1983, notes that in US it is 'usually rendered with a fake accent and written *vant*'.

I want to go places and do things. This is a c.p. (in US) only when used derisively: since *c.* 1930. (J.W.C., 1975.)

I want to know! In *Am.* 1859, J.R. Bartlett quotes this passage from Sir Charles Lyell (the famous British geologist), *A Second Visit to the United States of North America*, 1849:

Among the most common singularities of expression are the following: 'I should admire to see him' for 'I should like to see him'; 'I want to know!' and 'Do tell!' both exclamations of surprise, answering to our 'Dear me!' These last, however, are rarely heard in society above the middling class.

Apparently current *c.* 1800–90.

In John Neal, *The Down-Easters*, 1833, at chapter I, p. 3, the following occurs:

How? – *snacks* [shares] – hey? I don't understand you – I never heard of this before. I *want* to know! exclaimed the other down-easter [I.E. New Englander]. Well, you *do* know, replied the southerner, in perfect good faith, mistaking a northern exclamation for a formal interrogatory.

In short, the meaning is 'What you've just told me is remarkable *or* exciting *or* exceptionally interesting.'

In T.C. Haliburton, *The Clockmaker*, 3rd Series, 1848, concerning a young US girl being flattered by means of phrenology, Sam Slick of Connecticut remarks, 'And she keeps a-saying – "Well, he's a witch! well, how strange! lawful heart! Well, I want to know! – now I never! do tell!" – as pleased all the time as anything.'

A C20 example occurs in Gelett Burgess, *Love in a Hurry*, 1913, '"I want to know!" said Rosamund, with lively sarcasm' and indignation at a studied insult.

The phrase is recorded by Berrey, 1942, as an exclam. of 'surprise or astonishment'. Contrast **you wouldn't want to know.**

I was amazed! 'Frankie Howerd explains that when he was starting in radio just after [WW2] he thought a good gimmick would be for him to give unusual emphasis to certain words. Hence "I was a-*mazed*' and 'ladies and gentle-*men*', George Robey also used to say, 'I'm more than surprised – I'm amazed' (*VIBS*).

I was doing it when you were running up and down your father's backbone was a Services', esp. the British Army's, c.p. of WW1 and WW2; a WW1 var. of **before you came** (or **come**) **up.** The *it* is any activity whatsoever.

The civilian version is *when you were a gleam in your father's eye*, which occurs allusively in Harold Pinter's *The Homecoming*, 1965, 'That night ... you know ... the night you got me ... what was it like? Eh! When I was just a glint in your eye.'

This latter has engendered offspring of its own, as in '18 months ago, the new company plant was merely a twinkle in someone's eye' (Playfair, quoting *The Times* of 26 Oct. 1977).

See also **you were just a gleam ...**

I was there when they were needing 'em, not just feeding 'em. This old soldiers' gibe at peacetime soldiers, including National Servicemen home-stationed, arose long before

WW2 – approx. the early 1930s. The neatness of this c.p. indicates that it was not always merely contemptuous; occ. it connoted a tolerant, though wry, humour. (Elab. of a P.B. reminder.) UK only.

I washed my hair (or **me 'air**) **last night** (chorus) **and** (**now**) **I can't do a thing with it.** From the world of BBC entertainment. Russell Davies, in *New Statesman*, 9 Sep. 1977.

I wasn't born yesterday. I'm not a fool: C19–20. It lies on the border between c.p. and proverbial saying: *ODEP* cites from Marriott, 1837, 'The widow read the letter and tossed it into the fire with a "Pish! I was not born yesterday, as the saying is." ' It passed into US usage.

I weep for you! is a var., more US than Brit., of the satirical **my heart bleeds for you.**

I will ... See also entries at **I'll ...**

I will be hang'd and my horse too. See the quot'n from S at **at a church with a chimney in it.**

I will knock out two of your eight eyes is a mid C18–early C19 Billingsgate (London) fishwives' c.p. The other six, as Grose, 1788, enumerates them, are the bub*ies*' (nipples, 'eyes' of the breasts) – the naval ('eye' of the belly) 'two pope's eyes' (? the anal and urinal orifices) – and '***** eye', presumably the sexual aperture.

I will not make a lobster-kettle of my cunt. 'A reply frequently made by the nymphs of the Point at Portsmouth, when requested by a soldier to grant him a favour' (Grose, 1788): *c.* 1750–1850. Cf the slang *lobster*, or *boiled lobster*, a soldier, from his red coat (or jacket).

I will pay you as Paul did the Ephesians is a raffish c.p. of *c.* 1750–1850. (Grose). The explanation lies in the words usually added: **over the face and eyes and all the damned jaws.** An elab. of *pay*, to beat, to punish – cf the later form of the phrase, *I will pay you over face and eyes.*

I will work for my living. An underworld c.p., expressing the ultimate in improbability: since *c.* 1950 or a few years earlier. In effect, a preliminary *when* that happens has been implied.

I wish I had a man: I wouldn't half love him! A service-women's declaration of amorous longing: WW2.

I wish I had as many shillings! Frank Worsley, in *Itma*, 1948, says:

Tommy's [i.e., Tommy Handley's] remark, 'I wish I had as many shillings!', for instance, became quite a rage apart from Funf's incursion into the language, and 'I always do my best for all my gentlemen' was soon heard on all sides. They were the first of the many ['ITMA' 'gags'] to be adopted as part of everyday conversation.

And not only during ITMA days (1939–48) but for some years afterwards.

'Said ... in response to a remark such as "now I have a million eggs". This was a conscious borrowing from Jimmy Learmouth, a northern comedian of Handley's youth' (*VIBS*). See also TOMMY HANDLEY.

I wish I may die!, a c.p. of emphatic assertion, seems to have covered most of C18, as well as C19–20. It occurs in, e.g., George Colman, *The Jealous Wife*, at V, ii, where Toilet, a lady's maid, says to her mistress, 'I wish I may die, Ma'am, upon my honour, and I protest to your ladyship, I knew nothing in the world of the matter, no more than a child unborn.' As that quot'n implies, it is predominantly a lower- and lower-middle-class expression.

Also C20 US; variants: *I wish I were dead* and *I wish I was dead and buried.* (A.B., 1978.) In C20 usage, a cliché.

P.B.: app. a var. of **may I die!** q.v.

I wish I may never hear worse news! S, Second Conversation, has the following:

FOOTMAN: Madam, Dinner's upon the Table.

....

NEV[EROUT]: I wish I may never hear worse News.

Partly a c.p., not quite † in C18, partly a conventional courtesy – as it presumably was at first.

I wish my head will never ache till that day. See S, First Conversation:

LADY ANSW[ERALL]. Why, you must know, Miss is in Love. MISS: I wish my Head will never ache till that Day. [i.e. I'll be lucky if my first headache doesn't come before that.] It seems to have fallen out of, at least, frequent use by the end of C18.

I wonder what they will (or they'll) think of next! See what will they ....

I wonder who's kissing her now was orig. the title of a song that was sung, 1909, in a very popular play, *Prince of Thought*, as W.J.B., citing Edward B. Marks, tells me. The song became 'the rage' all over the English-speaking world and, in the US at least, gained some sort of currency as a c.p.

I won't be shat upon! I will *not* be 'squashed' or browbeaten or silenced: raffish: since *c.* 1930. By a punning blend of *sat upon* and *shit upon*. Contrast **I don't mind being shit on ...**

I won't play. See I shan't play.

I won't put a churl upon a gentleman. S, Third Conversation has:

LORD SM[ART]: Tom Neverout, will you taste a Glass of the *October*?

NEV: No, my Lord, I like your Wine; and I won't put a Churl upon a Gentleman: Your Honour's Claret is good enough for me.

This c.p., *c.* 1550–1850, means 'I won't drink ale or beer immediately after wine' – the implication being that whereas wine is a gentleman's drink, ale or beer is a yokel's; but that didn't prevent the gentlemen from drinking the latter.

I won't say I will, but I won't say I won't, mostly US, dates from 1923, when Irene Bordoni sang it in *Little Miss Bluebeard*; words by De Sylva and music by Gershwin. Noted by Edward B. Marks, *They All Sang*, 1934. (W.J.B.)

I won't, slightly. I certainly shall!: a military c.p. of *c.* 1925–39. It may have lasted a little longer, but I never heard it during my army service (Sep. 1940–Jan. 1942): but this sort of feeble jocularity does tend to have a short life.

I won't take me coat off, I'm not stopping is a music-hall 'gag' become a general-public c.p.: 'North of England comedian Ken Platt in radio comedy shows, post-WW2' (Noble, 1975). Cyril Whelan, 1975, says that Platt enjoyed a short flurry of success in the mid 1950s; he's remembered only for this tag, belongs to the world of 'Workers' Playtime' and 'Come-friendly bombs and drop on Slough', and was a paler image of Al Reed, a phlegmatic Northern comedian who enjoyed quite wide popularity for 'Right, monkey' and 'Give over'.

I won't work has, since *c.* 1912, been applied to a member, or members, or the corporate body, of the *Industrial Workers of the World*.

I work like a horse, (so) I may as well hang my prick out to dry! is a good-humoured excuse for – or palliation of – either an accidental or a ribald exposure: late C19–20.

US variants: *I work*, or *have to work*, *like a dog* or *a mule*: 'Feverish activity, in general. Probably since early C20 '(A.B., 1978). But Berrey, 1942, records the *horse* version.

I would ... See I'd ...

I wouldn't be caught dead doing that is a US c.p. applied to an aversion from, a detestation of, some action or practice: since *c.* 1920 – or a decade earlier. (W.J.B., 1977.) Cf:

I wouldn't be found dead in it! I certainly shan't wear that hat or that dress or skirt 'or whatever': feminine: C20. 'Much more usual to say, "I wouldn't be seen dead in it",' (Daphne Beale, 1976), although, as Playfair remarks, 1977, 'There is much more point in [the *found*] form, of which [the *seen*] is a decayed derivative'. P.B.: poss. relevant to the discussion is the well-established feminine principle of always trying to have on clean underwear, 'in case you get run over by a tram' (or any later form of vehicle).

I wouldn't be in it. 'Not for *me*!'; 'You can have it!': Aus.: since *c.* 1950. (Ralph W.V.Elliott, 1977.)

I wouldn't believe (him, etc.) **on a stack of Bibles.** ' "He *is* a liar!" ... Not credible, no matter how many Testaments he swears on. [US.] From 1930s or earlier, now becoming ob. (R.C., 1978).

I wouldn't bet on it! You would be foolishly rash to count (rely) on it: since late C19. Orig. among (horse-)racing men. It has, in US, an equally common var., *don't bet on it!* (J.W.C., 1977); and, occ., *I wouldn't do that on a bet* (A.B., 1978). P.B.: if orig. c.p., by mid C20 at latest, become cliché.

I wouldn't call the Queen my aunt is a Brit. 'expression of contentment' (Skehan, 1977), the particular monarch being, I think, Her Majesty Queen Elizabeth II, who assumed the throne in 1952, rather than Queen Victoria, who reigned 1837–1901.

I would't climb over her ... See I wouldn't kick her ...

I wouldn't give you the sweat off my balls or the steam off my shit. This disagreeably low Can. c.p., belonging to C20, expresses a pretty thorough detestation. P.B.: but as *he ... his ...* it expresses contempt for utter meanness. R.C., 1978, notes that the former version is also US usage. Cf **I wouldn't piss ...** and **wouldn't give you ...**

I wouldn't have to bite on a bullet. 'That would cause me no pain – indeed, I'd enjoy it.' An Aus. meiosis, dating since *c.* 1945. A ref. to the old tradition that, anaesthetics being unavailable for arr urgent surgical operation, a sailor or soldier bit on a bullet to stop himself yelling with pain: cf Kipling, *The Light That Failed*, 1891, 'Bite on the bullet, old man, and don't let them think you're afraid'. Elab. from a note sent me by Neil Lovett, of Adelaide, 1978. Later, Mr Lovett instanced a friend, 'in speaking of his desire to mate with a lady of glamorous reputation, [he] said cryptically *I wouldn't have to bite on a bullet*'.

I wouldn't kick her out of bed. A normal healthy male's comment on seeing the photograph or a picture of an attractive female: since *c.* 1920. It has, for some years, been current also in US. J.W.C., 1977, comments, 'Oftener ... the woman herself. And, without the stress on "her", it means "She's no prize, but still, I ... ".' Sometimes *that* for *her*: 1940s–early 70s. (A.B., 1978.) P.B.: a joc., raffish Brit. var. is as in 'Well, let's put it this way: I wouldn't climb over *her* to get at *you*!' Cf **I'd rather sleep ...**

I wouldn't know! Orig. – ?*c.* 1925 – a US c.p., it came to UK in the late 1930s, the migration being a natural one, for the phrase means 'I couldn't say' or simply 'I don't know'. In a Brit. film of 1940, *Pimpernel Smith*, Leslie Howard re-marked, 'In the deplorable argot of the modern generation, "I wouldn't know".'

The phrase has been much used ever since. Foster thinks that it is a translation of *ich wüsste nicht*, taken to US by Germans settling there.

Often it implies 'It's outside my territory – not my subject'. Not merely a disclaimer of competence but a proud claim to ignorance of a subject that doesn't interest one. Occ. a 'brush-off' or a 'get-out' or a facile avoidance of a necessarily long or tedious explanation.

The nuance 'I'm in no position to know' or 'I can't be expected to know' is appositely exemplified by that master of coll. English, Denis Mackail, in *Where Am I?*, 1948: 'Perhaps this accounts for the weather that we have been having lately. Well, *I* – to use the modern, familiar, and rather desperate phrase – wouldn't know.' (The essay in which the c.p. occurs is titled 'The Word for It.')

It carries also the further nuance, 'I don't know – and I don't much care'. (Owed to Winston Graham, the novelist, 1977.)

I wouldn't know him from a bar of soap is an Aus. c.p., sometimes elab. to *... from a bar of Monkey Brand*. (Lovett, 1978.) It has a var., *I don't* (or *didn't*) *know him* (or *you*, etc.) *from a bar of soap*, recorded by Wilkes for 1938, but existing certainly since *c.* 1920 and prob. since *c.* 1910. P.B.: if this is a c.p., what about the equally Aus. synon. (e.g. I didn't) *know him from a crow*?

I wouldn't like to meet him in the dark is, in gen., applied to any formidable or dangerous or sinister man and, among the womenfolk, a probably rather too venturesome fellow: C20.

It has, in US, the var. *I wouldn't like* (or *come*) *to meet him in* (or *up*) *a dark alley*: A.B., 1978, says 'current'.

I wouldn't piss on him if he was on fire. An Aus. expression of extreme dislike: 'I have no memory of having heard it before the early 1970s' (Lovett, 1978). I suspect that it was prompted by contact of Australian servicemen with Cockney servicemen during WW2, and that it was a semi-consciously deliberate adaptation of a even coarser UK original (applied to a female). P.B.: E.P. quotes it in his notes; I won't, *pace* his anon. Welsh contributor. Peter F. Reynolds reports (via J.B. Smith, Bath) that Northern Irish girls in the late 1970s were saying, simply and elliptically, of an unattractive male, *I wouldn't put him out* [sc. if he were on fire].

I wouldn't say No! Yes, *please!*: since *c*. 1920. 'He said, "I suspect you might find a drink helpful." – I wouldn't say no."' Rather coy. Cf **don't say No ...**

I wouldn't stick (or **put**) **my walking-stick where you stick** (or **put**) **your prick** (or **you stick ... where I wouldn't ....**) A medical c.p. addressed by physicians to men going to them with venereal disease; or by Services' medical officers to servicemen assembled to listen to a brutally, yet salutarily, frank talk upon the dangers of consorting with either prostitutes or 'enthusiastic amateurs'; commoner in WW1 than in WW2 – I myself heard it at such a gathering in Egypt very soon after we arrived there in 1915.

It prob. dates from late C19. In 1959 John Winton, in *We Joined the Navy*, records it as having been used by a MO addressing a group of midshipmen and saying, 'Tomorrow we'll be getting to Gibraltar ... and I've no doubt that some of you'll be putting your private parts where I wouldn't be putting my walking-stick' – for fear of rapid corrosion. Cf:

I wouldn't touch her with yours 'seems more offensive and effective than any talk about red-hot pokers or barge-poles' (Kingsley Amis, in *Observer*, 4 Sep. 1978). Yes, indeed! The phrase dates from *c*. 1950. Cf prec.

[**I wouldn't touch it with a barge-pole.** The US version, *with a forty-foot pole*, is at least semi-proverbial, as Fain has cautioned me. P.B.: in later C20 both versions are occ. combined in Brit. usage ... *with a forty-foot barge-pole.*]

I wouldn't trust him (or, the occasion demanding, **her**) **as far as I could throw** (occ., **blow**) **him** (or **her**). This c.p., applied to a spectacularly unreliable person, dates from *c*. 1870. It is still, later C20, the predominant form, but it has collected a number of humorous, even greater, exaggerations and qualifications: e.g., in Can., as noted by Leechman, 1967, *... as far as I could throw an anvil in a swamp*; in S. African, *... throw a piano*, 'which I heard from a Springbok in the Western Desert in 1942' (Yehouda Mindel, 1975); in the UK, *... as far as I could throw the Kremlin*, 'used of extreme politicians' (Sanders, 1978); in US, *... throw a pregnant elephant*. (A.B., 1978). But note that W.J.B. maintains, 1977, that 'the predominant American form is ... throw an anchor', while J.W.C. says '... a stick'. P.B.: finally, there is the rider, *... and I wouldn't even bother to pick him up.*

Cf two further variants: *I wouldn't trust him with a kid's money-box* (specifically, utterly dishonest), C20; and *I wouldn't trust him with our cat* (of a man with an unsavoury sexual record): C20.

I wouldn't walk him round a herring barrel. 'A Northern Irish girls' contemptuous rejection of the suggestion that she should go out with a particular young man' (Peter F. Reynolds): mid C20. Cf:

I wouldn't wear it to a dog-fight is applied to 'A distasteful article of clothing. Probably from before *c*. 1920. Still fairly common [in US]' (J.W.C., 1977). Peter F. Reynolds notes, 1979, that *I-wouldn't take him to a dog-fight* is a Northern Irish girls' contemptuous remark about a young man she does not fancy.

I'd do the same for a white man. 'Like many catch phrases, it doesn't mean anything much. It's used to staunch a profuse display of gratitude. I first became conscious of its use in *c*. 1970' (Lovett, 1978): Aus.

I'd hate to cough! is, with wry humour, said by one who is suffering from acute diarrhoea: C19 – 20. (I heard this, several times, on Gallipoli, 1915: both diarrhoea and dysentery were distressingly common – and severe.) It springs from the marked effect coughing has, as an aid – among the constipated – to defecation.

I'd have to be lifted on (and off). 'Worldly weariness of old, or older, man at unfledged youth's enthusiasm for a girl's charms' (L.A., 1974): C20.

I'd have you to know! Let me tell you!: US: C20. Berrey, 1942, classifies it as an 'expression of affirmation – decidedly emphatic. A.B., 1978, notes that it is sometimes varied *I'd like to have you (to) know*. Cf the idiomatic or cliché Brit. *I'd* or *I'll have you know!*

I'd like a pup off that indicates a male's sexually covetous approbation of an attractive female: Services': since *c*. 1930. That is, out of that bitch. Lovett, 1978, writes, 'In Australia *out of* is preferred to *off* and the desired object need not be female. I've heard it used of a wallet and of an electric drill – on such occasions it meant "I admire (the object) and covet it"'.

I'd like to get you on a slow boat to China (*from England* understood). I'd like to have enough time with you to influence you slowly and gradually: a nautical c.p., mostly joc.: C20.

P.B.: it may perhaps have been a nautical c.p., but as Benny Green pointed out in his review of the first ed. of this book, in *Spectator*, 10 Sep. 1977, it 'owes its popularity to a successful song of that name of Frank Loesser in 1948'. The second line is 'All to myself alone', and R.C., 1978, notes that this has always been the US implication, "'I'd like to be alone with you for a long time" – i.e. for romantic and/or sexual purposes'.

I'd love to be a fly on the wall. I should very much like to see and hear what is going on without being seen: mostly Aus., yet also common in Brit.: C20. (B.P., 1974.) P.B.: it has, *c*. 1980, given rise to the name for the 'fly-on-the-wall technique' of TV, for the filming of 'candid', documentary features, in which the subjects are supposed to be unaware of, or unconcerned about, the presence of the camera.

I'd rather have him inside the tent is applied to an influential, very intelligent man one wishes to keep an eye on. 'When J. Edgar Hoover was seventy, a lot of pressure was put on President Lyndon Johnson to have him resign. President Johnson ... said No ... Someone asked him why, and President Johnson said, "I'd rather have him inside pissing out than have him outside the tent pissing in!"' (Irving Wallace, *The R Document*, 1976). Lyndon B. Johnson (1908–73) was President of the USA 1963–9; Hoover (1895–1972) directed the FBI 1924–72. *Si non è vero, è ben trovato*. If the President did say it, he didn't, I feel reasonably sure, invent it: he was prob. using a folk-saying he had heard during his childhood and youth and later. It could have had a brief life as a c.p. in Washington, DC, and perhaps nationally, say 1965–70.

I'd rather keep you a week than a fortnight is directed at a consistently hearty – or, a greedy – eater: in the main, Aus.: since *c*. 1870; by 1976, slightly ob.

I'd rather sleep with her with no clothes on than (with) you in your best suit. 'Said by one man to another of an attractive girl either out of earshot or, preferably, assumed not to understand English' (Kingsley Amis, in the *Observer*, 4 Sep. 1977). Mr Amis added that he had 'heard it only once, in 1944.' I can at least assure him that it was current as early as the early 1930s; and am grateful to him for jogging my memory. Cf **I wouldn't Kick ...**

I'd rather you than me! See **rather you ...**

I'd watch it! I certainly won't! Certainly not! According to Manchon, this is a low c.p.:? *c*. 1910 – 40. But also, since *c*. 1930 at latest, a menacing 'Look out!' or 'Be very careful!' J.W.C., 1977, 'In the US, the first meaning is unknown; the second is very common and, without *I'd*, almost a threat, meaning "Watch your language!"' P.B.: the threat, without *I'd*, is of course also the predominant, if not now (later C20) the only, form in UK; it may be uttered not only against language, but against any action offensive to the speaker.

I'll 'ave to ask me dad. Concerning 'ITMA' in late 1944, Francis Worsley, *Itma*, 1948, writes:

Practically the only person untouched by her [Miss Hotchkiss's] domineering ways was the Ancient Mark Time, who, when taxed with any question, invariably replied: 'I'll 'ave to ask me dad!' This saying caught on with the public, and was being heard on all sides in a very short time. Sometimes ... it caused some embarrassment, one such case being, I'm told, at the General Election [of 1945] when Randolph Churchill, being heckled by his audience, was asked a question and, before he could reply, was greeted with loud yells of 'He'll have to ask *his* Dad!'

This c.p. prospered from Nov. 1944 until the end of 1945, and was still heard occ. until at least 1950; twice or thrice since (*c.* 1955 and *c.* 1967) I have heard it.

P.B.: as *VIBS* emphasises, the whole 'point of [the c.p.] was that it was spoken by a character who sounded about a hundred years of age'. See also TOMMY HANDLEY.

[**I'll be a ding-dong daddy.** 'This phrase probably started in Texas or Louisiana. Movie, radio and TV celebrity Phil Harris made his reputation with a theme song that began "I'm a ding-dong daddy from Dumas". Everyone in US is familiar with that song. Dumas is a Town in Texas' (W.J.B., 1977). The point of the c.p., I suggest, is that Dumas is situated in country noted for its cattle and its 'oil-wells – hence, for its 'he-men'. The c.p. was current in 1916, the period of Glendon Swarthout's *The Tin Lizzie Group*, 1972.

But Col. Moe has proved that *ding-dong daddy* is merely one of a cluster of anyone – or anything – phrases, and he compares 'I'll be a sonovagun' (son of a gun) ... 'a rootin', tootin' cowboy' ... *ad infinitum*' *I'm a Ding-Dong Daddy* is only one of several American ding-dong songs, esp. *ding-dong baby* and *ding-dong boogie*. In short, *ding-dong* connotes, when it doesn't firmly denote, 'dashing' or 'dashingly excellent'. Not even one of the *ding-dong* phrases can, he suggests, be seriously proposed as a genuine, incontrovertible c.p. (Based on the lists he supplied me in 1977.)]

I'll be a monkey's uncle! – often prec. by **well** – expresses astonishment: Can.: since *c.* 1945; adopted from US, where current since the 1930s, if not considerably earlier. 'This has been common in Australia for at least thirty years. It probably came from the US in films' (Lovett, 1978).

[**I'll be fucked if I do!** This late C19 – 20 ribald refusal becomes a c.p. once when it is employed joc. and allusively, as in the wittily bawdy semi-chant:

'Roll over,' said the Duke.

'I'll be fucked if I do,' said the Duchess.

'You'll be buggered if you don't,' said the Duke.]

I'll be hanged! An exclam. of either severe reprobation or profound astonishment: C16 – 20. Nathaniel Field, *Amends for Ladies*, written *c.* 1612, but not pub'd until 1618, at IV, ii has, 'I'll be hanged, if you were not busy too soon.' The *OED* cites an example from Addison, 1711.

But strictly, and to prevent a misapprehension, the construction *I'll be hanged if* ... is a cliché; it is the elliptical *I'll be hanged!* which is a c.p.

I'll be laughing haversacks indicates an anticipated pleasure that will ensure upon the fulfilment of certain conditions: the three Services': since *c.* 1930. (L.A.) It has the var. (*kit-*) *bags* or, in Lancashire dialect, *I'll be laffen bags*. (Jack Slater, 1978.) P.B.: may also be *you'll, they'll, we'll*, etc., *be laughing* ... Short-lived variants in the 1950s – 60s were ... *little oil-bombs*, and ... *Naafi-breaks*.

Mr P.V. Harris records, 1978, that he first heard the expressions *laughing haversacks* and *laughing bags* while serving with the East Lancashire Regt. in Mesopotamia, 1917.

I'll be one (or **a marble**) **upon your taw**. I'll pay you out!: respectively from *c.* 1770 and *c.*1780; † by 1890, except among schoolboys. (Grose, 2nd edn, 1788; Vaux, 1812 – pub'd 1818.) It derives from the game of marbles, a *taw* being the large and usually superior marble with which one shoots.

I'll be seeing you. See **be seeing you.**

I'll be the bunny. 'I'll be the mug: so *you* tell me!': Aus.: since *c.* 1940. (Lovett, 1978.) From *bunny*, an easy dupe, as in, e.g. Wilkes. Mr Lovett later amplifies thus: 'I'll take the unwanted task'; he admits that he can cite no printed example; I tentatively propose usage since *c.* 1970 at latest.

[**I'll believe it when I see it**, 'a c.p. used by a doubting Thomas' (B.P., 1975), stands on the vague border separating some proverbial sayings from c.pp.: it certainly goes back as far as late C19 – and perhaps very much farther.]

I'll bet! A var. of **I bet!**

I'll bite (or **I'll buy**) **it** (or **that**); **no! I'm not selling: serious!** 'All right! Tell me what the answer – esp. what the catch – is'; also, just plain 'I'll accept, *or* I accept, that': C20. Clearly *I'll buy it* (or *that*) was prompted by *I'll bite*: of the C18 *bite!*, 'caught you or tricked you'. *I bite*, when understood as meaning, or when misunderstood for, *I'll buy it*, generated the further c.p., *no! I'm not selling – serious* (for *seriously*) – itself hardly before 1930. In *The Judas Mandate*, 1972, Clive Egleton exemplifies the fact that *I'll buy it* is often used as a c.p. reply to 'Have you heard the story about – – ', thus: 'His face broke into a beaming smile. "At least we shan't be able to offer little Willie's excuse." Garnett said patiently, "Go on, I'll buy it."' Cf **I'll pay you that one!**

It is also US. In E. V. Cunningham, *Millie*, 1973, we read:

'And I am afraid. There's something ignominious about being afraid.'

'There's also something ignominious about the way you were before.'

'I'll buy that. If I can stay alive without being this nervous, well, it might work.'

One of E.P.'s American contributors (name omitted from the ms notes) wrote, 'The current US senses are quite different. "I'll bite" almost always means "I can't solve the riddle you propose"; "I'll buy it" = "I'll accept your proposition, or theory" [as in the quot'n from *Millie*].'

I'll come quietly! See **I'll go quietly.**

I'll cut you off with a shilling. See **I'll strike you out of my will.**

I'll dance at your funeral. See **dance at** ....

I'll do Justice Child. I'll turn King's Evidence: an underworld c.p. of late C17 – earlyish C18. 'I'll ... Impeach or Discover the whole gang, and so save my own Bacon' (BE). The ref. is to Sir Francis Child the Elder (1642 – 1713), who became High Sheriff, and later the Lord Mayor, of London.

I'll do (or **fix**) **you!** I'll settle your hash! Often joc.: ... **do** ... , since *c.* 1910; ... **fix** ... , since *c.* 1920. Spoken to a girl, it carries a playful sexual threat.

I'll draw you off a goffer. A RN c.p., challenging an angry man: *c.* 1910 – 40. From *goffer*, a bottle of aerated water, tending to bubble – hence, a man bubbling up into a bad temper, hence becoming angry. F&G.

I'll drink all the mistakes is an 'American, always jocular, offer to one's host to consume all the drinks wrongly mixed – in addition to the offerer's usual ones: since *c.* 1960' (J.W.C., 1977).

I'll drink to that! – indicating a genially hearty assent – is an alternative of **you can say that again**, dates from *c.* 1950, and was orig. US but by 1955, also Can.; not unknown in Brit., yet hardly a c.p. there. Mr Ben Traver calls it 'a celebration image' – cites *Addiction*, a monthly newsletter, Feb. 1975, and adds that it 'May be one of the most powerful phrases in the language' (early 1976). *VIBS* pertinently notes that the phrase was given further currency by the US TV comedy series, Rowan & Martin's *Laugh-In*, late 1960s.

I'll eat my hat! is not a c.p. when it is followed by 'If I'll do this or that', it is a cliché. But it is a c.p. when, late C19–20, it expresses surprise at what *has* been done.

I'll expect you when I see you is addressed to one whose announcement of a visit or a meeting isn't to be depended upon: late C19–20. A late occurrence: the TV serial, 'Coronation Street', episode of 15 Oct. 1973. (Thanks to Mr A. B. Petch.) P.B.: prob. as frequent in the form (you'll have to) *expect me* (or *us*) *when you see me* (or *us*). And Playfair, 1977, comments, 'Still in vigorous use, not obsolescent as your entry implies. But the present-day nuance is different: no suggestion of undependability, but agreement between the speakers that it is not practicable to fix an exact time for the addressee's arrival'.

I'll first see thy neck as long as my arm! I'll see you hanged first: *c.* 1650–1750. Ray,. 1678; Apperson.

I'll fix you! See **I'll do you!**

I'll forget my own name in a minute! 'The nameless Man from the Ministry (played by Horace Percival) in *ITMA*' (*VIBS*). See TOMMY HANDLEY.

I'll give it foire! 'A real rarity–a catchphrase launched by a member of the public. Not that Janice Nicholls a Brum [i.e. Birmingham] girl conscripted on to the pop jury of ABC's *Thank Your Lucky Stars*, could avoid a peculiar form of celebrity for long. Awarding votes to new releases [of records] in her local dialect and declaring (as if in mitigation for some awful vocal performance), "But I like the backing!" she became a minor celebrity and even made a record herself called–wait for it–"I'll give it five" ... of which almost everyone else declared, "I'll give it about *minus* five"' (*VIBS*): *c.* 1970.

I'll give you Jim Smith! I'll give you a thrashing: proletarian; mostly London streets': 1887–*c.* 1890. Ware, 1909, tells us that a pugilist so named was prominent in 1887.

I'll give you my mother for a maid was, *c.* 1700–40, a c.p. used by London fashionable society. S, Dialogue I, has:

MISS: ... It is better to be an old Man's Darling, than a young Man's Warling' (despised person; later, ... *young man's slave*).

NEV[EROUT]: Faith, Miss, if you speak as you think, I'll give you my Mother for a Maid.

The implication being that Miss's continued spinsterhood is as widely improbable as the speaker's mother's virginity.

I'll go he! is a NZ c.p. exclam. of surprise: since *c.* 1920. From those children's games in which one participant is either blindfolded or otherwise made the 'victim'. Cf:

I'll go hopping to hell! – esp. when prec. by **well**, an addition that affords a vigorous rhyme. Indicative of astonishment – or of profound admiration – or of both: C20. See **well, I'll go to Hanover!**

I'll go out into the garden and eat worms. I'll now eat humble pie: often ironic. Probably rural in origin, it arose *c.* 1880. More a feminine than a masculine c.p. Also US: A.B., 1978, recalls that it was still current among American children, and that, in the 1940s, there was a song that began with the piteous words, 'No one loves me./Everybody hates me,/I'm going to the garden to eat worms'. P.B.: the 'song' continues, as I am informed by a former Girl Guide from Derby, who remembers it as current in the 1950s: 'Long, thin slimy ones slide down easily,/Short, fat hairy ones always stick./Nobody loves me, everybody hates me,/So I'm going down the garden to be sick'.

To Mrs Mary Irwin and Mrs Stella Waring I owe thanks for a printed source: Elsie J. Oxenham, *The Two Form Captains*, 1921, p. 297, 'Nobody love me! I'll go into the garden and eat worms!' Perhaps the c.p. should realy begin *nobody love me*, and what we have here is the truncated form.

I'll go quietly is both Brit. and US in its joc. 'I won't cause any further trouble' sense, derived from the lit. meaning, as applied to a criminal or to a prison, or a 'nut-house' inmate who has been having an outburst, a tantrum, and is about to be subdued by the guards or attendants. 'Now a humorous

greeting among friends' (W.J.B., 1977): prob. since the 1930s. P.B.: sometimes, in UK, as a joc. burlesque, 'All right, Officer, I'll come quietly!'; and occ. as a joc. invitation, 'Are you coming quietly – or do you want a thick ear?'

I'll hand it to him! 'An idiomatic way of prefacing a compliment, often reluctantly. E.G., "I'll hand it to him, he is often generous," In use in New Zealand since about 1930' (Arthur Gray, of Auckland, 1969). And not unknown in Britain, where 'more often "I/you must ... " or "I/you've got to ... "' (P.B., 1976). At least equally common in US is the 'you've got to hand it to him (her, them, etc.) version. Cf **I have to hand ...**

I'll hate myself in the morning. See **you'll hate yourself ...**

I'll have a basinful of that! is applied to a new word or a long one: mostly lower and lower-middle classes': since the early 1930s. A synonym recorded in Michael Harrison's novel, *Spring in Tartarus*, 1935, and current since *c.* 1910, is *I'll have two of those;* the *basinful* version is still current in the 1970s, the other was ob. by *c.* 1970.

I'll have to ask me dad. See **I'll 'ave to ....**

I'll have two of those! See **I'll have a basinful of that!**

I'll have your balls for a necktie is 'commonly used in the sense ... *guts for garters* [q.v.]' (Cdr C. Parsons, RN, ret., 1973): Services': since before WW2 – ? *c.* 1910. P.B.: a version of this was used in the film *The Young Winston*, 1972.

I'll have your gal! 'A cry raised by street boys or roughs when they see a fond couple together' (B & L): mostly Londoners': *c.* 1880–1914.

I'll have your guts for garters! A threat, orig. serious, latterly humorous: mid C18–20. In C20, it has been a racecourse and low Cockney c.p. Cf Desmond Bagley, *Landslide*, 1967, '"Your father isn't going to like that. He'll have your guts for garters, Howard. I doubt if he ever ruined a deal by being too greedy."' [P.B.: it was in great favour with NCOs in charge of National Service recruits, 1948–62.]

Yet, since WW2, the phrase has gradually mounted the social scale – not that it has yet (1976) become either aristocratic or cultured. In Tim Heald's engaging 'thriller', *Deadline*, 1975, we read of a journalist declaring, 'If this doesn't work, then I think Parkinson [his 'boss'] will, as they say, "have my guts for garters".'

But it must have gone underground for a century or more: Robert Greene, *James the Fourth*, at III, ii: 'I'll make garters of thy guts, thou villain'; and Jack Lindsay found, in an early C17 parish register, *I'll have your guts for garter points.*

'Walter Scott, somewhere, "I'll have his entrails to garter my hose"' (S. C. Dixon, 1978). An odd sort of euph.

In 1969, L.A. glossed the present usage thus: 'The garters not so much historical as English homely phrasers' love of alliteration and assonance.'

I'll have your hat! A street c.p. – a mild, semi-comical threat. (B & L) Approx. latter half of C19: *Punch*, 12 Dec. 1869, has the caption 'I'll Have Yer Hat' to a cartoon showing a bear at the zoo, having grabbed the topper off a 'swell', much to the amusement of the onlookers. (P.B., 1976.)

I'll hold him. In a note from L.A., 1969, occurs a salutary warning that certain apparently homosexual c.pp. are merely ironic or facetious, as when one man, angry and irritated, says to another, 'I'll fuck you!' he merely expresses mood; and a third man will interpose a mock-encouraging *I'll hold him* – a genuine male c.p. current throughout C20.

I'll hold your bonnet. See **go it, Susan.**

I'll hold your coat! Among schoolboys in the 1940s a palliative, a joc. turning away of wrath: in full *wanna* (= do you want to *or* a) *fight? I'll...* Cf **go it, Susan.** (P.B.)

I'll knock seven kinds of shit out of you! A low, mainly Services' and perhaps orig. RN threat: since *c.* 1920. The non-c.p. slang is *knock the shit out of* someone, to thrash him, of which the c.p. is patently an elab.

I'll lay you six to four. 'This improper fraction is often used to enforce argument by non-punters' (Shaw), esp. among would-be sporting characters, and implying a temperate degree of assurance: since middle 1940s and perhaps since as early as 1930. 'Many variations in the numbers, "two to one" being the most popular over here' (the US: A.B., 1978). Cf **five will get you ten.**

I'll leave it all to the cook. I won't take that bet: a sporting c.p. of *c.* 1815–40. (Egan's Grose, 1823.) A cook is a good judge of meat, but it takes an experienced betting man to judge horseflesh on the hoof.

I'll leave it to you to choose, to decide, etc: C20. Noël Coward's earliest pub'd, although not earliest written, play was called *'I'll Leave It to You.' A Light Comedy in Three Acts,* performed on.21 July 1920 at the New Theatre, London, and pub'd two or three months later. Act I ends with the phrase being used lit.:

SYLVIA: What we want to know, uncle, is how on earth we are to start? (*They all nod.*)

DANIEL: (*smiling benignly , arms outstretched*) I'll leave it to you!

A.B., 1978, notes, 'There's a US country/Western song entitled "I'm leavin' it all up to you" – written, I think, in either the late 1950s or early '60s' – a combination of the phrase with the idiomatic 'it's up to you'.

I'll let you off this time, from being a teacher's condonation of a pupil's misdemeanour, has, since *c.* 1950, been a c.p., as employed – and in the *milieu* there indicated – in: 'Widely used by the boys my wife has to teach. "All right, Miss, let you off this time!" they say, to excuse some stupidity of their own' (P.B., 1975). The *milieu* was much more gen. than E.P.'s interpretation of my earlier note allows; the phrase is now, 1983, heard less frequently. (P.B.)

I'll love you and leave you. See **I must love you**...

I'll make (or **I think I'll make**) **a separate peace.** See **separate peace** ....

I'll make you sing 'O be joyful!' on the other side of your mouth – the orig. from; in C20, *O be joyful* has been omitted. A mid C18–early C19 threat. Grose, 1788.

I'll nark yer! This Aus., mainly urban, c.p., dating from *c.* 1905, combines the sense of slang *nark*, to annoy, and *nark*, to foil. Lavett has pointed out that the illiterate would pronounce both *yer* and *you* as *ye'* (short *e*).

I'll pay you that one! I 'bought' that – I admit I've been 'had': Aus. since *c.* 1920. In, e.g., Kylie Tennant, *The Honey Flow*, 1956. Cf **I'll bite.** Hence, that's a good story – that's a very good joke: Aus.: since *c.* 1945. (B.P.) Contrast **I owe you one!**

I'll pull your whatnot as long as my arm! 'A Royal Navy lowerdeck threat, 1940s' (Peppitt) – and presumably from a decade earlier and until a decade later. Lit., 'until it's long ... '; unexpectedly euph.

I'll push your face in and I'll spit in your eye and choke you are working-class threats, often used playfully: late C19–20. Cf:

I'll put you where the rooks won't shit on you. A joc. version of *I'll kill you* used humorously: army: since *c.* 1935. The implication is 'I'll put you underground'.

I'll rattle the bars of your cage. See **if I need you**...

I'll saw your leg off! See **my word! if I catch you** ....

I'll say! An enthusiastic Aus. affirmative: since *c.* 1930, but by 1965, slightly ob.; also Brit., since *c.* 1925. Adopted from the US: McKnight notes its US college use; Berrey records it as a gen. Americanism. A very neat US example occurs in Edward Albee, *The Sandbox*, written in 1959 and pub'd in 1960:

YOUNG MAN: (*Flexing his muscles.*) Isn't that something?

GRANDMA: Boy, oh boy; I'll say. Pretty good.

YOUNG MAN: (*Sweetly.*) I'll say.

A c.p. in the first line and two in the second, with the third c.p. ironically repeated and emphasized in the third line. A characteristically subtle, yet outright, example of Albee's utterly sincere, (here quietly) shattering satire.

As a Briticism, it is perhaps elliptical for 'I'll say it is!' rather than for *I'll say so!*

I'll say so! is, by H. L. Mencken, in 1922, included in a short list of US army c.pp. already falling into disuse. It passed into Brit. slang. Dodie Smith's *Call It a Day*, performed in 1935 and pub'd a year later, at I, II, has

DOROTHY: (*looking at the photograph*) Look at your superb waist-line.

MURIEL: And was it agony? I'll say so...

I'll see you further, with or without the addition of **first. I** certainly *won't*!: since *c.* 1840 – it occurs in, e.g., Mayhew's *London Labour and the London Poor* (at chapter I, p. 29), 1851. In C20, *first* is omitted. 'Originally, I would guess, a counter to "I'll see you in hell!"' (R.C., 1978).

I'll see you in church (or **in court**) or **in gaol (jail).** See **see you** ...

I'll see you in hell first. A predominantly Anglo-Irish, yet also a fairly common UK, c.p. of 'vehement refusal' (Skehan, 1977) – dating from latish C19. P.B.: but see also **I'll see you further.**

I'll see you in the funny papers (later, **the funnies**). See **see you in the** ...

I'll see you under the clock. See **see you under** ...

I'll shit! is an emphatic and vulgar expression of deeply felt indignation or contempt or disgust: US: since, I think, the 1940s. Recorded in *DCCU.*

I'll shoot through the barrel and drown you. Behind full water barrels placed at intervals along the street against fire, bystanders shattered against a gunman on the rampage. This threat became 'common in the West', (Ramon F. Adams.) Very approx. *c.* 1850–1900.

I'll show you mine if you'll show me yours. 'A phrase used by children comparing genitals' (B.P., 1974): dating from at least as early as late C19, and prob. from fifty – a hundred – years earlier. Only the most starry-eyed of parents believe in the innocence of children. Frederick Forsyth, *The Dogs of War*, 1974, has:

'Have you any scars from wounds? ...'

'Some.'

'Show me,' she said. '... Go on, show me. Prove it.' ....

'I'll show you mine, if you'll show me yours,' he taunted, mimicking the old kindergarten challenge.

Charles Loughlin, conductor at the last night of the 1982 'Proms' (Henry Wood Promenade Concerts) season, used the phrase to good effect in his valedictory speech.

I'll strike you dead with a shilling; also, **I'll cut you off with a shilling.** 'Jocular use among workingmen who have little or nothing to leave' (Petch, 1974): since the middle or late 1940s. P.B.: prob. earlier, and, in the latter version, as often ... *without a shilling.*

I'll swing for you if you don't! – if you don't agree – if you don't do it – etc. A proletarian threat of *c.* 1820–90. (Hotten.) The implication, obviously, is 'I'll be hanged for murdering you.'

I'll take a rain check. I'll accept, another time, if I may: US: since late 1940s (it's not in, e.g., Berrey, 1942), W & F recording it in 1960 as, ' ... promise to accept an invitation at a later date'. A *rain check* is a ticket, or the stub of a ticket, valid for the replay of a game cancelled or abandoned because of bad weather, usu. because of persistent rain. P.B., 1976: 'Heard in UK too, often with the addition *on it,* perhaps influenced by the verb = preposition, "to check on". It may also occur as, e.g., *let's take* ... , or *you'll have to take* ... '

I'll take vanilla is either an elab. or the orig. of *vanilla!,* of which W & F, 1960, note that it is a usu. joc. expression of disbelief, 'used when the lie or exaggeration is of no great consequence'.

In 1975, Col. Moe wrote: 'The phrase is usually intended to convey an attitude of indifference or to exhibit a lack of concern ... The meaning = it makes no difference.' But he also quotes from Carl Sandburg, *The People, Yes*, 1936: 'The city editor managed to have the final words. "I'll take vanilla horsefeathers!"' – that is, 'Nonsense!' And R.C., 1978, amplifies, '(Ice-cream understood.) "I don't care for the proposal under discussion": US; early C20; † by *c.* 1950'.

I'll tear your arm off and beat you over the head with the soggy end! Fearsome favourite threat of British Army drill instructors, very popular (among *them*) 1960s: prob. orig. in the Guard's drill depot at Pirbright. Cf **I've seen more...**

I'll tell it to nobody (or **no one**) **but friends and strangers** is a C18 c.p., at first of the fashionable world of London. S, in Dialogue, I, has:

NEV[EROUT]: Miss, I'll tell you a Secret, if you'll promise never to tell it again.

MISS: No, to be sure, I'll tell it to no Body but Friends and Strangers.

That is, everybody.

I'll tell the cock-eyed world! and **I'll tell the world!** The former, an elab. of the latter, is recorded by Berrey, and dates from *c.* 1930. The latter, anglicized in 1930 or 1931, goes back to *c.* 1917, occurs in HLM, who includes it as one of the favourite affirmations of the US Army in 1917–18; W&F describe it as 'now archaic'. A.B., 1978, notes that other adjectives, blasphemous or obscene, may replace *cock-eyed* – 'gosh-darned' was the most 'ordinary'.

I'll tell the vicar. See **I** *am* **the vicar!**

I'll tell you one thing, and that's not two; in C19–20, often **... and that ain't two**. The former, C18–20, appears in S, Dialogue I:

LADY SM[ART]: I'll tell you one thing, and that's not two; I'm afraid I shall get a Fit of the Head-ache To-day.

I heard it, in the street, so recently as 13 June 1972. It may last for years yet, for it's a pleasantly positive, without being too aggressive, way to emphasize one's point or statement.

I'll tell you those! is a US, notably a Chicagoan, emphatic var. of **I'm telling you:** *c.* 1890–1910. George Ade, *Artie*, 1896, '"Say, I like that church, and if they put in a punchin' – bag and a plunge they can have my game, I'll tell you those."' The phrase, which occurs several times in *Artie*, became so popular that it could be varied, thus: '"They've got me entered, but I don't know whether I'll start or not. I'm leary of it; I don't mind tèlling you those"' (ibid., p. 60). Elliptical for 'I'll tell you those things.'

I'll tell you what!: late C17–20; hence, **I tell you what!:** C19–20; hence, **tell you what!:** mid C19–20. I'll tell you something. The first occurs in Shakespeare and Tennyson; the second, in Violet Hunt. 'I tell you what, Janet, we must have a man down who doesn't shoot – to amuse us!'; the third, in Baumann. (With thanks to the *OED*.) It's an 'introducer': and it lies on the borderline between cliché and c.p.

But the best example I've found comes in Elizabeth Inchbald's *I'll Tell You What*, 1786. The Prologue, written by George Colman, begins:

Ladies and Gentlemen, *I'll tell you what!*

Yet not, like ancient Prologue, tell the Plot – and ends:

But hold – I say too much – I quite forgot – And so I'll tell you – NO – SHE'LL tell you what.

It still prospers, as in

'Can you help me, George?'

'Don't think I can, Bill! No, wait a moment, I'll tell you what! Come and see me tomorrow – I may, by then, hàve news for you.'

I'll tell your mother is addressed to a young girl – or ironically to a girl not so young – out with a boyfriend: late C19–20.

See **anything like that...**

I'll try anything once has, since *c.* 1925 in both Brit. and the US, been affected by the adventurous and the experimental, sometimes joc., sometimes satirically. Frank Clune's very readable autobiography, pub'd in 1933, bears the title *Try Anything Once*. The phrase was anticipated by Miles Malleson in *Conflict*, 1925, II, iii:

DARE: He can't *eat* me.

MRS TREMAYNE: I'm not so sure of that.

DARE: I've never been eaten before; I'll do anything once.

It is 'also anticipated by the naughty novel that made James Branch Cabell [1879–1950] notorious, *Jurgen*, 1919, in the form "I'll try any drink once"' (Shipley, 1977).

'Also in the form *I'll try anything once, except sodomy and British sherry* (or *pasteurized beer*, or *processed cheese*, or any other mild dislike). *Sodomy* used for emphasis and, perhaps, to shock' (Sanders, 1978).

In some contexts, it is virtually synon. with **there's always a first time.**

I'll venture it, as Johnson did his wife, and she did well. A semi-proverbial c.p., implying that sometimes it pays to take a risk: *c.* 1650–1800. (Apperson cites Ray, 1678, and Fuller.)

There's a prob. apocryphal story about a clergyman named Johnson suspected of having murdered his wife – returning from safety – and finding her alive and well. The orig. has perhaps some relation to some anecdote; but the balance of opinion agrees that it was a proverb: see, e.g., *ODEP*.

I'll walk off. See **don't take it out...**

I'm a ball of muscle: if I was any better, I'd be dangerous is a self-derisive Aus. c.p., heard by Jack Slater in Sydney, 1966–67, and presumably current for some years before and since.

I'm a bit of a liar myself. This US c.p., prob. dating from the 1880s or rather earlier, was *c.* 1900, adopted in the British Empire. P.B.: I have heard that, during WW2, certain bright sparks, fired by 'line-shooters', had cards printed with the legend 'I'm a bit of a bull-shitter myself – but do carry on!' One hopes they had the desired deflationary effect.

I'm a ding-dong daddy. See **I'll be a....**

I'm a Dutchman if I do!: since *c.* 1850; **I'm a Dutchman:** since *c.* 1830. If somebody else = disbelief; as in 'If there's anything there, I'm a Dutchman.' By 1940, ob.; by 1970, rare.

I'm a lover, not a fighter. A peace-preferring youth, declining a fist fight: St Paul schools. Minnesota, and prob. elsewhere: since *c.* 1950. (J.W.C., 1977.) P.B.: *pace* J.W.C.'s (or E.P.'s) dating, more likely to stem from the *make love, not war* peace-movements' slogan from the mid 1960s.

I'm a stranger here myself. This pellucid statement, which circumstances oblige us to make often enough, has, both in Brit. and in US, become a c.p. either humorous or ironic or both: since *c.* 1950. Paul Kavanagh, *Such Men Are Dangerous*, 1969 in US and very early 1971 in UK has:

'Is it like this all vinter long?'

'I'm a stranger here myself.'

A pleasant Brit. example occurs in Dorothy Halliday, *Dolly and the Cookie Bird*, 1970:

'Well done, I suppose you don't know where he's hidden the rubies?'

'I'm a stranger here myself,' said Derek, who still looked as if he had had four gins in a row. It was the first joke I had ever heard him make, which explains its unremarkable nature.

Connotation: 'I'm no more likely to know than you yourself are'; hence, 'I don't know what's going on and I shouldn't care to guess'. In short, from being a plea of specific ignorance, it has, as a c.p., become a sort of gen. excuse for inability, or unwillingness, to help.

I'm a tit man myself. I'm far more interested in a girl's breasts than in her legs: US: since the late (? middle) 1940s. Oddly, it hasn't become at all common in Britain – not, at least, up to 1976. 'Not at all common in Britain? But it *is* a Services' c.p. and has even been elaborated into a joke: about two mice watching a line of chorus-girls. One says, "Lovely legs they've got, haven't they?" To which the other replies, "Ah, but I'm a tit-mouse myself" – a double pun' (P.B., 1976).

I'm a true dog of the game, or else take away my gun. I'm an honest fellow and I 'shoot straight' or 'play the game': a rural, sporting, upper-middle- and upper-class c.p. of *c.* 1670–1750, perhaps orig. and predominantly in Ireland. See Charles Shadwell (a younger son of laureate Thomas) in his comedy, *Irish Hospitality: or, Virtue Rewarded*, pub'd in *The Works*, 2 vols. 1720, at I, i, where Sir Jowler Kennel, who thinks almost more highly of his dogs than of his neighbours, asks Sir Patrick Worthy to be allowed to pay court to one or other of his two daughters:

SIR PAT: I hope, Sir Jowler, you won't act like a *Poacher*, but give 'em – when married – Law enough.

SIR JOW[LER]: Pshaw, pshaw, no, no, I'm a true Dog of the Game, or else take away my Gun, as the saying is.

(Perhaps with the innuendo '....or may I be castrated!')

I'm always out of the picture, just clambering round the frame was 'current [among RN personnel] in the Indian Ocean *c.* 1942–1943' (Rear-Adm. P.W. Brock, 1975). A 'local catch phrase', yes; yet illustrative of the fact that a local, short-lived c.p. may be a good one; He adds: 'I believe someone, perhaps a Royal Marine, wrote a song with this motif.' Cf **I feel like a mushroom...**

I'm all right, Jack! See **fuck you, Jack...**

I'm Anne, fly me! – or any other girl's name, 'From the airline advertisement. Used when introducing oneself' (Simon Levene, 1977). P.B.: Nigel Rees, in *Slogans*, 1982, writes of the orig., 'I'm Margie. Fly me': 'National Airlines; US, current *c.* 1971. The campaign, also using *I'm Going to Fly You Like You've Never Been Flown Before*, aroused the ire of feminist groups. Later, Walls Sausages sent up the slogan with *I'm Meaty, Fry Me'*.

I'm as mild a villain as ever scuttled a ship is a c.p. applied to oneself in a tone of joc. reproach and not entirely condemnatory disapprobation: since *c.* 1821; little heard since WW2, but not yet† even by 1975. It garbles Byron, *Don Juan*, Canto three: 'He was the mildest-manner'd man,/That ever scuttled ship or cut a throat,/With such true breeding of a gentleman,/You never could divine his thought' – as Oliver Stonor reminds me.

I'm bomb-proof. Var. of **I'm fire-proof.**

I'm down, but not out. '"I've suffered a defeat, but not necessarily a final one." From a boxer knocked down but still conscious' (R.C., 1978): predominantly US: C20.

I'm dreaming oh my darling love of thee! 'Cyril Fletcher recalls that he was persuaded to broadcast "Dreaming of Thee", a poem by Edgar Wallace, in 1938. He did it in an extraordinary voice – a cockney caricature – and the constant refrain at the end of each verse, "I'm dreaming oh my darling love of thee", got yells of delight. It "made" him, he says, and later when he returned to London for a repeat performance he was on a bus and the conductor was saying "Dreaming of Thee" to every passenger, with a passable imitation of Fletcher's funny voice, as he gave them their tickets' (*VIBS*).

I'm fire-proof. Short for **fuck-you, Jack, I'm fire-proof!** – the RAF's adaptation of **fuck you, Jack, I'm all right!**: since *c.* 1930. Cf the civilian pun on the RAF motto, *per ardua ad astra: per ardua and aspidistra*. P.B.: there is, in the Services, the equally hubristic var., *(fuck you) I'm bomb-proof.*

I'm from Missouri. *D.Am.* at 'Missouri' states that the phrase, in full, is *I'm from Missouri [and] you'll have* – or *you have* – *to show me*; that it apparently dates from *c.* 1880 or a year or so earlier; that it occ. has *I come* for *I'm*; and that a demonstration is necessary, the speaker being either extremely sceptical or extremely reluctant to believe, without it. The second half, *you've got to show me*, has occ. occurred by itself. The earliest printed use Col. Moe has found is the song, 'I'm from Missouri and You've Got to Show Me', words by Lee Raney and music by Ned Wayburn; apparently the first dictionary to record it was Funk & Wagnall's *New Standard Dict.*, 1913. Fain has suggested that the c.p. prob. comes, ultimately, from the Missouri Compromise of 1820. W.J.B., 1969, says:

'I'm from Missouri' and its corollary 'You've have to show me' qualify for a c.p. tag. We call Missouri the 'Show Me State'. We Missourians (yes, I was born there) wish to have proof of something before we believe it. We are not easily fooled or taken in. 'I'm from Missouri' is now used by Missourians as an expression of skepticism.

I'm going down now, sir. See **don't forget the diver!**

I'm going to die is 'said twice, plaintively, followed by a pause, and then resolutely, in a Cockney accent, **nah, fuck it! I'll go tomorrer**' (P.B., 1976): since *c.* 1919.

I'm going to do a job no one else can do for me. Used among men when one of them excuses himself to go to the lavatory: since *c.* 1950. (Petch, 1974.) P.B.: hardly, perhaps, a c.p., but since E.P. put it in the first ed., then logically all the various synon. phrases should be included. Merely representative are: *I'm going to* (or, often, *I must*) *water the dragon* or *the nag*; and .... *shed a tear for Nelson*. Then there are ....*strain the greens* and ...*squeeze the lemon* – and many, many others. See also **point Percy at the porcelain**, and **shake hands....**

I'm going to get my head sharpened. I'm going to get a haircut: RAF: *c.* 1950–70.

I'm Hawkshaw the detective, usu. completed rather than elab. by – **he took a sly glance at me**: *c.* 1864–1914. From melodrama and burlesque, notably of the Transpontine sort. 'He was a character in Tom Taylor's *The Ticket-of-Leave Man*' (1863) and the implication of the c.p. is that 'someone is behaving like a copper's nark' (Shaw, 1968).

Tom Taylor (1817–80) wrote many successful plays, of which the *The Ticket-of-Leave Man* was perhaps the best and was spectacularly successful, and during his last six years he edited *Punch*.

I'm in condition to-night! I feel good tonight: *c.* 1955–70. Either from a 'quack' muscle-builder's advertisement or, as P.B. has suggested, 1975, from 'a TV comedian of the early 1950s, as he flexed non-existent muscles'. Cf **you too can have a body like mine.**

I'm in the boat! push off! was used by the army in WW1 and up to *c.* 1939. (B&P.) The equivalent of **fuck you, Jack, I'm all right.** Cf:

I'm in the lifeboat, Jack: pull up the ladder. A frequent var. of the prec.: not confined to the RN; it occurred often in the Army of WW2 and after. Cf:

I'm inboard: fuck you, Jack (or **fuck you, Jack: I'm inboard**). Synon. with prec.: RN: C20. Cf **I'm fire-proof.**

I'm it is 'used in derision of the "Great I am" type of actor' or music-hall, or variety, performer: since *c.* 1920. (Petch, 1974.)

I'm Jolly Jack the Sailor just come home (or **in**) **from sea.** Of the approx. period 1880–1914, it orig. in the music-halls. (Shaw, 1968.) Prob. connected with – perhaps even the predecessor of – **Ballocky Bill the Sailor.**

I'm just as happy.... See **happy as a dead pig....**

I'm keeping the tax-collector happy. 'Sometimes said by an elderly man when asked whether he has retired' (Petch, 1978): since *c.* 1950. P.B.: might also be the excuse of an incorrigible smoker: Albert Petch and Eric Partridge between them, even.

I'm Kruschen, the man who took R out of 'shirt' was 'used throughout Britain 1920–40' (Jack Slater, 1978). It referred to Kruschen's Salts, the refreshing and stimulating morning laxative.

I'm like all fools; I love everything that's good belongs to C18 and occurs in both Dialogue I and Dialogue II of S, 1738; thus in the second:

LADY SM[ART]: MR *Neverout*, do you love Pudden?

NEV: Madam, I'm like all Fools; I love every Thing that is good. But the Proof of the Pudden, is in the eating.

I'm nice. I feel very well: US negroes': since *c.* 1960. CM, 1970.

I'm not angry. See **I'm not mad....**

I'm not having any. See **I'm not taking any.**

I'm not here. See **I am not here.**

I'm not just a pretty face, often extended by **you know.** I'm not merely pretty (or occ. of men, handsome) – I do possess *some* intelligence. 'A feminine c.p. addressed to a crass male. "I have brains as well as looks"' (Granville, 1968). Since *c.* 1965 or a very few years earlier. It occurs in Miles Tripp's psychological 'thriller', *Woman at Risk*, 1974, thus: '"She's not just a pretty face," Philpott went on, "she's clever too"', which supports my own opinion that, strictly, the c.p. is *not just a pretty face*, and that this can be and is, often prec. by *I'm* or *She's*.

But the c.p. is also used joc. 'among men (from women's protest that they have ability, brains, as well as beauty) at proved acumen, handyman's help in the home, or when hunch is proved right' (L.A., 1975). Cf James Fraser, *Death in a Pheasant's Eye*, 1972: '"'Greenfingers Brown', they'll be calling you next," Bill Aveyard said. "You're not just a pretty face!"' (A police superintendent to his sergeant).

'I have often heard this followed by "Not *even* a pretty face"' (Derek Parker, 1977).

I'm not mad (angry), **I'm just terribly, terribly hurt.** 'Semi-humorous response to some such [question] as "You're not mad at me, are you?" Originating in the 1920s, probably as a "straight" line from some now forgotten play. Mainly sophisticated usage; now very obsolescent' (R.C., 1978). P.B.: also, with *angry* for 'mad', Brit., and in the same milieu. I remember a cartoon of the later 1940s, prob. in *Punch*: a mother, arrow through chest, to small boy clutching a bow, saying, 'No, Mummy's not angry, just terribly, terribly hurt'. The line is occ. reversed: see **more in anger...**

I'm not made of money. See **you must think....**

I'm not out for chocolate; just had grapes! No, thank you!, used intensively and rather contemptuously: c.p. of *c.* 1905–14. It occurs in W.L. Geroge's penetrating and perspicuous novel, *The Making of an Englishman*, 1914.

I'm not so green as I'm cabbage-looking. See **not so green....**

I'm not taking (or **having**) **any.** Not for me: respectively since *c.*1895 and since *c.* 1890; the latter occurs in J. Milne, *Epistles of Atkins*, 1902.

I'm not that kind (or **sort**) **of girl.** 'Originally the feminine response to a [sexual] proposition; later in general use as a jocular response to any mildly dubious proposal. Now, somewhat obsolescent, perhaps many more girls are [or are prepared to admit that they are] that sort of girl' (R.C., 1978.) Current all over the English-speaking world throughout C20 and perhaps since *c.* 1880.

I'm not tight, but I've taken up a lot of slack refers to being, not drunk but merely on the way to becoming so: mostly Can., I rather think: at a guess, since *c.* 1970. (Leechman, 1977.) But contrast **he's not tight,...**

I'm off in a cloud of dust and **pardon my dust!** These US phrases have a slightly different connotation from the next entry. They precede WW1, for they arose during that period when automobiles were ousting the horse and buggy, and before dirt roads were being hard-surfaced. People in horse-drawn vehicles found themselves covered with a choking cloud of dust every time an automobile passed them. (W.J.B., 1977.) Cf:

I'm off in a shower (or **cloud**) **of shit.** I am departing – Goodbye! 'Some US currency, 1930s. Low parody of the racetrack announcer's "They're off in a cloud of dust" [but cf. prec.]' (R.C., 1978). It was a Can. Army c.p. of WW2, and occ., among civilians, since 1945. P.B.: I heard it used by Australian servicemen during the 1960s.

I'm on agen with Monaghan and off agen with you had a brief life (English), 1910–*c.* 1914, and was adopted from a song-title that, in 1910, was sung by Maggie Cline, Edward B. Marks, *They All Sang*, 1934. (Thanks to W.J.B.)

I'm only asking. I'm merely asking a simple question, not expecting some benefit; I merely wish to know; I ask out of curiosity, nothing more: since *c.* 1910. P.B.: sometimes completed, ...**because I want to know.** See also **I only asked.**

I'm only here for the beer. I've no right to be here – all I want is a bit of fun; I'm not a serious person: from late 1971 or very early 1972. From a beer advertisement – for Double Diamond – of 1971.

Often shortened to *only here for the beer*, which has become so widely accepted that, in the *Sunday Times* Magazine of Sep. 1973, a summer-resort article can be headed 'Only Here For La Bière'.

I'm proper poorly and **I've been poorly, proper poorly.** 'Some clash of attributable dates and sources: I suspect, but no more, both [late] C19 music-hall and [a] revival perhaps on radio. Cf (even... significantly) George Formby, Senior (1871–1921), who made a gag, "Coughing better tonight", etc., out of his fatally consumptive element' (Wedgewood, 1977). Variant, maybe. Shaw, 1968, thought the first arose in the 1930s; Ronald Pearsall, however, suggests that it was popularized by Reg Dixon in the late 1940s or early 50s; Peter Herbert supports this latter opinion and adds that Dixon used it in the form *I'm not well, I'm proper poorly*. P.B.: cf the (? mainly Northern) domestic phrase *poorly sick in bed with a shawl*. (With thanks to Mrs Patricia Pinder.) It follows a long history of humour at the expense of those who 'enjoy ill health'.

I'm shipping out. See **fuck you, buddy...**

I'm skinning this cat, often elab. by the addition of **and you are not paid to hold the tail.** Mind your own business!: US: since *c.* 1920; by 1970, somewhat outdated. (Berrey.) Lovett, 1978, adds, 'I've heard in various parts of Australia *who's stuffing this cat*? – meaning "Who's doing this job?" – often followed by *who's holding its tail*? – "Whose assistance is essential?"'

I'm so empty I can feel my (or **me**) **backbone touching my** (or **me**) **belly button.** An uncouth, undeniably humorous, c.p.: C20. In, e.g., Alexander Baron, *There's No Home*, 1950. R.C., 1978, writes: 'Cf the eloquent "blues" metaphor'

> Oh, I been broke – I didn't have no grub,
> Backbone and navel – doing the belly-rub'

Cf also the next, and **I could take up the slack...**

I'm so hungry I could eat a shit sandwich, only I don't like bread is 'a rather repugnant self-explanatory c.p., which is not used in vice-regal circles' (B.P.): Aus: since *c.* 1950. A.B., 1978, provides the US variants *I'm so hungry I could eat a horse (and wagon) and (then)*chase the driver, and *I'm as hungry as a bitch-wolf in mating season.*

P.B.: in Dave Dutton, *Lanky* [i.e. Lancashire] *Spoken Here*, 1979, are listed [I translate from the dialect spelling]: *...so hungry I could eat a scabby pig without bread; ...a flock bed; ...a cow between two bread vans.* And *New Society*, 28 May 1981, quoted a lorry-driver saying that he 'could eat a scabby horse between bedrags'.

Lovett notes, 1978, that the innocuous *I could eat a horse...driver* is also current in Aus. as *I could eat a horse and then chase the rider.*

Cf **I could take up...** and **my stomach...**

I'm sorry I came in! An ironic, almost resigned, c.p. 'spoken by one who, expecting quiet, enters a room where there's a lot of human noise' (Shaw): since the late 1940s. Cf **sorry you spoke...**

I'm speaking (or **talking**) **to the butcher, not to the block.** 'Putting 'em in their place! If the boy speaks up before the workman can frame a reply, or if Jack's missus joins in the (acrimonious) argument: but it *can* be used jocularly' (Julian Franklyn, 1962): Cockneys: C20. P.B.: I have also heard *I'm talking to the (engine-) driver, not his oily rag.*

I'm telling you indicates emphasis: adopted, in early 1920s, in Britain: from US, where used since *c.* 1910. Supp. 1 of HLM notes that it is one of 'a number of familiar American phrases': for which the erudite Dr Roback had argued a Yiddish origin; and Berrey includes it in a long list of 'expressions of affirmation'. Cf **I'll tell the (cock-eyed) world!**

I'm trying to give them up. See **no, I'm trying...**

I'm willing, but Mary isn't, with *I* and *Mary* strongly emphasized. Used by a dyspeptic or other stomachic sufferer when some food is offered: C20. This is, of course, *little Mary*, the stomach.

I'm with you, pal – or with *pal* omitted – is a US c.p. of agreement, not, it is true, wildly enthusiastic, yet genuine: since *c.* 1920. Berrey.

I'm worried about Jim. In the *Daily Telegraph*, 23 Feb. 1977, Gillian Reynolds ('Radio Review') writes, 'It says a lot for the potency of radio that comedians can still raise the occasional laugh with a harp glissando and the words, "I'm worried about Jim...", the catchphrase which came to represent "Mrs Dale's Diary" in much the same way as "Play it again, Sam" [q.v.] did the film "Casablanca".' *VIBS* amplifies: 'Ellis Powell as the eponymous heroine of radio's *Mrs Dale's Diary* (referring to her doctor husband). Although she may not have uttered the phrase very often, it was essential in parodies of the programme'. This very British, middle-class soap opera was first broadcast in Jan. 1948 – and ran for 21 years.

imbars bidbib. An Army 'motto', current in WW2 and composed of the initial letters of *I may be a rotten sod, but I don't believe in bullshit*.

I've... See also entries at **I have...**

I've arrived: and to prove it, I'm 'ere (or **here**), Cyril Whelan, 1975, writes:

> Despite much raiding of the memory banks and a fairly rigorous inquisition of friends, I'm afraid I'm unable to remember the origin of [this]. It was certainly a comedian of the 50: and I think the fact that the tag is remembered independently of the individual makes quite a pertinent point. This kind of expression becomes popular and is used *ad nauseam* within groups of friends, newspaper headlines, etc., for a short, intense period while the radio or television show retains popularity or novelty. The impetus then seems to wear off, but the phrase is retained in the lower strata of the collective memory for use at much later dates and often quite far removed from the original context.

Which, you'll admit, is subtly and pellucidly expressed. 'I wish I had said that,' remarked Wilde. 'You will, Oscar, you will,' retorted Whistler.

Well, since then I've been told that the c.p. was orig. by that accomplished entertainer, Max Bygraves, in 'Educating Archie', a radio show based on the ventriloquist's doll Archie Andrews, which ran from 1950 to 1953 (BBC Written Archives Centre, Caversham Park, Reading).

I've been left out in the cold before, but never again! 'I have been abandoned, but I've learned my lesson!': US: since *c.* 1920. (A.B., 1978; he compares the *non-c.*p. 'He's left out in the cold' or ostracized.) Cf **out into the cold, cold snow.**

I've been poorly, proper poorly. A var. of **I'm proper poorly.**

I've been there. See **oh, yes, I've...**

I've been through the mill, ground and bolted. I'm much too experienced to believe, or to do, that: nautical mid C19 – early C20. (B & L.) When the last three words are omitted, it is a cliché.

I've been swaying with an old mess-mate. See **swaying...**

I've been thrown out of better joints than this. A derogatory description of, e.g., a bar or restaurant. Heard by me in early 1950s, but prob. dating since *c.* 1945. (A reminder from John Skehan, 1977.)

I've done (or **had**) **more sea miles than you've had** (or **eaten**) **pusser's peas** is a naval boast, dating since *c.* 1917 and claiming a comparatively long service at sea. (A *pusser* is, of course, a purser.) Cf **get some service in!** and **I've had more women...**

I've eaten a hundred like you for breakfast and had a dozen more as afters is a c.p. boast so exaggerated as to be genuinely funny and comical: rare, I believe, before 1950 and not very widespread until *c.* 1955. (Petch, 1974.)

I've got (or **I've**) **a bit of string with a hole in it** is a facetious would-be witty reply to a request for something-or-other quite different: C20.

I've got a duke's mixture. See **who dealt this mess?**

I've got a feeling in my (or **me**) **water,** with **I've** often omitted, is used as a c.p. reply to, e.g., 'Well, what makes you think it'll be all right this time?'. It means 'I can't give you a precise reason, yet I strongly feel that it *is* so': C20 and prob. back to 1850, if not further. (P.B., 1975.)

I've got a million of 'em seems to have been one of Max Miller's

'gags': 1940s and 1950s. (Noble, 1975.) See **I gotta million of them.** But the precise interrelationship is obscure.

I've got an 'orse! (Often rendered *I gotta norse!*) The cry of that black prince of race-course tipsters Ras Prince Monolulu (born Peter Carl McKay, † 1965): 'His famous catchphrase – coined while trying to outdo a race track evangelist carrying a placard "I got Heaven" – was "I've got an 'orse"' (Frederic Rolph, in *Weekend*, 31 Aug. 1983, p 21).

I've got (illiterately **I got**) **news for you.** I have something important – *or* startling *or* contradicting what you've just said – to tell you: US: since early 1950s. In *The Zoo Story*, performed in Berlin 1959, in New York 1960 (which was also the year in which it was published), Edward Albee causes Jerry to remark to Peter: 'Hey, I got news for you, as they say.' A.B., 1978, notes the extra emphatic var., 'Boy, do I have news for you!', with heavy stress on nearly every word; while R.C. added 'Have *I* ever got news for you!' [see also **have I got...**]. E.P. also noted the essentially Brit. var. *I have news for you!*, adding, in the first edn of this book: Since the late 1940s. On 1 Sep. 1975 I saw a *Daily Mail* poster that read, 'We have news for you': clear evidence of establishment.

'I've got the time', as Big Ben said to the leaning tower of Pisa. A joc. elab. on the 'time' theme, without the innuendo of the next: Brit.: C20. (Eric Fearon, 1984.)

I've got the time if you've got the inclination. Besides the ordinary usage, i.e. of sexual innuendo, which, clearly, is not a c.p., there exists a derivate sense, current since *c.* 1950: a 'retort to ejaculations of surprise or indignation (e.g. *bugger me!* or *fuck me!*) A gently pink' – suggestive – 'contrast between impulse and sobriety' or caution. (L.A., 1974.) R.C., 1979, provides a gloss for the reverse, *I've got the time but not the inclination*: 'I don't feel like doing it just now, in some situations "with you" being implied. General US from at least [as early as] 1930s. Originally, perhaps a "soft answer" to a sexual advance, but predominant usage has long been in non-sexual contexts'. And A.B., 1978, writes, 'I recall a song, *c.* 1952, entitled "If you've got the money, honey, I've got the time"'.

See also **any day you 'ave the money...**

[**I've got to do my thing** – 'very recent hippy talk, "I must express myself"' (Leechman, 1969) – is not a c.p., but a cliché: every 'hippy' has to do this and insists on telling you so, in any grammatical tense and number. P.B.: it became a 1970s poster slogan in the form *I gotta be me.*]

I've got to saddle up is a C20 Western Americanism for 'It's time for me to be going' and is 'often heard at parties or other social gatherings' (W.J.B., 1977). Clearly, at first a rural, perhaps a cowboys', expression.

I've gotter motter... See **cheer up, cully,...**

I've had a full, rich day. See **full, rich day.**

I've had (or **I had**) **a shit, shave, shower, shoe-shine and shampoo.** See **shave, a shilling....**

I've had more sea miles.... See **I've done more sea miles....**

I've had more women than you've had hot breakfasts or **dinners** is an older man's cynically joc. boast to a younger, clearly much less experienced, man: C20. The female counterpart, from 'knowing' woman to comparatively inexperienced girl is...*more men than....*

I've had more women... has become so incorporated into the language that there can naturally occur such allusions as this in Act I of John Osborne's *Inadmissible Evidence*, prod. 1964, pub'd 1965:

> BILL [speaking of a typist]: She looks as though she could do with a bit [of fornication]. She's got the galloping cutes all right. Joy. *She's* had more joy sticks than hot dinners.

The phrase had, during WW2, in the Army, the var. *I've had more women than you've had Naffy* [= NAAFI] *suppers*, cited, 1978, by Brian W. Aldiss, who comments: 'Whereas hot dinners are – supposedly, at least – enjoyable, and preferable to cold dinners, Naffy suppers were always considered revolting'.

P.B.: although usu. in this sexual context, the phrase may sometimes be heard applied to other desirables. The *dinners* version is the commoner.

I've had my moments. See **I have had...**

I've heard that one before. Noël Coward, *Waiting in the Wings*, 1960, has at II, i:

> PERRY: There's no need to get into such a fizz. She's promised to let me see whatever she writes before it goes in.
>
> MISS ARCHIE: I've heard that one before.

To attempt to date a c.p. of this sort would be to attempt the impossible. At a guess – a wild, wild guess – I'd hazard 'Since the 1890s, perhaps the 1880s, possibly the 1870s': and then, as likely as not, be a generation astray.

I've never met one before. See **I've read about people...**

I've not seen you since last year, 'a tiresome "gag" many use on January the 1st each year' was recorded, as Frank Shaw informed me in 1969, as far back as the *Comic Calendar*, 1841.

I've only got four minutes. The Australian comedian Bill Kerr used to preface his turn on BBC radio variety shows, *c.* 1950, with this drawled and lugubrious introduction, perhaps influenced by the 'four minutes' warning' the UK was supposed to have before an atomic attack on the country. B.K. went on to become perhaps more widely known for his part, teamed with Sid James and Tony Hancock, in 'Hancock's Half Hour'. (P.B.)

I've said nothing. See **mind you, I've...**

I've seen better things on Christmas trees is derisively applied, rather by women to men than vice versa, with ref. to genitals: since *c.* 1965.

I've seen 'em come and I've seem 'em go. 'Said of those (manager, n.c.o., officer) who start new job like a whirlwind and end with over-zealous mistake, hoped for by staff' (L.A., 1975): dating since the 1920s. A cynicism prompted by the proverbial 'A new broom sweeps clean'.

I've seen 'em grow and I've shit 'em! are army c.pp. used in WW1, the former indicating contempt for someone's rapid promotion, esp. a junior's; the latter scorn for soldiers of another regiment. The polite one appears in F & G, the rude one in B & P. Cf **scraped 'em off me puttees** and **soldiers? I've shit 'em.**

Of the *I've shit 'em* version, Jack Slater has (1978) remarked that it is 'used to create a situation of umbrage or as a retort about someone when the speaker can't find anything more unpleasant to say'.

've seen more order in a fire drill in a Chinese insane asylum is an NCOs' sarcasm directed at a sloppy fall-in, or other parade-ground manoeuvre, recalled by Ashley from the RCAF of the 1950s. Cf **I'll tear your arm off...**

've something to do (that) nobody else can do for me. I must pay a visit to the lavatory: never euph.; always – rather laboriously – joc.; C20. (A reminder from Petch, 1966.)

I've started, so I'll finish. From 'Mastermind', the BBC TV quiz, an annual series started in 1972. 'The presence of Magnus Magnusson [the question-master]...sternly administering the rules that he himself must keep ("I've started, so I'll finish") adds to the ambience' (*Guardian*, 22 Dec. 1981); the phrase is used if M.M. is caught by the time signal when halfway through posing a question to a contestant. The phrase has had some, usu. joc., out-of-context use among the population at large. (P.B., with thanks to Mrs Daphne Beale, and Allan Chapman, FLA, 1984.)

ice(s). See: **stinks; that cuts; Walls.**

ice-boxes. See: **could sell.**

ice-hockey. See: **pretend.**

ice it (or **that**)! 'An imperative to reduce [e.g., excitement, anger, noise] in intensity' (*The Third Ear*, 1971): a US Negroes' var. of **cool it!** (Paul Janssen.)

ice-man. See: **how'd you like.**

idea. See: **good idea; that's a very; well, it seemed; what's the big.**

idea is cold – the. 'It is of no further use' (Berrey, 1942): US: *c.* 1920–50.

identical. See: **very identical.**

if (or **when**) **all else fails, read the instructions!** This implies, of course, that the know-all who has blinded straight into trying to assemble or operate an unfamiliar device, and failed, should have given the matter some thought first: the phrase seems to have been nearing c.p. status during later C20, and may by now, 1985, have reached it. (P.B.)

if, (and it's) a big if supplied a cold *douche* to a very improbable, and startling, supposition or hypothesis: C20; by 1976, slightly outmoded. P.B.: but cf the later C20 slang use of *iffy* applied to anything doubtful, from a deal to a motorcar.

if anything can go wrong, it will. See **anything that can...**

if at first you don't succeed, suck a lemon. This 'Job's consolation' dates from *c.* 1910 and became slightly ob. *c.* 1975. The punning use of *a lemon* invites comparison with (the) **answer is a lemon.** (A reminder from Jack Slater, 1978.)

if ever! See **well, if ever!**

if ever a man suffered! See **ee, if ever...**

if God wanted to give the world an enema... See **arsehole of the world.**

if he doesn't like it he may do the other thing! 'The other thing' is 'lump it' – put up with it. Recorded by Baumann, it belongs to the approx. period, 1860–1914. Cf **if you don't like it, you can lump it.** P.B.: also applied to others, e.g. *if they* (or *you*, etc.) *don't...*

if he fell in the shit, he'd come up smelling of violets, and variants on this theme. See **could fall in the shit...**

if he had the 'flu, he wouldn't give you a sneeze has, since *c.* 1920, imputed extreme meanness. Prob. occasioned by the great influenza epidemic of 1918–19. Cf **so mean that...**

if he's not careful he'll shit himself. See **shot himself!**

if I am a dog, shake hands, brother! S, Dialogue III, has:

> NEV[EROUT]: ...Why, Miss, if I spoil the Colonel, I hope you will use him as you do me; for, you know, love me, love my Dog.
>
> COL: How's that, *Tom*? say that again. Why, if I am a dog, shake Hands, Brother.

Belonging to C18, this is 'one of the animal – human group of witticisms patterned by the Classical retort of old woman herding asses to pert youth, "Good morning, mother of *asses*. – Good morning, my *son*."'

if I die for it, short for **even if I die for it,** was current *c.* 1660–1760. In the final scene of Act III of Susannah Centlivre, *Marplot in Lisbon*, 1711, the egregious Marplot exclaims, 'Egad I'll not tell where Charles lives, if I die for it.'

if I disremember correctly is a US c.p., glossed by Berrey, 1942, as meaning 'if I have not forgotten'; prob. since *c.* 1920; by 1975, somewhat outmoded.

if I don't see you through the week, I'll see you through the window. A punning *au revoir*: Liverpool (and for full effect, best uttered in a true Scouse accent): later C20. (BBC Radio 4, 'You and Yours', broadcast 23 May 1984. With compliments to Ms Pattie Coldwell. P.B.)

if I had a dog with no more wit, I would hang him occurs in the opening Dialogue of S, and can prob. be dated C18 – early C19:

> NEV[EROUT]: Alack a day, poor Miss, methinks it grieves me to pity you.
>
> MISS: What, you think you said a fine thing now; well, if I had a Dog with no more Wit, I would hang him.

if I have breath is a c.p. of asseveration, synon. with **as I live and breathe:** current *c.* 1660–1750. Thomas Shadwell, in *The Lancashire Witches*, 1680, at II, i, causes the love-sick maid Susan to exclaim, 'Mother *Demdike* shall help me to Morrow: I'll to her, and discourse her about it: if I have breath, I cannot live without him.' Some C20 US variants and survivals: *as long as I have breath (in me)*: *well! as I live* *and breathe*; (e.g. *you won't do that*) *so long as I live and breathe* (A.B., 1978).

if I have the name, I may as well have the game, late C19–20, is a feminine, c.p., used by a woman unjustly accused of promiscuity. Contrast **name of the game.**

if I hit you, it's the graveyard; if I miss, it's pneumonia is a picturesque comic US threat: *c.* 1910–60. Berrey.

if I knew you were (or **was**) **comin', I'd've baked a cake.** Part of the chorus of a very popular song written and composed by Al Hoffman, Bob Merrill and Clem Watts; orig. US, it was pub'd in UK by Chappel's in 1950, as 'I'd've Baked a Cake'. (With thanks to Mr Williams of that firm.) It quickly became a c.p., 'sarcastically addressed to an arrival demanding too much attention…or [by a girl] to an arrogant marauding male' (R.S.). P.B.: or simply as a greeting to a surprise visitor; always joc., though there was sometimes some 'edge' behind the parody…, *I'd've greased the stair.* Still heard occ. in early 1980s.

if I live and breathe. See **as I live and breathe.**

if I lose my stick, I must have a shy for it. 'I will have a fight before I give up my right' (Egan's Grose, 1823): underworld and near-underworld: *c.* 1810–50.

if I need you, I'll rattle the bars of your cage. See **that really rattled his cage.**

if I stick a broom up my arse, I can sweep the hangar at the same time. This RAF c.p., dating since *c.* 1925, is uttered, with a bitter humour, by one who has been assigned a string of tasks that will keep him busy for hours.

The US equivalent is *stick a broom up my ass and I'll sweep the floor* (R.C., 1978). Australia offers the picturesque var. *you'd better give me a ball and chain to stop me breaking into a gallop,* 'I'm too heavily laden' or 'I've been given too many tasks' or even 'I'm only human – and so subject to error'. It has the shortening, *can I have a ball and chain*? Lovett, 1978, recalls having heard the full form in 1950, the shorter in 1971.

if I was as big as you, I'd challenge Dempsey. A US c.p. of the 1920s. Ring W. Lardner, *What of It?*, 1925, article titled 'Lay Off the Thyroid'. Jack Dempsey won the world heavyweight championship on 4 July 1919 and lost it to Gene Tunney on 23 Sep. 1926.

if I were near you, I wouldn't be far from you. If I were near you, I'd deal with you vigorously; if near at all, very near indeed: C18. In S, Dialogue I, Miss says this to a screaming child.

if in danger or in doubt/run in circles, scream and shout! Since *c.* 1925. Used as in Roger Busby, *A Reasonable Man*, 1972, 'The incident room was now buzzing with activity, detectives from all over the city frantically trying to look busy, fearful of the wrath of the CID chief. What was that old Navy saying? "If in danger or in doubt…shout!"' Cf **when in danger….**

if in doubt, toss it out! See **when in doubt….**

if it ain't good *to* you, it must be good *for* you. 'The unpleasant things which are supposed to be blessings in disguise' (*The Third Ear*, 1971): a US Negroes' semi-proverb: since *c.* 1950. This reminds one of the myth that, the more disagreeable a medicine or a treatment, the better it is for the patient.

if it feels good, do it! 'Expresses the hedonistic philosophy of some 1960s counter-culturists. Now obsolescent, along with the philosophy it aphorizes' (R.C., 1978): US.

if it had been a bear…. See **if it were a bear….**

if it had teeth…. See **it's staring you in the face.**

if it isn't one thing it's another! often prec. by **well** – is a C20 c.p., both US and Brit. In *Blue Goops and Red*, 1909, Gelett Burgess writes:

When Aunt Ethel and Mr Jack called to take Alonzo and Peter and Bessyrose out to ride in the automobile, you would have thought that they would behave nicely. But they didn't…. That rather frightened Peter and Alonzo and Bessyrose, so after that they kept very quiet and still and began to enjoy the ride….All the same, pretty soon a

tire was punctured, and Mr Jack said, 'Well, if it isn't one thing, it's another!'

if it moves, salute it; if it don't, paint (occ. **whitewash**) **it!** was the army's and RAF's advice to recruits and, in a way, motto: middle and late 1940s and 1950s.

J.W.C., 1968, writes, 'it was certainly common in the U.S. Armed Forces in 1944–46, and still understood, but I question whether it's a c.p. outside of military circles.' Correct! Never a c.p. outside of the British and US fighting Services. A.B., 1978, writes, 'My father, after his return from WW2 (African and Italian campaigns, 1942–45), told this one to me: "If you can lift it, carry it; if you can't lift it, paint it; and if it moves by itself, salute it".' Prof. Brown adds that the phrase was 'often put up on paper board as a motto' – I presume, during the last year of the war, and for a few years afterwards Ashley, 1984, provides the even more pointed *if it moves, salute it; if it doesn't move, paint it; if you can't paint it – fuck it!*

There is, however, an Aus. derivative var.: *if it moves, shoot it; if it doesn't chop it down,* a c.p. used to satirize 'the philosophy of those who are trigger-happy and axe-happy' (B.P., 1975). Wilkes's earliest quot'n for this comes from Alan Ross, *Australia*, 1963, 'The country had still to be conquered. The general attitude was: "If it moves, shoot it. If it stands still, chop it down".' But the predominant c.p. form seems to be B.P.'s, to which the *Sydney Morning Herald*, 4 May 1964, refers thus: 'So goes the old Australian saying'. But the orig. is, very clearly, the much older UK version.

See **if it's too big to shift…**

if it takes a leg! 'Threat of a desperado, in search of revenge' (George P. Burnham, *Memoirs of the United States Secret Service*, 1872): US underworld: *c.* 1850–1910. Even at the cost of a leg. P.B.: cf the later C20, orig. US, (*it'll cost an*) **arm and a leg,** q.v., for something outrageously expensive.

if it was raining… (Aus.: since the late 1940s) has several completions, all noted by Wilkes: *if it was raining pea soup, I'd* (or *he'd*) *get hit on the head by a fork* or *I'd* (etc.) *have only a fork; …palaces, I'd get hit on the head with the handle of a dunny door* – a *dunny* being a *dunnaken*, a privy, lit. a place (*ken*) for human *dung*; or …*virgins, we'd be washed away with a poofter* (or *poofta*), a passive male homosexual. Contrast this pessimistic outlook with the good fortune implied in **could fall in the shit…** P.B.: for an interesting adumbration, cf the Swift dialogue at **straight as my leg…**

if it were a bear, it would bite you; also if it had been a bear, it would have bit you. A semi-proverbial c.p., applied, C17–18, to 'him that makes a close search after what lies just under his Nose' (BE, 1698). It occurs also in Draxe, 1633, and in S, as Apperson tells us. P.B.: the second form, at least, lingers in the Provinces: I heard it used quite naturally, *c.* 1980, by an East Midlander in his 60s. Cf:

if it were a black snake, you'd be dead. See **it's staring you in the face.**

if it works, it's already obsolete forms the c.p. version of a modern US proverb, *if it works, it's obsolete,* which Lord Mountbatten quoted, 1961, in a speech containing the memorable phrase, 'the rapacious march of science'. With thanks to *ODEP*, 3rd ed.

if it's h-h-hokay with you, it's h-h-hokay with me! 'The stuttering catchphrase of one Tubby Turner, Lancashire music-hall artist, born 1882' (*VIBS*).

if it's too big to shift, paint it. The RN lowerdeck version, perhaps the orig., of **if it moves…,** q.v. As *Sailors' Slang* puts it, 'used when any awkward job confronts the men, or when taking heavy stores on board.' Prob. throughout C20.

if it's Tuesday, this must be Belgium was the title of a US comedy film, 1969, about a very fast package-tour of Europe. As Skehan remarks, 1977, it, and variations of it, have become something of a c.p. to satirize what he calls 'the blue-rinse tours', in ref. to cultural tours organised esp. for middle-aged women. But it is used also of fast travel anywhere, or about confusion over the day of the week. (P.B.) As Patricia Brent, beginning a travel article in *Illustrated London News*, Mar. 1981, had, '"If it's Tuesday, it must be Würzburg!" I wrote on a postcard from Franconia.'

if my aunt had been a man, she'd have been my uncle; also **if my aunt had been an uncle, she'd have been a man.** A mid C17–mid 20 semi-proverbial c.p., applied derisively to one who has, at length and most tediously, explained the obvious. It also, in C19–20, rebukes someone who has used a most unrealistic conditional, e.g. 'I could have done it if...' (Apperson.) A scabrous late C19–20 var. is *if my aunt had been a man* or *if my aunt had been an uncle – she'd have had a pair of balls under her arse*.

Yet another version, *if your aunt had balls, she'd be your uncle*, was 'current at least by [the] 1930s as a bawdy version of [the proverb] "if wishes were horses...".' G.E.R. Gedge quotes in the *sotto voce* of a young undersecretary on Mr Chamberlain's complaint, "If only Herr Hitler would be reasonable!" (*Betrayal in Central Europe*)' (R.C., 1976).

if not pleased, put your hand in your pocket and please yourself! is a mid C17–18 c.p. retort to a grumbler. Like the prec., it occurs in Ray.

if only I had some eggs, I'd make (occ. **cook**) **eggs and bacon** (pause) **if I had the bacon,** with several slight variations, is an army c.p. of WW1: wistful if applied to oneself, mildly satirical if to another.

By far the commonest 'American variant was "If we had some ham, we'd have some ham and eggs, if we had some eggs." (And no pause before the second "if")' (J.W.C., 1977). The US version has, R.C. tells me, 1978, been 'current from [the] 1920s; now obsolescent'. Cf *if I were thirsty, I'd go buy a beer, if I had a nickel*: US: since *c.* 1920. (A.B., 1979.)

if that don't pass! See **well, if that don't pass!**

if that's nonsense, I'd like some of it! retorts upon one who has just reproved a man for talking smut: since *c.* 1925.

if the devil cast his net is a prob. mid C19–20 c.p. sent to me by the late Frank Shaw, 1969, with this comment:

The jovial fellow suddenly coming on a group of jolly, half-drunk fellows like himself comes out with it as if nobody had ever said it before; he makes them feel very devils themselves and they receive the witticism, as if it was new [to them] also. 'What a capture he'd have!' understood. I just don't, at the moment, know how old; I definitely suspect Irish origin; origin, anyhow, in old folk yarn.

Mr Shaw added, 'We see the devil as a diabolical fisherman.'

if the camels die (dramatic pause) **we die.** 'A glimpse of the obvious. A line of the dialogue lifted from the film "Lawrence of Arabia," 1962. Probably first used in the earliest Westerns as "if the horses die, we die". Jocular' (Sanders, 1978).

if there's one thing worse than chaos, it's organised chaos. This is a Services' c.p., prob. orig. in WW2, used esp. if the staff has had a hand in things. (P.B., 1976.)

if they're big enough, they're old enough is a callous and cynical masculine c.p., referring to the nubility of *young* teenage girls: C20. With an allusion to the age of consent. P.B.: there are a number of even more coarse, brutal, and insensitive variants, on both sides of the Atlantic, that I decline to include. Those who know them, need no reminder; those who don't are better off without.

if this keeps on, someone is bound to (or **will** or **is going to**) **get hurt** is a cliché when used lit. and seriously, but when, as often, used humorously, esp. when ruefully and ironically, it has been a c.p. since late C19, as when Wilfred Saint-Mandé, *War, Wine and Women*, 1931, wrote, concerning an episode in WW1: 'Our camp was a mile from the town, and we got back just as our companions were examining a huge hole that a bomb had made. "'Ow would you like that on your nut, Charlie?" asked a man at my side. "If this keeps on,

someone's bound to get hurt," replied his pal, repeating an ancient joke that always raised a laugh.'

if we had some ham... See **if only I had some eggs...**

if wet: in the vicarage is 'facetiously used when making any arrangement' other than church arrangements; the ecclesiastical usage obviously orig. the profane: C20. (Shaw, 1969.) For origin, cf **good time was had by all–a.**

if you are angry, you may turn the buckle of your girdle behind you. Addressed to 'one Angry for a small Matter, and whose Anger is as little valued' (BE, 1698): late C16–mid 18. Merely signifying '... for all it matters and if *that*'ll help you'.

[**if you blind me, you must lead me** is perhaps not a proverbial saying but a c.p.: C18. S, near end of Dialogue I has:

MISS: Poh; you are so robustious: You had like to put out my Eye: I assure you, if you blind me, you must lead me.]

if you call yourself a soldier, I'm a bloody Army Corps! This was a WW1 military c.p., virtually extinct by 1940. It implied a vastly superior soldierliness in the speaker. B&P, 1931.

if you can name it (or **tell what it is**) **you can have it** refers to an odd-looking person or thing: C20. Cf **things you see....**

if you can pee (or **piss**) **you can paint.** A c.p. of the building trade – house-painters are meant: C20. 'Painters get knocked because their work is thought easy ("if you can pee you can paint")' (Colin Sheffield in *Telegraph* Sunday mag., 18 Dec. 1977). Not true.

if you can walk away from it, it's a landing is 'said of a makee-learnee airman who comes in to land with every indication of a crash or at least a heavy landing which is likely to cripple the aircraft or the pilot' (Granville, 1970): RAF: since (?) *c.*, 1950, P.B.: cf the old flying axiom, 'Every landing is a controlled crash'.

if you can't be good, be careful. See **be good,...**

if you can't beat (or, US and Aus., **lick**) **'em** (or **them**), **join 'em** (or **them**)! 'Since the early 1940s in Britain' (Shaw) – or was it not rather the mid 1950s? It seems to have orig. in the US: in the poem 'Laments for a dying language', forming part of *Everyone but Thee and Me*, 1962, the lamented Ogden Nash writes:

We're in an if-you-cannot-lick-'em-join-'em age,
A slovenliness-provides-its-own-excuse age,

It is also recorded by Safire. It could, I suppose, have arisen in politics and been applied to areas where one party is crushingly predominant. [E.P. guessed well: the first citation in *Concise Oxford Dict. of Proverbs* is Quentin Reynolds, *Wounded Don't Cry*, 1941, 'There is an old political adage which says "If you can't lick 'em, jine 'em".']

An excellent English example occurs in Nicholas Freeling's *Over the High Side*, 1971:

He buzzed round to Belgrave Square, but none of the lovely ladies were in: pity, that – he wondered whether they knew all about Stasie's little ways. If you can't beat them, join them. If you can't join them, there are even simpler verbs. He wasn't altogether happy about all these Anglo-Saxon monosyllables.

Cf Derek Robinson, *Rotten with Honour*, 1973:

'It wouldn't do any good.'
'Then what would?'
'Avoiding the whole smaller issue.' He turned smartly down a side street. 'If you can't beat 'em, don't join 'em.'

if you can't fight, wear a big 'at. Current among Cockneys during the 1930s – and presumably earlier – to judge by Jim Wolveridge's little book, *He Don't Know 'A' from a Bull's Foot*, 1978: 'If [a Cockney] had a new hat he was likely to be greeted with "'At done it" or "If you can't fight, were a big hat", and the very few overdressed would be accused of "looking like a pox doctor's clerk"'. The taunt lingered in the Army until at least the early 1970s, directed at a soldier in best uniform, where this includes 'a big 'at' (P.B.).

if you can't get a girl, get a (named school) **boy.** Aus. schoolboys': since *c.* 1930. The implication being that, at the rival school particularized, many of the boys are homosexual.

P.B.: cf the mid C20 Public Schools' and Services' chant:
If wine and women lose their joys.
Try bottled beer and little boys.
If for these you have no use.
Then – lemonade and self-abuse!

if you can't stand the heat, get (loosely, **keep**) **out of the kitchen.** If you can't stand the pace or the strain, don't get involved! US, since *c.* 1950; Brit. since *c.* 1970. Political in orig. Indeed it was Harry S. Truman (born 1884) who orig. the saying; he used it frequently in public speech and in conversation – and in print, e.g. in his *Mr Citizen*, 1960. (Bartlett.)
An indication of Brit. usage occurs in Julian Symons, *A Three Pipe Problem*, 1975:

Val spoke without looking up from her paper. 'If you don't like the heat you should get out of the kitchen.'
'I don't know what you mean.'...
'I think you do.... If you don't like the noise, why come and live here [in Baker Street, London].'

if you can't take a joke, you shouldn't have joined. 'Addressed to anyone temporarily dissatisfied with Service life; e.g., after having his weekend leave cancelled' (P.B., 1974): perhaps since *c.* 1930; certainly since *c.* 1950. Also used to a complaining fellow-workman.
The WW1 soldiers' version of this occurs in Olive Dent, *A V.A.D. in France*, 1917: '"Pinching" is always quite an accepted state of affairs.... All the consolation the late owner of any article may receive is the overworked tag, "You're unlucky, mate. You shouldn't have joined,"' (With thanks to Mrs Barbara Huston.)

if you don't like it here.... See **why don't you go back....**

if you don't like it, you can lump it (or... **you may do the other thing**) and one or two other variants, but these are or have been insufficiently general for them to rank as c.pp. 'If you don't like it, you'll just have to put up with it.' The two recorded forms date from at least as early as *c.* 1860; Hotten, 1864, records the derivative... *you may do the other thing*, which seems to have fallen into disuse by 1914 at latest. Dickens, 1864, 'If you don't like it, it's open to you to lump it.' The *lump it* version was adopted from the US, where it had been current for at least a generation.
There is – inevitably – an earlier version: it is *if you don't like it, you can stick it up your arse* (or, US, *ass*), which arose prob. *c.* 1890, or poss. even *c.* 1880. John T. Fair, who is exceptionally well qualified to speak about the vernacular, for reasons too numerous to mention, tells me, 1976, of the US usage, 'It became *you know what you can do with it* and, finally, a whole group like *stick – stuff – jamb – cram – shove – up it, up yours*, etc. Sometimes this is only a gesture ... pointing one's index finger up in the air. The only place I can remember seeing it [the orig. US form] in print is in *The Egg and I* by Betty MacDonald, 1945'.
Of the shortened variants he has mentioned, all are familiar in UK except *jamb it* (unknown) and *cram it* (rare). [P.B.: E.P. has failed to include the very common Brit., and Irish, *work it*, as in 'If he doesn't like it, you can tell him, from me, to work it – right up!']
Perhaps *you can put it where it will* (or *it'll*) *do the most good* is a jocularly deliberate euph. for *you can stick it up your arse* or *ass*; it is both US (Berrey records it) and Brit. (I first heard it during WW2). Cf **put it where the monkey put the nuts**, which in part overlaps this entry.

if yo don't want the goods, don't muck 'em about! orig. among Cockney stall-holders, apparently in latter half of C19, and came to be transferred to other activities; extant. (With thanks to Cyril Whelan, 1975.) 'Better *muck 'em abaht*: it's generally said – or chanted – in a Cockney accent. Note the var. *whelks* for *goods*. There is a song with the refrain consisting of the words forming the c.p. and having the addition "for if *you* don't want 'em, uvver people may"' (P.B., 1976). A US var.: *if you don't want any sugar, don't finger the bowl*: since late 1940s at least. (A.B., 1978.) Cf **if you vant to buy a vatch...**

if you feel froggish (or **froggy**) **leap!** (or **take a leap!**) This is an urban Negro challenge to fight: 'If you think you can beat me, come ahead' (CM).

if you had as much brains as guts, usu. followed by **what a clever fellow you would be!** was, *c.* 1760–1820, addressed to a man both fat and stupid. Grose, 1788.

if you have... See **if you've....**

if you have to ask, you'll never know the answer. 'If you're *that* ignorant, explanations would be pointless. Some American use from 1960s' (R.C., 1978).

if you haven't been to Manchester, you haven't lived! See **if you've never....**

if you haven't tried it, don't knock it. 'Answer to anyone adversely critical of something of which he knows nothing' (Skehan, 1977): since *c.* 1943. Cf the 1973 slogan for Guinness, 'I've never tried it because I don't like it' (P.B.).

if you know(s) of a better 'ole, go to it! Often prec. by *well*, and with *go to it* omitted. Often, too, in trivial circumstances. I'd guess that, in the shorter form, it dates from *c.* 1920, becoming ob. *c.* 1946, yet, not even by 1980, entirely †. The source was a cartoon, 1915, by Capt. Bruce Bairnsfather (1887–1959), who created the immensely popular 'Old Bill' cartoons, reprinted in Vol. I (*The Better 'Ole*) of *Fragments from France*, 1915 †. The more famous of these cartoons very soon became as famous among civilians as in the Army. P.B.: there was, as late as 1970 (? is still) a 'pub' near Fan Ling, in the New Territories of Hong Kong, called 'The Better 'Ole'.

if you know what I mean is a c.p. only when it is used ironically, as in Noël Coward, *South Sea Bubble*, performed and pub'd in 1956, at I, i:

CHRISTOPHER: And sometimes, some of the things he says, sort of shakes 'em up a bit. If you know what I mean.
BOFFIN: I do, I do, indeed, I do.

It seems to have arisen early in C20.
Edward Albee, *Quotations from Chairman Mao Tse-Tung*, performed in 1968: when, in her third speech, the Long-Winded Lady uses it, *she* is manifestly using a cliché, but the dramatist is, I think, suggesting to the audience that *he* is using it as a c.p.: 'I try to imagine what it would have been like – *sounded* like – had I not been... well, so involved, if you know what I mean.'
P.B.: in its cliché-role, as verbal padding in the speech of the unsure and the inarticulate, it reached epidemic proportions in the later 1970s and early 80s, and was compressed in extreme cases to a mere *nota mean*? Cf **well, this is it**, and contrast **see what I mean?**

if you like it, you may! is a c.p. of late C16–mid 17. In James Shirley's *The Witty Fair One*, performed in 1628 and pub'd in 1632, we hear, in II, ii, Worthy saying of a witty poem by the ineffable Sir Nicholas Treedle: 'Ay, marry, sir' – to which Treedle replies, 'Now, if you lik't you may.' Edmund Gosse, in the Mermaid edn, remarks, 'This is from the prologue to Ben Jonson's *Cynthia's Revels*, and was popular as a playful defiance.' The full title of the Jonson piece was *Cynthia's Revels; The Fountain of Self-Love. Or Cynthia's Revels. A Comedy*, 1601.

if you looked at him sideways, you wouldn't see him refers to a very thin man: C20; but little used after WW2.

if you say so. If you *say* so, it must *be* so: since *c.* 1950, as an established c.p.; often heard well before that date. 'In the US, connotes rather "I don't choose to argue the point" – i.e., "I will accept your say-so, for practical purposes"' (R.C., 1978).

if you see anything that God didn't make, throw your hat at it! 'This c.p., current since *c.* 1930, deprecates undue modesty' (L.A., 1967).

if you vant to buy a vatch, buy a vatch: (but) if you don't vant to buy a vatch, keep your snotty nose off my clean window! A semi-joc. Jew-baiting c.p., sometimes shouted by (Mostly London) boys outside a jeweller's shop: C20. R.C. adds, 1978, 'Some American use, 1920s, but concluding "Get away from the vinder – you take the sparkles off the vinders"'. Cf **if you're going to buy.... and if you don't want the whelks....**

if you want anything, just whistle. Perhaps not a full-blown c.p., except to Humphrey Bogart fans. *VIBS* gives the full quot'n from the film *To Have and Have Not*, where Lauren Bacall, as Slim, says to 'Bogey' as Steve: 'You know you don't have to act with me, Steve. You don't have to say anything, and you don't have to do anything – not a thing. Or may be just whistle. You know how to whistle, don't you, Steve? You just put your lips together and blow.' Wedge-wood, 1977, adds that the film was based loosely on Hemingway's novel, and that the phrase 'entered modern "folklore" because middle-aged Bogart and the intelligent new young actress fell in love during the making of the film; he gave her a small gold whistle as a memento. They remained happily married until Bogart's death'.

if you want to get ahead, get a hat! seems to have arisen in the 1930s; it has been remembered either as an Underground advertisement for a hatter or as a slogan used by the hat manufacturers when hat-wearing began to decline: but apparently it went out of fashion during WW2. P.B.: but I remember it from the early 1950s, and Nigel Rees, in *Slogans*, 1982, dates it, or at least a quot'n of it, as late as 1965; he attributes it to the Hat Council. Clearly, as E.P. noted, it owed much of its popularity to the neat pun.

if you will pardon my French. See **pardon my French!**

if your aunt had balls, she'd be your uncle! See **if my aunt....**

if your head was loose, you'd lose that too. Addressed to a very forgetful person, esp. a child: late C19–20. In US, '*head* is often replaced by *ass*, *butt*, *tail*, *nose*, *tits* – maybe, in some areas, by other parts of the anatomy' (A.B., 1978). Cf **you'd forget your head...** and **lose his arse...**

if you're close enough; there's room enough. 'If you want to fight, there's plenty of room right here': US: 1920s–30s. In, e.g. Dashiell Hammett's *The Whosis Kid*; 'now dead'. (R.C., 1978.)

if you're going to buy, buy; if not, would you kindly take the baby's bottom off the counter! A Can. c.p., addressed by butchers to customers: since *c.* 1920. (Leechman.) Cf **if you vant to buy a vatch....**

if you're so smart, why aren't you rich? 'Originally (? 1920s) the philistine's "put-down" [snub or deflation] of the intellectual or of any supposed "smart alec"; but for at least twenty years [i.e., since the latish 1950s] the intellectual's ironic "put-down" of the philistine. I suspect it remains current, in the original sense, among certain groups. American' (R.C., 1978).

if you've got the inclination or **... the money.** See **any day you 'ave the money...**

if you've never (or **if you haven't**) **been to Manchester, you've never** (or **you haven't**) **lived!** 'As true today as it was when uttered regularly by Tommy Trafford (Graham Stark) in *Ray's A Laugh* [BBC radio-comedy series, later 1940s]', notes Nigel Rees, of the *haven't* version, in *VIBS*. Jack Slater reminded E.P., 1978, of the *never* form; this is the more common, and is often adapted to other contexts, e.g. *if you've never eaten* or *drunk* or *slept with* or *seen*, etc., *...., you've never lived!* Occ., allusively, simply *you've never lived!* E.P. commented that it was perhaps evoked by 'What Manchester thinks today, the rest of England thinks tomorrow' (or some such words) – once a favourite quot'n, esp. among Mancunians.

ignorance. See: **brute force.**

ignorance is bliss is the c.p. form of what is perhaps now the best known quot'n from the works of Thomas Gray (1716–71), from his *Ode on a Distant Prospect of Eton College*, x: '... where ignorance is bliss, 'Tis folly to be wise'. Given great impetus as the title of a BBC radio comedy series, *c.* 1950, an uproarious parody of all 'sensible' panel discussions. The phrase is now, later C20, used disparaging-ly, derisively, of foolish, feckless, irresponsible deeds or

thoughts of all sorts – and of their perpetrators. (P.B.)

Ike. See: I like Ike.

Ikey. See: do it again.

illegal, immoral, or fattening. See **anything you like...**

illegitimis non carborundum! Lit., 'Let there not be a *carborun-dum*ing by the illegitimate!' – Don't let the bastards grind – hence, wear – finally, get – you down or break your spirit!: carborundum (silicon carbide), being extremely hard, is used in grinding and polishing: owing to its apparently having the form (*-undum*) of a L gerund, the word has prompted a piece of delightful mock-L. From being an army Intelligence c.p. of 1939–45, it became, as early as 1940, a more general army c.p., chiefly among officers. I have often wondered which Classical scholar, irritated and exacerbated almost to des-peration, coined this trenchancy; and I like to think it was my friend Stanley Casson, who, born in 1889, became Reader in Classical Archaeology at Oxford and who, after directing the army Intelligence School early in WW2, went to Greece to lead the resistance there and was killed mid-April 1944, a learned, witty, gallant scholar and man of action.

The phrase had by the late 1940s gained a fairly wide currency among the literate. In 1965, B.P. assured me that, in Aus., its use was by no means confined to those who had a little L.

In Martin Woodhouse's novel, *Rock Baby*, 1968, it occurs allusively thus: '*Nil carborundum* all right, I thought. Don't let the bastards grind you down, like it says in the book, but how was I to set about it?' And I am reminded by John Simon, in *Esquire*, Nov. 1977, of *Nil Carborundum*, the play by Henry Livings that the Royal Shakespeare Company put on in 1962.

'The form I'm familiar with is *ab illegitimis non carborun-dum est*, standard for the US' (J.W.C., 1977): but it's an ethic dative which is wanted, for the sense is not 'Don't be ground down *by* the bastards' but '... to the bastards profit or advantage'.

imagination. See: **use your i.**

immoral. See: **anything you like.**

impossible. See: **difficult we do at once; this should; why be difficult.**

imprisoned. See: **fart's.**

improved. See: **Uncle Joe.**

in (whichever is, currently, the world's most unpopular coun-try) **people are shot for less** is 'a c.p. (often jocular) implying that the hearer is living in such a tolerant country' (B.P.): Aus.: since the late 1940s. As in 'You're reading my book. In – –, people are shot' – or 'being shot' – 'for less.' P.B.: common also in UK, though ob. by *c.* 1980.

[**in a pig's eye,** at first merely euph. for **in a pig's arse** or **arse-hole,** was, *c.* 1945, adopted in Brit. from Can., which took it from the US (*in a pig's ass*); the vulgar form came from a bawdy song current since long before 1940. This violent negative – as in 'In a pig's eye you will!' – is only very doubtfully a true c.p.]

in a while, crocodile. See **see you later, alligator!**

in and out like a fart in a colander. See **like a fart in a colander.**

in and out like a fiddler's bitch. Constantly going in and out; applied either to a person or to some mechanical device: Services': mid C20. Cf the **up and down...** series. It presum-ably refers to the speed and dispatch of her copulations, but carries echoes of the low coll. *drunk as a fiddler's bitch* and *up and down like a fiddler's elbow*. (P.B.)

in Annie's room. See **Annie's room...**

in bed. See: **into bed.**

in charge. See: **Carl the caretaker.**

in everybody's mess but nobody's watch. Directed at a seaman both a cadger and chary of work: RN: *c.* 1880–1914. (Bowen.) Also in the US Navy: C20. Berrey comments: 'said of a busybody'.

in her (or **his**) **skin** is a pert – orig. a smart – evasive c.p. reply to 'Where is So-and-So?': C16–20. In George Gascoyne, *Supposes*, performed in 1966, at I, iv, begins:

DULIPPO: Ho, Jack Pack, where is Erostrato?
CRAPENO: Erostrato? Marry, he is in his skin.

In S, Dialogue I, 1738, we find:

COL[ONEL]: Pray, Miss, where is your old Acquaintance Mrs *Wayward?*
MISS: Why, where should she be? If you must know, she's in her Skin.

In C19–20, it has largely been one of the domestic c.pp.

in inverted commas (or **in quotes**) simply means either 'emphatically' or 'I'm quoting–for emphasis',. 'I didn't hear it until *c.* 1972. Often accompanied by the speaker's sketching quotation marks in the air with the forefinger of one or both hands.' (P.B., 1975). Ob. by early 1980s.

in like Flynn (– **he's**) has two independent usages, the US and the Aus., although with much the same meaning. Of the US, J.W.C. has said, 1977, 'He's an easy winner'; more widely, it means 'He's sitting pretty'; C20. Perhaps, as W&F, 1960, suggests, a rhyming slang extension of *in*, 'inside, safe', by way of *well in*, R.C., 1978, is more specific: 'Originally (1940s) New York City, but some general currency later, probably helped by the rhyme. The reference was to the late Ed Flynn, whose Democratic Party machine exercised absolute political control over the Bronx, N.Y.C.–hence, the candidates he backed were almost automatically "in"; and he himself permanently so'.

The Aus. c.p. emerged slightly later. It has been defined by Wilkes, 1978, as 'seizing an opportunity offered, especially sexual' in the *Dict. Aus. Coll.*, which goes on to adduce T.A.G. Hungerford, *Shake the Gold Bough*, 1963, for the gen. nuance, and two examples for the sexual: David Williamson, *The Removalists*, 1972, and Alexander Buzo, *Rooted*, 1973, Buzo glosses it thus: '*Flynn, in like* (also *in like Errol*) refers to the athletic and sexual prowess of the late Australian-born actor [Errol Flynn]'. Odd that these two playwrights should be the leaders of the vigorous, frank, disturbing new Australian theatre. (Note of 1 May 1978.)

in more strife... See **more strife than...**

in my way. See: are you in.

in spades! See **you can say that in spades!**

in the big league or **in the big time.** E.g., *he's*..., describes someone who is either rather grand, or full of self-importance. Very gen. since *c.* 1920. (Jack Slater, 1978.)

in the catbird seat derives from this bird's crafty habit of choosing 'a lofty perch to sing from and therefore has come to mean 'a position of great prominence or advantage' (*Webster's Third International*, 1961). Moreover, although the phrase's heyday may have been *c.* 1940–55, it has flourished ever since. It occurs in, e.g. Jame's Thurber's contribution, 1942, to *Short Stories from the New Yorker*, 1949. (Paul Janssen, 1978.)

W.J.B. wrote, 1969: 'If some player, let us say a pitcher, was in complete command of the game and was moving along to a sure victory, [Walter] 'Red' [Barber] would say to him 'He's in the catbird seat!'... In 1968 Doubleday in New York published a book entitled *Rhubarb in the Catbird Seat*, by Red Barber and Robert Creamer. I have glanced through this, did find a few of the [baseball] phrases, but no explanation as to their origins, etc.' Lit., a *catbird* is the black-eyed thrush, a US song-bird.

in the grip of the grape. This Aus. c.p., meaning 'tipsy', dating since *c.* 1950, and noted by Jim Ramsay in 1977, aptly–although unintentionally–recalls the subtle Japanese proverb, 'A man takes a drink, the drink takes a drink, the drink takes the man'.

in the same ball park is, in the US, applied to a financial offer not really, or to a guess, not really close: since *c.* 1960. 'Originates in baseball, with reference to a hit that is far from getting the ball to the desired place, but still not actually over the stands' (J.W.C., 1977). 'Very approximately correct. That is, it may not be a fair hit (in baseball), but it's at least in the ball park. American: since (?) late 1940s' (R.C., 1978). P.B.: but, I think, as often in the form *not in the same...*;

and presumably the orig. of the term 'ball park figure(s)' for 'a rough estimate' of the money, quantities of materials, etc., needed for a project. It was, as Mr John Davies told me, 'used to death' while he was working on a large water development scheme in NZ, late 1970s.

in the words of the Chinese poet expresses disgust on hearing bad news or on receiving unpleasant instructions: Can.: since *c.* 1910. If a friend hears one say this, he is expected to ask, 'What Chinese poet?' and thus to afford the opportunity of replying, 'Ah Shit, the Chinese poet'; *c.* 1919, also current in England, with the var. name, 'Hoo (or Who) Flung Dung'. Prompted by **Confucius he say.**

P.B.: *Ah Shit* could just be a rendering of a Cantonese name, but *Hoo Flung Dung* has always been impossible: no native speaker of Chinese could manage the combined consonants *fl*-. His legendary compatriot *One Hung Low* is, however, quite possible.

in your (pron. *ya* or *yer*) **boot!** An Aus. c.p. expression of either complete or disgusted disagreement: since the late 1940s. Jim Ramsay, *Cop It Sweet!*, 1977. Cf:

[**in your dipper!** is a defiant NZ expression that, used *c.* 1920–40, lies midway between a c.p. and a piece of slangy violence.]

in your eyes, gorgeous! See **where's the fire?**

in your hat! Nothing doing! I shall certainly do no such thing: a US c.p. of *c.* 1920–40. Clarence B. Kelland, *Speak Easily, c.* 1935, says: 'I found it impossible to make my way, though I requested sundry persons to let me pass. One gentleman thus addressed replied, cryptically, with the following sentence: "In your hat!"' Later in the same novel: 'To my letter the editor replied with a terse note, which read: "In your hat! You're getting off easy..."'.

Prof. Paul Korshin, in private conversation with me, 1972, dated the phrase as 'since *c.* 1890; by 1970, obsolescent'; he defined it as 'indicating a derisive refusal or rebuttal or general negative' and explained the semantics thus: 'You can put that in your hat and *wear* it!'

But R.C., 1978, says that it 'is rather, an elision of "Go shit in your hat!"', and A.B. adds, 'There are variations: *in your hat, Harry* was popular during the Harry S. Truman administration, 1945–52... *You can put that in your hat and keep it!* = "Shut up about that!" *Keep that in your lid and like it!*: 1920s.'

inboard. See I'm inboard; sod you.

inch. See: extra two inches; more wrinkles; two inches.

incident. See: here's incident.

inclination. See: I've got the time; yes, but not.

include me out! Leave me out–of the discussion or plan: US: since the late 1940s; by 1950, also Brit. One of the few genuine Goldwynisms; 'Most of the zany cracks attributed to Sam Goldwyn are the work of Hollywood gagmen', as A.B. Petch has remarked.

India. See: from Greenland's; rarest.

Indian(s). See: all chiefs; he's a regular; honest Injun; squeezes.

Indians about! Beware!–presumably of detectives or of rivals: US professional gamblers': *c.* 1830–1900. (Matsell.) Semantically cf **natives were hostile...**

indies. See: watch your i.

infinity. See: contemplating.

infirmary. See: answer is in the i.

influence in the right quarter, usu. prec. by **he has.** An ironic c.p., applied by NZ soldiers during WW1, to a comrade landed with a menial or distasteful job, e.g. cleaning out the latrines.

information. See: for your.

Injun. See: honest Injun.

innocent. See: she is so.

inoperative. See: statement.

ins-and-outs. See: you want to know.

inside. See: come inside; couldn't hit; don't laugh; get inside.

instructions. See: if all else.

insulated. See: am I i.; I resemble.

interest. See: no ambition; men are interested.

interesting. See: very interesting.

interferences. See: mind your own i.

International FYB Week. See what *is* this? International...

interrupt. See: I hope I.

into bed or out of barracks is 'the soldier's prescription for time off' (Skehan, 1977): current throughout C20, it arose in the Regular Army and may go back to *c.* 1860. This forms a motto-c.p. P.B.: by *c.* 1970 reduced to *in bed*...

into the woods? See **to the woods!**

introduce. See: never introduce.

intrude. See: I hope I.

inverted commas. See: in inverted.

Irene. See: good night, Irene.

Irish. See: no Irish; too bloody.

Irish wedding. See: you have been to.

iron lung. See: wouldn't work.

iron's down – the. Granville comments: 'Becoming obsolete, this catch-phrase means a bad or unresponsive audience. When the *iron* safety curtain is lowered the audience cannot be heard on the stage.'

irrigated. See: am I insulated.

Irving. See: when I was with.

is everybody happy? As a c.p., it means 'Is everybody satisfied? Comfortable?' Since the late 1940s and throughout the 1950s. R.S. associates it with such morale-boosting radio programmes (in WW2) as 'Workers' Play-time' (1975).

On the other hand, Cyril Whelan, 1975, thinks that, 'since long before WW2, it has been the traditional cry of the red-nosed comedian using an excuse to get some audience participation working, [in readiness] for the raucous chorus guaranteed to come rolling back at him from the stalls...The general area of my guess would be pantomime' – or perhaps rather pantomime and music-hall reacting upon each other. It seems that Mr Whelan is right about the date: in 1905 came a popular American song, words by Williams, music by Ernest Hoyan, *They All Sang*, 1934. With thanks to W.J.B.) The English vogue probably derived from the American.

Also, not altogether independently, it is the boisterously hearty query of the hosts at holiday camps, both over the microphone and personally to groups: and this usage has helped to promote the c.p.

(P.B., 1975.) Reviewing the first ed. of this book, Russell Davies, in the *New Statesman*, 9 Sep. 1977, wrote, 'Ted Lewis, the "top-hatted tragedian of jazz", surely deserves some credit for the survival of "is everybody happy?"' He certainly does!

To amplify the American ref.: In his *Vaudeville*, 1953, Joe Laurie, Jr, mentioned the comedian 'Harry Brown, the first to yell to the audience, "Is everybody happy? (That was in 1906.)' Elsewhere in the same book he wrote, 'And anybody who had a battered hat at home tried to imitate Ted Lewis saying "Is everybody happy?"' Upon which W.J.B. remarked, 1977, 'The phrase was the trademark of night-club entertainer Ted Lewis, who was, or appeared to be, drunk at every performance. He must have borrowed it from Harry Brown and imitators. He used the phrase on every appearance'. Moreover, Lewis was, with Maurice Rubens and Jack Caterman, the composer of the popular song *Is Everybody Happy Now*?...a hit of 1927; then, in 1929, he starred in an early sound film, *Is Everybody Happy?* (Eric Townley, 1978.)

is he with you? – No! I thought he was with you. An 'exchange between any two members of a party, *à propos* – and across the face of – a third friend, who has just made an exhibition of himself in some way; e.g., by making a foolish (or too clever) remark, breaking wind, etc.' (P.B., 1974): since 1950. Cf **excuse my pig...; you can't take him anywhere**, and **who's your friend?**

is it a mountain, or is it a mountain? This is a US 'tag' or,

rather, c.p., applied to 'any object of exceptional wonder' (Prof. A.C. Partridge, 1976): since *c.* 1950.

is it catching? A c.p. both Brit. and US, the question is facetiously asked when someone uses an unknown or rare or unusual or very long word somewhat out of place: in UK and the Commonwealth at least as early as *c.* 1910; I first heard it, in Australia, in 1913. (A reminder from Mrs John W. Clark, 1977.)

is it cold up there? is jocularly addressed to a very tall person: late C19–20; not much heard since *c.* 1960. Frank Shaw's comment, made 1969, was: 'To tall man by purveyor of stale wit.' J.W.C. adds, 1977, 'Universal American variant, "How's the weather up there?" Status the same as Shaw's for Britain'.

is it midnight already? 'Pretended wide-eyed innocence: from the story of the man found fornicating with a pumpkin in the park – an example of "quick thinking"' (Ashley, 1979): US: later C20.

is it my turn to utter? is 'an exaggeratedly comical catchphrase meaning "Do I speak next?" ...usually said of one who has not been paying attention at rehearsals and is caught "off"' (Granville): *c.* 1920–60.

is it possible (! rather than **?**); often shortened to **possible!** A US c.p., expressing amazement or admonition or consternation: C19–20. It occurs more than once in John Neal's *Errata; or, The Works of Will Adams*, 1823; his *Brother Jonathan*, 1825, has, at Act II, Scene 114;

'Nathan Hale! – is that you?'

'Is it possible?' said Hale, coming forward with great eagerness.

And at Act II, Scene 352, he has:

'To be sure! – we were at school together.'

'Possible! – why have I never heard of it?'

It also occurs in T.C. Haliburton, *The Clockmaker*, all three series, 1837, 1838, 1840.

is it true, what they say about Chinese girls (or women)? See **yes, and what they say...**

is (or was) my face red! and **was his face red!** are exclamations of acute embarrassment. US since *c.* 1930 (recorded by, e.g., Berrey, 1942); adopted in Brit. in the early 1950s.

is my hat on straight? How do I look? Noble, 1975, told me:

In *Fifty Great Years*, a booklet published by Kemsley Newspapers to mark the Golden Jubilee, 1947, of the *Evening Chronicle*, Manchester, I came across the following paragraph in reference to the female fashions of the early years of the century (1907 to 1914, it seems):

Hats were, at first, enormous. Their wearers had to sidle like crabs to get on trams. 'Is my hat on straight?' became a catch phrase.

I was born in 1908, but my recollection is of the First World War period when women's hats were considerably reduced in size, but the phrase remained in currency for 'How do I look?'

is my name mud: See **and his name is mud.**

is that a catch or a have? is a low and raffish admission that the speaker has been fooled: *c.* 1880–1910. Should the fooler attempt a definition, the victim turns the tables by exclaiming **then you catch (or have) your nose up my arse!**

is that a promise? and **that's a promise!** and – the most gen. – **is that a threat or a promise?** The traditionally licentious soldiery's stock retort to *fuck you!*: WW1 (and doubtless during the Boer War); and later. The currency has very prob. been much wider than merely in the army-in, e.g., the navy.

Of the three, the third has, throughout the C20, also been applied other than sexually: as Granville noted 1969 it is 'a question asked when a doubtful proposition has been made'. And in *A Three Pipe Problem*, 1975, Julian Symons exemplifies its usage, neatly, thus:

'Goodbye. I advise you to keep out of my way.'

...She smelt of cigarette smoke and gin. 'Next time, Mr Holmes? Is that a threat or a promise?'

Cf **promises, promises!**

is that all? An ironic comment, made in a sarcastic tone, when one has been asked an exorbitant price or to perform a long list of requests or duties: C20. (Petch, 1969.) P.B.: also used when, e.g., someone reads out an advertised price that is utterly beyond the reach of all but the most wealthy: 'Oh, is that all? Let's have two!

is that good? A question intended to disconcert one's interlocutor by its unexpectedness and by its at least partial air of a *non sequitur*: mostly among men of the law and among those who well could have been lawyers or barristers. I first heard it in the late 1920s, but suspect that it may already have been current for a generation. As in, e.g.:
'I won a hundred pounds on the Derby!'
'Is that good?'

is that so? See **oh, is that so?** It might be as appropriate here as anywhere else in the dictionary to quote Professor Emeritus F.E.L. Priestley's comment, 1975, 'What an enormous number of c.pp. there are, expressing agreement or disagreement, and nothing else!'

is that the way to London? See **that's the way to London?**

is the Pope Catholic? See AMERICAN RESPONSES.

is there a doctor in the house? is sometimes used joc. and non-lit. and therefore as a c.p. (as Mr Petch reminds me, 1974): since the late 1950s. P.B.: it may owe something, as E.P. suggested in the first ed., to the film title, following Richard Gordon's very popular novel, *Doctor in the House*, but the full phrase has long been a favourite inspiration for cartoonists.

is there a law against it? (Brit.) and **is there some kind of law?** (US): the former, since *c*. 1950, and the latter, rather later. Two facets of the same query. R.C., 1978, glossed the latter thus: 'That requires me to do thus and so. Implying "Your request is unreasonable, and I will assent only under compulsion" or simply "Why should I?" American from 1960s'. Ashley, 1984, notes the synon. *where is it written?*, which he glosses, 'who says it is compulsory? [Mainly] Jewish'.

is there any other kind? is the c.p. comment upon, or reply to, 'It's a dodgy business': since *c*. 1950.

is there room for a little (or **small**) **one?** – often shortened to **any room...?** or even to **room...?** – is addressed collectively – and either humbly or hopefully – to the occupants of a crowded vehicle [P.B.: or indeed in any situation where space, or sitting room, is already badly crowded]: C20. Often ironic, as when the suppliant is anything but small.

The phrase evokes from A.B., 1978, the comment: 'There is a variation of this. A tiny man is seen (in a cartoon) in an elevator with a rather tall, lovely lady. The caption reads, with the little man looking up to the lady and saying, "Do you have time for a small one?" This sexual reference derived from the boozers' question, "Would you have time for a small drink with me?" – "Do you have time for a small one?" or "Would you have just the one?" – glass of beer or whatever. Sometimes "Do you have time for a short one?" 1950s and onwards'.

is this a proposition or a proposal? Orig. – since the 1920s, or earlier – US (J.W.C., 1977); by *c*.1940, Can.; Brit. and Aus. since *c*.1943. Cf 'to *proposition* a girl' – to suggest sexual intimacy to her.

is this trip necessary? See **is your journey...**

is you *is* or is you *ain't*? Well, *are* you or *aren't* you, e.g. sure?: US: orig. negroes': since the middle 1940s; by *c*. 1970, ob. From the immensely popular song and gramophone record, *Is You Is or Is You Ain't My Baby* [my girl]?, written by Billy Austin and Louis Jordan, in very close collaboration in words and music, and pub'd in 1944. (With thanks to the Music Room of the British Library.) Eric Townley notes, 1978, that the record was released on 4 Oct. 1943.

Hence such allusive variants as *am I is or am I ain't?* and *are we is or are we ain't?* – as in Clarence B. Kelland, *No Escape*, 1951:
'What for do you want to know?' Pazzy asked.

'Curiosity.'
'Look,' said Pazzy, 'are we is or are we ain't pals?'
'We are,' Jonathan told him.

is your father a glazier? See **glazier....**

is your journey really necessary? was a WW2 slogan (1940–5); since as early as 1944 it has been used as a joc. c.p., by 1960 slightly, and by 1970, very, ob. An excellent example occurs in Wolf Rilla, *The Dispensable Man*, 1973:
'I have no intention of returning [to England], either myself or the money.'
Smith nodded, a little sadly it seemed. 'No, I suppose not.'
'In that case, was your journey really necessary?'
Smith's melancholy eyes suddenly lit up. 'You remember the war, then, do you? Is Your Journey Really Necessary? Careless Talk Costs Lives?'

It has its US counterpart: *is this trip necessary?*, 'with similar provenance and life history' (R.C., 1978).

is your rhubarb up (, old woman)? or **how's your rhubarb, missis?** Do you feel inclined to make love?: low: *c*. 1830–1900. Without the female vocatives, it can also apply to a man. Perhaps, as Leechmas has suggested, from a catch line in a comic song, and he cites the Can. var., *say, old woman, is your rhubarb up?*, which he calls 'another old timer'. Benham dates it as having arisen *c*. 1835, without giving any evidence: but, as Sir Gurney Benham was a conscientious as well as an excellent scholar, I accept the date. The form he quotes is simply *is your rhubarb up?*

'In US (from before 1900) applied to the male, not to the female. [A certain man, born 1876] used to sing, when somewhat "elevated",... this ditty:
Oh, the old man said, he was gonna leave the farm,
And the old woman said she didn't care a darn,
For the cats wouldn't kitten now and the pups (sic) wouldn't pup,
And the old man couldn't get his rhubarb up.
[Here,] *rhubarb* was certainly understood as "penis"' (J.W.C., 1977). An apt and very close visual image. P.B.: and one that was certainly still current is English school playgrounds in the 1940s, when I heard references to 'getting your rhubarb up', applied to the male. There was also a ditty with the same metre and rhyme scheme, even poss. the same tune (the one known as 'The Turkey Trot', a square dance):
Oh, the cow kicked Nellie in the belly, in the barn,
And the old man said it wouldn't do her any harm...

is zat so? is a joc. US var. of *is thasso?*, a slovenly form of **is that so?** Cf the *howzat?*, How's that?, of cricket. It occurs in Berrey and in, e.g., Clarence Budington Kelland's *Speak Easily*. *c*. 1935:
'G'wan,' said Sam.
'Is zat so?' said Sim.
'Yes, zat's so,' said Sam.

ish ka bibble! (or as one word)! I should worry! In the US it had a tremendous vogue *c*. 1913 and, via Can., reached UK *c*. 1925 and lasted perhaps a decade. Prob. adopted from the Yiddish, with *ish* representing Ger. *Ich*, I and the rest of the phrase a distortion. Berrey, 1942, records it without date or comment; HLM had briefly noticed it in 1922; W & F after stating the sense to be 'I'm not worrying' or 'I don't care', adduce two examples and then sum up by saying, 'A popular *c*. 1925 rejoinder' – even though HLM has implied a vogue beginning some five years earlier. J.W.C. adds, 1977, that it was very common in US *c*. 1910–25, but now 'Virtually obsolete. I should guess that it dates since *c*. 1890'.

island. See: keep it on.

isn't he a panic? See **you panic me.**

isn't it time you paid for them? 'Years ago, when cheap boots and shoes, often very poorly made, were common, they usually squeaked for some time when they were worn. Rude little boys were not unknown to shout things like: "Why don't you pay for them, Mister?"' (Petch, 1969). Period: *c*. 1890–1939. I first heard it *c*. 1910, but never during WW2 or since. It had several slight variations. P.B.: but the idea, if not the actual phrase, lingered for another three decades or so, among my own generation (born early 1930s). In the Wanchai district of Hong Kong there was a shop near the water front during the 1960s with the sign 'Genuine No Squeak Shoes'.

isn't that just dandy? can – of course – be literal and approbatory, but mostly it's ironic; sometimes bitterly ironic: US: since *c.* 1910. (Recorded by Berrey.) Cf **isn't that just too ducky!**

isn't that just like a man! and **isn't that just like a woman!** are the interlocking female and male comments upon the crassness and unpredictability of the opposite sex. Also, though perhaps less frequently: *oh, well! you know what men* (or *women*) *are!* A further US modification, applied to women, is *oh, well! you know how women are!*

In 1920, Irvin S. Cobb pub'd a book titled *Oh, Well! You Know How Women Are!* And in the same volume appeared Mary Roberts Rinehart's article, 'Isn't That Just Like a Man!' Within the volume occurs this passage:

'Kin you beat 'um?' says the conductor. 'I ast you – kin you beat 'um?' The man to whom he has put the question is a married man...Speaking, therefore, from the heights of his superior understanding, he says in reply: 'Oh, well, you know how women are!' We know how they are. But nobody knows why they are as they are.

Harold Pinter's *The Collection*, a TV play produced in 1961, a stage play of 1962 and a publication of 1963 has, at p. 31 of the Methuen edn:

JAMES: Mmm. Only thing...he rather implied that you led him on. Typical masculine thing to say, of course.
STELLA: That's a lie.
JAMES: You know what men are.

How far the c.p. goes back, I should not care to hazard anything more than: prob. since *c.* 1850. It seems to have been US before it became also Brit.; yet it could easily, except for the *how* form, have been the other way around.

Paul Janssen, 1977, adds that there was, in the late 1950s, a Fats Domino song, entitled *Ain't That Just Like a Woman?*

isn't that just too ducky! is, by Berrey, 1942, recorded as a US ironic c.p.; and by W & F, 1960, as *isn't that just ducky!:* apparently since *c.* 1930 and *c.* 1945 respectively. It reached UK by 1950 at the latest. Cf **isn't that just dandy!**

isn't that something (? or ! or both) was adopted by UK from US *c.* 1945. An expression of emphatic admiration, it means 'You must, like me, admire that – it's unique!' (Frank Shaw) or '...find it remarkable' (W & F at *something*). A good US example occurs in the Albee quot'n at **I'll say!** R.C., 1978: 'In US, usually *ain't that something* [q.v.], now obsolescent'.

Istambul. See: better than dog.

it adds up and **doesn't add up.** 'It makes sense' and 'It makes nonsense' – It fails to make sense: although occ. heard earlier, it was only in the late 1950s that the phrase became a genuine and gen. c.p. (L.A.) Either elliptical for *it adds up* (or *doesn't add up*) *correctly* or an extension of the coll. *add*, to yield the right answer. P.B.: also, of course *that adds up*. All are also US as R.C. notes, 1978; but the *adds* version are perhaps more the Brit. form of the characteristically US *it*, or *that, figures*, adopted from American servicemen *c.* 1944. *That figures!* is sometimes used not so much for 'It makes sense', but as a resigned 'Yes, that's just about how I expected it *would* turn out' – *Sod's Law*, q.v., has struck again; J.W.C. confirms that it often carries this nuance in US usage also.

it ain't all honey. It isn't all pleasure, or fun: *c.* 1904–14. Cf 'It ain't all honey and it ain't all jam,/Wheelin' round the 'ouses at a three-wheeled pram' – words adorning a music-hall song of Vesta Victoria's, *c.* 1905.

it ain't funny, McGee. 'From the old radio show, "Fibber McGee and Molly". Still heard occasionally' (Leechman, 1977); US, whence also Can.: since (?) *c.* 1935.

it ain't gonna rain no mo' (, **no mo'**) [= *more*]. Rather a quot'n than a c.p., sometimes prompted either by a downpour or by

steady rain. It orig. in a US popular song, and was already being parodied by American schoolchildren *c.* 1925; as a c.p., always rare in the US, and by 1978, † (R.C.). It 'was claimed to have been a modern (1923) version of a Southern [US Negro] melody, words and music by Wendell W. Hall, and because it was relentlessly plugged by the gramophone companies in time for the community-singing boom it was incorporated into the canon' (Ronald Pearsall, *Popular Music of the 20's*, 1976).

it ain't hay! See the more usu. **and that ain't hay!**

it ain't necessarily so. 'Either a famous quotation from the famous song [in Ira Gershwin's opera,] *Porgy and Bess*, 1935, or a c.p. Meaning anything from "You may or may not believe this" to "I don't believe a word of it!"' (R.C., 1978). It became a c.p., on both sides of the Atlantic, in the latish 1930s.

[**it ain't the 'untin' 'urts the 'orses 'ooves, it's the 'ammer, 'ammer, 'ammer on the 'ard 'igh roads.** Leechman records this as a c.p., heard by him in East Anglia, *c.* 1900. But it is a quot'n from Surtees, who re-edited his *Handley Cross* in 1854 from an earlier edition of 1843 (Arthur C.L. Grear, 1978); in the form 'It ain't the 'unting as 'urts 'im, It's the 'ammer, 'ammer, 'ammer along the 'ard 'igh road!', it appears, attributed to a Veterinary Surgeon, in a *Punch* cartoon, 31 May 1856, p. 218 (P.B.).]

it all depends on what you mean! is a derisive or a smilingly joc., often temporizing, c.p.: since 1941, and, as Noble remarked, 1974, Older people still use it in conversation, as it's lingered in their minds'. Strictly, it is a very gen. derivative from the stock challenge, or modification, by 'Professor' C.E.M. Joad (1891–1953) on the BBC 'Brains Trust', 'It all depends what you mean by (whatever the statement was)'; the derivative became the predominant form used by the public, for the very simple reason that it is self-contained. 'The Brains Trust' covered the period 1 Jan. 1941–1949; Joad did not appear after 12 Apr. 1948. See esp., in *Listener*, 18 May 1978, the anonymous article titled 'The Brain, the Tongue, and the Heart of the Brains Trust', and notably the sentence, 'As for the resident members of the panel, Joad, [Commander A.B.] Campbell and [Prof. Julian] Huxley – they had become such national celebrities that their tricks of speech, like the catch phrases of ITMA, went into the national vocabulary: Joad's "It all depends what you mean by...", Compbell's "When I was in Patagonia...", even Huxley's "Surely..."! P.B.: the programme was a panel of experts, with a chairman, answering questions sent in by the general public, similar to the BBC's later 'Any Questions?'

it all rubs off when it's dry. Don't take harsh words or summary punishment too hard: naval: late (?mid) C19–20. Rear-Adm. P.W. Brock adds, 'I've read this in the memoirs of some Victorian admiral who said it was about the best advice he ever had, and I found it so.' The mud that sticks – but not for very long. P.B.: even earlier: it occurs in 'Bill Truck', *The Man-o'-War's Man* serialized in *Blackwood's Magazine*, 1821–6, about the Navy of 1811–5, where 'It will all rub off when it's dry' is put into the mouth of an Irish seaman. Cf **it'll all come out in the wash.**

it bangs Banagher. See **bangs Banagher.**

it beats a kick in the head. See **better than a dig in the eye.**

it beats the hell out of me and **it beats working.** See **beats...**

it bombed. See **it went like a bomb.**

it came from a hot place belongs to C18. In Dialogue I of S, 1738, we see:

LORD SP[ARKISH]: This Tea's very hot.
LADY ANSW[ERALL]: Why, it came from a hot Place, my Lord.

A particularity that became a generality; roughly; = 'And for a very obvious reason'.

it can't be did! A joc. perversion of 'It can't be done': late C19–20; ob. by 1940, virtually † by 1960. Also US, with the complementary *it can be did.* 'Still current over here' (A.B., 1978). Cf **can do!**

it can't happen here. This bitterly satirical c.p., dating from *c.* 1936, was promoted from the status of age-old occasional comment, complacently uttered by self-deluding optimists, into a ruefully aware irony; suddenly thus promoted by the success, the bite, of Sinclair Lewis's novel, *It Can't Happen Here*, which, appearing in 1935, both in US and UK, 'dramatized the dangers of the Nazi technique as it might be applied in the United States' (*Encyclopedia Britannica*). It is extant as a c.p. – and still heard as a solemnly pompous statement. Cf **famous last words.**

it come off in me 'and, ma'am (or mum) – less frequent, yet common enough, it was broke already, mum. Domestic servants' c.p., dating from mid C19, perhaps earlier. Shaw, 1969, says: 'If a housewife breaks something, she has, since the late 1940s, tended to declare, **I never liked it anyway**' [which see separately]. P.B.: variants, *it come* (or *came*) *to pieces in me 'ands*, still heard occ., Rarely 1980s.

it comes from a hot place. See **it came from a hot place.**

it couldn't happen to nicer chap and it couldn't have happened to a nicer guy. Generously congratulatory, whether in address or in ref.: the former, Brit., arose in the late 1940s; the latter, US, arose, I believe, during WW2. The fame of incorporation into a free syntax is exemplified in Mickey Spillane, *The Erection Set,*1972, thus: 'A financial whiz kid. He parlayed a small bundle into a fat fortune and it couldn't have happened to a nicer guy.'

In the US it is at least as often used ironically as congratulatorily of one who, in the speaker's view, is anything but a 'nice guy', the 'it' being a misfortune (J.W.C.,1977). R.C. confirms: 'Basic meaning is still "He deserved it"'.

it curdles one's milk. See **curdles...**

it didn't fizz on me. This affair, this action, etc., had no effect on me: Can. c.p., since *c.* 1945.(Leechman.) From soft drinks: 'It fell flat'.

it didn't go into his boots. There was an effect, inevitable yet not immediately obvious: mostly Cockney: C20. It did at least go *some*where. 'Probably "it" refers originally to "piss"' (Fain, 1977). For 'probably' read 'certainly'.

it didn't strike on my box. it left me indifferent; it didn't make a good impression. 'His opera *Porgy and Bess* has never struck on my box, as they say' (a contributor to the *Daily Telegraph*, 17 Oct. 1977). The c.p., with variants *doesn't strike* and hasn't struck, didn't become fully established until *c.* 1960, and is now (Nov. 1978) slightly ob. The ref. is of course to safety matches.

it does your eyesight good. See **it'll do your eyesight good.**

it doesn't add up. See **it adds up.**

it doesn't grow on trees. See **grow on trees.**

it doesn't stand up and it won't get off the ground are c.pp. applied to a plan, a scheme, an experiment, that has nothing to commend it: the former, since *c.* 1940, the latter, since 1942 – and orig. of prototype aircraft that don't achieve flight.

it dries me up. It angers or exasperates me beyond words – deprives me of speech; as in 'It *dries me up* when I think of the terms he offered for the part': theatrical: C20. (Granville.)

it fell off (the back of) a lorry. See **did it drop...**

it figures! See **it adds up.**

it fits him like a duck's ass is applied to clothing that is too tight: US: since *c.* 1920. (Fain, 1977.) i.e., it's water-tight: the same simile, *tight as a duck's arse* or *ass*, is applied also to meanness with money, or, less often, to drunkenness. (P.B.)

it fits where it touches; of trousers, they fit where they touch. This joc. c.p. is applied to loose, very ill-fitting clothes: latish C19–20. (Jack Lawson, *A Man's Life*, 1932.) Since *c.* 1960, to suggestively tight clothes, esp. trousers.

it had my name (or number) on it was, in WW1, applied by a soldier to the bullet that wounded him. (F & G.) Revived in WW2, (PGR.) Cf **bullet with my name ... and when yer name's on it ...**

it happens all the time, which is equivalent to **it's just one of those things**, q.v., dates from *c.* 1925. The easy philosophy of the (for *some*) lighthearted 1920s. In later notes, E.P. changed his mind slightly about the status of this phrase, and wrote, 'This affords an excellent example of a cliché being used "in quotes" with a gently ironic intonation and a shrug. Yet perhaps too dignified, too understated, to be a fully qualified c.p.'

[it happens in the best-regulated families (UK) or ... in the best, or best of, families (US). In Brit. usage, it orig. referred to unmarried pregnancy and, in the main, it still does: prob. since, at latest, mid C19. But in the US, it is 'usually a way of minimizing a minor mishap or misdemeanor' (R.C., 1978).

This may be regarded as the c.p. form of the proverb usu. quoted as *accidents will happen in the best-regulated families*, which occurs, perhaps most influentially, in Scott's *Peveril of the Peak*, 1823, 'Nay, my lady, ... such things will befall in the best regulated families', and in Dickens's *David Copperfield*, 1850, '"Copperfield," said Mr Micawber, "accidents will occur in the best-regulated families."' See esp. *ODEP* at *accidents* and, even more fully documented, in *Stevenson's Book of Proverbs, Maxims and Familiar Phrases*. Yet, whatever the form, it remains, I think, predominantly proverbial.]

it is... See **it's...**

[it is a fine moon, God bless her! stands midway between proverbial saying and c.p.; well, perhaps nearer the former than the latter: mid C17–20; ob. by 1930. Apperson.]

it is as good to be in the dark as without light is a semi-nonsensical c.p. that, occurring in Ray, 1670, recurs in Dialogue III of S, 1738:

LADY SM[ART]: It is as good to be in the Dark, as without Light; therefore, pray bring in Candles. They say, Women, and Linnen, shew best by Candle-Light.

It is easy to dismiss this kind of wit as childish: examined, it emerges as proto-Learish and almost Lewis-Carrollish.

it is sitting up and begging. See **he can make it sit up and beg.**

it must be the heat, 'originally a corny riposte to "I'm off", now leads an independent life' (Russell Davies, in *New Statesman*, 9 Sep. 1977). A neat pun on 'I'm off', I'm about to depart, and 'It's off', elliptical for 'It's off', applied to, e.g., milk turned sour, it dates from the 1920s, perhaps during the wonderful summer of 1921; and the 'independent life', referring to a headache, a general irritability, etc., began, I think, very soon after 1945.

it must be the landlady. An ironical c.p. used by actors (esp. in touring companies) 'receiving faint applause on a line that usually gets a good hand. Cf **God bless you both!**' (Granville). Complimentary tickets have always been freely distributed among theatrical landladies.

it must have been something they put in the tea or something he ate which accounts for his health or his mood: since *c.* 1950. 'The former is based on the rumour that bromide was the only way to keep a good soldier down, and there was a ref. to the latter in Donald Swann and Michael Flanders's song "The Reluctant Cannibal": "It must have been someone he ate"' (Simon Levene, 1977). Also, the latter may refer to a 1960s' 'sick' story about a man with cannibalistic tendencies eating the psychiatrist he consulted.

it never got off the ground. See **it doesn't stand up.**

it only wanted a man on the job. A joc. c.p. uttered by a willing helper as devoid of modesty as he is rich in kindliness: late C19–20.

it puts years on me is a late C19–20 c.p. of rueful disparagement.

it rattles like two skeletons .... See **noise like ....**

it rots battleships (or your socks). Water, as opposed to beer, is harmful: publc.-house c.pp.: C20. (L.A.)

it seemed like a good idea at the time. See **Well, it seemed ...**

it sends me! 'Having established the toothsome, faintly posh schoolgirl, Monica, in [the BBC radio comedy series] *Educating Archie*, Beryl Reid wanted to find another character from a different social class. This turned out to be Marlene (pronounced "Marleen") from Birmingham, complete with Brum accent and girl friend Deirdre. She helped establish what was in any case an archetypal 1950s phrase for the effect of music on the hearts and minds of the young' (*VIBS*). She was also responsible, in the same show, for the even more widely-imitated *it's terrific!* (pron. *turreefeek*): Ibid. Cf **it turns me on.**

it shouldn't happen to a dog! See **shouldn't happen…**

it sits up and begs. See **he can make it sit up and beg.**

it smells. See **it stinks.**

it snowed! is lower-and lower-middle-class c.p. indicative of misery or even of disaster; adopted, before 1909, from the US. (Ware.) 'Dead in US for *c.* 50 years' (R.C., 1978).

it stinks is the intensive of – and much commoner than – **it smells**; adopted, *c.* 1945, from US, where, recorded by Berrey in 1942 and by W & F in 1960, it arose *c.* 1930; applied in general to anything offending one's intelligence, honesty, sense of taste and, in particular, to inferior entertainment, e.g. a film.

it sucks. A more recent var. of the prec.; it 'had a tremendous vogue from *c.* 1960 to early 1970s, esp. in "underground" circles, among students, musicians, drug-addicts, then some gen. use since *c.* 1970 up to now' (Paul Janssen, 1977). The fact that the c.p. has generated a 'free' usage, e.g. 'Life sucks', 'America sucks', etc., doesn't invalidate, but corroborates, its popularity. P.B.: did it refer orig. to 'the hind tit', 'a dry tit', or to fellatio?

it takes all sorts is the c.p. form of the proverbial *it takes all sorts to make a world*: late C19–20. A good example occurs in Peter Driscoll's novel, *The White Lie Assignment*, 1971: 'I paid the driver and he swung away, shaking his head. It takes all sorts, he'd be thinking, and I suppose it does.'

it was adopted by the US *c.* 1900 (W.J.B., 1977).

it takes one to know one. You're as bad as the person you're criticizing: late (?mid) C19–20. '"He's a thief." – "It takes one to know one."' (B.P., 1974). 'In US, almost always applied to (male) homosexuals' (J.W.C., 1977); 'now obsolescent' (R.C., 1978).

The saying owes something, I surmise, to the true story of Francois Jean Vidocq (1775–1857), a thief on the grand scale, whose talents so impressed the French authorities that he was recruited into government service, where he rose to the command of a highly special section of detectives. Cf the proverb *set a thief to catch a thief*. In the early 1920s, a very popular film series, *Les Aventures de Vidocq*, was being shown; it may have contributed to the genesis of the c.p.

it takes two to tango. Premarital coition, like the begetting of large families, requires active co-operation between the sexes: a mainly feminine c.p., implying that either of these two activities is not operated only by selfish males: mostly Aus.: since *c.* 1935. 'From a popular song thus named' (B.P.); *DSUE*. By 1974, slight outmoded.

'In US, where it was usually employed with *to tango*, it arose during the very early 1920s, [or even] as old as the dance. Still current, although not widely' (J.W.C., 1978). In the US, however, it had by *c.* 1950 added the sense, 'with general reference to any dubious transaction (e.g. a bribe) between two persons – i.e., if one is guilty, both are' (R.C., 1978) – and this observation is true also of UK usage (P.B.).

it takes you. 'An Army, esp. a Guards, usage perhaps best exemplified by these examples from Roger Grinstead, *Some Talk of Alexander*, 1943: "It'll take you instead of me" – you, not I, will be on duty; "It takes you for a casual day" – you'll be on this duty for a day, in addition to your usual work; "Soon be taking us to storm the shores of France" – we'll soon be due to invade France' (*DSUE*). By the early 1950s it had spread in the Army beyond the Brigade of Guards, and to more trivial uses, in addition to the above, e.g. 'it (just about) takes you' – to hand round your cigarettes, pay for the next round of drinks, etc.; i.e., 'it is your turn'. (P.B.)

it took you longer to get here, or **do that, than to get born.** This

US reproach – or reprimand – to someone very tardy or unconscionably slow, dates from the 1930s. (J.W.C., 1977; but the dating is mine.)

it turned out a lemon. See **answer is a lemon ….**

it turns me on. It gives me a thrill: gen. US, yet predominantly teenagers', since *c.* 1967, but at first (the 1950s) drug (esp. marijuana) addicts', as recorded by W & F, the ref. being, as in the slangy *switch on*, to 'turning on the light'.

In a Philadelphia newspaper of late May or early June 1970, Sidney, J. Harris, in a witty poem entitled 'This Cat Doesn't Dig All That Groovy Talk', declares that, in the scale of condign punishment, he would reserve

The royal dungeon for the peon
Who dared exclaim 'it turns me on'.

The phrase had, by mid-1977, outlawed itself by becoming entirely 'free' as opposed to 'tied'; it had also acquired an opposite, *it turns me off*, likewise entirely 'free'. During the last few years of their c.p. status, they were 'predominantly used of sexual arousal' (J.W.C., 1977).R.C., 1978, remarked that it was, by then, as much adult as teenage. P.B.: cf the earlier *he* or *it doesn't bring me on one little (fucking) bit*, 'he (it, etc.) has an adverse effect on me', an Army phrase from the Korean War (1950–3); the implication here was also orig. sexual. Cf **it sends me.**

it was broke already. See **it come off in me 'and.**

it was on for young and old is an Aus. c.p. for a general outburst of high spirits, whether innocuous or obnoxious: since the middle 1940s. Wilkes cites examples for 1951–75. There is an implication of widespread agreement. Indeed, the expression amplifies *it is*, or *was*, *on*, agreed, acceptable. P.B.: or is it more simply *on*, meaning 'occurring' or 'arranged'?

it was one of those days. See **it's just one of those days.**

it wasn't there is a C20 theatrical 'reproof addressed to a stage manager who *pinches* a curtain call on a dead house. The applause wasn't there' (Granville).

it went like a bomb. It was a tremendous success. It began, in the late 1940s, with cars possessing an extremely rapid acceleration and a fine turn of speed; by the early 1950s, it had been taken over by the world of entertainment; by the late 1950s it was being applied to. parties, love affairs, what-have-you, as in Mary Stewart, *The Gabriel Hounds*, 1967:

'A sort of Grand Tour, wasn't it, with Robbie?'
'Sort of. Seeing the world and brushing up my Arabic … Oh, it all went like a bomb.'

Obviously from the explosion of large bombs.

Contrast the orig. and mainly US theatrical *it bombed* or *it was a real bomb*, 'It (e.g., a theatrical production) was a total failure – i.e., like a bomb, it left things in ruins': US, from 1960s, now somewhat obsolescent' (R.C., 1978). Cf **went over like a lead balloon.**

it will … See it'll …

it will be long enough is one of the comparatively few c.pp. that contain a genuinely clever pun: C18–20; by 1940 †.

As in S, Dialogue I:

LADY SM[ART]: Colonel, methinks your Coat is too short.
COL: It will be long enough, before I get another, Madam.

it will (or **it'll** or **'twill**) **last as many nights as days** is a pert answer or comment upon durability: C18–20, although seldom heard in C20, and † by 1950. It occurs in Dialogue I of S, and, on the ladder of wit, it stands alongside **as old as my tongue and a little older than my teeth.**

it won't do! is the signal for desisting from a burglary: underworld, esp. burglars': *c.* 1800–80. It occurs in, e.g. the anon. book *The London Guide*, 1818.

it won't get off the ground. See **it doesn't stand up.**

it won't wash. See **that won't wash.**

it would make a cat laugh. See **cat laugh.**

it would make a man piss. Esp. of a person's lies and effrontery: it revolts me; it fills me with contempt. In, e.g., Pepys's Diary, 15 Nov. 1667. (With thanks to R.S.) Apparently since (say) 1640; at some time, it became *it* *would* (or *it'd*) *make a man piss blood*, which is extant. Very much a male c.p.

it'd blow a dog off a chain. This Aus. c.p. is applied to very windy weather and it dates since *c.* 1930. Ross Campbell, in *The* (Sydney) *Bulletin*, 5 Nov. 1977, called it 'this traditional form of speech'.

it'd give you a pain where you never had a window – that is, in the arse – is an Anglo-Irish c.p., prob. throughout C20. (Skehan, 1977.) A neat pun.

it'll all be put down down in evidence against you is joc., dating since *c.* 1935. Obviously from police procedure. P.B.: perhaps influenced by the immense popularity, and flowering of, detective stories between the two World Wars.

it'll all be the same in a hundred years is a consolatory c.p., prob. dating from the 1890s and, by 1940, verging on the status of an accepted proverb. Partly an elab. of 'Why worry?' but strictly the c.p. form of the proverbial *it will all be the same a hundred years hence* (C19–20; by 1970, ob.) Earlier forms of the proverb itself are *'twill be all one a thousand years hence* (S, 1738) and *all will be one at the latter day* (Day of Judgement). With thanks to *ODEP*.

it'll all come out in the wash. It'll all be discovered eventually; *hence*, It'll all be settled eventually; *hence*, Never mind – *or* don't worry – it doesn't matter: C20. It is recorded by that acute observer of everyday speech, W. L. George, in his best novel, *The Making of an Englishman*, 1914.

By 1920 or so, it had become also US (Berrey), but is, for the US, tentatively dated (by J.W.C., 1977) at *c.* 1890, and defined as 'It's trivial and easily remediable'.

Cf **it all rubs off when it's dry.**

it'll all come right on the night. See **all right on the night.**

it'll be a cold day in hell appears, W.J.B. tells me, in Glendon Swarthout's novel, *The Tin Lizzie Group*, pub'd 1972 but dealing faithfully with the year 1916. It usu. precedes *before* or *when* something happens; the essential c.p. implies the fill-out. R.C. proposes for inclusion the weaker, perhaps orig. euph., *it'll be a mighty cold day*. The former implies 'never'; the latter, 'not soon, if ever'. Col. Moe suggests that *it'll be a cold day in hell* is equivalent of the Brit., later also US, **that'll be the day!**

it'll be over by Christmas. Which Christmas? A c.p. heard, not in 1914, during WW1, mostly in the Army – mostly among the Other Ranks. (Petch, 1969.) In ironic ref. to the fatuously optimistic Press forecast that the war would end by Christmas 1914. Cf **B.E.F. will also go home.**

it'll cost yer! See **cost yer!**

it'll do your eyesight good is applied to something well worth seeing: late C19–20; by 1950, virtually †. A C20 US var. is 'it will (or would) do your old eyes good to see' (A.B., 1978); not unknown in UK also.

it'll last my (or **our**) **time**, the cautious person warily – or perhaps wearily – adding, **I hope.** A 'famous last words' c.p., dating since *c.* 1945 but gen. only since *c.* 1948, it is less cynical than nostalgic, and therefore not to be treated as exactly equivalent to *aprés moi le déluge*. Cf **it'll see me out.**

it'll look well on the train call is a theatrical c.p., dating *c.* 1890–1940 and then becoming more and more ob. Granville, a book that has unfortunately been allowed to go out of print, says:

In the days when the Sunday trains were full of touring companies and the changes *en route* were frequent, the parading of golf clubs, the carrying of fur-collared overcoats, etc., gave an air of opulence to the company, and a harp, displayed on the staron platform, … set a hallmark on a musical comedy troupe. This catch phrase greeted any request to tour an awkward piece of luggage. 'It'll look all right on the train call. I suppose' (the ref. being to the informal roll-call a little before the train left).

it'll make a man of you. 'Originally (?1920s) applied literally to joining the armed services. Later, ironically to any probably unpleasant experience' (R.C., 1978). US; heard, in its derivative sense, occ. in the British Commonwealth.

it'll never get off the ground. See **it doesn't stand up.**

it'll pass with a push. An expression of grudging approval, of bare toleration: since *c.* 1930 in UK; since *c.* 1950 in Aus. Dorothy L. Sayers, in *The Nine Tailors*, 1934, uses the elab. *it'll pass in a crowd with a push.* (*DSUE*; B.P.) P.B.: was there perhaps in the longer version a pun WW1 slang *push* = crowd)? Cf the idiomatic (hardly a c.p.) *it'll do at a pinch.*

it'll put hair on your chest. See **that'll grow more hair on your chest.**

it'll see me out. A var. of **it'll last my time**, although, as B.G.T. remarks, 1978, 'perhaps oftener *it'll see you out'.* Contrast the implication behind **another clean shirt...**

'ITMA'. See **it's that man again!** and also TOMMY HANDLEY CATCH PHRASES.

it's... If a c.p. is not listed at *it's*, try **it is...**

it's a bastard (often **a proper bastard** or, Aus., **a fair bastard**) is very common among both working men and servicemen for anything very difficult or extremely exasperating: C20. Cf the Aus. *it's a fair cow*, late C19–20. Adam J. Apt, 1978, tells me that it has also some US currency. P.B.: it is odd that E.P. included this very common expression, yet disqualified the equally widespread *it's a lugger*, *a sod*, etc.

it's a breeze. This c.p., derived prob. from sailing, is applied to anything easy: US and Aus.: since before 1945. (R.C.; J.W.C.; B.P.) P.B.: cf the synon. Brit. Services' *it's a doddle*. Also, of course, in other moods and tenses.

it's a bugger up a teapot! A 'jocular elaboration of "It's a bugger" [not itself a c.p.] = a quandary with little or no choice' (L.A., 1976). Currency, esp. in London and since *c.* 1920. Cf **it's a bastard.**

it's a can of worms. See **can of worms.**

it's a case of the tail wagging the dog. See **case of the tail...**

it's a deal. Agreed!: late C19–20. '"Come to dinner tomorrow night." – "Love to, it's a deal!"' = an example of post-WW2 usage sent to me in 1969. Prompted by 'We've made a deal', an agreement. 'In US, now often abbreviated to *Deal!*' (R.C., 1978).

it's a different ball game. See **different ball game.**

it's a different drummer. 'Life is more peaceful here, people are more relaxed ... Have citations (mainly mid-60s, early 70s) ... Title of a 1971 record, Warner Brothers' Lyrics: Fred Werner'. Paul Janssen, 1978, quotes from a 1972 source, ' ... Relax, and don't start worrying ... They've got a different drummer in San Francisco'. US: since *c.* 1965.

In its full form, *if a man does not keep pace with his companions, perhaps it is because he hears a different drummer*, it began as a famous quot'n from the conclusion of Henry David Thoreau, *Walden*, 1854; the passage ends, 'Let him step to the music which he hears, however measured or far away'. The complete passage, too long to have become a c.p., remains a famous quot'n. But the first sentence, esp. in the shortened *perhaps he hears a different drummer*, occ. with *perhaps* omitted, has been resurrected, implying (perhaps) his entire attitude, his criterion of life, the principle he lives by, differ fundamentally from those of others. (Based on a reminder from Paul Janssen, 1978.) P.B.: it may be that it was really only the *different drummer* bit that became a vogue phrase: I remember an American cartoon of the late 1960s, in which a smooth womaniser is flattering a girl at a cocktail party with words to the effect 'You and I are the same type. We march to a different drummer'.

Different Drummer, a new ballet by Kenneth MacMillan inspired by Büchner's drama *Woyzeck*, was advertised by Royal Opera House, Covent Garden, for 24 Feb. 1984.

it's a doddle is applied to anything very easy to do: since *c.* 1945 in the RAF and, by 1950, widespread among civilians. (Simon Levene, 1977.) Cf **it's a breeze** and **it's a piece of cake.**

it's a dog's life is 'said of a rotten job, or life on the breadline, the dole, etc. A life you wouldn't wish on a dog.' (Granville,

1969.) Despite the violent change of sense, this c.p. prob. derives from – or, at the least, was prompted by – the C17–19 proverb, *it's a dog's life, hunger and ease.* Cf **it shouldn't happen to a dog!**

it's a fair cop was orig. an underworld c.p., addressed to a policeman: since *c.* 1880. (Ware.) Hence, since *c.* 1920, a general humorous c.p., equivalent to 'All right! you've caught me *or* caught me out'. See, in E. H. Hornung's famous *Raffles*, 1899, '"All right, guv'nor," drawled Raffles, "don't excite. It's a fair cop."' Frank Shaw has noted its prevalence in Edwardian English comics. And in *Cecilia*, 1932, Allan Monkhouse writes in Act II:

CECILIA: And yet you'd reck on me pretty good at asserting myself.

DAN: Before a sympathetic audience – yes.

CECILIA: You think I'm caught?

DAN: Fair cop, as the criminals say.

it's a fair cow. See **it's a bastard!**

it's a freak country and **it's a free country.** Of the former, Petch wrote thus, 1966: 'Sometimes heard in respect of the "sights" we see nowadays, like the dirty, long-haired teenagers. From the other expression, *it's a free country*': the former since *c.* 1960, the later since late C19, as a characteristically British expression of tolerance.

'US, since before 1930s', writes R.C., 1978, of *it's a free country*, 'first as an expression of tolerance, but, since [during the] 1950s, sometimes ironic, since it has become apparent that we are not quite so free as we thought'. P.B.: the same, alas, holds true for UK: the phrase has an increasingly defensive and intolerant tone to it, as in the all-too-familiar exchange, e.g. 'Excuse me, but would you mind *not* smoking in here, please' – ' 'Sa free country, innit?' But in our modern world we may well ask not, like Pilate, 'What is truth?', but 'What is freedom?'; the adage 'Freedom for the pike means death to the minnow' birds fair to become a c.p. of the early 1980s.

it's a game! It doesn't make sense: a British Army c.p. of 1915–18, 'applied to the war and to the military machine' (B&P). P.B.: the phrase was civilianized and may still be heard occ. in the early 1980s, usu. in the form 'It *is* a game, isn't it!', applied with rueful, resigned acceptance to the minor trials of modern life, like battling with bureaucracy or any other inefficient machinery. See also **it's only a game,** and cf **what a game it is!**

[**it's a gas** (or a **gasser** or a **gig** or a **giggle**). It's very funny indeed: the first two, Aus.: since *c.* 1961, B.P. tells me. The latter pair Brit.: since *c.* (1945 at first, as in Frank Norman, *Bang to Rights*, 1958, low slang, then, *c.* 1955, the smart young set, then gen. What causes giggling; *gig* shortens *giggle*. But, like *it's a doddle*, it's very easy to do, it's a walk-over, these potential c.pp. depend far less on their popularity as c.pp. than on the wax-and-wane of the nouns *doddle, gas, gasser, gig, giggle*, and so they hardly qualify.]

it's a gift! Well, that has been very easily obtained, *or* That presented no difficulty – as easy to accept as a gift: late C19–20; by 1950, slightly ob. 'In US, "It's a natural talent" – usually sarcastic' (J.W.C., 1977).

it's a go! Agreed: mostly US, since *c.* 1890 (Berrey, 1942, records it), but, by *c.* 1978, ob. or even † (R.C.). Also Aus. and NZ since some years before 1914.

it's a good flat that's never down. Even the biggest fool or dupe (a flat) finally has his eyes opened: *c.* 1790–1870. (Vaux, writing in 1812, calls it 'a proverb among *flash* people' – the underworld.)

it's a good game, (if) played slow or **slowly** is an 'ironic c.p., evoked by repeated manual maladroitness, repeated inconvenience, idling, or imposed tedium of waiting, etc.' (L.A., 1959): fighting Services': WW2.

it's a great life if you don't weaken. Arising among British soldiers very early in WW1, it survived into civilian life; it occurred in, e.g., George Ade's excellent and shrewdly prophetic essay 'Golf', in *Single Blessedness and Other*

Observations, 1922: 'A great life, my friends, if you don't weaken, and you can't weaken where the match is all square and a small bet riding' – which tends to show that it was familiar also to Americans, prob. via the US soldiers on the Western Front in 1918; in G.D.H. and M. Cole's novel, *Burglars in Bucks* (Buckinghamshire), 1930; and it is still heard quite often. It has always been joc. – sometimes ruefully so.

It has an offshoot: *it's a great life if you weaken often enough*, 'chiefly among girls, but copied by men in WW2' (Sanders, 1978) – and since; decreasingly heard after *c.* 1965. As so often, the US version is more succinct: the remark is capped there by *but greater still if you do.* Yielding to temptation has its points! Cf Wilde's 'I can resist anything except temptation', and someone else's 'The quickest way to overcome temptation is to yield to it'. Ashley adds, of the original, 'So familiar as to be parodied in "Knock, knock" – "Who's there?" – "Cigarette" – "Cigarette who?" – "Cigarette life …"'

it's a great war was an often joc. but usu. ironic c.p. of WW1, although not before 1915; as used by the army, it could be extremely bitter.

it's a great way to go! See **what a wonderful way to die!**

it's a hard life! Used lit. it is clearly *not* a c.p.; but it's often used joc. or ironically, and then it is a c.p.: late C19–20. In *The Law Divine*, performed on 29 Aug. 1918 and pub'd in 1922, H.V. Esmond writes in Act II:

EDIE (*going to door*): Well, after this little social intercourse, I must love you and leave you.

JACK: Upstairs again?

EDIE: Upstairs again. (*She laughs.*) It's a hard life.

'In the US, often as ironic sympathy responding to some complaint, e.g., "It's a hard life for you – just like the rest of us!"' (R.C., 1978).

it's a job. See **it's a living, already.**

it's a lemon. See **answer is a lemon . . . . .**

it's a little bit over is an Aus. butchers' c.p. of the C19–20. Butchers in Australia always try to sell you more meat than you asked for, and apprentices are taught to use the phrase as an excuse for an apparent mistake. (A valued correspondent.) Lovett, from Aus., notes, 1978, 'Not restricted to butchers'. P.B.: but no doubt butchers in Britain were practising this 'hard sell', as they still do, long before the days of Captain Cook, or even of Van Diemen.

it's a living, already is 'a mock-Jewish expression of fatalism about any job. Or it can be used ironically, implying an obsession'. P.B., 1975, cites 'Don't you ever get fed up, messing about with all those squalid words and phrases?' – to which the answer may be, 'It's a living, already'. Prob. from the US, but, there, without *already*: 'It (a job) has few attractions other than a modest paycheck. Resigned, not jocular. Also *it's job*. That is, better than no job' (R.C., 1978). Both of these c.pp. had reached the UK by *c.* 1960, at latest.

it's a long lane that has no pub is a jovial, even a joc., c.p. that twists the old proverb ' … that has no turning': C20. (Shaw.)

it's a long time between drinks. Bartlett tells us (p. 824 *b*, footnote) that the most reasonable tradition is that John Motley Morehead, Governor of North Carolina in 1841–5, was visited by James H. Hammond, Governor of South Carolina in 1842–4. When in a discussion the latter grew heated, Morehead exclaimed, 'It's a long time between drinks', and thus restored amity and calm.

From being a famous quot'n, as indeed it still is, it became also a c.p. But don't expect me to tell you when – at a very rough guess, I'd say *c.* 1880 or 1890; but at least I can state that, already by 1908, it had become so well established that it could be employed allusively thus, in Chapter IV ('He Discusses Finance') of *The Genial Idiot* by John Kendrick Bangs (1862–1922), the US humorist and wit, better known as the author of *A House Boat on the Styx*:

I honestly don't like to lend money, believing with

Polonius that it's a bad thing to do. As the Governor of North Carolina said to the Governor of South Carolina, who owed him a hundred dollars, 'It's a long time between payments on account', and that sort of thing breaks up families, not to mention friendships.

The c.p. came to Britain and, among the educated and the well-read, has been widely understood although not widely used. I occ. try it out on writer friends and acquaintances afflicted with a literary conscience and say, 'The only adverse criticism I have to make of your books is that "it's a long time between drinks".'. Sometimes I'm treated to a blank and glassy stare, sometimes to an appreciative grin.

A link between quot'n and phrase is provided by James Maitland, *The American Slang Dictionary*, 1891: he cites *between drinks, a long time*, as a slangy synonym of 'a long time'. A.B. notes, 1978, that in the US, since *c.* 1930, often *it's been a long time*... See also **as the Governor**...

it's a lulu! It's a beauty, a 'humdinger': US: since *c.* 1890. Perhaps from the font-name *Lulu*, a reduplication of the *Lou* of both *Louis* and *Louisa* or *Louise*. (Based partly on my *U* and partly on W&F.) Ashley, 1979, notes the US synon. *it's a doozie!*

it's a monkey's wedding is a C20 S. African c.p., 'applied to weather characterized by a drizzling rain accompanied by a shining sun' (Prof. A.C. Partridge, 1968). 'Cf the US counterpart, *the Devil is beating his wife*, rain while sun is shining. Possibly Southern, but some [gen.] currency since *c.* 1900; now obsolescent or [even] dead' (R.C., 1978).

it's a new ball-game. See **different ball-game**.

it's a new one on me. See **new one**...

it's a nice place to live out of. See **nice place to live out of**.

it's a nice place to visit but I wouldn't want to live there. 'A c.p. often used of "perfect" cities like Canberra' (B.P., 1974): Aus.: since *c.* 1955. It is current also in US, where the "place" was originally, and still usually, New York City' (J.W.C., 1977). 'The ... *but I wouldn't want to live there* is sometimes intensified as *but it's a hell of a place to live in*. Inevitably then inverted, as by dyed-in-the-wool New Yorkers, such as yours truly: "It's a great place to live, but I wouldn't want to visit there"' (R.C., 1978). Cf **nice place to live**...

it's a nice place you have here. See **nice place you have here.**

it's a piece of cake. It is, was, will be something very easy to do, a 'snip'; occ., It's a wonderful opportunity: RAF: since *c.* 1938; by 1946, widely used by civilians. It is recorded by W.J. and by EP in *A Glossary of RAF Slang*, 1945, as well as by PGR. Origin: 'as easy to dispose of as a piece of cake'. By late 1960s, ob.; and by early 1970s, †.

it's a poor arse that never rejoices. A C20 c.p. uttered, when someone breaks wind, by a member of one of those 'gangs' or cliques or fraternities of would-be wits in which public-houses abound. Cf Grose's *ars musica*, dog L for *ars musicalis*. Based on the proverb, 'It's a poor heart that never rejoices'. Cf:

it's a poor belly that can't warm its own lies in the no-man's-land between potential proverb and domestic c.p.: current late C19–mid 20. That is, 'its own food'. With thanks to Mr Robert Robinson who, on 17 Oct. 1977, spoke of it in the BBC radio programme, 'Stop the Week'.

it's a poor soldier who can't stand his comrade's breath is an army – orig. the Regular Army – c.p. dating from late C19 and defiantly offered by the culprit when his companions complain of an offensive fart. Cf **it's a poor arse**...

it's a rumour! (often **'s a rumour!**), an army c.p. of 1915–18, was a retort on 'an opinion expressing a very well known fact or [on] a statement emphatically and usu. disagreeably) true' (B&P).

[**it's a screech** falls into the same category as **it's a gas**, q.v.]

it's a shame! was, in WW2, an Aus. var. of **it's a rumour!**

it's a small world, Brit. and US, dates since *c.* 1890 and is brightly proclaimed at an unexpected meeting either between two persons belonging to widely separated countries

or between two compatriots meeting far from their own country.

George Ade, *In Pastures New*, 1906, writes:
'It's a small world.' This is one of the overworked phrases of the globe-trotter. It is used most frequently by those who follow the beaten paths. In other words, we find it difficult to get away from our acquaintances.... To the ordinary traveller it is always a glad surprise to find a friend coming right out of the ground in a corner of the world supposed to be given over to strangers.

Thus begins the amusing chapter XI, titled 'Cairo as the Annual Stamping Ground for Americans and Why they Make the Trip'. P.B.: since *c.* 1920, often allusively, as in, e.g. 'Well, well! Small world!', and in references to 'the small-world club'.

it's a snice mince-pie. This c.p. arose *c.* 1916, was ob. by 1937 and † by 1945. It was suggested by the sibilance of the words a *nice mince pie*, esp. when prec. by *it's*. Weekley once noted: 'As I write [1917] there is a slang tendency to say *snice* for *nice*, etc.'

it's a state secret has, since *c.* 1933, been, though rarely since *c.* 1950, either prompously or joc. used by someone who refuses to disclose information no matter how trivial. Cf **don't make a Federal case out of it!**

it's a term of endearment among sailors. See **term of endearment**.

it's a way they have in the army was, in 1915–18, an army, mostly officers', c.p. But even then it was a revival of a c.p. current since *c.* 1880 or even earlier and deriving from a popular song that, *c.* 1880, opens thus. But I never heard it used during my army service in 1940-early 1942 and I doubt whether it was used at all during WW2; certainly not since.

P.B.: a cartoon in *Punch*, 1 Sep. 1877, p. 94, bears the title 'The Way We Had in the Army'.

it's a weird scene. A var. of **it's weird, man.**

it's a whole new ball game. See **different ball-game.**

it's a whole new can of beans. See **that's another can**...

it's a wonder that didn't choke you! She **choke you**...

it's agony, Ivy! See **ee, it's agony**... Ashley, 1979, notes a US var., *Antigone, it's agony!*

it's all a bit of buck! 'A c.p. used *ad nauseam* in a certain Signals Regt. in Cyprus, late 1950s, to indicate an attitude of "couldn't care less" and general fatalism' (P.B., 1974) – and to Servicemen stationed there at that time, the whole business [*Enosis*, EOKA, etc.] must have been intolerably frustrating. *Buck* was here an abbr. of *buckshee(s)* something not worth bothering about.

it's all bob. See **Bob's your uncle!**

it's all clever stuff, you know (or **y'know**), 'Often shortened to *it's all clever stuff* or even *all clever stuff*, it is a stock response to anything slightly baffling' (P.B., 1978): since *c.* 1950.

it's all coming out now is 'said by a participant, or a spectator, when an argument reaches the stage where people lose all their inhibitions and bring out all those things that have been rankling and niggling for years' (Simon Levene, 1977): C20.

it's all go. P.B., writing in 1975, says: A neutral c.p. indicating that life is a constant round of activity, which may be pleasant or otherwise. 'There's a dinner in the mess Friday, drinks with the other lot Saturday lunchtime, off to Dave's in the evening, down to the coast Sunday ... cor, it's all bloody go, I tell you.' Or conversely: "Ere I was on guard Monday night, then again We'nsday and Sat'day, and now the bastards've got me for bleedin' fire picket. It's all go in this lousy outfit – and no mistake.'

it's all good clean fun. 'Palliation of making a butt of a person, or persons, in a group – or when fun has been fast at others' expense; not necessarily free from impurity' (L.A., 1974); since *c.* 1955. Cf **it's good clean dirt.**

it's all good for trade, often prec. by **ah, well!** A 'concluding conversational phrase [– a gambit –] when options are best left open; what the boss said, what she said; the final (? bathetic) outcome. (I always felt some trade between the sexes was [sometimes] hinted at. [I first heard it in an] officers' mess, 1943 – 4.)' (L.A., 1974). In 1969, either L.A. or another friend, R.S., had written: 'The opting-out rejoinder. Your friend or his wife has paid too much, or another friend has been unfairly used. Best sum it up, [for] regret won't alter it: "It's all good for trade!"'

It goes back, I think to commerce during the 1920s or, at latest, the 1930s.

it's all happening is hard to nail down, its sense ranging from '(But) it all *is* happening, you know' to '(But) it really *is* so, whatever you may think' and to 'Wake up and face the reality!' Patricia Newnham, 1976, writes, 'I have heard this as a semi-laconic response to someone marvelling at an event or [at] a display of some kind'. Since at least as early as 1939 in Brit. and late 1941 in the US. Contrast – and cf – **it can't happen here.** (A reminder. 1975, from Fernley O. Pascoe.) R.C., 1978, notes, 'In US, always rare; now dead', and Michael Goldman, 1978, says of its UK use, 'a lot of things are going on; e.g., it might be said to a late [-arriving] guest at a party in full swing'. P.B.: since then it has become a, usu. joc., c.p. uttered when merely more than one thing happens at a time, often in the most trivial of circumstances, and sometimes, to emphasise, by sarcasm, that very triviality. *VIBS* says of *it's all been happening this week*, 'Stock phrase of Norman Vaughan during his TV Palladium days (from 1962)'. Contrast **it's happening.**

it's all in a lifetime. Why grumble? It's no use doing so: late – ? rather mid – C19–20.

[**it's all in the day's work** is far more a cliché than a c.p.]

it's all in the mind, you know! 'Convincing explanation of anything heard in *The Goon Show* – often said by the announcer, Wallace Greenslade' (*VIBS*). P.B.: Since the early 1950s, used in all possible circumstances and contexts: only recently (1983) I heard it applied to some particular vile weather, and, as E.P. commented when I suggested the c.p. for inclusion here, 'Too often, however, it's *not* in the mind only. Whenever somebody says to me "Things are *never* as bad as they seem', my retort is "No, they're often a bloody sight *worse*"'. Richard MacKarness, fighter against the over-use of drugs in medication, wrote a book, pub'd 1976, entitled *Not All in the Mind*.

it's all (or it all comes) in the seven. That's to be expected; it's a matter of course: army: (?late C19–20). 'In allusion to the soldier's term of service with the colours' (F&G) – that is, on continuous service.

it's all in the twelve is a 'remark levelled against any sailor who bemoans his lot or grumbles at Service conditions. It means that "he shouldn't have joined if he couldn't take a joke"' (*Sailors' Slang*). Cf the prec. entry and **if you can't take a joke....**

it's all lies, I tell you! Unconvincing defence frequently shrieked by 'Neddie Seagoon' (Harry Secombe) against all aspersions on his dubious character: almost as often heard from fans of the GOON SHOW, q.v. (P.B.)

it's all money dates since *c.* 1945 and serves as a c.p. reply to one who apologizes for paying in small coins or in more coins than are either necessary or sensible.

it's all over bar the shouting. See **all over bar the shouting.**

it's all over now, ducks (or love), **you can pull up your knickers** or drawers). 'An unpleasant experience has ended. Jocular or facetious. Said to have been used on the beaches at Dunkirk whenever the last of a line of Stukas [German dive-bombers] had dropped its bombs, it was fairly common during the Blitz [on 1940–41] when the "all clear" sounded' (Sanders, 1978). Clearly, it had existed before WW2; nor is it extinct at the end of the 1970.

it's all right by me. I agree: a US c.p., perhaps of Yiddish origin, as mentioned in HLM, Supp. 1. Mencken cites an article pub'd in 1941 by Dr. A. Roback, the predecessor of Mr Leo Rosten in the field of Yiddishisms, and mentions that 'a Yiddish popular song often sung in 1938 was "Bei Mir Bist Da Scheen" (By Me You Are Beautiful)' – that is, in my opinion. By 1945, heard occ. among Britons; by 1950, heard frequently. A var. of **okay by me,** q.v.

it's all right for some (or you). See **all right for....**

it's all right if it comes off. This mainly Aus. c.p. dates from *c.* 1930 and applies to an apparent attempt at a swindle. (B.P.)

it's all right, Ponsonby, 260 are in front. Writing of the British Forces' retreat in the Western Desert, early 1942, Barker Beresford is quoted by C.H. Ward-Jackson in *Airman's Song Book*, 1945, as saying [260 Squadron, RAF] were left behind at Benghazi to cover the 4th Indian Division, and very nearly spent the rest of the war in a prison camp... We had a catchphrase, "It's alright, Ponsonby, 260 are in front," as the Air Force were always the rearguard'. *Ponsonby* is here used as a generic for Army staff officers.

it's all Sir Garnet. See **all Sir Garnet!**

it's all systems go. See **all systems go.**

it's all up here. Often accompanied by tapping one's own forehead: since *c.* 1910. A version of **it's up there,** or **that's where, you want it,** *it* being, of course, brains, common sense, the ability to think.

it's (or that's) all very fine and large. See **all very large and fine.**

it's always jam tomorrow (but) never jam today dates, as a mainly civilian c.p., since *c.* 1917. The immediate occasion was prob. the sugar shortage experienced during WW1, but its ultimate source was 'Jam yesterday and jam tomorrow, but never jam today' in Lewis Carroll's *Through the Looking Glass*, 1871. It should be compared with **pie in the sky when you die.**

it's an old army game. 'And don't let anybody tell you that the expressions, "It's an old army game" and "Go away, boy, you're bothering me" belonged to W.C. Fields. It was Charles Kenna who used both these expressions in his act many many years before Fields even walked on the stage' (Joe Laurie, Jr, *Vaudeville from the Honky-Tonks to the Palace*, 1953; with thanks to my friend, W.J.B., writing, like the other contributors to this entry, in 1975). Therefore *it's an old army game* is a US c.p. and can be said to date from early in C20.

Yet another US friend, Col. Albert Moe, says that the meaning 'It's the system and therefore hard to beat or circumvent' (my own definition) 'does not seem to go back any further that WW2, and, chronologically, seems to be the last of several meanings that are associated with the phrase'. He continues: 'Prior to WW2, I had heard it used ranging from a major swindle to a minor deceit, i.e. to take advantage of someone's trust or gullibility. It was used to explain or justify the manipulating of any situation to the advantage of the manipulator, whether it be fleecing a lamb (pigeon) or finding a scapegoat.' Moreover, he has found that the earliest recorded evidence – John Quinn's *Fools of Fortune*, 1890, and Herbert Ashery's *Sucker's Progress*, 1938 – refers to such gambling games as chuck-a-luck and stud poker; both games are either 'designated' or 'called' not *a*, but '*the* old army game'. P.B. writes:

My friend Mary Priebe from Seattle.... Her interpretation is that it can be heard to excuse some crafty wangle; one, usually, that has been successful, or to describe any slightly devious ploy....I recall that there was a British TV comedy series a few years ago.... called 'The Army Game'.

And Prof. Harold Shapiro tells me that *he* has always heard it as *it's the old army game* and that it's still in use, although he'd be surprised to hear it from someone under say thirty-five.

It always seems to imply 'the system' – either as it affects someone or as someone attempts to beat the system, and always seems to imply the usual foul-up (on the part of the system), or a 'con' or dodge (on the part of the system or the part of the individual).

J.W.C. confirms *the.* See also **old army game....** and, at the end of that entry, the reason why I've allowed two entries for what, to some, will be one c.p.

it's an old Belgian custom is 'an occasionally heard American substitute for an apology when someone belches, whence the pronounced and written variant *Belchin''* (Adam J. Apt, 1978): since *c.* 1940(?). Obviously formed on:

it's an old Southern custom. This line from a popular song became a c.p.in 1935 and by the end of the year (in fact by Oct.) other words began to be substituted for *Southern*, but no var. has ever achieved c.p. status. In the *Evening News* of 4 Jan. 1936, I read an account of a man who, on being upbraided for kissing a girl in a square in London W2, explained that 'It's an old Bayswater custom.' The explanation, one regrets to say, was not accepted. R.C., 1977, confirmed J.W.C.'s observation that in US the custom is more frequently *Spanish*, and this dates from *c.* 1920. Cf prec.

it's apples. See apples...

it's as cheap sitting as standing. Why stand when you can sit?: C17–20. Dialogue I, has:

LADY ANSW[ERALL]: Well, but sit while you stay; 'tis as cheap sitting as standing.

One of the domestic c.pp., which tend to wear so well.

it's (as) cold as a witch's tit. See cold as a witch's...

it's 'as I roved out'. It's of no consequence, no more than those songs so often starting "as I roved out'' (Shaw, 1968): C20. Perhaps these *roved out* songs were supplemented by the carols beginning 'As I rode out'.

[**it's as simple as that!** 'As you see, it's really very simple': since *c.* 1944. Originally, I think, an Armed Forces', mostly an instructors', c.p., from a blackboard, or a mechanical, demonstration. (With thanks to Prof. T.B.W. Ried, 1972; the fact, not the theorizing, is his.)

It went to Aus. in, I think, the latish 1940s; in 1975 B.P. commented thus: 'A c.p. that some people introduce into every conversation'.

Clearly however, it is, esp. when used lit., also a cliché. P.B.: but it is noticeable that, for the person addressed, 'It' rarely is 'as simple as that'.]

it's awfully Aquascutum of you! 'A light-hearted way of thanking somebody... A way of passing off the thanks, is all part of the Austin Reed service' (Anon., 1978). Cf *just part of the Austin Reed service. Aquascutum* is a brand-name raincoat. I feel fairly sure that the *Aquascutum* c.p. arose later than the *Austin Reed* one. Another (? the same) anon. informant, 1979, mentions *that's terribly Aquascutum of you* as having some limited currency, 1970s, in the Metropolitan Police.

it's bad manners to speak when your arse is full. A C20 proletarian c.p., addressed to someone who farts noisily in company. An earthily humorous ref. to the domestic adage, 'It's bad manners to speak when your mouth is full'.

it's baloney.... See it's boloney...

it's been a very good year for girls has, since *c.* 1960, been a presentable young males' c.p. of gratification at the constant compliance of presentable young women. (Fernley O. Pascoe, 1975.) In jesting allusion to good years for wines.

it's been known. It's not unknown: often ironic: since the middle 1940s. Elliptical for 'It *has* been known to happen'.

it's been real is a US 'expression said on leave-taking... indicating the speaker's enjoyment of the time spent together or at a social function. *Orig. from* "it's been *real fun*"' (W&F, 1960) – or perhaps 'a real pleasure'. *DCCU*,derives it from 'It's been real nice' (enjoyable). Hence, ironically, 'It's been real dull' or 'very boring'. Both sets of US editors supply no date, however roughly approximate, so I'll hazard the guess that the earlier sense arose *c.* 1945–6, as a result of WW2's impact upon the national consciousness, and that the derivative sense arose *c.* 1955.

'Perhaps originally as stated, but influenced (and given currency) during [the] 1960s by emphasis on authenticity of feelings, etc. – hence "a real experience" – "a real relationship" – etc. Now usually ironic – "it wasn't all that real" – or simply a consciously cliché'd farewell' (R.C., 1978).

it's being so cheerful as keeps me going. In his book *Itma*, 1948, Frank Worsley mentions that a great success of 'ITMA' in 1946 was Joab Harben playing the part of

Mona Lott [punning *moan a lot*], the depressed laundry-woman, with her incredibly unlucky family always involved in some fearful disaster of other.... But, with true British grit, poor Mona sticks it out, for 'it's being so cheerful as keeps her going'. This type of unhappy comedy has always been popular in this country.... Mona Lott appealed to everyone's sympathy, but especially to that of woman listeners.

it's boloney (or bologny or baloney), no matter how thin you slice it. It's utter nonsense, no matter how hard you try to prove the opposite. US, dating since the middle or late 1930s and recorded by Berrey, 1942. Orig., an illiterate pron. of Italian *bologna*, the sausage so named, as W&F have noted.

'Perhaps taken over from a popular US jingle, current *c.* 1930, which, after enumerating all the things might be done to "disguise" boloney, concluded: "Dress it in silks and make it look phoney,/No matter how thin you slice it, it's still boloney". The last line is the standard US form – now often abbreviated to *no matter how thin you slice it'* (R.C., 1978).

Sometimes the nuance is 'It's shit [bad business] no matter what *you* call it' (A.B., 1978).

it's brutal! and **it's murder!** are both US in orig.: and the former immediately, the latter soon, became also Brit. The former was suggested by the latter: and the latter, dating from *c.* 1910 or earlier, was anglicized by 1920. The application ranges from brutally hard ('murderous') work to harsh treatment, to extortionate prices.

In Britain, there exists the var. *it's sheer murder.*

In US business, the former means 'business is poor'; the latter, 'business is good' – almost too good. (Berrey, 1942.) Period: *c.* 1930–50.

it's cheap at half the price. See cheap at half the price.

it's enough to... See enough to...

it's dead, a theatrical c.p. of C20, means 'The applause has died down' (Granville).

it's for the birds. See that's strictly for the birds.

it's Friday, so keep your nose tidy is a non-cultured, non-educated, late C19–20 c.p. (but † by 1970), uttered only on a Friday, a day that, in folklore, is – or was – thought to by unlucky; it means 'Keep out of trouble' and implies 'Mind your own business!'

it's getting deep in here. The company's deteriorating, the conversation's becoming more and more affected or in sincere: US, and rather low: since *c.* 1945. It = 'the shit'. (Fain, 1969.) J.W.C., 1977, adds that the phrase is often accompanied by tapping one's foot, explaining that 'the amount of bullshit (figurative) being spread around here, it's a good thing I have my shoes on'.

it's gone over Borough Hill after Jackson's pig. It is lost: a rural, esp. Northamptonshire, c.p. of mid C19–20; ob. by 1930 and by 1970 rarely used. (Apperson.) P.B.: perhaps orig. the Burrough Hill in East Leicestershire, to the North of Northamptonshire, a prominent landmark.

it's good clean dirt. 'Domestic c.p., used in ref. to, e.g., a morsel of food dropped on the floor, but picked up and eaten. Current from before 1920, but now ob.' (R.C., 1978). Also in the British Commonwealth, where, however, it is regarded as a cliché. Cf *it's all good clean fun.*

it's good enough for *Punch* (for inclusion in that very English periodical with its very high standards): since, I'd guess, late C19 and certainly not later than *c.* 1908, when I first heard it used. (Reminder, 1975, by Fernley O. Pascoe.) P.B.: cf the late C19–earlier 20 very British threat 'I shall (*or* I've a good mind to) write to *The Times* about it'.

it's goodnight from me/And it's goodnight from him! 'Ronnie Corbett and Ronnie Barker, sending up the contrived way TV co-presenters can sign off, in their BBC TV series *The Two Ronnies*' (*VIBS*).

173

it's got a back to it. I'm lending, not giving, it to you: Londoners': C20. A pun on 'You must give it *back*'.

it's got bells on. That's a *very* old story! I don't remember having heard it before 1930, but I suspect that it goes back to *c.* 1920 – or even to *c.* 1900. Perhaps a ref. to the 'chestnuts' told by medieval, notably the court, jesters, who wore cap and bells; or perhaps to the bell of a town crier. Cf **tell me the old, old story.** (Owed, in part, to Frank Shaw, 1968.) See also **pull the other one...**

'Cf the even more graphic US counterpart: *it's –* or *that's –* got whiskers on it, i.e. that joke's reached a ripe old age' (R.C., 1978). But the latter is also Brit. and goes back to, at least, late C19. An example occurs in Dorothy L. Sayers, *Gaudy Night*, 1935.

it's half-past kissing time and time to kiss again. See **kissing time....**

it's happening, occ., with semi-vocative *man* added, was 'widely used throughout the 1960s (though rare in print before the mid 1960s). In the underground, its sense was "it's modern"...; it's the thing to do; it's all the rage; it's successful". I remember... "Why do you smoke pot?" – "Because it's happening, man"; "Dylan has a new song out, it's happening"... J.L. Simmons & Barry Winograd's excellent book, *It's Happening: A Portrait of the Youth Scene Today*, 1966, undoubtedly helped to popularize the expression' (Paul Janssen, 1977). US in orig., but eagerly adopted in UK.

Cf **it's all happening.**

it's hell in there or **it must be hell in there,** sometimes prec. by *gad!*, or prec. or followed by *I tell you.* A c.p. from 'The Goon Show' (see GOON...), adapted to all sorts of contexts and circumstances, and usu. following explosive sound effects, either as of bombs or intestinal, it became widely popular and is still occ. heard, 1983. (P.B.)

it's in the bag. It's a certainty; 'victory is certain, or already won' (J.W.C., 1977). Orig. Brit. (*c.*1925), but very soon also US (*DSUE*). From game-shooting.

it's in your eye! is an exclam. uttered 'when an opponent's bowl comes to rest in the line of draw to your jack': S. African bowls players': C20. (Prof. A.C. Partridge, 1968.)

it's jake. See **she'll be jake.**

it's just my alley marble or **cup of tea** or **handwriting.** See **just my...**

it's just one of those days, sometimes with *it's* omitted and usu. uttered in a resigned or rueful or mock-despairing tone, is applied to a day on which nothing appears to go right and much does go wrong. I cannot date it, except that I do remember it in the 1930s and rather think that it arose during the 1920s. P.B.: occ. *just* is omitted, or the phrase is reshaped to *it just isn't my day*, or *this is definitely not my day.* See also **one of those fine days.**

it's (or **it was**) **just one of those things** is applied to something inexplicable, esp. if that something simply has (or had) to happen: since the middle 1930s. Nevil Shute, *The Chequer Board*, 1947, 'It wasn't his fault he got taken by the Japs. It was just one of those things.' Popularized by an extremely popular Cole Porter song of the 1930s thus titled. In II, i, of *Relative Values*, performed in 1951 and pub'd 1952, Noël Coward writes:

NIGEL: But he was such a mild, inoffensive little chap. What on earth did he do?
FELICITY: We have no proof that he actually did anything. It – it was just one of those things.

it's kissing time, See **kissing time....**

it's later than you think was orig. a monitory thought often seen inscribed on sundials. But it became a c.p., perhaps from its being used in one of Robert W. Service's early (1907–13) extremely popular collections of ballads; and was prob. reinvigorated by being quoted by Evelyn Waugh in *The Ordeal of Gilbert Pinfold*, 1957. As a c.p., it has been mostly employed 'to induce...a sense of urgency in political matters' (P. Daniel, 1978).

it's like a nigger girl's left tit: neither right nor fair. A Can. c.p., apparently in the main, feminine rather than masculine: since the middle or early 1960s. A correspondent tells me he heard it in 1968. P.B.: a Brit. var., since *c.* 1950 at latest, features *a nigger's left ballock* or *knacker* or *testicle.* See also **it's not right,** which this parodies.

it's like money in the bank. 'It (a financial scheme of some sort) is certain to succeed – i.e., its expected proceeds are as "real" (if not quite as negotiable) as funds actually on deposit: US: C20. Cf *you can bank on it*' (R.C., 1978).

it's like that, is it? and **so that's the way it is** are almost exactly synon. c.pp. dating from very soon after WW2. Slightly cynical, more than slightly resigned yet ruefully humorous, acceptances of fate.

it's London to a brick (on such and such a racehorse). See **London to a brick.**

it's made round to go round. It's so made that it'll circulate the more easily; that is, it's money – and therefore to be spent: Aus.: certainly in the 1960s and prob. continuing into the 1970s and perhaps arising in the latish 1950s. (Jack Slater, 1978.)

it's money for jam and **it's money for old rope.** Both refer esp. to payment for work done, but they are not perfectly synon., the former being applied to money very easily earned, the latter to money paid for nothing or almost nothing; the former arose *c.* 1900, and its derivative sense, 'It's too easy!' arose *c.* 1910 and was very common in the army of WW1 (see, e.g., B & P), and the latter, orig. low, *c.* 1905, occurring in, e.g., James Curtis, *The Gilt Kid*, 1936. By *c.* 1950, however, these two c.pp. were virtually interchangeable – and were possessed of the same social status; to Granville, writing in 1968, they were indistinguishable, one from the other. And then, in 1975, L.A. supplied this gloss: '(Mainly Services) of favourable duties, especially those which earn privilege; also of winning streak at, e.g., card games.'

it's more fun than a barrel of monkeys. See **more fun than...**

it's murder! See **it's brutal!**

it's my story. See **that's my story.**

it's naughty! It's dangerous: an underworld c.p., dating since *c.* 1920. *U.*

it's naughty but it's nice refers to sexual intercourse. In the US, some time in the 1890s, Minnie Schult sang – and popularized – the song so titled; the c.p. arose therefrom and reached UK by *c.* 1900. Cf Marie Lloyd's song, 'A little of what you fancy does you good' – which likewise generated a c.p.

it's nice to get up in the morning, with its rider, **but it's nicer to lie in bed,** understood, comes from perhaps the most popular song by Harry Lauder (1870–1950): since the fairly early 1900s; by 1960, ob. – except when used ironically. (A reminder from Oliver Stonor.)

it's nice to have a peg to hang things on! has, in C20 although not much since *c.* 1960, been the natural plaint of one who, in business, has to pay the penalty of a superior's mistakes.

[**it's no go.** It's no use – a waste of time. Current in Britain since *c.* 1820 or a little earlier, and in US, less commonly, since *c.* 1900, it does not fully qualify: it's a piece of straightforward slang, with no derivative and deviant meaning.]

it's not cricket! See **not cricket.**

it's not done and **it isn't done** date, the latter since *c.* 1870 (see the *OED*), the former since the 1880s, and mean 'It is bad form or behaviour unacceptable in good society. It could be described as an upper-class counter. Collinson writes, 'To reprobate unseemly conduct we now currently employ the expression "it's not done"...with the jocular variant "it's not a done thing".' He supports *it's not done* by references to John Galsworthy's *The White Monkey*, 1924, and H.G. Wells's *Christine Albert's Father*, 1925.

it's not much if (occ. **when**) **you say it quick** or **quickly.** Applied to a large sum of money or a very high price or charge: since *c.* 1910 or perhaps a decade earlier.

[it's not my bag. It's not my concern or 'line' or current interest: not a c.p., for it can be *anyone's* 'bag' in any tense or number.]

it's not my day. See it's just one of those days.

it's not my end. The sailor's way of disclaiming responsibility: 'It's not my end, chum, I'm not carrying that can back': lower-deck RN: since *c.* 1925. (PGR.) Cf the underworld *end*, share of the loot.

it's not my scene. Sometimes 'It's no concern of mine' 'I'm both disinterested and uninterested in the whole business' – but more often 'It doesn't attract me' or 'It's not the sort of thing I'm interested in'. Adopted, *c.* 1972, in Britain from the US, where widespread by 1970. Orig., *scene* was used by US negroes in the 1940s–50s for 'the main area of popular group activity, such as a street corner, a bar, a poolroom' (CM, 1970). The variants, *it's not me* and *it's just not me*, indicate that it is not something I would do, or wear.

it's not off the ground he licked it is 'said of anyone who acts and thinks as his parents would. Probably Anglo-Irish and rural' (Skehan, 1977), Prob. also C19–20.

it's not on. It's extremely inadvisable; it's impossible: since *c.* 1964, as a c.p., although one had heard it being used as early as *c.* 1960. In its May 1971 issue, the *Spectator* noted it as the average Briton's reaction to the Common Market. Short for *it's not on the cards*. There are two variations: *it's just not on* and *it's simply not on*, both with *on* emphasized. P.B.: in some contexts, almost synon. with it's not done, q.v.

it's not right, it's not fair is a derisive c.p. addressed to a complainant and applied to his complaint: mainly the Armed Forces': since *c.* 1905. See also it's like a nigger...

it's not so much the cross we have to bear: it's the flaming splinters on it! It's the *little* things we find the hardest to bear: mostly, perhaps orig., RN: C20. (Rear-Adm. P.W. Brock, 1968.)

it's not the bull they're afraid of: it's the calf is an Aus. c.p., applied to girls and implying that they fear not the loss of virginity, but pregnancy: C20.

it's not the end of the world is 'said of some minor mishaps or disappointment. "Even if the book is rejected, it's not the end of the world"' (Granville, 1969); 'A consolatory expression heard today' (Petch, 1974): since *c.* 1945.

it's not what you know but who you know is sometimes a merely cynical, but usu. a 'sour grapes', c.p., dating since *c.* 1945. 'Speaker, hopeless, anyhow. Equally hopeless hearer nods solemn assent' (Shaw, 1968). Current in Aus. as well as in Brit.: 'Influence is more important than ability' (B.P., 1975): and no less common in US (J.W.C., 1977). As R.C., 1978, remarks, 'Wide American currency from *c.* 1930 or earlier; the "Old-Boy network" and "Old Pals' Act" being as operative these as anywhere else'. Tom Ash, in *Childhood Days*, (n.d., late 1970s) notes its use among London dockers concerning the allocation of lucrative work.

it's OK by me! See okay by me!

it's old hat, often shortened to old hat! A condemnation of something very much outmoded: late C19–20. I heard it used in 1973 by a distinguished Professor of English Language. Decreasingly employed since *c.* 1955. (A reminder by Fernley O. Pascoe, 1975.)

it's on us. The police – or, in prison, the warders – are here, i.e. at the scene of the crime or the trouble: underworld: since *c.* 1920.

it's only a game becomes a c.p. when it is applied to some incident or situation that's anything but a game: since the late 1940s. (Skehan, 1977.) See also it's a game!

it's only human nature, after all! L.A., 1975, writes, '[A] Palliation of "youthful indiscretion" or [of] coarseness in social context. [Perhaps] from well-known verse:

It's only human nature, after all,
For a boy to take a girl against the wall,
And increase the population
Of the rising generation,
By rubbing embrocation

Into her communication –
It's only human nature, after all.
I can vouch for [its currency during] the 1920s: and in all probability going back to [late] Victorian times'. R.S., who added lines 5 and 6, dates them as current in the late 1920s. Here, *communication* is elliptical for *communication trench*, thus clarifying the pun. Therefore, the c.p. prob. dated, among the soldiery, in 1916 or even 1915.

For the period, cf here you are then!, and for semantics, cf man can't 'elp 'is feelings, can 'e?

it's only lent. 'A nonchalant acceptance of defeat, either physical or moral. It is sometimes embellished with the addition, "I'll get my own back"' (Julian Franklyn, 1962): mostly Cockney: since *c.* 1920. Semantically cf it's got a back to it. 'Said to a reluctant spender or party-sharer' (Leechman): orig. (?c. 1945) Can.: by 1955, also current in UK. Also a Can., hence also Brit., c.p. 'addressed to one [including oneself] suddenly confronted with an unexpected expenditure': since the latish 1940s.

it's only money! – with 'and money is for spending' either stated or understood – is a usu. care-free, although sometimes rueful, c.p. dating from *c.* 1925; sometimes heard before the great economic depression of late 1929 – *c,* 1934; then, with irresistible optimism, revived, although not very noticeably before the mid 1940s, when, moreover, it was adopted in Britain. 'It may have been helped by the great hit, *Beggar on Horseback*, by George S. Kaufman and Marc Connelly, 1924, London, 1926' (Shipley, 1977); J.W.C. contributing.

it's polite to wait until you are asked. See don't say No....

it's pretty soft. That's very foolish; that's crazy: US: since *c.* 1912; ob. by 1945. Cited by S.R. Strait in 'Straight Talk' in the *Boston Globe* of *c.* 1917. (W.J.B.)

it's pussy and parsley. 'Two different things (based on the understanding that "nobody likes parsley")' (Ashley, 1983).

it's rabbits out of the wood. See rabbits....

it's raining in London. 'And, speaking of affecting British mannerisms and habits, who remembers when cuffs on a man's trousers brought down the jibe: "It's raining in London"?' (Robert Benchley, *My Ten Years in Quandary*, 1936, in the article headed 'As They Say in French'): US: ?c. 1920–9.

it's right up (someone's) street. 'Surely this is a common c.p.?' (Michael Goldman, 1978). It most certainly is – and since the 1920s. Cf just my alley marble.

it's rough on rats. See rough on rats.

it's sheer murder! See it's brutal!

it's showery! See what a shower!

it's snowing down south is an Aus. feminine c.p. addressed to one whose slip is showing: during the late 1940s and the 1950s, but rapidly less since then. Perhaps it was suggested by the English schoolchildren's it's snowing in Paris, current since *c.* 1919 and recorded by Iona and Peter Opie in *The Lore and Language of Schoolchildren*, 1959; on the other hand, it may have gone to Aus. from the US (Berrey). 'It was current in New Jersey in the 1930s, as a feminine c.p.' (R.C., 1978). But much more widely known than that in the US: for instance, Raymond A. Sokolov, reviewing the first ed. of this book, in *The New York Times*, 2 Oct. 1977, says 'I can confirm, from personal experience, that the phrase was also current then [*c.* 1950] among children in Detroit'.

it's so cold it'd freeze the balls... See cold enough...

it's staring you in the face; if it had teeth it would bite you; if it were a black snake, you'd be dead. 'The three phrases are used when a person is looking for an object in plain view' (B.P.): C20. The first, going back, I suspect, to mid C19, is English; the third is Aus.; the second is fairly gen. – and should be compared with if it were a bear, it would bite you, recorded separately.

it's that man again! was, during the late 1930s, frequently applied to the machinations of Hitler, the *Daily Express* always referring to him as *that man*: and when Tommy Handley, aided by his brilliant script-writer, Ted Kavanagh, and the equally brilliant producer, Frank Worsley, inaugurated his radio show under the title of 'ITMA' ('It's That Man Again') these words immediately achieved national fame – and the linguistic status of Catch Phrase; the radio show ran from 19 Sep. 1939 until Handley's death in latish 1949. See esp. Ted Kavanagh's biography, *Tommy Handley*, 1948, and Frank Worsley's *Itma*, 1948; and cf the entry TOMMY HANDLEY CATCH PHRASES.

In his instructive and entertaining *Laughter in the Air*, 1976, Barry Took writes what serves as a chronologically modificatory note: 'The show [ITMA] was called after the 1939 catchphrase that related to Hitler's sinister antics of the time: whenever the Führer made a new threatening speech or made some new territorial demand, the newspapers would head the report "It's That Man Again"' and Francis Worsley seized on this as his title'. In short, the almost immediate success of the show reinforced the impact of the journalistic c.p.

'I never see recorded...that this well-known Hitler and, ultimately, ITMA, gag did not spring out of thin air in reference to Hitler, but was adopted from a 1930s' American line which...floated in and out of my awareness; never a by-word in this country before it became enshrined as an anti-Hitler joke. The joke-reference had to do with the basic situation of mummy's boy friend being innocently identified by a child – "Mummy, it's that man again" – as once more he comes calling while daddy is out' (Wedgewood, 1977). But then Shipley writes, 'My recollection [of "Mummy, it's..., in the US] is that it began, not as a story or a joke, but as a caption to a cartoon' – which he cautiously dates as belonging to the early 1930s.

it's the beer speaking or **talking** is C20 public-house wit addressed not only to one who breaks wind in public-house company but also to one who speaks boastfully or extravagantly. A.B. notes of the belch or fart provoked phrase, that it may be elab. to *there's more room for it out here than in there* (speaker pointing to, or patting, the stomach): commoner in US than in UK: Prob. throughout C20. P.B.: the Brit. version of the latter is more succinct: *better out than in*, q.v. at **better an empty house**... Cf **it's a poor arse**...

it's the berries. It's superlative or remarkable: US, 'common *c.* 1920 – *c.* 1930 student use....Archaic' (W & F). It passed to Can., where apparently extant: 'By no means recent' (Leechman, 1968). Perhaps from the attractive colour of many berries. 'And taste! Now dead in US' (R.C., 1978).

it's the change before death. 'Very ironical. Someone has eaten out of character, e.g. a mean man generously. A Liverpool usage still' (Shaw, 1968): C20. A play on 'the change of life'. P.B.: surely rather on 'a death-bed repentance'.

it's the gipsy (or **gypsy**) **in me** is a C20 US c.p., applied to impetuous acts, such as an impulse to carry on a wild, reckless love affair, but also to an insatiable desire to travel or to be constantly on the move. (W.J.B., 1977.)

it's the greatest thing since sliced bread. A 'c.p. to describe any useful novelty. Current and widespread in the army (? and beyond) for at least fifteen years' (P.B., 1974): yes, beyond, although never very widespread: since, I think. *c.* 1950.

It has the variants ...*chewing gum* or ...*fried bread* or ...*canned beans*, though none is perhaps as common as the, prob. US, orig. Skehan, 1977, adds what he ranks as the best, ...*a leather arse*, which he thinks might be an infantryman's admiration for a cavalryman 'of long sitting'.

Sanders, 1978, notes pertinently that this c.p. has another aspect: 'Often ironic, sliced bread being a convenience food that is not to everyone's taste'.

See also **best thing since**...

it's the only game in town. 'The course of action under discussion is attractive, but there's no alternative. From the classic anecdote of the faro addict who announces that he plans to sit in on a particular game. His friend points out that the game is notoriously crooked. "I know," is the rueful answer, "but it's the only game in town." Although faro is

now virtually extinct, [the c.p. presumably dates from 1900 or earlier] the phrase itself is "alive and well" (R.C., 1978).

it's the pits. 'Referred first to a place, but now to almost anything, e.g. a plan of action, regarded by the speaker as the ultimate in objectionableness...I am pretty sure that it was originally a euphemism for – or rather, a mollification of – "It's the ass-hole of the universe", *pits* being *armpits*. Never *armpits* and never *pit*, and never *of the universe*' (J.W.C., 1979): US, since *c.* 1976; some use in UK since *c.* 1980. P.B.: but *armpit* was in use in the US in the 1970s: *The Second Barnhart Dict. of New English*, 1980, cites examples from 1973, 'the armpit of America', and 1978, 'the armpit of Indiana'.

it's the poor as 'elps the poor is a Cockney c.p. that, prob. dating from *c.* 1850, became, *c.* 1920, a Cockney proverb – though I shouldn't swear to it that it has yet been enshrined in the dictionaries of proverbs. Cf the Japanese proverb, 'It's the poor who give alms to the poor'.

it's the poor what gets the blame. L.A., 1977, reminds us that this c.p. is 'unadulterated Cockney', from the dirge – always, in later C20, sung with an exaggerated Cockney accent – concerning that poor but honest maiden who succumbed to the Squire's whim, lost her honest name, was taken further advantage of by a bloated bishop and a labour leader, and finally ended her tragic life by jumping into the Thames at midnight. The chorus goes:

It's the same the whole world over:
It's the poor what gets the blame.
It's the rich what gets the pleasure;
Ain't it all bloomin' shame.

Dating is prob. from late C19, to judge from the *dramatis personae*. The first line of the chorus is also something of a c.p. (D.R. Bartlett; P.B.)

it's the same difference, often shortened to **same difference!** and even to **same diff!** There *is* no difference – it's precisely the same thing!: the long forms are Can. and date from *c.* 1940, the shortest are Aus., since *c.* 1945. (The first, Leechman; the latter, B.P.) Lovett, 1978, remarks that a mostly Aus. nuance is 'Don't expect me to share your pedantic concern for the distinction'. P.B.: the first two forms are also of course Brit. R.C. suggests an orig. in the conflation of 'It's the same thing' and 'there's no difference'. See also **no difference!**

it's the same the whole world over. See **it's the poor**...

[**it's the thought that counts,** said when a gift is of very little value, is a conventional cliché that, by the late 1960s, was fast becoming a satirical cliché.]

it's time I wasn't here. I ought to have departed before now; also *it's time you weren't here*, you ought...: an expression often used, e.g. when one is still present after 'knocking-off time': C20. (P.B.)

it's time to get the shit out of Dodge. See **who wouldn't sell a farm**...

it's two bob to a pinch of shit. See **it's London to a brick**...

it's turned out nice again! 'George Formby disclaimed any credit for originating the phrase with which he always opened his act and which became the title of one of his films in 1941. "It's simply a familiar Lancashire expression," he once said' (*VIBS*). The phrase is forever connected in my mind with a seaside postcard remembered by my father: it formed the caption to a sketch of a dog smugly regarding a fresh turd on a pavement (P.B.).

it's up for grabs. See **up for grabs.**

it's up there you want it. See **that's where you want it.**

it's weird, man!; var. **it's a weird scene!** 'Hippie-type slang that caught on with more conservative types in the 1960s to the present' (A.B., 1978).

it's what your right arm's for is addressed to someone raising a flagon or a large glass (a 'jar') of a 'long' drink, notably beer: since, if I remember rightly, the 1920s. (Mrs Shirley M. Pearce, 1975.) Nigel Rees, in *Slogans*, 1982, writes, 'Courage Tavern; UK, current 1972. Although this line became a popular catchphrase it risks being applied to rival products, whereas the earlier *Take Courage* (current 1966) clearly does not'.

it's winning the war, often prec. by **anyway,** is an ironic, usu. cynical, often bitter c.p. applied to anything, esp. an order or a task, disliked intensely: army: 1915–18. F&G.

it's wonderful how they make guns, let alone touch-holes. 'A c.p. used by women ... to deflate male superiority, especially about sex' (L.A., 1967): mostly in Service circles: late C19–20. The erotic imagery of gunnery (as e.g., in the WW2 film. *Target for Tonight*) is involved: *gun*, penis, and *touch-hole*, vulva.

it's your ball. The initiative lies with you: Can.: since *c*. 1946. From ball games: 'The ball's in your court, so play it.' (Leechman.) It has a UK counterpart: *your bird, I think*, which comes from grouse-shooting, but is, as R.C., 1978, opines, 'only marginally a c.p.' P.B.: E.P. was rather behind the times here: *your bird* is ob., if not †, and belonged to a restricted social milieu, whereas *the ball's in your court* has been very widely used – *ad nauseum* in the Forces, mid-1950s–mid 70s–though may now, early 1980s, be on the wane.

it's your corner. It's your turn to pay (for, e.g., a round of drinks): underworld and near-underworld: since *c*. 1930.

(Powis, *The Signs of Crime*, 1977.) For *corner* itself, see *Underworld*.

it's your funeral. See **your funeral.**

it's your pal you have to watch is applied to the act, or the words, of a friend: since the late 1940s. Shaw, 1969, compares Richard Crossman's remark, made in that year, about Labour MPs: 'With friends like mine, you don't need enemies' – itself an allusion to the proverb, 'With a Hungarian for a friend, who needs an enemy?'

'Crossman's remark ... in fact embodies the "standard" US version: *with friends like that, who needs enemies?* [q.v.] ... current since the 1940s; now often curtailed to *with friends like that*. Probably adopted from Yiddish: cf "God save us from our friends, we can take care of our enemies!" Here, however, the reference is not to treachery but to counter-productive "help". Some American use since 1930s, but now obsolescent' (R.C., 1978). To which might be added two related comments: Chaucer's famous 'The smylere with the Knyf under the cloke', and C.J. Dennis's 'Never introduce your donah [girlfriend] to a pal' – which has been an Aus. c.p. since 1915 – or earlier. P.B.: therefore see **never introduce ...**

it's your pigeon. See **your pigeon.**

itch. See: does your nose; my nose; standing; what's itching.

J

Jack. See: can't sleep; come ashore; fuck you, J.; high, low; hit the road; like Jack; sod you; swing that.

Jack doesn't care and Jack loves a fight are C20, mostly RN, c.pp., referring, the former to the seaman's infectious insouciance, the latter to his love of a scrap, esp. fisticuffs.

jack-knife carpenter! is 'a cry of derision hurled at a man, especially a carpenter, who uses a pocket knife in an emergency. Legend has it that all jack-knife carpenters end up in hell' (Leechman): Can.: since c. 1910; by 1960, ob.

Jack loves a fight. See Jack doesn't care.

Jack's come home is a theatrical c.p., applied to a happy-go-lucky, slapdash hotel or boarding house: C20. It occurs in, e.g. Ngaio Marsh, *Vintage Murder*, 1938.

Jackson. See: it's gone; jammed; steady, J.

jails. See: all the jails; forty exits; see you in court; worse in.

Jake. See: she'll be j.; that's jake.

jam. See: all jam; d'you want; it's always; it's money; kick out; that accounts; what do you want.

James. See: home, James.

Jameson. See: whoa, J.

jammed like Jackson. A late C19–20 RN c.p., used when something leads to disaster or goes less, although still, seriously wrong; rather less common since c. 1945. From one John Jackson who, in 1787, refused to listen to his pilot and consequently went close to wrecking his ship. (F&G) The earliest record of the c.p. I have occurs in W.N. Glascock, *Naval Sketch-Book* (chapter II, p. 136), 1826, 'Jackson's story is elaborated in the *Letters and Papers of Admiral of the Fleet Sir Thomas Byam Martin GCB* (Navy Records Society, 1903, pp. 106–7): – as Rear-Adm. P.W. Brock informs me. Cf up Shit Creek.

Jane. See: me Tarzan.

January. See: molasses in.

jar. See: wouldn't that jar.

jaw. See: like a sheep's.

jazz. See: and all that j.

jealous. See: you're jealous.

Jeeves. See: carry on.

Jericho. See: well, I'll go.

Jerry. See: stick it, J.; walls of.

Jerusalem. See: all jam; since Jesus.

Jessie. See: more arse.

jest. See: I love my j.

Jesus. See: since J.

Jesus saves, (but) Moses invests is 'an irreverent answer' to the over-evangelistic: US: later C20. (Ashley, 1984.)

Jesus wants me for a sunbeam, and a bloody fine sunbeam I'll be is 'the troops' [soldiers'] version of a sacred hymn' (anon., 1978): since the 1930s(?). P.B.: the hymn parodied is by Nellie Talbot; it appears, e.g., as No. 100 in *The Methodist School Hymnal* (Primary Department and Infant School), where occurs also, as No. 73, 'Jesus loves me! this I know,/For the Bible tells me so', altered by 'the troops' to *Jesus loves me! Yes, I know! So does Ragtime Cowboy Joe*. No. 73 is by Anna Warner. Hymnals such as this would, in the days when attendance at Sunday School was much more widespread than it is now, have provided a common background of musical experience for many servicemen. I surmise that the dating of these parodies is earlier than E.P. allows, perhaps pre-WW1.

Jew(s). See: cold enough; some of my.

jib. See: long may; more wind; never let it.

jig is up – the. The game is up – All is discovered: US: c. 1860–1920. George P. Barnham, in his very readable *Memoirs*, 1872.

Jim. See: hello, Jim; I'm worried.

Jim Smith. See: I'll give you.

jingle. See: hasn't got a ha'penny.

job(s). See: blue-stockinged; gissa; it only wanted; just the job; that job's; there's another; wish I; you'll do; you're fond; and:

job and finish. 'When a ship did not have much cargo the dockers would work the holds until the job was done, [thus] getting a double stamp on their [pay-] books' (W. Ash, glossary to *Childhood Days* [n.d., late 1970s], on life as a London docker). Not peculiar to dockers, of course; used in other occupations where piece-work is the rule.

jobs for the boys has become a lighthearted c.p., synon. with 'nepotism'. But orig. it was a political, hence soon a semi-political, c.p., that was current while Leslie Hore-Belisha was Minister of Transport (1934–7); it could, however, have arisen early, for every Minister and every Government is, by the nature of things, wide open to such charges; some, admittedly, more than others. (David Hardman, 1974.)

'A c.p. that is used by and of members of the Australian Labor Party' (B.P., 1975).

Jock(s). See: stand to; stop yer.

jockey(s). See: Confucius; them's the j.

Joe. See: get up, J.; have a go, J.; just tell 'em; knock three times; not for Joseph; say it ain't so; Uncle Joe; what do you know, J.

Joe Miller. See: I don't see.

Joe sent me. See knock three times ...

John. See: easy as shaking; old John; speak for.

John Bull. See: write.

John Hughes won't save yer! See LIVERPOOL CATCH PHRASES.

John Orderly! (or Audley!) is a US circus people's command to hurry: C20. (Recorded in Berrey and elsewhere.) By a sort of hasty or slapdash disguising of *order!* – i.e., come to order, and get moving!

John Whoball. See: he is none.

Johnnie Walker. See: still going strong.

Johnson. See: I'll venture.

Johnstown flood. See: don't spit.

join. See: George!; if you can't beat; if you can't take; she's joined; you shouldn't have.

join the army and see the world: the next world! A ruefully joc. gibe uttered by disgruntled soldiers: since *c.* 1948. Poking fun at the recruiting slogan, 'Join the army and see the world'.

'In the US 1920s, it was "Join the Navy and see the world" (on recruiting posters), which seems to have become a short-lived c.p.' (R.C., 1978). P.B.: so cf the chorus from the musical show *Anchors Aweigh*, 1945: 'We joined the Navy to see the world; and what did we see? We saw the sea!'

join the back of the queue! is addressed to someone slow – esp. if exceedingly slow – in the uptake: since *c.* 1948; by 1970 ob. (Petch, 1966.) Exactly synon. is **go to the back of the class!** Prob. since the 1920s and certainly possessing greater vitality.

join the club! Mrs Camilla Raab comments, 1977: '1. An invitation to join a group, for drinks, or in a discussion, "or whatever". – 2. An expression of sympathy over a commonly held experience ("I had to wait ages" or "The boss was mad at me", etc.)' Both Brit. and, slightly more often, US: since late 1940s. (R.C. and, independently, A.B, 1978.) Perhaps orig. from that 'club' listed at **she's joined ...** , q.v. Cf **get on line!**

join up! Get some service in!: fighting Services: since *c.* 1925. An elab. of the simple synon. injunction, *join!* H&P.

join? when I get out of this (lot), they won't get me to join a Christmas club! Forces': WW2.

joined the club or **the family – she's** (occ. prec. by **that girl's**). See **she's joined....**

joint(s). See: I've been thrown; let's case; what's a nice; and:

joint is jumping – the. The place – the building or the hall – is very lively: among US 'pop' music lovers, esp. teenagers: late 1930s–40s. (Berrey.) Mr Eric Townley, author of *Tell Your Story: A History of Jazz and Blues Recordings, 1917–1950*, 1976, amends the entry thus: 'Not really US "pop" lovers but swing music enthusiasts'. Cab Calloway includes it in his *New Hepster's Dictionary*, 1944.

joke. See: couldn't see; if you can't take; that's a j.; you're joking; and:

joke (or joke's) over! This **and when do we laugh?** are sarcastic c.pp. addressed to the maker of a feeble witticism: since *c.* 1925. The former is sometimes said by the joker himself when he sees that his wit has misfired.

joker. See: some deck.

jolly D! See **oh, jolly D!**

jolly hockey sticks! Mr Peter Sanders, in 1968, says:

One c.p., a great favourite in the family, is 'Jolly hockey-sticks!'–our 16-year-old daughter's riposte to anything smacking of tradition or convention. She picked it up last year at her school, Dartington Hall. 'Jolly-hockeysticks' was recently used as an adjective 'The jolly-hockeysticks image...' (of compulsory games) in the *Sunday Times*, 13 October 1968.

The phrase is mildly derisive of the jolly, hearty, games-loving atmosphere encouraged in many British girls' Public Schools: and it provided the title of a 'middle' in the *Evening News* of 7 May 1973.

Nigel Rees, in *VIBS*, gives its source: 'originally an expression used by Monica, Archie's schoolgirl friend, in *Educating Archie* [, the BBC radio comedy series of later 1940s– early 50s]. Coined by Beryl Reid, the actress, who modestly proclaims: "I can't write comedy material ... but I know what sort of thing my characters should say!" In this case she lighted upon a masterly phrase which has passed into the language'.

Jolly Jack. See: I'm Jolly.

Jones. See: keeping up; that boy.

Joseph. See: not for J.

Josephine. See: not tonight, J., pas ce soir.

Josephus Rex. See: you're joking.

journey. See: is your j.

joy. See: any joy; dirty mind; lady with.

joy-ride. See: give your face.

judge. See: gentleman; here come; silence.

Judy Fitzsimmons. See: don't make a J.

Jumbo. See: lend us your breath.

jump. See: go jump; joint is; spring; take a running; when he says.

jumper. See: oompah.

June too-too belongs to the year 1897 only: 22 June was the sixtieth anniversary of Queen Victoria's reign: a non-aristocratic, would-be smart-set c.p., punning '22' and satirizing the 'too-too' vogue initiated by the Aesthetes and promptly aped by social aspirants. Ware.

Jupiter Pluvius has got out (or **put on** or **turned on**) **his watercan** is a c.p. circumlocution for 'It is raining', applied mostly to a heavy shower: since *c.* 1870; ob. by 1920 and † by 1940.

[**jury – hang half and save half.** The jury may be **a Kentish –** or **a London –** or **a Middlesex** jury: respectively C18–19, late C18–mid C19, C17–19. The implication, as dramatist Middleton suggested of the prototypal third form is: 'Thou ... will make haste to give up thy verdict, because thou wilt not lose thy dinner.' Recorded by Apperson, it is either a semi-proverbial c.p. or orig. a proverbial saying that became also a c.p.]

just. See: it's just; sleep of; yes, but only.

just a crazy mixed-up kid. See **crazy mixed-up kid.**

just a trick of the light. See **oh, it's nothing ...**

just fancy (or **just fancy that!**) A c.p. either indicating one's own astonishment or admiration or inviting one's interlocutor to admire or to be astonished by something or other: C20. In either sort, it is sometimes very ironical.

In *Design for Living*, written *c.* 1932 and pub'd 1933, Noël Coward, in III, i, has:

HELEN [*social poise well to the fore*]: It's funny how people alter; only the other day in the Colony a boy that I used to know when he was at Yale walked up to my table, and I didn't recognize him!

LEO: Just fancy!·

Helen is American, and Leo maliciously ironic. A c.p. dating from *c.* 1880 – or perhaps much earlier. Both forms are elaborations of the exclamatory *fancy!*

just for the hell of it. See **for the hell of it.**

just for the record. Let me make – *or* thereby to make – my position clear; Let's get things straight!: since *c.* 1955 in UK. Cf the Standard US 'I wish to go on record as saying ...'; this, as R.S. points out, 1977, 'is verbatim Standard German *Ich möchte zu Protokoll geben*, but which came first, I do not know'. But the prob. genesis is this: *to keep the record straight*; then more colloquially, *just to keep the record straight*; whence the entirely coll. *just for the record*. Petch remarked, 1969, that it seems to have orig. among policemen.

just goes to show (you) – it or **that.** A C20 cliché (the US version more commonly *it all goes to show*, when, as J.W.C., 1977, remarks, 'it does nothing of the kind'), included here only because of the joc., deliberate perversion current in UK and Aus. since *c.* 1930: *it* or *that just* or *only shows to go* (*you*).

just give me the facts, ma'am. See **all we want is the facts ...**

just got off the boat, usu. prec. by **he** or **she** or **they.** 'Said of someone just arrived and ignorant of the place': US: perhaps since *c.* 1890. 'It is still used, but infrequently now' (A.B., 1978). Cf **came over with the banana boat.**

just in time; or, born in the vestry! is, obviously, applied to a wedding held only just in time to prevent the coming child from being adjudged illegitimate: C20. It 'has lost some of its sting now that legitimacy no longer depends on being born in wedlock' (Sanders, 1968). P.B.: perhaps modelled on typical Victorian novel-titles.

just like a midshipman's chest: everything on top and nothing handy is the full, orig. version of **everything on top and**

nothing handy: RN, mostly officers': since *c.* 1890. Recorded in *SS*, the shorter form; the full form was communicated to me, 1968, by Rear-Adm. P.W. Brock.

just like Roger was a short-lived voguish c.p. of the 1870s. Benham glosses it thus: 'In reference to the Tichborne trial, 1872.' A famous trial, spectacularly notorious.

Just like that! See **not like that...**

just my alley-marble or **cup of tea** (or **cuppa**) or **handwriting!**, sometimes prec. by **it's** or **that's.** I can do that with the utmost ease; but also 'That's right up my street', it suits me, pleases me, I'm delighted with it: C20. Also applied to other people, and used in other tenses or moods: *that'd be just her cup of tea*; *it was just his alley marble*; etc. Cf **just the job** and **right up my alley**, and see also **that's just my handwriting.**

just one of those days. See **it's just...**

just one of those things. See **it's just one of those things.**

just part of the Austin Reed service, I suppose? was current in the 1930s: and it arose in, as well as partly making good-natured fun of, Messrs Austin Reed's advertising slogan. Since *c.* 1950, the predominant form has been **it's all** (or **just**) part of the service.

just start something! That is, 'If you're looking for trouble': US: C20; adopted in UK *c.* 1944. Cited by S.R. Strait in 'Straight Talk' in the *Boston Globe* of *c.* 1917. (W.J.B.)

just tell 'em Joe sent you. A US c.p. of the early 1920s. 'Probably an instruction on how to get into a speakeasy during Prohibition' (fain, 1969).

just the hammer! Contemporaneous var. of:

just the job! That, or this, is exactly what I need (or needed) *or*

want (or wanted): fighting Services: since *c.* 1935; by 1950, in fairly gen. civilian use. H&P.

just the job for my brother from Gozo. Try to get someone else – Not for *me*!: RN: *c.* 1860–1914. Gozo is one of the Maltese islands – and many Maltese were, until *c.* 1970, employed by the navy. Cf **not me, Sare....**

just the ticket. A var. of **that's the ticket.**

just under the wire. See **got in just...**

just watch it, that's all! '[The comedian] Eric Morecambe admonishing Little Ern [his partner Ernie Wise] and grabbing him by the lapels' (*VIBS*). From the familiar blustering threat of the lower-class bully. (P.B.)

just what the doctor ordered is a c.p. of unqualified approval, applied to anything particularly suitable or relevant, or to anything exceptionally good or unexpectedly agreeable: C20.

In his *Itma*, 1948, Francis Worsley wrote, concerning 'ITMA's' visit to Scapa Flow in January 1944, 'Everything we did on the spur of the moment seemed to be just what the doctor ordered, and from then on we knew we had the best audience in the world': a quot'n that, better than any generalization, exemplifies how very much part of the language this particular c.p. had become.

A US example occurs in Jean Potts. *An Affair of the Heart*, 1970: ' "Thanks for everything, Gene. You're just what the doctor ordered." ' And on 26 Feb. 1972, it figures in an advertisement in the *New Yorker*.

Justice. See: there ain't no. J.

Justice Child. See: I'll do J.

jute mill. See back to the J.

K

Kaiser. See: 'alf a mo; hang the K.
Kamerad! See ONE-WORD CATCH PHRASES.
kangaroos in (one's) **top paddock**; esp. *he has ... his ...* To be very eccentric or extremely silly; to be crazy: Aus.: C20. Wilkes quotes the *Australian Magazine*, 1 Nov. 1908, 'If you show signs of mental weakness, you are either balmy, dotty, ratty or cracked, or you may even have white ants in your attic or kangaroos in your top paddock'; S.J. Baker lists it in 1947; Dal Stivens employs it in one of his stories, 1946. By 1970, it had become ob. Perhaps because, at times, to jump about like persons restlessly nervous. P.B.: or simply an inventive Aus. var. of the synon. Brit. *bats in the belfry.*
keep. See: fetch; I'd rather k.; I'm keeping; if this keeps; it's being so; you'll keep.
keep a cow. See: why buy a book.
keep 'em barefoot and pregnant! 'Semi-proverbial recipe for marital happiness ... [an example of] masculine collousness towards women – now, happily, all but extinct' (R.C., 1978): since *c.* 1915. Cf **catch 'em young ...**
keep him (or it) **in: he'll get pecking if let out** is a low, mostly N. Country c.p. addressed to a man with his flies open: late C19–20. A pun on *cock*; cf the US sense of *pecker*. In the US, 'Sometimes followed, or displaced, by *The barn door is open ...* dating back to the 1930s, at least' (A.B., 1978). Clearly rural in origin, it prob. goes back to late C19.
keep it clean! and, later, **keep the party clean!** The former, since the early 1920s and ob. by 1960; the latter, since *c.* 1930. Don't talk smut or tell dirty stories; don't act loosely or indelicately. A correspondent, *c.* 1965, commented thus: 'But the speaker often does not quite mean it. "Give me my hat and knickers," she said, "I thought you were going to keep the party clean."'
   The first form is, in US, 'far from obsolescent, though the variant "Let's keep it clean" is a good deal commoner. Almost always, jestingly, used especially when one has inadvertently used a *double entendre*' (J.W.C., 1977).
keep it dark! Keep it secret: underworld: *c.* 1830–70. Cited in *The Vulgar Tongue*, by 'Ducange Anglicus', i.e. John Camden Hotten, in 1857; this little-known work amounted to a 'trial run' for *The Slang Dictionary*, 1859. See also **hush! keep it dark!**, and cf **keep that under your hat.**
   In the US, 'sometimes "keep jark!" – from Mark Twain's *Tom Sawyer*' (A.B., 1978). Ob. by late 1970s. This *jark* is something of a mystery: just possibly a rhyme on *keep it dark*, or perhaps going back to Brit. *jark it* (see *Underworld*).
keep it on the deck! and **keep it on the Island** (or, later, **island**)! are synon., the former RN only, the latter RN in orig. and gen. in usage.
   The former, C20; the latter, since *c.* 1895. 'Naval football supporters' cry when the ball goes too often into touch' (Granville, for *deck*); and for *Island,* Granville remarks that 'When football matches were played on Whale Island,

Portsmouth, in the old days, the ball occasionally went into the water when it found touch.' On 17 Jan. 1944, Frank Butler, in the *Daily Express*, spoke feelingly of 'That monotonous "Keep it on the island" when the ball is banged into the grandstand to clear a dangerous position'.
keep moving! See **push on, keep moving.**
keep off the grass! Be careful!; Be cautious! – often in playful sexual ref. to a male paying attention to a girl regarded by the speaker as his own property: late C19–20; by 1960, ob.; and by 1970, virtually †. Orig. it was proletarian. It derives from notices in parks and elsewhere.
keep on smiling! See **keep smiling!**
keep on truckin'! As the Salvation Army puts it, 'Keep *on* keeping on': since the 1930s. Basically 'Keep moving!' Ben Grauer, on Christmas Day 1975, explained it as 'Keep on doing what you're doing; especially, encouraging or approving a vigorous or self-assertive action'; he adds, 'Originated by Negro dancers and spread to Whites.' US: it derives from the name of a dance popular in the 1930s. Writing to me in 1974 and 1975, Norris M. Davidson and Joseph T. Shipley say it is a † phrase. 'Comes from the great marathon dance contests that were a part of our 1930s scene, when all the partners clung to one another, half-asleep, but on and on moving around the dance hall through the night, like the great trucks that go endlessly across our continent through the dark hours, as they "keep on truckin" for the prize' (Shipley, 1975).
   'Little used by educated people, even in their relaxed moments; I think they merely regard it as vulgar and tiresome...I should classify it as merely (voguish and probably evanescent) slang ... Current among the vulgar and the young' (J.W.C., 1975). And later in 1975, John Browning, US citizen, London bookseller, two-worlds poet, classified it as (having become) a hippies', as well as a teenagers', c.p.
   J.W.C., writing on it again in 1977, noted, '*pace* Davidson and Dr Shipley, far from obsolescent', a point confirmed by Paul Janssen, 1978: 'My Californian pen friend John H. Escalona ... used it to conclude his letter of May 23. He adds, "Not considered vulgar among young relaxed, hang-loose Americans". (John in 23.)'
   But Eric Townley, 1978, disagrees with the orig. proposed above: '*Truckin*' was a song written for the "Cotton Club Parade of 1935" by Ted Koehler and Marty Bloom and the dance was originally at the Cotton Club, but soon became very popular with Negro dancers generally. All that about marathon dances is incorrect, as *Truckin*' was a fast-tempo dance which could not be performed by anyone half-asleep; and, by that time (1935), marathon dances had, I am reasonably sure, died out. Later, the word *truckin*' was used was used for any sort of lively dancing.'
   A notable example of its post-1970 usage occurs in Cyra

McFadden, *The Serial: A Year in the Life of Marin County* [in California], pub'd on 23 June 1977 and attaining its 7th printing in the following September: at once a glorious 'send-up' and a true-to-life satire:

'... Calling over her shoulder her thanks for the lift [in his car] and an uninflected "Keep on truckin'"'.

Yet there *is* a link with *truckers* (long-distance lorry drivers): 'The 1970s vogue for pick-up trucks (light-weight lorries with closed cab but open back) has given this [c.p.] a new lease on life, as, for example, a bumper-sticker – seen 1977' (R.C., 1978) – and seen *c.* 1980 in UK (P.B.).

keep (or **keep on**) **smiling!** was a sort of morale-boosting slogan during WW1, but some of us got a little tired of it and used it, either ironically or bitterly, in direct allusion to the slogan, with the implication 'That's kids' stuff!'. Rather like being expected to *grin and bear it* (cliché) – as if, often, it's more than enough, just having to experience and suffer it.

[P.B.: as E.P. wrote, indomitably, during his last illness, 'I can bear it – but I don't have to damn' well grin!']

'There was a song in the 1940s (I think) with this title. I heard Bing Crosby and the Andrews Sisters sing it on Crosby's "Philco Radio Time" show. Others sang it too; Nat King Cole made a recording of it in the 1950s' (A.B., 1978).

keep taking the tablets! Apparently from either a radio or a TV show: 'The Goon Show' or Morecambe and Wise: ?late 1960s or early 1970s. P.B.: in the late 1970s advertisers for Pilsener Lager used the allusive slogan 'Keep on taking the Pils!'

keep that in ... and at the matinée! That's worth repeating: theatrical: since *c.* 1910. 'This greets the introduction of any felicitous gag, or business that amused the company at rehearsals or was tried out during a performance'; *and at the matinée* is 'employed if the gag is exceptionally brilliant' (Granville).

keep that under your hat! That's strictly confidential: late C19 – 20; by 1975, slightly ob. – like hats.

Also *keep it under your hat*, which was 'a repeated phrase in a song recorded by Jack Hulbert and Cecily Courtnidge' – *c.* 1925. Lovett, 1978, quotes:

'Keep it under your hat!
You must agree to do that.
Promise not to breathe a word,
In case it should be overheard.
I saw a horseshoe by the way.
You picked it up without delay!
No, the horse stood on it the whole damn' day!
But keep it under your hat!'

'Keep it under your hat (in US, Stetson)!' was, like 'keep it dark!', a security slogan of WW2 when 'Walls had ears'. (Nigel Rees, *Slogans*, 1982.)

keep the change! You're welcome! *or* Not at all!: US: since early C20; ob. by 1977. (J.W.C., improving upon Berrey.)

keep the faith, baby. 'Be hopeful and steadfast!' A US c.p., uttered at a parting, esp. between friends: popularized, W&F tell us, during the mid-1960s, by Adam Clayton Powell after his expulsion from Congress; they add that the phrase was orig. Negro. But surely the orig. was religious, and prob. it was evangelical, not, as such, necessarily Negro. 'However current it may have been for a short while, I don't think it is[so] now' (J.W.C., 1976); 'Rarely heard during the past several years' (Moe, 1976).

It often occurs without *baby*, as, for instance in Hank Searls, *Pentagon*, 1976, '"Keep the faith, Morrie. That's all I can say."' Only one year earlier, Stanley Ellin, *The Man from Nowhere*, has one insurance investigator say to another: '"I'll leave it to you, Jake," ... "Keep the faith, baby."'

keep the party clean! See **keep it clean!**

keep the tambourine a-rolling! Keep things moving and lively: Londoners': *c.* 1830 – 70. See the Surtees quot'n (*Handley Cross*, 1854) at **all round my hat!**

keep this shut and those open. 'Keep your mouth shut and your eyes open!' – with appropriate gestures. 'Mainly in underworld use as advice' (Petch, 1969). Since *c.* 1945 (?). Cf **keep your bowels ...**

keep up, old queen! was, in late C19 – mid C20, but ob. by 1930 and † by 1940, a c.p. of farewell 'addressed by common women to a sister being escorted into a prison van' (Ware.)

keep up your pecker. Occ. for **keep your pecker up!**

keep yer 'earts up, lads! As an expression of civilian goodwill shouted to soldiers on leave in 1914 – 18, it clearly isn't eligible; but abused, among soldiers, by the soldiers themselves, it does qualify, for it was then ironic and was often accompanied by a muttered *if yer belly trails the ground.*

keep your bowels open, your mouth shut, and never volunteer! Advice, *c.* 1920 onwards, to someone joining the Army. Distilled wisdom from memories of WW1. (A reminder, 1979, from Yehouda Mindel.) Quite independently, Ashley attests for the US, 'Advice to soldiers in WW1 (and after)'. P.B.: by *c.* 1950 at latest, reduced, in the British Forces, to *never volunteer for anything!*

keep your eye on the sparrow! A 'new c.p. from America. Presumably something to do with being aware of the evil things life and men do' (Gareth Murshallsea, assistant editor of *Books and Bookmen*, in a private communication, 1976): since 1975 or, at earliest, 1974. Clearly an allusion to bird-droppings at awkward moments – a splendid deflater of pomposity.

'Probably *not* an allusion to bird-droppings; in the US, *that* bird is the pigeon! Perhaps an allusion to Him who sees a sparrow fall' (Shipley, 1977). In short, a New Testament allusion. Cf this, from R.C., 1978: 'Certainly never common. A more likely origin is the well-known Biblical "Not a sparrow shall fall". Given new currency by the autobiography of the singer Ethel Waters, *His Eye Is on the Sparrow* [UK ed., 1951]. Any fecal hazard in American cities would far more likely come from pigeons'.

keep your eye on uncle and **watch your uncle**, where *uncle* = me. Uttered by the leader of a group, either in banter or as a leg-pull: since *c.* 1930; by 1970, rather 'old hat'.

keep your fingers crossed! dates from *c.* 1920 in UK, where it means Pray for me! *or* wish me luck, for I'll badly need it *or* let us hope that this venture will prove successful, and from *c.* 1930 in US, where – whether 'lighthearted or serious' – it means Wish me luck! (as Edward Hodnett tells me, 1975). Prob. it was orig. prompted by *make the sign of the Cross* in order to ward off bad luck.

J.W.C., 1977, amends: 'The US meaning is more commonly "I wish *you* luck"; variant, "I'll keep *my* fingers crossed"'; and R.C. remarks, 1978, 'Perhaps influenced by its use in several children's games: with one's fingers crossed, one was "safe"' – and, thus protected, one could (? can) every tell lies with impunity: 'But you said ...' – 'Ah, but I had my fingers crossed'. Also in UK, 'I wish you luck' may be expressed by 'I'll keep my fingers crossed for you' (P.B.).

keep your hair on! was, *c.* 1867 – 1913 (to judge from the evidence afforded by Benham, by Ware, and by B & P), a c.p. applied, sometimes with ludicrous incongruity to any mishap. Cf **keep your wool on!**

'As children in the 1940s we were still using these expressions a good deal' (P.B., 1976); and both of them have, in the US, acquired the widely current senses, 'Don't get excited, or unduly indignant' (J.W.C., 1977).

keep your hand on your ha'penny (till the right man turns up) is 'an old piece of advice to an unmarried girl' (Petch, 1969): *c.* 1880 – 1970, but little used since *c.* 1960. Lit. 'Keep your hand over your genitals until ...' The orig. is of linguistic interest, for Grose, 1785, has *money*, as in a domestic nurse's admonition to a female child, 'You're showing your money', in the sense 'vulva'. There is a var., *three penny bit*; and the expression acquired a secondary meaning: 'Be careful or you'll find yourself expensively involved': C20; by 1970, ob. (Skehan, 1977.)

keep your head up and your tail over the dashboard! A US c.p. of latish C19–early 20. Fain writes, 1978: 'An old horse-and-buggy expression, meaning "A good horse should keep his tail up, and when he defecates, his tail should be well up so that it won't get messy and smelly". As a c.p., it seems to have meant originally something like "Walk proud, but don't get into any trouble". In the 1920s, it was used as a goodbye expression, like "Don't do anything I wouldn't"...'or "Be good"...or the modern American equivalent, "Have a good day" Not known to the present generation....It was not semi-proverbial and not predominantly rural, though not used in mixed company in those days'.

keep your legs together! is a C20 Aus. c.p., 'used to a girl. It is equivalent to "Be good!"' (B.P.). Shipley recalls that Billy Sunday (William Ashley Sunday, 1863–1935) – after a successful baseball career – became, in 1896, 'a widely known international evangelist, an earlier Billy Graham', who 'used to say, to his feminine audiences, "Cross your legs...Now that the gates of hell are closed"'. (P.B.: another version has him say, to a mixed audience, 'Ladies, cross your legs! Gentlemen, the gates of hell are now closed'.]

'Also, *keep your legs together, coming home from the Wake*, the last line of a rugger song about Mabel, who didn't and became "preggers"' (Sanders, 1978). Moreover, 'Current in US since at least the 1930s with the general sense "Don't let yourself get screwed – literally or figuratively [i.e., swindled]. Now probably obsolescent' (R.C., 1978).

keep your mind out of the sewer! See: wipe the shit off your face!

keep your nose clean, orig. proletarian and not unknown among criminals, was also an army c.p., with the special sense, 'Avoid strong drink – it gets you into trouble': late C19–20. But, by c. 1920, the army nuance had become simply 'Keep out of trouble!' – often, with an undertone of 'Mind your own business!'. All, however, are predominantly valedictory.

'Nowadays, often in advice, [as in] "I'd had enough of fooling around then, so I kept my nose clean for the next few months and along came my promotion. Now, you keep your nose clean a bit and you'll have it made"' (P.B., 1976). It is used also in the US, although not in the nuance 'Mind your own business'. (J.W.C., 1977.)

keep your pecker up! 'Don't lose courage!': since c. 1840. The *SOD* has *pecker*, courage, resolution, for 1848, and the phrase occurs in Cuthbert Bede' (Edward Bradley), 1853, 'Keep your pecker up, old fellow'; and Mr Colin Clair tells me that 'in 1857 Dickens was using the very same phrase in one of his letters'. Ernest Weekley proposed an orig. in the alert sparrow keeping its beak, hence its head up. This distinctively Brit. (metaphor and) c.p. took a long time to become a US c.p., because in American slang *pecker* has always predominantly signified the penis. So much so that, in 1976, my learned American contributor Robert Claiborne was able to describe the phrase as 'one of history's more famous (? unintentional) *double entendres*' and to add that 'this phrase was the peroration of W.S. Churchill's speech to a joint session of the US Congress and Senate during WW2. He (presumably) meant simply "maintain a courageous posture", but most of his hearers would have taken it in the American sense of "maintain an erect posture" (cf *pecker*, 4, in [*DSUE*]). At any rate, the adjuration brought down the House – and the Senate as well.' A.B., 1978, informs me that the phrase, as used in the US, has the occ. var. *keep up your pecker*, and that it is there used both sexually and non-sexually.

keep your shirt on! Don't lose your temper!; don't get over-perturbed!; don't be impatient!: throughout the English-speaking world: late C19–20. R.C., 1978, 'Ultimately, from stripping before a fight. That is, "don't be in a hurry to start fighting"'.

keep your thanks to feed your chickens! I neither need nor want your thanks: C17–mid C18; proverbial. Apperson.

keep your wool on! Don't get, or be, angry: c. 1880–1914. (B &

L.) Cf **kep your hair on,** much the commoner, more lasting, expression.

keep yourself good all through! Be – in *every* way – good: a society c.p. of 1882 – c. 1890. Ware.

keeping it. See: are you keeping.

keeping the fire warm? 'Said ironically to someone sitting so close to the fire that very little heat gets through to anyone else' (B.G.T., 1978): a domestic c.p., esp. in the country (the rural districts of England): (? mid) C19–20.

keeping up with the Joneses arose very soon after WW2 and signalized, as well as characterizing, the rapid revival of snobbery. On the marriage of Mr Anthony Armstrong-Jones, in 1960, to HRH Princess Margaret, it almost immediately, from being a cliché, became a c.p., the process accelerating on his elevation, in 1961, to the peerage.

It is perhaps the stupidest of all the stupid aspects of the social scene, this fear of possessing fewer 'status symbols' (esp. motor cars) and of otherwise appearing to be less well-off, less important, less smart, than one's neighbours and associates.

'In common US use by the 1930s and, I suspect, very much earlier. In US, "upward mobility" has always been largely a function of money, hence of visible possessions' (R.C., 1978). Mr Claiborne is right: so early as 1913, *The Globe* (New York) had the comic-strip title, 'Keeping up with the Joneses', as the *OED Second Supplement* informs us.

kefoofle. See: you'll bust.

Kelly. See: game as Ned; has anybody; Mistress K.; Ned K.; slide; you must know.

Kemp's shoes. See: would that I had.

kennel. See: back to the k.; who kicked.

kerfuffle. See: you'll bust.

kettle. See: Polly.

key. See: lost the key.

keystone under the hearth (, keystone under the horse's belly) – the second part often ommitted – was a C19 smugglers' c.p. that became proverbial, the ref. being to the concealment of contraband spirits below the fireplace or in the stable. Apperson.

kick(s). See: better than a dig; don't tear the; hope your; I only do; I wouldn't k.; no heart; there's no k.; they gotta; who kicked; and:

kick, bollock and bite! 'A character in Bethnal Green when in his cups and immediately prior to falling down the stairs at Liverpool Street Station used to holler "Kick, bollock and bite" as a warning *cum* battle cry. He was renowned for this, and the phrase attained a moderate currency in the building trade' (C.A. Worth, 1975): Londoners': C20 – probably c. 1925–50.

kick for touch! is an intimation that 'Here's a tricky situation' and a warning that 'You had better try to extricate yourself from it as soon as possible': a c.p. among Public School men and the young people moving in smart sets: since c. 1920; by 1970, slightly ob. From Rugby football. (Granville, 1968.)

kick out the jams! 'Behave freely, without inhibition!' – 'Be your natural self and to hell with it!' This, mainly youthful, US expression is recorded by W&F, 1975, and Paul Janssen, 1977, remembers seeing it often during the late 1960s, in both US and UK pop-music periodicals.

kid(s). See: crazy mixed-up; flippin'; here's looking; I kid; I love my wife; many all your k.; more kid; oh, you k.; you kid; you tell 'em, k.; you wouldn't k.

kidding. See: are you k.; cut your; no kidding; who're you k.; you're joking; you're not k.

kill. See: hate; I must have killed; lend us your breath; my feet; rectum?; that kills, that wouldn't then comes; 'tis not; you kill; you'd be killed; and:

kill another canary and give the cat a treat! Mainly a N. Country rather than a Southern Counties English c.p., dating from, roughly, the 1930s. (Ian Sainsbury, in the Sheffield *Morning Telegraph*, 5 Sep. 1977, reviewing the first ed. of this book.) Almost a domestic c.p. 'It sounds to me as though it originated in the patter of a music-hall comedian' (I.S. in a letter to me a month later). P.B.: this is a var. of **give the cat another goldfish**, q.v.

kill that baby! Switch off the spotlight: film industry: since *c.* 1930. *A baby* because it's only a small light.

kill who? was, *c.* 1870–1914, a proletarian 'satirical protest against a threat' (Ware.). Semantically of the same order as **you and who else?**

killing a snake? is a Can. golfing c.p., joc. addressed to a player taking many strokes in a sand-trap: since *c.* 1930.

Kilroy was here was at first a US WW2 c.p., recorded in HLM, Supp. 2; Mencken mentions that he knows of three theories of origin, but wisely hazards none of his own. W & F comment that it arose in 1940 and was in wide use immediately before the US entered WW2, the phrase coming to mean 'the US Army, or a soldier, was here' and it could be applied to any place anywhere. It caught on in UK and spread rapidly; by 1942, it was written on walls or other convenient places by British and US troops, no matter where they were stationed or fighting. For a tolerably credible theory, see the Appendix to *DSUE*, [E.P. later added:]

There must have been *some* topical reason for the choice of the surname *Kilroy*: and I still think that the orig. mentioned in *DSUE* is as probable as any, despite Mr R.W. Burchfield's animadversion in his review in the *New Statesman*, when the 7th ed. appeared 1970. I happen to be one of those irresponsible fellows who believe that it is better to have tried and failed than never to have tried at all.

Kilroy was here belongs to the thought-pattern type of c.p.–cf *does your mother know you're out?* Very probably the Roman legionaries scribbled *Marcus* (or whoever) *hic fuit*, and the Greeks and perhaps even the Hittites their equivalent. On the eve of banishment from Eden, Adam perhaps scratched on the bark of that apple tree *his* version of 'Adam and Eve were here'.

kind. See: as you go up; thank you for those.

kind thoughts. See: have you any.

kindly leave the stage! See **I say, I say, I say!**

kindness. See: all done by.

King. See: 'balls!'; for king; *must* is for; once a knight; one hand; shit! said; true, O king; you break.

King Kong. See: what's your song.

King of the Road! See **get off and milk it!**

King's horse – you shall have the. A c.p. directed at a liar: *c.* 1660–1840. (Apperson.) Implying that a statement, esp. a claim, was either grossly exaggerated or utterly false.

kingdom. See: horse, a horse.

kipper(s). See: couldn't knock; doesn't do; giddy.

kiss. See: fresh kiss; gi'us a k.; hear my tale; I wonder; match!; still alive; you can k.

kiss me, Hardy! is a joc. c.p. of late C19–20. Although indubitably a c.p., it has never been wildly popular. From Nelson's dying words, which certain historians suppose to have been '*Kismet, Hardy*', which I find most improbable.

In 1968, Mr Peter Sanders, who served in North Africa and elsewhere, wrote thus to me: 'How about counter catch phrases, if such beasts exist? I know one – the rude soldiery's counter c.p. to "Kiss me, Hardy!" which is "Kiss my arse, I'm next for admiral!" Fairly common in WW2, but I suspect it is much older' – so do I, but cannot, at present, prove it. P.B. added, 1976, 'The retort nowadays is more likely to be phrased, "Kiss you, my arse! I'm next in line for admiral!" – i.e., for promotion'.

L.A. wrote, 1976: 'I have heard this saying only as "Kiss me, 'Ardy, and I die 'apply" (always unaspirated), a jingle used by the barrack-room extrovert, who needs to make himself heard – never anything to do with kiss or Hardy or dying, or even happy'.

kiss me, sergeant! was, in the British Army during WW1, 'a common piece of facetiousness, uttered after a sergeant had been more than usually officious; and often in camps, to the

orderly sergeant after he had commanded "Lights out!"' (John Brophy in B & P).

WW2 produced a var. quite early on, with the very popular satirical song 'Kiss Me Goodnight, Sergeant-Major', which Martin Page used as the title for his collection of WW2 Service songs, pub'd 1974.

kiss my arse (US and Can. **ass**)! has been a c.p. either of entire incredulity or of profound contempt or, more gen., an intensified negative: Brit., mid C19–20, the others since *c.* 1860: but all three perhaps a half-century earlier. Often shortened to *my arse*! as in Ernest Raymond, *A Song of the Tide*, 1940:

'More like ten past [eight o'clock]'
'Ten past, my arse.'

Cf **kiss my Parliament!**: the 1660s. This rude c.p. was based on the *Rump* Parliament. Ernest Weekly once quoted Pepys's *Diary* for February 1660, 'Boys do now cry, "Kiss my Parliament."'

Also cf **kiss my tail!**: a violently contemptuous retort of C18–20; by 1930, ob., and by 1960, virtually †.

P.B.: in C20, sometimes elab. *you can kiss my arse*, or *he can*..., as in 'Well, if he thinks he can (whatever), he can bloody well...' cf that parody of the 'Red Flag' anthem: 'The working class can kiss my arse: I've got the foreman's job at last'. [E.P. later added:]

It has the frequent var. *kiss me arse*!, not only in Cockney, which is often elab. to *kiss me arse and call me Charley*, itself eminiscent of *gi' us a kiss and call me Charley*. (L.A., 1977.) Fain informs me that the orig. c.p. is very much older: it occurs in *The Towneley Play*, late C15, as 'Com kis myn arse'. And A.B., 1978, tells me that, in the US, it is 'sometimes truncated to *kiss ass*! or altered to *kiss my butt*!' Cf:

kiss my elbow. See **never said so much as...**

kiss my foot! Rubbish: mostly Aus. and Can.: latish C19–20. But much less common than the prec. Also *my foot*!: late C19–20.

kiss of death – the, has, since mid-1940s in UK, and a few years earlier in US, been applied to a fatal – or, at the mildest, an extremely dangerous contact. Foster quotes *The Observer*, 18 Sep. 1966, as saying 'Allying with Churchill was regarded as the political kiss of death even in 1939'; and Safire defines it as 'unwelcome support from an unpopular source'. The *OED Second Supp.* cites N. Shute's novel *No Highway*, 1948, as an early source.

Obviously from Judas Iscariot's kissing of Christ, in the great betrayal scene; thence to any other callous betrayal; and perhaps with a famous US thriller, *The Kiss of Death*, intervening.

kissing time – it's or **it's half-past kissing time and time to kiss again.** The former is a shortened version of the latter, and the latter must date from at least as early as *c.* 1850; during the approx. period 1870–1914, it was, mostly among Londoners, a low c.p. reply to a woman asking a man the time, and said to derive from a very popular ballad; the longer form has also, like the shorter, been, in C20, addressed to children continually asking one the time, as HLM records in 1922.

Cf the C18 **an hour past hanging time** and **half-past...**

kit-bags. See: I'll be laughing.

kitchen. See: if you can't stand.

kitchen sink. See: everything but; you've forgotten.

Kitchener wants you was, during WW1 – more precisely, in 1915–18 – an army c.p., addressed to any man selected for a filthy job or for very arduous, or perilous, work. It was prompted by a very famous enlistment poster, showing a sternly pointing Lord Kitchener captioned with these words, a poster frequently reproduced ever since. In Alec Waugh's famous novel, *Jill Somerset*, 1936, we read that 'All those [men] who had attested under the Derby Scheme should wear khaki armlets; there'd be no more embarrassments; no more soldiers jeering their "Kitchener wants you".' (B & P.)

A US correspondent wrote, late 1970s, 'Exactly paralleled in US (1917–18) by a similar poster, "Uncle Sam wants *you*". Both poster and slogan were inevitably revived during the Vietnam War [1965–72]; it thus became a c.p.'

kite. See: can't fly; go fly.

knackers! and – orig. a euph. for that term – **knickers!** are obviously not, in themselves, c.pp., but the responses to them certainly are: *knackers!*, synon. with *balls!* ('Nonsense!'), evokes **yours or mine**? (q.v.); and *knickers!*, mostly a feminine exclam., often supposed to be indicative of annoyance or feigned annoyance, evokes *yours – or clean ones*?, with emphasis on *clean*. I had heard the former response, but I owe the latter to Mr Fredrick Leech, who, in 1972, sent me a valuable list of slang words and phrases. Neither of these linked mutually evocative responses is used by the more fastidious members of society [P.B.: is very much in this book?]. I cannot date them precisely, but I'd guess; since the late 1940s.

knave. See: one of you; walk, knave.

knee. See: straight.

knee-buckles. See: there's a pair.

knee-caps. See: muscles.

kneel. See: you're kneeling.

knees. See: bee's knees; down on; get off your; get your k.; and:

knees up, Mother Brown! 'Courage!' or 'Be cheerful!': since the early 1940s. From the extremely popular song so titled. (Petch, 1969.) Not much heard since *c.* 1970.

knickers. See: come home with; don't get your arse; get a grip; get your k; it's all over now; red hat.

knife. See: false; hard in; sailor without; tinkle; you say true.

knife-box. See: you're so sharp.

knight. See: once a k.

knit. See: put that on.

knitting. See: her knitting.

knob(s). See: get in, knob; same to you; with knobs; you wouldn't k.

knob of a chair and a pump handle – a. A lower-middle class reply to the enquiry 'What is there to eat?': since *c.* 1890; by 1975, decidedly ob.

knock. See: come in: don't k; couldn't knock; do you hear anything; don't knock; I will knock; I'll knock; if you haven't tried; longest; now then, shoot; what's knocked.

knock! knock! dates from mid-Nov. 1936, and derives, in UK, from its effective use by Wee George Wood in a radio music-hall programme on the night of Saturday 14 Nov. 1936. Orig., it has been said, it was a US c.p. It is used by someone about to tell a smutty story or, esp., to make a pun in dubious taste. In this sense, ob. by 1975. A correspondent, Mr Alan Smith, wrote, in 1939: 'It is possible that this derives from the Porter's scene in *Macbeth*, Act II, Scene iii.' But from *c.* 1960 onwards it has also been used by a person knocking on a door, saying *knock! knock!* and, without further ceremony, entering the room.

[E.P. later amended:] Nowadays it is 'nearly always taken to refer to the series of "knock, knock" jokes, eternally popular among children' – nor only children – 'and was given a new impetus last year with the publication of the Puffin "Crack-a-Joke" book, which devoted a whole section to them' (P.B., 1979).

This c.p. effectively derives from 'a game played in Victorian England' – see Joseph T. Shipley, *In Praise of English*, 1977, p. 166. R.C., 1978, recalls it as having its US orig. in a craze of the 1930s. P.B.: the craze continues, as I wrote earlier, and, just in case there remains a reader unaware of what is meant, I should explain that the perpetrator of the pun starts by saying 'Knock, knock!', as if at a door. The willing stooge answers, 'Who's there?' The reply which I have most enjoyed recently, exemplary for the extravagance of its awfulness, is 'Mayonnaise'. Again, the willing stooge: 'Mayonnaise who?' – 'Mayonnaise have seen the glory of the coming of the Lord!' See also **it's a great life!**, last para.

knock (on) wood. The US version of **touch wood**.

knock three times and ask for Alice is 'a jocular c.p. – used, for example, to short-circuit someone else's long drawn-out directions as to location' (L.A.): C20; orig. Cockneys', but since 1939, mostly the Armed Forces'. P.B.: the number of knocks, and the name of the person, may vary, but the c.p. goes on. For instance, Skehan, 1984, notes the var. *knock three times and ask for Joe*, and *Joe sent me*, 'On entry into an unfamiliar place. Probably stems from the days of Prohibition in the US'.

knocked-knees and silly and can't hold his water. A Public Schools' pejorative c.p. of late C19–20.

knocker. See: brass knocker.

knot. See: don't get your arse; six knots.

knot-hole. See: pulled.

know. See: do you k.; do you think you'll; doesn't know; don't I know; don't know; don't want; d'you know; easy as you; God knows; have a go, Joe; he knows; I didn't know; I don't know; I know; I say, I say; I want to k.; I wouldn't k.; I'd have you; if I knew; it takes one; it's been known; it's not what; maybe they; next time you see; not that you; knows; one never; put her down; regurgitate; she knows; she wouldn't; ship; tell me something; that's a rhyme; that's all I wanted; that's for me; well, what; what do you k.; what he doesn't; yes, I also; you better k.; you don't k.; you know; you must be; you never k.; you sure k.; you tell me and; you want to k.; you won't k.; you wouldn't want; you'll never; and:

knows all the answers (– he). 'He is' – or 'pretends to be' – 'very knowledgeable': US: since *c.* 1930. 'Originally, either from school or perhaps criminal – i.e., he knows how to give non-incriminatory answers to police interrogators' (R.C., 1978).

Know-All. See: Ole man.

Kruschen. See: I'm K.; that K.

L

L. See: going through.
la! la! See **oh! la! la!**
lackey. See: who was your l.
lad(s). See: away, the lads; come on, my; harm; now then, me.
ladder. See: I'm in the life-boat.
ladies, lady. See: all fine l.; don't tear it; gangway; gentlemen present; Henry's; horses sweat; like the ladies; little old l.; long nose; make way; officers and their; preparing; that's no l.; waltz; who's your l.
Lady Agatha. See: pleasure.
lady with whom he shares his joys but not his sorrows – a. 'An Edwardian *mot*, prim and *juste*, to mean a man's mistress as contrasted with his wife' (L.A., 1976).
Lafarge. See: no Tich; pas de L.
laid. See: often laid.
laid 'em in the aisles. See **I had 'em rolling...**
laid, re-laid and parlayed. 'Sexually very active and satiated': entirely US: since the 1930s. R.C., 1977, adds: 'There is a pun involved, since a *parlay* is a series of bets laid on several horse-races, with the winnings (if any) cumulated. Hence a certain implication [triggered by *laid*] of successive intercourse with several women (more often, several times with one woman). Perhaps even a second pun, on "relay race", with the baton (!) passed from one runner to another. Cf **stewed, screwed...**'
lake. See: go jump.
lamb. See: mutton.
Lammie Todd! I would – if I got half a chance!: tailors': *c.* 1860–1940. Prob. from the name of a well-known tailor.
lamp. See: dim as a Toc-H; oil; swing that.
land. See: how lies; six foot.
land-office business. See: they're doing land.
landing. See: if you can walk.
landlady. See: it must be the l.; you have a heart.
lane. See: it's a long l.
language. See: we speak.
larceny. See: full of l.
lareovers for meddlers was, late C18–early C19, 'an answer frequently given to children or young people, as a rebuke for their impertinent curiosity' (Grose); the earliest recording comes in BE underworld glossary, *c.* 1668; then dialectal usu. as *layers for meddlers*, or even, occ., *lay horses for meddlers*, a piece of folklore that seems to belong esp. to Westmorland, as Mr Allan R. Whittaker informs me. Nevertheless *lareovers* .2.. has survived in the form *lay-overs for meddlers*. *Lareovers* is 'a contraction of *lay-overs*, i.e. things laid over, covered up, or protected from meddlers' (Apperson).
P.B.: this curious, well-known and widely used phrase has, like the equally enigmatic '(I'm making) a whim-wham for a goose's bridle', been the subject of extensive newspaper correspondence, esp. in the *Guardian*. It was even 'in the

form "larroes to catch meddlers" current in (Southern) US in 1920s, but even then, I suspect, obsolescent' (R.C., 1978). For a quite different explanation, I quote a letter to E.P. from Mrs Pam Brewer, of Richmond, 1980:

My grandparents, Derbyshire dales folk, always said 'Lay holes for medlars to keep folks fat'. As I never saw it written, the word might have been 'holds', as they spoke in dialect. When I pressed for explanation, they said that medlars, being inedible until they are frosted or half rotten, the fruit was laid in barn lofts or in boxed-in trenches in the ground until it reached a fit state for consumption.

G.K. Colton, writing to the *Guardian*, Dec. 1978, also recalls, from Oldham, Lancashire, the pronunciation *lay 'oles*, 'i.e. untimely graves for those who do not mind their own business. I wonder, 'he adds, 'if this is a piece of industrial folk wisdom about the dangers of tampering with machinery.' And R. Stonehouse has another theory, in the same paper: *his* Salford grandmother pronounced the *lay overs* 'without the letter "v" and [they] referred to goods in shops on which one put a small deposit to hold them for future purchase'.

Gentle reader, yer pays yer money, an' yer takes yer choice! And there's plenty more where that came from! – see, e.g., **weaving leather aprons.**
large as life and twice as natural – as. It may astonish and even surprise many Britons to learn that this was orig. US: T.C. Haliburton in *The Clockmaker*, 1837 (Series I, pp. 159–60), has his central character, Sam Slick of Slicksville, say, 'He marched up and down afore the street door like a peacock, as large as life and twice as natural'. The expression caught the public fancy and became a c.p., adopted by Britain well before the end of C19. It survives; indeed, it has – and enjoys – good health. Such is its vitality that it has fathered the frequent var. (which I owe to Cyril Whelan): *as large as life and twice as ugly*, which is Brit. and hardly earlier than *c.* 1910.
As Mr Benny Green suggested in his review of the first ed. of this book, in *Spectator*, 10 Sep. 1977, the orig. version was prob. popularised in UK by Lewis Carroll's use of it in *Through the Looking-Glass*, 1871. A.B., 1978, adds there is a US var., *as big as life...*
large mouth, large cunt; often **big** for *large*. An example of not entirely scientific male folklore: ?mid C19–20; certainly C20. Cf **big conk...**
lark. See: all's to that; fuck that for a l.; result; up with the l.
Larkin. See: down to.
larks in the night – the. A 'jocular c.p. for birds which are regarded as responsible for more births than the stork' (B.P.): Aus.: since *c.* 1930. A pun on a *lark* or a bit of fun, and *bird*, a girl.
[lass in the red petticoat shall pay (or piece up) all – the. Dating

c. 1660–1800 and occurring in, e.g., J. Wilson, *The Cheats, 1664*, and recorded by Apperson, it is prob. to be classified rather as proverbial than as c.p.]

last. See: it'll last; leave the deck; nice guys; who was your; who were.

last drop. See: good to; when you dance.

last of the big-time spenders (– **the**). This playfully ironic c.p. is applicable either to others or to oneself, and it has flourished, in UK, since *c*. 1945. P.B. exemplified it thus: 'D' you want any raffle tickets?' – 'Yes, give us 5p worth – the last of the big-time spenders, that's me!' It was very prob. adopted from US servicemen *c*. 1944 and has almost certainly arisen in US during the early 1930s – during the Great Depression. (Based on a note from Harold Shapiro, 1977.) R.C., 1978, thinks the ref. is to 'the big spenders of the 1920s boom years [ended by that almighty crash of late Oct. 1929]. Now obsolescent'.

In the UK and the Commonwealth, also *last of the big spenders*; and, in US and Can., *great spenders*, usu. 'self-deprecating; for example, speaker orders ginger ale when others are on [hard] liquor' (Hugh Quetton, of Montreal, 1978).

last of the Mohicans – the, and, derivatively, **the last of its tribe**, applied to the last of a series, a packet, etc., as, e.g. the last cigarette in a packet: C20; the former, in the US and then in UK, the latter in Aus. From James Fenimore Cooper's most famous novel, *The Last of the Mohicans*, 1836; but in UK, the former, as Frank Shaw once remarked, is often used by people who've never heard of Fenimore Cooper's book, and, in the US, it is used of 'any sole survivor in any group, or any vanishing group... and everyone gets the point, for Cooper's book is universally known. I have heard the expression all my life' (W.J.B., 1975 – and that would lit. mean since, say, 1915). It has been a c.p. – well, prob. since latish C19.

[**last one home is a cissy** is an English schoolchildren's taunt, and, like **last out, lousy!** – a children's late C19–20 c.p., applied, esp. in Aus., to games – is traditional: therefore, not a c.p. The same applies to **last one in is the cow's tail**, applied, as Leechman reminds me, to a bathing scene. Also US: *last one in is a rotten egg*: juvenile: late C19–20 (A.B., 1978).]

Last Supper. See: mashed.

late. See: call me anything; couldn't see; first term; too late; ve get; you've dropped.

late for (one's) **own funeral.** In, e.g. *you'd be late...*; *he or she'd be...*: addressed, or applied, to one guilty of chronic and irritating unpunctuality: gen.: C20. Cf *too slow to go to a funeral*. (P.B.)

lately. See: getting any; have you heard any; read any; yes, but what.

later. See: dig you l.; it's later; plant.

latest. See: have you heard the l.

lathed. See: roofed.

Latin. See: brandy; tace.

latter end. See: remember your.

laugh. See: ain't that a l.; anything for a l.; away you go; cat laugh; don't laugh; don't make I l.; don't make me l.; enough to make; face that; I haven't laughed; I'll be laughing; joke over; little Audrey; only when; stop laughing; talk about l.; that will stop; they laughed; you make me l.; and:

laugh? I thought I should have died dates from *c*. 1880; orig. gen., but by *c*. 1930, the standard of syntactical literacy having deteriorated, it was, in the lower and lower-middle class, superseded by *laugh? I thought I'd died!*

An excellent example occurs in Miles Malleson's play, *Black 'Ell*, written and pub'd in 1916, but the first edn copies were promptly seized by the police on the grounds that it was subversive, and the second edn was not pub'd until 1925; a housemaid says, 'There was a young chap on the platform makin' a speech or something... they pulled 'im orf... and 'is glasses fell orf an' 'e trod on 'em 'isself... LARF!!!! I thought I should er died.'

This c.p. prototyped two that Russell Davies, reviewing the first ed. of this book, in *New Statesman*, 9 Sep. 1977, rightly thought much stronger: *laugh? I nearly bought my own beer*, very much a public-house witticism, and *laugh? I nearly fell off the wife*, raffish; they go back to the 1920s. Cf *I nearly dropped...*

The Canadian Army, WW2 and after, version was *laugh? I thought my pants would never dry!* (Hugh Question, 1978).

P.B.: E.P. seems to have been unaware of the prominence accorded to this phrase in what was perhaps the most popular of all Albert Chevalier's (1861–1923) coster songs, 'Knocked 'em in the Old Kent Road'.

laughter. See: shrieks.

laundryman. See: only your l.

law(s). See: is there a law; there ought; there's an 'oss; you break.

lawn. See: going home.

lawnmower. See: your ass is grass.

lay low. See: Brer Rabbit.

lay of the land: See: do you want to know.

lay of the last minstrel – the. A cultured Can. c.p., dating from *c*. 1960 and applied to a particularly unattractive girl. (Leechman.) In allusion to Sir Walter Scott's famous poem and with a pun on the slangy US-become-also-English *lay*, a partner in sexual intercourse. Cf **do you want to know the lay of the land?**

lay off the comedy! Stop trying to be funny!; Be serious!: US: since *c*. 1930. In Noël Coward's *Relative Values*, prod. 1951 and pub'd 1952, at II, ii, Don Lucas, a film star, irritably exclaims, 'Lay off the comedy a minute, will you? This means the hell of a lot to me.' A var. of **can the comedy**, q.v., which was prob. the orig.

lay six to four. See: I'll lay.

layers (or **layovers**) **for meddlers.** See **lareovers...**

laying or **lying?** (– usu. prec. by *are they*). 'When hens are heard loudly cackling, somebody may say "Are they laying or lying?"' (Petch, 1969). Prob. current throughout C20. A pun on 'laying eggs' and the illiterate use of the intransitive 'to *lay*' for 'to *lie*' – as well as one *lie*, to speak an untruth.

lazy-tongs. See: take that fire-poker.

lead. See: get the lead; if you blind; like a rope; shake the l.; that'll grow; went down.

lead me to it! With pleasure!; That'll be easy, or a great pleasure: C20. Dorothy L. Sayers's *The Nine Tailors*, 1934, has:

    'Can you ride a motor-bike?'
    'Lead me to it, guv'nor!'

lead on, Macduff! is a late C19–20 c.p., based upon the very frequent misquotation of 'Lay on, Macduff' in Shakespeare's *Macbeth*, at V, vii, line 62. The c.p. occurs in, e.g. Edward Burke, *Bachelor's Buttons*, 1912.

Leechman 1969 defines its Can. nuance as 'All right, let's go, get started, etc.'.

leader. See: take me to.

leader of men (pause) **and follower of women – he's a.** A derogatory response to the admiring, e.g 'He's a born leader of men!': later C20. (Ashley, 1982.) P.B.: cf the ironic use of the term *beloved leader* (which occ. dovetail, *'bleeder' for short!*) and **dear Sir...**

league. See: in the big.

leak. See: when it don't.

leaky. See: old ships.

lean forward and shove! 'A cowboy's order to someone to get out of the way in a hurry' (Adams): US: C20.

lean on your chin-straps! was, 1915–18, heard in the army when the troops were either marching up a very steep hill or finishing a long and arduous route march. (F&G; B&P.) Contrast **get off your knees!**

leap. See: he'll leap; if you feel.

learn. See: that'll learn; you were born.

leather. See: nothing like; weaving; well, I never.

leather arse. See: it's the greatest.

leave(s). See: fuck 'em and; I must love; I'll leave; talks like; why don't you l.; why girls; and:

leave it all to the cook – I'll. See **I'll leave** ....

leave it for the cleaners! 'A c.p. often heard when someone drops small change on the floor' (B.P.): Aus.: since the late 1940s.

leave it out! Do not say, or do, that!; desist!: underworld and its fringes, creeping up into gen. popularity: early 1980s. Superseding the earlier *lay off!* or *belt up!* (P.B.)

leave me alone for that! See **let me alone for that!**

leave the deck to the last! is an ironic shout, greeting 'that hapless rating working aloft who has spilled paint on to the deck' (*Sailors' Slang*): RN: C20.

leave the garbage out! 'The beginning of wisdom for every drinking man takes place when he ceases to bray "leave the garbage out!" at the bartender mixing his Old Fashioned and yields that call to bumpkins and louts who don't know any better': *Cavalier*, Nov. 1963. (Paul Janssen, 1978.) Raffish: since *c.* 1960, or a little earlier.

leave the sea and go into steam! Transfer to a steam-driven ship!: sailing-men's c.p. of *c.* 1860–1900. Bowen.

leaves his fiddle behind the door (or he hangs up his fiddle) when he comes home – he. He is great fun, and very witty, when he's out of the house but not when he's is in it: *c.* 1800–1940. It prob. derives from the synon. C18–20 Derbicism, *to hang the fiddle at the door.*

left. See: army left; good men; I left; I've been left; no, half; over the l.; she wobbles; there are only.

left field. See: you're way out.

left hand down a bit! 'As far as I can discover, "The Navy Lark" script-writer coined the phrase in its nautical application, and within two years it was a standard piece of Navalese ... The phrase was, in the programme, used by Sub-Lieutenant Philips ... played by the actor Leslie Philips [as] a rather vague chinless-wonder type, who obviously could not remember the nautical term "Port a little". The phrase, I thought came from car driving. When instructors teach you to reverse, they use "left hand down" to indicate that you pull down your left hand hard and swing the back of the car to the left ... But a professional instructor for the Army At Aldershot thinks that driving instructors picked up the phrase from "The Navy Lark". It could thus be a felicitous invention of the script-wider's!' (Lt Cdr F.L. Peppitt, RNR, 1977). This quot'n from an authority on naval speech exemplifies the fact that many c.pp. arise and 'Catch on' in this, or some similar, rather haphazard, happy-go-lucky way. The BBC radio comedy series 'The Navy Lark' began its career in 1959, and the c.p. soon became gen. and widespread. P.B.: poss., as Peppitt suggests, from driving instructors, or lorry-drivers' mates helping drivers to park – my father, an Army Mechanical Transport Officer in WW2, was using the phrase long before 'The Navy Lark' – but perhaps, even earlier, from furniture removals men.

left-handed corkscrew. See: queer as a.

left-handed screwdriver. See: go and fetch.

left her purse on the piano! was, late C19 – early C20, a 'satirical hit a self-sufficiency' (Ware). Non-aristocratic, non-upper-middle class, it implied that a woman visitor, boasting of her efficiency and excellent memory, departs without her purse.

left out in the cold. See **I've been left** ...

leg(s). See: arm and a leg; break a leg; cheers; could eat; crutches; cut off; go it, you; he'd drink; he'd fuck anything; he's got his; I can always; I can't go; I have a bone; I nearly; if it takes; keep your legs; oh, my leg; saw; she has legs; she wobbles; shoot it; short, fat; show a leg; straight; what's the difference; yes, a cat; and:

leg over and you're away, often prec. by *get your*. This c.p. bears the primary meaning, 'Get your leg over and you're well on the way to "making it" with a girl'; secondarily, 'Be resolved and audacious, and you'll succeed': since the 1920s. (Owed, in part, to L.A., 1976.) P.B.: but contrast (e.g. he's)

got a leg over, he is confused, mistaken, has made a hopeless mess; from a horse with its leg over the trace.

legs grew in the night, therefore he could not see to grow straight (– his). A jeering c.p., addressed to a bandy-legged man: *c.* 1760 – 1820. Grose, 1796.

Leicester. See: you have a heart.

lemon. See: answer is; I'm going to do; if at first; like a spare.

lend his arse and shite through his ribs – he would. A c.p. applied to 'anyone who lends his money inconsiderately' (Grose, 2nd edn, 1788): *c.* 1770–1860. Here, inconsiderately = unthinkingly.

lend us your breath to kill Jumbo! A proletarian c.p. of 1882–*c.* 1910, it was a 'protest against the odour of bad breath' (Ware). 'Chiefly in allusion to a famous elephant at [the London] Zoo (d. 1885)', says Ware at *Jumbo*.

lend us your pound! Pull your weight on the rope: joc. nautical, esp. late C19–mid C20. owen.

Lendum's very bad. See **Givum's dead** ...

lent. See: it's only lent.

Les be friends! 'A mixture of a bad joke [a pun on *Les*, a Lesbian, and *le's*, illiterate for *let's*] and a catch phrase- ... more generally used than one would expect' (a correspondent, 1965): since the early 1960s.

less. See: couldn't care less; I could; I couldn't; in (–) people; little less; and: **less of that** (or **this**), **and more of the other.** 'Usage here [in Dublin] is obscure. Normally said by a man to a woman, in reply to a chaffing or mocking remark, (Skehan, 1977): since *c.* 1925. presumably 'the other' = amiable or appreciation speech. P.B.: but in English raffish register, 'a spot of the other' has an intentionally indefinite sexual significance, a vague ref. to intercourse.

lesson. See: here endeth.

let battle commence! See **gradely lads** ...

let 'em all come! arose in 1896, was at first proletarian, but by 1912, gen.; and it expressed a cheeky defiance. Ware attributes its origin to the way in which Britons received the following trio of setbacks in world popularity: the German emperor's congratulatory message to Kruger on the Boers' repulse of the Jameson Raid; the USA's communication about the British boundary dispute with Venezuela; and the shortly ensuing tricolor'd agitation in the Fr. press. The c.p. was noted by Collinson and recorded by Benham.

P.B.: cf Shakespeare's *King John*, V, vii: 'Come the three corners of the world in arms, and we shall shock them.'

let 'em sweat! 'Let them remain in suspense for a while (i.e., while we decide what *we* want to do): US: since late 1940s. Perhaps orig. Services'. "Sweat", of course, as a metaphor for nervousness' (R.C., 1978). Cf **let it sweat.**

let 'em trundle! Clear out! or Run!: apparently *c.* 1695–1730; occurs in Congreve, *The Way of the World*, 1700 (cited by McKnight). Presumably a ref. to the game of bowls.

let 'er go, Deacon! (or **Gallagher!**) See **let her go.** ...

let 'er rip. See **let her rip!**

let George do it! – roughly, Let someone else do it!. A journalistic c.p., dating from *c.* 1910 and applied to the enlistment of an unnamed expert or authority and the putting of the writer's own words into his mouth, and prob., as HLM pointed out in 1922, deriving from the synon. Fr. *laissez faire à Georges*, which goes back a long way, had an historical source, but 'later became common slang, was translated into English, had a revival during the early days of David Lloyd George's career, was adopted into American without any comprehension of either its first or its latest significance, and enjoyed the brief popularity of a year'. W&F pinpoint it to *c.* 1920 and note that it was popular during WW2, when it 'implied a lack of responsibility in helping the war effort': clearly the phrase was gen. enough during all the intervening US years. Fain, 1977, glosses it for the US as 'I won't do it, I'm not responsible', having noted earlier, in 1969, that 'it can still be heard'. In UK, it had, by 1950, become very ob. – and by 1970, I'd say, †.

P.B.: it was given a new twist and lease of life in WW2

when the 'automatic pilot' in aircraft became known as George.

let her cry: she'll piss the less was a semi-consolatory c.p. of mid C18–early C20, supposed to have been orig. addressed, as *the more you cry the less you'll piss*, by sailors to their whores – or so Grose, 1796, tells us. The third-person form verges on the proverbial.

let her (or **'er**) **go, Deacon (, she's headed for the barn)!** and **let her** (or, better, **'er**) **go, Gallagher!** are Western US 'calls to a "bronco-buster"' (Berrey): the former of C20 and perhaps a little earlier; the latter, recorded by HLM in 1922, is far the more gen. and has long had a much wider application, with the predominant sense, 'Let's begin!' – and dating from *c.* 1880, for it occurs in, e.g., James A Herne, *Mary the Fisherman's Child*, performed in 1888 and later called *Drifting Apart*, near end of Act II:

HESTER: Ready, Mary.
MARY: All ready?
SI[LAS]: Let 'er go, Gallagher. [*Song and dance.*]

In Gene Fowler, *Timber Line, A Story of Bonfils and Tammen*, 1938, we read that Bonfils sometimes visited prize fights. 'He frequently attended the Coliseum, a temple of fistiana presided over by Reddy Gallagher, a quondam athlete of Cincinnati, and of whose right fist the saying originated: "Let 'er go, Gallagher".' W.J.B., 1975, tells me that Bonfils and Tammen ran the newspaper the *Denver Post* and Gallagher was in Denver around the 1890s:

I have known the expression all my life....If someone gives vent to emotions, makes a verbal attack against some person or thing, becomes exercised over an injustice and speaks out with force, we are likely to exclaim in a humorous and approving manner, 'Let 'er go, Gallagher!'

See also **hi ho, let her go.**

let her (or **'er**) **rip!** Let her go freely! Damn the consequences!: mid C19–20. Prob. US in orig., as both Ware and Thornton believe. Cf:

let her rip, Macduff! A frequent US var. of **lead on, Macduff** (A.B., 1979).

let her went! Let it go! – 'a slang expression indicative of surrender and abandonment' (Farmer, 1889): *c.* 1885–90. This kind of facetious c.p., based upon a deliberate grammatical solecism, is usu. shortlived; cf such slang inanities as *used to was*, used to be, and (the orig. negro) **is you is or is you ain'?**, are you or aren't you?

let him alone until he weighs his weight! is a Bow Street Runners' c.p., to the effect that a criminal is not yet worth arresting, his offences being so small that no reward attaches to his apprehension, whereas a capital crime will produce a large reward: *c.* 1770–1830. Vaux notes that if a criminal *weighs forth*, there is a reward of £40 attached to his capture.

let him pick the bones out of that! See **pick the bones....**

let him up, he's all cut. See 'TAD' DORGAN ...

let it all hang out! Orig. a US negroes' c.p. of the 1960s–70s, according to CM and meaning 'Be free!' or 'Be uninhibited!' – it gradually gained a much wider acceptance; in Can., a rapid acceptance. I notice that Donald MacKenzie uses it in *The Spreewald Collection*, 1975. W.J.B., 1974, wrote to me thus:

We have a phrase going in the US that has caught on and is used widely. 'Let it all hang out.' It has had wide media exposure during the past two years. How it started, I do not know....The meaning is: Make a full confession, don't hide anything, be nakedly frank and honest. Come clean. Tell the truth. I suspect it had some reference to the male sexual organ to begin with.

That and shirt-tails too, I'd say. In a later letter, W.J.B. informed me that his friend Martin Goldman, editor of *Intellectual Digest* magazine, had written to him: '*Let it all hang out* may have dirty-linen connotations, but that may be a matter of laundering the language. Methinks the phrasing has sexual origins.' Glossed in *DCCU* as 'Tell the truth, the whole truth, and nothing but the truth.'

Mr. D.J. Barr, 1976, has confirmed that it was well established in Can. by 1975; L.A. that, since late 1975, it has, in UK, acquired an elab. and a fresh nuance: *and who knows what will show up,* 'in favour of accepting whatever developments may be revealed'. That prob. by 1976 and certainly by 1977, it was well established in UK, seems to be corroborated by this passage in Miles Tripp's *The Wife-Smuggler*, 1978: a woman says to her husband, 'Why can't you relax? Let it all hang out'.

A fairly early example occurs in *Playboy*, Sep. 1972: an article punningly titled 'Student Bodies' bears the sub-title 'the campus trend is obvious – let it all hang out', in which both the denotation and the connotation are 'nudity as generalized sex'. And an earlier issue (Dec. 1970) of that periodical shows a group of girls, bare-breasted, sitting around a Christmas brazier, with a sort of versified caption, '...Since liberated Christmas belles/ Say, "Let it all hang out"' (Both references owed to Paul Janssen, who remarks, 'Let's not be "sexists" or "male chauvinist pigs" and let's admit that the *popularization* of the c.p. owes much to the Women's Liberation Movement'. He dates the c.p. as originating in the very late 1960s.)

Carence Major's claim that the c.p. was orig. US *Negro* is corroborated – *not* that corroboration is needed – by *The Third Ear*, 1971.

P.B.: the phrase was ob. by *c.* 1980.

let it spread! (– aw,). 'Abandon care about over-eating and one's spreading waist-line'. (L.A., 1974.) US and Brit. since the middle or late 1960s. In the *Observer* Review, 7 May 1971, Katherine Whitehorn asks, 'And what about the "Aw, let it spread" attitude to fat?

let it sweat! Let things now take their usual course – don't interfere any more!: since *c.* 1920; by 1970, slightly ob. Perhaps suggested by the army's WW1 expression, *sweat on the top line*, to be in eager anticipation, esp. if one is about to obtain something very much desired or needed. Cf **let 'em sweat.**

let me alone for that! – often shortened to **let me alone!** Take my word for it!; You can depend upon me for that!; You don't need to worry about *me*, I'll manage: very common in Restoration Comedy and, indeed, until *c.* 1880.

Thomas Shadwell's play, *Bury Fair*, 1689, at II, i, has the pretended Fr. count say, 'Is ver well: lette me alone for dat' – and this from a man whose English is, in gen., very faulty, yet retentive of a phrase he must often have heard.

In his *Square of Alsatia*, 1688, Act V, in the setting of Mrs Termagant's fine lodgings, we find:

CHEAT[LY]: Madam, you must carry yourself somewhat stately, but courteously to the Bubble [i.e. the dupe].
SHAM[WELL]: Somewhat reservedly, and yet so as to give him Hopes.
TERM[AGANT]: I warrant you, let me alone; and if I effect this Business, you are the best Friends.

A rather earlier example had occurred in Edward Ravenscroft, *The London Cuckolds*, performed in 1681 and pub'd in 1682, at II, iii.

JANE: You must not stay long: therefore who you do, do quickly.
TOWN[LY]: Let me alone.

Still earlier was George Villiers, Duke of Buckingham, who, in *The Rehearsal*, prod. in 1671 and pub'd in 1672, a play of which 'the first draft ... was written and ready for the boards in the summer of 1665' (Montague Summers, editor), has at I, ii:

SMI[TH]: This is one of the richest stories, Mr *Bayes*, that ever I heard of.
BAYES: I [= ay], let me alone, I gad [= begad], when I get to 'em; I'll nick 'em, I warrant you.

At this point, it might be noted that during the Restoration period of this c.p., it sometimes bore the connotations, 'Oh, stop fussing! *I* can attend to this' and 'Don't be so concerned, so anxious – I'm not the fool you seem to think me' and 'Don't worry – *I* know what I'm doing'.

In William Burnaby, *The Modish Husband*, 1702, at V, ii (p. 337, lines 18–21, in F.E. Budd's edn, 1931, of Burnaby's plays), we find:

LIO[NEL]: But where is the Person; mustn't I know her before I marry her?

CAM[ILLA]: No, nor after neither, I'll pass my Word.

LADY R: O! let me alone for that –.

Susannah Centilivre's *The Man's Bewitched*, 1710, has at I, the scene in the churchyard:

SLOUCH: Ay, and his Man *Staytape*, too; and he works like a Dragon – My Master will soon be fit [i.e. fitted] Forsooth.

MARIA: Fit, quotha! For what? ha, ha.

NUM: For what! Nay, let me alone for that, an [= if] I don't show her for what, when I have her once, I'll be flea'd [i.e., flyed]

And in the next Act, scene 'the outside of Trusty's House', has:

MANAGE: Well, Sir, what am I to do now?

CONSTANT: Why, go watch about *Sir David's* Door, and as you see occasion, employ your Wits.

MANAGE: Very well, Sir, let me alone for that; your humble Servant, Gentlemen. (*Exit.*]

In *The Drummer*, 1716, IV begins:

VEL[LUM]: John, I have certain orders to give you – and therefore be attentive.

BUT[LER]: Attentive! Ay, let me alone for that.

Isaac Bickerstaffe, in *The Maid of the Mill*, 1765, uses the shorter form, and in his collaboration with Samuel Foote, *Dr Last in His Chariot*, 1769, II has:

ALL[WOULD]: But, Prudence, art thou not afraid, that her very thinking me dead will break her heart?

PRU[DENCE]: To be sure, sir, if you should keep her in her fright too long.

AIL[WOULD]: O, let me alone for that. . . .

The c.p. occurs as late as David Garrick and G. Colman's *The Clandestine Marriage*, 1766, at III, i:

STERL[ING]: But, Sir John! one thing more. [Sir John *returns.*] My lord must know nothing of this stroke of friendship between us.

SIR JOHN

Not for the world. – Let me alone! Let me alone. [*Exit hastily,*]

And later still in Richard Brinsley Sheridan, *St Patrick's Day or, The Scheming Lieutenant,* prod. in 1775 and pub'd in 1778, where I, i, has:

THIRD SOLDIER: . . . If we be to have a spokesman, there's the corporal is the lieutenant's countryman, and knows his humour.

FLINT: Let me alone for that, I served three years, within a bit, under his honour in the Royal Inniskillions.

Mrs Hannah Cowley, in *Which Is the Man?*, 1783, uses the occ. late var. *leave me alone for that* – which occurs also in Prince Hoare's *Lock and Key*, 1791.

Mrs. Elizabeth Inchbald (1753–1821), actress, novelist, playwright, also uses it, in *Such Things Are*, 1788, at II, i:

MEAN[RIGHT]: Yet do it nicely – oblique touches, rather than open explanations.

TWINE[ALL]: Let me alone for that.

Even later comes Arthur Murphy, *The Way to Keep Him*, 1794, at II, ii:

LOVE[more]: Sly, sly. – You know what you are about.

SIR BASH[FUL]: Ay, let me alone. – [*Laughs with Love-more.*]

In *The Marriage Promise: A Comedy*, 1803, John Till Allingham, at I, end of i, makes Tandem, steward to a country estate, boast:

I put some brandy into his beer . . . and then won all his money from him at cribbage – that's the way to get on. Oh, let me alone – I am a man of business.

In 1808, George Colman the Younger, in *The Review, or the Wags of Windsor*, at II, i, writes:

BEAUGARD: Zounds! get along; and come with the chaise, as you will.

LOONEY: Let me alone for that. (Going.)

In the astonishing late source, Benjamin Webster's *A Bird of Passage: A Farce*, perform'd in 1849, the admittedly late form *leave me alone for that* appears in its short form, thus:

MRS R: Not a word of what we've been talking about, or he'll imagine – –

CHICK: Leave me alone!

A year later, Morris Barrett and Charles Mathews, *Serve Him Right! A Comic Drama*, early in I, repeat the *leave* form, Harry Bellamy exclaiming, 'Suspect? Of course she does – but not *me* – no, no, leave me alone for that.

And the latest instance I've found: Richard Jones, *The Green Man: A Comedy* – adapted from the Fr. of MM. D'Aubigny and Funjol – 1862, where, in II, iii, we find:

GREEN: What, you are already provided with a writ.

CLOSE: Let me alone for that, and it shall be put in force, too.

Clearly, *let me alone for that* merits the comment, 'One of the two or three most widely used and longest-lived c.pp. in the language'. (Nor did I watch for it, much less seek it out. Its ubiquity spoke for itself.)

let me be hanged! is an occ. Restoration var. of **let me die**! It occurs in, e.g., *The Braggadoccio*, 1691, 'By a Person of Quality', at III, i:

CAROL: I am sorry for your misfortune.

BRAV: Let me be hang'd, if I was not baited by a pack o' slaves.

In the same play, at I, iii, there is another occ. Restoration var., **let me die in a ditch!** P.B.: the latter reminds me that my father used to recall a Kentish yeoman, at whose farm he stayed as a boy, *c.* 1915, who would genially abuse his children with the phrase, in dialect, 'Ah, you'd leave your old father to die in a ditch, you would!'

let me chat yer (or you). Let me tell you! An Aus. and NZ soldiers' c.p. of WW1; at least, from 1915. Backer; also in his *NZS*.

let me die! belongs to two widely separated periods and has two distinct senses: the earlier, *c.* 1660–1850, is a c.p. of asseveration, roughly 'Let me die if I lie', hence 'I assure you'; the later, *c.* 1860–1914, means 'You'll cause me to die laughing' – cf **you'll be the death of me!** and **carry me out!**

In Thomas Shadwell, *The Volunteers*, prod in 1692 and pub'd in 1693, at I, ii (lines 491–2 of the D.M. Walmsley edn), we find:

WIN[IFRED *to the dancing master*]: Go, go, get you gone, let me dye, you have the Charmingest way with you.

Used also by men, as for instance, by Sir Nicholas Dainty in II, ii (lines 68–9): 'Yes, Puppy and Fool, and Impudence, are familiar Names: let me die.' It may also occur at the beginning of a sentence, as when, in III, i (lines 191–2), Teresia exclaims, 'Let me die, I never saw anything so fine.'

Cf Colley Cibber, *The Comical Lovers*, prod. *c.* 1707, in I:

PHILOTIS: Count Rhodophil's a fine gentleman indeed, madam; and, I think, deserves your affection.

MELANTHA: Let me die but he's a fine man; he sings and dances, *en Français*, and writes the *billets-doux* to a miracle [i.e., miraculously].

She repeats the phrase on several occasions within this one scene.

And at V, i, Melantha, again speaking, says: 'O, here's her highness! Now is my time to introduce myself, and to make my court to her; in my new French phrases. Stay, let me read my catalogue – *Suite, figure, chagrin, naïveté*, and *let me die*, for the parenthesis of all.'

A decade earlier, Colley Cibber, in *Women's Wit: or, The Lady in Fashion*, 1697, had written (II, the scene between Lenora and Longville, the former speaking): 'Let me die, but you are a second *Phaeton*! This equipage and chariot were enough to set the whole beau-monde on fire.'

Arthur Murphy, in *The Upholsterer* (1758), a brisk farce, opens thus: 'BRISK: Mr Belmour! – Let me die, sir – as I hope to be saved, sir.'

In 1762, George Colman's *The Musical Lady*, in II, opening scene, has:

SOPHY: Nay, now, I'm sure you flatter me! Is my style so purely Italian? have I quite got rid of that horrid English cadence?

MASK: Let me die, madam, if your whole conversation and behaviour do not make me fancy myself in Italy; Signora Lorenza at Florence was the very type of you.

David Garrick, in *Neck or Nothing*, 1766, at I, ii, writes thus: 'MARTIN: A fine creature! [*Salutes her.*] Madam, I have seen the world! and from all the world, here would I chuse a wife, and a mistress – a family of beauties; let me die!'

In *The Sultan*, 1784, Isaac Bickerstaffe, at II, i, has Roxalana say: 'What, do they think we are going to prayers? Let me die, but I believe it is their dinner.'

The 'catalogue' in *Woman's Wit* suggests that the origin may lie in the Fr., *que je meure, si...*.

let me die in a ditch! A var. of the prec. See **let me be hanged!**

let me out! I'm not barmy; also **let me out! I'm barmy.** An Armed Forces' pantomime c.p., expressing a lively desire to be rid of Service restrictions: 1939–45.

P.B.: by the mid–1950s, this has become simply *let me out!*, accompanied by a loose lacing of the fingers in front of the face, to indicate the bars of a cage.

let me perish! is synon. with **let me die!**: *c.* 1660–1710. In II, i, of *Love in a Wood*, performed in 1671 and pub'd in 1672, William Wycherley writes: 'DAPPERWIT: 'Tis no fault of mine, let me perish!'

And in *The Double-Dealer*, 1694, William Congreve, at II, i, has:

LADY FROTH: ...Mr Brisk, you're a judge; was ever anything so well bred as my lord?

BRISK: Never anything but your ladyship, let me perish!

let me shake the hand that shook the hand of Sullivan! had a brief vogue (from 1898, when Johnny Carroll sang it, until, say 1905). The ref. is to John L. Sullivan, who held the world heavyweight championship from 1892, and who died, aged seventy, in 1918. But a c.p. only when *not* used literally; it connoted a derisive irony. (W.J.B. 1975.)

let me tell you! – recorded, as a Brit. c.p., by HLM, Supp. 2, – has existed, as an emphatic tag, prob. since *c.* 1700, but, as a c.p., only since 1944. The radio programme, *Happidrome*, popularized it: in every instalment, Enoch says, at least once, 'Let me tell you, Mr Lovejoy', with every word emphasized. Cf. **ee, if ever a man...**

Derek Parker, in his review of the first ed. of this book (*The Times*, 15 Sep. 1977), remarked that the phrase was very common among schoolboys during the 1930s and perhaps the early 1940s. It formed a usu. amicable assertion and asseveration.

let the dog see the rabbit! Get out of the way! Get out of the light!: common among dog-track frequenters of *c.* 1938–50; but also common in the fighting Services, 'in reference to one who wishes to do or see something' (L.A.).

A good example occurs in Angus Ross, *The London Assignment*, 1972:

This [room] was locked, and this time Billie had no key. She swore violently.

'Just step aside, love,' I said. 'Let the dog see the rabbit.'

Loosely, **show the dog the rabbit!**

let the good times roll! '(1900s–1920s) a cry for enjoyment: music, talk, drinking. etc.' (CM); US negroes'.

let the moths out of your wallet (or **purse**)! Don't be so niggardly, so mean with your money!: semi-joc.: since *c.* 1950. (Petch, 1969.)

let the peanut roast! 'Let the fool stew in his own juice and suffer from his own stupid mistakes!': (? mainly Western) Aus.: mid-C20. (P.B.)

let us proceed with the libretto. See **on with the motley!**

let you off this time! See **I'll let you off....**

let your braces dangle, usu. completed by **and let yourself go** and often prec. by **you want to** (i.e., need to). Relax and enjoy yourself: since *c.* 1945. Contrast **don't let your braces...**

let's appeal against the light. Let's object, for the hell of it: Aus: since *c.* 1950. Satirizes the gamesmanship of batsmen appealing unnecessarily at cricket.

let's be having you! See **let's have you!**

[**let's call it a day!** is almost certainly a cliché, not a c.p.]

let's call it eight bells. See **call it...**

let's case the joint! '"Let's see what we can find in the refrigerator to eat", for example. Originally burglars' [cant], meaning preliminarily and clandestinely inspect premises they think of robbing' (J.W.C., 1977): US; as a gen. c.p., since the 1930s, but as an underworld phrase, prob. since *c.* 1900.

let's face it was orig., '*c.*, I believe, 1957' (Mr A.L. Hart, Jr, 1972); US; it became Brit., Aus., NZ, within a year or two. Here, 'it' is the current situation, whether international or national or local, and whether collective or individual. Predominant meaning: Let's be *honest* about it! Late in 1974, L.A. glossed the c.p. as a 'palliation of introducing an aspect or topic hitherto avoided out of tact'. Later, E.P. added:

It is rather older than I had thought. Thanks to Mr Benny Green (reviewing the first ed. of this book, in *Spectator*, 10 Sep. 1977), it can be dated for 1941, when Cole Porter used it as the title of a revue written for Broadway in that year. Historically ironic, for on 7 Dec., the Japanese attacked Pearl Harbor.

P.B.: but Hart's dating is good for the expression's c.p. status; it was *c.* 1960 that it started to become mere 'conversational noise' and soon a cliché: cf **well, this is it.**

let's feel your pulse is a joc. c.p.; vague in sense and application: late C19–earlier 20.

let's get down to brass tacks and **let's get down to cases.** Whereas the former was orig. (late C19–20) Brit. rhyming slang on 'hard facts' and then adopted in the US, the latter is pure American and dates from the 1920s; both mean 'Let's focus on the concrete facts of the matter', the latter bearing 'an even stronger implication that the discussion has insisted on generalities' and referring orig. to legal cases, i.e. 'actual citations as contrasted with general juridical principles' (R.C., 1978). Cf:

let's get down to the nitty-gritty. Let's get to the nub of the conversation: a very slangy US c.p., dating since *c.* 1965, Mr Norris M. Davidson tells me. It was indicted by Sydney J. Harris – See **right on!** By *c.* 1972, adopted in UK. [P.B.: by 1982, very *vieux jeu*, and used only joc.]

It soon dwindled to *get down to the nitty-gritty*. 'Much used in business circles' (Playfair, 1977). The *OED 2nd Supp.* amply illustrates how the shortening operated; and Paul Janssen, 1978, opined that it is of 'US Negro origin. Semantics obscure, but probably referring to unpleasant (*gritty*) but basic realities'.

let's get it all together! See **get your act together,** of which it forms a var.

let's get on with it! 'Nat Mills and Bobbie were a variety act that flourished in the 1930s and '40s portraying "a gumpish type of lad and his equally gumpish girl friend". Nat recalls: "It was during the very early part of the war. We were booked by the BBC to go to South Wales for a *Workers' playtime*. Long tables had been set up in front of the stage for the workers to have lunch before the broadcast. On this occasion a works foreman went round all the tables shouting 'Come on, let's get on with it', to get them to finish their lunch on time. I was informed he used this phrase so many times the workers would mimic him among themselves. So I said to Bobbie, 'You start the broadcast by talking to yourself and I'll interject and say, "Let's get on with it".' Lo and behold it got such a yell of laughter we kept it in all our broadcasts,

Even Churchill used our slogan to the troops during the early part of the war"' (*VIBS*). The 'gag' was developed later to Nat saying, 'gumpishly', 'Let's get on with it', and Bobbie would bleat in answer, 'Yes, let's get *on with it!*, *with the o-o-o-on* dragged out in a quavery voice; it was really this pron. that 'made' the c.p. (P.B.)

let's get the show on the road! A US c.p., dating from perhaps as early as *c*. 1910 and certainly very common since *c*. 1930, and orig. as a theatrical or other show-business, esp. touring companies', exhortation to stop wasting time and to 'get moving'; by *c*. 1940, also Brit.

Ellery Queen, *Cop Out*, 1969, has the following: '"Okay, okay," Furia said. Malone could have sworn he was grinning under the mask. "Let's get the show on the road, as they say."' In the very next year, Stanley Ellin uses it in *The Man from Nowhere*. Cf its allusive employment in Michael Butterworth's English novel, *The Black Look*, 1972: '"Never mind about the slim quarto volume of arty pictures that's going to win you immortality, love," said Sonia Hammersley. "Let's get this bloody show on the road."' Allusive also is the following example from Thomas Patrick McMahon's very American novel, *The Issue of the Bishop's Blood*, 1972:

'It won't get you in trouble?'

'What doesn't?' he said cheerfully. 'Let's get the show on the road.'

let's give it the old college try or ...**the old one-two.** See **give it the old...**

let's go back to square one. See **back to square one!**

let's go for broke! 'Let's risk everything! We'll end up either rich or [bankrupt].' American: since WW2, when, I believe, it originated (possibly US Air Force). Now slightly obsolescent' (R.C., 1978).

let's go home! is a US negro c.p. of *c*. 1920–40: 'an agreement among jazzmen to do the final chorus of a number'. A blend of two ideas: the joy of going home and the relief of finishing something. CM.

let's go to Lily White's party! US domestic c.p., 'Said to a child about to be put to bed. (Lily White is, of course, the bed-sheets.) Not commonly used now, but popular in the 1930s–1940s' (A.B., 1978). I suspect that it long antedates 1930. P.B.: cf the Brit. near-synon, *climb the little wooden hill to Bedfordshire*, which dates back at least as far as mid-C19.

[**let's have one!** At **how will** (mostly **how'll**) **you have it?**, Lyell gives, as the commonest coll. invitations to take a drink, the following, all of late C19–20, except the last two (rarely heard before *c*. 1910): *what'll you have?* and *what's yours?* and *what is it? – how'll you have it?* and *let's have one! – name yours – what about a small spot?* and *d'you feel like a small spot?* Cf **name your poison!**

But I feel that full c.p. status should be denied to these drinking terms.]

let's have some light on the subject! Turn on the lights!: C20 (I can remember it from at least as early as 1910). An example of an uncommon-sense development: that from the figurative to the literal instead of the other way about. '*Let's shed some light on the matter* is a frequent alternative' (A.B., 1978) in the US. A further Brit. var., prob. as common, is *let's cast...*

let's have you! and **let's hear from you!** are non-commissioned officers' c.p. calls, the former to men due to turn out for a parade or a fatigue, and dating from *c*. 1910; the latter – 'Hurry up!' or 'Look lively!' – dates from the late C19, was esp. common in WW1, and derives from the vocal numbering of a rank of soldiers. (F & G for the later.)

The former may well have come from *let's be having you!* – a foreman's summons to his gang or party to start work.

let's keep it clean. See **keep it clean!**

let's live it up! See **live it up!**

let's make like (e.g. *horseshit*)... See **pretend you're a bee...**

let's make the scene! Let's share in what's going on: US: since *c*. 1965. Orig., hippy talk. Indicted by Sydney J. Harris in the

poem quoted at **right on!** It is 'now often [used] with specifically sexual connotation' (R.C., 1978).

let's not, and say we did! 'Negative response to the suggestion "Let's do" something or other. The implication is that "it" is not worth the exertion involved, plus a veiled suggestion that *saying* that one has done something may be as rewarding (i.e., in prestige) as actually having done it. American, mainly juvenile, from *c*. 1925; probably long extinct' (R.C., 1978).

let's not open that can of worms! '"Let's not introduce additional complications into an already complicated situation." A can of fishing worms is about as complicated as you can get. American: since *c*. 1940. It occurs in Raymond Chandler, *The Little Sister*, 1949' (R.C., 1978). See also **can of worms.**

let's not play silly buggers! 'Although you have this in the positive sense [see **let's play silly...**], in the negative it has a quite different meaning, identical with "Let's not play games"' (R.C., 1977) – i.e., an appeal to be serious about a matter. A var. is **don't play...**

let's re-invent the wheel! 'Let's not waste time by discussing things we all understand. Educated US, 1970s. A rather neat metaphor describing the not uncommon bureaucratic tendency to begin (and sometimes end) a discussion of some problem by belaboring the obvious' (R.C., 1978).

let's play it by ear!, with *let's* often omitted. 'Let's not plan our strategy [or our tactics] in advance. Extremely common since, *c*. 1960' (J.W.C., 1977). But arising, in the US, *c*. 1945 and adopted in the UK by the middle 1950s.

let's play silly buggers! Let's pretend we're mad *or* that we don't understand *or*, playfully, Let's do something silly: a proletarian c.p., dating from early in C20 and, by late 1914, adopted by the British army. B & P have suggested that this c.p. was prompted by a lot of wistful and, from the angle of reality or even of realism, rather silly talk about the possibility of being released from service.

let's run it up the flagpole! see **run it up the flagpole!**, and cf **let's spitball...**

let's see the color of your dough! Let's see your money! – either to ascertain whether one can pay or to demand immediate payment: US: C20. (Berrey.) P.B.: in UK, *let's see the colour of your money!*

let's spitball it into a windmill and see if... See **run it up the flagpole...**

letter(s). See: **deliver**; **Y is**; **you've been reading**; **Zed.**

letter in the post office – a (in full, **there is a...**). Refers to the monthly period: late C19–earlier 20.

[**lettuce, turnip and pea** indicates not even one vegetable 'but a natural need, thinly disguised. Daring of the frailer sex, I heard it during the 1930s, but it may go back to WW1' (L.A., 1976). It *did*; I heard several functional puns while on leave or in hospital in 1916 and 1918: it had prob. arisen a generation earlier. '*Let us turn up and pee.*' Not one of them is a genuine c.p., but I make the entry as a warning that a mere pun obviously does *not* form a c.p., although a c.p. may, and often does, incorporate a pun. P.B.: the legendary Lottie Collins is credited with 'She sits among the cabbages and peas'.]

liar. See: **I'm a bit**; **prove it.**

liars can figure. See **figures can't lie...**

library. See: **why buy.**

licence. See: **flying low**; **have you a**; **where did you get your l.**

licence to print money – not a. 'Coined by Lord Thomson in relation to commercial television, has, 1976 onwards, been a c.p. applied to any business venture likely to do well' (Skehan, 1977, and confirmed by Leonard Pearce, financial consultant). But the true c.p. form, obviously, is *this* (or *that*) *isn't a licence to print money.* (Lord Thomson seems to have used it in the positive, rather than in the negative, as Sir Edward Playfair has pointed out, and as Mr C.K. Patey writes that Thomson 'made the assertion...when he was awarded his first [Southern Television] franchise'.)

'Mobil [Oil] North Sea Ltd have published a series of 7 information broadsheets...Each has a catchy headline; one is "It's hardly a licence to print money". The affirmative version = "It's a bonanza"' (P.B., 1977). Note that (*it's* or *it is*) *hardly a licence... is a fairly frequent modification.

But the origin is much earlier than most people had thought: and I can hardly do better than to quote a comment by Vernon Noble, himself a BBC man for some years after WW2. A 'witticism perpetrated by Roy Herbert Thomson (later Lord Thomson of Fleet) which has taken up as a c.p. to denote the easy acquisition of riches; usually employed ironically in conversation. The remark was made by Thomson when commercial television was introduced into England in 1954 and he described the franchises for running such stations as "a licence to print money". Lord Thomson was a highly successful businessman and "Press Baron", a Canadian who became a British citizen in 1963' (1977). R.S. dates the c.p. as from 1955, but it didn't attain its heyday until *c.* 1970.

As an example of allusive employment: Ronald Pearsall, *Popular Music of the 20's*, 1976, 'Certain revues were not a licence to print money'.

lick. See: if you can't beat; it's not off; smear; we'll soon; you can't fight.

lid. See: that's put; there's a lid.

lie(s). See: and that's no lie; I cannot; I don't lie; it's all lies; that ain't no; you lie; and:

lie back and enjoy it! A c.p. allegedly used as advice to girl when escape from rape is impossible' (B.P., 1974): since *c.* 1950. 'The US version is "relax and enjoy it" – originally, I think, one of the **Confucius, he say** [q.v.] series, "When rape inevitable, relax and enjoy it". Now sometimes applied to any unpleasant but presumably inescapable prospect' (R.C., 1978). P.B.: the Brit. usage is also *lie back...*

lie down and I'll fan you! is a reply to any such request for service as the addressee feels to be unjustifiable: RAF, esp. among NCO Regular Servicemen: since *c.* 1925. With an allusion to the ministrations of punkah-wallahs in India and with an implication that the requester must be either feverish or distraught to have made the request at all. PGR.

lie of the day – the. An outrageous or monstrous or ludicrous untruth, spoken by one who is almost *splendide mendax*: *c.* 1760–1810. *The Morning Herald* of 7 Mar. 1786 offers 'Mrs M-ll, the elder, has herself as *ventilator principale* [sic], in circulating a certain report which long since was scouted as "the life of the day"'. On 17 March in the same year, *The General Advertiser* has 'This is so comical, that when folks hear of it, [they say...]'; John O'Kieffe, *The Toy*, III, ii, in his *Works*, 1798, uses it – but, in a shorter form, *The Toy* had been pub'd as *The Lie of the Day*, performed on 19 Mar. 1796. (Owed to Miss Patricia Sigh, who, 1977, notes that the *OED* cites Admiral Nelson's use of the phrase in 1796.)

lies, damned lies, and statistics neatly indicating an ascending order of mendacity, began its contemporary vogue during Clement Attlee's Labour Government of 1945–51 and increased its popularity during Harold Wilson's in 1964–69. Of its post-1945 currency, Mr Leonard Pearce thinks that it was a Treasury epigram, condemning the political economy of those outside, non-Parliamentarian authorities who were recruited by both those Prime Ministers. (Based on a talk with L.P., 1977.)

It has been attributed to Henry Labouchère – 'Labby', the writer (1798–1869); to Abram Hewitt (1822–1903); and, far more prob., Benjamin Disraeli (1804–81), who is quoted by Mark Twain (1835–1910) as saying 'There are three kinds of lies: lies, damned lies, and statistics.' I've failed to discover the date of Disraeli's *bon mot*, but would guess it to have been *c.* 1870; but its life as c.p. is prob. co-extensive with the C20. J.W.C. dates its US currency as from 1924, when Mark Twain's *Autobiography* appeared.

lieutenants might marry, captains may marry... occurs in full in Gavin Lyall's 'thriller', *Blame the Dead*, 1972, where one WW2 'type' says to another, '"Lieutenants might marry, captains may marry, majors should marry, colonels must marry," he quoted': army officers': since *c.* 1930. (I have to admit that as a GSO 3 (Education) in 1941 I never heard it.)

It evokes from Mr John Skehan, 1977, this pleasing reminiscence: 'I remember another gradation of rank, which was supposed to be current in the Indian Army in the days of the Raj... It was said that Routine Orders would refer to *officers and their ladies, Warrant Officers and NCOs and their wives, other ranks and their women*, which, as a fact, is mythical but, as a witticism, ranked as a catch phrase'. P.B.: Skehan's 'witticism' was still remembered, occasionally with some bitterness, in the Army of the 1970s.

life. See: all human *l.*; all part of life's; as I have breath; best things; hay, lass; how's your love; it's a dog's; it's a great *l.*; it's a hard *l.*; large as *l.*; living the *l.*; may you live; my life; not on your *l.*; nothing in; sit down; story; such is *l.*; thanks for saving; there's life; this is the *l.*; we ain't; what a *l.*; what do you want from; where have you; while there's *l.*; and:

life begins at forty (or **40**) was generated in the 1940s by a much-read book so titled – and by a popular song. P.B.: the phrase has become so embedded in the language that by the mid-1950s, at latest, the number 40 at Tombola (later known as Bingo) could be called simply 'Life begins', as an alternative to 'Four Oh: blind forty'.

life gets tedious (or **teejus**, occ. **tasteless**), **don't it?** An expression of resignation, a quiet acceptance, not despair, of inevitable monotony: since *c.* 1930. (Anon., 1978.)

life is just a bowl of cherries has been a US c.p. since 1931, when the song so titled was sung by Ethel Merman in *Scandals*; words by Brown, music by Henderson, as Edward B. Marks tell us in *They All Sang*, 1934; 'Marks sometimes omitted first names' (W.J.B., 1975). Pearl Harbor bombing, 7 Dec. 1941, rather jolted this rosy view of life: after that date, it tended to be ironical and to become ob. Introduced to me by Mr Ben Grauer during a long chat in 1974.

Cf Peter Cheney, *Never a Dull Moment*, 1942: 'I light a cigarette an' go on my way. I start whistlin' an old song – "Life is just a Bowl of Cherries". An' who says it ain't?' It is still current enough, in its ironic use, to be played with: R.C. cites the title of Irma Bombeck's, *If Life Is a Bowl of Cherries, What Am I Doing in the Pits?*, the Book of the Month Club's Publication No. 520, as advertised in *The New York Times Book Review*, 21 May 1978, where it puns the *pits* or stones of cherries and the slang *pits*, the very nadir of anything.

life is, or **life's, just one damned thing after another**, with **just** often omitted, and with **damn'** very often substituted for *damned*. Concerning the form *life is one damn' thing after another*. Mr Derek Parker, 1977, wrote to me thus: 'Don't know origin, but certainly extremely well known by 1926 when John Masefield published his novel *Odtaa* (the initials of the phrase). This must surely be the best known catch phrase which you missed [in the first ed. of this book].'

This is a 'triangular': famous quotation-become-cliché become (as *just one damn(ed) thing after another*) a c.p. The orig. form is as in the lemma, which, by *The Penguin Dictionary of Quotations* is attributed to Elbert Hubbard (1856–1915) in *A Thousand and One Epigrams*, and, by the 14th ed. of *Bartlett's Familiar Quotations*, to Frank Ward O'Malley (1875–1932); Bartlett does, however, add 'Also attributed to Elbert Hubbard'. It therefore seems likely that Masefield's book converted a famous quot'n and ensuing cliché into a c.p. – and popularized it.

What seems to be very much less well-known is that this c.p. acquired a dovetail: *and love is two damned things after each other*, which I first heard during the 1950s but which could easily have orig. during the late 1920s. A dovetail that is true of mere passion or lust but which is patently untrue of true love.

life is too short. 'It [whatever 'it' is] may be do-able, but the results won't be worth the effort: US: from 1960 or earlier'

(R.C., 1978). Much earlier, I'd say. Some currency in the UK also, usu. as *life's too short*.

life's *like* that! belongs to the 1920s and 1930s, although it's still heard occ. – hardly as a c.p. A Noël Coward sketch titled *Travelling Light*, written in 1924, ends thus:

ATTENDANT: You rang, Madame?

WOMAN: Shh! He's asleep.

ATTENDANT: Very human, Madame. Life's like that.

life's rich pattern. See: all part of life's.

lifeboat. See: I'm in the l.

lift. See: I lift; I'd have to be.

light. See: it is as good; let's appeal; let's have some; oh, nothing; once before; one of ours; put the lights; where was Moses; wouldn't give.

Light Brigade. See: charge like.

light the blue touchpaper and retire immediately! 'The firework instruction used as a catchphrase by Arthur Askey in *Band Waggon* on Guy Fawkes Night and used subsequently when withdrawing from confrontation with Mrs Bagwash' (*VIBS*). 'Band Waggon', starring Arthur Askey and Richard Murdoch, was BBC Radio's first real comedy series, and run through the late 1930s. Whether A.A.'s use of the phrase impressed it into the general consciousness, or whether nowadays it is simply associated with fireworks rather than with 'Band Waggon', the phrase is still current; as Simon Levene noted in 1977, 'Said when doing something risky'. *Retire immediately* is sometimes changed to *stand well clear*. (P.B.)

lights of Piccadilly Circus shining out of his (or **your**) **arsehole – he thinks he's (got)** (or **you think you've got)** the. A low c.p., dating since *c.* 1920, used mostly by the Services, and applied to someone's somewhat noticeable self-esteem. It adapts and elaborates the older and much more widely used *she thinks the sun shines out of his arse* or *arse-hole*, she regards him almost idolatrously: late C19–20, for certain, but perhaps dating since late C16, for it's the earthy sort of c.p. one could expect to have existed for centuries without getting into print or, at the least, into respectable print.

lights up! was, *c.* 1900–14, a playgoers' way of intimating their condemnation. Ware.

like. See: I like; I never liked; if he doesn't; if that's nonsense; if you don't l.; if you like; life's like; not like; one word; over you go; pink; some like; somebody up; stop it, l.; take that and; tell it l.; that's something l.; there are two; well, I l.; you still; and:

like a bandicoot on a burnt ridge. Extremely uncomfortable, perplexed, 'lost': Aus.: late C19–20. Henry Lawson used it in 1900. By 1978, ob. (Wilkes.) P.B.: an Antipodean 'cat on hot bricks'?

like a barber's cat... See **like a snob's cat....**

like a bastard at a family reunion or **a whore in church.** Said of a person glaringly out of place: US: C20. (Fain, 1977.) Cf **like a spare prick...**, **demure as a whore....** and **happy as a bastard....**

like a beer bottle. See **shag on a rock.**

like a blue-arsed fly. See **rushing around....**

like a cow's, or **a donkey's, tail.** See **all behind....**

like a fart in a colander. Applied to someone rushing, or tearing, around, esp. if to little effect, and in an anxious way: C20. B.G.T. remarks that, '"You're in and out like a fart in a colander" was said, in the 1920s, to a child running in and out of the house.' A var. is *like a fart at a fair*, and I have heard *like a fart in a bottle*. See also **much chance as a fart....** (P.B.)

Mr. F.M. Smith, Librarian of the British Transport Staff College, recalls, 1977, that *rushing around like a fart in a colander* was an RN expression for speedy and complicated action, esp. a sudden, or an unexpected, one; perhaps from as easily as the 1920s, and certainly pre–WW2. Cf **rushing around....**

like a fight between.... See **fight between....**

like a lily on a dirt-tin. See **shag on a rock.**

like a mercenary from the Cod War. 'Dressed in sea boots, submariners' sweater and Balaclava helmet': *My Old Man*, ITV comedy, 7 June 1974. 'This has become an "in" naval catchphrase' (Peppitt, 1976). 'The Cod War' refers to the *quasi* hostilities caused by the cod-fishing dispute between Britain and Iceland, mid 1970s.

like a moll, (or **a streetgirl) at a christening,** Wilkes defines it as 'ill at ease, flustered, confused', adduces examples covering 1954–73, and implicitly derives it from **demure as a whore**, q.v., and, by so doing, virtually dates it as having been in oral use throughout C19–20. Cf **like a whore....**

like a one-armed paperchangers with crabs. See **busy as a one-armed....**

like a pakapoo, ticket. See **pakapoo ticket.**

like a possum up a gum tree. See **possum....**

like a rope-dancer's pole: (with) lead at both ends (—usu. *he's*) was, *c.* 1770–1830, applied to a dull, sluggish fellow. Grose, 1785.

like a sheep's head: all jaw. Belonging to mid C18–20, although slightly ob. by 1935 and almost † by *c.* 1970, it has been scathingly applied to an excessively talkative person. Grose, 1788.

like a snob's cat: all piss and tantrums was a low c.p. of *c*, 1820–50. (JB). This snob is a cobbler or shoemaker. Extant is *like a barber's cat – all wind and piss*, applied, late C19–20, to a man all talk and no performance.

like a spare prick at a wedding, often prec. by **standing about.** Unwanted, useless, idle, esp. with a hint of painfully embarrassed superfluity: low: since, at least, 1920, when I first heard it, but prob. dating since *c.* 1880 or 1890.

In Act I (p. 40 of the Faber edn) of John Osborne's *West of Suez*, 1971, we find:

EVANGIE: Besides, you do, at least, seem to enjoy every-thing....

ROBERT: Instead of looking like a professional spare prick at a wedding.

And Prof. Laurie Taylor, in *New Society*, 4 Nov. 1982, p. 205, uses the shortened form: 'Wherever we went [in underworld circles], I continued to stand out like a spare prick.'

P.B.: the distinguished writer Miss Rosemary Sutcliff, OBE, reminded me, 1977, of the more ladylike version, *standing around like a lost lemon*.

like a steer, I can try. ' A cowboy saying applicable to many forms of conduct' (Adams): orig. cowboys', soon gen. in US rural usage: (?) late C19–20;. From the fruitless, frustrated mountings of castrated bulls.

like a whore at a christening. Cf **demure as a whore....** Common in the Merchant Navy since *c.* 1950–and prob. earlier; but in the sense 'clumsy, out of place' (Peppitt, 1976). See also **like a moll....**

like a winter's day: short and dirty. This prob., at first, rural mid C18–mid C19 c.p. is recorded in Grose, 1788. Cf the dialectal *winter Friday*, a cold and wretched-looking person. R.C. notes that C.S. Forester, in *Ship of the Line*, 1938 (period: Napoleonic Wars), uses the var. *short, dark and dirty*.

like all fools I love everything that's good, late C17–20, occurs in e.g., S, 1738, Dialogue I:

LADY SM[ART]:.... Colonel, do you like this Bisket?

COL[ONEL]: I'm like all fools, I love every thing that's good.

The *ODEP* classifies it as a proverb in the form. 'I am a fool: I love anything (*or* everything) that's good.'

like Aunt Fanny, often prec. by **you're,** is disparagingly addressed to someone either inexperienced or very clumsy with tools: workmen's: C20. Contrast **my Aunt Fanny!**

like Barney's bull. C.p. applied to one who is physically exhausted or otherwise distressed: Aus. and Eng.: C20. In Aus., either *bitched, buggered and bewildered*, or (*well*) *fucked and far from home* may be added; but in rural England 'I feel like Barney's bull' often suffices – as B.G.T. notes, 1978, of the Northamptonshire usage, 'heard to describe extreme weariness and disinclination to do any-thing'. This prob. derives from the *Barney's bull* that was **all behind**, q.v., and is not to be confused with its opp., the extremely fit and 'rarin' to go' *Mallee bull*.

like being caught up in a circular saw. 'An Australian metaphor for female promiscuity' (Wilkes): since mid C20.

like Dick's hatband. See **queer as Dick's**....

like flies.... See **flies around a bull's arse**.

like hell I will! An intensive refusal, 'I certainly will not!': since the middle 1940s, (Petch, 1974, says: 'heard on and off'.) 'Sometimes *like shit I will*' (A.B., 1978): US. P.B.: and, of course, with other, stronger intensives.

like it! See **and like it!** and **I like it!**

like Jack the Bear: just ain't nowhere. A US negroes' c.p. of *c*. 1930–50, indicating extreme disappointment or frustration or wounded vanity. CM.

like MacArthur I shall return. This mainly Aus. c.p. dates from 1942 and denotes that 'one's absence will only be temporary, especially if it is suspected that one is trying to escape hard work'. It derives from General Douglas MacArthur's famous promise to the Filipinos 'to return and liberate them from the Japanese'. (B.P.) A.B., 1979, adds that 'when he did return, he said "I *have* returned". These remarks are still in use [in US] but are fading from currency'. The two relevant dates are 11 Mar. 1942 and 20 Oct. 1944. Cf **Marines have landed**....

like one o'clock half-struck. 'Familiar in my youth, i.e. *c*. 1929–36. Somebody gormless, probably momentarily – "Well, don't stand like one o'clock half-struck" and varia-tions as necessary' (Wedgewood, 1977). Mostly N. Country, I'd say, with currency very approx. *c*. 1910–40.

like something the cat's brought in or, in Aus., **like something the cat brings in on a wet night**, usu. prec. *look* or *looking*. Applied to one who looks utterly bedraggled or very disreputable: since *c*. 1920. In US,... *cat dragged in* (J.W.C.); 'Not much used now' (A.B., 1978). Also **look what the cat's brought in!** As e.g., a young bird, rain-heavy. Cf **look what the wind's blown in!**

like the butcher's daughter: dripping for **it** is self-explanatory in its application to a liquescent woman: perhaps mostly, yet far from being only, Aus.: C20.

like the ladies of Barking Creek. Of women (esp. of girls still virgin) excusing themselves from intercourse on the grounds of having their period: since *c*. 1910; by 1920, also Aus. From the well-known limerick about the ladies of Barking Creek – who have their periods three times a week.

[**like the man said.** 'No particular man, any man. A throw-away introduction to a remark' (Noble, 1974): US: less of a c.p. than a cliché, it dates from the 1950s.]

like the man who fell out of the balloon: he wasn't in it refers to one who stood no chance whatsoever, as in an undertaking, an adventure, a boxing match, an athletic event: C20. The *Humorist*, 28 July 1934.

like the man who fought the monkey in a dustbin, or it may have been ... **in the dust-hole**, after the Queen's, later the Prince of Wales's, Theatre in the Tottenham Court Road, London: *c*. 1830–late 1880s. Meaning, vague: perhaps 'in an awful mess' – clothes torn, face and hands scratched. (Jack Eva, 1978.) John Harris, *The Sea Shall Not Have Them*, 1953, a flight sergeant addressing an aircraftman recruit: 'What are you? Armourer? Electrician? Sanitary wallah? Or just the man who fought the monkey?'

like the story of Pharaoh's daughter, who, you may recall, found the infant Moses in a basket: 'a well-known Australian c.p.', B.P. tells me, of C20. For its dry scepticism, cf **you'll be telling me**....

like there was no tomorrow, or occ. and formally, **as if there were (to be) no tomorrow**. A phrase expressing excess and recklessness of action, in such contexts as 'They were swarming at the sales, spending their cash like there was no tomorrow': orig. US; adopted in UK later 1970s. (P.B.)

like to bet on it? Are you absolutely sure it won't happen?: C20.

(Granville, 1969.) Prob. elliptical for 'Are you so sure it won't happen that you'll bet on it?'

like Tom Trot's dog: he'd go a bit of the road with (Anglo-Irish **wid**) **anyone**. 'He's too easy-going, anxious to please, of no fixed principles' (Shaw, 1968): Anglo-Irish: ?mid C19–20; then, by 1900 or a little earlier, also English. The *Trot* is not merely alliterative, but also allusive to such a phrase as *always on the trot*, restlessly active and busy.

likely. See: not bloody.

likewise, I'm sure! 'I reciprocate your sentiments. Prob. orig. Jewish-American, from 1940s; later, some general use; now somewhat ob.' (R.C., 1978). P.B.: not a c.p. in Brit. Eng., but 'genteel', and in use prob. throughout C20, if not considerably earlier: lower and lower-middle class.

lily. See: gild; shag.

Lily White. See: let's go to L.

lime. See: green lime.

limit. See: ain't that the *l*.; sky's the *l*.

line. See: get on; holding.

lines like a butter-box (–**she has**) is a nautical c.p. that has, in latish C19–20, been applied to 'a clumsy, full-bodied ship' (Bowen). Since it refers mostly to sailing-ships, it became, *c*. 1930, ob., and by *c*. 1950,†.

lining. See: every silver.

lion tamers. See: we'll soon.

lions. See: they tame.

lip(s). See: don't make me laugh; more lip; my lips; you are a mouth; your lip's.

lips that touch liquor shall never touch mine – the. 'Taken from a Victorian song. Addressed to a female in mock warning' (Skehan, 1984). The quot'n is from the song thus titled, words by G.W. Young, the relevant couplet running 'Though in silence, with blighted affection, I pine,/Yet the lips that touch liquor must never touch mine!' (P.B.)

liq. See: what will you.

liquor. See: lips that.

list. See: on my shit.

little. See: Eric; is there room; nothing for; only a *l*.; pain in his; with a *l*.; you know what; you little.

listen (sometimes **look**) **who's talking!** is addressed derisively to one who, in the circumstances, really shouldn't be talking at all, esp. in such a censorious way: lower and lower-middle class: C20. (Petch, 1974.)

The US form is *look*..., vouched for by Moe, 1975.

little Audrey laughed and laughed and laughed (–**and**) has been current since the late 1920s, and is applied to a fit of laughter arising for a reason either inadequate or not immediately apparent to others. 'There was a longish series of letters about this in *The Times* two years ago' (Simon Levene, 1977). It enjoyed very considerable popularity *c*. 1933–39 and orig. formed the 'lead-in to a frightful (and often scabrous) pun... perhaps in a Radio series by Leslie Sarony or some other such comedian.' To exemplify: One day, little Audrey, smug and knowing, wandered into the bathroom while her uncle was having a bath [and listening to the radio]. Seeing the symbol of his masculinity, she asked what it was. Her embarrassed uncle replied that it was his Bush, a well-known make of radio in those days, *and little Audrey laughed and laughed, because she knew it was Ferranti*, another make of radio: pun on *for Aunty* (R.S., 1977). 'I remember there *were* "little Audrey" jokes, and probably Leslie Sarony capitalized on them' (Barry Took, 1977).

[**little bird told me – a.** A semi-proverbial c.p.: C18–20. It replies to the (not necessarily expressed) query, 'Who told you?' Rather more of a proverbial saying than of a c.p.]

little bit of all right. See **this is a bit of all right**.

little bit of him, or **her**, **goes a long way with me – a.** This expresses dislike: US Negroes': since late 1940s. (*The Third Ear*, 1971.) But, esp. as *a little of*..., this c.p. has been current in Brit. since at least as early as the 1920s.

little bullshit goes a long way – a. It pays to flatter – to boast – to 'con' people: Aus.: since 1919. (B.P.) P.B.: prob. the inspiration of the story current in the later 1940s, of the robin, who, having eaten his fill from the stockyard floor, flew to the nearest high point and sung his contentment to the world. Whereupon he was in turn eaten by a passing eagle. Moral: a little bit of bullshit may get you to the top of the tree, but there is no need to make a song and dance about it.

little, but, oh my!, usu. prec. by **he is** or **he was**. In *Mr Bonaparte of Corsica*, 1895, John Kendrick Bangs says, '"Did you ever hear that little slang phrase so much in vogue in America," queried Napoleon, coldly fixing his eye on Barras – "a phrase which in French runs, '*Petit, mais O Moi*', as they have it, 'Little, but O My'? Well, that is me."' Apparently it was current in the US in the 1890s and early 1900s, for witness also Guy Wetmore Carryl, *Grimm Tales Made Easy*, 1902, in the poem titled 'How Hop O' My Thumb Got Rid of an Onus':

The youngest of the urchins heard,
And winked the other eye;
Hise height was only two feet three.
(I might remark, in passing, he
Was little, but O My!)
He added: 'I'd better keep mum.'

(He was foxy, was Hop O' My Thumb!)
The phrase travelled to UK and to Aus.; I heard it in the latter country in 1912 or 1913. Nor is it yet defunct.

What does need to be added is that this c.p. was mostly employed with a waggish imputation of sexual prowess and mischief.

R.C. compares the line from *Porgy and Bess*, 1935, 'Little David was small, but oh my!'; and J.B. Smith, of Bath, notes, 1979, that it has the German equivalent *Klein, aber oho*. He adds that Rölrich 2,516, doesn't trace the history of this common expression.

[**little fields have big gates.** Is this a c.p. orig. rural, or an unrecorded rural proverb of (?) C19–20? It refers to the fact that many small women bear many big children, the reason pretty clearly being that they possess an invincible vitality.]

little girl. See: and whose.

little green men is a Can. c.p., alluding to mysterious beings reported to have been seen emerging from flying saucers: since 1957. (Leechman.) Influenced by 'horror comics' with their pictures of little men from outer space. P.B.: equally well-known in UK, and prob. the rest of the English-speaking world.

little less off and a little more on – a, is the 'sarcastic injunction to a "dressing-room" star who is full of facetiousness and arrogance, but has no marked talent to justify the attitude' (Granville): theatrical: C.20.

little man, you've had a busy day dates in the UK since the 1930s, but may be much later in the US; it comes from a very popular song, addressed by mother to very young son and, as a c.p., is spoken with ironic pity to someone who has had a very tough day. (I've known the c.p. for some forty years, but was apprised of its US currency by Mrs John W. Clark and had the origin confirmed by Mr Michael Lane, Director of Music at Dartington Hall, Devon, 1977.) This 'sentimental popular song' appeared in 1934, words by Maurice Sigler and A.R. Hoffman, music by Mabel Wayne. (Courtesy of the Music authority at the Enquiries Desk, main reading room, the British Library; triggered off by Mrs Mollie Stonor.)

little of what you fancy does you good – a. In *Waiting in the Wings*, 1960, Noël Coward has, at III, i:

MAY: Only a very little. (*He goes round filling glasses.*)
ALMINA: Oh no, I daren't. really I daren't.
PERRY: Come on – a little of what you fancy does you good.

'Marie Lloyd sang and winked as she sang it, and it was for long a c.p.' (Noble, 1973): C20 – and extant! Marie Lloyd (1870–1922) remains a lively legend; this song she sang dates from *c.* 1897.

It is frequently misquoted as *a bit of what...* or *a spot of what...* Cf **it's naughty but it's nice**.

little old ladies in tennis shoes. This US c.p., apparently dating from *c.* 1920, is applied, says J.W.C., 1968, to:

bourgeois beldames – fussy, self-important, naïve, ignorant, self-confident, self-righteous, gullible, conventional, conservative, old-fashioned, prudish, unfashionable, and typical rural or small town. They wear tennis shoes because their feet hurt and they don't care how they look.

Ashley, 1979, instances 'the little old lady from Dubuque who wouldn't like anything risqué', in the *New Yorker* Magazine.

[**little poontang now and then is cherished by the wisest men – a**. It occurs in Glendon Swarthout's novel, *The Tin Lizzie Group*, 1972, set in the year 1916. *Poontang* may, as W & F propose, derive from French *putain*, a prostitute, via the Creoles of New Orleans, but I doubt it. Rather a chant than a true c.p., it parodies 'A little folly now and then/Is cherished by the wisest men'. R.C., 1977: 'The version I know is *a little kissing...* New obsolescent if not dead.']

little rabbits have big ears. A C20 Aus. warning to speak more quietly or less frankly in front of children. Partly a c.p., but partly also a mere modification of the proverb, *little pitchers have big ears*. (B.P.)

little things please little minds. Since mid C20 at latest the commoner version of **small things...**

live. See: come on, my; don't ask me; follow your own; I don't make; I live; I should *l.*; if I have breath; if you've never; it's a nice place; may you *l.*; nice place to *l.*; and that lives; sure as thou; we will.

live it up!, often prec. by *let's*. 'Let's enjoy ourselves, regardless of expense' – but now usu. ironic, in respect of some very minor expenditure. (R.C., 1978.) Cf the synon. *live (it up) a little*, same meaning, but less ironic; in the same class as *give the cat another goldfish!*, and *last of the big-time spenders*. (P.B.) Orig. US, soon also Brit.: since *c.* 1945. See quot'n at **be a devil!**

liver. See: wants his.

LIVERPOOL CATCH PHRASES. In 1968, the late Frank Shaw, author of, *inter alia*, *Lern Yerself Scouse*, wrote to me thus:

'**There's hair** [pronounced *durs ur*] **on baldy!**' – shouted derisively by Liverpool street girls *c.* 1924.

'**John Hughes won't save yer!**' – shouted after eligible-for-Service types *c.* 1917. A shopkeeper named John Hughes was alleged, in a court case, to have found ways of getting exemption from conscription for young men (often Irish) in his employ. Lasted, with origin forgotten, into the 1920s.

Buy a book (pronounced *bewk*), **Where's yer white stick?** (suggesting blindness), and other taunts to unpopular soccer refs, I quote in *Lern Yerself Scouse*. Used for decades to a defective kicker, **Here's yer bewk.** [i.e. Book of Rules.]

There he is – wheel him in. There he is – bail him out. The girls again won't let the boys alone. 1920–30? Or just *Bail him out* – shouted after any unpopular person.

A month later, Mr Shaw told me the Liverpool equivalent of *Bob's your uncle* has, since *c.* 1920, been **you're laffin bags**, where *bags* = '*very much*'.

Note also **make yer name Walker** and **muck in! yer at yer granny's.**

Liverpool landing-stage. See: only stage.

living. See: I will work; it's a *l.*; pardon me; that's the *l.*; there must be.

living bloody wonder – a. An Aus. c.p. of ironic appreciation: since *c.* 1930. (B.P.)

living doll – he's or **she's** or **you're a.** This US c.p., dating since latish 1940s and partly adopted in the UK, is glossed by J.W.C., 1977, as '(He's) a very kind and obliging and generous person' – to which I'd add 'likeable'. P.B.: popularized in UK by a love song, the chorus of which ran 'She's a walkin', talkin',... livin' doll!'

living high off the hog's back, or simply **...off the hog.** Living very well, almost in luxury. 'Contrasting ham, and pork chops, with the animal's lower cuts.. and especially salt pork, which were the traditional diet of the poor Southerner.

Originally Southern US from...C19, but long general, though [now] becoming uncommon. Cf the Irish *on the pig's back*' (R.C., 1978).

living in seduced circumstances is a raffishly joc. c.p., applied to a pregnant unmarried girl or woman: since *c.* 1920.

living on the bone of his arse and ...**on the smell of an oily rag,** or **oil-rag.** These are Aus. c.pp. indicating a condition of extreme poverty. Both from Lovett, 1978, who tells me that he first heard the *bone* version in 1953 – I had never heard it; but I've known the other since during WW1.

living the life of Reilly – *I'm* or *you're*, etc. A C20 Anglo-Irish c.p., denoting *la dolce vita* or, at worst, having a 'good' life. Adopted in US by *c.* 1935, often with sense '"Everything is all right with me"; in the form *Riley*; William Bendix played the part of Riley on both radio and TV; 1950s' (A.B., 1978).

living with mother now is addressed by females to a man either proposing or 'propositioning': 1881 – *c.* 1914. Ware noted that, orig., these words formed the refrain of a rather doubtful song.

Livingstone. See: Doctor L.

Liza. See: he's saving; outside.

Lizzie. See: Henry's.

load. See: get a load; take a l.; that's a l.; they go better; what a l.

lobby Lud. See: you are Mr.

lobster-kettle. See: I will not.

lodge. See: you can't l.

lodger. See: Roger.

logging. See: now you're l.

Lombard Street. See: all Lombard.

London. See: carry on, L.; don't turn; it's raining; that's the way to L.; Walker, L.; you could ride.

London to a brick (a *brick* being Aus. slang for £10 in the old currency). Orig., and still, racing odds; as an Aus. c.p., since *c.* 1955, an expression of (virtual) certainty. The phrase was orig., and, in his race-course announcements much used, by Ken Howard (1914–76), who, asked where the phrase came from, wrote, in 1974, that he thought he had picked it up in the billiard halls when he 'was younger'. (Wilkes.) Prob. the phrase was modelled on **all Lombard Street to a china orange.** Lovett, 1978, recalls Howard's name as John, and compares the phrase's popularity to that of the synon. *it's two bob to a pinch of shit* [P.B.: in UK that is usu. *a pound to a pinch...*]

Lone Ranger rides again. See **rides again.**

long. See: how long; I should live; I'll pull; it will be I'll be; it's a long; little bit of him; now we shan't; she hasn't had; too short; what's the odds; you're a long; you've come; and:

long and slender like a cat's elbow. A C18 – mid C19 saying, midway between c.p. and proverb. Fuller.

long as a piece of string (–as). 'A teasing reply (mainly) to questions about length of time, e.g. "How long will you be?"' (L.A., 1974). Cf **how long is a piece...**

long as a whore's nightmare, occ. prec. by *as*. Very long: US, 'I first heard it in 1953, in ref. to a very big automobile. I think it is not frequently used now' (A.B., 1978).

long-boat. See: three turns.

long day. See: been a long day.

long may your big jib draw! This is a Newfoundland c.p., C20, expressing good wishes for the addressee's future. Presumably it orig. among trawlermen. (Maxwell Taylor, 1977.) Prob. it has, among the raffish, attracted a sexual innuendo.

long nose is a lady's liking – a. A low c.p. of C19 – early C20. In a male, a long nose is, in popular mythology, said to denote a long penis. Fain thinks it is a C18 c.p.; this could well be so; it might even have occurred in Restoration comedy. It has, moreover, a proverbial tang. Cf **big conk...**

long short'uns or short long'uns? is an Aus. c.p. addressed to a male wearing trousers that fail to cover his ankles: since *c.* 1930. (B.P.)

long splices. See: different ships.

long-tailed bear – **a,** often prec. by **that's.** You're lying: not

used in the more cultured circles: late C19 – early C20. Ware gives, 'Bears have no tails.'

long time between drinks. See: **as the Governor...**

long time no see! I haven't seen you for ages: Brit. and US: since the early 1900s. In Brit. usage, it derives from Far East, specifically Chinese, pidgin; it came to UK by way of the Merchant Service, reinforced by the RN; Granville, 1967, says that it is a 'Chinaside locution akin to such phrases as *no can do, chop chop, no wanchee,* etc. Naval officers used to greet "old ships" who'd been on China Station with "Hullo, old boy, long time no see."' [P.B.: it is in fact a literal translation of a very common Chinese greeting, *hao jiu mei jian.*]

The US and Can. use of the phrase prob. comes from the same source but has been strongly influenced by two or three very widely distributed popular anecdotes. Leechman, 1967, writes: 'I first heard it about 1910.... Very common out here' (British Columbia). Berrey, 1942, lists it as a greeting. W&F gloss it as 'A common student and young adult greeting *c.* 1940 – *c.* 1945', but it's very much older than that; and in the British Commonwealth it is still going strong, as indeed it is in the US – witness the allusion in Jack D. Hunter, *Spies, Inc.*, 1970: '"Well, well, well," Carson beamed. "Long time no behold. How are you, Mr Fitch?"' Rather oddly, the oldest printed record I have of it is afforded by Harry C. Witwer's *Love and Learn*, 1924 (p. 73). Perhaps slightly on the wane since *c.* 1972. Nevertheless, this is one of the most widely used of all c.pp. whatsoever, despite the fact that many of us find it tiresome.

The US currency goes back to the late C19, to judge by the fact that the *OED New Supp.* can cite a Red Indian as saying 'Long time no see you'. P.B.: there have been Chinese living and working up and down the West coast of North America since the Gold Rush days of mid C19, and before. Petch noted, 1969, that the phrase had, since *c.* 1960, often been shortened to *long time*. It even features in the awful pun, 'As the Kipper bone said, "Long time..."' (*The Old Joke Book*, compiled by J. & A. Ahlberg, 1977). Cf:

long time no see: short time buckshee (i.e. free)! 'Services', Far East. Wishful thinking for a prostitute's greeting (P.B., 1975): since *c.* 1950.

longer. See: difficult we do; over you go.

longest pole knocks down the persimmon – **the.** This US c.p. [P.B.: or proverb?], throughout C20 and prob. dating from *c.* 1850, is a homespun version of 'The best man wins'. Recorded by the *DAm* from 1863 to 1914, but no orig. given; there could poss. be a ref. to the long pole used in the navigation of big rivers. But why *persimmon*? Some old sport?

look. see: don't look; good soldier; have a good l.; he's been looking; here's looking; if you looked; it'll look; lost his hat; no harm; over you go; pay up; pissed on a nettle, she's looks; things are looking; wreck.

look, do me (or us) a favour, will you? See **do me a favour.**

look, Ma (or Mum), no hands! See:

look, no hands! is often applied to something done cleverly, yet no conspicuously, if indeed at all, useful: since *c.* 1910. From the proud, showy claims of a child riding a bicycle with no hands on the bars. A good example occurs in Lesley Storm's comedy, *Look, No Hands!* which opened at the Fortune Theatre, London, on 19 July 1971; and a significant allusion had occurred in Peter O'Donnell, *A Taste of Death*, 1969: 'This is vox-operated transmission... the set automatically switches to send when... and to receive when...No hands.'

But perhaps the best example of all is the allusion in Terence Rattigan, *Variation on a Theme*, 1958, at I, ii, where Ron, a ballet dancer, rehearses teenaged Fiona, who's not very good, in a ballet routine.

He lifts her on to his shoulder with practised ease. Still giggling, she clutches first at his neck. Then she removes her hands precariously and waves her arms triumphantly in the air.

FIONA: No hands!

It has a US var., *look, Ma, no hands*, which occurs, wittily, in Hank Searl's *Pentagon*, 1971 (Moe), itself perhaps suggested by the Brit. var.. *look, Mum, no hands*, adduced by Skehan, 1977, who remarks: 'Said in a self-deprecatory sort of way when doing something difficult.' It has, of course, been used in a number of sick jokes: representative is its appearance as caption to a picture of the Venus de Milo (P.B.)

look on the wall and it will not bite you was, *c*, 1660–1914, addressed derisively to a person 'bitten with mustard' (Ray).

look (occ. **see**) **what the cat's brought** (or, in US, more often **dragged**) **in!** See **like something the cat's...**

look what the wind has (or **the wind's**) **blown in!** See **who's arrived!**: joc.: C20. Cf **like something the cat's brought in!**

look who's talking! see **listen who's talking!**

look you! is applied to Welshmen by all other nationals when they wish to allude to, or to impute or imply, any decidedly Welsh characteristic: C19–20. It is a Cymricism well known since C16 at latest; so much so that it occurs frequently in the plays by James Shirley (1596–1666), as, e.g., in V, iii, of *Love Tricks, or, The School of Compliment*, where Welshman Jenkin says, 'Hark you, is there another Selinas? Bless us awl, here is very prave Love-tricks, look you.'

'More to the point, it occurs very frequently indeed in Shakespeare's *Henry V* (1599): eleven times in the scene in which Fluellen makes his first appearance' (Prof. D.J. Enright, in *Encounter*, Dec. 1977).

look, you rhwew now! You surprise me! Colloquially: Well, I never!: late C17–mid C18. Sir John Vanbrugh, in *The Confederacy*, 1705, at I, i, where Mrs. Cloggit, a woman of the people, uses it twice.

MRS AMLET:...Would you believe it, Mrs Cloggit, I have worn out four pairs of patterns with following my old lady Youthful, for one pair of false teeth, and but three pots of paint.

MRS CLOGGIT: Look you there now!

looking at me? See **are you looking...**

looking for maidenheads is a c.p. directed at someone looking for something either unprocurable or, at the least, exceedingly scarce: since *c*. 1890; since WW2 becoming increasingly difficult to find, hence the phrase is now somewhat nostalgic and ob.

looking like a pox doctor's clerk. See **all dressed up like a dog's dinner.**

lookit. See: gee, lookit.

looks as if (or **though**)... Some similes will be found at their keyword, e.g. **lost a pound...**; **pissed on a nettle**; **Whelan the wrecker...**

looks good to me, elliptical for 'It *or* that looks good to me', is US, dating since *c*. 1910 and mentioned in 'Straight Talk', by S.R. Strait in the *Boston Globe* of *c*. 1917. (W.J.B.)

looks like a bag o' shit tied up with (or **wi'**) **string – he** or **she**, recalls **rides like a bag of flour**, but has a wider application, to persons shapeless and untidy: C20. (P.B.)

looks like a million dollars – he or **she**. 'Looks extremely attractive, as a million dollars certainly is. But with a suggestion that part of his money has been spent on expensive clothing' (R.C., 1978): since *c*.1920, at latest. Cf *a million-dollar figure*. 'The female form of divine' – as Mr. Claiborne adds. P.B.: also, *I feel like a million dollars*, I could not possibly be any happier, I am absolutely at the topmost pinnacle of enjoyment.

looks like a wet weekend (– **it**). This Aus. c.p., dating since *c*. 1930, has been used both by girls menstruating at the weekend and, since *c*. 1940, addressed by males, most of them expectably teenaged, to a girl carrying a packet that, to judge by its size, may well contain a carton of tampons or sanitary pads. P.B.: specialization of a simile earlier applied, in UK, to a particularly gloomy-looking person.

looks (or **it looks**) **like rain** refers to the probability of an imminent arrest: US tramps': C20. U.

look like something the cat's brought in. See **like something...**

looks like the wreck of the Hesperus. See **wreck of the Hesperus...**

looks towards you. see **I looks...**

loose. See: hang loose; how ya; if your head; lose his arse; stay loose; turn me; and:

loose as a goose (-**as**). A US c.p., from before 1960 (W & F) – say, late 1940s. An elab. of *loose*, (of a female) promiscuous: cf the Standard American, ex Brit. Standard American, ex Brit. Standard English, 'a woman of *loose* morals'.

lootenant. See: aw, shit.

Lord. See: praise.

Lord Mayor's show. See: after the Lord.

Lord Roberts. See: I have a picture.

lordship. See: one lordship.

lorry. See: coming up; did it drop off.

lose. See: cross, I win; don't lose; if I lose, if your head; we don't want; what can you l.; you win.

lose his arse if it was loose – he would. This refers to a careless, esp. very forgetful, person: *c*. 1770–1860. (Grose, 2nd ed., 1788.) Later, and still current, is the more polite (e.g. *you'd*) *lose (your) head if it wasn't screwed on (tight)*, q.v. at **if your head...**

loss is (sometimes **was**) **ours – the.** In S. 1738, Dialogue II opens thus:

LORD SM[ART]: I'm sorry I was not at home this Morning, when you all did us the Honour to call here. But I went to the Levee To-Day.

LORD SP[ARKISH]: O, my Lord; I'm sure the Loss was ours. This courteous c.p., perhaps orig. a witty convention, has survived from late C17 to the present.

lost. See: get lost; half an hour is; we are l.

lost a pound and found (a) sixpence – he or **she looks as if he** or **she has**; occ. **lost a shilling and found a ha'penny.** (He) looks either ruefully pleased or, more frequently, very miserable: C19–20; † with decimalization, 1971, but David Short, 1978, noted their use into later C20.

lost his hat and got off to look for it is 'said of a rider who has been thrown from a bucking horse' (Adams). An ironic excuse by onlookers: US cowboys': (?) late C19–20.

lost the key of the 'angar door. An RAF c.p. dating from the 1920s or the early 1930s. From a topicality explained in Flying Officer B.J. Hurren's *Stand Easy*, 1934.

lot. See: and that's your lot; cop that lot; greedy; how nice; not a lot; when you've seen; and:

lot of water has flowed under the breeches (or **britches**) – **a.** 'A low parody' (Petch, 1969) that has become a low c.p.: since *c*. 1950.

loud and clear. See: message.

Louis. See: drop the gun.

louse. See: he'd skin; never louse.

love. See: ain't love; face that; how's your l.; I love; I must l.; I wish I had a man; I'm dreaming; I'm like; like all fools; Mademoiselle; make love; sir, you are; somebody up; who loves; and:

love and a nickel seegar is, like **till hell freezes over**, a letting-ending c.p.: US: *c*. 1920–30. (J.W.C., 1977.)

love 'em and ride on. See **fuck 'em and leave 'em.**

love 'em (or **you**) **and leave 'em** (or **you**). See **I must love...**

lovely. See: 'e's lovely; everything in the garden; everything is lovely; oh, wouldn't; that's lovely; what a l. and:

lovely bit of boy – a. is a Servicewomen's c.p., applied – since 1939 and esp. throughout WW2 – to a man of whom they physically approve.

lovely grub! is another WW2 (and after) c.p., meaning 'Very nice indeed!' and applied to anything – from tasty food (*grub*) to a furlough or any other agreeable experience. *VIBS* amplifies: 'Said by George Gorge (played by Fred Yule) in *ITMA*. "The greediest man ever to have two ration books" used to say it, smacking his lips – as also did Charles Hill during his stint as the Radio Doctor (without smacking his lips)'. See also TOMMY HANDLEY.

lover. See: I'm a lover.

low. See: flying; riding his.

low ebb. See: he that is.

low man on totem pole – the. The lowest-ranking, least successful, etc., individual in a given group. *Low Man on a Totem Pole* was used as the title of a book by H. Allen Smith, 1941 (pub'd in UK, 1947), hence US from 1940s or earlier. If you need information about totem poles among the Indians of the NW USA and SW Can., go to any good encyclopaedic dictionary; the c.p. ignores the ethnological facts. P.B.: so well-known had the phrase become, in UK as well as US, that Charles Schulz could, 1982, have the loud-mouth-sister dominated Linus suffer, in the 'Peanuts' strip-cartoon, 'I was hoping to lie in the beanbag, and watch TV...' – 'Too bad,' says Lucy, 'I got here first.' – 'That's the story of my life....Low man on the beanbag!'

lower than a snake's belly (or **hips**) is, in Aus.. orig. and still mostly, applied to a person, or an act, utterly contemptible and despicable. Wilkes's earliest example comes from Leonard Mann, *Flesh in Armour*, 1932, but I heard it during WW1 – and, even then, it was clearly a well-known expression. By WW2 it was in use among Britain's Armed Forces. Hence, since *c.* 1945, the shortened *lower than a snake* and, since *c.* 1947, *he'd* (or *he could*) *crawl under a snake's belly with a top hat on* (L.A., 1959). US supplies the variants: *lower than a snake's elbows* and, of a very close-fisted person, *lower than a snake's vest-pocket*; also *he's so low a snake couldn't crawl under him*. None arising later than *c.* 1950. (A.B., 1978.)

luck. See: best of; devil's own; half your; over the top; shit out; up you go; you never know your; and:

luck of Eric Connolly – the. 'A byword for luck in betting, from a noted gambler (d. 1944): Aus.: since *c.* 1925. The earliest ref. I've seen to Eric Connolly occurs in the late Lawson Glassop's novel *Lucky Palmer*, 1949. Frank Hardy refe: two or three of his humorous works, to Connolly' (Wilkes,

[**luck to him! – bad** (or **good**). A pejorative or an approving c.p., which can, on occasion, be meant either ironically or jocularly congratulatory: C19–20. On the borderline between c.p. and cliché, but rather the latter than the former. Cf **best of British luck.**]

lucky. See: be lucky, come on, my; could fall; I should be; now then, me; so lucky; we lucky; you lucky; you should be; you'll be l.; and:

lucky Pierre (always in ze middle) is applied to someone getting more than his fair share of the 'action': since mid C20. From a scabrous joke, as Ashley, 1984, reminds me. (P.B.)

lucky as a bastard on Father's Day. See **happy as a bastard...**

lucky old saddle! 'This is a "naughty boys" chant or shout at a girl on a bicycle' (P.B., 1977): going back to early C20. The ref. is manifestly physiological. Cf **get off and milk it.**

lucky one – aren't I (but also **aren't you...**, **isn't (s)he...**, etc.). 'Congratulations, either sincere or sarcastically meant' (P.B., 1975) – or, of course, ironic: although I heard it during the 1920s, I rather think that it didn't become very widely spread before the 1930s. 'Non-U'. Cf:

lucky you!, often **lucky old you!,** is, C20, used in admiration or in envy – or both. (Petch, 1974; Mrs Margret Thomson, 1975.)

lugger. See: once abroad.

big'oles. See: pin back.

lulu. See: it's a lulu.

lump. See: happy in the Service; hokey-pokey; if you don't like.

lunch. See: I married; out to l.; who's opened.

Lushington. See: Alderman L.

lyddite. See: what's the dynamite.

lying. See: must have been l.

lyonch. See: gone to lyonch.

M

M.F.U. See: snafu.

Mabel. See: go easy.

MacArthur. See: like MacArthur.

Macready pauses is, in theatrical circles, applied to an actor who, either on this one occasion or habitually, pauses too long after a telling speech or line or witticism: since *c.* 1855. William Macready (1793–1873), the great mid C19 actor, had a bad habit of pausing inordinately long in any dramatic or emphatic or unusually eloquent speech. (With thanks to the late Wilfred Granville.)

Macduff. See: lead on.

McGee. See: it ain't funny.

McGinty. See: down went; up goes.

McGoo. See: give us a little.

McGregor. See: Shice.

McGuinness. See: good night, M.

Macy's. See: does Macy's.

mad. See: don't get mad; I'm not mad; my pocket; say when you're; went for; you are of; you don't have to be; and:

mad as my old Aunt Hattie. Utterly insane: US: since *c.* 1930. An allusion to the Brit. cliché *as mad as a hatter.* (A.B., 1978).

mad, married, or Methodist. 'Said of Sapper (Royal Engineers) officers. Could it be because the Sappers were the first fighting soldiers to need brains? From before WW1; possibly as early as the Peninsular War' (Sanders, 1978).

mad woman's shit. See: all over the place.

made. See: you have it.

made my day – that's, or **it's,** or **you've.** That incident, ranging from flattery to sincerity, from the trivial (e.g., a small gift) to the important (a bequest, a large cheque, the unexpected visit of someone dear), has made me happy or restored my confidence: since the late 1940s. But latterly, it has often formed an ironic comment on an unexpected, esp. if unwelcome, incident (Prof. Emeritus A.C. Partridge, 1978.) ᴾ.B.: in the latter nuance, in Brit. usage, often (*just about*) *made my day, that has,* for emphasis.

mademoiselle, I love you well (rhyme: *selle – well*) was in late Victorian and Edwardian times – say, rather, *c.* 1880–1914 – 'verse of courtly gallantry, which, however, continued: "Pray, let me kiss your toe"/"No, no, monsieur (pron. m'seer),/My bum's too near/If you should stoop so low." Older ladies could quote the first two lines at parties' (L.A., 1974).

madman. See: dear sir, much wit.

Madras for health, Bengal for wealth. George Colman's *The Man of Business* performed and pub'd in 1774, shows Tropick, a ship's husband back from India, and Fable, a businessman, after greeting each other, early in Act III talking thus:

FABLE: Excellent! – And his elder brother, that was placed at Madras, is he removed to Bengal yet, as he proposed?

TROP: He is, he is: but—

FABLE: That's right: Madras for health, Bengal for wealth – that's the maxim there, you know. ['There' being India.]

TROP: Very true, very true: but—.

Whence it appears that *Madras for health, Bengal for wealth* was a c.p. in the East India Company among the merchants and bankers dealing with the merchandise of India: *c.* 1740–1820.

Mafeking is (or **has been**) **relieved.** The former is an Aus. c.p., in use among shift workers on being relieved and, vulgarly, among workmen, after defecation: C20. (B.P.) Norman Franklin, 1976, says that in 1940, he heard 'Buller, the relief of Ladysmith; cascara, the relief of Mrs Smith'; the ref. being to the Boer War and to the laxative.

The latter is a Brit. sarcastic reply to someone, 'usually a gossiping busybody who says "Have you heard the latest?"' He adds that, on 23 Oct. 1969, he heard the shortened *the relief of Mafeking* employed by Jimmy Jewel in an episode of TV's 'Nearest and Dearest'. This ref. to a highlight of the Boer War (1899–1902) implies 'That's stale news' – in the comic mode of the proverb 'Queen Anne's dead'. Cf **Dutch are in Holland.**

Maggie. See: where Maggie.

Maggie's drawers. See: give him M.

maggot. See: fool at one end and a m.

mahogany. See: you shock.

Mahony. See: ring Mahony.

maid. See: I'll give you my.

maidenheads. See: looking for.

make a good trumpeter.... See **good trumpeter....**

make-and-mends. See: we want m.

make it easy on yourself! 'Modern, US. [UK usage would be *for yourself.*] Take the easy way, don't make life difficult for yourself; perhaps specifically, e.g. co-operate with the police, etc.' (Wedgewood, 1977): since *c.* 1960.

make like a.... See **pretend you're a....**

make love, not war! Orig. a slogan of US, it soon became one of Brit., youth: and, as such, it is ineligible. But, among true adults, it developed, in the late 1960s, into an allusive, gently mocking c.p., doomed, I'd suppose, to become ob. by 1980. Raymond A. Sokolov, 2 Oct. 1977, in a review of the first ed. of this book for the *New York Times*, noted the phrase's omission.

make money of that! S, in Dialogue III, causes Miss to say, 'Well, but I was assured from a good Hand, that she lost at one Sitting, to the Tune of a hundred Guineas, make Money of that.' General sense: 'That's a lot of money' – 'That isn't chicken feed' – 'And that ain't hay'. Apparently late C17–18.

make no mistake! In Act III of Leonard Grover's US comedy. *Our Boarding House,* prod. 1877, although not pub'd until 1940, Colonel Elevator on several occasions uses this predominantly US c.p.as in e.g.: 'Colonel M.T. Elevator is always the highest-toned gentleman, make no mistake' (and, make no mistake, 'M.T.' *is* a pun on 'empty'): since *c.* 1850. P.B.: in C20 Brit. Eng., rather mere idiom than c.p., and often in the form *and make no mistake about it*, which may introduce a sentence as well as suffix it.

make out. See: I got mine; and:

make out like a bandit—I or you; or, of course, **he makes.** To 'enjoy notable success, orig. sexual, now of almost any kind. Orig. (1960s) working class, now general, as in the *Wall Street Journal*, 6 Oct. 1978: "The tendency to think you part of the country isn't getting its just due and somebody else is making out like a bandit' (quoted from a member of a governmental advisory commission).... And nobody says "No" to a bandit' (R.C., 1978).

make use of it or that! A 'c.p. of rejection (ex Yiddish *Mach shabbos davon*): "Have a good time with it!" "It (whatever you are saying) is not reasonable." *Shabbos* is Saturday, the Jewish Sabbath; cf English "You get on with it!"' (L.A., 1976). Almost 'That's nonsense!' Used mostly by Jews: C20.

make the cheese more binding. See to make the cheese....

make way for a (or the) lady with a baby (or pram)! Adopted by Australians, during WW2, from US servicemen, it is semantically equivalent to **gangway for a naval officer!** Of its Aus. usage, Lovett, 1978, comments, 'In the war years and shortly after, this saying had a great vogue as the wag's shouted warning to crowds in department stores and on pavements.... One occasionally hears it still from people over fifty.' Cf:

make way for a naval officer! See **gangway for a naval officer!**

make way for Woolwich Arsenal! – often shortened to **Woolwich Arsenal!** was, in WW1, applied by satirical, not unkindly, onlookers, to 'the Poor Bloody Infantry', more heavily laden than a Christmas tree – cf the slang *in Christmas-tree order*, in full marching order.

make yer name Walker! Run away! Go away. A Merseyside c.p., dating from the early 1920s. (Shaw, 1968.) Cf **my name's Walker** and **Walker, London.**

make yourself at our house! Make yourself at home: joc.: C20; by *c.* 1945 slightly, and by 1970 very, ob.

make yourself comfortable! is ironically addressed to one who farts audibly: US: since the 1920s. (Fain, 1977.)

makes you see double (grumbling) **and wish you were single** (wistfully) is a US c.p. applied to strong drink: *c.* 1910–42. (Berrey.) Coined presumably by some bar-room wit.

makes you shit through the eye of a needle. See I could shit through the eye....

makes you think, doesn't it (or – often joc. – **makes you think, don't it?**) A humorous c.p., dating from the 1930s in the Armed Forces (H&P) but gen. since the 1920s, and, as *makes yer think, don't it?*, current among Cockneys much earlier – prob. since the 1870s or 1880s. A late example occurs in Philip Gleife, *The Pinchbeck Masterpiece*, 1970: 'Then she looked at me, solemn and round-eyed like a beautiful owl. "Makes you think, don't it?" Her enunciation was still clear but she spoke slowly.' But a better example occurs in another novel pub'd in the same year, John and Emert Bonett's *The Sound of Murder.* They describe the usual courtroom ghouls thus:

As he came level with the group, a shrill, grinding voice, redolent of malice and marital infelicity, was saying, 'And, mark you, *she* was in the flat when *'e* fell out of the winder.'

Her listeners nodded in venomous concert. 'Makes you *think*, don't it?' came the comment, and the vulture heads nodded again.

making a trundle for a goose's eye or **a whim-wham for a goose's bridle.** See **weaving...**, and:

making dolls' eyes and **putting spots on dominoes** and the † **putting holes in pikelets** (muffins or crumpets) are evasively pert answers to a query as to what one does for a living: C20. Cf prec.

making his (or **her**) **will – he** (or **she**) **is**; also **he's (she's)**.... Joc. applied to one who is writing a letter or making notes or merely filling in a form: C20. (Petch, 1966.) 'Also, joc. ref. to someone [staying] a long time in the lavatory' (Wedgewood, 1977; he dates this sense back to *c.* 1930).

Malley's cow is an Aus. c.p., used of someone who has departed and left no indication of his present whereabouts. From a piece of Aus. folklore. (Baker.) Wilkes quotes Ernestine Hill, *The Territory*, 1951; implies that the c.p. belongs esp. to the Northern Territory; and shows that can be applied also to animals, e.g. a horse or cow. P.B.: could this be the mate of the beast to be found at **fit as a Malley bull**....

malt's above the water – the. He is drunk: a semi-proverbial c.p. of *c.* 1670–1770. (Apperson.) Cf the equivalent proverbial *the malt is above wheat with him* of mid C16–early C19.

'Implying, I suspect, that his belly's full of beer and his bladder full of "water"' (R.C., 1978).

mama's home. See **papa's home.**

man See: big man; bigger the balls; go and find; go, man; holding; I have to see; I wish I had; if my aunt; isn't that just like; it only wanted; it'll make; it's that man; like the man; little green; see a man; tell a green; that's the man; that's what the man; where men; white man; who stole the donkey; you a better; you're a good man; and:

man outside Hoyt's – the. 'The commissionaire outside Hoyt's Theatre in Melbourne in the 1930s, so elaborately dressed as to seem a person of consequence, and jocularly referred to as the authority for various reports' (Wilkes, *Dict. Aus. Coll.*, where are cited sources 1953–75): Aus.

man robbed himself – the. 'Someone in the house assisted the thieves' (Matsell): an ironic US c.p. of *c.* 1840–1900.

man the pumps! 'Bear a hand!' or 'Help! Help!': rather more general in the US than in the British Commonwealth: C20. Clearly from the literal nautical sense. (J.W.C., 1968.) A.B., 1979, adds, 'I've often heard this preceded by *all hands on deck and...*, or varied as *all hands on deck and batten down the hatches.* Both meaning "Let's get to work!"' *Man the pumps!* became more pertinent and pointed and catch-phrasal in J.W.C.'s later comment, 1977: 'Perhaps most commonly by a man of weeping women'.

man wasn't meant to sleep at home every night – a: 'Applied to men (as sex) credited with roving eye. [E.g. on p. 100 of] *God Stand up for Bastards*, [by] David Leitch, 1973' (L.A., 1974): certainly since not later than *c.* 1910 and prob. current since late C19.

man who fought the monkey. See **like the man**....

man's gotta do what a man's gotta do – a. US: since *c.* 1945. As a piece of homespun philosophy, spoken 'straight', it is merely that: homespun philosophy. But when it is 'guyed' or 'sent up', it becomes a joc. c.p. sometimes applied to the most trivial occasions.

'But did it become general after John Wayne [alias 'The Duke', great 'he-man' film actor d. 1982] said it or did John Wayne say it when it was already general?,' asks Ian Sainsbury in the Sheffield *Morning Telegraph*, 5 Sep. 1977. I can't answer that one, but I should suppose the latter, with J.W. re-invigorating it. P.B.: Cf **when you gotta go...**, with which it is sometimes synon.

[**man's the only animal that can be skinned more than once.** This semi-proverb, semi-c.p., occurs in Adams: used, very approx., 1880–1960, esp. among cowboys.]

manager. See: never be rude.

Manchester. See: if you're never.

mangle. See: has your mother; hell! said; I haven't laughed.

manners. See: after you is; it's bad m.; one lordship.

manslaughter. See: from marbles.

mantelpiece. See: who looks.

manufacturing. See: she's gone.

many are called lies midway between allusive cliché and, when used playfully, genuine c.p.: C20. (Shaw. 1968.) Elliptical for the famous Biblical quot'n, 'For many are called, but few are chosen' at St Matthew, xxii, 14.

'Mrs Wiggs, in *Mrs Wiggs of the Cabbage Patch*, a humorous novel [written by Alice Hegan Rice and pub'd in 1901] and very popular perpetrated the complex pun, "Many are cold, but few are frozen" but [now] almost extinct, not so much... because the generation that read *Mrs Wiggs* is dying off as because the one that knew The Bible is [doing so]' (J.W.C., 1977).

many faces as a church yard clock (– **he has as**): He's thoroughly unreliable: C19–early C20. 'Old navy' (F & G).

many, many times! 'Innuendo from Lady Beatrice Counterblast... (played by Betty Marsden) in [the BBC radio comedy series, later 1960s] *Round the Horne*, originally referring to the number of times she had been married. Barry Took, co-scriptwriter with Marty Feldman, recalls an audience at [the musical] *The Sound of Music* falling about [= laughing immoderately] when the phrase was used in all seriousness during the run of the radio show' (*VIBS*).

mapsticks. See: cry mapsticks.

marble(s). See: from marbles; I'll be one; take the m.

march. See: Scotch.

mare. See: as Moss caught; 'gip'; whoa, mare; whose dog.

Marine(s). See: by the grace; send for the M.; tell that to; and:

Marines have landed – the, often completed by **and the situation is well in hand:** Help is coming *or* Help has arrived: U.S.: C20. Cf Britain's **cavalry are coming** (or **are here**).

It has become so well known in the US that it can be – and often is – employed allusively, as in Clarence B. Kelland, *Speak Easily*, 1935:

I... gave her the number.

'Keep on being compromised until I get there,' she said, 'but let it go at that. The marines are about to land.'

The c.p. comes from the (in the US) famous quot'n, 'The Marines have landed, and the situation is well in hand': commonly said to have been orig. by Richard Harding Davis, in a cable sent from Panama in 1885. But Col. Albert Moe, late USMC, who had always been sceptical of this origination, went into the matter and discovered that 'Davis was in college in 1885. He had no connection with the landing at Guantanamo in 1898 (it was unopposed) – he was observing the Rough Riders at San Juan' (Letter, 1975).

Cf **like MacArthur**, and **Navy's here.**

marline-spike. See: every hair.

married. See: mad, married; that's the man; two brothers; why don't you two; and:

[**married but not churched**, late C19–20, is almost a c.p. Cf the next.]

married on the carpet and the banns up the chimney. Living together as if man and wife: C19–20; by 1930, somewhat ob.; by 1950, †.Cf prec.

marry. See: I married; lieutenants; Punch's; would you like your; and:

marry, come up, my dirty cousin! Addressed to one who affects an excessive modesty: mid C17–18; then dialectal. Apperson.

marry poor blind Nell. See **and did he marry....**

Martha. See: I don't know whether.

Martin. See: all my eye.

Mary. See: carrying the news; hop along; I'm willing.

Mary Cook. See: and Bob's.

[**m'as tu vu?** 'A common French-Canadian expression used by one proud of his performance, and who hopes it was noticed. Such a one is often referred to as a *m'as-tu-vu*? [or 'Hast thou seen me?']' (Leechman, 1969). For the formation, cf the derivation of the Fr. (and English) *vasistas* from Ger. *was ist das?* – 'What is that?'.]

mashed the potatoes for the Last Supper – he (or she). This Can. c.p. dates from *c.* 1940 and is used thus: '*Know* him? He helped me mash the potatoes for the Last Supper! Known him for years' (Leechman).

mason. See: once a knight.

mast. See: I am becalmed; shoe.

masters. See: have among you; his master's.

masthead. See: blue shirt; she carries.

mat. See: enough to give.

match me, big boy! A request for a match: since *c.* 1930: US become, *c.* 1940, also Brit. (Berrey.) Ob. by 1960, † by 1970.

match! quoth Hatch (or **Jack** or **John**) **when he got his wife by the breech** (or **when he kissed his dame**) – **a.** This c.p., recorded by Ray and 'Proverbial' Fuller, was current *c.* 1660–1750. Apperson.

matchsticks. See: here's a couple.

mate. See: hate; oh, mate; 'ow you goin'; top mate.

matinée. See: keep that in.

matron. See: run away.

matter. See: no matter; what does it m.; what's the m.

maturing in the wood. This joc c.p., dating since *c.* 1950, is applied 'to men whose heads are full of ideas that never get any further than their heads' (Petch, 1966). With a pun on liquor maturing in the cask – and a slyly humorous allusion to wooden heads.

'I believe this is a variation on a motto used by the "Old Granded" whiskey company in the US, i.e. "Aged in the wood", meaning, of course, that the bourbon whiskey was kept in casks of charred oak; over here [US] the meaning is the something or someone has richly ripened. Since the 1890s, I'd say' (A.B., 1979).

mauve one! – a. 'Frank Muir describes this [BBC radio comedy series, late 1940s – early 50s] *Take It From Here* catchphrase as "the genuine article... a meaningless catchphrase, first used by Jimmy Edwards when selecting a wine-gum and given such a risible inflection by Jim (a *mauve* one) that Denis Norden and I worked it into a vast number of shows thereafter to describe (for example) a stamp, a businessman's face, a suit, etc. This is almost a perfect example of a catchphrase in that it was not imposed upon the listeners but chosen by them to be a catchphrase."

Jimmy Edwards recalled an occasion in May 1952 when, as Rector of Aberdeen University, he went to Buckingham Palace. A courtier remarked that Jim's academic robe was magnificent but that he should do a swap with the Dean of Westminster, who was also present. When Jim asked why, the courtier replied, "His is a *mauve* one!"' (*VIBS*).

maximum. See: cussedness.

May. See: sell in May.

may all your kids be acrobats! A theatrical 'trouper's expression of provocation' (Berrey): US world of entertainment: since *c.* 1920.

A.B., 1979, comments that it passed into rather more gen. currency. Almost certainly based on the cliché *may all your troubles be small* (Brit. *little*) *ones!*, as a toast, or as a later well-wishing, to a bridal, or a newly-married, couple, the ref. being obviously to children.

may all your roosters lay eggs! 'The best of luck to you!': Aus.: C20. Ms Jay James, in the Sydney *Sun-Herald*, 2 Apr. 1978.

may all your ups and downs be between the sheets! A US c.p., uttered on parting from a friend: among males: since *c.* 1960, or perhaps a decade earlier.

may be trusted alone – he. He is very experienced and shrewd: *c.* 1800–50. Recorded in Pierce Egan's enlargement, 1823 – one cannot call it an improvement – of Grose. It sarcastically suggests that he can safely go anywhere alone.

May bees don't fly now (or **all the year long**). Addressed to one who begins his sentences with 'It may be': the forming, late C17–18; the latter, mid C18–20. The latter occurs in Grose, 1788; the former occurs in S. 1738, in the Dialogue I, thus:

MISS: May be there is, Colonel.

COL[ONEL]: But *May-bees* don't fly now, Miss.

Perhaps the commonest form is *May bees don't fly this month*. Not often heard since *c.* 1914, it is extant.

There is a pun on *maybe*, perhaps, and a *May bee*. The

Scots form is *maybes* – or *May-bees* – *are no aye honey-bees*. Apperson.

may he dance at his death! 'May he be hanged!' (Matsell): *c*. 1840–1914. That is, at the end of a rope.

may I die! is a C18 c.p. used either in vehement protestation or in vigorous asseveration. In Act I of Charles Macklin's lively *Love à la Mode*, prod. 1759 but not pub'd until 1782, Mordecai – concerning Sir Archy Macsarcasm – says.

The man indeed has something droll – something ridiculous in him... his strange inhuman laugh, his tremendous periwig, and his manners altogether, indeed, has something so caricaturely risible in it, that – ha, ha, ha! may I die, madam, if I don't always take him for a mountebank doctor at a Dutch fair.

P.B.: app. a var. of **I wish I may die!**

may I have the touring rights? 'If anyone makes a good joke, or tells an original story, the hearer might say: "I like that, it's good. May I have the touring rights?"' (Granville).

Joc. on the lit. sense – 'the rights to tour a version of a London show': theatrical: C20.

may I never do an ill turn! A C18 c.p. of emphasis, as in Isaac Bickerstaffe, *Love in a Village*, 1763, at III, i, where Sir William says: 'May I never do an ill turn, if I knew what to make on't' and, later, 'And, may I never do an ill turn, but I am very glad to see you too.'

may I pee in your cap? (or **hat?**) is a N. Country working men's c.p., addressed to someone taken short: C20; by 1975, ob. P.B.: presumably as an irritating taunt, putting the words in the sufferer's mouth.

may the Force be (or **go**) **with you!** 'Picked up from *Star Wars* – now jocular for "God bless you"' (Ashley, 1983, from US). The *Star Wars* series of films burst upon the world from Hollywood in the late 1970s; in UK the phrase may have enjoyed much quot'n, but never really became a c.p., except perhaps as a punning ref. to the Police Force. (P.B.)

may you live all the days of your life! In Dialogue II of S, 1738, the Colonel, drinking to Miss Notable, says, '"Miss, your Health; may you live all the Days of your Life"' – which, not a mere, somewhat elementary jocularity, connotes 'Live fully, not merely exist!'

may your chooks grow into emus and kick your dunny down! See **hope your rabbit....**

[**may your prick and your purse never fail you!** is half a toast, half a c.p., of C18–mid C19. James Dalton, *A Narrative*, 1728, has: 'They bid the Coachman drive on, and civilly saluted the Player, wishing *his – and Purse might never fail him.*'

In his *In Praise of English*, 1977, Joseph T. Shipley shows that it was already in use as early as the reign, 1603–22, of King James I of England.]

may your rabbits flourish! 'May you prosper!': Aus.: since *c*. 1930. Primarily a popular farewell, secondarily an ironic allusion to the fact that, for a long time, rabbits were a pest in Aus. (Mrs Camilla Raab, 1977.) But see also **hope your rabbit dies.**

maybe. See: **and I don't mean; and:**

maybe they know something we don't. 'A c.p. of rather indefinite meaning: "They're doing A; how come we're doing B?" comes fairly close. It is one aspect of the rather generalized, free-floating paranoia of the 1960s and 1970s, implying that "they" always have inside information while "we" don't, but may also be used ironically, implying that their information may not be as good as they think. General, but predominantly middle-class US from 1960s' (R.C., 1978).

me and my big mouth! '"I shouldn't have said that" – implying that the speaker has revealed something the hearer wasn't supposed to know, e.g. **a secret**. Probable Negro origin, 1920s or earlier, but general US since *c*. 1940. I suspect that it was spread by some Negro or dialect comedian. Now somewhat obsolescent' (R.C., 1978). P.B.: common also in UK, often prec. by *whoops!* or *oh dear!*, etc., as an apology

from one who has just 'opened his mouth and put his foot in it'.

me and you! is a US negroes' c.p. dating since *c*. 1950. One negro writer, CM, glosses it thus: 'Short for: "It's going to be me and you" – a way of saying, we're going to fight'; and another, Edith A. Farb, in a cyclostyled thesis, 1972: 'A challenge to fight: "there's just me and you, so let's fight".'

me Tarzan, you Jane. '"You are a woman, I am a man": from film versions of Edgar Rice Burroughs's stories. So far as I know Tarzan never actually spoke this like in any film; what he did say was just "Tarjan. Jane." This seems to be one of those improvements that the general public make on famous phrases – cf, e.g., *come up and see me sometime*; *come with me to the Casbah*; *play it again, Sam*, and *you dirty rat!* [qq.v.] All these are US c.pp. still' (Ashley, 1983).

meal. See: **boys call; don't make a meal.**

mean. See: **if you know; it all depends; see what I; so mean; what do you m.**

mean as pig-shit (–**as**). Applied usu. to financial tight-fistedness, occ. to a particularly unpleasant person capable of mean actions; sometimes, like **common as cat-shit**, q.v., elab. by the addition of *and twice as nasty*: Services' (? wider spread): since mid C20, at latest. (P.B.) Cf **soft as shit....** and **so mean....**

mean to do without 'em (**– I**). Elliptical for .... *without women*, this c.p. was popularized on the music halls by Arthur Roberts in 1882 and went out of use *c*. 1910. Ware.

means. See: **his means; ve haf.**

meanwhile, back at the ranch. This forms a c.p. when used to recall one's listeners, one's *vis-à-vis* to the central point in the conversation, hence in any similar situation. The origin lies in the old silent 'Westerns'. While stirring fights with the Indians were going on, the film-viewers were shown flashbacks to the ranch, following the caption, 'Meanwhile, back at the ranch' – US and still current in late 1970s, it must have arisen quite early in the 1920s. (W.J.B., 1977.) P.B.: equally well known and used in UK, and often evoked merely by another speaker's use of the word 'meanwhile'. The location is occ. varied for joc. effect.

meat. See: **all that m.; angle of dangle.**

meat-pie. See: **Australian.**

medal(s). See: **didn't win; fall out and; you're showing.**

meddlers. See: **crutches; lareovers.**

meet. See: **I wouldn't like; parson would.**

meeting like this – we can't go on, or **we must stop.** Orig., presumably, a line uttered by star-crossed lovers meeting in secret, in some melodramatic play or film, it has become a later C20 c.p. evoked by any two people meeting again within a short time, and coincidentally, in somewhere inappropriate, e.g. a crowded lift, a public convenience, etc. As a cartoon caption it has been used for a variety of amusing illustrations. (P.B.)

Melbourne. See: **all behind.**

mellow. See: **stuff is here.**

melon-patch. See: **there's a nigger.**

melt. See: **don't come the tin; you won't m.**

memory-powder. See: **you want a little.**

men are interested in only one thing, (i.e. sexual intercourse.) A cynical feminine c.p., dating from *c*. 1920; or, rather, that was when I first heard it – but it prob. goes back to *c*. 1880 or perhaps even earlier. And so are women. But neither sex to the extent the c.p. implies. Cf **it takes two to tango.** P.B.: as often in the form *men are only interested in one thing*, or, to an individual male from a reproachful girl, *you're only...*

Martyn Harris, in an article about London kerb-crawlers, *New Society*, 1 Mar. 1984, p. 318; 'A man tried to steal the money she [a prostitute] carries in a concealed pocket in her skirt.... "Men are only after one thing," she says, and I don't like to ask whether it's money or sex that she means.'

men before monkeys. See **age before beauty.**

men over forty don't double is a RN c.p. – 'a sneering remark addressed to a youngster with a tendency to skulking and slackness' (*Sailors' Slang*): C20.

mensh. See: don't mensh.

mention. See: don't mention.

mercenary. See: like a m.

merciful. See: as you are stout.

Mercury. See: one night.

mercy. See: God have.

Meredith, we're in! A c.p. uttered when one succeeds in getting into a place, e.g. a tea-shop, just before closing time: since *c.* 1910. It occurs in, for instance, C.F. Gregg, *Tragedy and Wembley*, 1936. *VIBS* provides its origin: 'a music-hall sketch "The Bailiff" (or "Moses and Son"), performed by Fred Kitchen, the leading comedian of Fred Karno's company, and first produced in 1907. The phrase was used each time a bailiff and his assistant looked like gaining entrance to a house.'

merry and bright. See: always merry.

merry Christmas. See: and a merry.

mess. See: another fine; in everybody's; who dealt.

mess-kit. See: don't shit; put that in your m.

mess-mate. See: swaying; top mate.

message received loud and clear (often shortened to **message received**). I understand what you're getting at; I get the point – there's no need to go on and on about it!: since the middle 1940s. From the literal phrase much used by the Services, esp. the RAF, during WW2.

'Alternatively, *I read you loud and clear. From the* standard Services' radio query, "How do you read (=hear) me?"' (R.C., 1978).

messing about. See: stop message.

Methodist. See: mad, married.

methods. See: you know my.

mew! mew! Tell that to the Marines!: tailors': *c.* 1860–1940. Contrast **miaouw! miaouw!**

Mexicans don't count. A Southwest gunmen's boast that, in their tally of men killed, they didn't bother to include Mexicans (or, come to that, Indians) – a ref. to the fairly common practice of making a notch on their gun stocks for every victim, a practice more gen. in fiction than in fact, as Adams tells us. Apparently *c.* 1860–1900. P.B.: is this an echo of the fighting Indian Chief Geronimo's claim that he fought Mexicans with rocks and sticks, saving his cartridges for his white American enemies?

miaouw! miaouw! has, since the early 1920s, been addressed either by a third party to two persons engaged in malicious gossip or by one party reproving another for such gossip. The remarks are *catty* and the claws are out. Indeed it was prob. prompted by 'Don't be so *catty!*'

Also, since *c.* 1945, US. (W & F, who list it on p. 605, as *meow* (*-meow*).) Mostly used by and of women (J.W.C., 1977).

Michael. See: hip.

middle. See: lucky Pierre.

middling. See: fair to.

midnight. See: is it m.

midshipman. See: just like a m.

midshipmen have guts, ward-room officers have stomachs, and flag officers (have) palates is a RN c.p., dating since *c.* 1860; by 1965, ob. (Bowen: *Sailors' Slang*.) Cf **horses sweat...**, and **officers have....**

mighty white of you! – it's or that's. That's very decent or forgiving or generous of you: C20. Orig. Southern US, it soon became gen. US, and has been heard in UK since the 1930s, often with an understood implication of its origin. Of the US usage, J.W.C., 1977, has noted that 'it was, at first, used seriously – "like a white man, not like a Negro", Now used everywhere, by everyone to anyone, but always jestingly (and sometimes sarcastically), and with full consciousness that it is a provincial expression – and *not* racist'. P.B.: sometimes, in the Services, parodying the legendary British Empire builders, *Sir, you're a white man!* Cf **damn'**

white....

mild. See: I'm as m.

milder. See: have a gorilla.

mile. See: one that lives; she's a hot; within.

mileage. See: there's no m.

miles and miles and bloody miles of sweet fuck-all or, more politely, **of bugger all,** jocularly and ruefully describes either the African desert or the Canadian prairies: the former is a soldiers' description, WW1 and again in WW2; the latter a Can. civilian description, since *c.* 1919. (The latter comes Leechman; the former from my own experience). R.C. adds, 1978, that 'John Manifold, in *Poems*, 1947, gives the North African [WW2] version, "Miles and miles of shit-colored fuck-all"'. P.B.: Mesopotamia (modern Iraq) was described by those who had the misfortune to fight there in WW1 as *miles and miles of bugger-all with a river running through* (or *up*) *it.* Cf the earlier Aus. **so bare....**

Miles's boy is spotted. We know all about *that!*: addressed to anyone who, in a printing office, begins to spin a yarn: since *c.* 1830. From Miles, a Hampstead coach-boy. 'celebrated for his faculty of diverting the passengers with anecdotes and tales' (B & L). By 1970. ob.

milk. See: curdles; get off and m.; that accounts; who's milking; why buy.

milk in first! A domestic c.p.: C20. Sometimes allusively – and, only then, a true c.p. (S.G. Dixon, 1978.)

milk in the coconut. See **that accounts for the....**

mill. See: I'll been through; trouble.

miller. See: stout.

millionaires. See: half-crown.

million(s). See: first million; I believe you, but; I gotta; I've got a m.; looks like a m.; one that lives; and:

millions of moola (**h**). This had a brief currency during the mid 1950s – early 1960s and came from the BBC's GOON SHOW, q.v. It 'implies the easy life, along the lines of Paris or the spring, fat cigars and fat ladies' (Simon Levene, 1977). *Moola(h)* was adopted from a US slang term for money.

millstone. See: seaman.

mince-pie. See: it's a snice.

mind. See: do you m.; don't mind; I don't care; I don't m.; I have made up; it's all in the m.; never mind; not if you; she didn't; strong back; what's on; who's minding; with thumb; you can't tell; you must be out; you're out; you've got a one; your tiny; and:

mind boggles – the. A c.p. comment upon any marked absurdity: since the late 1950s but had been occ. heard for at least a decade longer. 'Popularized, and possibly even originated, in the strip cartoon "The Perishers", written by Maurice Dodd and drawn by Dennis Collins, which has appeared in the *Daily Mirror* since the late 1950s' (P.B., 1974). Nichol Fleming, *Hash*, 1971, has:

'I believe the old buffer was . . . cashiered for some kind of behaviour unbecoming to an officer.'

'The mind boggles.'

mind how you go! A c.p., common only since *c.* 1942, bearing the gen. meaning 'Look after – take care of – yourself', and addressed also to someone either caught in traffic or slipping on, e.g., a banana skin, or indeed to someone setting forth on a journey, e.g. to a distant country; hence, since *c.* 1945, also psychologically or morally. In V.C. Clinton-Baddeley, *To Study a Long Silence*, 1972, occurs this fragment of dialogue:

'Good night,' said Davies.

'Good night, guv,' said the bus conductor. 'Mind how you go.'

And it may have been orig. a bus conductors' warning to passengers as they step off a bus.

'The original [Yates Wine] lodges were great barns, ...primitive posters were stuck up on all the walls: "Mind How You Go", "Silence is Golden" ...' (Ray Gosling, 'Port and Sardines' in *Listener*, 22 July 1982, p. 8). The first YWL was started in Oldham, 1884.

'Given a new lease of life by Jack Warner in *Dixon of Dock Green*' (*VIBS*).

The var. *watch how you go* has been common in the Services since *c*. 1935 and became general a decade later, although little used since the late 1960s.

mind my bike! From the BBC radio comedy variety show, 'Garrison Theatre [which] belonged to January–May 1940. "Mind my bike" was a cheerily inconsequent remark which cropped up almost by accident when [Jack] Warner, seeking a new and aural way of making an entrance, thought of the sound of a bicycle bell, and the phrase "Mind my bike" to go with it' (Barry Took, *Laughter in the Air*, 1976). The phrase was aspic'd in amber by Stephen Potter in his *The Sense of Humour*, 1954. Like Warner's **not blue-pencil likely**, it became very well known indeed.

mind the barrow! In *The Spanish Farm Trilogy*, 1924, R.H. Mottram wrote:

Outside, the NCOs were 'falling-in' the men under the shelter of the embankment, in the gathering dusk. From without came a North-country voice growling: 'If A catches them, A'll slog 'em, bah gum!' and a Cockney: 'Mind the barrow, please! The Sergeant said I was to have my little spade, but 'e won't let me take my little pail. ...'

The Cockney catchword he had heard in the dusk had caught on, and all about him, shopmen and clerks, labourers, mill hands, miners were bellowing at the top of their voices, 'Mind the barrow, please!' as they skidded and waded, fell and died.

Apparently only during WW1 – and afterwards, for a while, among ex-Servicemen. (The quot'n, I owe to Mr A.B. Petch.)

mind the Brussels! See – at **did you enjoy your trip?** – the note on *mind the Brussels*; and add these details. The phrase may go back beyond 1900. In 1974, Christopher Fry provided me with evidence that this c.p. was still current then, and commented thus: 'The humour of it, of course, is in giving a cheap floor-covering the grandeur of a Brussels carpet.'

mind the dresser! See **up and down!**

mind the (or *your*) **step!** Look after yourself: the former addressed to a departing visitor, and dating from *c*. 1880, and recorded by Ware in 1909, soon developed a non-literal application, but ob. by 1960; perhaps orig. an admonition to a drunkard. The C20 *mind your step* has always been predominantly metaphorical and, by *c*. 1930, it had almost entirely ousted *the*. Cf **mind how you go!**

'In US, "mind your step" is much commoner; both literally and metaphorically' (J.W.C., 1977).

mind you, I've said nothing. Perhaps I shouldn't have said that, so don't quote me: Anglo-Irish: C20. This is the title of a book by Honor Tracy sub-titled 'Forays in the Irish Republic' and pub'd in 1953.

mind your backs! may qualify as a c.p. when used joc. for 'excuse me, I wish to pass you', esp if speaker is encumbered by a load, a wheelbarrow, etc.: earlier C20. From the usage of railway porters moving good or luggage. Cf **pass along the car ...** (P.B.)

mind your eye! Be careful: C18–20. The *OED* quotes a passage belonging to 1727. By 100 years or so later, it had become also US. In 1844, T.C. Haliburton, in *The Attaché* (one of the Sam Slick stories) in the 2nd Series, vol. I, p. 64, writes, ' "Mind your eye" is the maxim you may depend, either with man or woman', and then, at p. 77, 'It's the language of natur', and the language of natur' is the voice of Providence. Dogs and children can learn it, and half the time know it better nor man; and one of the first lessons and plainest laws of natur' is, "*to mind the eye*".'

Cf **mind how you go!** and **mind your helm!**

mind your fingers! (pause) **Clang!** An Army c.p. of approx. 1955–75, invoked by any ref. to detention in the guardroom cells, as in 'He wants to watch it: if they catch him at that lark, it'll be mind your fingers, clang, for him'. A slightly earlier version was a joc. imitation of the irate sergeant-major's call, rising to a bellow: 'Open the door [of the cell], Provost

Sergeant: he's comin' in!' (P.B., with thanks to P.J. Emrys Jones.)

mind your helm! A nautical version of **mind your eye!**: C19–20.

mind your own beeswax! See **none of your beeswax!**, reading via:

mind your own interferences! Mind your own business!: joc.: since early C20; by 1960, ob., and by 1970, virtually †. See prec., and:

mind (occ. **tend to** or **stick to**) **your own potatoes!** Mind your own business!: US: C20. Berrey.

mind your pockets! 'A c.p. uttered in a queue for the men's urinal; the speaker needs relief so badly he may not be able to wait for the proper place' (P.B., 1974): prob. orig. among civilians, from notices about pickpockets, but perhaps popularized in the Services during WW1. I don't remember hearing it until my King's Royal Rifles days, 1940 – early 41.

Cf *watch your pockets, lads!*, which was noted in the 1st edn. of this book as a humorous, unmalicious c.p., directed at any new arrival, with millieu 'mostly among workmen and WW1 British soldiers'.

mind your three S's! Bowen records this as a simple RN rule for promotion: Be sober, silly (simple – not offensively intelligent). civil: mid C19–20.

mind your worm: here comes a blackbird. Addressed to boys fishing with a line baited with a worm; but also, sexually, by a group of much older girls coming upon a group of young boys bathing naked: proletarian, esp. Londoners': late C19–20. It occurs in e.g. Alfred Draper, *Swansong for a Rare Bird* (1970, at chapter V).

minds. See: great minds; small things; two minds; you are of; you can hear.

mine. See: don't go down.

mine's up! I've a 'cushy' job (e.g., administration rather than labour): among prisoners of war in the Far East during the years 1942–45. From '*I'm* all right, Jack!' P.B.: or rather, from synon. *pull up the ladder, Jack, I'm inboard*.

mink. See: they think.

minnow. See: it's a freak.

minstrel. See: lay of the last.

minute. See: there's one born; worth a guinea.

miracles. See: difficult we do; do you think I can.

miraculous pitcher that holds water downwards – the is a conundrum c.p. ('What is the miraculous pitcher ... ?') – the answer being the female pudendum – of mid C18–19. Grose, 1788.

mirrors. See: all done with m.

miss. See: one you m.; what you don't; you missed.

Miss Otis regrets has been turning up, over and over again, in my post-1934 reading of American novels, short stories, humorous sketches, light-hearted plays, clearly used as a catch phrase. I thought from a play or a film, but no! as since Christmas 1975 I've surmised, from a song. No less clearly, it never gained a very wide acceptance: not one of half a dozen well-educated and cultured Americans could tell me the source. Only a week ago, I went to the wonderful British Library catalogue of modern music: the *Miss* ... volume had gone to the binders for repair: so I asked at the Enquiry Desk, and their 'musical expert' immediately said, 'It *may* have come from a play or a film; all *I* know is that it's the title of a song.' Then, yesterday morning, I was shown the score; the song begins, 'Miss Otis regrets she's unable to lunch today'. That score forms part of Messrs Chappell & Co's series, *Melodies Made Famous by the Years*, London, 1962. Forefronting the score itself was the information 'copyrighted 1934' – words and music by Cole Porter. The amiable fellow added, 'It has been revived by a "pop" singer.' The very next day – this morning in short, I received an air letter, dated 14 April 1976, from Dr Joseph T. Shipley, who, after confirming the British Library's information, reported thus, 'Written not for one of his musical comedies, but for the private entertainment of his friends. Monty Woolley (well-known play-director [and actor]) dressed up as a butler, and while Cole played the piano, Monty sang it. For a year or more, Monty delighted in dressing as a butler and singing the song at parties.'

'The song was included in the "hit" film biography of Cole Porter, *Night and Day* [the title of one of the best-known of C.P.'s songs], 1946, and became widely known. [C.P., 1893–1964.]

'*Miss Otis regrets* was a humorous way of expressing one's distaste, or refusal to accept unwanted overtures, invitations, and the like.'

In other words, Dr Shipley implied that, as a c.p., it was †. But is it? In a novel by Hugh Pentecost, *Girl Watcher's Funeral*, 1969 (US) and 1970 (UK), occurs this passage:

'Good evening, Captain Pappas,' Pierre Chambrun said. He looked at what must have been my pea-green face and smiled. 'Miss Otis regrets –' he said.

I think that this c.p. has reached a state of advanced obsolescence, but that it lingers in the memories of all Cole Porter lovers and that the 'pop' singer's revival of it may considerably delay its passage to obsoleteness.

(Written during the early afternoon of 21 April 1976. I admit to a small, unsquashable self-congratulation on my persistence – call it obstinacy if you wish 'and see if I care'.)

And then, on 26 April, I received, from Miss Katherine Hartley of CBS News the information that the song was dedicated to Miss Elsa Maxwell, the famous columnist, and that it was sung publicly in England before it was thus treated in America – by the once well-known Douglas Byng in the revue *Hi Diddle Diddle*, 1934. On 28 April the afore-mentioned musical authority at the enquiry desk told me that this information about the British performance is included in the Modern Music Catalogue entry 'To coin a phrase' – such is life!

The song *was* orig. a 'private' or party piece, but it was first sung publicly in the US in the same year as in London: 1934.

In America, it formed part of the musical comedy, *Anything Goes*. In Britain, by the way, *Hi Diddle Diddle* was performed at the Comedy Theatre on 3 Oct. (1934).

Cf **anything goes.**

P.B.: The *Guardian*, 2 Feb. 1984, recorded the death, at 89, of 'Bricktop, the singer and cafe owner who was the toast of 1920s Paris and about whom Cole Porter wrote his song *Miss Otis Regrets*. ... The red-haired singer['s] real name was Ada Beatrice Queen Victoria Louise Virginia Smith'.

Miss Scarlett. See: I don't know nothin'.

Miss Weston. See: my oath Miss; oh, Miss.

mission accomplished. The job has been done; or, the purpose has been fulfilled. US, since 1942; adopted, although less generally, in UK, 1944. Orig. a military formula. Jean Potts, *An Affair of the Heart*, 1970, has, 'Mission accomplished, and very neatly too.'

Missouri. See: I'm from M.

mistake. See: and no M.; I'll drink all; make no M.; this week's.

Mister and Mrs Wood in front. It's a nearly empty house: theatrical: C20. Plenty of seats, few people. In *Showman Looks On*, 1945, C.B. Cochran (remember Mr Cochran's young ladies) has the var. *Wood family in front*. From the wooden seats or wooden parts thereof.

Mister Nash.... See **Nash is concerned.**

Mister Nonesuch. See **Non such...**

Mister Palmer. See **Palmer is concerned.**

Mister to you! See **ne'er an M under your girdle?**

Mistress Kell(e)y.... See **you must know Mistress Kell(e)y.**

Mistress Kell(e)y – but in the form **Mrs Kell(e)y – won't let young Edward play with you** is a derogatory c.p. addressed to a child either ill-behaved or dirty: Aus.: since c. 1925. The allusion is to bushranger Ned Kelly, as much a folk-hero in Aus. as, say, Jesse James is in the US. (B.P.)

mix me a hike! Pay me off, *or* Give it to me: US tramps': since c. 1920. (See 'Dean Stiff's' *The Milk and Honey Route*, 1931.) This is the 'walking' sense of *hike*, noun and verb.

mixer. See: away with.

mixing the breed! is uttered by someone using another's hairbrush and comb or by another (whether owner or not) watching him: non-U, non-cultured, non-tactful: late C19–20.

mixture as before – the. Orig. and still 'the same again' – a drinking c.p. in reply to 'What'll you have?' Hence applied to acceptance of the offer of anything already had; hence, 'the same old ingredients, the same old features, the same old programme as before – as, e.g., in an electoral campaign: since c. 1920, Brit. and, since c. 1930, by adoption US ('Not common in this country,' says J.W.C., 1968). Prob. from the phrase used lit. on a chemist's or druggist's bottle of, e.g. cough mixture. In 1977, J.W.C. added, 'Didn't this perhaps start with *Pickwick Papers* [1836–37], ch. 30, in one of Bob Sawyer's false prescriptions? "Draft to be taken at bedtime – pills as before – lotion as usual – the powder from Sawyer's; late Nockemorf's. Physicians' prescriptions carefully prepared".'

moan. See: that moan's.

mob. See: one of my; what do you hear.

mock. See: don't mock.

mogue. See: and no mogue.

Mohicans. See: last of the M.

mokter nix. See **mox nix.**

molasses in January – (s) **he's as slow** or **dumb as.** Slow witted or stupid: US: late (? mid) C19–20. (A.B., 1978.) Cf:

molasses won't run down his legs is a US c.p., 'said of a lazy person' (Berrey): since c. 1920; by 1970, somewhat ob.

moll. See: like a moll.

Mollie. See: backwards.

moment(s). See: at this moment; I have had; never a dull; we all have.

momma(h). See: how's the m.; not you, M.

Monaghan. See: I'm on agen.

Monday. See: Sunday saints; swing it till.

money. See: any day; come home with; doesn't care; don't applaud; flings; for the widows; give him the m.; goes for; grow on trees; has more; hold up; it's all m.; it's like m.; it's money; it's only m.; licence to print; make money; put your m.; ready whore; shame to take; shoving; sold again; spends money; that was real; throws his; we ain't; what do you want if; you must think;

money can't (or **won't**) **buy you happiness: but it helps you to be miserable in comfort.** 'Possibly the first part is a proverb, but the elaboration is a c.p.' (Ashley): since mid C20, at latest.

money for jam or **old rope.** See **it's money for jam.**

money talks is a semi-proverb, a c.p., but perhaps justifiably classified as a c.p. based on, or arising from, such adages as Torriano's 'Man prates, but gold speaks' in 1666. In 1915 P.G. Wodehouse wrote, 'The whole story took on a different complexion for John. Money talks' – cf also A. Palmer in *The Sphere*, 1925, 'Money talks.... So why not listen to it?' (Partly Apperson.)

Also cf the US c.p. extension, *money talks turkey even in Greece*, with a pun on *Turkey*, on *talk turkey*, to talk good, hard commonsense, and on the grease used in, or caused by cooking.

monkey(s). See: as the m.; board the m.; cartload of m.; cheeky monkey; cold enough; couldn't give; does your mother like; don't monkey; have a gorilla; hog-law's; I'll be a m.; it's a m.; like the man who fought; more fun; pay over; put it where the m.; right, monkey; silence; softly; well, I never; who boiled; who put.

Monkey Brand, as Collinson remarks, is 'often applied derisively to an ugly face'. It derives from the well-known advertisement of a Lever Brothers' kitchen soap: a monkey gazing at itself in a frying-pan. As a c.p.: the 1920s–30s.

S.G. Dixon adds, 1978, that the phrase *Monkey Brand won't wash woollens*, popular in earlyish C20, lingers among the elderly. See also **I wouldn't know him...**

monkey got 'em. See **hog law's got 'em.**

monkey on horseback.... See **who put that monkey....**

monkey see, monkey do! A Can. and US c.p. 'addressed to one who imitates the actions of another, or as warning not to do such and such because someone (usually a child) might follow suit' (Leechman): since c. 1925. By c. 1950, also English, but, according to P.B., 1974, rather to describe the learning of a process, which, although performed thereafter with reasonable competence, is never actually understood. 'They're trying to teach us computer programming. I can write it out OK, but really it's "monkey see, monkey do": I haven't a clue what's actually happening inside the bloody machine or what I'm really doing it for.'

monkeys is the craziest people. This is a 'famous line of comedian Lew Lehr, who used it repeatedly. It was picked up by the American public [in the] late 1940s–1950s' (W.J.B., 1977).

Mons – gassed at and **on the wire at Mons** are WW1 soldiers' replies to enquiries about someone's whereabouts: both 1916–18. There was, of course, no gas used at Mons; nor, come to that, any barbed-wire entanglements during the Retreat from Mons. F & G record the latter. B & P both. Cf the more gen. **hanging on the (old) barbed wire,** and see also **biggest fuck-up...**

MONTY PYTHON CATCH PHRASES. 'Monty Python's Flying Circus', a surrealist TV comedy series was '*the* comedy show of the the 1970s' (P.B., 1978) – an opinion shared by many, many others. Several of its c.pp. gained a wide currency. I select two: *thank you, Karl*, 'from a recurring skit in the form of a panel quiz in which the "contestants" are [Karl] Marx, Engels, Mao, Stalin, *et al*. At one point, Marx *sotto voce* exclaims 'Ah, shit!" and the question-master, in a Nanny's "that's not quite nice" voice, says "Thank you, Karl". Hence, the boys (my informants at Loughboro' Grammar School) use "Thank you, Karl" as a rejoinder to any verbal infelicity'. The second is *you're not even a proper woman. Anyway, your hair's too long to be a vicar*, 'used as a derisive retort to anyone doing anything silly or ridiculous'. (The quoted passages came from P.B.'s letter.) See also **nudge, nudge...**

mooching. See: halt; here they come.

moola. See: millions.

moon. See: it is a fine; take a running.

moose. See: can a m.

mop. See: that's the way.

more. See: any more; are there any m.; I couldn't agree; never no; say no; that's all there; there's more; you can't have m.

more arse, or **cheek,** or **hide, than Jessie,** the first being the orig. and most frequent. The particular arse was that of Jessie, the very popular elephant that died, aged 67, at Taronga Park, NSW, in 1939. Although apparently unrecorded before 1951 (Dal Stivens), it must have been current during the animal's lifetime, since *c*. 1910 or perhaps a decade earlier. There is, of course, a pun on the Aus. slang term *arse*, impudence, for, as not every schoolboy knows, the triune c.p. epitomizes a quite spectacular effrontery. Based on, and owing most to, Prof. G.A. Wilkes. I must admit that, before I read his *Dict. Aus. Coll.*, 1978, I had supposed Jessie to be a notorious prostitute notoriously wide-beamed.

more bollocks than brains 'was applied [in the British Infantry, WW1] to any hefty character with little "malum" (knowledge or know-how)' (P.V. Harris, 1978).

more beef! A c.p. cry for the help of one or two more men when a heavy load or a very hard task demands it: Can.: since *c*. 1910. (Leechman.)

more curtains! 'Shouted by leary Cockney girls when a person clad in an evening frock passes by' (Julian Franklyn, 1939): since *c*. 1910; by 1950, ob., and by 1970, †.

more dirt, the less hurt. In *Handley Cross: or, Mr Jorrock's Hunt*, 2 vols, 1854, in the chapter entitled 'Another Sporting Lector' (lecture), during a disquisition on the c.pp. of the sporting set at that time, the jovial lecturer tells us that '"More dirt the less hurt!" is a pleasant piece o' consolation for a friend with a mud mask' (from a fall on the hunting field). A year earlier, in chapter XXIII ('The Great Run') of *Mr Sponge's Sporting Tour*, 1853, occurs this brief exchange:
'You're not hurt, I hope?' exclaimed Mr Puffington....
'Oh no!' replied Sponge. 'Oh no – fell soft – fell soft.

More dirt less hurt – more dirt, less hurt.'
This is a C19 fox-hunting c.p.

more firma, the less terra – the. 'A c.p. used by those who distrust air travel' (B.P.): since *c*. 1950. A pun on *terra firma*, land as opposed to sea, and on *terra*, land, and *terror*.

more fun than a barrel of monkeys, usu. prec. by *it's*. Tremendous fun: prob. common before 1920, and still common, in US. (Prof. and Mrs John W. Clark, 1977.)

more guts than you could hang on a fence, with *he has* understood. 'A cowboys' expression for someone with unusual [i.e., exceptional] courage' (Adams): Western US: late C19–20.

more hair on your chest! See **that'll grow more hair on your chest!**

more hair there than anywhere. Usu. in the form of a dialogue: 'There's more ...' – 'where?' – 'On a cat's back.' As Leechman adds, 1977, 'Said to a girl in a suggestive way', and he notes, 'Heard in East Anglia *c*. 1898'.

more holy than righteous is a domestic c.p., dating from late (? mid) C19 and applied to a very *holey* pair of socks – socks rather than stockings; nor is the phrase solely feminine. Not much used since *c*. 1960.

more in anger than in sorrow is a 'cynical, or humorously grim, reversal' of the cliché *more in sorrow than in anger*: US: since *c*. 1950. In 1975. J.W.C. notes also the 'closely parallel reversal. "Mother is not hurt; she is just frightfully angry."' See also **I'm not mad...**

more kid in him than a goat in the family way. Incurably addicted to 'kidding': Aus.: since *c*. 1930. Baker. 1959.

more like a foot than a hand. A card-players' rueful comment on being dealt a poor hand: C20. (P.B.)

more lip than a muley cow. Applied, among Western US cowboys, to anyone who talks too much: late C19–20. (Adams.) Here, *muley* = hornless.

more money than I could poke a stick at. See **has more money....**

more power to your elbow! expresses encouragement: late (?mid) C19–20. Anglo-Irish in origin, it is both Brit. and US: recorded by M.

more R than F was, *c*. 1860–1910, a c.p. directed at someone more rogue than fool; esp. at a servant appearing much more foolish than he is.

more room out there. See **better an empty house...**

more strife than a pregnant nun – in. In dire trouble or difficulty. Jack Slater wrote to E.P., 1978, that he had heard this earthy phrase in the Aus. Outback during the late 1950s; I heard it in th British Army during the 1960s, so it is by no means solely Aus., as E.P. conjectured in his notes. J.S. notes also a companion phrase *in more strife than a pork chop in a synagogue*, to which the same remarks apply, though the latter is more usu. in *as popular as*: see **pork chop...** (P.B.)

more strokes than Radmillovic – he has. He is very resourceful and many-skilled: Anglo-Welsh: since *c*. 1930. The saying, orig. Cardiff and lit., soon became gen. 'Radmillovic was swimming champion of Wales at the time when the crawl-stroke was first used. He was a trudgeon-stroke exponent, but was able to change to the crawl and still retain his championship, hence his mastery of the strokes' (Sidney Morgan, 1977). Radmillovic captained the Welsh Olympic swimming team from 1908 to 1928.

more than somewhat, lit. 'more than rather much', seems to have, *c*. 1925, become a US c.p. – meaning 'very much' or 'decidedly' – as a result of Damon Runyon's frequent and effective use of it, during the 1920s and early 1930s, in his newspaper columns; and to have become an English c.p. in 1932, from its occurrences in the book that made him internationally famous in 1932, *Guys and Dolls*, as e.g., in 'Social Error': '[Handsome Jack] is sored up more than somewhat when he finds Miss Harriet Mackle does not give him much of a tumble.' And in 'Butch Minds the Baby': 'I am now more nervous than somewhat.' And in 'Romance in the Roaring Forties': 'Dave somehow thinks more than somewhat of his dolls.' The impact was reinforced by Runyon's *More than Somewhat*, 1937, but the war of 1939–45, esp. America's entry in Dec. 1941, deadened the impact: yet the c.p. was, in (say) 1950, no more than moribund; by 1955, however, it was generally regarded as an antique.

more than that! This lower-deck RN c.p., dating from *c.* 1930, emphasizes that one's job or pay or whatever exceeds anything that can be opposed to it. In short, 'a fabulous amount', says Granville, who, in a letter, cites a derivative in 'Some lovely dames at the dance last night, lusher than that'.

[**more there's in it, the more there's on it – the.** In the Dialogue II of S, 1738, occurs this example:

NE[VEROUT]:Why then, here's some Dirt in my Tea-Cup.
MISS: Come, come; the more there's in't, the more there's on't.

A 'lost' saying, of which the sense is obscure. Perhaps it is a proverb, perhaps a c.p.]

more war! was, seemingly in 1898 only, or maybe for a year or so longer, a Cockney c.p. applied to a quarrel, esp. among women. Ware says that it referred to the Spanish-American War.

more where that came from. See and there's more ...

more wind in your jib! Used by the sailors in a ship in foul wind on meeting a ship in a fair wind: mid C19–early 1920. The wishers' ship hopes that thus she will gain a fair wind. Bowen.

more wrinkles than inches is applied to a man who is feeling extremely cold: perhaps orig. RN, but by mid C20 gen. in all Services'. Cdr C. Parsons, RN ret., dates it from the mid 1930s, and adds, 'from the supposed appearance of the prepuce'. P.B.: why 'supposed'? It's a physiological fact. Cf the cold weather male boast, 'Normally I'm seven inches and a wrinkle: now I'm one inch and seven wrinkles'.

Moreton. See: oh, get.

morgue. See: city morgue; what a dump.

morning. See: good morning; it's nice; one of these fine m.; you'll hate; you'll wake.

morning after the night before – the. is applied to the effects of a drinking-bout or to the person showing those effects: C20. Very common in Aus.; almost equally common elsewhere. P.B.: by mid C20 at latest, every bit as common elsewhere! A.B., 1978, notes that it is 'sometimes truncated to (*it's*) *the morning after*'.

morning glory. See: what's your story m.

morons. See: tell that to.

Morris. See: 'tis not.

Moses. See: Jesus saves; roll on, my; where was M.

Moss. See: as Moss caught.

mother. See: and her m.; black over; can you 'ear; cat's mother; Charley's dead; come home, all; coming, Mother; dead! and; dear Mother; does your m.; face that; go and get your m.; go home; has your m.; have a go, Joe; he never had; his mother; how's your m.; I have no pain; I haven't laughed; I'll give you my; I'll tell your m.; living with; my mother; never let; oh, mother; or your bitch; please, mother; pull a soldier; remember I'm; 'she' is a cat's; shit, mother; so my m.; some mothers; take your washing; tell your m.; thank your m.; throw your; who would be; wouldn't that jar; wrapped; you may have; you missed; you ought; your mother.

Mother Brown. See: knees up.

mother, is it worth it? A 'women's c.p., when anything goes wrong, particularly sex-wise. From the agonies of childbirth. Used ironically of things that go wrong in domestic life' (Granville in a letter): C20. And cf **oh mother ....**

mother of that was a whisker – the. That's a most improbable story!: *c.* 1850–1900. Cf the mainly dialectal synon. *the dam of that was a whisker*, which was, however, applied to a big lie.

motion. See: sharp's.

motley. See: on with.

motto. See: speak as.

mountain. See: is it a m.

mounted. See: one of the.

mourning. See: you're in m.

mouse. See: are you a man; dun; tight as; why is a m.

moustache. See: your fadder's.

mouth. See: all mouth; don't let your m.; every time; give your arse; I don't let; it's bad manners; keep your bowels; large m.; me any my; put your money; shut mouth; shut my m.; take the marbles; wouldn't say; you are a mouth; and:

mouth is full of pap – his. Applied to one who is still childish: mid C18-early C19 (Grose. 1788). *Pap*, babies' food.

mouthful. See: Queen; you said a m.

moves. See: got all; if it moves.

mox nix. It makes no difference; it doesn't matter; it's a trifle: US, orig. and mostly the post-WW2 Army in Germany, thence, *c.* 1950, not negligibly, among civilians. A Hobson–Jobsoning of Ger. *es macht nichts*, itself prob from Fr. *ça ne fait rein*. (Recorded by W & F, 1966.) More precisely, the Ger. is *das*, that, or *es*, it (coll. shortened to *'s*) *macht nichts*, and the orig. form of the Americanization seems to have been *mox nix for old ish* (Ger. *Ich*, I), 'It makes no difference – it doesn't matter – to me'; and 'it is usually associated with the G.I. who has served in Germany in contrast to the G.I. who has served in Korea, Japan or Vietnam' (Moe).

Of the pron. *mox* for *markts* (*machts*), J.W.C. notes that the change of *a* (oh) to *o* 'would be owing to the common [esp. the demotic] American unrounding of short *o* to *a*, with the result that the German *a* gets wrongly written *o* – most notably in *lox* for *lachs*, (smoked) salmon'.

P.B.: but my British Army comrades, who had had the good fortune to be stationed in Austria in the early 1950s, used the synon. var. *mokter nix*, which they had 'borrowed' unaltered from the natives of Graz. (with thanks to Pat Fox and John Goldsmith.)

Mr .... See **Mister ...**; **Mrs ...** See **Mistress ....**; and:

Mr Brown. See: how do you do.

Mr Sharp. See: has Mr.

Mrs Astor's horse. See: all dressed.

Mrs Calabash. See: good night, Mrs C.

Mrs Hoskins. See: 'e's lovely.

Mrs Kelly. See: you must know.

Mrs Moore. See: any more.

Mrs Pettibone. See: now, Mrs Rowbottom.

Mrs Rowbottom. See: now, Mrs R.

Mrs Wood. See: good evening, Mrs W.

much. See: not much; this is too.

much chance as a fart in a windstorm (– as). No chance whatsoever: Can.: C20. But *like a fart in a windstorm* is Brit. for 'puny' – hence 'incommensurate' or 'ineffectual' (cf **like a fart in a colander**): low; C20.

Both expressions are US as well' (R.C. 1977). A.B., 1978, adds the US variants *... in a hurricane* or even *... in an elevator*; and then, he remarks, there are *as effective as ...* and *about as much use as ...* with any of these completions. Harold Shapiro supplies a further var. from US: *... in a blizzard.* Moreover, in the UK, the *windstorm* often becomes a *thunderstorm*, as Michael Goldman reminds me, 1978. (What one owes to one's friends, including those one will never meet!) Cf:

much chance as a snowball in hell. None at all: late C19–20: US, hence Can., hence Brit. (in narrower sense – usu. as *snowflake*), hence Aus. and NZ. Prob. the prompter of the prec. P.B.: in later C20, sometimes, elliptically, '(e.g. you) haven't a snowflake's'. Cf **no more chance ...**

much use as a (sick) headache. See headache.

much use as my arse (– you're as). A low and abusive expression: since late C19.

much use as two men gone sick. See **about as much ...**

much wit as three folks, two fools and a madman (– as);

allusively, the first part only. (He's) a fool; but also, (he's) rather cunning: C17 – mid 19. (Grose, 1796.) Said, by Apperson, to be mostly a Cheshire phrase; bordering on the proverbial.

muck. See: bricks; he's a fine; if you don't want.

muck in! yer at yer granny's. You're welcome: Liverpool: C20. From, of course, the lit. sense: 'Eat up – after all, you're at your grandmother's'. (Shaw, 1969.) Cf **dig in ...**

muckhill on my trencher. See **you make a muckhill....N.L.**

mud. See: and his name; clear as mud; happy as a dead; there's shit; you're full.

Mudros, Chios: and chaos was a 1915 Services' c.p., satirizing the fact that the Mediterranean Expeditionary Force at that time had three separate authorities (or commands) and bases. Mudros and Chios were Gr. islands not very far from the Turkish coast (and Gallipoli).

mugs away! An expression used 'in various games such as darts and pool to mean that the previous game's loser or losers start the next game first' (Jim Ramsay, *Cop It Sweet*, 1977); or the losers of the toss, or whatever method is used to decide who shall start the first game: Brit. and Aus.: since mid C20 (? earlier). *Mug* here = fool or dupe. Cf:

mugs for luck! 'Said commonly and a little sourly when someone has a stroke of (undeserved) fortune' (B.G.T., 1978): prob. throughout C20. Just possibly prompted by the standard comment, *beginner's luck*.

mule. See: only a fool; three acres.

mulligrubs. See: you are sick.

mum. See: be like dad; here we come.

mum, me bum's numb – ee is a c.p. orig. – *c.* 1910 – N. Country, but by 1920 very widely distributed. It humorously alludes both to childish frankness and to dialectal pronunciation.

[**mum's the word!** Don't say a word, keep it secret!: this borderlines cliché and c.p. and is, I think, rather the former than the latter. Orig., a literal warning.]

murder. See: it's murder.

murder is out – the. The mystery has been solved: C20; by 1970, ob. From the proverbial *murder will out*.

'murder!' she cried was, *c.* 1910 – 30, the c.p. of any girl luckless enough, at a dance, to encounter a clumsy, heavy-footed, partner.

murdered. See: have you heard the news.

Murdoch. See: get in there, Murdoch; oh, get.

Murphy's been at it again. See **anything that can go wrong ...**

muscles. See: I'm a ball; this training.

muscles like sparrows' knee-caps. 'A disparaging way of commenting on the strength of somebody else' (anon., 1978): C20. P.B.: but may also be said in self-mockery. Did it prompt, or did it derive from, the schoolboys' parody of Longfellow's *The Village Smithy*, 'And the muscles of his brawny arms/Are strong as iron bands', which became '...arms/Stood out like sparrows' knee-caps'?

mush. See: you'd be far.

mushroom. See: I feel like.

music as a wheelbarrow – as good. See **you make as good ....**

music's paid – the. 'The Watch-word among Highway-men, to let the Company know that we're to rob, alone, in return for some Courtesy' (BE): late C17-early C19. From the harp on the reverse of an Irish farthing or halfpenny.

musical farce. See: for a musical.

must. See: there's no 'must'; this I must; you must.

[**must be hurt for certain, for you see her** (or **his**) **head is all of a lump,** usu. prec. by (**he** or) **she,** as in S. 1738. It may be an ostensibly callous c.p., but is more prob. an integral part of a normal conversation. The words are spoken, of Miss Notable, by the gallant old colonel.]

must be hurtin' for certain – he. Unlike the prec., is indubitably a US c.p., 'A military [and thence, more gen.] phrase, as I've heard it, meaning "he's in trouble" or "he's far behind with his work". I have no date for it. I guess C20' (A.B., 1978). I have read it in American fiction at least as early as 1950 and

think it goes back to the early 1930s: 'in financial trouble'. Rhyme has been at work and perhaps hurting, *penniless*, has intervened.

must have been drinking out of a damp glass. See **from drinking out of ...**

must have been lying in bed barefoot (– **you**); and **you must have been sleeping near a crack.** A usu. male rejoinder to one who has complained of being afflicted with a bad cold: the former, late C18–20, and lower and lower-middle class and raffish of almost any class; the latter, perhaps from much further back, even as far as C17 – even though I lack examples. The former occurs in, e.g., Ernest Raymond's novel *Mary Leith*, 1931. Among the raffish, there is always an innuendo concerning the anatomical cleft.

The latter reason for a severe cold in the head is either jocosely advanced by the sufferer or slyly imputed by a friend (Shaw, 1969). Cf prec., and **caught cold ...**

must have been something he ate or ... they put in the tea are merely the coll, forms of it **must have been ....**

must have worms – he (or **she**), is applied to a fidgety, restless child: mid C19–20. (Petch, 1974.)

must have stood too far off (with the shotgun) – he. The cook has put too few currants or raisins into a *brownie*, a sort of cake: Aus.: C20. (Brig. C.M.L. Elliott, OBE, 1970.)

must I spell it out for you? See spell it out for you?

[*must* is for the King. S, 1738, near the beginning has:

COL[ONEL]: Tom, you must go with us to Lady *Smart's* to Breakfast.

NEV[EROUT]: Must! why Colonel, *Must* is for the King. Only kings have the right and the privilege to be so peremptory. C17–18 as a c.p., rather longer as a proverb. (*ODEP*.)]

must you put in your two cents' worth? See two cents' worth.

must you stay? can't you go? appeared in *Punch* on 18 Jan. 1905 and has certainly been a c.p. ever since. 'Referring to the prolonged stay of the Russian Admiral Rodjestvensky, at Madagascar on his way to meet the Japanese Fleet' (Benham). But I suspect that this caption merely exemplifies a.c.p. that had existed from a few years earlier: and *ODQ* has a record of it as having been used before 1897, the year in which its originator, schoolmaster Charles John Vaughan, died: it was his customary speeding-up of departure to boys 'too shy to go' after a 'guest' breakfast, although in the form 'Can't you go? Must you stay?' – as recorded by G.W.E. Russell in *Collections and Recollections*, 1898, 2nd Series, 1895.

mustn't grumble. See can't complain.

mutton. See: who stole the m.

mutton dressed (or **dressed up**) **as lamb,** has, since latish C19, been directed at middle-aged and elderly women dressing in an unbecomingly youthful fashion. Drawn from the terminology of the butcher's shop.

my answer's in the infirmary. See answers ....

my arse and your face. See yes, my arse ....

my arse is dragging. I can hardly walk; indeed, I am completely exhausted: Can.: since *c.* 1915. (Leechman.) Also US, but, of course, *ass* (J.W.C., 1977). US variants: *my butt,* or *tail,* is dragging or *my ass,* or *butt* or *tail, is busted;* sometimes *my balls are hanging low* (A.B., 1978). All: prob. since *c.* 1910. P.B.: is the last an echo of 'Poor old Joe', who was comin', 'though my head is hangin' low'?

my Aunt Fanny! used as a suffix, e.g. 'Back-ache, my Aunt Fanny! He's swinging the lead again', expresses incredulity: C20. Contrast *like Aunt Fanny,* clumsy, and the idiomatic *my sainted Aunt!* expressing surprise; cf *my granny,* or *grandmother,* used synon. with *my A.F.!,* in e.g. Richard Blaker's novel of WW1, *Medal Without Bar,* 1930. (P.B.)

my back teeth are afloat (occ. **floating**) or **awash** implies a need – a strong desire – to urinate: mostly male, low: C20; by 1960, slightly ob. In US, however, as Berrey, 1942, records, the *floating* version meant 'I feel dead drunk'.

my belly button's playing hell with my backbone. I'm damned hungry: mostly lower-middle class: C20. Cf **my guts ...** and **my stomach ...** and:

my belly thinks my throat is cut. See **my stomach ....**

my bloody oath! – commoner than *my oath!* – is, apart from the (orig. mere) ejaculation, an Aus. c.p. meaning 'I certainly agree', and dating from early C20. Thus prompted by P.B., I now remember hearing it in the A.I.F. of WW1.

my brother from Gozo. see **just the job for ....**

my country cousin is here. See **country cousin ....**

my cup of tea. See **just my ....**

my dogs are barking. 'My feet are giving me hell'. A US c.p., dating from well before WW2, and soon adopted in UK and the Commonwealth by certain Servicemen near the end of that war, and by a few others several years later. Once *dogs*, human feet, arose in US slang, the c.p. was sure to follow: the only astonishing thing is that it took so long to do so. Cf **my feet ....**

[**my ears are burning,** proposed by several correspondents, is ineligible, for it is proverbial – a modern version of that very old proverb, *if your ears glow, someone is talking of you*: see *ODEP;* P.B.: however, the comparable Army and RAF retort to the observation 'my arse is itching', the scurrilous *a sailor must be thinking of you*, may perhaps qualify.]

my elbow!, as in 'True? My elbow!' A US emphatic negative: late (perhaps mid) C19–2. (Fain, 1977.) A derivative from **all my eye,** q.v. often aligned alliteratively with *elbows* as (*all*) *my eye and my elbow*, likewise US: (Prof. James R. Gaskin, in *The Sewanee Review*, mid 1978.) P.B.: Brit. Eng. prefers *my foot!*, and all are prob. euph. for *my arse!*

my eye and Betty Martin. See **all my eye and ...**

my feet are killing me. A mostly feminine c.p., dating since *c.* 1890 in Brit., it became, *c.* 1900, also US: it occurs in e.g. Damon Runyon, *Take It Easy*, 1938. The dictionaries of (Brit.) English language and quotations are singularly reticent about this phrase, but at least we may compare the c.p. **how's your poor feet?**

In the title story of Noël Coward's *Pretty Polly Barlow.* 1964, a British sailor speaks up for one of his four parrots: '"Gladys don't swear," said the giant defensively. "She only says 'Action Stations' and 'My feet are killing me'."' As so often, Noël Coward supplies a very neat example.

Cf **my dogs ...**

my friend (or **little friend**) **has come.** See **friend has come ....**

my gate's shut. See **gate's shut.**

my goodness is coming out. In Dialogue I of S, 1738, occurs this passage:

[*Miss feels a Pimple on her Face.*]

MISS: Lord, I think my Goodness is coming out: Madam, will your Ladyship please to lend me a Patch?

She implies that she is simply – or more precisely, pimply *because* she is chaste.

This c.p. was, I think, current throughout C18–19 and early C20; I first heard it just before WW1 but have not heard it since WW2.

my guts begin (or **are beginning**) **to think my throat's cut** is a (low) c.p. of *c.* 1750–1914. (See esp. *DSUE* at p. 363.) The predominant C20 form is, among men, *my belly thinks ...* and, among women and 'old women', *my stomach ...* , q.v.

But P.B., 1976, writes: 'Not dead yet, by a long chalk. I heard it all through my Service life, up to early 1970'.

my heart bleeds for you. Despite its 'My withers are wrung' overtone, it is often ironic – often bitterly so: since the late 1940s. 'Probably by a wincing reaction against that gushing sympathy which is insincere and, indeed, hypocritical – and wouldn't part with a penny. A variant c.p., more US than British, is *I weep for you*' (*DSUE*). In *Samantha*, 1968 (Brit. edn), E.V. Cunningham makes his very likable Japanese detective say to his chief: '"With all respects to my esteemed boss ... I am aware of his financial difficulties. My heart bleeds for the poverty of those who guard the wealthiest city in the world."' In the same novel occurs the further var. *you're breaking my heart.*

'Nowadays almost invariable heavily ironic. Perhaps worth noting are two shades of meaning: "It's not *my* problem" and "That's *your* hard luck" – the latter often implying that the person addressed is by no means as much in need of sympathy as he pretends' (R.C., 1978).

my hero! is, as Granville told me in a letter, 1964, a c.p. 'that greets a diver who breaks surface with small green crabs or perfectly useless fish, such as wrasse': since the late 1950s. It prob. derives from the ironic use of the phrase by girls satirizing the mushier sort of film. Cf this passage in P.G. Wodehouse's *Aunts Aren't Gentlemen*, 1975, in which the immortal Bertie Wooster offers to do something brave for his hard-bitten, sharp-tongued, bullying Aunt Dahlia:

'It will merely be one more grave among the bulls. What did you say?'

'Just "My Hero",' said the aged relative.

It possibly echoes a memory of Oskar Straus's *The Chocolate Soldier*, 1908, which was based on G.B. Shaw's *Arms and the Man*, 1898. (A blending of information from Maurice Wedgewood and Ronald Pearsall.)

my life. The unnamed witty author of 'Complete Vocabulary of Spoken English' in *Punch*, 10 Oct. 1973, has this entry: 'My life = *I am about to tell a Jewish joke*': since the late 1960s, when Yiddish humour, slang, c.pp. began to hit the Gentile headlines. P.B.: an occ. var. is *my life, already!*

my lips are sealed. A statement made, more than once, by Prime Minister Stanley Baldwin during the abdication days of late 1936–early 1937; upon King Edward VIII's abdication, feeling ran high for a period of some months. The first such statement: 'My lips are sealed. I am bound to keep silence.'

Occasionally it is impossible to distinguish between overworked quot'n – outright cliché – and genuine c.p. But in its wider application, this is a genuine c.p.; that is, when it substitutes for 'I'd rather not say' or 'I shan't answer *that* one', uttered with a smile that does duty for 'if you don't mind' or 'with respect': usu. humorous or wryly ironic or both.

my long-lost che-ild. 'Theatrical rant is commonly burlesqued by such phrases as "my long lost che-ild" (Collinson): *c.* 1890–1914. Like **dead and she never called me mother,** it satirized the Surrey-side or Transpontine melodrama of *c.* 1860–1914.

my moments. See **I have had my moments.**

my mother sews too. 'Heard on 21 February 1969. First pupil: "So?" [= so what?] Second pupil: "*My* mother sews too."' (Mr. D.J. Barr, schoolmaster): Can. schools' punning retort to someone saying *So?:* since *c.* 1965. But I suspect that it has a far wider distribution and that it goes back to late C19 – it not, indeed, to C17.

my mother told me there'd be days like this, but she didn't say there'd be so many. Applied to a 'tough' time, esp. in the army: Can. soldiers': WW2. An oblique ref. to menstruation. (Leechman.) But also US, with occ. variants *my father* or *someone* (A.B., 1978).

P.B.: a particularly moving account of the phrase's use occurs in Martin Caidin, *The Ragged, Rugged Warriors*, 1966, where, at the end of a description by an on-the-spot, anonymous historian of the intolerable conditions endured by the men of 67th Squadron, USAAF, at Guadalcanal, 1942, it is written, 'The phrase then was, "my mother told me there would be days like this but she didn't tell me there would be so many of them"' (Ch. 16, p. 301 of the UK ed., 1980).

my mother would have a hairy canary if I did that! She'd 'have a fit': Can. schoolchildren's: since *c.* 1955. (D.J. Barr, 1969.) Cf **my mother sews too.**

my name is Benjamin Brown, Ben Brown. 'Bend down, a formula pleasantry when there is no inspiration and meant to be outrageous, but is merely tedious' (a correspondent): since *c.* 1950 – perhaps much earlier.

my name is Haines! Farmer writes: 'A slang intimation of an intention to depart quickly .... This expression is similar in character to "There's the door, and your *name* is Walker!" It is said to have originated in an incident in the life of President Jefferson.' Therefore C19. Cf **my name's Walker!**

This US c.p. has been recorded earlier in V., and Ashley explains, 'the story behind it being that someone of this name who had greatly criticized Pres. Thomas Jefferson met the President (or ex-President – the story varies) in person, and when told "I am Thomas Jefferson", gave this reply and fled'.

my name is Twyford. I know nothing about it: semi-proverbial c.p. of *c*. 1680–1830. Used by Peter Motteux in 1694 in his completion of Urquhart's translation of Rabelais and recorded by 'Proverbs' Fuller in 1732 and referred to by Charles Whibley in his essay on Rabelais: all cited by Apperson. In the *New Statesman* of 20 Feb. 1937, David Garnett writes: 'Josiah Twyford, 1640–1729, learned a secret process in the manufacture of glaze by persistently feigning stupidity and was thus ... able to lay the foundation of the famous firm of sanitary potters.' So apparently not *all* 'don't knows' are stupid.

my name is 'Unt, not cunt. I'm nobody's fool or dupe: mostly RAF: since the middle 1940s. An elab. of the slangy *Joe Hunt*, that man who, in the Services, gets all the dirty work.

my name's Simpson, not Samson is a 'workmen's c.p., uttered when one is confronted by work too heavy for one person: C20. It was either orig. by some humorist named *Simpson* or derived from a scabrously witty limerick concerning a young woman named *Ransom*.

my name's Walker! I'm off: mid C19–20; by 1975, ob. Cf the var. noted at **my name is Haines.** There are several explanations about the origin of *Walker*; my favourite is that it's merely a pun on *walker*, one who walks, hence esp. one who walks off.

Arthur C.L. Grear notes, 1978, that it occurs in Dickens's *A Christmas Carol*, 1843, in this form, although the orig., recorded in 1811, was 'Hookey Walker'. P.B.: may there then be some connection with the old (formerly Standard English, in C19 become slang) term *hook*, to twist, jerk, hence depart? Cf **make yer name ...**

my nose itches is a C18–20 invitation to kiss, the dovetailed reply being as in S, 'I knew I should drink wine, or kiss a fool'; or, C18–20, 'I knew I would shake hands with a fool'; or, in C19–20, 'I knew I was going to sneeze *or* to be cursed, *or* kissed, by a fool'. But by *c*. 1945, ob. Cf **does your nose ...**

[**my oath – my Colonial oath – my bloody oath.** These picturesque Aus. exclamations are clearly not c.pp. at all: mere oaths don't even begin to qualify, any more than *good God!* They have almost become part of Aus. folklore. But see also **my bloody oath.**]

my oath, Miss Weston! On my honour *or* Cross my heart!: RN (lower-deck): C20, but little used after the 1930s. 'An expression originating in the lifetime of Dame Agnes Weston, the widely known and honoured foundress of hostels for bluejackets at the naval ports, in connection with temperance pledges' (F & G). Noted by John Laffin in his *Jack Tar*, 1969.

my part! Ironic for '*I* should worry!': since *c*. 1926. Perhaps elliptical for 'It's *not* my part – share – duty – to look after that'. Cf **my troubles!**

my pocket thinks my hand's gone mad. 'I'm spending money very freely' or 'I'm being very generous with my money': since the 1920s. Robert Robinson, in the BBC programme *Stop the Week*, 17 Oct. 1977, apropos the first edition of this book, tells us that this was what his father used to say when he was handing out money. (With the kind permission of Mr Robinson and the BBC.)

my prick's a bloater. See **or my prick's ...**

my problem! 'Used, without *it's* or *that's* in front, to mean "You

needn't bother, *I*'ll deal with it"' (Playfair, 1977): since *c*.1970.

my rents are coming in. 'I have torn my Pettycoat with your odious romping; my Rents are coming in; I'm afraid I shall fall into the Ragman's Hands': thus exclaims Miss Notable in Dialogue I of S: C18. Puns on rents in one's clothing and the old-clothes-man.

[**my son the doctor.** J.W.C., 1975, suggests that this phrase orig. as a cliché, based on Yiddish and first used by proud Jewish mothers, but is now used by others; and that it has come to be employed humorously and derisively and, by being so used, has taken on the status of a c.p., with the users' full knowledge that it originated as a cliché. I'm not entirely convinced, but I'm perhaps being a foolish 'doubting Thomas', for John Clark very, very seldom errs in such delicate discriminations. He adds, 1977, 'There is an additional c.p. (if it is one) based on this: "My son the dentist and my son the C.P.A. [Certified Public Accountant = Chartered Accountant]". The latter suggests with humorous pathos somewhat humbler aspirations and achievements'.]

my spies are everywhere. A 'facetious response to questions such as "How did you know it was my birthday?" Probably from spy films: US: from (?) 1940; now ob.' (R.C., 1978). Cf the Brit. **I have my agents.**

my stomach thinks my throat is cut. 'I have the very devil of an appetite' or 'I'm perishing of hunger': a semi-proverbial c.p.: C16–20. Recorded as early as 1540 by Palsgrave. (Apperson.) In late C19–20, mainly rural. Two frequent variants are **my belly thinks my throat is cut.** C18–20, and **my guts ...**, *c*. 1750–1914. See also **I'm so empty ...** and **I'm so hungry ...**

my troubles! is the Aus. version of '*I* should worry!': since *c*. 1890, or a decade earlier; Wilkes, in *Dict. Aus. Coll.*, records Cornelius Gowe, *The Australian Slang Dictionary*, 1895, as giving ' ... my troubles" what do I care'. Wilkes, moreover, notes the much later Aus. synon., *my worries!* – as in Alan Marshall's *How Beautiful Are Thy Feet*, 1949. Perhaps elliptical for 'That's not one of my troubles *or* worries'. Cf **my part!**

my watch runs upon wheels was a c.p. of very late C17–late C18. In S, near the end of the Dialogue I, we find:

col[ONEL]: Pray, my Lord; what's a Clock by your Oracle? [What time is it?]

LORD SP[ARKISH]: Faith, I can't tell; I think my Watch runs upon Wheels.

my wife (less commonly, **husband**) **doesn't understand me** is used repeatedly by men – or women – seeking sympathy and, sooner or later, sexual relations outside marriage: prob. almost immemorial, both in Britain and in the US.

What are *they* complaining about? It would be damned awkward for the speakers if they *were* understood!

'In a pre-WW2 musical comedy (one of Leslie Henson's?) a line that brought down the house was "My trouble is that my wife understands me"' (Sanders, 1978).

my word, if I catch you bending! In the London streets of *c*. 1895–1914, it was a semi-sexual c.p.; but then it became much more general in use and bore an additional meaning – 'The answer is, "I'll saw your leg off"' (all from a song)', as Julian Franklyn once phrased it: a humorous threat. L.A. adds that it has a wider application: ' "If I catch you when I can take advantage of you, look out!" I think this c.p. is not only sexual ... If it is, many people, especially women, did not think in this [the sexual] sense'. Cf the next – by which it was, I'd say, prompted. See also the var. **don't let me catch ...**

my word, if you're not off! is a c.p. of either dismissal or deterrence and was current *c*. 1890–1914; during its last four or five years, it was, like the prec., often augmented thus: *if you're not off, I'll saw your leg off.*

my worries! See **my troubles!**

N

N.A.B.U. See T.A.B.U.

N.B.G. No bloody good: C20. This affords a useful example of that phenomenon whereby, although the full phrase has not achieved the status of c.p., the abbr. has done so.

N.C. A fairly common abbr. of **no comment.**

N.C.A.W.W.A.S.B.E. See TOMMY HANDLEY, and **ta-ta ...**

N.C.D. See **no can do.**

N.F.L. See: welcome to the.

Naafi-breaks. See: I'll be laughing.

NAAFI suppers. See: I've had more.

nail(s). See: another nail; chews nails; couldn't drive; steal; up your tail.

name. See: all that the n.; and his n.; any publicity; bullet; I never remember; I'll forget; if I have the n.; if you can n.; it had my n.; make yer n.; no name; take his n.; that's the n.; what a ghastly; what is your; what was; when yer n.; who's that; wire up; you name; and:

name of the game – the, implies 'the precise meaning of which is –' and 'not to beat about the bush, the word is –': orig. US, but not at all gen. before *c.* 1965; Leechman in late 1968 glossed its Can. usage thus: 'The name of the game is murder – for instance. Very recent.' It did not become Brit. until 1973. In American fiction, I have noticed that Stanley Elliot uses it in *Strong-hold*, 1974. In the *Daily Telegraph*, 7 Aug. 1975, David Holloway, reviewing Edwin Newman's *Strictly Speaking*, says, 'Mr Newman protests properly about the use of "the name of the game"'; and, one day earlier, P.B. had written, 'I feel that it's a newish c.p., probably originating in sports journalism. It annoys me because it's one of the smug and "knowing" ones.'

The particular sense noted above has widened to 'the predominant factor – the true purpose, the plan, the crux' and various nuances thereof, e.g. 'what is really, not what is apparently, happening'.

It had been recorded for, and in, 1971; W & F, 1976, define it as the prec. para. But in the US, 'There is an early example (1962) in "Multiplication", a song recorded by actor-singer Bobby Darin. The lyric began: "Multiplication, that's the name of the game,/And each generation does it just the same"' (Janssen, 1977). So we can safely date its orig. at 1961.

name your poison! What will you drink?: joc. invitation, in UK from the 1920s but by late 1970s virtually †; in US, current late C19–early 20 (J.W.C., 1977). 'I suggest an origin in the Wild West, perhaps reflecting the Temperance Movement slogan, "Alcohol is poison". Of course it is, but what a wonderful way to go!' (R.C., 1978). Note also:

name yours! and **give it a name!** What'll you drink? (Water is honourably excluded.) Both: late C19–20; but rare after 1940. (See Lyell, a too little known book, pub'd in the Far East.)

Talking of *what'll ...*; when I was a post-graduate at Oxford in 1921–3, my College had a small drinking club, which called itself 'the *What' lling* Club'.

Nannie. See: not on your N.

Nanny Goat Lancers. See: charge of the N.

Napoleon's greeting to his troops: Good morning, troops. John Brophy, in 'Chants and Sayings', Appendix A of B & P, 1930, says: 'The headlong descent from the heroic strain was another form of stock humour. As, imitating a reciter's announcement of the title of his "piece":

Napoleon's Greeting to his Troops –

"Good morning, troops."'

The c.p. apparently dates from late C19 and became † *c.* 1940.

napoo finee. No more – finished!: army: 1914–18. A tautological elab. of *napoo*, nothing more, no more, and *finee*, finished: Fr. *il n'y en a plus, fini*, lit., 'there's no more of it, finished'. The British soldier dealt no less heroically with foreign languages than he did with the enemy.

Of *napoo*, B & P write: 'The word came to be used for all the destructions, obliterations and disappointments of war, e.g. "The bread's napoo"; "The S.M.'s [Sergeant-Major's] napoo"; "Napoo rum".'

nappies. See: go and get your mother.

napping. See: as Moss caught.

nark. See: I'll nark.

Nash (usu. Mr Nash) is concerned was an underworld c.p. of late C18–mid C19 and it meant that So-and-So had departed, or, as Vaux, professional criminal sent to Australia for his country's good, wrote as an exiled convict, 'Speaking of a person who is gone, they [his underworld companions] say, he is nashed.' Here, *Nash* or *nash* derives from the Romany *nash, nasher*, to run.

nasturtiums. See: are you casting.

nasty. See: cheap and n.; common; rough as; soft as shit; something n.

natives are restless (to-night) – the. A var. of the next, this c.p. vaguely alludes to the unrest of the emergent African and Asian peoples, but is also used in ref. to unfriendly audiences, whether of theatre or vaudeville, of radio or TV – or of political gatherings. It has spread to the US. In John Crosby, *The White Telephone*, 1974, we see: 'He [a not entirely apocryphal President] picked up the phone. "The natives are getting restless," said Miss Doll' [about some second-echelon Federal men].

Perhaps from the restless natives of the North-West Frontier of India during British rule; perhaps, too, it owes something to Rudyard Kipling's tales of India. R.C. remarks, 1978, that it 'originated long before the emergence of "the Third World" – from various films about pukka sahibs drinking sundowners on the veranda. Cf "Those drums, Carruthers, those damned drums!"'

'Also used humorously in the Gin-and-Jaguar Belt [the

most affluent, outermost suburbs of London], where established residents can be very clannish and resentful of newcomers. Current' (Sanders, 1978).

natives were hostile – the; occ. **are** for **were**, and **pretty** (or if the flak had been very heavy and severe, **bloody**) **hostile** for the unmodified **hostile**. 'Anti-aircraft fire was heavy': RAF aircrews, reporting a raid over Germany: 1940–5. (PGR) A characteristic meiosis, based on 'The natives were hostile', occurring so frequently in books of travel and exploration, esp. of Africa. The c.p. passed, *c*. 1945, into civilian and gen. use. Cf John Mortimer's moving play, *The Judge*, 1967, at II, viii.:

SERENA: You did that to me! Picked me up out of the cold hotel ... and dumped me into *this!*

JUDGE: To make it up to you.

SERENA: This outpost! This desert! This frontier! Alone! With the natives hostile! Cf prec.

NATO forces. See: from Greenland's

natural. See: large as life; not on your n.

naturally. See: do what.

nature. See: ain't nature; Gamp; it's only human.

naughty. See: it's naughty; you have been doing; and:

naughty, naughty! 'Used in admonishment among adults nowadays' (Petch, 1968), but rarely in other than non-U circles: since *c*. 1950. Adopted from the disapproval uttered to a child.

naval officer. See: gangway.

navel. See: carry the banner; contemplating.

navy. See: thank God; that's the old N.

navy's here – the. '– and all is well, for we've been rescued'. This became a c.p. almost immediately after the press and radio reported the freeing of 299 British seamen from the Ger. supply ship *Altmark* in Jossing Fjord, Norway, by the Royal Navy's destroyer *Cossack*, whose boarding party was led by Lieutenant Bradwell Turner. He shouted these reassuring words to the prisoners. The *Cossack* was commanded by the intrepid Philip Vian, who described the incident in his stirring memoirs, *Action This Day*, and who died with the rank of Sir Philip Vian, Admiral of the Fleet.

Cf **Marines have landed.**

nay, nay, Pauline! In Act III of *Father and the Boys* (A Comedy-Drama), 1924, the inimitable George Ade has:

LEMUEL [the father]: What's the kick? Everybody told me, 'Take a vacation – circulate – have some fun – cut loose –.' ...I've got out and cut loose – and now you're trying to head me off. Nay, nay, Pauline!

Gen. sense: 'certainly not!' or 'nothing doing!' In 1946, Peter Tamony traced *Nay, Nay, Pauline* to J.S. Wood's *Yale Yarns*, 1895; and HLM, Supp. 2, lists it among US c.pp. derived from songs.

Cf **not to-night, Josephine**, which may, I suspect, have prompted the US song and saying.

'nay, nay!' quoth Stringer, when his neck was in the halter was, *c*. 1660–1750, a semi-proverbial c.p., applied to one speaking too late. It occurs in Ray's and Fuller's books of proverbs and has been included in Apperson.

Prob. from a topical instance, perhaps of an innocent man, but possibly suggested by *string up*, to hang someone.

near. See: if I were n.

near enough is good enough has, since *c*. 1945, been an Aus. c.p. 'Applied to a very common attitude' (B.P., 1975). This might easily become a proverb.

near the foreman, near the door is a tailors' c.p., dating from *c*. 1850 and implying that it is best to keep as far away from the foreman as possible; by 1940, virtually †. B & L.

nearly bought my own beer. See **talk about laugh!**

neat but not gaudy, orig. serious, and Standard English, *c*. 1800 took an ironical turn and had, by 1838, when Ruskin, in the *Architectural Magazine* for Nov., could write, 'That admiration of the "neat but not gaudy", which is commonly reported to have influenced the devil when he painted his tail pea green' (Apperson) become a c.p. A var. by elab.,

current by 1860, is *neat, but not gaudy, as the monkey said, when he painted his tail sky-blue*, with the final clause often omitted. (F & H.) A further var. is *neat but not gaudy, as the monkey said when he painted his bottom pink and tied up his tail with pea-green*, not much used after *c*. 1900, but in the latter half of C19 was often applied to old ladies – and to some not so old – dressed flamboyantly. A C20 var., rare after *c*. 1960 and † by 1970 is *neat but not gaudy, chic but not bizarre*.

'Orig. serious' refers to the fact that the Rev. Samuel Wesley, in *An Epistle to a Friend Concerning Poetry*, 1700, wrote, 'Style is the dress of thought; a modest dress,/Neat, but not gaudy, will true critics please'. (Thanks to Sir Edward Playfair.) But, 'Surely,' writes R.C., 1978, 'the ultimate source is *Hamlet*, I, iii, "Costly thy habit as thy purse can buy:/But not expressed in fancy: rich, not gaudy"?'

But this note merely touches the surface of a c.p. that merits an article or even an essay.

necessarily. See: it ain't n.

necessary. See: is your journey.

neck. See: cow calves; get off my n.; I don't wish; I'll first; 'nay, nay!'; shit in the n.; stout; wind in; you've got it all.

necktie. See: I'll have your balls.

Ned. See: go it, Ned.

Ned Kelly. See: game as Ned.

Ned Kelly was hung (literately **hanged**) **for less.** This Aus. c.p., a mildly joc. reproof or complaint (e.g., of excessive taxation), has been current since the 1930s, as B.P. tells me. The ref. is to the famous bushranger, who has become something of a hero to many Australians.

Neddy. See: time for your.

need. See: I need; I was there; if I need; thanks, I needed; that's all I n.; who needs; you need.

need I say more! See **nudge, nudge, wink, wink.**

needle(s). See: I could shit; put that on.

needle, nardle (or **neidle** or **noddle**), **noo!** A recurrent nonsense line from the BBC radio surrealist comedy series 'The Goon Show', was a sort of chanted exclamation. Occ., if there was a 'Scottish' flavour to the programme, e.g. when the script-writers had parodied William McGonagal, the c.p. would emerge as *needle, nardle, McNoo!* This show ran through the 1950s, but is still remembered with great affection by its many fans. (P.B., 1983.) See GOON SHOW.

ne'er an M under your girdle? Have you no manners? – *esp.*, Haven't you the politeness to say 'Master' (or 'Mistress' or 'Miss'): *c*. 1540–1850. Apperson cites Udall's comedy, *Ralph Roister Doister*, Swift, and Scott. In the Dialogue I of S, we read:

NEV[EROUT]: Come then, Miss, e'en make a Die of it; and then we shall have a burying of our own.

MISS: The Devil take you, *Neverout*, besides all small Curses.

LADY ANSW[ERALL]: Marry come up: What, plain *Neverout*, methinks you might have an M under you Girdle, Miss. Cf the C20 '*Mister* to you!'

ne'er stir! See **never stir!**

negidicrop dibombit! See **eyaydon ...**

neglected. See: education.

neighbourhood. See: consult.

neither right nor fair. See **it's like a nigger ...**

Nellie. See: not on your N.; since Auntie; sitting by N.; up in Annie's; whoa, Emma.

Nelson. See: fuck 'em all; I'm going to do; and:

Nelson's dead. That's stale news, or that's nothing new: prob. since mid C19; not yet †, though very ob.: Noble quotes Elizabeth Mace, *The Rushton Inheritance* (a children's novel), 1978: 'Tilda lifted her head, listening. "Baby's crying," she said. "Nelson's dead," Tom grunted. "What's news?"' A satirical comment, based on the C18–20 proverb *Queen Anne is* (or *Anne's*) *dead*, itself prob. from *Queen Elizabeth is dead* (*ODEP*).

Nenagh. See: cheer up, there's.

nerve. See: of all the n.

nervous. See: are you n.; real nervous; titter.

nest. See: couldn't pull; have you found.

nettle. See: pissed on a n.

neutral. See: with thumb.

never a dull moment! This RN c.p., dating since 1939, is used ironically in moments of excitement or danger, but also in moments of personal, incidental, stress, as when one's leave has been cancelled for some usually unexplained reason. From *c.* 1945 onwards, it has been widely used among civilians too – usu. on much less exciting or dangerous occasions.

never be rude to the stage carpenter. He might be your manager next week. In a letter, 1968, Granville says:

> Dating from the fit-up times [the period of the portable theatres], when the carpenter seemed to be the only one with any money and could be relied upon to weigh in with a few quid when the company was at dry-up (closure stage) point for lack of funds. *c.* 1880–1920.

P.B.: cf that splendid piece of advice in one of 'Saki' [H.H. Munro]'s stories of Edwardian mores, 'Never be flippantly rude to elderly strangers in foreign hotels. They always turn out to be the King of Sweden.'

never buy your candy... See **never shit where you eat.**

never called me 'mother'. See **dead! and she never...**

never darken my doors (US **doorstep**) **again.** 'In old time melodrama [*c.* 1860–1914] the classic injunction to the erring daughter; later, facetious phrase of dismissal, now very obsolescent' (R.C., 1978). P.B.: in UK, as often *doorstep*, and the whole often prec. by *go! And never...* Cf **out into the cold, cold snow.**

never does anything wrong – he! ironically or satirically implies that he never does anything right; arising on 'the halls' in 1883 (Ware), it soon became gen., and by 1920 †. Another source, however, puts the origin in a Gaiety Theatre play that enshrines the song containing the optimistic words, 'In me you see the Rajah of Bong/Who never, no never, did anything wrong.'

[**never explain and never apologize.** the maxim of the Royal Navy's officers, is said to have been originated and 'promoted' by Admiral 'Jacky' Fisher: C20. (*Sailors' Slang.*) Almost a c.p.]

never fear: [the speaker's name] **is here.** Sometimes this is a cheerful greeting, at other times a jovial and friendly reassurance: since the middle 1940s, perhaps much earlier (say *c.* 1920). P.B., 1975, reminds me that the lure of rhyme or, rather, of a jingle has always been current among those who would never dream of reading poetry; nor only among the youthful.

never give a sucker an even break! (See the Carl Sandburg and the Fredenburgh quotations in the latter paragraphs of **old army game.**) This is a famous quot'n become, by 1920 at latest, a c.p. Although 'often attributed to W.C. Fields [1879–1946]' – as Bartlett informs us – it is more credibly attributed to a remark made by Edward Francis Albee (1857–1930). From the US it went to Aus. in the mid-1940s and it occurs in, e.g., Frank Hardy's *Billy Barker Yarns Again,* 1967, early in the story. 'Cheats Never Prosper – If They Have Principles'. It had reached Britain by 1944 – *via* the US Army.

'I think you're right about W.C. Fields and Albee, but I'd be willing to bet that this derives from P.T. Barnum, "There's a sucker born every minute", which practically became his motto' (A.B., 1978). Bet not accepted.

never had it so good, usu. prec. by **you've** (less often by **they've** or **we've**); in US usage, **never had it so good – you** (or **we** or **they**). So far as UK and the Commonwealth are concerned, it was 'sparked off' by Prime Minister Harold Macmillan (1957–63): 'Our people have never had it so good', which, by the educated and the cultured, is occ. rendered into L: *nunquam id habuistis tam bonum.* (For the Latinity, cf *excrementum tauri* and, as a c.p., **non illegitimis carborun-**

dum.)

But 'the Americans were using this idiom by the end of the Second World War, and possibly long before that. In German it is old established, while in modern German it is heard a dozen times a day': and this, adds Foster, seems to indicate that 'we are dealing with an idiom carried over into American English by the speech habits of German immigrants'. (Cf **I wouldn't know.**)

never had no mother. See **he never had...**

never introduce your (or **yer**) **dona(h) to a pal!** has been an Aus. c.p. throughout the C20. *Dona(h)* was taken to Australia by Cockneys, who themselves borrowed it from parlary (the theatrical lingua franca based on Italian): lit. 'woman' or 'lady', it came to mean one's girl or sweetheart: but things tend to come full circle: [name omitted in E.P.'s notes] sent me, 1977, the Londoners' version, *never introduce your pal to your donah* and glossed it, ' "Don't take the risk of losing your girl to your friend" – which is of course the Australian sense too'. Cf **it's your pal you have to watch.** P.B.: both of these seem to me to be not so much c.pp. as sheer commonsensical maxims.

never let it be said was orig. a lower-class genteelism, and as such it was used by W.L. George in *The Making of an Englishman,* 1914: C20. By *c.* 1920, it had, socially, become much more gen. and no longer regarded as a genteelism. Its meaning, 'I feel so discouraged that I could give up': 'Never let it be said'. Semantically cf **never say die.**

never let it be said (that) your mother reared a jib! – i.e., a coward, or, at best, a timid man – is an Aus. c.p. that can be used by itself but is often prec. by **have another drink!:** orig. and mostly W. Aus., esp. among cattlemen and horsemen: heard by Jack Slater in 1958. Orig. a *jib* was a horse tending to jib. There exists the var., *never say your mother bred a jibber,* 'Summon up your courage and do it!' – lit., 'Don't jib at it' (Jack Eva, 1978).

never louse a greasy head of his own – he will. He will never live to be old: C18–early 19. Grose.

never mind buying the bye: buy the bleedin' beer! was, *c.* 1890–1914, a mainly Cockney c.p., uttered as a comment when someone had remarked 'Oh, by the bye'. Leechman, 1969, noted, 'Heard in England before 1904'.

never mind, it'll soon be Christmas. 'Catch-phrases like *Never mind, it'll soon be Christmas* often fill gaps in drinking sessions, just as *Put another pea in the pot and hang the expense* can be said apropos of nothing' (Anthony Burgess, in *TLS,* 26 Aug. 1977).

How I came to miss *never mind...,* I shall never know! Perhaps it's because the subconscious mind dredges up trifles only when a suitable occasion sets memory working. This c.p. has been familiar to me since during WW1. I had never heard *put another pea...* ; it sounds like a late C19 expression and it remains actively extant. P.B.: with the latter, cf **give the cat another goldfish,** which is sometimes prec. by *hang* (or something stronger) *the expense;* in the former *never mind* is often replaced by *cheer up!*

never mind the quality: feel the width! At first perhaps simply an ironic parody of street-market salesmen's patter or spiel, since mid C20, it has come, in later C20, to be used more seriously in such contexts as, e.g. the necessity of eking out meagre resources of government aid to cover an impossibly large and neglected field. (P.B.)

never no more! Never again: humorously emphatic: late C19–20. Occurs in, e.g., Somerset Maugham, *The Casuarina Tree,* 1926.

It has, as Camilla Raab tells me, 1977, from a line of the chorus to the very well known ballad, *The Wild Rover,* been made into a semi-joc., semi-ironic c.p. of deliberate illiteracy and exaggeration of Standard English *nevermore,* never again, perhaps a conscious parody of the famous and formerly much recited poem *The Raven,* 1845: 'Quoth the raven, "Nevermore" '. When these fateful words became a c.p., I don't precisely know: since *c.* 1910, I'd say.

never said as (or so) **much as 'Kiss me elbow'** (– usu. he) has, throughout C20, although less common once 'the permissive society' became, *c.* 1960, well established and the orig. *he … 'Kiss me arse'* came back into favour, been 'heard among working-class women' (Petch, 1969). Why elbow? Prompted by *(he) doesn't know his arse from his elbow.*

never say die! From being a motto, it has, since *c.* 1915–esp. when used humorously – become also a c.p., as in the final speech of Terence Rattigan's *Who Is Sylvia?*, performed in 1950 and pub'd in 1951; Mark, after half a lifetime of 'leading two lives' and being routed by his wife, says, 'Pity. It was fun. Oh, well, never say die, I suppose. (*They move towards doors. Oscar turns off lights.*) Come on. Oscar. (*They go out into the hall together.*)'

never say your mother bred a jibber. See **never let it be said your …**

never shit where you eat! 'A semi-proverbial [admonition] against carrying on sexual intrigues at one's place of employment. A milder version is *don't buy your candy where you buy your groceries.* Both from 1940s or earlier' (R.C., 1978). And both US. P.B.: the earthy Brit. equivalent is **(you) don't** (or **never**) **shit on your own doorstep!**

never stir!; in C17; **ne'er …!** A c.p. of emphasis or confidence; of assurance or reassurance: *c.* 1660–1785; it is equivalent to 'Let me never stir again if I lie to you or mislead you!' In III, i, of Thomas Shadwell's *Epsom Wells*, performed in 1672 and pub'd in 1673, Bisket, a comfitmaker, to Tribble, a haberdasher, says: 'I vow she has had more temptations than any Woman in *Cheapside*, ne're [*sic*] stir' (lines 457–9 of D.M. Walmsley's edn); and in *The Miser*, 1672, and in *The Volunteers*, IV, ii, performed 1672, pub'd 1673, he employs a var.: Sir Timothy Kestril exclaims, 'Oh, what a Devil ailes you. Let me never stir I meant her no more hurt than my own soul.' And also in *The Virtuoso*, prod. and pub'd in 1676; and yet again in *The Scowrers*, 1691.

William Wycherley, in *The Country Wife*, performed *c.* 1672, pub'd in 1675, has:

HARCOURT: … I would be contented she should enjoy you a-nights, but I would have you to myself a-days, as I have had, dear friend.

SPARKISH: And thou shalt enjoy me a-days, dear dear friend, never stir.

In the same year, he uses it again – in *The Plain Dealer*, at II, i. The phrase was, indeed, much favoured in Restoration comedy. For instance, we find William Congreve, in *Love for Love*, performed and pub'd in 1695, at ii of II, having Mrs Frail say of Miss Prue, '…She's very pretty! Lord, what pure red and white! – she looks so wholesome; – ne'er stir, I don't know, but I fancy, if I were a man――.'

And here are several examples from the next century. In 1763, Isaac Bickerstaffe, in *Love in a Village*, at III, iii, causes Hodge to exclaim, 'Know you! ecod I don't know whether I do or not; never stir, if I did not think it was some lady belonging to the strange gentlefolks.'

In 1770, Samuel Foote, *The Lame Lover: A farce*, at III, i, final grouping, Jack says: 'Father, never stir if he did not make me the proof … of a new pair of silk stockings.' But eighteen years earlier, Foote had shown that the phrase was so gen., so very familiar, that it could already be incorporated into the very syntax of coll. English; in *Taste*, at Act II, Caleb, a boy, excited by cries, says: 'Mother! – father! never stir if that gentleman ben't the same that we see'd at the printing-man's, that was so civil to mother': a quot'n that shows how far down the social scale the phrase had slipped. The fashionable world had long ago discarded it. Foote uses it again in *A Trip to Calais*, 1778.

Like so many other Restoration comedy c.pp., it owed its long life mainly to its neatness and compactness.

never tell me! See **don't tell me!**

never the better for you. See **none better for your asking …**

never trust me! A c.p. of asseveration, roughly equivalent to 'Never trust me again if this doesn't happen as I say it will':

lower and lower-middle class: late C19–20; somewhat ob. by *c.* 1935; by 1970, more than somewhat.

never up, never in! A US golfing c.p., indicative of pessimism: since *c.* 1920. Lit., never up to the hole with the first putt, nor into it with the second. Hence, almost immediately, a scabrous c.p. 'with sexual side-glance' (Fain, 1969).

new. See: see something; this won't buy; what else is; what's new; and:

new one on me – a (usu. prec. by **it's** or **that's**). This is the first time I've heard of, or seen, *that* being done: since *c.* 1920.

Newgate. See: he that is.

Newhaven. See: we bombed.

Newmarket Heath. See: fine morning.

news. See: carrying the n.; do you hear the n.; have I got; have you heard the n.; I wish I may never; I've got n.; now for; tell me n.; we asked; what's the good n.; what's the n.

Newt. See: hold her.

Newton. See: old Newton.

Newton Abbot! It means, and rhymes on, **you can have it,** q.v.; implies 'I don't want it'; and, as a c.p., had a very brief currency, *c.* 1935–40. In its phonetics it recalls **Abyssinia.** (Sanders, 1978.)

Newton got (or **took**) **him.** See **old Newton …**

next. See: what will they; you're not on.

next object is … See **and the next object is …**

next time you make a pie, will you give me a piece? is a male hint to a girl that she should sexually co-operate with him: Can.: *c.* 1895–1914.

next time you see me, (I hope) you will know me – the. In T.C. Haliburton's *The Clockmaker*, 3rd Series, 1840, we find:

At last one of the dancin' girls came a-figerin' up to me … and dropt me a low curtshee.

Well, my old rooster, said she, the next time you see me, I hope you will know me; where did you learn manners, starin' so like all possest.

Orig. US and dating from *c.* 1820, it had, by *c.* 1850, become also Brit., often in the var. form, *well, the next time you see me, you'll know me, won't you?* Cf **do you think you'll know me again?**

next way, round about, is at the far door – the. You're going a long way round: C17 semi-proverbial c.p. Recorded in *P.* Here, *next* = nearest, i.e. shortest.

nice. See: how nice; it's naughty; it's nice; it's turned; oh, oh that's; turned out; very nice; what's a n.; you have a n.; and:

nice bit o' cloth you got there, my boy, often accompanied by the speaker's rubbing the new lapel between his fingers. Addressed to a male wearing a new suit, jacket, or overcoat. That it is prob. of radio or music-hall orig. appears from the fact that a Jewish or, rather, 'fake' Jewish accent is used – perhaps started (I'd guess) by a Jewish comedian. (Based on a note from P.B., 1976.)

[**nice 'ere, innit?** Nice here, isn't it? Current since latish 1960s, (*Daily Mirror*, 12 Sep. 1977.) Lit., a mere illiteracy; but it has come to be used allusively, thanks to the media. Cf **nice place you have here.**]

nice going! An interjection of approval, approbation, congratulation: US, since *c.* 1910; Brit., since *c.* 1920. (Berrey) Orig. applied to athletics, hence to games, it soon came to be applied also to artistic or musical or literary or theatrical performance.

nice guys finish last. This wry US c.p. 'can be dated from a column by a sports writer named Frank Graham in the New York *Journal American* in the summer of 1946. [It was orig. by Leo Durocher (born 1906) who] was manager of the [Brooklyn] Dodgers from 1938 to 1948, with 1947 excepted; in that year he was under suspension by the Commissioner of Baseball' (Prof. James Gaskin, in a private letter, 1977). In his notice of the first ed. of this book, in *The Sewanee Review*, Prof. Gaskin adds, 'The conversation from which the "nice guys" statement was lifted, and perhaps corrupted, took place in July 1946'. Used orig. among baseball players and 'fans', it caught on, has been widely employed ever since, and has been canonized by inclusion in Bartlett. 'A common US variant is *nice guys don't win ball games*' (Michael Goldman, 1978).

nice one, Cyril! That's neat or brilliant or most effectual. It arose either from the slogan for Wonderloaf bread, as one correspondent claims, or, as seems to be the predominant opinion, in the world of entertainment, in a gramophone record made early in 1973 by Tottenham Hotspur Football Club in appreciation of a player's – Cyril Knowles's – footballing ability, the full version being:

Nice one, Cyril.

Nice one, son!

Nice one, Cyril,

Let's have another one!

From being local, it rapidly became a national c.p. (With thanks to the Rev. Christian Bester of Cotton College, Staffordshire, which is where I first heard it used.) The *Evening News* of 17 July 1975 has: 'Knowles – the song Nice One Cyril was dedicated to him – would welcome a transfer back to his native Yorkshire.'

The wording of the full version has, perhaps inevitably, acquired an indelicate meaning.

P.B.: as usual, Nigel Rees, in *VIBS*, sets the record straight: 'Originating in a TV commercial for Wonderloaf, in which bakers congratulated each other on their wares, this phrase was taken up by supporters of Spurs footballer Cyril Knowles ... this is one of the most successful – and certainly one of the best – catchphrases to have entered the language from TV advertising'. A decade later it sounds very dated indeed.

nice pair of eyes. See **beautiful pair ...**

nice place to live out of – (it's) **a.** Indicating unpleasantness, it was current *c.* 1890–1940. (Ware.) Fain, 1978, adds the US variants, *nice place to work out of* or *to be from*, commenting, 'dates from 1915 or so. Typical of expressions that get their memorable quality from a play on words'. Cf synon. **good place to be from,** which shows how the idea lingered. Cf **it's a nice place to visit ...**

nice place (but esp. **nice little place) you have here** (or **you've got here**); often introduced by **it's.** Applied literally, it clearly isn't a c.p. – and nobody would suggest that it was – but applied ironically to a dead-beat hovel or room or, more often, to a very grand place, it is certainly one: and, as such, it dates from *c.* 1942. In his book *Itma*, 1948, Frank Worsley recalls how, when Itma performed at Windsor Castle on 21 April 1942, lunch was served in the apartment of the Gentlemen of the Household, with the gentlemen waiting to welcome the players. 'The ice was broken at once by Tommy [Handley] who looked round and remarked "H'm, nice little place you've got here!" Everybody laughed.' The remark caught on almost immediately.

It soon became familiar in the US, where, as in the British Commonwealth of Nations, it has remained so. In *Spies, Inc.*, 1969, Jack D. Hunter writes, 'I folded myself into a big Dixie cup I assumed to be a chair and said, "Nice place you have here." ... His handsome face registered undisguised satisfaction. "Yeah," he said. "Not bad for a South Philly [Philadelphia] paisan, eh?"' Cf Ed McBain, *Hail, Hail, the Gang's All Here*, 1971: 'A criminal bargain basement, awaiting only the services of a good fence. "Nice little place you've got here," Carella said, and then handcuffed Gross to Goldenthal and Goldenthal to the radiator.'

An apposite English example occurs in Catherine Aird's *The Complete Steel*, 1969, a police photographer saying to his superior, in a room at a Stately Home, ' "Nice little place you have here, sir." "And a nice little mystery," rejoined Sloan tartly.'

An occ. var. is *quite a place you have –* or *you've got – here*, as in Philip Quaife's speech-alert, speech-sensitive novel, *The Slick and the Dead*, 1972, 'I ... looked around at the soft, black-velvety comfort ... "Quite a place you've got here," I remarked.'

One of the most successful and urbane c.pp. existing in and since 1942. P.B.: and much to be preferred to **nice 'ere, innit,** q.v.

nice to see you: to see you, (pause) **nice!** Bruce Forsyth, as compère and master of ceremonies in his very popular BBC TV show 'The Generation Game': 'The first half spoken by himself, then the whole of the second, or perhaps the word "nice", invited from and supplied by his audience, in unison' (Derek Parker, in *The Times*, 9 Sep. 1977). Noble notes that it was firmly established as a c.p. by 1976.

nice weather for ducks! is applied humorously to wet weather – the wetter, the likelier. In this novel, *Experiment at Proto*, 1973, Philip Oakes writes:

'Right you are,' said Mark. Another formula uttered, he thought. Conversation on this level was like swapping coloured tokens, a kind of linguistic barter. At first he had been derisive, but lately he had found himself collecting banalities to trade. 'Nice weather for ducks' and 'it'll get worse before it gets better'; he was becoming used to serving them with a flourish.

It arose prob. fairly late in C19, and rather, I think, a c.p.than a cliché. J.W.C., 1977, vouches for its continued wide currency in US, and A.B., 1978, adds, 'Sometimes *fine weather if you're a duck* and similar variants, e.g. *only ducks would like this day*. Sometimes not so humorously applied; e.g. *not even a duck would go out on a day like this*, said to someone about to venture out on a stormy day'.

P.B.: but pride of place in this 'family' must surely go to the splendid Aus. hyperbole, said of soggy ground: *it's wet enough to bog a duck*, recorded by Wilkes, with examples from late C19 to the present day. Cf **fine day for the ducks.**

nice work! and **nice work if you can get it!** Expression of warm approval of a good piece of work or of a very favourable and agreeable arrangement: the former, since *c.* 1930; the latter, an obvious extension, since *c.* 1942. I remember that, very soon after WW2, the radio commentator Ronnie Waldron, in judging a beauty contest, remarked 'Nice work – if you can get it!'

The latter was promptly adopted in the US where it is still used frequently. Clarence Budington Kelland, *Stolen Goods*, 1951, has:

'What's an assistant buyer?'

'A cross,' said Roger, 'between a whipping boy and a doormat.'

'Nice work if you can get it,' the pudgy young man said. He grinned again. 'That,' he explained, 'is a cliché. Make the most of it, you intellectuals.'

The earliest printed record I've found of the longer form occurs in Noël Coward's *Peace in Our Time*, 1947, at I, ii: GEORGE: Good for you – nice work if you can get it.

A number of helpers were quick to comment. 'Cf the Frank Sinatra song which has this as its refrain, concluding "... and you can get it if you try"' (P.B., 1976). 'It was a popular US song of the 1930s, though the phrase probably preceded it. Hence, US origin' (R.C., 1977). That song was composed by G. and I. Gershwin, in 1937, (as Robert Burchfield, CBE, reminds me) and was written for a Fred Astaire picture called *A Damsel in Distress*. Ira Gershwin has since credited the phrase to the *Punch* cartoonist George Belcher, according to Benny Green, reviewing the first ed. of this book in *Spectator*, 10 Sep. 1977.

nicely. See: **that will do.**

nicer. See: **it couldn't happen.**

nicest. See: **you say the n.**

nick, nick, nick! 'Jim Davidson providing a vocal counterpart for the revolving light on top of a police vehicle' (*VIBS*). P.B.: not only aptly 'echoic', but wittily so, *nick* being common slang for a police station, as well as, earlier, a cell or prison in general.

nickel(s). See: **don't take any; if only; love and; squeezes.**

niet dobra! 'No good!': current at the latter end of WW1 among members of the North Russian Expeditionary Force; 'usually with an intermediate English expletive' (F&G), as in *niet bloody dobra*. Adopted from Russian.

nigger. See: another push; it's like a n.; sweating; there's a n.

night. See: all night; all right on the n.; every night; fine night; good night; it will last; legs grew; like something; man wasn't morning; once a knight; one consecutive; one of these dark; only birds; pity the poor; tonight's; 'twill; who were; and:

night's a pup – the. It's (still) too early to leave. esp. to go home: Aus.: C20. In, e.g., Henry Lawson, 1915, and Hal Porter, 1975. Wilkes, *Dict. Aus. Coll.*

nightie. See: off like; up and down.

nightmare. See: long as a whore's.

nikky, nokky, noo! 'Nonsense phrase devised by Ken Dodd, "Humour is anarchic, I suppose," he says, "So, like a child, from time to time you revolt against the discipline of words and just jabber!" ' (*VIBS*). P.B.: but cf **needle, nardle, noo.**

nil carborundum! A terse derivative of – and much less common than – **illegitimis non carborundum**, q.v.

nimble. See: quick and n.

nine-bob note. See: queer as a.

ninepence. See: tell your mother; that won't pay.

[**ninepence for fourpence.** According to Collinson, this was a political c.p. of 1908–9. From national health insurance. But surely a slogan?]

nineteen. See: he'll make; now then, only.

ninety-nine, a hundred, change hands! is a RN (lower-deck. of course) c.p., scurrilously imputing self-abuse: C20.

ninety-nine and forty-four hundredths per cent pure, often written **99 and 44/100ths % pure.** US. 'Much less common since Ivory Soap no longer uses it in its advertisements, where it started, probably some 50 years ago' (J.W.C., 1975). 'This usually meant (no longer much in use, except by us "oldies" [over 40] that someone's statement was almost perfect. It was a slogan of the Procter and Gamble Company, U.S.A. Properly "99 and 44/100% pure!" Harley Procter named "The White Soap" – as it was at first called – "Ivory", after hearing a sermon in church based on *Psalms*, 45 : 8: "All thy garments smell of myrrh, and aloes, and cassia, out of the ivory palaces, whereby they have made thee glad". Date [of origin]: 1880s' (A.B., 1979).

nit! nit! – in the language of convicts in British prisons – means 'Stop talking, someone's listening!' and it dates from *c.* 1930 or a little earlier. Lit., 'nothing! nothing!'; *nit* being a var. of *nix*, nothing.

nitty-gritty. See: let's get down to the.

no. See: don't say No; I wouldn't say No.

no ambition and fuck-all interest. Since *c.* 1950, perhaps earlier, the Services' slanderous interpretation of the initials NAAFI, the Navy, Army, and Air Force Institute – a fine organisation without which the lives of servicemen, despite their ritual grumbling, would be a great deal less bearable. Peppitt supplies a late printed source: M. Nelson, *Captain Blossom*, 1973. In the WW2 RN, a *naafi rating* meant, by the same process, a seaman having '*no aim*, ambition or fucking initiative'. (P.B.)

no back talk! Farmer says of it: 'A slang catch phrase indicating that the matter in question is closed to discussion: there's nothing more to be said': *c.* 1880–1910.

no better for your asking. See **none the better for your asking ....**

no, but I'm breathing hard or, **no, just breathing hard.** 'A common Service reply to the innocent question, "Are you coming?" is likely to be "no: just breathing hard" or "no: but I'm breathing hard" ' (P.B., 1975): since *c.* 1950. A sexual pun, of which a more decisive, more elegant var. is *no, just changing hands*, an emphatic ref. to masturbation.

no, but I've got a picture of Lord Roberts ... See **I have a picture ...**

no! but you hum it and I'll pick up the tune. A c.p. orig. and still addressed by a public-house, or a smoking-concert, pianist to a member of the audience asking 'Do you know such-and-

such song or tune?'; hence, by anyone asked to the person asking, 'Do you know whatever-it-happens-to-be?': late C19–20. A good example occurs in chapter VI of Alfred Draper's *Swansong for a Rare Bird*, 1970, concerning a 'pub' pianist:

'Do you know the arse is hanging out of your trousers?' Well, we all knew what was coming because it happened every Saturday night. Gloria [a queer] swung around on the stool and said, 'No, but you hum it and I'll pick up the tune.' Naturally, everyone laughed like a drain. Even me, though I'd fallen out of the cradle laughing at the joke.

There's a slightly shorter form often preferred: *you hum it and I'll pick up the tune.*

Ashley, 1979, notes the slight var., in answer to, e.g. 'do you now this building is on fire?': *no, but you hum it and I'll fake it.* P.B.: a well-known pub joke has the stooge asking 'Do you know your monkey's pee-ing in my beer?'

no can do. I can't do it *or* That's impossible – no means of doing it: orig., at least since *c.* 1850, but prob. *c.* 1830, pidgin English of the Chinese ports; by *c.* 1890, *passepartout* English and by *c.* 1900, a c.p., whence the Royal Navy's refusal, at the officer level, of an invitation: *NCD*.

Collinson said that the c.p. *no can do* was created 'in imitation of Pidgin', but *no can do* certainly was – it still is – genuine pidgin and is simply the negative of *can do* and perhaps earlier than *can do* itself.

A fairly early printed record of the negative occurs in Charles R. Benstead's *Retreat: A Story of 1918*, pub'd in 1930.

See also **can do.**

no chance! (Usu. with emphasis on a rather drawn-out *no*.) An emphatic negative: in gen. use since early 1970s, but superseded to some extent by the more flexible synon. **no way!** (P.B.)

no comment! I have no comment to make: a suave and elegant snub, this is 'a jocular catch phrase in imitation of politicians and prominent people who often say this when they are being pestered by reporters and TV interviewers' (Petch): since *c.* 1950 as a c.p. B.P., 1975, comments thus: 'It is unfair, but true, to suggest that this c.p. usually means, "Your allegations are correct, but I am not going to admit it yet". '

It may well have arisen in diplomatic circles before passing to the politicians, radio and TV, film stars and other such 'personalities'.

Jon Cleary, *Man's Estate*, 1972, has:

'But you still haven't told me what you're here for. Or is that an undiplomatic question?'

'No comment,' said Roth, with his gentle smile. 'Another cliché.' [But c.p., not cliché.]

no complaints! See **can't complain.**

no compree! I don't understand: a military c.p. of 1914–19. A sort of Hobson-Jobson for the Fr. *je n'ai pas compris.* (F&G.) Hence, 'No thanks – I don't want any': likewise military: 1915–19. (*Ibid.*)

no cups outside! 'Said [rather, bawled] in an Ulster accent by Ruby Rockcake (Mary O' Farrell) in *ITMA* – reflecting her early upbringing in a railway refreshment room' (*VIBS*). See TOMMY HANDLEY.

no dice! Not a chance!; no luck!; *or* It won't work: US and Can.: since *c.* 1925 (? much earlier). Recorded by Berrey, 1942, and by W&F, 1960. Still common in Aus., notes Lovett, 1978 [and known also in UK, esp. around mid C20: P.B.]. Obviously from gambling.

no difference! It doesn't matter which – or, come to that, who or when or why: US: since *c.* 1945 – perhaps very much earlier. Elliptical for *it makes no difference.*

John Godey, in his magnificent novel, *The Taking of Pelham One Two Three*, 1973, has:

'I want two policemen to walk down the track. One to carry the bag with the money, the other to carry a lit flashlight. Acknowledge.'

'Two cops, one with the money, one with a flashlight.

What kind of cops – Transit or NYPD?' [New York Police Department.]
'No difference.'
Cf **it's the same difference.**

no, don't applaud (or clap), **just throw money!** See **don't applaud ...**

no! don't tell me: let me guess or **I'll guess.** See **don't tell me: let me guess!**

no error! An occ. var. of *and no error*, q.v. at **and no mistake.**

no flies on him occurs in **there are no flies on him** or **me** or **you**, etc.: in combinations, none of which can fairly be classified as a c.p. But there's an extended form with variable *him* or, less often, *her:* and that elab. form is clearly a c.p.: *there are no flies on him – but you can see where they've been*, which goes back at least to *c.* 1920 and prob. to Edwardian or even very late Victorian days. Worth noting also is *no flies on me!*: current in US since *c.* 1910. Recorded by S. R. Strait in 'Straight Talk' (the *Boston Globe, c.* 1917).

'It may earlier have sometimes meant "He has no faults" [rather than the current 'He is sharp, wide-awake and aware of all the tricks and dodges'] – if the legend (which I heard 50 years ago) is true that there was a Salvation Army hymn, "There may be flies on some of you guys, but there ain't no flies on Jesus" ' (J.W.C., 1977). Also Aus. (Jim Ramsay, *Cop It Sweet*, 1977); Wilkes notes that there was, *c.* 1840–60, the slight var. *about* for *on*. Fain, 1977, mentions a punning US var., *no flies on her balls*, dating from *c.* 1920. P.B.: There was, mid C20, a var. which may qualify as a c.p.: *no flies on Auntie*, which could refer equally to oneself, or to another person.

See also **and no flies.**

no flowers, by request! This joc. c.p. means 'no complaints, *please!*': C20; by 1945, slightly ob., and by 1975 virtually †. From a frequent enjoinder in funeral notices.

no fooling or **no foolin'** is a humorous US way of affirming something: since *c.* 1910. Berrey.

no further seaward than the harbourmaster's cat. A nautical, esp. a RN, c.p., applied to in-shore vessels: since *c.* 1940 (?). Recorded by K. Duxbury, *Seamanship in Small Boats*, 1971. (Peppitt.) Joc. rather than arbitrary.

no future at all (or simply **no future**) **in it**, either form is often prec. by **there's.** These are fighting Services, esp. RAF, c.pp., dating since 1939. Whereas the former implies danger in the raid or sortie concerned, the latter either does the same or merely hints that the task is a thankless one. (*Observer*, 4 Oct. 1942, both phrases; and in H&P and C.H. Ward Jackson's *It's a Piece of Cake*, 1943.) Deriving from earlier familiar Standard English, *there's no future in it (at all)*, as applied to a hopeless love affair, it naturally became also a civilian c.p. as early as 1944 – and it still is.

no go; often prec. by **it's** – and when it is, a c.p.: it's no use; it's impracticable; it's impossible: since *c.* 1820; by 1940, somewhat outmoded; by 1975, decidedly ob. (Moncrieff, the playwright, 1830.) P.B.: inshrined in C20 English literature by Louis MacNeice's despairing 1930s verse about the Hebrides, *Bagpipe Music*, with its constant refrain, 'It's no go the ... , it's no go the ... ', e.g. 'Government grants' and 'elections'.

no good for the white man is a gen. disparaging remark, self-consciously parodying the old-fashioned Empire-builders, about any uncongenial situation, as in 'Good Lord, this place is an absolute midden. Definitely no good for the white man, old boy!': since *c.* 1950: mostly Services', prob. mainly army. (P.B.)

no good to Gundy. Very unsatisfactory; applied to anything adverse: Aus.: C20. It seems to have orig. among 'the Diggers' serving in WW1, and certainly I heard it used by them. Wilkes, *Dict. Aus. Coll.*, 1978, declares it ob. Baker, in the 1959 ed., notes the var. *no good to gundybluey*, which looks like an elab.

But who was this Gundy? My loyal and learned contributor R.S. wrote to me in 1973: 'Could this character be related

to that Solomon Grundy who, in the rhyming tag, was born on Monday, passed through the vicissitudes of a lifetime in six days, and was buried on Sunday?' Well, stranger things have happened.

no good to me! That won't satisfy me – by a long way! Since *c.* 1880; by 1940, slightly ob., and by 1970 very much so. An early example occurs in F. Anstey's entertaining and valuable dialogues, *Voces Populi*, Vol. I. 1890.

no grease! is an engineers' c.p., imputing a lack of *polish* or of good manners: *c.* 1880–1914. Ware.

no, half left (**and a bit in the centre**)! Mostly children's c.p. answer to questions containing the word 'right', e.g. 'Is that all right?' or 'Is that right?': since mid C20, perhaps earlier. (P.B.)

no hands. See **look, no hands.**

no harm in looking. As B.P. once remarked, this is 'the motto of husbands and boy friends whose eyes wander': perhaps esp. Aus., since late C19. But, as used by window shoppers, it is common in UK. P.B.: I have heard also the tolerant response from wife or girl friend, 'Can look – but mustn't touch!'

no harm in trying; often prec. by **there's**, and followed by **that's how** *I* **got it!**; illiterate and pseudo-illiterate variants are **no 'arm in tryin'** and **that's ow** *I* **got it.** To which should be added **God loves a trier**, with the proviso that the third lies on the borderline between c.p. and not yet fully accredited proverb; it is also sarcastic, as indeed are the other two. All three are applied to petty theft or to the giving of wrong change, or to a perhaps accidental or absent-minded pocketing of something merely lent, as a lighter or a box of matches; all three are almost as often used defensively by the offender as accusingly by either the victim or an observer; and all three go back at least as far as 1900 – *God loves a trier*, prob. much farther and the other two, perhaps a little farther. (An amplification and elab. of a note sent to me, 1968, by the late Frank Shaw.)

no heart to appeal to and no arse to kick. 'A committee may have, as they say, no heart to appeal to and no arse to kick' (Katharine Whitehorn in the *Observer*, 5 Nov. 1967): since the middle or late 1950s. L.A., who sent me the quot'n, commented in 1969, 'Deplores the impersonal in shared authority in specific instance'.

no hide, no Christmas box is an Aus. c.p., dating since *c.* 1930 and referring to a specific instance of 'hide' (brazen impudence or aureate self-confidence) and meaning 'I certainly won't!' or 'No hope of that'. Presumably a pun – a rural pun, at that. Cf **more arse ...**

no hits, no runs, no errors, from being a literal statement in baseball, has – because of the varying situations in that game – acquired three different shades of meaning, always clear in the context, in C20 US c.p. usage, as Moe pointed out in a letter, 1975:

(1) failure, bad job, strike-out, fizzle, no go; or decisive defeat ... (2) uneventful, in which everything went like clockwork, no hitches developed, and no mistakes were made ... (3) perfection, overwhelming success; or ... satisfying accomplishment. As an example of (2), this quotation from *The New York Times* of Sunday, 2 September 1945. Rear-Admiral Oscar C. Badger reporting to Admiral Halsey on the uneventful passage of fleet units (Task Force 31) into Tokyo Bay (after the Japanese surrender): 'No runs, no hits, no errors' [*sic*].

Col. Moe later contributed a verse, author unknown, which occurred in a 'Dear Abby' column conducted by Abigail Van Buren:
'Here lie the bones
Of Betty Jones;
For her, life held no terrors:
A virgin born,
A virgin died,
No hits, no runs, no errors.'
He added that Berrey's 1942 equation of the c.p. with

failure and 'decisive defeat' does not seems to fit the above.

For J.W.C., 1975, the predominant sense is 'a perfect performance', and he comments later that the catch-phrase uses are technically inexact: but then, c.pp. often are, on the surface, inexact or illogical, yet they possess a strange linguistic logic all their own.

no, I'm not selling, serious. See **I'll bite.**

no, I'm Reddy's brother is the stock response – the c.p. reply – to 'Are you ready?': 'not rare in Canada. Since about 1910 in my experience' (Leechman, 1969).

no, (or no, thanks,) I'm trying to give them up was orig., in the BBC radio comedy series 'The Goon Show' (c. 1951–62), the reply to (here,) **have a gorilla** [q.v.]; it became an all-purpose facetious or joc. refusal, everybody being aware of its source and the 'gorilla' gag: only slightly ob. by early 1980s. (P.B.)

no, I'm with the Woolwich. This was, briefly, mid 1970s, the smart reply to 'Are you with me?' – i.e., do you understand me? Orig. a TV advertisement, it became, c. 1975, a c.p. The ref. is to the Woolwich Building Society. (With thanks to Mr R. Line of Orpington, 1978.)

no Irish need apply. Popular in late C19 – early 20, when so many Irish people fled to the USA because of the recurrent potato famines in Ireland. Orig. used by businessmen advertising for employees, it soon became a c.p., meaning 'Don't bother trying for that job – you won't get it!' (A.B., 1978.)

no, just breathing hard or **... changing hands.** See **no, but I'm ...**

no kidding? or! Truly? or!; honestly? or!; I'm not fooling!: US (latish C19–20); then, c. 1910, Can. (Leechman), whence, by c. 1920, also to UK, whence the rest of the Commonwealth. (Berrey.) W&F note that, used interrogatively, it forms 'a somewhat doubting response to a statement that seems not entirely credible'.

In Edward Albee's *Who's Afraid of Virginia Woolf?*, 1962, Act I has:

NICK: It was probably more in the principle of the thing.
MARTHA: No kidding. Anyway ...

An excellent late US example comes in John Lange's novel, *Binary*, 1972:

She stopped when she saw them.
'I took the wrong turnoff. Can I give you fellows a lift?'
'We're going to Phoenix,' Peters said.
'No kidding,' the woman said. 'That's my home town.'
'No kidding,' Peters said. 'Which part?'
'The right part,' she said.

no lumps in the custard? See **happy in the service.**

no matter for that, you shall carry the rake. 'If you tax a Girl with playing the loose [i.e., being unfaithful], she shall immediately reply, *No matter ...* ', as we read in Anon., *Tyburn's Worthies*, 1722: an Essex c.p. of c. 1710–50. An example of rural imagery: 'You shall have the raking, the harrowing, even though you "missed out" on the ploughing' (cf the Lucretian metaphor, *to plough the fields of woman*).

no matter how thin you slice it .... See **it's boloney ....**

no more chance than a cat in hell without claws and **no more chance than a snowball** – or **snowflake** – **in hell.** No chance whatsoever: the latter, late C19–20; the former, c. 1750–1850, and Grose, 1796, says of it that it was applied to one 'who enters into a dispute or quarrel with one greatly above his match'. See **much chance ...** P.B.: the usu. later C20 form of the first is the elliptical *not a cat in hell's chance.*

[no more to be said! – elliptical for 'There's no more to be said' – seems to have, c. 1660–1750, been a c.p. It occurs frequently in the comedies of 1660–70, and later; for example, in those of Thomas Shadwell, e.g. *The Scowrers*, 1691, Act V, has the following in the final scene:

SIR WILL[IAM]: Sirrah, Coxcomb, if you speak one Word, I'll slit your Wind-pipe.
WHACH[UM]: Very well, very well! no more to be said.

Cf **say no more!**

no more use than a sick headache. See **headache ....**

no name, no pull. If I don't mention names, there should be no offence taken, hence, e.g. no action for libel or for slander: tailors': c. 1870–1914. Cf:

no names, no pack drill. Use no names and you'll be all right!: the British Army: since c. 1890. In B&P, 1930, its WW1 use is glossed thus: 'Used by a soldier relating something and wishing not to involve another by mentioning his name; it was taken over from the Regular Army.'

It recurred, although rather less frequently, among the army's Other Ranks in WW2. Moreover, it has been used fairly often by civilians from 1919 onwards; it has achieved print, as in Kenneth Giles, *Death and Mr Prettyman*, 1967, a crook speaking: 'O₁right I'm giving it to you straight. There's a boy I know. No names, no pack drill. It was on the night of September eight – remember, she done a bloke in outside a station?'

It occurs also in, e.g., Laurence Meynell, *The End of the Long Hot Summer*, 1972. Indeed, it is extant and not even (1976) ob., although the young might declare it to be slightly archaic.

In WW1 (and before), drill with a heavy pack 'up' was a common military punishment.

no, no, a thousand times no (: I'd rather die than say 'Yes')! 'Doubtless spoken first in response to an improper suggestion, but popularly applied whenever an emphatic negation was indicated' (P. Daniel, 1978).

no offence meant evokes the c.p. reply, *(and) none taken, I'm sure.* Sometimes, however, the two coalesce to form a c.p.; by itself, the former does not qualify. Since c. 1935; perhaps from some popular radio programme. (Mrs Ursula Roberts, 1978.) P.B.: in later C20, often uttered in a mock-genteel tone of voice. Quite coincidentally, and serendipitously, as I reached this entry in E.P.'s manuscript notes towards this second ed., I chanced upon this quot'n in Richard Blaker's fine novel of the Field Artillery in WW1, *Medal Without Bar*, 1930, p. 368, a comment on a sudden, whirlwind, enemy shelling on the Western Front: ' "No offence meant," as an onlooker from a comfortably deep and distant hole once observed, "and no 'arm done".'

no one loves me. See **I'll go out into the garden ...**

no order! 'An expression indicating disgust at the unconventional or unbecoming behaviour of others' (*The Third Ear*, 1971): US Negroes': since c. 1955 (?). P.B.: cf the similar, and almost synon. 'That's a bit out of order', used since later 1970s by the Brit. underworld and its fringes, and hence by some teenagers.

no percentage is elliptical for 'There's no percentage in it' – no profit, no advantage: US: dating since c. 1945 and adopted c. 1960 in UK, as in Tom Barling's dangerously readable underworld-and-police 'thriller', *Bergman's Blitz*, 1973, where the speaker, a London professional criminal, remarks, 'You'd have me back inside whatever I said. So why say anything? No percentage.'

no poes emptied, no babies scraped. (Here, *poes* is the plural of *po*, a chamber pot, French *pot de chambre*.) See **eleven o'clock ....**

no possible probable shadow of doubt, no possible doubt whatever, taken from Gilbert and Sullivan, is a cultured c.p. of late C19–20; it is either independent of, or in retort on, confirmation, perhaps rather an elab., of Standard English *of that there is no possible doubt.*

P.B.: the source is their *The Gondoliers*, 1889, and the full quot'n is, 'Of that there is no manner of doubt,/No probable, possible shadow ...., etc.'

no prizes for guessing is elliptical for *no prizes given for guessing the answer to that one,* 'where the answer is obvious, or the question is merely rhetorical' (P.B., 1978): since the late 1940s.

no problem. 'Not a c.p. in its literal sense, but is one, I think, as a recently (the last two or three years) frequent euphemism for "no offense"' (J.W.C., 1975).

no rats! A proletarian c.p. of *c.* 1890–1930, it means 'He (or, of course, she) is Scottish'. Ware remarks, 'A Scot is always associated with bagpipes, and ... no rat can bear ... that musical instrument.'

no remarks from the (peanut) gallery! and **no remarks from the gallery, please!** ' "Be silent!" ' – addressed to a younger member of the company: US: since *c.* 1930 (?). Originally the gallery of some motion picture theatres was set aside for children, at least during certain hours. "Peanut" from the common designation for children (cf. the well-known comic strip of that title), but also, perhaps, reflecting the eating of peanuts in the gallery in question – sometimes accompanied by the casting of the shells onto the lower and older members of the audience' (R.C., 1978). R.C. glossed the second version as 'a jocular forestalling of unwanted comments from the uninformed': both Brit. and US: the former, C20 and by *c.* 1970 ob.; the latter, since the 1920s and 'now virtually extinct'. The ref. is to derisive or derogatory calls from the gallery of, e.g., a music-hall.

no rest for the wicked! – occ. prec. by **there's.** Uttered either by or about a person not wicked at all but kept extremely busy: late C19–20. Partly in humorous irony and partly in ref. to several Biblical passages, in fact, as P.B. reminds me, 1976, it could be called the c.p. form of the cliché *no peace for the wicked*, which paraphrases *Isaiah*, 8, 22. P.B.: *no rest for the wicked* appears a number of times in 'Bill Truck', *The Man-o'-War's Man*, serialized in Blackwood's Magazine, 1821–6. A.B., 1978, notes the US var., *no rest for the weary*.

no return ticket. He's – or she's – mad. This lower-class c.p. of late C19–20, although little used since *c.* 1940, shortens *He's going to Harwell* [a lunatic asylum] *and has no return ticket,* itself a c.p. no longer used after *c.* 1910. (Ware.) P.B.: it is perhaps noteworthy that Harwell, in Oxfordshire, is now the headquarters of the UK Atomic Energy Authority.

no second prize! is an Aus. c.p., dating since the late 1930s and 'used when someone makes an unoriginal suggestion' (B.P.).

no shit! also **that's no shit!** The commoner form means 'That's the truth'; *no shit!* means 'Is that truly so?' This US c.p. apparently dates from the 1930s. (W&F.) Used interrogatively, it is synon. with **you're joking,** q.v. A.B., 1978, notes the elab. *no shit, Sherlock!,* ironic surprise at a very obvious remark': 1950s–early 60s. Hardly less obviously, a ref. to Conan Doyle's Sherlock Holmes.

no show without Punch, often prec. by **there's.** Applied to a person who is constantly popping up, no matter where you are: late C19–20. A ref. to the 'Punch and Judy Show'.

no sir! and **no sir(r)ee!** with emphasis on*-ree.* This emphatic US negative, recorded in Thornton for 1847 and prob. going back at least a decade, became, *c.* 1920, an English c.p., still used occ.

In Edward Albee's disturbing, salutary, deeply moving play, *Who's Afraid of Virginia Woolf?,* 1962, George – quietly the pivot and pilot of the entire play – remarks to Nick: 'I don't mean to suggest that I'm hip-happy ... I'm not one of those thirty-six, twenty-two, seventy-eight men. No-siree ... Not me. Everything in proportion.'

no skin off my nose (– **it's** or **that's**). It's not my responsibility that this should have happened *or* It doesn't affect me adversely *or* It doesn't harm me in any way – financially, morally, physically: since *c.* 1925, at the latest; I remember it from well before WW2 but neither before nor during WW1. It had become also US some years before WW2: *teste* Berrey. It almost certainly comes from boxing or, anyway, fisticuffs. R.S., 1975, relates it to the toast, 'Here's (to) the skin off your nose!'

It has the var. *no skin off my ass,* the predominant US from among males, as at least two alert American scholars have assured me. And another (Fain, 1977) instances a var. of that US var.: *no skin off my balls,* dating since *c.* 1920.

no soap! The deal's off!; Not a hope!; You're wasting your time: since *c.* 1945; adopted from US, where current since *c.* 1920 and where it also bears the meaning, 'I don't know' –

esp. when this is an evasive answer. The US usage is recorded by Berrey and by W&F; the Brit. is exemplified – as Frank Shaw once told me – in a short story ('Wedlock') by 'George Egerton'. A rhyme on *no hope.* Cf **no dice!**

J.W.C., 1977, comments on the US usage, 'I have never heard the second meaning, except in answer to a plea for information or help'. Of Brit. usage, there exists an excellent high-level example, which I owe to Playfair; it runs thus:' ... Even then, in spite of all the miracles fusion power can achieve, the answer will be the same – no soap' (Lord Rothschild, in a lecture delivered on 23 Oct. 1975, and quoted in *The Times* on 6 Sep. 1977).

Concerning the meaning 'no money', Eric Townley, 1978, notes that there was a 1939 recording, with this title, by Erskine Hawkins and his orchestra.

no speaka da English. 'A phrase that is often used about foreigners' (B.P.: Aus.: since *c.* 1920, although occ. heard earlier. For the UK, where common only since late 1940s although, again, occ. heard earlier, and 'probably obsolete by now' (Playfair, 1977), L.A., 1976, writes, 'a c.p. said jocularly of foreigners who don't quite get round syntax or pronunciation; mock-Italian English'.

'In US (where often *no spikka,* etc.) meaning "I'm not talking" – i.e., "I don't choose to understand what you say" ' (R.C., 1978). W&F say of *spic,* orig. (early C20) a derogatory US term for an American of Italian ancestry, 'Shortened from "spaghetti", reinforced by the traditional phrase "No spika da English'.

no sweat! It is – or was or it will be – no trouble: US: dating since *c.* 1935, if not a lustrum or even a decade earlier; during the 1960, much favoured by 'hippies'. Elliptical for 'It causes (*or* caused, *or* will cause) me (or you) no sweat – no undue exertion'. (Fain, 1969.)

It exemplifies, very neatly, how a meaning or a nuance develops and changes: ' "Anxiety" quite as commonly as "exertion". And it is beginning to be used as a sort of euphemism for "no harm done" and even "no offence" ' (J.W.C., 1977, of US usage). P.B.: the 'don't be anxious' nuance is quite common in UK also. See also **don't sweat it!**

no tell is a frequent reassurance made by someone asked to keep a secret: since *c.* 1945. Perhaps of joc. imitation of pidgin.

no thank you, I've had some! I don't believe what you've just said: US: since *c.* 1925. (Berrey.) From 'No thank you – I've been caught before, but never again.' Cf:

no thanks! You don't catch me in that way: society: *c.* 1885–1905. (Ware.) Cf the prec. entry. But, in C20, this c.p. meant something very different: like **not now** or **not now – later,** it is, among the raffish, a standard retort to a man saying *fuck me!*

no, thanks, I bruise easily. Since *c.* 1920: Michael Warwick says, in 'Theatrical Jargon of the Old Days', *The Stage,* 3 Oct. 1968:

'Come into the office, darling', once the approach of amorous theatrical agents, is succeeded by the more modern references to 'casting couch', a rather abused term, and the astute reply of one old-time actress, 'No, thanks – I bruise easily', is often joked about.

no, thanks, I'm trying to give them up. See **no, I'm trying ...**

no Tich! No talk, *please,* about the Tichborne case!: society: the 1870s. The notorious Roger Tichborne case of fraudulent claim was perhaps the best-known *cause célèbre* of the era. Ware, at *pas de Lafarge.*

no tickee, no washee. Lit., 'No ticket – no laundry', a Chinese laundry's refusal to work without being paid, but soon came to be applied to any situation where credit is unjustifiably asked for or even expected: US: late C19–20. (Moe, 1975.) J.W.C., 1977, explains, 'This refers to a claim-ticket which the owner has lost or a false claimant pretends to have lost'.

But Shipley, 1977, recalling the phrase from his childhood (born 1893), remarks, 'It did *not* mean "No credit". When you brought the laundry, a ticket was given you as a receipt;

you could not collect the laundry without the ticket – which was always one half of a long colored slip, the other half being kept by the laundry and put on the completed bundle of wash. The paper was torn and the halves had to match... In other words, nothing without proper identification'.

no wanchee! 'Pidgin English for "I don't want it, thank you"' (Granville in a letter): much used in the RN, esp. on 'China side' or the China Station: late C19–20. Rather less used since *c.* 1945.

no way! It's impossible – can't be done! US: since *c.* 1969. (Not in W & F, enlarged edn, 1967). Elliptical for 'There's no way to get out of it or avoid it'. By 1974, adopted in UK. (Cyril Whelan, in a letter, and Philip Stahl of Bronxville, over lunch: both 1975.)

J.W.C. however, also 1975, convincingly writes: 'Hardly a c.p., I think, any more than "Hell, no!" (which means no more and no less). I should call it nothing but a tiresome vogue slang phrase. Seldom heard among the educated, except in mockery.' He adds: 'I first heard it in California three or four years ago; within the last year or so it has begun to be heard in the Middle West.' (John Clark lives in Minneapolis.)

Later, E.P. added: But in its derivative or extended sense 'absolutely not', which, as R.C. remarked, 1978, 'can apply equally to the validity of a statement or to the speaker's willingness to perform some action', it has certainly qualified as a c.p. since the middle 1970s. W&F include the phrase in their third ed., 1975.

no worse than a bad cold (– **it's**). 'Meiosis applied to gonorrhea. Originally false; since [the discovery of] penicillin, an understatement. (Gonorrhea) can [now] be cured much more easily than a bad cold.) With the emergence of penicillin-resistant strains of gonococcus, becoming false once more. From 1920s; now obsolescent' (R.C., 1978): both US and Brit. Penicillin was discovered in 1928, but not fully developed until early 1940s.

Noah. See: since Jesus.

nob. See: that's where the big n.

nobody. See: ain't nobody; I'll tell n.; I've something; that devil; and:

nobody asked you, sir, she said is taken from the old comic song, 'Where Are You Going, My Pretty Maid?', pub'd 1878. It became a c.p. late in C19. Harold Brighouse, *The Game: A Comedy in Three Acts*, one of *Three Lancashire Plays*, pub'd in 1920, presents, in Act II, uncle and niece:
EDMUND: You needn't flatter yourself you've talked me into consenting to this marriage.
ELSIE: Nobody asked you sir, she said.

nobody can say black's my eye occurs in S, 1738, where, in the Dialogue I, occurs this passage:
NEV[EROUT]: Oh, Miss! I have heard a sad Story of you.
MISS: I defy you, Mr *Neverout*; no Body can say, black's my Eye.
A proverbial saying of C15–19; in C18– mid C19, also a c.p. Elliptical for '...black is the white of my eye'. Cf **black is your eye.**

nobody here but us chickens. See **ain't nobody...**

nobody home. See 'TAD' DORGAN.

nobody hurt. Was 'said of an inconsequential event' (Berrey, 1940): US: *c.* 1920–50.

nobody is going to sell me wooden nutmegs. This is a N. Country, esp. Yorkshire, boast of one's own alertness and freedom from gullibility: since *c.* 1830. Joan Fleming, *Screams from a Penny Dreadful*, 1971, has this passage: 'Better, I thought, take him home and introduce him first to Nanny whose boast always was that "Nobody is going to sell *me* wooden nutmegs".' For both the sentiment and the form, cf the US c.p., **don't let anyone sell you a wooden nickel** (or **don't take any wooden nickels**), perhaps prompted by the Brit. c.p.

nobody loves me. See **I'll go out into the garden...**

nobody's minding the store. See **who's minding...**

noise like two (or **a pair of**) **skeletons fucking on a tin roof – a**; also, **it rattles like two** (or **a pair of**) **skeletons....** This c.p. arose *c.* 1920 at latest, perhaps *c.* 1900, in the US, passed rapidly to Canada, whence, *c.* 1940, to the British Isles and other members of the British Commonwealth.

A muted noise is, in the US, c.p.'d as *a noise like two eels fucking in a barrel of grease* (A.B., 1978).

none of your beeswax! – None of your business! – is 'a line spoken by Nanette in the musical *No, No, Nanette* (Youmans, Harbuch and Mandel, 1925). Had a vogue in the [later] 1920s' (Derek Parker, in *The Times*, 9 Sep. 1977). In 1942, Berrey mentions *beeswax* as a slang synon. of business – an obvious pun – but does not allude to the c.p., but W & F, 1960, glos *beeswax* thus: 'Usually in "Mind your own beeswax"... *Common in child speech since c. 1920; also some adult euphemistic use*'. P.B.: certainly in use among Brit. children in the 1940s, and prob. considerably earlier. Cf **mind your own interference.**

none of your fancy fours and fives. In 1952, Granville wrote, 'It is now a catch-phrase in the provincial theatre' and cautiously notes that this was orig. a 'remark alleged to have been made by an agent to a leading touring actor being offered a part in a play, and meaning "You can have the part, providing you'll accept a reasonable [*sic*] salary – no four or five pounds a week".' The c.p. itself has existed since WW1; the alleged incident must date from a little before it.

none taken, I'm sure (– **and**). See **no offence...**

none (or **no** or **never**) **the better for your asking.** An abrupt rejection of conventional solicitude: the first, late C17 – early 18, and occurring in e.g. S, early in Dialogue I; the second, late C18–20; the third, late C18–20, but slightly ob. by *c.* 1970. Cf **not you by your asking.** P.B.: cf also the (usu.) Joc. greeting, current early 1940s, *and how are* you *– as if I cared a damn!*

Nonesuch, he's a Mr. He's very conceited: *c.* 1870–1914. Recorded by Baumann in 1887.

nonsense. See: if that's n.

noose is hanging – the. Everything is ready and everyone expectant. US: 'Some far-out and beat use since *c.* 1955' (W & F). A cool ref. to the ghoulish eagerness of crowds awaiting a hanging.

But as R.C. remarks, 1978, 'Certainly very rare...and now indubitably dead'. A.B. adds, 'Variant (for a miscreant): *he's looking for a high noose*, he's going [or likely] to be hanged in a while'. (?) Late C19 – earlier 20.

normal. See: subject.

north. See: he's gone.

nose. See: does your n.; everybody's doing it; follow your n.; go stick your n.; hang crape; have you bit; his nose; I didn't blow; I didn't think; if you vant; it's Friday; keep your n.; long nose; my nose; no spin; your nose.

Nosey. See: play up; up a.

not a bad drop, this! This is excellent liquor: Aus. drinking c.p.: C20. (Frank Hardy, *Billy Borker Yarns Again*, 1967.) P.B.: cf *a fabulous drop*, Aus. servicemen's appreciative phrase applied to an extremely attractive girl, 1960s.

not a cat in hell's chance. See **no more chance...**

not a dry seat in the house is 'an indelicate catch-phrase, meaning that the scene, or [the] comedian, was so funny that the audience was utterly helpless with laughter' (Granville): theatrical: since *c.* 1930. The c.p. plays on the cliché of dramatic critics, 'There wasn't a dry eye in the house'and was presumably suggested by the vulgarism, 'I pissed myself laughing.'

not a heel! Nobody: Cockneys': *c.* 1880–1920. Edwin Pugh, *Harry the Cockney*, 1912, has this exchange:
'Seen anybody?'
'Not a soul. And you?'
'Not a 'eel.'
'That's odd.'

not a lot! In full, *you're going to like this – not a lot, but...*: orig. by Paul Daniels, the Yorkshire comedian and conjuror, and popularised esp. by his TV series, 1981. The *not a lot* tag caught on, and cropped up in all sorts of contexts. Cf the use of **with difficulty**. (P.B.)

not a million miles from... See **one that lives...**

not a pretty sight. A c.p. arising *c.* 1980. prob. from the 'stiff-upper-lipped Empire-builders' skits and sketches of the ‚extremely popular British comedians Eric Morecambe († 1984) and Ernie Wise, but very soon of universal application. D.A.N. Jones, writing in the *Listener*, 16 Oct. 1980, has 'But if any gatecrasher gets in, they jump on him, hard, just like SAS [Special Air Service] men. Not a pretty sight.' (P.B.)

not a word of the pudding! Say nothing about it!: late C17–mid C18. (BE, at *mum-for-that*.) Why *pudding*? Cf the next two entries.

not a word to Bessie about this! This phrase began as a 'gag' of Kenneth Horne's in the radio programme 'Much Binding in the Marsh', which adorned the war years of 1939–45, and quickly spread to the general public as a humorously monitory c.p., not yet (1976) quite extinct. (P.B.'s reminder.) Cf the prec. c.p. and the one following this.

not a word to the vicar! Mum's the word! *or* Keep it dark!: since *c.* 1925; by 1965, slightly ob. (With thanks to Richard Merry.) The now obscure ref. being to some such enormity as brandy on the plum duff or rum in the coffee. Cf the prec. two entries.

not 'alf (pron. *arf*)! See **not half!**

Not bloody likely! and **not Pygmalion likely!** The latter is a cultured var. of the former and, with the Cockney girl Eliza Doolittle's startling use of the phrase, it arose when G.B. Shaw's *Pygmalion* appeared and rendered popular the late C19–20 existing Cockney c.p. *not bloody likely*, emphatic for the simple 'not likely'.

'Eliza Doolittle's "Not bloody likely" is very common in US among sophisticated people – only among those of them who know its literary source, and know their hearers know it' (J.W.C., 1975).

A modern US example of *not bloody likely* occurs in Joseph Hansen's novel, *Fadeout*, 1970:

'Do you know these lines, Madge? "The weight of the world is love. Under the burden of solitude, under the burden of dissatisfaction, the weight, the weight we carry is love...".'

'I wanted to set the weight down,' she said.

He shook his head and gave her a small regretful smile. 'Not bloody likely,' he said.

P.B.: Mr Robert Barltrop, an authority on Cockney usage and mores, remarked in a letter to me that he felt that Eliza, 'in real life', would prob. have been more likely to say 'No bleedin' fear!'

not blue-pencil likely! Jack Warner's c.p., modelled on the prec., which he used in the WW2 radio programme 'Garrison Theatre', Jan.–May 1940, in ref. to the strict BBC censorship of the time. 'So, when Warner said "Not blue pencil likely!", everyone knew what he really meant, and the phrase was used everywhere and by everyone' (Barry Took, *Laughter in the Air*, 1976). By 1975, it was becoming slightly ob., but I last heard it in 1976.

not cricket! – **it's** or **that's** means 'It's unfair!' and was adumbrated in 1867 (See W.J. Lewis, *The Language of Cricket*, 1934) but did not become a widely accepted c.p. until the very early 1900s. In Act III of *The Partners*, performed in 1913 and pub'd in 1914, Stanley Houghton wrote: 'It may even enable you to take high place in the ranks of the emancipated – but it is not playing the game. In other words, Cynthia, it is not cricket.' This phrase has always puzzled Americans and foreigners: and has delighted the few it no longer puzzles. In one of his *Inside...* books, John Gunther wrote a perceptive paragraph about it: clearly he had 'done his homework'.

Mr John Morris, CBE, formerly Director of the BBC's Third Programme and the author of several notable books, tells an amusing story concerning an incident, *c.* 1950, at the

Lawn Tennis Championships at Wimbledon. When a very fine player, afflicted by a diabetic seizure of cramp, lay writhing on the ground, an irate English colonel exclaimed, 'Oh, I say! It just isn't cricket!'.

not enough sense to pound sand in a rat hole! 'Extraordinarily stupid, since stopping rat-holes is not a job calling for any skill: US: C20, now slightly obsolescent' (R.C., 1978). P.B.: or because, if you don't stop up the rat-holes, you'll be in trouble?

not for Joseph; not for Joe. The former, which appears in C. Selby's *London by Night*, 1844, was current *c.* 1830–1920; it gradually gave way to the latter form, recorded in 1867 and current since *c.* 1860 – a form worthily 'enshrined' in Galsworthy's *Swan Song*, 1928, thus: 'Not if he knew it – not for Joe!' and honoured by a place in Benham.

Not for Joseph received a vigorous fillip from the music-hall song of this title, as composed, written, and sung by Arthur Lloyd, who, making his debut in 1862, died in 1904; this, his big song hit, was still being sung by others almost until WW1 (1914–18), as I learn from Ronald Pearsall's *Edwardian Popular Music*, 1975, and from his *Victorian Popular Music*, 1973: Arthur Lloyd 'had a vast repertoire, including the incredible best-selling "Not for Joseph" (80,000 copies of the sheet music sold)'.

Why *Joseph*? Perhaps in ref. to the famed Joseph of the Old Testament. Cf:

not for this child. Not for me: since *c.* 1890; ob. since *c.* 1940, but not yet (1976) †. Collinson records this c.p.; and *this child* (I or me) was adopted, *c.* 1890 or a little earlier, from the US.

not greedy, but he (just) likes a lot (– **he**, or, of courses **she**) is a late C19–20 c.p., sarcastically implying greediness.

not guilty, my lord. Not *my* fault! *or* No, not *I*! A c.p. current since *c.* 1890, but just beginning to become ob. as early as *c.* 1945, and by 1970 very much so. In *What's Bred in the Bone*, prod. in 1927 and pub'd in 1928, Harold Brighouse, in the second act, writes:

LEONARD (*close to her*): Have you been pawed by a nigger?

AUDREY: Not guilty, my lord.

Clearly taken from the law courts.

not half! is an exclamation of emphatic assent: orig. (*c.* 1905) and still mainly Cockney; very common in the British Army of WW1. '"Did you like it?" – "Not half"' It has gained a place both in B & P and in Lyell's glossary of roughly the same period; also in Manchon. A good example of Cockneys' ironic meiosis. Cf **you ain't 'alf a one.**

not if I am in orders for it! is a military c.p. of refusal, dating since *c.* 1930 (if not very much earlier), but little used since *c.* 1950. Lit.: 'I sha'n't [or 'wouldn't'] do it even if I were, in Daily Orders, instructed to do so.'

E.P. added, for this second ed.: This is misleading: no man of any sense would disobey orders: he would merely vent his strong feelings, his unwillingness, his criticism, by expressing them in these words. P.B.: or did (I never heard it in my service, begun 1953) it mean rather, 'I'd risk summary punishment', for this is the consequence of being 'put on orders'?

not if I can help it. You certainly *won't* – not if *I* can do anything to prevent it: C20. A clear allusion occurs in John Osborne's *A Sense of Detachment*, prod. late in 1972 and pub'd in 1973, in Act I (on p. 23 of the Faber edn):

GIRL: Don't tell me. I'll guess. Not that *you* could, anyway.

BOX MAN: I'll see you later.

GIRL: Not if I can help it.

not if I know it! 'I certainly sha'n't be *or* do it – at least, not if I'm conscious'; 'Not if I can avoid it': since *c.* 1860. (The *OED* quotes Thomas Hardy, 1874.)

not if I see you first. See **See you!**

not if you don't is the c.p. rejoinder to **do you mind?** (which see!) and it dates from within a year of the latter's promotion to c.p. status. It is used as, e.g., in James Barlow's *In All Good Faith*, 1971:

Eithne was standing in her pants in the dirty bathroom. She was plucking her eyebrows or something. She objected, 'Do you mind?'

'Not if you don't, he countered, equally automatic.

not in (all) your puff! Synon. with the orig. **not on your life!** and comparable with **not on your Nellie!**, it arose, if my memory serves me faithfully, during the 1930s.

not in front of the children! When used lit., it is not – obviously – a c.p. But it has, since *c.* 1920, often been used either ironically or joc. In *I'll Leave It to You*, performed on 21 July 1920 at the New Theatre, London, and pub'd two or three months later, Noël Coward, in this, his earliest performed comedy, has, in the opening scene, employed a var.:

SYLVIA: Knowing you for what you are – lazy, luxurious –
BOBBIE (*pained*): Please, please, please, not in front of the child. (*Joyce kicks.*) It's demoralizing for her to hear her idolized brother held up to ridicule.

It has a humorously cultured var.: *pas devant les enfants* (occ. *l'enfant*), a warning 'so much more useful when spoken in a foreign language' (Camilla Raab, 1977). I have known this French version since the late 1930s.

not in these boots (or, more often, **trousers**)! Joc. 'Certainly not!': respectively, *c.* 1869–1900, and recorded by Benham; and, arising *c.* 1920 but ob. since *c.* 1960, and recorded by Collinson, and glossed thus by Julian Franklyn (1969): '*not in these trousers*. Since *c.* 1920. Expressive of unwillingness to perform some action: make a journey; become involved in a scheme; etc. Used both seriously and joc. often reduced to *not in these*, deliberately, saucily, by women.' He thought that the phrase orig. in some music-hall comedian's gag.

not just a pretty face. See **I'm not just a pretty face.**

not like that, like *that*! This was a TV gag of Tommy Cooper's. 'Tommy Cooper is a magician whose tricks all go wrong (or seem to, until they come triumphantly right). He shows his audience how to go about the trick, and in the course of this spiel was his little phrase. It's delivered at staccato rate and comes out as *not like 'at, like 'at*, without a pause. [As a c.p., it is] used when showing anyone how to do anything' (Skehan, 1977): 1970s. P.B.: but even more frequently heard is Cooper's *just like that!*, which 'said in the appropriate gruff tones and accompanied by small paddling gestures,...is of course a gift to mimics. Inevitably the phrase is used by Cooper as the title of his autobiography. There is also a song incorporating it' (*VIBS*).

not me, Chief, I'm radar (or **asdic** or **gunnery** or...) is a c.p. 'used by a rating when given an order to do something not connected with his usual job, or if volunteers are asked for' (Granville, letter, 1962): RN: since *c.* 1946. The specialist's revolt against generality. This 'Chief' is the Chief Petty Officer.

not me, Sare (or **Senew**), **my brother from Gozo** is 'supposed to be the standard Maltese alibi against any charge. "Sare" and "Senew" were, of course, phonetic for "Sir", "Señor", and Gozo is the second largest island of the Malta group' (Rear-Adm. P.W. Brock, 1969): late C19–20. But Playfair, 1977, comments, 'I don't think "Senew" can come from Spanish "Señor": there is no obvious contemporary connection between Malta and Spain. Why not derive it from Maltese "Sinjur", itself derived from Sicilian "Signuri"? It seems more obvious and the sound is closer'. Well, I do so *now*! And am most grateful to Sir Edward.

Cf two other fellows from Poona and Kipling's var. *me, sar?* *not me, sar. My brother Manuel, sar,* in *A Fleet in Being,* 1898, and **just the job for my brother from Gozo.**

not *my* ball game (– **it's**). 'It' – usu. a dispute – 'is no concern of mine. Very common during the past five years or so' (J.W.C., 1977). Cf **different ball game.**

not much! dates, in UK, from *c.* 1885 and means 'Not likely!' or 'Certainly not!' – a sense † by 1940 at latest. It was adopted from the US: Farmer writes: 'Not at all. A common colloquialism': dating since the 1860s and † by *c.* 1920. From

before WW2, it has predominantly meant 'You certainly *did* (or *were*) – or do (or *are*) – or *will*!' and was, in the Services during WW2, used with heavy irony. Cf: **not much you didn't** (or **don't**, or **wouldn't**)! The first two (*didn't, don't*) are clearly a mere extension of **not much**; the one – meaning 'You certainly *would*!' – more strongly and worthily carries the escutcheon of catch-phrasery and may have been US and Can. before it was Brit. Of the basic and orig. *not much*, a splendid – almost a 'splendiferous' – example occurs in the verse of that delightful, often exquisite, US author of light verse (and prose) and artist Oliver Herford; in *The Bashful Earthquake and Other Fables and Verses*, both written and illustrated by him, and pub'd in 1899, there is a poem titled 'The Silver Lining' containing these lines:

I too found refuge from Despair
  In sonnets to Amanda's fair
White brow or Nell's complexion rare
  Or Titian hair –

Which, when she scorned, did I resign
  To flames, and go into decline?
Not much! When sonnets fetched per line
  Enough to dine.

not now, later. See **no thanks!**

not on your life! Certainly not! Since the late 1880s, or perhaps a few, or not so few, years earlier. It seems to have become, *c.* 1900, also US: I've noticed it recorded in, e.g., A.H. Melville's article, 'An Investigation of the Function and Use of Slang' in *The Pedagogical Seminar*, March 1912; in HLM, 2nd edn, 1922; in Berrey; W & F; and, indeed, Edward Albee uses it in Act II of *Who's Afraid of Virginia Woolf?* 1962:

MARTHA: (*Loud: a pronouncement.*) And Daddy said– ...Look here, kid, you don't think for a second I'm going to let you publish this crap. Not on your life, baby...not while you're teaching here.

But why *life*? Simply, I'd suppose, because it is one's most notable possession. Cf the Fr. intensive *jamais de la vie!* Contrast the triviality of **not on your tin-type!** More influential, prob., was the cliché 'not even if your life depended on it!' Cf the next five entries.

not on your life, boy! is a Can. – apparently only Can. – intensive of the prec.: *c.* 1920–30. 'With a pun on *Lifebuoy Soap*' (Priestley, 1975).

not on your Nannie! (or **Nanny!**) is an occ. var. of **not on your Nellie**, which is a development from **not on your life!** Anglo-Irish and dating since *c.* 1950. Prof. Alan Bliss tells me, 'A very common expression in Dublin is "not on your Nannie!" Has this the same origin as "not on your Nellie"?' (Letter, 1961). Julian Franklyn thought *Nannie* a mere arbitrary alteration of *Nellie*. So do I. Cf also:

not on your natural! Certainly not! C20. That is, 'Not on your natural life'. There may be an allusion to imprisonment 'for the term of his natural life'. Cf the prec. two, and the following two, entries.

not on your Nellie! (or **Nelly**) 'Not on your life!' An intensive tag, dating since the late 1930s. Used by, e.g., Frank Norman in his very readable *Bang to Rights*, 1958. Short for *not on your Nellie Duff!*; and *Nellie Duff* rhymes on *puff*, breath, breath of life, life itself. Therefore cf **not on your life!**

In 'Me and the Girls', one of the stories in Noël Coward's *Pretty Polly Barlow*, 1964, occurs this passage: '"None of those pony-tails and tatty slacks for George Banks Esq. Not on your Nelly. My girls have got to look dignified whether they like it or not."'

Cf the prec. three entries and also:

not on your tin-type! (also written *tintype*). Certainly not!: US and Aus.: *c.* 1880–1925, but surviving for another (say) fifteen years; it occurs in, e.g., Christina Stead's *Seven Poor Men of Sydney*, 1930. The ref. is to an old-fashioned type of photograph and there seems to be a feeble pun on **not on your life!**

With *Tessie* added, it was common in the US during the 1940s. This Tessie 'was a character in Ernie Bushmiller's cartoon strip, *Fritzie Ritz*, at that time, but was almost immediately applied to anyone putting on side, or overdressing' (:A.B., 1978).

not Pygmalion likely! See **not bloody likely!**

not quite quite – 'not quite the thing' or 'Not acceptable in polite society' – is a very Brit., esp. English c.p., as in 'Well, he's not quite quite; a bit of a rough diamond, you know; one of nature's gentlemen' – which Wilde once called the worst kind; or as in 'Her behaviour? Well, not quite quite, do you think?' Very late C19 and early C20; revived during the 1920s and lasting until *c.* 1940. I had thought it long †; yet, as someone much better versed in such matters than I has, 1977, remarked, although he himself thought likewise, his daughters have assured him that 'it is alive and well' in upper middle class society.

not so as (or **so's**) **you would** (or **you'd**) **notice** (it); var., **not that you would** (or **you'd**) **notice** (it). Well, not noticeably; *or* I'd hardly have said (*or* thought) so: since the late 1920s.

In his earliest play to be prod. and pub'd *'I'll Leave It to You'. A Light Comedy*, 1920, Noël Coward writes, at Act II:

MRS CROMBIE: I take it that yours is a gold mine.
DANIEL: Not so that you'd notice it.

And Alan Hunter, in *Gently by the Shore*, 1956, has (one policeman to another):

'You haven't traced that taxi?'
'Not so's you'd notice it.'

R.C., 1978, adds, 'Perhaps the original US form, but for at least 40 years, *not so's you would notice it*'.

not so daft as I'm cabbage-looking. A N. Country var. of the next. (Shaw, 1969.)

not so green as I'm cabbage-looking, often prec. by **I'm.** I'm not such a fool – such a simpleton – as I look (*or* as I seem): mid C19–20. In 1853 appeared a novel of English undergraduate life: Cuthbert Bede's *The Adventures of Mr Verdant Green*. Some years ago, I noticed its use by Ernest Raymond in his novel, *Mary Leith* (1931). From the entirely natural and proper equation of immaturity, hence daftness, with the colour green; one of the world's oldest metaphors. Cf **not so daft....**

not so old nor yet so cold. S, 1738, in Dialogue I, has:

NEV[EROUT]: Miss, what do you mean? you'll spoil the Colonel's Marriage if you call him old.
COL[ONEL]: Not so old nor yet so cold——You know the rest, Miss.

An already long-established proverb had, it seems, become something of a c.p. by *c.* 1700; but apparently, as a c.p., † before the end of C18. Not so old as to be impotent nor yet so unloving as to fail to keep his wife warm in bed.

not so scarce as all that! See S, 1738, in Dialogue I:

NEV[EROUT]: Come, come, Miss, make much of naught, good Folks are scarce.

Young Neverout implies that good *men* are scarce: and 'Good folks are scarce' is a C17–20 proverb. The women, so admonished, reply 'But not so scarce as all *that!*'; which is a late C19–20 c.p., not very much used since *c.* 1945.

not so you'd notice it! The US form – employed by, e.g., S.R. Strait in 'Straight Talk' (the *Boston Globe*) *c.* 1917 – of **not so as you would notice (it).**

not that you know of is defiantly addressed to one who has referred to something he either proposes, or is about, to do: *c.* 1740–1820. The *OED* cites novelist Samuel Richardson's 'As Mr B. offer'd to take his Hand, he put 'em both behind him. – "Not that you know of, Sir!"' Cf **not today, baker!**

not that you'd (or **you would**) **notice** (it). See **not so as you would notice (it).**

not to worry! Don't worry – there's nothing to worry about: current, since the middle 1930s, in the Services, and then, suddenly, in 1957–8, it began to be generally and very widely used; P.B., 1975, remarks that it 'was often qualified by "unduly"; and *not to worry unduly, old boy* was a common

Services' phrase in the ten years or so around 1960'. Leechman thinks it goes back to *c.* 1935; it may well have done so, and has certainly been current in the Services since the middle and prob. the early 1940s. Sanders tells me that the phrase was current in the War Office and the Ministry of Defence at the time of the Korean War (1951); in 1967, Granville writes: 'It is old hat. I first heard it, *ad nauseam*, in Admiralty about ten or twelve years ago, when I was researching the RNVR book'; and, late in 1968, B.P. informs me that it is also Aus.

The Services used to base it upon a Maltese analogy; Italian scholars compare *non tormentarsi!* and suggest that British officers returning from the Italian campaign and from the British occupation of Italy in 1944–5, brought it to England; Colonel Archie White, VC, suggests that it may, in form, have been influenced by such locutions as *ce n'est pas* – colloquially *c'est pas – à refuser*, but, more pertinently, why not by *ce n'est pas* – or *c'est pas – à s'en faire?* Those analogies may have intervened, it is true; yet I prefer my own theory – that *not to worry!* merely truncates, or is elliptical for, *you are not to worry*, there's nothing to worry about.

To quote two examples from among so many. John Arden, in *Wet Fish: A Professional Reminiscence for Television*, written 1960, prod. 1961, pub'd 1967, gives this one:

GARNISH: Miss Walters? No panic after all, dear. Not to worry.

Alistair Mair, *Where the East Wind Blows*, 1972, has: 'Oh, I say! I'm terribly sorry – –'
'Not to worry.'

J.W.C., 1977, notes that it is 'never heard in US except from Britons or [used] by sophisticated or affected imitators'.

not today, baker! refuses an offer or a suggestion: Can.: since *c.* 1945. Connoting (Leechman tells me) 'Oh, no! you don't catch me like that!' Cf **not that you know of.**

But Leechman, in 1968, says: 'In England, used by my mother, say 1895. Meaning "Not this time, thank you!"' Moreover, in the England of 1885 (and prob. for some years longer), *not to-day, Baker* was being addressed to any young man paying, to a young woman, court obviously undesired by her: and, according to Ware, the ref. was to a thus surnamed military man 'given into custody for pressing his attentions upon a young lady travelling by accident alone with him'.

Benham offers rather different evidence.

'The incident [referred to by Ware] was very well known at the time. It took place in 1875, which helps to date the c.p. See the *DNB* [at] Valentine Baker' (Playfair, 1977). The c.p. itself was perhaps further popularized by the song, *The Kiss in the Train*, which topically appeared immediately after the charge was brought; Colonel Valentine Baker's career was ruined by that case. (Ronald Pearsall, *Victorian Popular Music*, 1973.)

The c.p. has long connoted any kind of refusal and possessed the var., *not today, baker; crusty one tomorrow*, and is still extant in some parts of South-East England (David Short, 1978).

[**not tonight, Gunga Din** is, by Keith Bloggs in the London *Evening News* of 5 Sep. 1977, credited to Rudyard Kipling and said to have been current for a long time as a var. of the next. I don't refute the statement: stranger things than that have happened in the strange world of c.pp. I merely doubt it.]

not tonight, Josephine is a c.p. used by husbands, lovers, boy friends, to wife or mistress or girl friend, in refusal of a nudge, a hint, even a virtual request for sexual intercourse: always humorous or, at least, semi-humorous: late C19–20. Apocryphally attributed to Napoleon Bonaparte, said to have been given to decline Josephine's expressed desire. Hence, since *c.* 1970, it has been used in other and often trivial circumstances and without regard to sex, as in the loose var. exemplified by 'Care for a drink?' – 'Not today, Josephine.'

This last (supplied by B.P.) seems to be confined to Aus. R.C., however, later commented, 'The usage "without regard to sex" is by no means confined to Australia but has for at least 30 years been the predominant usage in US. Indeed I would guess that it's sexual usage is rare here. Folklorically, at least, it is the (American?) man who proposes and the woman who disposes, on the plea of a headache, a new hair-do, etc.'

Of **not tonight, Josephine,** Noble, 1974, remarks that it 'originated from music-hall fun based on romanticizing of Napoleon's relationship with Josephine, the widowed Viscountess de Beauharnais, whom he married and divorced. The legend of Josephine's sexual appetite produced the catch-phrase current in England' – and, in C20, elsewhere. Mr Noble suggests that George Robey may have done something to increase the popularity of the phrase.

Mostly – and, I'd suppose, firmly – ignored by the editors of dictionaries of quotations, it has nevertheless got itself into J.M. Cohen's alert and catholic *Penguin Book of Quotations*, 1960, Mr Cohen quoting the pseudonymous Colin Curzon's infinitely moving verses:

I'll tell you in a phrase, my sweet, exactly what I mean...
Not tonight, Josephine. [In a poem thus titled.]

Napoleon's name is also enshrined in **Napoleon's greeting to his troops.** See also **pas ce soir...**

not waving but drowing. In a letter dated 10 April 1970, the late Miss Stevie Smith, author of *A Good Time Was Had by All*, 1937, wrote to me: 'One of my later titles – "Not Waving but Drowning", published about 1958 – does seem to have passed into a sort of general use, at least I have heard people using it and have even seen it used as a column heading (with acknowledgements to me) in the *Evening Standard.*' But this phrase, as opposed to *a good time was had by all*, never attained a general currency. Perhaps, however, one might go so far as to say that, in literate and cultured, certainly in literary, circles, it was a c.p. of *c.* 1958–70.

It passed, *c.* 1960, to the same circles in the US. Frank Ross, *Sleeping Dogs*, 1978, has, on p. 102, 'Helen raised a red polka dot headscarf and waved to her vigorously. Margo walked round the end of the pool...and stopped. "Not waving, but drowning," she said acidly.'

not what it's cracked up to be (– it's). It falls short of its reputation: since *c.* 1910. Often applied to compilation. P.B.: where it presumably orig. in a physiological pun. A frequent var. is *not all it's cracked up to be.*

not what you know but who you know. See **it's not what...**

not yet dead, a theatrical c.p. of 1883 – *c.* 1920, was applied to 'an antique fairy' in pantomime. Ware.

not you by your asking. A c.p. reply to 'Who owns this?': late C18 – early C19. Cf the far better known **none the better for your asking.**

not you, Momma, siddown! 'A c.p. from the Ben Lyons, Bebe Daniels, Vic Oliver wartime [WW2] radio show, "Hi, Gang!"' (P.B., 1975). Not yet (1975) entirely dead. P.B.: indeed, Nigel Rees, in *VIBS*, 1980, notes, 'once reported as having appeared as a piece of graffiti on the underside of a train lavatory seat'. 'Ben Lyon was constantly afraid that his mother-in-law in the audience might take umbrage at any insulting lines from the stage' (Leslie Halliwell's *The Filmgoer's Book of Quotes*), but, as Wedgewood remarked, 1978, it was 'usable in a variety of circumstances' by the general public.

not your Uncle Dudley! '"You can't fool me!" ...said in New England in early C20...and [revived] on the Fred Allen radio show ("Allen's Alley" skit) in the 1940s' (A.B., 1978).

note. See: on that; that's a hell.

nother. See: that's a whole.

nothing. See: ain't saying; ain't that n.; everybody's pulling; everything in the shop; formerly; free, gracious; I don't know from; oh, it's n.; on a hiding; thank you for n.; there's nothing; they're eating; thin edge; think nothing; you ain't heard; you can always; you were born; and:

nothing below the waist is a tailors c.p., dating from before 1928 and meaning 'no fool'. *The Tailor and Cutter*, 29 Nov. 1928, has: 'Took me for a josser [a simpleton]. Nothing below the waist, me. I'm not to be rubbed about.' From a process in tailoring.

nothing but. 'Used to emphasize or conclude a preceding remark' (Berrey): US: since the 1920s. Cf **and how!**

nothing, but he's got it there. See **what has she got...**

nothing but up and ride? Is that the end?; Is there nothing else?; Why! Is it all over?: a semi-proverbial c.p. of *c.* 1620–1750. Recorded by Clarke, 1639; Ray; Fuller, 1732. (Apperson.) From horse-racing?

nothing doing! Certainly not! – in retort upon an invitation to amorous dalliance or to an unattractive or shady offer or suggestion: since the 1890s. In 1927, a schoolgirl, writing about Elizabeth I, evolved this masterpiece: 'Philip of Spain asked her hand in marriage, but she replied, "Nothing doing!"' Prob. developed from the coll. *there's nothing doing*, there's-no business being done.

In Act of Alfred Sutro's *Living Together*, performed and pub'd in 1929, the following occurs:

JULIA: I don't walk off with another girl's chap...
TONY: We're free, aren't we?
JULIA: [*Shaking her head.*] Nothing doing, Tony.
TONY: This is ridiculous...
JULIA: I've told you, nothing doing.

The phrase had reached the US by the late 1920s; Berrey records it in 1942.

It passed, fairly early, to Can. Sandilands, 1913, wrote, 'Nothin' doin', an expression that has become a by-word. Though originally it was a boss's reply to applicants when he had no works to offer them, it has become a frequent reply to an applicant for alms, to a drummer [= commercial traveller] for whom there is no order, to suitor whose attentions are not desired, or to anyone who is not to be granted what they desire. It has become a denial and a refusal in all sorts of circumstance, and even if you tell your choicest story, an unappreciative listener may mutter "nothin' doin'" and pass on. He means...the smiling line'.

nothing for nothing, and very little for tuppence-ha'penny, often prec. by **you get.** A c.p. dating since *c.* 1910 and orig. by George Bernard Shaw. 'Shaw's coinage,' writes R.S., 1974, 'is reminiscent of *Punch's* "Nothink for nothink 'ere, and precious little for sixpence" (vol. LVII, 1869), also used by Kipling (nautically adjusted) in *The Ship That Found Herself*, 1895'.

nothing happening is a US negroes' c.p. of *c.* 1940–60. Clarence Major glosses it thus: 'Often a response to "What's happening?" The implication is that things are more than simply slow' – in short, 'dead'. Contrast **it's all happening.**

nothing in my young life, usu. prec. by **he's or she's.** He means nothing to me: since *c.* 1930. Orig. among the youthful and concerning a member of the opposite sex. It occurred, for instance, in a story by Achmed Abdullah in *Nash's Magazine*, Feb. 1935.

nothing like leather is applied to anything that recalls and emphasizes, esp. if one-sidedly or tendentially, the doer's – or the speaker's – trade (orig., of course, that of a currier): since *c.* 1670, as, e.g. in L'Estrange, 1692, and Mrs Gaskell, 1855. (Apperson.) Since the late 1920s, the phrase has been a leathersellers' and shoemakers' slogan: and the slogan has repopularized the c.p. Folk-etymologically, the saying orig. in an anecdote about a certain cobbler's praise of his own wares.

nothing that you oughtn't answers the question, 'what shall I do?' and has, at the lower social levels, been current throughout C20. (Petch, 1976.)

nothing to cable home about. It's – *or* that's – ordinary, usual, unremarkable, unexciting: Aus.: since *c.* 1914 or 1915. It arose, I believe, in the Australian expeditionary force during WW1.

More widely used is *nothing to write home about*, which

dates from late C19 and is common to all English-speaking peoples, including – by *c.* 1918–the US; Berrey records it and notes the (US) var., *nothing to wire home about.* Cf **nothing to make a song about.**

nothing to do with the case! is often a polite way of saying 'That's a lie' and it dates from Gilbert and Sullivan's *The Mikado*, first produced on 14 March 1884. By 1935, a trifle ob. but not yet †. We still, even although only occ., hear the words from which the c.p. has been distilled: 'The flowers that bloom in the spring, tra-la, have nothing to do with the case', sung, as Ware tells us, with an alluring liveliness by the inimitable George Grossmith. From the phraseology of the law-courts – cf **not guilty, my Lord.**

nothing to make a song about. Nothing to make a fuss about; nothing in the least important: mid C19–20. Cf **nothing to cable home about.** P.B.: sometimes elab. *... song and dance about.*

nothing to wire (or **write**) **home about.** See **nothing to cable home about,** second paragraph.

nothing up my sleeve, sometimes prec. by *look* (and *ladies and gentlemen*), 'introduces any feat of skill' (Skehan, 1977) and apparently dates from *c.* 1930. From the conjurer's patter.

notice. See: I must have n.; not so as; sit up and take.

now can you? 'From *c.* 1914 divorce case in which a witness had overheard these words issuing from the bedroom. "Now can you (get in)?" It became a c.p. among youths who called after girls thus to cause a few giggles or, more hopefully, dates. Mostly working-class' (Granville, 1969).

now **for the bad news,** is applied, to the unfavourable as opposed to the preceding good news, by the communicator: since the late 1960s in the UK and perhaps *c.* 1970 in the US. From the news announcers' and commentators' general practice. P.B.: as often in the form *first, the bad news,* and, of course, among those who see the brighter side of things, the *good* news receives the emphasis.

now **he tells me!** In 1969, Mr D.J. Barr, a Canadian schoolteacher (of Hillsport, Ontario), wrote to me: 'One student used it after a spelling test, as if he [had] expected me to tell him his mistakes during the test.'

It had travelled, during the 1950s, to both Can. and UK as a US export: in the US, it began as a Hebraism and, among Gentiles, became a c.p., with the gen. sense 'And he thinks of telling me – when it's too late to be of use'. In Gavin Lyall's 'thriller', *Blame the Dead*, 1972, occurs this piece of dialogue:

He'd heard that Pat Kavanagh was last heard of working for Dave Danner.
'Now he tells me.'

Expectably and predictably, it has – or could be said to have – the var. *'now* you tell me!'. It occurs in, e.g., Blaine Littell, *The Dolorosa Deal*, 1973:

'Forget it! It happened in Bangkok. You're going to Jerusalem.'
'When did it happen?'
'Two weeks ago.'
'*Now* you tell me?'

Mason heard Webster's familiar chuckle at the other end of the line. 'Mazel tov! You're off to a good start. You even sound Jewish.'

P.B.: when I first heard this c.p., in the early 1960s, it was often a mock Italian accent, *now he tellsa me!,* with an accompanying shrug of the shoulders.

now I'll tell you one (emphasis on *you*) expresses 'incredulity at telling of scandalous, titillating, but unbelievable episode, or news in one's circle' (L.A., 1975): since *c.* 1932. Earlier (1974) L.A. had commented thus: 'In response to a witticism, tall or funny story, boast, etc. since early 1930s: adopted from US via "talkies", where informed incredulity was a mark of wise-guy sophistication'.

now I've heard (or **seen**) **everything!** is an ironical, yet usu. good-natured, c.p., expressing a mock admiration or wonderment: since the middle 1940s. An Aus. example

(*heard*) comes in Frank Hardy, *Billy Borker Yarns Again*, 1967. Cf **this I must hear** (or **see**).

now, Mrs Rowbottom, *if* **you please!** I'm ready when *you* are: Can.: since *c.* 1930. (Leechman, who adds: 'Of anecdotal origin'.) It went to Can. from the US, where 'c. 1930, the late Dwight Fiske performed and recorded a mildly salacious, "Mrs Pettibone", in which this line occurred as "Now, Mrs Pettibone, *if* you please!" ' (R.C., 1978).

now, now, come, come, don't dilly-dally! 'Charley Come-Come in *ITMA' (VIBS).* See TOMMY HANDLEY

now she bumps. See **bumps ....**

now she knows (all about it)! (or **she knows all about it now!**) is, not unexpectedly, applied to a bride any time shortly after the bridal night: C20, but not much used since *c.* 1950, virginity being no longer regarded – by most females – as advisable or even desirable.

now she's talking! is a nautical, esp. a naval, c.p., 'said of a ship's boat as she begins to more through the water which begins to slap her strakes' (*Sailors' Slang*): late C19–20.

now tell me another! See **now you tell me one.**

now then, me lucky lads! is a workmen's ironic c.p., applied, since *c.* 1910, to work and deriving from showmen's and three-card tricksters' and racing tipsters' invitation to the 'mugs' to enter or to participate. Cf Tommy Trinder's gag., **You lucky people!,** and **come on, my lucky lads ...**

now then, only another nineteen shillings and elevenpence three farthings to make up the pound before I begin the service. A military c.p., dating since *c.* 1908 and used by someone desirous of raising a loan or of starting a 'bank'. (B&P.) P.B.: ob. by mid-C20, and, of course, † with the decimalization of currency, Feb. 1971.

now then, shoot those arms out! You couldn't knock the skin off a rice pudding! has, since *c.* 1910 or a little earlier, been used by drill sergeants and physical-training instructors, at first in the army (see esp. B&P) and then, after WW1, also in the RAF. See also **couldn't knock ...**

now then, what's all this 'ere? Apropos of **hello, hello, hello!** and **you can't do that there 'ere:** 'A policeman's c.p., covering everything from a lost cat to mass murder' (Sanders, 1978). Often shortened to *now then, what's all this? ?,* q.v. at **hello, hello, hello!**

now, there's a funny thing: there *is* **a funny thing** is one of far too many domestic c.pp., and even this one verges on the potential proverbial saying, belonging, I'd guess, to late C19–20. I cannot do better than to quote R.S., who, in 1975 and in answer to a query, writes: 'I remember from my earliest days (putting my perceptive memory as starting *c.* 1910), as indicating that my mother's suspicions were beginning to be awakened by some unlikely coincidence or circumstance. So it must have been current then' – to judge by at least two other correspondents, early 1975, it still is. 'The meaning *funny-peculiar,* rather than *funny-haha.*'

But it was also – or, rather, it became – one of Max Miller's gags, as Vernon Noble tells me, 1975. And a few days later Cyril Whelan amplifies it by writing: '[This] was the "filler" used between shots by Max Miller, the celebrated Cockney comedian who pushed open vulgarity to the limit before it was modish to do so.'

Oddly enough, Sir John Betjeman – on Radio 4, 12 Apr. 1975 – played a Max Miller record that, in the 1920s, included the phrase. (Thanks again to R.S.)

There exists no contradiction here. Max Miller didn't just 'pluck it out of the air': perhaps quite unconsciously, he prob. drew on a childhood memory – what we used to call the tribal memory – and utilized it, revived it, popularized it.

now we shall be sha'n't. This joc., non-cultured perversion of **now we sha'n't be long** arose in Dec. 1896 and was prob. dead by 1900. Ware notes that it is purposely meaningless. This meaningless type of c.p. is fortunately as short-lived as it is tedious.

now we sha'n't be long is an 'intimation of finality' – of obscure origin, although 'probably from railway travellers' phrase when near the end of a journey': 'people's, 1895 on'; ob. by *c.* 1915 and virtually † by *c.* 1930. (Ware.) It occurred in the *Daily Telegraph* of 8 Sep. 1896 and in Somerset Maugham's *Liza of Lambeth*, 1897.

now we're busy was, earliest, a c.p. implying action and dating from 1868, but – as a c.p. – † by 1914. From the 1880s, it was also 'an evasive intimation that the person spoken of is no better for his liquor, and is about to be destructive' (Ware); † by *c.* 1920. See also **we're in business.**

now what have you (got) to say for yourself? was, *c.* 1920–60, a c.p. of humorous, semi-ironic greeting. P.B.: perhaps as often *and what have* ...

now you see it, now you don't. is a facetious reply to 'How are you?' (Russell Davies, in *New Statesman*, 9 Sep. 1977). It implies 'Oh, up and down; some days good, some days not so good': a 'rubbish': sort of c.p., dating since *c.* 1930. From conjurors' patter. P.B.: but as Ashley notes, 1979, it is of course used much more specifically, 'when anything (or anyone) suddenly disappears' – and he is writing of US usage also. Sometimes elab. ... *the quickness of the hand deceives the eye.*

now you tell me! See **now he tells me!** – final paragraph.

now you tell one and **now tell me another** date from the early 1920s; Shaw, 1969, derives it from 'a tearful 1920s "love" song'.

now you'll think I'm awful. 'A c.p. used by women after making an uncharitable remark or after spreading a rumour. It is also said to be used after a casual sexual encounter' (B.P., 1974): very widely employed, orig. as a cliché: late C19–20; a c.p. by *c.* 1910, esp. if humorously rueful. A US var. is *I*, or *I'll, bet you think I'm awful* (J.W.C., 1977).

now you're asking. is a var. of **that's asking!** It dates from the late 1890s and occurs in, e.g., Leonard Merrick's once famous *Peggy Harper*, 1911. A better example comes in Francis Clifford's *Act of Mercy*, 1959: there the sense 'That's a very difficult question' (cf **that's a good question**) emerges very clearly:

'What we can't grasp,' Susan said, 'is why there's been a revolution in the first place. I mean – what brought things to a head so suddenly?'

'Ah,' Swann sighed. 'Now you're asking.'

now you're cooking with gas. 'Now you are on the right track'; now you've got the right idea: prob. since *c.* 1940, for it resulted from an intensive Radio and Press campaign, carried on by the gas industry during the middle and late 1930s to combat the rapidly increasing use of the electric range (stove): Ben Grauer, in letter written on Christmas Day 1975. He notes the intensive var. *now you're cooking on the front burner* and the 'moderator', ... *on the back burner.* He further remarks that *now* is often omitted. Recorded by Berrey, 1942, and by W&F, who, in 1960, have glossed it thus: 'Originally swing ['pop' music, especially jazz] use. Fairly well known *c.* 1940, still some use.' It promptly travelled to Can. as Prof. F.E.L. Priestley informed me in 1975.

It has the exact synon., *now you're cooking on all four burners*, which J.W.C., 1977, glosses thus, 'Now you're doing a good, through, expert, exciting job' – and he amplifies the W&F ref. to 'pop' music by saying, 'Jazz musicians, originally praising one of themselves distinguishing himself by a remarkable improvised solo performance'; and

when J.W.C. talks about music, he richly knows what he is talking about.

The var. (*now*) *you're cooking on the front burner* occurs in S.J. Perelman's witty farce *The Beauty Part*, prod. 1962 and pub'd 1963, at II, 6, but in the form 'You sure are cooking on the front burner'.

'With all respect to my late friend Ben Grauer, I suggest [that] a more likely origin is a comparison of the gas range with the older and less convenient wood or coal range ... An occasional intensified version (1940s–60s) is "cooking with radar" ' (R.C., 1978).

now you're logging! A Western US loggers' (or lumberjacks') 'expression of commendation' (Adams, *Western Words*, 1968): late C19–20. Cf:

now you're railroadin'! 'You speak truly' (Berrey, 1942); also a c.p. 'of approval and admiration' (*ibid.*) or an expression of commendation, no matter what one is doing' (*ibid.*): a US railwa : c.p. of C20.

now you' e talking! Now you're saying something worthwhile (or arresting): since *c.* 1880, a date based upon the *OED*. Adopted *c.* 1900 by US; recorded by Berrey (as an interjection of 'approval and admiration'). It travelled early to Can. (Priestley, 1975).

now you've been and gone and done it. See **been and gone** ...

nowhere. See: flattery; horses that; like Jack.

nowt so queer as folks. See **there's nowt** ...

nudge, nudge, wink, wink, (often followed by **need I say more!**)! Orig. in the surrealist-comedy TV series 'Monty Python's Flying Circus' of the early 1970s, where *wink, wink, nudge* ... was the version used. By late 1970s, a widespread c.p. alluding to any doubtful situation, sexual, mildly criminal, etc., so that Jill Tweedie, in the *Guardian*, 24 May 1979, could write: 'Woman – a sexual object to be lusted after– , ... whistled at on the silver screen and nudge nudge wink wink'd in every comedy series ...'

The last element soon acquired a var. **say no more!**, q.v. (P.B.)

nuff said. A comic perversion (*nuff sed*) or var. of **enough said:** US origin, according to Ware, on whose evidence its Brit. use could be dated as from *c.* 1870; but John Brougham, in his farce, *Po-Ca-Hon-Tas or, The Gentle Savage*, performed in New York, 1855, has this passage at I, i:

COL: *Conclude* it done! The deadliest weapon I can find, I'll name.

OPO: Nuff said, old top, I'll go it blind!

But the *OED New Supp.* quotes a US newspaper as using it in 1840.

number(s). See: come in, number; get some service; I got your; it had my; safety; since Pontius; take his name; three is.

number one. See: public.

nun. See: more strife.

nurse. See: good night, n.; hello, baby.

nut. See: you some.

nutmeg. See: don't let anyone.

nuts. See: put it where the monkey; she goes; where the nuts.

nutted 'em! is an exclamatory c.p., uttered when the pennies turn up two heads at the gambling game of two-up: Aus. and NZ: C20. From slang *nut*, the head.

nutty as a fruitcake, usu. prec. by *he's*, or *she's as.* Crazy; extremely eccentric: US, since *c.* 1920; adopted in UK *c.* 1945. (J.W.C., 1977.)

O

O.B. See: same O.B.

O.B.E. See: time for your.

O be joyful. See: I'll make you sing.

O begga me! or O Bergami! is the way Ware presents these variants, but what he should, I think, have written was *O Bergami!* and its derivative *oh, beggar me!*, with *beggar* for *bugger*, naturally. Ware classifies it as 'London people's' – i.e., proletarian – and dates it at 1820; he adds: 'Still used in the streets as intimating that the person addressed is a liar, or worse. From one Bergami – a lying witness at the trial of Queen Caroline – whose denial of everything brought about this phrase, with his eternal "non mi ricordo" [I don't remember].' At *non me* in his very valuable book, Ware notes that the *non mi* of the It. *non mi ricordo* became, c. 1820–30, the London proletariat's synonym for a lie and was used thus: 'That's a *non me* for one' – 'That's a lie, to start with'.

O.K. See: okay; you're O.K.

oak. See: one that lives; within.

oak chest. See: on second.

oakum boy. See: ever since.

oar. See: perched.

oath. See: my bloody; my oath.

object of the exercise. See: that is the o.

oboe. See: play that.

observed. See: hist!

obsolete. See: if it works.

obvious. See: for obvious reasons; glimpses.

och man, you're daft! '(followed by a laugh "like a tinkling bell, rippling up the scale") – Molly Weir as Tattie MacKintosh in ITMA' (*VIBS*). See also TOMMY HANDLEY.

odd-come-shortlies. See: one of these o.

odds. See: what's the o.

of all the dumb tricks! is described by Berrey as an 'interjection of personal displeasure': US: since c. 1920 and prob. earlier. The corresponding Brit. exclam. would be 'Of all the bloody stupid things to do, *that* is the stupidest!' – which, however, doesn't qualify as a c.p. A.B., 1978, notes that the US often substitutes *stunts* for *tricks*.

off all the nerve!; what a nerve!; you've got a nerve!; your nerve!; I like your nerve!; also of all the gall! All were, orig., US; but, whereas the last has always been solely US, the others became, c. 1918, also Brit. As Americanisms, they are impossible to date with any accuracy; I'd hazard 'since the 1890s'. J.W.C. notes, 1977, that *of all the nerve* is now 'very rare in US'.

off. See: come off; get them; got it off; I'll let you; little less; my word, if you're; and:

off again, on again, Finnegan is a US c.p., deriving from an old song and has come to mean 'intermittent' or 'capricious' or 'fickle': late C19–20. But at first it was a 'railroad expression as old as 1890 and referring to minor train wrecks: off the track and then back on the track. *Finnegan* has no significance, I believe, except that it makes a good rhyme' (Fain, 1978). J.W.C., 1977, had remarked that it is 'applied to someone dashing in and out. Common [c. 1911–16, if not earlier, but] now seldom heard'.

P.B.: I have heard the more elab. *on again, off again, on again, Finnegan*, and am reminded of the children's repetition song, one verse of which goes:

There was an old man called Michael Finnegan,
He grew whiskers on his chinnegan,
The wind came out and blew them in again.
Poor old Michael Finnegan! Begin again!
[and so on.]

off and on! See off yer and on yer!

off like a bride's nightie. (Departing) promptly; speedily: Aus.: since c. 1960. Wilkes, *Dict. Aus. Coll.*, records it as being in print in 1969 – a book by Christopher Bray. Cf up and down like ... *Nightie* is, of course, domestic coll. for 'nightgown'.

off (or it's off) the record. See record.

off to Durban! 'A music-hall gag for any person going on a gallivanting holiday. Since c. 1920' (Prof. A.C. Partridge, 1968): S. African.

off with his head: so much for Buckingham! This was perpetrated by Colley Cibber in his 'improvement' of Shakespeare's *Richard III*, where the simple *off with his head* had occurred (1592–93): and, however long Cibber's elab. lasted, the c.p. has, in C20, usu. existed in the shorter form. (Enlargement of a note from Mr P. Daniel, 1978.) P.B.: in C20, surely as likely to derive from the awful threat *off with her head*, in Lewis Carroll's *Alice in Wonderland*.

off yer and on yer! – sometimes shortened to off and on!, and itself elliptical for off yer (or your) fanny and on yer (or your) feet! 'The limited use of the shortened phrase – i.e., *off and on!* – by Marines was as a command by the "non-com" to "turn-out" – or to resume activity after a rest period even though every individual was already standing' (Col. Moe, 1975). The two longer phrases were presumably current in both the navy and the army; and the longest passed into some gen. currency: late C19–20.

offence. See: no offence.

officer(s). See: fall out, the; gangway; midshipmen.

officer, call a cap! See TAD DORGAN.

officers and gentlemen has, during WW2 and National Service (ended 1962) and decreasingly since, been used as a c.p.

officers and their ladies, NCOs and their wives, privates and their women (folk) 'has, with many variants, been in existence since heaven knows when, I see, from yesterday's *Daily Telegraph*, 6 Dec., that, years ago, there were "men of the Merchant Navy, officers of the Royal Navy, and gentlemen of the P.&O." [the Peninsular & Orient Shipping Line]' (anon., 1978). Cf:

officers have abdomens, sar'n't majors have stomachs and other

ranks have bellies. One of the variants referred to in prec.: Army: (?) since late 1940s. (Mrs Camilla Raab.) Cf **midshipmen have guts ...** and **horses sweat ...**

officers: I've shit (or **shot**) **'em!** An army other ranks' c.p. of WW2 (and before) and during National Service: c. 1930–60. (Anon., 1978.) Obviously patterned on WW1 *soldiers! I've shit 'em.*

often. See: do you come here; vote early.

often trod but never laid. (Of women) often 'mauled' but never slept with: since the late 1940s. Here, *trod* = trodden on; and *laid* comes from 'to *lay*', to copulate with. P.B.: there seems to be a pun on hens.

oh, after you! That'll do! *or* Stop talking!: tailors' c.p., dating since c. 1870 and always used ironically. (B.&L.) Cf **after you, Claude ....**

oh, baby! was current among US students esp. in 1920–2, and decreasingly throughout the remaining 1920s. (McKnight.) It was apparently influenced by the much-longer-lived and far more widely distributed **oh boy!**

oh, bishop. See **bishop.**

oh, bloody good, wacco, (or **whacko,**) **Pup!** 'And after shooting down a Jap plane: "Oh, bloody good, wacco, Pup!" which was a queer New Zealand whoop of triumph the squadron had adopted': Kenneth Hemingway, *Wings over Burma,* 1944, – as P.B. describes it, 'an informal account of the author's experiences with 17 Squadron, RAF, during the retreat from Rangoon to Calcutta, February – April 1942 .... Their "in" phrase was, wherever possible, "Have a snort!" – not necessarily of alcohol', but clearly a cliché, not a c.p.

oh, boy! and **boy, oh boy!** and **oh, boy – did I!** Very gen. among US soldiers in 1917–18; arose c. 1910, if not a little earlier; current in England during the 1920s and after, but virtually † by c. 1970. Of its English use, R.S. writes (1969): '*boy!* or *oh boy!* Indicative of anticipation or satisfaction, as in "Boy! D'you see what I see?" or "What a party! Oh boy! Oh Boy!"' Or, of course, you can trust the urbane P.G. Wodehouse, master of limpid, effortless English, to provide a satisfactory example. In *Aunts Aren't Gentlemen,* 1974: 'E.J. Murgatroyd [a Harley Street consultant] would have been all for it. "Oh, boy," I could hear him saying, "this is the stuff to give the typical young man about town." The air ... seemed to be about as pure as could be expected, and I looked forward to a healthy and invigorated stay.'

McKnight quotes from the *Kansas City Star* (date not given) this example of a returned US soldier's language:

'Did you git clean over, Pink?'
'Oh, boy, did I?'
'Git sick on the ocean?'
'Oh, boy, did I?'
'Didya go over the top, Pink?'
'Oh, boy, did I?'
'How did it feel?'
'Oh, boy, believe me.'
'Pink, didya kill any Germans?'
'Oh, boy.'

In his *Hand-Made Fables,* 1920, George Ade writes:
They began to make out the White Houses and the big Red Barns and the Fat Stock ...

'How do they look to you?' asked the Conductor.
'Oh, Boy!' was all the Eb could exclaim.

The phrase was still going strong in the middle 1930s, as in Clarence B. Kelland, *Speak Easily,* c. 1935: '"You mean," said Mr James, "that you hooked this yegg with your umbrella and grabbed off the ruby. Oh, boy! Where's the photographers? Won't I do a job with this!"'

A year or so earlier, Alec Waugh, *Wheels within Wheels,* causes an American to exclaim, '"Oh, boy, if you could see the look on my mother's face at times! She think she's living in a fairy tale. And as for that girl, oh boy and how! You should just see her!"'

In Ed McBain's *Shotgun,* 1968, we find this lovers' tiff:

'... Go ahead, go home, what do I care?'
'Oh, boy,' he said.
'Sure, oh boy.'

And again in his *Jigsaw,* 1970, when still healthily extant. The var. *boy! oh boy!* occurs in, e.g., Morris Farhi's novel, *The Pleasure of Your Death,* 1972:

'Did you know, in the summer, now, the sun shines twenty-four hours a day?'
'No kidding?'
'And that nobody goes to bed. At least, not to sleep.'
'Boy, oh, boy.'

Another 1972 instance is afforded by Martin Woodhouse's *Mama Doll.*

To emphasize the longevity – of, at the least, its extraordinarily widespread use – the *New Yorker* of 19 May 1973 presents an elderly man as employing it in addressing his elderly wife.

But the popularity of such homely, apparently very ordinary, c.pp. is impossible to explain: yet I do not doubt that some 'smart Alec' will, in a learned and unreadable thesis, think it necessary to go beyond the natural explanation that such popularity was rendered possible, and was perhaps in the fact caused, by the homeliness and ordinariness and artlessness of the phrase.

[Later, E.P. added] It may have been influenced by *oh, man!*, which, popularized by the famous American comedian (male) cartoonist, Clare D. Briggs (1875–1930), may itself have briefly been a c.p. Note that, in 1970, J.W.C. could still write of *oh, boy* that it was 'for from obsolete or even obsolescent in US'. Cf **there's at least one in every club.**

oh, brother! is an exclamatory c.p., indicative less often of surprise or astonishment or assent or relief, than of dismay or wry comment or rueful afterthought: US: C20. Apparently suggested by the more naïve, less intelligent, yet more popular **oh, boy!** A late example occurs in Judson Phillips, *Nightmare at Dawn,* 1970:

'Jane!' he said softly.

'Oh, brother!' the girl said, 'I thought you'd gone away. Where are you?'

oh, calamity! 'Expression so often used by lugubrious characters in farce played by Robertson Hare (1930s on) that it became adopted in jocular conversation,' as Vernon Noble tells me, 1975; or, as P.B. puts it: 'Robertson Hare's woeful c.p. from the pre-war Aldwych farces, e.g. when [he was] de-bagged once again.'

oh, chase me! A satirical – or ostensibly satirical – invitation, issued by a girl to a youth, to run after her and kiss her. It arose, in the streets (orig. those of London) in 1898, but it had disappeared by the end of WW1.

'Cf *chase me* – described as an "old cockney expletive" by Margery Allingham, *More Work for the Undertaker,* 1947' (R.C.). It may have been prompted by the late C19 – early 20, 'Chase me, Jimmy,/I've lost my shimmy/and half the leg of my drawers' (B.G.T., 1978). See also **cor, chase me ...**

oh, come on! An exhortation to show some intelligence or evidence of thought; to react sensibly to the obvious: *on* heavily emphasised, a popular vogue phrase of c. 1983–4. See, e.g. *The Times,* 17 May 1984, where that witty columnist Miles Kington puts this very English phrase into the mouth of an American talking to a Russian. (P.B.)

oh, come on: be a devil! See **be a devil!**

oh, definitely! seems to have arisen c. 1919, and by the end of 1920 it had begun its inane yet spectacular career. It notably occurs in, e.g., Sutton Vane's play, *Outward Bound,* 1924; satirically in A.A. Milne's *Two People,* 1931, and, above all and *ad nauseam,* in Maurice Lincoln's novel about 'the smart young things', *Oh, Definitely!,* 1933. The following example comes from Lincoln's book:

'What do you think of her?'

Peter considered the question for a few moments. 'She's dumb,' he said at length.

'Dumb?'

'Dumbest thing I ever met. If you forbade that girl to say "marvellous", and the stooped her from saying "definitely", she couldn't speak at all.'

oh, Gertie, get off my neck! See **get off my neck!**

oh, get in there, Moreton! was comedian Robert Moreton's c.p., c. 1947, in the BBC radio comedy series 'Educating Archie', 'telling slightly incoherent stories from his Bumper Fun Book and from time to time saying [this] after some telling thrust' (Jack Eva, 1978). P.B.: the phrase was always uttered in a 'silly ass' voice, and as if the speaker were surprised at himself for being so 'with it'. Perhaps suggested by the earlier **get in there, Murdoch!** Nigel Rees says of this entry in his *VIBS*, 'Quite the saddest of the catch phrases in this book. Robert Morton had a brief taste of fame as tutor in *Educating Archie* ... After only a year he was dropped from the show, was unable to get other work, and committed suicide'.

[**oh, I believe you: Canadas, oceans, tons and eddies, I believe you!** 'At the Girls' High School, Longhborough, Leicestershire' used 'as a sarcastic expression of utter disbelief' (P.B., with thanks to Miss Jane Long, 1978). Normally, I shouldn't include a c.p. so very local and prob. ephemeral: but its expressiveness, its picturesqueness, justify this brief mention.]

oh, I say, I am a fool! 'The pay-off line of Dudley Davenport (Maurice Denham) in [the BBC radio comedy series] *Much Binding in the Marsh*. ... (Ken Platt uses the shorter, "oh, I am a fool!")' (*VIBS*): late 1940s. P.B.: the line was always spoken in a 'silly ass' voice, followed by a 'silly ass' laugh.

oh, I say, I rather care for that! 'Flying Officer Kite, the ex-RAF officer, complete with handlebar moustache and varsity accent, played by Humphrey Lestocq in [the BBC radio comedy series] *Merry Go Round*. ... After many a "wizard prang!", Eric Barker [see **Steady, Barker!**] would slap Kite down, but [the latter] would only roar "Oh, I say, I rather care for that" in return' (*VIBS*): later 1940s. P.B.: the remark was, perhaps intentionally, a contemporary opposite of **I couldn't care less**, q.v., and 'Kite' was a caricature of a very noticeable 'type' of the immediate Post-WW2 years, the demobbed pilot. The c.p. was always followed by a braying laugh, in an invariable rhythm: as near as can be caught in print, *haha, h-haa ha!*, hearty but meaningless.

oh, is that so? Farmer writes:

This expression ... serves the true-born American as a pendant to whatever observations may be addressed to him. It is both affirmative and negative, according to the tone of the speaker's voice; in the former case it takes the place of 'indeed!' or 'really!'; in the latter it does duty for 'not really!', 'surely not!'

It is an educated c.p.; moreover, it is also Brit., and it must date – from *when?* 1850 at the latest, I'd say; and perhaps from very much earlier. Cf **you don't say so.**

As late as 1923, in Robert Benchley's *Love Conquers All*, occurs this gem:

Among the more popular nuggets of repartee, effective on all occasions, are the following:
'Oh, is that so?'
'Eugh?'
'How do you get that way?'
'Oh, is that so?'
'Aw, have your hair bobbed.'
'Oh, is that so?'
'Well, what are you going to do about it?'
'Who says so?'
'Eugh? Well, I'll Cincinnati you.'
'Oh, is that so?'

See also **is zat so?**

[**oh, it's nothing: just a trick of the light**, explaining anything quite fantastic, occurs in three of seven scripts forming the body of *Round the Horne*, ed. by Barry Took and Marty Feldman, pub'd 1975, being excerpts from the radio comedy show that, so titled, was broadcast in 1965–67. It could

perhaps be claimed as a c.p., heyday c. 1966–68, with occ, use until c. 1977. P.B.: *Just a trick of the light* was certainly a well used quot'n, if not a c.p., from this very popular show.]

oh, jolly D! A gag uttered by the character 'Dudley Davenport' (played by Maurice Denham) in Kenneth Horne and Richard Murdoch's radio show. 'Much Binding in the Marsh' (c. 1944–5). The words represent a Public School version of *oh, jolly decent!* – and there's a double pun in the name of the show: on picturesque English place-names and on the WW2, esp. RAF, slang term *binding*, (constant) complaining or complaints.

oh, la! la! and Anglicized **oo-la-la!** During WW1, *oh, la! la!* was a military c.p., used far more by officers than by Other Ranks; it expressed either joviality or a delighted astonishment. (B&P.) In a way it extends the c. 1590–1930 *la! la!*, which expressed derision. Cf the slangy 'a bit of *oo la la*', a leg-show.

oh, Miss Weston! is a RN c.p., expressing disapproval – usu. a pretended disapproval – of strong language: since c. 1910. 'Dame Agnes Weston was a great stickler for propriety' (PGR). Cf **my oath, Miss Weston!**

oh, man! See **oh, boy!**

oh, mate! 'was an expression of humorously resigned expostulation ... Very popular c. 1970 but quite short-lived' (P.B., 1976). As with so many c.pp., intonation was of the essence.

oh, mother, is it worth it? – C20 and perhaps almost immemorial – originated and is extant, as a feminine *cri de coeur*, and, as such, obviously not a c.p. But it has, in C20, been used with rueful humour and irony, mostly (of course) by women, mostly young women and girls – and then it is, no less obviously, a c.p. Its c.p. status has prob. been reinforced by Arnold Wesker's little pamphlet, *The Modern Playwright or 'Oh, Mother, is it worth it?'* – referring to his early uphill struggle to make a living with his plays, and pub'd in 1960. Cf **mother, is it worth it?**

oh, mummy, buy me one of those! This c.p., mostly Can. and dating since c. 1920, recalls the much older **I (really) must have one of those!**, q.v. at **I must have ....** An earlier C20 Brit. version was *buy me one of those, daddy!*

oh, my achin' back! 'Poking fun at the Japanese: Second World War [mostly in 1944–5]: South Pacific and US' (Leechman, 1973). Allusive to an old Brit. c.p., **every picture tells a story.**

Orig., it seems, US. According to Miss Mary Priebe of Seattle, who was in the American Red Cross with the US Army from early 1940s for the next eleven years, the phrase swept through the US forces like an epidemic. She doesn't know the origin, but explains it as a mild expletive of exasperation .... She says it was sometimes, later, elab. to *oh, my achin' back, sack, company!* but can't explain the significance of this. (P.B., 1975.) R.C., 1978, notes that it is 'obsolescent but not yet dead in US'.

oh, my giddy aunt! 'I think from Brandon Thomas's long-running farcical comedy, "Charley's Aunt" (1,466 performances on its first production starting in December 1892); countless revivals since then – and the "Aunt" is still running' (Noble, 1974). Usu. uttered with a ruefully humorous smile or laugh, it occurred very frequently in, e.g., schoolgirl stories of c. 1946. Cf the var. *oh, my sainted* (less often, *sacred*) *aunt!* 'Long remembered but now seldom heard' (Leechman, 1977).

oh, my leg! was, c. 1810–50, addressed to someone recently freed from gaol. (JB.) A gibe allusive to the ex-prisoner's gait, caused by long confinement in fetters. Cf **clank, clank.**

oh, my poor (or **pore**) **feet!** Cf **how's your poor feet?**, by which it was prob. occasioned c. 1910. 'My three daughters assure me that *oh, my pore feet* is still alive and in use, though they would more naturally say "My feet are killing me"' (a distinguished contributor, 1977).

oh, oh, Antonio! This almost meaningless c.p. of c. 1912–30 vaguely expresses excitement and owes its existence to the once extremely famous song so titled.

oh, Pollacky! (stressed on the first syllable) – often shortened to

Pollacky! or **pollacky!** – was, *c.* 1870–1900, an 'exclamation of protest against too urgent enquiries' (Ware). From the advertisements of a 'foreign' detective resident at Paddington Green. Ignatius Paul Pollacky, by birth an Australian, who established his agency in 1862. He achieved a fame embracing London as a whole: W.S. Gilbert's *Patience*, first performed on 23 April 1881, included among the qualities necessary to make a good heavy dragoon, that of 'the keen penetration of Paddington Pollacky'; he often advertised in the 'Agony Column' of *The Times* and when he died, aged ninety, that newspaper accorded him, on 28 Feb. 1918, a well-deserved flattering obituary. (I owe most of this information to the staff of that courteous journal.)

oh, rather! is a var. – an elab. – of *rather!*, meaning 'I should think so' (in reply to a question) and used by Dickens in 1836 (*OED*); late C19–20. Denis Mackail, *Greenery Street*, 1925, has '"Rather," said Ian enthusiastically, "Oh, rather!"'

Clearly not a c.p. when used as a conventionalism, a cliché; no less clearly and decidedly a c.p. when used ironically and satirically or when used in burlesque or 'send-up' or derision, and, as Playfair notes, 1977, when used as a c.p., it lays emphasis on the *-ther* of *rather*.

oh! sorry and all that! is a c.p. extension of the conventionalism *oh, sorry!* – itself an elab. of *sorry!* Both Brit. and Can. ('Heard long ago, but can give no date'; Leechman, 1968) – and also, I believe, but do not assert, Aus. and NZ. I heard it in England as long ago as the early 1920s. P.B.: in later C20, it sometimes hints at some insincerity in the apology.

oh, that's nice! forms a quietly severe comment on the far too frequent use of this feeble and inadequate remark evoked by some occurrence, where the expression sometimes verges upon the irrelevant and the incongruous, as in '"Mrs Huggett? I'm from the Gas Board." – "Oh, that's nice."' (John Sparry, 1977). The c.p. was occasioned by 'Meet the Huggetts', the 'saga of a working-class family' in which, 1953, Jack Warner and Kathleen Harris starred: a radio programme based on a series of popular films; the programme had 'a long and successful career' (Barry Took, *Laughter in the Air*, 1976). The c.p. was ob. by *c.* 1970; yet it is still [1978] heard – nostalgically.

oh, to be shot at dawn! 'A jesting colloquialism for anyone (including oneself) in trouble: ... shootings for desertion, cowardice, etc., taking place at that time' (B&P): military; Other Ranks': 1917–18. Cf **you'll be shot** ...

oh, well! back to the grindstone! 'indicates that it's time to resume work after a break' (Mrs Shirley M. Pearce, 1975): C20 and perhaps since *c.* 1880. Cf **back to the drawing board!**

oh, well, it's a way they have in the army. See **it's a way** ....

oh, well, you know how women (or, come to that, **men) are.** See **isn't that just like a man!**

oh, Willie! Willie! was, in 1898–*c.* 1914, a c.p. of 'satiric reproach addressed to a taradiddler rather than a flat liar' (Ware). Cf **Willie, Willie! wicked, wicked!**

oh, Winifred! was, during the 1890s among the lower and lower-middle classes, a c.p. expressing scepticism and disbelief. Ware derives it from the reputedly miraculous cures effected by the water 'from St Winifred's Well, in Wales'.

oh, wouldn't it be loverlee! was, in 1958–9, a c.p. beloved by teenagers of both sexes and by shopgirls and office girls. It comes from the title of one of Eliza Doolittle's songs in *My Fair Lady*. (Michael Gilderdale in his valuable 'Glossary for Our Times' pub'd in the *News Chronicle* on 22–3 May 1958.)

oh, yeah! Oh, no! *or* You think you know all about it. In *my* opinion, you don't. Adopted *c.* 1930, via 'the talkies', from the US; Brophy recorded it as a US c.p., but in the longer – perhaps the orig. – form, *oh, yeah! says you!*, and remarks 'An expression of scornful disbelief'. On 28 June 1934, the *Daily Mirror* headed an item 'Oh Yeah!'

HLM very briefly mentioned it in the definitive 4th ed., 1936; Berrey lists it thrice – once as synon. with 'I don't believe it!', then includes it among 'disparaging and sarcastic flings', and finally as a threat; W&F, 1960, without dating it in any other way than by inclusion in their dictionary, gloss it as 'an expression of challenge, incredulity, or sarcasm. In 1969, Leechman noted that in Canada it was 'very popular for a short time, *c.* 1940' and defined its Can., usage as 'an expression of complete disbelief, uttered in an exaggerated tone'. In an article pub'd late in 1972 and captioned 'Slang is Imaginative, Picturesque', Prof. S.J. Hayakawa included it in a short list of 'counter-words' (*sic*) or 'repetitively-used expressions that are a substitute for thought. A few years ago it was "Oh, yeah!"'

But the US use goes, I think, back to the middle, or even the early, 1920s. A good, fairly early example occurs in Clarence B Kelland's novel, *Speak Easily, c.* 1935: 'It was magnificently absurd.... I said as much to Mrs Post. "Oh, yeah?" she responded.' Which further exemplifies the fact that the ironical usage is emphasized by casting *oh, yeah* in the interrogative.

oh, yeah! says (often written **sez) you!** See prec. entry, opening paragraph.

oh, yes. I've been there. I know what I'm about: 'a popular slang expression and usage' (Farmer): US: *c.* 1875–1914. Of women, 'sexually experienced'; of men, 'shrewd; much-experienced'. Adopted in UK *c.* 1900; by *c.* 1940, †.

oh, you are awful! See **you're awful, but I like you.**

oh, you beautiful doll! began, in the US, as a song title, words by A. Seymour Brown, music by Nat D. Dyer, and composed in 1911. (Eric Townley, 1978.) As a c.p., it was still heard occ., even in UK, where it was, although not very gen., current for 25 years or so.

oh, you kid! In HLM, Supp. 2, Mencken excoriates its users in the judgment,

> the numerous catch phrases that have little if any precise meaning but simply delight the moron by letting him show that he knows the latest, *e.g.* 'How'd you like to be the ice-man?' – 'Wouldn't that jar you?' – 'O you kid' – 'Tell it to Sweeney' – 'Yes, we have no bananas' – 'Ish ka bibble' (and its twin, 'I should worry') – and 'Shoo fly, don't bother me'.

Apparently *c.* 1925–35, although it lingered on for some years, to give way, briefly, to *oh, you kiddo!*, recorded by Berrey, 1942, in a long list of interjections 'of approval and admiration'.

See also **I love my wife** ...

oi, oi!, used in a particular tone of voice, interrupts or remonstrates with a speaker who is laying down the law. (Camilla Raab.) This entry elicited from Playfair, 1977, an amplification I cannot resist quoting: 'I would regard this as an exclamation rather than a c.p. In either case, it has really two separate uses. The English one, expressing incredulity (as often as not, mock incredulity), is spoken rather slowly: "'Oy, oy, what's going on here?' they joke" (*Guardian*, 5 Sep. 1977). The US Yiddish one is spoken rather fast, with a multitude of meanings, which are dealt with fully by [Leo] Rosten, *The Joys of Yiddish*, [1968,] pp. 280–1. The spelling *oy* is probably preferable – certainly the *Guardian* thinks so.'

oil-bombs. See: I'll be laughing.

oil for the lamps of China. 'This used to be said (I remember it in the 1940s – not much since) when you received a windfall of any sort, particularly on winning a big pot at poker. Of a small pot won, they would say "little fishes are sweet"' (Skehan, 1977). My own memory of it belongs to the 1920s, and as already familiar. But why China? I don't know: I merely guess that the ref. is to famous Chinese ware. P.B.: *little fish are sweet* is listed in the *Concise Oxford Dict. of Proverbs*, with first citation 1830. Cf the old phrase, more or less synon., *corn in Egypt*.

oild, oild story – the, refers to the drivel drooled by the drunk: since *c.* 1950. This c.p. is at once a pun on 'the old, old story' and on the slang '(well) *oiled*', tipsy.

oilskins. See: surprised?

oily rag. See: I'm speaking; living on the.

okay, baby! This US c.p., dating since at least as early as 1920, had become at least partly adopted in UK by 1932 or 1933; there was, for instance, a letter pub'd in the *Daily Mirror* of 7 Nov. 1933, apparently indicating anglicization. R.C., 1978, notes, 'Long dead in US'.

okay by me! – it's. Another US c.p. adopted in UK at the same period as *okay, baby!* It had been adopted in Can. by *c.* 1930. The interrogative **okay by you?** might also be classified as a c.p. 'The "by me" marks it as one of the many loan translations from the Yiddish (*bei mir*)' (R.C., 1978). P.B.: Playfair maintains that it was never naturalized in Britain, but I have heard it often enough here, as well as the perhaps more usu. form *okay with me*, to think it was. But both are surely simply idiomatic rather than c.p.

okay, sheaf. An Aus. pun on, and a synon. of, *okay, chief:* since *c.* 1930. Baker notes that it is a New South Wales 'advertising slogan that has won some currency. From Tooth's Sheaf Stout'. By 1970, very slightly ob.

okey-doke! A teenagers' and semi-literates' reduplication of slang *oke*, itself a var. of *okay*. Orig. (*c.* 1938) US, it reached UK *c.* 1940. In Terence Rattigan's *Separate Tables*, 1955, in the section titled 'Table by the Window', when Doreen – a maid in service at Miss Cooper's Beauregard Private Hotel – enters the dining room, the following exchange takes place:

DOREEN: Yes. miss? (*Seeing John.*) Oh, you back? I suppose you think you can have breakfast at this time?
MISS COOPER: Just some tea, Doreen – that's all.
DOREEN: Okey doke.

Shipley, 1977, notes, 'Often extended to *okey-dokey*'; in UK too, but there regarded as somewhat trivial. Also 'extended to *okey-dokey, pokey-lokey*, when someone seems to be intentionally slow to act' (A.B., 1978).

old. See: if they're big; it was on; not so old; too old; ve get; and:

old army game – it's an (or **the**). J.W.C. thinks it orig. in the army and referred to some simple but tricky card game popular among soldiers. He also says: 'It became extended (in this country [i.e., the US]) to any unfairness or favouritism committed (often maliciously or venally) by military superiors, especially in the manipulation of red tape, and even to red tape ... itself; then to any such thing, *not* military' (1975).

Through Col. Moe, 1975, Mr Jonathan Lighter quotes George William Small, *Story of the Forty-Seventh* (47th Coast Artillery, 1918), pub. in 1919: 'Name: Mech. Johnson. Nickname: Adley. Favorite Saying: "The Old Army Game".' And Carl Sandburg, *Good Morning, America*, 1928, Has:

Since we have coined a slogan. Never give the sucker an even break and the Old Army Game goes—
Let the dance go on...

It also occurs in Theodore Fredenburgh, *Soldiers March*, 1930:

'Do you get the idea?'
'Sure I get the idea. It's the old army game: first, pass the buck; second, never give a sucker an even break ...'

And Leonard Hastings Nason, in *A Corporal Once*, 1930, uses the phrase *the old army game* at least three times.

Mr Lighter, by the way, says, 'As far as I know, it's always *the*, never *an*' – to which Moe rightly rejoins that he has, over many years, 'heard "an" as frequently as "the" in [this] phrase' and implies – what I'm pretty sure is the correct view – that, as is entirely expectable, whereas *the* is generic, *an* is particular.

But the whole matter is so complicated that this entry should be compared with **it's an old army game.**

old as my tongue and a little older than my teeth (– as). A smart – orig. a fashionable, evasive – reply to 'How old are you?': late C17–20; by *c.* 1930, slightly old-fashioned but far from †. Recorded in Grose, 1788, it had already been

aspic-in-amber'd by S, 1738, in the opening Dialogue, where the pertly charming Miss Notable uses it. 'Current in US from before 1900; now either ob. or †' (R.C., 1978).

old college try. See: give it the.

old enough to know better is a predominantly feminine reply to 'How old are you?': since late – ? rather, mid – C19 – 20. 'Occasionally dovetailed with *but young enough to do it anyway*' (R.C.) or '... *young enough to do more*' (A.B.: both, 1978). Cf the prec. entry.

old hat. See **it's old hat.**

old John, always on blob (or **ready to spit**; or **with a wet nose**): a low naval c.p., directed at a mature rating of unhygienic habits. P.B.: the refs are to gonorrhoea.

old man. See: can't have; ole; so is your; you dirty; your old; and:

old man is allowed (occ., **accorded**) **two privileges: a bad memory and a weak bladder – an.** I remember it since *c.* 1920 and would suppose it to have arisen early in C20.

old man must be working overtime – the. In ref. to a man with a very large family: mostly lower-middle class: C20. Here, the *old man* is 'husband'.

old Mother Hubbard. See **that's old Mother Hubbard.**

old Newton got (or **took**) **him:** with *old* occ. omitted. He crashed, esp. if fatally: RAF c.p. applied to a pilot suffering this fate: since *c.* 1925. Isaac Newton discovered the laws of gravity: and the pull of gravity is implacable.

old, old story. See **oild, oild story – the.**

old one-two. See: give it the old.

old ships, leaky ships. In the RN this has, since the late 1940s, been the standard, often derisive, reply both to the rather older *a last ship's the best ship*, dating from, I think, WW1, and to nostalgic reminiscences about 'the good old days', an ageless cliché that must, in sentiment, go back to tales about the sea-worthiness of Noah's Ark. (The factual element: Peppitt, 1976.)

old soldier: old shit; and old soldiers: old cunts. A Regular, then gen., Army c.p.: since 1914. A gloss on the latter: an exacerbated sergeant or sergeant-major often adds, 'You ain't even that: a cunt *is* useful.' The former 'was the usual reply to a man who tried to claim superiority by reason of his long service' (Frank Roberts in PGR). Cf the second verse of the song in the next entry.

P.V. Harris recalls, from his WW1 service, that 'Young soldiers were said to use "Old Soldier, old shite", to which the veteran would reply, "Young soldier, have a bite!"'

old soldiers never die: they simply fade away has been extracted from the British Army's C20 parody of the song 'Kind Thoughts Can Never Die' and the tune adopted from it:

Old soldiers never die,
Never die,
Never die,
Old soldiers never die –
They simply fade away.
Old soldiers never die,
Never die,
Never die,
Old soldiers never die –
Young ones wish they would.

This immortal ditty appeared in B & P and has been preserved in *The Long Trail*, lamentably out of print in Britain, but to be reprinted in the US.

It was 'given its first familiarity in US in a speech by General [Douglas] MacArthur on his recall from Korea; still not forgotten' (J.W.C., 1977). R.C. fixes the date of the speech thus: 'Its most famous usage being at the conclusion of [MacArthur's] "farewell address" to the US Congress, 1952. Often humorously paraphrased, as in "Old golfers never die: they just lose their balls"'. P.B.: *only* is often substituted for *simply*, as in another parody, 'Old soldiers never die: they only smell that way'.

old soldiers: old cunts. See **old soldier ...**

old Southern (or **Spanish**) **custom – it's an.** See **it's an old ...**

old woman. See: every little helps; that won't pay.

ole man Know-All died las' year. A US c.p. of late C19–early 20. A gentle intimation that the addressee shouldn't think he 'knows it all'! Source: Joel Chandler Harris's Uncle Remus stories (1881–1906). Remus, a gloriously natural 'old darkie', uses it esp. to Br'er Rabbit and other characters. (Shipley, who dates it for the year 1881, and says, in 1977, that he heard it 'a couple of years ago, used to check an over-positive man'.)

olive oil! A c.p. perversion of *au revoir!* According to Ware, it orig. in a music-hall in 1884; ob. by 1937 (see *DSUE*); † by 1960 at latest. Some currency in the US during the 1930s–40s, and closely comparable with *au reservoir!* (Fain, 1977.)

olly, olly! was, among Cockney schoolchildren of c. 1870–1920, an invitation to a friend, or a companion, to play a game with, or to accompany, oneself; occ. a farewell.

Hence, among all Cockneys, 'a shout of greeting or recognition, usually with a broad, rumbustious, freebooting leer to it' (L.A.): C20.

Perhaps from *ho there!* or from Fr. *allez* (or even both) – rather than from Spanish *olé! olé!*

P.B.: Iona and Peter Opie, in their masterly study *The Lore and Language of Schoolchildren*, 1959, list *olly-olly-ee* among a number of terms used to claim a truce or 'breather'; some others were *creamos, creamy-olivers* and *ollyoxalls*. Their source for this set was the Southern Grammar School for Girls, Portsmouth. My wife, who spent her young childhood in North London, remembers, from the 1940s, a call to end a game *all-y, all-y , all in free*, and to judge from one of Charles M. Schulz's 'Peanuts' cartoon-strips, a version of this exists in US.

omelette. See: day the o.

on a cat's back. See more hair there...

on a hiding to nothing, usu. prec. by *he's* or *they're.* Bound to be defeated: (?) since c. 1960, but very much in the vogue early and mid 1970s. 'Common. I suspect mainly political or business. It appeared in a headline in *The Sunday Times*, 25 Sep. 1977' (Playfair).

on a wing and a prayer. See **we got back on a wing...**

on behalf of the committee-ee! 'Colin Crompton as the concert chairman of ITV's *Wheeltappers And Shunters Social Club*. Colin says: "Letters by the score told me my catchphrases were a schoolteachers' nightmare"' (*VIBS*).

on behalf of the working classes! 'Music-hall comedian Billy Russell (1893–1971)' (*VIBS*).

on for young and old. See **it was on for...**

on guard!, from fencing or sword-play, often accompanies a mock-threatening thrust with ruler, stick or other makeshift 'weapon'. In the British Army, 1950s–60s, it was as frequently countered by the neatly punning riposte, *can't! I was on guard last might.* (P.B.)

on my shit list – he's (or occ. **you're** or **they're**). 'Condemnation of fellow-worker or Serviceman who plays underhand trick on [one of] the group' (L.A., 1974): since c. 1940. A pun on *be on the short list* for an appointment to a job or for promotion. P.B. comments, 1976, 'The "old soldier" RSM of a large Signals unit, mid 1950s, was remembered for some years after his departure for two phrases: "You're right at the top of my shit-list, bruvver!" and the (?) semi-proverbial "Brasses cleaned by candlelight should be inspected by moonlight"'.

R.C., 1978, writes: 'US also since c. 1940 or earlier. I question the derivation (at least so far as US is concerned), since "short list" is strictly British. Rather, "He's on my list of shits" or possibly "list of those to be shat upon at every opportunity". The late sensational newspaper publisher, W.R. Hearst [1863–1951], was notorious for keeping "shit lists" of public figures who displeased him and whose names were therefore forbidden for mention in his newspapers'. J.W.C.'s gloss, 1977, is well worth quoting: ' "He's my enemy," often with implied determination to get even; but

the reason for the enmity is not necessarily an *underhand* action, but merely hostile, or even one not favoured by the speaker'.

P.B.: I'd always thought of it as a vulgar version of the gangsters' *hit-list*.

on parade, on parade; off parade, off parade, with *on* and *off* emphasized. A Regular, then a general, Army c.p. of late C19–20: 'or, in ordinary speech, "Keep your mind on your job"' (B&P). The literal sense is clearly: formal on duty, informal off it. (BBC radio programme 'Stop the Week', 17 Oct. 1977.)

on pleasure bent. A Can. c.p. applied to a bandy-legged girl or young woman: since c. 1920. A crooked *gradus ad vulvam.* P.B.: cf the equally bawdy term applied to a bandy-legged man: *bollocks in parenthesis.*

on second thoughts I thought it best to put it in the old oak chest was 'heard during WW2 when the speaker was in danger of losing his temper or of over-hasty speech' (Sanders, 1974).

It comes from the chant very popular with British soldiers during WW1 and dating back, I gathered during that war, some ten or twenty years earlier. Those words, however, formed only part of a mock-heroic chant that ran:

Today's my daughter's wedding day.
Ten thousand pounds I'll give away.
(Three ironic cheers from the audience.)
On second thoughts I think it best
To put it away in the old oak chest.
(Audience): Yer mingy bastard! Chuck him aht!, etc.

on that (rousing) note I will close. 'Originally, the orotund conclusion of a public speech. Later (? 1920s) a facetious way of ending a conversation. Now obsolescent' (R.C., 1978): US.

on the Erie. Shut up! Someone's listening: US underworld: since c. 1920. With a pun either on the *Erie* Canal or, as R.C. suggests, the Erie Railroad [E.P.'s orig. idea was on Lake Erie], and esp. on slang *eary,* with ears straining – usu. applied to habitual eavesdroppers. The genesis may, by association both phonetic and semantic, have been *on the eary – eerie – Erie.* (For sources and quotations, see my *U.*) R.C., 1978, amplifies his amendment thus: 'I suggest the reference is rather to the Erie Railroad, during its life normally referred to as "The Erie" – as Lake never was or is. In late C19, the railroad won much notoriety as the scene of financial manipulations spectacular even for The Gilded Age'.

on the stairs! was, c. 1860–1914, a tailors' c.p. in reply to a call for someone to do a particular job. Cf **up in Annie's room.**

on the wire at Mons or **Loos;** hence, **on the old barbed wire.** See **hanging on...**

on the wrong side of the fence or **hedge.** See **wrong side of the hedge.**

on with the motley! is a quot'n become c.p., used as an encouraging signal to begin a party, an expedition to the theatre, etc.: C20. It comes from Leoncavallo Ruggiero's opera *I Pagliacci*, 1892: 'Camio's grief over his betrayal by Nedda finds expression in one of the most famous numbers in Italian opera, "Vesti la giubba" (On with the motley), with its tragic "Ridi Pagliacco" ... it is the old and ever effective story of the buffoon who must laugh, and make others laugh, while his heart is breaking' (*Kobbé's Complete Opera Book*, rev. ed.).

The synon. *On with the show!* 'has been "guyed" as *let us proceed with the libretto*: US: since c. 1970' (A.B., 1978).

on you! Hullo!: Aus.: since c. 1925. As in
'Hiya, Curly. Hi, Ronnie,' I said...
'On yuh, Terry,' said Curly.
Perhaps from *good on you!,* 'Well done!'

on your (often yer) bike! Off you go! Go away!: since c. 1960. (Anthony Burgess, in the *Listener*, 2 Mar, 1967.) With an intimation that promptness and speed are advisable. P.B.: given fresh popularity by some political slanging matches under Mrs Thatcher's government of the early 1980s.

The now ob. US version is *on your horse* (R.C., 1978).

once. See: I'll try.

once a knight, always a knight: twice a night, dead at forty! A witty c.p., the 'twice a night' referring, of course, to sexual intercourse and the implication being 'as a regular thing'. Since *c.* 1950 at latest, but prob. from at least fifty years earlier. P.B.: a version current in the mid-1950s was *once a king, always a king: but once a (k)night and you'd be dead within a fortnight* (fings, obviously, ain't wot they useter be!); A.B., 1978, notes the US *once a knight, always a knight: but once a night's enough*. E.P. added that there is implied a pun on 'sexually *mounted*' – well, perhaps.

J.W.C., 1977, however, for the US provides *once a Mason, always a Mason, once a Knight's enough,* the ref. being to Freemasons and to Knights of Columbus, two organizations that, formerly, were mutually exclusive, but adds, 'In these ecumenical days, Roman Catholics are permitted to become Masons'.

once aboard the lugger and the girl is mine. A male c.p., either joyous or derisively joc., of late C19–20. It is based on a passage in Ben Landeck's melodrama, *My Jack and Dorothy*, which, prod. at the Elephant and Castle theatre *c.* 1889–90, ran for many years, as the late Julian Franklyn, who knew a great deal about the 'Transpontine' or Surreyside theatres, once informed me. In 1908 A.S.M. Hutchinson's novel, *Once Aboard the Lugger – the History of George and Mary,* strengthened the impact made by the play. By 1970, very slightly ob.

Cohen attributes it to John Benn Johnstone (1803–91) in *The Gipsy Farmer,* in the passage: 'I want you to assist me in forcing her on board the lugger; once there, I'll frighten her into marriage'; and says that this has since been quoted as 'Once aboard the lugger and the girl is mine.'

once before we fill and once before we light was a drinking c.p. of early C18. Ned Ward recorded it in *The London Spy,* 1709.

once is enough! has, throughout the C20, been applied by widowers, a few widows and divorced people – to marriage. It was canonized when, in 1938, one of Frederick Lonsdale's witty comedies was prod. as *Once Is Enough*. (The year before, it had appeared in New York as *Half a Loaf*.) It is sometimes elab. *once around is enough,* and may of course be applied to experiences other than marriage.

once is funny, twice isn't. 'Comment on a belabored jest. Current from 1920s, but now ob. or even †' (R.C., 1978).

once round auntie, twice round the gasworks (occ., **gasometer**) is applied to a woman enormously fat: mostly urban: C20.

once wounded, twice as windy was, in 1915–18, current among British soldiers, esp. the Other Ranks. This is the slang *windy,* 'having the wind up' (timorous, very much afraid), so widely used during, and for some years after, WW1. P.B.: a warriors' version of the old proverb *once bitten, twice shy*.

once you've seen one, you've seen the lot. See **when you've seen one, you've seen the lot.**

one-armed. See: busy as a one-; like a one-.

one at a time. A (mostly fox-) hunting c.p. of *c.* 1820–70, if not much longer. In R.S. Surtees, *Handley Cross; or, Mr Jorrocks's Hunt,* 2 vols, 1854, we read, at the chapter titled 'Another Sporting Lector' (lecture): 'And "One at a time, and it will last the longer!" is a knowin' exclamation to make to a hundred and fifty friends waitin' for their turns at an 'unting wicket.' (A sort of turnstile.)

'During, and for a while after, WW2 current with the tail, *gentlemen, please,* relating to a mythical Land Girl (member of the Women's Land Army], knocked unconscious with a swish of its tail by the cow she was milking' (R.S., 1978).

one consecutive night was, *c.* 1890–1915, a Society and theatrical c.p., meaning 'enough'. Ware cites the *Daily News* of 15 Aug. 1890.

one damned thing after another. See **life is just one...**

one drink and the boat sails is writes Ashley, 1979, applied, in the US, to a person easily inebriated. Cf the Brit. *one sniff at the barmaid's apron.*

one-eyed. See: there's a one-.

one flash and you're ash. 'A c.p. used about the atomic bomb and the hydrogen bomb' (B.P., 1974): Aus.: since 1945.

one foot in the grave and the other on a banana skin. See **you've got one foot....**

one for the book, often prec. by **that's.** As an RAF c.p., it dates from the early 1920s and refers to *the lines,* or *line book,* which was kept in the Mess for the recording of gross exaggerations made by its members and was 'sometimes called a "Shooting Gallery"' (C.H. Ward-Jackson, *It's a Piece of Cake,* 1943); the latter name for the book derives from RAF slang *shoot a line,* to boast, to exaggerate shamelessly.

But much better known is the gen. c.p., (*that's*) *one for the book,* applied to 'a joke so funny or an event so extraordinary, that it deserves inclusion in "the book" – Joe Miller's Jest Book' (Leechman): orig. US, Berrey recording it in 1942 as meaning 'that is something of account', it had, by the late 1950s, become popular in Can. and, by *c.* 1955, in UK. In Clarence B. Kelland's amusing novel, *Speak Easily, c.* 1935, occurs this example:

'Sam slapped Sim on the back, and Sim countered by slapping Sam. 'That's one for the book!' said the latter.
'Ain't he the wise-crackin' kid!'

Since the late 1950s in Can., and by *c.* 1962 in UK, the phrase had acquired the var., (*that's*) *one for the record,* – with ref. to a book of records (in e.g. athletics).

Contrast **what a turn-up for the book!**

one for the road (– and) is a C20 – orig. commercial travellers' – c.p., either applied to the last of several drinks or proposing a final drink to keep one warm on the journey. The RN has the derivative *one for the gangway,* applied to a drink offered a guest just before he leaves the ship by the gangway (Granville). See also **satu empat jalan.**

one from column A, one from column B. 'A selection: after [uninformed] choices in a Chinese [restaurant] men' (Ashley, 1982): US: later C20.

one hand for the King (or **Queen**) **and one for oneself; and two hands for the King** (or **Queen**). These are C20 RN lowerdeck mottoes. In 1968, Rear-Adm. P.W. Brock wrote to tell me that he dated the two phrases as arising in mid C19; he added: 'In contrast to the maxim attributed to the Merchant Navy, "One hand for the ship and one for yourself", meaning that a man aloft should keep one hand on the jackstay for his own safety and use the other for handling the sail.' Of *two hands for the King* (or *Queen*), he remarked that it 'was used by a young officer or rating showing undue caution aloft'. The Merchant Navy's phrase appears in Bowen.

one hundred and twenty (usu. written **120**) **in the water bag.** An Aus. c.p. current in C20 and applied to an extremely hot day (120 degrees Fahrenheit).

one-legged. See: tell that to a o.

one lordship is worth all his manners. 'His manners are perfect, but a lordship counts for more than manners.' An English c.p. of C17 – the pun clearly being on *manors*. It occurs in Ray.

one never knows, does one? You never can tell!: a playfully ironic c.p., dating from the later 1930s; slightly derisive of its literal, pompous use. Benny Green, reviewing the first ed. of this book, in *Spectator,* 10 Sep. 1977, writes that it 'is the title of a song written by Harry Revel and Mack Gordon for a 1936 [motion] picture called *Stowaway*; it was later apotheosized by the great jazz singer Billy Holiday'.

one night with Venus led to a lifetime with Mercury. 'Heard in the days when mercury was the cure for venereal disease. From an article in *The Freethinker* of Sep. 1968' (Petch). Perhaps *c.* 1860–1910 and prob. either a medical or a raffish club-men's c.p.

one now and again would break the monotony. See **you can't win them all.**

one o'clock. See: like one.

one (or **two** or **three...**) **o'clock at the waterworks.** An Aus. warning that one or more of one's fly buttons are undone: C20. Waterworks = one's urinary apparatus. cf. synon. **medal showing!**

one of my mob (**– he's**). 'He's my sort of person' or 'He and I have much or, at least, something in common': Aus: since the late 1940s. Written by Fred Parsons for Roy Rene – 'a headliner from 1920 to 1955' as a stage comedian and then also a radio star. As Roy Rene orig. used it, it applied to a fellow-Jew, but it 'came to mean to the [Australian] public someone with whom you have something in common', as I learned from Mr Harry Griffiths, who had played the part of 'Young Harry' in Rene's 'Mo' sketches in the *McCackie Mansions* radio series, part of the *Calling the Stars* programme. (In a long, delightful, instructive letter, 1978.) Cf **cop this, young 'Arry.**

one of ours; and **put that light out!** From the WW2 remark and the WW2 order, came these two c.pp. uttered when a sudden, loud (esp. if very loud) noise is heard; but whereas the former fell into disuse *c.* 1960, the latter is still, in 1976, no worse than ob. Although *one of ours,* one of our heavy shells, had arisen in WW1, or one of our aircraft, or one of our bombs, arose in WW2, the phrase didn't – at least, so far as I remember – become a c.p. until *c.* 1944.

Of *one of ours,* it is to be noted that the phrase started during the Ger. air-raids on Britain during 1940–1, to be reinforced when well-meaning air-raid wardens reassured the timorous by suggesting that the crump of a bomb was merely the bark of an anti-aircraft gun – as if anyone but a fool could confuse the two sounds.

But *put that light out!* had enjoyed – and I mean *enjoyed* – an entirely independent existence and sense, usu., as *put the light out!*, since late C19. When, at a private party or even a social gathering, a couple showed unmistakably that they wished they could be alone, some wag, usu. male, cried, 'Put the light out!' – which became, in certain circumstances, rather a c.p. than either a cliché or a piece of low IQ'd traditional waggishness.

Eric Fearon adds, 1984, that the 'RAF WW2 answer to *put that light out!* was often a chant, at first in a squeaky imitation of a female voice, and then a gruff one: "It's the moonlight, flight-sergeant." "I don't give a damn, put it out."'

one of the mounted is a raffish c.p., dating from *c.* 1945 and applied to a female successful in 'getting her man'. Clearly a punning ref. to the old saying – prob., at first, a proud claim – that 'the Mounties always get their man', the Mounties being the Royal Canadian Mounted Police.

one of these dark nights, with *there'll be dirty work at the crossroads* placed either before or after: since *c.* 1910. The connotation is sexual, the tone joc. Cf **dirty work...**, both in this book, and in *DSUE*.

one of these fine days, with slight emphasis on *one*, is ironic for 'That's *most* unlikely to happen': since *c.* 1950. Cf *that will be the day* or ... *the frosty Friday*, and *I should live so long!* (Camilla Raab, 1977.) Contrast **one of those fine days.** *One of These Fine Days* was chosen as the title of her memoirs, 1982, by Myfanwy, daughter of that fine poet Edward Thomas.

one of these fine mornings you'll wake up and find yourself dead. An Anglo-Irish C20 c.p., either joc. or derisive – or both.

one of these odd-come-shortlies. In Dialogue I of S, 1738, we find:

COL[ONEL]: Miss, when will you be married?
MISS: One of these odd-come-shortlies, Colonel.

Current throughout C18–19 and, although ob. by 1920, not yet quite †, the phrase means rather 'oh! some day, I suppose' than 'some day soon', even though, lit., it must orig. have meant 'one of these odd days shortly to come'. It is applied to an event one cannot yet date.

one of these wet days. 'Said by a busy housewife when she is asked when she is going to get round to doing some neglected

chore' (Petch, 1978): since *c.* 1910 – and not only among housewives.

one of those days, frequently intro. by **it was** or **it has been** (or **it's been**) or **it is** (or **it's**). Elliptical for 'one of those days, when everything goes (or has gone) or went wrong'; or merely 'a hectic day': since the 'smart young things' of the 1920s. John Wainwright's exciting 'thriller', *Cause for a Killing*, 1974, begins thus: 'It was (as the saying goes) one of those days'. Cf **it's just one of those days.**

one of those things. See **it's just one....**

one of us. See: **he's one.**

one of you two are both knaves. S, Dialogue III, 1738, has:
LORD SM[ART]: But, pray Gentlemen, why always so severe upon poor Miss. On my Conscience, Colonel, and *Tom Neverout*, one of you two are both Knaves.

That is, 'both of you are Knaves': a witticism of *c.* 1700–50. This c.p. belongs to those trenchantly illogical witticisms exemplified by 'There are two fools born every minute – and he is all three of them'.

one of your team is playing a man short, often intro. by **I see** (**that**), has, since *c.* 1920, been joc. addressed to a youth sporting an eleven [hairs]-a-side moustache. It derives rather from Association football than from cricket.

Cf **swear it with butter...**

one squint is better than two finesses. This is, in the game of bridge (at not quite the highest levels), a c.p. warning one's partner that their opponents are trying to see his hand: mostly Anglo-Irish: since the early 1920s.

one star: one stunt was, in 1916–18, an extremely frequent c.p. of the entire British Army, but esp. among officers: a newly promoted officer's uniform singled him out in any raid or attack. In WW2, the officer's battle-dress was the same as the Other Ranks'. P.B. it refers of course to the extreme vulnerability of newly commissioned second lieutenants.

one that got away – the. At first, early in C20, derisive of anglers boasting about the fish that escaped and, oddly, remarkable for its size or its speed or its cunning; and then, since *c.* 1945, applied to someone who has providentially escaped some great danger, as, for instance, a bachelor from a female predator. 'In US, I'd say 1920s to 1950' (A.B., 1978).

one that lives within a mile of an oak. Not far away. See S, 1738, towards the end of Dialogue I:

MISS: Well, who was it?
NEV[EROUT]: Why, one that lives within a Mile of an Oak.
MISS: Well: go hang yourself in your own Garter...

Current for a very long period: late C16–mid C19. The c.p. derives from the proverbial saying. (Apperson and others.)

P.B. an early 1980s version is (*some*) *one not a million miles away from* (named location): affected by gossip-columnists, sports writers, and the like.

Cf **within a mile...**

one toot and you're oot. Not a word from *you*, please!: current in UK since *c.* 1910 (as R.S. assures me) and in Aus. since *c.* 1950 (B.P.). Mock Scots dialect: the genuine dialectal form is *ae toot and ye're oot,* orig. 'uttered by an elder of the Kirk to an old lady who appeared in a church with her ear-trumpet' (James R. Sutherland, 1977). R.S. thinks the joke may have appeared in *Punch,* and Ashley, 1979, from the US, recalls 'an old man with an ear-trumpet'. The scene of the story varies: Sir Edward Playfair recalls his mother telling it in the 1920s about the chairman of a meeting to a member of the audience with, of course, an ear-trumpet.

one-track mind. See: **you've got a....**

[ONE-WORD CATCH PHRASES are not entirely a contradiction in terms, for usually they represent, either punningly or elliptically or formatively, a true phrase; or, expressed differently, when they stand, either phonetically or semantically, or both, for a true phrase.

Eleven that come immediately to mind are: *Abyssinia – Arboath* (ephemeral) – *attaboy,* q.v. – *curtains!* (see **cur-**

tains for you!) – *ishkabibble* (see **ish ka bibble**) – *period*, q.v. – *quoz*, q.v. – *Roger*, q.v. – *scrubbers*, q.v. – *snap*, q.v. – *wilco*, q.v.

These being *marginalia* to the subject, there clearly must be a limit to the inclusion of this particular freak. But I cannot resist the temptation to quote P.B., 1977: 'A couple more of your favourite paradox, the one-word c.p. [These were] used by Radio/TV comedian Norman Vaughan in his Sunday evening TV shows, late 1961–early 1962:
Swingin: accompanied by a thumb-up gesture of the right hand, held fairly low and moved from side to side in approbation, and
Dodgy: disapprobation.
P.B.: another one, missed by E.P., that ought to be in is *pass!*, the formula by which contestants show inability to answer the quiz-questions in 'Mastermind' (See **I've started, so I'll finish**); now used (early 1980s) in 'real life'.]

one word from you and he (or **she**) **does as he** (or **she**) **likes.** (Other pronominal variations are obviously possible – and no less obviously employed; but they're very much less employed.) He or she ignores your commands or orders or instructions: C20. Sarcastically derived from 'One word from me (etc.) is enough' or, less frequently, 'one word from me and he obeys'.

one you miss is the one you never get – the. A somewhat ambiguous, because slovenly, way of saying 'The one you regret is the one you missed' (failed to achieve, forwent) – or, as B.P., 1975, neatly put it, 'A sexual opportunity neglected is gone for ever': C20: perhaps orig. Aus.

onion boat. See: came over.

[**only a fool argues with a skunk, a mule, or a cook,** used among cowboys, lies midway between a potential proverb (homespun philosophy) and a c.p. It occurs as the epigraph to the letter *C* in Ramon Adams's fascinating *Western Words* without mention of authorship or other source and no indication of its period of currency, so one could only hazard 'late C19–mid 20'.]

only a little clean shit is derisively addressed to one who has been either bedaubed or self-fouled with excreta: C19–20. In Scotland, they understandably prefer . . . *dirt*.

only a rumour! It's much worse than that! Aus.: since c. 1919. (Baker.) Cf **it's a rumour**.

only another penny (needed) to make – or **make up** – **the shilling.** Used mostly by persons collecting money, esp. for a good cause: C20. With the advent of metrication, already 'on the way out' by 1974.

only asses make passes at lasses who wear glasses. Since c. 1960. An alteration and elab. of Dorothy Parker's 'Men seldom make passes/At girls who wear glasses'. (Petch, 1974.)

only birds can fornicate and fly (with 'simultaneously' understood). 'Just an old saying the unromantic RAF had: "only birds can fornicate and fly. And birds don't booze"' (Gavin Lyall, *Shooting Script*, 1966): WW2 – and after.
'Cf the usually exasperated and heartfelt, rather seldom jocular, "Go and take a flying fuck (at yourself)"' (P.B., 1976). The latter is not a fully qualified c.p., but merely a ribald and elab. objurgation.
Cf, with the orig., *birds and fools fly, and birds don't fly at night*: RAF: 1930s and prob. before. 'Familiar among nightflying crews' (ex Sqn. Ldr. Vernon Noble, 1978). Ashley, 1982, attests the use of this dictum among members of the RCanAF, with *airmen* substituted for *fools*, and J.E. Horrocks, of Cumbria, in a letter to the *Guardian* (date now lost), quotes the phrase as *only birds and fools fly – and only owls would fly at night*.

only eating a good soldier's rations was, in 1914–18, applied by British, esp. English, soldiers to inferior soldiers; implying that that's all they were good for.

only here for the beer. See **I'm only here...**

only place you'll find sympathy is in the dictionary. See TAD DORGAN.

only pretty Fanny's way. Characteristic: Parnell, c. 1718, has

'And all that's madly wild, or oddly gay,/We call it only pretty Fanny's way' (cited by the *OED*): C18–19. Prob. a topical elab. of 'only her (*or* his) way'.

only river in the world that flows upside down – the. The Yarra River: Aus., esp. in NSW and particularly in Sydney: since the mid 1940s. Explained thus in Jan Smith's *An Ornament of Grace*, 1966, '...Melbourne, the only city in the world where the river flows upside down with the mud on top' (Wilkes, *Dict. Aus. Coll.*). Cf **stinking Yarra!** and **too thick to drink**, qq.v.

only stage you'll ever get on is the Liverpool landing-stage – the. A theatrical c.p., addressed to an aspirant: C20. Gladys Cooper in a BBC TV interview, 3 Oct. 1976.

only way to tell their sex is to get them in the dark – the. 'Heard today in reference to the difficulty in telling whether youngsters are male or female' (Petch, 1974): since the early 1960s. Sanders, 1978, adds, 'Also, "to tell them apart, you need a search warrant"—used of schoolchildren before it was common for boys to wear their hair long and for both sexes to wear jeans'.

only when I laugh (often written – heaven know why! – *larf*). Elliptical for the literal 'It hurts only when I laugh'; but as a c.p., gaining a wider applicability, it has an overtone of irony: as a c.p., not much, if at all, before c. 1950. In 1968, Len Deighton increased the popularity of the phrase by titling one of his novels *Only When I Larf*. It was the title of a Brit. film released in the same year. Ashley, 1979, comments, 'from a joke about a stoic Briton speared in darkest Africa' – i.e. it mocks traditional British 'stiff-upperlippery'.

only your laundryman knows for sure – whether you wet or foul your underpants, your pyjamas, etc.: applied to, e.g., 'scared shitless' during air raids over Vietnam: US: since c. 1965. Paul Janssen cites Tom Wolfe, *Mauve Gloves*, 1976. P.B.: for the phrase's prob. origin., see Nigel Rees, *Slogans*, 1982, p. 57, concerning the genesis of the US hair-tinting manufacturer's Clairol's slogan, current from c. 1955: 'Does she...Or doesn't she?/Only her hairdresser knows for sure'. Rees's postscript to the story is worth quoting here: '"J" underlines the double-meaning implicit in the slogan with this comment from *The Sensuous Woman*: "Our world has changed. It's no longer a question of 'Does she or doesn't she?' We all know she wants to, is about to, or does." A New York graffito, quoted 1974: "Only *his* hairdresser knows for sure".'

oo-la-la! See **oh, la! la!**

ooh, an' 'e was strong! 'From a late '40's radio show, I think "Ray's a Laugh". A weekly "situation" was made to lead up to this c.p.' (P.B., 1975); the 'gag' became – promptly became – a c.p. *VIBS*, however, attributes the phrase to comedian Al Read.

oompah, oompah, stuff (or **stick**) **it up your jumper!** A joc. derisive declaration of contempt for a crazy suggestion; an expression of defiance or of lighthearted dismissal. It arose during the 1920s, occurred frequently throughout WW2 and is still (1978) extant, although mostly archaic and somewhat nostalgic. From the blare of trumpet, trombone, brass or other noisy band.
By itself, *Oompah, Oompah* 'was a song written and sung by Leslie Sarony and Leslie Holmes in the 1930s' (Anon., 1978). The orig. pronunciation, as in this song, was apparently *umper, umper*, to accord with *jumper*; if this pron. was indeed so, the *oompah* version was, at first, a 'take-off', perhaps even mock-affected, as the same anon. contributor has suggested.
On the other hand, Noble, 1978, very firmly comments, '[It] was popular in WW2, as you say, but I really couldn't acknowledge this as a c.p.: it's just a comic repetition of a jingle without significance'. Perhaps we have here yet another instance of *Quot homines, tot sententiae*.
P.B.: *oompah, oompah* may now be very dated, but *stick it up your jumper!* is alive and well, certainly among the

middle-aged, as a polite euph. for 'I don't want it. You know what you can do with that: you can stuff it up your fundamental orifice!'

[**oops-a-daisy!** A consolatory cliché, rather than a c.p., uttered as one picks up a child that has fallen: late (?mid) C19–20. A baby-talk alteration of *up-a-daisy* or *upsadaisy*. See also **upsy daisy!**]

open. See: bar's open; box open; canteen open; don't open; I can always; keep this; keep your bowels; let's not o.; please, mother; that dame; they've opened; who's opened; your store.

open a can of worms. See **can of worms** and **that's another can…**

open season for birds (– it's). Girls everywhere are available or, as it has, since *c.* 1955, been customary and almost fashionable to say, 'There's plenty of local talent': since the 1930s, but little used since *c.* 1960, the girls themselves having openly indicated that this is so. (A reminder from Petch, 1974.)

open the box! Make your mind up! 'Contestants in the old ITV quiz *Take Your Pick* were given the option of opening a numbered box (which might contain anything from tickets for a holiday to Ena Sharples's [a well-known character in the long-running TV soap opera *Coronation Street*] hairnet) or "taking the money". The studio audience would chant their advice to hesitating contestants. When the host, Michael Miles, died, it was said that his funeral had been interrupted by the congregation shouting, "Open the box! Open the box!" The show ran for almost twenty years from 1955' (*VIBS*).

open the door, Richard! is an Aus. c.p., dating since *c.* 1930. and 'used when someone knocks on an unlocked door' (B.P.).

Did this phrase inspire, or should it be dated later because it derives from, the 'American song composed by Jack McVea and Dan Howell with lyrics by Dusty Fletcher and John Mason…popular in the US in 1947 and probably the same year or 1948 [in the UK]' (Eric Townley, 1978)? *VIBS* notes that the song was 'first sung in Britain on ITMA'; and David Dalton refers to it in *James Dean, the Mutant King*, 1974, as being one of the hit songs during Dean's youth (Paul Janssen, who adds that in those days a hit song remained a hit song for years).

operation. See: since Auntie.

opinion. See: would you like a.

opportunity is (or **opportunity's**) **a fine thing, miss** (or **madam**). See **chance is a fine thing**.

or my pick's a bloater. 'A most unlikely alternative to the proposition just set out, which is by implication a dead certainty. "A fine pair o' knockers? Rubbish! Them's falsies, or my…"' (P.B., 1974). Cf **pound to a pinch…**

or out goes the gas. A threat, current *c.* 1880–1905, 'to put an end to whatever is going on' (B & L).

[**or what have you?** lies midway between a c.p. and a cliché; both Brit. and US; it arose during the 1930s. I feel that it is very much rather cliché than c.p. P.B.: in later C20, at least in UK, usu. replaced by *or whatever*.]

or would you rather be a fish? 'A c.p. quip after proposed line of action (the more at the odds the better). To the response "Yes", the rejoinder is: "You haven't far to go"; rebutted by "No, it's too wet"' (L.A., 1959). This set of witticisms – cf the 'chants' so popular among British soldiers in WW1 – dates from *c.* 1945 and springs from, indeed it forms an elab. of, the c.p. **which would you rather – or go fishing**, which I remember as existing already in the late 1920s and which occurs in one of Dorothy L. Sayers's two or three best novels, *The Nine Tailors*, 1929. (Patricia Newham thinks that it comes from a famous song: that is true, in so far as the song reinforced the c.p. that prompted it.)

And Eric Townley authoritatively writes of that song, 1978: '"Swinging on a Star" was composed by Jimmy Van Heusen with lyrics by Johnny Burke for the movie musical of

1944 *Going My Way* in which [it] was sung by Bing Crosby'. A sample verse, recalled by Camilla Raab, is:

Would you like to swing on a star?
Carry moonbeams home in a jar?
And be better off than you are?
Or would you rather be a fish?

Cf **which would you rather be – or a wasp?**, current among London schoolchildren *c.* 1905–14, as Julian Franklyn once recalled; he added, 'So far as I remember, there was no standard reply.' Cf also such c.pp. as **how high is up?**, **how old is Ann(e)?**, **why is a mouse when it spins?**.

or your bitch of a mother. 'The most excoriating catchphrase I have ever come across was in a footnote in [Richard Ellman, *James Joyce*, 1959]. It was a translation of a phrase current in Trieste while Joyce was there. To anything you didn't like, you added the rider *or your bitch of a mother*' (Robert Robinson, in the radio programme 'Stop the Week', 15 Oct. 1977). Joyce († 1941) was in Trieste *c.* 1914. The phrase's circulation must have been somewhat restricted; certainly I never heard it. A good example would have been: 'This threat of war, or your bitch of a mother'.

orchestra. See: this is an o.

orchids to you, dear! was, *c.* 1935–55, a 'polite' var. of 'balls to you!' (*not* a c.p.). Based upon an etymological pun (someone with a curious mind really ought to collect such witty cerebrations) – of which most users of the c.p. were blissfully unaware.

In the US, 'often used another way. Campus (and other) newspapers are fond, at term's end, of awarding "orchids and onions" to professors, administrators and fellow-students: orchids for praise, onions for disapprobation' (A.B., 1978). Since before 1942, when *orchids to you!* signified 'Congratulations' (Berrey). P.B.: cf the British service officers' synon. use of 'strawberries' and 'raspberries'.

order(s). See: give order; just what; no order; not if I am.

order, counter-order, disorder. The late Col. Archie White, VC, historian of the Royal Army Educational Corps, wrote to me 1969, that it has been a common saying amongst officers since long before my time – and that is now 60 years. The NCOs' more cynical version: 'Never obey an order: it will be cancelled before you finish it'.

I think I saw it in one of the Hornblower books [by C. S. Forester], and I've seen it a number of times in Victorian memoirs and in French military memoirs.

You would, I think, be accurate in saying that it is a sequence so inevitable where staff work is not of the best that it came to birth long ago in many armies and navies – and that the Air Forces of the world have doubtless heard of it.

The saying may also have sprung from the confusion that almost inevitably results from an excess of orders.

In Evelyn Waugh's satirical novel about army officers on Home Service, *Officers and Gentlemen*, 1945, we meet with this dialogue:

The Adjutant…suddenly said; 'Sergeant-Major, couldn't we have recalled Mr Crouchback here and given him the address ourselves?'

'Sir.'

'Too late to change now. Order, counterorder, disorder, eh?'

'Sir.'

To indicate the degree to which this c.p. has become incorporated in the language, it will perhaps suffice to quote from the following passage on the opening page of Henry Cecil's novel, *The Wanted Men*, 1972: 'What they would have been like together in real war will never be known.… But if their behaviour at croquet is any guide, the proverbial order, counter-order and disorder might well have prevailed.' (But it never has been a proverb nor even a true proverbial saying.)

Orderly. See: John Orderly; rise and shine.

orders is orders. This joc. c.p., orig. an army sergeants', became a gen. civilian c.p. very soon after WW1 – in 1919 or 1920. Like the prec., it has been incorporated in coll. English. Always with a humorous tone and undertone. P.B.: or with resignation by the one ordered, 'Oh well, orders is orders, I suppose' – there's no use arguing.

orft (= off) **we jolly well go** (**, then**)! 'One of a number of verbal tricks performed regularly by Jimmy Young after his switch from singing to radio deejaying [acting as a *disc jockey*]. Note also his frequent recourse to the phrases "You see!" and "I ask myself "[q.v.]' (*VIBS*). Often imitated, sometimes without the *jolly well*. (P.B.)

organ. See: he's not so.

organize. See: couldn't organize; if there's.

O'Riley. See: blimey.

orphans. See: for the widows.

other(s). See: bit of how's; do the other; if he doesn't; if you don't like; is there any; less; plus; pull the o.; since when; two other; with a five-; you should see; you're blind.

other half. See: come in and see.

ought to be bored for the hollow horn and **ought to be playing with a string of spools.** Both of these cowboys' expressions mean a crazy, or a feeble-minded, or an extremely ignorant person; the latter can also mean 'young and foolish': respectively late C19–20 and C20. The former has its orig. in the practice of boring a small hole in the horn of a cow suffering from 'hollow-horn', a run-down condition, as Ramon Adams tells us.

our 'Arbour! and **our bridge!** These two gibes at Sydneysiders by those Australians who aren't, and esp. by Melbournites, have existed, the former since 1900 or even earlier; the latter, since *c.* 1935. It *is* a beautiful harbour; it's also a spectacular bridge over it. The retaliatory gibe is **stinking Yarra!**

A friend, who shall be nameless (and it's no good your guessing) has sent me, in 1977, what was, in the early 1970s, known as 'The Sydney Prayer' – a wittily irreverent parody of the Lord's Prayer in the demotic of that period. I retain his approximately phonetic spelling:

'Our 'Arbour, wot art in 'Aiven, Good-o be thy naime. Our bridge we done, in 1930 and '31. Give us this dai our daily [diley] Bradman. Forgive us our trespasses and we forgive those caows in Melbourne. Lead us not into taxation and deliver us from stroikes. For ours is the 'Arbour, the bridge and the Bradman, For ever and ever. *Too* roight!' (Bradman is, obviously, 'the Don' – the greatest batsman cricket has ever known.)

ours is a nice 'ouse, ours is. It the main, bitterly ironic, esp. in the form *so it's a nice 'ouse, ours is.* Mostly Londoners' – indeed, chiefly Cockney – it is applied to 'one big happy family' that's anything but happy. (I've known it since *c.* 1925.) It arose as the first line of a nonsense song; the second is 'What a nice little (h)ouse ours is!' After *c.* 1940, rarer and rarer. Noble, 1976.) *VIBS* attributes it to the comedian Cyril Fletcher.

out. See: another clean; does your mother; don't tear the; everybody out; gas; get out!; how much; I'm down; it'll see; it's all coming; it's the beer; leave it out; or out; take it out; there he goes; who let; you must be out; your custom; and:

out in the woodshed behind the axe-handle. 'Just use your eyes and you'll see it' or 'Why don't you use your eyes?' A C20 US rural response to the inquiry 'where is something or other?' (J.W.C., 1977.)

out into the cold, cold snow lies half-way between a chant and a c.p. It has been current since very early in C20: and, as one might guess, it derives from the language of melodramatic and unblushingly sentimental ballads and plays.

'In your deriving the c.p. from melodrama, I take it to come from the specific instances of (e.g.) stern father banishing his erring daughter with her babe out into the cold, cold snow – "and never darken my doors again"' (Wedgewood, 1977). Correct! Cf **never darken...**

out of this (or **the**) **world.** 'Of exceedingly high quality. An

elaboration of "heavenly" and/or the speaker's response to whatever-it-is. Orig. (? 1930s) jazz musicians', but soon applied to anything by anyone. US, but I would expect also UK' (R.C., 1979). P.B.: Claiborne is right about use in UK, where also there was some affection, late 1960s, of the orig. US (? Negro or hippie) synon. *out of* (usu. rendered *outta*) *sight* (*, man*)!

out to lunch – he's or **she's.** This implies that the person concerned is either extremely eccentric or plain mad. Col. Moe heard this in 1978 and, on making inquiries, was informed that it, and several variants, had been used, at least in California, for a number of years. P.B.: some use also in UK, early 1980s.

out where the bull feeds. See **where the bull feeds.**

outside. See: no cups; step outside; they don't pipe.

outside, Eliza (or **Liza**)! Ware defines it as 'drunk again, Eliza' and says that it's 'applied to intoxicated, reeling women'; the implied meaning is 'Get out of this! It is a low or streets' c.p. of mid C19–early C20. *Liza* is – or used to be – generic for 'females of the London proletariat': cf Somerset Maugham's title, *Liza of Lambeth*, his earliest and perhaps most compassionate novel. As J.W.C. has proposed, Eliza Doolittle in G.B. Shaw's play *Pygmalion*, 1912, may have been a late coming in the phrase's currency.

Ovaltineys. See: we are the O.

oven. See: there's a bun.

over goes the show! This proletarian c.p. of *c.* 1870–1900, recorded by B & L, comments upon either a disaster or upon a sudden and dramatic change. It prob. refers to the overturning of a Punch and Judy outfit.

over-laid. See: under-paid.

over-paid, over-sexed, and over here was a fairly gen. c.p. applied by British Isles Britons, male and female, to the GIs stationed in Britain during 1943–5. Far more joc. than derogatory. (Mr Y. Mindel, 1972.) In Australia it was revived and applied to American forces personnel who spent 'rest and recreation' leave there during the Vietnam War.

R.C. adds, 1978, 'Often with the addition of "over-decorated", US servicemen being, in fact, far more decorated than those of their allies, to the point where old soldiers sported banks of ribbons referred to as "fruit salad"'. P.B.: the term *fruit salad* is a well-known slang expression among British servicemen too.

Eric Townley, 1978, provides the Americans' retort, justified on two counts anyway: 'The counter catch phrase was *you're underpaid, under-sexed, and under Eisenhower*'. 'Ike' was indeed the Supreme Commander of all Allied Forces in Europe.

over the left shoulder!, often shortened to **over the left!** (or even **over!**) This c.p. negatives one's own or another's statement and indicates derisive disbelief, the thumb being sometimes pointed over that shoulder. The full form is C17–20, but by 1930, slightly, and by 1970 very, ob.; *over the left!* is C18–20; *over!* is mid C19–20. Recorded at least as early as Cotgrave in his justly famous French–English dictionary, 1611. (Apperson.) Prof. Harold Shapiro notes that Dickens gives an account of the gesture in *Pickwick Papers* (pub'd 1836–37), at ch. 42.

In 1870, H.D. Traill, 'Don't go? It's go and go over the left...it's go with a hook at the end.' (F & H; *OED*.)

There is some reason to believe that it is, in UK, a predominantly Cockney usage. Charles Smith Cheltnam, in *Mrs Green's Snug Little Business,* performed on 16 Jan. 1865, has:

RAPPS: ...Never you take nothing upon your individual self, but just call for me *Joe.*

JOE: Oh, very well. (*Aside.*) Over the left!

The usage travelled to the US. Mencken records it in the definitive edn., 1936, of HLM, and again in Supp. 2, 1948; and so does Berrey in 1942. However, R.C. comments, 1978: 'Certainly never common [in US]. I have never heard it or read it in forty-odd years'.

Apparently from the centuries-old custom of throwing salt over one's left shoulder in order to avert bad luck.

over the top and the best of luck to you! – the last two words being usu. omitted as grimly superfluous. An encouraging convention for the comfort of infantrymen about to leave the comparative shelter of a trench to deliver a frontal attack, the *top* being the parapet: it arose in July – Aug. 1916, during the great Battle of the Somme – where one needed and occasionally met with good luck. The soldiers' song 'Over the Top', one of the 'Mademoiselle from Armenteers' group, begins thus:

Over the top with the best of luck.
Parley-voo!
Over the top with the best of luck,
Parley-voo!
Over the top with the best of luck,
Our number's up if we don't come back,
Inky-pinky parley-voo!

It is recorded in B & P, 1931, a book that reappeared a generation later as *The Long Trail*. J.W.C. notes that the last line had, among US infantrymen, the var. 'inky-*dinky*'.

In his novel, *Circle of Squares*, 1969, Bill Turner writes: 'I felt a sensation like cramp in my stomach as our car stopped, but there was no backing out now. Hirst opened the rear doors for us. "Over the top and the best of luck," Crossley muttered, getting out.' (Crossley was a veteran of WW2, not of WW1.)

There was a var.; F & G have this entry: 'OVER THE BAGS: Leaving the trenches to attack – going over the sandbags of the trench parapet. "Over the bags and the best of luck!" was a common phrase in this connection.'

John Gibbons, John Brophy, EP – these three knew all about it at first hand and on several occasions.

P.B.: E.P. was himself one of the soldiers fighting on the Somme – see esp. his contribution to *Three Personal Records of the War*, pub'd by his own firm Scholartis in 1929, and the moving chapter on comradeship in his *Journey to the Edge of Morning*, 1946. John Gibbons is the 'G' of 'F & G'.

By the early 1980s the memory was beginning to fade of the phrase's orig. significance, and *over the top* began to be applied, in UK, to anything excessive or exaggerated: 'I say, that's a bit over the top!' could refer equally well to too steep a price, too tall a story, or too violent an action or re-action.

over you go: the longer you look, the less you'll like it! 'may be 'ollo'd to a friend looking long at a fence' – as Mr Jorrocks tells us in 'Another Sporting Lector' (lecture) in vol. I of R. S. Surtees, *Handley Cross; or, Mr Jorrocks's Hunt;* 1854, an expansion of *Handley Cross or The Spa Hunt,* 1843: a foxhunting c.p. of c. 1820–80, and perhaps very much longer.

overhauling. See: give yourself.

overtime. See: can't have; old man must.

overweights. See: go and fetch.

'ow are yer? all right? 'of Wilfred Pickles' radio programme "Have a Go" with which the morale of the ageing was boosted in the late 1940s–50s' (R.S., 1975).

Besides this greeting, *VIBS* lists the alternative, '"Ladies and gentlemen of Bingley [Yorkshire], 'ow do, 'ow are yer?" – this is how Wilfred Pickles introduced the first edition of *Have a Go* in 1946 [in his broadest native Yorkshire accent, of course]. Within a year the show [one that aimed 'to bring the people to the people': P.B.] had an audience of twenty million and ran for twenty-one years. Pickles died in 1978'. He is remembered also with affection by those who heard him as one of the BBC's most distinctively-voiced WW2 news broadcasters – if he had ever had to broadcast anonymously, there would have been very little doubt in anyone's mind about the identity of the speaker. (P.B.)

'ow you (or **yer**) **goin', mate?** How are you?: NZ: since c. 1920; also Aus., where it is usu. followed by 'orright?' [For those who query the precedence, remember E.P. was born in NZ, 1893, and the family moved to Queensland when he was about 12.]

In the Aus. *National Times*, 23–28 Jan. 1978, Neil Lovett deprecates the omission, from the first ed. of this book, of 'Willy Fennel's *'ow are you, mate?* with its drawled, cracked vibrato with which one was greeted everywhere 20 or so years ago'.

owe. See: do I owe; I owe.

owl. See: only birds.

owsat or **owzat?** – strictly, but, in practice, only occ. *how is that?* – is 'a general plea for recognition and applause for a neat action – like **look, no hands**' (Levene, 1977): since c. 1950. Orig. in the cricket appeal from wicketkeeper to umpire. The shorter form of the c.p. is the more humorous.

oy, oy! See **oi, oi!**

P

p is silent, as in batheing – the. (And variants.) See silent, like the p...

p.o.e.t.s. See t.G.I.F.

pack drill. See: no names.

packed. See: so round.

paddle. See: up Shit.

paddle your own canoe! 'This encouragement to self-reliance was the last line in the chorus of a sentimental music-hall song by the eminent Victorian "comic" singer Harry Clifton (1824–72). It was taken up as a catch phrase and it persisted right into Edward times' (Noble, 1977, who remembers it as late as his schooldays in the 1920s). The phrase appears in *Harper's Monthly*, May 1854, as by 'Anon.' (*Bartlett's Dict. of Familiar Quotations*). A rather more likely source that 'I think it much better that every man paddle his own canoe' in Frederick Marryat's *Settlers in Canada*, 1844, cited by the *ODQ*. Although decidedly ob., it has by implication, survived in the mock-French *pas d'elle yeux Rhône que nous*, current during my own schooldays, 1900–10, but itself *vieux jeu*. (Note written 1978.)

paddock. See: kangaroos.

Paddy Doyle. See: when Paddy.

padre. See: speak up; went for.

page. See: he's in the book.

paid out with spit is a c.p. ref. to a small salary or low wages: US theatrical, since *c.* 1920; partially adopted, *c.* 1932, among English 'theatricals'. P.B.: in later C20 UK, miserly payments are usu. made in 'peanuts' or, since *c.* 1970, in 'shirt buttons' – presumably the latter are the smallest 'viable' buttons.

pain(s). See: bringing; feeling; I have no; it'd give; you give me the; and:

pain in his little finger, or occ. toe (– he has a). Applied to a malingering Serviceman or workman: C20. One who runs to the medical officer or a civilian doctor on any excuse – or none.

paint. See: go and fetch; if it moves; if you can pee.

painters. See: rags on.

pair. See: there's a pair.

pakapoo ticket, esp. as in, e.g. 'It looks like a pakapoo ticket'. Lit., indecipherable; hence (as. a c.p.) extremely untidy or confused: Aus.: C20; by 1978, ob., Wilkes observes. 'Pakapu is a Chinese gambling game, not unlike housie. A pakapu ticket, when filled, is covered with strange markings' (Edwin Morrisby, 1958). Indeed, S.J. Baker, in *The Drum*, 1959, gives the var. *marked like a pakapoo ticket*, 'confusedly or incomprehensibly marked'. Being merely on approx. transliteration of unfamiliar Chinese sounds, there are of course many var. spellings.

pal(s). See: dear old; it's your pal; never introduce.

palate. See: midshipmen.

pale people. See: pink pills.

pall-bearers. See: fuck 'em all.

palm. See: cross my p.

Palmer is concerned – Mr. Applied, *c.* 1790–1850, to one who offers, or one who takes, a bribe: the underworld and its fringes. (Vaux.) A pun on *palmy* – to pass slyly.

panic. See: pro bono; you panic.

panic stations! is a c.p. only when *not* used literally; esp. when employed humorously: since 1939 or 1940. From the navy's *be at panic stations* – to be prepared for the worst.

   L.A. adds, 1976, 'Said when unthinkable mistake or omission has been made, or an impending inspection by authority – originally in the Services – is announced and the comfortable has to be reconverted to regulation good order'.

   'Also, "Don't hit the panic button!" said to someone about to do something disastrous, or potentially so...From the 1950s worry about nuclear war' (A.B., 1978): US. It is relevant to remember that almost endemic death wish in the US and, much less, in UK, *c.* 1948–62, which coloured many novels, plays, films, of the period. P.B.: and *c.* 1980–? See **don't push...**

pantry. See: half-crown.

pants. See: don't pee; get the lead; laugh?; when you dance; when you were wearing.

panty lines. See: your old man.

pap. See: mouth.

papa. See: come to papa; and:

papa's home, the seat's up and Mama's home, the seat's down. Orig. applied lit. to the seat in a water-closet, then to one or the other parent's being at home, it is now a joc. expression heard at homes everywhere in the US. (W.J.B., 1977.) It is extremely difficult to date domestic c.pp., but it's fairly safe to hazard the guess that it arose during the 1920s. P.B.: in UK, and with *Dad* and *Mum* substituted, from at least as early as *c.* 1910, to judge from my father's recollections.

paper(s). See: all I know; 'book!'; go peddle; see you in the funny; sounds; you don't have p.

paper-bag. See: couldn't knock.

paper-hanger. See: busy as a one-; like a one-.

par for the course. See: that's about.

Parachute. See: that dame.

parade. See: on parade.

paranoids. See: even paranoids.

pardon me for living! is 'an elaborate mock-apology, used by one checked for some minor error' (Leechman): Can.: since *c.* 1945. It was very soon adopted in UK: witness, in Noël Coward's 'A Richer Dust', one of the six stories comprising *Star Quality*, 1951, 'He jumped violently, and said in a voice of bored petulance, "Lay off me for one minute, can't you." Discouraged, she withdrew her hand as requested, muttered "Pardon me for living", and took a swig of tomato juice...' 'The US form is *excuse me*...' (J.W.C., 1977).

Pardon my dust! See **I'm off in a cloud of dust.**

pardon (or **excuse**) **my** (or **the**) **French!** Please excuse the strong language! Dating from *c.* 1916, it was a non-cultured, non-Society c.p. A good example occurs in Michael Harrison's *All the Trees Were Green*, 1936, '"A bloody sight better (excuse the French!) than most."' Prob. it was indebted to the British soldiers' experiences in the war-torn France of WW1, yet I cannot still an uneasy feeling that it arose during the Edwardian period.

The US form is either *excuse my French* (Col. Moe. 1975) or *if you will* (or *if you'll*) *pardon my French*, although *pardon my French* also exists in US, W & F citing Tennessee Williams, 1957. *If you will pardon my French* occurs in John Mortimer's *Collaborators*, prod. and pub'd in 1973, where Sam, an American, asks: 'Does she cut ball? – if you will pardon my French.'

Cf **you should excuse the expression.**

Paris. See: fought; it's snowing.

parish. See: his stockings.

park. See: result; that's gone.

parlayed. See: laid, re-laid.

Parliament. See: kiss my arse.

parlour. See: come into; will you walk.

parrot. See: bring us.

[**parrot must have an almond – the.** This c.p. – very common *c.* 1520–1640 – was applied, whether equivocally or unequivocally, to incentive or reward or bribery. Bordering on a proverb, it is well covered by Apperson, who cites esp. Nashe's *Almond for a Parrot*, 1590. It alludes to a parrot's delight in almonds.]

Parsees. See: R.C.s.

parsley. See: it's pussy.

parson. See: Davy.

Parson Mallum and **Parson Palmer. See remember Parson Mallum.**

parson would have said, I hope we shall meet in heaven – a. The opening dialogue of S. 1738, takes place in St James's Park, Lord Sparkish meeting Colonel Atwit:

COLONEL: Well met, my Lord.

LORD SP: Thank ye, Colonel; a Parson would have said, I hope we shall meet in Heaven.

Dating from late C17, it is still (1975) not quite extinct. Sometimes prefaced by *as* and sometimes modified to . . . *would say* . . . .

part(s). See: good for What; good in; how are they hanging; my part; refreshes; till death.

party. See: I took my harp; keep it clean; let's go to; and:

party's over – the is 'often heard when something come to an end has been anything but a party' (Petch, 1976): since *c.* 1945.

pas ce soir, Josephine! is an English 'translation' into Fr. of **not tonight, Josephine!**, q.v. An embellishment and a politesse, it has been much less used than the English form; I doubt whether it has been used at all since 1960 or, at latest, 1970.

pas de Lafarge! Don't be a bore! Don't you know that's a forbidden subject – that everybody's sick of it?: a Society c.p., current, during the 1840s, in London, to which it came from Paris. It alludes to a notorious murder case: 'Did or did not Madame Lafarge murder her husband?' (Ware.)

pas devant les enfants. See not in front of the children.

pass. See: it'll pass; ONE WORD; we'll cut; well, if that; and:

pass along the car, please! Asking for elbow room in a crowded place: 1920s–30s. From the tramcar conductor's request to passengers bunching up near the exit. (Sanders, 1978.) It could be characterized as urban lower-middle class. P.B.: also *pass right down the car, please!* Cf **mind you backs!**

past your heart: hold your hat on! is a coarse male exaggerative priapic boast to his female partner *in coitu*: raffish and 'pubby': the 1920s, says L.A.; I remember hearing it used during the 1930s, but not since.

Patagonia See: when I was in.

[**Patience is a virtue; virtue is a grace; Grace was a little girl who wouldn't wash her face,** the first line being a quot'n, the second a naughty childish addition. 'This was certainly heard and said by us as children, in a sickeningly pious and provoking manner – guaranteed to needle even further anyone who was feeling rattled or impatient' (Miss Penny A. Cook, 1975).

Yet clearly this is a chant, not a c.p., but it does show how thin, sometimes, is the borderline between the two.]

patter of tiny feet – the. 'A satirically saccharine reference to the joys or imminence of parenthood: US [and UK]: from 1920s; now slightly ob.' (R.C. 1978). P.B.: in UK, sometimes consciously – and truthfully – perverted to *the thunder of tiny feet.*

Paul. See: I will pay; what do you know, Joe.

Pauline. See: nay, nay, P.

pause. See: Macready; and:

pause that refreshes – the. A joc. ref. to urination, inspired by the famous Coca-Cola slogan, launched in 1929 and publicized world-wide. (Ashley, 1979; Nigel Rees, *Slogans*, 1982.)

pawn. See: who pawned.

paws off, Pompey! Don't paw me about! A proletarian c.p. of *c.* 1910–40. (Manchon.) As if the girl were talking to the dog Pompey. Perhaps the sailors at 'Pompey' (Portsmouth) have had a say in the origination, as Patricia Newham has suggested.

pay. See: God pays; I will pay; I'll pay; isn't it time; music's paid; since Jesus; someone forgot; that won't pay; what's to pay; when Paddy; who's dead; who's up; you couldn't pay; you pays; you should pay; you're not paid.

pay-book. See: he's been looking.

pay-day. See: golden, roll on, pay-.

pay for a room. See: are you going.

pay over face and eyes, as the cat did the monkey, slang for 'to give someone a terrible beating about the head', became a c.p. when, as so often it was, it occurred in the form, **he paid me** (or you)...or **I paid him** (or you).... Hotten records it in the 2nd edn, 1860, and it seems to have covered the very approx. period, 1840–194.

pay the woman or leave the bed! 'Get on with it!' or 'Do what you should do, without shilly-shallying!': since, I'd guess, *c.* 1920. (Owed to John Skehan, 1977.) Cf **shit, or get off the pot!**

pay up and look pleasant or **pretty** or **big.** An injunction to look pleased (the first version) when one pays a statutory or otherwise unavoidable sum, as, for instance, one's income tax: since the mid 1940s. (A reminder from L.A., 1976.) Perhaps suggested by the cliché *grin and bear it.* There was, however, an earlier form, *pay up and look pretty*, applicable to a woman; it occurs in George Sala, 1894. P.B. remarks of . . . *big*, 1977, that it is 'a gently joc. invitation to fork out some small amount, or a mock-rueful acceptance of a social duty, as in "Oh, Lor'! They're having a collection. Oh, well, pay up and look big, I suppose".' I don't recall hearing it before *c.* 1950; perhaps adopted from US.

pea-patch. See: tearing.

peace. See: separate.

peaches. See: everything is p.

peanut. See: let the p.

peanut gallery. See: another voice; no remarks.

pearl barley. See: remember pearl barley.

Pearl Harbor. See: remember Pearl.

pears. See: apples a pound.

Pears soap. See: good morning, have; preparing.

peasants are revolting – the. 'A *double-entendre*: covers everything from strikes generally to a librarian's jaundiced observation on the public at large. Since mid 1950s, if not earlier. One of the (US) "Wizard of Id" strip-cartoon books by Brant Parker and Johnny Hart, a collection first pub'd in 1971, was so titled' (P.B., 1979).

peck. See: keep him.

pecker. See: keep your p.

Peckham. See: holiday.

peculiar. See: funny peculiar.

pedal. See: back pedal.

peddle. See: go peddle; and:

peddle your own fish! 'Mind your own business!': US: C20, and prob. late C19. (Fain, 1977.) Cf **go peddle your papers!**

pee. See: doesn't know; don't make I laugh; don't pee; he squats; he thinks; if you can pee; may I pee; soldier's s.

pee-time. See: I look like.

[**peek-a-boo!** orig. in 1881, as an American song, sung by William Scanlon in *Friend and Foe*. It may have become a c.p. in the US, but not in UK, where it has merely been a rather tiresome cliché.]

peel me a grape, 'like *come up and see me sometime*, is owed to dear Mae West in *I'm No Angel* (? early 1930s). Coolly dismissive of a display of hysterical fuss. After a frantic and enraged admirer has slammed out, she turns to her Negro maid with a shrug and: "Beulah, peel me a grape"' (R.S., 1975).

Joseph T. Shipley – the eminent US historian of the US theatre – writing in 1975, modifies and amplifies thus: 'Apparently first spoken by Mae West in her play *Diamond Lil*, which opened in New York on April 9, 1928.... Diamond Lil is a member of the demimonde who affects the manners (as she understands them) of the haut monde – the height of pseudo-sophistication.' And, by the way, Dr Shipley then mentions another line from the same play, the famous 'Come up and see me sometime', which was, as he puts it, to become her 'trademark'. He has further allowed me to quote from his *Guide to Great Plays:*

As actress and author, Mae West (b. 1892) occupies in the American theatre a special niche that she has carved for herself. She swaggers in it superbly, the tired businessman's bosom friend. To establish herself as prime exponent of one aspect of our life, she had not only to develop her special type of performance, but also to write the plays to which that performance added body and form. No picture of the American theatre would be complete without Mae West.

J.W.C., however, 1975, writes: 'Perhaps rather a universally familiar quotation... than a real c.p.; it is always, that is, allusive to her, and to her use of it, not applied to other situations.' Ben Grauer, however, writing on Christmas Day 1975, signalizes it as a c.p. encapsulating 'upstart insouciance and feigned elegance'.

Moreover, in the US there appeared, in 1967, Joseph Weintraub's anthology, *The Wit and Wisdom of Mae West,* which, in 1975, was pub'd in UK as *Peel Me a Grape,* thus placing the witticism high in the hierarchy of her sayings: there's canonization, almost a sanctification, of one of her wittiest and deftest c.pp.! (With thanks to John O'Riordan, 1976.)

peg. See: it's nice to have.

pencil. See: that'll grow.

pennants. See: who's hoisting.

penn'orth. See: had your p.

penny. See: has the penny; only another; putting your; steal; they're two; and:

penny bun costs twopence – a. Expenses rise as soon as one marries: N. Country: *c.* 1905–65. P.B.: perhaps a retort to the old fallacy that 'two can live as cheaply as one'.

penny has dropped (most frequently, **penny's dropped) – the,** sometimes prec. by *at last*, and often by an exclamatory *ah!* of satisfaction or relief. It is applied when someone has belatedly realized either what was meant by another's witticism or, occ., the true significance or urgency of a situation. (Playfair, 1977.) I remember it from the 1920s, but it prob. dates from very early C20.

But this deft c.p. merits a second comment from a lively mind: '"At last you understand what I said *or* meant" or "At last you've got the joke". From the early penny-in-the-slot machines that needed a jog to make them work. Still current' (Sanders, 1978), indeed, very much so. See also **has the penny...**

penny (or **twopence** or **threepence) more and up goes the donkey! – a.** This lower-class London c.p. expresses derision, arose a few years before 1841, and fell into disuse either during or just before WW2. From an itinerant, esp. a street, acrobat's stock finish to a turn.

people are shot for less. See **in** (such or such a country) **people are shot...**

percentage. See: no percentage.

perch. See: come off your.

perched on an oar like a budgerigar is a Sea Cadet Corps description of a youngster 'too small to handle an oar efficiently' (Peppitt): since *c.* 1965.

Percival purchased a new aeroplane, based on a song title, was in 1912–13, a c.p. (The late Dr Lindsay Verrier, 1976; he added, 'I saw Gustave Hamel loop the loop in 1912'.)

Percy. See: point Percy.

performance. See: all promise; how did it go; what a p.; what do you do.

[**period!** is that absurdity, a one-word c.p. Frank Shaw, 1969, writes: finally; without extension or elaboration or modification, palliation or appeal: originally (*c.* 1945) typists', journalists', authors', broadcasters'; only since *c.* 1955 has it been at all general. 'Dead as a door-nail? Just dead. Period!' From a person dictating, and saying 'period' (full stop). Early BBC comic 'Stainless Stephen', ex-teacher, gave the whole idea of speaking punctuation signs a comic twist some imitated.]

perish forbid! 'This conflation of "Perish the thought!" and "God forbid!" was constantly uttered by Archie the bartender in a radio serial called *Duffy's Tavern*. Used as an echoic c.p. by aficionados of the program, of whom there were millions; but now [ob. – prob. †.] The program was ousted by the growing popularity of TV' (J.W.C., 1977): latish 1920s–30s.

Persian Gulf's the arsehole of the world. See arsehole of the world.

persimmon. See: longest.

person. See: as I am a p.

Peter the Painter. See: here's Peter.

petticoats. See: up with p.

pew. See: you're in the wrong.

phantom (something) **strikes again – the.** Applied to any recurrent horror, e.g. serial murder, a sequence of bomb outrages, a continuing spate of 'poison letters' or of robberies: since the 1920s, perhaps from titles of early film serials. That it has become a variable, with the 'phantom' specified, does not invalidate its status as a c.p., although it does, clearly enough, expose it to the risk of becoming a cliché. (Prompted by a note from P.B., 1977.) P.B.: and all that, because I told him the story of the unfortunate kindergarten teacher who kept finding stray turds under desks, accompanied by the scrawled legend, 'the phantom arsehole strikes again!' Cf **rides again...**

Pharaoh's daughter. See: like the story.

Pharisees. See: R.C.s.

Phildadelphia. See: this must.

Phoebe. See: don't force it.

phoney. See: queer as a.

phrase. See: to coin.

pianist. See: don't shoot.

piano. See: left her purse; play that; they laughed; try that; you've forgotten.

Piccadilly Circus. See: lights of.

pick. See: don't pick; he broke; plays as fair; you can always; you've picked.

pick a bloke from the Smoke! 'Cockneys' reminder to escape routine, gain reward. They have the gift of making little of obstacles' (L.A., 1974): Londoners': since *c.* 1930, perhaps since as early as 1910 or even 1900.

pick a soft plank! Sleep easy: a nautical c.p., addressed to young seamen sleeping on deck for the first time (Bowen): mid C19–20; ob. by 1930 and † by 1950.

pick him up and pipe-clay him and he'll do again was *c.* 1860–1910, a naval seamen's sarcastic remark directed at a Royal Marine fallen on the deck – esp. if he had fallen hard (Bowen).

pick on somebody your own size! Brit. and – with *own* sometimes omitted – US: late C19–20. The gen. sense is 'Pick a quarrel with ...'.

In an article titled 'Lay Off the Thyroid' in *What of It?*, 1925, Ring W. Lardner mentioned 'the old stand-bys like pick somebody your size and you must be a good dancer, you are so tall, and if I was as big as you I would challenge Dempsey'.

It would seem that, nowadays, *own* is never omitted in the US. (J.W.C., 1977.) There, sometimes *fight (with) somebody your own size* (A.B., 1978).

pick the bones out of that! – **let him** (or **he can**). I'd like to see – or hear – him reply convincingly, or retaliate successfully, to that!: C20. Also used in direct address, as to, e.g., the victim of a particularly crafty snooker, or round the card-table. 'I've heard this used by low types who have just hawked and spat rather horribly. They might also say, instead, "Get out and walk (, you bastard)!"' (P.B., 1976).

Pickford's. See: coming up.

pickings. See: how's pickin's.

pickle. See: come and have.

picnics and parties. See: balls, bees.

picture(s). See: every picture; I have a p.; whistling.

picture-frame. See: I shall see; I'm always.

pie. See: next time you make; there'll be pie.

piece. See: still all.

piece of cake. See: cut yourself.

Pierre. See: lucky P.

piffle. See: balderdash.

pig. See: brandy in Latin for pig; brinded pig; dear Mother, it's a bugger; excuse my pig; happy as a dead; home and dried; how's your belly; I'm so hungry; in a pig's; it's gone; silk; then comes; well, I'll go; what can you expect; What? have; you pig; where the pig; you're on the pig; and:

pig on pork implies 'too much of the same thing. I think particularly common in financial circles, e.g., lending to a man on the security of the shares in a company which he runs. If he cannot pay his loan back, it is unlikely that the shares will be worth much' (Playfair, 1977): since late 1960s.

pig-shit, See: mean as.

pig-sty. See: who kicked.

pigeon. See: your pigeon.

pike. See: it's a freak.

Pike's Peak or bust! (Rather similar to **California, here I come!**) The earliest record of the phrase occurs in the *Nebraska City News* of 28 May 1859, in ref. to the gold discovered in the Cripple Creek – (now) Colorado Springs – area in that year; Pike's Peak was named after the explorer Zebulon L. Pike. In the gold rush, prospectors from the East and Middle West started across the Great Plains in their covered wagons, headed for the roadless, rugged and almost uninhabited foothills of the Rocky Mountains. See notably B.A. Botkin's, *A Treasury of American Folklore*, 1944, p. 310. W.J.B., to whom I owe this information, 1975, writes:

'Pike's Peak or bust' has become such a familiar expression no explanation is needed in the United States – everyone knows it means a determination to reach an objective, not necessarily a geographic one. It expresses hope, may imply difficulty of achievement; it always implies a buoyant, adventuresome, devil may care desire and determination to reach the top, to scale the mountain, to reach the decided-upon goal. The booming optimism of a young and cocky nation feeling its oats, tinged with braggadocio, chauvinistic.

P.B.: E.P. omitted to note that in UK, and no doubt also in US, the *or bust* is sometimes tacked on to other placenames or objectives, pointing out a determination to reach them: e.g., one might see, painted on a vehicle whose occupants intend to cross Europe, the slogan 'Istambul or

bust'. In a somewhat different category is the adjectival phrase used to describe an impulsive, stubborn person given to trying desperately hard, who will do a thing and damn the consequences: *shit or bust* – which is, of course, *not* a c.p.

pile. See: cross, I win; you can only.

pills. See: pink pills.

pilot. See: since Pontius.

pimple. See: easy over.

pin. See: that'll pin; there's no point.

pin back your lug'oles! (= ear-holes, ears.) 'Cyril Fletcher's conversation-stopper is in decay, but once ruled O.K,' (Russell Davies, in the *New Statesman*, 9 Sep. 1977, reviewing the first ed. of this book. I owe much to Mr Davies – and all of it so agreeably conveyed, so good-humouredly, uncensorily expressed!) P.B.: As *VIBS* notes, it was 'Cyril Fletcher's customary cry before embarking on one of his Odd Odes'; these very characteristic monologues, peculiar to C.F., formed a very popular part of his broadcasts in the decade around 1950.

pinch. See: pound.

pink I do like forms the c.p., the essence, of a woman's monologue overheard in a bus, *c.* 1925, in Glamorganshire and adjacent parts: 'Pink I do like; puce I do rather; but I do go fair mad over a little bit of blue'. As Dr Lindsay Verrier, 1977, told me, 'The first four words were a c.p. that called for the rest in chorus'. How far beyond Wales this one spread or how long it lasted, neither Dr Verries nor I know. P.B.: this reminds me of a family saying, a quot'n from a Tunbridge Wells haberdasher's assistant, 'It comes more of a beige', which we used in much the same way as Dr Verrier's example.

pink pills for pale people. From the wording of a much-advertised remedy or tonic, comes this humorous c.p. interjected into talk about patent medicines: late C19–20; by 1940, ob., and by 1950, †. P.B.: but still firmly ingrained in the memories of the older generation, early 1980s. In full, *Dr Williams' pink...*

pint. See: couldn't knock.

pip, pip! arose either during or a few years before WW1 – perhaps from a musical comedy – and was, esp. during the 1920s, used – always trivially – both as cheerful greeting and more freely as a cheery 'Good-bye!' I remember hearing it during WW1, but never during WW2; and Leechman recalls it as having been also Can. Dead by 1950. R.S. quotes from 'Bartimeus', *The Long Trick*, 1917, in which a young girl, asked how she'd reply to a rough calling *yah-boo!*, says, 'How thrilling! Why, I'd say "pip-pip".' It had become slightly ob. by *c.* 1925; yet Patricia Newnham 'when young' heard it during WW2 – in the version *toodle-loo pip, pip!* 'jokingly said'. Camilla Raab remembers it as simply *toodle-pip!* P.B.: cf the equally nonsensical, contemporaneous exclam. *chin-chin!* used as a farewell, occ. as a toast.

R.S. (1975) adds that it was often used in reply to the farewell *tootle-oo* and thinks that it may have, ultimately, been 'based on early bulb-blown motor-horns, when the road-hogs deep *tootle-oo* was answered by the perky *pip-pip* of the smaller car'.

pipe(s). See: here they come smoking; put that in your p.; take your p.; they don't p.

pipe-clay. See: pick him.

pips. See: six pips; squeeze till.

piss. See: all wind; dogs are pissing; every little helps; he never had; he pisses; I wouldn't p.; if you can pee; it would make; let her cry; like a snob's; pot; such a reason; wish in; you can't p.; you could p.; you don't p.

piss-holes. See: eyes like.

piss off. See: enough to p.

piss, or get of the pot, usu. prec. by *look* or *now, either.* A var. of **shit, or get off the pot,** 'than which it is *much* more prevalent, [has] much greater stamina; and, I believe, because of its alliterative element' (Fain, 1977). Also, prob. because it is rated as less vulgar.

piss-up. See: couldn't organize.

piss when he can't whistle – he will (or **he'll**). He will be hanged: perhaps orig. an underworld c.p.: mid C18–19. (Grose.) A ref. to the *post-mortem* release of waste.

pissed in the sea.... See **every little helps....**

pissed on a nettle – (usu. **he**) **looks as if he had** is 'a c.p. evoked on seeing a doleful countenance' (Leechman): late C19–20. From the coll.—later, dialectal – mid C16 – earlier 20 expression, *to have pissed on a nettle*, to be ill-tempered, or very uneasy.

pissed on (or **upon**) **from a great height – he should be.** He's beneath contempt: R Aus. N: WW2 and after. I cannot prove it, but I'd say that this c.p. was prompted by the RAF's *to shoot* (someone) *down from a great height*, to defeat him in argument or on a matter of procedure or protocol.

R.S. later added a further gloss: He should be officially or semi-officially reprimanded by a high-ranking officer: RAF: latter half of WW2. See Paul Brickhill, *The Dambusters*, 1951, where he relates the very amusing incident that originated it. But it passed to the other Services and became fairly common among civilians.

P.B.: this seems to me to be merely a 'politer' version of the common Services' and low phrase *shat* or *shit on* or *upon from a great height*, also meaning to have trouble, in whatever form, visited upon one from higher authority. Perhaps inspired by the idiomatic *sit* or *sat upon* (someone) *firmly*, repress(ed) him by admonition; not restricted to the third person, since it may just as well be *I was shat...*, *you'll be shit...*, etc. See also **shit on...**

pistol. See: hot as a dimestore.

pit. See: do they have.

pit-pat's the way! Don't stop! Go on! A proletarian c.p. of *c.* 1870–1914. Recorded by B & L.

pitch. See: get in there and.

pitcher. See: miraculous.

pits. See: it's the pits.

Pitt Street or Christmas. See **doesn't know...**

pity about you! An almost hilariously derisive c.p. directed at a person either boastful or irritating or self-seeking – or to a person either constantly or excessively querulous: C20. P.B.: or simply used as a gratuitous insult, to provoke a response. Also in var., *it's a shame about you!*

pity the poor sailor on a night like this! A semi-humorous, semi-compassionate c.p. that has, since the 1880s or 1890s, been uttered *à propos* of a stormy night. Perhaps prompted by *The Book of Common Prayer's* 'For Those in Peril on the Sea'.

'Also "God help sailors on a night like this!" used ironically by sailors in peril, if we are to believe C.S. Forester in *Flying Colours*, 1938' (Sanders, 1978). Nor should we disbelieve him! The ref. is to the Napoleonic Wars.

'In US, more often "God help the poor sailors..." Now becoming ob.' (R.C., 1978).

place. See: good place; has his; it's a nice p.; nice place; that grabs; this is no; what a funny; what's a nice; where the dogs; yes, but in; you have a nice; you make the p.

plan. See: according to p.; what's your song.

plank(s). See: pick a soft; thick as.

plant you now and see you later. I must – or I'll leave you now and see you later: US underworld since *c.* 1930; by 1960, slang. (John Martin Murtagh and Sara Cowen Harris, *Who Live in Shadow*, 1960.)

'Although this may have been the original form, the only form I recall hearing is *plant you now, dig you later*' (Shapiro, 1977). P.B.: this *dig* may however be a pun on the later 1960s hippy use of *dig*, to understand, to enjoy.

plantain root. See: born near.

plastered. See: roofed.

plates. See: turtle.

play. See: as the man in the p.; don't let's p.; go and play; he's playing; I don't want to p.; I shan't p.; I took my harp; it's a good game; let's not p,; let's play; one of your; ought to be;

since Jesus; so you want; then the band; they laughed; you can't p.; you play; and:

play it again, Sam! It 'has virtually replaced the old cry of "Encore!" Attributed to Humphrey Bogart in the film "Casablanca", made in 1943. In fact, he did not use these exact words, but he might as well have used them, because everyone else does' (Skehan, 1977). And *VIBS* says, of this c.p.: 'At one point Ingrid Bergman says, "Play it once, Sam, for old time's sake", and later on Bogart says, "You played it for her, you can play it for me. Play it!" But, what the hell – the phrase exists!' The 'it' that Sam was requested to play on his piano in that Casablanca nightclub was 'As Time Goes by'.

Cf **me Tarzan...**

play it by ear. See **let's play it...**

play *that* on your oboe (or **piano** or, the least used, **harpsichord**)! All three, put together, are less used than **put that in your pipe and smoke it,** q.v. The three lesser forms do not mean, however, 'Think it over!' but are 'triumphant conclusions of withering plain-speaking or of an (in the opinion of the speaker) crushing rejoinder; [they] are obsolescent and seem a little quaintly old-fashioned, but they are not obsolete, unless among the young' (J.W.C., 1977). Date? Prob. since the later 1930s. John Le Carré, in *The Honourable Schoolboy*, 1977, has 'Play that on your Aunt Emma's piano!'

play the game, cads! 'The Western Brothers (who were, in fact, cousins) would begin their act with "Hello, cads!" and end it with "Cheerio, cads, and happy landings!"' (*VIBS*). It was, of course, parody: DSUE glosses *play the game* thus:

To act honourably, to 'do the decent thing': coll.: since latish C19; in later C20, a concept too personal to be treated other than humorously. *Daily Chronicle*, 2 May 1904, 'Men do not talk about their honour nowadays – they call it "playing the game"' (*OED*). Lit., playing to the rules; cf *it's not cricket*.

P.B.: the phrase and, some would say, the concept declined with the sunset of the British Empire. The Western Brothers, who performed on the halls and broadcast in variety shows until *c.* 1945, always immaculate in white tie and tails, carried on a serial song, their signature tune, from act to act, and the chorus was '(I say,) play the game, you cads, play the game!' It was sung in a burlesque of Public-School English; most people would have recognised the source being imitated by those using it as a c.p.

play trains. See **run away and....**

play up, Nosey! A traditional London cry from 'the gods': late C18 – early C20. From Cervette, that famous 'cellist of Drury Lane Theatre who, because of his very large nose, was called 'Nosey'. ('John o' London in his *London Stories*, 1911–12.)

player. See: every player; trap for.

playing hell with himself. See **he's playing....**

playing it on the heart-strings, often prec. by *that's*, less often by *it's*. That's – or you're – being sentimental instead of realistic (L.A., 1974): since *c.* 1920.

[**playing with a full deck,** 'possessing all one's faculties': US: since *c.* 1930 at latest. Cf Dashiell Hammett's 'How do you figure her [a very disturbed young woman]? Only fifty cards to her deck?' *Deck* = a pack of playing cards (R.C., 1978). Cf *he's got a few loose seeds in his gourd*, 'popularized by "Grannie" on the TV show, *The Beverly Hill Billies*, 1960s–70s' (A.B., 1978). But I'm very doubtful about the eligibility of these two phrases; surely merely ordinary slang idioms.]

playmates. See: hello, playmates.

plays a game of hide-and-seek – he or she. He or she is a secret drinker: since *c.* 1950. (Petch, 1971.) Obviously a pun on the children's game. But *he plays at hide and seek* was, *c.* 1750–1880, 'a saying of one who is in fear of being arrested...and therefore does not choose to appear in public' (Grose, 1785).

plays as fair as if he'd picked your pocket (– he) was, in C19, applied to a dishonest gambler.

pleasant. See: pay up.

please. See: if not pleased; we aim; and:

please, I want the cook-girl! was, c. 1895–1914, either directed or 'said of a youth haunting the head of area steps' (Ware) – the household staff being 'below stairs'. Cf:

please, mother, open the door! was, c. 1900–14, a Cockney c.p., spoken admiringly to a pretty girl. They have winning ways, these Cockneys.

please, teacher! and **thank you, teacher!** The former indicates that the speaker wishes to make a remark (he requests permission to speak); the latter connotes irony or even derision towards someone who is either permitting condescendingly or explaining pompously or in excessive detail: C20. Both – obviously – from the schoolroom. To which should be subjoined the contemporaneous *please, teacher, may I leave the room?* employed joc. by adult humorists of retarded intelligence.

pleased. See *will be pleased!*

pleasure, Lady Agatha – a. Apparently a C20 Society c.p., but seldom heard since WW2. Perhaps from one of Oscar Wilde's comedies or from some other early C20 drawing-room piece. As Mr Brian Bliss has pointed out to me, it occurs in, e.g., Act II of Noël Coward's *Private Lives*, 1930:

AMANDA: Do you mind if I can come round and kiss you?

ELYOT: A pleasure, Lady Agatha.

plot thickens – the. 'The work at the crossroads is getting dirtier. [See **dirty work**...] Used seriously in Victorian [and Edwardian] melodrama and modern "comics"; otherwise jocular' (Sanders, 1978). Clearly, only when it is either joc. or ironic does it quality as a c.p. It has thus qualified since latish C19. The phrase has long been a cliché; the cliché itself was adumbrated in George Villiers, Second Duke of Buckingham's famous comedy, *The Rehearsal*, 1671, at III, ii, 'Ay, now the plot thickens very much upon us'.

Of its US usage, R.C., 1978, says, 'Things are becoming more complicated, hence (perhaps) more interesting: C20, perhaps earlier; somewhat ob.'

plough. See: I might as well; too thick.

plum-tree. See: have at.

plums. See: poke full.

plural. See: answer is in the p.; singular.

plus a little something some (loosely the) **others haven't got.** This joc. (and self-explanatory) c.p. dates from a motor-oil advertisement issued early in 1934 by the Shell-Mex and British Petroleum Company.

pneumonia. See: if I hit.

po. See: after you with the po; eleven o'clock; no poes.

pocket(s). See: death adders; dipped into my; his pockets; if not pleased; mind your p.; my pocket; plays as fair; snake; wanted.

poet. See: in the words.

poet and didn't (occ. **doesn't** or **don't**) **know it.** See **that's a rhyme.**

point Percy at the porcelain, (of males) to urinate, usu. prec. by *I must (just) go and...*, is an Australianism introduced by the actor comedian Barrie Humphreys via his comic-strip 'hero' Barrie MacKenzie in the satirical magazine *Private Eye*. The phrase swept into great popularity among the raffish in the early 1970s. (P.B.)

point taken. Acceptance of a point in an argument or a discussion, as in 'You've put a very good case. Point taken!' [P.B.: it may be used as an acquiescent response to a rebuke seen as justified: 'Point taken! It won't happen again, I promise you.'] Now that Playfair, 1977, has drawn my attention to a reprehensible omission, I remember first hearing it in the early 1950s, but I rather think that it arose during WW2.

poison. See: name your.

poke a stick at. See: has more.

poke in the eye with a burnt stick. See **better than a dig...**

poke full of plums! – a. An impertinent reply to *which (is the) way to (such and such a place)?*: c. 1570–1680. It occurs in Brian Melbancke, *Philotimus*, 1583, and Giovanni Torriano, *A Dictionary of Italian and English*, 1609, and is treated by Apperson.

poker. See: don't chant; wouldn't touch it.

pole. See: like a rope; longest pole; low man; wouldn't touch it.

policeman. See: better than a drowned; I think your; tell your troubles.

polish. See: clean and p.

politic. See: how does your body.

Pollacky. See: oh, Pollacky.

Polly put the kettle on and we'll all have tea comes from an old nursery rhyme, reinforced by Dickens's song 'Grip the Raven' and, as a c.p. dates from c. 1870. (Collinson.) Since WW2 it has become increasingly ob. [and recognised rather as a quot'n from the nursery rhyme: P.B.].

po'ly, thank God! See **poorly**...

Pom. See: punch a Pom.

Pompey. See: paws.

pond. See: run it up; tap run.

ponies. See: do they have.

Ponsonby. See: it's all right, P.

Pontius. See: since Pontius.

poodles. See: raining.

Poona. See: Gad; two other.

poontang. See: little poontang.

poor. See: it's the poor; rich; she's good.

poor blind Nell. See: and did he.

poor chap, he hasn't got two yachts (or **Rolls-Royces**) **to rub together** is 'said of a rich man complaining of his poverty' (Sanders, 1974): since the late 1960s. Cf the ironical 'Poor devil – down to his last million', which hasn't yet (1976) become a c.p., although it deserves to do so. 'Certainly (*he's*) *down to his last yacht* has been in American use for at least 20 years' (R.C., 1978).

poor old thing or **soul.** See **pore...**

poor soldier. See **it's a poor soldier...**

poorly. See: I'm proper.

poorly (or, illiterately, **po'ly**), **thank God!** 'Southern US (from c. 1910) response to an inquiry as to how one does. The implication is "Thank God I'm no worse!" Now almost certainly extinct' (R.C., 1978).

pop goes the weasel! – occ. prec. by **and** – has, since c. 1870, been regarded as a c.p.: orig. proletarian, mostly Cockney. Ware remarks:

Activity is suggested by 'pop', and the little weasel is very active. Probably erotic origin. Chiefly associated with these lines –

Up and down the City Road.

In and out The Eagle.

That's the way the money goes.

Pop goes the weasel!

The City Road, a famous London street; The Eagle, a very well-known public-house in Shepherdess Wall. The *ODQ* attributes the song to W.R. Mandale and dates it 'Nineteenth Century'. In her *Song Index*, Minnie L. Sears classifies it as 'Children's Song'. The British Library's Music Index records *Pop Goes the Weasel* as 'an old English Dance', pub'd in 1853. Perhaps, therefore, the song was composed to be sung to a dance that had existed long before, and continued to exist for some time after, 1853. Julian Franklyn (b. 1899) remembered it, as a Cockney c.p., at least as early as 1910; EP (b. 1894) remembers that the c.p. was freely used in NZ before 1910.

Noble, 1977, however, suggests a different orig. for the two key words, *pop* and *weasel*. 'The "weasel" was the nickname for a flatiron with its sharp, thin face, similar to that of a weasel. It was a domestic commodity that could be spared, hence it could be pawned, or "popped". After spending money in The Eagle, [one had] nothing left for food, so "pop" goes the weasel.'

'The Eagle' was in the City Road, London, and the 'weasel' was a special tailoring iron. (Ms Joanna Dessau, historical novelist, 1978.)

Whatever the orig., it is a very English c.p.

Pope. See: enough to piss; trot.

popping. See: how are you p.

poppy show. See: all dressed.

poppycock. See: balderdash.

popular as a pork chop... See **pork chop...**

population. See: what's that? the p.

porcelain. See: point Percy.

pore ole thing, she'll 'ave ter go was a 'gag' employed by Frankie Howerd, in ref. to his accompanist. It passed into gen. use to fit any vaguely similar circumstance or situation; occ. as *she's a poor old* or *pore ole...* (P.B., 1975.) *VIBS* notes another version, *poor soul, she's past it.* Perhaps it was reminiscent of, and even prompted by, **don't shoot the pianist, he's doing his best.**

pork. See: pig on.

pork chop in a synagogue. Either as a vivid simile for something very badly, esp. embarrassingly, out of place, as in, e.g. 'The suggestion went down like a pork chop...', it was so badly received that it ought never to have been made; or, more usu. since c. 1950, applied to anything unpopular or unwelcome, (*about as*) *popular as a pork chop in a synagogue*, because, of course, pork is forbidden to Jews. See also **more strife...** (P.B.)

pork chops are going to hang high. Very US, this c.p. predicts a hard winter. A Westernism. Berrey.

porridge. See: you have your glue.

portholes. See: you want p.

portrait. See: have a gorilla.

Portsmouth. See: consider.

posh. See: gone for a posh.

position. See: I left.

possible. See: is it possible; this should.

possum up a gum tree – like a. An Aus. c.p. applicable to a person exceptionally, or completely, happy: C20. (Jim Ramsay, *Cop It Sweet,* 1977.) Clearly rural in orig., opossums being arboreal marsupials; and a gum tree being a eucalypt; and gum tree; this engaging creature's natural habitat. Baker, 1942.

post-office. See: letter.

postage stamp. See: what he doesn't.

posted. See: get in, knob.

pot. See: come on, stew; piss, or; put a stone; shit, or; there'll be a chicken; there's a lid.

pot to piss (euph. **pee**) **in – he doesn't** (or **didn't**) **have a.** Indicates extreme poverty: mainly US and Can.: dates since c. 1905. Often expanded by addition of **and not even a window to throw it out of.**

potato(es). See: all that meat; mashed; mind your own p.; take a red.

Potomac. See: all quiet.

pound. See: lend us your p.; lost a pound; now then, only; you don't get.

pound note. See: you don't happen.

pound of tea. See: given away.

pound to a pinch of shit – it's. A low expression of complete confidence: since late C19. Sometimes *it's... that...,* but often prec. by *I bet* (*you*) or *I'll lay a pound...* 'In Australia, boundless confidence is sometimes asserted by *it's two,* or *ten, bob to a pinch of shit*' (Lovett, 1978). Less frequent is the negative, *I wouldn't bet...* – but the loser's end is always a *pinch.* Cf **or my prick's...**

Powder River! Let her buck! 'A cowboys' shout of encouragement... A cry of derision... hence this is a very familiar cry throughout the southwest cattle country.' It orig. in an accident happening in 1893. (Adams.) The Powder River flows through Oregon.

power. See: more power.

pox-doctor's clerk. See: all dressed.

practice. See: this practice.

[**praise the Lord and pass the ammunition!** stands half-way between a cliché and a c.p. But it began as a famous quot'n. 'Said at Pearl Harbor [7 Dec. 1941]' by Howell M. Forgy (b. 1908), as Bartlett tells us.]

prang. See: wizard.

prawn. See: don't come the raw.

prayer(s). See: Gawd; she will say; we got back.

praying. See: that's past.

pregnant. See: keep 'em; more strife; worried.

preparing to be a beautiful lady. This Pears' Soap advertisement became a c.p., 'still sometimes used in a slightly unkind way' (Anon., 1978). The archives of Messrs A. & F. Pears Ltd. tell me that 'the advertisement captioned "Preparing to be a beautiful lady" first appeared [in] 1932'. With thanks to Miss L. Mary Barker, *Pears Cyclopaedia,* 21 July 1978. Cf **good morning, have you used Pears' soap.**

preserves. See: wouldn't that jar your.

press on regardless!, often shortened to **press on!** In his play *South Sea Bubble,* 1956, at II, i, Noël Coward uses the shorter form:

SANDRA: There are a million things I want to ask about – I don't know where to start.

GEORGE: Press on, my love. You're not doing badly.

As a c.p., it dates from the middle 1940s. Of its origin. Vernon Noble, a squadron-leader and one of the Air Ministry's four Official Observers (the other three were John Pudney, the late H.E. Bates, John Bentley) during WW2, has, 1973, recalled that the orig. form, *press on regardless,* 'was one of those joking phrases, defiant of all adversity, minimizing hardships, like "the gremlins have got into it", offered as an explanation for the inexplicable troubles with an aircraft'.

Common among flying, esp. bomber, crews during the war, it refers to the determined prosecution of an air-raid over Germany, despite losses before the target was even reached.

And not only RAF: 'Used in the [N. Africa] desert (1940–43) as a spur to keep advancing, however hard the "going" or heavy the opposition. A "press-on type" was a good soldier' (Sanders, 1978).

See also **we must press on....**

press the flesh! Shake hands!: c. 1910–40. It was recorded by A.E.W. Mason in his novel, *The Sapphire,* 1933.

E.P. 'killed' it too early. As R.S. remarks, 1977, 'Much heard during President Carter's electoral campaign of 1975; candidates appear to lay much importance on physical personal contact. Cf **give me some skin**'. That admirably observant cartoonist and chronicler of our times, Ms Posy Simmonds, includes this phrase, *c.* 1980, in the somewhat dated repertoire of her boozy, pub-loving, whisky salesman character, Edmund Heep. (P.B.) See also **slap me five!**

pretend you're a bee, and buzz. This Aus. c.p. of dismissal dates from *c.* 1950 and clearly puns *buzz off,* run away. (B.P.) It belongs to a small group of such punning phrases. A.B., 1978, adduces three, all US, and assigned by him to the 1950s–60s:

Let's make like horseshit and hit the trail!
Let's make like radiation and fall out!
Let's make like snow and drift!

This last I would guess to be the earliest. I don't think that these three are fully qualified c.pp.; but they are, at least, witty.

P.B.: E.P. seems somewhat inconsistent in his judgments here, but never mind, eh! He misses a rather rude Canadian Army version I heard *c.* 1960:

Why don't you make like an ice-hockey ball, and puck off!

prettiest. See: I am the p.

pretty. See: I'm not just; pay up; who's a p.

pretty Fanny's way. See **only pretty Fanny's way.**

prevents that sinking feeling (– **it**) is 'one of those advertising slogans (like **Guinness is good for you**) which the public adopted for its own jocular purposes. This one accompanied a picture of a cheerful little man [in his pyjamas] clinging to a huge jar of Bovril [the well-known meat extract] afloat on a rough sea. The c.p. was current for a few years after the advertisement made its first impact – in the 1920s' (Noble, 1977).

That information was soon supplemented by this from the Bovril Bureau, Miss Judy Regis writing thus: '"Bovril Prevents That Sinking Feeling" was designed by H.H. Harris and first appeared in 1920. You may be interested to know that the slogan was said to have been produced several years earlier, but was withheld because of the Titanic disaster'. The 45,000-ton liner *Titanic* sank on her maiden voyage in 1912 with the loss of nearly 1500 lives.

Cf **alas, my poor brother.**

price. See: cheap at half; two for; what's that got; what's up.

prick. See: all mouth; big man; clumsy as a cub; I work; I wouldn't stick; like a spare; may your p.; or my p.; short and; standing; with a five; wouldn't give.

pride. See: fie.

prince. See: some day.

print. See: licence to p.

private peace. See **separate peace.**

privates sweat, officers perspire, ladies glow. A British Army officers' c.p.: C20. (P.B., 1976.) Cf **horses sweat…**

privilege. See: old man is; what is rank.

prize. See: every player; no prizes; no second.

pro bono publico, no bloody panico! For the public's sake, no panic, please: orig. and still, in the main, theatrical, used to prevent or to allay panic or alarm in an emergency, for instance, a fire or a sudden death at a public performance or even a minor emergency at rehearsal: C20. Note that the L. *pro bono publico*, in the public interest, is reinforced by the It. *panico* and perhaps also by the *-o* (a very, very common It. suffix) of English *no*.

In Laurence Meynell's *Die by the Book*, 1966, the actor 'hero' says: 'The taste of the tobacco steadied me. "Pro bono publico, no bloody panico," I reminded myself. The great thing was not to flap.' In 1968, Granville noted that, during the 1920s – 40s, it was often used, joc., in the RN. He added that **'not to worry!'** (q.v.) would be the modern version.

problem. See: my problem; no problem; we have a p.

procedure. See: standard.

production. See: big production; don't make a p.; for a musical; you're holding.

profit. See: all profit.

promise. See: all promise; is that a p.; she wants.

promises, promises! P.B., writing in 1975, says:
[A] c.p. within the past 2 or 3 years, used either sarcastically or jokingly (the soft answer turning away wrath); e.g., 'If I find this is a bum steer, I'll blood from well *do* you!' – 'Nyah, promises, promises!' The answer might as likely have been 'Is that a threat or a promise?' which is fairly common in Service circles still.

promotion that cometh neither from the south nor from the east nor even from the west. Patronage dispensed by Lord North. Cited by F.W. Mant in *The Midshipman*, 1876. (Peppitt.) This was that Lord North (1732–92) who, a notorious last-ditcher and a compliant Prime Minister (1770–82), did more than anyone else to lose the American colonies. The saying would therefore seem to have orig. during the middle or latish 1770s – and to have survived for perhaps a century in the RN.

prop. See: buy a prop.

proposition. See: consider; is this a p.

prosper. See: cheats.

prostitution. See: all that's between.

protection. See: free trade.

protocol, alcohol, and geritol. 'Attributed to Adlai Stevenson (1900–65) as a summary of the diplomatic life (for an ageing man) when he was ambassador to the UK from 1961 to the end of his life' (J.W.C.) – and not yet †. (*Geritol* is a tonic.)

One of the comparatively few c.pp. of an upper professional stratum, it nevertheless spread to the educated and cultured public in the US and is, or was, not unknown in the UK. Moreover, it merits commemoration as a testimony to Adlai Ewing Stevenson's brilliant wit and intelligence; he is perhaps the greatest American to have never been elected President: and those of us who know about such matters know why he wasn't.

proud. See: are you getting too p.

prove. See: I've arrived; you can't p.

prove it, liar! 'Spoken quickly, the point of this was it peremptorily insulting quality [and] its very outrageousness. The same is true, as to outrageous insult, of the even cruder *you think you're tough, but you only smell stronger*', or *he thinks he's tough, but he only smells stronger*: schoolboys': c. 1910–40. (Mr. P. Daniel, 1978.)

proverbs. See: raised.

prunes. See: raised.

pub. See: go to the pub; it's a long lane.

public enemy number one was orig. applied to 'Kill Crazy Dillinger' – a once-famous Midwest US outlaw (as Berrey reminds us); it became a US c.p. It reached England after WW2. Mr A.B. Petch, 1974, reminds me that it is 'sometimes used for the Prime Minister in office' and that it was 'used by Jimmy Jewel in *Spring and Autumn*, a comedy series in 1973'.

'The FBI keeps a list of the "Ten most wanted criminals" posted in Post Offices throughout the country. As a result, there were a radio, and then a television, show with that title. John Dillinger *was* on the list for a while, but the listing continues to be current. The phrase now means "anyone I don't care for", as in *he's on my shit-list* [q.v. at **on my shit-list**]' (A.B., 1978).

publicity. See: any publicity.

pudding. See: hungry; not a word of; put your p.; she's joined; what would shock.

Pudsey. See: well, I'll go.

puff. See: not in all.

pulheems. See: don't push.

pull. See: I'll pull; it's all over; no name, no p.; who pulled; and:

pull a soldier off his mother – he wouldn't (occ. prec. by **pull?**). Directed at a very lazy or slack man: orig. (*c.* 1880) nautical, esp. RN, it became, *c.* 1900, also Army.

pull down the blind! was, *c.* 1880–1940, a London lower classes' c.p. addressed to couples making love. (Ware.) B.G.T. (b.*c.* 1921) recalls, 1978, that her grandmother used to sing:
Oh, what a little short shirt you've got,
Jimmy, pull down the blind!

pull down your vest! In M, 1891, James Maitland scathingly glossed it as 'a stupid expression which originated a few years ago, became a catch phrase on the streets and then faded into deserved oblivion'.

Fourteen years earlier, in the 4th edn of *Am*, I see it glossed thus: 'A curious flash expression of recent origin, without meaning. It is heard on all occasions, coming alike from the lips of the street-boy, who would "shine your boots", and a fashionable attendant of the clubs [club member, not club servant]; yet no man can tell whence it came.' Bartlett quotes, from *Burton's Events of 1875–76*, pub'd either very late in 1876 or, less prob., very early in 1877, the following verses written by H.G. Richmond.
Flash sayings, you know, now-a-days are the rage,
They're heard in the parlor, the street, on the stage,
'You're too fresh' and 'Swim out, you are over your head';
But a new one's been coined, and the old ones are dead.
'A Centennial crank' is one that is new,
And 'Crawl out of that hat' is quite recent too;
But the latest flash saying with which we are blest
Is to tell a man quietly, '*Pull down your vest*'.
J.W.C., 1975, writes:

Common here as a c.p. up to, say, 20 or 30 years ago, when 'vests' (waistcoats, remember) 'went out'. Men's clothing makers have tried during the last 15 years or so to bring them back 'in', but with only very moderate success, and the phrase has never regained its wide currency. Its commonest – perhaps its only – use was as an irrelevant interruption, meant to be distracting and disconcerting, of a long-winded bore's tiresome discourse.

As it happens, Col. Moe had, only a week or thereabouts earlier, noticed what he judged to be a merely 'nostalgic', and predicted to be a brief, revival.

A.B., 1978, adds a helpful note: 'Mark Twain used this expression in one of his stories about the Western USA, about a "talking" blue jay bird, who tills a man "pull down your vest!" – quit being pretentions. Not current, since vests are not!'

pull in your ears (– you're coming to a bridge)! occurs in a long list of 'disparaging and sarcastic flings' recorded by Berrey: US: since c. 1930; little used since c. 1960.

pull the chain!, often, as P.B. tells me, 1976, 'accompanied by gestures of holding one's nose and "pulling the chain"', expresses the greatest contempt for a feeble joke or stupid remark: perhaps orig. among schoolboys: since c. 1940 (?earlier) by 1965, ob., and by 1970, virtually!. There is – obviously! – a witheringly cloacal ref.!

pull the ladder up, Jack, I'm all right! is a late C19–20 var. of **fuck you, Jack….**

pull the other one, its's got bells on it!, occ. prec. by *now*. 'A rejoinder to a fanciful statement or a tall story. "We don't believe it. Pull the other leg, it has bells on it"' (Granville, 1969).

Frank Shaw attributed it to the 1920s.

It has become so widely accepted that it sometimes occurs allusively, as in Karen Campbell's 'thriller', *Suddenly, in the Air*, 1969, 'Or was it my little joke! If so, I could pull the other one – it had bells on.' This shorter form recurs in the anon. 'Complete Vocabulary of Spoken English' in *Punch*. 10 Oct. 1973; the writer glosses it thus: 'There seem to be some flaws in your argument.'

Presumably from pictures of court jesters, wearing cap and bells.

A derivative ar. is *pull the other leg!*, as in Robert Crawford, *Kiss the Boss Goodbye*, 1970:

'In the frames, you see, are jewels.'

'Go on,' I said, 'pull the other leg.'

Miles Tripp, *Five Minutes with a Stranger*, 1971, has:

'I'm on a research project,' I said.

She paused. 'Researching what?"

'Charitable deeds and the motives behind them. You almost qualified as a Good Samaritan.'

'Pull the other leg,' she said.

See also **it's got bells on.**

Pull up a bollard and sit down. A c.p. invitation from the extremely popular radio-comedy series of the 1950s, the 'Goon Show'. Often, when used by the general public, it accompanied **hello, Jim!** See GOON SHOW.

pull up your socks! '"Take heart, and try harder." Very common, and for at least 20 years,' writes J.W.C., 1975, of its US currency. Adopted from Britain, where it has been current since, I think, c. 1910, but where it has, since c. 1945, become increasingly outmoded. P.B.: the Brit. version is almost always (**Oh, come on!**) *pull your socks up!*, or allusively, *he* (or *she*) *must* (*try to*) *pull his* (or *her*) *socks up*, said of one considered to be slacking.

pull your ear! Try to remember!: lower classes': c. 1860–1910. Ware.

pull your finger out! See **take your finger out!**

pull your head in! You're sticking your neck out – i.e., Be careful, you're talking foolishly or wildly: Aus.: since c. 1930, often in the allusive var. *pull it in!* An ephemeral Sydney version, c. 1948–51, was *pull your skull in!* (Sidney J. Baker, in a letter, 1950; Kylie Tennant, *The Joyful Condem-*

ned, 1953.) Prob., as B.P. told me some years ago, 'from the habit of army men sticking their heads out of troop trains and making smart remarks: the origin was "Pull your head in, or people will think it's a cattle train."'

pull through a (clothes) wringer or **a knot-hole** – (usu. **he**) **looks as if he had been**. This US c.p., applied to a lanky, tall, thin person, prob. goes back to the latish C19, but is 'still in use' (J.W.C., 1977). The *through a knot-hole* form is recorded by Berrey, 1942, and may be older.

pulling. See: everybody's pulling; harder.

pulling the right string? See **are you pulling…**

pulse. See: let's feel.

pump(s). See: go to hell; hokey-pokey; man the; your pump.

pump handle. See: knob.

punch. See: couldn't punch; devil a bit; it's good enough; no show; and:

pull a Pom a day! – i.e., a *Pommie*, i.e. an Englishman. A xenophobic c.p., used by New Zealanders and, I rather think, Australians: since c. 1950. 'It seems to owe something to slogans such as "Drinka pinta milk a day" and "Eat an extra egg a day"' (B.P., 1975).

Punch has done dancing. I can no longer dance to your tune – a tune of requests and solicitations: c. 1870–1910, perhaps with a decade added at either end. 'It was said with bitterness when good-natured helpfulness was felt to be taken as a matter of indifference over the years, and so, at another call, was brought to an end by the person concerned. It was used by my father, who was born in the early 1860's (L.A., 1974). This was the Punch both of Punch-and-Judy puppetry and of general folklore.

Punch's advice to those about to marry, as in 'Remember *Punch's* advice…: Don't!' This is the c.p. form of 'Advice to persons about to marry – Don't!' (*Punch*, 1845, VIII, 1). The witticism has been attributed to Henry Mayhew; and the c.p. has existed since very soon after 1845.

punched. See: doesn't know.

puns are punishable is a c.p. that – obviously – is itself a pun: mostly Aus.: since c. 1930. The dovetail rejoinder is *there is no punishment when no pun is meant.* (B.P., 1975.)

punt. See: when in doubt, p.

pup. See: I'd like a pup; night's; oh, bloody; since Hector.

pure. See: ninety-nine and.

purpose. See: accidentally.

purse. See: left her p.; may your prick; silk.

push. See: after you with the p.; another push; did she fall; don't push; I'll push; it'll pass; when push; and:

push in the bush is worth two in the hand – **a.** A working-men's erotic parody – since c. 1925 – of the proverb, *a bird in the hand is worth two in the bush*, with a pun on *bird* and a ref. to female pubic hair.

In the US, this form is never heard: there, it is *two in the hand is worth one in the bush*, 'common, and probably 40 years old at least' (J.W.C., 1977).

push on! keep moving! (See the Gifford quot'n at **what's to pay.**) Orig. a quot'n from Thomas Morton's *A Cure for the Heart Ache*, 1797 (II, i), it immediately 'caught on' with the public – in other words, became a c.p., but, to judge by the absence of other references, had, I'd say, a very short life, perhaps a mere two or three years and almost certainly not more than ten (1797–1806).

push the boat out! God ahead – *I'm* all right!: military: WW1. Cf **pull the ladder up!**

pusser. See: I've done.

pussy. See: it's pussy; you never get.

put. See: you're putting.

put a cross (or an X) on the wall! 'Addressed to someone who has done something out of character, or when something strange or unexpected happens' (B.P.) Aus.: since the late 1940s. To mark – to record – the event. Cf **chalk it up!**

put a galley down your back! Such-and-such a superior wishes to see you: printers': since c. 1860; ob. by 1930 and by 1950.

A galley would serve as a screen – or, rather, as a protection against a metaphorical caning.

put a sock in it! 'Oh, do stop talking about it, you've been going on and on about it for far too long.' As an Army (Other Ranks') c.p., it has been current since latish C19; but since the late 1940s, it has been much more widely used, as Mr. Alan Steele has reminded me, 1977. Here, *it* is obviously '(your) mouth.'

put a stone in the pot with 'em, and when it's soft, they're cooked! This C20 Aus. c.p. is applied to food that remains tough, however long it's cooked. Jean Devanney, *By Tropic Sea and Jungle*, 1944, has, 'The old saying applied to them [galahs]...'

This c.p. is also Brit. – a famous recipe for cooking porcupine. *In extenso*, When it's soft, throw the porcupine out and eat the stone' (Leechman): late C19–20 and apparently the orig. c.p. Strictly, there are no porcupines, only hedgehogs, in the UK; there has long existed this loose usage of the two terms.

put an X on the wall! See **put a cross...**

put another in the pot and hang the expense! See **never mind, it'll soon be Christmas.**

put another record on! and **change the record!** A C20 c.p., addressed to one's wife, or to anyone else, 'going on about something'; 'Heard as "For God's sake, put another record on, will you?"' (Petch, 1966). Socially, lower-middle class. A gramophone record, of course.

A.B. remarks, 1978, for the US, 'I've heard also "Why don't you change the [gramophone] needle, baby!" In little use now'.

put crape on your nose... See **hang crape...**

put (one's) foot down with a firm hand. A mixture of metaphors that has become a c.p. in later C20, along the lines of 'every time he opens his mouth he puts his foot in it'. (P.B.)

put her (or him) down, you don't know where she's (or he's) been. 'A jocular c.p., addressed to a friend who is demonstrating affection for a friend of the opposite sex, kissing, walking arm in arm, etc.' (P.B., 1975): since the 1950s or a little earlier. From Mother's remark to thoughtless child, carrying or hugging, e.g., a doll or a ball picked up in the street: 'Put it down, darling, you don't know *where* it's been!'

put in a good word for me! Addressed facetiously by scoffers and agnostics to a person seen going to church on Sunday: since *c.* 1920 – if not twenty-or-so years earlier. (Petch, 1974.) A subconscious insurance against eternal punishment. Cf **say one for me.**

put it on the back burner! 'Shelve it for the moment'; 'Don't give it a high priority': US: 'since perhaps *c.* 1930' (J.W.C., 1977). Cf **now you're cooking with gas.**

put (or shove) it where the monkey put (or shoved) the nuts; also **you can put (or shove) it...** Go to blazes! *or* Go to hell! Or, more specifically, addressed to one who refuses to share, or to hand over, something expectantly requested by the speaker. In *Ulysses*, James Joyce has the ver. ... *where Jacko put the nuts,* Jacko being a favourite name for a monkey. A low c.p. of late C19–20. Obviously the ref. is anal, the vulgar equivalent being 'You can stick (or stuff) it!' and the polite; **'You know what you can do with it'**, q.v. As Mr. Y. Mindel reminds me, the phrase 'contains a physiological inexactitude: strictly the monkey puts his nuts in his cheek pouches'. He adds, 'The innuendo is probably intended, anyway.' What's a scientific inaccuracy to the coiners of graphic, earthy phrases?

Occ. *nut-shells*, which perhaps makes better sense; also occ. – but only very occ. – *monkeys*; often... *the monkey puts (or shoves) its (or his) nuts*; rarely, *that* for *it*. Cf **if you don't like it...**, and:

put it where the sergeant put the pudding. You know what you can do with it. A low c.p. of late C19–20. The physiology of this phrase seems to be even more slapdash than that of the prec. phrase.

put it where the sun doesn't shine. Hide it quickly: US: since *c.* 1920. (A.B., 1978.)

put me in! Let me join you!: prison cant: since *c.* 1925 – perhaps from a decade earlier. Lit., '*Include me!*'

put more water in it! – with *water* emphasized – has, since *c.* 1880 or so, been humorously addressed to someone tipsy or well on the way to becoming tipsy. (I was reminded of this one by the generous Mrs M.Thomson of Bray-on-Thames, 1975.) Prob. from the, at first, serious advice tendered by teetotallers to those less total. Cf **take more water with it!**

put that in your mess kit! Think that over!: US Army: C20 (Berrey.) A deliberate var. of:

put that in your pipe and smoke it! Make what you can of what I've just said!: Digest that, if you can!; Put up with (or tolerate) that – if you *can*!: since early C19. Peake, 1824; Dickens in *Pickwick Papers*; 'Ingoldsby' Barham: Miss Mary Braddon (1837–1915), the now forgotten bestseller of late C19. (With thanks to *OED* and *ODEP*.)

It's a fact worth noting: that, despite its continuous currency and continual – indeed, constant – use, very little attention has been paid to this phrase, which is, I'd say, rather more of a c.p. than of a proverbial saying.

And, by the way, it derives from the very widely held, not entirely erroneous, belief that pipe-smoking and meditation go together.

Sanders, 1978, adds, 'Also "put that in your sock and suspend it". From a Leslie Henson comedy of the 1930s'. Too witty to have survived WW2. P.B.: and not many men nowadays wear sock-suspenders.

put that light out! See **one of ours.**

put that on your needles and knit it! This forms the feminine counterpart of – or rather, complement to – **put that in your pipe and smoke it!**: latish C19–20. (B.G.T., 1978.)

put the lights out! is perhaps more frequent than **put the light out**, q.v. at **one of ours**, third paragraph. L.A., 1976, rightly points out that **put the lights out!** was usu. completed by *they want to be alone*. He cites 'From the back of the hall a drunken voice shouted a favourite cliché [read 'catch phrase']: "Put the lights out! They want to be alone." [J.A. Cuddon, *The Bride of Battersea*. 1967]: of two boxers hugging in a clinch'. I first heard it *c.* 1912; it prob. goes back to the 1890s – perhaps to the 1880s.

put the wood in the (h)ole! Shut the door!: by later C20 this had become the gen. shape of the earlier *put a bit of wood in it!* recorded by DSUE (at **wood**, 6) as earlier C20 Services' usage, itself from the Yorkshire dial. version *put a piece of wood in the hole!* (A reminder from J.B. Smith of Bath, 1979.) Cf **were you born in a barn?**

put them in a field and let them fight it out! or, more coll., **put 'em in a field and let 'em fight it out;** there is also the more positive var. **...and make them (or force them to) fight it out.** Let the Heads of State fight out between (or among) themselves the wars they start, and thus prevent millions of innocent and rightly reluctant men and women and children from getting killed: Servicemen's (hence others') in WW1 and again in WW2. War is probably mankind's most spectacularly stupid folly: and one can only conclude that the age of miracles is *not* passed, the greatest, most mysterious miracle of all being that the human race has, so far, survived the human race.

put this reckoning up to the Dover waggoner! was. *c.* 1810–40, usu. addressed to the landlord of an inn. JB says. 'The waggoner's name being Owen, pronounced *owing*.'

put up or shut up! Prove what you say or be silent: orig. US: late C19–20. Back your assertion by putting up money – or shut up! (W & F: Berrey.)

Hence, in C20, also Brit., but often apprehended as 'Put up your fists and fight, or shut up! Desmond Bagley, in *Landslide* (set in Canada), 1967, has: 'Now, put up or shut up. Do you have anything to say? If not, you can get the hell out of here....'

'Or, in an automobile, *put out or get out! 1950s [onwards]'*

(A.B., 1978). To *put out* is US and Can. slang for 'to comply sexually' – as applied to the girl, of course.

put your feet up. 'Sit down and make yourself comfortable': US: used lit., (late C19–20), not a c.p. but a conventionalism; but seldom – since *c.* 1910, anyway – so used. When employed ironically, it verges on c.p. status. (Based on a note from J.W.C., 1977.)

put your money where your mouth is! Back your words with cash: Brit. and Aus.: since *c.* 1945. (B.P., 1973; John Braine, *The Pious Agent*, 1975, but ostensibly dated 1960.) Its complete incorporation into British speech-ways was, in Sep. 1975, confirmed when a very widely displayed Government poster began to advise all good citizens, 'Put your money where your mouth is' above a smaller-lettered line advertising the National Savings Bank Accounts Department and, by so doing, forestalled the Trustee Savings Banks.

Adopted from US, where current since *c.* 1930, if not earlier. (Col. Moe, 1975.)

put your pudden up for treacle! 'Encouragement to be forthcoming; with a suggestive strain to give a double edge. Used, 1917–18, by officers in the Royal Naval Air Service' (L.A., 1974).

'I met the phrase in the Army in 1914 and my informant told me that it relates to prison. If you were unwise enough to "hold your pudden out for treacle" it would have been swiped by another inmate, who "knew the ropes" better than you did' (Edgar T. brown, 1977). God bless the general intelligent public! It has so often helped me...

Putney. See: well, I'll go.

puts years on me. See: it puts...

puttees. See: scraped.

putting spots on dominoes. See making dolls' eyes.

putting their things together or, in full, **they're** (occ. **they are**) **putting...** 'When a wedding reception is nearing the end, and the happy pair have gone to change before leaving on their honeymoon, (a male guest] may ask, "Where have they got to?" and another will likely reply, "They're upstairs, putting their things together" – which will probably encourage another male to say, "Have they started already?" (Petch, 1976): lower-middle and middle-middle class?: since early C20, I'd guess. A pun on the euph, *things*, sexual parts: cf the Shakespearian 'to *exchange flesh*'.

putting your two penn'orth in (Anglo-Irish): or **coming in** (or **you must come in**, or **must you come in?**) **with your two eggs a penny.** A scathing comment upon a paltry contribution to the conversation: respectively latish C19–20 and C18–early 20. In Dialogue I of S, 1738, Swift has:

> NEV[EROUT]: Come, come, Miss, make much of naught, good Folks are scarce.
> MISS: What, and you must come in with your two Eggs a Penny, and three of them rotten.

There is a C18–19 var.: '...*five eggs, and four of them rotten*'. Semantically cf the C20 'There are two fools born every minute' (or 'Two fools are born every minute') with its witty addition, 'and you are all three of them'.

Also cf the US **two cents' worth**.

putty won't stick. A US underworld c.p., applied, apparently *c.* 1850–1910, to 'any attempted deceit that miscarries'. George P. Burnham, *Memoirs of the United States Secret Service*, 1872, has, 'This kind of "putty won't stick" much with him' – This kind of trick won't fool him.

Pygmalion. See: not bloody.

pyramids. See: hence.

Q

Q.E.D. *Quod erat demonstrandum,* which was, or had, to be shown or proved, and now *has* been: educational world: C19–20, although not much used since *c.* 1960. A tag of Euclidean geometry; a tag used humorously, often with a mockpompous intonation.

Also, naturally, *quod erat demonstrandum* itself.

quack. See: you can't q.

quail. See: seaman.

quality. See: never mind the q.

quarter. See: influence.

quarter flash and three parts foolish. A fool with a dangerous smattering of worldly knowledge: raffish, mostly London: *c.* 1810–50. (Pierce Egan, *London,* 1821.) Cf the † slang *fly flat,* a would-be expert.

queen. See: 'balls!'; eh! to me; I wouldn't call; keep up; one hand; true, O King.

Queen Victoria. See: have a gorilla; hey, Johnny; sorry, no.

Queen, you've spoke a mouthful was a c.p. of 1929–30 and prob. for a few years earlier and later. Harold Brighouse, *Safe amongst the Pigs,* performed 1929 and pub'd 1930, has the following in Act II:

> ROBERT: ...You may have uses for more money than you've got.
> CELIA: Queen, you've spoke a mouthful.
> ROBERT: This is serious, Celia.

The above is valid for the UK, but the c.p. represents a slight adaptation of the slightly earlier US *Queen, you spoke a mouthful,* 'As soon as was practical after the Armistice [11 Nov. 1918: WW1], the King and Queen of the Belgians visited this country. They were taken on a tour by the mayor of New York....The great sight, of course, was the look down the island to the sky-scrapers....The Queen remarked on the impressiveness of the scene, and the mayor answered her in those immortal words. That must have been about 1921–22. The story went all round the country and the phrase became famous' (Prof. Emeritus S.H. Monk, 1977).

queen. See: there's nowt.

queer as a... (–as). There are a number of phrases, similes, beginning thus and applied to homosexuals; perhaps the best known in later C20, current since *c.* 1955, is (*as*) *queer as a clockwork orange,* which seems to have orig. either in the East End of London or the Lowerdeck of the RN. It was given a gen. widening of popularity by Anthony Burgess's strange and moving novel, *A Clockwork Orange,* 1962, later filmed. Derivatives from it are ...*as a four-speed walking-stick,* used, and perhaps invented by, the well-known raconteur and bawdy anecdotist 'Blaster' Bates, 1970s, and ...*as a left-handed corkscrew,* also early 1970s.

Applicable to things odd and strange (and also, occ., to homosexuals) are *queer as a nine-bob note* or *a three-pound note,* or *a two* (or *nine*) *bob watch:* mid C20; they became ob. with the decimalization of currency in Feb. 1971. There was

no such note as a nine shilling or a three pound one, and a watch so cheap would be suspect, or phoney, indeed. These perhaps stem from the N. American *queer as a three-dollar bill,* current in Can. since late C19; in US, also *phoney as...,* and R.C. remarks, 'Often in the sexual sense, In *phoney as...,* the bill is often a *nine-dollar* denomination – equally fictitious, of course'. Cf:

queer as Dick's hatband (–as). Very odd indeed: mid C18–mid 19, and still 'alive and well' in the dialects of the Northern half of England. Grose, *The Vulgar Tongue,* 2nd ed., 1788, has it; so has Southey; so too G.L. Apperson's *English Proverbs and Proverbial Phrases,* 1929, a book that has never received its dues.

In C19, sometimes (*as*) *queer as Dick's hatband that went round nine times and wouldn't meet;* slightly less extravagant is B.G.T.'s version from Northamptonshire, 1978, *it's like Dick Clark's hatband, went round twice and wouldn't tie,* with the connotation 'however hard she tried, she couldn't get her job done. She said, "It's like..."'. Wedgewood, too, from Yorkshire, remembers from his youth, early 1930s, 'something about "going twice round like Dick's hatband"'. P.B.: I have heard the suggestion, unsupported by anything firmer than tradition, that Dick is Oliver Cromwell's son Richard.

question. See: ask a silly; good question; I forgot; I must have notice; that's a good; that's the sixty-four.

queue. See: join the back.

quick. See: sharp's; you couldn't be served.

quick and dirty. P.B., 1975, writes:

> I heard it in 1973 from a retired colonel, talking about intelligence reports which were produced fast and without scrupulous accuracy. I heard it again recently, used by a computer expert to describe 'initial print-outs', before 'the program has been de-bugged'. One might use it as well to describe a first edition on which proof-reading has been skimped to meet a publishing deadline.

P.B., 1983: I suspected at the time that this might be of US orig. the Colonel having served in Washington, and R.C., 1978, confirms that belief: 'Current in US magazine and magazine-publishing from before 1960, when I first heard it'.

quick and nimble: more lik a bear than a squirrel was, C18–mid C19, addressed to, or directed at, someone moving slowly when speed was required. Fuller; Grose, 1788.

quick (or **smart**) **as a rabbit** (–as). 'He's on the ball! Fast thinker!: US: late C19–mid 20' (A.B., 1978). P.B.: ?Brer Rabbit or Bugs Bunny.

quickly. See: it's not much.

quickness. See; now you see.

quid est hoc? Hoc est quid! A punning c.p. of mid C18–late C19. (Grose, 1796.) As Hotten explained, the question *quid est hoc? –* What's this? – is asked by one man tapping the bulging cheek of another, who, exhibiting a 'chaw' of tobacco, answers *hoc est quid* – 'This is what' – a *quid* of tobacco.

quiet. See: all quiet; anything for a q.

quiet as it's kept. 'Used prior to revealing what is assumed to be a secret' (CM, 1970): US negroes': since *c.* 1960.

quietly. See: I'll go q.

quilt. See: trying.

quite. See: not quick.

quite a place you've got here. A var. of nice place...

quite a stranger, often prec. by **well!** Addressed to a person one hasn't seen for some time: C20. R. Blaker's novel, *Night Shift*, 1934.

quius kius! Hush! *or* Cease!: theatrical: *c.* 1875–1910. (B & L.) Mock L. for 'Quiet please!.', the second element perhaps suggesting *please*, the first prob. representing *quietus*.

quod erat demonstrandum. See the first Q entry.

quodding dues are concerned. This is gaol matter – i.e. an offence that, detected, involves imprisonment: *c.* 1780–1850. Vaux.

quoth the raven 'was the code sign for actors to beware of certain digs' or lodgings, as Michael Warwick tells us in his article 'Theatrical Jargon in the Old Days', in *The Stage*, 3 Oct. 1968: in short, a theatrical c.p. of *c.* 1890–1940. As such, it prob. arose less from a concensus of actors' and actresses' literary knowledge than from the vogue for Edgar Allan Poe's poem *The Raven*, with its famous line, 'Quoth the Raven, "Nevermore"', a vogue which started with the recitations of it by Sir Henry Irving (1838–1905).

[**quoz!** is that not entirely absurd contradiction in terms, a single-word c.p. It was included by Mackay in his wonderful pioneering article. 'Popular Follies of Great Cities' – in effect, London and its c.pp. It was employed to intimate incredulity; I suggest that, approximately, it synonymized **sez you!** P.B.: or, as one might say to the Raven (see prec.), *quoth you!*]

R

R.C.s, Parsees, Pharisees and Buckshees indicates 'the Sergeant-Major's view of all those religious sects and oddities who do not conform to the Established Church and who can refuse to attend church parades, or could, when there were such things' (P.B., 1974); army: since *c.* 1945.

An anon, correspondent, 1978, expands and varies: *Chinese, Japanese; R.C.s, Parsees; Standatease and One-Two-Threes*, which arose in the Regular Army during the 1930s, or perhaps during the 1920s. Cf **Sudanese, Siamese...**

R.S.V.P. Ribbons showing very plainly – e.g., of lingerie: UK Society girls' c.p. of *c.* 1920–60. (Mrs David Hardman, 1977.)

rabbit(s). See: does your mother want; hope your r.; let the dog; little rabbits; may your r.; quick as; thank your mother; white rabbits.

rabbits out of the wood (–it's). It's splendid – sheer profit or a wonderful windfall: racing c.p., dating since *c.* 1920. Such rabbits cost nothing, whereas those in a butcher's shop *do.* P.B.: perhaps a poachers' memory.

racket. See: wrong business.

radiation. See: pretend.

Radmillovic. See: more strokes.

Rafferty (or **Rafferty's**) **rules.** Either no rules whatsoever, or rules applied haphazardly and arbitrarily: Aus.: I seem to remember hearing it 1915–18. Wilkes's citations in *Dict. Aus. Coll.* range from *The Bulletin* of 5 Jan. 1928 (the former) to *The Bulletin* of 18 May 1974 (the latter). Orig. obsucure; Wilkes very ingeniously proposes the English dialectal *reffatory*, refractory [P.B.: cf obstreporous to *obstropolous* to *stropy*]; I suggest some forgotten boxing referee named *Rafferty*, just poss, influenced by *reffatory* and by the (Marquess of) *Queensberry Rules* (1867) of boxing.

rag. See: takes the rag.

rag on every bush – (oh,) he has a. He is (or he's in the habit of) courting or 'chasing' more than one girl at a time: *c.* 1860–1914. Cf **takes the rag...**

rags on – she has (or she's got) the; and **she's got the painters in** or **the painters are in.** She is having her period: mid C19–20; the *painters* versions ob. by 1950. None could be called cultured or even tactful. Lovett, 1978, adds the Aus. var. *the painters haven't turned up* (when expected). Cf **red sails in the sunset.**

railroad. See: what a way.

railroadin'. See: now you're r.

rain. See: I think it's; if it was raining; it ain't gonna; it's raining; looks like rain; when it don't; you win.

raincheck. See: I'll take a r.

raining cats and dogs– it carries the c.p. 'gag' addition *and there are poodles in the road* 'to mock the cliché' (Ashley, 1984): US: later C20.

raining palaces or **pea-soup.** See **if it was raining...**

raised on prunes and proverbs. 'A cowboys' expression describing a fastidious and religiously inclined person' (Adams): hardly before late C19. It strikes me as being rather too literary, and too polite, for the average cowboy; indeed, it evokes the idea of Bostonian wit or perhaps of academics at their ease in the Senior Common Room.

rake. See: no matter for.

ran (or **run**) **away with another man's wife.** See **fine night...** and **you know what thought did.**

ranch. See: meanwhile.

rang a (or **the**) **bell.** See **does that ring...**

rank. See: what is rank.

raptures. See: roses.

rarest thing in India: Guardsmen's shit – the. Orig., **what is the rarest thing in India? – Guardsmen's shit,** shouted by Regular Soldiers not Guardsmen at a Guards unit or section as it passed: late C19–earlier 20. In ref. to the fact that Guards regiments never served in India in, at least, peacetime. (With thanks to Mr Y. Mindel.)

rarin' to go is a prob. late C19–20, certainly C20, c.p. – US, of course, and orig. Western – but only when it is used joc. or ironically. It indicates an impatient eagerness to get started and, when used lit. and therefore not as a c.p., it was applied to a high-spirited horse: dialectal for *rearing to go.*

'Current in the US and kept so by a [diminutive, mustachio'd] cartoon character named "Yosamite Sam" on the Warner Brothers' show, Bugs Bunny. Sam is a Westerner, although not all the cartoons in which he appears are necessarily Westerns' (A.B., 1978).

rat(s). See: bangs like; no rats; not enough; rough on; this is rat; you dirty rat.

rat shit, cat shit, and several kinds of bat shit. A nonsense response evoked by any mention of a 'ratchet' e.g.a ratchet screwdriver: Army (though very parochially): 1960s. (P.B.: with retrospective thanks to Capt. Peter Goonan.)

rather. See: oh, I say, I r.; oh, rather; or would you; would you r.

rather keep you for a week than a fortnight, the *for* often omitted. See **I'd rather keep you....**

rather you than me! Dating from *c.* 1930, it predicts – as *and the best of British luck!* predicts – the possibility – even the probability – of failure. US version: *better you...* (R.C., 1978). Also *sooner you...*

rations. See: came up with; only eating.

rattle. See: standing; that really rattled.

rave. See: what's the r.

rave on! Just go on talking nonsense! A US students' c.p. of the early 1920s (McKnight) Cf the coll. *raving mad*, very crazy indeed.

raven. See: quoth.

raw prawn. See: don't come the raw.

razor. See: I cut.

razzle-dazzle. See: give 'em.

reach. See: excuse me; I feel for you.

reaches the parts... See **refreshes the parts...**

read. See: can read; I read; if all else; you wouldn't r.; you've been reading.

read (rarely, **have you read**) **any good books lately?** In the 1920s and, slightly less, the 1930s, this was often employed as a social gambit and it was occ. varied to *seen any good plays lately* or *recently?* Then, in the BBC radio comedy series *Much Binding in the Marsh*, 1945–46, Richard Murdoch revitalized *read any good books lately?* by using it in any awkward situation, esp. when he was 'confronted by the unanswerable' (Barry Took, *Laughter in the Air*, 1976); R.M. spread it among a later generation. [*VIBS* instances the following exchange between R.M. and his fellow star Kenneth Horne:

K.H.: One of the nicest sandwiches I've ever had. What was it, Murdoch?

R.M.: Well, there was–er–have you read any good books lately?

K.H.: I thought it tasted something like that.

VIBS notes further that the phrase was 'also used in *Band Waggon* [Murdoch's late 1930s radio show with Arthur Askey], and air-force *Merry Go Round*'.]

Although decreasingly used, it was, even by 1978, not yet†. This particular c.p., like so many others, exemplifies the fact that, when dealing with the subject, the historian desperately needs a strong sense of perspective. To me, the phrase had long been so familiar, that in the first ed. of this book I forgot to refer to *Much Binding* at all. To those born (say) c. 1920–39, only Richard Murdoch's use of the phrase has, naturally enough, any validity. [P.B.: and that almost precludes its use, without apology or disclaimer, as a genuine, polite question.]

The stock reply, whether among authors anywhere or at literary cocktail parties, has, since the late 1940s, been, 'No! but I've written one'. And, 'at the height of the cold war (1945–55) the witty question to ask the Security Service or Special Branch was "booked any good Reds lately?"' (Sanders, 1978).

DSUE, at **crook**, adj., 5, after explaining the Aus. *go crook*, to give way to anger, has 'Hence the c.p., *have you read the* (or, more gen., *that*) *little red book?*; if the man thus addressed looked interrogatively, one added *that little red book, "Why Go Crook?"*: c. 1910–20'.

read 'em and weep! is, among US gamblers of C20, a dice-thrower's 'threat that he is going to throw a winning number' (Berrey). Not, since the middle 1940s, unknown among Brit. gamblers.

'Originally, I think, from poker – i.e., when laying down a (presumably) winning hand: read those cards – and weep. Whence, in crap, but now general, concerning any material (e.g. a financial statement) likely to distress the recipient' (R.C., 1978). Cf **eat your heart out!**

read me and take me! was a Restoration Period c.p., used in ref. to riddles and meaning, approx., 'Get me?' *or* 'Get me!' It occurs in, e.g., Dryden's *Marriage à la Mode*, performed in 1672 and pub'd in 1673.

ready. See: who got.

ready whore, ready money. It's easy to find a prostitute if you have the cash on you: raffish: c. 1660–1800. In Thomas Shadwell's *The Amorous Bigot*, 1690, at Act II, the scene in the Parks, Tope, a roistering adventurer, exclaims, 'These damn'd young Fellows... will snap up all Adventures: they have the better of us at cruising, we have no Game to play at but ready Whore, ready Money.'

real. See: it's been real.

real money. See: that was r.

real nervous (or, more often, **'way out**), **dad.** A jazz-lovers' adjectivally admiring c.p., dating from c. 1950. (*Observer*, 16 Sep. 1956.) Perhaps from 'It makes me real nervous [excited]' and *way out*, notably eccentric or unusual. Patricia Newnham, 1976, writes, 'I think there is a link with drugs.

Very much in use with teenagers today.'

'I suspect that "nervous" was merely a clique synonym for "excited"... Never used, to my knowledge, by US teenagers in the 1970s; far more likely would be "far out!" or "outasight!"' (R.C., 1978).

reason. See: such a reason: theirs not.

received. See: message; small contributions.

recommends. See: we want make.

record. See: just for the r.; put another.

record – (it's) off the. This C20 US – and, by 1960, commonly used in UK – c.p. 'stems from statements made by high government officials to members of the news media; [meaning] that what the officials have just revealed is "off the record" – implying that it would be against the public interests if they printed it. It amounts to a sort of gentlemen's agreement, which is seldom broken. In common speech it simply means, "Forget you even heard it!"' (W.J.B., 1978). Contrast **no comment.**

rectum? Damned (or stronger) **near** (or **nigh**) **killed 'em!** 'In the Services, any conversational ref. to, or use of the word, *rectum* has, since c. 1950, evoked this punning ("wrecked 'em?") response' (P.B., 1976).

red. See: better red; is my face; two white; up she; when roses; would you rather be; you've got a big.

Red Baron. See: curse you.

red fence. See: she wants.

red hat and no knickers (or **drawers**) is applied to 'a fashionably dressed woman whose appearance covers vulgarity. My wife says this originated in an Alan Bennett TV show, but I seem to remember it from earlier' (Derek Parker, 1977). Perhaps Alan Bennett heard it, liked it, used it. Certainly it epitomizes feminine vulgarity in dress and, by implication, in social and sexual life, ostentatious vulgarity. It dates from c. 1920. In G.F. Newman's police novel, *Sir, You Bastard*, 1970, occurs this example: 'A woman in a red hat darted in front of him: "Red hat, no drawers". He couldn't call that out now. He was in uniform...' And on the opposite page: 'Thinking about [it], he wondered what her reaction would have been to that expression'. Sanders, 1978, comments, 'A wishful thinking c.p. of the 1920s [and '30s], when one could be sure that every woman wore a *hat*'. Equally well-known, at least in Lancashire – and just as down-to-earth – is the version *fur coat and no knickers* or *drawers* (Mrs Malvene Richards, 1983); and, in 1984, Skehan notes, of *fur coat and no drawers*: 'It was used in the city of Cork quite frequently, but a Dublin friend tells me that he has been familiar with the phrase all his life'.

red herring ne'er spake word but e'en, 'Broil my back, but not my weamb (or **womb**)'. A c.p. of c. 1650–1700: *womb* being belly, *weamb* a dialect version of that word. Apperson.

red-hot. See: take a red; wouldn't touch it.

red-hot stove. See: steal.

Red or dead. See **would you rather be...**

red sails in the sunset orig. in the title of a very popular song and became an Aus. c.p., a caustic ref. to excessive sentimentality. (Neil Lovett, in the *National Times*, 23–28 Jan. 1978.) But it also means that a female is menstruating and therefore unavailable for sexual intercourse; cf **rags on.**

Reddy. See: no, I'm Reddy's.

Reds under the bed was of political origin and applied to excessive suspicion of Communist influence. It has been applied – as a c.p. – to any excessively or pathologically suspicious attitude. It arose in the US, during Senator McCarthy's Communist witch-hunt in the 1950s and soon reached UK, (R.S., 1975.) where it has been very common indeed during the 1970s.

Redskin. See: another Redskin.

refrain. See: desist, refrain.

refresh. See: pause.

refreshes the parts that other (something) **cannot reach.** Orig., 'Heineken [Lager]. Refreshes the parts that other beers cannot reach', a slogan invented by Terry Lovelock of

Collet, Dickenson, Pearce & Partners, and in use to advertise the drink since 1975, accompanying a series of humorous illustrations. But it is wide open to *double entendre*, which of course is part of its strength as a slogan, and so, without ref. to Heineken, sometimes with *reaches* substituted for *refreshes*, it soon became, if not a c.p., at least a widely-recognised and much plagiarised pattern, as in, e.g. the compliment paid by a fellow cleric to the introductory prayers of the Rev. Kenneth Cracknell at a conference, 1983: 'Opening devotions that reach the parts other opening devotions don't reach' (Nigel Rees, *Slogans*, 1982, the facts; P.B., the comment.)

regardless. See: press on; we must.

regards. See: give my regards.

REGIONAL CATCH PHRASES are sparsely represented in this dictionary. Lancashire comes off best: cf **Blackpool**... Most tend to be parochial; a few, esp. if used freely by music-hall and radio/TV comedians – for instance, George Formby, Senior and Junior, both delightfully Lancashire – yet gaining a much wider audience. An eligible couple: *kick him in* (or *into*) *touch!* = 'He should be dismissed' or 'He shouldn't be in our company *or* group'; and *stay like that for an old hat!*, common around Manchester, Oldham, Ashton-under-Lyne and nearby towns, applied to a woman caught, by a man, bending over with her bottom in the air, the hat being a policeman's helmet, referring to the nob or *glans penis*. (Jack Slater,1978.) Cf **right, monkey!**

P.B.: I'm sure E.P. has merely skimmed the surface here, and that (to blend two or three c.pp.), 'there's a whole new can of worms just waiting to be opened'. To forestall justifiable trans-Atlantic criticism, I plead that it would be an impertinence to tackle a field about which I know far too little: that such a field exists in the US is made abundantly evident by, among others, Bob Bowman, whose intriguingly titled *If I Tell You a Hen Dips Snuff*, 1981 (completed within ..., *you can look under her wing*, and glossed 'You can rest assured I'm telling you the truth'); Jim Everhart's four-volume *Illustrated Texas Dictionary*, 1967; and *Texas Talkin'*, 1981, by Kay Russell and Nancy Jones, were all obtained for me in the Lone Star State by my friend, visiting from Lower Galilee, Yehouda Mindel. I was interested (and heartened) to find how many of the phrases, esp. in the first mentioned, come from old British stock.

regurgitate all you know upon (or **about**) the following. An academics' c.p., cynically summing up all the questions likely to be asked about any particular subject in 'finals' examination: 1970. (P.B.)

Reilly or **Riley.** See: living the life.

re-invent. See: let's not r.

rejoice. See: it's a poor arse.

relations have come. See **country cousins**...

relic. See: rub.

relief. See: for this relief.

relieved. See: Mafeking

religion. See: it's against my.

remark. See: I resemble; no remarks.

remember. See: I never r.; you ought to; you play ball; and:

remember Belgium! was heard with ironic and bitter intonations in the muddy wastes of the Salient' – the Ypres salient. 'And some literal-minded, painstaking individual, anxious that the point should be rubbed well in, would be sure to add: "As if I'm ever likely to forget the bloody place!"' (John Brophy in B & P). Cf **give it to the Belgians.**

remember I'm your mother and get up them (or **those**) **stairs!** was often used by the British soldier during WW1. A memory of childhood. (B & P) For this phrase's later life see **get up them stairs!**

remember Parson Mallum! and **(remember) Parson Palmer!** Pray drink about, Sir!; Don't keep the bottle, or the decanter, in front of you! The former: late C16–18: the latter, C18–19. The latter carries the rather special sense of a reproach to 'one who stops the circulation of the glass by

preaching over his liquor' (Grose). Both of these admonitions verge on the proverbial. Apperson.

remember pearl barley! An Aus. perversion of the next, 'meaning it's happened before' (Jim Ramsay, *Cop It Sweet*, 1977). The semantics: 'It *has* happened before, and *could* happen again, so don't be so cocksure!'

remember Pearl Harbor! was, in WW2, an Aus. c.p., often prec. by **don't panic** (joc. **don't picnic**) and used in much the same way as the **remember Belgium!** of WW1. (B.P.) P.B.: known and used, if perhaps not frequently, in the British Forces, post-WW2. I first heard it late 1950s.

Whether it has ever been a US c.p. seems open to question: some Americans say 'Yes, but only among Servicemen – and perhaps among journalists'; other hotly deny that it was ever a c.p. even in those two categories; a temperate US view is that it does figure prominently in the lectures, talks, seminars of staff instructors at Service colleges, but '[now] heard even less than often than [the next]' (J.W.C., 1975).

remember the Alamo! was occasioned by the massacre, in 1836, of a small US force by General Antonio Santa Ana, at that time President of the emergent independent Mexico: a warning, even if in jest. (R.S., 1975.)

I could hardly do better than quote what J.W.C. writes, 1975: 'A c.p., certainly in US, but now *never* used a chauvinistic battle cry or with real reference to the Alamo, or otherwise than humorously. Universally understood, but not really very frequent.' Nor better than to add W.J.B.'s slightly later comment: '"Remember the Alamo!" was the great-grandfather of "Remember the *Maine*!" and "Remember Pearl Harbor!" and could have gained currency any time [after 1836]. Even at this late date it is still in use, and heard more often than the other two exhortations.'

Cf the Brit. **remember Belgium!** of WW1 and the Aus. and perhaps US **remember Pearl Harbor!** of WW2.

remember the girl who went out to buy a knicknack and came back with a titbit. A low or, at best, a raffish Can. c.p. of *c*. 1935–55. For the benefit of the innocent, *with a titbit* puns on *with a tit* (nipple) *bit* or *bitten.*

remember the Johnstown Flood. See **don't spit**...

remember the starving Armenians! This c.p. is US and, if I remember correctly, also Brit. It arose *c*. 1925 and 'had some currency... to tell someone to stop laughing in church or in any other unsuitable place' (J.W.C., 1977). Fain, however, 1977, thinks that it was 'a WW1 c.p., used when people left too much food on the plate or took too much to start with'. I think that the earlier date is the correct one: but there were so many Armenian disasters during the approx. period 1890–1925, that I haven't been able to pinpoint it. P.B.: I think that the UK equivalent – at least, the one used to exhort me as a child, late 1930s, to clear up my plate or to tackle something I found unpalatable – was *think of all the poor starving children in China*!

remember there's a war on! '"Don't waste time; don't be frivolous; let's get back to our real job." A popular admonition to "scroungers" and "gossips"' (John Brophy in B & P): WW1. Yet more frequently: **don't you know there's a war on?**, which was mildly revived during WW2.

When used lit., it clearly isn't a c.p. – but it was very frequently employed with joc. irony, e.g. for 'hurry up!' or as a palliative, 'After all, there is a war on'.

Frontline troops would observe bitterly of base 'types' that 'They don't know there's a war on.'

remember you next astern and beware of your latter end are RN c.pp.; the former, meaning 'Do unto others as you would have them do unto you', deriving from the literal advice to ships in station, 'Keep a good look-out both on the ship ahead and the ship astern... and so avoid collision' (*Sailors' Slang*); and the latter, 'Watch your step!' – esp. towards the end of one's Service career (*ibid.*): late C19–20.

rent. See: did you get; my rents; who's up.

repairs. See: road up.

repel. See: stand by to.
reply. See: shrieks.
resemble. See: I resemble
reservoir. See: an reservoir.
rest. See: and the rest; give it a r.; give us a r.; no rest; when you're talking; you'll have no.
restless. See: natives are.
result of a lark in the park after dark – the. Applied jocularly and insensitively to a pregnant girl: public-house and raffish wit: since c. 1930. (Petch, 1974.)
retire. See: light.
retreat? Hell, no! We just got here! has, from a famous quot'n (the US Captain Lloyd S. William, at Belloar, on the Western Front, 5 June 1918, to the retreating French who advised him, just arrived, to turn back), become a c.p., 'used when someone may suggest that a task be abandoned before completion, or to give up or quit on some endeavor. It has been heard at athletic contests, even when it is late in the game and your team is hopelessly behind' (Col. Moe, 1975).

A comparable morale-booster, perhaps inspired by this one, is recalled in *Time* (Europe), 9 Jan. 1978: ' "Retreat, hell! We're just advancing from another direction." Uttered by General Oliver Prince Smith when, trapped by 8 divisions of Chinese Communists in North Korea in the Fall of 1950, he led the 20,000 man 1st Division on a bloody, 13-day, 70-mile break-through to the sea and rescue'. (Cited by Paul Janssen.)

return. See: like MacArthur.
rev up. See: why don't you just.
revolting. See: peasants.
rhubard. See: is your r.; and:
rhubarb, rhubarb, rhubarb. This elab. and intensive of the Brit. underworld – and-its-fringes' *rhubarb*, 'nonsense', derives 'from the mutterings of actors when simulating the sound of a crowd' (David Powis, *The Signs of Crime*, 1977): since c. 1950. *VIBS* calls *rhubarb!* 'The heroic cry, further popularised by *The Goon Show*'. See also *is your rhubarb up?*, and, in *DSUE*, the note on *rhubarb* in the Appendix.
rhyme. See: that's a r.
ribbin runs thick (or thin) – the. There is – or he has – much (or little) money: late C17–mid C19. (BE; Grose.) By itself *ribbin* or, later, *ribbon* was an underworld term for money.
ribbon. See: all wrapped.
ribs. See: lend his.
ribs have slipped (a bit) – his, your, my is applied to someone developing, or who has developed, a notable paunch: joc. male: c. 1960. P.B., 1977.
rice-pudding. See: couldn't knock; now then, shoot.
rich. See: if you're so; too rich.
rich get richer and the poor get poorer – the; with a joc. var.: **the rich get richer and the poor get children.** The former was orig. (? late C19) a bitter cliché, which later (?c. 1920) was employed humorously; the latter (C20) has always been humorous – admittedly somewhat wry-mouthed.

J.W.C., 1977, notes that the *poor get children* verious was, in the 1930s, revitalized by its occurrence in the still popular song with the title (and often repeated line) 'Ain't we got fun?', also a musical comedy.

P.B.: the original has, as the C20 draws on, reverted to bitter, because all too true, cliché; it may even qualify as a proverb.

Richard. See: had the R.; open the door; too short.
[Richard's himself (or, in Cockney, **hisself) again!** In III, iii, of *Susan Hopley: or, The Vicissitudes of a Servant Girl: A Domestic Drama*, performed in 1841, George Dibdin Pitt writes:

GIMP: Poor young man! What an awful situation!
DICKY: No such thing – Richard's his-self again!

It is a quot'n from Colley Cibber (1671–1757), *Richard III altered*: after his ghostly nightmare, Richard is made, in Cibber's V, iii, to say, 'Conscience avuant, Richard's himself again' (*ODQ*). I think that this became a cliché, enjoying a

special popularity during the period c. 1830–60 – or perhaps merely a conventionalism.]

ride. See: go and have; he'll do; nothing but up; squeezes; they that ride; went for; you could r.; and:
ride 'em, cowboy! and **ride her** (strictly, **'er), cowboy!** 'Never heard in the longer version [*ride 'er, cowboy, ride 'er*]... Rodeos were held annually at least since 1844, to round up and brand the new horses running wild, the unbroken broncos (Spanish *bronco*, unruly). The custom became a show at least as early as 1883, when the army scout William F. Cody ("Buffalo Bill") organised *Buffalo Bill's Wild West Show*... The particular event that created the phrase in question is the bronco-riding contest... the object is to stay on a full minute... If a man stays on 20 seconds or so, the crowd cries: "Ride 'er, Cowboy!" If he sticks on, in another 20 seconds or so, the cries go on: "Ride 'er!" ...and more tumultuously as he approaches the bell or whistle that announces the minute-span... The expression means about the same as "Go to it!"' (Shipley, 1976). Cf W.J.B.'s comment, 1977, 'Now a general saying, a shout of encouragement to anyone in a situation as hazardous as [that of] a cowboy atop a bucking bronco'. Obviously it is this gen. application that has, in C20, become a c.p.
rides again – Destry and **the Lone Ranger.** We owe these two c.p.s to 'Western' film titles. The gen., rather than vague, sense is that someone formerly famous, has, after a long interval, come back in his well-remembered role. In 1938–39, by one of those quirks and chances which do occasionally occur in the world of motion pictures, there appeared two very successful films: *Destry Rides Again*, starring James Stewart and Marlene Dietrich, and *The Lone Ranger Rides Again*, a serial starring Bob Livingston. WW2 somewhat reduced their very considerable impact. Then, in the 1950s, there were remakes of both films, with shortened titles, *Destry*, 1955, with Audie Murphy, and *The Lone Ranger*, 1956, with Clayton Moore, who reappeared, 1958, in *The Lone Ranger and the Lost City of Gold*, less successful and soon forgotten.

The earlier films did not generate a c.p. in UK and only an incipient one in US. The remakes, however, did so affect Britain that it became the fashion to say *Destry rides again* or, more often, *the Lone Ranger rides again*, with the var. *the Lone Ranger strikes again*, when some crusader intervened effectually – or when some monomaniac exacted revenge, more than once, in a somewhat spectacular manner. Something of the sort happened also in the US. So far as I have been able to ascertain, in neither country did these c.pp. achieve a currency either exceptionally widespread or very long-lasting. By 1970, they were fading from public memory, yet, in UK at least, the *Lone Ranger* versions, esp. the *strikes again*, lingered on, nostalgically, among the long-memoried. (I owe the film chronology to those devoted, far too little recognized, servers of the public's curiosity, the Enquiries staff of the British Library.) From the same source, basing its reply on Jim Harmon & Donald F. Glut, *The Great Movie Serials*, 1973, I learned that *Destry Rides Again* was apparently made first in 1933, with Tom Mix in the star role.

On the subject of *The Lone Ranger*, Harmon & Glunt point out that he had appeared first in a radio serial in 1932, six years before Republic Pictures produced *The Lone Ranger* as a film serial in 1938; their introductory remarks are very well worth quoting: 'The most famous masked hero of the West has been the Lone Ranger... The masked rider of the plains was the culmination of nearly a century of frontier fiction... Although created for radio drama, the Lone Ranger nevertheless presented a vivid memorable visual image – a tall man in a black mask on a great white horse'. Harmon & Glut conclude thus: 'The Lone Ranger rode beyond the limits of popular entertainment, and became an imperishable part of Americana' – which, instead of being perhaps exaggerated, could turn out to be true. They reveal that the star of *The Lone Ranger* was Lee Powell, but that, in

The Lone Ranger Rides Again, he was passed over in favour of an established Western star, Bob Livingston.

To summarize: after being a radio serial of 1932, *The Lone Ranger* became a film in 1938, with the sequel *The Lone Ranger Rides Again* in 1939. The white stallion was named Silver, which, at critical and at wistful times, the Lone Ranger addresses in the memorable words, **hi-ho, Silver**, q.v. P.B.: I have never heard either phrase used as a c.p., but only as conscious quot'n. In late C20, however, other names, nicknames and so on, are often used with *...rides again*, sometimes with *...srtikes back*, but esp. with *...strikes again*: see **phantom strikes...** The old L.R. himself is still, 1983, alive and well, with Tonto and Silver, in a newspaper comic strip syndicated worldwide.

rides like a sack of flour is applied to a poor horseman: Can: prob. throughout C20. (Leechman, 1968.) Perhaps euph. for the vulgar Brit. *...like a bag of shit*.

ridge. See: like a bandicoot.

ridiculous. See: vergin'.

riding his low horse is a joc. c.p., dating since *c.* 1930; referring a tipsy, or a half-tipsy, fool either boasting very rashly or otherwise acting foolishly; not very common. (Petch, 1966.) P.B.: perhaps orig. an allusion to one 'coming down off his high horse' or 'getting on his high horse'.

riding out of town with nothing but a head is 'used of a cowboy the morning after a big drunk' (Adams) and it implies a head aching badly and pockets empty of money: late C19–20.

right. See: army left; customer; dropped; has his; how right; it's all r.; it's like a nigger; it's not r.; it's what; she's right; straighten; we've got; when my wife; yes, but in; yes, stung; you couldn't be more; you're happy; and:

right, but only just, orig. and still predominantly prec. by *that's*. A shopkeeper's, barmans' and similars' facetious remark when one pays the exact price: since *c.* 1930, if not twenty years earlier. I heard it as recently as 21 July 1976.

right, monkey! '"She said, 'Did he say anything about the check suit?' and I thought, 'Right monkey!'" – Al Read. Gerry Collins of Manchester's Music Hall Association adds: "My mother used to say this to me *years* before Al Read's pro-time. When I refused to go an errand because I was busy playing, she'd say, 'Right, monkey, wait till your father comes home' – which shows how talented Al Read was, to store up in his mind all these real Lancashire gems and, in after years, be able to reproduce them"' (*VIBS*). The northern comedian's speciality was reporting domestic chatter, and he had a particular, almost (to Southerners) inimitable, intonation for phrases like this one, and for **you'll lucky**, q.v. For me, one sketch remains outstanding in memory: Al Read on the radio evoking a small boy, taken for a haircut by his father and saying, of the customer already in the barber's chair, 'Dad! Dad, if 'e cuts 'is ear off – can I'ave it?' (P.B.)

right old commercial going on – a. There's a right old brawl' or quarrel taking place: Suffolk: C20.

right on! 'has come to mean something like "you're on the right track" – "continue your present course" – or simply "OK"' (Norris M. Davidson, 1971): US – perhaps orig. US negro – since *c.* 1960, in full force, yet already common enough during the 1950s.

In a Philadelphia newspaper of late May or early June 1970, Sidney J. Harrison, in a witty poem entitled 'This Cat Doesn't Dig All That Groovy Talk', declares that:

By fearful tax I'll put the bite on
All the squares who gargle 'right on!'

In the *New York Post* of 20 Feb. 1976, Max Lerner, in a most entertaining and instructive article, wrote that 'A striking phrase emerged in the '60s: "Right on". Alas, it has all but disappeared. I am sorry to see it go. It had warmth, humor, camaraderie.'

By *c.* 1970 the phrase had been adopted in Can.; in 1974, Leechman defined its Can. currency as 'precisely correct, exactly it'.

In 1979, E.P. added this note: A US adaptation of the RAF's *bang on!*, 'That's dead right! That's fine!' From US airmen it passed to other servicemen and then to the general public; numerous American friends have attested its continuing currency – until 1979, at least. That it has 'caught on' with US Negroes is interesting, but not central. P.B.: theirs could, of course, have been an independent coinage.

right up my alley. That's something in which I'm deeply interested or concerned or, esp., familiar with or good at: US: C20. (J.W.C., 1977.) Cf **just my alley-marble**, q.v.

right you are! All right!; Agreed!; mid C19–20. (Hotten, 1864; Churchward, 1888.) 'Right you are; I don't think I'll go up,' is an example quoted by the *OED*. Apparently prompted by the coll. *all right!* and the Standard English *you are right*. It evokes from Shipley the comment: Pirandello wrote a play *Cosi è se vi pare*, 1918, Englished as *Right You Are If Think You Are*. Pirandello (1867–1936) was a truly witty playwright; I once saw, at the Atelier theatre in 1922, a comedy of his played in French: subtle delectation.

righteous See: more holy.

rights. See: bang to rights; may I have.

Riley. See: living the life.

Rin-Tin-Tin. See: tin that.

ring. See: does that r.; don't ring; sing; sing; you can put a r.; and:

ring Mahony's bell! 'A lodger in one sub-let room of a single flat in an apartment house with one doorbell to an apartment – an instruction to his intending visitors. Prob. since *c.* 1930... Heard now and then' (J.W.C., 1977).

ring-tailed bustard. See: he'll spit.

ring up the Duchess!, and, with the same meaning but from a different angle, **I must ring up the Duchess**. Applicable to the resolution of a doubt or to the solution of a problem, this c.p. arose in Jan. 1935 from the play *Young England*; orig. and predominantly a society c.p., it had a very lively, yet very brief currency, for it was, by the end of 1936, already, yet very brief currency, for it was, by the end of 1936, already ob. and, by the outbreak of WW2, already †.

rings a bell. See **does that ring...**

rinse a sock – I must go and. I must go and urinate: raffish male: later C20.

rip. See: let her rip; wouldn't it.

rise and shine (naval and hence also military) and **rouse and shine** (naval). An order (become a c.p.) to get out of bed: respectively late C19–20 and C19. F & G give this definition for *rise*...: 'A barrack-room orderly corporal's call, on reveille sounding for the men to rouse out'; Bowen at *rouse*...cites the version, which John Brophy in B & P, 1931, glosses as follows:

the disagreeable or the amusing reality of the orderly-corporal's rousing cry in camp, billet or barracks:

Show a leg! show a leg!,

which dates from the early nineteenth-century Navy. Two popular variants were

Rise and shine,

and, no matter if the sun were not due to appear for some time,

The sun's scorching your eyes out (*or* burning a hole in your blanket).

An enlightening quot'n is this from Douglas Reeman, *The Destroyers* (a naval story of WW2), 1974: '"Wakey, wakey, lash up an' stow. Rise an' shine, the sun's scorching your bleeding eyeballs out." The age-old joke at half-past five of a spring morning.'

E.P. later added: This is the shortened, the c.p., form of *rise and shine*, *rise and shine – hands off your cocks, pull your socks – orderly room's at nine* – or, rather of *rise and shine, rise and shine*, often heard as an entity, precisely as *hands...socks* is an entity; put *orderly room's at nine* isn't one, for it is merely the final member of the orig. triad, mentioned by Anthony Burgess, who, 26 Aug. 1977, adds [reviewing the first ed. of this book in *TLS*] *out of them bloody wanking pits.*

'An interesting example of US usage occurs in "Reveille Rock", an instrumental record issued in 1959 (Johnny and the Hurricanes). During the "intro", an NCO's bulldog" voice thunders: 'All right, you guys, rise and shine!'" (Paul Janssen, 1978). 'In the Southern US, it is often thus: "Good mornin' Glory; it's time to rise and shine'" (A.B., 1978).

To cap it all, here's an Anglo-Irish example. 'Brendan Behan, *Borstal Boy*, [1958, concerning the late 1930s] continues it: "Rise and shine, the day is fine, the sun will scorch your balls off"' (Levene, 1979): and I feel reasonably sure that Brendan Behan did not invent the expansion. During WW1 I often heard ... *the sun will scorch your eyes out.* P.B.: in the 1950s, ... *scorch your eye-balls out,* a mixture of the two. See also **wakey, wakey!**

river. See: could fall; he'll do; miles and miles; only river; so lucky.

rivet. See: watch out.

road. See: hit the r.; let's get the show; like Tom; one for the r.; tell that to a one; up the road; and:

road up for repairs! In society – a very long way from being Society – indicates that the female at whom the c.p. is directed is having her period: latish C19–20; by 1950, ob., and by 1970, virtually †. In long-outmoded unconventional English, *road* is the female pudendum.

roast. See: let the peanut.

rob. See: who's robbing; you wouldn't fuck.

robbed. See: man robbed; we was.

robbing a bank. See: been robbing.

Robin Hood. See: they used to call.

Robinson Crusoe. See: you're not R.

rock(s). See: between a r.; don't knocks the r.; don't shag; this channel; wouldn't it; you got rocks; and:

rock on, Tommy! Started by the Lancashire comedians Bobby Ball and Tommy Cannon: 'The catchphrase "Rock on, Tommy "emerged naturally one night while his [Ball's] partner was singing. Now when fans recognise them in the sheet they chant it like a password entitling them to membership of some secret society' (Alan Road, 'Why Cannon and Ball are finally calling the shots', in *Observer* colour sup., 31 May 1981). Seen as a slogan-sticker on a large lorry, summer 1980. P.B.

rocking the boat. See: sit down, you're.

Roger. See **just like R.**

[**Roger** – a one-word c.p. for 'That's understood and agreed' and 'That's OK' – was orig. an RAF then general Armed Forces' 'code word' of acknowledgement: Brit., and by adoption, US. 'Considerable civilian use after WWII' (W & F). J.W.C. has added what I should have stated: 'This stood for "right" and was modified in the US Forces in WW2; designed to make the letters of a spelt-out word intelligible through static'. P.B.: perhaps more of a c.p. when, as in the British Services, given the joc. duplication of sound in *roger dodger!* The letter R became *Roger* in the phonetic alphabet introduced in 1941; it had previously been *Robert*, and stood, in this context, for 'Received (and understood)'.]

Roger lodger is a c.p. that has, since *c.* 1925 been directed at, or in allusion to, a male lodger who makes love to the mistress of the house. *Roger,* not merely because it rhymes on *lodger* but also because it puns on *roger,* (of the male) to coit with, 'from the name of Roger, frequently given to a bull' (Grose). This Roger has long been, not only in the UK but also in Aus., the subject of a famous limerick, during WW2 and after, that has reinforced the popularity of the c.p.:

There was a young lady named Nodd
Who thought that all kids came from God.
But 'twas not the Almighty
Who lifted her nighty,
It was Roger the lodger, the sod!

Thus Sanders, 1978; P.B. remembers a var. first line, 'There once was a girl at Cape Cod', and comments that,

strictly speaking, the verse is a paradox.

roll. See: heads will; I had 'em; let the good; wagons; wait till.

roll on! is the very gen. shortened form, both of **roll on, duration!** (see next entry) and of **roll on, time!,** q.v.

roll on big ship (or **that boat**) and **roll on, duration!** Military c.pp. of 1917–18, expressing a fervent wish that the war might end. The ship is, of course, that which all take the weary troops home. But the *that boat* c.p. came a little later – since *c.* 1925 – and belonged to the RAF. The commonest was *roll on, duration,* which derived from the fact that 'the volunteers of 1914–15 enlisted for three years or the duration of the war' (B & P).

P.B.: on biting cold February day I was just thinking 'Oh, roll on, Springtime!' as I entered a chemist's shop – there to be confronted with a small container, labelled 'Roll-on anti-perspirant'. Moral: don't wish time away!

roll on Blighty! A military c.p. of 1915–18, equivalent to 'When this bloody war is over,/Oh, how happy I shall be!' *Blighty,* England, home, comes from Hindustan *bilayati,* foreign, esp. European.

roll on, cocoa! A prison c.p., expressing a desire for the evening meal to arrive with bedtime to follow: since *c.* 1918. (James Curtis, *The Gilt Kid,* 1936.) Imitative of **roll on, duration!**

roll on, death! May this monotony, this feeling of desperation, end! 'The cry of the "fed-up", or of the instructor whose pupils are slow in responding to his teaching' (PGR): mostly army: WW2. P.B., 1976, notes: 'Sometimes elab. to "...and let's have a bash at the angels"'.

The c.p. has evoked from Anthony Burgess, reviewing the first ed. of this book in *TLS,* 26 Aug. 1977, the notable comment: '*Roll on, death* (which can be followed by *And let's have a go at the angels*) has a situation context so wide – being in the Services and being frustrated by it – that it can easily be extended to encompass the whole of life".

Shipley, 1977, relates all the *roll on* c.pp. to W.S. Gilbert's 'Bab' ballad, *To the Celestial Globe:* 'Roll on, than ball, roll on!' – which ends: 'Never *you* mind! Roll on! (It rolls on.)'

roll on, duration! See **roll on, big ship!**

roll on, my bloody twelve!; in full, **I heard the voice of Moses say, Roll on...!** A very common RN lower-deck c.p. of C20. 'Active service ratings are "in" for twelve years and as often as they are "chocker", they give vent to this expression' (Granville in PGR).

roll on, pay-day! A workmen's c.p., uttered by those with (almost) no money left: since *c.* 1919. Influenced by the Service c.pp. of WW1 – see **roll on, big ship!** Hence, since *c.* 1925, used by those who, weary of their present job, are looking for a better one.

roll on, that boat! See **roll on, big ship!**

roll on, time! May my sentence end!: a prison c.p., dating since *c.* 1880; not entirely †. It occurs in, e.g., A. Griffiths, *Secrets of the Prison House,* 1894. Cf:

roll round!, with the year of release stated, is the US equivalent of **roll on, time!:** since *c.* 1880 at latest. An early example of its use occurs in Hutchins Hapgood, *The Autobiography of a Thief,* 1904.

rolling. See: give him a r.; I had 'em r.; keep the tambourine; take a running; thousand.

Rolls-Royce. See: poor chap; you don't have.

Romford. See: you could ride.

Rommel. See: that'll push.

roof. See: come off the r.; could fall; fall of the; noise like; when it don't.

roofed, lathed plastered. extremely drunk: US: late C19 – mid 20. Glendon Swarthout, *The Tin Lizzie Group,* 1972, but set in 1916 with dialogue faithful to the period. (W.J.B., 1977.) P.B.: elab. of the slang *plastered* = drunk.

rooked. See: we was.

rooks. See: I'll put you.

room. See: better an empty; I prefer your r.; if you're close; is there r.; it's the beer; please, teacher; there's more r.; Tommy make; up in Annie's.

rooster. See: don't crow; and:

rooster one day and a feather duster the next – a. An Aus. – mainly political and journalistic – c.p., prob. dating from *c.* 1960, to judge by A.A. Calwell's *Be Just and Fear Not*, 1972, 'Years ago I told the House of Representatives a basic truth that I had read in a United States publication. The writer said that a politician is "a rooster one day and a feather duster the next".' Four years later (in the *Sun-Herald*, 25 Apr. 1976) a journalist phrased it as 'Today a rooster, tomorrow a feather duster', and added, 'It's another was the late Arthur Calwell'. (Wilkes, *Dict. Aus. Coll.*) clearly the phrase must have had some US currency.

root. See: wouldn't it.

root, hog, or die! Fend for yourself and earn your own living – or take the (dire) consequences: US: C19–20. In the chapter titled 'The Sixth Ward in the Old Days' (apparently the 1860s and 1870s), of *The Mulligans*, pub'd in 1901 and written by Edward Harrigan (1845–1911), occurs his passage: '... Bimble's Band, that discoursed at intervals such airs as "The Solid Men of the Front!" "Root, Hog, or Die!" "Ham-Fat!" "When This Cruel War Is Over!" each selection, when finished, being cheered to the echo.' The *DAE* quotes the famous Davy Crockett as writing in 1834, 'We therefore determined to go on the old saying root, hog, or die', and an Iowa agricultural report, pub'd in 1866 as stating, 'It has been a common practice with farmers ... to turn them [i.e., pigs] out into the woods or onto the prairies to get their own living.' Both a cowboy and later a minstrel song were thus titled: see Minnie Sears, *Song Index*, 1926, and its Supplement; and in 1975 W.J.B. glossed it as an 'early Negro minstrel song'. Eric Townley, 1978, notes that it 'was the title of a jazz recording made in 1937'.

rope. See: it's money; you can't piss.

rope-dancer. See: like a rope.

rope yarn. See: every hair.

rosaries all the way. A Protestant c.p., slightly disparaging, to Catholic processions: C20. This, clearly, is a pun on the cliché, *roses all the way*, orig. applied to the roses strewn on the road, the street, taken by a triumphal procession.

roses. See: could fall; everything is r.; when roses; and:

roses and raptures was, *c.* 1830–1900, a literary c.p., applied, Ware tells us in 1909, to the *Book of Beauty* kind of publication – what has, since *c.* 1960, become known as 'coffee-table books'. Very nice too, if you can afford them! 'There could be more to this than a literary c.p.,' writes Sanders, 1978. 'Swinburne [in *Dolores*, 1865] wrote "Change in a trice/The lilies and languors of virtue/For the roses and raptures of vice." (*Vice* for the rhyme: the right term would have been 'sexual freedom' or some such euph.]' The roses and raptures are a lot more fun that the lilies and languors. Or, as Ogden Nash [1902–71] put it, "Virtue/Won't hurt you,/But vice/Is nice", '

roses grow on you! 'An advertising slogan for Cadbury's Roses chocolates' (*VIBS*). It was popularised by the comedian Norman Vaughan in a short series of TV advertisements; in them he made his famous thumb-up gesture (see *swingin'*, in ONE-WORD CATCHPHRASES) and a bunch of roses sprouted from his thumb: mid 1960s. (Mrs Janet Bowater, 1977.) Nigel Rees quotes Vaughan, in *Slogans*, 1982, as saying that, even as late as 1979, 'people still ask me, "Where are your roses?"!'

Rossa. See: where did you get the R.

Rot 'em. See: Starve 'em.

rot your socks? – wouldn't it. See **wouldn't it make you ...**

rotate. See: wouldn't it Rock.

rotten. See: how's your dirty; something is; you dirty r.; you must come.

rough. See: that's rough; things are r.; and:

rough as bags and twice as dirty (or nasty). An Australian soldiers' c.p. of 1915–18, it was applied to the prostitutes frequenting the neighbourhood of Horseferry Road, London, where the AIF headquarters occupied a building. Cf the Aus. simile (*as*) *rough as bags* and the Eng. (*as*) *rough as a sandbag*, uncouth.

rough on rats – it's. That's tough luck!: since *c.* 1890; by 1960, †. From, I vaguely remember, an advertisement for rat poison.

round. See: it's made round; roll round; so round; wait for your; your wheel's; and:

round the back for a quick brandy (sometimes prec. by **right, lads,**)! An urgent shriek from Harry Secombe/'Neddy Seagoon' in the BBC radio comedy series 'The Goon Show', 1950s, usu. in the background as the interval music started to play. Taken up and used in all sorts of contexts by the show's devotees, and still heard occ., early 1980s. (P.B.)

round the corner was, in WW1, 'the soldier's normal reply to "How far is it to ... ?" It might be several miles' (B&P).

rous mit 'im! Throw him out!: *c.* 1920–50. Berrey says 'From German "*hears mit ihm*".'

Rouse. See: bravyo.

rouse and shine! See **rise and shine!**

routine. See: back in the old.

Rover. See: down, Rover.

row of tents. See: camp.

rub. See: it all rubs; spare a rub; and:

rub of the relic – a. This phrase 'derives from the practice of touching wounds with religious objects to effect a cure'. It became a c.p. when it was 'used with sexual overtones' (Skehan, 1977): orig., *c.* 1960, in Eire; by 1970, some use in UK.

rub together. See: poor chap.

rubber duck. See: you can't quack.

rubber hammer. See: go and fetch.

rubbish. See: what a load; what do you think of the show.

Ruffians (or Ruffins) Hall. See: he is only.

ruffin cook ruffin, who scalded the devil in his feathers. A c.p. applied, *c.* 1750–1830, to a bad cook. (Grose, 1788.) *Ruffin* or *Ruffian* was, C13–early C16, the name of a fiend; hence, C16–early C19, the Devil.

rug. See: all's rug; gone for a Burton.

rules. See: I don't make; Rafferty.

rum, bum and bacca. See **beer, bum and bacca.**

rumour. See: it's a r.; only a r.

rump. See: he hath eaten.

run(s). See: no hits; she's got her; still running; top run; titter; won't run.

[**run away and play marbles**; and **run away and play trains** (with the var. **go and play trains**), signifying a contemptuous dismissal – the former, of late C19–early C20, and the latter, C20 – are not, I think, true c.pp.]

Run Away, Matron's Coming was, in WW1, an army c.p. directed at the *Royal Army Medical Corps*. Not very general. (F&G.)

run in circles, scream and shout. See **if in danger ...**

run it down! 'Tell it like it is!': US Negroes', since *c.* 1965, at latest. *The Third Ear*, 1976.

run it up the flagpole (and see who salutes) – let's. 'Let's try it out and see what reactions are. Educated US from *c.* 1950; originally *in extenso*, but soon becoming familiar enough for the shortened version to serve. The most familiar of a number of "Madison Avenue" (i.e., professional advertising) c.pp. to the same general effect (e.g., "Let's put it on the train to Westport and see who comes down to the station" – Westport being a NYC suburb densely populated with advertising and media personnel). Of the same vintage as *That's the way the cookie crumbles* [listed below at **that's how ...**]. Now hackneyed enough to make for usual usage between (implied) inverted commas' (R.C., 1978).

A further version, cited by Janssen from Tom Wolfe, *The Pump House Gang*, 1968, was *why don't we throw it and see if it skips across the pond?* Then there's *let's spitball it into a windmill and see if it hits a wave* (A.B., 1978): since early 1960s.

259

run that (one) by me again! has two meanings: 'Please repeat' and 'Give me another chance': US: 'current during the 1960s, when TV re-runs and instant replays were developed' (A.B., 1978).

run up a tack and sit on it until I call you! Oh, stop talking nonsense and be quiet for a while!: US students': early 1920s (McKnight).) Cf **go sit on a tack.**

rush. See: don't all r.; you'd be killed.

rushing (or **tearing**) **around like a blue-arsed fly** is applied to oneself, or to others, rushing around in a frenzy, usu. when trying to complete a task before a deadline; sometimes – not always – a certain ineffectuality is implied, like that of the blind dashing of a bluebottle against windows and other obstacles: C20. Cf **like a fart in a colander.** (P.B.)

Russian. See: come to the R.

rusty. See: you're swinging.

S

S.A.B.U. See T.A.B.U.
S.N.A.F.U. and S.N.F.E.U. See snafu.
S.O.L. See shit out of luck.
S.O.P. See standard operating procedure.
S.O.S. See Charley's dead and same old shit.
sack of flour. See: rides like.
saddle. See: get a s.; her clothes; I've got to s.; lucky old.
safety in numbers, orig. and still often prec. by there's. 'Used jocularly, and mainly, as opposed to "two's company", meaning that courting couples will not get up to anything while others are present' (Petch, 1969): late C19–20.

I first heard it at least as early as 1910. But also used by one person, either to herself (formerly) or to himself (as, frequently, nowadays), or to another, and meaning 'I don't very much want to find myself alone with him (or her)': since c. 1930. Both, by an extension of the cliché.

said. See: enough said; never let it be; never said; no more to be; nobody asked; nuff; stand always; that's as well; well, you s.; what the soldier; you said; you've said; and:
said he. In 1927 Collinson, in his invaluable book, recorded this example,

'Do you like that?'
'No, said he frowining.'

Current since the early 1920s and, although somewhat 'old hat', still far from†. It derives, I'd say, from a novelists' trick that is also a journalists' mannerism.

It is spoken in, as it were, italics. 'Perhaps influenced by literal translations of French texts, as in *Non, dit-il, en se refrognant*' (Janssen, 1978). P.B.: occ. varied by the use of the earlier generation of historical novelists' *quotha* or *quoth he*.

said the spider to the fly. See come into my parlour.
sail(s). See: I am becalmed; one drink; red sails; she sails.
sailing for China with a load (or cargo) of tea. A 'kidding of new entries' on Training Ships: late C19–earlyish 20. Peppitt quotes J.R. West, *T.S. Indefatigable*, 1909.
sailing ship coming up astern, sir. A 'contemptuous reference to the slow, unreliable steam ships' (Peppitt, citing D. Phillips-Burt, *The History of Seamanship*, 1970): apparently, therefore, a nautical, esp. a RN c.p. of c. 1845–60 and perhaps, joc., applied to any slow vessel.
sailor(s). See: as the girl said; Ballocky Bill; hello, sailor; I'm Jolly Jack; pity the poor; save a s.; term; and:
sailor must be thinking of you. See my ears are burning.
sailor without a knife is like a whore without a cunt – a. This nautical, prob. orig. RN, c.p. implies both an extreme improbability, and an unthinkable lack of common-sense and foresight: late C19–20. (Peppitt, 1977.)
sailors don't care – natural enough, with their girls in every port: latish C19–20. Canonized by inclusion in Benham. But L.A.'s 1975 gloss is valuable: 'Among soldiers, airmen and others, apt when what is in hand is not likely to be

straightforward if niceties are allowed to get in the way; e.g., trespassers will be prosecuted, but if it's a short cut ...' And, late in 1974, L.A. had glossed the c.p. thus: 'Quip to reject or mitigate undue caution'.
sailor's farewell – a, occ. with to you added. A nautical, including RN, parting curse: late C19–20. Perhaps suggested by the apparently slightly earlier (and much sooner†) nautical coll., *sailor's blessing*. But the best comparison is that to be made with soldier's farewell. Cf also best of British luck (to you)!
saint(s). See: shore; Sunday saints.
St. Swithin's. See: effort.
sainted. See: oh, my giddy.
salt. See: I could eat; she looks; we sha'n't.
salt mines. See: back to the s.
salute. See: if it moves; run it up.
salute this happy deck. See Christians, awake...
Sam. See: play it; and:
Sam got you. 'You've been drafted into the Army' (Cab Calloway, 1944): US: since 1942. Uncle Sam has caught you, or caught up with you.
same. See: it'll all be the s.; they're all the s.; time's always; what's the difference; and:
same diff. is the Aus. counterpart of the next: since c. 1945. (B.P.)
same difference. See it's the same difference.
same here! I agree: US: C20. (Berrey.) For 'It is the same here, i.e. with me'; 'I think the same as you do'. The drinking sense, 'I'll have the same [drink] as you' is hardly a c.p.
same in a hundred years. See it'll all be the same....
same OB. The usual price (for a ticket of entry): lower classes': c. 1880–1914. (Ware.) for *same old bob* (shilling), the usual entrance fee for most popular entertainments and pastimes during the period.
[same old faces! 'The cry that always greets winners of raffles, tombola, dance prizes, etc., as they go up to collect their "loot" at Service, esp. Sergeants' Mess, social functions' (P.B., 1975): since late 1940s. On the borderline between c.p. and cliché.]
same old shit, but (or only) more of it – the. The Canadian Army's version of snafu: WW2.
same to you and many of them! – the, politely synon. with the phrases immediately following this and is, so far as I've been able to ascertain, rather earlier, for it seems to have arisen c. 1880. In Act III of Stanley Houghton's *The Perfect Cure*, prod. in 1913, we find:
    CRAY: Confound Mrs Grundy! Confound Madge! Confound – yes, hang it, confound you, Martha.
    MARTHA: The same to you, and many of them.
same to you with knobs on!; or the fairly common var....with brass fittings! The same to you – only *more* so!: both belong to C20 and were prompted by – were, orig., perhaps euph.

261

for – the low-slang expression, '*balls* to you!' Clearly, how-ever, there is ref. to brass knobs on a bed, as Norman Franklin has reminded me.

The *knobs on* form was, at one time, very common in schools; it occurs in, e.g., Frank Richards, *Tom Merry & Co. of St. Jim's*, as Mr Petch tells me. Cf the prec.

The *brass fittings* version was common in the US, and *with brass fittings* by itself 'is still widely current in the general sense "with costly (and useless) decorations" or, more loosely, "in an extreme degree" – e.g., "He's a son of a bitch, with brass fittings"' (J.W.C., 1977).

See also **with knobs on**.

Samson. See: my name is Simpson.

san fairy Ann (seldom **Anna**); occ. **send for Mary Ann** (and **Aunt Mary Ann**). It doesn't matter, *or* It's all the same, *or* Why worry?: late 1914–18, then nostalgically; not, so far as I know, used during WW2, except among a few 'old soldiers'. B&P say:

> An extremely popular phrase, approximated into English form the French *ça ne fait rien*.... As the intelligence of the soldier penetrated year after year the infinite layers of bluff and pretentiousness with which military tradition enwrapped the conduct of the War, so his cynicism increased, became habitual.... Naturally he adopted a fatalism comparable to that of the Moslem murmuring his enervating '*Maalish*' – It does not *matter*.... Let anything happen, the only appropriate comment was – *San Fairy Ann*.
>
> Naturally, the phrase had its lighter uses, especially in defiance of the warnings of friends. It was so much used that variants were almost as popular – chiefly *San Fairy* and *San Fairy Anna*.

And B.G.T., 1978, recalls yet another: *san fairy dustbin*. Hugh Kimber ends his war novel *San Fairy Ann*, 1927, thus: 'There is a magic charter. It runs, "San Fairy Ann".'

sand. See: you've got s.

sandals. See: hands off your.

sandman (or **the dustman**) **is coming** – **the**, has, the latter since *c*. 1810, as in Egan's *Grose*, 1823 and the former (*teste OEd*), since *c*. 1850, been either addressed to or directed at children beginning to rub their eyes and yawn. From their rubbing their eyes as if sand were in them; the same applies to dust in the eyes.

sandpaper. See: get the cat.

sandwich. See: I'm so hungry.

Santa Claus. See: yes, Virginia.

satisfied. See: you never get.

satu empat jalan is, in Malay, lit. 'one four road', punned among Servicemen and other 'expats' for use as **one for the road**, q.v., a c.p. of genial farewell, 'very popular in Malaya in the 1950s' (P.B., 1974). On 26 Aug. 1977, Anthony Burgess, reviewing the first ed. of this book in the *TLS*, courteously reprimanded me for having omitted this phrase.

Saturday. See: t.G.i.F.

saucepan. See: your saucepan.

sausage. See: I didn't get.

sausage and mash. See: bang, crash.

save. See: Jesus saves; saving; states; you've saved; and:

save a sailor! is a RN officers' c.p., employed when, in the mess bar, a glass gives off a ringing sound: late C19–20. This sound is, in sailors' superstition, thought to augur a sailor's death by drowning. To prevent this misfortune, one places a finger on the glass, thus stops the ringing – and thus redeems the sailor. (*Sailors' Slang*.) P.B.: in C20 this has become a domestic superstition too, if a glass is knocked at the meal table, 'save a sailor from drowning!'; cf the superstition that crossed knives on the table mean death.

save the last dance (or **waltz**) **for me** 'almost invariably implies sexual intercourse... The Drifters' song thus titled has: "But don't forget who's taking you home/And in whose arms you gonna be./So, darling, save the last dance for me" (late 1950s).' The film *Juggernaut*, 1974, showed Richard Harris as

the leader of a mine-clearance squad. 'As he's trying to neutralize a highly sophisticated bomb, he mutters "Save the last waltz for me" just before cutting one of the two remaining flexes, not knowing which wire triggers off the detonator' (Paul Janssen. 1978).

save the surface and you save all is a US 'sarcastic or cynical c.p. of general application' – derived from a varnish manufactur-er's slogan; since the 1920s and 'still heard, though less than formerly' (J.W.C., 1975). 'Now obsolete', declares R.C., 1978.

saved by the bell. Saved, or spared, by a lucky accident or intervention: UK and the Commonwealth: late C19–20. In boxing, the bell indicates the end of each round. Also US (Ashley, 1982).

saved my life! is short for **you've saved my life!**

saves the washing-up (–**it**). 'A domestic, or a cook-house, dining-hall c.p. cry when anybody drops and breaks some crockery' (P.B., 1976): since *c*. 1920 at latest.

saving. See: hang saving; he's saving; thanks for s.; what are you s.

saw. See: I see; and:

saw your legs off, you're swinging like a rusty gate. 'You're getting old, your bones are creaking.' A derisive Aus. sporting c.p., dating since late 1940s. 'It is shouted regularly at any player who has kicked for goal and missed' (Lovett, 1978). Cf, and contrast, **my word, if you're not off.**

saxophone player. See: tell a green.

say. See: I say; I should say; I'll say; if you say; let's not, and; now what; oh, I say; smile when; step outside; what say; what they say; what you say; when he says; when I say; who did; you can say; you could say; you don't say; you know what; you say; and:

say anything but her prayers. See **she will say....**

say au revoir (also, slangily and facetiously, **au reservoir**) **but not goodbye!** We are not parting for ever – we'll see each other again: since *c*. 1910; the facetious form became ob. by 1930 and † by 1950. J.W.C., 1977, adds that there was, in US, prob. in (1917–) 1918, a popular song containing this line and referring to partings between conscript and sweetheart. P.B.: in late C20, occ. parodied by 'Not au revoir – just, goodbye for ever!'

say, bo! A US form of address, prob. at first (? *c*. 1880) among tramps and then more and more gen.; by 1900 or very soon after, also Brit. For *bo*, see esp. Irwin, both at *bo* and at *hobo*. P.B.: since 'Irwin' is not readily available to the casual reader, I will note here that he suggested, 1931, two possible etymologies for *hobo*: one, from Latin *homo bonus*, good man; the other, from post-Civil War US, 'where soldiers walking home through the country replied, "Homeward bound", when questioned as to their destination'.

say 'cheese!' See **watch the dicky bird**.

say hey! is a US c.p., and included in W&F's list of 'synthetic fad expressions', 1960.

An American authority writes (1977) to tell me that a famous baseball player, Willie Mays, who played for the New York Giants in the 1950s–60s, was nicknamed 'the *Say Hey* Kid' by the New York sports writers because he always used the expression 'Say hey' when he got excited, prob. echoing a phrase in vogue among Southern Blacks.

Moreover, *say hey* has an elab.: *hello, and if you see Susie, tell her hey for me!* (Fain, 1977).

say it again! I entirely agree with you: a tailors' c.p.: *c*. 1870–1920. (B & L.) A forerunner of **you can say that again!**

say it ain't so, Joe! W.J.B., 1975, writes:

> [It] is a phrase that came out of a baseball scandal, 1920–21. The Chicago White Sox were bribed by gamblers to 'throw' a game in the World Series – or in a game leading up to that series. A small boy, who worshipped the team, is said to have approached one of the stars after the scandal broke and blurted tearfully, 'Say it ain't so, Joe', and from the sports pages to common speech was but a

quick jump. When we face any situation with unbelief we say, 'Say it ain't so, Joe'.

From an academic angle, it may be suggested that this phrase merely extended the C20 synonym, not c.p., *say it ain't so!*: and the rhyming *Joe* – cf the Brit. *have a go, Joe* – helped to perpetuate it. In the review of the first ed. of this book, in *Guardian*, 8 Sep. 1977, it is noted that 'the most recent literary occurrence… is in Malamud's novel, *The Natural*,' a novel that, mainly about baseball, appeared in 1952.

say it, don't spray it. Don't spit while you're talking: Aus.: since the late 1940s. (B.P., 1968.) P.B.: UK equivalents are *spray it again* and *you can spray that again*, punning *say it again!*

say it with flowers! 'National Publicity Committee of the Society of American Florists; US, from late 1920s. Henry Penn of Boston, Mass., originated the phrase as chairman of the committee' (Nigel Rees, in *Slogans*, 1982, quoting I.E. Lambert, *The Public Accepts*, 1941): the phrase/slogan soon crossed the Atlantic, and came to mean simply, 'Say it nicely!'

say no more! The 'Quote, Unquote' quiz programme (BBC Radio 4), 6 July 1977, with its catch-phrase quotations, cited this in context of 'The Monty Python' show, and played a recording of an eerie voice (Eric Idle) saying: 'Is your wife interested in photography? Nudge, nudge, wink, wink – if you know what I mean! Say no more!' P.B., 1977, adds: 'And the "Say no more" was in the exact intonation I've heard from several different sources since then'. See also **nudge, nudge…** and cf the C17 version **no more to be said.**

say nothing when you are dead! Be silent!; Be quiet! A subtly trenchant c.p. of *c.* 1650–1750. Ray.

say, old woman, is your rhubarb up? See **is your rhubarb up?**

say one for me! Addressed to someone kneeling otherwise than in prayer: late C19–20. Perhaps mostly in Australia. (B.P., 1974.) P.B.: equally common, and current (early 1980s) in UK, addressed to someone known to be on the way to church. Cf **put in a good word….**

say 'shit' even if he had his mouth full. See **wouldn't way…**

say something, even if it's only 'Goodbye'! 'A fairly common exhortation to anyone not bothering to reply to one's questions' (P.B., 1976). I have known it since the 1920s, so it may date from the very early C20; and usu. delivered in a mock-pathetic tone and with an assumed expression and gesture of wistful appeal.

say 'Ta'! 'Say 'Thank you'. Orig. – ? late or even middle C19–nursery, but often used by adults in fun' (Leechman): UK and the Commonwealth: since *c.* 1920 at latest.

say 'uncle'! E.P.'s orig. gloss was, 'A US formula, to which the required statement of surrender is *uncle!* A convention, not a c.p.' But this drew an expostulation from Playfair, 1977: 'I would firmly claim that this is a c.p., if only because I often use it in ordinary coversation, meaning "admit defeat", not as a formula nor as part of a game or expecting the answer "uncle". I must have heard it from others as a c.p. I have never heard it in its primary sense. The form I use is *cry uncle*' To which E.P. added apologetically, 'Peccavi!'

say what? '"*What* was that you just said?" – sometimes lit., but more often with the implication "Did you really say what I think you said?", in which case that *what* is of course strongly accented. Fairly gen. use from mid-1970s, earlier in the ghetto, where it orig. (Should be distinguished from **says what?**, which means rather "Who say so?")' (R.C., 1984): US. The almost synon., aggressive use of the Brit. idiomatic *you what?* is comparable. (P.B.)

[**say when!** has, since *c.* 1880 been a drinking cliché rather than a c.p. In *Modern Society*, 1889 (June 6):

'Say when,' said Bonko… commencing to pour out the spirit into my glass.

'Bob!' replied I.

The 'dovetail' was outmoded by *c.* 1914.]

say when you're mad! Tell me when you're ready to lift: Can. workmen's, one to another: since *c.* 1930. (Leechman.)

Says me! is the 'correct' reply to **says who?**: US: *c.* 1930–50. See the two quotations from Clarence B. Kelland at **says who?**

says what? is a var. of the contemporaneous **says which?**; and both forms were prompted by **says who?** In Clarence B. Kelland's *Dreamland*, 1938, we see:

'Yes, sir,' he said, 'I defy all of these personages and organizations and – and Mussolini.'

'Says what?' asked Algernon Swinburne's heavy, sleepy voice… 'What's Mussolini done?'

Contrast **say what?**

says which? 'What did you say?': US: *c.* 1930–50. Clarence B. Kelland, in *Speak Easily*, *c.* 1935, writes:

'I trust,' said I…'that the studies you are undertaking under Mr. Greb are – ah! – proving of both interest and profit?'

'Says which?' she rejoined, and then very quickly she assumed a posture of elegant nonchalance.

Cf **says what?** and:

says who Who says so? – addressed, in a truculent mode, usu. to one's interlocutor: (W & F, without dating; Berry roughly equating it to 'I don't believe it!' and, elsewhere, including it in a long list of 'disparaging and sarcastic flings'.) But two good – and earlier – references occur in a couple of Clarence B. Kelland's novels. *Speak Easily*, *c.* 1935:

'Alexander the Great'll see you through.'

Says who?' asked Miss Espere.

'Says me, speaking up like quartette.'

And *Dreamland*, 1938:

'Miss Higgs, you are guilty of reprehensible waste.'

'Says who?'

'Says me,' retorted Hadrian.

This c.p., dating since the early 1930s, is the progenitor of **says me!** and **says what?** and **says which?** See also **sez you!** **says you!** See **sez you!**

scabby. See: I'm so hungry.

scarce. See: good men; not so s.

scatty. See: catty.

scene. See: it's not my s.; it's weird; let's make.

scholar. See: gentleman; good a s.

school. See: depending; we went; went to night.

schoolgirl. See: that schoolgirl.

science. See: blinded.

scone. See: who stole your.

scoop-shovel. See: couldn't hit.

score. See: what's the s.

Scotch Greys are in full march by the [e.g.] **Gown Office – the.** The lice are crawling down his, e.g., head: a low c.p. of *c.* 1800–30. This particular regiment was chosen for no better reason than that body lice are predominantly *grey* in colour. (Recorded *LB*, which, pub'd in 1811, would have more fittingly been called Grose's *Vulgar Tongue*, 4th ed.)

Scotch mist. See: what do you think that is.

Scotland. See: stands Scotland.

scout's hono(u)r! 'You can take my word for it' – based on the assumption that a Boy Scout would not lie on oath. Both Brit., since *c.* 1910, and US a few years later; by 1950, slightly ob., yet even by 1979 not entirely †, although, since the earlier date, tending to be joc. Lord Baden-Powell (1857–1941), after many adventurous years, founding the Boy Scouts in 1908 and, with sister Agnes, the Girl Guides in 1910. (Thanks to a reminder by R.C., 1978) Cf **honest Injun!**

scoutmaster. See: balls on him.

scrambled, like your brains! See **how do you like your eggs…**

scraped 'em off me puttees! was, during WW1, a British soldiers' contemptuous ref. to other soldiers; esp., perhaps, the Staff. (B & P.) Cf **I've seen 'em grow** and **they've opened another tin**, which are not at all points synon.

The allusion is to *shit*, whether literal or figurative.

scraping. See: wants his.

scratch. See: have a scratch; and:

scratch his arse with – he hasn't a sixpence to. A low c.p. of mid C19–20; ob. by 1930 and† by 1950. Cf **hasn't got a ha'penny...**

scratch my breech and I'll claw your elbow. Partly a proverb and partly a c.p.: C17–19. An earthy synonym of the entirely proverbial, and politer, *scratch me and I'll scratch thee* and, its modern form, *you scratch my back and I'll scratch yours.*

scream. See: cheers for now; dragged screaming; when in danger.

screw. See: first turn; you'd forget.

screw and bolt. See **fuck 'em and leave 'em.**

screwed, blued and tattooed. See **stewed, screwed...**

scrub round it! 'Originating in the Services [during WW2], where it was easier to clean around an object than to move it, and adopted in civilian life to enjoin the avoidance of an unpleasant task or doing unnecessary work' (Noble, 1978). Cf:

[**scrubbers!** is a 'one-word c.p.', not a fully qualified c.p. It means 'That's finished' or 'That no longer exists': RAF: since *c.* 1930. (Examples can be found in, e.g., C.H. Ward Jackson, *It's a Piece of Cake*, 1943.) It may derive from the turf *scrub 'er*, to sponge off the big odds on one's (bookmaster's) board. P.B.: prob. by the Oxford and RN – *er*(s) word-formation, on *scrub*; cf prec.]

scuttle(d). See: I'm as mild; three turns.

sea. See: down went; every little helps; I'm Jolly Jack; leave the sea; shore; there's sorrow; who wouldn't; worse things.

sea-boot. See: 'fuck me!'

sea-miles. See: I've done.

sea-time. See: get some sea.

seal. See: all right, you did hear.

sealed. See: my lips.

seaman, if he carries a millstone, will have a quail out of it – a. A mid C18 – mid C19 semi-proverbial c.p., alluding to seamen's traditional resourcefulness and ingenuity, esp. in the matter of acquiring food or drink. Ray.

search me! Aso **you can** (or **may**) **search me!** Orig. US and Can. (since *c.* 1900), it became, *c.* 1910, also Brit.: 'But you won't find it' (a solution, an answer) is understood. The earliest ref. I've discovered is in Gelett Burgess's essay, 'A Defence of Slang', in *The Romance of the Commonplace*, 1902. W & F cite a US book title, *You Can Search Me*, 1905; Sandiland, 1913, comments, 'Literally, search me all over for the information you require' and notes the synon. *you have me there* and *you have me beat*; S.R. Shait, in 'Straight Talk' (*Boston Globe*, *c.* 1917), includes it in a list of c.pp. of the day; McKnight notes that it was very common among US students of *c.* 1920–2; George Ade uses it in his 'comedy-drama', *Father and the Boys*, 1924, in the form, *you can search me!*; Terence Rattigan, *While the Sun Shines*, performed on Christmas Eve 1943, and pub'd in 1944, has in Act III, near end:

HORTON: Who is his lordship marrying in three minutes?
MULVANEY: Search me.

His distinguished contemporary, Noël Coward, in *Nude with Violin*, 1956, causes one of his characters to say, at II, ii, 'In the idiom of our American cousins, Miss Jane – "search me!"'

The form *search me!* occurs in Hugh Pentecost's novel, *The Gilded Nightmare*, 1968, and in the *New Yorker*, 31 Jan. 1970, where one of two visitors from outer space says to the other, 'Search me!'

An amusing 1960s Brit. example of *search me!* comes in Ruth Rendell's novel, *Wolf to the Slaughter*, 1967:

'My daughter Sheila's having a jam session.'

'No,' said Burden with a smile, 'they don't call it that any more.'

Wexford said, belligerently from behind his beer, 'What do they call it, then?'

'Search me.'

Sears Roebuck. See: where did you get your licence.

season. See: open season.

seat. See: in the catbird; not a dry; papa's; up and down; you want the best.

second coming. See: you are slower.

second-hand car. See: would you buy.

second opinion. See: would you like a.

secret. See: it's a state.

seduced. See: living in s.

see. See: can't see; do you see; don't fire; hello yourself; I don't see; I see; I'll be seeing; I'll expect; I'll see; I've not seen; I've seen; if I don't see; if you see; it'll see; long time; monkey see; next time you see; nice to see you; now you see; plant; something nasty; suck it; things you see; this I must; wait and; well, I never; what you see; when you've seen; why should; wouldn't be seen; you can see; you couldn't see; you going; you should see; you're blind; and:

see a dog about a man – I have to (or **I must**), recorded by Berrey, but also Brit., dates from the 1930s and is a joc. var. of:

see a man about a dog – I have to (or **I must**); also **I'm going (out) to see...**; and the full, the orig., form, **I have to** (or **I must**) **go to see a man about a dog.** I must visit a woman – sexually: late C19–20. Hence, I'm going out for a drink: late C19–20. In C20, often in answer to an inconvenient question about one's destination; I must go to the water-closet, usu. to 'the gents', merely to urinate. Cf prec., and see **excuse me, I have...**

see anything green? 'Asked, if somebody is staring. Also if something is unnoticed, something that has been changed or re-arranged, or something new. I heard it in 1915 and still hear it [in US] occasionally' (Fain, 1978. Cf **do you see any green in my eye?**, from which it just poss, derives. (P.B.)

see how the poor live. See **come in and see...**

see something new? is a C20 Suffolk c.p.: refers to someone who, usually pretty helpless and hopeless, has done something remarkable. (A Suffolk correspondent.)

see the chaplain! Turn to **go see the chaplain!**

see what I mean? is, naturally, a cliché when it is used lit., but a c.p. when it bears the sense, 'I told you what would happen That's how it goes' (Granville, 1969): C20. Contrast **if you know what I mean.**

see what the boys in the back room will have. See TAD DORGAN.

see what the cat's brought in! A var. of *look what...*, q.v. and like something the cat's...

see what the wind has blown in! See **look what the wind...!**

see ya! (or **see yer!**) is a post-1945 English, esp. Londoners', illiterate version of:

see you! I'll be seeing you, *or* Au revoir: orig. and mostly Aus.: since *c.* 1930. (Baker.) In the late 1930s, also Brit. (a good example occurring in Peter Dickinson's moving novel, *Sleep and His Brother*, 1971), the counter or 'dovetail' being **not if I see you first**, as Sanders has reminded us, in ref. to the var. *see you soon;* and by the late 1940s – not necessarily independently of Aus. or Eng. usage – also US: W & F remark, 'Very common, esp. among students and younger people. Almost as common as "so long" or "good-by".'

I cannot resist an impulse to quote from Arnold Wesker's *I'm Talking about Jerusalem* (the new Jerusalem, a modern version of Utopia, prod. and pub'd in 1960, at II, i, where Ada says to Dave about his friend Libby: 'He stood out here and he looked around and he said: "It's all sky, isn't it?" and then he stalked off with "see you".'. Cf:

see you around! A valedictory c.p., dating since *c.* 1930, slightly more frequent ('Very common', says J.W.C., 1968) in US that in the British Commonwealth. Cf **see you!** and:

see you bright and curly. 'I suspect a Canadian background for this farewell. *Curly* obviously change for *early*' (P.B., 1974): since *c.* 1955.

see you further. See **I'll see you...**

see you (or I'll see you) in church is a 'common valedictory – always ironic' US phrase (J.W.C., 1968): C20; but 'a good deal less often heard than, say, thirty years ago; seems to have come to be felt to be hackneyed and unimaginative, and perhaps bucolic', he adds in 1975. Recorded by Berry, 1942. Like the next, also – since *c.* 1910 – Aus. P.B.: well known in UK too, at least since mid C20. Cf:

see you (or **I'll see you**) **in court** (or, less frequently, **gaol, jail**) is another valedictory c.p., mostly Aus.: since *c.* 1910. Humorous and occ. ironic. Frank Shaw, 1968, provides a Liverpudlian var.: *see yer at the Assizes!*; and R.C., 1978, says of the *court* version, 'Certainly current in US during the 1920s and 1930s. It occurs, for instance, in D. Hammett's *The Maltese Falcon*, 1930'.

see you in hell first. See **I'll see you...**

see you in the funny papers (– often and orig. *I'll*). 'This jocular farewell suggests that the person addressed is rather laughable: US: 1920s; extinct by the 1950s' (R.C., 1978). Perhaps adopted in the UK from American servicemen *c.* 1943. By *c.* 1955, (*I'll*) *see you in the funnies.*

see you later, alligator! A US, Can. and Eng. c.p., to which the 'dovetail' or response is (**yeah, see you) in a while, crocodile**: *c.* 1950–60 and then derided as outmoded, yet still used. This sort of rhyming was, *c.* 1935–60, a vogue; a vogue that has left only a very small residue of phrases, which, after their vogue, strike me as being even more tedious and monotonously painful than one had felt them to be in their prime. In 1975, W.J.B. described it as being, among teenagers, 'still heard'. P.B.: *VIBS* points out that it was, of course, 'from the title of a Bill Haley hit in the film *Rock Around the Clock* [1956]', one of the best known of all the early rock in films, and one that produced hitherto unknown excitement and rioting in those cinemas that showed it – others banned it in trepidation. Dennis Bloodworth, in *An Eye for the Dragon*, 1975, writing about riots in Singapore, says: 'In 1956...in swinging Singapore the current chant ran, "See you later – agitator"', to which the 'with-it' response was, 'when it's quieter – rioter'. Cf **what o'clock, cock?; dig you later!**, and see the entry **don't knock the rock!**

see you soon! See **see you!**

see you under the clock! A lighthearted ref. to an agreed meeting soon to take place, but not to any particular clock: the Brit. use of this c.p. prob. dates back to the mid 1940s, for it had been adopted from the US, prob. via American servicemen during the latter part of WW2. W.J.B., 1977, tells me that the US ref., from the 1920s, is to the clock at the Biltmore Hotel, which was connected with the Grand Central Railroad terminal. Young people arriving from the suburbs walked through a tunnel and met their 'dates' under the clock in the hotel lobby.

seeing you! See **be seeing you!**

seen one, you've seen 'em all. The clipped version of **when you've seen one...**

seen something nasty in the woodshed. See **something nasty.**

seizing. See: hard in.

sell. See: could sell; couldn't organize; don't let anyone; don't sell; how do you sell; I'll bite; nobody is; who wouldn't; you're selling; and:

sell in May and go away was, during the inter-war years of 1919–39, a Brit. stockbrokers' saying, which was temporarily killed by WW2. The going away referred to a long holiday in, e.g. the south of France. (Skehan; period indicated by Leonard Pearce; both, 1977.) 'The chairman of an investment trust tells me it is still understood in the City, though the doctrine is obsolete. In the days when individual investors dominated the market, it was thought that share prices dropped in the holiday season for lack of buyers. So you sold in May, held onto the cash, and went away. Later, you could buy at lower prices, at the end of the holidays. If this was ever true, it isn't nowadays, since the institutions dominate the market – and they never go away' (Playfair, 1977).

sell the pig and buy me out! See **dear Mother, it's a bugger!**

selling tickets is a c.p. only when it is used derisively or contemptuously or pityingly as a comment on overt, blatant

publicizing or promotion: US: since, at earliest, mid 1976. (Paul Theroux, 1977.)

semper fi. See **I got mine...**

send. See! it sends; when I want; and:

send for Gulliver! was, 1887 – *c.* 1985, a Society c.p., referring to 'some affair not worth discussion., From a cascadescent incident' in Swift's Gulliver's Travels, Part I. (Ware, 1909.)

send for Mary Ann. See **san fairy Ann!**

send for the green van! 'Indicating that someone was going crazy or thought to be behaving strangely and requiring immediate removal to a mental hospital: 1950s' (Mrs Shirley M. Pearce, 1975). The US version is *send for the (padded) wagon!*: since 1930s. (R.C. 1978.) Cf **another one for the van!**

send for the Marines!, 'Often preceded by *you'd* (or *we'd*) *better...* Help is needed – not necessarily military aid, but assistance of any sort and in a hurry! I recall this from the 1940s–1950s, with variations' (A.B., 1979). Manifestly prompted by *(the) Marines have handed.*

send for the overweights. See **go and fetch...**

send her down, Hughie! (and ..., **Steve!**) This Aus. – hence also NZ – c.p. of late C19–20, the *Steve* var. being used during WW1, expresses a fervent desire for rain. (*AS.*) Variations of the next, *her* for *it* being characteristically Aus.

send it down, David (with var. **Davy lad**)! The var. belongs to the Regular Army; and the basic *send it down, David* is often intensified by the addition of a repetitive *send it down*: late C19–20. In the army, esp. during WW1, it was used to implore David, the Welsh patron saint, to send a preferably very heavy shower, notably when it might cause a parade to be postponed or cancelled. Parts of Wales have a notoriously wet climate; and, what is more, Wales is 'the Land of *Leeks*' (leaks). Both F & G and B & P are eloquent about this c.p.

sense. See: not enough.

sent to dry us. 'Used to be said when prohibition was a leading topic' in Britain, esp. during the ten to fifteen years preceding WW1 and during the early 1920s. A pun on the cliché 'sent to try us.' (Petch, 1974.)

sentiments. See: them's my s.

separate (or **private peace – I'll make a,** occ. prec. by **I think.** A wistful yet joc., deeply felt yet lightly expressed, British soldiers' c.p., much used during the war-weary years of 1917–18. (B & P.)

separate the men from the boys – that'll (or **this'll**). This crisis or national emergency will serve to determine who are the real men: much used by businessmen and orators: since *c.* 1930 in US and since the late 1930s in UK; not much used since the 1960s. (Shaw, 1969.) A var. is *sort out the men from the boys.* And see **this is where the men are separated...**

September. See: frozen.

serene. See: all serene.

sergeant. See: kiss me, s.; some say; take his name.

Sergeant-Major. See: carry on, Sergeant; officers have; take his name.

sergeant-pilot. See: I don't want to be.

servant. See: what did your.

served. See: yes, but beautifully; you couldn't be s.

service. See: are you nervous; happy in the s.; now then, only; you haven't been.

set 'em up in the other alley! This mostly printers' c.p. – mainly Can. at that – has, in C20, been used 'when a task is accomplished. "O.K. So that's that. Now set 'em up in the other alley"' (Leechman). In other words, 'Well, *that's* done. What's next?' Its far from certain that there is a ref. to ninepines.

But, of its US currency (since *c.* 1920), R.C. tells me, 1978, that 'the derivation from bowling (tenpins) is almost inescapable. That is, we have knocked down one set of pins, so put up another'. Yet the constradiction may be only apparent: a c.p. *can* have independent origins in two different countries.

set-up. See: you have a nice.

sets. See: these sets.

seven. See: it's all in the s.

seven and six, was she worth it? This is a Services' c.p., dating from WW2 players of housey-housey, which was retained in Bingo. (Mr R. Line, of Orpington.) In Great Britain, the sum of seven shillings and sixpence, was, for many years, the normal charge for many kinds of licences, including esp. the marriage licence. P.B.: sometimes reduced to just *seven and six, was she?*, or even just *was she?* in Service messes. I don't know why E.P. chose to include this one call, out of all the scores available; for a reasonably full list of the traditional housey-housey, tombola or bingo (call it what you will) substitutes for straight, dull numbers, see *tombola* in the Appendix to *DSUE*, 8th ed.

sew. See: my mother sews.

sewer. See: wipe the shit.

sex. See: how's your love; only way; and:

sex and beer soup are too good for the people indicates a 'mock-Marie Antoinette disdain for the senses of the people. Beer soup is a German dish made from beer, eggs and milk; of pleasing delicacy of flavour. Among a few of the British Forces in Germany' (L.A., 1974): c. 1945–60.

sex is all right, but it will never replace the bicycle. A c.p. 'used to stop those endless discussions of sex. From c. 1960' (Sanders, 1978).

sex rears its ugly head, very common in the late 1930s and throughout the 1940s, although used decreasingly since, was, when employed to mean 'Sex has (again) become operative', a cliché; but when – esp. perhaps in Aus. – used as a synonym for *cherchez la femme*, it is a c.p., † by 1970 at latest.

'With various changes in tense (e.g., *is rearing*) current in the US since the 1930s. Now extinct – perhaps because the near-omnipresence of sex in advertising, etc., makes it otiose' (R.C., 1978).

Allan Chapman cites the *Guinness Book of Film Facts and Feats*, 1980, which attributes the phrase's origin to James R. Quirk, in an editorial about *Hell's Angels* (the US film, 1930) in *Photoplay* (no date given).

Sexton Blake! See **I'm Hawkshaw the detective.**

sez how – sez which or **why.** See **says...,** and:

sez you! is that 'conventional' unconventional spelling of *says you* which assigns it to slangy usage. This derisive c.p., orig. US, became also Brit. c. 1930 and was signalized by Brophy; but in UK, gradually – since c. 1950 – yet slowly, becoming more and more ob. To paraphrase W & F, it arose in US 'since before c. 1925' and has been employed either to express a belligerent doubt of the addressee's knowledge or opinion or, at another level, authority or to indicate disbelief, esp. when the speaker does not wish to have to agree. It is also recorded by Berrey.

Noted in Bernham and in other reference books, this snappy phrase has inevitably been used by hundreds of writers (the majority, very properly, US): for instance, Clarence Budington Kelland, who had a very sharp and sensitive ear for his compatriots' coll. and slangy words and phrases; as in *Speak Easily* and *Spotlight*, both in the middle 1930s. The English novelist, Philip Macdonald, *RIP*, 1933, assigns it to an Englishman in the form *says you*, which recurs in, e.g., Selwyn Jepson's *The Angry Millionaire*, 1969.

In the *Kansas City Star*, 23 Feb. 1930, appeared an article titled 'Sez the Wise – Crackers', which begins: '"Sez which," scoffs the 1930 youth and pats himself between the shoulder blades for having employed perhaps the most up-to-the-minute expression in collegiate parlance; doubtless, also, to the extreme discomfiture of the one addressed. Perchance the phrase is "Sez how?" or "Sez why?" or "Sez" something else. Regardless of what is said, however, "Sez" is always spelled with a "z" and pronounced with a mockingly exasperated half-sneer and a sound similar to that emitted by asthmatic Frenchman reading an article in Castillian Spanish'. Later, 'Oh, yes!' and 'Oh, yeah!' are adduced as comparables, and the writer remarks, 'Apparently "Sez

you", "Oh, yeah?" or some other phrase of identical connotation, is necessary in the word box of the modern boy or girl approaching manhood or womanhood'. Later still: 'At all events, indicates are that the use of "Sez which?" – "Sez you" and "Sez" everything else... will soon be a thing of the past and that some substitute phrase will appear'. (Thanks to Col. Moe.) Note, however, that, even as late as 1978, *sez you* is merely ob., not †.

shabbos. See: make shabbos.

shade. See: up a s.

shadow. See: creeps out; no possible.

shag. See: he'd fuck; stag.

shag on a rock – like a, usu. *standing (out)*, or occ. *sitting, like...; ...like a lily on a dirt tin*; rarely, **like a beer bottle on the Coliseum.** The first, meaning 'lonely' or 'isolated' and 'desolate' is recorded for 1845 as having existed much earlier in the form *miserable as a shag on a rock*; the second, meaning 'conspicuous' since c. 1935; the third, meaning 'incongruous', since c. 1945. (Mostly, G.A. Wilkes's admirable *Dict. Aus. Coll.* Australia, like the US, excels in picturesque c.pp.)

Shah. See: have you seen.

shake. See: easy as shaking; if I am; let me s.; that shock; what shakes; what's shaking.

shake a stick at. See: has more money.

shake hands with the wife's best friend – I must (go and) or **I'll go and.** 'I must go to the Gents': male, mostly raffish: since c. 1930, at latest. It occurs in, e.g., Anthony Grey, *The Chinese Assassin*, 1978. P.B.: another version is *I must go and shake hands with a very old friend*, which leads to the ritual exchange: 'Known him long?' – 'I've known him longer!': C20, perhaps earlier. Cf the synon. **Shed a tear for Nelson;** see **a man about a dog;** and see also **I'm going to do...**

shake the lead out of your ass! (or **arse!**) A US and Can., mostly workmen's, 'Get a move on!': since c. 1930. A US var. is *get the lead out*: W & F. Cf **get the lead out of your pants!**

shake your ears! – often prec. by **go.** A 'sick' joke of c. 1560–1790: advice to one who has lost his ears. It can be found in, e.g., Gabriel Harvey, 1573; Shakespeare; Mrs F. Sheridan, 1764. Apperson.

shall I put a bit of hair round it for you? is a crude question posed to a workman having trouble inserting something into something else, the 'dovetail' or usual response being, **yes, if you've got the right kind:** Can.: C20 Analogous to **don't look down....**

shall I spell it out for you? See **spell it out....**

shall us? let's! Shall we do it? Let's!: Current, esp. among juveniles, c. 1895–1914. Prob. suggested by Cockney *shall us?* for *shall we?*

shall we dance? 'Often said by two people dodging in a doorway, narrow corridor, etc., each uncertain of which side to pass the other. Perhaps prompted by (if not pre-dating) the song of this title from the very popular musical show and film *The King and I*, 1956' (P.B., 1976).

shame. See: ain't it a s.; pity about; standing; and:

shame on your shimmy! A partly facetious pun on 'Shame on you!': lower-middle class: since c. 1930. Here, *shimmy* is a slang form of *chemise*.

shame to take the money – a, sometimes prec. by **it's.** That's money very easily earned or otherwise received, esp. for work one has enjoyed doing: late C19–20.

shape. See: there's a shape; we'll soon; you shape; and:

shape up or ship out! Straighten up and fly right; snap out of it; get on the ball; a threat to get rid of the person so addressed unless he shows an improvement in the performance of his duties. Milieu: orig. army usage during WW2...but not restricted to armed forces' usage (Arthur M.Z. Norman, 'Army Speech...', in *American Speech*, May 1956): 'The soldier's language is cemented by more or less ephemeral idioms: *You've had it* (a promise of punishment); *Shape up or ship out* (start soldiering or be sent to a combat zone)' (Col. Moe, 1975). Note that W.J.B., 1975 writes: 'Navy slang. Now used by any employer who warns employee to "get with it"...or pick up his check.' R.C., 1978, adds, 'Certainly used extensively by, and possibly originating among, WW2 merchant seamen'. Nautical, anyway.

share. See: lady with; thank you for sharing.

share that among you! was, during WW1 – or, at least, 1915 – 18 – a soldiers' c.p., uttered as one hurls a hand-grenade into an enemy trench or dug-out; 'he might be quite jovial about it' (B & P), for the action released him from tension and frustration. Cf the centuries earlier **have among ye, my blind harpers!**

sharks. See: too late.

sharp. See: 'e be arf; you're so s.; and:

sharp's the word and quick's the motion, often shortened to **sharp's the word.** A c.p. implying that a person is 'very attentive to his own interest' (Grose, 1788): since c. 1660; by 1930, slightly ob., yet not, even in the 1970s, †. An elab. of *sharp's the word*, an enjoining of promptitude. In Sir John Vanbrugh's *The Mistake*, performed in Dec. 1705 and pub'd in 1706, Lopez speaking an aside to his master, Don Lorenzo, in III, says: 'Are you thereabouts [i.e., near the mark], i' faith? Then sharp's the word.'

In S, 1738 (but begun thirty years earlier), in Dialogue III, we see:

LADY ANS[WERALL]: Upon my Word, they must rise early that would cheat her of her Money. Sharp's the word with her: Diamonds cut Diamonds.

Here, *sharp* bears the two meanings, 'prompt' or 'very quick', and 'shrewd'.

In Richard Brinsley Peake, *Ten Thousand a Year: A Drama* (adapted from Samuel Warren's famous novel), performed in 1842, at I, i, Titmouse, formerly a linen-draper's assistant, addresses his former close companion thus abruptly: 'What d'ye want with me, sir? Sharp's the word.'

When Sharp's Toffee launched their advertising campaign, many years ago, their publicity man brilliantly introduced the slogan, 'Sharp's a word for toffee'. Mr A.C. Drew of Trebor Sharp's Ltd, as the old firm became during the 1960s, says that 'Sharp's a word for toffee', as a slogan, was first used in 1927, so far as he knows. Edward (later Sir Edward) Sharp began to manufacture this famous toffee in 1880, at Maidstone. The slogan did much to revive the c.p. *sharp's the word*.

In 1976, Christopher Fry wrote to tell me that '"Sharp's the word, quick's the action" was often said to me when I was small' (c. 1910 – 14) – that is, *action* rather than *motion*. P.B.: my mother-in-law, Mrs Arthur Hughes, slightly older than C.F., uses *sharp's the word and quick's the action*, for 'Let's get a move on!' Both I, and Nigel Rees in *Slogans*, 1982, recall the toffee slogan as 'Sharp's the word for toffee'.

shat. See: have you shat; and:

shat who? 'What are you talking about?': US: since 1920s; obsolete' (Fain, 1977). Yet another var. of *sez who?*, q.v. at **sez you!**, using a joc. past tense of *shit*.

shave, a shilling, (and) a shove ashore – a; also **shit, shave, shove ashore.** This RN (lower-deck) c.p. was applied to the procedure and priorities of short leave. The *shove* synonymizes 'a short time' or expeditious copulation. The var. *shit, shave, (and) shove ashore* likewise describes a matlow's evening-leaver routine; and it has two elaborations: *I've had – or I had – a shit, shave, shower, shoeshine and shampoo*, a Can. c.p. that, arising c. 1930, was very gen. among Canadian soldiers during WW2, implying as it did, a 'heavy date', and the Brit. *shit, shine, shave, shampoo and shift*, where *shift* = a prompt and speedy departure. Lately, P.B. writes, *I've had* tends to be dropped, and the phrase starts simply *Time for a shit*... In the *TLS*, 26 Aug. 1977, Anthony Burgess notes an elab., *shit, shave, shampoo and piss buckets out of the window*, which I've never heard. Doubtless there are still other variables.

shaved. See: go to Bath.

Shazam! Orig. S.H.A.Z.A.M. Often prec. by *holy moley!*, a mere euph. expletive ('Holy Mother' or 'Holy Moses'). A US expression of astonishment, very popular during the 1940s – mid 1950s, when there was a vogue, almost a cult, of Caption Marvel 'comic' books. 'For instance, the Gomer Pyle TV show made much use of "Shazam!" When Billy Balson said the word, it turned him into Captain Marvel – like Superman.' Thus A.B., who 1978, explains *Shuzam* as:

S = wisdom of *S*olmon;
H = strength of *H*ercules;
A = stamina of *A*tlas;
Z = power of *Z*eus;
A = courage of *A*chilles;
M = speed of *M*ercury.

Prof. Brown has provided me with a wealth of further information; but what precedes is richly sufficient, so I must regretfully abstain from using it.

she can put her shoes under my bed... See **he can put his shoes...**

she carries the broom (at the masthead). She's a whore: a seaport c.p. of c. 1810 – 90. (JB.) The ref. is to that broom which, attached to the masthead, indicated that the ship had been sold.

she couldn't cook hot water for a barber has, since c. 1880, been applied to an inferior housekeeper, esp. to a girl unlikely to be able to 'feed the brute' satisfactorily.

she didn't seem to mind it very much. A proletarian c.p., grimly ironic, implying considerable jealousy in the female concerned: c. 1880 – 1910. Ware.

she dunno where she are. See **'e dunno where 'e are.**

she goes as if she cracked nuts with her tail was, C19 – early C20, directed at a woman with a provocative gait. Cf **she walks...**

she had a hair across her arse is 'said of a perpetually bad-tempered woman, it being suggested that this minor irritation accounted for her evil temper. Recent' (Leechman, 1968): a Can. c.p.

'A variation: *she had a wild hair up her ass!* – meaning that she had a peculiar idea or driving whim – she did something without thought. I heard this in the 1950s in the Southern US' (A.B., 1979).

she has a bun in the oven. See **she's joined the club.**

she has a face like the back of a bus (or tram). See **face would stop a clock.**

she has (or **she's got**) **a nice pair of** (pause) **eyes.** See **beautiful pair...**

she has (or **she's**) **been a good wife to him** is an ironic proletarian c.p. 'cast at a drunken woman rolling in the streets' (Ware): since c. 1905; by 1940, ob.; by 1975, virtually †.

she has everything has, since c. 1945, been applied to an exceptionally – and, esp., physically – attractive girl or woman. Also **she has two of everything**; well, not quite everything.

she has (or **she's got**) **legs up to her bum.** A mid C19–20 c.p., slightly ob. by 1970, addressed by men to boys in order to imply a common humanity: 'She has legs too, you know; just like you, son.' P.B.: but also used appreciatively, as in, 'Ginger bint, she was, with legs right up to her bum. Wiggle, wiggle, wiggle; cor, smashing!' which I heard in the late 1950s from a Londoner.

she has (or **she's got**) **round heels** is, in Canada, directed at a very accommodating female, her heels being so round that a mere nudge will put her on her back.

she has seen something nasty in the woodshed. See **something nasty...**

she has swallowed a stake and cannot stoop. See **swallowed....**

she has two of everything. See **she has everything.**

she hasn't had it so long, sometimes prec. by **nothing, but.** A reply to the oft-heard complaint, 'What has *she* got that I haven't (got)?' Since the 1940s.

'she' is a (or **the**) **cat's mother.** One of the two or three best-known of the domestic c.pp., this has, mid (?early)

267

C19–20, been addressed, usu. by a parent, to a child, whether very young or teenaged, referring thus to his or her mother. By 1960, slightly ob.

There is a var.: *who is 'she'? the cat's grandmother?*: late C19 – mid C20. (Prof. T.B.W. Reid, 1972.) In Dodie Smith's play, *Touch Wood*, 1934; at II, iv, there is the following exchange between Nonny, a little girl, and Elizabeth, a spinster, aged thirty-eight:

NONNY (*with a jerk towards Elizabeth*): Perhaps she'd play.

ELIZABETH: In my young days I was taught that 'she' was the cat's grandmother

– which exemplifies the entirely natural extension of the relationship.

she is in her skin. See **in his skin.**

she is so innocent that she thinks Fucking is a town in China; occ., **she was...that she thought...was a town....** This is a mostly Londoners' c.p., dating since *c.* 1940. The geographical ref. is to Chinese *Fukien*, a south-eastern maritime province.

she knows about it now. See **now she knows about it.**

she knows, you know occurred in Eric Barber's radio comedy programme *Just Fancy*, broadcast 4 Sep. 1959:

MRS AIGBURTH: We nearly got turned out at Blackpool – laughing so much.

MR AIGBURTH: Hylda Baker!

MRS AIGBURTH: She knows, you know.

In 1977, P.B. commented, 'It enjoyed something of a vogue in the 1960s and is still around'. He added that this is Hylda Baker's own c.p. and that it became one not only because she used it, but also because, for the *Daily Mirror*, Dennis Collins drew a comic strip, called 'Hylda Baker's Diary'; P.B. cited Denis Gifford's *Stap Me!: The British Newspaper Strip*, 1971.

Of this c.p., Russell Davies, reviewing the first ed. of this book in *New Statesman*, 9 Sep. 1977, remarked that it 'spent about a decade turning up in conversation (though seldom with the original's awful landlady-like inflection followed by the nudge in the hapless stooge's ['her mute giraffe-like butt, Cynthia' (*VIBS*)] ribs and the wild yell of "DON'T YER?")'. R.D. even titled his article 'He Knows, Yer Know'.

she looks as if she could eat me without salt. In S, 1738, Dialogue I, Neverout says: 'But. pray my Lady *Smart*, does not Miss look as if she could eat me without Salt?' – that is, finds me so delightful that she could eat me. A c.p. current throughout most of C18. Cf the C19–20 coll.: (a person) *good enough to eat*. Cf **I could eat...**

[**she rapes awful easy** is a jocularly sardonic US c.p., applied to girls not so very reluctantly admitting that they've been 'raped' once again: since the middle 1940s, if not a decade earlier. But 'this is just an example of a pattern; "I scare easy" is commoner' (J.W.C., 1975, who adds that the *awful* is usu. omitted). Not, therefore, a true c.p.]

she sails. A US underworld c.p., dating since the 1920s and applied to a compliant or accommodating girl or woman. (Berrey.) Cf the British tramps' **she's all right.**

she smokes and **she's a smoker.** She performs penilingism: low: C20 Cf synon. French slang, *elle fait des pipes* (Janssen, 1972).

she stacks up. See **she's class.**

she thinks she is wearing a white collar. She's putting on 'side': a Women's Army Auxiliary Corps c.p. of 1917–18. Among the 'Waacs' a white collar was worn by NCOs. B & P.

she walks like she's got a feather up her ass. This C20 Can. phrase is applied to a woman noticeable for her self-conscious, mincing gait. 'In the southern US, the phrase usually goes, *she walks* (or *looks*) *like she's got a corncob up her cunt* (or *ass*). William Faulkner makes use of this in a very literal fashion in his worst novel, *Sanctuary*, 1931. Probably throughout C20' (the name of E.P.'s informant is missing from the ms notes). P.B.: it is of course too picturesque not to be also low Brit., as is the vulgarly allusive *She walks like she's still got it in*, in the same sense. Cf **she**

goes...

she was so innocent... See **she is so innocent...**

she wants (or **he promised her) the (whole) world, with a little red fence around it.** A humorously dry observation on pre-marital feminine ambition and masculine optimism; a cynical, or a mock cynical, comment on 'love's young dream' and Virgil's *omnia vincit amor*. US: since the 1920s, I'd guess. (C.P. owed to J.W.C., 1977.) By 1976, slightly moribund.

she went out to buy a knickknack and came back with a titbit – is an occ. var. of **remember the girl.**

she will (or more commonly **she'll) die wondering.** An Aus. C20 c.p., referring to a virgin spinster. Hence the c.p., *at least she won't die wondering*, applied, since *c.* 1920, to a spinster marrying late and badly. (B.P.)

she will go off in an aromatic faint was, in 1883 – *c.* 1886, a Society gibe at 'a fantastical woman, meaning that her delicate nerves will surely be the death of her' (Ware).

she will say anything but her prayers, and those she whistles. She never says her prayers: current, late C17 – mid C19, it was partly a proverbial saying and partly a c.p. S, 1738, Dialogue I, gives:

LADY SM[ART]: Well said, Miss: I vow Mr *Neverout*, the Girl is too hard for you.

NEV[EROUT]: Ay, Miss will say anything but her prayers, and those she whistles.

Apperson.

she wobbles like a drunken tailor with two left legs was a C19 – mid 20 nautical c.p., applied to a ship that steers erratically. Bowen.

she would sell her hole for half a dollar is a contemptuous ref. to a girl lacking in self-respect: C20.

she would (or **she'd) take you in, and blow you out (again) as** (or **in little) bubbles.** This 'men only' c.p. is, in C20, deflatingly directed at men addicted to amorous boasting. P.B.: or, in ref. to a particularly large and well-built woman, 'My word, she's a hefty girl! I'll bet she could take...'

she wouldn't know if someone was up her. A low, mostly Aus., c.p. referring to a remarkably stupid girl: since *c.* 1910.

she'll be apples. See **apples – it's** or **she's,** and cf:

she'll be jake (or **right) Jack** (or **mate).** It'll work, *or* All will come right, be right, etc.: virtually the NZ national motto; known also in Aus., where used by, e.g., Nino Culotta (Aus.), *c.* 1920, *very* approximately. (Mrs Hazel Franklin, 1975.)

This use of *she* for *it* was orig. Aus., but it soon found a home in NZ too. See also **she's right!** and **that's jake...**

she'll be right. See **she's right!**

she'll die wondering. See **she will die wondering.**

she'll never drown is equivalent to **you don't get many of those to the pound,** and is shouted at an actress: since *c.* 1965(?). Perhaps – well, just possibly – deriving from the use of *Mae West* for a life-jacket. (Levene, 1978.)

shell-like See: **world in your.**

Sherlock Holmes! – often abbr. to **Sherlock!** – has, since *c.* 1898, been ironically directed at detectors of the obvious: ob. since *c.* 1960, but not yet †. Obviously in ref. to Conan Doyle's detective, the most famous of all fictional sleuths. In 1968, Julian Franklyn told me that, because he smoked a bent meerschaum, he sometimes had *Sherlock!* or *Sherlock Holmes!* shouted at him by children in the street.

she's a hot member for a mile, she is and no mistake is a horse-racing c.p., dating from *c.* 1920 and obviously applied to a filly very fast indeed up to that distance. (Shaw, 1969.)

she's a smoker. See **she smokes.**

she's all right is a British tramps' C20 c.p., applied to a female sexually willing. (Hippo Neville, *Sneak Thief on the Road*, 1935.) Cf **she sails,** and contrast **she's right?**

she's been a good wife to him. See **she has been....**

she's been fucked more times than she's had hot dinners or **she's had more fucks than you've had hot dinners.** A low, proletarian c.p. of late C19–20. The male counterpart is **I've had more women than you've had hot dinners,** q.v.

she's class and **she stacks up** are synon. US c.pp applied to an attractive female, esp. if young: the latter implies an impressive frontage: since *c.* 1920. Berrey.

she's gone into the manufacturing business is a US euph. c.p. applied to pregnancy: *c.* 1950–70. 'Probably not current' (A.B., 1979). Neither pithy enough nor, perhaps, earthy enough; and, I suspect, too witty to reach middle, much less old, age. Cf the Brit. **she's joined the club**, and similar insensitive variants.

she's good (or **very good**) **to the poor** has, since *c.* 1910, been a prostitutes' 'catty' c.p., applied to one who cuts her price, and thus lets the sisterhood down.

she's got... entries. See the **she has...** (or **she has got...**) entries.

she's got her run on. A Public School senior girls' statement of a menstrual period: C20.

she's had more fucks than you've had hot dinners. See **she's been fucked...**

she's jake. See **she'll be jake** and **she's right.**

she's joined the club. She is pregnant – applied esp. to an unmarried girl: C20. This somewhat inexclusive club is *The Pudding* – or, in proletarian circles, *Pudden – Club*, which dates from latish C19. To *put in the pudden club*, to render pregnant, is extant; it was used in, e.g., James Curtis's remarkable novel of the underworld, *The Gilt Kid*, 1936. By itself, *pudden*, seminal fluid, which had, in C19–early 20, the synonym, *marrow pudding*, seems to have existed since Restoration times.

There is a var. applicable to any pregnancy: *she has a bun in the oven*: C20. This again has the occ. allusive var., *she has one in the oven* (J.W.C., 1977).

she's making her will. See **making his** (or **her**) **will.**

she's right! That's *most* satisfactory!; *but also* That's all right, *or* Don't mention it!: both NZ and Aus.: since *c.* 1925 or a little earlier. (J.H. Henderson, *Gunner Inglorious*, 1945, for NZ; Nino Culotta and, in sense 'All's well', Alexander Buzo, *Norm and Ahmed*, performed in 1968, for Aus.) This coll. *she* may stem from *she* for a ship.

Of the NZ use of *she's right*, Mr Arthur Gray of Auckland, NZ, wrote to me, 1969:

Sometimes *she's all right, Jack* [prompted, doubtless, by **I'm all right, Jack**] implies that all is well with the speaker, and others' interests can be disregarded. Often considered to be a comfortable cynicism on the part of New Zealanders, and increasingly quoted as a criticism of their attitude since the Second World War.

In Aus. *she's apples!* and *she's sweet!* are synonyms. *she'll be right!* is a common reassurance.

Cf the Aus. **she'll be jake.**

she's sitting on a goldmine. A 'men only' c.p., usu. applied to an attractive, demure girl apparently unaware of her own charms. 'The ref. is to prostitution, of course. Services', certainly during my own time (1953–74), and prob. long before' (P.B., 1977). It was current during WW2, but often referring to part-time prostitutes or to 'enthusiastic amateurs', as the phrase went.

she's very good to the poor. See **she's good...**

sheaf. See: okay, sheaf.

shed a tear for Nelson. See: I'm going to do...

Sheean. See: absolutely, Mr. Gallagher.

sheep. See: hasty; like a sheep; two heads.

sheets. See: may all your ups.

shell. See: that's shell.

shell-like. See: word in your.

sheriff. See: I shall see.

Sherlock. See: no shit.

Shice McGregor's about today. 'Trade is very slack': among market-traders throughout England, esp. in London: prob. since late C19. Patrick O'Shaughnessy, pithily introducing 'A Glossary of Market Traders' Argot' in the July 1975 issue of *Lore and Language*, defines and partly explains it as 'Personification of slack trade'. Why *shice*? Because, orig.

language of the underworld, then low slang, then Cockney market-traders', grafters' and barrow-boys', it derives, via Yiddish, from German *scheisse*, excrement. And why McGregor? It is a derisive allusion to the common practice of using 'good old Scottish names to intimate a shining commercial and financial rectitude'. (The entry is owed to Vernon Noble.)

shift. See: if it's too big.

shilling(s). See: I wish I had as; I'll strike; only another; you'll be telling; and:

shilling (since 1971, e.g. **ten p.**) **to get in; how much to get out** **(again)?** – *a.* 'Heard in reference to charity fêtes, church money-raising events, etc.' (Petch, 1969): C20.

shimmy. See: shame on; and:

shimmy on your own side! 'Get out of my way!' hence, 'Mind your own business': US: 1920s–early 30s. (Fain.) From a style of dancing popular during the 1920s; W & F cite the song, 'I Wish I Could Shimmy Like My Sister Kate', *c.* 1927. P.B.: presumably the next generation's 'rationalisation' of **shimmy...**

shine. See: lights; rise and; when do you.

shinny on your own side! 'Stop interfering with me' (implicitly, 'Mind your own business'). From the game of *shinny*, a form of hockey – i.e., 'You are off-side'. 'Still current in the 1920s, when I heard it from my mother, but now, along with the game, extinct' (R.C., 1978). Therefore earlier than and entirely independent of **shimmy on...** The *D.Am.* records it for 1866. P.B.: this is the Celtic game known also as *shinty*.

Shinola. See: can't tell; doesn't know.

ship(s). See: different ships; don't give up; I love my jest; I'm as mild; old ships; roll on; sailing ship; shape up; who pawned; who wouldn't; you'll have no; and:

ship is known by her boats – a. A RN c.p.: late C19–20. 'Emphasized by Lord Charles Beresford in his command in the early 1900s, but an unofficial c.p. before that' (Rear-Adm. P.W. Brock, 1969). Only as 'an unofficial c.p.' does it, of course, concern us: as an official one, it would be either a motto or a cliche or a sage piece of traditional advice (Lord Charles Beresford lived 1846–1919).

Shipka Pass. See: all quiet.

ships? I see no ships: only hardships! A mostly Services' c.p. uttered (the speaker sometimes clapping an imaginary telescope to his eye) by anyone hearing a mention of ships – or of hardships: since *c.* 1950, at latest. (P.B.)

shirt. See: another clean; blue shirt; close as God's; do as my shirt does; I'm Kruschen; keep your s.; six hat; tail of my; that's up your.

shit. See: all over the place; all shit; aw, shit; between a s.; big shot; can't tell; common; could fall; do you think I can; doesn't know; don't get your arse; don't let your braces; don't shit; eat shit; free as; get your ass; go and eat; golden; gone for a; good shit; happy as a pig; have you shit; I could shit; I don't mind; I need a; I won't be; I wouldn't give; I'll knock; I'll put you; I'll shit; I'm Kruschen; I'm off in a shower; I'm so hungry; I've seen 'em grow; in the words; it's London; lend his; like hell; looks like a bag; never shit; no shit; officers, I've; old soldier; on my shit; only a little; pissed on from; pound; rarest; rat shit; same old shit; shot himself; so thin; soft as s.; soldiers?; sticks; t.G.i.F.; telegram; that's a real; there's shit; they think; this training; tin that; tough shit; up shit; went for; what do you expect; when I say: when shit; who wouldn't; who's shit; wise the shit; wish in; wouldn't say; yeah, you; you don't s.; you wouldn't s.; you're all about; you're full; and:

shit (or **fuck**) **a day keeps the doctor away – a,** is an Aus. c.p., dating from the mid 1920s: a joc. adaptation of the proverb *an apple a day keeps the doctor away.*

shit a seaman's turd – he'll never. He'll never be a good seaman: RN: late C19–20.

shit and corruption! and **shit and derision!** These expletives were feelingly uttered by RAF aircrews throughout WW2; they were applied to 'bad weather, with rain and flak' or to mere 'clouds and rain'. They, esp. the latter, soon acquired everywhere, a more gen. meaning, as appears in John Skehan's gloss, 1977: '*shit and derision*, often used as an exclamation of bafflement or [profound] disappointment. Stems from the story of (I think) the wagga-wagga bird, which flies round and round in ever-decreasing circles until it finally disappears up its own arse, from which lofty eminence it hurls *shit and derision* upon its baffled pursuers'. P.B.: this 'recitation' appears in slightly different words, but with the same import, at *oozlem bird* in *DSUE*, 8th ed. A rare var., that I owe to Mr. Bob Tanner, sometime airborne wireless operator for Imperial Airways, is *shit and molasses*, with which cf:

shit and sugar mixed is a vulgar reply to the query, 'What are the ingredients?' of this or that dish: C20. An offensive var. of an *ad hoc* 'That's none of your business'.

shit-cart. See: after the Lord Mayor's; could fall.

shit doesn't stink. See **they think their shit doesn't stink.**

shit, eh? (or !) Isn't that just too bad!: an Australianism, dating from *c.* 1945.

shit for the birds. See **that's for the birds.**

shit from a goose. See **shit off a shovel.**

shit from shinola. See **doesn't know...**

shit hits the fan.... See: **when (the) shit hits the fan.**

shit in it! 'This I recall from school (Framlingham) in the mid-1930s. The over-talkative were often told to *shit in it!* – a frequent Army usage of the 1940s' (Brian W. Aldiss, 1978). P.B. and of the 1950s–70s. Also used in the sense 'I don't agree with your argument', and usu. prec. by a disgusted *ah!*

shit in the neck – (usu. he) **has.** Refers to a conceited person: US high schools' and colleges': *c.* 1918–30. (Fain, 1978.)

shit list. See **on my shit list.**

shit, lootenant... See **aw, shit...**

shit me easy! (**I'm one of the boys.**) 'Take it easy – I'm one of you'. 'Don't try to con *me*!': US: since *c.* 1950, if not a generation earlier. Cf **you wouldn't shit me.**

shit, mother, I can't dance is a vulgar c.p., Can., and, as a distinguished correspondent puts it, used 'just for something to say'· since *c.* 1920. See **aw, shucks, ma...**

shit off a shovel or **shit from a goose – (more) like.** 'Both of these [phrases] are used as a command, with *move* sometimes rapped out in sergeant-major style'; that is, 'Get a move on!' into position or readiness; or in a talk on tactics. Jack Slater, 1978, tells me that he heard them in the Lancashire Fusiliers, 1952–54. But they date from before WW2 and go far beyond Lancashire. Cf **when I say 'shit'...**

shit on (often **upon**) **from a great height.** Usu. in such contexts as 'he ought to be...', 'they deserve to be...', or 'I shall probably be..., if I...', where it means 'to get into serious trouble from, to be reprimanded by, someone in higher authority', although in the first two instances it may simply be an expressed wish that condign punishment shall fall upon those who are out of one's favour: in RAF use since *c.* 1925, soon spreading to the other Services; the Canadian Army in WW2 employed the form *shat*, and that too has enjoyed much use in the British Armed Forces all through the post-war years. In the first ed. of this book E.P. listed an Aus. Services' var. *pissed on from a great height*, but whatever the form of excretion, the general malevolence in the same. (P.B.) See also **pissed on...**

shit: or get off the pot! Get on with the job or let someone else do it or, at the least, try to do it!; Either do it or get out of the way and let someone else try!; or, simply, Make up your mind! (R.C., 1966.) US: C20.

This homely and humorous c.p., which must verge upon being a US proverb, is so general that it can be employed elliptically and allusively, as where, in Robert Rostand's novel, *Viper's Game*, 1974, a frank secretary says to a dithering consul, 'Oh, come on, Walter. Let's get off the pot' – and make a decision. I notice that it has been enshrined in *DCCU*, 1971.

Adopted in Canada; during WW2, it was, in the army,

directed at a player unable to 'crap out'. The c.p. became, *c.* 1944, also English (as L.A. informed me, 1967) – thanks to the pervasive influence of the US Armed Forces.

Since *c.* 1940, there has been a 'refined' Can. var.: *spit – or get off the cuspidor.*

There is a synon. companion, **piss or get off the pot**, q.v.: 'Conceived of as addressed to a man, not a woman, *shit*, I am sure, is the original form; but in the polite civilian society in which I move, the form with *piss* is invariable, and I have never heard the form with *shit*' (Playfair, 1977). 'In the US, much more commonly *piss*, not because *piss* is not quite so vulgar as for the sake of alliteration' (J.W.C., 1977).

shit out of luck, often shortened to *S.O.L.*, is 'sometimes euphemized as *short on luck*, in an extremely unfortunate position: US services (WW2 or earlier), then general' (R.C., 1978). P.B.: in Brit. forces, shortened to, e.g. *you're shit out.*

shit! said the king – often elab. to... **and all his loyal subjects strained in unison**, or **and ten thousand loyal subjects shat.** An Aus. c.p. – of the same semantic order as **hell! said the duchess.** P.B.: by no means confined to Australia: in UK hyperbole goes further, '...and forty thousand arseholes strained in the dust', while for the US, A.B. writes, 1979, 'This goes on: "ten thousand loyal trousers hit the floor"; then "Fuck the queen!" said the king, and ten thousand loyal knights headed for her room. Or: "She's in bed with laryngitis," said the royal chamberlain. "What," said the king, "is that Greek bastard back in town?" 1950s, I'd guess'. Such is the fascination that court life holds for the commoner. 'Shit! said the king' provides the lead-in to the climax of that bawdy monologue about the prophet Daniel and the king, a fairly complete version of which is to be found on p. 130 of Martin Page's *For Gawdsake Don't Take Me!*, 1976.

shit, shave and shove ashore and **shit, shave, shower, shoeshine and shampoo** and **shit, shave, shampoo and shift.** See **shave, a shilling, (and) a shove ashore.**

P.B.: and cf *I didn't know whether to shit, shave, shampoo, or blanco up*, which indicates a state of indecision: Army: late 1940s onwards. To 'blanco up' is to apply a latterday form of pipeclay to one's uniform accoutrements.

shit weighs heavy! A vulgar, either brutally sarcastic or jocularly ironic Can. c.p., directed, since *c.* 1890, at a boaster.

shithouse. See: bangs like a s.; brass knocker; built like; floats; stands out; up and down.

shity cloth. See: he'd drink.

shock. See: what would s.; you shock.

shocking. See: what a s.

shoe(s). See: baby wants; drop the other; he can put; this won't buy; try some horse; would that, you've got sand; your mother wears; and:

shoe is on the mast – the. If you want to be generous, here's your opportunity: a C19 nautical become gen. proletarian c.p. Ware explains the orig. thus: in C18, 'when near the end of a long voyage, the sailors nailed a shoe to the mast, the toe downward, that passengers might delicately bestow a parting gift' – something that, after so delicate a hint, they could hardly refrain from doing.

shoo, fly! or, in full, **shoo, fly don't bother me!** This, one of the most famous of all US c.pp., seems to have been first been reputably noticed by a famous man as early as 1893 – in the redoubtable Brander Matthews's article on slang in the July issue of *Harper's Magazine*, where he signally failed to foretell, and to estimate, its durability, for, as W & F remark in 1960, it 'has reappeared from time to time, usually without much specific meaning' – nevertheless, predominantly in the sense, 'Stop bothering me, and go away!' It kept on reappearing, too, in HLM, from the early ends until the definitive 4th in 1936, and again in Supp. 2, when he dealt with it at some length.

In 1968, Prof. S.H. Monk wrote to me thus (alluding to **twenty-three, skiddoo**):

Another phrase for getting rid of small brothers who were

bothering their elder sisters was 'Shoo, fly, don't bother me'. This I know definitely came from a soldiers' song in the Spanish–American War, when flies and the yellow fever mosquito were the serious enemy. The song is nonsense 'Shoo, fly, don't bother me' repeated three times and then the final line, 'For I belong to company G'.

That song revived and reinforced the popularity of a phrase noted as early as 1889 by Farmer: 'An exclamation of impatience. . . . *Fly* is not the insect as some have supposed, but simply a pleonastic addition to – *sh-sh-fly*, i.e. fly away! be off! The full phrase is now familiarly colloquial.' Farmer prints it as *shoo! fly! don't bother me.*

Yet *fly* is very probably the insect, after all.

But the phrase seems to have arisen much earlier than all those other historians and lexicographers had supposed, for Edward B. Marks, in *They All Sang*, 1934, records it had been sung by Bryant's Minstrels in 1869, with words by Billy Reeves and music by Frank Campbell; exactly a decade later, the same recorder, in *They All Had Glamour*, has this entry: '1869 Shoo Fly – Don't Bodder [*sic*] Me. Words – Billy Reeves, sung by Cool Burgess'. (I owe both of these references to my exceptionally well informed friend, W.J. Burke, who, moreover, has been indefatigable – and prompt – in his assistance to me.) In 1978, W.J.B. added the complementary information: 'In George M. Baker's *The Handy Speaker*, 1876 (p. 65), is this: *The Deutsch Maud Muller*, by Carl Pretzel:

Maud Muller, von summer afternoon,
Vast tending bar in her father's saloon.
She sold dot bier, and singed 'Shoo Fly'
And vinked at der men mit her left eye.

Proving that "Shoo Fly" was a popular song even before 1876, for the book quoted is an anthology, and its selections were popular before publication date'.

shook. See: have you shook; ten days; that shook.

shoot. See: did you shoot; don't shoot; I'll shoot; if it moves; them's shooting; will you s.; and:

shoot him in the pants... See **good goods.**

shoot it in the leg, your arm's full is recorded by HLM, 1922; but without comment. I make none myself, except to say that it sounds like either a 'smart Alec' nonsense c.p. or (Patricia Newnham, 1976) a c.p. suggested by drug injections.

shoot that hat! and **I'll have your hat!** were, *c.* 1860–72, common, esp. in London, as derisive retorts. Cf **what a shocking bad hat** and **where did you get that hat?**

shooting fish in a barrel – it's like. ' "It's dead easy" – often with the implication that it is so easy as to be unfair, or not worth doing. This robust and (probably) rural simile has been current in US during C20 and probably earlier, though by now something of a cliché' (R.C., 1978).

shop. See: everything in the s.

shore saints and sea devils was, mid C19–early C20, a nautical c.p., applied to those sailing-ship skippers as were lambs with their owners and lions with the crew.

short. See: grass is getting; life is too; like a winter's; long short 'uns; long time; one of your; thick as; too short; Virgin; when you were wearing; will you short; and:

short and thick, like a Welshman's prick. A vulgar saying applied, mid C19–20, to a short person, usu. a male, very broad-bottomed. Yet another of those pieces of physiological folklore which are as inaccurate as they are earthy.

short life and a gay one. See **cheer up, cully.**

short, fat, hairy legs! 'Applied to Ernie Wise by Eric Morecambe in contrast to his own long, elegant legs. Ernie says that this emerged, like most of their catch phrases, during rehearsals – particularly during their spell with ATV' (*VIBS*).

Short's in the Strand. See: cheap and nasty.

Shorty. See: cut off.

shot. See: big shot; in (–) people; oh, to be; they've shot; went for; what's the damage; who shot; you'll be shot; you've shot; and:

shot – that'll (or **that would**) **be the;** and **that's the shot.** That will – or would – or most satisfactory, *or That's* the idea!: Aus.: both since *c.* 1945, at latest; the former from Nino Culotta, the latter in A.M. Harris, *The Tall Man*, 1958. Semantics: that hits – will or would hit – the target; 'bang on'. Cf **shot to you!**

shot at dawn. See **you'll be shot at dawn,** and **oh, to be shot . . .**

shot himself! If someone breaks wind in or near a group of men, it often elicits this comment, to which there is, from another member of that group, the 'dovetail' or response, **if he's not (bloody) careful, he'll shit himself:** late C19–20.

shot to you! You score there – a c.p. 'aimed at indifference or complacent cocksureness [occasioned by] a lucky chance or when sharp practice has triumphed' (L.A.): in the Armed Forces: since 1939 or *c.* 1939 Cf the semantics of **that'll be the shot.**

shotgun. See: couldn't hit; must have stood.

should be sawn off at the waist has, since *c.* 1930 and in the RAF, been applied to a stupid girl.

should be so lucky! See **I should be . . .**

shoulder. See: over the left.

shouldn't happen to a dog – it or that. It's too unjust or disagreeable to be wished on even a dog; occ., however, applied to persons, as in 'He's one of those unpleasant fellows who shouldn't happen to a dog' (Granville, 1969).

Terence Rattigan's play *Variation on a Theme*, 1958, at I, ii, has:

FIONA: The last doctor's put her on a very strict régime. He even says she might have to . . . go to Switzerland . . .
MONA: Switzerland? That shouldn't happen to a dog.

R.C., 1978, from US, adds that there is sometimes the form . . . *to my worst enemy;* and of the *dog* version, 'current from 1930s; almost certainly from Yiddish'.

shout. See: all over bar; they can hear.

shove. See: lean forward; when push; who are you shoving; and:

shove it! Of *shove it* itself, R.C., 1978, says: 'Standard US violent rejection of a proposition, money or whatever. Sometimes *take it and shove it!*' Elsewhere he compares Dashiell Hammett's 'You know where you can stick it'. Both R.C. and A.B. (1979) have noted that the full expression is (*you can*) *shove it up your ass.* P.B.: in the short form it hardly qualifies as a c.p., because, for one thing, there are – at least in UK – so many violent and vulgar variants: *work, stick, stuff,* and *poke* all spring at once to a mind sludged with the struggle through *DSUE*, and there are doubtless many others. Cf **you know what you can do with it.**

shovel. See: before you bought; get the s.; shit off; when I say.

shoving money upstairs is a mainly N. Country c.p. of C20 and is used thus: 'When a man is worrying about going bald, someone tells him banteringly it must be with "shoving money upstairs" ' (Petch, 1946). The implication is that it would be much safer to put the money into a bank.

Julian Franklyn once told me that, among Londoners, it has, since *c.* 1920, been predominantly applied to 'spending money on useless "cures" ' – esp., one would suppose, to the quack cures for baldness.

show. See: after the Lord; all show; for show; he's the whole; I'll show; just goes; let's get the s.; no show; on with; over goes; sing, sing; stopped; there's another s.; what do you think of; you're showing; your slip; and:

show a leg! Get out of the bed or hammock!: nautical, esp. naval, since early in C19; by early C20, also military. Lit., to show a leg from under the bed clothes. In his *The Conway*, 1933, John Masefield noted that on that training ship, from before 1891, the full call has been

Heave out, heave out, heave out! Away!
Come all you sleepers, hey!
Show a leg and put a stocking on it.

The earliest record I've come upon (and that was sent to me by Col. Moe) occurs in Alfred Burton's *Johnny Newcome*, 1818. Orig., the call was shouted in order to ascertain whether the occupant of the bed was male, not an unofficial bedwarmer. 'Short for *show a leg or a pusser's stocking*, a naval phrase dating from the time when women went to sea in HM ships, and a bare leg or a purser's stocking guaranteed a lie-in until "Guard and steerage" was called. Nowadays the cry means *hurry up; get a wriggle on*, etc.' (*Sailors' Slang*).

show-biz. See: that's show.

show must go on – the, has long been 'the traditional slogan [perhaps rather motto or c.p.] of the troupers'. Whatever misfortune or illness befalls, 'it is a point of honour not to let the other players down by deserting them when no understudy is available' (Granville.)

Common also in Aus. and US. Cf **on with the motley.**

show the dog the rabbit. See **let the dog see the rabbit!**

showdown. See: hustlers.

shower. See: didn't come down; I'm off in a s.; what a s.

showing next week's washing. Your shirt is showing (at the flap): not entirely proletarian, nor in the least aristocratic or cultured: C20; by 1970, however, somewhat outmoded.

P.B.: used also, of course, of a girl's slip or petticoat showing below the hem of her skirt – in the olden days when it was unfashionable for it so to do. Cf **Charley's dead, your washing is hanging out,** and for a male failure to 'adjust one's dress', **you're showing an Egyptian medal.**

shred. See: you shred it.

shrieks of hysterical laughter; and **shrieks of silence was the stern reply.** The former is mostly Aus. and used when someone has advanced an untenable proposition or made a ludicrous suggestion, as in:

'I'm going to sell this car. Should get about eight hundred for it.'

'Shrieks of hysterical laughter.'

Clearly taken from dramatic and film critics' commentaries.

The latter, wholly Aus., provides an ironic synonym of 'No one replied, or said a word'.

Both date from *c.* 1950 and both were supplied to me by Mr Barry Prentice, whose ear for the Australian vernacular is exceptionally acute. P.B.: but the latter, without *shrieks of*, is very well known in UK also. It sounds like a quot'n – but where from?

shrift. See: he hath been.

shrimps. See: can't you feel.

shucks. See: aw, shucks.

shut. See: box open; gate's; keep this s.; keep your bowels.

shut mouth never fills a black coffin – a. Keep your mouth shut and you'll never die untimely! Common among US gangsters since the early 1920s. Recorded in a very rare book, *Yankee Slang*, privately printed in London, 1932, by one who thought it best to use a pseudonym: 'Spindrift', whom the British Library catalogue reveals to be Ernest Tooné.

Beginning as an underworld c.p., it began also as a motto, a warning, and passed into the ranks of the very few underworld proverbs.

shut my mouf! Col. Moe, writing to me in 1975, says: 'When a person is astonished or surprised, he is very likely to allow his jaw to sag and to permit his mouth to be … agape, e.g. to manifest open-mouth wonderment'. Harold Wentworth, *American Dialect Dictionary*, 1944; '1940 [from] *Negro*; Shut ma mouf.' Said by a negro (or, in imitation, a black-and-white minstrel) who realizes that he has said too much, or the worse thing. Meaning 'I should have kept my mouth shut.' (Shipley, 1975.)

shut my mouth and call me Shorty! – often prec. by **well.** See **cut off my legs …**

shut that door! 'Larry Grayson, fending off rheumatism again. Larry Grayson's rise to fame in the early 1970s stemmed from a four minute TV spot he was offered out of the blue. This was the first time he used the phrase "shut that door!" He said, "It's so draughty in here. I've got my surgical stocking on and it's not working!" Within a year he was in the cast of the Royal Variety Show' (*VIBS*).

shut up. See: put up or; stand up, speak; and:

shut up and give your arse a chance. See **give your arse a chance!**

shut up, Eccles! See GOON SHOW. It must always be uttered in the adenoidal tones of Peter Sellers as 'Bluebottle', and formed part of the perpetual lunatic arguments with the ponderous, dim-wittedly voiced 'Eccles', played by Spike Milligan, who would reply, as often as not, 'Yeah, shut up, Eccles!'

shut up, you little bastard. See **what did you do …**

shut your eyes and open your hands. See **close your eyes and guess …**

shut your eyes and think of England. See **close your eyes and think …**

shut your mouth and give your arse a chance. See **give your arse …**

shy. See: if I lose.

sick. See: about as much; headache; you are sick.

side(s). See: don't turn; d' you want; shimmy on; wrong side.

side-pocket. See: wanted.

sideways. See: if you looked.

Sidney. See: George, don't.

sign. See: I live at.

sign of a mis-spent youth – the or **a.** Inevitable comment on anyone displaying any proficiency at billiards or snooker: common in Army or RAF, and prob. wider: since *c.* 1950, at very latest. (P.B.)

silence. See: shrieks.

silence in court: the cat is pissing (or **the monkey wants to talk** or **speak;** or **the judge wants to spit**). These cogent enjoinders are addressed to anyone requiring or demanding or blatantly expecting silence: *c.* 1760–1850. Gross, 1785, for the first. The second is juvenile Aus. (*talk*) and Brit. (*speak*): C20. (B.P.; P.B.) The third is US: C20. (Berrey, 1942, includes it in a list of slangy phrases synon. with 'Be quiet' or, esp., 'Shut up!'.) B.G.T., 1978, for UK, recalls, '*While the judge blows his nose* was our schoolroom wit'.

This is one of the more entertaining deflaters of pomposity.

silent. See: strong, silent.

silent, like the *p* in swimming. This fairly common c.p. has, since *c.* 1914, been used in less-than-academic exposition of a difficulty in pronunciation. 'Her name is Fenwick, where the *w* is silent – like the *p* in swimming.' To explain the obvious: there is a pun on *pee*, to urinate. Yet even in academic or, at lowest, scholastic circles, it occasionally serves to lighten the depressingly dogmatic assertions of manic phoneticians, who sometimes blindly and unsuspectingly, excel in a ludicrous putting of the cart before the horse.

'Also, *the P is silent as in batheing*. Used when spelling words beginning with *psy*, etc.' (Sanders, 1978). P.B. notes, sometimes elab. '… *mixed batheing*'.

silk purse on a pig – (that's) a. 'That's sheer waste': Aus.: since *c.* 1950. (Jim Ramsey, *Cop It Sweet*, 1977.) Prompted by the proverb *you cannot make a silk purse out of a sow's ear*.

silly. See: knocked-knees; let's not play; you silly; and:

silly (occ., **crazy**) **as a two-bob watch** or **a wheel** (**– as**). Extremely silly or very stupid: Aus.: since *c.* 1940. (*Dict. Aus. Coll.*) Owing to the change in monetary denominations, the *wheel* form seems the more likely to survive. But why a wheel? Presumably because it 'goes round and round in circles'. Cf the similes at **queer as …**

[**silly old moo;** and **silly moo.** In the *Daily Mail* of 2 Nov. 1968, at 'Comment', concerning the under twenty-fives, we read about what they, in their turn, 'will bore their children with': 'They'll recall old television programmes like…, forgotten personalities like…, try to remember catch-phrases from old comedy shows like "Sock it to me" and "Silly old moo".'

The phrase *silly old moo*, where *moo* is a euph. for the vulgar *cow*, was, as Noble writes, 1974:

applied by actor Warren Mitchell as the Cockney character Alf Garnett to his wife (played by Dandy Nichols) in long-running comedy series 'Till Death Us Do Part' (by Johnny Speight) on BBC television. Dandy Nichols said that the epithet was called to her affectionately in the streets when people recognized her.

But, strictly, this isn't a c.p. Those who need further information could do far worse than to consult *DSUE*. The same exclusion applies to *silly old mare*.]

silver. See: cross my palm; every silver; hi-ho, Silver.

similar. See: you mean.

Simon. See: sup, Simon.

simple. See: it's as simple.

Simpson. See: my name is S.

since AMOs were carved on stone. See **since Pontius was a pilot.**

since Auntie had her accident and **since Nellie had her operation.** For a very or a fairly long time: the former is Aus., as in 'I haven't been to Melbourne since Auntie had her accident', and it dates since *c.* 1920. (B.P.) The latter is English, dates since *c.* 1910, and is 'a burlesque c.p., marking banteringly a certain lapse of time' (L.A.). Cf **I haven't laughed so much...; since Willie died,** and:

since Hector was a pup. 'Since way back when' – a very long time ago: a US equivalent of the surrounding entries: since *c.* 1920. (W.J.B., 1977.) '*Hector* is a rather common name for a mastiff or other large dog. Meaning is, I suppose, "I'm as close to him as I am to my dog" – man's best friend' (A.B., 1979).

since Jesus Christ played half-back for Jerusalem. Synon. with prec.: since 1920s: obviously ex 'soccer'. An older, MN version occurs in Thomas Wood, *True Thomas*, 1936, *since Noah touched his pay.* Cf:

since Pontius was a pilot, as in 'He's been with that mob since Pontius was a pilot' (punning *Pontius Pilate*): RAF: since *c.* 1944. Belonging to the same semi-erudite – or, rather, mock-erudite – order, are, since *c.* 1946, *since the Air Ministry was a tent* and, referring to Air Ministry Orders, *since AMOs were carved on stone*, both of which, however, enjoyed only a very restricted currency, yet are perhaps worthy of inclusion as examples of what could be classified as armchair ingenuity rather than scene-of-action humour. P.B.: Army hyperbole in the same vein has *my first charge was for a dirty bowstring* and *when I joined, we didn't have* [service] *numbers, we all knew each other*. Ashley, 1983, recalls from the 1950s RCAF, *since we didn't wear blue, we were painted blue.* See also **when Adam...**

since when I have used no other has, since 1884 or 1885, been applied to any (usu. domestic) article in common and frequent use. From the witty Pear's Soap advertisement showing an unmistakably grubby tramp, who says 'Two years ago I used your soap, since when I have used no other'. Cf **good morning! have you used Pear's Soap?**

The tramp advertisement dates from the 1890s and was based upon a commissioned painting of Phil May's. Intervening – prob. originating – was *Punch*, 1884 (LXXXVII, p. 197), I used your soap two years ago; since then I have used no other.

since Willie died is a C20 Can. counterpart of **since Nellie had her operation,** q.v. at **since Auntie had her accident.** '"We haven't had so much fun since Willie died" – said in approbation of a good time' (Leechman).

sing. See: don't chant; for God's sake; I'll make you; what do you mean; and:

sing, sing: or show your ring! 'Invitation to perform at an informal troop concert: the assembled company cheers at the victim, who either then does sing or drops his trousers' (P.B., 1975): an Army c.p., prob. throughout C20. The 'ring' is ('Well, naturally!') the anus.

sing us a song! This is 'a call from the gallery when an artiste is disapproved of: music-halls: late C19–20; by 1970, ob. Granville adds that 'this exhortation is euphemistic for something grosser'.

single. See: makes you see.

sings more like a whore's bird than a canary bird (**–he**). He has

a strong, manly voice: *c.* 1760–1820. (Grose, 1788.) A *whore's bird* is a debauchee.

singular or plural? was, in late 1914–18, an army c.p.: hospital enquiry when eggs appeared on the dietary. B & P.

sink. See: didn't you sink; everything but; I love my jest.

sinking feeling. See: prevents.

sinner. See: as I am a s.

sir. See: dear sir; no, sir; nobody asked; unhand; yes, sir; and:

sir, I see someone has offended you, for your back is up is one of the earliest 'sick' jokes: it was, *c.* 1750–1850, addressed to a humpbacked man. Grose, 1785.

'sir' to you. A c.p. of mock-offended dignity: prob since *c.* 1830. My earliest record (so far) occurs in R.H. Barham, *The Ingoldsby Legends*, Third Series, 1847, at the piece titled 'Jerry Jarvis's Wig':

At this moment neighbour Jenkinson peeped over the hedge.
'Joe Washford!' said neighbour Jenkinson.
'Sir, to you,' was the reply.

Admittedly, however, the expression seems here to be literal and respectful. An unquestionable example, however, does appear in the inimitable P.G. Wodehouse's *The Pothunters*, 1902; a later example in H.A. Vachell, *Vicar's Walk*, 1933. By 1970, slightly ob. Cf **dear sir** (spelt 'C-U-R').

sir, you're a gentleman... See **gentleman...**

sir, you are speaking of the woman I love originated as a cliché in the 'Transpontine', or Surrey-side, drama during the 1880s and 1890s, and in corresponding US melodrama of the same period, as well as in Horner's Penny Novelettes, a genre enlarged and immensely improved in the novels by Charles Garvice, a man of culture and sensitivity; its pomposity rendered it a phrase of fun, used therefore as a c.p. from *c.* 1890 onwards in both countries. P.B.: I have heard this raffishly parodied as 'Careful! You are speaking of the whore I love!'

Sirgarneo. See **all Sir Garnet!**

sister. See: harder; key, Johnny; how's your s.; sorry, no; who pawned; your mother wears; and:

Sister Anna shall carry the banner. Apropos of what he calls a 'catch-phrase dialogue' – strictly, a chant – Anthony Burgess, in his *TLS* review of the first ed. of this book, 26 Aug. 1977, writes: 'Then there is *Sister Anna shall carry the banner*, a whole sad story when done in full'. I had never heard it, nor seen it in print, therefore I'm wildy guessing when I add: 'C20, perhaps arising in a Salvation Army instruction concerning a public procession; and never widely used'. P.B.: E.P. is half right: the dialogue does start with a parody of a Salvation Army instruction, but there can be few who served as Other Ranks in the Armed Forces, certainly since *c.* 1945, and remained unaware of Sister Anna or Hannah:

'Sister Hannah, you'll carry the banner!'
'But I carried it *last* time.'
'You'll carry it every time.'
'But I'm in the family way.'
'You're in every bugger's way...'

And so on, becoming more and more obscene. But I have always felt the ref. to the 'Sally Army', though mocking, to be affectionate and aware of the Army's real worth, as in the line handed on to me by my late father, therefore to be dated earlier C20: 'Right! One more verse of "'Oly, 'oly, 'oly", and then we'll bugger orf'.

Cf **carry the banner...**

Sister Mary. See: hop along.

sit. See: he can make; I don't lie; it's as cheap; not you, Momma; pull up a; she's sitting pretty; so dumb; they sat; and:

sit down and make your miserable life happy! This domestic and amenities-of-life c.p. affords a good example of those catch phrases which seem to be – and often are – impossible to date satisfactorily and are occ. difficult to classify definitely. I'd say that it prob. dates mid C19 – mid 20 and isn't yet entirely †, and also that sociologically it belongs to the ordinary (not upper) middle class and, by absorption, to the lower-middle. It is cheerful and friendly, never bitter, although it can be kindly-exasperated, as in 'Oh, things can't be as bad as all that: sit down and make your miserable life happy!' It isn't a cliché; it is almost proverbial. Whence prob.:

sit down and rest your brains! A joc. US, thence Can., c.p.: since (?) 1950. Cf:

sit down and take a load off your feet. See **take a load off your feet.**

sit down, you're rocking the boat! Don't disturb the *status quo!* Both Brit. and US: since *c.* 1920. Applied mostly to sociological or economic or political affairs. (For US use: Moe, 1975.) Also **don't rock the boat!** – an 'exhortation to someone about to disturb a comfortable situation'. (Norman Franklin, 1976.)

P.B.: *sit down, you're rocking the boat!* was the title, and formed the refrain, of a song sung with tremendous verve by that generously-built American comedian Stubby Kaye as 'Nicely Nicely Johnson' one of the compulsive gamblers in the musical 'Guys and Dolls', based on Damon Runyon's stories. The show started in New York in 1950, and in London in 1953. The true US equivalent of *don't rock the boat!* is, as R.C. notes, 1978, *don't make waves!*, which arose slightly later, giving rise to (? or arising from) the punchline of a scatological joke.

sit on a tack! See **go sit on...**

sit up and beg. See **he can make it sit...**

sit up and take notice! Wake up!: US: since *c.* 1910. Recorded by S.R. Strait in 'Straight Talk' (*Boston Globe* of *c.* 1917); † by 1942.

sitting comfortably. See: **are you sitting.**

sitting (occ. **standing**) **by** (or, more usu. **with**) **Nellie.** From the song 'On Mother Kelly's Doorstep', sung by Randolph Sutton at 'The Old-Time Music-Hall' TV programme from Leeds or Bradford. In this, Nellie is (like 'Sally in Our Alley') the smartest girl. This phrase is very popular in northern mill towns in common parlance, and the general inference is that Nellie is the most competent and experienced mill hand, who can demonstrate to a new-comer how the loom, or whatever, works.

'In teacher-training, at present the process of learning by observation is referred to as "sitting by Nellie"' (a lecturer at De La Salle College, Middleton, Manchester). P.B.: the phrase, hardly a c.p., has been current and in fairly gen. use, since *c.* 1960 at latest, for any in-service training.

situation is well in hand. See **Marines have landed...**

six. See: **don't tell more.**

six foot of land, that's all the land you'll get has, in C20, been addressed to one who expresses a desire to 'own just a bit of land'. Cf the WW1 *became a landowner,* to die.

But usu. either a threat ('You do that and I'll kill you', *six foot of land* for a grave) or a mostly well-intended warning – a pronouncement on a person's fate for continuing a present foolish activity or embarking on a foolish action or course of action. (With thanks to Mr Robin Leech of Edmonton, Canada.)

six hat and a fifty shirt – a. A US underworld c.p., dating from the 1920s and applied to one who, weak in the head, is strong in the back. (D.W. Maurer in *The Writer's Digest* of Oct. 1931.) His hat is only a six-incher, but he needs a fifty-inch chest measurement in shirts. R.C., 1978, notes, 'Never general; now long gone'.

six knots and a Chinaman. (At) an unknown speed: RN: (?) late C19–20. 'A Chinaman, using the ship's log, caught his foot in the line and was dragged overboard before fixing the speed' (Peppitt, 1976).

six pips and all's well! Six o'clock and all's well: in, and since, 1933. There's a ref. both to the BBC's radio time-signal and to the nautical *six bells and all's well.*

sixpence. See: **all Lombard; bang goes; hasn't got a ha' penny; lost a pound; scratch his.**

sixty-four, ninety-four was a WW1 army c.p., canonized in

R.H. Mottram's *The Spanish Farm Trilogy,* 1927, thus: 'You see, I don't know the man's name. His number was given as 6494.'

'That's a joke, of course. It's the number that the cooks sing out, when we hold the last Sick Parade, before going up the line.'

'Of course it is. You're right. I ought to have remembered that, but I've been away from my regiment for some time.' (With thanks to Mr A.B. Petch, 1969.)

Mr P.V. Harris, who served with the King's (Liverpool) Regt. in WW1, writes, 1978: 'To the sick call on the bugle we sang

Sixty-four, ninety-four,
Won't go sick any more;
The poor bugger's dead!'

sixty-four-thousand-dollar question – the. See **that's the sixty-four-thousand-dollar question.**

sixty-nine! 'There shearers' code-warning that ladies or visitors are approaching and language is "out of order"' (*Straight Farrow,* a magazine, 21 Feb. 1968): NZ: C20.

size. See: **ah there, my s.; pick on; that's about the s.; that's just about your; that's my s.; try this.**

skeleton. See: **noise like.**

skiddoo. See: **twenty-three.**

skin. See: **cheaper; couldn't knock; give me some; he'd skin; I'm skinning; in his skin; no skins; now then, shoot; slap; wouldn't give; you can't have more.**

[**skip it!** Don't bother with it! Forget it! A Brit. and US borderline between ordinary slang and c.p.: not, so far as I remember, common before *c.* 1930. Berrey, 1942, records it and Noël Coward, in *Peace in Our Time,* 1947, at II, ii, has:

FRED: What a pity! He won't have much time to learn now, will he?

GLADYS: How do you mean?

FRED: Skip it.]

[**skipper's never wrong, mate's seldom wrong, bosun's sometimes wrong, deckie's always wrong.** (*Deckie, -y,* deck hand.) 'Deep-sea fishermen's pecking order' (Peppitt, 1976): late C19–20. This traditional saying almost ranks as a c.p.]

skunk. See: **only a fool.**

sky. See: **there'll be pie; what's up; and:**

sky's the limit – the is a US c.p. of C20. Orig. a gambling term, meaning 'no limit to the size of a bet', it soon became used more gen. and is still current. (W.J.B., 1978.) It appears in the magnificent *Webster's Second International,* 1934, and in Berrey, 1942. R.C. glosses it as 'There is no restriction on what you wish to do'.

skylark. See: **any more.**

slack. See: **cut me; he's not tight; I could take; I'm not tight.**

slam the door in the doctor's nose. See **good night, sweet repose...**

slanging dues concerned; in full, there has (or **have**) **been....** In late C18– mid C19, this was an underworld-and-its-fringes c.p. uttered by one who felt that he had, esp. by his mates, been defrauded of his rights or of his fair share of the booty. (Vaux.) From *slang,* to cheat (someone); *dues* occurs in several underworld phrases of the same period.

slap across the belly – a. See **better than a dig the eye...**

slap me five! and **slip me some skin!** '"Shake hands!" Both are American Negro in orig. (*c.* 1950), the latter being adopted by white jazz musicians and eventually youth and "hip" culture generally. [Now] obsolete' (R.C., 1978). The former is of the 'same meaning, origin, culture. The reference is to the "handshake" used (orig. and still predominantly) among Negroes in which one person slaps with his fingers the outstretched (five) fingers of the other' (Ibid.). Cf synon. **press the flesh** and **give me some skin.**

slaughter. See: **fattened.**

slaves. See: **Britons.**

slaving. See: **here am I.**

sleep. See: **I can't sleep; I'd rather s.; man wasn't; must have been lying; talk a glass.**

sleep of the just and the sleep of the just after. The former is exceeded only by the latter (the sleep that, for many, rapidly follows copulation): since *c.* 1960.

sleep tight! mind the fleas don't bite! A children's goodnight to parents, brothers and sisters, friends: certainly of late C19–20, but perhaps existing very much longer: this is the sort of phrase that, naturally enough, escapes the attention of lexicographers, even the light-hearted.

'The full children's version with which I am familiar is "Goodnight,/Sleep tight,/Mind the fleas don't bite"' (B.G.T., 1978). P.B.: and another is *'Night 'night, sleep tight! Mind the bugs and fleas don't bite!*

The US form is *goodnight, sleep tight, don't let the skeeters* (or *the bedbugs) bite*, 'Now obsolescent. Mosquitoes and bugs are commoner pests than fleas here' (R.C., 1978). Cf **good night, sweet repose...**

sleeping near (or **next to**) **a crack.** See **you must have been lying....**

sleeve. See: nothing up.

slender. See: long and.

slice of the action – I want a. This forms an elaborative c.p. based on *slice of the action*, '"a share in the equity of a venture". Very common business c.p. Heard at a board meeting [recently]' (Playfair, 1977).

sliced bread. See: best thing; it's the greatest.

slide, Kelly, slide! A short-lived US c.p., from the song, so titled, sung, and pub'd, in 1889. It is recorded by Edward B. Marks in *They All Sang*, 1934, with the gloss, 'J. W. Kelly'.

This 'is not short-lived', objects Shipley, 1977. 'In 1961, a college...went to a court to change his name. He came before an Irish judge, who, citing Cardinal Kelly and other distinguished Kellys, bade him go home. The newspapers picked it up; one Catholic weekly ran a long poem, which ended with the man, dying, "going...on the slippery sluice of pride/And the Devil will say,/In my cheering way,/Slide, Kelly, slide".'

slightly. See: I won't, s.

slightly oiled. See: clean, bright.

sling. See: ass in a s.

sling 'em out! is the c.p. – almost the 'signature tune' – of *the dhobeying firm*, a partnership of two or more naval ratings undertaking to do their messmates' washing. 'An unofficial ship's laundry and a very lucrative business if the "firm" is an energetic one' (Granville, in PGR, 1948). The *'em* refers to the dirty clothes.

slingshot. See: doesn't know.

slip. See: your slip.

slip me five! See **slap me five!**

slobber. See: you sure s.

slotted jobs. See: blue-stockinged.

slow. See: molasses; too slow.

[**slow down!** is an Afro-American greeting, as in 'Hey, Paul, *slow down*, man! What you been doing?' It suggests 'Let's talk for a minute or two' and dates from *c.* 1960. Recorded in *The Third Ear*, 1971. Cf:]

slow down a bit! Don't try quite so hard to do the right thing, *or* Don't be so very formal: since *c.* 1945. (Granville, 1969.)

slower than the second coming of Christ. See **you are slower....**

slowly. See: it's a good game; twisting.

slug. See: cant a slug.

smack it about! Get a move on!: RN: C20. 'From the vigorous smacking-about of brushes when painting the ship's side' (*SS*).

small. See: it's a small.

small contributions gratefully received is a Brit. and US c.p. dating from *c.* 1900: it means what it says, but in an ironic tone of voice and often ludicrously applied to all contributions. In *The Heart Line*, 1908, Gelett Burgess writes:
'I believe that I might go so far as to imprint a salute upon your chaste brow!'
'I accept!' said Fancy Gray.
He stooped over and kissed her. She was graciously

resigned.
'Thank you, Frank,' she said demurely. 'Small contributions gratefully received.'
From the advertisements of charitable societies. See also **all contributions...**

small print. See: always read.

[**small things amuse small** (or **little**) **minds** is, I should, unthinkingly perhaps, have said, is a proverb – or, if not a proverb, a cliché; yet several very intelligent friends of mine have proposed it as, unequivocally, a c.p. For instance B.P. writes, 1975: 'This is an extremely common c.p. in Australia. It is unknown elsewhere, as it occurs in [e.g.] *A Woman on a Roof*, a short story by Doris Lessing...reprinted in *A Man and Two Women...* 1963....The c.p. is often used when a person is doing something that seems childish.' I've known it all my life, in NZ, in Aus., in England. The 'dovetail' reply is **and only small minds would notice!** (Thus E.P. in the first ed. Later he added:)

'Oh, no! This wouldn't ring at all true to English kids. We said, "Little things please little minds", to which the dovetail response was and is, "While bigger fools look on". But even while I'm writing this, another childish dovetail pops up out of my subconscious, 'And little trousers fit little behinds"' (P.B., 1976). Among Aus. schoolchildren, the *small* form has acquired the var. *little things please little minds, and large things* (or *persons) have large behinds*. Moreover, Mrs C. Raab adds an *in sympathy* to P.B.'s *bigger fools look on*.

The *Concise Oxford Dict. of Proverbs* lists *little things...*; it notes that Disraeli, in *Sybil*, 1845, has 'Little things affect little minds', and even finds the same idea expressed by Ovid.]

small world! See **it's a small world!**

smart. See: don't get s.; if you're so; ve get.

smart as a rabbit. See **quick as...**

smarter than the average bear, Booboo. Early 1970s: P.B., 1975, says:
[This is a] c.p. from the US cartoon series 'Yogi Bear' shown on TV in this country. Used by Yogi Bear (named presumably after the baseball star Yogi Berra) whenever he outwits any other character in the film. Booboo is his little satellite bear-friend. The phrase can be and is translated into all sorts of situations.

smasher. See: I say, what.

smear it with butter and get the cat to lick it off! A Cockneys' shattering deflation of the aspirations of youths desirous of growing a beard and signally failing to do so: late C19–20. Cf **one of your team ... and get the cat to lick it.**

smell. See: good trumpeter; he who; he's had; it stinks; living on the; so thin; there's a s.; wake up; you can smell; and:

smell my finger! A vulgar male – youths' rather than men's – c.p. with an erotic implication: late C19–20.

smelling of (or **like**) **roses** (or **violets**). See **could fall in the shit ...**

smile. See: don't make me laugh; Eliza; fuck me, I'll; I should s.; keep smiling; you've got a s.; and;

smile, damn you, smile! Concerning such optimistic clichés as 'It won't hurt none to try', HLM, 1922, says, 'Naturally enough, a grotesque humor plays about this literature of hope; the folk, though it moves them, prefer it with a dash of salt. "Smile, damn you, smile!" is a typical specimen of this seasoned optimism.' So far as I've been able to discover, this US c.p. has been current throughout the century; Benham, 1948, glosses it as known in England since '*c.* 1907'. P.B.: also heard sometimes as *smile, darn you, smile*, which formed the title of a popular song.

smile, please! Watch the birdie! '*ITMA*, from the traditional photographer's instructions' (*VIBS*). See TOMMY HANDLEY and **watch the dicky bird.**

smile when you say that, stranger is explained by a quot'n from Desmond Bagley's novel *Running Blind*, 1970:
'...I still love you, you silly bastard.'
'Smile when you say that, stranger.'

As Rear-Adm. Brock has reminded me, 1977, a version occurs in Owen Wister's romantic 'Western', *The Virginian*, 1902, where 'what the Virginian said was "When you call me that, smile" – *vide* the heading of Wister's chapter II. "That" was given in those days as "a son of a b –" [bitch]'. Orig., and still predominantly, it refers to one man's calling another a *bastard*, or using similar insult, and was orig., still is predominantly, US. Ashley notes the occ. use of *pardner* (or *partner*) for *stranger*, and Edward Hodnett, 1975, observes that it was reinforced, *c.* 1920, when, in US, it was 'picked up in mock-solemn echo of Grade B Western movies'.

smile, you're on 'Candid Camera'! is 'from Allan Funt's long-running hidden-camera show – now used for: smile, you've been tricked, etc.' (Ashley, 1984). Brit. TV of course had to pick up this nasty US idea of cashing in on the victims' embarrassment. (P.B.)

Smith. See: I refer.

smock. See: wrapped.

smoke. See: pick a block; put that in your pipe; she smokes; watch my dust; and:

smoke that in your pipe! The US form of **put that in your pipe and smoke it!**: late C19–20. Recorded by Berrey, 1942, as a synonym of 'Think that over!' and attested to by J.W.C. and W.J.B., 1968.

smoking. See: carry on; here they come s.; when it's s.; who's smoking; you'll be s.

snaffler. See: that's the s.

snafu phonetically shortens and typographically 'solidifies' *SNAFU*. There's an occ. var., *SNEFU*; cf also *MFU*. The *FU* part is pron. *foo*.

Snafu was, by HLM in Supp. 2, 1948, described as 'one of the few really good coinages of the war'; it represents 'Situation normal, all fucked up' (politely '... fouled up'); coined by British soldiers, it was, in 1943–5, well known, and used, in the US Army. The Brit. var. *snefu* (*SNEFU*) = 'Situation normal, everything fucked up' – not very common, and mostly officers'; another Brit. var. was *MFU*, a 'military fuck-up', indicating that someone had blundered, and this had its own modification: *Imfu* (*IMFU*), when the blunder was on an 'imperial' scale – used only among officers.

From both the British and the US Army, *snafu* spread to the other Services.

From various sources [wrote E.P. later] I have been able to complete – well, perhaps rather, nearly complete – the forms listed above. These complementary terms are:

COM(M)FU: complete (monumental) fuck-up; *FUBAR*: fucked-up beyond all recognition; *FUBB*: fucked-up beyond belief; *FUMTU*: fucked-up more than usual; *JANFU*: joint Army–Navy fuck-up; *SAPFU*: surpassing all previous fuck-ups; *TARFU*: things are really fucked-up; *TUIFU*: the ultimate in fuck-ups.

JANFU is exclusively US; the rest are predominantly so. I owe one, at most two, to W&F; the rest to Peter Sanders, 1978. Cf also *FYFAS*.

snake(s). See: he'd fuck a s.; I stepped; it's staring; killing; lower than; there's no s.; and:

snake in your pocket – a? or, in full, **have you got a ... ?**, often shortened to **got a ... ?** This Aus. c.p. has, since *c.* 1920, been addressed to one who is reluctant (and very slow) to buy his friends a round of drinks, esp. when his turn to do so has come. The implication is that the snake will bite him when he puts his hand in his pocket to get at his money. Cf synon. *death-adders ...*, a more specific version.

snake's belly. See **lower than ...**

[**snap**] is – to be 'Irish' – a one-word c.p., deriving from the parlour game so named. It occurs frequently in N.F. Simpson's perturbing play, *The Hole*, performed in 1958.]

snatch. See: they think.

sneeze. See: if he had.

snice mince pie. See **it's a snice mince pie.**

sniff. See: he's had.

sniper. See: went for.

'sno use (it's no use) was the c.p. of Harry Weldon (1881–1930) – 'with the "s" uttered with an ear-drum-piercing whistle without which Weldon could pronounce no "s"' (Mathew Norgate, 1977). Weldon was a music-hall star before Radio undermined 'the halls'.

snob. See: like a snob's.

snow. See: eyes like; it snowed; it's snowing; out into the cold; pretend.

snow again! We didn't get your drift, often abbr. to **snow again!**; var., **snow again, kid! I've lost your drift.** This US c.p., signifying 'Say that again! I didn't get your meaning' and punning on *snowdrift*,' arose *c.* 1910 or a little earlier, to judge by the ref. in HLM, 1922; it is recorded by Berrey, 1942, as *snow again, baby, I've lost your drift* and glossed as 'Explain yourself, I don't know what you're talking about'; and Leechman, 1969, records its (derivative) Can. currency as '*c.* 1910'.

'Much commoner than any of these in US are *that snows me* = 'that's too complex or learned for me to understand" and *he gave me a snow job* = "he confused and mystified me with (usually intentional) gobbledygook"' (J.W.C., 1977). *Snow again*, indeed, is 'extinct in US' (R.C., 1978).

Cf the *snow* line at **pretend you're a bee ...**

snowball. See: much chance as a s.; no more chance.

snowbank. See: couldn't drive.

snub squash flat. 'This schoolchildren's c.p. of the 1930s was a gibe, intended to underline the victim's discomfiture when unexpectedly humiliated. You might translate it as "Consider yourself so severely snubbed as to be metaphorically squashed and flattened' (Peter Daniel, 1978).

snuff. See: spends.

snug's the word! Say nothing about this! Let's keep things comfortable and say nothing about the matter: late C17–mid C19. The *OED* cites William Congreve and Maria Edgworth and Lover's *Handy Andy*, 1848. Cf *mum's the word.*

so are you! – often **so're you!** This c.p., common all over the English-speaking world – and going back to heaven knows when – is used in defiance or bravado (or both). Robert Benchley, in *Love Conquers All*, 1923 includes it in the delightfully satirical list quoted at **oh, is that so?**

Cf **and you too!**

so bare (that) you could flog (occ. **hunt**) **a flea across it** is an Aus. 'outback' or remotely rural c.p. applied feelingly to land drought-bare of grass and other vegetation: used by Rolf Boldrewood in 1866, by which time it had clearly been in use for a generation; no less clearly, it was ob. by *c.* 1950. (Dict. Aus. Coll.) Cf the later **miles and miles and bloody miles ...**

so busy I've had to put a man on (to help me). See **getting any?**

so confused.... See **doesn't know ...**

so crooked he couldn't lie straight in bed (– **he's**). Directed at a thoroughly unscrupulous and dishonest fellow: Aus.: since the early 1920s. (B.P.) It expectably occurs in Frank Hardy's *Billy Borker Yarns Again*, 1967 – with the frequent illiterate var., *lay* for lie.

so dumb she thinks her bottom is just to sit on. This raffish, mostly male, c.p. dates from when? I first heard it *c.* 1945, but suspect that it goes back to late C19.

Equally caustic is this, also US, and since the mid 1920s, noted by A.B., 1978: *so dumb he couldn't find his butt* [= his posterior] *with both hands.* With *drunk* substituted for *dumb*, this phrase may be applied to intoxication.

so empty I can feel my backbone touching my belly-button. See **I'm so empty....**

so fast his feet won't touch. As P.B. has (1975) put it:

Army and possibly RAF. Always in connection with 'putting a man inside' for some misdemeanour. 'Cor, he'll neet to watch it. If the RSM cops him at it, he'll have him inside so fast his feet won't touch!' (Deck, ground or floor understood.) Quite common. Current.

As an army c.p., with variations, it goes back to well

before WW2 and was, if I remember correctly, often used during WW1; prob. late C19–20. See also **your feet won't touch.**

so fools say! is a mostly Cockneys' retort to 'You're a fool': since *c.* 1880; by 1970, slightly ob. It occurs *passim* in the novels and stories by Edwin Pugh.

This c.p. has an elab.: *you ought to know – you work where they're made*; ob. by *c.* 1960.

so glad! – elliptical for 'I'm *so* glad' – arose in 1848 as an ephemeral London c.p. orig. by the French King and revived by William Brough's *Field of the Cloth of Gold*, 1867, and still current in 1909, as Ware intimates.

[**so help me, Hannah!** A US c.p. of affirmation or asseveration: C20. (Norris M. Davidson, 3 November 1968.) Either an elab. of *so help me!* or a euph. for *so help me, God!* Hardly a true c.p.]

so is Christmas. See **coming?**

so is my (earlier **mine**) **arse** and **kiss my arse!** Coarse exclamatory phrase, indicative of contempt or incredulity – or both: the former, C17–20, and occurring in, e.g., Ben Jonson; the latter, C18–20, and occurring in, e.g., Swift. Cf **ask my arse!**

so is your old man, but usu. **so's your old man!** Arising in UK *c.* 1900, it was mildly ob. by 1935 and not yet entirely † by 1976. The implication of impudent scepticism and, sometimes, a hearty derision, is well exemplified in Ngaio Marsh's novel, *Tied up in Tinsel*, 1972:

'.... so I said: Do me a favour, chum. You call it what you like: for my book you're at the fiddle!'

'Distinguished and important collection!'

'Yeah! So's your old man!'

In the US, it arose *c.* 1915; 'Originally West Coast use' (W & F), and recorded by Berrey, 1942, as a slangy synonym of 'I don't believe it!' It passed Canada early in the 1920s, as Leechman told me late in 1968.

In 1969, my friend Professor Fain glossed the US use of the c.p., thus: '(*c.* 1920 – *c.* 1940). "Your old man is a son of a bitch, too", or something like that. Typical expression when people sat around and "played dozens" – that is, tried to "put each other dawn" or get the better of, to silence, one another.'

In *Mr Deeds Goes to Town*, 1937, Clarence B. Kelland wrote:

'What's wrong with common people? That's what I want to know.'

'They are vulgar,' said Mr Bengold.

To this the only apt reply Longfellow could think of at the moment was to say, 'So is your old man,' but he did not feel that he knew his secretary well enough to make so flippant a rejoinder, so he kept silent.

Four years earlier, Philip Macdonald, in *RIP*, had put the phrase (*so's...*) into the mouth of a Canadian.

so lucky that if he

so lucky that if he fell in(to) the river he'd only get dusty (– **he's**). Attributing exceptionally good luck: C20. See **could fall in shit...** for a number of other synon. phrases.

so mean that... There are a number of phrases applied to someone exceptionally mean, close-fisted and stingy: some are ... *that he* (or, of course, *she*) *wouldn't give you the time of day* or *give you his cold* or *wouldn't give anyone a fright;* then there is ... *wouldn't spit in your mouth if your threat was on fire* (which has several very low variants), and the low Can.... *wouldn't give you the steam off his shit* (again, with variants): nasty phrases for an unappealing trait, they were mostly in use by WW1, at latest. See also **wouldn't give...,** and **mean as...**

so my mother tells me, dating since *c.* 1700 or even a decade or two earlier, corresponds to the old proverb, 'Ask the mother if the child be like the father'; by 1950, slightly ob. In Dialogue I of S, 1738, we find:

NEV[EROUT]: Pray, Mrs *Betty,* are you not *Tom Johnson's* daughter?

BETTY: So my Mother tells me, Sir.

so round, so firm, so fully packed. 'Originated in the advertising of a cigarette... Applied salaciously to women's figures. No longer used in advertising, and less heard now than twenty or thirty years ago' (J.W.C., 1975):

US: since (say) the middle or late 1940s. P.B.: the orig. 'Lucky Strike' slogan went on ... *so free and easy on the draw*; it is listed in William Sunners, *American Slogans,* 1949 (together with 12,999 other slogans).

so stupid that he (or **she**) **can't chew gum and walk straight at the same time,** usu. prec. by **he's** or **she's.** Current since *c.* 1960, it occurs notably in John Braine, *The Pious Agent,* 1975: 'Not only is he so stupid that, to adopt a famous saying, he can't chew gum and walk straight at the same time, he's also illiterate.' Its American usage has been 'revived with President Ford' (Norman Franklin, 1976).

'The description of President Ford attributed to Nixon is "He's played too many football games without a helmet; he's so stupid he can't chew gum and fart at the same time". Heard on BBC TV. Has the Beeb at last realised that we are not rendered insensible by everyday vulgarisms?' (Sanders, 1978). *Beeb* = the BBC.

so sue me! Then do something about it! Sometimes it means little more than 'So that?' This US c.p., dating from the early 1950s or a little earlier, occurs in, e.g., Jack D. Hunter, *One of Us Works for Them,* A US novel of espionage, 1967:

'That's one of ritziest neighbourhoods this side of Chevy Chase.'

'So sue me.'

See also **sue me!**

so that's how the jam got into the doughnut. See **that accounts for the milk...**

so thay's the way it is. See **it's like that, is it?**

so they tell me is a c.p. only when used ironically or as a 'dry counter to a verbal "facer"; [made] to disarm malice and retain poise': heyday, 1930s; seldom heard before 1930; still heard occ. among people aged 16 or over by *c.* 1940. (L.A., 1974.)

so thin you can smell the shit through him (– **he's**). This low, mostly Cockneys', c.p. dates from *c.* 1880 and is applied to an extremely thin man. (Julian Franklyn: communication.)

so well; and **so what?** The former, which had only a brief career (I myself never heard it), arose in or about 1936 and seems to have been a deliberate var. of the latter, which, in 1936, was adopted in UK from the US: the former was Cockney, the latter (in UK) at first Cockney but very soon gen. Meaning either 'That doesn't impress me', or merely 'I'm simply not interested', **so what?** arose in US *c.* 1930 so far as I have, so far, discovered. W & F give no date, nor, of course, does Berrey, 1942; the latter synonymizes it with 'What does it matter?'.

In HLM, Supp. 1, Mencken notes that *So What?* was the title of a book by an Englishman, pub'd in London in 1938; and 'So What?' is a chapter heading in Michael Burt's novel, *The Case of the Angel's Trumpets,* 1947. A good example occurs in Janet Green's remarkable novel, *My Turn Now,* 1971:

'You'll ruin me. Ruin my career.'

'So what? You've had your day. It's my turn now.'

But more effective is this, in Noël Coward's *Peace in Our Time,* 1947, at I, iii:

ALBRECHT: I know that you are too stubborn to believe me, Mr Shattock, but I assure you that my intentions are friendly.

FRED: All right – so what?

so what does that make me? See **what does that make me?**

so what else is new? See **what else is new?**

so you want to play ball. Often shortened to *so you want to play!* Dating since late 1930s, this a 'c.p. of threatened retaliation to a man [or, come to that, a woman] who irritates or interferes in jest, e.g. with sly punches, [disarranging] e.g.

papers on one's desk' (L.A., 1977). Prompted by the slangy *play ball*, to co-operate.

so's your Aunt Susie! is classified by Berrey as one of the humorous 'disparaging and sarcastic flings' and is there synonymized with **so's your old man!** Very approx. 1930–50.

so's your grandfather! See **all my eye and my elbow!**

so's your old man! See **so is your old man!**

soak. See: go and soak.

soap. See: how are you off; I wouldn't know him; no soap; while there's life.

sock(s). See: bless your little cotton; come on, let's; hands off your; it rots; pull up your; put a sock; put that in your pipe; and:

sock it to him! or **sock it to them!** but esp. **sock it to me!** (with or without **baby** added).

The first occurs as long ago as 1889, when, in chapter 33 of Mark Twain's *A Connecticut Yankee in the Court of King Arthur*, the Yankee, who is, naturally, the narrator, gets into a sociological argument with the smith and says:

'Well, observe the difference. You pay eight cents and four mills, we pay only four cents.'

I prepared, now, to sock it to him. I said: 'Look here, dear friend, *what's become of your high wages you were bragging about a few minutes ago*' – and I looked round on the company with placid satisfaction.

Here, clearly, the sense of the phrase is 'to apply the *coup de grâce*, the final demolishing blow'. (I was alerted to this remarkable adumbration of the *sock it to ...* series by Mrs Barbara Lock Goodman, early in 1969.) Now it is worth noting that, in Mark Twain's *Life on the Mississippi*, 1883, appear these fateful words: 'A rich man won't have anything but your very best [coffins]; and you can just pile it [the price] on too, and sock it in to him – he won't ever holler.' Yet even earlier, *Am*, 1877, exemplifies *sock*, to strike, thus: 'Two loafers are fighting; one of the crowd calls out, "*Sock it to him*."' Can any origination be better supported than by this great scholar and that great writer?

The second occurs in Clarence B. Kelland's novel, *Spotlight*, 1937:

'People who work with me,' said Hadrian, 'need their health.'

'Boy, you had me fooled,' said Mr P[eak]. 'More power to you. Sock it to 'em, lad. I'll be getting along.'

Here clearly, the sense is, 'Give them hell!'

The third occurs, at first (I think), as either a 'teenybop-per' (teenage hellion) cult expression of unpolarized violence and vague meaning: 'Liven things up!', or, as W.J.B. in 1968 suggested, was 'originally a jazz term': and, as he amplified in 1969, '"Sock it to me", now having a vogue in the Rowan & Martin hit "Laugh-In" (NBC), is a phrase borrowed from the vocabulary of Negro jazz musicians. "Laugh-In" started two years ago.'

Adopted from the US, in 1967 or 1968, it was propagated, to the limit of the ludicrous, by disc jockeys. In 1968, Dr Douglas Leechman of Victoria, British Columbia, Canada, wrote to me thus: 'To-day's c.p. here is "Sock it to me (or them ...)". It can be given a variety of implications, depending on who uses it and in what circumstances. Quite recent and heard often on the air.'

And then, later in 1968, the late Norris M. Davidson, a US commentator (and another good friend), wrote:

There is a current revival of a phrase which, I am told, once had a obscene meaning. On our current 'most popular' TV comedy show – Rowan and Martin's 'Laugh-In' – the most repeated phrase is 'Sock it to me!'. And the one speaking the phrase always suffers instant retribution in the form of a clubbing, a bucket of water over the head, a drop through a trap door, etc.

A column in the *Philadelphia Evening Bulletin* of November fourth by Merriman Smith, United States Press International Writer, is captioned: 'Sock it to 'em, Boys' and it turns out to be a rather lengthy treatise [*sic*] on the resurgence of that phrase. He cites the fact that the Rowan & Martin television show has given the phrase new life and that no less a person than Hubert Horatio Humphrey used it literally in several of his later campaign speeches and added the work *baby*, so that it came out 'Sock it to 'em, Baby!'. He cites the fact that Nixon also had used it at an earlier date in his speeches – without the *baby*. The column ends: 'Sadly, no one thought to say a kind word for Mark Twain in whose writings the phrase first appeared many years ago.' Unfortunately Mr Smith did not identify the precise work in which Mark Twain used the phrase.

Prob. it was prompted by the basic (Brit. and) US slang 'to *sock* (someone)', to punch or strike him hard. Note that both the Rowan and Martin show and the phrase 'became exceedingly popular here [UK] too a few years ago' (Patricia Newnham, 1976).

[A later note by E.P.:] It has inevitably attracted considerable comment. In Feb. 1969, *Playboy* had a full-page Berk Brown cartoon of a very old married couple sitting on the stoop of their cottage and the wife turning to her husband and saying, 'You never sock it to me any more'. (Paul Janssen.)

Among American Negroes (witness *The Third Ear*, 1971) the nuance is that of urging and encouraging someone to give of his best, in circumstances ranging from the trivial to the important: since *c.* 1950. Of gen. US usage, A.B., 1979, thinks – no doubt, rightly – that its use in baseball, and prob. in boxing, helped to spread its popularity long before the days of TV

P.B.: I cannot resist adding, as a colophon, the remark made by my friend Alistair Sinclair, while we were sharing a Japanese-style meal in Hongkong, *c.* 1969: 'It may be Japanese rice wine to *you*, but it's saki to me, baby!'

[**sod me up and down!** On the borderline between a picturesque oath and a c.p. of Cockney amazement, late C19–20; more the former than the latter. P.B.: there is of course also the inevitable and alliterative *sod me sideways!* Contrast the next.]

sod you, Jack, I'm inboard! is a RN lower-deck var. of **fuck you, Jack, I'm inboard!** – than which it is felt to be slightly less coarse, slightly less offensive, and slightly more polite: C20.

[**Sod's Law**, like *Parkinson's Law*, is clearly not a c.p.; the former does, however, the more nearly approach the dividing line. In *The Times Literary Supplement* of 19 Oct. 1973 there was a review of Richard Swinburne, *An Introduction to Confirmation Theory*. That review opened by saying, 'Philosophy, like life, is subject to what is vulgarly known as Sod's Law. In life, Sod's Law takes the form of doors opening the wrong way, love being unrequited, and so forth.' This provoked a correspondence; someone claimed to have written about Sod's Law in the *New Statesman* of Oct. 1970.

My friend Paul Beale tells me that he first heard of it in mid 1972 and adds: 'Sod's Law is that which places mankind at the mercy of the small gods of minor misfortune and trivial annoyances. It decrees that if something *can* go wrong, it will.'

Obviously the form *Sod's Law* was prompted by *God's Law:* and hardly less obviously the sense of the phrase owes much to the sense of 'It's a fair sod' – synon. with 'It's a proper bastard'.

P.B., 1983: the phenomenon is still with us – naturally – but the term is now slightly ob. Perhaps the most irritating current exemplar is the way the 'Autobank' is always 'out of service' just at those times when one needs one's own ready cash most urgently – are you listening, High Street Banks?]

sodomy. See: I'll try.

soft. See: hard or; it's pretty; pick a soft; put a stone; and:

soft as a whore-lady's heart (– **as**). Not soft at all; hardhearted: C19–20. Contradictory to the legend that prostitutes have hearts of gold.

soft as shit and twice as nasty (– **as**) is a rural c.p., belonging to

S-E England and applied by rustics to those pasty-faced and loose-living urban owners of weekend 'cottages' in the country: late C19–20. (First heard by me in Kent, during the summer of 1932.) Contrast the workman's *soft as shit*, which they apply to a man habitually speaking without filth and occasionally thinking of something other than booze and soccer and 'birds'; but cf the Cockney's prob. derivative C20 **common as cat-shit and twice as nasty**, applied either to a social inferior or, less frequently, to a very inferior article. Cf also **mean as pig-shit**...

softly. See: speak softly.

softly, softly, catchee monkey. 'Gently does it!': prob. late C19–20. In Benham, 1948, it is given as a proverb, in the form *'Softly, softly' caught the monkey* and glossed as being of negro origin. But as *softly, softly, catchee monkey* it is a c.p. and used as in, e.g., Laurence Meynell's novel, *Die by the Book*, 1966: 'In my time I had made one or two blunders by rushing my fences and I didn't propose to make the same mistake again. "Softlee, softlee, catchee monkey".'

In 1969, Granville glossed it thus: 'Stalk your prey carefully; or, generally, to achieve an object by quiet application.'

In Michael Delving's novel, *The Devil Finds Work*, 1970, a detective says: 'I don't want to make him edgy.... I've got to be very careful. Softly, softly, catchee monkey, you know.'

This well-known phrase has, except for Benham, been neglected by the editors of the relevant works of reference; and I haven't been lucky enough to find an early quot'n.

P.B.: 'Softly, Softly' was the title of an extremely popular and long-running BBC TV series based on the Lancashire Police, 1960s; the title was inspired, so the *Concise Oxford Dict. of Proverbs notes*, by the whole phrase's being 'the unique motto of the Lancashire Constabulary Training School'. E.P. later noted that Warwick Deeping, in his once famous novel *Sorrell and Son*, 1925, used the rarish var. *softlee, walkee, catchee monkey.*

sold again and got the money was, c. 1840–80, a costermonger's c.p., uttered upon having bested someone in a bargain. (Hotten, 1859.) Cf the London simile current in late C18–mid C19: *sold like a bullock in Smithfield,* thoroughly duped or badly cheated.

sold the farm or, in full, **he has**... 'He has given an opponent an easy chance to win' – esp. in billiards or pool: Aus.: since late 1940s. Jim Ramsey, *Cop It Sweet*, 1977.

sold to the man in the (e.g. bowler hat, false moustache, etc.) or **the lady in the** (e.g. red wig, etc.) 'C.p. from auctions, used to mean "you've got it", "That's perfectly correct", etc.' (Ashley, 1979): US and Brit.: C20. P.B.: The facetious examples are my own, recollected from schooldays, 1940s, when we used it to mean 'the object is yours'; I presume that Prof. Ashley implies the same sort of thing.

soldier(s). See: as I am a gentleman; as the girl said; brutal and licentious; don't come the tin; fuck that for a lark; good soldier; harder; I didn't raise; if you call; it's a poor s.; old soldier; only eating; pull a s.; that's gone; what the s.; and:

soldier on, chum! was, during WW1, frequently heard among British, esp. English, soldiers, one to another. See the entry at **dear Mother, it's a bugger**...

soldier said – as the. See **what the soldier said.**

soldier's farewell (to you understood and occ. expressed – **a**). Orig. – from before 1909, when Ware recorded it – military and meaning 'Go to bed!', with various ribald, not to say bawdy, additions and ornamentations. But in WW1 and after, although still military, it meant 'Good-bye and bugger you!'. In *Oh! Definitely*, 1933, Maurice Lincoln writes: '"Good-bye...!" he yelled.... "Soldier's farewell," he said amiably.' Synon. is (*a*) *sailor's farewell*, q.v., a parting curse, both naval and, by adoption, military.

In B & P, John Brophy remarked that *a soldier's farewell* 'was originally invective.... But its chief use was as a jocular exclamation made very loudly for the benefit of others.'

soldiers? I've shit 'em! 'An expression of contempt for another

unit (esp. if slovenly)', as John Brophy explained in B & P, 1930: British soldiers': WW1 – and doubtless afterwards.

soldier's supper: pee (or **piss**) **and turn in** – **a**. A RN c.p. of the 1970s and prob. a little earlier. Soldiers don't get an official supper. (Peppitt.)

some call him Robin Hood... See **some say**...

some children don't half have them (or **'em**)! See **some mothers...**!

'some day my prince will come,' said the Princess, idly stirring her tea with the other hand. Since c. 1910. 'This punning innuendo of masturbation was probably suggested by the companioning *'fuck me,' said the Duchess*' (P.B., 1977). See also **'you're a long time coming'**...

some days you (just) can't make a dime. Some days, *nothing* goes right: US: from 1930s. (R.C., 1978.)

some deck is shy a joker, lit., 'Some deck, or pack, of cards is short of the Joker', this is 'a cowboys' description of an outlandishly dressed person, usually a tenderfoot' (Adams): since late C19.

some hopes! It's *most* unlikely or improbable! This c.p. arose at the beginning of C20 and was very generally used in the British Army during WW1; far more so than the synon. *what hopes!*; equally popular, however, was **what a hope!**

some like it hot became a c.p. c. 1960, its meaning, 'Some people like things, especially if sexual, to be hot.' Popularized by the world of entertainment; orig. it was applied to fast-tempo'd, exciting, jazz music, now often described as 'cool', as Patricia Newnham reminded me in 1976. See esp. W&F at *hot*, sense 10, and *cool*, adj., 3.

Ultimately, as R.C. reminds me, 1978, from the nursery rhyme *Pease Porridge Hot*: 'Some like it hot, Some like it cold; Some like it in the pot, Nine days old'. And as Prof. D.J. Enright pointed out, in *Encounter*, Dec. 1977, its popularity as c.p. arises from its being the title of an immensely popular film, made in 1959, starring Marilyn Monroe, Jack Lemmon and Tony Curtis. P.B.: Halliwell's *Film Guide*, 2nd ed., lists another film with the same title, a Bob Hope comedy released in 1939.

some mothers (or **movvers** pron. and often written **muvvers**) **do have 'em!** is 'invariably Cockney, whether native or assumed' (L.A., 1974): since c. 1920. A BBC series in 1974 'Some Mothers...' was for a wide audience: and it thoroughly popularized the c.p. The implication is that some children are either idiotic or thoroughly intolerable. But it also, e.g. among workmen, furnishes a jeer at clumsiness and among schoolboys and youths when someone has blundered. [This appeared in the first ed. of this book, but earlier in the book E.P. had noted *don't some mothers 'ave 'em!*. He'd got it rather wrong, so here is Nigel Rees's version from *VIBS*:]

'An old Lancashire saying popularised by Jimmy Clitheroe in radio's *The Clitheroe Kid*, which ran from 1958 to 1972 (when the little lad died at the age of fifty-seven). Later, as *Some Mothers Do 'Ave 'Em*, the title of Michael Crawford's TV series.' Noble, 1973, notes that the *don't*... version was familiar also in Yorkshire.

Cf **some people rear awkward children.**

The popularity of this c.p. has generated the parody, *some children don't half have them*, 'used derisively of parents who are "squares"' (Petch, 1974).

some of my best friends are Jews (or, derivatively and far less commonly, almost any group or class or religion or race you happen to be prejudiced against) is 'a c.p. used just before making a disparaging remark about some segment of the human race' (B.P., 1969) – it is, therefore, employed to 'excuse bigotry' (B.P., 1974). Moreover, it is, of course, a Gentile c.p., current among those who secretly think – or, at any rate, feel – that Jews are not merely different, hopelessly different, from, but also socially inferior to, Gentiles. Common to the entire English-speaking world, it dates from not later than 1940 and has prob. been current since the early 1930s, with equivalents in other European languages. It orig. perhaps rather in US than in UK. So enshrined is it in US folkways that it can be employed allusively, as in Alfred Marin, *Arise with the Wind*, 1969:

'I was never against those people [the Jews],' Weber said with feeling.

'Sure, some of your best friends were Jewish,' Clay said bitterly.

Indeed, as a friend of mine, a Gentile, once remarked, 'Makes you want to vomit, doesn't it?' Sometimes one wonders why, there being so much racial prejudice and even hatred about, there haven't been even more wars. The true miracle, the enduring miracle, the greatest miracle of all, is that, so far, the human race has succeeded in surviving the human race; clearly the age of miracles is *not* past.

Used as a plain statement, it is obviously not a c.p. But, esp. since the middle 1940s, it has been so derided, by both Jews and Gentiles, that it has come to be used jocularly – by, for instance, a Jew to a Gentile friend. It's rather like saying 'Some of my best friends are human beings – well, almost.' Indeed, Leo Rosten, author of the splendid *Joys of Yiddish*, sub-titled a later book *Passions and Prejudices*, 1978: *Some of My Best Friends Are People*.

some people (occ. **parents**) **rear** (or **raise**) **awkward children,** with **do** sometimes inserted before *rear*. This c.p. dates, I'd say, since *c*. 1880, if not earlier, and is either addressed to or directed at someone who has been very clumsy. By *c*. 1960, it was showing signs of becoming a proverb, but it has not yet (1975) become one. Cf **some mothers do have 'em!**

some say 'Good old sergeant!' This military c.p., dating since *c*. 1890, perhaps earlier, was either spoken or shouted by privates within the sergeant's hearing. Of its use in the British army during WW1, John Brophy (in B & P) wrote,

There were thousands of really good sergeants, respected and liked. On the individual's conduct and character it depended whether the private shouted:

Some say 'Good old sergeant!'

Others say '—[i.e., fuck] the old sergeant!' with rancour or with quite affectionate jocularity.

This c.p. itself engendered, from *c*. 1919 onwards, the much more widely employed *some say 'Good old* [e.g., *Smith*]' – *some* (or *I*) *say 'Blast* (much more commonly '*Fuck*) *old* (Smith)'*!*

'Amongst children and young people it was also common to hear *but others tell the truth*' (Patricia Newnham, 1976): *c*. 1920–60. Cf **they used to call him Robin Hood …**

somebody('s) and **someone('s)** are interchangeable in the next four entries.

somebody up there likes (or **loves**) **me** (or **you,** etc.). 'I am very fortunate at the moment'; 'you are obviously in favour with the right people': adopted as a c.p. from the US *c*. 1960. The ref. is to heaven, but the phrse may be used less fig., with direct ref. to higher authority. Halliwell's invaluable *Film Guide*, 2nd ed., describes the film *Somebody Up There Likes Me*, 1956, starring Paul Newman and Pier Angeli, as 'a sentimental fantasia on the life of [the boxer] Rocky Marciano'. (P.B.)

somebody's dropped his false teeth. Uttered apropos of a sudden noise, esp. a crash: since the early 1920s. In 1939–45, an Armed Forces' c.p. apropos of a bomb or a shell exploding some distance away.

A.B., 1979, writes, 'It has, both in US and UK, acquired a much wider currency. With such variants as *I nearly dropped my teeth!* and *if my teeth had been false, I'd have dropped them*, it expresses mouth-wide-open amazement or utter surprise. Also said to someone who openly yawns, "Watch that you don't drop your teeth!": a sort of admonition'.

someone forgot to pay the washerwoman and **someone's taken the water away.** These RN (lower-deck) c.pp. of of C20 are applied thus: the former is a 'remark made on a wet day': the latter, a 'self-conscious observation made by a member of a pulling-boat's crew when he misses the water and catches a crab' (*Sailors' Slang*).

someone must have died in this chair is 'said by card-player who is having bad luck' (Skehan, 1984): Anglo-Irish: C20.

someone's been looking in my pay-book! See **you've been reading my letters,** second paragraph.

something. See: ain't that s.; do you know s.; don't just; d' you know; go do me; good morning, sir; I guess; I've something; isn't that s.; it must have; like something; maybe they; plus; say something; tell me s.; that's another s.; that's something; want to make; you want to start; you'll get s.; you've dropped; you've got s.; and:

something completely different. See **and now for something …**

something is rotten in the state of Denmark. This famous quot'n (*Hamlet*, I, iv, 90) 'must have been understood as a c.p. even in Shakespeare's time. Denmark was always a big cheese-exploiter, I believe' (Fain, 1977). This would make it almost the longest-lived of all c.pp. The misquotation *there's something rotten … * occurs almost as frequently as the correct form.

something like. See **this is something …**

something nasty in the woodshed – he (or **she**) **has seen.** Applied – in ironic derision of too many psychiatrists' too glib explanations – to 'a crazy, mixed-up kid': Brit. and Aus.: since the mid 1930s.

'This c.p. was originated by Stella Gibbons in her immortal *Cold Comfort Farm*, 1932, the satire that put an end to a vogue for novels of rural passions and dominant grandmothers' (R.S., 1959).

An anon. correspondent, 1978, notes that there is a var., *seeing something nasty in the woodshed*, 'every girl's ambition, or fear'.

something the cat's brought in. See **like something ….**

something to hang things on. An infantryman's self-description, rueful yet humorous: WW1. As F & G phrase it: 'In allusion to the paraphernalia of his heavy marching order kit.' Whatever one looked like, one certainly did not feel in the least like a Christmas tree.

something to write home about. See **nothing to cable …**

sometimes I wonder! Deriving from – and meaning – 'Sometimes I wonder whether you are entirely sane', *or* '… are right in the head': prompted by a stupid or very silly remark the addressee has just made; often delivered in a reflective tone and with a rather puzzled air: C20. (B.P.)

somewhat. See: more than s.

somewhere in France was, in 1915–18 and by the British army and by the Australians, Canadians, New Zealanders and others, put to joc. uses or arbitrarily, even senselessly, varied: and thus it became a c.p. (B & P.) From the heading of most Western Front letters home.

son. See: good idea; hello, my old; my son; that's a joke; this is no.

song. See: nothing to make; sing us; what's your s.

soon. See: tinkle; ve get; women are; you would not be.

sooner you than me. See **rather you …**

soppy. See: you soppy.

sore. See: done up like a sore.

sorrow. See: lady with; more in anger; there's s.

sorry. See: I'm s.; oh! sorry; you'll be s.

sorry I spoke! See **sorry you spoke …**

sorry (, no); but I've got a sister in the WAACs [Women's Auxiliary Army Corps] (Army, WW1); **… a granite bust of Queen Victoria** (RN, 1940s). Answers to a request one cannot fulfil. (Peppitt, 1975.) See also **I've got a bit of string …** and **I have a picture …**

sorry to keep you up. An Aus. ironical c.p., addressed to someone who yawns: C20. (B.P., 1974.)

sorry you spoke? – aren't you arose very early in C20 and occurred in e.g., W.L. George, *The making of an Englishman*, 1914; by 1950, ob., and by 1976 virtually †. Addressed to someone who has spoken hastily and unjustly and who is clearly embarrassed at having done so.

P.B.: but the corresponding (*Oh!*) *sorry I spoke* (, *I'm sure*)! is still current, early 1980s, occ. in genuine emollient contrition, but more often used ironically – not sorry at all, the thing needed to be said; or with offended dignity, after a cool reception to what the speaker had thought was a harmless remark.

sorry you've been troubled! This is the title of a Noël Coward sketch, written in 1923 and ending thus: '(*The telephone rings violently. POPPY snatches up the receiver, listens for a moment, then hurls the instrument to the floor.*) (Through clenched teeth.) Sorry you've been troubled!'. Dating from *c.* 1910, it obviously derives from telephone operators' often perfunctory apologies.

sort. See: that's your sort.

sort 'em out! A 'cry of derision evoked by a clumsy attempt at changing gear on a motor vehicle; sometimes extended to **sort 'em out – they're all there**. Another jeer at crashed gears is *d' you want/need a knife and fork?*' (P.B., 1975). Since *c.* 1950.

soul. See: pore ole thing.

soul on! This US negro c.p. has been glossed by CM, 1970, as a 'phrase of encouragement to be authentic', i.e. sincere, to be a man of integrity, one of the *hommes de bonne volonté*: app. since *c.* 1960.

P.B.: W & F, 1975 edn, define *soul, adj.*: 'Negro; pertaining to or having the essence of things, feelings, moods, etc., that are considered to be basically Negro.' See, if poss., their complete entry, helpful and enlightening.

sound. See: wired.

sounds OK on paper is a US c.p., meaning 'But will it work in practice?' and dating since the early 1930s, prob. during the Great Depression. J.W.C., 1977, notes also its acronym, *SOKOP*.

soup. See: that's the ticket for.

south. See: it's snowing.

Southern custom. See: it's an old Southern...

sovereign's not in it – a. Applied to a person, esp. a sailor, suffering from jaundice: nautical, from before 1909 (Ware), and ob. by 1940, † by 1950. In ref. to the gold coin worth £1 sterling and to the patient's dark yellow complexion.

sow. See: her clothes.

spades. See: you can say that in s.

Spanish custom. See: it's an old Southern...

spare. See: home, James; like a spare; woodman.

spare a dime. See buddy, can you...

spare a rub? Let me have some, *or* After with it!: tailors': *c.*1880–1950 (very approx.). (B & L.) A ref. to pipe-tobacco.

spare me gory details. 'I need no further details, thankyou': later C20. (Ashley, 1982.)

spare my blushes! A c.p. response to an embarrassingly flattering statement or compliment: *c.* 1880–1940. In Arthur Wing Pinero's *Letty*, 1903, we read, in Act II, where a photographer is posing a group:

PERRY: Ladies – Mr Irdish – Mr Neale – I have pleasure, and pride, in informing you that there is every prospect of my obtaining an effective picture, a strikingly beautiful picture –

NEALE: Spare my blushes!

(Neale is a commercial traveller, unlikely to blush.)

spare prick at a wedding – a. See **like a...**.

sparrow. See: keep your eye on the; muscles.

sparrow (or **geese**) **flying out of one's backside** (– **like**) is a picturesque Aus. c.p., descriptive of the male orgasm: app. since *c.* 1950, to judge by the printed records (notably Wilkes), but perhaps a decade or two earlier.

speak. See: can I speak; couldn't speak; did you say; don't all s.; Funf; I'm speaking; it's the beer; sir, you are speaking; stand up, s.; this is your captain; unaccustomed; you'll speak.

speak a little louder: I'm deaf in that ear. 'I know I was wrong, but please don't let's talk about it: what you are saying embarrasses me.' R.S., 1975, dates it at *c.* 1918; I heard it during the years 1922–29.

speak all American, with a big 'A'! 'So that I can understand' implied. This 'was a line from one of Spike Jones's records in the immediate post-WW2 years, now [still] remembered, along with his City Slickers by some' (Anon., 1978). P.B.: so that's where it came from! Listed among E.P.'s notes towards the 2nd ed., it reminded me that we were familiar with the phrase at school, 1946–7, in the form *America, with the big 'A', 'A', 'A'!*

speak as you find, that's my motto! 'This was the catchphrase of Nola, the stubbornly unmarried daughter of Mrs Purvis, the studio cleaner, in Arthur Askey's radio show *Hello Playmates!* [early 1950s]. Bob Monkhouse (who wrote it with Denis Goodwin) called them "a truly marvellous pair of characters who sprang into life fully-blossomed in our first script for the show. They were played by Irene Handl as the mother, ... and Pat Coombs as the curiously self-composed Nola, whose smug excuse for the appalling insults she hurled was, "Well...speak as you find, that's my motto"' (*VIBS*).

speak for yourself, John! 'has been used to encourage an individual to speak up in his own behalf. It is variant of "Why don't you speak up for yourself, John?" ...popularized by Longfellow in *The Courtship of Miles Standish*, 1858. Longfellow did not originate the phrase,... I ran across in an 1830 account' (Moe, 1978).

speak softly and carry a big stick. This US c.p. was popularized by Theodore Roosevelt (1858–1919) in a speech he made on 2 Sep. 1901: 'There is a homely adage which runs "Speak softly and carry a big stick; you will go far". Whence it becomes clear that an American proverbial or semi-proverbial saying became almost immediately a c.p. Notified to me by W.J.B., 1977, but I owe the Roosevelt quot'n to *Bartlett's Familiar Quotations*, the best of all American dictionaries for the United States – and very nearly as good for Britain.

speak up, Brown! is a Londoners' and Armed Forces' c.p., dating since *c.* 1930 (or a few years earlier) and addressed to one who has farted very noisily. I have also heard *did you speak?*, but rather doubt whether it ever became eligible.

P.B.: variants are *speak up, Ginger* or *Padre*, and *you're through!* may be added to any.

speaking of oars... See **how's your sister?**

speaking to the butcher or **the engine-driver.** See **I'm speaking...**

Special Branch again! – the. An 'ironic phrase used when an eccentrically dressed or filthy person is seen' (David Powis, *The Signs of Crime*, 1977): later C20. Cf *the Umbrella Brigade*, an ironic ref. to the Special Branch of the CID itself (Ibid.)

speech. See: usual s.; you have made.

speed. See: built for; watch my.

spell it out for you? – do I have to or **must I** or **shall I.** Surely it's clear (or obvious enough?: since *c.* 1950. In 1968 Granville commented thus: 'Gives further emphasis to what now is already clear enough.' Sanders, 1978, adds the var. **...draw a diagram?**

P.B.: cf the cliché use of the phrase in *New Society*, 26 Apr. 1984, concerning London road and rail schemes: 'Both...will re-orientate London to some extent. Martin Elson, reader in town planning at Oxford Polytechnic, spelt it out in his evidence to the Commons environment committee...'

spend. See: doesn't care; you have to s.; you'd only.

spenders. See: last of the big-time s.

spends money as if it were going out of fashion or **style** (– **he**); (**he**); **throws money around like snuff at a wake.** He spends it recklessly, as if it were either worthless or soon to become so: the former common to UK and Ireland; the latter, Anglo-Irish: respectively since *c.* 1930 and *c.* 1910. (Skehan, 1977.) Americans prefer ... *out of style*, current since *c.* 1970 or a little earlier (R.C., 1978). P.B.: common also to US and UK since *c.* 1975 is (e.g., spends money *like there was no tomorrow*.

spin. See: why is a mouse.

spirit. See: that's the old Dunkirk; that's the old Navy; and:

spirit of the troops is excellent – the, was, in late 1916–18, a military c.p., 'taken from newspaper blather and used in jocular, and often in bitterly derisive, irony' (John Brophy, 3rd edn, of B & P).

spit. See: do you spit; doesn't it make; don't spit; he'll spit; I'll push; paid; silence; wouldn't it make; and:

spit and polish! no wonder we're winning the war! See **clean and polish** ....

spit on the deck and call the cat a bastard! This Brit. c.p. of the merchant marine belongs to C20 and is exemplified thus by my friend P.B., 1975:

In Richard Gordon's *Doctor at Sea*, 1953, chapter I, occurs this phrase used by a crew member to welcome the new doctor aboard a merchant ship: '...Liberty Hall, this hooker. Make yourself at home. Spit on the deck and call the cat a bastard.' This vivid phrase has the ring, I feel, of genuine reported speech.

Not much doubt about that.

Cf **he'll spit ...**, another version.

spiteful See: white and.

spits rust. See: chews nails.

splinter. See: it's not so.

split. See: God knows.

split lip. See: don't make me laugh.

spoil. See: that's where you s.; there's nothing spoiling.

spoke. See: English; Queen; sorry you s.

spoon(s). See: start; tinkle.

spot(s). See: how's your belly; X marks.

spot on! Right on the spot, orig. dead centre on target: RAF: WW2 and after. Adopted by civilians in UK, in Aus., in S. Africa. Cf **bang on!** and **right on!**

spotlight on charm! See **I say, what a smasher!**

spray it again, will you? Say it again, please: Aus. used when someone emits saliva or, frankly, spits in pronouncing *p*'s: and *s*'s: since the 1940s and mostly in Sydney, where Jack Slater heard it in 1962. Cf *say it, don't spray it.* P.B.: the version *you can spray that again* has been current in UK since *c.* 1950 at latest.

spread. See: let it s.

spring to it!, a military order, became, either in 1918 or certainly not later than 1919, esp. (of course!) among ex-Servicemen, a joc., at first allusive, recommendation to 'Look lively!' Not quite †, even by 1975. P.B.: but in later C20, usu. replaced by *jump to it!*

say. See: spies.

square. See: form s.

square an' all! 'Of a truth; verily' (C.J. Dennis): Aus., orig. proletarian: C20. An elab. of the Standard English, then coll., *square*, 'straightforward'.

square one. See **back to square one.**

square your own yardarm! See **that's your worry!**

squash. See: snub.

squat. See: he squats.

squattez-vous! Please sit down: late C19–20. It occurs in, e.g., Kipling's *Stalky & Co.*, 1899. Although ob. by 1950, it was still, as Petch remarked in 1974, 'sometimes heard for "Be seated" or "Take a pew"'. A blend of *squat* and *asseyez-vous.* Cf **twiggez-vous?**

squeak. See: are you a man; squeeze till; tight as.

squeeze. See: hold 'em.

squeeze him and 'e'll fill a bucket is the c.p. equivalent of saying that he's as wet as a scrubber – a complete 'ullage', a thoroughly dim-witted, or useless, rating: RN (lower-deck): C20. (Granville, in letter, 1968, but also in his *SS.*)

squeeze the lemon. See **I'm going to do ...**

squeeze till the pips squeak. To extract the utmost from: a political c.p. concerned with retribution, or sheer envy. Arthur Marwick, in *The Deluge: British Society and the First World War*, 1965, provides a source: 'Sir Arthur Geddes, one of the leaders of the generation of business experts and political incompetents of 1916, produced the delightful metaphor of "squeezing Germany until the pips squeak".' A footnote to this gives refs to *The Times*, Nov.–Dec. 1918, passim. The metaphor arises from an old-fashioned lemon-squeezer. In 1918 it applied to reparations; in later C20, politicians seem to use it for taxing those they envy most.

Only secondarily does it apply to obtaining information. (P.B.)

squeezes a nickel until (or **'till**) **the Indian is riding the buffalo** – he or she. 'He (or she) is tight with money': US: C20. (Ashley, 1983.) A ref. to the emblems on the coin.

squib. See: his mother.

squid. See: you can't tell.

squint. See: one squint.

squire. See: have you heard the news.

squirrel. See: quick and nimble.

stab yourself and pass the bottle! Help yourself and pass the bottle: theatrical: *c.* 1850–1930. (Hotten, 1864.) From dagger-and-poison melodrama.

stables. See: his horses.

stacks. See: she stacks.

stacked like a brick shithouse. See **built like ...**

stag or shag? With or *without* a female companion? Aus.: since the late 1940s. A pun on *a stag party*, males only, and *shag* (of the male), to copulate with, a copulation.

stage. See: I say, I say; only stage.

stairs. See: get up them; I'll go hopping; if I knew; on the s.; remember I'm; we are lost; well, I'll go.

stake. See: swallowed.

stamp. See: couldn't knock.

stand. See: don't do anything; I grow; if you can't s.; it doesn't s.; it's as cheap; like a spare; while I'm standing.

'stand always!' as the girl said. A mid C19 – early C20 c.p. with a punning ref. to a physiological erection. This young woman seems to have belonged to the Ransom persuasion:

There was a young woman named Ransom
Who was screwed seven times in a hansom.
When she turned to her swain.
And said, Let's do it again,
He said, My name's Simpson not Samson.

stand and grow good! See **I grow while I'm standing.**

stand by to repel boarders! A RN officers' c.p.: C20. Used when visitors, esp. if unwelcome, have been announced. P.B.: has wider and more (usu.) joc. usage than E.P. allows here, i.e. it may be spoken at, rather than said to, visitors already within earshot.

stand by your beds! This c.p. mimics and mocks self-importance, the speaker pretending that he is arousing the occupants of a room to activity – or to greater activity: Armed Forces': 1939–45. 'From disciplinary order of superior on entering a barrack room' (L.A.). But see also **any complaints?**

[**stand closer, it's shorter than you think.** 'A non-cultured notice that is put near the WC in some homes ... to urge or shame males into standing closer so that they will not wet the floor. *Ladies, please remain seated during the entire performance* is much rarer' (B.P., 1975). The phrases occur together on printed cards to be bought in joke shops (Camilla Raab). This *might* some day rise from raffish witticism to raffish c.p.] Cf **we aim to please ...**

stand on a fag-paper! Advice to someone unable to reach up to something, esp. if he's rather short: mostly Londoners', and Cockneys' at that: since *c.* 1920.

stand on me for that! – often shortened to **stand on me!** You can take my word for it: sporting circles: since the 1920s, if not a decade or two earlier. The longer form is recorded in EP, *Today and Yesterday*, 1933; the latter in Frank Norman's *Stand on Me*, 1959.

stand out. See **stands out like ...**

stand to, boys, the Jocks are going over! In B&P, 1930, John Brophy remarked that it 'belonged to the latter half of the war' – i.e. 1917–18. He added that it was 'a fairly kindly way of making fun of killed soldiers and of the excessive popularity they enjoyed with journalists and women; spoken with exaggerated and comic respect on the advent of Highland troops – but without any mean feeling of jealousy'. The 'going over' refers to going over No-Man's-Land in an attack. Whereas on Gallipoli (and later) it was the 29th

Division (English), on the Western Front it was the 51st Division (Scottish), which the very critical Australian infantry men the most admired; not, however, that there weren't others.

stand up and be counted! Show your true political colours; hence also in other contexts: since *c.* 1920. (Petch, 1974.) P.B.: in later C20, and often in political rhetoric, 'It is time to stand up and be counted'.

(stand up, speak up: and shut up! This famous advice to all post-luncheon and post-dinner speakers has become almost a c.p.; almost, not quite.]

stand well clear. See **light the blue**...

standard operating procedure. Often shortened to *S.O.P.*: 'the expectable, routine way of doing things: US Services', WW2, then general' (R.C., 1978).

standing about (or **around**) **like a spare prick** (or **a lost lemon**). See **like a spare**...

standing by Nellie. See **sitting by Nellie**.

[**standing prick has no conscience – a**; often elab. with complementary animadversion, **and an itching cunt feels no shame.** Prob. mid C18–20; certainly at least mid C19–20. A low c.p. that, because of its verity and its force, had, by 1920 at latest, become a proverb – not, of course, to be found in the standard books of quotations and dictionaries of proverbs, yet none the less a proverb, for all that. Cf those other unrecorded proverbs, *Let your wind go free,/Where'er you may be*, with its var. *Let wind go free,/Where'er you be*, which, in its longer version, I heard from a septuagenarian parson excusing himself, somewhat perfunctorily I thought, to me after dinner one night in the summer of 1927 [P.B.: the couplet should be followed by *In church or chapel,/Let it rattle*; the whole is attributed, with what truth I know not, to Robert Burns – prob. a case of 'If he didn't write it, he should have done']; and *Short and thick/Does the trick; Long and thin/Goes right in*, which I heard from an Oxford don early in 1940; and **as soft as shit and twice as nasty** recorded separately in this dictionary. There are, I believe, two or three others, but if I ever heard them, I've unforgivably forgotten them.]

stands out like a shithouse in the fog (**– it**). There are several c.p. similes for 'the patently obvious': among them this low Can. version; vulgar Brit. equivalents are ...*like cods*' (or, more logically, *a dog's*) *ballocks* (occ., a bulldog is specified). Referring esp. to eyes naturally protuberant, or made so by emotion, is the perhaps orig. N. Country *stand out like chapel hat-pegs*. (P.B.)

stands Scotland where it did? This famous quot'n from Shakespeare's *Macbeth*, IV, iii, line 164, became a c.p. not later that I, think, the 1880s or 1890s. Cf S, Dialogue II:

COL[ONEL]: And, pray, Sir *John*, how do you like the Town? You have been absent a long time.

SIR JOHN: Why, I find little *London* stands just where it did when I saw it last.

(Thank God, he – this bluff Derbyshire squire – at least, didn't call it 'little old London'!) This quot'n from Swift very clearly suggests that the phraseological pattern may have become gen. early in C17.

star(s). See: one star; teeth; you're starring.

start. See: I've started; just s.; what you don't; you want to s.

start to count the spoons!; variants, **count the spoons!** and **we'll start to**...This is a said, either partly or wholly as a jest, when we've seen depart a person, a couple, even a small group of persons whom we don't trust. A domestic c.p. very difficult to date. I hadn't heard it before the late 1940s. On the Radio programme 'Stop the Week' 17 Oct. 1977 Anne Lesley remarked, 'It always makes me laugh because it implies something about your social economic status which is that you have spoons worth stealing...family silver'. (With the kind permission of the BBC.)

starter. See: cheated.

Starve 'em, Rot 'em and Cheat 'em is a naval (hence also military) c.p. of *c.* 1750–1880. Recorded at one end by

Grose, 1785, and at the other by Hotten, 1864, it refers to the unfavourable reputation of the barracks, and the publichouses and brothels, at Strood, Rochester and Chatham.

In *Sailors' Slang*, 1962, Granville called it 'a good-natured libel' of these Medway towns.

starving. See: remember the s.

state secret – a. See **it's a state secret.**

statement is inoperative (**– this** or **that** or **the**). '"I lied": from the Nixon administration' (Ashley): a US c.p. thrown up by the Watergate scandal of the mid 1970s. Cf **twisting slowly**...

states can be saved without it was, according to Ware in 1909, a political, thence also an educated and cultured, c.p., expressive of ironic condemnation; current in the 1880s.

station. See

statistics. See: lies, damned.

stay. See: must you stay; will you have.

stay and be hanged! Oh, all right – if you must!: a mostly lower-middle-class c.p. of C19 – early 20. Ware.

stay in your own backyard! was a c.p., implying 'I don't want your company' and sometimes 'Mind your own business!' Period 1899 – *c.* 1916. The song thus titled was pub'd and first sung by J.P. Witmark in 1899; words by Kennett, music Udall. (Edward B. Marks, 1934, cited by W.J.B.)

stay loose! A 'valediction, orig. = "Keep your bowels open", but now usually innocently, "Keep relaxed, keep on taking it easy", and hence more widely used than in its orig. sense. Since *c.* 1960. Probably Harlem Negro. Still not common among adults of the "respectable" classes, but common enough among their adolescent offspring' (J.W.C., 1977). Cf **hang loose.**

steady. See: halt.

steady, Barker! was, *c.* 1941, adopted from the navy's version of the BBC radio programme 'Merry-Go-Round', as Campbell Nairne, formerly editor of the *Radio Times*, informed me while I was preparing 'Those Radio Catch Phrases', pub'd in that weekly on 6 Dec. 1946. *Steady, Barker!* was obviously prompted by **steady, the Buffs!**

P.B.: the whole point was that it belonged particularly to the star of the show, Eric Barker, who used to utter it in a slightly apologetic, though would be resolute way, to admonish himself for, e.g. becoming over-excited by the attractive proximity of his co-star, Pearl Hackney. It really caught the public fancy, and was heard in all kinds of contexts; it was, 1956, the natural choice of title for Barker's autobiography.

steady, Jackson! 'Take it easy' (Berrey): US: C20; by 1960, somewhat ob. I suspect that this c.p. may be ironic – prompted by the military tactics of General 'Stonewall' Jackson. R.C. comments, 1978, 'I'd say extinct by 1960s, certainly now'.

steady, the Buffs! A c.p. of self-admonition or self-adjuration or self-encouragement: late C19–20: military and – rather later, by adoption – RN; and finally among civilians. From an incident in the history of the East Kent Regiment, the nickname *the Buffs* perhaps orig. in the fact that they were the first regiment to wear buff, or buffalo, leather accoutrements. (F&G.) Perhaps the c.p. arose when, in 1888, Kipling popularized the phrase in *Soldiers Three*.

Thus, a man aware that, tipsy, he is walking unsteadily, might say to himself, 'Steady, the Buffs!'

P.B.: not always only to oneself: the phrase may be used to 'steady' others too.

steal. See: ah there, my size.

steal anything that's not too hot or too heavy (**– he**, etc., **will** or **would**). Applied to anyone notoriously 'light-fingered'; the N. Country form is (e.g., he'll) *lift out that's not too heavy or too hot*, and the gen. form has been traced back to Chaucer (J.B. Smith cites J. McKelvie, *Lore & Language*, 1, 2, p.3). A US version is *he'd steal anything that isn't* (or *that's not*) *nailed down*, while an earlier, *c.* 1840–1900, form was (he) *wouldn't steal a red-hot stove*, implying that such a person will steal anything else. R.C., 1978, notes that the Abolitionist Thaddeus Stevens said it of Abraham Lincoln's First Secretary of War, Simon Cameron, and was forced to retract the slander.

Another, similar set of phrases is applied to extreme meanness, as 'he's so mean, he'd...', or to someone particularly unscrupulous and dishonest. *He'd steal the coppers* (or *pennies*) *off a dead man's eyes* is, as Ashley, 1979, writes, 'from the custom of placing coins in the coffin with the corpse, harking back to the fare provided in ancient days for the Styx boatman, Charon'. An even more offensive elab. is *he'd dig up* (e.g. *his grannie*) *just to steal...*

A further series, applied mainly to the ease of a proposed dishonest action, runs 'it's (or it'll be) as easy as' *stealing* (or *taking*) *pennies from a blind man*, and ...*candy* (or *sweets*) *from a child*.

D.B. Gardner of Preston supplies a fine Anglo-Irish example, heard on the RTE programme 'Sunday Miscellany', 16 Oct. 1977, for a thoroughly fiendish daredevil: *he'd steal the grace out of the Hail Mary!* (P.B.)

steam. See: forty pounds; I wouldn't give; leave the sea.

steel helmet. See: get your steel.

steer. See: like a steer.

step(s). See: can't sleep; I stepped; mind the s.; there's shit.

step outside and say that! Otherwise phrased, **them's fightin(g) words.** 'Literally, a threat of violence if "that" is repeated, but now more often jocular' (R.C., 1978): US: since early C20. P.B.: some joc. use in UK also, via the influence of 'the movies' and TV, esp. Westerns.

step-mother. See: colder than.

step right up, ladies and gentlemen... See **go away, boy,...**

Steve. See: come on, S.; got me, S.; I get you; send her down.

stew. See: come on, stew; buck 'em.

steward. See: don't crack.

[**stewed, screwed and tattooed** – or sometimes **screwed, stewed and tattooed.** 'Strictly soldier – sailor lingo of the kind heard in dockside saloons the world over' (W.J.B., 1975): US: Cf the Brit. **bitched, buggered and bewildered (and far from home).** But Mr Burke implies – and I rather agree with him – that *stew...* is hardly a true c.p.

A.B. adds, 1978, 'This must be a naval term concerning what happens to a sailor on shore leave (in the orig. use, anyway). In current use, although rare; it is akin to your [Brit.] **fucked and far from home'.**

P.B.: the *bitched* version is a parody of the popular song from the musical show *Kismet*: 'Bewitched, Bothered and Bewildered'.]

stick. See: better than a dig; go stick; has more; if I lose; oompah; putty; speak softly; that's my story; they think.

stick a broom up my arse. See **if I stick...**

stick around, fellers, maybe I'll use yer! 'Mae West's notable scripted line to extras who wanted to play in one of her films; said by that lady from her motion picture *persona*' (L.A., 1974): US: (post-1932, when she went to Hollywood). A *double-entendre* that rapidly became a c.p.

stick it, Jerry! An army c.p. of *c.* 1914–18: and not necessarily nor probably in allusion to *Jerry*, a Ger. soldier: in the *Daily Express* of 6 Nov. 1939, there is an 'item' pointing out that Lew Like, a Cockney comedian, originated a sketch, 'The Bloomsbury Burglars', featuring Nobbler and Jerry; as Nobbler, Lew Luke would, as they hurled missiles at off-stage policemen, shout to his partner, 'Stick it, Jerry!'.

stick it up your jumper! See **oompah, oompah...**

sticks like shit to a blanket (– he). This earthy c.p. is applied to someone you can't get rid of: 'local [i.e., Oldham, Lancashire] expression for generations; heard also in Sydney, Australia, in the 1960s.' It is, in fact, a frequent expression throughout UK and the Commonwealth. P.B.: the phrase is applied as often to any viscous, clinging stuff, 'gunge', and is sometimes expressed *it clings like...*

stiff upper lip. See **carry on, Jeeves!**

still (occ. **all**) **alive and kissing – she's.** 'Used of a sexy girl'

(Petch, 1974): since *c.* 1950. A pun on *all alive and kicking*, orig. the street cry of a fishmonger.

still all in one piece. 'Used when someone has been in an accident and yet has sustained little, or no great, harm: since *c.* 1919' (Petch, 1974).

still going strong, like Johnnie Walker. A c.p. taken from the famous advertisement of a very famous whisky, it was recorded by Collinson, 1927. Nigel Rees, in *Slogans*, 1982: 'In 1908, Sir Alexander Walker decided to incorporate a portrait of his grandfather in the film's advertising. Tom Browne, a commercial artist [well known at the time for his theatrical portrait sketches], was commissioned to draw the founder as he might have appeared in 1820. Lord Stevenson, a colleague of Sir Alexander's, scribbled the phrase "Johnnie Walker, Born 1820 – Still Going Strong" alongside the artist's sketch of a striding, cheerful Regency figure. [The slogan, and a stylised version of the sketch have] been in use ever since'. Often in the form *like Johnnie Walker, still going strong*; both are an elab. of *to be going strong*, to be vigorous, to be (very) prosperous. It may sometimes appear allusively, as in Prof. Randolph Quirk's chapter on 'Dictionaries', in his *Style and Communication in the English Language*, 1983: 'English lexicography knocks Johnnie Walker into a tricuspidal fedora. Over four hundred years, and going stronger than ever'. (P.B.)

still he is not happy! Applied to one whom nothing satisfies and nothing pleases: *c.* 1870–5. Ware, following the *Daily Telegraph* article of 28 July 1894, attributes its popularity to a phrase uttered more than once, in a Gaiety Theatre burlesque in 1870.

still running, like Charley's Aunt is a C20 c.p. applied to plays and then also to films, implying a long 'life'; occasioned by the continuing popularity of that evergreen farce, *Charley's Aunt*. The c.p., however, has been comparatively little heard since *c.* 1960. See **where the nuts came from.**

stink. See: he's a fine; it stinks; they think.

stinking Yarra! An insult hurled by Sydneyites at Melbournites: C20. The retort is **our 'Arbour!**, q.v. The allusion is to the myth that the Yarra is the only river that flows upside down – it is very muddy! Neither phrase has been very much used since the 1950s.

Cf **too thick to drink...**

stinks on ice (– **he**)! 'Intensive of "He stinks!". He would be rotten even under refrigeration: US: from 1920s(?). Now extinct' (R.C., 1978).

stir. See: never stir.

stir it up! – often accompanied by a mime of someone stirring a huge cauldron – is a third party's remark upon, and fomenting of, a quarrel either already in progress or clearly brewing: since *c.* 1955. (L.A.)

Contrast the US use of *let's get stirring* ('Let's get moving!') or, as an imperative, *get stirring* ('Get moving!'), noted by A.B., 1979, as having been current since the 1930s at latest. But are they c.pp.? I doubt it.

stirring her tea with the other hand. See **'You're a long time coming'...**

stockbroker. See: as the Windmill.

Stockholm tar. See: every hair.

stockings. See: his stockings; tie up.

stole. See: who ate; you are a thief.

stomach. See: midshipmen; my stomach; officers have; your eyes.

stone(s). See: easy over; put a stone; will she.

stood. See: I should have; must have s.

stoop. See: swallowed; you can always.

stop See: face would; full stop; I won't take; meeting; that will stop.

stop it, Horace! Dating since *c.* 1930, this, as one of my most valued correspondents puts it, is 'shouted in a squeaky, semi-lisping, high-pitched voice after any refined-looking "delicate" young man: it does not mean Stop anything' – prob. it derives from a George Robey 'gag'.

stop it! I like it! Mostly directed at giggling teenage girls pretending, neither very long nor very convincingly, that they dislike their boy friends' caresses: since *c.* 1920 or maybe a decade or two earlier. Cf Harry Lauder's famous song, 'Stop your tickling, Jock!'

stop laughing! Stop complaining! An Aus. irony, dating since *c.* 1930, it is recorded by Baker; and it occurs in Jon Cleary's *Back of Sunset,* 1959.

Neile Lovett, in the *National Times* (Australia) of 23–28 Jan. 1978, comments, 'It would have been pleasing to see some reference to Stan Cross's famous "For Gorsake, stop laughing, this is serious",. P.B: with the ironic use, cf the Brit. sarcasm 'What are *you* laughing about?', and the address 'Similar', to any extremely gloomy-looking person.

stop me and buy one! belongs to 1934–9 and sprang from the very well known slogan used by Wall's Ice Cream. Contrast **buy me and stop one!**

stop me if you've (or **you have**) **heard it** (or **this one**) is the usu. mock-considerate, certainly imminent, inveterate funny-storyteller's stock preamble: since the 1920s. If you try, it's at your own risk; if you succeed, you lose a friend.

In Noël Coward's *Star Quality,* 1951 one of the short stories is titled 'Stop Me If You've Heard It' and it contains this trenchant comment:

'Stop Me If You've Heard It.' That idiotic insincere phrase – that false, unconvincing opening gambit – as though people ever had the courage to stop anyone however many times they've heard it.

The sad, little story ends, '"I've got something to tell you," she said. "Stop me if you've heard it."'

stop messing about! (– **no, no,** or **come on.**). 'Kenneth Williams in his nudging voice. The phrase started when he was a supporting actor in *Hancock's Half Hour.* Later the title of a radio series in which he starred' (*VIBS*).

stop-out. See: you're a dirty.

stop rocking the boat! See **sit down, you're rocking...**

stop that dancing up there! is said by 'someone pretending to hear noises in his head, to be crazy' (Ashley, 1984): US.

stop the world, I want to get off. 'I'm tired of life' – intended serio-ironically, not in genuine despair. As a c.p., only since 1962. From the title of an Anthony Newley stage-show. An article in *Punch,* 13 Oct. 1976, was titled 'Stop the Miss World, She Wants to Get Off' – in ref., naturally, to the beauty competition. (Thanks to P.B., 1976.) As Noble has put it, 'This was too evocative a play title to be neglected as a catchphrase; it had a vogue from the early 1960s and until the early 1970s; nor is it yet obsolete. The musical play was by Anthony Newely and Leslie Bricusse, and Newley took part in it, 1961–62. There was a New York production, 1962–63'.

stop yer tickling, Jock! is a C20, non-aristocratic Brit. c.p., current in and since 1904, but little heard after *c.* 1945. From Harry Lauder's song thus titled – pub'd in that year – written by Lauder himself in collaboration with F. Folloy; technically, perhaps Lauder's cleverest and most exacting song. Cf **stop it! I like it!**

stopped the show – he or **she.** 'Not a negative, but praise for a biliant actor. Generally theatrical or cinema – since the 1920s, I suppose' (A.B., 1979). Prob. at first, US; then, by late 1930s, UK, Can., Aus., elsewhere. It may have been prompted by the older, more widely known, (he, she) *stole the show,* which is not a c.p.

store. See: who's minding; your store.

storm in Channel, Continent isolated. The Channel being the English, the Continent Europe: satirical of British insularity during the years when Britain dominated the seas, and the *Raj* still existed: late 1940s; by 1955, rarely used except derisively. (Based on a L.A. note, 1976.) P.B.: also in form *fog in...*; alleged to have been seen as newspaper headline or placard.

story. See: big production; but that's another; do you know any; every picture; full stop; have you any; have you heard any; like the s.; oild; tell me the old; that's a different; that's my s.; what's your s.

story of my life! – (that's) the. A rueful, usu. resigned c.p. applied by the speaker to any of life's small setbacks, disappointments, half-expected failures, with a spark of humour not entirely quenched by pessimism: later C20. See quot'n at **low man...** (P.B.)

stout. See: as your are s.; collapse; and:

stout as a miller's waistcoat, that takes a thief by the neck every day (– **as**). This C18–early C19 c.p. glosses the proverb, *many a miller, many a thief,* and that other about a miller, a tailor, a weaver, in a bag. Apperson.

stove. See: here am I.

straight. See: is my hat; legs grew; so crooked; and:

straight as my leg: and that's crooked at knee (– **as**). In S, pub'd 1738 but concerned mainly with the language of Queen Anne's reign (1702–14), we find in the first conversation this exchange:

LADY ANSW[ERALL]: But, Mr *Neverout,* I wonder why such a handsome strait [*sic*] young Gentleman as you, does not get some rich Widow.

LORD SP[ARKISH]: Strait! ay, strait as my Leg, and that's crooked at Knee.

NEV[EROUT]: Faith, Madam, if it rain'd rich Widows, none of them would fall upon me...

The phrase was prob. current well into C19 and may therefore have prompted the late C19–20 synon., (*as*) *straight as a dog's hind leg,* as B.G.T. reminds me, 1978. P.B.: for a modern use of Neverout's formula, cf **if it was raining...**

straighten up and fly right! Orig. Marine Corps, since the early 1940s, and then Air Force, this US c.p. means 'Snap out of it – and get on the ball!'; hence, 'Act like a *true* Marine, or a *real* airman!' Synon. with **shape up or ship out,** q.v. (Moe, 1974.)

Basically an elab. of the coll. *straighten up* (both transitive and intransitive), to reform.

There is, however, another aspect: Eric Townley tells me, 1978, that 'There are two jazz blues recordings, *Fly Right, Baby* by Lonnie Johnson, recorded Feb. 1943, and *Straighten Up and Fly Right* by Tiny Bradshaw, recorded 1944. He thinks that the c.p. is Negro is origin and altered through misunderstanding by white Americans, the former meaning 'Behave correctly and honestly and live according to acceptable social standards'.

strain. See: don't s.; he'd drink; and:

strain the greens. See **I'm going to do...**

strand. See: cheap and nasty.

stranger(s). See: I'll tell nobody; I'm a s.; quite a s.; smile when; that's fighting.

strategic advance to the rear. See **according to plan.**

straw's cheaper! has, since *c.* 1920, been current among S. African children, but apparently ob. since *c.* 1960. A rejoinder to the exclamatory address *hey*! (Keith Sutton, in the *Eastern Province Herald,* Dec. 1977.) Cf **hay is for horses!,** and 'eh!' to me..., q.v.

strawberry. See: don't do that.

street. See: dogs are barking it; farther down; house devil; it's right; York.

streetcar. See: women are like.

streets paved with coppers. 'A modern idea of London': since *c.* 1960. An allusion to Dick Whittington's rapidly dispelled belief that London's streets were paved with gold. There is also a pun on *coppers* = policemen. P.B.: the pun is the main point. Cf the late 1970s expression for extensive police presence, *wall-to-wall fuzz.*

strength. See: give me strength; what's the s.

stretch. See: you break.

strictly for the birds. See: **that's for the birds.**

strife. See: more strife.

strike. See: I'll strike; it didn't s.; phantom.

strike a blow (for freedom), often prec. by **let's,** means 'We had better start work *or* make a move from our resting place': heard by Jack Slater in NSW and the Northern Territory, Australia, in 1957–69.

strike on my box. See: it didn't strike...

strike, or give me the bill! Mind what you're doing!: *c.* 1660–1750. From an injunction to a man clumsy with this ancient military weapon, used later by the constabulary. Apperson.

string. See: all done with mirrors; are you pulling; funny as a piece; how do you sell; how long is; I've got a bit; long as; books like a bag; ought to be.

stringer. See: 'nay, nay!.

stroke(s). See: different strokes; hot and; how strong; ooh, an'; still going; what's the s.

strong back and a weak mind – it takes a. A 'capsule description of a job requiring more brawn than brain; also, sometimes of a person peculiarly suited for such a job. General US, from 1930s or earlier, although now relatively uncommon – as are the jobs referred to' (R.C., 1978). A version of this occurs in a popular song of the early 1950s, of which the chorus was 'You load sixteen ton, and what do you get? Another day older and deeper in debt!': it was *strong in the arm and weak in the head*, which has also a Brit. N. Country ring to it. (P.B.)

strong, silent man (or **type – a** or **the**). Orig. a cliché of fiction, esp. among women novelists, e.g. Ethel M. Dell and Gertrude Page, it became, in the early 1920s, a mostly sarcastic c.p. By 1960 slightly – and by 1976, very – ob. P.B.: except in derision – perhaps from the realisation among more intelligent woman that such men can be, after all, pretty dull to live with.

stronger elastic. See: you should use.

stuck. See: wind changes.

stuck in. See: get stuck.

stuff. See: it's all eleven; that's the s.; where did you get that s.

stuff is here and it's really mellow – the. Among US 'pop' musicians and their devotees: this c.p. is glossed by Berrey, 1942, as 'likening "swing" to fine whiskey'; current, *c.* 1935–50 (*very* approx.)

'I have a record, "The Stuff Is Here and It's Mellow". The title has nothing to do with "swing" or "whiskey". It means "the marijuana is here and it's of excellent quality. It would not be understood by most white Americans' (Eric Townley, 1978). Well, that really sets me straight!

'stung' is right. See: yes, 'stung'...

stunt. See: one star.

stupid. See: how s.; so s.; very interesting; you were born.

stutter. See: you tell 'em, kid.

style. See: spends.

subject. See: let's have some light; and:

subject normal! refers to smutty talk or esp. to its resumption: Armed Forces, since *c.* 1939; by 1944 or 1945, it had become gen. 'The lowest common denominator' – a mathematical term used derivatively for 'what is understood or accepted by the most people' – has also been called 'the one safe subject'.

sublime. See: from the s.

succeed. See: if at first.

such a dawg! was, in the theatrical circles of 1888–*c.* 1914, applied to a tremendous 'masher', as the knowledgeable Ware noted in 1909.

such a reason my goose pissed (or ...**pissed my goose**). This was, in latish C18–earlyish C19, the standard retort made to one who, as an excuse, gives some absurd or extremely feeble reason. (Grose, 1796.) Geese don't piss.

such is life without a wife! has developed from the world-old, world-wide, world-weary truism, 'Such is life', as an elab. and as a c.p. of late (?mid) C19–20. The addition, bearing little relation to the facts, has generated a serio-cynical rider, **and a thousand times worse with one**, current among those who believe not merely that you can't win 'em all but that you can't win, 'period'.

such (perhaps rather more often **these**) **things happen** (or. more

usu. **will happen**) **in the best regulated families.** See: **it happens**...

suck. See: if at first; it sucks; that sure; thousand; you're full.

suck it and sea! This derisive retort, current in the 1890s, apparently went underground for almost a generation, to be revived, *c.* 1945–60, by Australian children – and by English children in the late 1930s and until *c.* 1950. It arose from the habit of sucking sweets, esp. those as hard as a bullet or, at the least, as a rock.

R.S., 1977, adds: 'It did not go to ground completely. In Hampshire *c.* 1913–20 it was known to me as the answer to a conundrum' – which, for racial reasons, can hardly be repeated here.

sucked that out of his (or **her**) **fingers – he** (or **she**) **hasn't.** That's not *his* idea *or* He hasn't thought of *that* all by himself; in a rather different nuance, He has mysterious – *or* closely-guarded – authentic information: mostly Londoners' and esp. Cockneys': late C19–20. I haven't heard it since *c.* 1950, but that's not to say that it doesn't linger on.

Cf the US he (*must have*) *sucked that out of his thumb*, which R.C., 1977, explains as 'The information in question is a product of imagination, not investigation. From the 1950s'.

sucker. See: never give; your pump.

sucking (on) the hind tit. It applies to anyone 'getting the most unfavourable draw, especially in horse-racing..., obviously rural [in orig. and] springing, I suspect, from pig-farming' (Skehan, 1977). In UK and Ireland; mostly Anglo-Irish: C20.

In Can. usage, *on* is omitted, and in US *the* also. Gen. sense: 'He's coming in late or in last place, or in arrears'. A.B., 1978, adds, 'This is a very common Southern US phrase. Andrew Lytle wrote a book of literary essays entitled *The Hind Tit*'.

Sudanese, Siamese, Breadancheese, Standatease. 'General round-up of all "the lesser breeds without the law"; our brown brothers' (P.B., 1974): mostly army: since latish 1940s. Cf **R.C.s, Parsees**...

sudden. See: this is so.

sue me! 'There's nothing I can do about it (i.e., even under the law's compulsion). Orig. (*c.* 1930) chiefly New York City, but from 1950s some general US use, propelled by the song of that title sung by "Nathan Detroit" in the musical comedy, later film, *Guys and Dolls*, one of Frank Loesser's masterpieces' (R.C., 1978). See also **so sue me!**

suffered. See: ee, if ever; when (name); who suffers.

sugar. See: aw, shucks; if you don't want;

sugar boat. See: captured.

suit. See: I like your company; I'd rather sleep; what s.

Sullivan. See: hop and; warm.

summer name. See: what is your.

sun. See: hard on; lights; put where the s.; thinks the s.

sun's scorching your eyeballs out! See **rise and shine.**

sunbathing, in, e.g. 'What do you think you're doing? Sunbathing?', an NCOs' traditional hyperbole hurled at a man on parade with a button undone, in recalled by Ashley, 1983, from his RCAF days in the 1950s. Cf **rise and shine.**

sunbeam. See: Jesus wants.

Sunday. See: fit as; hay, lass; and:

Sunday, *bloody* **Sunday!** has, prob. since the 1880s or 1890s, so much been the cry of those stranded in a strange city or even in their own, therefore including all such as have no true home of their own, that it became a c.p. during the 1960s. The c.p. was not produced by the play and film of that title. The c.p. afforded the playwright a wonderful title. Cf the Fr. *sombre Dimanche* (Paul Janssen, 1978).

Sunday saints and Monday devils indicts those who, pious on Sunday, go to church but who are thorough bastards the rest of the week. Jack Slater, of Oldham, Lancashire, describes it, 1978, as a local expression current for generations; but for generations current throughout England. I possess no early citation, but I feel reasonably sure that it covers most of C19–20. Cf **shore saints**...

sunlight. See: don't worry.

sunset. See: red sails.

sun-tan. See: I didn't think.

sup it out of a sweaty dog – he'd or **she'd.** This was, *c.* 1880–1940, a Lancashire c.p., applied to a drunkard. It occurs in Robert Roberts, *A Ragged Schooling*, concerning the first two decades of C20. Cf **tap the admiral.**

sup Simon: good broth! Dialogue II of S, 1738, has:
COL[ONEL].: O, my Lord, this is my sick Dish (the small quantity I eat when I'm feeling unwell): when I am well, I have a Bigger.
MISS: [*To Colonel.*] Sup *Simon*: good Broth.
An ironic c.p., current throughout C17–19, although in C19 mainly rural. Apperson.

supper. See: soldier's s.

sur le telephoneo! 'Said by Jimmy Young, who established himself as a radio personality, first by chatting to housewives on the phone, second by taking his show on a tour of European capitals to mark Britain's entry into the EEC, hence **sur le continong**' (*VIBS*).

sure. See: that's for s.; you sure.

sure as thou livest, then ... you live. A c.p. of assurance and esp. of reassurance: late C19–mid C17. Thomas Middleton, *The Merry Devil of Edmonton*, 1608, at I, i:
Nay, as sure as thou liv'st, the villainous Vicar is abroad at the chase this dark night.
This one I missed; I owe it to Col. Moe.

sure I'm sure! has, since not later than 1930s, been the US c.p. reply to 'Are you sure?' Cf:

sure thing! Surely, *or* Certainly, in reply to either a direct question or an implied doubt: US (late C19–20), adopted in UK by 1910 at latest. Cf the prec. entry and **that's for sure.**

surface. See: save the s.

surprise me! All right! Surprise me – show how intelligent, how original, you are! Both US, orig. (I think), and Brit. by adoption: respectively since late 1940s and middle 1950s. A Brit. example comes in John Mortimer's scathingly witty *Conference*, pub'd 1960, in *Sketches from One to Another*, written by John Mortimer, N. F. Simpson, Harold Pinter. The neurotic US tycoon is interviewing Jones, who can't get a word in edgeways (or in any other way), and finally interrupts himself on the telephone to speak to Jones: 'Carry on, Jones. Surprise me!'
Cf **astonish me!**

surprise! surprise! Either 'Here's a tremendous surprise for you', or, the surprised one speaking, 'Well! *What* a surprise!' Dating, I think, from the 1950s. Several examples: Noël Coward uses it in 'Me and the Girls', one of the stories comprising *Pretty Polly and Other Stories*, 1964. Dick Francis, in *Forfeit*, 1968, has:
'Try?' she said tentatively...
'Surprise, surprise.' It sounded more flippant than I felt.
'I thought it might be you,' she said.
Also US, as in Edward Albee, *The American Dream*, 1961, near the end of the play, when Grandma says (to the audience), 'Shhhhhh! I want to watch this. [*The young man is framed in the doorway.*]' And Mrs Barkar, the slightly sinister caller, says, 'Surprise! Surprise! Here we are!'
And as in Hillary Waugh, *Finish Me Off*, 1970: 'He sorted through the girl's items and found the injection paraphernalia in the kit. "A junkie," he said. "Surprise, surprise."' And also in Michael S. Lewin, *Ask the Right Question*, 1971:
'Oh,' she said... 'Can I help you with anything else?'
'Yeah. A little information.'
'Surprise, surprise.'
By 1971, both in UK and the Commonwealth and in US, the c.p. had become so embedded in coll. usage that it was occ. shortened to *surprise!*, as in John Godey's magnificent US novel, *The Taking of Pelham One Two Three* (1973), which ends with the sole survivor of the four 'talkers' of a New York underground train jumping off a fire escape into

the arms of a waiting detective: '"Surprise," Haskins said with a nice touch of irony.'
Of this c.p., one of the best and most widely used since *c.* 1950, P.B. has, 1975, penetratingly written:
[A] c.p., occasionally as a genuine expression of astonishment and pleasure, but more often sarcastically and in disappointment; the expected worst has come to pass.
Wife, who did't want to go out anyway: 'I'm awfully sorry, darling, but I've got this splitting headache.'
Husband, who has seen it coming [and] who very much wanted to go out, might respond in a deadened, unsympathetic and disenchanted tone: 'Surprise, surprise!'
'In a US television show entitled *Gomer Pyle* (a US Marine Corps Private), the actor, Jim Nabors, constantly used this expression' (A.B., 1979).

surprised? you could have fucked (in polite company, **kissed**) **me through my oilskins** was current among undergraduates at the University of Oxford during the 1930s and then with a wide acceptance; slightly ob. by *c.* 1950 – rather more so by 1965 – yet still, in 1975, extant. A valued and frequent contributor glossed it thus in 1972: 'Meaning – if it means anything much – that the speaker is *not* surprised.' Anthony Burgess, in *TLS*, 26 Aug. 1977, comments that 'it clearly has an earlier Naval origin', prob. since during WW1 or a little earlier.

Susan; Susie. See: go it, S.; say hey.

swallow. See: you say true; and:

[**swallow a sovereign and shit it in silver.** This C19–20 vulgarism lies on the borderline between a proverbial saying and a c.p. It indicates the very acme of convenience.]

swallowed a stake and cannot stoop – he (occ. **she**) **has** was, mid C17–mid C19, applied to an upright, stiff-mannered person. In C16–17 the form was *he has eaten a stake*. Apperson.

Swanee. See: down the S.

swaying with an old mess-mate; in full, I've been.... A RN (lower-deck) explanation of a boozy evening ashore: since *c.* 1860; by 1945, virtually†. F. Bowen, 1929.

swearing. See: forgive.

sweat. See: between a shit; don't sweat; horses s.; I wouldn't give; let 'ems.; let its.; no sweat; privates; shit, mother; sup it.

sweating like a nigger at an election predates WW2 and refers to the practice of taking Blacks to numerous polling places, for the purpose of 'stuffing' the ballot box – hence the fear of being found out: US: very approx., 1880–1930. (George Krzymowski of New Orleans, 1978.) Cf **vote early and often.**

Sweeney. See: tell it to S.

sweep. See: if I stick.

sweet. See: cop it; how s.; very tasty; you bet.

sweet repose.: See: goodnight, s.

sweetest. See: you say the nicest.

swell. See: does your nose.

swim. See: duck, silent, and:

swim out, you are over your head! was a US c.p. of the 1870s. *DAm*, 1877, quotes, from *Burton's Events of 1875–76*, by H.G. Richmond's verses about 'flash sayings' that 'now-a-days are the rage, –/They're heard in the parlor, the street, on the stage, –/"You're too fresh" and "Swim out, you are over your head"', but does not gloss this saying, which sounds, to me anyway, like an early example of the 'sick' joke – a callous, a fiendishly insensitive, a macabre, joke or witticism.

swine. See: you dirty rotten.

swing. See: I'll swing; saw; you're swinging; you've got a swinging.

swing it, baby! 'Usually said by a man observing the movement of a woman's hips while she's walking away from him' (A.B., 1979): US: since *c.* 1960.

swing it till Monday! – the motto of the Torpedo School, HMS Vernon – 'really meant "switch on and chance it"' (Rear-Adm. P.W. Brock, 1973): late C19–early 20.

swing that lamp, Jack! is, in the RN (lower-deck), addressed to a 'line-shooter' (or teller of tall stories) and a hint that he is showing very bad form: since *c*.1942. (Granville in PGR).

P.B. tells me that the saying has – since 1950, at latest – spread to all the fighting Services, and that *Jack* is often omitted. It is 'addressed by one listener to the rest of the company, as in "Oh, Lor', swing the lamp! Old George is starting one of his wories", as George tells of his military experiences. Another c.p. used in this situation is "Grab your steel helmets!" – less often, "tin hats" in these days. A *wory* blends war story'. Cf **get your steel...**

swingin'! See ONE-WORD CATCHPHRASES.

switched. See: well, I'll be be.

swoppin' sure for 'appen, exchanging 'certain' for 'perhaps'; 'forgoing certainty for a chance, from domestic affairs to political propositions. West Riding' (Noble, 1974): West Riding of Yorkshire: since *c*.1930.

Sydney or the bush! – it will be (or **it's**) (**either**). A momentous choice or a final decision: Aus.: late C19–20. Edward Shann, *An Economic History of Australia*, 1930 has, ' "Sydney or the bush!" cries the Australian when he gambles against odds.' Cf the US **that's strictly bush.** I.e., either the bright lights and luxury of city life, or roughing it in the wilderness hinterland.

synagogue. See: pork chop.

'SYDNEY FAD EXPRESSIONS' is W & F's classification (and condemnation) of the more trivial and transient of c.pp. In 1960, they listed seven (all US, naturally): **coming, Mother!; Hey Abbott!; hi ho Silver; I dood it; say hey!; what's up, Doc?; you're a good one!** (See the individual entries.) Such triviality and transitoriness are much less frequent than is generally supposed.

systems. See: all s.; you can't beat.

T

T.A.B.U.; N.A.B.U.; S.A.B.U.; also **T.A.R.F.U.** and **T.C.C.F.U.** Of these, the first four soon came to be written, and pronounced, 'solid' – that is, *Tabu, Nabu, Sabu, Tarfu,* with the *u* pronounced *oo*.

Respectively, a *typical army* balls-*up*: a *non*-adjustable balls-*up*; a *self* adjustable balls-*up*, where balls-*up* = confusion, 'mess': army, mostly officers', esp. in North Africa: 1940–5. *TARFU* is that state of confusion in which '*things are really fucked-up* (politely, *fouled-up*)'; *TCCFU* is a '*typical Coastal Command fuck-up*' and was employed in the RAF, esp. in Coastal Command itself, 1941–4.

Cf **snafu.**

T.G. – representing 'Thank God!' – is applied to cutlery and crockery left unused at table and therefore not needing to be washed up. What's more, the articles themselves become *T.G.s.* Domestic: since *c.*1940. (David Short, 1978.) Seemingly prompted by the next. P.B.: cf the Aus. use of *sunbeams* for the same thing (*DSUE*).

T.G.I.F. 'Thank God it's Friday!': perhaps orig. among teachers in primary and secondary schools, C20, but by *c.*1950, at latest, it had been taken over by all Monday – Friday workers. Common also in US (R.C., sometimes in the form *T.G.F.* (J.W.C.). P.B.: there arose in the Services, *c.*1960, a similar expression, *P.O.E.T.S.,* or *poets,* standing for 'push (or, vulgarly, piss) off early, tomorrow's Saturday', used by all those excusing themselves for skimping the Friday afternoon stint. (With thanks to P.J. Emrys Jones.)

A.B., 1979, adds another: 'My friend Richard French (sadly deceased) used to have a job with our [US] Navy Department. For some reason his week's work ended on Thursdays; so, when he wrote to me, he would abbreviate "Sure happy it's Thursday" – *S.H.I.T.*!' E.P. commented, '*S.H.I.T.* never became a c.p. – but that's how many c.p. originate.'

T.S. See **tough shit.**

T.T.F.N. See **ta-ta for now.**

T.V. See: **you're getting TV.**

ta. See: **say 'ta'!**

ta-ta for now! A c.p. form of 'Good-bye for the present!' – often 'initialled' to *T.T.F.N.*: esp. during the 1940s, it was instituted and popularized by the radio programme, 'ITMA': see TOMMY HANDLEY CATCH PHRASES. In Frank Worsley's *Itma,* 1948, we read that Dorothy Summers first appeared in ITMA on 10 Oct. 1940 and rapidly became famous in her role of Mrs Mopp and that, by mid-1943, 'Mrs Mopp's entrances and exits had become standardized. As she was going she bellowed *"T.T.F.N."'*

As the years went by, and the series continued in popularity, Tommy started to respond to *T.T.F.N.* with ever longer sets of initials, e.g. the exchange:

MRS MOPP: T.T.F.N.
HANDLEY: N.C.A.W.W.A.S.B.E.

MRS M.: What's that?
HANDLEY: Never clean a window with a soft boiled egg!

tab. See: **ain't coming.**

tablets. See: **keep taking.**

tack. See: **go sit; run up a; that, Bill.**

tact. See: **that, Bill.**

tace is Latin for a candle. Be quiet *or* stop talking!: mid C17–mid C19, then only among a diminishing number of scholars. In Thomas Shadwell, *The Virtuoso,* 1679, we find, at I, i:

LONG[VIL]: A Wit! 'faith, he might as well have call'd thee a Dromedary.
SIR SAM[UEL HEARTY]: Peace, I say; *Tace* is Latin for a Candle.

It occurs in Swift, Fielding, Grose (1788), Scott; then in dialect. (Apperson.) The pun is double; *tace* in L. = be silent; a candle is snuffed out or otherwise extinguished. Cf **brandy is Latin for a goose.**

TAD DORGAN'S CATCH PHRASES Thomas Aloysius Dorgan ('Tad'), born 1877 in San Francisco, became famous as a satirical cartoonist and, later, sports commentrator, first on the San Francisco *Bulletin* (1892–1902) and then on the New York *Journal* (1902 onwards). To the *New York Times* Magazine of 23 April 1978, that brilliant American humorist Sidney Joseph Perelman (b. 1904) who, in 1924, began his career on the old *Judge* weekly, contributed an entertaining, witty, affectionate memoir on 'Tad' as a man and as an artist and commentator, with particular attention to his single-term (ordinary slang) and his catch phrase innovations.

It was he who coined the phrases, 'Yes, we have no bananas', '23-skiddoo,' 'See what the boys in the back room will have,' 'Officer, call a cop,' and 'Let him up, he's all cut' [drunk]. Among the other apothegms he invented, still part of our common speech, were such daisies as 'The first hundred years are the hardest,' 'The only place you'll find sympathy is in the dictionary' and 'Half the world are squirrels and the other half are nuts.' [A pun on *squirrel,* a hoarder, and on *nut,* a crazy person, and *nuts,* crazy.] Tad evolved the catch phrase 'nobody home' to denote incomprehension, witlessness, or downright idiocy in those he was shafting. Dairly on the sidelines of his 'Indoor Sports,' there appeared one or another of his repertory figures uttering some fresh orchestration of the idiom, as, for instance, 'Nobody home but the telephone and that's in the hands of the receiver' or 'Nobody home but the oyster and that's in the stew' or 'Nobody home but the flatiron and that's got a pressing engagement.'

Mr Perelman also refers to the patterns *you tell 'em...,* as in 'You tell 'em, goldfish, you've been round the globe' and 'You tell 'em, corset, you've been around the girls', and *I'm the guy who...,* as in 'I'm the guy who put salt in the ocean', and 'I'm the guy who put pep in pepper'.

289

Nor should we omit this ultimatum: 'And no matter what innumerable scholiasts of humor contend, it was to him that we owe the immortal simile: "As busy as a one-armed paperhanger with the hives."'

To that article I owe the above-mentioned catch phrases with Mr Perelman's and the *New York Times*'s most generous permission.

tail(s). See: case of the t.; cats of nine; cross, I win; hasty; heads, I win; hear my tale; I need that; I'm skinning; keep your head; kiss my arse; long-tailed; my arse is; she goes; there's no point; up your t.; what a t.; who put; wrapped; and:

tail of my shirt looks like a french-polisher's apron: all brown (–the). As a correspondent has phrased it, this c.p. is 'a would-be kicked pleasantry at the expense of a comrade': RN: since *c.* 1930. The imputation is one of sycophancy.

tail will catch the chin-cough (–his). This mid C17–18 c.p. is applied to one who is sitting on wet ground. Ray, 1678.

tailor. See: she wobbles.

'tain't no big thing indicates 'insignificance' of a certain object or event' (*The Third Ear*): Afro-American: since *c.* 1960.

take. See: do you take; don't t.; it takes; read me; she would t.; that takes; what do you t.; you can t.; you can't t.

take a bow! Congratulations!: US: since *c.* 1925; by 1975, ob. (Berrey.) As if before a theatre audience calling 'Author! Author!'

take a carrot! A low, insulting c.p.: *c.* 1860–1940 (Hotten 1874). Orig. said to women and scabrously intended: cf **have a banana**, at first innocent, but soon, among the raffish, obscene. Cf the old Fr. *et ta soeur, aime-t-elle les radis?* By *c.* 1880, it also, among men and without sexual innuendo, signified 'I don't care!' by 1940, †. Baumann

take a dagger and drown yourself! was, *c.* 1880–1910, a theatrical retort. From the old coll. phrase, meaning 'to say one thing and mean another'. Cf **stab yourself and pass the bottle!**

take a load off your feet. Often prec. by **sit down and...** Make yourself comfortable. 'From (?) 1920s; now somewhat obsolescent. Both American and British' (R.C., 1978). See **sit down...**

take a red hot potato! was, *c.* 1840–60, a way of saying 'Be quiet!'–esp., 'Be silent!' (Duncombe, *Sinks of London*, 1848.) A very hot potato in the mouth is an effectual deterrent against talk, notably against loquacity.

take a running jump at yourself! (– **go and**), which E.P. noted in the first ed. of this book as 'not strictly a c.p.', is clearly in the same family as the Can. phrase supplied by Leechman, 1969, *take a running fuck at the moon!* – he dates it to the 1930s.

A more recent version, which I first heard in the early 1970s, and later found in print in Robert Prest's fine account of how he became a fighter pilot, *F4 Phantom*, 1979 is *take a running fuck at a rolling doughnut*. But this is not so much a dismissal, being usu. used as a description of something requiring appropriate ability and an exact sense of timing: Prest applies it to a fighter re-fuelling from an airborne tanker. (P.B.)

take all you want: take two! A US c.p., dating from at least as early as 1945 and applied to a qualified generosity. 'Originally, I am pretty sure, Yiddish – but used by Jews themselves in self-mockery – not anti-Semitic' (J.W.C., 1975).

take care! (or **take good care!**) This 'is now the fashionable last word on saying good-bye' (Leechman, 1974): Can.: arising late in 1973 or very early in 1974. Cf the English **mind how you go!**, and **have a good day**, which it sometimes precedes.

take eight! You've won, *or* I give in: a C20 military c.p. (F&G.) From points gained in some game or other.

But in Suffolk, since *c.* 1945, it has been addressed to someone breaking wind. Again: why precisely?

[**take five!** See **take ten!**]

take good care! See **take care!**

take his name and number! – with **Sergeant** often added. 'This

had a vogue as a popular catch phrase after the First World War' (Petch, 1966): say 1919–25. Humorously nostalgic. Cf **stand by your beds!**, and:

take his name, Sergeant-Major, take his name. An army c.p. of C20, but not very gen. before WW1. From the army order, issued by an officer, in precisely those words.

take in your washing! A nautical, esp. a RN, c.p. 'order to a careless boat's crew to bring fenders, rope's end, etc., inboard' (Bowen): late C19–20; by 1960, ob.

take it and shove it! See **shove it!**

take it away! Take the fellow away, he bores me with his nonsense: US, mostly students': 1920s (McKnight.) P.B.: the phrase was very popular in radio variety and comedy shows of the 1940s and early 50s, as an invitation to, or by, the band-leader to start the next piece of music.

[**take it easy.** See **take it slow!**]

take it from here! Let's begin at this point and ignore what's been said or done or is past: since *c.* 1955. P.B.: There was, in the late 1940s–early 1950s, a very popular BBC radio comedy series thus named, starring Jimmy Edwards, Dick Bentley, and Joy Nichols. It was written by Frank Muir and Denis Norden. I have always felt that the phrase could also mean, 'This is where to get your enjoyment, your inspiration, even!' Cf:

take it from me. See **you can take it from me.**

take it off your back! Don't worry about it!: RN (lowerdeck): C20. 'Borrowed from dock lumpers' (Granville, 1962) – i.e. stevedores working at a fish dock.

take it out of that! Fight away!: Londoners': *c.* 1815–60. JB adds: 'Accompanied by showing the elbow, and patting it.'

take me to your leader! is a world-wide c.p. used by the *little green men* – mysterious beings alleged, since *c.* 1950, to have been seen emerging from flying saucers: since the late 1950s. From comic cartoons about Martians landing on Earth and from Science Fiction. the linguistic lineage seems to have been: USA–Can.–UK–Aus. and NZ.

(Frank Shaw; B.P.; Leechman; and conversation.)

June Drummond's novel, *Farewell Party*, 1971, has:

'Come too,' I said.

'And the host will clap hands when he see me?'

'He won't mind...'

'Take me to your leader,' said Dave.

Wedgewood, 1977, tells me he is convinced that 'this is a much older reference that "little green men of *c.* 1950", and that *take me to your leader* has been adapted for this purpose from older story-cliché of exploring derring-do, meeting primitives, lost tribes, or whatever, and addressing first contacts thus'. I entirely agree; the c.p. may go back as far as 1860.

take me with you! In Beaumont and Fletcher's *The Noble Gentleman*, written not later than 1616, although not pub'd until 1640, at III, i, we see:

SHATTILLION: ...Which we will likewise slip. [I.e., omit.]

DUKE: But take me with you.

It had already occurred in Thomas Middleton's *A Trick to Catch the Old One*, 1606, as Col. Moe has informed me. Meaning 'Please explain in detail', belongs to the very approx. period, late C16–mid C.17.

P.B.: cf the later C20 expression of (still polite) puzzlement: 'Er... sorry! I'm not quite with you...?' = 'What the devil are you talking about?'

take more water with it! imputes clumsiness or incompetence or tipsiness, but mostly either of the first two as caused by the third: late C19–20. Orig. and esp. a joc. c.p. addressed to a sober person happening to sway or to stumble. Cf **put more water...**

take off. See: he'll take off; that takes.

[**take ten!** like **take five!** – meaning 'Take a rest of ten, or five, minutes' – is clearly not a c.p. but an ordinary colloquialism.]

take that and see how you like it. Put that in your pipe and smoke it! Think that over: apparently US rapidly become also Brit.: C20. Berrey.

take that fire-poker out of your spine and the (or **those**) **lazy-tongs out of your fish-hooks** (hands)! A nautical adjuration to rid oneself of laziness: late C19–early C20.

take the marbles out of your mouth! Speak more distinctly: an uncultured c.p. of late C19–C20.

take to the hills! A c.p. applied to more or less trivial alarms – or even to stir them up: since c. 1955. (P.B.)

take two. See: be content.

take yer 'at orf in the 'ouse of God... cunt! 'An army c.p., often attributed apocryphally to the fiercest RSM one has known. It is muttered *sotto voce* and then, after a slight pause, comes the viciously explosive epithet. Heard, of course, at church parade, but "for fun", anywhere. I first heard it in 1953.' (P.B., 1975).

take your change out of that! A C19 c.p. accompanying a blow, a neat retort, a crisply decisive act. Cf **pick the bones...**

take (or **pull**) **your finger out!** Get a move on! Get busy! Orig. (c. 1930) RAF, *as take...*; adopted in either 1941 or 1942 by the army, where often *pull* was preferred. Officers' deliberately pompous variants: *dedigitate* and, among RAF officers, *remove the digit*. An alternative, since c. 1944, is *get your finger out!* A further RAF var., WW2 and until 1950, was *he's got his finger wedged*. Granville has noted the RN var. *take your fingers out.* (EP, *RAF Slang*, 1945; PGR.)

P.B.: E.P. had written, for the first ed., that the semantics were, 'Stop scratching your backside and get on which the job'. While the book was still being proof-read, I wrote to him that 'many low-minded types understand that the removal of the male digit applies to a rather different locality, and on the female'. My suggestion was confirmed: in E.P.'s notes for this 2nd ed. appears: 'Kingsley Amis, almost as good a critic as he is a poet, novelist and scholar, says that the phrase contains no reference to backside-scratching. "The full reading is *take your finger out and get stuck in* and has to do with a courting couple." (I hope that I don't truly need to add that I agree with him.)

'In 1941, No. 23 Intruder Squadron, R.A.F. (offensive night fighters), then based at Ford in Sussex, had a colour facsimile of Leonardo's *St John the Baptist* prominently displayed, and much appreciated (because he *had* take it out) in the squadron intelligence briefing room' (R.S., 1977).

The phrase gained a much wider and late popularity by Prince Philip's use of it in a speech, 17 Oct. 1961, referring to British industry, his words being 'It is about time we pulled our fingers out!' (Wedgewood, 1977).

See also **extract the manual digit.**

take your pipe! Take it easy – have a rest!: among North Country miners and labourers: C20. 'Take your pipe out of your pocket and have a smoke.'

take your washing in, Ma: here comes the (whatever unit it may be). 'On the line of march, greetings were usually exchanged by meeting regiments' (B&P): military: late C19–20. No animosity felt and no malice intended.

A civilian var., prob. late C19–20, is ... *here come the gypsies* (with the Race Relations Board's permission); actively extant in 1977, but prob. 'threatened with in-built obsolescence'.

taken up a lot of slack. See **he's not tight.**

takes the rag off the bush – it or **that.** A US c.p. synon. with **that takes the cake**, q.v. Poss. of Texan orig., it seems to have arisen c. 1880 or, at latest, 1890. It occurs in a short story by O. Henry (d. 1910), *A Little Local Color*, and seems to have enjoyed a minor vogue c. 1895–1910. (Shapiro, 1977.) But the phrase travelled, for Leechman cites the Victoria, BC, *Daily Colonist*, 11 Sep. 1977: 'His teacher is well known for her bizarre judgements, but this one takes thr rag off the bush'. My own guess, admittedly a wild one, is that the phrase orig. in a competition forming part of rural festivities, as did *that takes the cake.*

P.B.: but cf **rag on every bush**, and the placing of pieces of cloth or paper on trees and bushes, as votive offerings, in primitive societies.

tale. See: hear my t.; tell that for.

talk(ing). See: all talk; are you talking; I'm speaking; it's the beer; listen; money talks; no back; now she's; now you're t.; that's fighting; ve haf; when you're t.; you talk; and:

talk a glass eye to sleep – he would (or **he'd**). A pithy and picturesque Aus. c.p., applied to a bore, esp. a monologuist, since c. 1960. Jim Ramsay, *Cop It Sweet*, 1977.

talk about laugh! I, we, etc., really did laugh heartily! Belonging to the popular speech current throughout C20 and prob. since c. 1860 or so, this is a non-cultured c.p., as can readily be perceived from the following piece of Services vernacular cited by a valued correspondent: 'Y'should've seen ol' Dodger; got half his pubes [i.e., pubic hairs] caught up in his [fly] zip. Talk about a laugh!'

A var. of this, 'current among RAF personnel at the time of the Suez crisis [1956] was "I nearly drank (or bought) my own beer!"' (Dr David Bridgeman-Sutton, 1978). Current among all the fighting Services since late 1940s, but not much heard since c. 1975. P.B.: this elab. is applied to astonishment as much as to amusement.

talk to me! is a US negroes' c.p. of the 1920s–1940s. 'When a jazzman is really communicating through his music, people often cry out "Talk to me!" Or they might say "He's saying something!"' (CM).

talking. See: talk.

talking of oars... See **how's your sister?**

talking to me or chewing a brick? See **are you talking...**

talking to the butcher, not to the block. A var. of **speaking to...**, q.v. at **I'm speaking....**

talks a good game – he. '"He talks very knowledgeably about [the subject] – but *can* he really do it?" (In the case of a woman, more often "*Will* she do it?")' (R.C., 1977): US: since c. 1950.

talks like a book with no leaves (i.e. pages) **in it(– he** or **she**). 'An old expression used in reference to a person full of empty talk' (Petch, 1976): mostly lower-middle class and public house: since c. 1920. Cf **you talk like a half penny book.**

tall. See: you must be a good; you'd have be.

tall, dark and handsome, only when used derisively and ironically, since (perhaps) c. 1910: both British and US: from cheap romantic fiction, where the hero was so often described thus. J.W.C., 1975, notes that its formation resembles that of **fair, fat and forty.** Cf **strong, silent man.**

tall weed in the grass, bud! was, in the 1930s, an intimation to a fellow convict that a 'stool pigeon' was within earshot: at San Quentin. Gladys Duffy, *Warden's Wife*, 1959.

taller they are, the farther they fall – the. See **bigger they are....**

tambourine. See: keep the t.

tango. See: it takes two.

tank. See: clank, clank, I'm; tiger; your mother wears.

tanner. See: he'd skin.

tantrum. See: like a snob's

tap run dry? (or **tap-water run out?**) A showmen's c.p., addressed to a quack doctor either unoccupied or idling while his fairground fellow workers are busy: since c. 1880. There is an implication that most of his medicines consist of (coloured) water. See Neil Bell, *Crocus* [quack doctor], 1936, for one example of this usage.

Of its US usage, A.B., 1979, wrote, 'I've heard it, with variations, as *has the well run dry?* or *has the pond dried up?* Meaning "Is money all gone?" or, in oratory, "Has he finished talking?" or "Can't he think of anything else to say?" Both these American forms are very old: C19–20, at latest'.

tap the admiral – he would (or **he'd**). He would do anything for a drink of strong liquor: RN: mid C19–early C20. According to Bowen, 'From the old naval myth that when Lord Nelson's body was being brought home, seamen contrived to get at the rum in which it was preserved.'

Cf **sup it out...**

tar. See: written.

tart shop. See: dragged.
tarted up. See: all dressed.
Tarzan. See: me T.
taste. See: I need a piss.
tasteful. See: that was not.
tasteless. See: life gets.
tasty. See: very t.
tata for now! See ta-ta for now.
tats and all! An underworld and fringe-of-the-underworld c.p. of *c.* 1780–1850. (Vaux.) It expresses incredulity at another's statement or, at the end of one's own, a contradiction of what has preceded the phrase, *Tats*, rags, small pieces of material; implication, 'worthless'.
taught. See: who told you.
tavern bitch has bit him in the head – the. He's drunk: late C16–mid C17. (Thomas Middleton, *A Trick to Catch the Old Ones* 1608; Apperson.) If ever you study the popular prints of C17–early C19, you'll notice how often a dog figures in the tavern scenes.
taw. See: I'll be one.
tax-collector. See: I'm keeping.
taxidermist. See: go and see.
tea. See: coffee; given away; it must have; just my; Polly; sailing for; some day; what's for; what's the got; you're a long; you're selling.
teacher. See: please, t.; this is the way; yes, t.
team. See: he's whole; one of your.
teapot. See: it's a bugger.
tear. See: don't tear; I'll tear; what does it matter.
tearing up the pea-patch – he's (or **they're**). He is, or they are, ruining the game or contest or competition; hence, 'going on a rampage' (W & F) – applied orig. to baseball: US: *c.* 1945–55, then decreasingly, although still heard at least as late as 1969. The expression was popularized by Walter Barber 'in his *c.* 1956–*c.* 1955 broadcast of the old Brooklyn Dodgers baseball games' (W & F).

Thanks to the generosity of my old and learned friend, W.J. ('Jerry') Burke, I am able to amplify. In a letter, 1969, he writes:

Sportscaster Walter 'Red' Barber began his Major League baseball broadcasting in Cincinnati, Ohio, in 1934. He was from the South, and most Southern boys lard their speech with homely colloquial phrases. Black-eyed peas are a favourite Southern dish, and almost everyone has a pea patch. If a stray dog or cow broke through the fence and got into one of these pea patches, a great deal of damage was done. One might hear such an expression as 'That critter is tearing up the pea patch!' It is an old expression down South and 'Red' Barber didn't create it. He popularized it. In describing a 'rhubarb' (baseball slang for a fight among players of opposing teams...) Barber would exclaim, 'They're tearing up the pea patch!' His listeners got the picture right away.

tedious. See: life gets.
teeth. See: all tits; I need a piss; it's staring; my back; old as; somebody's; with t.; and:
teeth like stars. Applied to false teeth – 'they come out at night'; ironic use of the cliché compliment: US: C20 (Ashley, 1983.)
telegram from arsehole: 'shit expected' is a var. of the theme expressed by **it's a poor arse that never rejoices**: raffish: since *c.* 1910.
telephoneo. See: sur le t.
tell(ing). See: are you asking; are you trying; catch 'em young; class will t.; do tell; does Macy's; don't tell; every picture; I am here; I guess; I hope to t.; I told; I'll tell; I'm telling; just tell; let me t.; no, don't t.; no tell; now he; now I'll; now you t.; so my mother; so they; they don't t.; you tell; you'll be telling; you're telling; your best friend; and:
tell a green man! Please bring me up to date, *or* Put me wise!: among US jazz players and jazz devotees: since *c.* 1950. (W & F.) Here, *green man* may, rather vaguely, refer to the

slang sense, 'a piece of paper money'.

'Also *tell it to the saxophone player*! Why that particular instrument, I don't know, unless it is because the sax-players are in the front row of a jazz band and they can easily take requests from the audience' (A.B., 1979).

But the c.p. also synonymizes **tell that to the (Horse–) Marines!**

P.B.: the *green* here is more prob. that of youthful ignorance: cf **not so green...** Perhaps even, in this context, a *greenhorn*, a novice.
tell 'em what I did to Colin Bell. 'Said on being congratulated for performing some feat.... Colin Bell was a boxing champion, killed, I believe, during WW1. The phrase was used by the music-hall comedian Harry Weldon, possibly before that war. Weldon used to appear in boxing gear on the stage, looking rather frail. When threatened by a large bruiser, he used to try to impress by appealing to his trainer, "Tell 'em what I did to Colin Bell". Usually when the bruiser had taken the hint and disappeared, Harry Weldon would add, "But don't tell 'em what Colin Bell did to me" ' (Jack Eva, 1978).

Vernon Noble has since informed me that Colin Bell was an Australian; he was heavily defeated by Bombardier Wells on 30 June 1914. 'Weldon coined the gag *remember what I did to Colin Bell*, taken up by the public and used in early part of WW1 and then lost.'
tell it like it is! Tell it naturally without the slightest elaboration of style or withholding, or manipulation, of the truth: US, orig. among negroes. CM (a negro author), 1970, inevitably includes it, but in this instance I find the explanation given by 'Whitey' the more valuable. In 1968, J.W.C. wrote to me thus:

Hardly older than 1960, but very common now. Originally used by negro agitators with reference to giving what they regard as the real facts about the negro situation. Now generally used with regard to any situation in which it is supposed that the real facts have been suppressed: 'Let's be honest and factual' (as people have not commonly been hitherto.)

A year later, Fain classified it as 'a hippies' c.p.' It reached Aus. early in the 1970s. B.P., 1975, wrote, 'Our gutter press assures us that they "tell it like it is".'

A valuable allusive example occurs in Ross Macdonald's *The Goodbye Look*, 1969: 'The question made her unhappy.... You want me to tell it like it is, like the kids say?" ' – which rather suggests that the c.p. had reached the juvenile public by (say) 1967.

The expression expectably corresponds to a human situation. In Irvin S. Cobb's *The Escape of Mr Trimm*, 1913, a poorly educated young woman says, ' "I'm goin' to tell you the whole story, jest like it was," she went on in her flat drone.'

On 21 Sep. 1977, a *Sunday Times* headliner contained the statement, 'State industry must tell it like it is' – which shows that the c.p. had become fully accepted in the UK. (Playfair.)
tell it not in Gath – when its meaning was, in late C19–early C20, being debased to 'Fancy *you* doing that!' or 'Fancy you doing *that*!' – a c.p., drawn from the cliché, itself drawn from the *Bible* (2 Samuel, i, 20).
tell it to Sweeney received from HLM, Supp. 2, a contemptuous inclusion among 'the numerous catch-phrases that have little if any precise meaning but simply delight the moron by letting him know that he knows the latest'. Berrey, 1942, had included it in a long list of slangy and c.p. synonyms of 'I don't believe it!' W & F, 1960, date it from '*c.* 1920; now archaic' and gloss it as = 'Go tell it to Sweeney. He may believe you. I don't.' But it's older than 1920. In *The Pedagogical Seminary*, March 1912, A.H. Melville mentions it in his article 'An Investigation of the Function and Use of Slang' as being current among teenagers. The evidence tends to show that Mencken erred in dismissing the phrase so

lightly. Perhaps orig. a tribute to Irish eloquence and powers of improvisation. The British form was *tell that to Sweeney*: c. 1922–39.

W.J.B. adds that it served as the title of John Chapman's book, subtitled *The Informed History of the New York Daily News*, 1961.

tell it to the Marines! See: **tell that to the Horse-Marines!**

tell me about me (or **myself**) (–now). Now gen. before 1945, it is a counting c.p., reassuringly joc., although it may have started off as a fatuously serious request.

tell me another! Tell me another story – I simply can't believe *that* one! *or* You don't (*or* you can't) expect me to credit *that*: C20. (W.L. George, *The Making of an Englishman*, 1914.)

It passed to US; Berry, 1942, records it as 'I don't believe it!' Yet it had been used much earlier by Alfred Sutro in his comedy, *Rude Min and Christine*, 1915 (but clearly written before the outbreak of WW1 on 4 August 1914), near the end:

CLAUGHTON: ...I say, Minnie and I are going to get married.
GEORGE: [*Laughing.*] Go on! Tell me another!

tell me news! (– that's ancient history). A retort upon an old story or a stale jest: C18–early 20. (S.) Cf:

tell me something I don't know! I've known that for ages: both Brit. and US: since late C19; ob. by later C20 (R.C., 1979.) An earlier form, perhaps since late C19, in *tell something new*! Lyell.

tell me the old, old story! comes from No. 681 in *The Church of England Hymnary*, although the c.p. is also very popular among Nonconformists; often heard at, e.g., political meetings, where hecklers favour it; apparently since late C19. Among soldiers in the ranks, during WW1 (from late 1915, onwards), 'all rumours of good times to come and promises from authority would be met by the singing of the first line of a Nonconformist hymn – Tell Me the Old, Old Story' (John Brophy, in B & P).

Frank Shaw, 1969, curtly glossed the saying, thus: 'He's going to lie again. From hymn.'

In Scene ii of John Mortimer's witty comedy, *What Shall We Tell Caroline?*, performed and pub'd in 1958, the following occurs:

TONY: ...But it's gone too far, you know – we should never have started it.
ARTHUR: Of course you shouldn't. Now there's a twinge of conscience.
TONY: You know as much as I do. There's never been a breath of anything amiss.
ARTHUR: (*singing bitterly*): 'Tell me the old, story...'

tell that for a tale, often shortened to **that for a tale!** I don't believe that – it's too far-fetched altogether: an expression of utter incredulity: the former, c. 1870–1940; the latter, C20.

tell that to a one-legged man so he can bump it off down the road denotes, among American Negroes, 'utter disbelief and scorn for the statement or story' (*The Third Ear*, 1971): since c. 1950.

tell that to Sweeney! See **tell it to Sweeney!**

tell that to the Horse-Marines!; but predominantly **tell that to the Marines.** Don't be silly – do you think I'm a fool? *or* I don't believe it – someone else may: C19–20. John Davis *The Post Captain*, 1806, has '*tell that to the Marines*'; in 1830, Moncrieff used the longer form – † by c. 1900. An early var. was that employed by Byron in 1823: *that will do for the Marines, but the sailors won't believe it.* It was, in the form *tell it to the Marines*, very early adopted in the US. Sailors always did rather make fun of the credulity of the Marines.

But the c.p. has become so enmeshed with naval and nautical folklore that it deserves, for interest, an article apart. The space cannot be spared here, but see Col. Moe's references to several specifically American connotations in his article in *American Speech*, Dec. 1961. Cf:

tell that to the morons is a hecklers' c.p., current since c. 1950.

Obviously a pun on **tell that to the marines** (see the prec. entry).

tell the world. See **I'll tell the cockeyed world.**

tell us something new. See **tell me something...**

tell you what. See **I'll tell you what.**

tell your mother ninepence!, sometimes prec. by a palliative **oh**. This c.p. expresses unwillingness to reply helpfully to a question requiring some thought, as in 'What a question! Tell your mother ninepence': mostly lower-middle and lower class: since c. 1912. Franklyn, 1968, opined that it arose soon after Davin Lloyd George introduced National Insurance 1911, with employees paying fourpence, and employers fivepence, a week: the masses were already realizing that Lloyd George was a 'fast talker'.

tell your mother she wants you! See **go home and tell...**

tell your troubles to a policeman! was a cynical US c.p. of c. 1919–29. HLM, 1922 edn.

telling – that would be (or **that's**); also **that's tellings!** A reply to a question one does not, or should not, answer; since c. 1830. The *OED* cites Captain Marryat, 1837: ' "Where is this...and when?" "That's tellings"' replied the man.' Often, in Aus., shortened to *tellings*! or *tellin's!*, as in Edward Dyson's *The Gold Reef*, 1901.

The form *that would be telling* seems to be C20 US. P.B.: but since mid C20, at latest, has been as often used – in an irritatingly smug tone of voice (cf the children's taunt, occ. borrowed by adults, 'I know something *you* don't know!') – in UK.

telly. See: **can't have.**

ten. See: **five will; two upon.**

ten bob each way. See **get you!**

ten days that shook the world has been a fairly common c.p. ever since the American John Reed's book thus titled appeared in 1919. In its literal sense it obviously became a cliché: but in its frequently ironic or derisive, it is no less clearly a c.p. P.B.: the book is a eye-witness account of the Russian Revolution.

ten shillings. See: **dear mother, I.**

Ten Sixty Six and All That: 'One still hears this famous title in conversation' (Leechman, 1969): and even now in 1976, although decreasingly since the publication, in 1930, of W.C. Sellar and R.J. Yeatman, *1066 and All That*, an immensely popular comic 'potted' history of England. As a c.p., it lightly, yet rarely contemptuously, dismisses any event preceding the speaker's birth as unimportant – 'old hat' and all that – 'Queen Anne's dead!'.

ten up! is a stockbrokers' c.p., directed at a broker whose credit is either shaky or, at the least, suspect: since c. 1870. (B & L.) From the enforced deposit of 10 per cent obligatory in these conditions.

tenant. See: **better an empty.**

tend your own potatoes! See **mind....**

tennis, anyone? and **who's for tennis?** These alternative c.pp. open a conversation or a flirtation: perhaps mostly Can.: since c. 1950. But they come from the much older Brit. usage: in UK the c.p. goes back to c. 1910 and is 'the hall-mark of that so familiar species of English "social comedy" where there are French windows upstage centre' (R.S., 1967).

The orig. form of the laconic *tennis, anyone?* was the slightly more formal *who's for tennis?*; and both have served not only to initiate a conversation but also to comment, either ironically or enviously, upon the pastimes of the leisured (or the comparatively or apparently leisured) classes. It seems, indeed, to have arisen as a good-natured comment upon lawn tennis as an adjunct of tea-parties in the vicarage garden or at country-house weekends.

There has long existed the intermediate form, *anyone for tennis?* Jessica Mann, in her novel, *Mrs. Knox's Profession*, 1972, treats us to this illuminating example:

She had never seen a play where an actor sprang through French windows calling 'Anyone for tennis?' but she suddenly realised that this catchword, a shorthand joke to her for everything that was reactionary and moribund in England, represented something as real as a kitchen sink. In Orton, matinee land was still going strong.

And, with that sense of linguistic opportunism for which he was justly famous, Noël Coward, in the section 'Monday' or 'Me and the Girls' in *Pretty Polly Barlow and Other Stories*, 1964, shows us George Banks, actor, reminiscing thus: 'I had a bang at everything, Young Juveniles – "Anyone for tennis?" – old gentlemen, dope addicts, drunks.'

The c.p. passed to the US in the early or middle 1950s, so far as I have been able to ascertain. In the *New Yorker* of 20 Sep. 1969, there was a wonderful 'picture' of a playhouse, the stage illuminating a small group of men and women in the nude, with one of the men brandishing a racket and addressing the drawing-room *ensemble*, 'Tennis, anyone?'

'The phrase "Who's for tennis?" which was – still is – used to represent the drama of the 1920s, *nearly* appears in Maugham's *The Circle*. Robert Gittings tells me that it really does appear in a, '20s comedy' (Christopher Fry, 1976).

tennis shoes. See: little old ladies.

tent. See: camp; I'd rather have him; were you.

Tenth don't dance – the. An army officers' gibe at the 10th Hussars. It originated in 1823, when the officers, at a ball in Dublin and after long experience of London and Brighton society, declined to be introduced to the ladies on the unconvincing plea, 'The Tenth don't dance'. (F & G.) P.B.: the saying prob. lasted at least until the end of C19. Kipling uses it in his short story *The Brushwood Boy*, 1895: the hero's mother asks him, after his return from arduous service in India, 'But you have met hundreds [of girls] in society and at balls and so on', to which he, 'the youngest major in the British Army', replies, 'I'm like the Tenth, Mummy: I don't dance.' (The story is actually far more interesting than this small excerpt might indicate.)

term. See: first term.

term of endearment among sailors – (it's) a, is a palliative c.p., excusing the 'use of swear-word bugger. Unfair to the Navy, but sailors have had worse than that to bear; soldiers, airmen, and the French laugh it off too: *dirty bugger* is, however, meant to have a sting' (L.A., 1967): current since *c*. 1890: joc.

terra firma. See: good old England; more terra.

terribly Aquascutum of you – it's or **that's.** See **it's awfully...**

terrific. See: it sends.

Tessie. See: not on your tin-type.

Thames. See: you didn't.

thank God! See: Christmas; poorly; and:

thank God it's Friday! See **t.G.i.F.**

thank God we have (or **we've got) a navy!** A C20 c.p., muttered by the army when things were going very badly wrong; esp. during WW1. F & G remark: 'Said to have originated in a soldier's sarcastic comment when he saw a party of the old Volunteers marching by one Saturday night.' I suspect that it's far older. In his *Charles I*, 1933, Evan John suggested that it was orig. by Sir John Norris in the days of that monarch. In a letter, 1968, the late Col. Archie White says, 'I have seen examples of this disparagement of the Army as far back as the S. African War. I shouldn't be surprised if it were of Crimean origin....I think I have seen it in letters from the Crimea.'

Of its WW1 use, John Brophy writes, ' "Thank Gawd, we've got a navy!" It was always "Gawd", even with north-country troops to indicate the burlesque of the original sentiment. This phrase was called into use whenever the incompetence of authority became more manifest than usual.'

Of its WW2 use, L.A. writes, 1975:

'Army and RAF NCOs' outburst of dismay when, e.g., a recruits' squad blunders out of formation in foot-drill; NCOs' exclamation when an "unbelievable" mistake or omission has been made in work or duty.'

thank God we have (or **we've got) an army!** An ephemeral and ironical army c.p., used when it heard the first official news of the Battle of Jutland on 31 May 1916. Obviously prompted by – and deliberately reminiscent of – the prec.

[**thank heaven for little girls!** – a song sung by Maurice Chevalier in *Gigi* (1958), based on Colette's novel – has remained a popular quot'n and has, I believe, failed to achieve the status of c.p.]

thank you and good night! R.S., 1975, writes: must surely come from the BBC Radio appeal programme 'The Week's Good Cause' (8.25 p.m. on Sundays) which ran for many years. It ended every appeal (except when rash innovators said: 'Good night and thank you for listening'); and as the majority of listeners' withers remained unwrung, is tantamount to 'Thank you for nothing' among the cynical.

thank you for nothing! I owe you no thanks for *that!*: C20. Shaw, 1969, cites the var. *thanks for nothing!*, which he glosses thus: 'Ironic thanks for an unexpected rebuff or rejection or disservice, often preceded by "well" ': since *c*. 1910.

thank you for sharing that with us is an urbanely ironic US comment on someone's 'sick' story or bawdy joke or unpleasant news: since *c*. 1960. (Levene, 1979.)

thank you for those few kind words! is a semi-ironic c.p., recorded earliest, I believe, in my *Slang Today and Yesterday*, 1933, but going back, within my own memory, to *c*. 1910, at latest. A good example occurs in Alistair Mair's *Where the East Wind Blows*, 1972:

'But the thing that wrapped it up was the stuff you gave me, especially the photographs. They were, if I may say so, bloody good.'

'Thank you for those few kind words,' I said. 'Nice to know I've been useful.'

This c.p. occurs also in plays. In H.M. Harwood's *The Old Folks at Home*, performed in 1933 and pub'd in 1934, I find, in the opening scene:

LIZA: ...Professor – don't you think I should make a very nice Viceroy's wife?

CHARLES: Well, if being ornamental is a qualification...

LIZA: Of course it is, especially with Orientals....And thank you for those few kind words.

J.W.C., 1977, notes that in US a very frequent form is 'thank you for *them* few kind words'. See also the var. **at for those few...**

thank you, Karl! See: MONTY PYTHON.

thank you, ma'am. See **wham bang...**

thank you, teacher! See **please, teacher!**

thank you very much – the *very* heavily emphasized, and the phrase often prec. by **well** – is, clearly, a c.p. only when it's ironic: C20. Philip Purser, *The Holy Father's Navy*, 1971, has:

'My own view was that it was – shall we say a little unambitious for a Colin Panton special?' That was the flashing candour bit.

'Well, thank you very much.'

R.C., 1978, notes that the US equivalent is *thanks a lot*, with 'lot' stressed.

thank your mother for the rabbit was brought to my notice by the late Frank Shaw in 1969, but without definition, date, *milieu*. I suspect that it belongs to the same class of c.p. as **don't tear it, lady!**, i.e. street vendors' humour; that it is Cockney; and that it arose late in C19.

thanking you! (pron. very genteely, *thenking yew*). After declaiming one of his 'odd odes', the comedian Cyril Fletcher would acknowledge applause by saying 'Thenking yew! Odd Ode number two comin' up', and would then launch into his next burst of doggerel: mid C20. Not to be confused with **Any thang yew!** (P.B.)

thanks. See: for this; for those; keep your t.

thanks, but 'No, thanks'! Prob. orig. more common in US than in UK and the Commonwealth: since *c*. 1955. 'A polite refusal, but often ironic – that is, the offer refused had been no favour' (R.C. 1978).

thanks for having me, with ironic emphasis on *having*, is the c.p. uttered by a boarder to the landlady of the seaside boarding-house where he has been holidaying: C20. A pun on *having*, boarding, and *having*, befooling, swindling.

thanks for nothing! See **thank you for nothing!**

thanks for saving my life; or alternatively **thanks! you've saved my life.** A joc. c.p., addressed to one who has just 'stood' a drink: since *c.* 1919. An example of mildly ironic exaggeration. The phrase, however, is often used of thanks for almost any minor hospitality or kindness.

Sometimes without the *thanks*, as in John Morgan's play, *The Judge*, 1967, in I, iii; Serena, having succeeded in begging a cigarette from a strange girl just arrived on the scene, exclaims: ' "Welcome child: you saved my life!" (Inhales deeply, coughs.)'

thanks for the buggy-ride! merely elaborates 'Thank you'; it is US in orig. (recorded by Berry, 1942): C20. It passed to Can.; Leechman glosses it as 'a c.p. expressing thanks for some small service; often ironical'. Cf prec. P.B.: in UK, still a sort of c.p., but most commonly used almost literally, as thanks for a lift in another's car; ob. in later C20.

thanks, I *needed* that! It's US currency has been largely caused by Don Adams's TV show *Get Smart*, late 1960–70s. (A.B., 1978.)

that accounts for the milk in the coconut, US var., **that explains....** That explains the puzzle or elucidates the mystery: US: mid C19–20. The *explains* form is recorded, 1912, by R.H. Thornton for 1853; James Maitland, 1891, 'When an explanation of something is given it is said "That explains the milk in the cocoa-nut" and it is sometimes added "But not the shaggy bark on the outside".'

This US c.p. passed, almost inevitably, to Canada. But it passed also – and very early – to UK, Hotten recording it in his 4th ed'n, 1870; so far as I've ascertained, it seems to have been current there *c.* 1860–1910.

'Also, *so that's how the jam got into the doughnut*, which must be a British native c.p., because American doughnuts don't have jam in them so far as I can remember' (Sanders, 1978). At a guess, since earlyish 1940s.

that adds up. See **it adds...**

that ain't hay. See **and that ain't hay.**

that ain't no lie. That's the literal – or the real – truth: US: *c.* 1880–1914. In the delectable George Ade's *Artie*, 1896, we read: ' "You know you've got me right, don't you? And I guess you have, too. That ain't no lie." '

that allows me plenty of scope. See **that gives me....**

that bangs Banagher. See **bangs Banagher....**

that beats... See **beats...**

that beats the Dutch. That beats everything! – It's incredible – or That's the limit!: late C18–20. The *Dutch* simply because Britons are so ready to recognize the worth of their opponents: and in the latter half of C17, the Dutch navy was extremely hard to beat: *to beat the Dutch*, to do something remarkable, is recorded for 1775.

It was early adopted in US. M. includes it and adds that the superlative is *that beats the Dutch and the Dutch beat the Devil*; and it had appeared two years earlier, in 1889, in Farmer.

that, Bill, is tack (or occ. and schoolmarmishly **tact**); often prec. by **and.** That C20 c.p., somewhat outmoded by 1970, reposes on the chestnut of the plumber explaining to his assistant that 'tack is when you find her ladyship in the bath and you get away quickly, saying "Beg pardon, my lord!" ' Var.: *and that what they call tact.*

that boy Jones again! The eruption, in Summer 1982, into the media of the case of the Buckingham Palace intruder prompted Richard Gilbertson, antiquarian bookseller in Cornwall, to send P.B. this extract from Charles Hindley, *The Life and Times of James Catnach*, 1878:
...innocent lunatics to force their way into Windsor

Castle, in each case around with nothing more deadly than a proposal of marriage:- notably the "Boy Jones", is respect of whom there was a street-saying much in vogue, of "That Boy Jones again", which was used to cover or account for all petty delinquencies in public or domestic life. The Boy Jones, like a Lord Byron before him, "awoke one morning and found himself famous."

that cut his water off. 'That stopped him from doing or enjoying what he was doing or saying' (Fain, 1977): US: since *c.* 1920.

that cuts no ice. That makes no difference or has no importance or doesn't impress or influence me: US: late C19–20; anglicized just before WW1. A Can. var., ? since *c.* 1910, is *that cuts no custard.* The American usage appears in, e.g., the witty S.R. Strait's 'Straight Talk' in the *Boston Globe c.* 1917, as W.J.B. tells me.

A US var. noted by R.C., 1978, is *that doesn't cut any ice with me*, still current although, as he points out, 'cutting ice (from ponds in winter) is a long-dead industry'. P.B.: this latter version is also fairly common is UK, and of course other names or pronouns may replace *me*: 'this feeble excuse cut no ice with the Governor'. And A.B. adds, ' "She (or he) don't cut no ice with me" was common amongst our Southern Negroes [in USA], I recall, from my childhood days, late 1930s–40s'.

that dame would make me a present of a parachute if she knew it wouldn't open. She hates me: US: 1920s. In Maurice Lincoln's *Oh! Definitely*, 1933, occurs (p. 216) this passage:
'...Sally happens to be fond of you.'
'Fond of me, indeed,' said Peter scathingly, 'Why, as they used to say in the States, that dame would make me a present of a parachute if she knew it wouldn't open'.

that devil nobody is applied to the culprit when, in an accident or an error, no one will admit culpability: C20. (Probably I'm wrong to suppose that originator of the c.p. was familiar with the C18 phrase *that devil Wilkes.*)

that doesn't cut it, does it? 'That's not the meat of the matter': US: current: prob. since *c.* 1970. In ref. to dull or blunt knives.

that explains the milk in the coconut. See **that accounts for....**

that figures. See **it adds up.**

that for a tale! See **tell that for a tale!**

that gets me! is recorded in HLM, 1922, as a 'picturesque' phrase. Meaning: 'That annoys me': recorded by the *DAE* for 1867; current in Britain *c.* 1919–39. P.B.: but still current, in UK, by allusion, in remarks like 'What gets *me* about it is the way she can so blatantly...'

A.B., 1979, Amplifies: 'Sometimes, *that really gets my goat!* [also Brit.] and [the later] *that really does piss me off.*, which is often truncated to *I'm really P.O.'d!*...I don't think the "got" one is largely current, but it isn't dead. Kin to *that's enough to piss-off the Pope!*'

that gives (occ. **allows**) **me plenty of scope** is the counter to **don't do anything I wouldn't.**

that grabs me in the right (or **the wrong**) **place** is the US dovetail to **how does that grab you?** The use of *right* or *wrong* 'depends on whether the response is positive or negative; *how does that grab you?* is not meant sexually, except in innuendo, and it means "How do you accept that?" ' (A.B., 1979).

that horse is troubled with corns, i.e., foundered: sporting world: C19 – early 20.

that is... See also the entries beginning **that's...**

that is (or **that's**) **me all over.** Just like me – to behave in such a way! A US c.p. of *c.* 1918–50. (Berrey.) It was launched by the publication, in 1918, of *Dere Mabie: Love Letters of a Rookie*, which sold 550 copies within a year.

that is (or **that's**) **the object of the exercise.** That's precisely why we're doing it! That's the general or, come to that, the specific idea behind it all: orig. army officers' in the 1930s and during WW1, but by the mid 1940s it had spread to civilians.

that job's jobbed. It's finished; it's all over: *c.* 1830–1960. The *OED* cites Marryat, 1840, 'That job's jobbed, as the saying is'. L.A. recalls it as having been used by his mother, born in the 1860s, and glosses it thus: 'Used when the job had called for more than usual enterprise and determination, and it was good to know that it was behind one, for whatever reason; or when it was a little personal triumph' (1971).

that kills it! That destroys my enthusiasm, interest, respect; that ruins it: US: since *c.* 1945. (W & F, 1960 'Now fairly common.')

that Kruschen feeling. An allusion to vigour and energy and verve: *c.* 1925–40. (Collinson.) From a famous advertisement put out by Kruschen Salts. Cf **I'm Kruschen...**

that makes the cheese more binding. See **to make the cheese...**

that makes two of us is addressed to someone who says that he doesn't understand what he has just heard or read: since *c.* 1940, or rather earlier.

that man wants burning! is a C20 Brit., esp. English, tramps' c.p. directed at anyone who has the audacity to disagree with one's own opinion.

that moan's soon made. That's a grief will soon be consoled; Scottish: since before 1885. Ware.

that must have been a butcher's horse by his carrying a calf so well was, mid C17 – mid C19, a c.p. jest made at the expense of an awkward rider. (Ray, 1678; Grose, 1788.) There's a double pun: *calf*, a dull, oafish young fellow, and the calves of the legs.

that rattled. See **that really rattled...**

that really does get (or **really gets**) **my goat** or **...pisses me off.** See **that gets me.**

that really rattled his cage. 'A friend of mine, from Florida, a psychologist, uses this expression when speaking either of an examination, or of a question, that shocked someone. "That upset him considerably" is a reasonable translation. I can't pin-point the date, but one hears this only rarely' (A.B., 1979).

P.B.: a few weeks before transcribing this note, 1983, I heard the taunt 'Who rattled *your* cage?' being directed at a young woman who had risen briskly – and predictably – to verbal provocation, in this instance to do with feminist attitudes, and A.B. confirms this version's fairly rare use in US, later C20.

Jan Sainsbury, the 1st ed. of this book, in the Sheffield *Morning Telegraph*, Sep. 1977, notes that *if I need you, I'll rattle the bars of your cage* was 'very popular in the dance halls of the [1950s] for getting rid of importunate partners', with which one might compare the equally unkind **who kicked** *your* **kennel?** and **who pulled** *your* **chain?**

Just within the same semantic family belongs the phrase noted by E.P. (and rejected by him as 'too brief to be worth recording, and too regional') *that rattled his furniture*, which he glossed as 'N. Country cricketing c.p.

that remains to be seen. See **as the monkey said.**

that rings a bell. See **does that ring...**

that schoolgirl complexion belongs to the approx. period 1923–39. From the inspired advertising poster of Palmolive Soap, as Collinson testified in 1927; the alert P.G. Wodehouse had mentioned the slogan in *Ukridge*, 1924; that slogan so captured the public fancy that it rapidly became also a c.p., among women and men alike.

that shook him; intensively, **that shook him rigid** or, less frequently, **rotten.** That astounded or greatly startled or perplexed or perturbed or baffled him: orig. WW2 Services', esp. the RAF; and then, by 1945, gen. (H & P.) Lit. caused him to shake with nerves.

P.B.: I recall a friend telling me of a sermon he had heard preached by an Army chaplain in the Suez Canal Zone to some British troops, *c.* 1950. Dealing with the flight of the Jews from Pharoah across the Red Sea, the padre described the Egyptian soldiers' reaction: 'They were shook (pause) RIGID!'

that shouldn't happen to a dog. shouldn't happen...

that sure made him suck air! That hurt him badly; also, that caused him to react violently or obviously, whether physical-

ly or mentally: Can: since *c.* 1960 or perhaps a decade earlier. Liet., it caused him to gasp. (Dr Robin Leech, Edmonton, 1978.)

that takes me off! is a theatrical c.p., expressing either defeat (as in an argument) or sheer incredulity. '"*That took me off* (the stage), I couldn't argue any longer." A reference to an exit line' (Granville). Brit. C20.

that takes the cake! Lit. 'That wins the prize', it came to mean 'Well, if that doesn't beat all!' – for, e.g., impudence, or wholly unexpected luck, good or bad, and simultaneously became a gen. US c.p. Of Negro origin, it arose thus: 'At a cake-walk, a cake was given as a surprise to the one who could "shout his stuff" the best' (Holt); this cake-walk was not, of course, the dance but the contest popular at rural out-door festivities. In 1891, M glosses the c.p. thus: 'Said of a tall fish story or of anything superlative'. From the negative evidence of its c.p. absence from *Am*, and from Farmer in 1889, I – perhaps rashly – deduce that it did not become an established c.p. until the late 1880s. On the other hand, it then passed very rapidly indeed to UK as early as 1895, the lively short-story writer, W. Pett Ridge, used in his *Minor Dialogues*, the derivative, allusive form *that takes it*.

P.B.: occ. variants are *well, that fairly takes the cake!*, used in indignant astonishment, and in the same mood, ...*biscuit!* Also, of course, the open-ended *well, if* that *doesn't take the cake!*

that takes the rag off the bush. See **takes the rag...**

that tears it and **that tore it.** See **that's torn it!**

that turned his water off. See **that cut his...**

that was about as successful, or **useful, as an open umbrella in an elevator.** See **went down like a lead balloon.**

that was interesting. See **what do you do for an encore?**

that was not very tasteful (i.e., that was in bad taste). On 21 April 1972, the *Australian Financial Review* reproduced a recent article pub'd in the *Wall Street Journal* and quoted Lily Tomlin's 'running gag', 'That was not very tasteful', on the Rowan and Martin 'Laugh-In' show. This 'gag' can, I think, be said to qualify as a US cultured c.p. of 1972 *plus*. (With thanks to B.P.) Cf **thank you for sharing...**

that was real money (, that was)! is applied to the old £. s. d. coinage: 1973 onwards. (Petch, 1974.) The UK currency 'went decimal' in Feb. 1971.

P.B.: the c.p. was ob. by 1980, at latest, even if the sentiment remains in the hearts of those who remember, for instance, 'a half o' bitter and a packet o' Woods for a tanner' (= a small drink of beer and five small 'Wild Woodbine' cigarettes, all for sixpence, or 2½p), or the cinema commissionaire's stentorian cry, 'Standing in the one and nines only' (= behind the seats costing approx. 9p).

Gerald Kaufmann, in *Listener*, 17 Feb. 1984, laments the dearth of nicknames for the decimal coins, as opposed to the wealth of names for the 'old money' – but familiar names for the 'real money' had decades, centuries, in which to develop. Only the egregious half penny, disappearing in 1985, attracted a soubriquet *daddler* or *tiddler* – too small, both in size and buying power, to be of much use except to advertisers.

that was the week, that was. (Occ., ...*the year*.) 'From the well-known TV programme [title], now a c.p. in ordinary use. Description of a week when everything went wrong' (Playfair, 1977): 1970s.

that went better in Wigan! A C20 Brit. theatrical c.p., 'A music-hall comedian's *sotto voce* remark when a gag fails to get over. Wigan is a music-hall joke that has become a national one in England, though why this Lancashire town should be so treated is not known' (Granville, 1952). Wigan, truly Lancastrian, is in fact rather charming.

Cf **comes from Wigan**, which helps to explain this ref.

that will... C.pp. beginning thus may also be found at **that'll...**

that will (or **that'll**) **be the day,** with emphasis on *that*, and with a decidedly ironic inflection; also the humorous var.,

that'll be the bloody day, boy! That's not very likely to happen:

since late 1917, or early 1918. After a longish interval, it passed, during the 1930s, to New Zealand – witness *NZS* ('Expressing mild doubt following some boast or claim') – and, at the same period, to Australia, as in Eleanor Dark, *Lantana Lane*, 1959; Mr Arthur Gray of NZ has expressed himself rather more emphatically than Mr Baker, thus: 'A fervent denial of a suggestion, or an expression of complete incredulity. E.g., "You could be elected captain of the team yourself." – "That will be the day."' And Mrs Hazel Franklin has reminded me that NZ usage offers the var., *that'll be the frosty Friday!* – which, if I remember correctly, dates from either 1915 or 1916. Deriving, I'd say, from army officers' 1915–18 *der Tag*, 'any much desired date or goal'; obviously satirical of Ger. *der Tag*, the day, historically 'the day when we Germans come into our own' – esp. 'the day we conquer Britain' (in WW1): cf the lively derision with which the ordinary soldier greeted Lissauer's *Song of Hate*, 'perpetrated (Aug. 1914) by one Lissauer' – as Weekley neatly and tartly put it.

Mr Dudley R.D. Ewes, formerly editor of the *Cape Times* tells me (17 Dec. 1968) that, in S. Africa, this c.p. has become so much a part of everyday speech that it's current also in Afrikaans as *dit sal die dag wees*. A S. African example of the c.p. occurs in James McClure, *The Gooseberry Fool*, 1974.

The phrase is still very much alive: it occurred also in, e.g., Noël Coward's *Relative Values*, prod. in 1951 and pub'd in 1952, and in Terence Rattigan's *Variations on a Theme*, 1958.

In UK, the c.p. has become so incorporated into the language that it can be employed allusively, as in Anthony Price, *The Alamut Ambush*, 1971: 'Roskill grinned at the incongruous idea of anyone outsmarting an alerted Shapiro. That, as old David was so fond of saying, would be the day!'

For a 'straight' example, cf this from C.P. Snow, *The Malcontents*, 1972:

'I thought you were going to cut the grass?' his wife said.

'I will,' he said, 'just let my lunch settle down... You don't want to give me indigestion, do you?'

'Indigestion,' she said, 'that'll be the day.'

Moreover, it seems to have reached the US during the 1930s and to have been thoroughly acclimatized by the early 1940s. In Tucker Coe's 'thriller', *Wax Apple*, copyright in 1970, we read:

Bob said, 'Maybe the person who did it will confess. He didn't really want to kill anybody, he just wanted to hurt people. Maybe this will shake him up, and he'll confess.'

'That'll be the day,' Karter said.

It occurs with complete naturalness and no sense of adoption in the American Charles Williams's novel, *Man on a Leash*, 1973.

'Popularity doubtless reinforced by the song "That'll be the Day" (Allison, Holly, Petty), 1957... Recorded by Buddy Holly and the Crickets. Since then, also recorded by a host of other singers or groups' (Janssen, 1978). It was also as *That'll...*, used as the title of a Brit. film, with a fairground story, 1973.

that will do nicely, sir! From a TV commercial: the grovelling acquiescence of an hotelier to the supposed power and status-symbolism of an American Express credit card. By 1984 the advertisement had begun to disgust and irritate enough people for them to start parodying the slogan and using it out of context, thus bringing it within the field of c.pp. And if the blatant sexuality and male-chauvinist-piggery of some of the phrases in this dictionary dismay you, what price the sheer immorality of the banker's invitation to 'Take the waiting out of wanting' by delivering yourself into the hands of usurers? (P.B., who, snobbishly, has managed so far to do without either TV or credit cards.)

that will stop him laughing in church. That will take the smile off his face – That'll fix him: since *c.* 1930. Cf the (?mainly Public School) boys' version: *that will teach him to fart in*

chapel or that'll stop their farting in chapel, 'That'll stop them from taking liberties.' All three: C20. The first is, I suspect, a euph. var. of the other two. (A combination of two contributions.)

that won't buy (the) baby a frock. See **this won't buy....**

that won't pay the old woman her ninepence, Ware (1909) tells us, was a Bow Street Police Court, London, c.p. condemning as evasive action: *c.* 1890–1914.

that won't wash! prob. dates from *c.* 1840, to judge by Charlotte Brontë's 'That willn't wash, miss' (1849), quoted by the *OED*. The semantic clue: 'As good fabrics and fast dyes stand the operation of washing' (F & H).

Noble, writing in 1975, says:

Originally indicated unreliability (as of a statement) but by latter part of C19 had taken on the meaning of something not up to standard, not durable, unconvincing. In a letter by Charles Kingsley, referring to Browning, he wrote deprecatingly, 'He won't wash'.

The predominant C20 senses are 'It won't work' and 'It won't stand up to examination.'

The phrase duly passed to the US. Berrey, 1942, records it, but A.B. notes that it was ob. by 1975.

that would be telling! See **tellings...!**

that wouldn't kill a brown dog! 'I first heard it used by Australian colleague of mine... in the context of an event not being too serious, or, he being a member of the boozy fraternity, anything less than a treble scotch: "Lord, THAT wouldn't kill a brown dog".' Thus the justly popular BBC Radio 2 broadcaster Ray Moore, in a letter to P.B., 1984, after being questioned on his own use of the phrase as comment on some uninspiring piece of pop-music. Mr Moore's many admirers are able to face the coming day the more cheerfully for having listened to what he calls 'my fevered ramblings at unearthly hours', and his use of this vivid idiom could help to turn it into a c.p. It has the feel of an Anglo-Irishism, or possibly, in view of the Aus. connection, the dog is brown in contradistinction to 'Yellow dog dingo'?

thataway. See **went thataway.**

that'll be the day! See **that will be...!**

that'll be the frosty Friday. See **that will be the day.**

that'll be the shot. See **shot – that'll be the.**

that'll grow (or put) hair (or more hair) on your chest; and that'll put lead in your pencil. That will render you potent *or* that will restore your virility: late C19–20. Both are applied to either food or liquor, the latter mostly to liquor; both are applicable at any time, but the latter esp. after illness or a sustained bout of lovemaking, even to a mere semblance of sexual fatigue; the former is used mostly by men, the latter by both sexes, among women not necessarily confined to what used to be called the lower-middle classes.

The first is mainly Aus. (Baker) and, as an invitation, or an encouragement to drink, it takes a shorter form, *more hair on your chest!* The second has been adopted in the US.

Cf **this will give you the cock-stand.**

that'll hold you! (– there,). J.W.C. provides two glosses for this phrase. The first is, 'That'll keep you going for the present, esp. in ref. to a drink, less often to a snack: American: since the late 1940s', and the second he defines as 'usually a rebuke or a retort – a "settler". Perhaps rather a perfectly normal and colloquial idiom than a c.p.: US: C20'. The second may well have given rise to the first.

that'll larn (or learn) you! The former is US, the latter Brit.: 'That'll teach you'!: late C19–20. Although in form solecistic or entirely illiterate, neither indicates illiteracy in the users, the phrase having always been joc., with occ. a genuinely monitory undertone. Since *c.* 1919, *larn* has, even in UK, predominated over *learn*.

A late example occurs in Len Deighton, *Yesterday's Spy*, 1975:

For a moment Ercole was taken aback. Then he roared, 'I hate you, I hate you,' and kissed Schlegel on the cheek.

'That'll learn you, Colonel,' I said softly.

In the US, the cinema, then radio, then TV have rendered the c.p. so general, so widespread, so popular, that it must rank very high in any hierarchy of c.pp. (A 'prompter' from A.B., 1979.) To a lesser degree, this is true also of the UK. P.B.: dialect rather than illiterate.

that'll pin your ears back! That'll be a real set-back for you!: since c. 1940: mostly in the Armed Forces. (L.A.)

that'll push (or **that's pushed**) **Rommel back another ten miles** was an army c.p. of 1941–42. Gerald Kersh, in *Slightly Oiled*, 1946, says: 'When in North Africa there was some extra bit of red tape or regimental procedure, we always used to say: "And that's pushed Rommel back another ten miles." Everybody said ... "That'll push Rommel back another ten miles".'

that'll put (more) hair on your chest, or ... **lead in your pencil.** See **that'll grow hair ....**

that'll put your back up! That'll make you amorous: since c. 1920. From cats fighting; cf informal Standard English *fighting-fit.*

that's a bad cough you have! See **you've a bad cough.**

that's a bit hot! That's unreasonable or unjust: an Aus. and NZ c.p.: since c. 1910.

that's a bit of all right. See **this is a bit ...**

[**that's a bit thick** (often prec. by **Oh, I say!**) in the UK counterpart of **that's a bit hot** and, in the sense of exorbitantly expensive, has synon. *that's a bit steep.* In the sense 'that's an unreasonable demand', there is also *that's a bit of a tall order.* (David Short, 1978.) But, after some thought, I've come to regard all these phrases as being, at best, borderlines.]

that's a bit under is an office girls' and shop girls' c.p., prompted by a *risqué* joke or remark: since c. 1950; by 1970, ob. 'Not infrequently the "under" is dropped in favour of a dipping action with the elbow' (Michael Gilderdale, 'A Glossary for Our Times' in the *News Chronicle*, 22 May 1958). P.B.: 'a bit of under', however, is a euph. for copulation.

that's a cough lozenge for him! He's been punished or 'paid out' or beaten: proletarian: c. 1850–90. From an advertisement for cough lozenges. Ware.

that's a different ballgame. See **that's another ballgame.**

that's a different story, and that's something else again, orig. US (Berrey, 1942, 'That's a different matter') and dating the former since c. 1900, and the latter since c. 1930, became also Brit., the former c. 1918 and the latter not until c. 1944.

that's a good one. See **that's a good 'un.**

that's a good one (or **that's one**) **on one!** 'That's a joke on me' (Berrey, 1942): since c. 1920.

that's a good question, often altered to **a very good question** or shortened to **a good question!** or simply **good question!** That's a sensible or shrewd or very pertinent question; often as a time-gainer when one's seeking for an answer to an extremely difficult question; indeed, it often implies 'That's a question *I* can't solve'; since the middle or late 1940s, but not very common before c. 1955. From radio and TV 'panels' and 'quizzes'.

J.W.C., 1977, notes that it is 'usually, in US, followed by the mendacious and dilatory stop-gap, "I'm (very) glad you asked it"'; and A.B., 1979, added, 'It occasionally evokes the response *that's a very poor answer*, commoner in US than in UK, but not very common anywhere. Since c. 1960'. See also **very good ...; good question** and cf **that's the sixtyfour thousand dollar question.**

that's a good 'un (or **one**). What a fib! Occ., 'That's an *excellent* story!': late C19–20. But the orig. sense was 'That's very witty' or 'That's an excellent joke': since c. 1660. It occurs in, e.g., William Wycherley's *The Country Wife*, performed in 1672 and pub'd in 1675, at III, ii, thus:

ALITHEA: I hate him because he is your enemy; and you ought to hate him too, for making love to [in the old sense of 'paying court to'] me, if you love me.

SPARKISH: That's a good one! I hate a man for loving you! If he did love you, 'tis but what he can't help; and 'tis your fault, not his, if he admires you.

It occurs again in Joseph Addison's comedy, *The Drummer; or, The Haunted House*, 1716, at I, i:

ABI[GAIL]: ... You first frightened yourselves, and then the neighbours.

GARD[NER]: Frightened! I scorn your words. Frightened, quotha!

ABI: What, you sot, are you grown pot-valiant!

GARD: Frightened with a drum! That's a good one!

And a final example: Joseph Ebsworth, in *The Rival Valets: A Farce*, performed in 1825, has, at I, i, this dialogue, where the 'smart Alec' valet, Frank, says to the well-meaning, rather clumsy, very unlucky valet, Anthony: 'Besides, my figure and appearance are so superior to your!' – to which Anthony indignantly replies: 'Come, damn it, that's a good one. You don't mean to say that you are more sightly than I am?'

that's a hell of a note! That's extremely and disagreeably surprising – extremely rude or impudent or insolent or insulting; 'What a plight or predicament!'; or, indeed, 'This is a very grave – even a disastrous – situation': US: since c. 1930. (Recorded by Berrey, 1942, and by W & F, 1960.) A (musical) note badly out of tune.

It spread, c. 1950, to Canada, where the predominant sense has been 'a grave situation' (Lechman), and, c. 1960, to UK, where, however, it has not firmly established itself – up to 1975, at least.

A.B., 1979, notes, 'Sometimes, for emphasis, "That's one hell of a note!" ... I'd date it 1930s [onwards]'.

that's a horse of another colour. See **horse of another colour.**

that's a joke, son (sometimes followed by **joke, that is**)! Used by the radio announcer and comedian Kenny Delman, in the Fred Allen show. He played the part of Senator Beauregard Claghorn (a caricature of the 'typical' Southern US politician), who lived in 'Allen's Alley'. The character appeared in Warner Brothers' cartoons as a loud-voiced rooster named Foghorn J. Leghorn. The radio show was broadcast in the 1940s; the phrase is still current, but fading out. (Based on a note from A.B., 1979.)

that's a laugh! That's ridiculous: since the 1920s. Berrey.

that's a load of old cobblers. That's utter nonsense: since the late 1950s. Often used by those who don't know that *cobblers* is rhyming slang, short for *cobbler's awls*, testicles.

It has, in all classes, been virtually superseded by *that's a load of old rubbish.* 'A Leyland worker, claiming to have been misled by the shop stewards, is reported as saying "That's a load of old rubbish, and they know it" (*The Times*, 17 Aug. 1977). Of course, he may have said something more obscure or more obscene, but the reporter used the familiar form' (Playfair, 1977).

that's a long-tailed bear. See **long-tailed bear.**

that's a promise! See **is that a promise?**

that's a real crock (of shit)! 'That's utter nonsense. Probably from the services, WW2, but general only since 1960s. Occasionally euphemised as "a crock of the well-known article"' (R.C., 1978).

that's a rhyme if you take it in time; also **he's (or you're) a poet but doesn't (or don't) know it.** (A form that fits all persons and numbers is **a poet but don't (or doesn't) know it.**) The former is directed at one who rhymes accidentally and the reply is *yes, I'm a poet and didn't ...*; the latter, in the *you're ...* form, elicits *yes, that's a rhyme ...*: mostly a lower-middle-class c.p.: since c. 1700. Cf *he's a poet,* directed – from c. 1850 until c. 1965 – at a long-haired male: and with this, cf *who robbed the barber?,* similarly directed, but dating since c. 1880 and not yet entirely †.

In the Dialogue I of S, 1738, we find:

NEV[EROUT]: Well, Miss, I'll think of this.

MISS: That's Rhyme, if you take it in Time.

NEV: What! I see you are a poet.

MISS: Yes, if I had but Wit to shew it.

The *a poet but don't* (or *doesn't*) *know it* version has long been also US. In, e.g., Ring Lardner's *The Real Dope*, 1919, occurs this passage (sent to me by a correspondent in 1975): 'Well, Al, I wish you could of seen how surprised she was when she read [the verses] and she says "So you are a poet". So I said "Yes I am a poet and don't know it" so that made her laugh.' Note also Ellery Queen's *The Last Woman in His Life*, 1970: ' "She can't hope to cope! I'm a poet and don't know it!" '

that's a sure card. That's a safe device or a shrewd expedient or one likely to succeed; and often applied to the person thinking of, or using, it: C16-20. (The anon. *Thersites, an Interlude, c.* 1537; BE.) Manifestly from card-playing.

that's a very good idea, turn it round the other way. 'Workshop engineer's dirge on realization that the job can be better handled from the opposite angle: to the tune of a well-known ditty: "In the middle of the night/When the bugs begin to bite,/Scratch 'em out with all your might ..." ' (L.A., 1974): since *c.* 1930, if not a generation earlier.

that's a very good question. See **that's good question.**

that's a whole new ball game. See **that's another ...**

that's a whole nother matter (or **question**) is 'a curious Americanism ... in which the word "whole" divides the word "another" in two! I've never seen this written ... but I suspect it is more often used by us Southerners than by our Northern neighbors. I cannot date it' (A.B., 1979). Nor can I. My guess, and it is no more a guess, in that if follows the pattern of the slangy 'abso-bloody-lutely', where the interpolation connotes a considerable emphasis.

P.B.: admirers of the 'little animal songs' of Donald Swann and the late Michael Flanders will be reminded of their verses about the gnu, pron. with hard *g* as *g-nu*: 'I'm a g-nu. A g-nother g-nu ...'

[**that's about it**; and **that's about right**, with emphasis in each case on *about*. That's exactly right: Aus.: since *c.* 1920. Clichés rather than c.pp.]

that's about (or **just about**) **par for the course.** That's pretty normal *or* That's what, after all, you can expect *or* might have expected: since *c.* 1920. From golf.

The predominant US form is *(that's) par for the course.* (J.W.C., 1975.) The c.p., when applied to an individual, suggests that the standard – the criterion – is rather low.

R.C. notes that 'ironically, "par" (usually 72 strokes for an 18-hole course) is *not* what one expects from the majority of golfers, the "no handicap" (i.e., par) player being rather a rarity'.

[**that's about right.** See **that's about it.**]

that's about the size of it, used for 'that describes the state of affairs fairly well' (Berrey, 1942), is a cliché, adopted from US *c.* 1915; but when it is 'accompanied by a gesture in which the forearm is allowed to fall forward and down, the palm of the lightly-clenched fist uppermost' (P.B., 1974), it is a sexual-inuendo c.p., dating since 1920.

that's all gay was, *c.* 1895-1915, a Cockney c.p., indicating a peaceable agreement. Used by, e.g., Edwin Pugh. But earlier, C19 underworld for 'The coast is clear'.

P.B.: this is of course using the old, Standard English sense of *gay*, 'joyful, happy'.

that's all I have (or **I've got**) **between me and the workhouse.** 'An old whine heard used by spongers and ear-biters' (persistent borrowers): late C19-20. (Petch, 1975.) Cf **all that's between ...**

that's all I need! Ironic for 'That's the last thing I needed or wanted'; 'That's the last straw!': since *c.* 1958; perhaps a lustrum or even a decade earlier.

The phrase has been 'US since 1950s' (R.C.), 'where *needed* is the more usual form' (J.W.C.).

that's all I wanted to know! The speaker bitterly confirms, and angrily resents, a thoroughly disagreeable fact or an exacerbating set of circumstances: since the middle 1930s. (L.A. Cf prec.

that's all she wrote; and **that's what she wrote.** W & F, 1960, gloss this US c.p. thus: 'That's all there is ... it's finished' and date it 'during and since WWII' and explain it as referring to a soldier's last letter from his sweetheart, telling him it's all over – what, in short, is known as a *dear John*.

The degree to which the phrase has become incorporated into conversation may be gauged by this quot'n from Charles Larson, *Muir's Blood*, 1976: ' ... Todd continued, "a cancellation coming on the heels of the last big deficit – well, that'd be all she wrote, boy." ' Cf:

that's all that's between me and prostitution. See **all that's between ...**

that's all there is: there isn't (loosely **ain't**) **any more.** That's all: US: since *c.* 1900. (Berrey, 1942.) 'Said by Ethel Barrymore at the beginning, or near the beginning, of her theatrical career, in response to repeated curtain calls' (J.W.C., 1968). But, in 1975, Prof. Clark told me that the phrase was 'less common than formerly, but by no means extinct', and amplified that Bartlett records *there's nothing more – that's all there is* as the correct form and as being a 'curtain line' contrived by Thomas Raceward's *Sunday* in 1906; he adds that he thinks the play was revived nearly thirty years later and that the c.p. arose then. With her first starring role, *c.* 1900, Ethel Barrymore (1879-1959) – who made her debut in 1894 – achieved fame in *Captain Jinks of the Horse Marines*; during the next five years, she appeared alongside Sir Henry Irving on one of his US tours – in 1905, in Ibsen's *The Doll's House* – and in 1906 in a Barrie play.

The var. *that's all there is – there is no more* was, on 20 Aug. 1973, satirized in a caption that runs, 'This is your anchorman, John Moore, saying "That's all there is. There is no more." Until to-morrow at the same time, when there will be more.'

P.B.: in UK, *that's all there is: there ain't no more.*

that's all very fine and large. See **all very large and fine.**

that's all we need! A natural var. of **that's all I need!**

that's another (or **a different**) **ball game.** See **different ball game.**

that's another can of worms. 'Usually said by someone dealing with a problem to someone else, who presents an additional, whether related or not, problem. I've heard this all my life' (A.B., 1979); that is, since the early 1940s. W & F, 1960, define *can of worms* as 'a very complex, unsolved problem', add 'Not common', and do not date it. P.B. notes, 1979, 'the clearly North American *can of worms* (the UK equivalent is surely "a bucket of bait") crossed the Atlantic in late 1977 or in 1978, particularly in the political phrase "that would be to open a whole new can of worms". Cf also **can of worms** and **let's not open ...**

that's another something 'denotes a complete change of subject or orientation' (*The Third Ear*, 1971): American Negroes': since *c.* 1960 (?). Cf **that's something else.**

that's anyone's bet. See **anyone's bet.**

that's as well done (or **said**) **as if I had done** (or **said**) **it myself** occurs in S, 1738. In Dialogue II Lady Smart speaks ill, and wittily, of oysters and Neverout remarks, 'Faith, that's as well said, as if I had said it myself.' They belong to C18-19. The C20 equivalent is 'I couldn't have done, or said, it better myself' – which, obviously, is not a c.p.

that's asking! You're asking when you shouldn't – *or* when I shouldn't answer: the C19-'20. Cf **that's tellings** at **telling – that would be.**

that's before you bought your shovel. See **before you bought ....**

that's better beer, out of the same barrel! 'Sometimes shortened to the first park of the phrase only; said when something not making good progress suddenly gathers momentum again, or when something has failed and a second "go" meets with more success' (B.G.T., 1978): rural England: C20.

that's better out than in! See **better an empty house ...**

[**that's chummy** (or **ducky**, or **just dandy**, or **(just) lovely**).

That's the last straw! All are Aus., dating since c. 1946, except the third, dating since 1944 and adopted from US Serviceman. The second and fourth are common in England. (B.P.) But it's rather doubtful whether these ironic locutions can justifiably be classified as c.pp. P.B.: see, however, **that's lovely ...**]

that's decent of you is a c.p. only when it is spoken ironically: since c. 1910.

'D'you know, I believe you're almost honest.'
'That's decent of you.'
Var.: *that's damn'* (or *damned*) *decent of you!*

that's duck soup. That's easy to do: US: C20. (Fain, 1977.)

that's enough to make a cat laugh. See enough to make ....

that's fighting talk is a joc. retort upon a pretended affront: C20. (L.A.) P.B.: an occ. var. is *them's fightin' words, stranger* (or *pardner*), in imitation of 'Western' film dialogue. Cf smile when you say that.

that's flat. See and that's flat.

that's for me to know and you to find out. A 'tart refusal to answer a question – usually said to or by a child. American: C20, now obsolescent. Most recently in the film *Pretty Baby* (1978, but set in 1917), where it struck me immediately as a familiar but long unheard c.p.' (R.C., 1978). Cf the smugness of *that'd be telling*, at **telling ...**, q.v.

P.B.; Gregory Benford, in his novel *Timescape*, 1980, places it as US teenagers', mid 1950s.

that's for sure! Certainly; Surely: US, since c. 1925; adopted, during WW2, in UK and the Commonwealth, and thoroughly naturalized by 1955 at latest.

that's for (or strictly for) the birds. Tell that to the Marines; but also – in UK, at least – 'That's of no consequence'; in both countries, 'That's entirely unacceptable or utterly unwanted'; in US only, 'That's corny'. Adopted, c. 1955, from US, where current since the late 1940s. W & F, 1960, quotes, 'I won't buy it. Or any part of it. It's for the birds' (J. Crosby, in the *New York Herald Tribune* of 8 Feb. 1952).

Leechman, 1969, notes the frequent Can. var. *it's for the birds.*

R.C., 1978, elucidates: 'from the by-products of horse-drawn transport, which once nourished a large population of, especially, sparrows. That is, "that's a lot of horse-shit". American, from 1930, or earlier'.

that's going some! indicates either approval or admiration – or 'That's going *too* far': US: C20. Recorded by S.R. Strait in 'Straight Talk', the *Boston Globe*, c. 1917, and by Berrey, 1942. Adopted in UK and the Commonwealth by 1910 at latest.

P.B.: Cf this, from Albert Smith's *Natural History of the Gent*, 1847: 'Other [gents] adopt large noses, and false mustaches, which they think is "doing it – rather!"'

that's gone, as the girl said to the soldier in the park was, in raffish circles, current c. 1890–1914. (Arthur Binstead.) Well, after all, there has to be a first time. See also **as he girl said ...**

that's him with the hat on! This humorous c.p. indicates the whereabouts of a man standing near pigs, monkeys, scarecrows and other disparate creatures: orig. farmers', then rapidly become gen. An agreeable example of rustic wit.

that's how I got it. See no harm in trying.

that's how the cookie crumbles. See that's the way ...

that's jake with me. 'That's okay by me' – 'It's acceptable' – 'I go along with that': US: since the 1920s, but ob. by c. 1955. (R.C., 1978.) Cf **she'll be jake.**

that's just about par for the course. See that's about par ....

that's just about your size! is included by Berrey, 1942, in a long list of 'disparaging and sarcastic flings' and it means 'One would *expect* that of you': since c. 1930s. Contrast **that's my size.**

that's just my handwriting; with waggish var., **that's just my bloody *écriture.*** This c.p., dating since WW2 (apparently since c. 1950), 'accepts [a] manipulated disadvantage in

arrangement and envisages resource that will turn discomfort against perpetrator' (L.A., 1975). See also **just my alley-marble.**

that's just too bad! This c.p., 'implying that an appeal to consideration or restraint has failed' (L.A.), was adopted, c. 1937, from US, where it arose during the 1920s and was recorded by Berrey in 1942.
Cf **that's too bad.**

[**that's life! or that's life for you!** 'That is, it's just one of those things [q.v.] – the thousand mortal shocks that flesh is heir to. Cf the French *c'est la vie!*' (R.C., 1978). It stand midway between cliché and c.p.

P.B.: cf the 'Ritual exchange' very popular among, e.g., schoolboys c. 1950: 'That's life!' – 'What life?' – 'A magazine' – 'How much?' – 'Ten cents' – 'But I've only got five cents' – 'That's life!' *Life* = the famous American magazine.]

that's lovely, that is! An ironic Aus. c.p., orig. by Fred Parsons for Roy Rene in the latter's radio series 'Mo' during the late 1940s and popularized by Rene himself. Cf the comment at **one of my mob.** (Thanks to Harry Griffiths, 1978.) P.B.: cf the Brit. use of the heavily sarcastic *charming!*, and **that's chummy!**

that's made my day. See made my day ...

that's more like it! That's better – more acceptable or reasonable: C20. Both Brit. (*DSUE*, 1937) and US (Berrey, 1942). Cf **that's something like ...**

that's my boy! An occ. var. of **attaboy!** It occurs, e.g., in Act I of John Osborne's *Look Back in Anger*, prod. in 1956. P.B.: ITMA had the c.p. *that's the boy!* (*VIBS*), and *that's my boy!* was the regular boast by the father bulldog of his puppy son in a series of US Warner Bros film cartoons of the 1950s–60s.

that's my size! That suits me; I am agreeable; 'that's the ticket' (Farmer): c. 1880–1914. Cf **ah there, my size ...**

that's my story and I'm stuck with it; or, in US, also ... **I'll stick to it.** Both forms are glossed by Berrey, 1942, as 'I mean it; I'm in earnest', but sometimes as indicating a stubborn unwillingness to retract. It came to UK in the middle 1930s; and during WW2 the Royal Engineers had a var.: *that's my story and I'm stuck all round it*, that's my explanation and I'm standing by it.

In *Relative Values*, prod. 1951 and pub'd 1952, Noël Coward writes (at 1 i):
PETER: Is it?
FELICITY: Yes, Peter, it is and you needn't look quizzical either. That's my story and I'm sticking to it.

Australia has had its own version, dating since the mid 1940s and prob. occasioned by US Servicemen there stationed during the latter half of WW2: *that's my story and I'm sticking to it*, is glossed by B.P., 1975, thus: 'You can believe it or not'.

'Quite often heard turned the other way, i.e. "That's your story and you're stuck with it". In fact, this is perhaps the more common construction nowadays' (P.B., 1975).

'"I'm stuck with it" doesn't mean "I'll stick to it" at all; it is rather a humorously rueful acknowledgment that one has been caught in a lie ... "I'm stuck with it" is said by a revealing (pretended) slip of the tongue by someone who wishes he could say "I'll stick to it"' (J.W.C., 1977).

that's my (or the) ticket! See that's the ticket.

that's no (or that wasn't a) lady: that was my wife, more often **that was no ....** Prob. it began as a music-hall joke (perhaps in a song) in the 1880s or 1890s. In Scene i, in the first dialogue (immediately after Refrain 1) of Noël Coward's *Red Peppers*, pub'd in 1936 and written c. 1935, we read:
LILY: Who was that lady I saw you walking down the street with the other morning?
GEORGE: That wasn't a lady, that was my wife.
Later, Lily includes it in a list of 'hoary old chestnuts'.

[**that's not hay and that's not peanuts.** See that ain't hay.]

that's not my department. 'That's not my responsibility: often with a sardonic twist' (R.C.): both Brit. and US: since late

1940s. I'd say that it orig. in the Civil Service as a characteristic 'passing the buck'.
P.B.: cf **just the job for my brother from Gozo** and **not me, Chief...**

that's old Mother Hubbard. That's incredible: a non-aristocratic, non-cultured c.p. of c. 1880–1910. From the nursery rhyme. Ware.

that's one for the book. See **one for the book.**

that's one for you! That settles *you! or* Put that in your pipe and smoke it!: C20. Fain, 1978, notes the US var. *... on you.*

that's one on me! See **that's a good one on me!**

that's one up against your duckhouse. 'I've got even with you': Aus.: since the late 1940s. Popularized by Roy Rene. (Harry Griffiths, 1978.) See comment at **one of my mob.**

that's past praying for. 'What's done cannot be undone': US and Brit.: C20, and prob. much earlier; but by late C20, ob.

that's pushed Rommel back.... See **that'll push....**

that's put the lid (or tin lid) on it. Nothing more to be said, *or* That's done (or, finished) it: late C19–20. A mainly Merseyside var., C20, is *that's put the top-hat on it.* (Frank Shaw.) P.B.: the version *... tin hat...* occurs in J. Milne, *The Epistles of Atkins*, 1902, soldiers' letters from the S. African War.

that's real George. '"That's okay!" – dating from the latish 1920s to the 1950s in the US. I suspect that it relates to St George or to one of the kings bearing the name' (A.B., 1978). P.B.: a young American expatriate friend of mine was still using it in the mid-1970s as an equivalent of the Brit. 'that's pretty good'.
Cf **everything is George.**

that's right, but only just. See **right, but...**

that's rough! (sometimes, for emphasis, with **R-U-F-F, rough!** added) conveys a lack of sympathy towards someone spinning a hard-luck story: mid-C20. (P.B.) Cf ironic use of **tough shit!**

that's Shell, that was! has, since late 1930s (but much less since c. 1960), been applied to any person or thing moving very fast. From a Shell (–Mex) slogan for the petrol they market. (A reminder from John Skehan, 1977.) The slogan appeared on hoardings showing a head swivelling through 180 degrees (in effect, a two-headed figure) and registering astonishment and admiration.

that's show-biz for you! That's how it goes: orig. applied to public entertainment, and US: C20. By the late 1930s, also Brit., and with a wider application, as in Laurence Meynell, *Death of a Philanderer*, 1968: '"Blue Plates" [an imaginary TV programme] finished, Pat[ricia] gone and my second novel the worst flop of all time. Which, as they say, is showbiz.'
It had in the 1930s, and prob. later, an off-shoot, *that's the picture business*, 'as used in Hollywood, as a tag-line to almost any situation reflecting the ups and downs and oddities of the Hollywood way of life' (Wedgewood, 1977).

that's something else – or, more emphatic, with **again** added. That's a (very) different matter: US: since the early 1930s; adopted in UK during WW2. (Berrey.)
The phrase is defined by *The Third Ear*, 1971, a glossary of American Negro speech, as 'something out of the ordinary, whether good or bad', and R.C., 1978, writes 'Now more often "something extraordinary" – often laudatory – i.e., far beyond common experience'. Paul Janssen provides the French synon. *voilà autre chose – coll., v'là aut' chose.* Cf **that's another something.**

that's something like it! That's as it should be, *or* that's *far* more pleasant, *or* That's come closer to what I expected: US: since the 1920s; adopted in UK during the 1930s. (Berrey.) P.B.: also, comparatively, in UK, **that's a (bit) more like (it)!**, q.v. – but both phrases are rather more idiomatic or cliché than c.p.

that's straight from central casting. Conventional or stereotyped; requiring no imagination: US film circles, and 'show-biz' in gen.: since mid-1960s, perhaps since very early

1960s. (Janssen, 1978.)

that's strictly bush (or **what a busher he is!**) is applied to someone whose behaviour is unmannerly: perhaps since soon after 1905, for in that year *big time* and *small time* arose as complementary terms applied to show business, that being the date when *Variety* (the periodical) first appeared – and when *Variety* fathered those complementaries. My friend Mr W.J. Burke writes, 1975:
> We also use 'Big League' to denote success, the term coming from Big League Baseball (The National League and The American League). Ball players who did not 'make' the Big League were said to be playing in the 'Bush League', and from that came the word 'busher', used to describe any person who had not made the grade, so to speak. ... Bush is associated with backwoods, or rural fringes. Your Australian Bush may suggest parallels.

And it does, for cf **it will be Sydney or the bush.** He refers to Joe Laurie, Jr, *Vaudeville: From the Honkey Tonk to the Palace*, 1953.
I'd say that whereas *that's strictly bush* is a c.p., *what a busher he is!* is not one.

that's strictly for the birds. See **that's for the birds.**

that's telling (or **tellings**). See **that's telling – that would be.**

that's telling 'em! – which in UK would have been *that's telling 'em where they get off!* US: since the 1920s. Berrey.

that's that. See **and that's that.**

that's the article is a var. of **that's the ticket.** That's the very thing we need: mid C19–20; ob. by 1940 and virtually† by 1950. An article – or commodity – of commerce. Also, by c. 1900, US. Berrey.

that's the barber was, c. 1760–1830, an approbatory street saying. George Parker, *A View of Society*, 1781; Grose, 1785.

[**that's the beauty of it:** mid C18–20. Samuel Richardson, *Sir Charles Grandison*, 1753–4, has 'That's the beauty of it; to offend and make up at leisure'. The most agreeable or valuable or pleasurable part or aspect of anything. Also US: C20. (Berrey.) A 'borderliner' between cliché and c.p.]

[**that's the bee's knees.** See **bee's knees.**]

that's the cheese. That's the best, *or* the fashionable thing: since c. 1815, but gen. only since the 1830s or very early 1840s. Anon (*The London Guide*, 1818; R.H. Barham, *The Ingoldsby Legends*, 1840; Charles Reade, *Hard Cash*, 1863); † by c. 1920. Perhaps from the Urdu *chiz*, a thing (see esp. YB).
Adopted in US c. 1870. In Farmer it is glossed as signifying 'excellent performance' or 'quite the thing'.† by 1914.

that's the end! See **that's the living end!**

that's the end of the bobbin! That's the end of it – that's finished: mid C19–early C20. Mostly lower-middle class. B&L comment thus: 'When all the thread is wound off a bobbin or spool.... It rose from the refrain of a song which was popular in 1850.' Also US, though ob. by 1979.

that's the give to stuff 'em. See **that's the stuff to give the troops!**

that's the (or **that's just the**) **hammer.** That is very good; that's exactly what is needed: army, and perhaps more widespread: late 1940s–1950s. (P.B.) Cf. the Aus. synon. *that's the shot*, q.v. at **shot.** Often shortened to **just the hammer!**

that's the living end! 'The utmost, in any situation. Recent' (Leechman, 1969): Can. An extension of the never very gen. English **that's the end,** itself c. 1915–40. See also **this is the end!**

that's the name of the game. Lit., that's what they call it; fig., that's what it's all about: since c.1965. 'We [industrial psychologists] guarantee the objectivity. Personally. That's what makes us worth a lot of money to any modern and properly objective management. Ergonomics, baby. *That's the name of the game*' (Desmond Cory, *The Circe Complex*, 1975). Cf **name of the game – the.**

that's the man as married Hannah; occ. **that's what's the matter with the man as married Hannah.** A proletarian c.p. of c. 1850–1905. (Hotten.) Orig. denoting a good, or a happy, beginning, it soon came to mean 'Good for you!' or 'Excellent!'; hence, simply a hearty agreement. Hotten implies that this c.p. migrated from Shropshire to, esp., London.

Just who Hannah was, history is apparently silent; prob. some forgotten song or ballad affords a clue.

P.B.: later still, at least in the N. Country, as Mrs Barbara Huston tells me, it came to be used as an expression of triumph when the right (perhaps previously lost) object, or apt phrase turned up just when needed: 'AH, that's the man...'

that's the old ball-game! 'Sometimes said joyfully, but usually ruefully, meaning "that's the way it goes". I think it must have derived from American baseball – or football – when a team lost and a fan lost his bet. It really now means "It's all over". Also "that's the *same* old ball-game" – that's the same old story!' (A.B., 1979). Contrast **different ball-game.**

that's the old Dunkirk spirit! 'Ironic. Directed at shirkers and lead-swingers. Since *c.*1940' (Sanders, 1978). For those who've never heard of it, even though they have immeasurably benefitted by it, the ref. is to the evacuation of the British Expeditionary Force, in very late May – very early June 1940, from Dunkirk, a feat unparallelled, for courage and endurance, in the entire history of war. Cf **biggest fuck-up since...**

that's the old Navy spirit. Col. Moe wrote to me, 1975:

At one time, there was a great deal of animosity between Marines and sailors. A sailor could always count on the phrase 'Why is a Marine?' to get a rise out of a Marine. Or he might merely say 'Twenty-eighty' to get the same result. (This was during the time when a Marine private's pay was $21.00 per month, which was reduced to $20.80 after the 20-cent deduction for the 'hospital' fund.) This jibe is meaningless today under the present pay scale. There were many retorts by marines, but one seems to have persisted and to have lingered on, i.e. 'That's the old navy spirit'. Just why [these phrases were so effectual] is something I have never understood. I only know that it worked. It was understood that the 'navy spirit' connoted 'I've got mine. How are *you* making out?'

I suggest that the sting in *why is a Marine?* lies in its literal meaning, i.e. 'Why does a Marine exist?' (at all).

R/Adml Brock reminds me that 'The hymn of the USMC – From the Halls of Montezuma to the Shores of Tripoli – tells us that.

"If the Army and the Navy ever visit Heaven's scenes. They will find the streets are guarded by United States marines."'

that's the shot. See **shot – that'll be the.**

that's the sixty-four thousand dollar question! I find the question very difficult to answer: US, since the early 1950s and, by adoption, Brit. since the late 1960s. From the US 'quiz game' – with a very much smaller top prize in UK and the Commonwealth. (Shaw, 1968.)

But this is itself a development from and an elab. of the purely US *that's the sixty-four dollar question*, which, as a c.p., date from *c.*1942. Webster's *International Dictionary*, 1961, tells me that *the sixty-four dollar question was* 'so called from the fact that $64 was the highest award in the CBS radio quiz show. "Take It or Leave It"' (1941–8). The meaning of both of these c.pp. is 'That is the crucial question – the most difficult one – a real puzzler.' It is still heard, 1975, occ. in UK, whereas it was already, in US, 1969, passing into history, as Prof. Emeritus S.H. Monk told me in that year.

The phrase 'was kept alive by the scandal when it was revealed that [a certain English teacher] had been given the answers, and coached how to hesitate and seem to ponder. That put the program off the air' (Shipley, 1977. See further Dr Shipley's *In Praise of English*, 1977.)

that's the snaffler! Well done! *or* Excellent!: naval, in the main: *c.*1820–70. (Wm N. Glascock, *Sketch-Book*, 2nd Series,

1834.) I.E., 'that's got it under control', as a snaffle does a horse.

that's the sort of clothes-pin I am. That's my nature! That's *me!*: among men only: *c.*1865–1914. One of the small group of domestic c.pp.

that's the stuff to give the troops! In B & P, 1930, John Brophy definitively wrote:

That's the stuff to give the troops was heard whenever rations or billets, rum or any other creature comfort turned out better or more plentiful than might have been expected. It was varied into *That's the stuff to give 'em!* and *that's the give to stuff!* and in this form would often be shouted approvingly to artillery in action.

It often became *that's the stuff!* – which, oddly enough, was current in the US as early as 1896 (*OED* Supplement).

Arising in 1915, the orig. form remained current among ex-Servicemen; the facetious form died with the war. In UK, the c.p. prob. (as L.A. has reminded me) orig. in the old music-hall song (*c.*1910–14):

That's the stuff for your Darby Kell!
Makes you fat and keeps you well,
Boiled beef and carrots!

that's the ticket! prob. goes back to *c.*1820; it occurs in, e.g., W.N. Glascock, *Sketch-Book*, 2nd Series, 1834, 'That's *you*, Ned – you has it – that's the ticket bo.' It soon migrated to US, 'Sam Slick the Watchmaker' Haliburton using it in 1838 (*OED*); and it is recorded in *DCCU*. And lest a misapprehension should arise, I should add that Thomas Chandler Haliburton (1796–1865) was, of course, Canadianborn; but his character, Sam Slick of Slickville, was an American salesman, whose brash, breezy, cheerful speech Haliburton delighted to record with complete fidelity. (See, e.g., *The Oxford Companion to American Literature*).

In *Please Help Emily: A Flirtation in Three Acts*, performed in 1916 and pub'd ten years later, H.M. Harwood writes, near end of Act I:

EMILY: We might send to Jessie to pack them. Couldn't you say I'd asked you to have them sent on?
TROTTER: That's the ticket. We'll do that. [The best idea or plan.]

The semantics are in dispute: either ticket is a corruption of Fr. *etiquette*, as Ware maintains, or it is a winning ticket in a lottery, or it's simply a ticket advertising the price of merchandise.

By 1940, slightly ob., by 1976, somewhat ob.

For the US, W & F gloss it thus: 'In the phrase "That's the ticket", *ticket* = That's what I meant or wanted'; they offer no dating. J.W.C., 1977, confirms a US meaning for *that's the* (or *my*) *ticket* as 'That's the opinion, or line of action, I endorse': late C19–20. From election procedure'. See also **that's the article,** and:

that's the ticket for soup. You've got what you came for – so now be off!: from the late 1850s until a few years before WW1. Hotten, 1860, wrote that the c.p. came from 'the card given to beggars for immediate relief at soup kitchens'.

But R/Adml. Brock adds, 'My mother (b. 1885 in Canada) used "That's the ticket for soup" in the sense of your "That's the ticket" [See prec.].'

that's the tip. That's right – very much so, *or* That's the thing, *or* that's the cheese: *c.*1860–1910. Hotten, 1864.

that's the tune the old cow died of. That's damned unpleasant noise!: *c.*1820–60. (Captain Frederick Marryat, *Mr Midshipman Easy*, 1836.) From an old ballad. (Apperson.) Hence, 'I asked for a loan or a small gift of money or provisions – not for a bloody sermon!': *c.*1880–1940.

It was current in the US from (?) *c.*1830 onwards, if one may judge by its occurrence in Mark Twain's *Life on the Mississippi*, which, appearing in 1883, 'harks back to the 1840s and 1850s' (R.C., 1978). Rural rather than urban.

In A.E. Housman's *Apologia* poem, 'Terence, this is stupid stuff', the lads have been listening to him reading his grim poems, and they ask him to write 'tunes to dance to' instead. They say to him, 'The cow, the old cow, she's dead;... and we poor lads, 'tis our turn now, To hear such tunes as killed the cow'. That A.E. Housman (1859–1936), a very distinguished classical scholar, whose *A Shropshire Lad*, 1896, and *Last Poems*, 1922, should have thus alluded to the old expression would seem to indicate that it prob. survived until *c*. 1900. P.B.: in later C20 perhaps ob., but still not †.

that's the way it goes is a c.p. of humorous resignation or of either rueful or defiant acceptance: mid or latish C19–20. It is prob. the earliest of the derivatives from the cliché *that's how it is*. P.B.: in later C20, sometimes with *kid* added. See also next two entries:

that's the way the ball bounces is synon. with the next. US: since *c*. 1954 (W & F) and adopted in both Can. and Aus. very soon after. (Leechman; B.P.) In Can., *that's how the ball bounces* is a frequent var.

that's the way (or **that's how**) **the cookie crumbles**
'There is a rather frequent expression here [in New York]: "That's the way the cookie crumbles" – meaning "That's how (this situation) has turned out" and there's nothing you can do about it' (Shipley, 1974); but, only a week later, Dr Edward Hodnett declared it to be old-fashioned. It has been a frequent c.p. in the US since the 1950s and in UK since the middle 1960s, the late Frank Shaw telling me in 1969: 'Recent'. Brit. usage permits the very occ., *that's the way the cookie drops* or *falls* (Noble, 1974). It gained a wide currency also in Can.; in 1975, Prof. Emeritus F.E.L. Priestley spoke of 'the now happily obsolete "that's the way the cookie crumbles"' and referred to 'the lovely take-off line in the movie *The Apartment* [1960] when Jack Lemmon says, "That's the way it crumbles cookiewise"' – when he is also deriding 'the horrible "-wise" jargon of about ten years ago' (F.E.L.P.).
In *The Zoo Story*, prod. in Berlin 1959, in New York 1960, and pub'd in 1960, Edward Albee employs the more usual form thus:

JERRY: And you have children?
PETER: Yes; two.
JERRY: Boys?
PETER: No, girls....both girls.
JERRY: But you wanted boys.
PETER: Well...naturally, every man wants a son, but...
JERRY: But that's the way the cookie crumbles?
PETER: (*Annoyed*.) I wasn't going to say that.

And Morris Farhi's *The Pleasure of Your Death*, 1972, has:
'I have no pals.'
'You poor bastard. Life's treated you pretty bad, huh?'
'That's how the cookie crumbles.'
'Ever ask yourself why?'
'No.'
'Time you did. Who'd trust you with a snake?'
'My mother.'

An early instance of its Brit. currency occurs in Patrick Campbell's *Come Here Till I Tell You*, 1960, '"Well...that's how the cookie crumbles." – "I beg your pardon?" – "It's a new American expression from the advertising boys on Madison Avenue. A philosophic comment on disaster. One can also say, 'That's how the grapefruit squirts'."' Well, the grapefruit var. never caught on in the UK and had, I gather, only the most ephemeral currency in the US. (Quot'n owed to Mrs Camilla Raab.)
'The phrase lent itself to variation, of course. A fairly common one in the 1950s–60s was "That's the way the mop flops"; and a very local, short-lived, one in Hong Kong, 1962, after a particularly devastating typhoon, code-named Wanda! "That's the way the typhoon wanders".' (P.B., 1976.) I record the latter, despite its emphemerality and obvious negligibility, because it does help to show how c.pp. proliferate and how topicality contributes. Lt. Cdr. F.L. Peppitt wrote, 1977, '"That's the way the mop flops" has, since *c*. 1969, been how the Royal Navy expresses "...the cookie crumbles".'

That's the way the cookie crumbles and **that's the way the ball bounces** are, according to W & F, 1976, the two commonest of a score of variant c.pp. for 'That's fate – that's the way things go, *or* the rub of the green'.

that's the way the mop flops. See prec.

that's (or **that is**) **the way to London?** (or **is that the way to London?**) A question disguising a nose-wiping on back of hand or on one's sleeve: mostly children's, but occ. an adult jocularity, without the action; but always a vulgarity: C20.

that's the whole ball of wax. 'That's it – that's the nub of the matter – that's all there is to it...1960s, I should think, and rather common, more often orally than in print' (A.B., 1978).

that's too bad! (– well!). In Act III of Terence Rattigan's *Love in Idleness*, prod. 1944, pub'd 1945, we find:
MICHAEL: ...You dislike me, I dislike you. Well, that's too bad, but we needn't act like primeval apes about it.
I'd say that this characteristically Brit. c.p., understated and ironic, goes back to *c*. 1880; but I've failed to record an early occurrence. Cf **that's just too bad.**

that's torn it. That has spoiled it. That's ruined everything: orig. (*c*. 1905), low, but soon gen., as in 'Ian Hay', 1909 (*OED* Supplement). A var. occurs in John Arden's *The Workhouse Donkey: A Vulgar Melo-Drama*, prod. in 1963 and pub'd in 1964, at I, ix:
BUTTERTHWAITE: Afraid? You don't mean the police?
HOSTESS: That's right.
HARDNUTT: Oh, my Lord, no....
HOPEFAST: I say, Charlie, that's gone and torn it, hasn't it?
The US form – which neatly exemplifies the US preference of the Preterite to the Present Perfect tense – is *that tore it*. A US correspondence writes, 'I suggest that it was first applied to a coïtal stroke so violent as to tear the condom.' But if the origin is sexual, which I doubt, it may equally well have been feminine: the tearing of the hymen. Prob. from a dress getting torn. R.C., 1978, notes that occ. it can also be *that tears it*.

that's up against you! What do you say – what, indeed, *have* you to say – to that? Aus.: late C19 – mid C20. Cf **that's one up...**

that's up to you! caps a (most) convincing argument: C20. Often accompanied by a coarse gesture.

that's up your shirt. That's a puzzler for you: mid C19 – early C20. F & H.

that's what gets me down! is a US expression of annoyance or irritation: C20. (Berrey.) Adopted in UK *c*. 1918. Cf:

that's what gets my back up. That's what angers me: since the 1920s. Perhaps from cats fighting. Contrast **that'll put your back up.**

[**that's what** *I* **say** is a grossly overdone conversation tag, half way between cliché and c.p.: late C19–20.]

that's what she wrote. See **that's all she wrote.**

[**that's what the man said.** 'Either "that's what he said, true or not" or "that's the way it's got to be". *The Man* is a not uncommon US synonym for anyone in authority: US: from (?) 1950s' (R.C., 1978). Some use also in UK (P.B.), very commonly also, 'Do as the man says'. Much more of a cliché, or even an everyday coll., than a c.p.]

that's what *you* **say!** I simply don't believe it: US: C20. (Berrey.) Contrast **that's what** *I* **say.**

that's what *you* **think!** That's your opinion, but you're almost certainly wrong – badly wrong!: tone: scornful or, at the very least, derisive C20. 'Derides ignorance of important factor [and implies] that projected action will be thwarted' (L.A., 1975).

that's where I am. 'That's what I enjoy, *or* believe, *or* do' – 'That's my thing' (*DCCU*): US: since *c*. 1960.

that's where it's at. That is a fair, a just, an accurate view of things: a somewhat illiterate, rather slangy, US c.p., dating since *c*. 1964 or 1965. (Norris M. Davidson, 1971.) –
Adopted in UK either in late 1972 or in early 1973: glossed by *Punch*, on 10 Oct. 1973, as 'I think you're right'.

Var., for emphasis, *that's where it's all at.*

that's where the action is. 'That's where important things are happening, the key area of activity...By the 1960s almost any sort of intense and engrossing activity, whether speculative, sexual, commercial or political. The c.p. has been current since then, though by now a trible hackneyed' (R.C., 1978). Cf **this is where it's at.**

that's where the big nobs hang out is 'a jocular comment when a man expresses intention [to go to the urinal]. Certainly 1939–45 in the Services and later, offices and factories [and public houses]' (L.A., 1969): since *c.* 1935. Here *nob* is a pun on the slang senses, 'important man' and 'penis', and, as Playfair pointed out, 1977, on *hang out*, in the lit. Standard English sense, and in the slang sense 'to dwell'.

that's where you spoil youself! was, in 1880–1, directed at a would-be smart, i.e. shrewd or crafty, person overreaching himself. Ware.

that's where you want it and **it's up there you want it**, with hand touching one's own forehead; *want* used in sense 'to lack'. You should use your brains! Lower and lower-middle class (since very early C20), become also WW1 military, and then civilian once more. In B & P, John Brophy comments: 'An expression of pride...to indicate intellectual superiority after one had "wangled" extra leave or a "cushy" job or some such privilege. Cf **this is where you want it.**

that's yer lot! See **aye, aye, that's...**

that's your best bet. That's your best way to do or achieve something, or to go somewhere: since the 1920s. From horseracing. P.B.: in later C20 more cliché or idiom than c.p., with var. *that'd be...* or *I tell you what'd be your best bet.*

that's your chicken and **that's your pigeon.** See **your pigeon.**

that's *your* funeral! See **your funeral.**

that's *your* hard (Brit.) (or **tough** (US)) **luck.** 'It's not my concern' (Berrey): C20.

that's your lot! See **aye, aye, that's...**

that's your pidgin. See **your pigeon.**

that's your sort! indicated, *c.* 1785–1930, approval, usu. of a specific action or method, only occ. of some object. (Holcroft, the playwright, 1792; Hotten, 1864.) By ellipsis.

It is to be noted that the phrase seems to have been already well known by 1792, when Thomas Holcroft's *The Road to Ruin: A Comedy* was performed; the actor William Lewis, playing Goldfinch, a raffish, sporting, esp. a horsey man, so popularized the saying that it enjoyed a furore. *c.* 1792–1800 and remained very popular for a generation longer, partly because this comedy proved to be enormously successful and was revived at Drury Lane in 1824 and again in 1826 – and at both the Haymarket and Covent Garden in 1825. In Act II, Goldfinch signals his meeting with the amiable young spendthrift, Harry Dornton, thus:

GOL: Hah! my tight one!

HAR: [*Surveying him.*] Well, Charles?

GOL: How you stare! – an't I the go? That's your sort! And a few lines further on:

HAR: You improve daily, Charles!

GOL: To be sure! that's your sort! An't I a genius? [*Strutting about.*]

HAR: Quite an original. – You may challenge the whole fraternity of the whip to match you!

GOL: Match me! Newmarket can't match me! – That's your sort!

In *Management*, 1793, Frederick Reynolds refers to Holcroft's phrase on three occasions.

The phrase, one perceives, is of vague sense – but tremendous significance. It's an intensive, with (apparently) the general meaning, 'I should *say* so!' It connotes an uncritical, warmhearted approval. Goldfinch's final words, in reply to a plea that he should now lead a sober life in trade, are: 'Damn trade...I'm for life and a curricle. A cut at the caster, and the long odds. Damn trade! The four aces, a back-hand, and a lucky nick! That's your sort!'

(I owe the Holcroft quot'n to Miss Patricia Sigl.)

The phrase recurs in R.H. Barham, *The Ingoldsby Legends*, Third Series, 1847, and in Surtees's *Mr Sponge's Sporting Tour*, 1853.

It seems to have reached the US during the 1870s or 1880s. In 1891, M glossed it as 'A term of approbation or encouragement'.

that's your story and you're stuck with it. See **that's my story....**

that's *your* tough luck! See **that's *your* hard luck!** Cf:

that's *your* worry! It has (more coll. it's) nothing to do with me. 'A disclaimer of responsibility ("Who cares?") or, as the navy says "Square your own yardarm!"' (Granville, 1969): C20.

thataway. See: went t.

thatta boy! is an occ. var. of **attaboy!** In Malcolm Bosse, *The Man Who Loved Zoos*, 1974, we read:

'Just so [i.e., provided] we don't lose it [i.e., confidence] in ourselves.'
'Thatta boy. What should I tell Hopkins?'
'Tell him...I'm not up a blind alley yet.'
'Thatta boy.'

theatre. See: funny thing.

theirs not to reason why has, in C20, been used as a c.p. From Tennyson's 'The Charge of the Light Brigade'. P.B.: but much more frequent is the misquotation, 'Ours is not to reason why'.

them as has, gits. 'Quite common in everyday speech. Refers to persons of great wealth....Saying now applies to almost anybody better off than the speaker. Often a "sour grapes" expression' (W.J.B., 1975): US: C20. P.B.: A paraphrase, intentional or otherwise, of the Biblical 'To him that hath shall be given'.

[**them wot's got boots wot lets wet.** 'The grammar of this is above my head, but it expressed effectively what the ordinary lads [conscripts in WW2] thought about the speech of the peacetime Regulars' (Anon., 1978).

P.B.: E.P. included this among his notes for a 2nd ed., but it sounds not so much a c.p. as the kind of quartermaster's assistant's obscurity that might baffle a well-educated young National Serviceman. Cf two instructions I heard at the N.S. intake camp, RAF Padgate of infamous memory, given by an elderly corporal in 1951. The first, an attempt to grade us recruits by medical categories, on the parade ground, ended 'Them wot's been vaccinated – in the rear!'; the second, dividing us up by religious denominations, was 'Right! We'll 'ave R.C.s on the left, Church of England on the right, an' Other Dimensions in the rear'. A further example from the same anon. source as 'boots' above is *them wot's keen get fell in previous.*]

them's fightin(g) words is prob. the orig. form of, as it remains more common than, **that's fighting talk:** late C19–20. Brit.; US (recorded by Berrey, 1942, *words*); Aus. ('In my experience, jocular, rather than illiterate': B.P., 1969); NZ – and elsewhere? Occ. shortened to *fightin'* (or *fighting*) *words*, as in Alistair Mair, *Where the East Wind Blows*, 1972:

'Alive,' I said. 'Which is more than you'll be if you don't clear out.'

Berchard smiled...'Fighting words,' he said.

them's my sentiments! is a c.p. of warmhearted agreement or approval: late C19–20. (John Galsworthy, *Swan Song*, 1928.) An excellent example of a famous quot'n – from Thackeray's *Vanity Fair*, 1848 – that took some time to become a c.p. Sometimes with *precisely* or *exactly*, or humorously, *persactly* added.

them's shooting words! is 'a phrase going back to the days of cowboys and gunmen on the American frontier. People from our Western States still say, when they take their leave after a visit, "It's time to saddle up", a hangover from the Wild West days' (W.J.B., 1975). Cf the Brit. **them's fightin(g) words!**

them's the jockeys for me! is a Can. c.p., dating since *c.* 1950 and applied to anything delicious or desirable. (Leechman.) Of anecdotal orig.: in 1969 Leechman wrote:

> Have you heard of the dinner guest, venerable, whitehaired, austere, silent, evidently a man of sense and dignity, perhaps wisdom, who remained silent throughout the conversation? When the desert was brought in, and the silver cover lifted, he cried aloud: 'EEE! Lookee! Little mince poies. Them's the jockeys for me!'

'Far from being a Canadian utterance of the 1950s, [the phrase] is to be found in Coleridge's *Table Talk* (1835) – relating to apple-dumplings' (Oliver Stonor, in *Books and Bookmen*, Oct. 1977). Clearly it was already a c.p. in the 1830s, must have persisted in UK for, say, a century, and was adopted in Canada.

then comes a pig to be killed! Expressing disbelief, used among the lower and lower-middle classes *c.* 1900–14. Ware says, 'Based upon the lines of Mrs Bond who would call to her poultry – "Come, chicks, come! Come to Mrs Bond and be killed!"'

then I will be hang'd, and my horse too. Equivalent to 'I'll be damned – *if* it's true': late C17–18. See the quot'n from S at **at a church with a chimney in it.**

then the band began to play (or **played**), both often prec. by **and.** Then the fat was in the fire – then the trouble began: the longer version, *c.* 1880–1914; the shorter, C20. Kipling, 1892, 'It's "Thank you, Mister Atkins", when the band begins to play'; D. Coke, in *Wilson's*, 1911, has 'then the band began to play'. Ware, 1909, adduces *then the band played*. Either from music played by a band at the end of a celebration or other public occasion, or, as Ware proposes, 'derived from the use of brass bands on the nomination day, which immediately sounded when the opponent of their employer attempted to address the people'. Cf **and the band played on,** and:

then the shit'll hit (or **then the shit hits**) **the fan!** See **when shit hits the fan.**

then the town bull is a bachelor! was, mid C17–mid C18, a semi-proverbial incredulous retort upon a woman's – or a man's – chastity (or other moral quality). Ray, 1678.

then you woke up! And then you came down to earth!: C20.

there ain't no justice! Less a c.p. than a simple, very common observation on the manifest inequalities and unfairness of life in general; almost proverbial, like *nothing is certain but death and taxes*, but perhaps verging on c.p. when used in conjunction with, e.g. **you can't fight City Hall**: since mid C20 at latest. (P.B.)

there ain't no more. See **that's all there is.**

there ain't no sech animal (or **animile**, or **animule**). I just don't believe it!: US: perhaps since *c.* 1880, and ob. by 1945, and † by 1970. (Berrey.) Said to be of anecdotal origin: a rustic, seeing a giraffe for the first time, exclaimed 'There ain't no sech animal (or -ile or -ule)!' – and who could blame him?

I first heard the expression on Gallipoli in 1915, from an Englishman familiar with US speech.

'"As "there ain't no sech critter" it is attributed to that Mid-Western former who was so notoriously unsophisticated' (Sanders, 1978). In 'Bartlett' it appears as 'There ain't no such animal', the farmer belonging to New Jersey, and the animal (in a circus) being a dromedary: credited to *Everybody's Magazine* by *Life*, which, on 7 Nov. 1907, had a cartoon illustrating the story. P.B.: but the allusive *no such animal* is still current in later C20.

there and back is a c.p. reply to the query, whether unwelcome or merely impertinent, 'Where are you going to?' Late C19–20 and always commoner among children than among adults; by 1950, ob., yet not † by 1975.

'The full version of the reply I've known since childhood is "there and back to see how far it is"' (B.G.T., 1978). That is so: I myself heard it, as a child [b. 1893] in New Zealand.

A.B., 1979, notes a somewhat different version, both in form and in meaning: 'Also, peevishly, "I'm going to hell and back again" or "I've been to hell and back again": it will

be – or was – a difficult journey, or unpleasant situation, I've experienced; I don't want to do *that* again'.

there are just two chances... See **Buckley's chance.**

there are only a few of us left does not, of course, qualify when it is used literally. When used joc. or ironically or 'deadpan', it became, *c.* 1965, a c.p. In Donald Mackenzie, *Postscript to a Dead Letter*, 1973, we encounter 'Jean Paul's one... who knows that what he's done is good and doèsn't bother to tell you. There are only a few of us left.'

This c.p. has the self-congratulatory var. *there aren't so many of us left, you know,* which, the earlier, may have arisen during the 1920s, in ref. to survivors of Mons or The Somme or Passchendaele or any other sanguinary battle of WW1. (Fernley O. Pascoe, 1975.)

Eric Fearon, 1984, notes the phrase's juxtaposition with a cliché: *he was one of nature's gentlemen* (pause) *there aren't many of us left.*

[there are plenty more fish in the sea (Aus.) or... **pebbles on the beach** (Brit.) lie at a point where proverb and cliché and c.p. meet. It has, throughout C20, been addressed to a girl when her romance comes to an end. (B.P., 1975.)]

there are two people I don't like and you're both of them. It arose early in the 1930s and may have been suggested by a silent-film subtitle. (Shaw, 1969.) I don't recall hearing the c.p. before *c.* 1937. Cf the witticism, 'There are two fools born every minute and you're all three of them.'

there are worse in gaol (or **jail**). See **worse in gaol.**

there aren't so many of us left, you know. See **there are only a few....**

there, boys, there. There, lads, enjoy yourselves! There, lads, isn't that (or this) fine! Late C16–mid C17. In Beaumont and Fletcher's, *The Knight of the Burning Pestle*, performed in 1611 and pub'd two years later, at III, v, Merrythought sings:

> If you will sing, and dance, and laugh,
> And hollow, and laugh again,
> And then cry, 'there, boys, there!' why, then,
> One, two, three, and four,
> We shall be merry within this hour.

there come de judge! See **here come de judge!**

there goes beef and beaver! 'An expression used by mountain men when they sustained a severe loss of any kind': US Westerners': *c.* 1870–1920. (Adams.) Here, *beef* = food and *beaver* = money; and clearly alliteration has woven its artful linguistic spell.

there goes his hotel! was, *c.* 1872–1920, a US professional gamblers' c.p., directed at one who goes on gambling until he loses even the money he had intended to reserve in order to pay his hotel bill (*U.*)

there has to be a first time for everything. See **there's a first time for everything.**

there he goes with his eye out! In his remarkable essay Mackay, after discussing (*Hookey*) *Walker!*, writes:

> The next phrase was a most preposterous one. Who introduced it, how it arose, or where it was first heard, are alike unknown. Nothing about it is certain, but that for months it was *the* slang *par excellence* of the Londoners, and afforded them a vast gratification. '*There he goes with his eye out!*' or '*There she goes with her eye out!*' ...was in the mouth of everybody who knew the town. The sober part of the community were as much puzzled by this unaccountable saying as the vulgar were delighted with it. The wise thought it very foolish, but the many thought it very funny, and the idle amused themselves by chalking it upon walls, or scribbling it upon monuments. But 'all that's bright must fade', even in slang. The people grew tired of their hobby, and '*there he goes with his eye out!*' was heard no more in its accustomed haunts.

The vogue of the phrase apparently belonged to the mid or latish 1830s. Note, however, that, early in chapter LIX of *Plain or Ringlets?*, 1860, Robert Surtees writes, concerning Mr Bunting: 'Four horses would be of no use to him with his mild style of riding, besides which he wouldn't like to go about with a man with one eye. The slang cry of "There you go with your eye out!" occurred to his recollection.'

I cannot avoid the *ignis fatuus* thought that perhaps this c.p. contains an allusion to some pertinent and widely quoted ref. to the crowd's seeing, a generation earlier, Nelson pass with his one eye.

P.B.: pursuing E.P.'s suggestion: it may be relevant that, while the construction of Trafalgar Square started in 1829 and went on for nearly 40 years, Nelson's Column was being erected 1840–43.

there he is! Wheel him in! See LIVERPOOL

there he stood with his finger in his ass, wondering what on earth to do: US: since the 1920s. (Fain, 1977.) Cf *with thumb in bum...*

there I was on my ditty box saying nothing to nobody. A US navy and Marine Corps saying: C20. 'Not in the mainstream of American speech' (W.J.B., 1975).

there is... See also entries at **there's...**

there is a letter in the post office. See **letter....**

there is always a tomorrow or **there will be (a) tomorrow** and the negative **there is–** or **will be–no tomorrow.** 'It is used to indicate that one has another chance to redeem a loss or a failure, e.g. to win a game or to succeed in a venture. The negative [indicates that] the defeat or lack of success is final and that there will be no opportunity to offset them' (Moe, 1978): US: since *c.* 1960 or perhaps a decade earlier. From the aphorism *tomorrow will be a new day*, based upon Spanish *mañana es otra dia*, and going back to Cervantes in *Don Quixote*. Contrast **like there was no tomorrow.**

there is no punishment when no pun is meant. See **puns are punishable.**

there is the door the carpenter made, usu. with *there* emphasized. You may go: lower-middle class: *c.* 1750–1800. It occurs in *Sessions Paper of the Central Criminal Court*, 1767, in the account of the trial of Rebecca Pearce. Cf **there's the door....**

there is York Street concerned. See **York Street....**

there must be an easier way (or easier ways) of making a living has, since the middle or late 1940s, been applied to difficult or dangerous, arduous or precarious, occupations, as in Brian Lecomber's exciting aviation 'thriller', *Turn Killer* (1975), where Ken Holland, stunt flyer, records, '...I was fighting down the hollow ball of fear in my stomach and listening to a still small voice somewhere in my head, saying for the thousandth time that there must be an easier way of making a living. I agreed with the voice...'

there ought to be a law against it! is a (mainly Aus.) expression of disgust: since *c.* 1960. As the contributor, B.P., adds, 1975: 'Self-evident in meaning, but very interesting sociologically'.

A.B., 1979, comments that the phrase is prob. from the pithier US *there ought to be a law*, which formed the title of a syndicated comic strip by the American newspaper cartoonist, Jimmy Hatto: 'I read it in the 1940s and 1950s in various newspapers, but I haven't seen it recently. The cartoon showed people in various situations, humorous of course, from which there seemed no way out.'

there she blows! is an impudent cry directed at a fat woman seen bathing: C20. From the whaler's cry upon sighting a whale. P.B.: often pron. *thar...*: cf the pron. in **there's gold...**

there she goes with her eye out! See **there he goes....**

there, that'll hold you. See **that'll hold you.**

there was a cow climbed up a tree. 'A retort, equivalent to telling a man that he is a liar' (F & G); John Brophy, in B & P), says:

If one were thought to be telling a lie, his mates either sang

Comrades don't believe him (*ter*):
He's such a bloody [or fucking] liar,

or chanted

There was a cow

Climbed up a tree:
Oh, you bloody liar (*fortissimo*).

It is to be noted that many of the longer sayings were occ. chanted.

In short, a C20 c.p., very popular in the British Army of WW1 – not much heard since *c.* 1950.

there was I at 20,000 feet... See **upside down in cloud.**

there were four turds for dinner – usu. amplified, **stir turd, hold turd, tread turd and must turd.** 'To wit, a hog's face, feet, and chitterlings, with mustard' (Grose, 1796): a low rebus c.p. of *c.* 1760–1830.

there you ain't was, *c.* 1870–1914, a proletarian, notably Cockney, declaration or imputation of failure. (B & L.) You're not on the spot when you're needed.

[**there you go!** Not a true c.p. – rather a cliché. US, it occurs in, e.g., Joseph C. Neal, *Peter Ploddy*, 1844, on p. 6.

P.B.: as a term of approbation, gen. of a specific action, method, etc., or as an expression of agreement or even thanks, it had a sudden brief popularity in UK *c.* 1980–1. Its status then might be said to have verged on c.p.]

there'll (or **there will**) **be a chicken in every pot.** Alerted to this c.p. by Skehan, I passed it to J.W.C. who, 1977, glossed it thus:

It was a Republican slogan in the presidential (and congressional) campaign of 1928 and was commonly attributed to the Republican candidate who had been in office since 1925. I doubt whether he himself actually used the phrase, but it was widely used by everybody else as summarizing the Republican promise. After the crash of 1929, it was dropped by the Republicans, in embarrassment, but widely [used] sarcastically by their opponents, who occasionally used the elaboration, [*and*] *two cars in every garage*. They have both long been obsolete, or virtually so, but everybody over 40 remembers them well, and they were certainly widely current as catchphrases. The heyday of (there will be) a chicken in every pot was late 1929 – (say) 1933.

P.B.: cf other such political boomerangs as **three acres and a cow**, q.v., and Lloyd George's promise in 1918, of 'a fit country for heroes to live in'. See also **there'll be pie...**

there'll be a hot time in the old town to-night. See **hot time....**

there'll be blood for breakfast. See **blood for breakfast.**

there'll be dirty work at the cross-roads. See **one of these dark nights...**

there'll be pie in the sky when you die; more usu. **you'll get....** A derisive and cynical US c.p. dating since *c.* 1907 and implying that a reward hereafter is an illusion and a delusion; apparently deriving immediately from the parody of a facilely promissory hymn and much influenced by the propaganda of the IWW – Industrial Workers of the World – movement. See esp. *Webster's New International Dictionary*, 3rd edn; and *DSUE* Supplement. Cf **there's a good time coming.**

Playfair notes, 1977, that in the *there'll be...*, not in the *you'll get...*, form, the phrase migrated to the UK *c.* 1943. In both countries, the shortening *pie in the sky* became very common since *c.* 1945.

there're gentlemen present, ladies! See **gentlemen present....**

there's a blow in the bell. There's something wrong, something suspicious, somewhere: US underworld: *c.* 1920–60. (Herbert Corey, *Farewell, Mr Gangster*, 1936.) Something that fails to 'ring true'.

there's a blue shirt at the masthead. See **blue shirt....**

there's a bun in the oven refers to a pregnancy: and the US form is *...cake...* Fain dates its US heyday as *c.* 1920–50. The Brit. form (frequently, *she's got a bun...*) dates from *c.* 1910 and is not yet (1978) quite †.

there's a deal (or **a lot**) **of glass about.** See **deal of glass...**

there's a deal of weather about. See **deal of weather....**

there's (or **there has to be**) **a first time for everything; also there's always a first time.** See Terence Rattigan, *Who Is Sylvia?*, performed in 1950 and pub'd in 1951, in Act I:

DAPHNE: Shall I let you into a little secret? This is my very first taste of caviare.
MARK: Well, there has to be a first time for everything, doesn't there?

But *there's always a first time* is mostly a mocking, occ. a consolatory, rejoinder to 'I've never done that before': it did not become gen. until *c.* 1945; it is both Brit. and US; and it has, one surmises, a sexual origin. In the main, it is still (1975) a c.p., although it has, since the late 1960s, shown unmistakable signs of becoming a proverb.

there's a good time coming is, used lit., a cliché; used ironically to one in trouble or danger – well and truly **up Shit Creek without a paddle** – it is, however, a c.p. – going back to when? I heard it, as a c.p., during WW1. Cf **there'll be pie...**

there's a joke. See **joke over.**

[**there's a lid for every pot** is applied particularly to 'seemingly strange marriages and generally in the sense "there's always some kind of solution possible". Also, somewhat sexual. I cannot date this, but I heard it from a German Catholic [American] from Southern Illinois' (A.B., 1979). It's prob. safe to place it as 'late C19–20' and to classify it as 'semi-proverbial'. That, admittedly, was a guess, but I did find it richly confirmed, exemplified, parallelled, in *Stevenson's Book of Quotations, Maxims and Familiar Sayings*, 1948, at p. 1427; and it goes back to at least C16.]

there's a nigger in the woodpile is recorded by HLM, 1922; and in Supp. 1 he both notes that this characteristically US phrase has been 'traced by the *DAE* to 1861' – respectably old – and that it is, by that eminent dictionary, defined as 'a concealed or inconspicuous but highly important fact, factor or "catch" in an account, proposal, etc.' Berrey cites it as having the var. *on the fence* and as connoting suspicion.

Current – surprisingly early – also in Can., where ... *nigger in the fence* is the commoner form (not *on*) and where *nigger in the melon-patch* also exists although less commonly than in the US. I have not found the third form recorded elsewhere, but the *D.Am.* records ... *in the fence* as early as 1850, with the definition much the same as that in the *DAE*. Cf:

there's a nigger in the woodshed (It's usu., since *c.* 1920,– shed, not – pile). 'Sometimes preceded by "there seems to be a" or "there must be a" or "there must have been a". In the Southern US, this tended (we no longer use it *openly*) to mean that something was either wrong or highly unusual about some situation. Sometimes it was used to question someone's ancestry, his racial origins' (A.B., 1979). The *D.Am.* provides early dates as 1852 and 1911 – both, however, as *woodpile*. Moreover, *Stevenson's Book of Quotations...*, 1948, has, as its earliest and predominant form, *woodpile* – which I have never heard in the UK or in Aus., but in both of which I've known the phrase since *c.* 1918, always as *woodshed*.

P.B.: but I, on the other hand, had always heard the *woodpile* form in UK; it seemed natural, because when I was a child there was a woodpile on my grandfather's farm. I have also often heard the phrase applied to a person upon whom suspicion rests, or is proved: 'So *he's* (or *he* was) the nigger in the woodpile!' Cf **something nasty in the woodshed.**

there's a one-eyed man in the game. 'Look out for a cheat!' – a warning uttered where cardsharps are about. Ramon Adams makes it clear that this c.p. arose thus: 'One of the most common superstitions in the early West was that bad luck would forever follow a man who played poker with a one-eyed gambler.' At a guess, the c.p. got started in *c.* 1860.

'there's a pair of us', as the Devil said to his knee-buckles. N.W. Bancroft, in *From Recruit to Staff Sergeant*, 1885, writing of the Governor-General of India, Sir Henry Hardinge, visiting the wounded after the battle of Ferozeshah, Sikh War, 1845, has 'If a poor fellow had lost an arm, the Governor-General would point to his own empty sleeve,... as much as to say – "There's..."'. (P.B.)

there's a shape for you! referred, *c.* 1850–1910, to a person – or a quadruped – extremely thin.

there's a smell of gunpowder is an oblique, unexpectedly polite, ref. to a breaking of wind: army: late C19–20.

there's a war on. See **remember there's...**

there's 'air! See **there's hair!**

there's always a first time. See **there's a first time for everything.**

there's always something to inconvenience – or to disappoint – you: since the late 1940s.

there's an awful lot of coffee in Brazil! Since *c.* 1948. Perhaps from a song popular in the late 1940s and early 1950s. Only when it's *not* applied to coffee is it a c.p. It ironically and tactfully condemns the utterance of a truism by the addressee.

there's an 'oss a-layin' down the law. 'When you see a lawyer floored, sing out, "There's an 'oss a layin' down the law!"' (R.S. Surtees, *Handley Cross; or, Mr Jorrock's Hunt*, 2 vols, 1854, vol. 1, the chapter headed 'Another Sporting Lector', i.e. lecture): a fox-hunting c.p. of *c.* 1820–80. Here, 'floored' = thrown off his horse.

there's another job needs doing. 'This has been heard used by overseas women of the moneyed type. When a male servant or [a visiting] workman has been doing jobs in a lounge or [a] drawing-room, the employer [reclining] on a couch may say this to him' (A.B., 1969): C20; but I cannot pinpoint the date.

there's another show. A racecourse cry, meaning that a 'tictac' man has signalled fresh odds: C20. (The *Cornhill Magazine*, 1932, in an article by George Baker.) Another – a different – showing of the odds offered by bookmakers on the course.

there's at least one in every club has, prob. since early C.20, been a Brit. c.p., applicable to bores and conversation-monopolisers, in short to the 'pew-emptiers'. That it became also a US, esp. New York and Boston and Washington, c.p. was largely due to a cartoonist, Clare A. Briggs (1875–1930), who thus titled one of his series. The President of the Gale Research Company, Mr F.G. Ruffner (orig. Jr), selected a number of cartoons for two of his Christmas leaflets during the early and middle 1970s: and in the Foreword he wrote: 'Think how often you hear the phrases "invented" – let's not quibble about "invented"! – by Briggs, "When a Feller Needs a Friend" – "Ain't it a Grand and Glorious Feelin'?" – "Somebody is always Taking the Joy out of Life – "The Days of Real Sport" – "Oh Man" – "There's at least One in Every Club" – whenever the actual situation before us takes on a comic aspect how readily these phrases of Briggs come tripping from our tongues.' Cf. *oh, man!* at **oh, boy!**

there's blood for breakfast. See **blood for breakfast.**

there's eyesight in it. That's evident or obvious: since the early 1930s. Clear to the view.

there's gold in them thar hills is a US c.p. (recorded by Berrey, who glosses it as 'there is good profit in that enterprise'), current throughout C20 and prob. also in latish C19, also deriving from the literal assertion dating, presumably, since the great gold rush of 1849; adopted in UK, although not very generally, during the 1930s and become fairly gen. during the late 1940s–50s.

Of its Brit. use, R.S. wrote in 1960: 'A c.p. from the Frontier days in the US [and] anglicized by early Western films. Over here it was ironical, impugning the probability of some extravagant hope; by 1960, it was virtually obsolete' – true; but it has certainly been fairly popular in England during the 1970s. The c.p. is revealingly employed by Noël Coward, *Waiting in the Wings*, performed and pub'd 1960, at II, i, where Zelda, visiting a charity home for aged actresses, exclaims 'There's certainly gold in these yar hills.' Note, too, the significance of the fact that on the front page of the *Sunday Telegraph*, 7 Apr 1974, appeared a small cartoon of two miners looking at a couple of great slagheaps and one of them saying, 'I'm telling you – there's gold in them thar hills' – the ref. being to a land-deal scandal relating to reclaimed land.

In respect of its US use, it is interesting to see how

Clarence Budington Kelland, an immensely successful not-very-good novelist with an acute ear for easy coll. everyday speech, uses it in *House of Cards*, 1941, in chapter XIV: 'If a bird from Chicago presents himself,' Ream said, please cherish him....'

She heard him chuckle. 'Thar's gold in them thar hills.' (The speaker is a contract bridge expert. He implies that there's a fortune to be made in that quarter.)

'I've heard physicians alter this, punningly, to "there's gold in them thar ills", meaning, I think, in times of epidemic disease, there's money to be made. [The *hills* form] is probably seldom used now, and I've heard it only infrequently' (A.B., 1979).

Not only in the US but also in the UK, this c.p. has become so much a part of everyday speech that it can be punned-on, as in Helen MacInnes, *Prelude to Terror*, 1978, 'He never enjoyed cutting anyone to knee-level, particularly a woman. One thing he had learned, though, in these recent months: to be on guard, don't trust completely, there are deep bogs in them thar meadows.'

there's hair (occ. **'air**)! There's a girl with a lot of hair!: London streets': *c.* 1900–10. (Ware.) Ware dates it at 1900 and refers it to the vogue that favoured 'packed masses, coming down over the forehead'; but the phrase lingered for perhaps a decade.

It developed into *there's (h)air–like wire!*, long and stiff: remembered by Colin Clair, the eminent biographer, and the historian of printing, as heard by him, at the mature age of six, in 1906, and recorded by Collinson in his alert, perceptive, shrewd book. Comparable is the Yorkshire, esp. the West Riding, simile applied to hair: *as straight as a yard of pump water*.

Cf the Liverpool c.p. *there's hair*–pron. *durs ur–on baldy*, 'shouted by L'pool street girls *c.* 1924' (Frank Shaw, the great authority on Merseyside speech and folklore, 1968).

there's life in the old dog (or **old girl**) **yet.** He or she is still very much alive, still capable of a love affair: late (? mid) C19–20. In H.V. Esmond, *The Law Divine*, performed on 29 Aug. 1918 and pub'd 1922, in Act II we read:

BILL: ...He's much too old to go messing about with widows.

TED: (*chuckles*): There's life in the old dog yet.

And then Noël Coward wrote in 1923 a dramatic sketch titled 'There's Life in the Old Girl Yet'– included in *Collected Sketches and Lyrics*, 1931.

there's money bid for you. See **hold up your head**....

there's more hair there than anywhere. See **more hair there**...

there's more in that head than the comb'll ever take out. 'An ironic Anglo-Irish c.p. with the overt meaning, "You're clever"' (Shaw, 1969): C20. The ref. to *comb* implies nits in the hair.

there's more room for it out here than (**there is**) **in there,** 'pointing to one's stomach. Said after someone has belched or farted' (A.B., 1978). Cf **better an empty house**...

there's no answer to that! (– **well,**). Miss Penny A. Cook, writing in 1975, says:

One punch line that seems to be catching on now is 'Well, there's no answer to *that*!' and there isn't– nor, of course, is there expected to be. It is the ultimate face-saver, leaving one with the last line, the last laugh, and without the necessity of having to think up an original retort to the preceding repartee.

Dating, I think, since late 1973 or early 1974. Supplementing that, is this: 'Eric Morecambe's catchphrase, meaning that the innuendo which can be read into the question makes an answer superfluous' (Mr D.R. Bartlett, MA, FLA, later in 1975). P.B. recalls 'the splendid Buckinghamshire dialect records of monologues by (Sir) Bernard Miles made before WW2, which used to end up with the discomfiture of "posh" village ladies, "...That 'ad 'er– unanswerable, that were."'

VIBS provides a genuine example: 'Eric Morecambe's standard innuendo-laden response to such comments as:

Frank Finlay (as Casanova): I'll be perfectly frank with you – I have a long felt want.'

there's no doubt about (significant pause) **you!** An Aus. c.p., expressing admiration and dating since *c.* 1925.

there's no future in it. See **no future in it.**

there's no kick (or **squawk**) **coming.** That's satisfactory. That's O.K. by me – no complaints at all. US: since *c.* 1920. Berrey.

there's no mileage in *that*, meaning 'there's no future in it', is a c.p. prompted by the slang become coll. *get no mileage out of*, no profit, no advantage: since late 1960s. (Mrs Camilla Raab, 1977.)

there's no 'must' about it, late (? mid) C19–20, is the c.p. that has emerged from a number of *there's no* (something or other) *about it*, which is a cliché pattern. Michael Arlen, *The Green Hat*, 1924, has for instance: '"You *must* do it." – "There's no *must* about it."' (cited by Collinson).

there's no point trying to pin the tail on the donkey, as in Glendon Swarthout's *The Tin Lizzie Troop*, 1972 (but valid for 1917): 'They were on their feet, fists raised, glaring at one another. "There's no point trying to pin the tail on the donkey", said Phipps. "We're all to blame."' The connotation is 'There's no point trying to pin the blame on any one individual'; from the children's party game of trying blindfold to pin a tail at the right place on a picture of a tail-less moke.

there's no show without Punch. See **no show**....

[**there's no snakes in Virginny** (Virginia). In full, if I don't do such or such a thing, there's no snakes in Virginny. I'll most certainly do it: US: very approx. 1800–90. 'I have encountered this expression, or a variant, at least half a dozen times in my readings in the nineteenth century' (Moe, who then cites a passage from Matthew Edward Barker's anecdotes, about the Chelsea pensioners in the *London Literary Gazette* of 3 Jan. 1824: 'Halloo!' – 'I say...if you ever send your Joey aboard of me again, and I don't break his neck, there's no snakes in Virginny.') Apparently it stands midway between c.p. and cliché, for it isn't entirely self-contained and free.]

there's no squawk coming. See **there's no kick coming.**

there's no two ways about it has, in C20, been a Brit. c.p., but it came from the US, where it may have been current as early as 1840, to judge by the fact that, in his *Am*, Bartlett has the entry: 'THERE'S NO TWO WAYS ABOUT IT, *i.e.* the fact is just so and not otherwise. A vulgarism of recent origin, equivalent to the common phrase, *"there's no mistake about it"* or "the fact is so and so *and no mistake"*.'

there's nobody here but us chickens. See **ain't nobody here**...

there's nothing like a good shit. See **good shit**...

there's nothing like it. A C20 c.p., as often as not used with little relevance or none. P.B.: perhaps ex the archetypal **nothing like leather** – or the prec.

there's nothing more: that's all there is is the textually correct form (as coined by Ethel Barrymore, 1879–1959, in 1906) of what has come to be rather more often used: **that's all there is: there isn't any more,** q.v.

there's nothing spoiling. There's no hurry – no urgency: C20. Of domestic origin; and often domestic in application. (Petch, 1974.)

there's nowt so queer as folk. There's nothing so odd as people: It's a queer world!: mid C19–20. Orig. and still a Yorkshire saying, verging on the proverbial: but since *c.* 1890, much used in other parts of England. The loose *there's nothing-....* is to be deprecated.

Cf the witticism addressed to me in 1917 by a fellow Brigade Observer on the Western Front: 'There's an awful lot of human nature in men, women, and children.'

there's one born every minute, to which they **say** is sometimes appended. Elliptical for 'one fool'. This c.p. implies that either oneself or another has been duped: C20. By *c.* 1945, it had begun to acquire, yet by 1975 it had still not yet attained, the status of a proverbial saying. 'From a saying attributed to

P.T. Barnum (1810–91), the circus magnate, "There's a sucker born every minute"' (Leechman).

'Elaborated by professional confidence men as "...and two to rope (entrap) him and three to trim (fleece) him" (D. Maurer, *The Big Con*, *c*.1950)' (R.C., 1978).

[there's only one way to find out – i.e., 'Try it!' – lies midway between cliché and c.p.: C20;? rather late C19–20. P.B.: by later C20, *there's* is often omitted.]

there's safety in numbers. See **safety in numbers.**

there's shit not far behind is a late C19–20 workmen's c.p., evoked by a loud breaking of wind – but, as Cdr C. Parsons, RN ret., tells me, 1977, it is not peculiar to workmen: the Services, esp. perhaps the RN, know it. The Navy's preferred version is *don't step back or you'll get your boots full of shit*. P.B.: cf the synon. (*that's*) *a bit near the mud*!

there's something rotten in the state of Denmark. See **something is rotten...**

there's sorrow on the sea. 'Traditional warning to one *who'd sell his farm and go to sea*' (Granville, 1962, but first recorded by him in 1949): prob. from as early as mid C19. More poetical than most c.pp.

there's the door: and your name is Walker! See **my name is Haines.**

there's the right way, the wrong way, and the Army way. 'Sardonic allusion to the fact that, in armies, efficiency (the right way) is less important than following orders (the army way). US Services', from 1930s or earlier; now obsolescent' (R.C., 1978).

these sets take a long time to warm up. Originated with Kenneth Horne, in concert with Richard Murdoch, in the radio programme 'Much Binding in the Marsh' during WW2. The gag, with its sly dig (cf that *Binding* = *binding*, RAF slang for complaining), became a c.p., which endured to *c*. 1960 and then passed into the faëry realm of nostalgic memories. P.B.: the sets referred to were of course the old-fashioned, pre-transistor age, valve radio sets, 'Wireless';. and Murdoch and Horne would accompany this c.p., 'Let's just see what's on the wireless...ah, these sets take a long time to warm up, you know', with imitation whistles, hums, squeaks and static before whatever it was they wanted to hear came on.

these things will happen (even) in the best-regulated families. See **such things....**

they came to do good...and they did well. 'Said of the C.19 US missionaries, to Hawaii, who having come to convert the heathen somehow ended up owning most of the land in the islands...: US: C. 20, now obsolete with the waning power of the Hawaiian "Big Six". Possibly a familiar quot., but if so I do not know the source. Cf. the familiar couplet about the Pilgrims of 1620, who "fell first upon their knees and then upon the aborigines".' (R.C., 1978).

they can do any bloody thing to you.... See **they can make you do....**

they can hear you, you needn't shout (or **there's no need to shout.**). 'Sometimes said to big-mouthed Yorkshiremen and Lancashire people when they boast that all their relatives are living in the north' (Petch, 1974): C20.

they can make you do anything in the air force except have a baby. 'A c.p. tribute to authority and discipline' (L.A.): RAF: since *c*. 1925. This is an adaptation of the army's (1914 onwards) c.p., which, obviously, substitutes...*in the army* – and which often adds and *they* (or *some of them*) *would have a bloody good try to do that*! Cf J.R.L. Anderson, *Death in the Thames*, 1974, 'The old saying that the army can do anything it likes with a man except put him in the family way expresses a pretty exact truth.' Among Australians, the predominant form was *they can do any bloody thing (at all) to you in the army except put you in the family way – and some of them would have a bloody good try to do that* (final word emphasized). Cf **they tame lions...** and **even the Admiralty...**

they don't grow on trees is a 'lament that few brilliant people or rare items are "in short supply" (few are in much demand)'

(Granville, 1968): since the late 1940s. This c.p. derives naturally, almost inevitably, from the much older *it doesn't grow on trees*, as applied to money.

they don't know there's a war on. See **remember there's a war on.**

they don't pipe dinner outside is a RN warning, whether to those who plan to desert ship or to those who, on completion of twelve years' service, rush unthinkingly into civilian life and thereby lose a number of benefits, such as duty-free tobacco and spirits: since *c.* 1930. (*Sailors' Slang*; 1962, and earlier Granville's book, *SS*.)

they don't yell, they don't tell, and they're very (very) grateful. A 'young men's tribute to love of good, mature women, and their supposed amorous response' (L.A., 1969): since *c.* 1920.

'The observation on gratitude was adumbrated in Benjamin Franklin's famous essay, "Advice to a Young Man on Choosing a Mistress"' (R.C., 1978). What a fellow he (1706–90) was! But was it not *Reasons for Preferring an Elderly Mistress*, 1745?

A.B. wrote, 1979, 'I have heard it this way: "I like women over forty: They don't yell – they don't swell – they don't tell – and they're grateful as hell". 1950s, I recall, but no longer current'.

they 'it where they touch. See **it fits where it touches.**

they give them away with a pound of tea. See **given away with...**

they go better loaded! (i.e., if loaded). 'Country humour; called in derision to someone [heavily] laden – the reference is, of course, to mules or donkeys' (B.G.T., 1978): rural England; prob. since latish C19 – or even earlier. Cf **clap your hands!**

they got (occ. **they've got**) **me**; also **they got me, pal.** 'A trivial c.p., uttered when one hears a peal of thunder or a loud explosion' (B.P.): mostly Aus.: since the latish 1930s. From the 'traditional' cry of the mortally wounded – at least in stories and films.

The third version (*they got me, pal*) is the earliest and widest-spread, for it is 'a mock-heroic c.p., burlesquing the gangster films of the 1930s. Speaker staggers, clutching chest, at noise like gunfire' (Shaw, 1969).

'More likely from Western, not gangster, films; the former not infrequently featured a touching farewell between the invulnerable hero and his vulnerable pal' (R.C., 1978). Contrast **you got me, pal.**

they gotta quit kicking my dawg around is US, 'from an American song. Probably *c.* 1912. Was used as a [political] campaign song' (W.J.B., 1975): *c.* 1910–40, then less and less.

they hosed them out. B.P., 1975, writes:

This grim [orig. RAF] c.p. was used during WW2. The claim was made that there was so little left of the bodies of rear gunners on bombers that they had to hose out the remains. A book about 'Tail-End Charlies' entitled *They Hosed Them Out* was published in Australia in 1965 and in England in 1969. It was written by John Beede.

The c.p. had soon spread to the air forces of the Commonwealth.

they laughed when I sat down at the piano. But when I started to play!; emphasis on *play*. 'That old advertisement has crept into the language as a standard cliché' (Monica Dickens in *Woman's Own*): not a cliché but a c.p.: since the 1920s. 'Usually, in US, "they all laughed"; "but when I started to play" is almost never added' (J.W.C., 1977).

'A classic advertising headline written by John Caples at Ruthrauff & Ryan [for the] US School of Music Piano tutor; US, from 1925. ..... The ad gave rise to various jokes – "They laughed when I sat down to play – somebody had taken away the stool" – and Caples also wrote a follow-up: "They Grinned When The Waiter Spoke To Me In French – But Their Laughter Changed To Amazement At My Reply"' (Nigel Rees, *Slogans*, 1982, q.v. for more on this famous advertisement – and on many, many others).

they must have captured a sugar-boat. See **captured....**

they sat on their hands is a C20 theatrical sarcasm, directed at an audience that has refused to clap. (Granville.)

they say the first hundred years are the hardest. See **first hundred years...**

they tame lions in the army was a Regular Army c.p. of *c.* 1890–1939. (Frank Richards, *Old Soldiers Never Die*, 1933.) The ref. being – or had you guessed? – to military disciplinary measures. Cf **we'll soon lick you into shape,** and **they can make you...**

they that ride on a trotting horse will ne'er perceive it. S, 1738, in Dialogue I has:

> MISS: [To Lady Answerall.] Madam, one of your Ladyship's Lappets is longer than t'other.
> LADY AND: Well, no Matter; they that ride on a trotting horse will ne'er perceive it.

The implication of this C18 c.p. is that only the idle notice trifles.

they think their shit doesn't stink; (he) thinks his shit doesn't stink. The former is applied to would-be superior girls: C20; the latter – in full, *he* (or *the sort of bloke who*) *thinks... but it does, all the same, like any other bugger's* has, since *c.* 1870, been applied to any conceited fellow. In Canada the shorter form, *his shit doesn't stink*, is used. Not a c.p. much heard among the educated and the cultured.

'More prevalent in the US of the 1930s was *he thinks his shit stinks* [presumably said of a man with an inferiority complex]. Then there's the American companion phrase *he thinks he's shit on a stick*, conceited' (Fain, 1977). R.C. noted, 1978: 'An occasional US variant: *she thinks her snatch* (i.e. vagina) *is lined with mink.* From 1930s; now ob. or †'.

For a good London example, there is Jim Wolveridge's *Ain't It Grand: This Was Stepney*, 1976, quoting a Jewish girl's reaction to her brother's taking a 'posh' stage-name: '"Al Feld", she'd grumble, "Where does he get that name from? Mr Big? He fancies his shit don't stink." Anyone in the East End who got too big for his boots got that one slung at him, it kept Al's kind in their place'.

they used to call him Robin Hood. New they call him robbin' bastard! 'A Services occasional c.p., particularly relevant in these days of leaping inflation, heard from time to time during the past couple of decades, *they used...* of anyone suspected of overcharging' (P.B., 1975).

Cf **some say 'Good old Sergeant'...**

[**they want their cake and a ha'penny** is a regional c.p., applied by North Country people to the Welsh: late C19–20. (L.A., 1976.) P.B.: this surely applies not only to the Welsh; let's be impartial in our prejudice while we still have the chance! *Bun* may be substituted for *cake* in the phrase, which is more semi-proverbial than c.p.; cf the old proverb 'you can't have your cake *and* eat it'.]

they want to be alone. See **put the lights out.**

they went that(t)away. See **went that(t)away.**

they're all in the box: just pick the right one. A Services' transport drivers' (esp. driving instructors') c.p., addressed to someone driving clumsily and chiefly if with a jarring of gears: prob. since the middle 1930s. (Y. Mindel, 1972.) Cf **sort 'em out!**

they're all the same with their head in a bag is synon. and approx. contemporaneous with **who looks at the mantelpiece...**, q.v. The implication is that a plain or homely-looking girl may be sexually desirable. (Skehan, 1977.)

they're all up at (old) Harwich. They're in a nice old mess: late C19 – early C20. (Manchon.) Why *Harwich*? Perhaps, folk-etymologically, from dialectal *harriage*, disorder, confusion.

they're better fuckers than fighters. See **better fuckers....**

they're both common has, since *c.* 1930, been a stock reply to 'What have they in common?' (Petch, 1978.) Here, *common* is used in the sense 'vulgar' – 'common as muck'.

they're doing land-office business. 'Their (commercial) affairs are exceptionally active and successful. American: late C19–20; now ob. From the days when farmland could be obtained, through the government or speculators, at modest or no cost; hence, an office that sold or allocated homesteads was expectably very busy' (R.C., 1978).

they're eating nothing. They'll sell later, esp., their business: tradesmen's: C20; they are doing so badly that they cannot afford to eat. By 1970, ob.

they're either all shit or all shine. See **all honey...**

'they're off', said the monkey. See **as the monkey said.**

they're only interested in one thing. See **men are interested...**

they're two a penny. 'Expendable; easy to come by; hardly worth notice. From a remark by Jesus (Matthew, 10) – "Are not sparrows two a penny. Yet without your Father's leave, not one of them can fall to the ground"' (Noble, 1975). Prob. since latish C19; my own memory of it goes back to *c.* 1910.

E.P. later added: Mr Kingsley Amis is right when, in the *Observer*, 4 Sep. 1977, he sternly comments 'I must take Mr Partridge severely to task. He says it comes from a remark by Jesus, and quotes, "Are not sparrows two a penny?" Accorded to St Matthew, what Jesus said was, "Are not two sparrows sold for a farthing?"' In the Authorised Version, 1611, that is so. As Mr Amis allows, the words I cited must have come from one of the C.20 versions; 'It was the travesty-merchant who tastelessly adopted the catch phrase, thereby giving Jesus's question a wholly inappropriate air of the chummily colloquial'. Seldom have I been thus chastised: and, although I'm no masochist, I admit to being grateful for the castigation.

P.B.: In fairness to E.P., though, it should be mentioned that St Matthew, Ch. 10. v. 29, does appear in the *New English Bible* as 'Are not sparrows two a penny?', while the *Revised Standard Version*, the *Jerusalem Bible* and the *Good News Bible* all equate the price of two sparrows, according to Jesus, to one penny. *N.E.B.* renders St Luke, Ch. 12, v. 6, as 'Are not sparrows five for twopence?', while the other versions give 'five for two pennies'.

they've opened another tin was current, among the army's Other Ranks, in 1915–18. 'An expression frequently heard... in a depreciatory sense, with reference to some recently arrived draft, or officer' (F & G). Presumably a tin of sardines.

they've shot our fox. 'My memory is... that this was Nigel Birch's exclamation when [in 1947] Hugh Dalton resigned as Chancellor of the Exchequer. Not very common, but persistent. After I had written it down to add to this list [1977], I heard it from the mouth of the Master of an Oxbridge College' (Playfair).

thick. See: **short and; too thick.**

thick ... and tired of it. 'Used in reference to a pregnant or [less usually, very] stout woman.' (Petch, 1969): since *c.* 1930. Obviously a pun on *sick and tired of it* (informal S.E.).

thick as a short plank – usu. prec. by either **he's, she's** or **you're, as** – and having the variants *as a four-inch plank* and even, to indicate extreme stupidity, *thicker than two four-inch planks*. 'In the Army, *thick as two Cavalry subalterns*, which is unkind and unjust – a Cavalry subaltern was bright enough to carry off the most eligible girl in the Kingdom' (Sanders, 1978). Since *c.* 1960 in the Services, but rather earlier among civilians. 'There is, of course, no such thing as a four-inch plank; it would be a beam or a joist' (Ibid.) P.B., 1979: During the past decade or so, the phrase as I have heard it has always been *as thick as two short planks*; there were also a couple of unkind Army variants in the Far East, 1960s – but with the seeming unkindness tempered by affection – *as thick as a Gurkha's foreskin* and ... *as the Brigade of Gurkhas in parallel*. In the shorthand of slang, the whole idea is now, early 1980s, reduced to the simple *planky*.

thicken. See: **plot thickens.**

thief. See: **you are a t.**

thimble on a bull's arse – (like) a. A North Country (and prob. elsewhere rural) description of a small cap on a large head:

C.20, and prob. since, say, 1850. (Edwin Haines, 1978.) Cf. **Tom Tit on a round of beef** and *pea on a drum*.

thin. See; cake is getting; it's boloney; ribbin; so thin; too thick.

thin as a boarding-house blanket (–**as**). Woefully thin, as of a person; also in the games of bowls, especially in S. Africa: C. 20. (Based on a note in A. Cooper Partridge's review in *English Usage in Southern Africa*, May 1978.)

thin edge of nothing – the. Applied, during the 1920s and 1930s, 'when people are very crowded and there is hardly room to sit' (Lyell).

thing(s). See: do your own t.; how's things; I haven't a t.; I know one t.; I'll tell you one; if it isn't; it's just one of those things; life is just one; pore ole t.; putting their; very identical; you say the nicest.

things ain't what they used to be. Implied at **fings ain't wot they used ter be**. It is rather the former than the latter which attracts the dovetail *were they ever?*

things are crook ... See **things is crook ...**

things are looking up! has, since *c.* 1925, been addressed to – or directed at – someone wearing a new suit or owning a new car. 'Jocular *double entendre* phrase: improvement in conditions; priapism' (L.A., 1975).

things are rough (or **tough**) **all over.** A sardonic rejection of someone's complaints about hard luck, the injustice of life, etc. In effect, 'things are no tougher for you than for anyone else': US: from (?) 1920. Cf **tough shit!**

things I do for England! – the. L.A. wrote, 1975:

Self-congratulation on achievements unrealized or unsung by others. Current in 1930s; quoted from film *The Private Life of Henry the Eighth* .... script by Lajos Biro. Prompted by first marital felicity with one of his less attractive brides. – Apt when act of grace is duty rather than pleasure.

But it has been occ. heard since the 1930s; it still is – I have myself heard it, more than once, during the 1970s.

Cf **close your eyes and think of England!**

things I do for you! – the. Orig. (*c.* 1955 as an established c.p.) and mainly Brit. Philip Purser, *The Holy Father's Navy*, 1971, has:

Affection needs love as much as love needs affection. .... I kissed her.

She said, 'What are you thinking of?'

'Guess.'

'You must be joking.'

'I'm deadly earnest. And Deadly Ernest.'

Every couple has its private, awful jokes. ...

She relaxed. 'The things I do for you.'

things is crook in Muswellbrook; and things is weak in Werris Creek. Aus. card-players' c.pp., applied to a poor hand; recorded by Baker: since *c.* 1920.

Mr Jack Slater, of Oldham, Lancs, wrote, 1978, that 'it had a local variation at Rum Jungle, Northern Territory, about 1961, *i.e.* "Things are crook at Tookarook and there's no bloody work in Bourke". I fancy that [this] did have some basis in fact, either from the shearers' strikes in 1890 or from the Depression of the [early] 1930s.' I'd say the latter. Wilkes indicates that ... *Tallarook* was a more often heard place-name, and that *are* is more usual than *is*; other place-names are used, provided they rhyme. What's more, they are all applied to 'any adverse situation'. Aus. c.pp. tend to proliferate in variants perhaps more than any other country's.

things you see when you haven't got your gun – the (exclamatory). For instance, an odd-looking man or an oddly dressed woman: prob. late C19–20, although I myself don't remember hearing it before *c.* 1920; by 1971, slightly ob., for, by that time *not* to be oddly dressed was, in itself, almost an oddity.

'I've heard, a couple of times, "The things you see when you haven't got your camera"; and this Christmas, on the Morecambe and Wise Shaw, Leonard Rossiter said, on being introduced to Eric Morecambe, "Oh, my God – the things

you see at Christmas!"' (Levene, 1979).

think. See: do you t.; don't look now; great minds; he thinks; I can't t.; I didn't t.; I don't t.; I think; it's later; lights; makes you t.; my pocket; now you'll t.; she thinks; that what you t.; they think; we don't want; what do you t.; what will they; yes, I don't; you can't t.; you must t.; you think; you're not paid.

think big! is characteristically US, and current since the early 1950s. 'It all began with business executives putting the slogan "THINK BIG!" on their office walls to inspire themselves and their staff to higher goals. It was picked up and used in cartoons in *The New Yorker* and other smart publications. Then it passed into common speech as a humorous admonition to anyone making a timid approach to something. Often used without any specific meaning, but just to get a laugh' (W.J.B., 1978).

think I've just been dug up? See **do you think....**

think nothing of it! This is both Brit. and US, dating since the 1940s, meaning 'Oh, that's all right', *or* 'You're welcome'; 'It's a trifle – let's not exaggerate!'

In Terence Rattigan, *The Sleeping Prince*, performed 1953 and pub'd in 1954; at I, i, we read:

NICHOLAS: (*To* MARY.) I shall not soon forget your kindness in this matter, Miss Dagenham.

MARY: Think nothing of it.

Ellery Queen, *Cop Out*, 1969, has:

'Thanks a lot, Tru ...'

Hyatt waved, 'Think nothing of it.'

Dominic Devine, *Illegal Tender*, 1970, also uses it:

'Thanks. I'm not holding you back?'

'Think nothing of it,' she said drily.

So does Val Gielgud, in *The Black Sambo Affair*, 1972:

'...No, Humphrey, you haven't wasted your time and effort.'

'Think nothing of it, Greg.'

It can also be found in Julian Symons, *The Players and the Game*, 1972, and Dick Francis, *Smokescreen*, 1972.

think of England! See **close your eyes ...**, and cf **things I do for England.**

think of the poor starving children in China! See **remember the starving ...**

thinking. See: good thinking.

thinks he holds it – he. He's conceited and vain: *c.* 1870–1930: orig. a sporting, soon become a gen., c.p. (Ware.) By *it* is meant either a championship or a prize.

thinks he's tough, but he only smells strong – he. See **prove it, liar.**

thinks his shit doesn't stink. See **they think ....**

thinks the sun shines out of her (or **his**) **arsehole** (or **arse**) – **he** (or **she**). He idolizes her, or she him: late C19–20– and perhaps from very much earlier. The phrase has become so embedded in the language that it can, with perfect naturalness, appear in Julian Symons, *A Three Pipe Problem*, 1975, thus: 'And you said yourself that those two old people thought the sun shone out of Gledson's backside.'

P.B.: applicable also to a person him-(or her)self, i.e. he or she is immensely conceited. Elliptical there for 'his own arse'. A rather charming, occ. heard euph. for the objective phrase is as in 'You think the flowers grow out of his head'. See also **lights of Piccadilly ...**

thirsty. See: if only.

thirty-five years!, long drawn out, expresses the idea of a very long time; it was orig. for the radio comedy programme 'Beyond Our Ken', starring Kenneth Horne and inaugurated in 1964. In it 'there was a character who every week was led up to saying, in a quavery, over-emphatic voice, something like "Thirty-five years I bin in this job. THIRTY FIVE YEARS!" I've heard the c.p. time and again, and it's still around' (P.B., 1977). Barry Took notes that Kenneth Williams, who played the part, excelled in old-man parts. Cf the Biblical use of *forty years* as a long, indefinite period.

this channel is full of rocks, I know them all: (significant pause)

and that's one of them. 'Royal Navy joke about Irish pilots, 18th Century' (Peppitt).

this has put the top-hat on it. See **that's put the lid on it.**

this hurts me more than it hurts you, a cliché – and usu. a barefaced lie – used by parents administering corporal punishment to their offspring, has come, in C20 (I myself never heard it so used before *c.* 1920), to be a scathingly derisive c.p. ref. to that very odd moral attitude which used to be taken by over-severe and, implicatively, sadistic, parents.

P.B.: the phrase was used to me, in all seriousness, by the headmaster of the preparatory school I attended, early 1940s, before he beat me for using 'dirty words'. Readers of this dictionary will appreciate the ineffectiveness of the punishment.

this I must hear, and ***this I must see*** express an amused intention, partly ironic and partly deprecatory: since the late, perhaps the middle 1940s. I can hardly do better than quote from a letter sent to me in 1969:

Based on 1930's joke, US – Yiddish origin. Eavesdropper by honeymoon bedroom.
'I'll get on top.'
'No, I'll get on top.'
'No, let's both get on top.'
Eavesdropper: '*This* I *must* see.'
Couple were trying to close suitcase. Collapse of stout eavesdropper.

'Widely current (and perhaps for twenty years) among all classes – perhaps especially the educated. A real c.p., I think, although only with the marked stresses' (J.W.C., 1975).

By the 1960s, also Brit. Alistair MacLean has *this I must see* in his espionage 'thriller', *Circus*, 1975.

'A variant – and the actual punch-line of the joke quoted, as I have heard it – is "*this* I got to *see*!"' (R.C., 1978).

this is (or **that's**) **a bit** (or **a little bit**) **of all right!** That, or this, is excellent; also applied to a pretty and compliant female: orig. and mainly Cockney: C20. An extension of the slang *a bit of all right*, something excellent or cosy or very welcome. The c.p. occurs in, e.g., Alexander Macdonald, *In the Land of Pearl and Gold*, 1907, ' "That's a bit of all right," said the guard, cutting a piece of the stem and putting it into his mouth.'

Occ. var., rare after *c.* 1930: ... *a bit of 'tout droit'*, from the mock or bogus Fr. *un morceau de tout droit.* (Manchon.)

this is all right! – meaning 'Things are all wrong', *or* 'Everything's wrong': *c.* 1896–1905. Ware quotes the *People*, 7 Nov. 1897, 'This is *all* right, nothing to eat or drink, and no one to speak to.'

this is an orchestra, not an elastic band. 'The classic observation by an exasperated musical director after trying in vain to keep pace with the woman vocalist who was hopelessly out of tune and time' (Granville): C20.

this is Funf speaking. See **Funf speaking** and TOMMY HANDLEY CATCH PHRASES.

this is it! and **this is mine!** are exclamations uttered when an approaching bomb or shell seems to portend one's imminent death: Armed Forces': 1940 onwards.

The former may have been adopted from US.

See **also well, this is it.**

this is me and you. This is between me and you – and no one else is to know: convicts': C20. An example occurs in Jim Phelan, *Lifer*, 1938: ' "This is me and you," Cobb went on, using the jail phrase demanding secrecy.'

this is mine! See **this is it!**

this is my day out is consecrated to those sacred occasions when one person 'stands treat' to a group in, or even to all the occupants of, a bar in a public-house: since *c.* 1930.

this is no place for a clergyman's son. 'Facetious remark made when conversation turns to sex [*the lowest common denominator*, as some wit has defined it]. Royal Navy, 1970s' (Peppitt). But long before 1970: within my own experience,

1921 at latest. And not only in the RN. Although it perhaps doesn't fully qualify, *clearly* (or *obviously*) *this is no place for a nicely brought up girl* formed, *c.* 1920–65, a feminine counterpart.

this is not (more emphatically; **definitely not**) **my day.** See **it's just one of those days.**

this is not only but also. In Dialogue I of S, 1738, Swift writes:
NEV[EROUT]: Miss, I want that Diamond Ring of Yours.
MISS: Why then, Want's like to be your Master.
[Neverout *looking at the Ring.*]
NEV: Ay marry, this is not only, but also; pray, where did you get it?

this is not only handsome but valuable is a C18 c.p. expressive of astonishment at, or admiration of, superlative quality. Characteristic of the polished eloquence of polite society in that century.

this is rat week: write to your M.P. 'A contemptuous c.p., dating from before WW2' (Sanders, 1978).

this is so sudden! is a C20 c.p., either joc. or ironic, and applied to any unexpected offer or, less often, gift. From the reputedly customary reply of a girl to an offer of marriage. (Collinson.)

US as well as Brit. See Clarence Budington Kelland, in *Dance Magic*, 1927:

'Petrie,' said Mrs Wilder, 'this is Jahala Chandler. ... I'm going to make a team of you and Miss Chandler. Petrie and Chandler! How will that look in electric lights?'

Petrie turned to survey Jahala and his eyes twinkled. 'This is so sudden,' he cried, and compelled Jahala to smile back at him.

In Noël Coward's first-written play (1920), not performed (up to 1923, anyway), but pub'd in 1925, Act III had contained this passage:
NAOMI: ... I want you to become a permanent member.
KELD: (*laughing*): This is very sudden.

And then in Act III of *This Was a Man*, pub'd in 1928 after it had been 'hurriedly banned by the Lord Chamberlain and forbidden production in England', Coward employs another slight variation:
EDWARD: If I were free, Zoe, would you marry me?
ZOE: Edward!
EDWARD: I suddenly thought of it.
ZOE (*laughing*): This is terribly sudden.

As B.P., 1975, remarks: 'This c.p. is used in the same circumstances as "I didn't know (that) you cared"'; that is, as in the opening paragraph of this entry. He adds: 'It is also used when someone accidentally touches a person of the opposite sex, in such a way that it could be interpreted as an embrace.' This usage – not only Aus., by the way – is the later of the two; not, I think, earlier than *c.* 1950, but, to be scholarly-honest, I didn't hear it before the early 1960s. P.B.: a Brit. var. of this latter is *I never knew you cared*, and it doesn't necessarily have to be a member of the *opposite* sex. E.P. later wrote of *this is so sudden*:

As a conventionalism-become-cliché it goes back heaven knows how far. Only when used ironically or as a 'dead-pan' joc. is it a c.p. Louisa May Alcott, 1832–88, has 'I am so young and this is so sudden'.

this is something like! Richard Brome's *The Covent Garden Weekend ... A Facetious Comedy*, written *c.* 1642, pub'd 1658, opens with Cockbrain – 'a Justice of Peace, the Weeder of the Garden' – saying to Rooksbill – 'a great Builder in Covent Garden' (a projector, a speculative builder): 'I Marry Sir [i.e., 'Aye, marry, sir!'] This is something like! These appear like Buildings! Here's Architecture exprest indeed! It is a most sightly situation and fit for Gentry and Nobility.' Rooksbill replies, 'When it is all finished, doubtlesse it will be handsome'; and Cockbrain asserts, 'It will be glorious.'

Prob. this has been a c.p. since early C17. In mid C19–20, often prec. by *well*.

Clearly elliptical for 'This is something like what we want, *or* what is needed.'

this is the day the eagle shits. See **golden eagle.**

this is the end! Not literally the end; merely intolerable or outrageous. Frank Worsley, in *Itma*, 1948, quotes part of a post-war, although still 1945, show:

> TOMMY: Yes, the [Crafty Clara] sailed through the side of the tent, slap into the bearded man. He turned a somersault, so she saw the picture right through.
> BRIGADIER (*furious*): This is the *end*.
> TOMMY: That's what Clara said when the tattooed man put his shirt on.

This c.p. may have arisen on the outbreak of war in 1914.

'It has the American variant, *this is the living end*, dating from the 1920s, and susceptible of untied usage, as in "She's the living end!" – said of a beautiful woman, or a very talented one. I heard it through the 1950s' (A.B., 1979). Presumably to distinguish it from *a dead end* (P.B.). See also **that's the living end!**

this is the life! dates from *c*. 1910 and was popularized by British soldiers (with American following suit) in WW1, often with the ruefully homorous addition, *if you don't weaken*. Also *it's a great life*, q.v.

this is the way we exercise (and teacher says we may.). 'A return [catch] phrase to a comment on [one's] activity, as much as to say "I'm working and there's not much more to be said about it". A phrase I knew as a child and thought it was meant to be suggestive' (L.A., b. 1904, in 1968).

L.A. added, 1976, that it could be very approx. dated late C19–early 20, and that it could be used by an unexpected caller or, usu., callers (or social interrupters finding the other party completely unready and perhaps embarrassed, and the visit therefore unwelcome), the greeting being brightly, cheerily, defensive.

Manifestly orig. in good schools for girls, it was an adult c.p., perhaps popularized by the mnemonic quality of its metric form.

this is the weather we signed on for is a C20 merchant navy c.p., applied to agreeably warm, fine weather and a calm sea. *Sailors' Slang.*

this is too much! A retort or comment upon an excessive inconvenience or demand or effrontery: since the mid 1860s. (F & H suggests that it echoes *Artemus Ward among the Shakers*, *c*. 1862.) Cf **this is the end!**

this is where it's at and **this is where the action is.** This is where things – esp., notable things – are happening; this is the place you seek, if you want excitement: US: since the late 1950s; adopted in UK in late 1960s. In the *New Yorker* of 17 Apr. 1971, a C.E.M. drawing shows a mother hen addressing a just-hatched chick, 'Just take my word for it, kid. This is where it's at.'

Jonathan George, *The Kill Dog*, 1970, has the following exchange:

> 'I want to stay here.' She tried to laugh.... 'This is where the action is,' she said brashly.
> 'Please?'
> ... She translated:
> 'It's a phrase. A bit dated, but ... well ...'

Cf **that's where the action is.**

this is where the men are separated from the boys (or ... **where they separate the men from the boys**). Now we'll see who the real men are; that is, where we can distinguish the genuine men from the 'phoneys': US: since before WW2, but I shouldn't care to guess how long before. (Moe, 1975.) Shipley, 1975, states that the former is the orig. shape and that it was coined by Mae West. Cf **come up and see me sometime.**, and see also **separate the men ...**

this is where we (hence also **I) came in.** We've come full circle, so we can leave now, cease now, etc.; I'm beginning to repeat myself, or someone else is doing so; I, we, have seen or heard all this before: US, then also Brit.: since the 1920s, and 'unquestionably a c.p., and vigorously alive' (J.W.C., 1975).

'It is, of course, in origin a remark made in the days of continuous showings of a film at motion-picture theatres, so that one went in at any stage of a film's progression – now used in any situation where something seems to repeat itself, and meaning "Let's go!" ' (Shipley, 1975).

this is where you want it, the speaker pointing at, or rapping on, his forehead. You need to have brains: late C19–20. The same gesture accompanies the C20 c.p., *he's got it up there*, he's very intelligent. Cf **that's where you want it.**

this is your captain speaking. 'From airline practice, but used generally' (Skehan, 1977); 'In imitation of Naval ship's or civil airlines captain's introduction' (Ashley, 1982). More fully, it became a joc., sometimes a mock-pompous, c.p. of assumed control of, and leadership, in any situation, however trivial, where either a definite announcement has to be made or decision taken. Although I didn't hear, much less see, it before 1973, it goes back, I believe, to *c*. 1965 or even 1960.

this isn't a licence to print money. See **licence to print ...**

this must be Philadelphia, Pennsylvania, seems to have been, *c*. 1898–1903 (perhaps rather longer), a US c.p., connoting sleepiness and a failure to keep up to date, for, in 'How a Beauty was Waked and her Suitor Suited', one of the poems in Guy Wetmore Carryl, *Grimm Tales Made Gay*, 1902, we read:

> There were courtiers without number,
> But they all were plunged in slumber,
> The prince's ear delighting
> By uniting
> In a snore.
> The prince remarked: 'This must be Philadelphia, Pennsylvania!'
> (And so was born the jest that's still
> The comic journal's mania!)

this one's on me, orig. a public-house conventionalism, became, *c*. 1950, a c.p. with special application: 'Said by a male guest when a lady[?] diner belches or makes a rude noise' (Petch, 1978): lower middle class.

this practice will now cease. 'A perhaps ephemeral c.p. accompanying, e.g., the repelling of an attacker by means of a left to the jaw. Current in 1930s in Dorothy Sayers and/or Margery Allingham [writers of detective stories], though I cannot give precise references. Clearly derived from the (obs.? extinct? [not in UK]) statement in correspondence columns of periodicals, "This correspondence will now cease"' (R.C., 1978.) The phrase as it stands was still appearing in army unit routine orders up until at least the early 1970s. (P.B.)

this should not be possible (or, more usu., **this should be impossible**). This quot'n from the *Royal Navy Gunnery Manual* has become a RN c.p., 'employed sarcastically when something has gone wrong' (Granville, 1962): *c*. 1910–35, and then used occ. by the older men; by 1960, †. It circulated only among officers.

That distinguished officer, Rear-Adm. P.W. Brock, wrote to me in 1971:

> It came from the gunnery drill books in force when I was a midshipman and acting sub-lieutenant, 1920–4. It concerned the tests of the safety arrangements that a gun's crew was expected to carry out on closing up at their quarters. There were various mechanical interlocks to prevent, for instance, closing the breech of a big gun before the power rammer was withdrawn, or firing with the breech not fully closed. The drill book instructed you to try to find a tube with the breech in this state, and went on to say 'This should be impossible'.

Sometimes *not* is changed to *no*, a change that invests the phrase with a pawky Scottish humour.

this side of the black stump. See **black stump.**

this town isn't big enough for both of us. 'Hard man' talk from Western films, e.g., the villain threatening the sheriff: some use as a joc. c.p. (Ashley, 1984.)

this training really toughens you: you get muscles in your shit. A WW2 c.p. employed by the Canadian Army.

this week's deliberate mistake! 'In an early broadcast of the 1930s radio series Monday Night at Seven (later Eight), Harry S. Pepper committed some ghastly mistake. Listeners immediately rang in and Pepper cleverly extracted himself from the situation by saying at the end of the show, "I wonder how many of you were clever enough to spot my deliberate mistake?"

There was a genuine "deliberate mistake" every week thereafter and the phrase has entered the language to some extent as a cover for ineptitude' (*VIBS*).

The idea was used again, by Ronald Waldman, in a post-WW2 run of the show, and that helped to consolidate the phrase with a younger generation. As P.B., 1974, writes of *you've spotted this week's* ..., it is a useful c.p. for any instructor caught out in writing an unwitting error on the blackboard.

this will give you the cock-stand is a male c.p., dating since *c.* 1910, and addressed to someone to whom one has offered a drink or a special dish. Cf **that'll grow hairs...**, esp. **that'll put lead in your pencil.**

this won't buy baby (or **the baby**) **a frock** (or **new dress**). But this won't do! I'm wasting my time (*or* being idle): C20. Leonard Merrick uses it in, *Peggy Harper*, 1911: 'This won't buy baby a frock.' Although with increasing rarity heard in UK since *c.* 1940, it remained popular in Aus., as James Aldridge mentioned to me in 1969, in the form *this won't buy the baby a frock.*

'I know this better as "This won't buy the baby a new bonnet" – which is more memorable because of the alliteration. I have known it for more than sixty years, and as my grandparents used the c.p., it must have been Victorian. It was uttered as an admonition against wasting time or relaxing from a prescribed task' (Noble, 1978). P.B.: the phrase is often prec. by a reluctant *well!* ..., and I have heard also the variants ... *a new pair of shoes* (or *boots*). See also **baby wants...**

thou shalt not be found out. 'This is known as the Eleventh Commandment. Another ten can be found in *The Latest Decalogue* by Arthur Hugh Clough' (B.P., 1975): very common in Aus. as well as in UK. Clough lived 1819–61. R.C. adds, 1978: 'In the form *thou shalt not get caught,* [it had] some currency in the US from 1930s'.

though I say it who shouldn't; and **though I says it as shouldn't.** See **although I say it** ....

thought. See: on second; two minds; what did t.; who would have; you know what t.

thought you'd never ask! (– I). An honest, joc., response to a long-expected or hoped-for invitation ('How about a drink?') or other query ('Well? How did you get on?') that has become, in the early 1980s, something of a gen. c.p. (P.B.)

thousand(s). See: farewell; handsome; I believe you, but; no, no.

thousand strokes and a rolling suck – a. A nautical c.p. of *c.* 1870–1930; applied to a leaky ship, the pumps requiring many strokes, and sucking – an indication that she is dry – only when the ship rolls. Bowen.

threat. See: is that a promise.

three acres and a cow satirized baseless or excessive optimism: Ware implies that it was current in 1887–*c.* 1889; but Collinson notes that it was revived *c.* 1906. The late Alexander McQueen thought it directed ironically at Joseph Chamberlain's Jesse Collings, who proposed that every smallholder should possess them – he became known as *Three Acres and a Cow Collings.* The slogan had been coined by Chamberlain himself, who may have drawn the phrase from a song popular in the 1880s. Yet another theory appears in Brewer.

Ashley, 1982, draws attention to the famous US slogan of C19, *forty acres and a mule.* See also **there'll be a chicken in every pot.**

three-badge budgie. See: chirruping.

three bags full. See: yes, sir.

three bears. See: have you any more; yes, I also.

three-cornered. See: when you were wearing.

three-dollar bill. See: queer as a.

three hearty British cheers! Ironical or 'grudging praise for a minor accomplishment. "I passed that exam after three goes at it." – "Three hearty British cheers"' (B.P.): Brit. and Aus.: since *c.* 1930.

three is an awkward number. An ephemeral c.p. of 1885–6, arising from Lord Durham's nullity-of-marriage lawsuit (Ware). It paraphrases 'two are company; three, not'; also it's an *odd* number. Cf **two's company....**

three on the hook, three on the book is a dockers' c.p. for half a week's work: since the 1920s (perhaps earlier). The hook is a tool of the stevedore's trade; the *book* refers to the dole.

three penn'orth. See: about as high.

three S's. See: mind your three.

three turns (in late C19–20, less often **two**) **round the long-boat and a pull at the scuttle** is a nautical c.p. (ob. by 1910, †by 1930) that, dating from before 1867, when recorded by Admiral Smyth in his dictionary of naval language, characterizes the (avoidance of) activities of an 'artful dodger' or skrimshanker. Bowen makes, 1929, the *two turns* phrase mean 'under sail, killing time'.

three weeks indicated, 1907–*c.* 1914, a sexual adventure either culminating within, or lasting, that time. It testified to the vast popularity of Elinor Glyn's novel, *Three Weeks,* 1907.

threepence more and up goes the donkey. See **penny more....**

three penny bit. See: couldn't speak; keep your hand.

throat. See: I have a bone; my guts; my stomach.

through the eye of a needle. See **I could shit...**

throw. See: I wouldn't trust; I've been thrown; run it up; spends; would that; you couldn't t.; you threw.

throw the baby out with the bath water. See **don't throw....**

throw your mother a bone! 'That is, you are the son of a female dog. Educated US, from 1930s; now ob. or†' (R.C., 1978).

throws a tread. See: Christian born.

throws money around like snuff at a wake. See **spends money as if it was going out of fashion,** and contrast:

throws (his) money around like a man with no arms (or **hands**). See **flings (his) money...**

thumb. See: every hair; sucked.

thumb in bum and mind in neutral. See **with thumb in bum and mind in neutral.**

thumbnail. See: written.

thump. See: ecky thump.

thunder. See: go to hell.

Thursday. See: t.G.i.F.; up the road.

thus spake Zarathustra. See **Confucius he say.**

Tich. See: no Tich!

ticker is diving – the represents a gallant depreciation of the seriousness of a heart attack: since either late 1929 or early 1930. 'Perhaps with a pun on the stock [market] ticker, which *c.* 1930 was indeed diving' (R.C., 1976) – the ref. being to the catastrophic suddenness of the stockmarket crisis, the monetary collapse that began in the US on 29 Oct. 1929 and was consequently hitting Britain very hard by as early as Jan. 1930. (Mr Claiborne was commenting on the entry in the 1970 Supplement to *DSUE*.)

ticket(s). See: no return; no tickee; pakapoo; selling; that's the article; and:

ticket – it's just the: and – which see also separately – **that's the ticket.** That is exactly what is needed, or exactly right of fitting or suitable: C19–20. Christopher Fry, 1974, remarked of both phrases: 'Often said to me in childhood.'

tickle. See: I didn't get; stop yer.

tickled. See: have you ever.

tidy. See: it's Friday.

Tie up your stocking! No heel-taps!; University of Oxford: late C19–early 20. Ware limits the phrase to the drinking of champagne. The semantic orig. is obscure.

tiger in the tank was a 'not quite succeeded' c.p. extracted by E.P. from the Esso Oil Company's famous slogan *Put a Tiger in Your Tank*. So perhaps it is to be considered as overlapping the bounds of both categories, for, as Nigel Rees, in his immensely browse-worthy *Slogans*, 1982, says, 'This was a slogan that really took off and gave rise to endless jokes and cartoons'. The cartoon tiger and his slogan were launched in US in 1964, in UK a year later, 'and it became a national craze, with countless tiger tails adorning the petrol caps of the nation's cars. ... The UK campaign ran for two years before it flagged' (Ibid.). Among the 'spin-offs' were 'the mocking, non-commercial *a weasel in the diesel*' (R.S., 1973), and the use of the abbr. *tiger tank* in rhyming slang. This is one advertising campaign that has certainly lingered in folk-memory – but did it actually sell much petrol? (P.B., 1983.)

tight. See: he's not t.; I'm not t.; sleep tight.

tight as a bull's arse in fly-time and **he's so tight he squeaks** (like a pair of tight shoes). He is incredibly mean with his money: Can. (the former line): since the early 1930s. (Leechman.) P.B.: to some 'family' such expressions, hardly to be classified as c.pp. as *tight as a duck's arse*, *and that's watertight*, for both mean and drunk, and the indelicate *tight as a mouse's ear 'ole*. The former was brought to E.P.'s attention by David Short, 1978.

A.B., 1979, added from the US: 'There are so many variations, such as *he's so tight, they'll have to split his ass so he can shut his eyes*'. Turning to inebriation, he cites *he's as tight as a tick*, and to politics, *he's as tight as a tick on a dog's ear*, 'a political statement meaning "he's close to the powerful people"'. On all three, he commented, 'I'd say C19 in origin; but not in current usage': E.P. thought mid-C19.

tight under the arms. See bit tight ...

'til (or till) death do us part. 'Possibly a c.p. [in the US] rather than a cliché, in that it is indeed sometimes used, not with reference to marriage but a (usually irksome) responsibility, or what not, that one cannot hope to escape from – e.g., a burdensome ... dependant, an unwelcome ... office in a society, or, somewhat different, an unconquerable addiction to drugs or drink....!' (J.W.C., 1975). That convinces me that, so used, it *is* a c.p. in the US: perhaps – mere guesswork, this – since c. 1965.

P.B.: E.P. had apparently missed the enormously popular British TV series, shown also in the US, *Till Death Us Do Part*, a title taken straight from the marriage service in the *Book of Common Prayer*. See **silly old moo.**

'til (or till) hell freezes over is a c.p. letter-ending: orig. N. American, and prob. US rather than Can. in origin: since late C19; virtually † by 1975. And used also in speech, not merely in letter-endings. My WW1 friend Howard Philips († 1918) often employed it as = for ever. It appears in *Bartlett's Familiar Quotations* as an anonymous saying, undated. It has a companion: *when hell freezes over*, as in 'I'll do it when hell freezes over' – that is, never: US: C.20, and still (1978) current.

P.B.: I surmise that H.P. was the 'Felipé' who was featured so affectionately in Eric Partridge's *Frank Honywood, Private*, pub'd by his own Scholartis Press in *Three Personal Records of the War*, 1929. E.P.'s middle name was Honeywood, and 'Felipés' name in the book is given as Jim Hicks, a much-travelled man, some ten years older than the young Partridge when they shared a dug-out at Gallipoli. The other two 'records' were by R.H. Mottram, of *Spanish Farm Trilogy* fame, and John Easton, another traveller. The whole forms a very moving volume, and is long overdue for reprinting.

'til (or till) who laid the chunk. This US c.p., dating from c. 1920, means 'in great excess', as in 'we've got copies of that book till who laid the chunk'. J.W.C. adds, 'I find it completely mystifying'. A chunk is a large, solid piece or portion of anything, e.g., a chunk of wood or bread, or as in the dialectal 'a great chunk of man' – a very big fellow. Semantically, perhaps, 'until somebody laid a stump or a log against the door to prevent

anyone, or anything, else coming or being brought in'.

time (s). See: any day; at this moment; be a good girl; come in, number; do your own time; every night; every time; feeding; get some service; gone to lift; good time; having a wonderful; hot time; how many times; I'll let you off; I've got the t.; in the big; isn't it t.; it'll last; it's a long t.; it's time; just in t.; kissing t.; knock three; let the good; long time; many many; next time; no, no; one at a t.; roll on, t.; so stupid; that's a rhyme; there's a first; there's a good; these sets; well, it seemed; what time; what's the t.; you'll be a long; you're a long t.; you've had your t.

time and tide wait for no man, (and) neither do Beecham's pills. A joc. c.p. of earlier C20. A ref. to the famous laxative, which prompted A.B. to write, 1979, of the var. *time and tide wait for no man, and for few women*, 'I still hear this every now and then, especially in English pubs and American taverns. The connotation here is "Let's get on with the show" – "Time's a-wasting" – and the like'.

time for a shit ... See shave, a shilling ....

time for your O.B.E., Neddy. A 'Goon Show c.p. uttered every so often by the villainous Grytpype-Thynne to Neddy Seagoon, as one might say "Time for your medicine". Was quite popular in the army, where people are more noticeably awarded decorations' (P.B., 1975). See GOON SHOW.

time, gentlemen, please: haven't any of you got a home? is often heard in public-houses when the customers are unwilling to depart: since c. 1925. (A correspondent; name unfortunately lost.) P.B.: another version is *ain't you got* (or *haven't you got*) *no homes to go to?*, which is occ. used, in other contexts, e.g. after a party, without the *time, gentlemen, please!*

Sanders, 1978, adds a var. of the pub version: '*Act of Parliament, ladies and gentlemen*, which is more recent, but heard before WW2'.

time I gave it the old one-two. See **don't forget the diver!** and **give it the old ...**

time of miracles is not past – the. See age of miracles ...

time on that! 'Wait a while, sir; not so fast' (Matsell): US underworld and fringe of the underworld: c. 1840–80.

time you had (or got) a watch! 'Sharp reply to "What time is it?"' (Shaw, 1968): C20. Cf:

time's always the same, lad: one, one-two! (or **one, tup-tree, one!**) – (the). 'An Army NCO's jocular reply to a private's artless query, "what's the time, please, Sarge (*or* Corp.)?" C20; by 1950, somewhat dated – long since worn threadbare' (P.B., 1975). A pun on the timing or cadence called or chanted by instructor, or the recruits themselves, while drill movements are practiced at 'square-bashing'.

Times, the. See: write.

tin. See: they've opened.

tin hat. See: get your steel; swing that lamp; that's put.

tin of Vaseline. See: black cat.

tin soldier. See: don't come.

tin-type. See: not on your t.

tin that Rin-Tin-Tin shit in – the. A British Army c.p. of the earlier 1950s; it was evoked from any Other Rank, esp. among National Servicemen, on hearing mention of the world *tin*, as 'Tin! What tin? The tin that ...!' From the well-known exploits of 'Rin-Tin-Tin the Wonder Dog', canine star of screen and comic. Cf **board the monkey ...**, and **ships? ...** (P.B.)

Tinker to Evers to Chance is the more usual form of **from Tinker to Evers to Chance**, which, however, see.

tinkle, tinkle, little spoon: knife and fork will follow soon. A nautical, esp. a RN, lowerdeck jingle: 'Sailors often tip cutlery over the side with the dishwater. Hence the RN slang *tinklers* = spoons' (Peppitt, 1977): C20.

tiny. See: your tiny.

tip. See: that's the tip.

tip the crusher. See **fear God and tip ...**

Tippecanoe and Tyler too was selected by W & F as one of two US political slogans that have taken on a 'generalized meaning and become popular ... still heard = "this is even more wonderful than I expected" or more recently, since the slogan has become so old, to = "that's very old-fashioned".'

D. *Am.* makes it clear that orig. the phrase was a rallying cry during the Log Cabin and Hard Cider presidential campaign of 1840 and that it promptly became the refrain of a popular song; also that John Tyler was a candidate.

'I have never, in 50 years, seen or heard this without a historical context – either the specific case of the 1840 campaign, or as an example of political sloganry' (R.C., 1978): that is, never as a true c.p.

P.B.: but I have heard it in England used as a children's nonsense jingle – it just sounds right, and no context is necessary.

tired. See: thick and; you make me t.

'tis better than a worse. It might be worse: C18. In S, 1738, Dialogue I, see:

COL[ONEL]: I'm like all Fools, I love every Thing that's good.

LADY SM[ART]: Well and isn't it pure good?

COL: 'Tis better than a worse.

Cf the next.

'tis indifferent, as Doll danced. See 'twill last as many days as nights.

'tis not every day Morris kills a cow. 'Favourable opportunity comes but seldom': (Maxwell Taylor, 1977): Newfoundland: C20. Apparently in ref. to some big farmer, who occasionally killed a cow in order to vary a hideously monotonous diet of codfish. Much the same sort of thing prevailed in rural districts of NZ in late C19–earlyish C20; there the staple diet was everlasting mutton.

'tis only I: be not afraid has, in C20, been 'an accusation of some (minor but impudent) trespass, in the form of an excuse; meant to discomfit intruder. For example, your neighbour is in your front doorway to look at a parcel left there in [your] absence' (L.A., 1968). Apparently it derives from 'It is I, be not afraid' (The New Testament, Matthew, 14, 27; Mark, 6, 50; John, 6, 20).

tit(s). See: all tits; hell! said; I haven't laughed; I'm a tit man; it's like a nigger; sucking; tough titty; useless; weak; with knobs; you're as much.

titbit. See: remember the girl.

titter that runs through the gallery – the. Example of party game to express a common phrase by mime for party to guess. One of the men who knew the game went from woman to woman touching them on their [breasts]. Film studio staff. Early 1930s.' (L.A., 1976.) A pun on *tit*, nipple, breast.

The phrase is current also in US; usage attested by Shipley, who writes, 1977: 'A *New Yorker* cartoon (can't remember the date) has a big-bosomed woman squeezing her way past seated persons in a theater row; caption: A big titter went through the audience'. A.B., 1979, explains further: 'Also *a nervous titter ran through the gallery* (or *audience* or *crowd*). It is also a pun on the giggling of an audience in a theater when an actor or actress makes a blunder. A sort of vicarious embarrassment'.

to coin a phrase is used ironically, to excuse and apologize for either the immediately preceding or the immediately ensuing triteness, esp. if it's a cliché; or disarmingly equivalent to 'to use a familiar, a well-known, phrase': orig. US: since *c.* 1945, yet not gen. in UK until the middle 1950s.

Clarence B. Kelland uses it in *No Escape*, 1951 (Brit. edn): 'Any port in a storm,' Jonathan said.

'To coin a phrase,' said Peggy.

Noël Coward, *South Sea Bubble*, 1956, at III, ii, has:

PUNALO (*inexorably*): ... I will show your wife's clip to the Press and, to coin a phrase, bust the works wide open.

In UK, the phrase became, as it were, canonized when, in 1973, there appeared a revision and enlargement of Edwin Radford's *Encyclopedia of Phrases and Origins*, 1945.

P.B.: but it was a c.p. in one of the 1940s BBC radio comedy series, or of a particular comedian. Can anyone remind me of title or name?

[**to cut a long story short,** clearly – at least basically – a cliché, verges on being a c.p. when used humorously.]

to-do. See: ee, what.

to-er is human. 'The slurred sound of dubiety punned with *to err is*

human or, in Latin, *Humanum est errare*' (L.A., 1976): since *c.* 1960 – or perhaps much earlier.

to hell with you, Jack, I'm all right! is a euph. var. of **fuck you, Jack** ....

to make a fool ask, and you are the first. s, 1738, Dialogue I, has:

NEV[EROUT]: Pray, Miss, why do you sigh?

MISS: To make a Fool ask, and you are the first.

Prob. current throughout C18.

to make the cheese more binding. In order to clinch a deal or other agreement: US: latish C19– mid 20, yet still extant: Glendon Swarthout, who always 'does his homework', employs it in his 1916-set novel, *The Tin Lizzie Group*, 1972. (W.J.B., 1972.) Fain, 1977, notes a further, extant, US sense: 'That makes the problem more knotty' or 'the situation is more difficult' or 'a further angle to be considered': since *c.* 1945.

In Can. usage, *c.* 1945–55, the var. *that makes the cheese more binding* meant 'That improves matters; that's just what we need'.

Cheese is notoriously *binding* or constipating.

to tell them apart. See **only way to tell their sex** ...

to the woods! An anon. correspondent, 1978, mentioned *into the woods!* as 'a more or less meaningless statement, usually with a girl is mind', but in fact it forms part of the 'ritual exchange' partly covered at **I *am* the vicar!**, q.v. One version goes 'To the woods, to the woods!' – 'No, no! If you do, I'll scream'; and another, 'The whip, the whip!' – 'No, no! Anything but the whip!' – '*Anything?*' – 'The whip, the whip!' All end 'I'll fuck you when I find you!' – 'I'm (hiding) in the cupboard – and the key's under the mat'. With such simple, and basically innocent, exchanges did the young Servicemen seek to divert the boredom of life in the barracks, mid C20. (P.B.)

toad. See: wanted.

toast your blooming eyebrows!, a proletarian c.p. of *c.* 1895– 1915, synonymizes the slangy *go to blazes!* – itself, clearly, a euph. of *go to hell!* Ware.

Toc-H. See: dim as a Toc-H.

today. See: it's always; not t.; tomorrow the world.

today a rooster, tomorrow a feather duster. See **rooster one day** ...

toe. See: done up like a sore.

toffee. See: don't give.

together. See: get your act; keep your legs; putting their.

told. See: who told.

Tom Collins. See: whether.

Tom Mix in 'Cement' was, *c.* 1938–52, a retort to 'What's on at the pictures?' A pun '*to mix* ...' and 'to *mix* cement'.

P. Daniel, 1978, adds that *Tom Mix and cement* would, on the RN lowerdeck, during WW2, 'be uttered whenever cement was in question, regardless of the fact that Tom Mix was a silent-film actor long forgotten by the 1940s'.

Tom Tit on a round of beef. A children's c.p., shouted at someone wearing a hat, or a cap, too small; also 'used of anything small on anything big, e.g. of a lonely cottage on a hill' (Peter Ibboston, 1963): C20.

'At school in Liverpool [during the 1950s], the matching, mildly abusive, c.p. was *a pea on a drum* ... [it] referred to boys in the upper years still wearing the cap, now shrunken, that they had had when they started at the school' (David Short, 1978). P.B.: *pea on a drum* should prob. be dated C20, if not earlier; it was used in the same sense in the Home Counties. Cf the more earthy simile, supplied from memories of childhood in Cumbria by my friend Eddie Haines, (*like a*) *pimple on a bull's arse*. I am not sure why E.P. gave *Tom Tit* its capitals; I have always assumed that it meant the familiar name of the little bird, the blue tit, *Parus caeruleus*. Mrs Patricia Pinder, 1984, tells me of a similar phrase, perhaps a private, family usage, 'Sitting there like Piffy on a rock bun', which apparently combines the incongruity of the previous examples with the ideas behind **like a spare prick** ...

Tom Trot. See: like T.

tomato. See: woo-woo.

tombstone. See: hasn't got a ha'penny.

Tommy. See: rock on; yo, T.

TOMMY HANDLEY CATCH PHRASES; that is, the c.pp. from 'ITMA', the most famous British radio show of them all, the show that did so much for morale, both at home and abroad, during the stressful years of WW2. In 1948, Frank Worsley could truthfully write,

Many of the 'ITMA' catch-phrases have passed into the English language. They reappear in advertisements, in pantomimes – always a sure sign of a successful saying – and even as captions for cartoons. There have been several series of comic postcards, and quite recently a progressive Brighton parson advertised as the subject of his Sunday Sermon: 'What me, in my state of health!'

They will be found, separately treated, in their alphabetical order. Perhaps the best known are **after you, Claude ... ; can I do you now, sir?**; **don't forget the diver**; **Funf speaking**; **I go – I come back**; **it's being so cheerful as keeps me going**; **it's that man again**; **ta-ta for now**; **what, me – in my condition** (or **in my state of health**)?

The famous radio comedian, Tommy Handley (1894–1949), is remembered chiefly for his radio show 'ITMA' – 'It's That Man Again' – which ran from 19 Sep. 1939 until his death ten years later. ITMA owed much of its vast and enduring popularity to its script writer, Ted Kavanagh, and to its producer, Frank Worsley, and to the rest of Tommy Handley's cast. Kavanagh wrote Handley's biography and Worsley the story of 'ITMA'; and both of these books were rushed out before the end of 1949. The former remarked:

The show's catch-phrases were, of course, the trade mark with which Tommy was greeted wherever he went .... Writers had to be careful not to use parallel phrases, and worse than that was to give a cue which could expect an 'ITMA' answer.

In his review of the first ed. of this book, in *TLS*, 26 Aug. 1977, Anthony Burgess, having spoken of 'unrelated and unmotivated catch phrases', adds: 'And, indeed, the whole point of a lot of the catch phrases made popular by ITMA was their floating quality, their Surrealistic freedom from context. One was *NCAW-WASBE* – a virtuoso effort admittedly, to be picked up only by the few, meaning "Never clear a window with a soft-boiled egg.".' Then, of **don't forget the diver**, with its pendant **I'm going down now, sir**, he says that 'it touched, appropriately, submarine depths in the collective unconscious'. After a ref. to Mae West's **peel me a grape**, which really demanded a context, he concludes his ITMA paragraph thus: 'Whitey whitey kay, provoking "What does that mean?" makes its own context. It means, of course, *YTYTK*, which in turn stands for "you're too young to know" – ITMA again.' That *of course* is an example of what I call 'doing a Macaulay', as in the hackneyed famous quotation-become-cliché, *as every schoolboy knows*.

Of the list of best known phrases, Mr Arthur C.L. Grear, 1978, writes: 'A c.p. often used by Tommy Handley and one of his best alliterations was: "Well, chuck a chicken up the chimney!" ', and P.B. remembers waiting, with uncharacteristic eagerness, for the beginning of a school term in the mid 1940s, just to be able to greet a friend in the words of 'Signor So-So', played by Dino Galvani: 'Dah! *There* you are, Mr Handlebar!'

Tommy make room for your uncle! was, from 1883 (*teste* Ware) until *c*. 1940, and then (*teste* Shaw) among a few oldsters right up to *c*. 1970 addressed to the youngest man in a group or to the younger man of two. From a popular song.

tomorrow. See: it's always; like there; there is always.

tomorrow the world, 'deprecating some minor achievement' (Skehan, 1977). P.B.: in full the phrase is *today* (somewhere), *tomorrow the world!*, which, applied to any project, means 'who knows what heights of success I/we may reach?' Prob. from show business, of young talent impressing 'today the home town, tomorrow ...'; adopted from US late 1960s. E.P. commented on John Skehan's note: for meaning cf **look, no hands**; for style, slyly satirizing pomposity, cf **stop the world, I want to get off.**

tomorrow will be Friday and we've caught no fish today. 'Just a way of saying something: before [WW2, it] used to be a fairly common, almost pointless comment, [uttered] especially on Thursdays' (Anon.): rough dating – the 1920s and '30s. P.B.: the ref. is to Friday as a day of fast, when fish was the only 'meat' allowed.

tongue. See: has the cat got; old as; white man; your t.

tongue is hinged in the middle and he (or **she**) **talks with both ends – his** (or **her**). Applied to an excessively loquacious person: late C19–20.

It has two US variants: R.C. notes 'a now extinct version: *her tongue is loose at both ends* [P.B.: applying perhaps rather to spiteful gossip?]. Probably late C19–early 20'; and Fain mentions the C20 *your tongue is on a hinge.*

tonight. See: I'm in condition; not t.

tonight's the night! indicates the imminence of something important. Since 1913, when Miss Iris Hoey starred in a musical comedy so named; for instance, the first night of a play. In Aus. it has rather tended to prophesy a successful culmination to a sexual association. P.B.; and not only in Aus.: rather, throughout the English-speaking world.

too bloody Irish (or **right**) (or **true**)! are picturesque emphasizings of the colourless *of course*. All three have been widely used throughout the C20 and prob. go back to *c*. 1870 or even earlier; the first two were favourites of English soldiers in WW1 and are duly recorded by B & P.

The late Gerald Bullett (in a letter, 1950) suggested to me that *too bloody Irish* merely extends the synon. *too Irish* and that *too Irish* is short for *too Irish stew*, rhyming slang for *too true*; he was probably right.

too damn' tooting! Certainly: C20. In Can. **you're damn'** (or **darn'**) **tooting**, you're absolutely right. (Leechman.) Moreover, **you're darn' tooting** is also US.

There may be a pun on *Tooting Common*, London, and *common*, general or usual. P.B.: I can't help feeling that E.P. was 'pushing his luck' here, with his creed that 'any etymology is better than none': *you're darn tootin* is recorded by Berrey, and what would the ordinary American know of Tooting Common? More likely is 'you're blowing the right tune on the trumpet'.

too late! too late! is a C20 military and, by 1930, gen. c.p., uttered in high falsetto and with a humorously derisive inflection. It derives from the story of that luckless fellow who lost his manhood in a shark-infested sea very soon after he had summoned help.

Also **help! sharks!**, the first word spoken in a normal voice, the second in falsetto. Clearly this secondary c.p. is spoken – or, like the first, chanted – with an impressive pause between the two words.

too old and too cold is either the 'traditional domestic excuse [made] by husbands for not being more demanding' (B.P.) or the customary slighting ref. mady by chagrined and frustrated wives 'afflicted' with such husbands: C20 and perhaps much older. Prob. suggested by **not so old nor yet so cold.**

too old at forty stands in a no-man's-land corner, contiguous to famous quot'n and to cliché and to c.p. Attributed to Sir William Osler (1849–1919), the famous quot'n was, in the fact, 'the uselessness of men above sixty years of age', which degenerated into *too old at forty*, which, by 1925 at latest, became a cliché, and, by 1930 at latest, also a c.p. – often used jocularly.

too rich for my blood! Too expensive for *me*!: C20. From the literal sense of the phrase (orig., I think, *too high*...): food (or wine) too rich for one's digestion.

But also *for his* (*your, their*) ...' and also US. Paul Janssen, 1978, cites *Playboy*, June 1975, '... Griscard is plainly a man of the world – one who would not find Emmanuelle's brand of eroticism too rich for his blood'.

too right! See **too bloody Irish.**

too short for Richard, too long for Dick is a 'Yorkshire expression for *N.B.G.* [no bloody good]; said to have reference to Richard III, who was known as Crookback' (Sir Archibald (later Lord) Wavell, 1 Aug. 1939, in a letter).

But how long it has been a c.p., I simply don't know. The saying, obviously, borders on the proverbial.

P.B.: it is noteworthy that A.P.W. should have taken the trouble, at this stage of world affairs (WW2 started for Great Britain on 3 Sep. 1939), to write thus to E.P. The two had corresponded about works ever since the publication of the 1st ed. of B. & P., and Wavell's (anonymous) contributions to earlier editions of *DSUE* were more than a few.

Much to E.P.'s regret, the two men were never actually to meet; but Eric told me that A.P.W. was instrumental – even in the midst of conducting the British campaign in the Near East – by writing to a very senior RAF officer, in getting the very junior Aircraftman Second Class Partridge, E.H., transferred from a dead-end stores job to a post in the Air Ministry. There he became clerk to RAF's Official Observers, a small, select group that included, among others, Squadron Leaders John Pudney, H.E. Bates, and Vernon Noble. Small wonder that FM Lord Wavell inspired so much affection among so many who knew him.

too slow to go to a funeral has, in the N. Country, been, late C19–20, often 'applied to one slow in the uptake or in his work or actions' (Petch, 1971). P.B.: cf the joc. remark concerning one guilty of flagrant unpunctuality, 'he (*or* she) would be late for his (*or* her) own funeral'.

too thick to drink, too thin to plough was *c.* 1900–50, although little after 1940, used by the inhabitants of New South Wales in derision of the Yarra River, which flows through Melbourne. Part of that not entirely humorous 'war' between Sydney and Melbourne which is characterized by the complementary c.pp., **stinking Yarra** and **our 'Arbour**. See also **only river...**

But the phrase was also known in the Wild West: American cowboys used it for muddy water that, for lack of clear, they were sometimes forced to drink if they wished to stay alive: late C19–earlier 20. Adams, who remarks that 'if he's thirsty enough, it's "damned good water"'.

too too (or **too-too**) and **too all but; too utterly too** and **too utterly utter.** The first is the oldest and the only one to have survived; the second, the shortest-lived, was described by Ware as 'resulting out of *Punch's* trouvaille "too-too"', which was 'first found in *Punch* in the height of the aesthetic craze' (1881).

The third, *too utterly too*, seems to have arisen in 1882; it certainly went close to rivalling the second for its brevity of life.

The fourth, *too utterly utter*, arose in 1883, according to Ware, who says that it was the 'final phrase resulting from the satirical use of "too-too"'; it lasted far longer than the second, and third, which hardly outlived 1884 or 1885.

James Redding Ware, it may be added, was in an excellent position to observe the speech of fashionable Society: all four phrases were originated by Society: and only the first seeped down into the next stratum. [E.P. later added:]

It doesn't stop there. As if to pile Pelion upon Ossa upon Olympus, Mr Peter Sanders has sent to me, 1978, this delectable offering: 'Also "(how) too, too utterly sick-making" and "(how) too, too utterly shame-making". Elaborations(?) on the catch phrases used by the Bright Young Things of Evelyn Waugh's early novels [*Decline and Fall*, 1929, and *Vile Bodies*, 1930]. In *Vile Bodies* is the paragraph: '"*Well!*" they said, "*Well!* how too shaming. Agatha darling," they said. "How devastating, how un-policemanlike, how goat-like, how sick-making, how too, too awful."' Evelyn Waugh was always quite first-class at dialogue.

took his (occ. **her) arse in his (her) hands and left.** 'Bathos for indignant, would-be-dignified, exit' (L.A., 1976): lower and lower-middle class: C20.

took three rounds to lick a stamp. See **couldn't knock the skin off a rice-pudding.**

toot. See: **one toot.**

tootin(g). See: **too damn.**

tootle-oo! See **pip pip!**

top. See: **all on top; can you top; go to the top; over the top; you're the top. top hat.** See: **fuck that for a comic; lower than; that's put.**

top mate before a mess mate, a mess mate before a ship mate, a ship mate before a station mate, and a station mate before a dog – a. This naval c.p., dating since *c.* 1860, was recorded by Captain George S. MacIlwaine, RN (a sub-lieutenant in 1860 and a commander in 1879), author of a 'a random assembly of notes that appeared in the *Naval Review* in 1930,' says Rear-Adm. P.W. Brock, who goes on to say: 'One has seen this with *and a dog before a soldier* added'; he calls the whole 'a common saying'. It indicates the descending order of preference in a rating's choice of associates.

top-sail. See: **first on.**

top that one! See **can you top that?**

top your boom! Go away: a nautical c.p., addressed to one who has 'forced his company where he was not invited' (Bowen): *c.* 1810–1910. It occurs in W.N. Glascock's *Sailors and Saints*, 1829.

toppled. See: **gyros.**

torn. See: **come home with; that's torn.**

totem pole. See: **low man.**

touch. See: **don't touch; I wouldn't it.; it fits where; kick for t.; lips that t.; since Jesus; so fast; wouldn't touch; your feet.**

[**touch pot, touch penny** is half proverb and half c.p.: mid C17–very early C20. It means 'No credit allowed' and is clearly of public-house origin. Apperson.]

touch wood! When intended literally, it is a superstitious cliché; when used joc., a c.p. Or, expressed otherwise, the proverb is *Touch wood,/It's sure to come good*; and the c.p. is *touch wood*, which can, as proverb, be short for the full version, and which, as c.p., is derivative therefrom. Both are precautionary: uttered to avert bad luck in general or to avert a reversal of the good fortune of which one has, just this moment, boasted; as in 'I've been lucky, so far – touch wood!'

For the various origins proposed for this phrase, you must consult the folklorists; the more, the greater fun. As merest layman and not all that seriously, I suggest that it originates in some half-buried myth about 'the Great God Pan', haunter of woods and forests.

The longer, proverbial form is excellently treated in the 3rd ed., 1970, of *ODEP*, which glosses thus: 'To touch wood is supposed to be a charm to avert misfortune, especially after untimely boasting'; its earliest ref. is to *Notes and Queries*, 1906. Yet I remain convinced that *touch wood!* existed in British folklore a long, long time before 1906 and that both the practice of touching wood and the accompanying words 'Touch wood!' originated the proverb, rather than the other way about. (Note of 22 Dec. 1977). Vernon Noble proposed, 1977: 'This is probably of ancient origin, or perhaps no further back than mediaeval times when relics were hawked about the country, including pieces of "the true cross". Those ... unable to buy splinters supposedly from the cross on which Jesus was crucified were probably allowed to touch them freely, as a gesture of piety and to bring them good luck or a blessing.'

In *Goodbye to All That*, 1929, Robert Graves wrote: '[When] he suddenly realised that he had said something unlucky, David said: "Touch wood". Everybody sprang to touch wood, but it was a French trench and unrevetted. I pulled a pencil out of my pocket; that was good enough for me.' Cf. Boyd Cable, *Grapes of Wrath*, 1917, '"Touch wood", said Pug warmingly. "Don't go boastin' without touchin' wood."' (Both owed, 1970, 1971, to Mr A.B. Petch, who has helped me so much and so long.)

Knock wood!, the American equivalent, is not, I notice, in the admirable *D.Am.*; nor in Berrey's, nor W & F. Yet it does, with var. *knock on wood*, occur in *Webster's International Dictionary*, 2nd ed., 1934, with definition 'To strike something wooden to avert loss of good luck' – classified as a colloquialism. I'd say that it goes back to 1850 at least, and prob. much further.

touch-holes. See: **it's wonderful.**

touchpaper. See: **light.**

tough. See: **things are rough.**

tough act to follow. See **act to follow.**

tough shit! Bad luck!; Hard luck!: a US c.p., indicating such indifference to the misfortunes and unhappiness of others as amounts to a callous denial of aid and comfort and an equally callous withholding of all sympathy or even ordinary human compassion. W & F and *DCCU* offer no dating, but the latter states that it indicates lack of interest and sympathy in and with the problems of the addressee. My guess is that, although prob. used before 1940, it didn't become a widespread c.p. until during WW2.

R.C., 1978, adds that this 'is now almost invariably abbreviated to *T.S.*, and has been since WW2.... Also abbreviated to the one word c.p., **tough!**' Cf:

tough titty! A Can. and Aus. c.p., synon. with the prec. and dating since *c.* 1930. It also has some negro use in the US, as CM shows. Frequently used ironically. Semantics: a tough teat is hard on the baby.

Fain, 1977, writers, 'It probably arose in US during the 1920s, where the full version was *tough titty breaks the baby's teeth*'; and A.B. notes, 'This was used in the American musical play *Gypsy*, and [was] spoken by the "tough" strip-teaser, Tessie. Late 1950s, I recall... Kin to [the derivative] *sugar tit*, which implies the opposite: "easy-going", "everything is great"'. J.W.C., 1977, says that in the US, 'It is by no means confined to... Blacks'. P.B.: it also had some usage in the British Armed Forces, later C20, and as *tough tit!*

tougher. See: farther down.

touring. See: may I have.

tow-rope. See: girls are hauling.

Tower Bridge. See: up and down.

town. See: hot time; it's the only game; riding out; she is so; this town; what you say.

Town Hall steps. See: can't sleep.

tra la la! – Goodbye! – was a proletarian c.p., slightly contemptuous and not too polite, of *c.* 1880–90. Ware says that it 'took its rise with a comic singer named Henri Clarke, whose speciality was imitating Parisians.... he made a great hit with it as the burden of a chorus'. One must, I think, assume that Clarke was familiar with the Fr. slang sense of *tra-la-la*, i.e. the posterior, if that be so, then the phrase approximately signified 'Kiss my arse!'

traces. See: drop your.

trade. See: how's the fag; it's all good for.

traffic. See: all the t.; go and play.

trail. See: pretend.

train. See: bugger this; wrong side.

train call. See: it'll look.

training. See: this t.

tram. See: face would.

trap for young players – (that's) **a.** A risk; a threat or a danger for the unwary: Aus.: since early 1950s. (Wilkes.) B.P. instances esp. marriage.

trap door. See: fall through.

trap is down! – the. The trick – the attempt to cheat me – has failed; It's no go: *c.* 1870–1910. An allusion to the fallen door of a trap for birds.

travel. See; have gun; you didn't t.

travelling. See: fine day for t.

tray bon for the troops. Excellent; (of a girl) attractive: British Army Other Ranks': 1914–18 and then nostalgically. (B & P.) Fr. *très bon.*

treacle. See: put your pudden.

tree(s). See: grow on t.; there was a cow; they don't grow; woodman.

trencher. See: you make a muckhill.

tribe. See: last of the Mohicans.

trick(s). See: for my next; how's tricks; of all the dumb; oh, it's nothing; standing.

trimmer. See: you little.

trip. See: did you enjoy; is your journey.

trod. See: often.

trooper's horse. See: you will die.

troops. See: don't bully; how are the t.; Napoleon's spirit; that's the stuff; tray bon; you wouldn't shit.

trot the udyju Pope o' Rome! Ware says:

This is very enigmatic English, composed of rhyming and transposition styles, and is generally used by one man to another when he wants the wife, or other feminine person, out of the way. Udyju is judy (wife) transposed [strictly, back-slanged – judy being very common for wife or mistress equally]. Pope o' Rome is rhyming for home. Cockney: *c.* 1860–1920.

trouble at t'mill, sometimes prec. by **aye, lad, there's...** '*Trouble at t'mill* appeared as the title of an article by Tony Aldous in *New Scientist*, 14 Apr. 1977, and reminded me that this is a sort of c.p. Usually pronounced with a mock-Northern accent (*trooble*), it covers all those stories of wicked mill-owner versus restive workers, from [the days of the Brontës] onwards. Cf *they went thattaway* for westerns, and '*unhand me, villain', she cried* for melodrama.' (P.B., 1977). Skehan adds, 1977, 'Usually said with a Geordie accent when a person [usu. male] is called away from a gathering.' E.P. glosses: Prob. of industrial origin and spoken either by, or of, a manager of sub-manager or head foreman: C20.

trouble(s). See: don't tell me your; my troubles; sorry you've; tell your t.; you have your t.; you think you; you'll be in.

trough. See: after you with.

trousers. See: all month; got a feather; not in these.

truck. See: and not a bone.

truckin'. See: keep on t.

true. See: you say it.

true for you! has, since *c.* 1830, been an Anglo-Irish c.p. of hearty agreement with another's statement. *OED* Supp.

true, O king! (or **O queen!**, as appropriate). 'I agree.' This one has existed since early C.20 and perhaps since late C.19, but is now used only by the elderly or the old. (Another emergence from the subconscious memory; caused, as so many of my own have been, by P.B.) It comes from historical novels and historical plays and semi-historical musical comedies.

truly as I live. See **as I am honest.**

trumpeter. See: good trumpeter.

trumpeter is dead – his (or rarely **her**). This was *c.* 1720–1940, applied either to a person boasting on a particular occasion or to an habitual boaster. Benjamin Franklin, *The Busy Body*, 1729; Grose, 1788, in the orig. form, *his trumpeter is dead, he is therefore forced to sound his own trumpet; DNWP.* Cf *King of Spain's trumpeter*, a braying ass: a neat pun on the pun: *Don Key* = donkey.

Although it occ. is *my* (or *your*) *trumpeter is dead*, the *his* form is that which has most securely attained the status of c.p.

trundle. See: let 'em t.

trunk. See: how fares.

trunkmaker's daughter. See: all round St Paul's.

trust. See: I wouldn't trust; may be trusted; never trust.

truth. See: ain't it a fact?

try. See: I'll try; if you haven't tried like a steer.

try a piece of sandpaper! See **get the cat to lick it off!**

try anything once! See **I'll try...**

try back! was, *c.* 1810–60, addressed to a person boasting. JB.

[try it on the dog! (– **let's**). Let us experiment safely: since *c.* 1890, and orig. theatrical. If it's a c.p. at all, it derives from an ordinary slang phrase: see esp. *DSUE.* I include it here only because that excellent scholar, elegant writer, alert observer, James R. Sutherland has, 1978, proposed it.]

try some horse-muck in your shoes! Workingmen's advice to undersized boys: C19–20. Horse-dung, often used as manure, would cause them to grow.

try that on your piano! is US and recorded by Berrey as synon. with 'Think that over!' – but also as 'Try that!' It seems to have been current *c.* 1930–50. R.S., 1978, notes also the comparatively short-lived var., *try that on your pianola*, earlier C20. Cf **play that on your oboe,** and:

try this (occ. **this on) for size!**, used in horseplay, often accompanies a playful punch, and has been current since *c.* 1930. It prob. derives from either drapery or hattery or shoeshop salesmen's jargon. Hence, since perhaps a decade later, it is often applied to contexts remote from horseplay: 'See whether you like this drink or cigar or book or what-have-you'; as in Miles Tripp, *Five Minutes with a Stranger*, 1971: '"I simply supply the drinks." She came across. "Try this one for size," she said.'

In the first sense, it had, *c*. 1935–50, a var. *how's that for centre?* – perhaps orig. army and derived from marksmanship. Never very widespread. I cannot remember having heard it more than once.

R.C. notes of *try this for size!* that it has long been current in US, and is often prec. by *let's*.

trying. See: no harm in t.; no, thanks, I'm t.

trying to find the long end of a square quilt aptly describes the frustrating, exasperating, maddening job of keeping a very large flock of sheep on the move in open spaces: Western cowboys': C.20. (Adams.) I should have thought that, even so, sheep were easier to herd than cattle. (Nor am I wildly guessing, for I spent my first ten years on a New Zealand farm.)

trying to tell me something? See **are you trying...**

tu l'as voulu, George Dandin 'was an intellectual's way, in the 1940s, of saying *you've had it*' (Anon., 1978.) The quot'n comes from Molière's *George Dandin, ou le Mari Confondu*, 1668, I, ix, but in the 1831 ed. of Lucien's *Oeuvres de Molière* it appears as '*vous l'avez voulu, George Dandin... vous avez justement ce que vous méritez.*' (With grateful thanks to Margaret Maison, who adds 'Don't know why G.D. addressed himself as "vous" – "Tu l'as voulu" seems better, but it's not in this text.') E.P. glosses the c.p.: surely rather *you've asked for it* or *them*.

Tuesday. See: boat sails; doesn't know; if it's T.

tune. See: that's the tune.

tune in, turn on and drop out. 'Summarized philosophy of the psychedelic drug culture of the 1960s, and coined, I believe, by the patron saint of that culture, Dr Timothy Leary. Now obs. or extinct, as is the culture itself – though the drugs, alas, are not. "Tune in" meaning "attune yourself" to what's new and (!) vital; "turn on" as the common US and British term for taking a dose of drugs...; "drop out" meaning, of course, abandon conventional "middle-class" society (in practice, often *any* society except the drug culture itself). A c.p. only when derisively or, at the least, ironically by the rest of US' (R.C., 1978).

tune the old cow died of. See **that's the tune...**

tuppence-ha'penny. See: nothing for; and:

tuppence-ha'penny looking down on tuppence is, as Skehan notes, 1984, a succinct deflation of self-aggrandisement. Cf **half-crown millionaires...**

turd. See: all honey; down in; fart's; hasty; he'd skin; there were four.

turkey. See: you're full.

turn. See: don't turn; if you are angry; is it my t.; it turns; it's turned; may I never; three turns; tune in; whatever turns; when father.

turn 'em upside down and they all look alike. 'Very low US version of [the proverb] *in the dark, all cats are gray* – "they" of course being women: 1930s; now (I hope) extinct' (R.C., 1978).

turn in her urn. See: enough to make my gran.

turn it round the other way. See **that's a very good idea.**

turn it up at that! All right, you may knock off (work) now and call it a day: RN: since *c*. 1925. 'From the "turning up" of a rope when belaying' (PGR).

turn me loose! '"Let me do just as I please, without any moral or social restrictions." As there is a recording with this title made, in February 1965, it [the c.p.] must have started before then' (Eric Townley, 1978): US.

turned on, tune in and drop out. The more logical and usual form of **tune in...** above.

turn-up. See: what a t.

turned out nice again! 'As used by George Formby [junior], a Lancashire comedian and comic singer, *c*. 1930s: example of

---

demotic literal usage [hence cliché], referring to the weather, being crystallized as a comedian's c.p. and thus returned to the streets as such, perhaps to be used ironically in its original sense, and sometimes slyly with a hint of double meaning, deriving from its adoption by Formby' (Wedgewood, 1978). One example of such *double entendre* was the McGill-type comic postcard depicting a large dog contemplating its own freshly produced turd: *turned out nice again!* was the caption. (P.B.)

turnip. See: lettuce.

turning in the wind. See **twisting slowly..**

turtle plates! R. Lancelyn Green, *Tellers of Tales: Children's Books and Their Authors*, 1946 (and later editions), referring to American humorist John Habberton, *Helen's Babies*, 1876, mentions 'phrases which have become parts of the English language: "Want to shee the wheels go wound" [in a watch], and the cry "Turtle plates!" when anyone looks at the maker's mark on table crockery'. The book, when pub'd in UK, became immensely popular both there and throughout the rest of what was then the British Empire. (I read the book in 1902.) Very soon, these two phrases 'caught on': the former was, by 1940 at latest, ob., yet even now (1979), not entirely †; the latter had a shorter life and was, I believe, † by 1930.

tweet tweet. See: I lift.

twelve. See: it's all in the t.; roll on, my.

twelve o'clock! It's time to be moving: working classes': *c*. 1890–1914. (Ware.) Noon being break-off time.

twenty-eighty. See **that's the old navy spirit.**

twenty-three (written **23**), **skid(d)oo!** – the full expression is, in fact, an elab. of **23**.

O'Malley's was a real drugstore.... It was devoted to the preparation and dispensation of prescription drugs and those few patent medicines that retained the stodgy respectability they had acquired in the days of twenty-three skiddoo [Jack D. Hunter, *Spies Inc.*, 1969].

This phrase has caused the recorders of US speech, beginning with HLM, and esp. the chroniclers of US slang (Berrey, 1942, onwards to W & F, 1960), much trouble and caused overmuch controversy.

To clear the ground a little, *skid(d)oo* derives from – and, in the imperative, synonymizes – *skedaddle*, to depart in haste or with at least an unseemly alacrity.

The earliest possible explanation I've seen is that advanced by Frank Parker Stockbridge (*teste* and editorial in the Louisville *Times* of 9 May 1929): that *twenty-three* or *23*.

was launched by *The Only Way*, a dramatization of Dickens's *Tale of Two Cities*, presented by Henry Miller in New York in 1899. In the last act an old woman counted the victims of the guillotine, and Sydney Carton was the twenty-third. According to Stockbridge, her solemn 'Twenty-three!' was borrowed by Broadway, and quickly became popular. He says *skiddoo*... was 'added for the enlightenment of any who hadn't seen the play'. [HLM, definitive edn, 1936.]

W & F quote C.T. Ryan as writing in *American Speech*, 1926,

[Approximately twenty-five years ago] appeared in my vocabulary that effective but horrible '23-Skiddoo'. Pennants and arm bands at shore resorts, parks and county fairs, bore either [23] or the word 'Skiddoo'. In time the numerals became synonymous with and connotative of the whole expression.

W & F themselves define the full phrase as, on the one hand, 'a mild expression of recognition, incredulity, surprise, or pleasure, as at something remarkable or attractive'; and as, on the other, 'an expression of rejection or refusal' – or, of course, mere dismissal, whether literal ('Run away' – 'Beat it') or figurative ('I don't care').

W & F then supply an invaluable gloss: 'Like "shoo-fly", "twenty-three skiddoo" was often used without specific meaning. It was in male use *c*. 1900–1910, originally among students and sophisticated young adults. It was perhaps the first truly national fad expression and one of the most popular fad expressions to appear in the US.' They add that 'Ironically it is now associated with the 1920s and is frequently used to convey the spirit of the 1920s in novels and plays of the period'; they also note that, even in 1960, although no longer much used, it was still very widely remembered and understood.

Valuable as their entry is (what, indeed, should we in Britain do without it?), it can be enlarged and perhaps slightly modified.

Opinions, even among the at least apparently well-informed, differ. For instance, Joe Laurie, Jr, in *Vaudeville from the Honky-Tonks to the Palace*, 1953, writes: 'Tom Lewis, the man who originated the catchword "Twenty-three", (they added skiddoo to it later) in George M. Cohan's *Little Johnny Jones* [prod. in 1904], was an old-time trouper from "Frisco".' (with thanks to W.J.B.)

The phrase, either in its full form or in one of its two shorter forms, remained popular until *c.* 1914 at least. In *The Pedagogical Seminary* of Mar. 1912, A.H. Melville, analysing the slang expressions common at a school, finds that, there, *skiddoo* is very widely employed, but *twenty-three, skiddoo*, never.

In 1910, Oliver Herford and John Cecil Clay, in *Cupid's Cyclopedia*, have, under *s*, this passage: 'Poor Adam! (Poor Us!!!) There confronting him was this word in fresh bright paint, "SKYDDU". That night it rained. Oh, how it rained!' (Here, painfully obvious, SKYDDU is a pun on *skiddoo* and *sky-dew*.)

In 1908, John Kendrick Bangs, author of that at one time world-famous *Houseboat on the Styx*, had written, in *Potted Fiction* (chapter VI, 'The Last Secret'): 'I am a Bravado, and our motto is "Sempre Bravado Sic Non Skiddoo".'

Still earlier, Bert Leston Taylor and W.C. Gibson had, in *Extra Dry*, 1906, in 'The Rime of the Water Wagon Mariner' (in part, a parody of Coleridge's poem), lyricized thus:

Hast thou the price, O Wedding Guest?
I know an onyx bar –
'Skiddoo!' replied the Wedding Guest,
And caught a Broadway car.

Much later than *c.* 1910-10 comes this illuminating example from Lyle Stuart, *The Secret Life of Walter Winchell*, 1953, in ref. it would seem, to the year 1923:

He was fast talking and persuasive. He snooped. He listened. But most of the time he talked.
'Listen, kiddo, how would you like to have your picture in *Vaudeville News*?' he would say.
'Twenty-three, skiddoo,' might be the response.
[Here = run away and don't bother me.]

In 1958, Clarence Budington Kelland, in *Where There's Smoke*, writes, in a manner implying that the phrase now belonged only to the older generation: '"You will leave the dishes," her father said in a voice of command. And then with ill-simulated humour, "Twenty-three, skidoo with ye."'

In 1967, Jack D. Hunter – I can't resist quoting him again – writes in *One of Us Works for Them*: 'I would have been very angry if I hadn't felt the sudden, heady realization that today was someday, now was the hour, no time like the present, first things first, live today for today, and twenty-three skidoo. I quit.'

To serve as a comment on the mistaken belief that the phrase belonged peculiarly to the 1920s, the lively little book EJ, pub'd in the US in (note the date) 1972, begins the second chapter ('Some Words Die Young; Others Just Hang Around') thus: 'About fifty years ago the "in" groups frequently used such expressions as *twenty-three skiddoo* and *vo-dee-o-do*.... Expressions like *so's your old man* and *oh, you kid* lingered late into the thirties and died.'

It is, I think, relevant to quote from Dr Douglas Leechman who, in 1969, wrote: 'It was much used just before WW1, especially in US' – and thus he implied a

limited Canadian currency. 'I believe it to be part of a long-forgotten telegraphic code, devised by one Phillips. Numbers took the place of frequently used phrases: thus, 30 meant "the end" and still appears on MSS; 23 meant "Away with you!" and 73, "best regards".' This code meaning of 23 could, just possibly, have been a contributory factor.

There are c.pp. serious; there are c.pp. semi-serious; there are c.pp. trivial; and there are c.pp. both trivial and either very silly or almost meaningless: proudly at the crest of the third group stands *twenty-three, skiddoo* as the finest of all US examples.

J.W.C., 1977, writes, 'Nobody, in U.S., ever any longer says the first part alone; the two parts together are [now] very rare; the "skiddoo" by itself, rather less rare.... I should say that, in U.S., all three have always been used only in the sense "Beat it!" [Go, or Run, away!]'.

See also TAD DORGAN
twice removed from Wigan is a disparaging c.p., used, since *c.* 1920, to describe Lancashire (hence, loosely, also Yorkshire) people living permanently in the south of England.
twiggez-vous? – also written **twiggy-vous** (or **voo**)? Do you 'twig' or understand?: *c.* 1892–1930. Kipling, in *Stalky & Co.*, 1899, has:
'Twiggez-vous?'
'Nous twiggons.'
(But *nous twiggons*, we twig, did not catch on.) From slang 'to twig'; on the analogy of Fr. *comprenez-vous*? For the form, cf **squattez-vous**; for the sense, cf the WW1 'Hobson-Jobson' *compree?*, do you understand?

But, in a letter, 1949, Leslie Verrier, MRCS, wrote to me thus enlighteningly: 'I suspect that by the time it had filtered down to Kipling's schoolboys, it was rather *vieux jeu* in the metropolis. It may have originated in the song of Marie Lloyd by whom it was first popularized in 1892.'

In *Edwardian Popular Music*, 1975, Ronald Pearsall confirms Verrier's claim made on behalf of Marie Lloyd 'whose first big hit came with "Oh, Mr Porter". Born in 1870 in Peerless Street, Hoxton, Marie Lloyd also immortalised "Then You Wink the Other Eye", "Twiggy-Voo" (giving a catch phrase to a nation), "A Little of What You Fancy Does Yon Good", and "One of the Ruins that Cromwell Knocked about a Bit".'

However, adds P.B., Kipling's *Stalky & Co.*, although published in 1899, was based, albeit loosely, on his own schooldays, 1878–82. Kipling had a superb ear for remembered speech, and I feel it unlikely that he would have permitted himself such an anachronism as back-dating a piece of well-known slang by twenty years. I therefore propose that *twiggez-vous*? really does date from the late 1870s at the latest.

'twill last as many days as nights is a characteristic C18 c.p., evasive and intentionally unhelpful; the vague general meaning is, 'for a (short) while', as in S, 1738, Dialogue I:
MISS: See, Madam, how well I have mended it.
LADY SM[ART]: 'Tis indifferent, as *doll* Danc'd.
NEV[EROUT]: 'Twill last as many Days as Nights.
twin. See: you must be a t.
twinges round the hinges through binges 'refers to "the screws" [rheumatism] – and one cause [thereof]' (Petch, 1974): since *c.* 1950.
twinkle. See: I was doing it.
twist. See: don't get your arse; get your knickers; you could t.; you silly.
twisting slowly, slowly in the wind 'is likely to be used whenever Presidents let their nominees go without support' (William Safire, 'Political Word Watch' in *The New York Times*, 19 Nov. 1978): US political: since *c.* 1975. Ashley recalls the phrase is *turning in the wind*; cf **statement is inoperative.**
two. See: I'll tell you one; it takes two; push in the bush; take all; that makes two; there are two; there's no two; they're two; thick as; we went; who asked; why don't you two; yes, a cat; you must come; you'll speak.

two cars in every garage. See **there'll be a chicken...**

two cents' worth – put in (one's). One's opinion or advice, for what it's worth – the implication being that it's worth precisely that; whence, loosely, an idle remark, also an unasked comment: US, hence also, since *c.* 1945, Can. I have no earlier record than 1942, Berrey offering the var. *one's nickel's worth*, which desn't seem to have lasted very well.

But clearly this is a c.p. only in the forms, *must you put in your two cents' worth?* or **who asked you to put in...?**

two eyes upon ten fingers. See **two upon ten.**

two for the price of one is 'said when a man marries a fat girl or woman' (Petch, 1976): mostly lower-middle class and public house: C20.

'I would have thought this [c.p.] restricted neither in meaning nor in class. I certainly use it and have often heard it used; but I have never heard of Mr Petch's restricted meaning' (Playfair, 1977). Yet Mr Petch's is the more pointed and undoubtedly a c.p.

two hairs past a freckle. 'When we [in our schooldays, *c.* 1958–65] were asked the time was, and we didn't have a watch, we'd look at the back of our wrists as if there was a watch there, and say "two hairs past a freckle"' (Levene, 1978). P.B.: the idea, if not the actual phrase goes back a decade or two earlier: our school version, earlier 1940s, was 'according to the hairs on my wrist...'

two hands for the King (or **the Queen**). See **one hand for....**

two heads are better than one, even if one is only a sheep's head. This c.p. is directed at or, usu., addressed to the second party to a plan or an undertaking; often in retort to the trite or proverbial *two heads are better than one*: C20, but perhaps going back to 1890 or even 1880.

two in the hand. See **push in the bush.**

two inches beyond upright was, *c.* 1900–14, applied to a hypocritical liar. Ware classifies it as 'People's' – that is, proletarian. He adds: 'Perversion of description of upright-standing man, who throws his head back beyond upright.'

two L.O. 'represents 2 LO and was, during the 1920s, used as a catch phrase dovetail to the greeting "Hello!". It obviously originated in the earliest days of broadcasting; 2 LO was a Marconi radio station which opened, broadcasting from the top floor of Marconi House [in Savoy Hill] in London, on May 11, 1922' (Derek Parker, 1977).

Prob. confined, in the main, to Londoners, as Noble has suggested; he adds that '2 LO, London calling' was the callsign, very familiar for some years.

two men gone sick. See **about as much...**

two minds with but a single thought! is frequently uttered in circumstances similar to those that call forth **great minds think alike**, q.v. It is a misquotation rather than a c.p., and comes from near the end of Act II of *Der Sohn der Wildnis*, 1842, by Friedrich Halm (1806–71), in the trans. by Maria Lovell: 'Two souls with but a single thought,/Two hearts that beat as one'. Perhaps the usual misquot'n has been influenced by the *great minds* phrase. (P.B..)

two other fellows from Poona or, in full, **it must have been....** A serio-comic denial of association, as, e.g., by one of two men seen drinking together or acting suspiciously: since *c.* 1910; but after *c.* 1960, *from Poona* has often been omitted. It occurs allusively in 'It Mush Have Been Two Other Fellows' – the opening story in Len Deighton's *Declaration of War*, 1971, with its key passage: 'The Colonel still looked puzzled and Wool said, "Oh, well, it must have been two other fellows, eh?" He laughed and repeated his joke slowly.' The 'two other fellows' in this story were the two

soldiers, Colonel and Lance-Corporal of twenty-five years earlier – so different, so (in some ways) superior to their present selves: in short, two other fellows.

Poona implies the old Regular Indian Army; a famous station.

Ashley, 1979, gives the US version as 'It wasn't me: it was a couple of other guys'.

two pun ten. See **two upon ten.**

two short planks. See **thick as...**

two tin fucks (about it) (**I, he,** etc.) **don't care** or **worry** or **couldn't give.** A low C20 c.p.; 'I couldn't care less!' As Wedgewood has reminded me, it is apparently suggested by the common idiomatic phrase *not to care two brass farthings*. Moreover, **brass** suggested **tin;** the *f* of **farthing** that of **fucking;** and *fucking* may well have prompted the idea of *fucks*.

two to one against you. The odds are very much against you getting your pledge back: a proletarian c.p. of *c.* 1890–1914 (Ware). A ref. to the pawnbrokers' sign: two blue balls over one.

two upon ten, often corrupted to **two pun ten;** in full, **two eyes upon ten fingers.** A trade c.p., dating since *c.* 1850. Hotten, 1860, explains the saying thus: 'When a supposed thief is present, one shopman asks the other if that *two pun'* (pound) *ten* matter was ever settled.' The full expression generated the short.

two white, two red, and after you with the blacking brush! Hence, **after you, miss, with the two two's and the two b's.** A London streets' c.p., addressed to a female excessively rouged and powdered: the 1860s. (Ware.) Two dabs of red, two of white, and a brush to tidy and heighten the eyebrows.

two with you! suggests a two penny drink: common in taverns, inns, other drinkeries, of *c.* 1885–1914. (Ware, who intimately knew his London and its lighter side.)

twopence. See: give her; penny bun; putting your t.; wash; and:

twopence to buy, and twopence to get rid of was, in the 1930s, applied to a cup of coffee at a Lyons, an Express Dairy, an ABC café, perhaps esp. in London. A ref. to the diuretic properties of coffee. I heard it in 1937.

[two's company, (but) three's a crowd is Brit. and Aus. proverb (late C19–20) rather than a c.p.: it answers to the † English proverb, *two is company, but there is none,* recorded by *ODEP.* (B.P., 1975.) R.C. writes, 1978, 'Also US, now obsolescent or simply a cliché? A cliché it is, but perhaps it qualifies for inclusion here in the US form noted by A.B., 1979: 'I've heard it this way in the 1950s: "One's enough – two's company – three's too many – and four, not allowed" (or "Four's a crowd")'.]

two's up. 'In the Services this has, since *c.* 1950, been a very common and widely used expression to claim next use of anything. E.g.: "Good book, this" – "Is it? Two's up, then", or "Two's up on that piece of porn[ography] you've got there, mate"' (P.B., 1974).

Twyford See: my name is T.

Tyburn. See: he that is.

Tyler. See: Tippecanoe.

typical naval argument: assertion, flat contradiction, personal abuse – a. A naval officers' c.p. of Service, and self, criticism: since *c.* 1930. (Rear-Adm. P.W. Brock, 1969. He queries the '*c.* 1930': the c.p. might, he thinks, have arisen a little earlier – or a trifle later.)

P.B.: I was strongly reminded of this phrase when reading (in Andrew Boyle's moving biography of *Trenchard*, 1962) about the post-WW1 efforts of the Admiralty to scotch the existence of an independent RAF.

U

umpah, umpah, stick in up your jumpah! See **oompah**...
umpire. See: how's that, umpire?
unaccustomed as I am to public speaking. This cliché has, since c. 1950, been used ironically and esp., quasi-apologetically, by people suffering from no such handicap. (Skehan, 1977.) P.B.: sometimes, just *unaccustomed as I am* is sufficient.
unbounded assortment of gratuitous untruths – an, was a Parliamentary c.p. of late 1885–mid 1886. Ware glosses it as 'extensive systematic lying' and derives it 'from speech (11 November 1885) of Mr Gladstone's at Edinburgh'. Cf Lord Randolph Churchill's justly famous definition of a lie as a 'terminological inexactitude'.
uncle. See: and Bob's; he has gone; I'll be a monkey's; if my aunt; keep your eye on u.; say uncle; Tommy.
Uncle Joe is much improved. He's – hence I'm – feeling much better, business or things are going much better: since c. 1930. Prompted by the 'improved' of an invalid's health and also by the second line of a raffish, once roguish, couplet, 'Since he had his balls removed'.
Uncle Sam. See: Kitchener.
uncomfortable. See: any B.F. can be.
under. See: get out and; that's a bit u.
under the bunk! Shut up! (esp. at night): US convicts': since c. 1920. As if 'Get under your bunk and keep quiet!'
under-paid and over-laid is a US off-shoot from the next and may, therefore, be dated as since latish 1940s. 'A strange expression', remarks A.B., 1979, when he noted it for me: 'Said by a man or a woman, petulantly, when asked "How are you doing?" casually. The implication is, "I'm not getting what I'm worth": *over-laid* means too much sexual activity, not much compensation, physically or economically – maybe even emotionally or psychically'.
under-paid, under-sexed, and under Eisenhower. See **over-paid**...
undercumstumble. See: I u.
understand See: my wife.
unhand me, villain (or, occ., **sir**)! Current since early C20, this c.p. describes and often amiably, derides the Surreyside, or Transpontine, melodramas. Cf the quot'n at **trouble at t'mill.** The phrase is often followed by *she cried.* The *sir* form, comparatively rare in UK, has been fairly common in US since early C20. Moreover, *unhand me, sir!* has acquired a joc. sense, 'Go away! Quit bothering me!' – used, for instance, by a young woman. The plays thus characterised were popular c. 1860–1914.
universe. See: cussedness.
unlike the home-life of our dear Queen. See **how different**...
unrelieved holocaust – an, was a Society c.p. of 1883 and applied to even a minor accident. Ware tells us that it was occasioned by its use by a writer in *The Times* to describe the destruction (1882) of the Ring Theatre in Vienna and of a

circus at Berditscheff in Russia, both fires being accompanied by a heavy loss of life.
unstuck. See: glue-pot.
untidy. See: you make the place.
up. See: are you up?; break it up; come up; cough it up; go up; it's all up; keep your pecker; may all your ups; mine's up; never up; nothing but up; penny more; she wouldn't; sorry to keep; stir; that's up; two's up; what goes up; what's up; who's up; with the corner.
up a—'s arse, and don't be (so bloody) nosey! 'A schoolboy's answer to the question, "Where is it?"' (Granville, 1969): late C19–20. The juvenile version, which omits *so bloody*, derives from the male, adult, proletarian, mostly N. Country version – the longer one; the latter version is also a reply to the more specific question, 'Where did you get that thing?'; neither has been much heard since c. 1960.
up a shade, Ada! has since c. 1950 in the RAF, esp. while it was stationed in Malta, been an appeal for more room ('Move up a bit there!'). Hence, also applied to a noisy collision between two persons.
up against you. See **that's up**....
up Alice's. A 'teasing evasion of questions such as "where did you get to last night?" — "You going out this evening?" Orig., and still mostly, N. Country: since c. 1910, ?ten or twenty years earlier. (L.A., 1974.) Not 'up at' nor 'along to', but 'up Alice's [vagina]'.
up and down like a bride's nightie; ... like a whore's drawers on (a) Boat Race night. The latter is a MN c.p., certainly of the 1950s (Peppitt); but I've heard it since the 1920s and it has been used since 1960: a humorous ref. to the traditional Oxford and Cambridge undergraduate jollification on the occasion.
  The former, the more widely known, is applied to someone very restless: since the mid 1930s. Levene, 1977, describes ... *like a bride's nightie* as 'terribly camp', but cf. *off like a bride's nightie.*
up and down like a fiddler's elbow is a lower-middle-class c.p. of late (? mid) C19–20 and applied to anyone very restless. Cf. **in and out like a fiddler's bitch.**
up and down like a shit-house seat was a Canadian Army c.p. of WW2 and referred to a gambler's luck. (Leechman.) Contrast the prec. and cf the next:
up and down like a yo-yo. This has been, since c. 1960 at the latest, and certainly in the Armed Forces, the most commonly used of all the *up and down* similes. Applied like the *bride's nightie, whore's drawers,* and *fiddler's elbow* versions, to someone very restless, it is used perhaps more of the those servicemen who, although quite frequently promoted, are just as frequently 'busted back down' again. Also allusively, as in 'He's been up and down to corporal more time than enough. Talk about a bloody yo-yo!' (P.B.)
up and down like Tower Bridge is a Cockney c.p. of late

323

C19-20. It has a 'scabrous innuendo' and is used 'in response to *How goes it?*' (L.A.) P.B.: Robert Barltrop & Jim Wolveridge, in *The Muvver Tongue*, 1980, maintain that it is simply a punning reply to a friendly enquiry, without any *double entendre:* life is changeable.

up and down! Mind the dresser! A C20 Anglo-Irish c.p. employed of a party held at a farmer's house. (The dresser is, of course, the piece of furniture, not a person.)

up for grabs. With ref. to the expression *it's up for grabs,* J.W.C., 1977, glosses, 'Whoever succeeds in grabbing it first, gets it (for good): American: since *c.* 1950. Very common'. P.B.: but a substantive may replace *it*, e.g. the piece of land; the commercial proposition; the idea. Perhaps rather idiom than c.p. Some use in UK in later C20.

up goes McGinty's goat. Things become exciting, e.g. as at a great explosion:? orig. Anglo-Irish: prob. latish C19-mid C20. In William Guy Carr's *Brass Hats and Bell-Bottomed Trousers*, 1939, but valid for the RN throughout WW1, we read that an enemy shell lands 'kerplunk' among a cluster of British lyddite shells 'and up goes McGinty's goat'. Cf **down went McGinty.**

up, Guards, and at 'em! is a c.p. of light-hearted or, at the least, nonchalant defiance, virtually synon. with **let 'em all come!:** late C19-20. Based upon a famous quot'n that is almost certainly apocryphal: in 1852, when asked what he had, in the fact, said at the Battle of Waterloo (22 June 1815), the Duke of Wellington replied to the anecdotist J. W. Croker: 'What I must have said and possibly did say was, Stand up, Guards! and then gave the commanding officers the order to attack.' (*ODQ.*) By 'what I must have said', he clearly meant 'If I said anything, it would have been "Stand up, Guards!"' Nevertheless, there is no need to deny that *up, Guards, and at 'em* long ago achieved full c.p. status.

up, guards, and atap! According to H. W. Fowler and I. P. Watt, in an excellent article pub'd in a ship's news-sheet of late 1945, among WW2 prisoners of war – in the Far East, 'Our officers spurred themselves to greater efforts in hut-building with the cry, "Up guards and atap!" [*Note.* All our huts were atap-roofed!] A debonair pun on **up, Guards, and at 'em!** Also noted that *atap* is a Malayan word for thatch made from napa palm leaves.

up in Annie's room. An Army c.p., slightly prec. WW1, but at its height during it, in answer to 'Where's so-and-so?' – esp. to an enquiring sergeant or corporal. In contrast to the sombre **hanging on the (old) barbed wire** and – orig., at least – implying that the sought one was 'a bit of a lad with the girls'. Hence, a double in the game of darts.

Often shortened to *in Annie room*, as F & G tell us. Occ. var.: **Nellie's,** as B & P inform us, and, as Rabbi Dr David Goldstein tells me, the *Annie* version has, as a civilian rather than an Army elab., the fairly frequent addition *behind the clock.*

up she comes and the colour's red is an exclam. uttered at a favourable turn of events, notably if the opposition suddenly collapses or an obstacle is unexpectedly removed: since *c.* 1945 or perhaps ten years earlier. Presumably from gambling.

up Shit Creek (or, euph.) **up the creek;** or even, derivatively, **up the well-known creek) without a paddle:** after *c.* 1950, occ..... **with a broken paddle,** which last I've never heard since *c.* 1960.

A C20 saying, perhaps orig. RN; certainly, by *c.* 1920, RAF; and, by *c.* 1945, very widely used. Orig. it denoted a being badly off course, with ne'er a paddle to steer by; hence, lost and in bad trouble; hence in bad trouble and no discernible or expectable relief at hand.

In 1969, concerning US usage, J.W.C. wrote to me: 'Sometimes, among people not acquainted with the full form, "up the creek".' In 1942, Berrey had listed *up salt creek* (but not *up Shit Creek*) and synonymized it with 'in a predicament'. In 1960, W & F remarked that 'Although the shortened form "up the creek" is common, the full original

term is seldom heard now' and glossed it as 'Originally from homosexual usage' – which may or may not be true of US usage, but is not, I believe, true of Brit. usage.

Prof. Clark added, 1977, '*up the creek* is the commonest form in the US, where *without a paddle* is usually omitted'; he refutes for the US, as strongly as I do for the UK and Commonwealth, the homosexual orig. The *without a paddle* version is occ. elab. *and the boat's leaking,* as noted by R.C., who, 1978, convincingly pleads that, in US at least, the originating form was *up Salt Creek* and that Salt River in Kentucky was the ultimate; the curious should consult B. Bolkin, *A Treasure of American Folklore,* 1944. A.B., 1979, supplies a further intensification: *up Shit Creek and neither a paddle nor a canoe.*

P.B.: the invariable use of *creek* seems to point to an orig. in the US, where 'creek' is the common term for many rivers smaller than, say, the Mississippi – unless somewhere specific in UK, e.g. Barking Creek (a tributary of the Thames below London), was meant. Harry Clifton's music-hall song, 'Paddle Your Own Canoe' (q.v.) may have helped to popularize the phrase in the UK and Commonwealth. Cf **jammed like Jackson.**

up the road and turn right next Thursday. 'The jocular c.p. used to anyone in the [Nile] delta asking the way to a unit in the desert [during the North African campaign, 1940–43]. There was only one road in the desert and that led – eventually – to Tunis, a longish drive. (Sanders, 1978. Mr Sanders once contributed to the *Sunday Times* a truly excellent, quietly humorous, dulcetly ironic article on the slang of the British Army during that campaign.)

up the Swanee. See down the Swanee.

up there, Cazaly! was, *c.* 1930–50, an Aus., but esp. a Melbourne, cry of encouragement. Baker, 1943, writes: 'Cazaly was a noted South Melbourne footballer, whose speciality was high marking.' (Australian Rules Football, of course.)

Roy Cazaly (1893–1964) occurs in Wilkes at *Cazaly*; cited for 1943–73. Clearly, I 'sold him short': the phrase for a long time.

[**up to you for the rent!; up you!** (Aus. **upya!**); **up your** (this or that)! are not true c.pp. but mere verbal violences.]

up, up, up! See **get off and milk it!**

up, up and away, a c.p. for 'let's get moving', orig. in the adventures of that all-American hero of mid–late C20, Superman, as Ashley tells me, 1983. ... *in my beautiful balloon* is a song-writer's embellishment. (P.B.)

up with petticoats, down with drawers! It orig. in a ribald couplet, dating since *c.* 1905,. I first heard it, in Aus., in 1913; but it is common too in UK (*teste* L.A., 1974). Often a 'dare' among mixed company friends in raffish or bibulous mood, often followed by the second line, 'you tickle mine and I'll tickle yours'.

up you go with the best of luck! 'The MO's benediction when sending you up the line after hospital' (B & P, 1931): British Army: WW1. Inevitably it incurred the odium of the soldier's derision.

P.B.: an early example in print occurs in Olive Dent, *A V.A.D. in France,* 1917. Recounting how a soldier up-patient helped her make the beds in a camp hospital, she wrote: 'he helped the young soldier sit up so that he could adjust the mattress, saying as he did so, "Up you go ... and the best of luck!" – he could not help completing the tag.' (With thanks to Mrs Barbara Huston.)

up with the lark, and to bed with the Wrens [WRNS]. An 'Armed Forces', esp. the RN's, officers' rather than ratings, c.p. of WW2. (Camilla Raab, 1977.)

up your tail with a rusty nail! is a US c.p. elab. of the vulgar phrase, *up yours!* App. late C19–20; by 1979, ob. (Owed to A.B., 1979; the 'ob'. is mine.)

upright. See: **two inches.**

uproar. See: **don't get your arse.**

Upsey. See: **down, Upsey.**

upside down. See: only river; turn 'em; and:

upside down in a cloud. 'Abbreviated version of "There we were, upside down in cloud, fuck-all on the clock [= the altimeter registering zero], and still climbing" – commonly used to check live-shooters [= boasters]': RAF operational : 1940–5 (Wg/Cdr R.P. McDouall, in a letter, 1945, while I was on 'the Writers' Team' in Public Relations at the Air Ministry.)

P.B.: with the slight elab. ... *fuck-all on the clock but the maker's name, and still climbing hard*, the phrase was still current, or at least well-remembered, in the RAF of the early 1950s. R.C., 1978, adds, 'Cf the American WW2 Air Force version, *there I was a twenty thousand feet*'.

upstairs. See: shoving.

[upsy-daisy! (See **oops-a-daisy**.) This is mentioned only because several respected scholars have urged its inclusion. But obviously it doesn't even begin to be a c.p. P.B. adds: true; but what about the parody **Ups** (or **oops**) **a bloody buttercup!**: (?) *c.* 1930–50?]

urn. See: enough to make my gran.

use. See: headache; stick around; you should use; and:

use your imagination, because (often written *becos*), followed by a brief significant pause. The c.p. consists of these four words only; it conveniently abridges the refrain of a 'saga': 'He was a very handsome young soldier, he was'. 'The c.p. was applied when a work-mate feigned innocence of the matter in hand' (L.A., 1976): since the early 1940s, but little used after early 1970s.

[use your loaf! – Use your head (*loaf of bread*, rhyming slang) or intelligence – has, since the mid 1940s, been so common as to cause me to wonder: but no! However popular, it's still ordinary slang.]

useless as tits on a boar hog. Utterly useless: US: C20. (George A. Krzymowski, 1978.) Cf the Can. *useless as tits on a bull* (or *a whore*): late C19–20. See also **you're as much use...**

usual grounds. See: I decline.

usual speech not required was, *c.* 1870–1920, a Brit underworld c.p., tantamount to 'No bill!' in ref. to the verdicts 'Guilty' or 'Not guilty'. Clarksom and Hall, *Police!*, 1889.

utter. See: is it my; too too.

VR, VR, VR was, at the time of Queen Victoria's Diamond Jubilee, June 1897, a Cockney c.p. It punned on *ve are, ve are, ve are*, we are (thrice), and *VR*, Victoria Regina. Ware.

vain. See: who's that.

valuable. See: this is not only.

valve. See: you'll bust.

van. See: another one; coming up; send for the green.

vanilla. See: I'll take v.

vas you dere, Sharlie? 'A radio comedian who called himself Baron Munchausen told tall stories to a "straight man" (Charlie), who expressed doubt. This was the gag line. It became popular for a while – if anyone expressed any doubt or scepticism, you said "Vas you dere, Sharlie?" in the 1930s' (Professor Emeritus F. E. L. Priestley, concerning its Can. usage). Berrey records its US usage.

'Jack Pearl created the character of Baron Munchausen in US radio, 1940s. He spoke with a pidgin German accent' (A.B., 1979) – so, understandably, there are var. spellings, *vass* or *wass*, and *dare*. Cf *how's the mommah?*

Vaseline. See: black cat.

ve get too soon old and too late s(ch)mart occurs in Glendon Swartout, *The Tin Lizzie Group*, a novel that, pub'd in 1972, is valid for the US of 1916 – and perhaps as far back as 1900. R.C., 1977, supplied the likely source: 'This and its occasional variant *vy do ve get so soon old and so late schmart?* are still sometimes seen, e.g. as a plaque on a bar-room wall. Dating probably from *c.* 1870, when German dialect comedy was in its heyday, due to heavy German immigration following the 1848 revolution. See, e.g., Charles Godfrey Leland's *The Breitmann Ballads*, 1871'. Cf *Si jeunesse savait, si vieillesse pouvait* (Henri Estienne, 1531–98), which might be rendered, 'If youth but knew, if old age but could!'

ve haf vays and means to make you talk, sometimes 'anglicized' – somewhat stupidly – **we have ways and means to make you talk.** 'Said always in a sinister mock-German accent to represent all the Gestapo films, Colditz, TV Series, etc. It gets misapplied and it is quite general and popular' (P.B., 1975). As a c.p. from (say) 1950 onwards. But note that 'it is also featured in the TV comedy show "Laugh-In" – as famous there [the US] as **very interesting'** (Patricia Newnham, 1976). In gen. use the *and means* is often omitted.

veal will be cheap: calves fall. A jeering ref. to a spindle-legged person: mid C16–18. Ray, 1678; Apperson.

veddy, veddy English. Obtrusively or conspicuously or unmistakably English: US: since late 1940s. Paul Janssen, 1978, cites Etienne & Simone's *Grand Dictionnaire d'Americanismes* (5 edd. 1956–73) listing it. He adds, 'Jocular or derisive of the way Englishmen are supposed to pronounce the letter *r*'. Largely a myth. P.B.: but listen to some of our politicians!

venture it as Johnson did his wife. See **I'll venture it.**

venture. See: I'll venture.

Venus. See: one night.

Vergin' on the ridiculous. Usu. prec. by *yes*, and following any mention of the word *virgin*, esp. when a girl's virginity is in question: Services' and raffish: later C20. Cf **Virgin for short.** (P.B.)

very funny! (With the first syllable always stressed heavily and long, and the phrase often prec. by **oh!**). 'Not funny at all' or 'very far from being at all funny': Brit. and US: since *c.* 1950. (A reminder from R.C., 1978.) P.B.: cf the Brit. later C20 use of *charming!* to mean its exact opposite, and stressed in the same way. This is presumably the same process that turned the C16–17 use of *rum*, meaning 'good', into its later meaning of 'strange, suspect, odd'.

very good question – a: See **that's a good question,** but add that in *The American Dream*, 1961, Edward Albee wrote thus:

MOMMY: Are you in the habit of receiving boxes?
DADDY: A very good question.

very how! A not infrequent answer to the Aus. greeting **'ow yer going, mate?,** q.v. (Mrs Camilla Raab.)

very identical thing – the! Just what I needed; exactly what I wanted; yes, *that's* what I asked for, or sought: *c.* 1830–90. J. E. Carpenter, *Love and Honour, or, Soldiers at Home – Heroes Abroad; an Original Domestic Drama*, performed in 1855, has at I, i:

BOLUS: This, gentlemen, I assure you is –
BRIEF: [*Drinking.*] The very identical thing!

This c.p. occurs many times in the play; always used by lawyer Briefwit. To me, it sounds like an echo of Dickens – ? Sam Weller.

very interesting! 'A few years ago,' wrote Vernon Noble in a letter, 1974,

an American comedy show – very successful on TV in the States – was shown weekly by BBC. It was called 'Rowan and Martin's Laugh-In'. A character in it, Arte Johnson (usually dressed incongruously as a German soldier) would exclaim 'ver-rr-y interesting!' This became [in UK] a catch-phrase introduced inconsequently and [it] lingered for a few months after the series ended.

The pron. was *vairee* – with a Ger. accent.

P.B.: the phrase in full is *very interesting... but stupid!*, and that was the title chosen by Nigel Rees for his 'book of catchphrases from the world of entertainment', 1980, a compilation and commentary that has been of considerable help to me in the preparation of the second ed. of this present collection.

very like a whale! was, in mid C19–early C20, applied to a very improbable, esp. to a preposterous, statement. Hotten recorded it in 1859 and, in his 2nd ed., 1860, noted the var. *very like a whale in a tea-cup*, which seems to have lasted for no more than a decade. From Polonius's phrase uttered while doing his best (*Hamlet*, III, ii, lines 392–8) to show a sycophantic approval of Hamlet's deliberately far-fetched similes.

very nice too! (– and) with emphasis on *too* and with the connotation, 'Well! Aren't you (isn't he, etc.) – *lucky!*' As in '"He's just come into a fortune." – "Very nice too!"' To a girl suddenly discovered in a state of entire or partial nudity, the polite man will say '(And) very nice too!': almost, in such contexts, a formula of courtesy. The phrase goes back to *c.* 1920 at least and prob. much earlier.

very tasty, very succulent! was, *c.* 1948–57, an Aus. c.p., popularized by the Australian comedian known as 'Mo'. (*AS.*) It elaborates:

very tasty, very sweet! was extremely popular in UK during WW2, when precious things *were*! By 1965, † – except as a rather self-conscious piece of nostalgia among older people. Yet it must be noted that as an erotic c.p., existing since *c.* 1900 (if not earlier), it is still very common.

Nigel Rees, in *VIBS*, notes that it was the c.p. of Nan Kenway and Douglas Young, variety stars, in the radio series *Howdy Folks*, etc.

vest. See: pull down.

vestry. See: just in time.

vicar. See: I *am* the v.; not a word to.

vicarage. See: if wet.

Victoria Station without the clock – like. 'Said of any over-crowded area, indoors or out. Probably antedates WW1' (Sanders, 1978). Brit., obviously; the ref. is to Victoria Main Line Station in SW London.

Vienna. See: goodnight, V.

villain. See: hemp; I'm as mild; unhand.

vim, vigor, and vitality. See the more usu. form wim...

violin. See: where's your v.

Virgin for short but not for long is a humorous C20 c.p., applied, punningly, to girls forenamed *Virginia*. Cf **yes, Virginia**... and **vergin'**....

Virginia Woolf. See: from Beowulf.

visitor. See: I have a v.

vive la différence! 'A c.p. used when someone has just said that there is hardly any difference between men and women' (B.P.): since 1919 or 1920. An adaptation rather than a simple adoption of the Fr. male toast.

To show how easy it is to err in 'coverage', another correspondent writes, 1974: 'Heard when somebody mentions that women are [in temperament] different from men.'

Fain, 1977, comments, 'This has taken on a new life since the women's liberation movement became so prominent.'

vo-dee-o-do. See **twenty-three, skidoo**, penultimate paragraph. Perhaps influenced by *vodudobo*, a curse, a word used in the Gullah – a negro – dialect of the Georgia and South Carolina coasts (Dr Lorenzo Turner, as glossed by HLM, Supp, 2, pp. 265–7); almost certainly, *vo-de-o-do* (often written *vodeodo*) has been chosen for its abracadabraic qualities.

'To my knowledge, this has been used since *c.* 1920 to indicate pleasure, [as in] "Did you like it?" – "Vo-dee-o-do!", and *do* rhymes with *o*, of course' (Fain, 1977).

voice. See: another voice; good voice; his master's; roll on, my.

volunteer(s). See: I want three; keep your bowels; you only v.

vote early and often. 'A c.p. used early in this century by political stalwarts. An indication that moral standards have risen in at least one area' (B.P., 1974).

'The truncated *vote early and often* is less common, less euphonious – and less correct, than *vote early and vote often*' (Michael Goldman, 1978). Playfair suggests that it is US in origin. Yes, indeed: 'Bartlett' records it for 1848. Cf **sweating like a nigger...**

vote for Boyle! According to PGR,

[A] catch phrase after the fall of Tunis [1943]. Hal Boyle, of the Associated Press, drove into Tunis chanting 'Vote for Boyle, son of the soil: Honest Hal, the Arabs' pal'. The Arabs, with their usual facility for picking up a phrase without knowing the meaning, puzzled the troops by greeting them with this cry, which they in turn adopted. British Army in N. Africa: 1943–4.

voulez-vous squattez-vous? Will you sit down?: since *c.* 1820; by *c.* 1940, decidedly ob. yet, even by 1975, not completely †. 'Started by [the world-famous clown] Grimaldi,' says Ware. Not, you'll notice, *squatter*; cf **squattez-vous!**, and **twiggez-vous?**

vous pouvez cracher! '*ITMA* did a skit on pre-war Radio Luxemburg and called it "Radio Fakenburg". "Ici Radio Fakenburg," the announcer would say. "Mesdames et messieurs, défense de cracher (no spitting)." Each episode would end: "Mesdames et messieurs, vous pouvez cracher!"' (*VIBS*). See **tommy handley.**

vy! vot a cake [= fool] **I've been!** appeared – Shaw vouched in 1969 – in the Comic Calendar of 1841. Prob. occasioned by some public event and prob. ephemeral.

W

wagging. See: end is a-wagging.

wagons roll! ' "Let's get started!" Popularised by the TV series *Wagon Train* in the 1950s' (Sanders, 1978). By the late 1970s, slightly ob.

waist. See: nothing below; should be sawn.

wait. See: hurry up and w.; time and tide; we want eight; will you have; and:

wait and see! Although prob. used twenty or thirty years earlier, it became a gen. c.p. in March–April 1910 when Asquith employed it in ref. to the date for the reintroduction of Lloyd George's rejected budget. Asquith was himself, 1910 onwards, called *Old Wait and See* and, on the Western Front, 1914–18, French matches, so often failing to ignite, were called *wait-and-sees*. Eric Partridge, *A Covey of Partridge*, 1933.

wait for baby! 'Said by someone who is late (not dilatory) in making his appearance. Meaning: "Please wait for me – I'm slow but I'm trying to catch up with you"' (Dr George D. Herving, New Jersey, *via* A.B., 1979): US: since (?) c. 1950.

wait for it! – properly, the phrase is rapidly repeated, as in the Coward quot'n below. If it derives from the army's *wait for it!*, wait for the word of command (e.g., to fix bayonets), it dates, as a c.p., since the latter part of WW1; if, however, it has a music-hall origin, the c.p. may go back to late C19.

In *Red Peppers*, written c. 1935 and pub'd in 1936, Noël Coward offers – immediately after 'Refrain 1' in the first dialogue, this vastly convenient example:

GEORGE: I saw a very strange thing the other day.

LILY: What was it?

GEORGE: Twelve men standing under one umbrella and they didn't get wet.

LILY: How's that?

GEORGE: It wasn't raining. (Wait for it – wait for it.)

That is, wait for the laughter to end before you resume the dialogue.

wait for your round! A theatrical c.p. of very approx. 1880–1940: Michael Warwick, in an article entitled 'Theatrical Jargon of the Old Days' in the *Stage*, 3 Oct. 1968, says:

Actor-proof parts could always be recognized by the number of laughs or rounds of applause in any given scene, and the term 'wait for your round' is dated as the Dodo. But in the old days anyone killing a 'round' by coming in too quickly with their lines came in for some crushing criticism.

The same principle applied to laughs.

wait till the clouds roll by! Inducive of optimism: 1884, Ware tells us; by 1915 it had become proverbial. Ware also tells us that it came 'from an American ballad'; and Ashley, 1979, suggests a conflation of two lines from the old song, 'Wait till the sun shines, Nellie,/And the clouds go rolling by'.

wake. See: don't wake; spends; you'll wake.

wake up and smell the coffee! Of this US c.p., J.W.C. wrote, 1968: 'Not, I think, in origin an advertising slogan. A derisive way of saying "You're dreaming" or "You're not facing the facts" or "You might as well be asleep". Fifteen or twenty years old, I should say, though possibly much older.' Perhaps, however, prompted by various aromatic-chromatic advertisements by coffee manufacturers.

wake up at the back there! 'Jimmy Edwards in *Take It From Here*. Frank Muir comments: "This was a line I always used in writing Jim's schoolmaster acts. It was technically very useful in breaking up his first line and getting audience attention." Bob Monkhouse adds: "Jimmy Edwards's roaring admonition 'Wake up at the back there!' had everything I felt a gilt-edged catchphrase should have. It was perfectly in character and it arose naturally from Jimmy's actual wrath with a sullen audience. It was short, funny in any setting and *useful* – the kind of all-purpose joke-saving line beloved of comedians who hate to hear a subtle gag go down in silence." Jim: They laughed at Suez but he went right ahead and built his canal – wake up at the back there!' (*VIBS*).

wake up, England! is a 'c.p. used by anyone cross with himself for not seeing at once something fairly obvious. Var.: "Wake up [name], England needs you" ' (P.B., 1974).

In 1911, there appeared a timely reprint of a speech that King George V had made, in Guildhall, on 5 Dec. 1901, on his return from a tour of the Empire (*ODQ*). Both his speech and the reprint, like the warnings of Robert Blackford, Kitchener, Winston Churchill, and others, were blandly ignored by the purblind politicians of the day: behaviour ever more stupidly duplicated during the 1930s.

P.B.: In Iona and Peter Opie's *The Lore and Language of Schoolchildren*, 1959, it is recorded as one of the phrases used to greet – and deride the bearer of – stale news.

wakey, wakey! Lit., as used in C20 by Services' non-coms, it obviously isn't a c.p.; but it inevitably became one. Deriving from the nursery, it was orig. neither tender nor affectionate, despite its intentionally heavy irony when it was used by those good-humouredly bossy fellows.

Since c. 1945, it has, partly because popularized by the band-leader Billy Cotton (1900–69) in his radio and TV *Band Show*, been very widely used figuratively in civilian contexts and not necessarily by ex-Servicemen: where the persons addressed merely seem to be asleep or are extremely slow in moving along or in getting something done. An elaborated version (I must admit that *I* never heard it in the army, 1940–2, nor in the RAF, 1942–5) was

Wakey, wakey, rise and shine!

Don't you know it's morning time?

P.B.: Cotton, whose *Band Show* ran from 6 Feb. 1949 almost continuously until his death, put an enormously cheerful, strident vulgarity into the phrase, which he used to open the show (*VIBS* tells why): 'wakey-WAkey!' But it may sometimes be used more gently, e.g. to someone a bit 'dozy' and slow to grasp the obvious, 'Oh, come *on* – wakey-wakey!'

walk. See: are you going; Felix; ghost; I wouldn't w.; if you can w.; she walks; so stupid; will you w.

walk, knave, walk! was, in C16–17, a c.p. taught to parrots – presumably in order to vex all who passed by. Apperson cites, e.g., 'Proverbs' Heywood, 1546; Lyly; 'Hudibras' Butler; The Roxburgh *Ballads*, c. 1685.

walk this way, please! See **excuse my wart.**

Walker. See: Hooky; make yer name; my name's still going; and:

Walker, London seems to have been a derisive street cry, like **get yer 'air cut,** of London street arabs; after, I think, a business's signpost. J.M. Barrie used it in *Walker, London*, "a farcical comedy in three acts", published in 1921. Could be associated with *make yer name Walker*, q.v.' (Shaw, 1968).

walking-stick. See: I wouldn't stick; queer as a.

wall. See: he never had; I'd love; look on; put a cross; whiter; you couldn't throw.

wall-stretcher. See: go and fetch.

Walls have ices was, c. 1930–45, a c.p. retort to *walls have ears* (very common as a government slogan in WW2), the ref. being to the London firm of Walls, famous makers of sausages, and musically inclined vendors of ice-creams. Sometimes the c.p. ran: *walls have ears and sell ice-creams.* During the war years of 1942–5, there existed a joc. var. (still remembered, although hardly used, by a few): *walls have ears and ice cream*, which refers to a famous spy-slogan and puns on the firm's name. But all three forms were somewhat ob. by the late 1960s and virtually † by the middle 1970s.

walls of Jerry and Co. falling, the. A ref. to *jerry*built houses, etc., with a pun on the Biblical Jericho: since c. 1950. (Petch, 1974.)

waltz. See: save the last; and:

waltz with the lady! 'A cowboy's shout of encouragement to a rider on a bucking horse' (Adams): c. 1870–1910. Not merely derisive, but conveying the advice 'Roll with it!' or 'Ease yourself to the horse's movements'. Cf **ride 'em, cowboy!**

wanna buy a battleship? is a slovened version of **want to buy a battleship?**, q.v. at **do you want . . . ?**

wanna buy a duck? (– orig., **do you**) 'It was a catch phrase coined, c. 1933, by a leading radio comedian named Joe Penner. Everyone [c. 1933–5] repeated it, although I doubt if anybody ever attached meaning to the phrase. Does a catch phrase have to have precise meaning?' (Norris M. Davidson in letter, 1968). The answer to his question is NO.

The phrase recurs in a Gilbert Shelton comic strip, 1971. See also **how's the mommah?**

want. See: Kitchener; that's where you w.; this is where you w.; what do you want; when I want; you wouldn't w.; yours if.

want to bet on it? (or **do you want . . . ?** or **you want . . . ?**) – with *bet* emphasized. Are you so sure that you'll bet on it?: since c. 1945. See, e.g., Berkeley Mather, *The Terminators*, 1971: 'He was good, but not that damned good, I told him. "Does the sahib ever value his house, his cattle and his wife?" which is the Pathan way of saying, "You want to bet on it?"'

want to borrow something? A short form of **do you want to borrow something?**

want to buy a battleship? See **do you want to buy a battleship?**

want to (or **wanna**) **fight?** See **I'll hold your coat.**

want to make something of it?, sometimes slovened to **d'yer wanna make . . .**, is a threatening response to criticism or insult: since c. 1925. Implying a readiness to punch the other fellow's nose. (L.A.) A neat example occurs early in Act II of John Mortimer's witty *Collaborators*, 1973:

SAM: All right, Hank. Where were you raised?

HENRY: The rough end of Godalming. Want to make something of it?

R.C. notes, 1978, 'Also US, from at least the 1920s. The

"something" is, of course, a *casus belli*'; and Fain adds that the US version is *want to start something?* 'Recently (1977) as an advertisement for a battery manufacturer'. See **you want to start . . .**

want to shee the wheels go wound. See **turtle plates.**

want to start something? See **want to make . . .**

wanted as much as a dog (or **a toad**) **wants a side-pocket** was, mid C18–early C20, applied to one who wants (desires) something he doesn't need. Grose, 1785, *toad*, and 2nd edn, 1788, *dog* and *as much need of a wife as a dog of a side-pocket*; Arthur Quiller-Couch ('Q'), 1888, has: 'A bull's got no more use for religion than a toad for side-pockets.' Apperson.

wants (i.e. needs) **his liver scraping!** (–*he*) has, by the Army, been applied throughout C20 to a superior who's in a particularly vile temper. (B. & P.)

'Probably from the expression "hob-nailed liver" – cirrhosis of (usually) alcoholic origin, hence a metaphor for ill-temper on "the morning after"' (R.C., 1978).

wants the world with a little red fence round it. See **she wants . . .**

war. See: back to the war; clean and polish; come on in out; come to the Russian; day war; for you; it's a great war; it's winning; make love; more war; remember there's; what a lovely; what did you do; when the Duke; where's the war.

ward-room. See: midshipmen.

['ware skins, quoth Grubber, when he flung the louse into the fire lies on the border between proverbial saying and c.p.: mid C17–mid C18. Apperson.]

['ware wheat! Don't step on my corns, or Be careful not to do so: apparently a c.p. current, mostly among young men of c. 1870–1910. Jerome K. Jerome, *Three Men in a Boat*, 1889, (Chapter 10): 'Harris, moving about, trod on George's corn . . . As it was, he [George] said, "Steady, old man; 'ware wheat".' A neat pun on corn in its sense 'wheat'. Possibly, however, an idiosyncratic witticism, as Mr D.B. Gardner, to whom (1978) I owe this quot'n, has pointed out. P.B. adds: could it perhaps be an adaptation of a warning cry of careful huntsmen, cross-country runners, and the like?]

warm. See: it's a poor belly; keeping the; these sets; you're getting w.

warm in winter and cool in summer is an Aus. c.p. applied to women *qua* physical contacts: since c. 1940. (B.P.) The origin, as Norman Franklin has proposed, could reside in the Aertex slogan of the 1930s.

warn. See: you have been warned.

warrant. See: death-warrant.

wart. See: excuse my wart; you still.

[warts and all. This nugget from Oliver Cromwell's instructions to the portrait painter Lely has been used so often in the early 1980s as to become almost a c.p. What Cromwell actually wrote, as reported in Walpole's *Anecdotes of Painting*, ch. 12, was, according to the Oxford and the Penguin Dictionaries of Quotations: 'Mr Lely, I desire you would use all your skill to paint my picture truly like me, and not flatter me at all; but remark all these roughnesses, pimples, warts, and everything as you see me, otherwise I will not pay a farthing for it.' The phrase is still used much in Cromwell's sense, though perhaps without his puritanical abhorrence of 'eyewash', for 'the plain truth'. Cf **tell it like it is!** A reminder from Mrs Joan F. Beale, 1984.)]

Warwick. See: you could ride.

was my face red? See **is my face red?**

was your father a glazier (later, **glassmaker)?** See **glazier . . . ?**

wash. See: eleven o'clock; he washes; I washed; it'll come out; that won't w.

wash and brush-up tuppence was, c. 1885–1915, a humorously muttered lower-middle-class comment made by host to friend about to wash his hands in the former's house. Its orig. lies, as Sir Edward Playfair reminds me, 1977, and I should have remembered, in 'the notice in all public [men's] lavatories in pre-inflationary days'.

wash-house. See: cor! chase.

wash your neck. See: come and have one.

washee. See: no tickee.

washerwoman. See: someone forgot.

washing. See: does your mother take; showing; take in; take your w.; your washing.

washing-up. See: saves.

wasp. See: which would.

watch. See: cough it up; doesn't know; I like work; I'd watch; if you vant; in everybody's; it's your pal; just watch; keep your eye on uncle; my watch; queen as a; time you; what's the time by; work! I.

watch how you go! (Whence, at first loosely and then usu., the weaker **mind how you go!**) Look after yourself, be very careful: common in the Services since the earlyish 1930s, but not in widespread gen. use until the late 1940s.

watch it! Be careful, you're running a risk: since the 1920s. (Sanders, 1968.) Prob. short for 'I'd watch it (*or* watch out) if I were you'.

J.W.C. adds, 1977, 'Almost always, in US, = "Don't go too far with me. You're breeding a scab at the end of your nose!"' P.B.: this is frequently also its Brit. meaning – a defensive threat as much as a warning, and sometimes stated as such: 'I'm warning you: just watch it, that's all!'

watch it and weep! A var. of **read 'em and weep!** (A.B., 1979.)

watch my dust (or **smoke** or **speed**)! All three are US (Berrey records them as boasts): the first is the commonest; the third the least used, and rare since *c.* 1960; the second is also Brit. – and seems to refer to the dust raised by the hooves of a galloping horse. Both the first and the second prob. go back to late C19.

The *watch my dust* version was also Can., late C19–20, though slightly ob. by 1970. Sandilands, 1913, 'Watch me hustle, or watch the dust at my heels, as the young man boastingly said when the went West, determined to make his fortune.' Sandilands explains the Smokey var. thus: '[Red] Indians surmise what is going on inside a teepee by the smoke issuing from the top of it; and, in their wayfaring days, smoke from fires lighted on the hill-tops was their method of signalling'.

watch out for the golden rivet is a homosexual c.p. that has developed from *Go and find* (or *look for*) *the golden rivet*, 'an order given to a Merchant Navy first-voyager ... he'd be sent to more and more inaccessible places in search of this non-existent treasure' (Mr G.P.B. Naish, a noted naval historian, in a letter, 1975, written to Rear-Adm. P.W. Brock, who passed it on to me). Nobody seems to know quite when the c.p. arose.

But the phrase has other senses: and I cannot do better than to quote from Cyril Whelan's letter, 1975.

Seemingly it shows up most often as a jokey and traditional valediction (*watch out for the golden rivet*) as the ship leaves the quay-side – but has a far wider allusive application.

My own suspicion is that reference to a golden rivet is sufficiently·unexpected and bluntly esoteric to make it a powerful emblem of the user's length of service and knowledge of the ropes. ... Because of this the phrase has, I suspect, acquired the real function of stamping the user as party to all the secrets and all the inner mysteries of life on board and is used literally self-consciously for that purpose.

P.B.: in explanation given to me, 1951, by an ex-RN stoker, the 'golden rivet' was always low down, and so the innocent novice would have to bend over and down to see it. However, an altogether more innocent context occurs in Tom Ash, *Childhood Days: the Docks and Dock Slang*, [n.d.,? *c.* 1980]: according to him, 'I've found the golden rivet!' was the glad cry raised by the first man, in a gang unloading a cargo-ship in London Docks, to remove that bale, chest, etc. covering the first sight of cargo hold's

'floor' – a cry of encouragement akin to 'We're winning!' and 'Now we shan't be long'.

watch the dicky bird! In UK, Aus. and NZ. (I distinctly remember it being successfully addressed to my brothers and myself in 1901, in Gisborne, New Zealand) – since late C19–20 – a 'photographers' c.p. used when photographing children, so that they will be gazing at the camera lens with a bright, expectant look' (B.P.)

The US version is *watch the birdie!* (R.C.), but it has, according to Shipley, 1977, been replaced anyway 'first by photographers, by "Say cheese!": now used whenever one wants to get someone to smile': US: since *c.* 1950. P.B.: but *say 'cheese'!* (a word which stretches the mouth into a grin) has been Brit. for a decade longer – or more. 'c. 1950' was E.P.'s guess for US. See also **smile, please ...**

watch your indies! 'Used when a man is lifting something heavy': since *c.* 1950. 'Indies = india-rubber balls, hence *balls*, testicles' (Jack Slater, 1978).

watch your pockets, lads! See **mind your pockets!**

watch your step! is an occ. var. of **mind the step!**

watch your uncle! See **keep your eye on uncle.**

water. See: come on in; he's fallen; hold your; I've got a feeling; knocked-knees; lot of w.; malt's; miraculous; put more w.; she couldn't; someone forgot; take more w.; that cut.

water the dragon or **nag.** See **I'm going to do ...**

water under the bridge – it's (or **that's**) **all.** Dismissive of things, affairs, over and done with, and no longer worth bearing in mind; with, however, the implication 'but there's plenty more where that came from'; C20. (Mrs Daphne Beale, 1979.)

water's wet – the. A joc., mock-helpful c.p., addressed to someone entering – at bath side or beach side – the temperature of the water with his toes: late C19–20. Prob. to be included among the small stock of domestic phrases.

water-bag. See: one hundred.

watercan. See: Jupiter.

watertight. See: tight as.

waterworks. See: one o'clock.

Watson(s). See: bets like; elementary; you know my.

Wavell. See: too short.

waving. See: not waving.

wax. See: that's the whole.

way. See: I could go; it's a way; little bit of him; make way; next way; no way; only way; pit-pat's; rosaries; that's the way; there's no two; there's the right; this is the way; ve haf; what a way; what a wonderful; you've come.

way out. See: real nervous; you're way.

way to go (, **fellow**)! See **attaboy!**

we aim to please, as in ' "That's very good of you, Bill." – "We aim to please," said I modestly', dates from the 1930s at the latest. From the newspaper advertisements and the brochures of travel agencies, employment bureaus, the great stores. In that slogan used joc. as a c.p., the 'we' is humorously royal.

In evoked from J.W.C., 1977, the pleasing reminiscence: 'A *graffito* common [in US] up to, say, 30 years ago, above the urinals in a men's toilet (esp. that of a bar or a restaurant) was "We aim to please; you aim too, please!" By no means forgotten in the UK, for Simon Levene wrote, 1978, to say that he had seen – and recently – this writing on the lavatory wall.

Cf **stand closer ...**

we ain't got much money, but we do see life! – often shortened to **we do see life!** and comparable with **this is the life!**: C20. In 1931, the Rev. Desmond Morse Boycott adopted it as the title for his book about tramps. Cf **we don't get much money.**

we all have our moments, bears two senses, the better-known being 'We've all had brief periods of sexual satisfaction or brief experiences of light-hearted physical love' and dating from, at latest, 1950; the other being 'We all have our odd ways and our aberrations', dating from *c.* 1920 (if not earlier) and, *c.* 1975, becoming ob. (I owe the latter to Mr A.B. Petch, the Bournemouth antiquarian secondhand bookseller and veteran of WW1. I have been in his debt since the middle 1930s.) See also **I have had my moments.**

we are all born and we are none buried. ' "All right, you bastard, there's plenty of time to get my own back!" Used by Cockneys and others since before 1910. ... I've seldom heard it since WW2, but when I was a kid [he was born in 1900] even schoolboys used it' (Franklyn, 1968). I long wondered whether this were a proverb, but, all the appropriate dictionaries ignoring it, I've concluded that this was a true c.p. Not, I think, since *c.* 1970.

we are coming, Father Abraham, three hundred thousand more (or later, occ. **strong**) 'During our Civil War, President [Abraham] Lincoln called for more volunteers for the Union Army after heavy losses to the Confederates at Bull Run and elsewhere. James Sloan Gibbins wrote a poem entitled "Three Hundred Thousand More", which was published in the *New York Evening Post* 18 July 1862. It began "We are coming, Father Abraham, three hundred thousand more". It passed into popular speech and was a morale builder, is still current in a situation calling for announced determination to support a person or a cause. Intended as a rallying slogan, it was to a considerable degree a c.p. and has remained one' (W.J.B., 1976).

'*Pace* Mr Burke, this is surely a very rare c.p. – I have never heard it outside its specific historical context – and at least in C. 20 limited to the educated public. I would guess that at least 99% of the American public today, asked to identify "Father Abraham", would either stare or guess the Biblical Abraham' (R.C., 1978).

we are just good friends. See **we're just ...**

'We are lost', the captain shouted, /As he staggered down the stairs. A US c.p., uttered by one who has had bad luck at cards: C20; † by *c.* 1970. 'Pretty certainly from a sensational ballad' (J.W.C., 1977).

we are not alone. 'Be quiet, I think someone is listening or is, at least, close enough to overhear us.' From its lit. use in old-fashioned melodrama, it has become an allusive c.p., 'not natural speech' (J.W.C., 1977) – rather a US than a Brit. c.p.; and dating, I'd guess, since *c.* 1910. Cf **hist! We are observed.**

we are not amused. Queen Victoria's famous snub has, in C20, been on the verge – has it not rather gone over it? – of becoming a c.p., as Vernon Noble reminded me, 1974. On the occasion of a private Palace soirée, when the Hon. Alexander Grantham Yorke, groom-in-waiting to Her Majesty, did an imitation of her. In imperial Russia he would soon have found himself banished to farthest Siberia. 'Some American use from *c.* 1920; now very ob.' (R.C., 1978).

we are the Ovaltineys was orig. the title of a song that, on Radio Luxemburg (1930s), advertised Ovaltine. It became a c.p., mostly in the form of a chanting film-making fun of a noisy group: approx. 1936 – 40. (Shaw, 1968.)

we ask ourselves. See **I ask myself.**

we asked for the news, not the weather. 'Used when somebody spits as he speaks' (Levene, 1977) and current since late 1960s. Prompted by 'It's spitting with rain'. Cf **spray it again,** or *you can spray that again.*

we bombed in Newhaven! We crashed – were an utter failure: US theatrical: since *c.* 1930. 'Plays are often "tried out" in large city centers before being put into a Broadway theater. To "bomb" in Newhaven is the essence of *failure.* It has come to mean utter defeat or failure of any kind' (A.B., 1979).

[**we breathe again** and, less commonly, **we live again** are partly clichés and partly c.pp. – the latter, only when used ironically and with a playful exaggeration: predominantly Aus. and dating since *c.* 1920. (B.P., 1974.)]

we can (or **will**) **live with it.** See **we will live with it.**

we can't go on meeting like this. See **meeting like this ...**

we do get them! We *do* see some very odd people: since *c.* 1870

(mere guesswork). Cf **we're got a right 'un 'ere!**

we do see life! See:

we don't get much money, but we do see life! 'First War [WW1] catch phrase meaning much the same as the Second War's [WW2's] *never a dull moment.* It was usually uttered in the middle of any form of panic or *flap* and was mainly of wardroom usage' (*Sailors' Slang*).

But, since the early 1930s, the predominant form has been *we haven't got much money, but we do see life!*: '[At first] said of jollification with "booze", piano and singing in poorer quarters of Edwardian London; almost certainly late Victorian [in origin]' (L.A., 1975). See also **we ain't got ...**

P.B.: in *The Dump*, XXIII Division's Christmas magazine, 1915, one eavesdropping telephone linesman to another: 'Well, we don't get much money; but we do hear life'. L.A. later noted that the full form, *we ain't got* or *we haven't got* or *we may not have much money, but we do see life* goes back to *c.* 1890 or perhaps a decade earlier.

Cf **ain't we got fun.**

we don't want to lose you, but we think you ought to go comes from a WW1 popular song, which faded out, even among civilians, soon after it and which, during it, had caused much ribaldry and – often bitter – irony among those who went, many of them never to return.

we got back on a wing and a prayer, whence the phrase *on a wing and a prayer,* 'trusting in the successful outcome of an endeavour, despite the slender chances. The originator of the sentence "We got back on a wing and a prayer" is unknown, but deserves to be commemorated – some unsung RAF flyer. The c.p. ... was current in Bomber Command from 1941, but may have started in Fighter Command during the Battle of Britain [1940]. It spread [*c.* 1946] into civilian life.' (Thus ex-Squadron Leader Vernon Noble, 1977.) Perhaps I should add that, orig., the c.p. was *we got back ...,* but that it inevitably became shortened to *on a wing and a prayer,* which, after being, in the RAF, a c.p., itself became a picturesque ordinary, not a catch, phrase. Its spread into civilian life was no doubt given some impetus by a song from the American composers Jimmy McHugh and Harold Adamson pub'd in 1943 and titled 'Coming in on a wing and a prayer'.

we had dozens of these, usu. with an expletive prec. *dozens.* 'Like who got yer (or you) ready? and **does your mother know you're out?,** this is a deflating c.p.: C20' (Shaw, 1968). Cf:

we had one, and (or **but**) **the wheel came off.** See **had one ....**

we have a problem here seems to have gained ascendency over **I have** (**he** or **she has; you** or **they have**) **a problem** (**here**), which are natural mutations of the cliché *to have a problem,* to be confronted with a difficulty, a grave embarrassment, etc., whether personal or public, individual or collective, and by gaining ascendency, to have emerged from the vagueness and pedestrianism of cliché into the more luminous and particular world of the c.p. *We have a problem here* became, I'd surmise, a c.p. during the years 1970–1.

[**we have met the enemy – and they** (or **he**) **– is us.** Col. Moe writes, 1975:

Originally 'he' was used in lieu of 'they' and [it] appeared in a comic strip. In popular usage, I have heard only 'they'. Meaning: A person's or group's own faults [or failings] are responsible for lack of success ... one's own worst enemy is oneself when one refuses to ... make any attempt to cope with [one's own shortcomings].

Walt Kelly's comic strip 'Pogo' began to appear nationally in May 1949; and in 1972 Kelly (1913–73) pub'd *Pogo: We Have Met the Enemy and He is Us.* Pogo, by the way, is a possum, but a possum who constitutes a powerful 'satire on the unnatural behaviour of human beings, who live like marionettes – slaves to the repressions of their society': he had earlier satirized the Communist-hunting Senator Joseph McCarthy as 'Simple J. Malarkey'. (With further thanks to Col. Moe.) But perhaps not a c.p., after all: Dr Joseph T. Shipley thinks not.

W.J.B., 1975, thinks it 'a corruption of "we have met the enemy and they are ours" [at our mercy], uttered by US naval hero Oliver Hazard Perry at the Battle of Lake Erie, Sep. 10, 1813.'

In *The New York Times*, 6 Nov. 1977, William Safire, in his lament 'Gasp! Sob! L'il Abner is no more' writes: '...the only quotation from the comics [i.e., the comic strips] that is intellectually fashionable any more is "We have met the enemy and he is us" from Walt Kelly's "Pogo" still quoted by people who never read "Pogo".' (Thanks to Dr Joseph T. Shipley.)]

we have ways and means to make you talk. See **ve haf vays** ....

we haven't got much money, but we do see life! See **we don't get much money** ....

we live again. See **we breathe again.**

we lucky! 'Drawn from the punchline of a quotation I first hard in the U.S. in mid-60's; at that time about a Japanese used-car dealer, but applicable in many businesses: "We buy your car for best price. We sell you new car for low price. How we stay in business? WE LUCKY!" Now used in business, self-deprecatingly usually, either the last two or just the final phrase' (Hugh Quetton, 1978).

we make 'em ourselves. Farmer says:

A street catch-phrase, which quickly spread throughout the Union, and was quickly supplanted by other slang expressions. [It] implies readiness to follow another's lead; or capacity to perform what others have done [usually the latter nuance.]

Dates from the middle 1880s.

we must press on regardless is the c.p. crystallization of *to press on regardless* and it means 'We have urgent work to do – and must get it done as soon as possible' despite all the difficulties and dangers; RAF: 1941 onwards (by *c.* 1946, also civilian). Communicated by Sqn. Ldr. Vernon Noble to AC2 E.H. Partridge in Feb. 1945, P.B.: occ., pedantically and joc., *let us press on* ... See also **press on** ...

we sha'n't take salt! Our box-office returns will be very small: theatrical: late C19–20; † by 1960. Ware glosses it as, 'We shall not take enough money to pay for salt, let alone bread'.

we speak the same language. We think and feel alike; we're 'on the same wave-length'; we're in complete accord. Educated and cultured, it became a full c.p. only *c.* 1965, although I've known it since the latish 1950s. Unfortunately I've never thought to record it, yet it has become so widely used, so incorporated into the language, that we can freely say, for instance, 'They speak the same language'. P.B.: E.P. wrote this note in 1977, and so I include it; but I think that both the key-phrase, and the 'wavelength' version, are idiomatic rather than c.pp.

we want eight and we can't wait. This is an ephemeral c.p. of 1909 when eight dreadnoughts were demanded for the Royal Navy.

We want make-and-mends, not recommends. A C20 RN lower-deck c.p. *A make and mend* is a naval half-holiday, originally for attention to one's clothing; a *recommend* is a recommendation (for promotion) red-inked on to a sailor's Service Certificate.

we was (or **wuz**) **robbed** (or, in Aus., occ. **rooked**). A joc. c.p. used when one has been either tricked or merely outsmarted: since the late 1940s. From the indignant and usually bogus claim of illiterate boxers when the referee has declared them defeated.

It is 'still very common in US; usually associated—and, I think, [it] began—with the loyal and contentious "fans" of the old [base]ball team the Brooklyn Dodgers. Older than 1940 by 10 or 20 years. Borrowed by the Australians [and by the British: P.B.], I suspect' (J.W.C., 1977).

Cf the quot'n at **I should of stood in bed.**

We went to two different schools together. is the 'dovetail' response to 'How did you two meet?': US: since *c.* 1920. A.B., 1979, relates its illogic to that in *what's the difference between a chicken?*

we will (or **we'll** – rather more often, perhaps, **we can**) **live with it.** A 'usually humorous acceptance of minor nuisance or disruption of plan. "They're asking if they can send those blokes to-morrow, instead of Friday" – "Oh, well, tell 'em yes; we'll live with it"' (P.B., 1974). Perhaps mainly Services': since *c.* 1960, if not 10 or 15 years earlier.

we won't eat you! We're not dangerous – we sha'n't harm you: C18–20, but very little used since *c.* 1960. S, 1738, Dialogue II, has:

SIR JOHN: What, you keep Court Hours I see. I'll be going ...

LADY SM[ART]: Why, we won't eat you, Sir *John*.

we'll be looking at each other and one of us won't know it. Berrey, 1942, has it as a c.p. that exemplifies 'prediction of death': US: *c.* 1916–42.

we'll cut them off at the pass. US c.p.: C20, and still current, according to Ashley, who says, 1983, 'perperated on the screen' – that is, in 'Western movies'. Its use out of context is of course joc. Cf *white man speak* ... I have also heard *we'll head them off* ... (P.B.)

we'll let you know. A synon. of **we'll write to you.**

we'll soon lick you into shape: we're lion tamers here. A sergeant-majors' and drill sergeants' pleasantry addressed to recruits undergoing their initial training, esp. in England: 1914–18. (Collinson.) Very seldom if ever (except with a nostalgic jocosity) used during 1939–45. See also **they tame lions** ...

we'll write to you! – lit., 'the stock promise to an *un*-promising applicant for an audition' – 'has become a theatrical catch-phrase, and is often directed at anyone singing out of tune in the dressing-room' (Granville). Cf **don't call us, we'll call you.**

we're all going to Brighton! Chanted, in a joggety rhythm, was a mainly Services' raffish c.p., mid-C20. It derived from a rude story about a girl caught 'in flagrante delecto' on a young man's lap in a railway carriage (and in the old days of jointed rails): this was her explanatory 'ad lib' – 'and, if you'll believe *that*, you'll believe anything ...' (P.B.)

we're all together, like Brown's cows. See **all together** ...

we're in! See **Meredith** ...

we're in business. According to P.B., 1975:

Not necessarily commercially. A fairly common c.p., indicating that the first stage of any enterprise has been successfully accomplished; e.g., even looking up something in a dictionary that provides a lead to something else. General. I first heard it consciously about three years ago.

I myself first heard it *c.* 1960, and it may easily go back as far as 1950; W.J.B., 1977, notes *now we're in business* as US, 'later half of C20'.

we're in, Meredith! See **Meredith, we're in!**

we're just good friends. Attributed, by newspapermen, to notorieties, usu. filmstars, disclaiming that there's anything in a close association with a member of the opposite sex, esp. during a 'lull' between marriages. 'Since the 1930s. Hardly used seriously now, and used in mockery to enquiring friends with a "No comment – mind your own business" intent, usually by ordinary folk' (Shaw, 1969); or, as Petch has put it, 1974, 'Heard when a couple often seen about together are asked if there is anything in it.' Common throughout the British Commonwealth; for instance, B.P., 1975, 'A c.p. that is used to kill rumours of romance.'

'In American use from 1930 or earlier – often a way of implying that the individuals in question were rather more than friendly. Now almost always with that implication – a way of "kissing"-and-not (-quite)-telling. But certainly now ob.' (R.C., 1978).

we're not going anywhere is elliptical for 'what's the hurry? We're not ...': a domestic c.p. current since *c.* 1955. (Petch, 1974.) Cf **where's the fire?**

we're winning. Things are going well for us – or me: from 1942, the ref. being to progress in the war, then quite gen. Also 'an evasive stock answer to "How're we getting on?" or "How goes it?"' (L.A.). Cf **are you winning?**

we're winning the war. See **clean and polish** ...

we've got a right one (or **'un) 'ere!** (occ. prec. by aye, aye). 'Usually A to B (official) about C' (Shaw, 1968): mainly Liverpool: since *c*. 1940. On the other hand, Noble writes, 1975: 'Bruce Forsyth in BBC TV "The Generation Game" in which the public (related, e.g., father and daughter) participated in contests, 1970s.' There's probably no contradiction: the c.p. may have been a recurrent, for another reliable source, Cyril Whelan, 1975, states that this was an aside consistently and constantly used by the late Tony Hancock, who preceded Bruce Forsyth. Ironic. Implication: a fool or a very odd person indeed. P.B.: Nigel Rees, in *VIBS*, takes the radio/TV use back further, to the 1940s, with Dick Emergy as Mr Monty in *Educating Archie*, which starred the ventriloquist Peter Brough and his schoolboy doll, 'Archie Andrews'. A curious notion, to have a radio comedy series like that, when surely the essence of ventriloquism is that the doll should be *seen* to speak.

weak eyes, big tits summarizes a popular example of fallacious folklore: Aus.: since *c*. 1920. (B.P., who comments: 'Often worded in other ways'.) Cf **big conk** ...

weaken. See: it's a great life.

wealth. See: Madras.

wear. See: don't wear; I haven't a thing; I wouldn't wear; she thinks; what the well-dressed; your mother; and:

wear it in health is, when used by Jews, a conventionalism, a cliché, certainly not a c.p., which it becomes only when used jocosely by Gentiles in making a present of an article of clothing or a piece of jewellery: since *c*. 1950. (J.W.C., 1968.)

'Mostly *wear it in good health!*: enjoy whatever you get – this includes gifts and such things as weather, opportunities, and experiences. It truly is a "catch-all" expression. I cannot date it, but surely current since [at least, late] C19' (A.B., 1979). B.G.T., 1978, wrote thus enlighteningly: 'When my mother, aged 16 (WW1), showed off her new shoes to a friend's Scottish mother, the comment was, "Well, I wish ye health to wear them, dearie!" Perhaps an old courtesy?'

wear it in a dog-flight. See **I wouldn't wear it** ...

wears a head. See: as wears.

weasel. See: pop.

weasel in the diesel. See **tiger in the tank.**

weather. See: cold enough; deal of w.; fine day; how's the w.; nice weather; this is the w.; we asked.

weaving leather aprons was, *c*. 1840–1940, an evasive reply given to someone enquiring what one has been doing lately or what one does for a living. (Hotten, 1864.)

There are many variants; among them are: *I'm a doll's-eye weaver* (Hotten, 1874), with which cf the old man's occupation, 'I hunt for haddocks' eyes ... And work them into waistcoat buttons' ('The White Knight's Song', in Lewis Carroll, *Alice Through the Looking Glass*, 1872); *making a trundle for a goose's eye*, or ... *a whim-wham to bridle a goose* (Hotten, 1864) – the latter also occurs as ... *a whim-wham for a goose's bridle*. The insistence on *goose* may fairly be assumed to imply that the enquirer *is* a goose (a silly person) to be asking such a question. In 'A List of Words Illustrating the Nottinghamshire Dialect', by E.A. Guilford, in *Trans. of the Thoroton Soc. of Notts*, LII, 1948, is noted *a whim-wham for a treacle mill*, and L.A., 1976, mentions *a whim-wham for ducks to perch on* (ducks can't perch). But see esp. John B. Smith's comprehensive article on 'Put-offs and related forms', which contains these and many more, in *Lore & Language* (Sheffield), vol. 3, no. 3, Part A, July 1980, and **lareovers for meddlers**, above.

John Skelton, in *Elynour Rumming*, *c*. 1500, lines 75–76, has 'with a whim-wham/Knyt with a trym-tram'.

wedding. See: it's a monkey's; like a spare; you have been to.

wedding dues are concerned. They're about to get married, *and*

It's time they got married: *c*. 1750–1840. For the form of the phrase, cf **Alderman Lushington** ...

weed. See: tall weed.

week. See: dear Mother, I; I'd rather keep; if I don't see; never be rude; showing next; this is rat; this week's; three weeks; what to you think this is; what is this?; wind enough.

weekend. See: looks like a wet.

weep. See: enough to make you; read 'em.

weight. See: have you got; let him alone; what's yer fighting.

weird. See: it's weird.

welcome. See: hello, good; and:

welcome aboard. In the US, this phrase is 'widely used as a greeting to a newcomer to an institution – or, for that matter, to a poker game. I found myself using it the other day in greeting a new English Department stenographer' (J.W.C., 1968): since *c*. 1946. As it chances, I have no printed record earlier than 'He put Hubbard's material in the envelope, hesitated, then scrawled across the front of it, "Welcome aboard!!!!! Fred Frick"' (John D. MacDonald, *A Key to the Suite*, 1962). Perhaps less prob. from the formal naval greeting than from the formal commercial-aircraft greeting, so rapidly popularized during the tremendous upsurge in civilian flying which took place very soon after WW2 ended in Aug. 1945. Col. Moe, however, assumes it to have been naval in origin, a point which J.W.C., 1977, confirms: 'I quite agree with Colonel Moe; and I think the expression is decades older than WW2 – in its literal naval sense, yes; yet not, I believe, older than the 1920s as a c.p. P.B.: some use also in Brit.: I have had it said to me both in the Army, and later, on taking my first civilian job, 1975.

welcome to the club! 'I (we) share the sentiments you have just expressed. In, e.g., W. Wager, *Viper Three*, 1971, "Maybe I'm scared ... a little." "Welcome to the club, Willie!" American, since *c*. 1978' (R.C., 1978). A var. of **join the club.**

welcome to the N.F.L. 'is a phrase used to point to unexpectedly rough treatment', esp. in games: a US sporting c.p.: since *c*. 1975. (William Safire, in the *New York Times Magazine*, 23 July 1978.) N.F.L. = National Football League.

well. See: didn't he do; he's not so; tap run; they came.

well, back to the (old) drawing board! See **back to the drawing board!**

well, ah'll go to Pudsey! See **well, I'll go** ...

well-dressed. She: what the well.

well? End it! (second word emphasized). A deflation of a poor storyteller, exhorted to finish his story when, in fact, he has already done so: since *c*. 1930. (Shaw, 1968).

well, for evermore! Yet another *ITMA* c.p., this one from 'Sam Scram' (played by Sidney Keith), Tommy Handley's Chicago-gangster bodyguard. See TOMMY HANDLEY.

well, I ask you! See **I ask you!**

well, I declare!; occ. var., **well, I'll declare!** A US c.p. of astonishment or shock: apparently since *c*. 1830; since *c*. 1920, very old-fashioned; by 1950, †. The *OED* records it as occurring in Longfellow's *Kavanagh, A Tale*, 1849, thus: 'Well, I declare! If it is not Mr Kavanagh!' A more enlightening example comes in George Ade's *Doc Horne*, 1899:

Suddenly Doc' straightened up in his chair and looked most intently at a passing man who carried a walking-stick and seemed to be in a hurry.

'Well, I'll declare!' he exclaimed.

'What's the matter, Doc'?' asked the lush.

Doc' continued to gaze at the pedestrian until he turned the corner.

'That's most extraordinary,' he said; 'I could have sworn that was Bridgeman.'

'Often *well, ah decleah* as a parody of the alleged speech of US Southern womanhood. Not, I think, utterly extinct, though certainly an ironic, self-conscious archaism' (R.C., 1978). P.B.: it also appears – at least in a few British books about the USA – as *well, I do declare!*, and my belief that this might be an accepted var. was confirmed by Prof. Ashley: 'It ought to be *well, I do declare* (very Southern US)'.

well, I like that! – often without *well*. An ironical c.p., meaning the exact opposite, often with the nuance, 'What cheek, you suggesting *that!*': late C19–20. (Granville, 1969.) In short, a derisive, or an indignant, 'Certainly not!'

It may have come to UK from US: See John Kendrick Bangs, *Toppleton's Client or A Spirit in Exile*, 1893:

'Don't look at me that way, I beg of you, Mr Toppleton,' said the spirit ... 'I don't deserve all that your glance implies, and if you could only understand me, I think you would sympathize with me in my trials.'

'I? I sympathize with you? Well, I like that,' cried Mr Toppleton.

In a synonym of equivalents to 'the insolence of it!', Berrey lists (*well*) *I like that!*

Semantically, cf **not half!**

well, I never! See **you don't say!**, and:

[**well, I never, did you ever see a monkey dressed in leather?** 'One very frequent catch-phrases in my early boyhood' was this, Christopher Fry tells me in 1976 – and *he* was born in 1907. I had known it since 1921, but only in the shortened form, **well, I never, did you ever?** I don't recall having heard it since 1950, although I think that the shorter version persisted until well into the 1960s.

P.B.: I remember this as a chanted couplet, and used it myself as a child in the late 1930s–early 1940s. In Iona and Peter Opie, *The Lore and Language of Schoolchildren*, 1959, the chapter on 'Wit and Repartee' and the Section 'Stale Jokes and Stale News' is: 'Should the slow one also think her news to be marvellous, saying, for instance, "Did you ever? Betty's come to school in trousers, did you ever?" [the other children] chaff:

Well I never! Did you ever.
See a monkey dressed in leather.
Leather eyes, leather nose,
Leather breeches to his toes.'

This version was recorded from Hayes, Mddx. Several other similar chants are also given. Does a children's jingle count as a catch phrase? I think not.]

well, I should smile! is an extended form of **I should smile!**

well, I suppose it's winning (or **helping to win**) **the war.** See **clean and polish.**

well, I'll be a monkey's uncle! See **I'll be a monkey's uncle!**

well, I'll be switched! 'Somewhat akin to "Well, I'll be damned – or hanged – if I do that!" An expression of either surprise or regret' (A.B., 1979). Mostly US: *c.* 1850–1960. Here *switched* prob. means 'caned; receive a beating'.

[**well, I'll go to Hanover!** or **to Jericho!** or **to Putney on a pig!** 'All [country] exclamations of amazement. Only this week, however, I've read of a Londoner's version: "Well, I'll go to Putney to see the boat race!"' (B.G.T., 1978.) Rural England is meant, and the period is C20. The boat race is the annual Cambridge *v.* Oxford event, and the London version may have been prompted by the fact that it commonly takes place in mid or latish March.

All three are based upon the exclam. 'Well, I'll go to hell!' Strictly, these expressions are borderline cases, as also, perhaps, is *well, ah'll go to Pudsey*, which has the strictly North country variants still commonly heard: ... *to our 'ouse* and ... *to the foot of our stairs* (P.B.; David Short). E.P. suggests that the speaker's agitation might be relieved by walking that far. See also **I'll go hopping to hell!**]

well, if ever! was, *c.* 1810–60, a US c.p. of either astonishment or admiration. John Neal, *Brother Jonathan: or, The New Englander*, 3 vols, 1825, at chapter I, p. 150, has ' "My stars!" cried Miriam, when she saw him in it [a calico waistcoat]. first: "My stars! – well, if ever!" – wiping her fat hands very carefully.'

Perhaps it is elliptical for 'Well, if ever I saw *or* heard such a thing!'

More usual is **if ever!**, as in *ibid.*, chapter II, p. 161: ' "... Ruth Ashley – my own child; why Ruth, if ever! – what's the matter now, maiden – give the lad thy hand." ' Neal uses it again in *The Down-Easters*, 2 vols, 1833 (at chapter I, p. 24).

well, if that don't pass! – with *well* only occ. omitted. That's amazing!: US: *c.* 1820 (? earlier) – 1890. It occurs in, e.g., T.C. Haliburton's three-volume work *The Clockmaker*, 1837–40; and also in his *The Attaché*, 1843, Series I, vol. 2, pp. 136–7, thus:

'Not hear of *Bunkum!* why how you talk!'
'No, never.'
'Well, if that don't pass! I thought everybody know'd that word.'

Elliptical for 'Well, if that don't (or doesn't) pass understanding (*or* the imagination)!'

well, if you knows of a better 'ole, go to it! See **if you knows ...**

well, it seemed like a good idea at the time orig. as a cliché: US; then, fairly soon, Brit. By being employed, humorously and ruefully, as a cliché, it has become, in the US at least, also a c.p., dating since the 1950s. J.W.C., 1975, adds that it is applied to 'one's own impulsive or, rather impetuous actions, now recognized as foolish – as, one confesses, they should have been at the moment of action'.

well, lump it! See **do the other!**

[**well, now, there's a thing!** 'An expression of mild surprise. General' (P.B., 1976) lies between c.p. and cliché – and nearer the latter, I'd say.]

well, that's that! See **and that's that!**

well, this is it. In 1974, P.B. wrote to me:
Suddenly, within the last few months, this seems to be everybody's stock response to a statement with which they agree, where before they might merely have said 'Yes', 'Yes, isn't it?' or 'Too true', e.g. 'It seems to me there are too many layabouts sponging off the social services.' – 'Well, this is it! I mean, you know, honestly, let's face it ... etc. (ad nauseam).'

'Originally, I think, U.S., from war and/or gangster films, spoken as the combatants go into action' (R.C., 1978); I remember hearing it in 1943, in ref. to a violent bombing attack on London. P.B. – the perpetrator of the orig. entry – adds: this is of course true of earlier usage, but there is a considerable difference between the intonation used in war, etc., when *this is it, men* (*lads, chaps,* and so on) is uttered grimly, with teeth clenched, and the 1970s usage, which tends to be much more a whining, resigned, fatalistic acceptance – all defiance gone. 'Let's do something about it' has given way to ' "They" ought to do something about it'.

[**'well, well,' quoth she, 'many wells, many buckets'.** Half-proverb, half-c.p., of C16; recorded by Heywood, 1546. Cf the C20 'catch': ' "Have you heard the story of three wells?" – "No; what is it?" – "Well, well, well!" '

'The childish mocking taunt used in the North [of England] when anyone was foolish enough to say *well, well* was: *two wells make a river*' (David Short, 1978).]

well, what do you know! expresses an incredulous or mildly ironic surprise: since *c.* 1920. (*NZS.*) Cf the Armed Forces' var., 1939–45: *well, Joe, what do you know?*, derisively addressed to anyone named Joe; but the orig. form had become common in UK by 1930 at latest and it occurred in, e.g., the film titled *Dunkirk*, 1958. As *well, what do you know*, it seems to have reached the US *c.* 1930, and Berrey, 1942, records the basic *what do you know?* which arose in *c.* 1910, S.R. Strait using it *c.* 1917 in 'Straight Talk' in the *Boston Globe*. In Ellery Queen's *The Blue Movie Murders*, 1973, we read: 'The eyes were at their widest when he opened the door of his flat and saw Hyde. "Well, what do you know?" '

More notably, Edward Albee uses it in Act II of *Who's Afraid of Virginia Woolf?*, 1962.

See also **what do you know.**

well, yer do, don't yer? A 'gag' in terse c.p. form, uttered by comedian Jack Storey. An earthy, not unkindly, 'putting-down'.

well, you *said* you could do it! was, in 1914–18, an army officers' c.p. reply to, or comment on, a complaint: and it has, in much wider circles, endured, as Julian Franklyn testified in 1969.

Welshman. See: short and thick.

went. See: let her went.

went down (or over) like a lead balloon (–it). It was a 'flop' – a *rank* failure, as applied to a joke, a play, a film, a plan, an act or action either hoped or expected to succeed. US: *c.* 1950–8; it gave way to 'It was a lead balloon'. As you will have guessed, a lead balloon wouldn't even get off the ground. Attested by W & F and by *DCCU*, 1971. P.B.: some borrowing of this colourful phrase in UK.

R.C., 1978, notes of the *over* form, 'still some currency [in the] 1970s, though now ob.', while A.B., 1979, adds, 'Also, *it went over like a pregnant elephant*. The reference here is to pole-vaulting ... Kin to *that was about as successful* (or *useful*) *as an open umbrella in an elavator*: from the 1950s, I think'.

went for a crap (or a shit) and the sniper got him, and **went (or gone) for a ride (or just shot through) on the padre's bike,** and **went mad and (or so) they shot him**; all are usu. prec. by **he**; the third is the commonest. All three, characteristically Aus. [but the third has certainly been 'borrowed' by the British: P.B.], supply joc. answers to a request for somebody's whereabouts, and date from *c.* 1940. (*Dict. Aus. Coll.*) Cf **hanging on the** (usu. **old**) **barbed wire** and the **gone for ...** entries for the merely apparent callousness. For orig., the first and second clearly arose during WW2; also prob. the third, although it may refer to the shooting of a rabid dog.

P.B.: was the first an echo of Kipling's WW1 *Epitaph for The Refined Man*:

I was of delicate mind. I went aside for my needs,
Disdaining the common office. I was seen from afar and
    killed ...
How is this matter for mirth? Let each man be judged by
    his deeds.
I have paid my price to live with myself on the terms that I willed.

went thataway (–**he** or **they**; the form **gone thataway** is rare). Lit., 'He (or they) went in that direction' – accompanied by an outstretched arm pointing, and usu. in ref. to departed thieves or robbers, it has acquired an allusive sense: either 'a Western novel' – employed by those elderly people to whom the novel meant more than motion pictures; or 'a Western film' – used by those to whom motion pictures, esp. 'Westerns', mean everything; or either, determined by the context; or both. It is a joc. literary, a cinematic, classification (cf **unhand me, villain**, used as the archetypal c.p. of a different genre). Only in this sense is it a c.p. For both novels and films it dates since the 1930s. (Based upon enquiries made, 1977, in the US by Col. Moe; and, for the UK, upon my own knowledge, *plus* a pertinent probe or two.)

went to night school and he (or she) can't spell in the daytime (–**he** or **she**). A C20 c.p. directed at a bad speller. (B.P.)

were you born in a barn? Addressed to one who leaves a door open, esp. when it's cold and windy outside: mid C19–20 – and, I suspect, fifty, or more years earlier. Of the same order of enquiry as *is your father a glazier?*, q.v. at **glazier**; in short, semi-proverbial. 'Even more typical of country humour is the version "you must ha' bin born in a field with the gate open!"' (B.G.T., 1978). The Aus. var. is *were you born in a tent?* (B.P., 1975); in US, *were you raised in a barn?* (Fain, 1977). P.B.: J.B. Smith suggests that *do you come from Yapton?*, and other local sayings recorded by Jacqueline Simpson in *The Folklore of Sussex*, 1973, appear to be equivalents of ... *barn*. Yapton is in that windswept, flat countryside between Downs and sea, east and south of Chichester. And Gerald Bramley, FLA, tells me that the same idea is conveyed in the Nottinghamshire coalfields by

the phrase *d'you come from Warsop* (pron. *Waas'p*)? This refers back to a particularly miserable miners' strike (long before 1984) during which impoverishment became so bad that strikers' families had to burn even their own house-doors for fuel.

west. See: go West.

Westminster Gazette. See: you are Mr.

wet. See: don't bother me; get your feet; if wet; looks like a wet; one of these wet; water's; you never get; you're all wet.

wet arse and no fish – a. A fruitless quest or a sleeveless errand: late C19–20. Clearly orig. either among trawlermen or among anglers.

P.B.: cf this entry from *DSUE*: 'Saltash luck. "A wet seat and no fish caught": RN: late C19–20. (Bowen.) Ex *Saltash*, a small town 4 miles NW of Devonport'.

wet grass. See: corvette.

wha' hap'? See **what's happening?**

whaddayasay? (what do you say?). 'A US proletarian c.p. of greeting. From *c.* 1940 or earlier – originally, I think, New York City' (R.C., 1978). 'What do you say?' = 'what do you say to that – Don't you agree?!'

whaddya want: eggs ... See **what do you want: eggs in your beer?**

whale? See: very like.

wham, bang, thank you, madam! Since the early to middle 1940s, orig. an Armed Forces' c.p.; applied to the rapidity of a male rabbit's breeding activities.

An adaptation of the US *wham, bam, thank you, maam!* – applied to hurried, almost mechanical, copulation with a strange woman: dated by W&F as 'since before *c.* 1895'. By itself, *wham-bam* means 'quickly and roughly' – brawnily, not brainily.

In Sidney Sheldon's *The Other Side of Midnight*, 1973 (UK, 1974), I've found this illuminating passage: 'Like most Frenchmen, Armand Gautier prided himself on being a skilled lover. He was amused by the stories he had heard of Germans and Americans whose idea of making love consisted of jumping on top of a girl, having an instant orgasm, and then putting on their hat and departing. The Americans even had a phrase for it. "Wham, bam, thank you ma'am".'

Cf the negro **bip bam, thank you, ma'am!**

what a beanfeast! '(*People's.*) Satirical exclamation in reference to a riot, [a] quarrel or [a] wretched meal: or other entertainment' (Ware): *c.* 1880–1914.

what. See: do you know w.; I'll tell you w.; it's not w.; just what; little of w.; now then, what's; say what; says what; tell 'em w.; who does; yes, but w.; you know w.; you what?; and:

what! a bishop's wife? eat and drink in your gloves! A semi-proverbial c.p. of mid C17–mid C18. (Ray, 1678.) Apperson glosses it thus: 'This is a cryptic saying'. But prob. it means 'You're quite the fine lady (now)!'

[**what a busher he is!** See **that's strictly bush.**]

what a drag! See **drag–it's a.**

what a common boy! An *ITMA* c.p.: see TOMMY HANDLEY.

what a drip! 'What an uncouth person!'; sometimes, 'what a bore [he is!]' Maybe 10 years old or so, in US. (Fair, 1978.) P.B.: but this was in English schoolchildren's usage in the 1940s–and perhaps earlier. Cf the RN slang or *drip*=to complain.

what a dump! and **what a morgue!** What a dead-and-alive, or what a dull, place! The former arose *c.* 1919, the latter *c.* 1945, to die out by the early 1970s.

what a funny little place to have one! Dating since *c.* 1890 and slightly ob. by *c.* 1970. In ref. to a mole; addressed to a woman; suggesting contiguity to *le petit coin*.

what a game it is! (often shortened to **what a game!**) A humorously, if wryly, resigned c.p., directed at life's little ironies and not quite so little vicissitudes: C20. Cf **it's a game!**

what a gay day! A c.p. used by the TV comedian Larry Grayson, 1970s. It can, of course, also be used with heavy irony, as, for instance, by our college commissionaire about a day of particularly vile weather during the caretakers' strike.

Local Leicestershire teenagers – and perhaps youngsters more widely – have added a dovetail response, 'but not *that* gay!', uttered with a lisp and a limp-wrist flip, i.e., the later meaning of *gay*. (P.B., 1979.)

what a *ghastly* name! 'Jimmy Edwards in *Take It From Here* [q.v.] Frank Muir comments: "A useful (albeit meaningless) line which could always be given to Jimmy when somebody else mentioned a name. In fact I suppose it was quite a funny, deflating way to react"' (*VIBS*).

what a hope you've got! (often shortened to **what a hope!**); also *you've got a hope* (*, you* have)! and **what hopes!** This, in all its varieties, affords an excellent example of how very difficult it is to date such c.pp. as these. I can but hazard a guess that they go back to *c*. 1870 – and that, orig. at least, they were Cockney. The first and the last seem to have been the most popular: cf John Brophy in B & P, 1930:

WHAT HOPES! – A retort expressing utter disbelief in some promise or prophecy of a future good (or not so bad as at present) time. A variation, addressed to a man confident of securing an advantage for himself, was *What a hope you've got!*

what a life! When used as a gen. animadversion on life as a whole, it is clearly not a c.p. but a cliché; when, however, it is applied to some trivial mishap or accident, esp. if in humorous disgust, it is no less clearly a c.p.: and it may go back to mid C19 or even fifty or, for that matter, a hundred years earlier.

In late C19–20, it has had the extension, *without a wife*, to which, in C20, the cynical add either *and even worse with one* or, more colloquially, *and a damned sight worse with one!* More common, however, is **such is life with a wife!** – q.v. Also US: Berrey synonymizes it with boredom.

what a load of rubbish! 'A modern c.p. chanted by spectators at football matches to show their disapproval of the players' performance; and thence, into all sorts of situations in "real life"' (P.B., 1975).

'In the US, it is more frequently heard as *what a load*, or *pile*, of *horseshit!* Sometimes *manure* is employed when the speaker wishes to be less offensive' (A.B., 1979).

P.B.: therefore cf **that's for the birds!** And I gather that the 'polite' US version may not always be understood: Dr Dwight F. Decker, of Providence, RI, tells me that he had some difficulty with the word interpreted as 'man you're' by New York City schoolchildren.

what a long tail our cat's got! See what a tail ...!

what a lovely war! has been an army, hence – in due course – a civilian, c.p. ever since 1915. The army's irony was directed at conditions in general; its sarcasm, at profiteers and 'cushy'-jobbers and baseline troops. In the early 1960s, this was extended to the title of a revue dealing with WW1.

It was 'adapted in the U.S. by Harry Belafonte and his singers ... and it first appeared in his album entitled *Cheers!* It was a show-stopper at Belafonte's performance at the Palace Theater. This American version was apparently written for Belafonte by Oscar Brand and Rosemary Primont. I heard it at Carnegie Hall in May 1960' (A.B., 1979).

what a morgue! See what a dump!

what a nerve! See of all the nerve!

what a performance! 'Sid Field, the comedian (died 1950)' (*VIBS*). P.B.: it was Field's intonation of the c.p., as much as its wording, that made it memorable to his listeners and imitators, late 1930s – earlier 1940s.

what a shocking bad hat! Mackay (1841), after noting that this succeeded *quoz!* as the phrase in vogue, remarked that

No sooner had it become universal, than thousands of idle but sharp eyes were on the watch for the passenger [i.e., passer-by] whose hat showed any signs, however slight, of ancient service. Immediately the cry arose, and, like the war-whoop of the Indians, was repeated by a hundred discordant throats. He was a wise man who, finding himself ... 'the observed of all observers', bore his honours meekly. .... The obnoxious hat was often snatched from his head and thrown into the gutter ... and then raised, covered with mud, upon the end of a stick, for the admiration of the spectators, who held their sides with laughter, and exclaimed in the pauses of their mirth, '*Oh, what a shocking bad hat!*' '*What a shocking bad hat!*' ....

The origin of this singular saying, which made fun for the metropolis for months, is not involved in the same obscurity as ... *Quoz* and some others. There had been a hotly contested election for the borough of Southwark, and one of the candidates was an eminent hatter .... Whenever he called upon or met a voter whose hat was not of the best material, or being so, had seen its best days, he immediately said, '*What a shocking bad hat you have got: call at my warehouse, and you shall have a new one!*' Upon the day of election this circumstance was remembered, and his opponents made the most of it, by inciting the crowd to keep up an incessant cry of '*What a shocking bad hat!*' all the time the honourable candidate was addressing them. From Southwark the phrase spread all over London, and reigned for a time the supreme slang of the season.

The phrase, which seems to have arisen *c*. 1838 or 1839, soon became transferred to persons with a bad reputation or the most shocking manners. It was so used by John Surtees in a novel pub'd in 1851–2 (see the quot'n at **I don't think**); and then, in 1892, in *Vice-Versa* Anstey wrote, 'Regular bounder! Shocking bad hat!'

It survived well into C20; by 1930, it was outmoded and by 1950, virtually † except among people seventy or more years old.

Cf **where did you get that hat?**

what a shower! and it's showery! The latter derived from the former and was an RAF saying, current during the approx. period mid 1930s to late 1940s.

But *what a shower!* arose, *c*. 1919, in the army, as an insult hurled at the members of another unit; later – in the RAF too – it would be directed at, e.g., an intake of recruits. In 1942, Gerald Kersh, in *Bill Nelson*, wrote, 'Some of the lousiest showers of rooks you ever saw': clearly *what a shower* was already being applied individually as well as collectively; for instance, it could be addressed to one who had made a bad mistake. It has survived among civilians, and indeed I heard it used so late as 26 Feb. 1975.

The shower is popularly – and prob. correctly – explained as elliptical for a *shower of shit*.

what a tail (often **what a long tail**) **our cat's got!** A mid C19–20 proletarian c.p. at a female 'flaunting in a new dress', the rear skirt of which she swings haughtily or provocatively. (Ware: the shorter, the orig., form.)

Later it could be used of either sex and be addressed to – or at – a person boasting vaingloriously: usu. in the longer form. Leechman vouches for its Can. usage.

But Simon Levene writes, 1979, to correct my dating: he cites Henry Carey, *The Dragon of Wantley*, 1738, at Act II, line 43: 'Lauk! What a monstrous tail our cat has got!', and then comments, 'I don't suppose that that was the exact wording people used, because it is an iambic pentameter, and rhymes with "Nay, if you brave me, then you go to pot"'.

what a to-do! See ee, what...

what a turn-up for the book! has, since *c*. 1955 or a little earlier, expressed 'pleasure at the unexpected. (The book is, of course, the bookmakers)' (Sanders, 1972). But it had orig. been an underworld c.p., as in Arthur Gardner, *Tinker's Kitchen*, 1932.

what a way (occ. **a hell of a way**) **to run a railway** (or **railroad**)! 'A c.p. directed at more or (mostly) less organized chaos: US, then UK. From an American cartoon of the 1920s: signalman coolly surveying a number of trains colliding beneath his box' (1969).

In 1973, Rear-Adm. P. W. Brock wrote to me thus:

I have a cartoon from a frivolous American magazine

called *Ballyhoo*, of 1932, showing an American railway signalman looking out of his signal box at two trains about to collide head on and saying 'Tch-tch – what a way to run a railway!'

A contemporary of my father said that it [this c.p.] was quite common in Canada at the turn of the century or thereabouts.

In *The General and the President* (MacArthur and Truman in opposition over Korea, 1951) the authors, Arthur Schlesinger, Jnr, and Richard Revere, remark – 'It is, *in the idiom of Missouri*, a hell of a way to run a railway'.

B.P., 1974, quotes it as current in Aus. in the form '...*railroad*', since *c*. 1950, if not seven or eight years earlier. In Alexander Buzo's *The Roy Murphy Show*, performed in 1971 and pub'd in 1973, Roy, a TV compere with a tendency to pronounced *r* as *w*, speaking of Australian Rugby League football, says, 'City selection blunders like the shock omission of veteran Ken Irvine and the surprise inclusion of tyro Kel Brown. What a way to wun a wailwoad!'

'Sometimes *that's a hell of a way to run a railroad!* Its U.S. origins may date back to late C.19, when some railroads were in the hands of financial manipulators whose last interest [and concern] was efficient or safe operation... In the 1960s, a book recounting the (often deliberate) mismanagement of U.S. railroads post-WW2 was published under the title *A Hell of Way to Run a Railroad*' (R.C., 1978). To which A.B., 1979, added: 'Sometimes expressed querulously, when *everything* goes wrong, or seems to, "Is this any way to run a railroad?" (or an airline or a bus line, depending on the size of the city one lives in. In the U.S., it is most commonly heard by people commuting from suburbs to a city. Current from the 1900s, I'd guess.'

what a wonderful (or **agreeable** or **pleasant** or the feeble **nice**) **way to die!** is a C20 'c.p. of consolation when someone has mentioned a death through drink, riotous living or other cause due to debauchery' (Granville, 1969). Whereas Wilfred Granville had always heard *nice*, I've always heard *wonderful*, as in.

'Poor old man! He died, making love to his young wife.'
'Poor! What a *wonderful* way to go!'

[Which reminds me of one of the most remarkable pieces of plain and lucid English I've ever heard. *Scene:* a police court. The magistrate asks a middle-aged prostitute about a male death that has occurred in her room. 'Well, yeronner, we lay down on the bed and go on with it. After a while, he gave a great sigh. I thought he had come – but he was gone.' (Related to me by a Savile Club friend in, I suppose, 1972.)]

R.C. adds, 1978, that the idea is, in the US, more often phrased *it's a great way to go!*

what about it? If you're ready, go ahead, *or* Let's go, let's get going (or busy): since *c*. 1914. In his *Carrying On*, 1917, Ian Hay (properly Ian Hay Beith) numbers it among the 'current catch-phrases.'

But in its perhaps predominant post-WW2 sense, 'Shall we make love?', it can hardly be called a c.p.

what about the workers? (usu. *wot abaht* ..., to give proletarian authenticity). This Labour hecklers' cry becomes a c.p. 'When used to parody the idea of public political meetings or, indeed, on any occasion when labour relations are concerned' (P.B., 1976): since the 1950s. See also **hello, folks!**

what am *I* supposed to do: cry? A US c.p., dating from *c*. 1930. Berrey treats it as a synonym of 'It's not *my* concern!' and '*I* should worry!'. Cf **what do you expect me to do: burst into flames?**

what **are you?** Implication: 'You're a fool (or worse)!': later C20. Elliptical for the Services' drill instructor's howl at a clumsy recruit, 'You're an 'orrible little man – *what* are you?', to which the hopeless recruit had to reply, 'I'm a horrible little man, sergeant'. In civilian use, usu. a humorous, though (still) pointed, rebuke. (P.B.)

what are you going to make of it? is an Aus. c.p., dating since *c*. 1930 and inviting the interlocutor to a bout of fisticuffs in order to settle the matter. (B.P.) Cf **want to make something of it?**

what are you saving it (or **yourself**) **for?** 'Said to a chaste or abstemious or non-smoking youth or young man, by his peers. Since 1930, at latest' (J.W.C., 1977). Cf **are you keeping it for the worms?**

what are you: some kind of nut? see **you some kind of nut?**

what can a poor girl do? 'Still occasionally heard in derision or as a jocular catcall (Petch, 1969): C20. 'Means that a "poorgirl" can only go on the streets.'

what can I (occ. **we**) **do you for?** has, since the early 1920s (I remember hearing it *c*. 1925), been a joc. var. of *what can I* (or *we*) *do for you?* Based in Brit. slang *do*, to cheat or to cheat out of.

what can you expect from a pig but a grunt? You can't expect civility from an ill-mannered person, usu. a man: late C. 19–20, but little heard since *c*. 1960. It occurs in Col. R. Meinertzhagen, *Army Diary: 1899–1926*, entry for 6 Feb. 1918. (Thanks to Mr Y. Mindel.) Prompted by the proverb *you can't make a silk purse out of a sow's ear.*

what can you lose? 'A c.p. implying either that a proposed course of action has few or no risks or that the person addressed has, in fact, nothing to lose, hence might as well try it' (R.C., 1978): US: since *c*. P.B.: the Brit. version is variable, e.g. *what is there to lose?* or *what have you* (*got*) *to lose?*, or even *there's nothing to lose*, and thus, in UK, cliché or idiom rather than c.p..

what cheer, my old brown son: how are you? See **hello, my old....**

what did Gladstone say in (e.g., 1879)? A political hecklers' c.p.: late C19–20; not much heard since 1939. If the question were serious, it wouldn't be eligible; but usu. it was either merely obstructive or goodhumouredly meaningless or, at the least, almost so. That great Gladstone scholar, Prof. M. R. D. Foot, thinks that the c.p. could have arisen at any time after Nov. 1879, when Mr Gladstone, as he was always known, conducted his famous Midlothian campaign. In a conversation in 1975, Prof. Foot very properly reminded me that here, although indirect, is yet another tribute to the immense personal popularity of the GOM.

what did Horace say, Winnie? comes 'from Harry Hemsley's music-hall turn in the 1940s, in which he "did" the voice of a whole family of children, the youngest of whom, Horace, was quite unintelligible and had to be interpreted by an older sister, Winnie' (P.B., 1976); it lasted into 1950s. As a c.p. it was used in any vaguely similar situation.

what did thought do? was a C18 c.p., exemplified in S, 1738, Dialogue I:

LADY ANS[WERALL]: I thought you did just now.

LORD SP[ARKISH]: Pray, Madam, what did thought do?

The orig. form of the C19–20 *you know what thought did!* – often extended by **kissed another man's wife**, to quote the polite version.

what did you do in the Great War, daddy? was orig. a recruiting poster of WW1. The British soldier seized upon it, derided it, repeated it 'scathingly in times of distress and misery' (John Brophy). In late 1917–18, 'there were many variations, some quite lengthy. We need cite but one reply: "Shut up, you little bastard! Get the Bluebell and go and clean my medals"' (EP, likewise in B & P). Poor daddy may have 'fought the war' at a base or been a general's batman. *Bluebell* is the brandname of a well-known metal-polish.

what did your last servant die of? is 'used when someone asks you to do something he could easily do himself. Winnie, our maid, has been using this,... to my grandmother's knowledge, for 65 years' (Levene, 1977). I remember it since *c*. 1910. As a domestic c.p., it has prob. been current since the 1890s, if not earlier; it has had a wider currency since *c*. 1920. A var. of **when did your last servant die?**

what do I owe? See **do I owe you anything?**

337

what do you do for an encore? 'A question that is asked when somebody does something foolish or drops something' (B.P., 1975): Aus.: post-WW2.

'In US, often with the approximate meaning, "What you propose may be feasible enough – but *then* what do you do?"' (R.C., 1978). P.B.: perhaps orig. from the story of the theatrical agent interviewing a performer who proposed to commit suicide on the stage. For a more light-hearted version, cf. **can you do anything with your ears?** Other sarcastic remarks in the same vein are *how about a repeat performance?*; *how did it go?*; and *that was interesting!*

what do you expect (or **want**) **me to do: burst into flames?** An RAF c.p. arising in 1940, but not much heard afterwards, it deprecates excitement. Obviously from aircraft catching fire after being hit by flak. (L.A.)

Two US equivalents: Fain, 1977, notes *Do I have to stand on my head?* = 'Yes, I heard you. So what?'; and A.B., 1979, adds, 'I've also heard it as "What do you want me to do, shit bricks *or* shit a brick?" I've known it since the 1940s'. Cf **I don't care if you burst into flame.**

what do you hear from the mob? 'Common. Goes back to the Al Capone era of gangsterism, during Prohibition period. A familiar expression currently meaning, "What do you hear from our old gang of buddies?"' (W.J.B., 1975).

what do you know? is the more abrupt, prob. also the orig., form of **well, what do you know?** In 'Watching a Spring Planting', forming part of his *Love Conquers All*, 1923, Robert Benchley writes: 'Then you can laugh, and call out to a neighbour, or even to the man's wife: "Hey, what do you know? Steve here thinks he's going to get some corn up in this soil!"'

Also Can.: late C19–20. Sandilands, 1913: 'A common salutation, meaning "Anything new?" or "What news?"' Cf:

what do you know about that? A C20 expression of surprise, neither aristocratic nor upper-middle class, nor cultured, it could not fairly be called proletarian. It achieved a considerable popularity in the Services – esp. the army – during WW2. (PGR.)

Moreover, this c.p.had reached the US very soon after WW1, presumably via the returning US soldiers. In Robert Benchley's *Love Conquers All*, 1923, 'The Score in the Stands' offers this passage: 'SECOND INNING: Scanlon yelled to Bodie to whang out a double. Turtelot said that Bodie couldn't do it. Scanlon said "Oh, is that so?" Turtelot said "Yes, that's so and whad'yer know about that?"'

E.P. later had second thoughts, citing Sandilands, 1913, '"What do you think of that?" It is, however, merely an an exclamation...', and adding: Can., adopted by the UK. Whether orig. Can. or US, I shouldn't care to assert, for the D.Am. gives the first US date as 1914.

what do you know, Joe? This c.p. possessed, in the WW2 Services, the dovetail response *damn* (or *bugger* or esp. *fuck*) *all, Paul!* – which soon became fairly gen. among civilians in public-houses and at such predominantly male concourses as a 'soccer' match. (Reminder from L.A., 1976; haven't, myself, although often encountering the orig., heard this response since c. 1960.)

what do you mean, your bird won't sing? 'Indicative of disbelief. Dates from the 1920s. I believe there is a story behind this phrase. Perhaps even a *Punch* cartoon' (Sanders, 1974).

what do you take me for? A usu. indignant c.p., roughly equivalent to 'What sort of a person do you think I am?' Esp. 'What sort of a rogue or fool – or girl – do you think I am?' Current throughout C20 and perhaps going back some decades earlier. Denis Mackail, *Huddleston House*, 1945, has:

'Going out' means [for a girl in WW2 London] a night of Cimmerian darkness, partly, quite often, of considerable danger, partly of a plush *banquette* or a scrap of parquet in a cellar, partly of shouting for taxis, and partly of saying 'What do you take me for?' inside them.

A.B., 1979, notes that the phrase sometimes has *a fool* added, 'which is the way it's used in the Broadway [and London] musical, *My Fair Lady*. Var.: *what do you think I am, a fool?*'

Cf **would you for fifty cents?**

what do *you* think? A late C19–20 c.p., implying 'You're too well informed, *or* too intelligent, not to know exactly what that, *or* this, means *or* meant.'

what do you think of the show so far?, with it's emphatic response, **rubbish!** 'Eric Morecambe's customary inquiry of audiences animate and inanimate' (*VIBS*): 1970s.

what do you think that is? Scotch mist? Var.: **what's that? Scotch mist?** Occ. var.: **what's that? fog?** A sarcastic c.p. of the Services, notably the RAF, dating from the mid 1920s; implying that the addressee is either 'seeing things' or, more usu., failing to see objects he ought to be able to see, 'Can't you see my tapes? What do you think they are – Scotch mist?' Hence, loosely, applied to noise. 'A bomb falls. "What was that?" – "Well, it wasn't Scotch mist"' (Wg/Cdr. R.P. McDovall, 1945). For the pattern cf:

what do you think this is? Bush Week? Var.: **what's this? Bush Week?** An Aus. c.p., addressed to a man making a (great) noise and a considerable fuss: since the 1920s. Baker records both forms and mentions that no such week exists. B.P. has pointed out that a commoner form is *What do you think this is – Bush Week or Christmas?* and that it is also 'used when someone has produced something very "fishy"'; it occurs in, e.g., Lawson Glassop, *Lucky Palmer*, 1949. This latter sense derives from the country agricultural and pastoral show, when the sharpers fleece the locals. Jim Ramsay, 1977, defines it as 'retort to a tall story'.

what do you think this is (or, more often, **you're on**) **? (your) daddy's yacht?** 'A very common Service c.p., esp. NCOs'. Still heard occasionally in the Army' (P.B., 1975). 'Where the hell do you think you are ? Aboard daddy's yacht?' occurs *passim*, and with variants, in Colin Evans powerful novel of National Service in the RN, *The Heart of Standing*, 1962; an example in print for the Army is in B.S. Johnson, ed., *All Bull: the National Servicemen*, 1973, '"Get back and get your uniforms on!" bowled the guard commander. "What do you think this is? Your daddy's yacht?"' Peppitt attests its use in the MN. Mostly late 1940s–late 1960s. A logical var. is *where do you think you are?* ... (P.B.)

what do you (or, illiterately yet frequently, **whaddya**) **want? eggs** (or **an egg**) **in your beer?** 'Usually said to someone who is bitching or griping without justifiable cause. I have heard this used only by Marines, but I strongly suspect that it was borrowed from civilian use' (Col. Moe, 1975). Therefore, tentatively: C20; civilian become, during WW2, Marine Corps.

'I heard this first in 1937, (as ... *egg* ...) and in a civilian context. Certainly it has been in general (*not* just USMC) use since then' (R.C., 1978). A shorter var. is *you want an egg in your beer?*; cf **what do you want? Jam on it?**

what do you want from my life? 'Just what *do* you want? (Implicitly, "I've already done or suggested everything a reasonable person would ask.") As a direct translation from the Yiddish (*Vos vulst du fun mein leben?*), current from c. 1930 among second-generation Jewish-Americans, whence some general use from c. 1940, primarily in New York and Los Angeles, our two main centers of Jewish population and – via "the media" and show-biz – cultural influence. Semantics unclear, but perhaps the phrase implies that only the speaker's life – i.e., death – will satisfy the person addressed. Or, possibly, "How much more of my life do you expect me to devote to satisfying you?"' (R.C., 1978).

what do you want if you don't want money? 'Title of a song, late 1940s – early 1950s. It became a meaningless c.p.' (P.B., 1975); little used after c. 1965.

what do you want? jam on it? A late C19–20 military c.p., addressed, as a rebuke, to a constant grumbler. As John Brophy wrote in B & P, 1930: 'But this was used just as often ironically, when extra fatigues or working parties took the place of a promised rest, or something fell short of the normal standard.' It had an occ. var., *d'you want jam on both sides?*, q.v. P.B.: fairly common also in civilian life, and sometimes as a comment on a 'pick-thank' person, 'You want bloody jam on it, you do!' Cf the US equivalent what do you want? Egg ..., and the Aus. **you want portholes in your coffin.**

what does 'A' do now? what does someone (usu. the speaker, referring to himself) do next – how should he respond?: since *c.* 1930; by 1975, slightly ob. Prob. ex question posed in earlier C20 detective stories. (P.B., 1975.)

what does a mouse do when it spins? An elaborated, conundrum version of **why is a mouse ...?** Cf **what was the name of the engine-driver?**

what does it (or **what's it**) **matter what you do, as** (or **so**) **long as you tear 'em up?** (Always uttered in a strong West Country accent.) 'In *Mediterranean Merry Go Round*, Jon Pertwee played a Devonshire bugler at Plymouth [RN] barracks who eventually became the postman in *Waterlogged Spa* [the post WW2 civilian version of the radio comedy series], not to mention thirteenth trombonist in the Spa Symphony Orchestra. At one concert he became bored with the slow movement of a symphony and broke into "Tiger Rag". When Eric Barker [see **steady, Barker**] remonstrated with him, he said: "Ah, me old darling, but it tore 'em through, didn't it?" Barker: "Well, er, yes ..." Postman: "Well, what's it matter what you do, as long as you tear 'em up?"' (*VIBS*).

Pertwee explained, in *Pick of the Week*, BBC Radio 4, 4 July 1975, that 'it was derived from a character he had known as a boy in the West Country, a postman who used to "get slewed out of his skull" [dead drunk] on scrumpy [cider] and throw all the letters away' (P.B., 1975).

what does that make *me*? (–**so**) expresses lack of interest or a refusal to participate or to become involved: since the late 1930s. (L.A.)

But it came to UK from the US, where it had been current since the early 1930s and often (as later in UK) used in the sense, 'How do I come out of that statement or argument?', or 'That statement or argument isn't very flattering to *me*, is it?' – as in James Eastwood, *The Chinese Visitor*, 1965, ' "All bureaucrats are cautious and unenterprising." The very senior Civil Servant ruefully commented, "So what does that make *me*?" '

what else did you get for Christmas? has, since *c.* 1965, been a 'sarcastic remark to someone showing off "a toy", e.g. in exasperation at a roadhog blinding down the outside lane of a motorway in his brand-new Jag, hooting and flashing his lights. General' (P.B., 1975). The ironic implication is that it isn't a *man*'s car but a *kid*'s plaything.

what else is new? (–**so**) is a sarcastic response to a piece of stale news, the sting being in the *else*: US and dating from perhaps as early as *c.* 1890. J.W.C., 1977, thinks that *so* prob. indicates a New York City Jewish orig. It may also have been prompted by the cliché *what's new?*

what gets me down and **what gets my back up.** See **that's what** ...

what gives? and **what gives out?** What's happening? The latter was the property of the RAF in North Italy, 1945. The former, becoming Brit. in or about the same year, had migrated from the US, where current since well before 1939; W&F, who note another sense, 'What did I do to make you say or do that?', suggest orig. in Ger. *was ist los?* – but doesn't it rather derive from Ger. *was gibt's*?

R.C., 1978, comments, "Your derivation, not W&F's, is undoubtedly correct – except that I think Yiddish a more likely immediate source than German."

what goes up must come down. Several of the friends I've asked about this truism replied, 'Oh, but that's a *proverb*!' Perhaps on its way to becoming a proverb, and certainly obvious and trite enough to have long since done so, it was orig. and is still predominantly a c.p., dating, I'd say, from *c.* 1870 (but

not improbably much earlier). R.S., 1969, describes it as 'a C19–20 c.p., commenting with cheerful Newtonian logic on a pregnancy, whether extramarital or not': which suggests that the ultimate origin does, in the fact, reside in the Newtonian dictum of the pull of gravity. B.P. remarks: 'A c.p. that is no longer true.'

P.B.: *The Concise Oxford Dictionary of Proverbs*, 1982, accords it a place (at *up*) with first citation in print dated 1939.

what has she (or **he**) **got that I haven't** (**got**)? A feminine c.p., orig. as an abandoned or jilted wife's or mistress's outcry against a successful rival: since the 1930s. As in the young wife's reproach to her soldier husband, returning from abroad, '*What had she* ...?' – and his engaging, if somewhat insensitive, reply, 'Nothing at all, my dear. But it was available.'

Sanders, 1978, supplies the reverse: 'In WW2, when a man received a "Dear John" (known at the time as "one of those letters") from his wife or sweetheart (or both!), his reaction was to ask "what has he got that I haven't?" – to which his comrades would reply, "Nothing – but he's got it *there*!" '

what have you done for me lately? See **yes, but what** ...

what? have you pigs in your belly? (Prob. *what* was often omitted.) Current in C18 and occurring in S, 1738, Dialogue I:

NEV[EROUT]: Miss *Notable*; ... pray step hither for a Moment.
MISS: I'll wash my Hands and wait on you, Sir; but pray come you hither and try to open this Lock.
NEV: We'll try what we can do.
MISS: We! what, have you Pigs in your Belly?

Miss Notable uses a c.p. to comment adequately upon young Neverout's rather pompous use of the plural 'we'. In gen., 'What's wrong with you?'

P.B.: but surely Miss Notable is not asking what is wrong, but is implying, quite strongly, 'We? I can see only one of you! Are there pigs ...?'

what he doesn't know, you could write on the back of a postage stamp, with a two-inch brush, the last four words being a RN elab., in the 1970s, of a popular c.p. (Pepitt.) Stemming orig. from H.C. Beeching's epigram, late 1870s, on Benjamin Jowett (1817–93), Master of Balliol College. Yet it was Jowett who is said to have reproved a bumptious undergraduate know-all with the caustically modest words, 'No one knows everything – not even the youngest of us'.

what ho! she bumps! See **bumps** ...!

what is ... See also entries at **what**

what is (i.e. what use is) **rank without privilege?** I first heard this joc., slightly cynical, rhetorical excuse for the irresponsible abuse of small powers, e.g. the 'pulling of rank' for personal advantage, or the acquisition of 'perks' (perquisites, or 'bunce'), in the Army *c.* 1960, but guess it goes back to (? much) earlier. (P.B.)

what is that (or **what's that**) **when it's at home?**; and **who is he** (or **she**) **when he's** (or **she's**) **at home?** C20 tags, implying either derision or incredulity, and signifying 'I've never even heard of her, him, it'. Edwin Pugh uses it in *The Cockney at Home*, 1914, and Dorothy L. Sayers in *Have His Carcase*, 1932, has: 'Haemophilia. What in the name of blazes is that, when it's at home?' Cf the oddly similar quot'n from Terence Rattigan, *Harlequinade*, prod. 1948 and pub'd 1949:

JACK: Social purpose, Mr Burton.
BURTON: Social purpose? Now what the blazes is that when it's at home?

It is, in short, directed esp. at someone employing an unusual or erudite or highly technical or scientific term in a *milieu* unlikely to know its meaning. Cf this, in Julian Symon's *The Players and the Game*, 1972:

'My belief is ... that this might be a case of *folie à deux*.'
'And what's that when it's at home?'

what *is* this? International Fuck Your Buddy Week? P.B., 1974, writes:

I haven't heard this phrase for some years now: I think it must have come into the British Army via those units which served alongside the Americans in Korea [1950–3]. It was a useful emollient c.p. in situations where people were getting 'narky' and edgy with each other. 'What is this then? International ...?' [That is, '–you, bud!']

It is therefore prob. that the saying had become current in the US Army in 1942–5.

'Sometimes just *National* – and the more cautious person might say ... *F.Y.B. week?* Current among college students here [in US]' (A.B., 1979). Evidently, therefore, the c.p. has long passed into US civilian use.

what is your summer name? A discreetly joc. question asked of a man who gives as his name one that the asker suspects is false: US Western: C20. Adams, at *summer name*.

what it is! 'An expression of greeting similar to "what's happening?"' (Folb): the US south-west.

what keeps your ears apart. See **I didn't ask ...**

what me! was, in WW1, a frequent greeting between two, or among more than two, soldiers. B & P, 1931.

what, *me*? In *my* state of health? Ted Kavanagh, the script writer for 'ITMA', tells us, in his biography, 1948, of Tommy Handley, that 'There was even a Brighton parson who announced that the subject of his sermon would be: "What *me*, in *my* state of health?"'

From Francis Worsley, the producer, we learn, in his *Itma*, 1948, that his was an 'ITMA' c.p. that caught on, *c.* 1946–50, with the general public.

See also TOMMY HANDLEY CATCH PHRASES.

what next, and next? is contemptuous of an audacious assertion: *c* 1820–1905. Ware.

what o'clock, cock? What's the time, chum?: since *c.* 1955; by 1970, virtually †. From an advertising campaign [P.B.: for 'Seven o'Clock' razor blades] in which, over several years, this sort of jingle occurred: cf **gently, Bentley** and **see you later, alligator.**

what say?; and **what say you?** The former shortens the latter, which dates from *c.* 1870, but was, by 1975, decidedly ob.: the former dates from the 1880s and occurs in those two masters of Cockney speech. W. Pett Ridge (*Minor Dialogues*, 1895) and Edwin Pugh (*Harry the Cockney*, 1912).

It passed into US speech as *what say?*: and Berrey equates it to 'What's the plan?' W&F state that it has been common since *c.* 1920 and that, to distinguish it from a true question, *say* is stressed.

what says the enemy? See **how goes the enemy?**

what shakes? What are the chances? Brit. underworld: *c.* 1830–1900. Hotten, 1859, gives: '"What *shakes*, Bill?" "None,"' – that is, there's no chance of our being able to commit a robbery here. From 'to *shake* the dice', to gamble.

P.B.: cf the idiomatic disparagement, *no great shakes*, which dates from early C19.

what (or **which**) **shall we do, or go fishing?** My old friend Archie Pearse attests, 1976, the Aus. currency of this loaded trick question so early as 1904. In one of her two or three best novels, *The Nine Tailors*, 1934, Dorothy L. Sayers offers this example:

'What shall we do, or go fishing?'
'I'm on; we can but try.'

Prof. Emeritus T.B.W. Reid, 1976, suggests that 'it must be a later derivative of *which would you rather be, or a wasp?* [q.v.], since this explains itself as an instance of a punning type of trick question ... popular among schoolchildren – I believe there are others of the type *be – bee* [and] *wasp – fly*'.

R.C., 1978, comments, 'As heard by me in 1920s, *what would you rather do or go fishing?* Long extinct in US, and I think never common'. P.B.: but enjoying periodic revivals in UK. See also **or would you rather be a fish?**

what suit did you give it upon? was an underworld and fringes-of-the-underworld c.p. of *c.* 1790–1850. Vaux.

what the soldier said isn't evidence, whence **as the soldier said**

used as a humorous tag: the former, since the latish 1830s, the latter from the same time or very soon after. The generative passage is this, in which Dickens's account of the trial of Mr Pickwick includes the cross-examination of Sam Weller, who spoke appreciatively of his master:

'"Little to do, and plenty to get, I suppose?" said sergeant Buzfuz with jocularity.

"Oh, quite enough to get, Sir, as the soldier said ven they ordered him three hundred and fifty lashes", replied Sam.

"You must not tell us what the soldier, or any other man, said, Sir", interposed the judge; "it's not evidence."'

The saying prob. did not arise during serialization (Apr. 1835–Nov. 1837), but on the publication of *The Pickwick Papers* in 1837. Either form implies that 'as statement may not be factual' or is 'merely used as a conversational "throw-away" ... It even crops up again today, a tribute to the tremendous impact of *The Pickwick Papers* ... The c.p. is allied to the modern **as the man said**, q.v.' (Noble, 1977). In 1837, Dickens was twenty-five years old. Cf also **as the girl said.**

what the well-dressed (...) is wearing! The orig. was prob. *... well-dressed gentleman ...*, but in c.p. form anything, derogatory or otherwise, may be substituted, e.g. airman, vicar, or twit, slob, camel, etc.: presumably from a once well-known tailor's or couturier's slogan: mid C20. Occ. in approbation, but usu. derisory, of, e.g., a recruit in ill-fitting denim overalls, or someone in fancy dress. (P.B.)

what they say about Chinese women (or **girls**). Uses of the phrase vary according to context, from the simple, allusive *you know what ...*, to the full *yes, and what they say about Chinese women is wrong too* (or *isn't true*, or *right, either*), which in general may be employed to support a statement or an admission, but, in particular, controverts **clever chaps, these Chinese.** The allusion is to the myth, apparently common on both sides of the N. Atlantic, that, in Chinese females, 'it' is lateral, not vertical: the phrase/idea has been current since well before WW2.

A.B., 1979, suggests that the theory 'arose from the fact that the eyes of Orientals appear slanted. I do not know why the comparison between the slant-eyes and the *labia majora* became made: perhaps it hearkens back to some medieval metaphor, as in Chaucer's descriptions in the "General Prologue" to *Canterbury Tales*, or to some of the "character" writers of the C17, Overbury, Hall, Burton, and others'.

R.C., 1978, notes: 'Certainly earlier in US than WW2, since I first heard it *c.* 1930 (in the form *is it true what they say about Chinese women?*). I suspect [that it was] originally a send-up, by old hands in the US and/or Royal Navy, merchant marine, etc., of the amazement of greenhorns who had never visited China'.

It received the accolade of literature when, in Act II of Edward Albee's *Who's Afraid of Virginia Woolf?*, 1962, George remarks to Nick, 'All's pretty much the same, anyway ... in spite of what they say about Chinese women'.

'A variant – for what it's worth – met (*c.* 1946) orally only was "and is it true about Western ladies, as Madame ... asked Mrs ..." This var. had a short, not very active life' (R.S., 1973).

Peter Sanders tells me that, at the end of some advice he drafted for British troops bound for Korea, *c.* 1950, he added, in an attempt to keep it light and to help morale, 'It is not true about Korean girls either' – but, sadly, some humourless type at the War Office deleted it 'as frivolous, not for the more valid reason that the troops would prefer to find out for themselves'. He goes on, 1978, that 'as a result of this semi-myth, the transverse engines to many motor cars these days are sometimes referred to as Chinese engines, to the bewilderment of those who don't know the facts of life'.

what time (or **when**) **does the balloon go up?**; with the reply, **the balloon goes up at** (a stated time). When does it happen? Esp., when does the barrage open or the attack begin: 1915, orig. military; then, 1919 onwards, also civilian. John

Brophy, in B&P, 1930, writes: 'What time does the balloon go up? was a favourite way of asking the time fixed for any special parade or "stunt". The balloon going up was equivalent to the chief event of the day.' The ref. is to the observation balloons often to be seen behind the lines. By 1935, slightly ob.; by 1945, almost †.

A.B. adds, 1979: 'I think most Americans would also understand this to refer to a New Year's Eve party, as well as the *dropping* of the lighted ball on *the New York Times* building at Times Square, N.Y.C., where more than a million people gather on 31 December to watch the ball descend. It was used also as a query at weddings, funerals, and other, similar occasions. We use it infrequently now.'

what time's Treasury? See **ghost walks...**

what was the name of the engine-driver? A Cockney c.p. either derisively or provocatively interrogative: C20. Used either to express boredom or to start a discussion or even a bad-tempered argument. It derives from the trick of asking many questions about speeds and times, as a mathematical exercise in school.

The Opies, Iona and Peter, ask, 1976: 'Are you sure *Watt* wasn't the name of the engine-driver?' Theoretically, it could have been [what about James Watt? P.B.], but I think not, the evidence supporting an origin in the general human tendency to ask either awkward or seemingly naïve questions. Prof. Emeritus T.B.W. Reid, 1976, wrote 'For me, this is not exactly a catch phrase: I remember it as the "spoof" conclusion to an elaborate pseudo-mathematical problem about train speeds and departure and arrival times'; and my old friend Oliver Stoner, also 1976, said 'My version of the engine-driver ends, after a series of unrelated data, with the question: "Now what was the colour of the engine-driver's whiskers?"' P.B.: variants include the substitution of a lift-boy for the engine-driver, and the colour required that of his eyes or his socks.

what *will* they think of next? A c.p. – perhaps exclamatory rather than truly interrogative – either of joc. astonishment or of mildly derisive admiration, when something new has been invented or announced. Occ. modified to **I wonder what they'll think of next!** It arose, I believe, as a humorous aping of a question often asked by the naïve: and therefore it is usu. spoken in a slightly ironic tone.

what will you liq? What will you drink? Ware's evidence tends to show that it didn't last very long; say 1905–14, if so long! A pun on *liquor* and *lick*.

what would happen if you were in an accident? is 'a proverbial c.p. used by mothers to children whose underwear is not in perfect condition' (B.P., 1975): common, I believe, to UK and to the entire British Commonwealth of Nations and to former Dominions, e.g. Rhodesia and S. Africa; prob. going well back into C19. J.W.C., 1977, states that it is 'equally common (and old) in US'. But applied by others than mothers to not only children but also to adult females.

what would shock me would make a pudding crawl. It takes an awful lot to shock me: predominantly feminine: *c.* 1880–1920. 'Men were supposed to be unshockable, anyway' (L.A., 1971).

what would you do, chums? dates from early 1939, and is still (1977) heard occ., although mostly in nostalgic reminiscence. Syd Walker, 'The Philosophic Dustman' who died of appendicitis during WW2, used, with these words, to pose various droll problems in the BBC's radio programme entitled 'Band Waggon'. (EP in *Radio Times*, 6 Dec. 1946.)

To amplify: Barry Took, in *Laughter in the Air*, 1976, notes that a 'regular feature [of the 'Band Waggon' show] was "Mr Walker wants to know", in which Syd Walker, playing the part of a rag-and-bone man, posed social questions of the day and asked the audience to supply the answers. His catchphrase, "What would you do, chums?" became nationally quoted. Mr Took adds that 'Band Waggon', in which the stars were Arthur Askey and Richard Murdoch, 'had been pre-war radio's biggest comedy success'.

what you can't carry you must drag was, mid C19–early C20, a nautical c.p., applied to clipper ships carrying too much canvas. Bowen.

what you don't start you don't miss is an Aus. c.p. used about alcohol, sex, drugs, etc.: C20. (B.P., 1975.)

what you say goes (pause) all over the town has, since the middle 1940s, been applied to gossips and rumour-mongers. (Petch, 1966.) The first part of the phrase = what you say carries great weight, or is unquestioned; there is a considerable pause before the second part is uttered.

what you see is what you get is, when used with humorous irony, an Aus. c.p., dating from *c.* 1920. (B.P., 1975.) R.C., 1978, adds, 'Also US, 1970s (*The Serial*, 1977) and probably earlier. Origin is perhaps a sales cliché of street pitchmen'.

'This was "reborn" in us on American television's National Broadcasting Company (NBC) *The Flip Wilson Show* early 1970s. Wilson, a Negro comedian, appeared in women's clothes in one of his routines, as a girl named Geraldina. The show is no longer on television, but Wilson still does his act in nightclubs and in guest appearances. He wears a woman's wig and, approaching someone, uses the expression flirtingly. It is not a very common expression any more' (A.B., 1979).

whatever turns you on (with 'is all right with me' understood) is 'a phrase accepting another's foibles, hobbies or interests, which do not coincide with one's own': since 1972 or early 1973. (P.B., 1975.) 'Among younger Canadians is always humorous, and usually a sexual allusion' (Hugh E. Quetton, 1978).

what's (or **what does**) **a man have to do to get a beer** (or **drink**) **around here?** 'Originates in whorehouses, where it is literal; but a c.p., I think, in US, and has been for some 40 years, when used by a friend dropping and not very soon being offered a drink' (J.W.C., 1977).

what's a nice girl like you doing in a place (or **a crummy joint**, etc.) **like this?** 'Now used mockingly or as a consciously silly conversational gambit' (Ashley, 1982): prob. orig. US, but soon well known in UK: since (?) *c.* 1950. Perhaps from a line in a second-rate motion picture, or a caption from a cartoon, but since used in all sorts of ludicrous contexts, and with absurdities replacing *girl*. (P.B.)

what's all this in aid of? See **what's this in aid of?**

what's bit (or **bitten**; or usu. **biting** or **crawling on** or **eating**) **you?** What's the matter? British soldiers' (1915) become, by 1920, gen. John Brophy in B & P, 1930, says:

Curiosity, though not necessarily sympathy, was conveyed by the query, 'What's biting you?' Varied by *What's bit you?* or *What's crawling on you?* – all obviously metaphorical from the spectacle of the gestures and grimaces of anyone tormented with lice.

Prob. it orig. in the US, there being a US example dated 1911. Berrey cites two forms, *what's eating you?* and *what's biting you?* The Can. currency of this phrase (in the form *what's biting you?*) is glossed thus by Leechman, 1969: 'What are you complaining about? *or What irritates you?* Not recent.'

A modern – since *c.* 1950 – US var. is *what's bugging you?* (Fain, 1977.)

what's cooking? What is happening?: Services', esp. RAF, since mid 1940; by 1946, a common civilian c.p. From 'What is that smell – what's cooking? – asked so very often by so many. In 1942–6, often amplified to *what's cooking, good looking?* – with the g's often dropped. Adopted from US, where it was employed both as a greeting and to mean 'What's happening?' *or* 'What's going on here? what's being planned?' Esp. in army, among students, among negroes. (W & F; CM.) P.B.: a late 1940s song from the US had the chorus, 'Hey, good-lookin'! Whatcha got cookin'? How's about cookin' somethin' up with *me*?'

what's for tea, Ma? A 'cheerful greeting coined by the character "Ernie Entwistle" of the Knockout Comic in the 1950s' (Mrs Shirley M. Pearce, 1975). The cartoonist responsible was Hugh McNeill (1910–79), and the popularity of this c.p. was noted in his obituary in *The Times*, 26 Nov. 1979.

what's eating on you? What's annoying you?: US: *c.* 1910–65. Superseded, Fain suggests, 1978, by *what's bugging you?*, q.v. at the Brit. synon. **what's bit you?**

what's going down? An Afro-American form of greeting: since *c.* 1960 (?). (*The Third Ear*, 1971.) Ashley, 1982, notes it as equivalent to the earlier:

what's happening? 'A form of congenial greeting meaning hello' (*The Third Ear*, 1971); with a 'deep' – Negro, quasi-dialectal var. *wha' hap'*? Whether the former was the earlier and better-educated form, debased by the illiterate, or whether *wha' hap'*? was the earlier, the natural form, 'cleaned up' by the educated, more cultured, I don't profess to know. Yet they could have arisen simultaneously, the one among one class, the other among the other class.

what's in the green bag? 'What is the charge being preferred against me?' (B & L). Since *c.* 1880; if not much earlier; by 1940,†. The brief-bag or -case carried by lawyers used to be coloured green.

what's it in aid of? See **what's this in aid of?**

what's it to you? – What concern is it of yours? – is a US c.p., dating from *c.* 1919, as in Robert Benchley's 'The Questionnaire Craze', orig. pub'd by the *Chicago Tribune* in 1930 and reissued in *Chips Off the Old Benchley*, 1949:

The first question is a simple one. 'How many hours do you sleep each night, on the average?'

Well, professor, that would be hard to say. I might add 'and what's it to you?' but I suppose there must be some reason for wanting to know.

Berrey, 1942, synonymizes it with 'Mind your own business!', and as A.B. notes, 1979, it is 'often followed by *Buster* or *Mac* or *Jack*.

what's itching you? is 'said to somebody tense or worried' (Petch, 1974): lower and lower-middle class: at least as early as *c.* 1920. A var. of **what's bit you?**, and cf **what's eating on you?**

what's knocked your donkey over? 'What has upset you?' – 'Why are you so disgruntled?' (R.S. reports its use on BBC radio, 19 Apr. 1978.) Since *c.* 1950, unless a decade or two earlier.

what's new? What's the news?: British Army: WW2. (PGR.) P.B.: in 1965 a US/French film, described as 'a zany sex comedy' by the invaluable Halliwell, appeared, called 'What's New Pussycat?'; this, with its popular title song, ensured that the phrase *what's new?* was usu., even so late as the 1980s, suffixed with *pussycat*.

what's on the table, Mabel? See **give him the money, Barney.**

what's on your mind? What's the trouble – your difficulty – the question you long to ask?: since the 1920s. From the lit. Standard English sense, 'What's worrying or preoccupying you?'

what's shaking? is a US negro form of greeting, roughly equivalent to 'what's happening?': the 1950s. (CM, 1970.) Cf **what's going down?**

what's that got to do with the price of eggs? In what way is that relevant?: US: since the 1920s, if not earlier. (J.W.C., 1977.) A.B., 1979, notes the var. *...of tea in China?*: since the 1940s – perhaps influenced by the expression, e.g. 'I wouldn't do that, not for all the tea in China'; and for Aus., B.P., 1975, supplies *what's that got to do with the price of fish?*, which is also Brit.

what's that in aid of? See **what's this in aid of?**

what's that? Scotch mist? See **what do you think that is...?**

what's that? the population of China? is an Armed Forces' c.p., arising in 1941 and 'deriding a comparatively high service or regimental number' (L.A.), i.e., one issued later than the speaker's.

what's that to me? 'A phrase so common that it shows it's a natural one, when people have no interest in a thing. Well, when a feller gets so warm on either side as never to use that

phrase at all, watch him, that's all!' (T.C. Haliburton, *The Clockmaker*, 1837). US, esp. New England: C19–20. Hence also Brit.: mid C19–20.

what's that when it's at home? See **what is that when it's at home?**

what's the big idea? (– hey!). What folly – or unpleasant, unwelcome plan – have you in mind? 'Anglicized' *c.* 1930, from US. (*OED* Supp.)

'Now and for some decades the predominant US [and Brit.: P.B.] meaning has rather been "By what right (*or* for what reason) are you doing that? – implying that the "idea" leading to the notion under discussion was erroneous or unreasonable. Cf [the cliché] (*just*) *what do you think you're doing?*' (R.C., 1978). P.B.: the remonstrance is always indignant, sometimes petulant; the phrase is now, early 1980s, rather ob. Might be used by, e.g. a girl unwilling (or pretending so) to be 'man-handled'.

what's the damage? What's the cost or expense?; How much do I owe?: mid C19–20. 'A humorous variation of the earlier *what's the shot?*' (Weekley).

Apparently it came to UK from US: *Am*, 1848, records it, and so does Farmer. 'This c.p. is extremely common in Australia' (B.P., 1975).

what's the diff? – Of what use? *or* What does it matter? – is a US c.p. of *c.* 1930–50, then rapidly decreasing in use. Berrey.

what's the difference between a chicken? A 'trick' or bogus puzzle question, to which the 'dovetail' or answer is: *One of its legs is both the same.* (P.B., 1976.)

Christopher Fry, 1976, writes: 'I always knew it as "What is the difference between a *duck*? One of its legs is both the same" – better, I think, than "chicken", which I never heard said. And you're right that it was prevalent in the 1930s'. P.B.: I heard the *chicken* version in 1951; with both, cf the illogic of **what shall we do or go fishing?** and **why is a mouse...**

what's the dirt? What's the scandal?; soon weakened to 'What's the news?': Society: since the very early 1930s. It occurs in, e.g., Evelyn Waugh, *A Handful of Dust*, 1934. In the weak sense, not much used since *c.* 1960.

what's the drill? A military version, dating since *c.* 1925, of **what's the form?** What's the procedure, the social custom, the method? Not very gen. army use until the late 1930s.

what's the dynamite? (or occ. **lyddite?**) What's the 'row' about?: Society: respectively 1890–9 and 1899–1900. (Ware.) The former derives from the dynamiters' activities in the 1880s; the latter arose during the Boer War.

what's the form? What's it like at, e.g., a house party?: Society: since the early 1920s. Evelyn Waugh, in *A Handful of Dust*, 1934, says of a household:

'What's the form?'

'Very quiet and enjoyable.'

During the middle 1930s, it became also an army officers' greeting and quickly spread to the other two Services; in the RAF for instance, it signified 'What is the procedure or tactics or strategy?'; and, more gen., 'How're things?' (PGR.) And adopted from army by navy. P.B.: the *form* was perhaps, orig. that of race-horses.

what's the good news? In Berrey we find it included in a list of invitations to drink; but the sense broadened to 'What's the news?' Cf **what's the news?**, and:

what's the good word? What's the news? – esp. 'What's the good news?' – US, it dates from *c.* 1910. In Ring Lardner's 'Thompson's Vacation' (Act I), forming part of *First and Last*, 1934 (he had died a year earlier), we find:

HAINES: Hello there, Thompson.

THOMPSON: Hello, Mr Haines.

HAINES: What's the good word?

THOMPSON: Well—

It occurs much earlier in John Kendrick Bangs, *A Line o' Cheer for Each Day o' the Year*, 1913; where the entry for 23 April runs:

THE ANSWER
'What's the good word?'
Now that's a phrase I truly love to hear,
And when 'tis heard,
I always smile and promptly answer 'CHEER!'
It holds more warmth and genial glow
Than any other word I know.
Damon Runyon and Howard Lindsay use it in *A Slight Case of Murder*, 1935.

'A var. from an American (Harvard and Government Service) acquaintance, late 1950s: "What's the glad word?" This somehow rings truer for Bible-punching Southern Baptists' (P.B., 1976)–yes, but prob. not elsewhere.

what's the mat? What's the matter?: English Public Schools': c.1870–1940. (Ware.) For truncation, cf **what's the diff?**

what's the matter with father? He's all right is a C20 Can. c.p. (Leechman, 1969.) Of vague denotation it has the connotation 'There's nothing really the matter with the person being referred to'.

'A US popular song of c.1920. No longer much heard' (J.W.C., 1977).

what's the matter with your hand? was, 1914–18, an army c.p.–addressed, joc., to someone lucky enough to be holding an article of food.

what's the news? What's the matter?: esp. 'What's the matter with you, all of a sudden?': late C16–mid C17. As if literal news has been very bad. In *A Woman Is a Weathercock*, 1612, Nathaniel Field, at IV, ii, writes:
STRANGE: She said you challenged her, and publicly Told you had lain with her: but truth's no wrong.
POUTS: Truth! 'twas more false than hell, and you shall see me
(As well as I can repent of any sin)
Ask her forgiveness for wounding of her name,
And 'gainst the world recover her lost fame.
Kind soul! would I could weep to make amends!
STRANGE: The more base villain thou. [*Strikes him.*]
POUTS: Ha! what's the news?
Cf **what's the good news?**

what's the odds, so (or **as**) **long as you're happy?** seems to have orig. as a c.p. (even if, as E.P. thought, it later became a cliché) in the early 1850s. It occurs in *Punch*, 25 Sep. 1852, p.143, and in the *Punch Almanack* for 1852, where the answer is given as 'Ten to one in your favour'. As R.C. notes, 1978, Kipling uses it in his *Stalky & Co.*, 1899, indicating its currency among Public Schoolboys in the late 1870s; George du Maurier has it in *Trilby*, pt I, 1894. It was still remembered in the 1940s, among the older generation, and perhaps survives even yet. (P.B.)

what's the rave? 'What's the main, or most exciting, topic of conversation?': US teenagers': since 1976 or '77. William Safire's sparkling article in *The New York Times Magazine*, 23 July 1978, '*Suave* kids enter the room with "*What's* the rave?"'

what's the score? What sort of weather is it?: RAF pilots': 1939 onwards, but decreasingly after c.1950. From the world of sport. Hence, 'What's the latest "gen" (information)?': RAF: 1941 onwards. Both sense spread to the Commonwealth wartime air forces.

Quite independent is the Suffolk male c.p., prob. of late C19–20, and addressed to a man playing or fumbling around his crutch, but within a trousers side-pocket. (A Suffolk correspondent.) From billiards.

what's the strength? What's the news?: Services, whether combatant or protective: 1940 certainly and 1939 prob. It occurs in, e.g., Allan A. Michie and Walter Graebner, *Lights of Freedom*, 1941. Contrast:

what's the strong of it? 'What's the truth?' *and* 'What's the gist of the matter?' Aus.: since c.1910. (I didn't hear it used until 1914.) Recorded by Baker.

what's the time? was, c.1880–1960, a juvenile c.p., directed–from the impudence ensured by either cover or distance–at

a man whose feet are exceptionally wide apart as he walks. The posture is variously described as *ten to two* (o'clock), (*a*) *quarter to three*, and (*a*) *quarter to one*. F & G, 1925, describe 'a man who turns out his feet more than [is] usual' as *quarter-to-one-feet*.

what's the time by your gold watch and chain? What's the time?: c.1880–1914. (Leechman, 1969: 'Heard often in England before 1908.')

'It had other implications, at least in the US. I remember a cartoon, c.1908, of a big threatening fellow, obviously with "mugging" intent, asking the question of a slim, frightened citizen with a gold watch chain across his belly' (Shipley, 1977).

what's this blown in? Whom have we here?: C20, but rarely heard after c.1950. Contemptuous. My earliest record is: W. L. George, *The Making of an Englishman*, 1914.

what's this? Bush Week? See **what do you think this is? Bush Week?**

what's this (occ. **that**) **in aid of?**; **what's all this in aid of?**; and **what's it in aid of?** The second is the predominant post-1945 shape of the first; the first dates from c.1918 and is also the usual US form, mostly used by people conscious of its Brit. origin, as J. W. C. tells me, 1968; the third has been common, esp. in the Services, since the early 1920s.

Meaning 'What's this about?', *or*, sometimes, 'What's the trouble?', the phrase derives from the popular street collections made, during WW1, in this or that good cause.

what's to pay? In *The Baviad and The Maeviad*, 1797, effectively the 2nd edn of both these satires (the latter, 1st edn 1795), William Gifford (1756–1826), editor of the *Quarterly Review* from its inception, 1809, until his retirement, 1824–reputed 'slasher' of Keats's *Endymion* and of other Romantics–considerable translator, esp. of Juvenal, asked, in a footnote on p.23, concerning the playwrights Holcroft, Reynolds, Mortin: 'Will posterity believe this facetious triumvirate could think nothing more to be necessary than an external repetition of some contemptible vulgarity, such as That's your sort! Hey, damme! What's to pay?' Keep moving, etc.!'

The phrase *what's to pay?* occurred in Frederick Reynold's *Fortune's Fool*, 1796, thus, 'Damme, "what's to pay" is my watch-word while I stay in London'–a sort of charm in every situation or predicament or against every misfortune–and was spoken by the famous actor, William Thomas Lewis (commonly called 'Gentleman' Lewis); it became a c.p. of c.1796–1810. (With thanks to Miss Patricia Sigl, 1975.) Cf **who's dead...**

[**what's up?**–What's the matter? What's the trouble?–cannot itself be regarded as a true c.p.: but it has evoked several 'near'-c.p. rejoinders, **the sky** and **the prices**, the former since c.1920 if not earlier, esp. among juveniles; the latter, since c.1960 and mostly among adults. (Petch, 1966.)]

what's up, Doc? 'In *Bugs Bunny*, a Warner Brothers cartoon feature in the 1940s and still very popular, one sketch has the rabbit playing straight man to comedian Elmer Fudd in a vaudeville show. Their act is a failure until... Bugs, gnawing on a carrot, says to Elmer, "Eh, what's up, Doc?"–upon which the audience roars, repeatedly. Mel Blanc does both voices (and many others). It is merely an "ice-breaker"; a "What's going on, old sport?" type of thing' (A.B., 1979). P.B.: the cartoons, on film and TV, are equally popular in UK, and in Hong Kong, in the 1960s, where I saw many of them, the local audiences loved them too. Bugs' (=crazy) intonation, which 'makes' the c.p., is unreproducible in print, unfortunately. Nigel Rees, in *VIBS*, notes that the phrase was subsequently used as the title of a film starring Barbra Streisand and Ryan O'Neal, 1972.

what's with you?–a US cp. of greeting–means no more than 'How are you?'. W & F think that it is of Yiddish origin.

what's yer fighting weight? and **what's your Gladstone weight?** I'm your man if you want to fight: respectively c.1883–1914, and of Cockney origin; and of 1885–6 only, but of political origin. (Ware.) Cf **what did Gladstone say...?**

what's your beef? is the Can. c.p. form of the slangy US, hence also Can., 'What are your beefing [complaining] about?' The US c.p. form is *what's the beef?* – which goes back to the 1920s.

[**what's your poison?** What would you like to drink? Like the virtually synon. *name your poison!*, it cannot, I think, be classified as a true c.p.]

what's your song, King Kong? is a US negro expression current during the 1940s and meaning 'How do you feel?', (CM, 1970.) A jingle.

'Equally popular at the time were *what's your story, Mornin' Glory?* [see below] and *what's your plan, Charlie Chan'* (Townley, 1978) – Charlie Chan was the star role in a series of films about a Chinese detective; Ashley, 1979, calls *what's your song...*, 'One of the *see you later, alligator* [q.v.] jazz expressions'. Cf:

what's your story? 'What's your excuse?' – hence, 'What have you to say for yourself?' and 'What do you want?', and finally in such loose extensions as 'How's tricks?' – i.e., 'How are you?': US: since late 1930s; by 1975, slightly ob. (Based on Cab Calloway, 1944.) Cf **that's my story**, and:

what's your story, mornin' glory? 'The recording with this title was made on 28 Feb. 1940, so this [predominantly US] catch phrase probably came into use in that year or a little earlier' (Townley, 1978). In his *Tell Your Story*, 1971, Mr Townley notes it as by Jimmie Lunceford and his Orchestra and glosses it thus: 'A form of greeting in rhyming slang popular in the 1940s and the equivalent of "How are you?"'. See the two prec. entries.

what's yours is mine, and what's mine is me own is a joc. comment upon have-it-both-ways greed and selfishness: late C19–20.

George M. Krzymowski, 1978, notes that the US version is *... and what's mine is mine*, and P.B. that a more usual later C20 UK var. is *... and what's mine I'm keeping*; both agree that the idea, however expressed, is applied to those Communist States where the communism practiced is less than ideal.

wheat. See: 'ware wheat; you shared it.

wheel(s). See: cartload of monkeys; had one; let's not re-invent; my watch; silly as; turtle; your wheel's.

wheel it on! Bring it on (*or* in); hence 'Let's have it!' It orig., during the late 1930s, in the RAF: and, not surprisingly, it then referred to aircraft; by the middle or, at latest, the late 1940s, it had become a fairly gen. civilian usage.

P.B.: cf the army usage, applied to a defaulter brought up on a charge before his senior officer, as in, e.g. 'Right, Sarn't-major. Wheel him in!', where the *wheel* is a drill manoeuvre usu. very necessary in the confined space of 'Orderly Room'.

wheelbarrow. See: you didn't; you make as good.

wheelchair. See: couldn't ride.

Whelan the Wrecker was here! (–it looks as though). This Aus., chiefly Victorian, c.p. is applied to 'a room, an office, in disorder; from a famous firm of demolition contractors who pull down all city centres' (Camilla Roab, 1977): since soon after WW2.

whelk. See: giddy.

when a girl has to go, she has to go! (To *the lavatory* understood.) A feminine c.p., ruefully frank and prettily innocent and usu. as 'phoney' as hell. Since during WW2 – let's say *c.* 1943. P.B.: merely a feminine var. of **when you gotta go...**, q.v.

[**when Adam was an oakum boy in Chatham Dockyard; when coppers** (or **donkeys**) **wore high hats**; and all other such phrases implying a vast antiquity. Not true c.pp.; therefore omitted. Several are genuinely funny; one or two, genuinely witty. P.B.: but see E.P.'s entry at **ever since...**, and cf the entries at **since...**]

when all else fails, read the instructions. See **if all...**

when are they goin' to burn yer? It 'was called sepulchrally after a rival gang of footballers on a Saturday morning after the callers had lost a match. I heard this in York *c.* 1919. Semantically, I suppose, it is equivalent to "Go to hell!"' (Wilfred Granville, 1973). North-east England: *c.* 1910–40. P.B.: there might be some ref. to Guy Fawkes's night, 5th Nov., when the guy burns on the traditional bonfire.

when did you blow in? 'In frequent use. Not recent' (Leechman, 1969): Can.: earlier C20.

when did your last servant die? Don't order me about: mid C19–20. 'Still used, esp. by adults to demanding kids' (Shaw, 1969). A var. of **what did your last servant die of?** Cf also **who was your lackey last year?**

when do we laugh? See **joke over.**

when do you shine? What time have you been called for?: US and Can. railroadmen's: C20. (Adams; Leechman.)

when does the balloon go up? See **what time does the balloon go up?**

when father says 'Turn!', we all turn, as a political c.p., was current *c.* 1906–8. It was occasioned by a political picture-postcard, depicting a family sleeping in one large bed, and it referred to a political leader. (Collinson.) But it took on a social connotation: 'A c.p. of father's authority as head of the house, or wife's tribute to, or mockery of, husband's domination' (L.A., 1975).

when he (or **she**) **says 'frog', she** (or **he**) **jumps.** '(Gender makes no difference.) The other person does what is demanded – or else! Mark Twain uses this idea in his first story, *The Celebrated Jumping Frog of Calaveras County*' (A.B., 1979). The theme, based on a piece of folklore, first appeared in print, 1853, in California; Mark Twain improved upon the story, which he too had heard, and pub'd it in a periodical of 1865 and, two years later, it formed the title of a collection of sketches and stories, his first book, 1867. (James D. Hart, *The Oxford Companion to American Literature*.) Cf the coarser **when I say 'shit'...**

when hell freezes over. See **'til hell...**

when hens make holy water. Never: rural: C16–17. The *OED* cites RH, 1631, 'As our Country Phrase is, When Hens make Holy-water, at new Nevermasse'.

when I come into my Yorkshire estates. When I have the means in a remote and doubtful future: *c.* 1840–1940. Hotten, 1860.

when I say 'shit', (you) jumps on the shovel! 'Like slippery – get a move on!' A MN c.p. of the 1940s at least; I'd say: *c.* 1930–70. Peppitt mentions the RN's slangy phrase, (like) **shit off a shovel**, q.v. P.B.: the phrase also had considerable use in the Army during National Service days, say late 1940s–early '60s, esp. among NCO instructors. Cf **when he says 'frog'...**, which may have prompted it.

when I want a fool I'll send for you. Occurs in S, 1738, Dialogue I:

NEV[EROUT]: So, Miss, you were afraid that Pride should have a Fall.

MISS: Mr *Neverout*, when I want a Fool I'll send for you.

This C18 (? until mid C19) c.p. may derive from the C17 proverb, 'He that sends a fool, expects one'.

when I was in Patagonia...! 'Commander A.B. Campbell was one of the regulars on BBC radio's *Brains Trust*, but it was on an earlier version of the programme, called *Any Questions*, that he came up with his famous phrase. Donald McCullough, the chairman, said: "Mr Edwards of Balham wants to know if the members of the Brains Trust agree with the practice of sending missionaries to foreign lands." C.E.M. Joad and Julian Huxley gave their answers and then Campbell began, 'Well, when I was in Patagonia...'"

In a book which used the phrase as its title, Campbell recalled: "I got no further, for Joad burst into a roar of laughter and the other members of the session joined in. For some time the feature was held up while the hilarity spent itself. For the life of me I could not see the joke... I got hundreds of letters and it cost me a small fortune in stamps... Even today (1951), years after, I can raise a laugh if I am on a public platform and make an allusion to it"' (*VIBS*)

P.B.: a very popular c.p. of mid C20, used to deflate boasting ('line-shoots') about experience in 'faraway places with strange-sounding names'. Cf **Gad, sir, when I was in Poona.**

when I was with Benson; and **when I was with Irving** are sarcastic theatrical c.pp.: rejoinders to boasters and liars among actors; clearly from the literal phrases. Granville comments,

In the old days the actor laddies [actors in Victorian melodrama] used to boast that they were in the same cast as Sir Henry Irving at the Lyceum. The stock comment was 'Walking on, I suppose'.

Irving (1838–1905) was, and off, at the Lyceum for many years.

Sir Frank Benson (1858–1939) was not a great actor: here, the ref. is to being a member of his famous Shakespeare company, 1883 onwards. It occurs in, for instance, Allan Monkhouse's *Nothing Like Leather*, 1913.

P.B.: cf the RAF's later C20 acronymic jibe WIWOL, directed at those pilots whose stories begin 'when I was on Lightnings...' These fighters were in front-line service approx. 1955–65.

when in danger, when in doubt/run in circles, scream and shout! This US cp., current in C20, may well have arisen in the Marine Corps; certainly it was, esp. in WW2, 'used by Marines to criticize some foul up in the navy'. Certainly, too, it passed from either the USMC in particular or the Fighting Forces in general to civilians; and both in the Forces and on the civilian front, 'its application has been to indicate a state of confusion, a general milling about, a lack of leadership, and an absence of definite or positive action ... I do not know if it is of British or American origin' (Col. Moe). Lt Cdr Peppitt, RNR, assumes that it is Brit. (and cf the synon. **if in danger ...**) and points out that it is 'a parody of the seamen's rhyme, "when in danger or in doubt, always keep a good look-out"'. A var. is ... *doubt,/yell and scream and dash about.*

P.B.: a later C20 Brit. synon. is the simple *all join hands and panic!*

when in doubt, punt! is not from Rugby football, but rather 'derives from American football back in the 1920s. (With the changes in the rules, the present-day game could *not* give rise to the expression ...) The general advice given to the quarterback (particularly to those of little experience or of little ability), before the team took to the field, was "When in doubt, punt". He was [by the coach] told that, as a consequence of "doubt", he might call a wrong play which could result in disaster for his team. The best thing to do ... was to punt and get rid of the ball, and then let the opponents do the worrying for a while. The usage today is in the sense of "If you don't know what to do about a problem, get rid of it"; that is, "pass the buck" and let the other person be saddled with it while you take the opportunity to study it and figure out what to do about it' (Col. Moe, 1977).

when (or if) in doubt, toss it out! A pharmaceutical, esp. Aus., c.p. of C20. (B.P.)

when it don't rain, the roof don't leak; and when it does rain, I can't fix it. '*Dolce far niente* as practiced in the American backwoods. Prob. from C19, and still current 1941 (R. Heimlein, *Methusaleh's Children*), but becoming ob. with general decline in rural and "hillbilly" humor since c. 1960. It seems likely, however, to retain a limited currency as a terse summation of an easy-going, not to say shiftless, life-style' (R.C., 1978).

when it's at home. See **what is that when it's at home?**

when it's smoking, it's cooking; when it's burning it's done. 'American forces' [servicemen's] commentary on mess cooks' attitude towards their duties: WW2; now ob. or †' (R.C., 1978).

when men were men ... See **where men are men ...**

when my wife is here, she is my right hand; when my wife is away, my right hand is my wife. A somewhat laboured c.p., applied to male masturbation: C20.

when Paddy Doyle gets paid for his boots (–yes,). Never!: used in the Training Ship HMS *Indefatigable*, c. 1909: perhaps since c. 1900 and certainly also later than 1909. (Peppitt.) Granville, in his *Dictionary of Sailors' Slang*, 1962, glosses Paddy Doyle: 'Detention barracks or cell. Perhaps from the name of a notorious defaulter.'

when push comes to shove. If worse comes to worst: US prostitutes': C20. (Murtagh and Harris, *Cast the First Stone*, 1958.)

But R.C., 1978, comments: 'Rather, I think, originally Negro than prostitutes', and with meaning closer to "when the situation is reduced to basics" – when you must really get out and push'.

when roses are red (a significant pause). When girls attain the age of sixteen, they are no longer too young for sexual intercourse: mostly Aus.: since the early 1920s. It was prompted by the – esp. in Aus. – widely known couplet:

When roses are red, they are ready to pluck;
When girls are sixteen, they are ready to fuck.

Cf the cynical, world-wide c.p.: **if they are big enough, they are old enough.**

P.B.: equally well-known, at least among low-minded little schoolboys of the 1940s, in UK; it was said among them – with what truth? – that it was the recitation of this couplet, with the ending ... *ready to* (pause) *good night, ladies and gentlemen*, that caused Max Miller ('The Cheeky Chappie') to be banned from broadcasting during the 1930s.

when she bumps she bounces occurs since c. 1920, either independently or, with prec. **and**, added to **what ho she bumps!** (Shaw, 1968.) See also **bumps ...**

when the shit (generic) (or **the shit** (specific)) **hits the fan**: also **then the shit'll hit the fan**; and **the shit hit the fan**; and **then the shit hits the fan**, apparently the predominant US form. Leechman says that it is 'a c.p. indicative of grave or exciting consequences': Can. and US: since c. 1930. 'Wait till the major hears that! Then the shit'll hit the fan!' Dr Leechman adds that 'the allusion is to the consequences of throwing this material into an electric fan'. But the orig. ref., as Norman Franklin reminds me, 1976, is to the agricultural muck-spreader.

In *Troubleshooter*, 1971, David Dody writes: '"Otherwise, I'm proud of you, pal. You really emptied your bowels on the table during that last scene. As we used to say in the [US] Navy [during WW2], the shit hit the fan. But good."'

In *Harlequin*, 1974, Morris West writes, '"We'll have it back on the wires in time for the Monday editions here. Same in Europe. Then the shit hits the fan. It might be wise if you went away."'

Col. Moe adds, 1977, that it had, by 1970, became so embedded in US coll. that it can occur in allusive form, as in Hank Searle, *Pentagon*, 1971: '"It's hit the fan, Morrie," Hardy told him. "Can you come down?"'

W & F cite an anecdotal origin [remembered independently by R.C., A.B., and P.B., covering mid 1930s–mid '50s], which is perhaps valid: a guest, unable to find the w.c., uses a hole in the bathroom floor and on rejoining the party, is asked, 'Where were you when the shit hit the fan?' *Si non è vero, è ben trovato.*

when (name) suffers, everybody suffers is 'a c.p. used when a person with a cold, etc., makes everybody else miserable' (B.P.): Aus.: since c. 1930.

when the (bloody) Duke (or Dook) puts his (bloody) foot down, the (bloody) war will be bloody well over. A WW1 c.p., peculiar to the 62nd Division, the ref. being to the divisional sign, a pelican with right foot upraised. F & G.

when the eagle shits. See **golden eagle ...**

when will the ghost walk? See **ghost walks on the walk.**

when yer name's on it, it's on was current in London during 'the London Blitz' of 1940–1. 'Genuine Cockney: if the bomb has

345

your name on it, it will get you, no matter what you do, so stop worrying' (R.S., 1975).

Cf **when you gotta go, you gotta go!**; **bullet with my name on it**; and **it had my name ...**

when you dance in France, the last drop always goes down your pants. This low Aus. c.p. dates from *c.* 1955 and has three stressed words, pronounced *dahnce – France – pahnts* in derision of those who say *dahnce* and *France*, regarded by most Australians as affected, even though they say *bahstard* and *cahstrated*. (B.P.)

On the other hand, 'an American (US) artist gave me this version *c.* 1925: "No matter how much you may wiggle and dance/The last drop inevitably falls in your pants." There was nothing of the long "A" [*ah*] in his version' (Leechman, 1967).

when you gotta go, you gotta go! The US usage (since middle 1930s) perhaps comes from the US gangster films of the 1930s; the Brit. usage (since the middle 1940s) perhaps from 'the London Blitz' of 1940–1 (cf **when yer name's on it, it's on**). 'In universal [US] use and, I think, a real c.p.' (J.W.C., 1975). But, it is 'now used exclusively – in the States – for going to the lavatory' (P.B., 1975). And see **when you've got to go ...**; **when a girl has to go ...**, and **man's gotta do ...**

when you were (just) a gleam in your father's eye. See **I was** [doing something or other] **when you were a gleam ....**

when you were wearing short (or, intensively, **three-cornered**) **pants.** When you were still a boy or (*three-cornered* = diapers) a baby: Aus.: since *c.* 1920. (B.P.) Prompted by the **before you came up** group of c.pp.

when your mother was cutting bread on you. A var. of **before you came up.**

when you're on (or **onto**) **a good thing, stick to it!** Dating from before 1920, it takes the *onto* (or *on to*) form in UK the *on* form in Aus.

when (or **while**) **you're talking about me, you're giving somebody else a rest.** This mainly Can. c.p., which implies slander, dates from before 1949.

when you've got to go, you've got to go. Duty calls: Aus.: since *c.* 1920. 'Often used in frivolous situations, e.g. *re* a visit to the toilet' (B.P., 1975). Cf **when a girl has to go ...** and see **when you gotta go ....**

But in the US, it rather means 'When you have to die, you have to die': since the 1920s. (J.W.C., *et al.*)

when you've seen one, you've seen the lot. They are all the same: C20. (B.P., 1975.) As a gen. statement, it would be a cliché; but it isn't a cliché when it is used by men of females, or by women of males, to mean that when you've seen one sexual organ, you've seen 'em all. (Which is far from being true.)

J.W.C., 1977, notes that Americans prefer '*em all* to *the lot*, and Janssen, 1978, remarks 'Cf the French *Quand on en a vu un, on les a vu tous*. Here, clearly used by males of females'.

where. See: **that's where**; **this is where.**

where did that one go? 'is actually short for *Where did that one go to, Herbert,/Where did that one go?* which comes from a popular wartime song: it was the abbreviation that the soldiers made into a well-used saying and sometimes followed up with: *Theirs or ours?*' (John Brophy, in B & P.) Current in 1915–18 and applied to a shell-burst near by.

where did they dig him up? 'Used in reference to a newcomer who acts queerly' (Petch, 1974): since *c.* 1945. Implying that he acts like a zombie.

where did you get that hat? was very popular in Britain *c.* 1885–1914. From a well-known music-hall song, 'Where did you get that hat?/Where did you get that tile?/[Tumpty-tum ...] just the latest style.' The words of another song so titled, words by Joseph J. Sullivan, started in the US, in 1888 and inaugurated a vogue there too. Cf **who's your hatter?** and **ah there, my size ...**

where did you get that stuff? What a crazy idea!; What crazy ideas!; Where did you hear such crazy nonsense? This US

c.p., apparently dating from *c.* 1919, may orig. have been students'– as McKnight suggested in 1923. In 1936, in the definitive edn of HLM, Mencken quoted a var., *where do you ...?* and included it in a list of c.pp. that possess some appositeness and sense.

'Sometimes *shit* instead of *stuff*. [The synon.] *where do you get off on that?* is common in the northeastern US, esp. New York City' (A.B., 1979).

where did you get the Rossa? – i.e., the borrowed plumes: current in 1885 only, and borrowed from a notorious New York police trial, Ware tells us.

where did you get your licence (, lady) ? Sears Roebuck? A US implication of very poor driving: since *c.* 1970; orig. directed at female drivers; by 1975, at any inferior driver. (Paul Janssen, 1979.) Sears Roebuck: one of the largest and best known of US mail order retailers.

where do flies go in the winter-time? A C20 c.p., drawn from an immensely popular song. In the *Spectator* of 13 Sep. 1935, a Swanage hotel's advertisement began with these fateful words.

where do we go from here? has two periods, set in two countries and bearing two different nuances. In UK, it dates from *c.* 1945, is serious; it applies to, e.g., in political or social or moral or economic state of the country, as in 'Well, you see what the situation is. So where do we go from here?'; 'In what directions can we improve matters and how shall we go about doing so?' It occurs in, e.g., Alan Gardner's novel, *The Man Who Was Too Much*, 1967, and perhaps more notably in Noël Coward's *Design for Living*, prod. in 1932 and pub'd in 1933, at I, i:

GILDA: Last year was bad enough. This is going to be far worse.

LEO: Why be scared?

GILDA: Where do we go from here? That's what I want to know.

But the better known sense, at least in the US where it orig., is 'What do we do next?' – as Berrey, 1942, explains it; a meaning loosely synon. with that of Brit. usage, but employed in very different, often rather trivial, circumstances.

In *DD* Oliver Herford refers to the US usage – to the matured years of that usage – with this entry: 'HEREAFTER. An evasive answer to the GREAT QUESTION: "Where do we go from here?"'

In *The Glory of the Coming*, 1919, Irvin S. Cobb wrote (very near the end of chapter I):

Not a man aboard the *Tuscania*, [carrying, in February 1918, a contingent of US troops for the Fr. front] whether sailor or soldier, showed weakness or fright. ... Descending over the side, some of them to be saved, those American lads of ours [glorified] what before then had been a meaningless, trivial jingle. ... Perry said: 'We have met the enemy, and they are ours.' Lawrence said: 'Don't give up the ship!' Farragut said: 'Damn the torpedoes, go ahead.' Dewey said: 'You may fire, Gridley, when you are ready.' Our history is full of splendid sea slogans, but I think there can never be a more splendid one that we Americans will cherish than the first line, which is also the title of the song now suddenly freighted with a meaning and a message to American hearts, which our boys sang that black February night in the Irish Sea when two hundred of them ... went over the sides of *Tuscania* to death: 'Where do we go from here, boys, where do we go from here?'

Related to Cobb's passage is this matter from, and about, J.P. Marquand's *H.M. Pulham, Esq.*, serialized, as *Gone Tomorrow*, in *McCall's Magazine*, in 1940, then pub'd as a book in 1941; matter I owe to Prof. Harold Shapiro, who, 1974, writes from the University of North Carolina at Chapel Hill:

J.P. Marquand, who always made very effective use of catch phrases in his novels, uses this one in Chapter

XXI...headed 'Goodby to All That'...The chapter opens: 'Now and then, even as late as 1920, it was not difficult to hear someone humming "Where Do We Go from Here"'–and continues with references to the song. But it is quite clear from the next page (p. 225) that the phrase had come into common use by 1920 quite apart from the song. (Marquand is ordinarily very accurate in such matters.) A character gets off the train in Boston and says: 'Well, where do we go from here?' Then the song is picked up again. There are further references later in the same chapter.

Clearly, therefore, the song had achieved an immense popularity by 1918; it was pub'd in 1917, with words by Wenrick and music by Johnson. For some further account of the song, consult–if you happen to be in the US–S.M. Smith and T. Morse's *Good Old Timers, c.* 1922, as Minnie Sears's *Song Index Supplement*, 1934, bids one do.

The song had become popular in Can. by late 1918. Rear-Adm. P.W. Brock tells me that he was familiar with it in late 1918 or very early 1919, while he was a cadet at the Royal Naval College of Canada; that it was sung on 16 Oct. by RNC cadets at Halifax; and that the last two lines of the chorus were

When Pat would see a pretty girl, he'd whisper in her ear
Oh joy! Oh boy! where do we go from here?

A.B., 1979, notes a US var., *which way from here?*

where do you get that stuff? See **where did you ...**

where do you think you are? On daddy's yacht? See **what do you think this is? Daddy's yacht?**

where have you been all my life? has expressed exaggerated flattery from a fellow to a girl, or occ. vice versa, since the early 1920s; it implies 'What I've missed in life until you came along!' Orig. US, it doesn't seem to have become well established in UK and the Commonwealth until *c.* 1942, but that it was very well established in US by *c.* 1925 at latest appears from the fact that it could be employed allusively as early as in Clarence B. Kelland's *Dance Magic*, 1927:

'Who is Leach Norcott?'

'Where have you been all our lives? Whoops, my dear! Leach is a bearcat and I don't mean maybe.'

Kelland used the phrase in other novels–e.g., *No Escape*, 1951.

An English example occurs in, e.g., James Eastwood, *The Chinese Visitor*, 1965: 'The girl was obviously attracted, receiving the Grade A treatment, eyes only for you, where've you been all my life, [all] done to a Duty-and-Love routine.'

In Thomas Shadwell's comedy, *Epsom Wells*, 1673, at I, ii (lines 540–1 in D.M. Walmsley's edn), occurs an adumbration. Two 'men of wit and pleasure' speak of two girls newly met and respectively admired:

BEV[IL]: By Heaven a Divine Creature!

RAINS: Beyond all comparison. Where have I lived?

The pairing affords an amusing example of the prevalence of thought-patterns in human communication: a mode of thinking determines a similarity in expression. Only an influence fanatic would suggest that someone reading Shadwell was thereby prompted to 'think up' *where have you been all my life?* Cf **does your mother know you're out?**

where I'm coming from. See **do you know where I'm coming from?**

where it gets dark. This evasive S. African underworld c.p., dating since *c.* 1920, if not a decade or two earlier, is explained in the *Cape Times* of 23 May 1946: 'If he'–a crook–'has no fixed place of abode, then he lives "where it gets dark".' Origin? Either 'in the native quarter' of a town or city; or semantically related to the NZ and Aus. cant phrase, *in smoke*, in hiding.

where it was to be had: where the devil had (or got) the friar. See S, 1738, Dialogue I, where Neverout, looking at Miss Notable's handsome ring, asks '...pray, where did you get

it?' and she pertly replies, 'Why where it was to be had; where the Devil got the Fryar.' This C17–18 c.p. is explained by a passage in Davenport, 1639: 'Where the devil had the friar, but where was he?'–wherever it happened to be. Apperson.

where it's at. See **where the action is.**

where Maggie wore the beads. She wore them where most women (and now men too) wear them, around the neck; hence 'in the neck', disagreeably, unfortunately, disastrously, fatally–'where', in short, 'the chicken got the axe', q.v. Current *c.* 1905–30. Weekley.

where men are men and women are glad of it (or **like it; or are double-breasted**) are c.p. expressions of the cliché *where men are men:* C20: predominantly US. (Col. Moe, 1975.)

Concerning early C20 Brit. use, however, Mr S.G. Dixon, 1978, recalls '*where men are men and Fred Barnes counts for sex*. Told me ...*c.* 1920. Fred Barnes was an undersized music-hall star'. Noble suggests that this version was perhaps occ. used in derision, and refers us to Daniel Farson, *Marie Lloyd and Music Hall*, 1972.

where (or **out where**) **the bull feeds** (or **gets his bleeding, or bloody, breakfast**). In the outback, the backblocks, a remote country district: Aus.: C20. Baker.

where the chicken got the axe is the originator of **where Maggie wore the beads**, q.v. Orig. US, it began life in 1892, in a song thus titled, the words being by Harry Mayo. It went to England *c.* 1893 and was slightly ob. by 1936, yet not extinct even by 1975, though noticeably moribund. (W.J.B., 1975, and Weekley.)

where the crows fly backwards to keep the dust out of their eyes. A joc. Aus. ref., late C19–20, to any godforsaken place in the outback (*the Woop-woop*, as it is often called). It orig. in a verse of the ribald recitation known as *The Showman*.

where the deception took place is a C20 c.p., applied to courtship and marriage. It is–as if you needed to be told–a pun on '...where the *reception* took place'. (Petch, 1966.)

where the dirty work's done. 'Office, workshop or room where any work or business is carried on. Mostly used jocularly' (Petch, 1946): since *c.* 1919.

where the dogs don't bite (–**the place**). Prison; in prison: English, mostly London, underworld: *c.* 1870–1960. Arthur Morrison *A Child of the Jago*, 1896, has, 'He was marched away, and so departed for the place–in Jago idiom–where the dogs don't bite.'

where the flies won't get it is used when one downs a drink: late C19–20. US before it became Brit., according to Ware in 1909.

where the nuts came from tends to be heard when either Barcelona or Brazil is mentioned: mostly lower-middle class. (Petch, 1974.) Obviously by association with 'Barcelona nuts' and 'Brazil nuts'. As Shipley points out, 1977, it could have arisen as early as 1893, for the farce *Charley's Aunt*, written by Brandon Thomas, 'opened in London on 12 Dec. 1892, and ran for a record 1406 performances. It has been played in 22 languages, including Esperanto. It was [converted] into a musical, *Where's Charley?*–still revived and popular at [US] summer theatres. In the play, Dona Lucia d'Alvadorez, left a fortune by her husband, is returning to England. Charley needs a chaperone to have the girls to his college rooms; and one of his undergraduate friends disguises himself as "Charley's aunt from Brazil–where the nuts come from"'.

Cf **still running** ...

where the pig bit yer! A vaguely minatory, slightly facetious, proletarian version of *bugger you!*: C20. (Shaw, 1969.)

where was Moses when the light went out? Granville, 1917, says:

A fatuous phrase that was coined, I think, during the First World War Zeppelin raid periods of 1915–16 when the street lights were dimmed and the youths in the 'monkey runs' of the main streets [of London] used to call [it] out when the dimming took place.

It was still heard occ. as late as the 1930s. But why *Moses?* But the c.p. may have come from the US. Dr Edward Hodnett tells me, 1975, that, in his childhood, if lights went out, children would chant:

Where was Moses when the light went out?

– Down in the cellar eating sauerkraut.

Derivatively, *where were you when the light* (US) – or *lights (Brit.) – went out?* is addressed to a couple obviously in love or suspected of venery, or to a male or a female missing a dance and not visible: C20. It occurs in, e.g., John Mortimer's *David and Broccoli*, 1960.

This derivation form prob. derives from the music-hall song, 'Where were you when the lights went out?'

But, in the US, much earlier, where clearly the whole thing orig. as a juvenile conundrum, as Mark Twain showed in *Huckleberry Finn*, 1884; and that conundrum, that joke, as J.W.C. has remarked, prob. existed decades earlier – and not only in the US but in the UK and throughout the Colonies; I heard it as a child [1890s]. The answer was *in the dark*. Levene, 1983, draws attention to Joyce's allusive use of the phrase in *Ulysses*, set in *c*. 1906: 'What selfevident enigma pondered ... during 30 years did Bloom now– ... comprehend? Where was Moses when the candle went out?', which, he adds, would take it back to 1876 at latest, given Joyce's care for period detail. When, precisely, childhood's conundrum became an adult c.p., I can't say – all I know is that I heard it as a c.p. as early as 1912 or '13. Cf **put the lights out.**

[where you stand is where you sit. In the *S.F. Chronicle*, 3 Jan. 1979, there is a short article titled 'Words that Irk the Unicorns' in which occurs the passage: 'A Washington Phrase Alert was issued for "Where you stand is where you sit." This new jargon apparently means [that] one's philosophy and opinions are based on one's job, said [Prof. Peter] Thomas.' Lit., therefore, 'where you stand (in life) depends on where you sit (at work)'. Clearly, it orig. among desk men, seat-of-pants polishers: the higher in the hierarchy, the larger the office, the better the carpet, the more comfortable the chair.

But this saying cannot be jargon: the language is far too simple and lucid. It could very easily, and very soon, fall into the waste-paper baskets; yet, in essence, it is a c.p., a good one, and, from potential, it could achieve the status of c.p. It will be interesting to see what has happened by the time the 2nd ed. of this book appears. (Note of 6 Feb. 1979.) P.B.: I can report, exactly 5 years later, following enquiry of knowledgeable US correspondents: nothing.]

where's George? See **George – let's join.**

where's he coming from? is an almost inevitable c.p. evolution from the coll. *where* (one) *is coming from*, a pompous verbosity for one's view-point or 'ego state', current in US mid 1970s. E.P. went to much trouble with this phrase, asked many learned American friends, and covered a sheet of foolscap with notes and names: but the whole reduces to no more than an ephemeral example of 'psychobabble', as implied in *Encounter*, July 1978: 'Fashionable phrases appear and submerge with startling rapidity in trendy U.S. society. The latest cool expression for "I understand" beats most. It is "I know where you're coming from"'. (P.B.)

where's the beef? I cannot do better than quote, with the very kind permission of the *Financial Times*, an article that appeared on the paper's front page of 5 Apr. 1984. Reginald Dale, the *FT*'s US Editor in Washington, wrote:

With her delivery of one short, sharp question in an American TV hamburger commercial, an 82-year-old grandmother has become overnight a national celebrity, entered into advertising folklore, and just possibly affected the outcome of this year's U.S. presidential election.

Mrs Clara Peller, a retired manicurist, stars as one of three elderly ladies presented with a sizeable-looking hamburger in a restaurant called 'Home of the Big Bun'. They admire the bun, but there is only a small sliver of meat inside. Mrs Peller picks up

the phone to the owner and with great, but controlled indignation, demands: 'Where's the beef?'

The aim of the 30-second spot was to increase what is known as customer 'size perception' in favour of Wendy's, the third biggest U.S. hamburger chain after McDonald's and Burger King. What it has done, as US. advertisers might say, is much, much more.

'Where's the beef?' has become the most faddish slogan in the nation. Last month, it burst into national politics when Mr Lane Kirland, president of the AFL-CIO, the country's largest labour federation, used it to attack what he regards as the insubstantial 'new ideas' politics of presidential aspirant Senator Gary Hart of Colorado.

Former Vice-President Walter Mondale re-plagiarised it the following day, putting the question directly to Mr Hart in the middle of a televised campaign debate in Atlanta. 'When I hear your "new ideas" I'm reminded of that ad, "where's the beef?"' he chided.

Since then, the slogan, or variations on it, has appeared on the covers of national magazines, in TV comedy shows and news programmes and on Mondale campaign tee shirts. Mondale supporters took to waving empty hamburger buns at campaign rallies. ... It is probably by far the most effective swipe that Mr Mondale has taken at his opponent in the campaign so far.

Mr Dale's article went on to discuss the slogan's commercial significance and future prospects. (P.B.)

where's the body? is US, glossed by Berrey as 'why so sorrowful?': *c*. 1920–70.

where's the fire? has, since *c*. 1930, been addressed, would-be humorously to someone in a tearing hurry. Perhaps orig. US; Dr Edward Hoodnett, 1975, writes: 'A common salutation by a motorcycle cop on overtaking a speeding motorist and waving him to a halt. By extension when someone is in an unseemly hurry or makes a hasty proposal.' A good example occurs in Hartley Howard, *Room 37*, 1970:

He did it as if he had no time to waste.

I said, 'Where's the fire?'

'Fire, sir?'

'You know darn well what I mean.... Anyway, what's all the rush?'

Cf Alan Gardner, *The Man Who Was Too Much*, 1967:

'I've been trying to find you for hours.'

'We open at nine-thirty and it is not yet midday,' observed Ivan. 'As my American friends might ask – where is the fire?'

But perhaps more revealing is the fact that, in *Still Life*, 1936, Noël Coward could write, in Scene III:

MYRTLE: ... I'll trouble you to get out of here double quick....

JOHNNIE: 'Ere, where's the fire – where's the fire?

'When used by a policeman to a woman driver, the answer is "In your eyes, gorgeous!" – but she has to be young and attractive to get away with it' (Sanders, 1978). This c.p. reply dates from *c*. 1950.

where's the kitchen sink? See **you've forgotten the piano.**

where's the war? was, in 1900–1, directed at a street wrangle: London streets'. From scattered fighting in the Boer War. (Ware.) Cf **come to the Russian war.**

where's yer white stick? See LIVERPOOL CATCH PHRASES.

where's your violin? – implying 'You need a hair-cut' – was an Aus. c.p. of the late 1940s, the 1950s, the earlier 1960s. From a tradition that male musicians wear their hair long. (B.P.) Once so many males of the Western World began to wear their hair long, such hairiness no longer caused any comment.

'It got to a point where I had to get a haircut or a violin': Franklin D. Roosevelt (1882–1945). See Nicholas Bentley's delightful anthology, *The Treasury of Humorous Quotations*, 1951.

whether or no, Tom Collins is a phrase among sailors, signifying, whether you will or not' (W. N. Glascock, *Sailors* *and Saints*, 1829, at chapter II, p. 7): very approx. *c.* 1820–50. A var., perhaps rather the orig., is *Tom Collins, whether or no*, occurring in Alfred Burton, *Johnny Newcome*, 1818. (I owe these to Col. Moe, 1959.)

which is where we came in. See **this is where...**

which shall we do, or go fishing? See **what shall we do...**, and cf:

which side do you shake it? See **do one for me.**

which would you rather be, or a wasp? A London schoolchildren's c.p. of *c.* 1905–14. Julian Franklyn compares **or would you rather be a fish?** and adds, 'So far as I remember, there was no standard reply.'

See also **what shall we do...**, and cf the var. of that, *which would you rather, or go fishing?*

while I'm standing I'm going was a smart c.p. of *c.* 1700–50. It occurs in S, 1738, Dialogue I:

COL[ONEL]: No, Madam, while I'm *standing, I'm going.*

The meaning: 'I'm able and ready to go'. Possible implication: 'I'm still alive'.

while the going is good. See **beat it!**

while there's life, there's hope; and while there's Hope, there's Crosby. A US c.p., going back to mid C20 and now†. A ref. to the long and entertaining partnership between the comedian Bob Hope and the crooner Bing Crosby. (From a young American, a few days before Bing died in Oct. 1977.) Cf:

while there's life there's soap is a C20 would-be joc. var., little heard after *c.* 1950, of the old proverb, ... *there's hope.*

while you're talking about me.... See **when you're talking....**

whim-wham for a goose's bridle;...for a treacle mill; for ducks to perch on, etc. See **weaving leather aprons.**

whip. See: Christian-born; fair go.

whirl. See: give it a w.

whisker(s). See: attitude; dam of that; enough to put; mother of that.

whiskers down to here (– he has, or he's got). A low c.p. (spoken only) of C20; rare after *c.* 1940; † by 1950. Simultaneously with the utterance of *here*, the speaker placed his hand on his trouser flap.

whiskers on it – it's (or that's) **got.** See **it's got bells on.**

whisky. See: gentleman.

whistle. See: and no w.; if you want anything; piss when; she will say.

whistling. See: can't believe; you ain't just.

whistling in the pictures, lit. at a cinema. A standard Aus. answer to a question the addressee doesn't wish to answer specifically: since *c.* 1960. (Jim Ramsay, *Cop It Sweet*, 1977.) Cf **weaving leather aprons.**

white. See: damn' white; I'd do; mighty white; no good for; she thinks; two white; who stole the donkey; and:

[**white and spiteful,** sometimes prec. by **all.** 'One of my colleagues [recently] returned to work after a bout of 'flu. Asked how she was feeling, she replied, "A bit better than I was, but still white and spiteful".' As applied to women, it orig. as a description of a physical and moral condition accompanying menstrual pains. Sometimes *all white and spiteful* refers to a child 'allowed to stay up long past its normal bedtime' (P.B., 1975): since 1945, at the least, and prob. since *c.* 1900. It teeters between cliché (menstruation) and c.p. (all other applications).]

white ants. See: doesn't know.

white man speak with forked tongue. 'A c.p. from old Western films' (Ashley, 1983). Prof. Ashley offers this as one of the 'genuine' quotations-become-c.pp. (as opp., e.g. **come with me to the Casbah**); spoken by 'noble savage' North American Indians – was it, perhaps, orig. a literal translation from one of the Indian languages, or merely inspired script-writing? – about the too often double-crossing European in-comers. Now applied, as c.p., to chicanery among the Whites themselves. (P.B.)

[**white rabbits!** – often shortened to **rabbits!** A South of England greeting on the first day of every month; equivalent to 'Good luck!' C19–20. Not a true c.p.: it's folklore. P.B.: not only South, but almost all UK. And not so much a greeting as a good luck incantation to be muttered to oneself before any other word may be spoken. See esp. Iona & Peter Opie, *The Lore and Language of Schoolchildren*, 1959, p. 300.]

white spruce. See: hop and.

white-topped. See: blue-stockinged.

Whitehall. See: he's been to W.

whiter than the Whitehouse on the wall. 'Used occasionally for those who support Mrs Whitehouse and Lord Longford' (Petch, 1974): 1973–4. In ref. to their campaign for purity in films, and in life in general: and with a pun on *whiter than snow* – on the *whiter than white* of detergents advertising – and on the coll. phrase, *whiter than the whitewash on the wall*. Like most such c.pp., it had a brief life.

whites of their eyes. See **don't fire...**

whitewash. See: if it moves.

whitey whitey kay. See TOMMY HANDLEY.

who, See: here's how; it's not what; kill who; says who; yes, but who; you, and who.

who am I to contradict (him, here, etc.)? (**—and**) is a c.p. only where, following praise of the speakers, it expresses *mock-modesty*, as in 'He claims I'm a genius—and who am *I* to contradict him?' Both Brit. and US: post-WW2 (Owed to R.C., 1978.)

who are these guys (anyway)? This question, in which the 'anyway' has no textual basis, arose from the film *Butch Cassidy and the Sundance Kid*, 1969, rapidly caught on among young people, esp. Americans, but seems to have died out *c.* 1976. Mr R.W. Burchfield, CBE, the very eminent lexicographer, interviewed on 'Kaleidoscope', 5 Sep. 1977, pointed to its absence from the first ed. of this book. (With the permission of the BBC, and thanks to the producer, Miss Rosemary Hart; and thanks also to R.W.B. himself.)

who *are* yer (or **you)?/Who are *you*?** An offensive enquiry and the truculent answer: London streets': 1883 (Ware); by 1950, ob. But, in this remarkable pioneering article, Mackay tells us that *who are you?* succeeded *does you mother know you're out?* as the regnant phrase and then says.

Every alley resounded with it; every highway was musical with it,

'And street to street, and lane to lane flung back The one unvarying cry.'

The phrase was uttered quickly, and with a sharp sound upon the first and last words, leaving the middle one little more than an aspiration. Like all its compeers which had been extensively popular it was applicable to almost every variety of circumstance.

Apparently *who are you* (or *yer*)? reigned in the middle and later 1830s, and then, as a c.p., disappeared to live, as it were underground, a more modest life; then it reappeared in 1883 and, in a second period of popularity, acquired the dovetail.

who are you calling 'dirty face'? See **who're you...?**

'who are you shoving (or **pushing)?' said the elephant to the flea.** A joc. c.p., uttered by a big – or, at the least, a noticeably bigger man – jostled, or knocked into, by a small man: since *c.* 1920 (Petch.)

who asked you to put in your two cents' worth? 'Who asked you for an opinion or advice?' – esp. when neither advice nor opinion had been sought: US: since *c.* 1945. (W & F.) See also **two cents' worth.**

who ate (or **stole) the cat?** Directed at pilferers: mid C19–20: ob. by 1920,† by 1950. Prob. from an actual incident.

who boiled the bell?; and who hanged (but usu. **hung) the monkey?** On the Clyde, both: in the N. Country, the latter, supposed to have derived from an incident at Hartlepool. Derisive.

who called the cook a *bastard*?**/Who called the bastard a** *cook?* 'Complementary, but scarcely complimentary, rhetorical remarks passed in disparagement of the cook's efforts' (*SS*): Services': since early 1900s. As a private in the Australian Army, WW1, I heard it rather often. During WW2 and esp. since *c.* 1950, a coarser, alliterative word has often been used for *bastard*.

who curled your hair? See **who's your hatter?**

who dat up dere? is 'the first line of a dialogue which must, I think, have originated with the... Nigger Minstrels of the 1880s, presumably in the US. Funny story about two Black men in the dark, one at the top of a ladder..., the other at the bottom. Dialogue: "Who dat up dere?" – "Who dat down dere saying who dat up dere?" – "Who dat up dere saying who dat down dere saying who dat up dere...", &c, &c, &c. I've heard this line very recently' (Derek Parker, 1977). P.B.: and, indeed, its popularity continues undiminished.

who dealt this mess? 'American card-players say this of a very bad hand; applicable to other situations as well. A synon. card-playing c.p. is *I've got a duke's mixture*, of obscure origin. Since *c.* 1930, perhaps earlier' (A.B., 1979). P.B.: cf the synon. Brit. *I've got a hand like a foot*.

who did yer (or **you**) **say?** Levelled at a person of evident, or self-asserting, importance, and uttered by one friend to another, during the 1890s, in the streets of language-inventive London. Ware.

who died and left you God? That is, in the will. 'Who gave you the right to behave so arrogantly?' One of the most trenchant of all c. pp., it has been current, although never quite a vogue, since *c.* 1930. (Thanks to Mr Simon Levene, 1977.)

who do you like? See **what do you think?**

[**who do you think you are?** Clark Gable? A feminine, esp. teenagers', gibe, addressed to a youth, or a young man, obviously fancying himself as a Lothario: since the 1930s; very common in the 1940s too, although declining in popularity since the famous US film actor's death. Gable had a dashing and debonair, self-assured manner–at least, in the majority of his films. Heard on British TV as late as early Jan. 1972. [E.P. later added:] It lies on the borderline between cliché and c.p. and is, I've come to think after much consideration, rather the former than the latter. The promoter of that re-thinking is J.W.C., who writes, 1977: 'Alone, or with any famous name, a cliché, universal, usually hostile or combative in tone, addressed to one putting on airs, assuming authority, or the like'.]

who does what, and with which...? 'A request for enlightenment in a confusing situation. From the last line of a famous limerick:

A Lesbian from Khartoum
Took a fairy up to her room.
As she turned out the light
He said, "Let's get this right:
Who does what, with which, and to whom?"

American: from 1920s or earlier' (R.C., 1978). *Fairy* in the slang sense, 'male homosexual'. P.B.: the limerick is equally well-known in UK, where *nancy-boy* often replaces *fairy*, and the first line is made to scan.

who d'you do? is a C20 Liverpool petty crooks' fraternal greeting. Lit. 'whom have you cheated or defrauded recently?' (Shaw, 1969)

who got yer (or **you**) **ready?** (The *yer* form belongs to Merseyside and several other parts of England.) Lit., 'Who took your ready money?' This is a scornful and deflating phrase: C20. (Shaw, 1968.) Cf **we had dozens of these.**

who has any land (or **lands**) **in Appleby?** See **how lies the land?**

who hit Billy Patterson? See **who struck...**

who ho she bumps. A joc. var. of *what ho...*, q.v. at **bumps.** (Leechman, 1971.)

who hung the monkey? See **who boiled the bell?**

who is at your elbow? A late C17–mid C18 warning to a liar. (BE.) The implication: 'There is One who hears.'

who is he (or **she**) **when he** (or **she**) **is at home?** See **what is that...?**

who is 'she'? A (or **the**) **cat's mother** is a var. of **'She' is a cat's mother.**

who kicked your kennel (or **pig-sty**)**?** Who asked *you* to interfere?, *or* Mind your own business! A lower-middle-class c.p.: C20. Cf **who pulled your chain?** and **who rattled your cage?**

who laid the chunk. See **from who laid...**

who let you out? 'When a person shows himself very cute and clever, another says to him, "Who let you out?" – an ironical expression of fun: as much as to say that he must have been confined in an asylum as a confirmed fool' (P. W. Joyce, *English... in Ireland*, 1910): Anglo-Irish: late C19–20; by 1940, slightly – by 1960, very – outmoded. Occ. heard outside of Ireland.

who looks at the mantelpiece when poking the fire? A common rejoinder to an adverse comment about a young woman's face. It has the air of a proverb, cf **a standing prick hath no conscience.** 'I have also heard more than once the callous "You could always stick a sack (or bucket) over her head"' (P.B., 1975).

Also, of course, in the form *you don't look at the mantelpiece when* (or *while*) *you're poking the fire*, where the ref. is specifically, as R.C., 1976, points out, 'to a woman of plain countenance but abundant other charms'. A fairly representative example of the kind of thing one overhears in a reputable 'pub'.

...*when you poke the fire* occurs in 'Number One' of John Osborne's *The Entertainer*, 1957.

who loves ya, baby? 'certainly caught on; though the time has now come when one wishes it would drop off', remarked Ian Sainsbury in the Sheffield *Morning Telegraph*, 5 Sep. 1977, reviewing the first ed. of this book, and after handsomely admitting that is was 'probably too recent to be included here'. It caught on, in UK, if I remember rightly, in late 1975 or early '76.

John Skehan, writing a fortnight later from Dublin, to exemplify his statement that 'Television is spawning a whole new batch' of c.pp., says, 'I think *who loves ya, baby?* may have been used for some little time, but it became common parlance as a result of its constant use by a TV character – a New York [City] police lieutenant called Kojak (played by the actor Telly Savalas)... Addressed to anyone in virtually any context, it could probably best be defined as a [phrase] of affectionate dismissal, not calling for any reply'. It has been so [much] used that it has already nearly lost currency'.

Col. Moe, noting that the first series of *Kojak* started 24 Oct. 1973. and the second, 2 Oct. 1977, adds that Lieutenant Kojak usu. closes each episode by consolatorily saying this to the person in trouble as he pats him on the cheek. Kojak turns away and the scene ends, with the manacled man, suspected of murder, or other grave crime, making no reply. The other memorable thing about the tough cop is his incongruous love of lollipops, which gave rise to a fashion among sweet-makers in UK.

who needs it? 'I neither need nor want it. By implication, nobody needs it. American: since *c.* 1950' (R.C., 1978).

who pawned her sister's ship? A Clare Market, London, c.p. of *c.* 1897–9, directed offensively at a woman. Ware shrewdly conjectured *shift* corrupted.

who pulled your chain? Who asked you to interfere?, *or*, less politely Mind your own ruddy business. It dates from *c.* 1910; it was much used by 'the troops' during WW1; and, *c.* 1919, from being somewhat low, it acquired a certain, although modified, social grace – as why should it not? It's genuinely witty. (B & P, 1930.) Clearly from the noise made by the pulling of a w.c. chain. Cf **who kicked...**

who put that monkey on horseback without tying his tail? A cheeky, London streets' insult hurled at a bad horseman: (very roughly) *c.* 1760–1830. Grose, 1788; but in the 3rd edn, 1796, Grose has *legs* for *tail*.

who rattled (or **who's rattling**) **your cage?** 'What's bugging you?' – 'What's disturbing – or perturbing – you?' See that really rattled... Cf **who kicked your kennel?**

who robbed the barber? See that's a rhyme.

who says so? See oh, is that so?

who shot the cat (or the dog)? A stock reproach shouted at the Volunteers: London streets': 1850s and 1860s – and presumably it went underground, to re-emerge in OTCs, where it remained extant until c. 1940 at least.

who shot who? 'Asked of a person who has attended a meeting at which the questioner seems to think that "the fur would fly", I heard it [in US] during the 1940s–60s' (A.B., 1979).

who stole the cat? See who ate...?

who stole the donkey? – to which a second person would sometimes add **the man in** (or **with**) **the white hat**; a man wearing such a hat as a donkey might, in a very hot summer, wear supplies the occasion: c. 1835–1900. (The late Prof. Arnold Wall, 1939.) Said to have arisen from a specific incident.

who stole the goose? '(*People's – provincial.*) Interjection of contempt, which appears to have some erotic meaning, probably of an erotic nature' (Ware, who gives no date):? C19–earch C20.

who stole the mutton? Jeeringly addressed to a policeman: c. 1835–60. From the failure of the police to detect the culprit in a theft of mutton. Brewer.

who stole your scone? 'What are you worrying – or making a fuss – about? The matter, or incident, doesn't affect you; indeed it isn't your concern, is it?' A C20 Scottish c.p. (Marjorie Crawford, 1977.)

who stuck Billy Patterson? In that invaluable work, *An American Glossary*, 1912, R.H. Thornton defines this as 'a ludicrous question admitting of no reply', and cites two references from *The Yale Literacy Magazine*: the earlier, of 1847, 'Di-lemma – *Who struck William Patterson?*'; the later, 1858, 'who was the Man in the Iron Mask? Was there ever such a book as "De Tribus Impostoribus"? Who struck Billy Patterson? Who hit dis nigger?' Note that *William* never formed part of the c.p.; it is here merely an academic jocosity. Clearly, by 1847, the c.p. was very well established – so well, that it had already to be regarded as a part of American folklore. I'd guess that this c.p. went back to c. 1820, if not as far as 1800. Cf:

who struck Buckley? was, in C19, employed to irritate Irishmen. The origin is obscure, even though Hotten offers a plausible and amusing story.

It went to Aus.: there recorded for 1885 in Steward & Keesing's *Old Bush Songs* (1957), and it occurs in that Aus. classic, *Such is Life*, by Joseph Furphy, 1903. (Wilkes, *Dict. Aus. Coll.*) I'd say that it was † by c. 1940.

who suffers? In II, ii, of *John Bull, or The Englishman's Fireside*, pub'd 1803, George Colman the Younger causes the Hon. Tom Shuffleton, a young man-about-town, to say to his rural friend, Frank Rochdale, 'Psha! damn it, don't shake your head. Mine's a mere *façon de parler:* just as we talk to one another about our coats: we never say, "Who's your tailor?" We always ask, "Who suffers?"' This, then, would seem to have been, c. 1780–1830, a c.p. current among young men of fashion. The tailors *suffered* because they had to wait so long for their bills to be paid.

who told yer (or **you**)? Ironic for 'We *all* know that' or 'Queen Anne's dead': since c. 1925. (Shaw, 1969.)

who told you to say that? A deflating remark 'to a chap trying to be witty. Liverpool: since 1920s' (Shaw, 1968) – but not only Liverpool: indeed, A.B., 1979, notes the US var. *who taught you...*

who took it out of you? A low London c.p., addressed, c. 1890–1914, to a man looking either utterly dejected or washed-out. (Ware.) Sexual implication?

who was that masked man? See hi-ho, Silver!

who was the best man here before I came in? A jocular expression sometimes heard when a man enters a pub,

canteen, etc.' (Petch, 1974): since the late 1940s.

who was your lackey last year? In *The Letter Bag of the Great Western*, 1840, T. C. Haliburton, 'Whenever I asked one of them [the crew of a passenger boat] to help me, he said, "It's my turn below": or, "It's my turn on deck"; and, "Who was your lackey last year?" or, "Does your mother know you're out?"' Clearly meaning 'I'm not a servant – do it yourself', this was an English c.p. of c. 1820–70. Cf **when did your last servant die?**

who were you with last night? This became a c.p. in 1915, orig. in the army. Soldiers derived it from the opening line of a very popular music-hall song dating from a few years before WW1. Although the c.p. hasn't been much heard since 1939, it is not yet (1976) † .

Who were you with last night,
Out in the pale moonlight?
It wasn't your sister
And it wasn't your ma –
I saw ya, I saw ya!

The troops sang it either vigorously or with a mock sentimentality. B & P, 1931.

who would be a mother?! Feminine: since c. 1920, if not very much earlier. (Fernley, O. Pascoe, 1975.)

who would have thought it? occurs in John Day's *Law-Tricks or, Who Would Have Thought It*, 1608; in *P*, 1639, and many times since, for it is characteristic of a fool to ask this question or to say 'I should not have thought it' (*Insipentis dicere, Non putarem*). See Stevenson.

R.C., 1978, notes Kipling's use of the slovened *who'd ha' thought it*, in his schoolboy stories of c. 1880, *Stalky & Co.*, 1899, and also 'the mock-rural (or perhaps mock-illiterate) version, *who'da thunk it?* [which] was current in US from c. 1930, but [is] now extinct'. In late C19–20 there was a further var., *whoever would have thought it?*, with – *ever* heavily stressed.

who wouldn't sell a farm and go to sea? and **who'd** (or **who'll**) **sell his farm and go to sea?** These are nautically synon. c.pp. spoken when something very unpleasant or extremely difficult has to be done. Bowen records the former: *Sailors' Slang* says of the latter: 'Old naval expression varied by *sell the pig and buy me out.*' They prob. date from c. 1870 and were not, even by 1975, † .

'Varied, in the US, to *who wouldn't sell out and the ship out?* or *!* Meaning "to liquidate all one's assets and take them away, going as far as possible". Or more vulgarly, *it's time to get the shit out of Dodge*, orig. a ref. to *Dodge*, a city in Nebraska, and *Dodge City*, one in Kansas. Both were frontier towns (forts, at first) in American migrations to the West' (A.B., 1979).

who'll sell his farm and go to sea? See prec.

who're you (or **who yer**) **calling 'dirty face'?** Writing about the latter half of 1916 in his WW1 novel, *Medal without Bar*, 1930, Richard Blaker, from the viewpoint of an Artillery officer, says: '"'Oo yer calling dirty-face" became a standardised pleasantry in the light of a lantern held to a cigarette-stump, from drivers turned muleteer ("the cavalry" as the gunners called them).'

who're you kidding? Who do you think you're fooling? US: C20. Hence Brit.: since c. 1919.

According to J.W.C., 1977, the more usual US form is *who do you think you're kidding?*, and A.B., 1979, adds, 'Popular among US teenagers is *who're you putting on?* or *who're you trying to put on?* Kin to the slangy *you're puttin(g) me on!* – implying "I don't believe you!" Current, but I can't date it before the 1960s'.

who's a pretty boy then? P.B., 1975, writes: 'Conventional form of address to the *psittaci*; may be misapplied' and thus become a c.p. 'I enjoyed a pocket-cartoon showing Count Dracula thus addressing a vampire bat.'

who's afraid of the big bad wolf? is a gen., rather vague c.p. of defiance: since 1933. It comes from Ann Ronell's popular song in Walt Disney's *Three Little Pigs*, 1933, according to

BQ. I think that Benham must be wrong when he cites 'Who's afeared of the Big Bad Wolf?' as a song written *c*.1936 by Frank Churchill (d. 1942), for W.J.B., 1975, glossed the *Three Little Pigs* song thus, 'This is the song that helped Americans lick the depression of the early 1930s.' The fame of that song – whatever its title – and, still more, the vogue of the phrase may have prompted the titling of Edward Albee's play, *Who's Afraid of Virginia Woolf?* – which, in 1962–3, met with a remarkable, and a remarkably well deserved, success. R.C., 1978, tells me that the song 'was actually sung during the play. During the rehearsal, the original Disney tune was used, but because of copyright problems, "Nuts in May" had to be substituted'.

who's been at the knife-box today? See **you're so sharp...**

who's counting? A Jewish c.p., as in:
'Have another cake, Mr Levy.'
'I'd love to, my dear, but I've already had three.'
'Excuse me, you've had four – but who's counting?'
One of those Jewish ironic, anti-self sayings which so spice a conversation; I owe this one to Mr Simon Levene, 1977. Prob. since late C19.

who's dead and what's to pay? What's all the fuss about? *or* Why all the fuss and noise? A US c.p. of *c.* 1820–90; by *c.* 1880, adopted in England, where it fell into disuse *c.* 1920. In the 2nd Series (p. 386), 1838, of T.C. Haliburton's *The Clockmaker*, occurs this passage: 'Stop, says I, and tell us what all this everlastin' hubbub is about: who's dead, and what's to pay now?'
R. S. Surtees, *Facey Romford's Hounds*, 1862 (at chapter LXII, 'The Beldon-Ball') has: "Who's dead, and what's to pay?" demanded Betsey Shannon, pressing forward through the crowd...' Cf **what's to pay?**

who's for tennis? See **tennis, anyone?**

who's hoisting my pennants? Who's talking about me?: RN (lower-deck): C20:. 'A seaman may ask this when he overhears someone talking about him' (PGR).

who's milking this cow? 'Mind your own business!', hence, 'Let me get on with the job': US (Berrey, 1942) and Aus. (Baker, 1959). A milder var. of **who's robbing this coach?**

who's minding the store? 'Who's actually in charge of this project or operation? Implied ref. is to the more-or-less routine functions which, however graveling to imaginative minds, are absolutely essential if imagination is to generate productivity. US, 1970s' (R.C., 1979). And of course, as Claiborne adds, the statement may be positive – or rather, negative – *nobody's minding the store*: the project is collapsing, leaderless.
J.W.C., 1977, however, places the c.p. from an earlier date, and with slightly different nuance: 'It is applied, for example, to the absence of all high officials from Washington over, e.g., a Christmas, or Easter weekend: since the 1930s. From the sort of question that is asked about stores, shops, that are under-staffed. It is true that, as soon as the nation had recovered from the *débâcle* of Pearl Harbor, some alert American journalist asked, "Who was minding the store? Will the full story ever be written or, if written, allowed to appear?"'
The Brit. version naturally uses *shop*, as in 'Shadow Chancellor Sir Geoffrey Howe offered two cheers for the IMF for "minding the shop" that Labour so nearly destroyed' (*Observer*, 18 Sep. 1977: Playfair).

who's opened his lunch? is addressed to – or directed at – one who has broken wind: later C20. (Mentioned by Russell Davies in his review of the first ed. of this book, *New Statesman*, 9 Sep. 1977.) Cf the more direct **who's shit?**

who's paying the rent? See **who's up who?**

who's robbing this coach? 'Mind your own business!': N. American and Aus.: prob. since late C19. Leechman, 1967, gave me:
'The anecdote from which this phrase derives: The train robbers were robbing the passengers and threatening to rape the women. An altruistic passenger cries, "Spare the women!" An elderly lady turns on him, exclaiming, "Who's robbing this train, anyway?"' It therefore rather looks as if the train, hence coach, version was US in origin and that it soon passed to Can.
B.P., 1975, supplies the Aus. version of the origin: 'Ned Kelly and his gang held up a coach. Ned gave orders to rape the men and rob the women. One of his off-siders said, "You mean, rob the men and rape the women". A male passenger with a squeaky and affected voice exclaimed, *"Who's* robbing this coach, anyway?"'
Cf **who's milking this cow?**

who's shit?, a low c.p., directed at one who has broken wind, elicits the reply *yours if you want it* [q.v.]. Almost entirely masculine and often heard in not quite the most respectable pubs: C20. (Frederick Leech, 1972.) Both the question and the reply have variants, occ. *who spoke?* or *who said that?*, to which the dovetail reply be vastly less decorous.

who's smoking cabbage leaves? A mostly Londoners' c.p., addressed to someone smoking a rank cigar: late C19–20. Cf the late C19 – early C20 jibe, *flor de cabbagio* (a not entirely unpleasing example of mock-Spanish).

who's that takes my name in vain? – in C19–20, usu. **who's (that) taking ....** Adopted from the Bible, this c.p. has been current since late C17 or very early C18. It occurs in S, 1738, near end of Dialogue I:
NEV[EROUT]: Pray, Madam, smoak [watch closely] Miss yonder biting her Lips, and playing with her Fan.
MISS: Who's that takes my Name in vain?

who's to pay for the broken glass? Who is to pay for the damage (*any damages*)?: late C19–20; by 1930, ob.; somewhat revived during the bombing, esp. of London, during WW2; by 1970, however, †.

who's up who? is perhaps more usual with the additional **and who's paying the rent?**, which Baker, 1966, defined as 'Just what is happening? Who's in control? ... said of a complete mess-up': Aus.: WW2, and since. Barry Oakley, 1970, uses it smoothly, as 'These days you don't know who's up who and who's paying the rent'; in 1971, Frank Hardy uses it allusively. Wilkes, *Dict. Aus. Coll.*, at *up who*.

who's which. See: **don't know.**

who's your friend? A sarcastic, retaliatory remark, from a third party, ostensibly to one of a pair, the other of whom has just committed some gaffe or, more usu., said something rude or otherwise provocative: since mid C20, at latest. Perhaps influenced by 'Beau' Brummell's alleged jibe at the Prince Regent, 'Who's your fat friend?', of which I am reminded, 1984, by Eric Fearon. Cf **is he with you?**, q.v. (P.B.)

who's your hatter? was, *c.* 1860–85, a London, esp. a Cockney, c.p. An early occurrence is in *Punch*, 16 Mar. 1861, p. 116.
P.B.: but the phrase had clearly spread by *c.* 1880, as this, from John Birch Thomas's autobiography, *Shop Boy*, written 1922 but not pub'd until 1983, show. He is describing how he had to push a barrow load of chamber-pots to a girls' home outside Swansea:
'But you wouldn't believe how those girls went on. They didn't seem to mind a bit about those things I had on the truck ... One of them snatched my cap off and said, "who's your hatter?" and another wanted to know if my mother knew I was out. Then she ruffled my hair all up and said, "Who curled your hair this morning, boy?" Then one said, "Let's help him push the truck, girls," and some of them got behind and pushed so that the truck moved very quickly, but after I'd gone a few yards they said, "Whoa, Emma," and pulled the truck back again.'
Poor little chap – he was only about twelve or thirteen then! Cf **where did you get that hat?**

who's your lady friend? This c.p., current since *c.* 1910, but † by *c.* 1950, derives from a very popular music-hall song of *c.* 1910–11.

whoa! carry me out is an occ. var. of **carry me out!**

whoa, Emma! This urban lower-class c.p. was, *c.* 1880–1900, directed at a woman 'of marked appearance or behaviour in the streets' (Ware, who gives it an anecdotal origin). Note, however, that the phrase more prob. arose in 1878 or 1879, for, in the former year, Henry Daykins's song, *Whoa, Emma!*, began with the words, 'A saying has come up', as Shaw has informed me, 1968. Cf **whoa, mare!** Benham cites the longer and perhaps earlier form, *whoa, Emma! mind the paint.* Hence, *c.* 1900–40, a warning to a person of either sex to be careful.

In 1923, McKnight mentions it as a US c.p. 'in vogue not long ago'. A.B., 1979, from US notes the occ. var. *whoa, Nellie* (or *Nelly*)! See the quot'n at **who's your hatter?**

whoa, Jameson! was, in 1896–7, 'an admiring warning against plucky rashness'. From the Jameson Raid, Ware tells us.

whoa, mare! Turn it up! *or* Desist!: *c.* 1920–70. From an old song – and probably of ultimately rural origin. (Shaw, 1968.) Cf **whoa, Emma!**

Whoball. See: he is none.

whole new ball game. See **different ball ...**

whole show. See: he's the w.

whole team. See: he's a w.

whore. See: demure; like a bastard; long as a whore's; ready whore; sailor without; sings more; soft as; up and down; you shape.

whoreson. See: Zed.

whose dog is dead? – variants, **whose dog is a-hanging?** and **whose mare is dead?** Also in the more coll. form, **whose dog's (whose mare's) dead?** What is the matter *or* fuss? The former dates from C17; † by *c.* 1940. Massinger, 'Whose dog's dead now/That you observe these vigils' is cited by the *OED.* The latter belongs to late C16– mid C18 and was used by Deloney and Shakespeare and Swift. Apperson.

whose little girl are you? See **and whose ...**

whose mare is dead? See **whose dog ...**

why. See: theirs not.

why be difficult when with a little effort you can be impossible? was proposed by Hugh Quetton, of Montreal, 1978. R.S. comments that it 'smells almost Churchillian'. I have heard it fairly often as ... *bloody impossible*, and am inclined to think that, even if at first a c.p., and, as E.P. put it, 'an urbane insult to a notoriously "difficult" person', it soon became, in later C20, merely a printed joke-motto, to be stuck up in offices, stores, etc. as a reminder to the incumbents that they could, if they so wished, exercise their tiny powers as offensively as possible. (P.B.)

[**why bring** *that* **up?** Isn't that entirely irrelevant? is the use when the question is indisputably a piece of literal Standard English: but when it is employed to mean 'Isn't it unkind *or* horribly tactless to mention that *or* to remind me (*or* people) of it', it has come to verge upon the status of c.p. – prob. from as far back as the 1890s.]

why buy a book when you can join a library? and **you don't have to buy a cow merely because you are fond of** (or **like,** or **need**) **milk.** Cynical male gibes at marriage: the former, Aus., dates from *c.* 1920; the latter, gen. since late C19. In the second, B.P. tells me, Australians prefer *just* to *merely*; they also prefer these interrogatives: *if you like milk, why buy a cow?* and *why buy a cow just because you like milk?* And R.C., 1977, adds the US var., by then ob., *why buy a cow when milk is so cheap?*

A friend tells me – I needed telling, for I had completely forgotten – that in *The Life and Death of Mr Badman*, 1680, John Bunyan offers some such adumbration as *you don't need to buy a cow merely because you like milk.* [Elsewhere in the 1st ed., EP. had noted *as long as I can buy milk I shall not keep a cow*, and dated it back to C17. Later he added:]

The *milk* version was even more impressively adumbrated by Samuel 'Erewhon' Butler (1835–1902) when, in his *Notebooks*, he wrote: 'The public buys its opinions as it buys its meat, or takes in its milk, on the principle that it is cheaper to do this than to keep a cow. So it is, but the milk is more likely to be watered'.

why curls leave home was a short-lived c.p. of *c.* 1950–60; it

referred to baldness. (Petch.) A pun on the literal use of 'Why girls leave home'.

why don't we throw it and see if it skips across the pond? See **run it up the flagpole ...**

why don't you drop dead? See **drop dead!**

why don't you get wise to yourself (and grow up)? A US fling – very sarcastic and *de haut en bas* – at someone acting childishly: *c.* 1930–45. (Berrey.) Cf. **get wise ...**

why don't you go back there? Addressed, often illogically, to a praiser of a country other than the speaker's: since the 1920s. (Shaw, 1969.) Cf:

why don't you go back where you came from? (– **if you don't like it here,**): 'Cliché'd retort to any radical critic of US conditions, policy, etc., since it was assumed (correctly or not) that any such critic must be an immigrant. Now all but extinct as conscious irony characterizing mindless rejection of all political dissent. It dates from 1920s or earlier' (R.C., 1978). Brit. as well as US: cf prec.

why don't you just hang it up? See **give us a rest.**

why don't you just rev up and fuck off? Run away and stop bothering me (or us)! Addressed during the latish 1950s to early 1960s by Servicemen to RAF apprentices: 'they wore little brass wheels on their sleeves ... I'm not sure why we bothered to elaborate so much' (P.B., 1975).

It 'has the US semantic equivalents *why don't you just beat it?* and *why not just get your ass out of here?* Both current, I believe' (A.B., 1979). But are they c.pp? I very much doubt it. Note the US slang use of *your* (or *my* or *his,* etc.) *ass* (= arse) for 'self', common since *c.* 1970, although W & F, 1975, do not mention it.

why don't you leave it out (, then)? (– **dwell,**) is the c.p. reply to 'Gee, it's nice out!' – i.e., outdoors; dating since 'the gay Twenties' and very popular, esp. among adolescents until Pearl Harbor. It failed to get itself adopted in UK; certainly *not* because it was highly suggestive. (Elab. from a note by J.W.C., 1977.)

why don't you two get married? A RN lowerdeck c.p. directed at two men fighting or wrestling or quarrelling: current during WW2, also before (? *c.* 1930) and after. (P. Daniel, 1978.) Cf *they want to be alone* at **put the lights out.**

why girls leave home has, since *c.* 1910 or a little earlier, been used to deride a good-looking, esp. if conceited, 'ladies' man'. Contrast **why curls leave home.**

why is a Marine? See **that's the old navy spirit.**

why is a mouse when it spins? has the 'dovetail' c.p. answer **because the higher the fewer** (occ. *because it is higher than up*). A further, rare, version has the less splendidly illogical *what does a mouse do when it spins?*; Mrs Dinah Murray, 1976, suggests that the orig. and predominant form was *why does a mouse ...*

In June 1919, the notable US novelist John Dos Passos (1896–19–), writing from Paris to a Yale freshman, expressed a hope that he was reading something better than the usual authors and ended the paragraph: 'But why in God's name Tennyson and Ruskin? – Why is a mouse when it spins?' I owe this quot'n based on *The Fourteenth Chronicle: Letters and Diaries of John Dos Passos*, ed. by C.T. Ludington and pub'd 1974 (p. 253), to Prof. Harold Shapiro, who, 1975, tells me that when he 'was in secondary school during the late 1940s', the phrase, in this form, 'was fashionable among some of us boys. There was an answer too: "Because the higher the fewer [q.v.]"'. Later, Shapiro added that, as Dos Passos was at school in England in 1906–7, he may have learnt the phrase at that earlier period.

Prof. Shipley, 1976, writes, 'it has always seemed to me a companion query to "which came first: the chicken or the egg?"'; the second deals with the *how*, the first with the *why*, of life on earth.' Note, however, that the chicken-egg question belongs to cliché, not to c.p.

Cf **how old is Ann(e)?; how high is up?; do they have ponies down a pit?; what's the difference between a chicken?**

why should I go to see (here insert the name of any soccer club

WHY WORRY?

that is doing badly)? **They didn't come to see me when I was ill** (or *sick* or *poorly*, according to which part of the UK the speaker comes from). Orig., I believe, a gag of Tommy Trinder's. (Sanders, 1978.) As a c.p., it dates from *c.* 1955.

why worry? See **I should worry!**

wicked. See: **no rest**; **Willie.**

wider the brim, the fewer the acres – the. The station-owner or farmer who wears an exceptionally wide-brimmed hat – known as a lunatic hat – tends to be only a small landowner: Aus.: since the 1930s. A lack of intelligence is implied. (B.P.)

widows. See: **for the widows.**

width. See: **never mind the quality.**

wife. See: anything for a quiet; 'dab!'; fine night; I love my w.; I'll venture; it's a monkey's; laugh?; match! my wife; officers and their; shake hands; she has been; such is life; that's no lady; what! a bishop's; when my w.; you can bet; you know what thought.

Wigan. See: comes from; that went better; twice removed.

Wilbur. See: **I told W.**

wild. See: **she had; and:**

wild, woolly, and full o' fleas. 'An early-day cowboys' expression for a genuine cowboy' (Adams): later C19–early 20. P.B.: cf the chorus of a scurrilous verse, attributed to Kipling: 'He was dirty, and filthy, and full of fleas,/And he loved his queens by twos and threes/– Hurrah for the Bastard King of England!'

Wilhelm II much. A bit too much of the Kaiser! – that is, we're getting sick of hearing about the Kaiser. A Society c.p. of 1898. (Ware.) From his numerous activities.

will. See: **I'll strike; making his.**

will a duck swim? See **duck swim . . .**

will be pleased! **– he** or **she** or **they.** This ironic c.p. dates from *c.* 1910.

will she take a stone in her ear? Will she fornicate?: a raffish c.p. of *c.* 1670–1720. In *The Scowrers, A Comedy*, 1691, Thomas Shadwell, at Act II, Scene in the Park, Tope says to Sir William Rant, a young hellion: '. . . Did you see who went off with your Aunt? is she given to stumble? Will she take a Stone in her Ear?' An ingenious physiological innuendo.

will you have it now or stay (or wait) till you get it? is addressed to someone either impatient or in a hurry: mid C17–20; the *stay* from belongs to C17–18; the *wait*, to C19–20. The c.p. occurs in S, 1738, early in the Dialogue I:

NEV[EROUT]: Pray, Miss, fill me another.

MISS: Will you have it now, or stay till you get it?

Dickens uses it in chapter X of *Pickwick Papers* (1836–7). Prob. domestic in orig. and certainly, in C20 at least, mainly domestic in usage.

Eric Fearon, 1984, notes that the var. *will you have it now or will you take it with you?* was 'said in the 1930s by [British] Midlands females who felt that they were being eyed too boldly'.

will you shoot? Will you pay for the drinks? Has, since *c.* 1920, been heard in Aus. hotel bars. (Baker.) Presumably a pun on slang *shout*, to stand drinks; perhaps, in part, suggested by the next – if, indeed, the next be authentic.

will you short? Will you pay for a tot of spirits? An Aus. c.p. of late C19–early C20. (Ware.) Cf prec.

will you walk into my parlour, said the spider to the fly arose in the 1880s, from a song thus titled and sung by Kate Castleton. (W.J.B., 1975.) From England, then the rest of Britain, it passed to some of the Dominions that grew into a Commonwealth; I heard it, in NZ, *c.* 1902. When exactly it became a c.p., I have been unable to discover; all I can be tolerably sure of is that it was † by the middle 1930s and that it was a c.p. only when applied by the prospective victim to a dubious invitation – or by others commenting on it.

But, as Prof. H. Shapiro points out, 1977, the line ultimately originates in the poem *The Spider and the Fly*, written by Mary Howitt (1799–1888), and adds, 'I used to hear that line from the poem frequently [in the US] in the 1940s as a c.p., and I don't think it is entirely dead yet'. It actually runs:

'Will you walk into my parlour?' said a spider to a fly:
'Tis the prettiest little parlour that ever you did spy.'

Cf **come into my parlour . . .**

will you *will* **or will you** *won't?* 'Make up your mind!' A US var. of **is you is or is you ain't?**: late 1940s and the 1950s. (W.J.B., 1977.)

Willie. See: **oh, W.; since W.; and:**

Willie, Willie! wicked, wicked! This was, *c.* 1900–14, a 'satiric street reproach addressed to a middle-aged woman talking to a youth'. Ware derives it from a droll law-suit. Cf **oh, Willie, Willie!**

wim, wigor, and witality (less often **vim, vigor, and vitality**) is a US c.p., current since *c.* 1930 and prob. occasioned by a considerable advertising campaign for some health food or some new beverage. (J.W.C., 1975.) 'Not current now, nor (I think) for many years' (R.C., 1978).

win. See: cross, I; didn't win; every player; Gipper; how to win; it's winning; you can't win; you win; you've got to be in.

wind. See: all wind; doesn't know; look what; more wind; standing; twisting.

wind changes, you'll get stuck like it – if the, or **mind, in case the**, or **wait till the**. The form of the admonition may vary, but the basic idea remains: orig. a nurse's threat to a child making a face, or squinting, it has become embedded in domestic folklore: since very early C20, prob. much earlier still. (Mrs Joan F. Beale, 1983.)

with enough to last a Dutchman a week. More wind than enough: nautical: *c.* 1820–1930. The American sailor, lawyer, author, Richard Henry Dana uses it in his sea classic, *Two Years Before the Mast*, 1840.

wind (v.t.) in your neck! has, in the Services (esp. in the RAF), been, since the 1930s, 'a polite way of asking someone to close a door' (H & P). Contrast *wind your neck in!* = stop talking!: id. P.B.: both ob. by 1950.

wind of change – the. A political c.p. soon, through over-use, become stale cliché: taken from the Brit. Prime Minister Harold Macmillan's speech at Capetown, 3 Feb. 1960, where he said, 'The wind of change is blowing through the continent [of Africa]'. Often misquoted as *the winds . . .*

windmill. See: **run it up.**

Windmill girl. See: **as the W.**

window(s). See: everything in the shop; glazier; half-crown; if you vant; it'd give; you make a better.

windstorm. See: **much chance as a fart.**

windy. See: **once wounded.**

wine. See: **I never drink.**

wing. See: **we got back; you can't fly.**

Winifred. See: **oh, Winifred.**

wink, wink, nudge, nudge. See **nudge, nudge . . .**

winking at you (**– it's**). It – esp. penis or vulva – greets you with a wink: a playful admission of either innocent, because unintentional, or unabashed exposure of the human body: C20.

Winnie. See: **what did Horace.**

winning. See: are you winning; it's winning; we're winning.

winter. See: like a winter's; warm; where do flies.

winter drawers on dates from late C19; I heard it, not in NZ but in my second country, Australia, *c.* 1908; very widely used, except among what one used to call 'the nobs', when the onset of winter necessitates a change from cotton to woollen drawers, underpants, knickers, panties, what have you, whether male or female. Obviously it puns the cliché 'winter draws on'.

winter's day. See **like a winter's . . .**

wipe the egg off your face! and **you've got egg on your face!** 'You've made an utter fool of yourself' (something said rather than done; often of a boast that remains unfulfilled): US, soon also Brit.: since *c.* 1965 and very common. (J. W. C., 1977.) Ob. by *c.* 1980 (P.B.). Perhaps suggested by:

wipe the shit off your face! and, more politely, *keep your mind* *out of the sewer!* are US rebukes to 'one who is using verbal obscenities' (W.J.B., 1977): dating, resp., from the 1920s and the 1930s. Excellent examples of what has been aptly called 'sewer(-)realism'.

wipe (or **wipe off) your chin!** is an Aus. c.p. addressed, since early in C20, to a person suspected of lying. To prevent the 'bullshit' he is talking from getting into the beer he is probably drinking.

But as a US c.p., used 'as a recommendation to be silent – from chin being used to mean speech' (Ware): *c.* 1860–1910. Berrey includes it among 'Disparaging and Sarcastic Flings'. A.B., 1979, notes the US var. *wipe your mouth off!*

'Oddly enough, *wipe off your chin* underwent a renaissance *c.* 1940 with a quite different meaning: "Stop drooling (over her)" – i.e., addressed to a man showing blatant sexual interest in a woman' (R.C., 1978).

wire. See: got in; hanging; Mons; nothing to cable.

wire in and get your name up! Have a go!: proletarian: 1862–*c.* 1914. Ware wrote thus: 'Recommendation to struggle for success, but originally very erotic' and quoted a non-erotic example from *The Referee*, 21 Oct. 1888.

wired for sound (– he's or she's or they're). 'As a c.p., "He's (etc.) a loud-mouth". Originally of movie houses in the early days of talkies' (J.W.C., 1977): US: since *c.* 1930.

wise. See: get wise; why don't you get.

wish. See: don't you wish; I don't wish; I say, I say: I wish.

wish I had yer job! is a C20 Cockney c.p., meaning 'I work – or, I have to work – much harder than you do' (Julian Franklyn).

wish in one hand and see which (hand) gets full first! is another C19–20 Cockney, low c.p.: a retort to someone expressing any wish whatsoever. (Julian Franklyn.)

But this is, I believe, a var. of what seems to have been the C18–early (? mid) C19 form, *wish in one hand and piss in the other – and see...*, if I read correctly this passage from Dialogue I of S, 1738:

NEV[EROUT]: You'll be long enough before you wish your skin full of Eyelet Holes. [That is, before you wish yourself dead.]

COL[ONEL]: Wish in one Hand –

MISS: Out upon you; Lord, what can the man mean?

Miss gives herself away by the haste with which she interrupts the Colonel. Admittedly, however, *piss* may rather have been *prick.*

George Krzymowski, 1978, notes that it has had some currency in the US, esp. in western Virginia and western Pennsylvania, since before 1935.

wish you were here! has a 'sarcastic twist to the unimaginative but familiar postcard message from the seaside, "Having a good time. Wish you were here", Edwardian, but still current (1978), as in a newspaper heading on a report of the Liberal Party conference at Southport when a controversial M.P. appeared on the platform, the c.p. being altered to "Wish you weren't here"' (Noble, 1978). See also **having a wonderful time.**

wit. See: if I had; much wit.

witch(es). See: all fine ladies; cold as a witch's; I think you; you have hit.

with a five-franc note in one hand and his prick in the other was, 1914–18 in France, a soldiers' c.p., applied to those who, immediately on receipt of their week's pay, hastened to a brothel.

with a hook at the end (of it) – accompanied by the speaker crooking a finger. Don't you believe it!: proletarian: C19–early C20. The shorter form is recorded by JB in 1823; the longer occurs in, e.g., Henry Daff Traill (1840–1900), *The New Lucian*, 1884.

with a little help from my friends, a US c.p., was 'originated or, at the least, popularized by the Beatles' song, "A Little Help from My Friends" (1 June 1967). Seems to have been – and still to be – a c.p. with vague meaning: "I'll cope, I'll get by, with..."; that is, with the aid of, e.g., drugs, alcohol,

money, etc. Can also be backstairs influence, political "clout" and so on. The lyric says:

"I'll get by with a little help from my friends,
I'll get high with a little help from my friends,
Going to try with a little help from my friends."'

(Thus my very good pen-friend, Paul Janssen, 1977, whose knowledge of popular musicology since *c.* 1960 is prodigious.)

P.B.: the phrase occurs also quite frequently in UK journalese, the *my* being varied to *his, your, their,* etc. to suit the context.

with bells on, hence also simply **with bells.** And *how!* – emphatically; in full force; in a joyous mood and dressed in one's best; and so on: US: since *c.* 1909 (W & F), but by 1960 archaic. But also and prob. orig. Brit., in nuance 'with lurid or, at the least, picturesque additions': *c.* 1880–1914. See Agatha Christie, *Nemesis,* 1971:

'How sad and tragic and terrible it all was. "With bells on," as you might say,' said Miss Marple, using a phrase of her youth [very late C19–early 20]. 'Plenty of exaggeration...'

Prob. from pictures of court jesters: cf **pull the other one: it's got bells on it.**

'In the US, not from court jesters [but from] the "surrey with the fringe on top", celebrated in the song by that title in the great hit and continuingly popular "Oklahoma" (March 31, 1943). Music by Richard Rodgers, book and lyrics by Oscar Hammerstein 2nd. It was on special occasions of joy or merriment pulled by a horse *with bells on* the harness. [The phrase was] very popular in the 1960s to indicate emphasis; still occasionally heard' (Shipley, 1977).

W & F list a joc. masculine US var., dating from *c.* 1950: *with balls on.*

Cf **with knobs on**, and **you can say that in spades.**

with brass fittings. See **with knobs on.**

with difficulty! The often correct, but also oblique and usu. joc. answer to questions beginning 'How', e.g. 'How do I get from here to the other side of Birmingham?' or 'Good heavens, girl! How *did* you get into those jeans?'; occ. qualified, as *with great* (or *considerable,* etc.) *difficulty:* since *c.* 1981. (P.B.)

with forty pounds of steam behind him. See **forty pounds...**

with friends like that, who needs enemies? 'Used whenever a friend is derogatory or uncomplimentary' (Skehan, 1977); or as a comment, by a third party, on some act of selfishness, unhelpfulness, omission, etc.: in UK, later C20; but Fain, 1978, from US, recalls, 'I've heard it since *c.* 1920'. There exists the var. *with such friends, who...*

This c.p. derives from a famous quot'n to the effect – I don't guarantee the wording – that 'He who has a Hungarian for a friend needs no enemy' or 'doesn't need an enemy', which I think is of Hungarian origin: compare such other self-derogations as those in which the Irish, the Scots, the Jews, and several other nationals indulge. But I've been unable to trace the proverb.

Cf **it's your pal you have to watch.**

with knobs on is used both adjectivally and adverbially: late C19–20: US, since *c.* 1930. Embellished or with embellishments; generous, generously; vigorous, vigorously; forcible, forcibly; emphatic, emphatically. W & F note: 'Often in "I'll be there with knobs on", in accepting an invitation. From "with bells on". Usually follows an accusation or oath.' Therefore cf **with bells (on).**

A vulgar, predominantly male, US var. is *with tits on* (W & F). 'I suspect "knobs" is a euphemism for "balls" – "I'll be there with all my equipment". Now rare or extinct [in US], as is the var. "with tits on" and the [subsequent] with "teeth" [see next]' (R.C., 1978). Patrick Leigh Fermor uses it comically in his enchanting *A Time of Gifts,* 1977.

J. W. C., 1977, notes a further US var., *with brass fittings,* dating from before 1930, and 'applied to anything extreme – especially extremely elaborate or fancy'.

P.B.: as a small boy at an English preparatory school in the early 1940s, I was very familiar indeed with the phrase; it was frequently used as a would-be forceful, but paradoxically feeble because merely self-defensive, retort, and elab. as in *and the same to you – with brass knobs on!* In those innocent days no suspicion of euphemism entered my mind; the phrase seemed to me eminently fitting, as I had spent so many nights at my grandparents' farmhouse, sleeping in a huge, double bed: it had a great brass knob on each bed-post, and varied sized ones along the tops of the bed-ends. Very traditional – and I'm sure the schoolboys' use of the phrase goes back much further than my childhood.

Cf **same to you**...

with me? See are you with me?

with teeth. J. W. C., 1975, says: 'i.e., before I become decrepit with age. Originally, I am pretty sure, said sarcastically by a woman whose fiancé keeps putting off the wedding, and to whom she says, "I want to get *married; with teeth*".' It is a US c.p. – dating since the 1930s – only when it is *not* used literally; when, in short, in roughly corresponds to the prec. entry.

with the corner up! Don't believe him: Brit. underworld: *c.* 1930–60. Occurs in, e.g., Robert Fabian, *Fabian of the Yard.* Origin obscure: perhaps cf the underworld *at the corner*, engaged in looking for 'mugs' at street corners in 'shady' districts. Cf **with a hook**...

with the help of God and a few Marines. See by the grace of God....

with thumb in bum and mind in neutral. P.B., who thought it was an Aus. c.p., wrote, 1974:

I first heard it from an Australian Army officer in the early 1960s – and have enjoyed it ever since as a very useful c.p. to describe an attitude of vacant-minded uninterest. 'What's the new bloke like, then?' – 'Hard to say; he just wanders around all day with his thumb in his bum and his mind in netural.'

Adopted, *c.* 1965, by the Services in UK and elsewhere, it has, P.B. notes, been applied rather to 'a "character" who knows how to relax – to let his mind lie fallow – and to refrain from worry and from excessive work'.

But, as Anthony Burgess corrects us in his review of the first ed. of this book, *TLS*, 26 Aug. 1977, 'Herman Wouk has it as one of [Captain] Queeg's insults in *The Caine Mutiny* [1951], thus placing it in the US Navy in the 1940s'.

within a mile of an oak is a derisive, purposely evasive reply to 'Where do you – or does he (etc.) – live?' Current in late C16–18. (Apperson cites several writers.) Oaks being in late C16 so plentiful in England that most country people did live within a mile of one.

Cf **one that lives**...

WIWOL. See: **when I was with Benson.**

wizard prang!, 'a spectacularly successful raid on an enemy target' (DSUE), a very widespread piece of RAF slang, soon became a RAF c.p. applied with emphatic derision to a (very) bad landing or accident or to a colossal mistake of any kind, and it spread, by 1943, to civilians; by 1960, however, it was†. (Noble, 1977).

wobble. See: **she wobbles.**

Wogs begin at Calais. 'Thus speaks the insular Englishman. There are some, more parochial still alas, who would contract the circle even further and say, "Wogs begin west of Offa's Dyke; West of Pompey; North of Cockfosters; etc." (P.B., 1974): since the middle, perhaps the earliest, 1950s.

That is, travelling *from* England, the prejudiced tend to think that foreigners – esp. coloured peoples – begin at Calais. Strictly, a *Wog* is an Indian of India; an Arab; a native of any country from the Levant (but excluding native Jews) to the Indian-Burmese border. The saying arose, I think, among army and RAF 'officer types'.

wolf. See: **who's afraid.**

woman. See: **isn't that just like; sir; you are; and:**

woman and her husband – a, was, *c.* 1770–1850, applied to 'a

married couple, where the woman is bigger than her husband' (Grose, 1788).

woman with skirts up run faster than man with trousers down. See **Confucius**...

women. See: **hot and; I've had more; leader; officers and their; pay the w.; time and tide; what they; where men.**

women and children first has, since *c.* 1914, been used joc. on occasions where no emergency exists.

A.B., 1979, adds, 'I've heard this with a sarcasm attached: *women and children first – after me, of course!* or ... *after me, that is*'.

women (oftener, **girls**) **are like buses: there'll be another coming along soon; women are like streetcars, always another one along.** The former is Brit., and dates since the 1920s; the latter US, since late C19 and therefore prob. the semantic source of the former. A consolation of the 'plenty more fish in the sea' type. Glendon Swarthout uses the US version in *The Tin Lizzie Group*, 1972, which trustworthily renders the everyday speech of 1916. (Based on a note from W. J. B., 1977.) R.C. comments, 1976, 'I know it as ... *there'll be another one along in a minute.* Now obsolescent, since a majority of Americans have never seen a streetcar (tram)'.

wonder. See: **choke you?; I wonder; living bloody; she will die; sometimes; what will they.**

wonderful. See: **it's wonderful.**

won't lie down. See **dead but won't**...

won't run to it! A racing c.p., applied to a horse that has insufficient staying power to gain a place, or even to reach the winning-post: C20; ob. by *c.* 1940 and † by *c.* 1950. Ware.

won't you come home, Bill Bailey? Used humorously during the first decade of C20. (Collinson.) From the lachrymose, extremely popular song so titled. (I remember my father singing it *c.* 1900–2.)

woo-woo, what a tomato! 'In the US satirical magazine *Mad* (UK edn., No. 172) an article on changing styles of US campus life characterizes the 1940s thus: "Students ... jitterbugged to 'Mairzy Doats' and 'Three Little Fishes' on the juke box, while saying things like 'Hubba-hubba' [q.v.] and 'Woo-woo, what a tomato!'"' (P.B., 1977, who comments, 'It has the right idiotic ring'). The song 'Mairzy Doats' [= Mares eat oats] came to UK and had a maddening success, yet it did possess an endearing lunacy.

wood. See: **maturing; Mister and; put the w., rabbits; touch wood; you can't get.**

wooden legs. See: **go it, you.**

wooden nickels. See: **don't take any.**

wooden nutmeg. See: **don't let anyone; nobody is.**

woodman, spare that tree! 'is a quotation, I know, but since it is so often addressed to people other than woodmen about objects other than trees, I thought it might qualify' (Levene, 1977). Correct! But it is a corruption – perhaps rather a popularization – of a line in a poem 'The Beech-Tree's Petition' by Thomas Campbell (1777–1844): 'Spare, woodman, spare the beechen tree'. As a c.p. it has, among the literate, been fairly common since the 1890s.

woodpile. See: **there's a nigger.**

woods. See: **to the woods; and:**

woods are full of them – the. '"They" (the people of a particular type) are abundant and easy to find. Ultimately, a hunters' metaphor. US; C20 (?19); UK from 1930s (M. Allingham, *The Fashion in Shrouds*) or earlier' (R.C., 1979). P.B.: also in the sense 'the place is infested with them', of, e.g. 'security agents'.

woodshed. See: **out in the w.; something nasty.**

wool. See: **keep your w.; and:**

wool is up and **wool is down** are Aus. ruralities, dating from *c.* 1860 but much less frequently heard after *c.* 1945, wool since then being less predominantly the staple product of Australia. B & L.

Woolwich. See: **no, I'm with.**

Woolwich Arsenal. See: **make way for W.**

woppity wop wop, cocking handle 'or the Gunnery Instructor's method of imparting instructional matter. Royal Navy, 1940s' (Peppitt). Satirical of a breezy man-to-man method of using jargon and technicalities that sounds more like 'talking down'.

word(s). See: can't believe; famous; for those; Greeks; in the words; my word; not a w.; one word; put in a good w.; sharp's; snug's; step outside; thank you for those; them's fighting; what's the good w.; you'll speak; and:

word in your shell-like – a, sometimes prec. by e.g. *may I have, he would like,* etc. Elliptical for *shell-like ear.* I have heard this curiously general, poetical phrase used for at least the past quarter-century, and sometimes to those of whom the 'shell-like' would appear to refer rather to artillery than to the graceful convolutions of a small pink seashell. (P.B., 1984.)

words fail me forms a good example of an irritatingly frequent cliché that has "acquired a c.p. flavour over the last, say, ten years. I found it used as a c.p. in a strip cartoon 'The Wizard of Id', 1968 by Brant Parker & Johnny Hart, American cartoonists. Cf the Morecambe & Wise c.p. retort *there's no answer to that'* (P.B., 1977, following a suggestion from Camilla Raab).

work. See: all my own; are yew werkin'; are you happy; beats working; dirty work; don't ask me; everybody works; how do you w.; I don't make; I like w.; I only w.; I will w.; I won't w.; I work; if it works; nice work; old man must; where the dirty; would you rather; wouldn't work; you don't have to be mad; you'll have your.

work! I could watch it all day; also **work? I could....** See **I like work...**

work (or **it's,** with ref. to work) **is the curse of the drinking classes.** A c.p. pun on the cliché (untrue since WW2 and grossly exaggerated since WW1), *drink is the curse of the working classes*: since the late or, at earliest, the middle 1940s.

work out! 'An expression used to encourage one [someone other than the speaker] in speech or course of action' (*Third Ear,* 1971): American Negroes': since *c.* 1960 (?). Perhaps elliptical for 'Work it out to the end!'

workers. See: what about the.

workhouse. See: that's all I have; you couldn't throw.

working classes. See: on behalf.

world. See: around the w.; bangs Banagher; eyes and ears; going round; how's the w.; I'll tell the cock-eyed; it's a small; it's not the end; join the army; only river; out of this w.; she wants; stop the w.; ten days; tomorrow.

worms. See: can of w.; digging; I'll go out; let's not open; mind your w.; must have w.; that's another can.; you've got a smile.

worried as a pregnant fox in a forest fire (– as). This picturesque Can. c.p. dates from *c.* 1920. (Leechman.)

'This would appear to be a var. of the US c.p. (*as*) *hot as,* or *hotter than, a freshly fucked female fox in a forest fire,* the heat in question being either sexual or meteorological' (R.C., 1976). The US form has prob existed since late C19. Note that *female fox,* instead of *vixen,* is used in order to increase, and thus emphasize the alliteration.

worry. See: don't worry; I should w.; I'm worried; not to w.; that's your w.

worse in gaol (or **jail**) (– **there are**). A C20 c.p., admitting that the person concerned might be worse; often self-deprecatory.

worse things happen at sea – in C20 occ. **can happen** – is a vaguely, often perfunctorily, consolatory c.p., half-serious, quarter-rueful, quarter-jocular; dating since *c.* 1840 if not earlier. It is recorded at 24 Aug. 1852 in a Diary quoted in Joan Fleming, *Screams from a Penny Dreadful,* 1971. (I believe this to be a serious dating.) A good modern example occurs in John Aiken, *Nightly Deadshade,* 1971: '"You mustn't be misled by cloistrophobia," I say to him. "Worse things happen at sea."'

Cf **pity the poor sailor on a night like this!**

worships his creator – **he** was a society c.p. of *c.* 1900–40; applied to a *self-made* man holding an excessive high opinion of himself. Punning on *the Creator,* God. Ware.

worst. See: first seven.

worst is yet to come. See **cheer up: the worst...**

worth (**it**). See: mother, is it; oh, mother; push in the bush; seven; yer blood's.

worth a guinea a minute. 'With reference to a pair (usually) of persons with a good line in humorous cross-talk. From the fee believed to have been paid by the BBC' (P.B., 1974). On the analogy of Beechman's Pills, formerly advertised as *worth a guinea a box.*

'Cf "His time is worth a thousand pounds a minute" (Lewis Carroll, *Through the Looking Glass,* 1872). Cf also Dorothy L. Sayers, *The Nine Tailors,* 1934: "At Southend you would call it ozone and pay a pound a sniff for it"' (R.S., 1977).

wotcher, cock, how's yerself! A Cockney c.p. of greeting, very common during the 1940s and 1950s. (Mrs Shirley M. Pearce, 1975.) I.e., *what cheer, cock....*

[**would!** – **he** (or she) or **you,** which is both Brit. and US, meaning 'That's only to be expected of him', cannot, I think, be adjudged a true c.p. But see also **would, wouldn't it.**]

would lend his arse! See **lend his arse...**

would Macy's tell Gimbel's? See **does Macy's...**

would that I had Kemp's shoes to throw after you! I wish I could bring you good luck: C17–early C19. (Grose, 1785.) From a lost topical ref.: I suspect to William Kemp (flourished 1600), comic actor and *dancer.*

P.B.: Will Kemp was famous for his feat, 1600, of morris-dancing from London to Norwich in nine days; his book, *A Nine Daies Wonder,* is a record of this early 'publicity stunt'.

would, wouldn't she (or **he, they,** etc.) – **she** (etc.), often prec. by **well.** Frequently, in print, in later 1970s–early 1980s, introduced by 'as Mandy Rice-Davis (might have) said', which refers back to a remark she made during the trial, 1963, resulting from a sex 'scandal' in high places. The c.p. acknowledges the exasperating, and predictably contrary, reaction of someone known to the speaker(s). 'I see that *Sunday Telegraph* critic was carping because you'd pulled the bumpy bits out of the original main text of the *Dictionary of Slang* and had gathered them into an appendix where people could actually find them.' – 'Well, he would, wouldn't he!' (P.B., 1984.)

would you believe. P.B. wrote, 1974:

A meaningless prefix (occ. suffix) to any statement, but usually an answer to a query. 'When am I on guard again?' – 'Would you believe – tonight!' It struck us like a plague in Hong Kong in 1969 or 1970, and I think it originated in some American TV show, possibly the Rowan and Martin 'Laugh-In'.

It occurs, as an Americanism, in David Fletcher, *A Lovable Man,* 1974.

A.B., 1979, amends: 'In an American TV show, *Get Smart,* 1967–69, which was a spoof on spy-type stories (and real activities), comedian Don Adams played the rôle of Max Smart ("Agent 86"). When he made some outrageous, exaggerated remark, he would use this phrase'. Cf **you better believe it!**

would you buy a second-hand car from this man? 'A phrase which bestowed a dubious immortality on Richard Nixon long before the Watergate scandal' (Skehan, 1977): Richard M. Nixon became the US President in 1969. P.B.: *The Penguin Dict. of Modern Quotations,* rev. ed., tells us that the phrase is attributed to the US comedian Mort Sahl. Later, loosely, ... *a used car...,* and applied to the photograph of any man that looks like a crook, or to the man himself; according to context, and in joc. use, the object sold may be something other than a car. As first used, by Sahl or whoever, it was a very effective smear.

would you for fifty cents? In HLM, 1922, it is listed in a group of c.pp. that, happening 'to strike the popular fancy, are

357

adopted by the mob' and therefore are 'soon worn threadbare and so lose all piquancy and significance'. Later in the same work, Mencken says:

[it] originated in the ingenious mind of an advertisement writer and was immediately adopted. In the course of time it acquired a naughty significance, and helped to give a start to the amazing button craze of the first years of the century – a saturnalia of proverb and phrase making which finally aroused the guardians of the public morals and was put down by the *polizei*.

P.B.: does this derive from, or did it originate, the anecdote of that witty man (some say it was G.B. Shaw) who, at a formal dinner, asked the lady sitting next to him whether she would sleep with him for fifty thousand pounds. After a moment's consideration, she replied that she might.

'In that case, Madam, would you sleep with me for, say, a shilling?' Outraged, the lady huffs, 'What do you take me for?'

'Madam, we have already established that. We are now merely haggling over the price.'

would you like a second opinion? A comment on, a response to, someone's self-praise: since *c*. 1960. A second medical opinion often differs from the first. (A reminder from R.C., 1978.)

[**would you like your daughter to marry one?** Would you like your daughter, who is white, to marry a black man. A piece of oft-quoted bigotry that is clearly not a c.p. but a cliché. 'Sometimes for *like*: *allow*, *let*, *permit*. I cannot date it, but [for the US] I suggest the early 1900s' (A.B., 1979).]

would you mind! is a polite var. of **do you mind!** It occurs in, e.g., Noël Coward's *Pretty Polly Barlow*, 1964.

would you rather be a fish? See **or would...**

would you rather be Red or dead? – that is '... communist or dead?' This mostly Brit. c.p. dates from *c*. 1970, but did not become very gen. until 1973, (Norman Franklin, 1976.) Cf **better Red than dead.**

would you rather do this than work? has, since *c*. 1920, been humorously addressed to one who is doing some manual work in his own free time – or, even more humorously, to someone busy at his usual job.

wouldn't be in it. with prec. I understood. 'I wouldn't take part in it!' An Aus. c.p., dating since *c*. 1945. (B.P.)

wouldn't be seen crossing (or **dead in**) **a forty-acre field with her** (speaker male) or **with him** (speaker female); with prec. I either expressed or understood. A c.p. contemptuous or derisive or both; mostly Cockneys'; late C19–20. To a Cockney, forty acres represent a considerable area. Why *forty*? Because it is often employed generically for a largish number.

wouldn't come! A C20 underworld c.p. applied to 'payment refused on the forged cheque' (Val Davis, *Phenomena*, 1941).

wouldn't give you a light, with **he** or **she** understood. He (or she) is extremely mean: Cockney: late C19–20. For one's cigarette or pipe.

The 'more usual version [is] "wouldn't give a blind man a light" [or 'a light to a blind man': P.B.] – stronger implication than your suggestion, perhaps' (B.G.T., 1978). Not 'perhaps', but 'certainly'. The c.p. prob. alludes to *The Book of Common Prayer*, at 'A Collect for Aid against Perils': 'Lighten our darkness, we beseech Thee, O Lord; and by Thy great mercy defend us from all perils and dangers of this night'; perhaps also to Cardinal Newman's 'Lead, Kindly Light, amid the encircling gloom', in *The Pillar of Cloud*, 1833.

P.B.: but cf the contemptuous dismissal of something worthless, 'Tain't worth a light', for the meanness, and:

wouldn't give you the skin off his prick (**– he**) is a low US comment on a man exceptionally mean: since *c*. 1930. (W.J.B., 1977.) Cf. prec., and the entries at **mean as...** and **so mean...** See also **I wouldn't give...**

wouldn't it! Elliptical for 'Wouldn't it make you angry or

disgusted!' Aus.: dating since *c*. 1925. (Baker.) Hence, since the 1930s, elliptical for 'Wouldn't it make you laugh?' – as in Jon Clearly, *The Climate of Courage*, 1954, 'Asking your wife if you can write to her. Wouldn't it?'

'"Wouldn't it" was [during WW2] one of the commonest [Aus. expressions of disgust or surprise, being an abbreviation of "Wouldn't it rock you?" and having many variations' (PGR, at the entry 'Digger Slang').

Wilkes defines it as 'an expression of exasperation' and notes the variations *wouldn't it rip you?* and *wouldn't it root you?* – the former in Lawson Glassop, *We Were the Rats*, 1944, about the Aussies at Tobruk, the latter as very common among them throughout WW2. Both Baker and Wilkes, however, clearly show that the predominant expression, esp. among civilians, has always been the simple *wouldn't it*, whether interrogative or exclamatory – or both. This cluster merits a well-considered article by some alert Australian scholar.

P.B.: the usual pron. is *wooden it*, with which cf the silly story of the two wooden puppets: one says, 'Wouldn't it!', to which the other replies, 'Wouldn't what?'

Cf the next two entries.

wouldn't it make you spit blood? (Eng.), or **... chips?** (Aus.), or **wouldn't it rot your socks?** This c.p. indicates, with some emphasis, a superb contempt. The variants date, respectively and only very approximately, from *c*. 1920 to *c*. 1900, to *c*. 1930. (Partly B.P.) Cf prec. and:

wouldn't it rock you? and **wouldn't it rotate you?** Wouldn't it disgust you?; Wouldn't it make you sick?. These phrases arose, *c*. 1941 and *c*. 1942 respectively, among NZ and Aus. soldiers and then passed to civilians. The earliest record I can supply is J.H. Henderson, *Gunner Inglorious*, 1945 (NZ). Clearly the latter c.p. merely elaborates the former; and the former derives from the slangy *rock*, to startle (someone). Cf the two prec. entries.

wouldn't say 'shit' even if he had his mouth full (or **a mouthful**) **of it – he.** This low Can. c.p. satirizes a man excessively mealy-mouthed: since *c*. 1930 or perhaps a little earlier.

wouldn't steal a red-hot stove. See **steal anything...**

wouldn't that jar you? In HLM Supp 2, it is included in a list of 'the numerous catch-phrases that have little if any precise meaning but simply delight the moron by letting him show that he knows the latest'; Mencken does not place it in time: was it the 1930s? For the meaning, cf **wouldn't it rock you?**, and **wouldn't that jar your mother's preserves?** A Can. c.p., expressing surprise and current *c*. 1910. 'Here *jar*. v[erb], means to preserve fruits and vegetables in air-tight jars, with a pun on "shake"' (Leechman, 1968). Cf **wouldn't it rock you?**

wouldn't touch it with a red-hot poker, with prec. I understood. An Aus. c.p., indicative of extreme aversion: C20. (Baker.)

With it goes **wouldn't touch her** (or **him**, or **it**) **with a forty-foot pole,** usu. with prec. **I,** Indicating utter contempt or extreme distaste, it isn't – *pace* Baker – solely or even mainly Aus.

P.B.: for what unfathomable reason did E.P. allow these two, and yet reject *wouldn't touch it with a bargepole* as a cliché?

wouldn't work in an iron lung – he. 'He is so lazy that he would not work [even] if his breathing were done for him' (B.P., 1975): Aus.: since *c*. 1950.

[**wouldn't you like to know?** (or **!**), in answer to a direct question: Brit. and US. *Not* a c.p. but an informal cliché.]

wounded. See: **once wounded.**

wounds. See: **died of.**

wow-wow(-wow)! and **bow-bow!** was a Slade School c.p. of the late 1890s; R. Blaker, *Here Lies a Most Beautiful Lady*, 1936, '"Wow-wow-wow" she gurgled; for "bow-wow" or "wow-wow" was currency in her circle at that time, to denote quiet contempt of an adversary's contempt.'

Contrast **miaow! miaow!**

wrapped (or **wrapt**) **up in the tail of his mother's smock** (**– he**

was). A c.p. of c. 1760–1830; applied to 'any one remarkable for his success with the ladies' (Grose, 1785). It evolved from *be wrapt* or *wrapped in his mother's smock*, to be born lucky.

'The ultimate derivation is surely from "born with a caul", i.e. still wrapped in the amniotic membrane, [which fact is] considered to be a sign of good luck' (R.C., 1978).

wreck of the Hesperus – he or **she looks like the**; or **you look** or **I (must) look like the.** In a sad state, or merely rather untidy: since late C19. Both Brit. and US, from a once very frequently recited poem, 'The Wreck of the Hesperus', 1841, by Longfellow; 'based on an actual incident off the coast of New England' (A.B., 1979). P.B.: in UK, ob. by later C20, though still heard among the older generation. Sometimes also *I feel like the wreck...*

wrecker. See: Whelan.

Wrens. See: up with the lark.

wriggle. See: you must w.

wringer. See: pulled.

wrinkles. See: I don't know whether I'm Angus; more wrinkles.

write. See: can read; nothing to cable; we'll write; what he doesn't.

write to *John Bull* (or *The Times*) **about it!** If you wish to complain, write to the newspapers: respectively c. 1910–30 (before *John Bull* turned genteel) and late C19–20. In short, *The Times* version prompted the *John Bull*.

write to your M.P. See: **this is rat week...**

writing. See: could I.

written. See: is there a law; and:

written with a thumbnail dipped in tar. A 'catchphrase for rough penmanship, from Paterson's "Clancy of the Overflow"' (Wilkes) – i.e., from that poem in A.B. Paterson's *The Man from Snowy River*, 1985. Wilkes omits to add that it has long been †. 'Banjo' Paterson (1864–1941) was the Robert W. Service of Australia.

wrong. See: anything that can; fifty; never does; skippers; you're in the w.

wrong business or racket – in the, prec. by **I'm** or **we're** or **you're.** Employed much less lucratively than one might be – indeed, could be, if one were less scrupulous; usu. said with rueful humour: orig., early 1950s, US, both forms; by late 1950s, UK, and nearly always *racket*. (A reminder from R.C., 1978.)

wrong side of the hedge when the brains were given away – he was. He is brainless or stupid or, at the very least, extremely dull: c. 1810–80. In late C19–20, the form has been *he was on the wrong side of the door when the brains were handed out.*

A.B., 1978, supplies a more up-to-date US var.: *when the brains were being passed out, he thought they said 'trains' and didn't catch one.*

wrote. See: that's all she.

X

X marks the spot. From being an almost obligatory caption to photographs of 'the scene of the crime', usually murder, it came to be applied to trivialities, e.g. one's room in hotel or boarding-house, and thus, by its frequency, became, *c*. 1925, a c.p.; my own memory of it hardly antecedes the late 1920s.

'Much earlier in US – probably since the beginning of newspaper photography' (J.W.C., 1977). 'There are also many literary uses, as in pirate tales where maps are used, as in E.A. Poe, *The Gold Bug*, 1843, and R.L. Stevenson, *Treasure Island*, 1883' (A.B., 1979).

[**X. Peary Enza does it** is 'a ridiculous malformation of the Latin tag [*Experientia docet*, 'Experience teaches' – 'We learn by experience']. I first heard it about 1912' (Leechman, 1969). This and the rather better-known *experience does it* didn't quite 'make the grade'. I've heard neither form since *c*. 1960.

'Mrs Micawber quotes her father as saying "Experientia does it"' (J.W.C.), the ref. being to Dickens's *David Copperfield*, 1849–50.]

Y

Y is a crooked letter. A reply to children continually asking 'Why?': Aus. domestic: C20, from trad. UK, dating, I'd guess, from at least as early as mid C19.

Y.T.Y.T.K. See TOMMY HANDLEY.

yabbadabba doo! A cry of exultation, uttered by 'Fred Flintstone' (the voice was that of Jackie Gleason: Ashley) in 'The Flintstones', 'one of the most popular cartoon series in the history of television' (W. Brasch, *Cartoon Monickers*, 1983). The series depicted current US suburban life translated back into a make-believe 'Stone Age', and was shown in many parts of the world: B.P. vouches for the c.p.'s use among Aus. surfers, and I for its popularity among British servicemen in Hong Kong, in the early 1960s. Cf **hubba hubba!** (P.B.)

yacht(s). See: poor chap; what do you think this is.

Yapton. See: were you.

yard. See: I don't want to play.

Yarra, stinking Yarra! See **stinking Yarra!**

ye gods and little fishes! was, c. 1884–1912, a lower- and lower-middle-class indication of contempt; from c. 1912 until c. 1940, a gen. exclam. either of derision or of humour. So lofty a phrase found its humble level by way of 'the Transpontine (or Surrey-side) Melodrama' or, as Ware puts it, 'mocking the theatrical appeal to the gods'.

yea big, yea high is a US c.p. – 'a sophisticated fad phrase since c, 1955' (W & F). Starting from the lit. 'thus big or thus high', indicated by the hands being spread laterally or raised, two contradictory senses derive: 'very large or high, overwhelmingly large or tall'; and, with suitably modified gestures, 'not very big or high' (W & F). Some occ. use in UK, late 1960s–early 70s (P.B.).

[yea(h), bo. Only doubtfully a c.p., of c. 1925–50; certainly two words, not one, as in a suggested derivation from the Zulu *yebo*, yes, which suggestion is simply incredible, since there is no likely channel through which a Zulu word could have reached the US – in 1925 or at any other time. (American Negroes originated in West Africa, 2000 miles from the Zulus.)

A far more plausible explanation is simply 'Yeah, bo', 'the latter word ... used in direct address to a man ... [Perhaps] a contraction of *boss*, often used as a respectful term of address – e.g. by Negroes to Whites' (R.C., 1978). The *D. Am.* proposes a shortening of *bozo*, perhaps from Span.; I think that it may come from Fr. *beau*. P.B.: or *boy*, or the old East Anglian *bor* ...?]

yeah, see you in a while, crocodile. See **see you later, alligator.**

yeah, you could shit a brick. Like hell you could!; Can.: since c. 1930. Suggested by the slangy *shit a brick*, to have an excessively hard stool after a long costive period.

year(s). See: Christmas; first hundred; first seven; it'll be all the same; it's been a very; May bees; ole man; thirty five; who was your.

yell. See: they don't yell.

yer blood's worth bottling! An Aus. c.p., indicating either very warm approval or hearty congratulations: since c. 1950. Russell Braddon, in his Preface to the English ed. (1958) of *They're a Weird Mob* (1957) has: 'To Nino Culotta, therefore, in thanks for this book, I say: "Thanks, mate. Yer blood's worth bottling."'

yer mother and father. See **your mother** ....

yes: a cat with two legs. A C18–20, by 1960 ob., domestic c.p. – the housewife's traditional reply to an errant housemaid; beautifully exemplified in S, 1738, early in Dialogue I:

LADY SM[ART]: Go, run Girl, and warm some fresh Cream.

BETTY: Indeed, Madam, there's none left, for the Cat has eaten it all.

LADY SM: I doubt it was a Cat with two Legs.

yes, and I know ... See **yes, I also know** ...

yes, and what they say about Chinese women ... See **what they say** ...

yes, but beautifully cooked (or **served**) is 'the dovetail retort to the cookhouse or mess complaint (among those at table) that "This food is shit!"' (P.B., 1974): Services': since mid C20 at latest, and prob. also US Forces' as well.

yes, but in the right place is a fast girl's, or a prostitute's, retort to the 'You're cracked' or 'You must be cracked': late C19–20. (I first heard it in 1922 from a man about town.) Cf **cracked in the right place** and

yes, but not the inclination is a joc. – or a saucy – reply, from either sex to the other, to the question, 'Have you the time?' Cf **yes, but who'll** ... and see also **any day** ...

yes, but only just, short for **yes, that's right, but only just** (with payment understood). In reply to 'Is that the right money?' First heard in 1949 or 1950, but not a c.p. until the late 1950s.

yes, but what have you done for me *lately*? 'Maybe 20 or 30 years old; but still widely current,' says J.W.C., 1975, adding:

Very specifically Jewish in *original* allusion, but the kind of Jewish joke that is not anti-Jewish ... and is first circulated among them, with humorous allusion to qualities particularly attributed to them – in this case, insatiable and single-minded rapacity. The specific story is essentially this. A (relatively) poor and uninfluential Jew visits a rich or influential one, a friend of his, to ask a favor. The friend, weary of his visitor's repeated importunities, names, with exasperation and sarcasm, the many favors he has done him in the past; to which the beggar replies with self-righteous indignation, 'Yes, but what have you done for me *lately*?' Now used here, as a c.p., of any such person, Jewish or Gentile, but always with allusion to this story.

Ashley, 1982, comments: 'heartless, inconsiderate attitude ascribed to show biz types (esp sharp Jewish Hollywood agents) – the anti-Semitism often underlined by an assumed accent – behind it is the joke about the man who applies for a job pleading he once saved the prospective employer's life, only to receive this reply'.

yes (or **yeah**), **but who'll hold the horses?** is a US dovetail to 'have you got the time?' It dates from *c.* 1910. (Fain, 1977.) Cf **yes, but not the inclination**. P.B.: a further var. is *yes, if you've got the money*: see **any day**...

yes, doctor. See **yes, teacher.**

yes, I also know the one about the three bears. 'A sarcastic remark to one who has purveyed a very old, very well known story: since the 1930s' (Franklyn, 1969). The ref. to the Grimms' tale 'The Three Bears' is clear enough. Cf **have you any more funny stories?**

yes, I don't think! In his *Chosen Words*, the late Ivor Brown mentioned this as a c.p. of the 1930s. Roughly equivalent to 'I'm damn' sure it isn't (*or* wasn't, etc.)'

yes, my arse and your face is the almost obligatory retort, in workshop and offices, to 'Got a match?' ('I want to light a cigarette, or my pipe.'): non-cultured, non-refined, 'pubby': C20. (L.A., 1974.) I had never heard it, even in the Australian army during WW1, until I came to England in 1921. And certainly not during my Oxford days, 1921–3. 'A Liverpolitan reply to "Have you a match?" obscene' (Frank Shaw, 1968, an authority on the speech and folklore of Liverpool. C20.)

yes, she gave me a farthing. See **does your mother know you're out?** Cf:

yes, she's with us is another smart stock reply to **does your mother know you're out?** It dates from *c.* 1920.

yes sir, no sir, three bags full, sir has, since *c.* 1910, been a – ? predominantly RN – c.p. applied to or 'describing an over–obsequious person' (Granville, 1969). But has been also used as 'an indignant reaction to someone being bossy but whom one has to obey' (Patricia Newnham, 1976). It intentionally alters the old nursery rhyme:

Baa, baa, black sheep.
Have you any wool?
Yes sir, yes sir,
Three bags full.

'Sometimes it is just used sneeringly as "three bags full" after somebody has given a doubtful explanation or alibi' (Petch, 1969).

yes, 'stung' is right! That is – or was – an extortionate price or charge: US: *c.* 1910–40. Recorded by S.R. Strait, 'Straight Talk', *Boston Globe* in *c.* 1917. (W.J.B., 1976.)

yes, teacher (or, occ., **yes, doctor**). A joc. ironic c.p., addressed to someone who delights in airing his knowledge of general matters or – the latter form – esp. of medical ailments and cures: since *c.* 1910. (Petch.)

yes, Virginia, there *is* **a Santa Claus** 'is still used to indicate that fair play or justice has been done, or that an unexpected gift or reward has been received. It appeared originally in an editorial by Frank Church – "Is there a Santa Claus?" – [in] New York *Sun*, September 21, 1897 ... A variant usage indicates that a truth or a fact exists, e.g. "Yes, Virginia, there is (are) ..."' (Moe, 1976). P.B.: Virginia = naivety and innocence?

yes, we have no bananas was, during the approximate lustrum or quinquennium, 1923–7, the most widely used of all c.pp. It is based upon that popular song which has, as refrain, those moving and eloquent lines:

Yes, we have no bananas,
We have no bananas today.

It arose in the US, as HLM remarks in the definitive edn, 1936, '[Tad Dorgan] also [besides several immensely popular neologisms] gave the world, "Yes, we have no bananas," though he did not write the song.' Yet it very rapidly caught on in UK, *teste* Collinson, who writes (in ref. to music-hall originations):

Of recent American importations the best (and worst) is perhaps, Yes, we have no bananas. It is interesting to note that this quaint phrase became so widespread as to

clamour for expression in circles where least expected, for in 1923 I heard a learned colleague perpetrate the phrase 'Yes, we have no aspirates' in a philological lecture.

But perhaps the most interesting and notable tribute to the song's popularity comes from Will Rogers. In *The Illiterate Digest*, 1924, a collection of humorous speeches and articles, is a piece titled 'The Greatest Document in American Literature'. It begins thus: 'The subject for this brainy Editorial is resolved that, "Is the Song Yes We Have no Bananas the greatest or the worst Song that America ever had?"' And it ends:

I would rather have been the Author of that Banana Masterpiece than the Author of the Constitution of the United States. No one has offered any amendments to it. It's the only thing ever written in America that we haven't changed, most of them for the worst.

The song was written by Frank Silver and Irving Cohn and pub'd in 1923. It is worth recording that the song was revived in Britain during the food shortage prevalent from mid 1940 until late 1946.

'... In 1923 "Yes, we have no bananas" was publicized by giving away free bananas ... It was so successful that there was a follow-up in 1926, "I've never seen a straight banana", and £1,000 was offered by Denmark Street [London] to anyone who could produce a perfectly straight one ... In the end, no absolutely straight banana was found' (Ronald Pearsall, *Popular Music of the 20's*, 1976).

See TAD DORGAN.

yes, your face ... See **yes, my arse** ...

yesterday. See: **I want it; I wasn't born.**

yo bad self! See **your bad self!**

yo, Tommy! is glossed thus by Ware: 'Exclamation of condemnation by the small actor [i.e., an actor in minor theatres] Amongst the lower classes, it is a declaration of admiration addressed to the softer sex by the sterner.'

York Street is concerned (or **there is York Street concerned**). Someone is looking at us very closely: either cant or low slang: *c.* 1780–1830. Prompted by cant *york*, to stare at, to examine.

Yorkshire estates. See: **when I come.**

you ain't 'alf (or **'arf**) **a one!** (or **a caution!**) Addressed to someone very odd, or very much a 'lad' (or female counterpart), or of a quirkish humour that elicits gentle mockery: mostly lower or lower-middle class: at least 1910 to 1930s (L.A., 1974); in fact *c.* 1890–1939.
P.B.: also *a proper caution*. Cf **you are a one**, which this entry perhaps, paradoxically, intensifies, and **not half!**

you ain't got the brains God gave a goose! See **you don't have the brains** ...

you ain't heard (or, the commoner, **seen**) **nothin' yet!** is a US c.p., recorded in 1942 by Berrey, who glosses it thus: 'it is greater, worse, &c., than you think'. Apparently it dates since 1927, for, as W.J.B. writes, 1976, 'Howard K. Smith, in a recent newscast on TV, used [this] old catch phrase ..., and he said it went back to the play *The Barker*, [written] by Kenyon Nicholson and produced on Broadway in 1927.'

According to the *ODQ*, however, the orig. form was *you ain't heard nothin' yet, folks*, a remark made by Al Jolson in the first talking film, *The Jazz Singer*. Kenyon Nicholson may, of course, have adapted the longer form: one cannot, or should not, be dogmatic about everything so insusceptible to strait-jacketing as a c.p. Jack Warner, d. 9 Sep. 1978, 'the last of the Hollywood moguls ... was a driving force behind the introduction of sound films with "The Jazz Singer" (1927), in which Al Jolson uttered the historic line: "You ain't heard nothin' yet"' (Ian Brodie, in the *Daily Telegraph*, 11 Sep. 1978).

It was adopted, in 1944, in Aus., rather in the nuances, 'There are still worse things to come' and, after *c.* 1950, 'There are even better – or more wonderful, more startling – things to come' (B.P., 1969); as you might expect, it occurs in Frank Hardy, *Billy Borker Yarns Again*, 1967. But in the

Australian Army song, 'Wait Till you Get to New Guinea', composed in 1944 by one of 'the Desert Rats' of Tobruk, occurs the verse

We like ourselves a little bit,
Until to Aussie we get,
'Wait till you get to New Guinea,
You ain't seen nothing yet.'

Recorded in Martin Page's splendid collection, *Songs and Ballads of World War II*, pub'd in 1972 and then as a Panther paperback. P.B.: I think E.P. sells the UK short here; the phrase has been every bit as common in UK, certainly since mid C20, in both the *heard* and *seen* versions. A comparable phrase is *you haven't seen anything* (or *the half of it*) *yet!*

you ain't just kidding. See **you're not kidding!**

you ain't just whistling 'Dixie'! is a c.p. Americans 'say to someone who has just made a statement with great emphasis and conviction'; the ref. is to the song 'Dixie', which 'was the rallying tune of the Confederate soldiers in our Civil War [1861–5]' (W.J.B., 1975).

'The tune of "Dixie" (the words came later) was written in 1859 by Daniel Decatur Emmett. It was, at first, intended as "walking-around music" for the then popular Negro Minstrel shows in some of our larger cities. People in the audience were encouraged to whistle along with the pianist playing the song, while the Minstrels strutted about on the stage. One definition (besides Prof. Burke's) is: "You aren't just saying it, you're *doing* it' (A.B., 1979).

you ain't seen nothin' yet. See **you ain't heard nothin' yet.**

you ain't the Lone Ranger. See **you're not Robinson Crusoe.**

you and me both! is a US c.p. of bonhomous agreement – but also of sympathy. 'You hear this expression every day' (W. J.B., 1975). It seems to date from the 1920s. (Berrey, 1942.) Cf **that makes two of us.** P.B.: some Brit. use, at least since mid C20. Cf also **join the club.**

you, and who else? [Brit. and, since *c.* 1930, also US) and **you and whose army?** (US, Brit. and Aus.) are phrases of derisive defiance addressed to a quarrelsome opponent: respectively C20 and since *c.* 1944. ' "I reckon I can fight you any day." – "Yeah, you and whose army?" ' (B.P.).

you are ... For further phrases beginning thus, see **you're ...**

you are a calf! You *do* weep a lot, don't you?: *c.* 1910–40. (Manchon.) Prob. influenced – perhaps prompted – by Fr. *tu pleures comme un veau*, you weep copiously.

you are a gentleman. See **as I am a gentleman ...**

You are a mouth and will die a lip was a low and obusive c.p. of *c.* 1850–80. (Hotten, 1864.) Apparently suggested by the †*mouth*, a noisy, prating, ignorant fellow, and esp. by *mouth almighty*, which, *c.* 1850–1910, signified a noisy and extremely talkative person. Here *lip* = impudence, 'cheek' – cf *lippy*, cheeky, impertinent.

you are a one! – with *are* and *one* emphasized. Either 'You're odd,' *or* 'You're droll,' or both: orig. and still mostly Cockney: since (I'd guess) *c.* 1880 and still extant, although perhaps in the main allusively, as in Charles Drummond's very entertaining detective novel, *A Death at the Bar*, 1972:

He laughed.... 'Fifty quid or one month under the lock.'
'You are a one,' camped Bertie. [Said Bertie in affected mimicry.]

P.B.: as Sanders, 1978, notes, it is often followed by *and no mistake*; and, at least in the 'camp' or mockingly imitative mood, prec. by *ooh!*

Cf **you ain't 'arf a one; you are awful,** and the US counterpart **aren't you the one!**

you are a thief and a murderer, you have killed a baboon and stole his face is a c.p. of vulgar and illiterate abuse, recorded by Grose in 1785 and current *c.* 1760–1830.

[**you are all for the hustings.** You're all due for trouble: mid C17–18. Partly a c.p., partly a proverbial saying, it prob. derives from *the Hustings*, long the supreme law court of London.]

you are another! (or, more frequently, **you're another!**) A retort, meaning 'You too are a liar', or a rogue, a thief, a coward, a fool, or what you will: C16–20.

R.S. Surtees, *Handley Cross*, 1854, in vol. I, at the chapter 'Serving up a Hunt Dinner', offers this gem:

Great was the rush! The worthy citizen... scrambled to his seat at the head of the table, amidst loud cries of 'Sir, this is my Seat. Waiter, take this person out.'
'Who are you?'
'You're another!

You're Another served as the title of a comedy by Leicester Buckingham; apparently not listed in the British Library Reference Division catalogue, it was included in Lacy's Acting Edition of Buckingham's *Faces in the Fire*, performed in 1865. In John Bridgeman's *I've Eaten My Friend! A Farce*, performed in 1851, there had been this illuminating passage:

WIG:... She only answered it by throwing in my teeth –
COC: The hair-brush.
WIG: No, a sort of 'you're another' answer about a certain Sarah Jane...

It occurs also, as recorded by Farmer and Henley, in Udall, Fielding, Dickens and Sir William Harcourt. In the third, thus: ' "Sir," said Mr Pickwick, "you're another." ' And in the fourth, thus: 'Little urchins in the street have a conclusive argument. They say, "You're another".' A late C19–early C20 var. is *so's your father*. Note, too, that *you're another* has, in late C19–20, been almost meaningless, yet slightly contemptuous.

you are awful (, but I like you! – oh!). 'Dick Emery, dressed in fearsome drag, engaged in a sketch about "her" relationship with "her" boyfriend. The straight man took the role of an interviewer, and asked a series of double-meaning questions. These culminated in some frightful suggestion or other, and then Emery would smile, give the interviewer a hefty push which caused him to disappear off screen, and deliver this line. The phrase is a classic among TV gags, and burlesques an ancient [? since late C19: P.B.] cliché common among females remonstrating with a sexual innuendo or indulging in an intimate touch or caress' (Skehan, 1977): 1960s–early 70s.

you are Josephus Rex. See **you're joking.**

you are Mr Lobby Lud (: and I claim the *Westminster Gazette* prize). In later C20, an occ. almost nonsensical c.p. of greeting, but orig., the key words in a publicity stunt launched by the paper on 1 Aug. 1927. 'The name Lobby Lud came from the *Westminster Gazette's* telegraphic address: Lobby because of Westminster [and Parliamentary lobbies], Lud from Ludgate Circus. The idea of the stunt was that on the day in question the mystery man called Lobby Lud would be in Great Yarmouth, on the run and with £50 on his head. His job was not to get caught. The readers' job was to spot him and stop him, challenging him with [these] words... The man who first "played" Lobby Lud was William Chinn' (*Radio Times*, 30 Apr. 1983, p. 19, an article on a programme about Chinn, still alive and well, and living in South Wales: P.B.).

you are of so many minds you'll never be mad was a semi-proverbial c.p. of mid C16–mid (or perhaps until late) C18. It occurs, as Apperson informs us, both in Ray and in S. Such vacillation precludes the mounting tensions of insanity.

you are sick of the mulligrubs with eating chopped hay seems to have been a c.p. in S's time, to judge by this passage in Dialogue I:

MISS: Indeed, Madam, I must take my Leave, for I an't well.
LADY SM[ART]: What, you are sick of the Mulligrubs with eating chopt Hay.

It implies, I think, an imaginary indisposition. Lit., *the mulligrubs* = a stomach-ache.

you are (or **you're** or **he's**) **slower than the second coming of Christ.** A drill-sergeants' 'gag': C20. As John Brophy remarks in B & P, 1931:

Those drill-sergeants were often violently objurgatory and their choicest clichés cannot be printed, but here are three of the more cultured:

You shape like a whore at a christening! –
You are slower than the second coming of Christ. –
(*At the fixing of bayonets*). Don't look down! You'd soon find the hole if there was... [hair round it].
I first heard it in Queensland in 1912.

[**you aren't** (or **you're not**) **the only pebble on the beach**, a C20 'deflator' of the addressee's conceit or self-esteem, both Brit. and US (W & F, *you aren't*...): more of a cliché, or even a proverbial saying, than of a c.p. See also **you're not the only pebble...**

Eric Fearon notes, 1984, that 'when a female says [you aren't...] to a male it invites (and often gets) the reply "No, but all the others are stony"'.]

you asked for it (, buster)! US: since '*c.*1950. Prob. out of gangster movies and TV, uttered in the act of blasting someone usually addressed as "buster"' (Edward Hodnett, 1975). You asked – i.e., sought – trouble: now you're getting it! My own impression is that it goes back to the 1920s. A.B., 1979, notes that *baby* is sometimes used instead of *buster*, as indeed are a number of other vocatives.

you astonish me! Well, that's pretty obvious, isn't it?: ironic: dating from *c.*1920 – or perhaps a little earlier.

you beaut! orig. – not later than 1925, but not, I think, earlier than *c.*1910 – indicates a warm approval or even a profound admiration; it came to be occ. employed in ironic derision. Aus. (Baker, 1943.)

[**you bet!**; **you bet your (sweet) life!**; also US **you bet you!** or **you betcha!** – meaning 'You may be sure' or 'Assuredly, surely, certainly' and dating probably since the 1860s in US and since the late 1880s in UK cannot strictly, I feel, be classified as c.pps. (but cf the next). A.B., 1979, adds that there are many US variants, e.g. *you can (just) bet your sweet ass on it*, very common in 1970s.]

you bet your sweet bippy! exemplifies the transiency of certain TV and radio c.pps. In the *Oxford Mail*, 8 Sep.1977, reviewing the 1st ed. of this book, Jayne Gilman writes, 'Doesn't anyone else remember "You bet your sweet bippy"? There was a time when everyone was saying it. Along with "Take it away, Goldie" ['Goldie Hawn, at one time the resident blonde dum-dum of *Laugh-In*': VIBS] and "Time to say goodnight, Dick" [response, of course, 'Goodnight, Dick'] and, particularly "Vairee eenteresting – but schtoopid" [See **very interesting...**] ... They were all catch phrases from an American TV import called "Rowan and Martin's Laugh-In"... screened in Britain in (I think) 1970'.

Jayne Gilman adds that 'a silly sentence like "You bet your sweet bippy" suddenly becomes part of the national vocabulary – and can just as suddenly disappear again'. This particular example made so little impact that I've never heard even one of my numerous friends and acquaintances use it, nor seen it in print. The same is true of the *Goldie* and *Dick* examples. The *very* (or *vairee*) *interesting...* c.p. had a wider and longer-lasting currency.

Robert Claiborne, writing from US, 1984, notes that *up your bippy!*, apparently a quasi-euph. for **up yours!**, had some currency during the 1970s but is now †.

you better believe it! An emphatic 'yes': US. I've seen it in novels of the 1960s – for instance, Dorothy Uhnak, *The Witness*, 1969. R.C., 1978, adds 'Often with the nuance, "It's very much to your interest to accept it". I suspect a TV origin'; Fain, 1977, says 'I've heard it since *c.*1940'. Leechman, 1968, and Priestley, 1975, confirmed the phrase's Can. use, but in the more literate form *you'd better believe it!*; Leechman notes 'quite recent'.

P.B.: I recall seeing in an American magazine, mid 1960s, an advertisement for a neck-tie: it began, 'Would you believe such a bargain for only $1–99? Better believe!' Cf:

you better know it! '"Are the white women better Twisters [i.e., copulators] than the men?" – "Baby, you better know it!"' *Cavalier*, Nov.1963. (A black waiter to a white journalist.)' So runs an anon. contribution, 1978, from US. In *The Third Ear*, 1971, a glossary of Afro-American, the

phrase is defined as 'a warning that is used for emphasis referring to something that will be firmly enforced'. Cf prec.

you break the King's laws, you stretch without a halter was a Society – and perhaps a donnish – c.p. of C18. See S, 1738, Dialogue I:

[Colonel stretching himself.]
LADY SM[ART]: Why, Colonel, you break the King's Laws, you stretch without a Halter.

In the last resort, only the Crown has had – in Britain – the right either to order or to allow a stretching (of the neck), i.e. a hanging.

you can always stoop and pick up nothing. A C20, mostly Cockney, saying, for instance by one friend to another after a quarrel or, esp., by a parent to son or daughter concerning the intended daughter-in-law or son-in-law. It is prob. to be included in the small, very revealing, group of domestic c.pps.

you can ax (or **axe**) **me** (occ. my) **arse**. A low verbal snook-cocking, a c.p. of defiance: mid C18–20; by *c.*1950, slightly ob., and by 1975†.

you can bet your wife! 'Heard on and off' (Petch, 1974): C20. A pun on *you can bet your life* – see **you bet!**

you can call me anything (or **what**) **you like**.... See **call me...**.

you can go off some people, you know is a remark that, dating since *c.*1960, is 'addressed to, or directed at, someone who has just said or done something to upset [the speaker]. Very common a few years ago, not heard so much now. Perhaps from some radio or TV show' (P.B., 1974).

[**you can have any colour you like, so long as** (or **provided**) **it's black** is a famous quot'n attributed to Henry Ford concerning the Model 'T' Ford automobile – not quite a c.p.]

you can have it! (I don't want it is understood. The emphasis lies on *you* and *I*.) I want nothing to do with it; *or* I think so little of it, I'd give it away.

Orig. Brit., with var. *you can keep it!*, it prob. arose during the 1890s: it certainly seems to have been current throughout the C20. In B & P, 1930, in the section on 'Chants and Sayings'. John Brophy writes:

Much more terse [than the 'Help, help, there's a woman over board!' concerted chant or collective serial c.p.] was the following dialogue:
A: This is a *bloody* war. What shall we do about it?
B: You can have it! (*or*, You can keep it!)

Americans adopted it, I'd say in 1918–19, from the British Army. Berrey records it as an interjection 'of disapproval'.

'Also "Newton Abbot" – but there must be some clue in the context to this obscure c.p.' (Sanders, 1978). It represents a phonetic pun, almost exactly comparable with *Abyssinia*, 'I'll be seeing you', thus: *Newton Abbot*, 'you can 'ab it', with *ab* clearly substituted for '*ave*. (Playfair, 1978.) The use of *Newton Abbot*, market town and well-known railway junction in Devonshire, enshrines no mystery: it merely provides a realistic convenience. Cf:

you can have it for mine! (– well,). 'All right for you, perhaps, if you like that kind of thing, but I'd hate it' (P.B., 1977): since *c.*1960. An elab. of the prec.

you can have my hat! See **carry me out!**

you can hear them change their minds. Dating from the late 1940s, this urban c.p. is applied to those who live in postwar flats and council houses, so thin are the walls.

you can keep it! See **you can have it!**

you can kiss the book on that. It's a dead cert!: a sporting c.p. that dates from late C19. The book is The Book, the Bible, on which solemn oaths are sworn.

you can only pile it so high. 'There is a limit to the amount of nonsense people can be expected to swallow. "It" is, of course, bullshit. American, from 1920s or earlier; now ob.' (R.C., 1978). P.B.: perhaps also an allusion to 'the straw that broke the camel's back'.

you can put a ring around that one. That's one thing you *can* be sure of: NZ: since *c.*1925. To 'ring' it – preferably in red – so that it stands out on the page.

you can put it where it'll do the most good appears in Berrey's synonymy of 'disparaging and sarcastic flings' (Section 296, paragraph 8, on p. 300, of the 1st edn, 1942). Cf:

you can put (or **shove**) **it where the monkey puts** (or **shoves**) **its nuts.** See **put it where….**

you can say that again, orig. US, soon became also Can., and then, during the late 1920s, Brit.; it also passed to Aus. and NZ, prob. during the late 1930s and certainly not later than during the latter half of WW2. It indicates a hearty, even a heartfelt, agreement, and amounts to an emphatic 'Yes!' W & F merely refer it to their entry at *you said it* (which they omit to date).

The phrase had by *c.* 1950 become so ingrained in US speechways that, in *Strong Cigars and Lovely Women,* 1951 (a collection of essays and articles reprinted from *Newsweek* of 1949/1950/1951), at the title 'Kefauver Conquers All', John Lardner, that brilliant son of Ring Lardner who died untimely young, could write, 'This year's drought has got real significance, and don't tell me that I can say that again. I know I can. It has got real significance.'

In 1961, Edward Albee, *The American Dream,* uses it thus:

DADDY: I do wish I weren't surrounded by women; I'd like some men around here.

MRS BARKER: You can say that again.

In the *New Yorker* of 28 Apr. 1973, the letterpress to a drawing of indignant husband saying to tactless – or perhaps merely embittered – wife, 'And when I make a self-deprecating remark, I would appreciate it if you would not join in so fast with "You can say that again!"'

Another good recent US examples comes in James Hadley Chase, *Goldfish Have No Hiding Place,* 1974:

I called her house.

When she came on the line, I said, 'Great news about Wally! You must be relieved.'

'Oh, boy! You can say that again.' Shirley sounded very elated.

The survival of **oh, boy!** is worth noting. Moreover, the alert reader will have noticed that, by 1974, both of these c.pp. were clichés as well. Perhaps, however, I may be permitted to interpose a general editorial comment (which the very severe, I think the *ultra*-critical, reviewer may regard as more properly belonging to the Introduction):

There is no such thing as an inviolable and immutable classification of *permanent* inter-distinction between any one and any other of the three groups: c.pp., proverbial sayings, clichés. What's more, the almost infinite number – hence also the variety – of contexts for familiar phrases (a very useful 'umbrella' term) means that a phrase *can* exist simultaneously in any two of these groups. Language, by its very nature, is insusceptible of being straitjacketed.

To take several Brit. examples: *you can say that again* occurs in P. M. Hubbard, *The Holm Oaks,* 1965; Anne Morice, *Death in the Grand Manor,* 1970; Douglas Hurd and Andrew Osmond, *Scotch on the Rocks,* 1971; Reginald Hill, *An Advancement of Learning,* 1971; John Mortimer, *Collaborators,* 1973; John Braine, *The Pious Spy,* 1975.

In 1969, Mr Arthur Gray of NZ described this c.p. as 'a strong affirmation of agreement with a speaker, probably introduced from America to NZ during the Second World War. E.G., "He is just a deliberate liar." – "You can say that again."'

Cf **that makes two of us** and:

you can say that in spades has, since *c.* 1945, been a c.p. of heartfelt agreement. John Welcome, *Beware of Midnight,* 1961, has:

He saw me properly then for the first time…. 'You looked bushed. You need a drink.'

'You can say that in spades,' I said.

R.C., 1976, adds: 'From bridge, in which spades is the highest ranking suit. Hence (in US) a general intensifier, as in "He's a bastard in spades", occ. with the addition of "doubled (and redoubled)"'.

'A variant is "He *did* it – in spades!" He triumphed royally! He not only did the job, he did it perfectly. Spades are the top cards in many games' (A.B., 1979).

you can search me! See **search me!**

you can see their breakfasts (their navels) is 'said of girls wearing very low-cut dresses' (L.A., 1974): perhaps orig. Glasgow, but, if so, it spread almost immediately: since the late 1940s (I myself heard it in 1949 or 1950). Noted in the *Observer* Review, 28 Jan. 1973, article 'A Glasgow Gang Observed'.

you can smell my bloody arse! 'A C19–20 Cockney c.p., intended as a crushing conclusion to an argument, but sometimes evoking the still more crushing retort, "I can – from 'ere"' (R.S., 1969).

Also used as a declaration of defiance. From the olfactory reconnaissance of two dogs becoming acquainted.

you can stuff it! See **shove it!**, and **you know what you can do with it.**

you can take it from me! You may accept – *or* take – my word for it: Brit.: since *c.* 1910, if memory serve me faithfully. Often shortened to *take it from me!*

Both froms are also US, with var. *take it straight from me;* they appear in a synonymy of 'Expressions of Affirmation' in Berrey.

I shouldn't care to 'stick my neck out' and assert which usage, the Brit. or the US, preceded the other: but then, it doesn't have to be either – they could be simultaneous flames from a red-hot spontaneous combustion.

See also **take it from here.**

you can't beat the system (, can you?) is a 'c.p. of grievance when authority is believed to oppress' (L.A., 1974): since *c.* 1955.

P.B.: less a c.p. than a commonly true observation, a Brit. version of **you can't fight City Hall.** Cf **there ain't no justice.**

you can't do that there 'ere! and **'ere, what's all this?** This pair of C20 c.pp. orig. in (often ironical) derision of the rather gen. illiteracy of the old-style police constable. Contrast **hello! hello! hello!**

you can't fight (less often, as in life, **beat** or **lick**) **City Hall.** W. J. B., 1975, writes:

It is used with a shrug of the shoulders and simply means to the person it is addressed to, that a citizen without political pull can't do a thing against petty regulations of Government, injustices, over-taxation, red tape, etc…. But City Hall may mean any bureaucratic organization in a loose sort of way.

B.P., 1974, had noted that it was 'An American c.p. that is widely known in Australia. The term "City Hall" is not used [officially] in Australia except in Brisbane'. Dr Edward Hodnett thinks that the US c.p. goes back to the corrupt days of Tammany Hall and that it wouldn't now, mid 1970s, be used by the younger generation.

you can't fly on one wing is a US and Can. invitation (Moe; Leechman) – and Brit. (P.B.) – 'frequently heard in bars and at cocktail parties' (W.J.B.), to one more drink before departure: since the early – mid 1940s. Cf the (mainly) Irish *a bird never flew on one wing,* a jocularly gracious assent to a pressing invitation to another drink (Skehan, 1977). The latter is semantically reminiscent of the †, perhaps mainly journalistic *birdman* for airman, and both, of the largely mythical tales of aircraft returning, from missions over Europe, on one wing. P.B.: did both phrases arise simultaneously, or is the Irish acceptance, as I surmise, the earlier version, and prompter of the invitation?

[**you can't get away with it,** current since the middle 1950s, occurs, e.g, in John Osborne's *The World of Paul Slickey* (1959), where it forms the chorus of Act II, Scene ix. But it is, I'd say, a cliché rather than a c.p.]

you can't get high enough was, mid C19–early C20, a low jeering comment on a man's failure to achieve something. 'Probably obscene in origin' (F & H).

you can't get the wood, you know. 'A nonsense c.p. from the

Goon Show; used nowadays to explain the lack of almost anything' (P.B., 1975): as a c.p., since the early 1970s. Usu. in the high, quavery tones of 'Minnie Bannister' or 'Henry Crun'; see GOON SHOW.

[**you can't grow hairs on a billiard ball**. It's no good trying to do the impossible or what's against nature: midway between a c.p. and a potential proverb: (?) late C19–20. (Proposed, 1977, by W. J. B.)]

[**you can't have everything** is usu. a cliché, but when used in lighthearted, often also ironic, allusion, it verges on the c.p., as in Noël Coward, *Nude with Violin*, 1956, in the opening passage of Act I:

CLINTON: You don't talk like a valet.
SEBASTIEN: You can't have everything.

Benny Green, reviewing the 1st ed. of this book in the *Spectator*, 10 Sep. 1977, points out that it is the title of a song, written by Harry Revel and Mack Gordon, and pub'd in 1937.]

you can't have more than the cat and his skin was, c. 1870–1920, a somewhat proletarian, somewhat proverbial, Londoners' c.p., on the theme of *having one's cake and eating it*. Baumann.

you can't keep a good man down is both US (Berrey) and Brit. If used lit. and seriously, it's an irrefutable cliché; if used humorously, ironically, esp. if self-deprecatingly, it is an irrefutable c.p. (My tentative datings would be: US, since c. 1900; Brit. since 1918, perhaps via US soldiers.) Edward B. Marks, *They All Sang*, 1934, mentions a song thus titled in 1900, words by M. R. Carey.

you can't lodge here, Ferguson (or **Mr Ferguson**) is a Londoners' c.p., but very short-lived: c. 1845–50; expressing either firm refusal or open derision. It arose from the well-publicized difficulties experienced by a drunk – not a drunken – Scot named Ferguson in obtaining lodgings.

you can't piss up a rope implies 'Why attempt the impossible?': US, certainly current during WW2 and prob. since c. 1900. Hank Searls alludes to it in his *Pentagon*, 1971. (moe.)

you can't play in my backyard is US, pseudo-children's, based on an early C20 (or late C19) popular song and become a humorous c.p., used by and to adults. (J. W. C., 1977.)

you can't play that on me! 'I am not to be thus deceived; I am not a tool or cat's-paw. This c.p. is of Shakespearian descent. "You would play upon me.... 'Sblood, do you think I am easier to be played on than a pipe?"' [Farmer]. Apparently current c. 1850–1900. The Shakespearean ref. is to *Hamlet*, III, ii, lines 380ff.

'This has been modernized to *you can't pull that (one) on me!* and *you can't put that across on me!* (A.B., 1979). But are these truly c.pp.? I feel that they are merely familiar slangy expressions.

you can't prove it by me. '"I can't confirm the statement in question – and am inclined to doubt it": US: from c. 1950' (R.C., 1978).

you can't quack me: I'm a rubber duck. 'I'm too long in the tooth to fall for that one. An "in" phrase, Royal Navy, 1974–5' (Peppitt). P.B.: prob. orig. a pun on childish pron. of *crack*.

you can't sleep here, Jack: Town Hall steps. See **can't sleep here**...

you can't take him (less often **her**) **anywhere!**: *without him embarrassing you* understood. 'Exclamation to the company at large *re* one's partner [or companion] who has just done or said something contrary to the accepted custom [or the social code]' (P.B., 1975). Cf **excuse my pig, he's a friend and is he with you?** It dates from c. 1945 at the latest.

you can't take it with you is directed at one who, saving money, loses happiness or, at the least, pleasure. Widely known, almost proverbial, c.p., prob. throughout the English-speaking world. Shipley, 1977, noting that it is very much alive in US, goes on, 'It was the title of a hit comedy by George S. Kaufman and Moss Hart, that, opening on Broadway, 15 Dec. 1936, has had frequent revivals all over

the [USA]. It played in England (Manchester, 13 Dec., London, 22 Dec. 1937). It won the 1937 Pulitzer Prize'.

But the c.p. long preceded the comedy and perhaps goes back to late or even mid C19, as J. W. C. has suggested, adding 'widely current, though perhaps *less*, not more, so before it became the title of the well-known play... I suppose it can be regarded as a vulgarization of "assuredly we can take nothing out"' (1 *Timothy*, vi, 7, and *Job*, i, 21–but very familiar from the introductory words of the Funeral Service: P.B.).

you can't tell the mind of a squid. 'This refers to an unreliable person. A squid can move backwards or forwards' (Maxwell Taylor, 1977). This C20 Newfoundland c.p. verges on the proverbial, yet it remains predominantly a c.p.

you can't: they go too fast forms the dovetail response to the cliché 'Time flies': earlier C20. A pun, in case you hadn't got there, on *time*, noun, and *time*, verb: it took me a little while when my father first used it on me in the 1930s. (P.B.)

you can't think! You couldn't possibly imagine it; *or* You'd never believe it; *or* It's incredible: orig. and still mostly proletarian Londoners': since c. 1770 or a little earlier. Frederick Pilon, *He Would Be a Soldier*, 1776, at III, i, Caleb says to Charlotte: 'Suppose you and I go this evening to Bagnigge Wells, and drink tea – the hot rolls are so nice there, you can't think!' In W. Pett Ridge's *Minor Dialogues*, 1895, we read, 'She took up such an 'igh and mighty attitude, you can't think.' This exclamatory c.p. derives from such a sentence as 'You couldn't imagine how I felt'.

you can't win! Orig. a US c.p. 'expressing the impossibility of coming out on top and the futility of kicking against the pricks' (Leechman, testifying to its Can. usage); Mrs Ursula Roberts in her column 'All About Words', in the Hong Kong *South China Morning Post*, late 1978, wrote 'I remember hearing it in America [i.e., the USA] then [c. 1950], and Harold Ross, the former editor of the *New Yorker* magazine, who died in 1951, is quoted as using it, in Brendan Gill's book, *Here at the New Yorker*'. R.C., 1978, tells me that the author of the quot'n 'The odds are 6–5 against life' was Shoeless Joe Jackson or some other US baseball player, in the period 1910–30; I had thought it might be Ring Lardner – but what spirited person would refuse to accept such odds?

By 1960, at latest, it had become a common Brit. c.p., soon incorporated into everyday speech and writing, as, for instance, in John Hillaby, *Journey through Britain*, 1968: 'From Cornwall?' he said. 'Do you mean to tell me you've walked all the way here?' I nodded. Shaking his head sadly, he said: 'Then all I can say is it's a pity you couldn't be doing something useful.' You can't win.

Cf this from Frederick Nolan's 'thriller', *The Oshawa Project*, 1974: '...The old army rule of Murphy's Law, in itself an extension of the philosophy best described in the words "You can't win"...'

In the *Bournemouth Echo*, 18 Aug. 1970, there is a short article headed 'You Can't Win', subtitled 'Council on the road to trouble': an official plaintively makes this poignant remark. (Petch.) Mr Arthur Gray, 1969, confirmed that the c.p. was actively current in NZ.

P.B.: in UK often, in mock or real despair, *you just can't win!*

Cf:

you can't win them (but usu. **'em**) **all!** You can't *always* succeed; You can't win every game or girl or contest or battle; or, as Edward Hodnett 1975 puts it, 'a philosophic acceptance of defeat, often self-mocking': a US c.p. dating from c. 1940 and adopted in UK c. 1955, yet not widely used there before c. 1960.

Brit. usage may be exemplified by the following quotations:

James Munro, *The Innocent Bystanders*, 1969, 'He hesitated just a split second too long, and was already starting to turn when Craig's voice spoke behind him. "Be sensible," said Craig. "You can't win them all. Guns on the bed, please."'

Michael Delving, *The Devil Finds Work*, 1970:

Chead was a hamlet.... The pub, Chead House, was neither old nor attractive....

'A quaint little place,' I said.

'Olde Englande,' said Bob, with a grin at me.

'You can't win 'em all,' I said.

In it carries the dovetail tag: **but one now and again would break the monotony.** (Cyril Whelan, 1975.)

US examples abound. One will suffice. In *Hail, Hail, the Gang's All Here*, 1971, Ed McBain writes:

'Anything?' Kling asked.

'You can't win 'em all,' O'Brien [a detective] said.

This is perhaps the most satisfactory joint US–British c.p. to have become very widespread since WW2 and looks (in 1976, anyway) likely to endure a long time.

It is well worth while to note J.W.C.'s comment, 1975: 'You can't win 'em all' is very common here [the US] as a sort of rueful and more or less humorous self-consolation for an occasional and usually rare defeat or frustration in any kind of contest or contest-like activity.... [Prob.] it originated in the language of usually successful (and often crooked) poker players.

Cf **you win a few, you lose a few,** and the prec.

you come home with your drawers (or **knickers) torn** .... See **you'll be telling me, like the girl, that you've fahnd** (or **found) a shilling** and **come home with your knickers torn.**

you could have fooled me, with emphasis usu. on *me*; often employed with (a mostly gentle) irony, to mean the opposite of what it says: since *c.* 1955. As in Angus Ross, *The London Assignment*, 1972, ' "I'd say you were a very active man. Me, I'm more of the – er – passive type." ... "You could have fooled me," I told him solemnly.'

Of its Aus. use, B.P., 1974, supplies the gloss, 'I am surprised by your story'; as L.A. remarks, 1977, it is 'particularly apt when what is told is in doubt or so impossible as to be unbelievable'.

It has the occ. var. *you could fool me*, 'an oblique way of expressing, or acquiescing in, doubt, e.g. "He says he's an expert – but you could fool me". Semantically, it apparently implies that the speaker could very easily be "fooled" into doubting the statement in question; in effect, "Even the most dubious [or] foolish evidence would convince me otherwise' (R.C., 1978, from US).

you could piss from one end of the country to the other. A c.p. ref. to the (comparatively) small size of England: naturally commoner among natives of the Commonwealth than among Britons: since *c.* 1910; also predictably: used rarely by women. P.B.: a politer version substitutes *spit*.

you could ride bare-arse from London on it is a West Country c.p., alluding to a very blunt knife: late C19–20. It has an agreeably rural tang. (With thanks to Mr D.B. Gardner.) Yet it may be urban, for in S, 1738, Dialogue II, occurs this adumbration:

LORD SM[ART]: [*Carving a Partridge*.] Well, one may ride to *Rumford* upon this *Knife*, it is so blunt.

Why Romford? Apparently for the alliteration.

Robert Barltrop, 1981, in a letter to P.B. recalls that as a boy in the 1920s, he used to hear London East End housewives say 'You could ride bare-behind to Romford on this knife'; Grose's comment, *c.* 1790, that 'Rumford was formerly a famous place for leather breeches', may or may not be relevant. A further regional var. comes from B.G.T., 1978: 'In my childhood [1920s], "You could ride bare-back to Warwick on it" ' – a form particularly suitable to children in the South and West Midlands.

you *could* **say that** is an understatement for 'You could have put it much more strongly and still not be exaggerating': perhaps going back to *c.* 1920, but I didn't hear it – or, rather, notice it as a c.p. – until WW2. (Mr A.B. Petch happily reminded me of it.)

It is as much US as Brit. Edward Albee, in *Tiny Alice*, performed on 29 Jan. 1964 and pub'd in 1965, has at I, ii:

JULIAN: I am a lay brother.

BUTLER: You are *of* the cloth, but have not taken it.

JULIAN [*none too happily*[: You *could* say that.

you could twist my arm. An understated, yet enthusiastic, reply to 'Have a drink!' – current since the 1940s. Also *you have*, or *you've talked me into it*: since late 1940s. (Shaw, 1969.)

The latter form occurs at the end of 'The World's Worst Urger' in Frank Hardy's *Billy Borker Yarns Again*, 1967.

'Also *you twisted my arm*, which is commoner in the US, precisely as *you talked me into it* is American for British *you've talked...*' (R.C., 1978). Of the *you twisted* version, Fain, 1978, writes, 'A rejoinder when someone has proved to you that you should do something. Sometimes ... humorously, to indicate that you would do it without any argument (as when only a suggestion has been made). Sometimes as an assurance that no [persuasion] is necessary, as in "O.K., but you don't have to twist my arm" '.

you couldn't be more right. This Aus. c.p., dating since the late 1930s, indicates the speaker's entire agreement. (B.P.) A var., prob. deliberate, of **I couldn't agree more.**

you couldn't be served quicker in a cook-shop! 'Housewives' own tribute (richly deserved) to promptness of catering. Edwardian [to my knowledge], but undoubtedly Victorian [in origin]' (L.A., 1975).

you couldn't blow the froth off a pint; or **you couldn't knock a pint back;** and **you couldn't fight** (or **punch) your way out of a paper bag.** See **couldn't knock ...**

you couldn't hit the side of a barn. See **couldn't hit ...**

you couldn't pay me enough '(to make me do it). "Under no conceivable circumstances would I – i.e., for no conceivable reward": US: since (?) 1940s' (R.C., 1978). P.B.: cf, from Kipling's *Captains Courageous*, 1897, but concerning an American fishing fleet of *c.* 1870, 'I tell you, Harve, there ain't money in Gloucester [Massachusetts] 'ud hire me to ship on a reg'lar trawler'.

you couldn't see his arse for dust. He departed very hastily indeed, or in a great hurry: late C19–20.

P.B.: but the speaker may apply this phrase to himself: *you won't see my arse ...*, merely a vulgarization of the cliché, as in, e.g. Leopold's farewell song in the musical 'The White Horse Inn', 'You won't see my heels for the dust'.

Cf **I'm off in a cloud ...**

you couldn't throw your hat over the workhouse wall. You have many illegitimate children in there: a Cockney c.p. of C20. The implication is that an attempt to retrieve one's hat thrown over the wall would be to expose oneself to the risk of recognition. Diminishingly popular since mid-1945: it's no longer polite or seemly or befitting human dignity to mention anything so vulgar as a workhouse.

you date! Well, you *are* out of date! – but with the connotation, 'You *are* a queer fish (*or* odd fellow)!': *c.* 1919–30. (Manchon.)

'In the US, "it (anything) dates" is much commoner – and still common' (J.W.C., 1977).

you didn't travel up the Thames in a wheelbarrow. 'You're no fool. This possible c.p. is taken from H. Carmichael, *Candles for the Dead*, 1973. Meaning is quite clear from context, and semantics are reasonably clear – i.e., anyone attempting to navigate the Thames in a wheelbarrow would indeed be a fool. It would appear to be either a c.p. (British, of course) or a remarkably eccentric original metaphor' (R.C., 1978).

you dirty old man! 'The younger Steptoe (Harry H. Corbett) to his father (Wilfred Brambell], in *Steptoe And Son*' (VIBS); an immensely popular BBC TV comedy series about a pair of London totters (rag-and-bone merchants): later 1960–earlier 70s.

you dirty rat! 'James Cagney claims he never said the words put in his mouth by countless impressionists. In [the film] *Blonde Crazy* [, 1931], however, he does call someone a "dirty, double-crossing rat" – which, I suppose, amounts to much the same thing' (*VIBS*). Cf **me Tarzan...**

P.B.: even so late as 1983, the *Mail on Sunday* magazine *You* (21 Aug.) could publish an allusive cartoon: two rats, one saying to the other, 'You dirty Cagney!'

you dirty rotten swine, you! (The *dirty* occ. omitted.) 'Bluebottle (Peter Sellers) in The Goon Show. Also, **you have deaded me!**' (*VIBS*). P.B.: this usu. followed some tremendous explosion or catastrophe, and managed to be simultaneously indignant and plaintive. See remarks at **shut up, Eccles,** and GOON SHOW.

you don't! See **you don't say so!**

you don't get many of those to the pound. Cyril Whelan, 1975, says that this orig. in

A rude joke shared between males as a particularly well developed pair of female breasts passes by. Like all bawdy jokes it became ubiquitous without any apparent process of communication and is almost impossible to place in time or location with any authority. Possibly, as with 'Kilroy was here', we need to return to the lees of Pompeii to find companion scribblings (sibling scribblings?) – *Marcus hic fuit* – to discover the proper origin.

Not, I think, pre-C20.

you don't (happen to) have a dirty pound note (on you), do you? A casual intimation that a small loan would be most acceptable: since the early 1950s. 'Also, "you don't have a Rolls-Royce with the ash-trays full?" From the joke about the enormously rich man who used to trade in his Rolls-Royces rather than empty the ash-trays. [Since] *c.* 1960' (Sanders, 1978). By *c.* 1975, slightly ob., whereas the *pound note* var. is – at least in 1978 – still 'going strong'. P.B.: by 1985, more likely to be *a dirty five-pound note* (or *fiver*), to keep pace with inflation. Another version is *you haven't a dirty pound note or two (that) you don't want, have you?* or *... I suppose?*; all can, of course, be simply a playful request made on the spur of the moment.

you don't have papers on me. You can't serve a writ on me, for, e.g., debt or, esp., for maintenance of an illegitimate child: earlier C20.

you don't have (illiterately, but very commonly, **you ain't got) the brains God gave a goose.** You're brainless, or exceptionally stupid: US, prob. rural in orig.: prob. from mid C19. A.B., remembers it from *c.* 1940 but thinks that it was used by Mark Twain in the 1870s–1880s. By *c.* 1970, slightly ob. 'There are variants, of course, especially in the sort of animal named – mule, pig, goat, rabbit, dog, etc.' Cf **you haven't got the brains...,** the Brit. version.

you don't have to be mad to work here, but it helps. As P.B. remarked, 1975: 'It's one of those things like *the impossible we do at once*, instantly memorable and spread through offices and workshops like wildfire. The sort of thing one can buy a printed sign of in a joke shop.' Since *c.* 1960.

You don't have to buy... See **Why buy.**

you don't know the half of it! was current among US university students during the 1920s (McKnight mentions it) and then more generally.

I don't know when it came to England, but I'd guess the 1940s. Petch noted, 1974: 'Heard on and off.

you don't know..., in expressions of contempt at ignorance and naivety. See **doesn't know...**

you don't look at the mantelpiece... See **who looks at...**

you don't piss hard against the ground yet. 'Although the initial pronoun can vary, this is always a masculine phrase. It is usually addressed by an older, experienced man to someone who is either literally immature or acting immaturely. I heard it in Tennessee in the 1950s, but I suspect it is not widespread' (A.B., 1979). P.B.: but I have heard it once or twice in UK.

you don't really love me. See **aw, gee, you...**

you don't say! – with emphasis usu. on *don't* rather than on *say* – is short for **you don't say so!** but it deserves a separate entry, for it has been current since late C19 in UK and perhaps earlier in US. It expresses astonishment, sometimes amazement, sometimes incredulity; often tinged with irony, as in ' "He's a great man." – "You don't say!" ' As a synonym of 'Fancy that!' it was satirized by *Punch* on 10 Oct. 1973 in the 'feature' titled 'Complete Vocabulary of Spoken English'.

It is recorded by Berrey as being so well established that it labels a brief synonymy indicating surprise or astonishment. A good example occurs in Tom Ardies, *The Man in the White House*, 1971:

'We writer fellows spend a lot of time meditating and contemplating.'

'You don't say?'

'I do say.'

Dr Edward Hodnett, 1975, however, explains its US usage as 'a sarcastic equivalent of **sez you!**' Its Can. usage is recorded by Sandilands in 1913, with the gloss, 'Exclamation of surprise – usually feminine'; Priestley adjudged it to be † in Can. by 1975.

you don't say so (! or ?) Orig. US, it became also Brit. in late C19. In *AM*, 1859, we find an entry 'YOU DON'T! for *you don't say so!* i.e. really! indeed! "Mr Grimaldi threw a back somerset out of a three-story window." Now, *you don't!*' Apparently *you don't say so!* dates from early in C19, for it occurs – as a New England c.p. – in John Neal's novel, *The Down-Easters*, 1833, at chapter I, p. 76, thus:

What I tell you is the truth, nevertheless –

Sneks an' spiders! you don't say so!

An early Brit. example comes in Henry Arthur Jones, *The Crusaders*, performed in 1891 and pub'd in 1893, early in Act III:

PALSAM: Sir, a very terrible scandal has occurred, which I shall be compelled to make public.

DICK: You don't say so?

There is even a facetious var., the joc. *you don't shay sho* (or *so*)*!*; C20. Parodying the drunken pron. of the phrase. This has a parallel, rather than a deliberate, var. *I should shay sho* (or *so*)*!* – as in Ian Hay, *David and Destiny*, 1934: 'I should shay sho! Go right ahead!' These jocularities signify, the former 'Really!' and the latter, 'Certainly!'

CF prec.

you don't shit on your own doorstep is a c.p. var., a realistic alteration, a down-to-earthing of the proverbial 'You don't foul your own nest': late C19–20. Cf **never shit where you eat!**

you figure it. '*You* explain what it means (i.e., since you don't find *my* explanation wholly convincing). US from (?) 1920s. From "standard" US coll. use (C20) of "figure" as synon. with "assess" or "reckon up" a situation or person. Cf *it figures*, and *it adds up*' (R.C., 1978).

you first, my dear Alfonso (or **Alphonse**). See **after you, Claude.**

you get my goat! was orig. US: *c.* 1905; recorded by S.R. Strait in the *Boston Globe, c.* 1917, and by W&F, who show it to have been extant in 1960; it still is in 1976, although less common than formerly. P.B.: but in UK, if ever a c.p., long since become cliché, or simply coll. idiom; much more often of a third party than directly accusing, as in 'His attitude gets my goat' or 'What really gets my goat is the way they...'

you get nothing for nothing... See **nothing for nothing...**

you get that. In 1977, Cdr C. Parsons, RN, ret., wrote to me about 'a c.p. which became almost wearisome by overuse... I am now so much retired (end 1969) that I cannot vouch for its present currency.

(1) you get that

(2) you get that – you're bound to

(3) you get that – you're bound to (get it) in a ship this size.

(3) presumably started it and, with familiarity, it dwindled through (2) and (1).

Its origin I don't know, but it could well have been a skit on the favourite utterance of, perhaps, the Executive Officer of what, at the time, was one of the largest ships in the Royal

Navy. One can picture him explaining ... the inevitability of some particular circumstance of discipline, welfare, ship-handling in confined waters or in a high wind, attributable to the unique size of the monster to which Their Lordships, in their infinite discernment, had been pleased to appoint him. His scurrilous juniors would have pounced upon it with gleeful repetition on the occasion of any trivial mishap to a brother officer – even, for instance, a bridge player having his ace trumped on the very first round'.

you getting too proud to speak to anyone now? See **are you getting** ...

you give me the balls-ache! (or **you give me a pain in the arse** or **back**, or **balls**, or **neck**, or **penis**, or in one or two other parts or otherwise-named parts of the body not here specified!) I utterly disapprove of your behaviour; I thoroughly disagree with your point of view; or, most frequently, 'You make me tired' – i.e., impatient, disgusted, etc.: C20. The first, third, fourth, sixth being low (yet 'educated' for *prick*): mostly Londoners'.

P.B.: an Australian Army friend of mine, later 1960s, would describe anyone, male or female, that he found offensive, as 'a pain in the bum'.

you going to see the Dook and complain? 'Are you intending – *or* do you propose – to complain to a high-ranking officer?' An Army (Other Ranks') c.p., dating from 1814, when Sir Arthur Wellesley was created Duke of Wellington, until *c.* 1870. In Ronald Pearsall's *Tides of War*, 1978, a private, speaking to a lance-corporal who has just lost his stripe: '"You going to see the Dook and complain?" asked another.' Apparently *and complain* was sometimes omitted.

you got me, pal! 'I simply don't know' or 'That's a puzzler': US: *c.* 1910–60. (Berrey.) P.B.: the Brit. shape is usu. 'You've got me there (, I'm afraid)'; contrast **they got me**. Sandilands, 1913, gives Can. synon. *you have me beat* and *you have me there*. Cf *search me!*

you got rocks in the head? 'Usually said to one who has made a ridiculous or audacious suggestion or proposal' (W&F, who cite two examples of its use in 1951): US: since the middle 1940s. P.B.: the idiom sounds Yiddish.

you got to spend a dollar ... See **you have to spend a dollar** ...

you guessed it! is a US expression of affirmation, recorded, 1942, by Berrey, but going back, *I'd* guess, to early C20.

you had a mother once. See **you ought to remember** ...

you have (or **you've got**) **a heart like a Leicester landlady.** You're hard-hearted and without romance: since *c.* 1920. In, e.g., Douglas Hayes, *Quite a Good Address*, 1073. (L.A., 1976) Ex touring repertory actors. P.B.: was this a gen. denigration of provincial landladies, with Leicester chosen as representative for alliteration's sake, or was it a specific accusation?

you have (or **you've got**) **a nice place** (occ. **set-up**) **here**, 'here' being a house or flat or room or office: US, since the late 1940s, with *place* predominating from *c.* 1965 onwards. See also **nice place you've got here**, the prob. orig.

you have another guess coming! You are mistaken, 'You're all wrong!': US: since the 1920s, if not a decade or two earlier. P.B., 1976, pertinently asks, 'What does this make "If *that's* what you think, [then, I'm afraid] you've got another think coming?" A potential, perhaps even an incipient, c.p.

you have (or **you've**) **been doing naughty things** is a tediously arch C20 bourgeois c.p. addressed to a young couple when, clearly, the wife is pregnant.

you have been to an Irish wedding was, *c.* 1750–1850, addressed to one who has a black eye. Grose, 1788, says, '... Where black eyes are given instead of favours'.

you have been warned is a joc. c.p., current since the 1930s. From the wording of a familiar police admonition. (Petch, 1974.)

you have deaded me. See **you dirty rotten swine.**

you have grown a big girl since last Christmas! is a C20 c.p., hardly a cultured address to a girl or even a woman, the ref. being to somewhat noticeably large breasts. (Occurs in, e.g.,

R. Blaker, *Night-Shift*, 1934.) Cf **you don't get many** ... , and **you're a big girl now.**

you have hit it: I believe you are a witch is given by *ODEP* as a proverb, but I'd have said that, orig. at least, it was a C18 c.p. Usu. ironic, as in S, 1738, Dialogue II:

LADY SM[ART]: Well, but do you hear, that Mrs *Plump* is brought to bed at last?

MISS: And pray, what has God sent her?

LADY SM: Why, guess if you can.

MISS: A Boy, I suppose.

LADY SM: No, you are out, guess again.

MISS: A Girl then.

LADY SM: You have hit it; I believe you are a Witch. The C20 equivalent is **how did you guess?** See also **I think you are a witch.**

you have (or **you've got**) **it made.** You're on the point of succeeding: US: since *c.* 1920. Adopted in UK and Aus. and NZ by *c.* 1944. It has a synon., current since the middle 1960s (or a little earlier): *everything is marvellous for you.* (A reminder, 1976, from Patricia Newnham.) Esp., however, it is addressed to someone who is constantly saying 'It was marvellous' – 'That's marvellous', and in this nuance the *you* is either heavily or, more deadly, lightly yet incisively, emphasized. P.B.: but the initial pronoun may change, for ref. to others: 'she's got it ...', etc.; in UK, at least, it now means rather, 'You have succeeded'.

you have made a fair speech was, *c.* 1660–1770, a c.p. uttered 'in derision of one that spends many words to little purpose' (BE). Cf **you sure slobbered** ...

you have me beat (or **there**). See **you got me.**

you have (or, more coll., **you got**) **to spend a dollar to earn a dollar.** A modern US version of 'nothing venture, nothing gain': since *c.* 1950 or earlier. (R.C., 1978.) P.B.: more proverb or folk-wisdom aphorism than c.p.

you have your glue (or **often, porridge**). 'A c.p. much in use, among my friends at least, in my native city of Dublin ... It's roughly cognate with **you'll be lucky** and might be used in response to, say, "I'll have a large brandy" or "I want to borrow a tenner"' (Ian Sainsbury, 1977).

you have your troubles and I have mine is a US c.p., orig. in a wartime story (*c.* 1940) of three sailors who succeed in prying a barman loose from a free drink apiece, with the third one facing the barman's indignation by saying, 'Look, buddy, you've got your troubles and I have mine. Now, give me my change and I'll get the hell out of here.' As a c.p., it arose during the late 1940s and is 'used to dismiss someone with a tale of woe' (Edward Hodnett, 1975.)

Cf. **you think you got troubles,** of which this is prob. a var. Janssen, 1978, notes that 'this was doubtless reinforced by the Fortunes' tremendous hit, "You've Got Your Troubles", highly praised by *Special Pop*, Oct. 1967. All members of the Fortunes group are British'.

you haven't a dirty pound note ...? See **you don't have a dirty** ...

you haven't been in the Service half a dog-watch. A C20 RN c.p. addressed, esp. during WW2, to a newcomer. *SS.*

you haven't got the brains you were born with! A derisive C20 c.p., addressed, usu. in exasperation, to an exceptionally stupid person.

A.B., from the US, adds, 1979: 'Sometimes ... *the brains God gave an apple.* This phrase still "lives", but I don't hear it very often now'. Cf **you don't have the brains** ...

you haven't seen anything (or **the half of it**) **yet.** See **you ain't heard** ...

you hear me! Writing in 1889, Farmer says: 'A pleonastic ejaculation of Californian origin. Used to emphasize a statement already made, and to which assent has been given. "Will you go to-night?" "Yes, that's so." "Wa'al, *you hear me!*"' Apparently only *c.* 1880–1910.

you heard! You heard me all right, so don't pretend you didn't! *or* Oh, you understand, so stop pretending!: US, since *c.* 1935; adopted in UK not later than the middle 1940s.

Contrast **I hear you!** In Hugh C. Rae, *The Marksman*, 1971, we read:

'...Ever since I first thought of it.'

'But you didn't think of it, Jack,' Weaver said quietly. 'What!'

'You heard. It's not your idea...'

But a much earlier example appears in John Mortimer's endearing short play, *Conference*, which forms part of an avant-garde symposium of plays: *Sketches from One to Another*, pub'd in 1960 and written by John Mortimer, Norman F. Simpson, Harold Pinter:

JONES (*in the call-box*): This Jones speaking.

TYCOON: Jones, doll, I appreciate your calling. long time no hear. Have you lost your love for me, Jones?

JONES: Yes.

TYCOON (*appalled*): What did you say? Guess this is a bad connexion.

JONES: You heard.

It also occurs in John Osborne's *A Sense of Detachment*, prod. 1972, pub'd 1973, early in Act I:

GIRL: You would, you filthy old woman.

OLDER LADY: What did you say?

GIRL: You heard.

P.B.: it may have been earlier still in UK. E.P.'s date for its adoption was orig. mid 1950s, but I remember it being used to me during WW2. In fact, the Brit. usage may be of independent origin, a shortening of *'you heard, you ain't got clorf* (Cockney), or *cloth* (more gen., yet still predominantly proletarian) *ears*: fairly common 50 years ago' (Sanders, 1978); E.P. thought that this form might well have gone back to very early C20.

you hum it and I'll pick up the tune. See no! but you hum it....

you kid me not! You're telling me! *or* Don't I know it!: US: since *c.*1940. Adam Hall, *The Berlin Memorandum*, 1965, 'I'm hot,' I said....

'You kid me not,' he grinned quickly.

Cf **I kid you not.**

you kill me! An ironic 'You're so *very* funny!': since the middle 1930s. Also, since early 1940s, *you slay me!* Adopted from US, where current since *c.*1930. Carolyn Weston, *Poor, Poor Ophelia*, 1972, has:

Then he grinned at Krug. 'Just like the bluebird of happiness, Al – it's right here in our own backyard.'

'You kill me, you know that? Bluebird! You really kill me. Okay,' Krug said briskly, 'let's go.'

An English example: Anne Morice, *Death of the Dutiful Daughter*, 1973:

'In the first place you could hop over to Dedley and crack the case yourself, thereby releasing Robin for more important duties.'

'You kill me, Toby.'

In the title story of Noël Coward's *Pretty Polly Barlow*, 1964, an American says to (English) Polly, '"You slay me!" Rick Barlow laughed, "The way you say things, sort of deadpan."'

You slay me had, by 1975, become sadly outdated; and *you kill me*, slightly do.

you kill my cat and I'll kill your dog. An exchange of social amenities, in the lower strata: late C19–20; ob. by *c.*1950, well-nigh † by 1976.

you know me, Al is a US c.p., meaning 'You can trust me' (Berrey) or 'You can depend on me'. In 1915, there appeared in US a book that almost immediately became famous: Ring Lardner's collection of baseball stories, *You know me, Al* (*A Busher's Letters*)–where *busher* = a 'Bush League' (i.e., inferior grade) baseball player; Al was the recipient of the letters. In 1923, McKnight's excellent book set it on the academic map.

You know me, Al thus extends the synon. *you know me* (and can therefore trust me), which is itself much rather a cliché than a c.p. The somewhat boastful, entirely self-delusive writer of these letters keeps on saying 'You know

me, Al' – as in the letter of 13 May, which ends: 'I will get back in the big league and show them birds something. You know me, Al.'

you know my methods, Watson. The late Prof. W.E. Collinson, while at Dulwich College (1901–7) read 'especially the *Sherlock Holmes* stories then appearing in the Strand Magazine.... Holmes supplied us with the oft repeated phrase: "You know my methods, Watson, – apply them."' The phrase is extant. Cf **elementary...**

you know the old saying: the Persian Gulf's the arsehole of the world... See **arsehole of the world.**

you know what men (or women) are! See **isn't that just like a man (or a woman)!**

you know what they say about Chinese women. See what they say...

you know what they say about little men. 'Heard now and then. Appears to mean that they are big elsewhere [i.e., the genitals]' (Petch, 1969). Cf **big conk.... and little, but oh my!**

you know what thought did is a mid C19–20 c.p. If one's interlocutor asks 'What?' one replies **ran away with another man's wife.** This is a euph. version of the C18–mid C19 form recorded by Grose, 2nd edn, 1788: *'What did thought do? Lay in bed and besh*t himself, and thought he was up*; reproof to anyone who excuses himself for any breach of positive orders, by pleading that he thought to the contrary.' Cf **what did thought do?**

A C20 var. is recorded by Franklyn, 1968: 'The pert Cockney boy's response is, "No, 'e never! 'E only thought 'e did!"'

you know what you can do with it (or... **what to do with it**) but *with it* is often omitted. 'I don't want it, *you* can stick (*or* shove) it' (in the usual anatomically fundamental nuance): low: since the early 1920s, if not since *c.* 1900 or even earlier; became, in WW2, very popular in the British Armed Forces, whence, on the Exchange system, it passed also to the US Army; hence to US civilians – that is, if they too hadn't already known it. (W & F include, but do not date, it.) Cf the predominantly US euph. **you can put it where it will do the most good.**

R.C., 1978, helpfully confirms my suggestion of early US knowledge, and use, of the phrase: 'See D. Hammett, *The Glass Key*, 1930, hence current from *c.* 1920'. He adds that the US possesses a var.: *you know what you can do.* A.B. noted, 1979, a song that was current, entitled 'You Can Take This Job and Shove It'. R.C. had earlier pointed out that, whereas in UK a distinction is very rarely made, in the US it is observed: 'Despite their close similarity, these expressions have quite different meanings: *you know what you can do with it* is, indeed, "shove it"; *you know what you can do* is "go fuck yourself"'. (Yet another example of what I owe to Mr Claiborne's clearheadedness and wide knowledge.)

P.B.: may also occur with other pronouns or names, e.g. *they know what they...* Cf **shove it!**

you know where you can put it. A US synonym (Berrey) of **you can put it where it will do the most good,** q.v. at prec.

you lie like a dockyard clock. You're an awful liar: RN, mostly lowerdeck: C20. (Daniel Farson, 1977.)

you little trimmer! 'A joyous exclamation of appreciation of beauty' (Harry Griffiths, 1978): Aus.: since the late 1940s. Coined by script-writer for use by Roy Rene in the *McCackie Mansion* radio series; Rene popularized it, as he did *Young Harry, cop it!*, which became the c.p. **cop it, young Harry,** q.v.

you look good enough to eat has, in late C19–20, been addressed by males to attractive or very pretty females. Cf **he (or she) looks as if he (or she) could eat me without salt.**

It goes perilously close to being a cliché – and it may have been patterned on French, for Janssen has adduced examples from Molière, 1662, Madame de Sévigné, 1679, and Balzac. P.B.: and a genuine cliché – or should it be proverb? – is *the way to a man's heart is through his stomach.*

you love your mother better than your father. See **Charley's dead.**

you lucky people! is that music-hall and BBC comedian Tommy Trinder's 'gag' become a c.p.: since the 1940s (? latish 1930s).

you make a better door than a window. Addressed to a person obstructing the light: US (Berrey, 1942) and NZ (*NZS*), both since *c*. 1920 at latest. Cf **is your father a glazier?**

John B. Smith, 1979, recalls an English version: *you make a very good door, but a very bad window.* J.W.C., 1977, doubts that the phrase was ever much used in US.

'you make a muckhill on my trencher,' quoth the bride. You carve a great heap of food for me: *c*. 1650–1750. Ray, 1678; Fuller (Apperson).

you make as good music as a wheelbarrow was, in C18, addressed to one who plays a musical instrument very badly, hence also to one who is disagreeably noisy. Fuller.

B.G.T., 1978, adds, 'My grandfather's version: "You could (*or* you'd) charm the guts out of a wheelbarrow"': English Midlands: since mid C19.

you make me laugh! – late C19–20, sometimes joc. varied, *c*. 1905–40, to **you make I laugh!** Whereas the former is contemptuously ironic, the latter tended to be mild and good natured. Cf **don't make I laugh,** and

you make me tired! You bore me to tears: a US c.p. introduced into Britain in 1898 by the Duchess of Marlborough, 'a then leader of fashion' (Ware). It was glossed thus by M, 1891: '...said to one who tells a stupid story or who bothers a person'; and some fifty years later by Berrey, with the var. *sick*. It is recorded also by Sandilands, 1913, as Can. usage. Fain, 1977, provides a (? later) US var., *you make my ass tired.*

you make the place untidy. An ungracious or joc. invitation to be seated, as in 'Well, sit down then. You...' (Clement & La Frenais, *Going Straight*, 1978): later C20. (P.B.) Petch, 1969, records the var. *you're making the place look untidy.*

you may fire, Gridley, when you are ready. See AMERICAN HISTORICAL BORDERLINERS. Cf the ref. in the Irvin S. Cobb quot'n made at **where do we go from here?**

you may go back again like a fool as you came was a Society c.p. of C18. See S, 1738, Dialogue I:

NEV[EROUT]: What's the Matter? Whose Mare's dead now?
MISS: Take your Labour for your Pains, you may go back again like a Fool as you came.

Apparently prompted by the C16–19 proverbial *have nothing but labour for one's pains.*

you may have broke (or you broke) your mother's heart but you (bloody well) won't break mine! A C20 military c.p. that may have gone back to the Napoleonic Wars, when the drill-sergeants worked miracles upon Wellington's army. As John Brophy remarked in B & P, 1930, it

was originally a stock phrase of drill-sergeants taking recruits in hand. It was intended both to intimidate and to reassure the new soldiers that the tyrant of the barrack-square was human underneath. A jest widely appreciated and often repeated by privates.

you mean 'similar', sir. 'Eternal barmaid's retort to "same again"' (Shaw, 1968): a public-house c.p.: C20.

you missed that, as you missed your mother's blessing. You're unlucky: C18. Near the end of Dialogue I of S, 1738, we read:

[*Miss tries to snatch Mr* Neverout's *Snuff-Box.*]
NEV: Madam, you miss'd that, as you miss'd your Mother's Blessing.

you must be a good dancer you are (or you're) so tall. A US c.p.: C20. Addressed to any tall man. Cf **who is the weather up there?**, q.v.

you must be a twin: no single person could be so barmy (or stupid)! A sergeant-majors' and drill instructors' c.p. of abuse, perhaps borrowed from Cockney where it was prob. more gen.: WW2, but ob. by *c*. 1950. (Lt. – Gen. Chaim Laskov, former Chief of Staff, Israeli Defence Forces, and

sometimes major in 'The Buffs': via Mr Y. Mindel, 1979.) For the idea, cf **much wit as three folks...**

you must be a witch! See **I think you are a witch** and cf **you have hit it....**

you must be joking or **kidding.** See **you're joking.**

[**you must be out of your cotton-picking (or tiny) mind!** These US expressions date from *c*. 1945 at the latest. The latter is the kind of c.p. you see in the *New Yorker* – the kind that Thurber would have adorned. Orig., it belonged either to academic circles or to smart Society; as nearly always happens, it spread both downward and outward, like women's fashions. The former expression is not in the least cultured. But J.W.C. has made it clear that they are clichés and can be used in any person or tense, and are therefore *not* c.pp. Cf, however, **you're out of your tiny Chinese mind.**]

you must come in with your two eggs a penny and three of them rotten was current throughout C18–19 and into C20. It has the var....*five eggs and four of them rotten.* S, 1738, in Dialogue I, has:

NEV[erout]: Come, come, Miss, make much of naught, good Folks are scarce
MISS: What, and you must come in with your two Eggs a Penny, and three of them rotten.

Very pertinently cf the US *must you come in with your two cents' worths?* – q.v. at **two cents' worth.** The c.p. implies that the most frequent and copious contributors to a general conversation are precisely those who have the least to contribute and that what they do contribute is, more often than not, totitesticular.

you must hate yourself! 'Don't be so conceited!' (Berrey, 1942): US: since the 1920s. Var.: *you sure hate yourself!*

you must have been drinking out of a damp glass. See **must have been drinking....**

you must have been lying in bed barefoot and **you must have been sleeping near a crack.** See **must have been lying...**

you must have been lying in bed barefoot; and **you must have been sleeping near a crack.** A usu. male rejoinder to one who has complained of being afflicted with a bad cold: the former, late C19–20 [P.B.: but see E.P.'s entry at **caught cold...**], and lower and lower-middle class and the raffish of almost any class; the latter, perhaps from much further back, even as far as C17–even though I lack examples. The former occurs in, e.g., Ernest Raymond's novel *Mary Leith*, 1931. Among the raffish, there is always an innuendo concerning the anatomical cleft.

The latter reason for a severe cold in the head is either jocosely advanced by the sufferer or slyly imputed by a friend. (Shaw, 1969.)

you must know Mrs Kell(e)y is a c.p. 'with no particular meaning' – addressed to 'a long-winded talker' and deriving from a 'phrase used for two years at all times and places by Dan Leno' (Ware): *c*. 1898–1905.

Often in the longer form: 'Mrs Kelly – you *must* know Mrs Kelly' (Daniel Farson, 1977).

you must put in your two cents' worth. See **two cents' worth...**

you must think I'm made of money! and **do you think I'm made of money?** A late C19–20 c.p. rebuke – or an exacerbated remark – either to an importunate borrower or to an extravagant wife. A var. is *you seem to think money grows on trees* or *it doesn't grow on trees* (with, *you know* sometimes added).

you must wriggle your arse...! See **for a musical farce...**

you name it! – as in 'He's had a year of mishaps and misfortunes – you name it' (with 'he's experienced it' understood) – has been rather widely used since *c*. 1955, but esp. from 1970 onwards. Very prob. elliptical for *you have only to name it.* Contrast:

you name it: we have it. 'Literally, a claim by a firm that they stock everything'; 'hence, we can do anything you need or anything you want done' (Granville, 1969): since the late 1940s. It sounds as if it might have been prompted by the **'You want the best seats – we have them'** slogan of a well-known London firm.

you need eyes in your backside! A proletarian c.p. for 'You need to be very wide awake': C20. (Petch, 1971.)

you need your head examined! You must be out of your mind! I suspect that it may go back to the 1890s–early 1900s, when phrenology became fashionable and the science humorously named 'bumps'. In 1971, I had thought it at least ob., yet I found the c.p. used in Francis Clifford's then recently pub'd novel, *The Blind Side:*

He took his time. 'You can't seriously –'
'Oh, yes.... Why not?'
Howard snorted. 'You need your head examined.'
'Perhaps. But it doesn't alter the facts.'

There is a frequent var. *you want your head read!* – current since *c.* 1910 and perhaps mostly Aus. Then there's the US var., recorded by Berrey, 1942: *you'd better have your head examined*: C20.

A.B., 1979, offers a whole nother lot of US synon. phrases: *you need to have* (or *get*) *your brains examined*; *you're not playing with a full deck of cards*; *you've got a few loose shingles on your roof*; *you've got some loose seeds in your gourd*; *you're nutty as a fruitcake*: all, as he says, difficult to date accurately, but certainly C20. Later he added, 'Many variations, e.g. *you ought to* (or *should*) *have your head examined* and *you should take your head to the laundry*. These also mean, "You should see – go to – a psychiatrist". Finally, *you need to have your head shrunk*, from slang *shrink* [a shortening of *head-shrinker*], a psychiatrist'.

'Cf the apocryphal Goldwynism, "Anyone who consults a psychiatrist needs his head examined"' (P.B., 1976). How very true of so many psychiatrists – and how unjust to the genuine able ones!

you never did is a Cockney (hence gen. lower-strata) c.p. expressive of humorous appreciation or approval or amazement; elliptical for you've never heard or seen the like of it – anything so oddly strange, so very funny, etc.: apparently dating since the 1860s or 1870s, it appears in composition (and therefore not, there, strictly a c.p.) in A. Neil Lynon's *Matilda's Mabel*, 1903, 'My dearest Tilda. Such a go you never did! Mr Appleby proposed to me this afternoon!'

P.B.: but this hardly constitutes a c.p., since it merely changes the pronoun in the idiomatic exclam. of surprise *well, I never did!* Cf **well, I never, did you...**

you never get a satisfied cock without a wet pussy is a low C20 c.p., of which L.A., 1975, has shrewdly remarked, 'The crude and the undeniable in juxtaposition are a frequent astringent herb of popular speech'. P.B.: it may well have been orig., or at least simultaneously, US; A.B., 1979, quotes a rather contrived anecdote, a 'dirty story' of which this is the 'moral'. E.P. commented, 'I think the c.p. suggested this pleasing example of folk-etymology'; cf the story arising from the phrase *a little bit of bullshit may get you to the top of the tree...*

you never know (, you know). You never know what may come of it, you can't lose 'em *all*: mid C19–20, for the shorter form, C20 for the longer. Cf:

you never know your luck is an elab. of the prec.: C20. Strictly, it lies on the boundary between proverb and c.p.; Benham calls it a proverb, Apperson and *ODEP*, 3rd edn, omit it.

The Aus. form tends to be a restrictive elab., *you never know your luck in a big city* (B.P., 1975); in pre-war London they preferred *you never know your luck till the ball stops rolling.*

you only volunteer once is a sergeant-major's – or a drill-sergeant's – reply to a recruit's remark that he has enlisted voluntarily, the implication being that, once in the Service, he'll obey orders: WW1, and after.

you ought to remember that, once, you had a mother; with variants..., **that you too...,** and **...even you...** This c.p. has, C18 (perhaps late C17) – 20, been addressed to a man speaking ill, cynically, callously, of women. In the Dialogue I of S, 1738, we find:

LADY SM[ART]: But, Colonel, they say that every married Man should believe that there is but one good Wife in the World, and that's his own.

COL[ONEL]: For all that, I doubt, a good wife must be bespoke; for there is none ready made.

MISS: I suppose, the Gentleman's a Woman Hater; but, Sir, I think you ought to remember that once you had a Mother.

you panic me. I think that you – your way of life – your problems and difficulties – are ludicrous: US: since *c.* 1950. W & F, 'The remark is meant to be cruel.'

But R.C., 1978, doubts the 'cruelty': 'Not necessarily, nor even, I think, usually; for instance, as used ironically in response to an unfunny joke. Essentially, no more than "you make me laugh heartily" – from the slang *panic*, to make (someone) laugh uproariously; semantically, to render them hysterical with laughter'. And A.B., 1979, notes: 'Also *you really do put me in a panic.* This can also mean "You really upset me!" or, ironically, "You really don't make any impression on me!" Not much used now'.

Cf this, from *VIBS*: **isn't he a panic?** A submerged catchphrase from [BBC Radio 4]'s "The Burkiss Way" [mid-late 1970s] – by which I mean that it was known only to cast and writers. But there it was in the dialogues between Fred Harris and Eric Pode of Croydon (Chris Emmett)'.

you pays your money and you takes your choice appeared first – as you might have supposed had you remembered that this weekly has always been prompt to record the customs and curiosities of Cockney speech – in *Punch*; what surprised me is that it came so early as 1846 (X, 16). Used lit. (a stallholder's cry to prospective customers), it is obviously not a c.p.; used otherwise, it is. A notable characteristic of this c.p. – an instance, by the way, of what Mr Cyril Whelan has, 1975, called 'costermongery' – is its popularity among literate and illiterate alike.

R.C., 1978, writes, 'Certainly current in US by 1920s, and, I suspect, much earlier. Now ob. or at least archaic'; but, A.B., 1979, of the more American *you pay*(s), *your nickel, you take your choice* (or *chance*), says, 'this is still in use in some of our larger cities'.

you play ball with me, and I'll play ball with you. Only (or **just**) **remember: it's *my* ball.** 'Let us co-operate by all means, but always be aware that it is I who am in charge': Services', esp. senior NCOs and drill instructors'. I first heard the *only* version in the Army *c.* 1958; the *just* occurs in Strong & Hart-Davis, *Fighter Pilot*, 1981. (P.B.)

you play like I fuck. You're a poor sort of card-player: Can. Army: WW2, and in gen. low Can. use for some years earlier, and ever since.

you play the cards you're dealt. You do the best you can with what you have – physically and mentally, socially and financially: US, esp. in the West: since *c.* 1910. '"I'm a Western nut. The rituals are relaxing, I find. In every other Western [film] there's a line – 'You play the cards you're dealt'"'. Thus Brian Garfield, *Death Sentence*, 1975. Mr Garfield is not only an eminent writer of 'thrillers'; he's an authority on this particular branch of cinema, as he has ably shown in his *Complete Guide to Western Films*. Cf the informal Standard English *the luck of the draw*, and the phrase recorded in *ODEP, to play one's cards well*, glossed as 'to make good use of one's resources or opportunities', with first citing at 1702.

you really do take the cake! and **now doesn't that just take the cake!** US variants of **that takes the cake!** (A.B., 1979.)

you said a mouthful! Now you really have said something witty or important or strikingly pertinent or otherwise agreeable! In the definitive edn, 1936, of HLM, the author, who said a multitude of worthwhile mouthfuls, includes this c.p. in a brief list of phrases possessing some degree of sense and appositeness and incidentally makes it clear that it had been current since before 1932. Both Berrey, 1942, and W & F, 1960, duly record it.

In Ring Lardner's *First and Last*, 1934 (a year after his death), we read: '"Well Lardy we will have to make it some other time," said Gerry. "You said a mouthful Gerry" was my smiling reply.' This had been anticipated by five years in Irvin S. Cobb's *This Man's World*, 1929. Prob. the phrase goes as far back as *c.* 1920, if not a decade, or more, earlier.

Equally mentionable is the fact that as late as 26 May 1973 the *New Yorker* shows, in a saloon, a maudlin, sombre drunk paraphrasing John Donne's 'No man is an island' and the barman admiringly commenting, 'Friend, you sure said a mouthful!'

The phrase was adopted, very late in the 1920s or very early in the 1930s, in UK, where it tends to become *you've* (said a mouthful), as in H. M. Harwood. *The Man in Possession*, 1930; in II, i, where Clara, the maid says to her mistress, 'It *will* be a great change for you, madam' and madam elegantly replies, 'Clara! You've said a mouthful.'

Cf the next, which had prob. fathered it, and also **Queen**....

you said it! was adopted in UK *c.* 1931, via 'the talkies' (as they were then called). It occurs in Dorothy L. Sayers, *Murder Must Advertise*, 1933:

'The idea being that...?'
'You said it, chief.'

In 1937, Dodie Smith, *Bonnet over the Windmill*, at II, i, has:

BILLIE [*a woman of 40*]: Funny – anyone can see you're potty about her, but you don't really like her, do you?
BRIAN: You said it, lady.

In 1942, Evelyn Waugh uses the fairly frequent Brit. var. *you've said it*, thus in *Work Suspended*:

'There's not the money about.'
'You've said it.'

Adopted from US, where it arose *c.* 1900.

In Lillian Mortimer's play *No Mother to Guide Her*, performed in 1905 (not published until 1940), in Act II, we read:

MOTH[ER] J: You have many sweethearts.
SILAS: You said it.

Already in 1922, HLM, 2nd end, remarked, 'The favourite affirmations of the army, "I'll say so," "I'll tell the world," "You said it," etc., are...passing out'; in the definitive edn, 1936, of that famous book, he notes that Tad Dorgan, q.v., who died in 1929, appears to have been its begetter; Berrey, 1942, includes it in a synonymy of 'You are right; you speak truly' phrases; W & F, 1960, gloss it 'Emphatically yes: "I agree with you"; "You are right"' – but say nothing of its duration.

P.B.: just a couple of footnotes: A.B., 1979, remarks, 'often with *buster* or *baby* or *sister* or *chief* added' – true of UK usage too; and Janssen, 1978, suggests an orig. in Fr. *Tu l'as dit*, which is very old. See also **you've said it!**, and:

you said it, I didn't (with *you* and *I* strongly emphasized). 'If someone speaks insultingly or disparagingly about someone known to the speaker, who probably feels the same way but does not have the guts to say so, this is the rejoinder. That makes one person liable, absolves the other. One hears the expression quite often.' (W. J. B., 1975.) Prob. since early C20.

That is the US usage. In UK, the predominant usage is exemplified when someone addresses the c.p. to one who has spoken derogatorily of *himself*. (The Briticism, as opposed to the Americanism, has been sent by Patricia Newnham, 1976.)

P.B.: cf Jesus's answer to Pilate's 'are you the King of the Jews?', at, e.g., *Mark*, 15, 2.

you said you could do it. See **well, you said**....

you saved my life. See **you've saved**....

you say (occ., **you do say**) **the *nicest*** (or **the *sweetest*) things.** Obviously, when used lit. this is merely a conventionalism, a polite reply to flattery or high compliment. But it is, no less obviously, a c.p. when used with graceful irony or with

deliberately simpering jocularity; it may sometimes be almost bitter: both Brit. and US: since perhaps as early as *c.* 1930, though examples in print come later. See, e.g., James Eastwood, *Little Dragon from Peking*, 1967:

As the music stopped, he [a Japanese] said, 'Very nice, very pleasant. You do not dance like virgin.'
'Why, thank you,' Anna said. 'You say the nicest things.'

And in Hartley Howard, *Nice Day for a Funeral*, 1972, we find an American private investigator saying to an American police officer:

'Worried in case something might happen to me?'
'Unofficially, my only worry is that something might not. Officially, I have to treat you as though you were a civilised member of society.'
'You say the nicest things,' I said.

(Hartley Howard has a lively sense of dialogue and a very acute ear for nuance in spoken English. True, it's as good for literate as for less literate speech. But then, it hasn't yet become a crime to be well-educated, nor an offence to be intelligent.)

you say true; will you swallow my knife? Current *c.* 1890–1940. 'I doubt it!' – applied to an impossible story or assertion. The 'swallowing' implies an 'acid test'.

you seem to think money grows on trees. See **you must think**...

you shall have the King's horse. See **King's horse**....

you shape like a whore at a christening is a lower classes', whence also an army, esp. a drill-sergeants', c.p., addressed to a (conspicuously) clumsy person: since the 1890s, if not very considerably earlier – to judge by *as demure as a whore* (or *an old whore*) *at a christening* [q.v., at **demure as...**] which was recorded by Grose in 1788 and goes back even earlier.

you shock my mahogany, current only *c.* 1935–50 and, indeed, very little used after 1945, is an example of those sillier c.pp. which the empty-headed affect. It means 'You shock my morals'.

you should be so lucky! 'It's cheek that you have the luck. Present day' (L.A., 1977): since *c.* 1945. See **I should be so lucky!**

you should excuse the expression. 'Interjection immediately before or after a word or a phrase expected to distress the hearer, usualy because of its profanity or obscenity [or sheer vulgarity]. Cf **pardon my French!** American Jewish from *c.* 1930 [and] general since, at least, the 1950s' (R.C., 1978).

you should pay for them has, since late C19, been addressed to one whose footwear squeaks, supposedly in protest; it is – or was – so well known that a self-conscious wearer may forestall that comment by remarking (*I*) *haven't yet paid for 'em*.

P.B.: in Hong Kong, 1960s, there was a shop on the Wan Chai waterfront that proudly displayed the sign 'Genuine no squeak shoes'.

you should (or, US, **ought to**) **see the other fellow** (occ. **man**)! (– **but**). Used after a bout of violent fisticuffs and implying that the opponent is in even worse shape: C20 (? also late C19). John Rossiter, *The Victims*, 1971:

'You've been fighting,' she said.
'Yes,' he admitted. 'But you should see the other man.'

'Also *you should see what the other fellow looks like!* This is mostly used to explain an obvious bruise or broken bone. Sometimes a person will employ it as a question put to someone who has an obvious injury, "Well, what does the other fellow look like?" I suspect it arose, in the US, in the 1920s' (A.B., 1979).

you should use stronger elastic! 'From the first major radio series for the troops after [WW2], *Calling All Forces*. Ted Ray was the star host and Bob Monkhouse and Denis Goodwin... teamed up to script the comedy sequences. In the first show, broadcast live [3 Dec. 1950], the guests were Jimmy Edwards, Jean Kent, then a major British film star, and Freddie Mills, the world light-heavyweight champion.

Mills, departing from his script, told of one punch he received when he lowered his gloves. He added, quite seriously, "My trainer nearly fainted when he saw me drop 'em. I didn't mean to drop 'em." Ted Ray heard a ripple of laughter as the audience perceived a double meaning and immediately responded, "You should use stronger elastic." The roar of laughter this line provoked sent Monkhouse and Goodwin hurrying backstage to augment the script for a Napoleon and Josephine sketch. They gave Jean Kent an extra line – "I have only flimsy defences against your passionate advance and I can't even keep them up!" – so that Ted Ray, as Napoleon, could repeat his ad-lib line from the Mills interview. This he did. The laughter and applause stopped the show for a full minute and the two young writers, aged twenty one, were severely reprimanded by the Director of Variety, for circumventing the censor.

By mid-week, however, the phrase had caught on. A cartoon appeared in the *Daily Sketch* depicting Clement Attlee in drag, tripped up by a pair of bloomers around his ankles bearing the unlikely phrase, "The National Health Act", while a chirpy Winston Churchill leaned out of Broadcasting House window and called out, "Caught you with your plans down, Clem! You should use stronger elastic!"... Bob Monkhouse seven years later heard it as an automatic answer, at Kempton Park races, to the cry, "They're off!'" (*VIBS*, which adds a number of other amusing instances of the phrase's use): still heard occ. from the generation that knew it; in the early 1980s.

[**you should worry!** Ironic: C20. Mostly Brit. A mere off-shoot from *I should worry* and therefore not strictly a c.p.]

you shouldn't have joined! was a WW2 British Armed Forces' c.p., current since *c.* 1930, addressed to a complainer against the Service. (Prob. the poor devil had no choice.) Cf **if you can't take a joke**....

you shouldn't have joined if you can't take a joke. See **if you can't take a joke**....

you shred it, Wheat. I agree with you – heartily; *or* How very true!: Can. adolescents': *c.* 1946–7. (In an article pub'd 24 Oct. 1946 in a Toronto newspaper.) A pun at once on *you said it, chief!* and on *shredded wheat*, the breakfast cereal. P.B.: also some late 1940s use in UK; see **you said it.**

you silly twisted boy! 'Usually said [by 'Grytpype-Thynne', always in a very 'superior' voice] to Neddie Seagoon' (*VIBS*); and hence in gen. Brit. c.p. use since the early 1950s. See GOON SHOW.

you slay me! See **you kill me!**

you some kind of a nut? 'A rhetorical question put to anyone whose behaviour or appearance seems odd. Derisive, of course. I have heard it for years' (Leechman, 1969): US, since *c.* 1915 (a deduction from the entry in W & F); Can. since *c.* 1920. Why *nut*? Because, I'd suppose, it's so often *cracked*.

P.B. amends, 1976: 'In Brit. usage perhaps more often heard now as "What are you: some kind of nut?" *Nut* = *nut case* = lunatic, with something wrong inside his *nut*, head'.

you stick your.... See **I wouldn't stick my walking-stick**....

you still wouldn't like it on your eye for a wart is a low C20 c.p. 'retort to imputation of undersized penis, but, even more, with boring suggestiveness and knowing wink when anything is thought' – perhaps rather, said to be – 'not big enough' (L.A., 1967). One of those playfully arch ribaldries which arouse contempt rather than amusement.

you sure know how to hurt a guy! 'Usually said jocularly – or ruefully – when an expected compliment is not forthcoming': since *c.* 1925, but app. little used since WW2. In, e.g., Peter de Vries, *Forever Panting*, 1973, '"Edward G. Robinson? Tallulah Bankhead? You sure know how to hurt a guy!"' (Col. Moe, 1977.) Cf **guy could get hurt**....

you sure slobbered a bibful is a Can. var., since *c.* 1938, and NZ var., since *c.* 1943, of the US *you slobbered a bibful* (, *baby*), which, recorded by Berrey, 1942, was itself a modification of

you said a mouthful. (Mrs Hazel Franklin of Christchurch, NZ, supplied the NZ usage, 1974.)

R.C., 1978, comments 'No version of this was ever common in US'. P.B.: but it was always felt to be essentially American, and sometimes uttered in a would-be American accent, as to me by a schoolmaster, *c.* 1949, after I had 'flannelled' my way very unconvincingly through a piece of vile translation into French.

you take the calls. You're hard to beat; You're formidable: US; *c.* 1900–40. (Edward Hodnett, 1975.) From the theatre, where, during and after tumultuous applause, the player solely or mainly responsible comes to the front of the stage.

you talk like a halfpenny (or **a penny**) **book** was, *c.* 1880–1914 and esp. among the lower-middle class, addressed to an affected or pedantic or pompous, or a merely very fluent, speaker. But, Frank Shaw once told me, it was (in the *half-penny* form) current in Liverpool, late C19–mid C20, to mean 'You talk (very) foolishly or stupidly'. In the US, this becomes, naturally, *a dime novel*, 'not much in use now' (A.B., 1979). Cf **talks like a book**....

you talked me into it. See **you could twist my arm.**

you tell 'em! You're dead right!: US, whence also Can.: in vogue during the very approx. period, 1924–41; and with an increasingly limited currency right up to the present (mid 1976) – or, in the words of J. W. C., 1975: 'a c.p., but dead, or nearly so, for, say thirty years, because of overuse'. Prob. the orig. on which the next has been elab.

In Philip Hart Dunning and George Abbott, in Act I of *Broadway, A Play*, 1926, used by speakeasy-owner Dolph, to bootlegger Steve, as Col. Moe tells me.

See also TAD DORGAN.

you tell 'em, kid, you tell 'em: I'm bashful is a US c.p. listed by Berrey, in a synonymy of phrases equivalent to an expression 'of approval and admiration': mid 1930s–40s; The var. '*you* tell 'em, Harry – *I* stutter' seems to have worn better.

you tell me! I haven't the faintest idea. Why don't you tell me about it – implying either an answer to a straight question or a denial by one wrongly accused: since the late 1920s. (Prompted by Granville, 1969.)

you tell me and we'll both know – '*I* don't know' – is used when one has been asked a question one is unable to answer: mostly Aus.: since *c.* 1950. (B.P., 1975.) P.B.: not unknown in UK, where it occurs usu. as *you tell me and then we'll both know.* Cf **that's asking!**

you think *you* got troubles (? or!) 'What are *you* complaining about? If you had *my* troubles, you'd have good reason to complain': orig. *c.* 1930, during 'the Great Depression' – and still predominantly – US (R.C., 1978, suggests poss. Jewish), it had, by 1945, passed, often in the form ...*you've got*..., to UK and, by the late 1940s, to the British Commonwealth and RSA. (Prof. A.C. Partridge, 1977.) Cf **you have your troubles**..., of which this is prob. the orig. shape.

you think you've got the lights of Piccadilly Circus shining out of your arsehole. See **lights of Piccadilly Circus**....

you threw me a curve indicates surprise or irritation or a sense of unfairness, is US, dates from *c.* 1950, and derives from baseball.

you too can have a body like mine is a c.p. only when used ironically, as when the speaker is frail or delicate or puny: mid 1930s–*c.* 1970. (I once heard it used with a sort of humorous, self-deprecating boastfulness by an extremely fit, very likable, physical training instructor, in a hut at Technical Training Command, Reading, in 1943.) It comes – as Frank Shaw told me, 1969 – from a magazine advertisement of Charles Atlas's body-building course.

It had, by 1957, become so widely known that it could be used thus in John Osborne's *Look Back in Anger*:

JIMMY: .... Should I go in for this moral weight lifting...? I was a liberal skinny weakling. I too was afraid to strip down to my soul, but now everyone looks at my superb physique in envy.

P.B.: since *c.* 1950 at latest, often carries the suffix, voiced either by the speaker or his audience, ... *if you're not (very) careful!*

you twisted my arm. See **you could twist...**

you wanna buy a duck? See **wanna buy a duck?**

you want a little memory-powder. Your memory is bad: Londoners': *c.* 1880–90. Baumann.

you want an egg in your beer? See **what do you want?...**

you want portholes in your coffin! A C20 RN lower-deck c.p., addressed to a man extremely hard to please. F & G.

you want the best seats: we have them has been a c.p. since the latish 1920s, as in Stuart Jackman, *Guns Covered with Flowers*, 1973,

She jumped to her feet and joined the other girls [dancing the can-can] as they lined up across the stage, turned their backs, flipped up their skirts and bent over.

'There's a sight for sore eyes, squire,' Meyer said happily.

'You want the best seats, we have 'em.'

An allusion to the slogan used by Messrs Keith Prowse, the agents for theatrical – and other – seats. On 18 April 1975, they very kindly sent me a postcard: 'Above phrase first used about 1925. Cannot be more precise. Still in use today.'

you want to get some sea-time in! See **get some sea-time in!**

you want to know all the ins-and-outs of a nag's arse! 'You're bloody inquisitive!': low Cockney: late C19–20.

P.B.: but used also of a third party, e.g. 'She wants to know...'; the *arse* may belong also to a cat or a duck.

you want to start something? 'We [in the US] have a common saying: "you want to start something?" We use it when addressing some truculent person who has said something we resent. It is a challenge to put up or shut up. Someone spoiling for a fight is often warned and rebuked by the [use of the] phrase, but it can be uttered in fun, and usually is. It has been around for a long time, a good part of this century no doubt. It is currently being used in a TV commercial, by actor Burgess Meredith' (W.J.B., 1978).

Cf **want to make something of it?**, the Brit. version.

you want your head read! See **you need your head examined!**

you were born stupid, you've learnt nothing, and you've forgotten (even) that! A scathing comment: C20. Perhaps predominantly, but far from being only, Aus. (B.P., who adds that 'it is known in Austria and Germany').

In the US, since the mid 1940s, *you were born stupid and you've lost ground ever since.* 'I recall that in the Jack Benny – Fred Allen feud show, Allen says "Benny was born stupid, and he's lost ground ever since" (A.B., 1979, who adds 'not common now, but heard occasionally').

you were bred in Brazen Nose College. You are impudent: C18 (? also late C17). (Fuller.) A pun on *brazen-face*, an impudent fellow, and Brasenose College, Oxford.

you were just (Brit., **you were (still) only) a gleam in your father's eye.** That was, or that happened, before you were born: US and Brit., since the crazy 1920s; but which of the two peoples can claim for it the honour of primogeniture, I haven't been able to discover. The *New Yorker*, 17 July 1971 (p. 31), has 'Of course, at that time you were just a gleam in your father's eye': Mother to barely teen-aged son, in presence of Father, both parents looking as if they were too bored and stodgy ever to have admitted or responded to such concupiscence.

The phrase is adaptable, as in 'Know him? I've known him since he was just a gleam in his father's eye', or 'Oh, that was when you were just...'

See also **I was doing it...**

you weren't born: you were pissed up against the wall and hatched in the sun. See **he never had no mother...**

you what? – with emphasis on *what*. Literally, this c.p. is elliptical for 'You mean – *what?*' Hence, 'What do you mean?' Hence also 'What did you say *or* do *or* think?' and 'What do you want?' It dates since *c.* 1950 and belongs, socially, to the lower and lower-middle classes and, occupa-

tionally, to the fringe of the underworld; it is also affected by those who'd like to be regarded as belonging to the underworld or, at worst, its fringes.

If considered uncritically, it looks like an ordinary ellipsis, yet, as a c.p., it is used derisively and trenchantly.

Laurence Henderson uses it in *Cage until Tame*, 1973:

'All right,' his voice was tired, 'how much?'

'A hundred grand.' Tolly took pleasure in saying it.

'You what?'

'Yeah,' Tolly grinned, 'give or take a bit.'

An example can also be found in one of Ted Lewis's novels about roughs and toughs, *Jack Carter's Law*, 1974:

'What's the matter? Rather switch than fight?'

'You what?'

'Forget it.'

you will catch cold at that. A warning to desist: mid C18–mid C19. Grose, 1788.

you will die the death of a trooper's horse. This joc. c.p., current prob. throughout C18 and into early C19, means 'You will be hanged'. Grose, 1785, explains it thus: 'That is, with your shoes on'.

Cf, therefore, **you will ride a horse foaled by an acorn**, which was an underworld witticism of mid C18–early C19; recorded by Grose, 1788, 'The gallows, called also Wooden and Three-legged mare'.

A grim, a decidedly macabre, sense of humour these Augustan Age criminals had!

you win a few, you lose a few is a wholly US var., dating since *c.* 1945, of **you can't win 'em all.** (Moe, 1975.) It can even be employed allusively as on the last page of Charles Williams's novel, *And the Deep Blue Sea*, 1971: 'She stopped, arrested by something in the attitude of the two figures leaning on the rail, and shrugged. You won a few, you lost a few.'

J.W.C., 1975, says:

Current, and for perhaps 30 years. Having originated as a 'philosophical' or fatalistic remark by a gambler who has just lost a bet (or a games player who has just lost a game...), it has a raffish aura rather than a sentimental one... and its persistence is perhaps owing to that fact. Equivalent to 'You can't win 'em all' – which I think is now commoner.

'Have heard. Common gambling observation or experience. A perfectly legitimate item in everyday speech' (W.J.B., 1975).

Fain, 1977, notes the var. *you win some, you lose some*; and A.B., 1979, adds *win some, lose some, some rained out*, with the comment that it orig. in bets on baseball games: prob. since the 1920s.

you won't know yourself! A C20 c.p.: 'You just won't recognize yourself.' Either independently or (as in 'Try on this overcoat – you won't know youself!) semi-independently.

you won't melt! One of the domestic c.pp., it is addressed to a child objecting to going out, and esp. to running an errand, in the rain: C19–20 and perhaps older.

P.B.: in full, either pre-fixed or suffixed by *you're not made of sugar!*

[**you won't, you know!** is a sturdy proletarian retort to, e.g., 'I'll do something or other': prob. going far back into C19. But a conventionalism, rather than a c.p., I think. Cf the next.]

[**you would!** is elliptical for 'You would go and do that, curse you!' or 'That's the sort of thing you *would* do!' Prob. goes back to C18; a cliché or a conventionalism rather than a c.p. Cf prec.]

you would (plus phrase). See also **you'd...**

you would not be so soon in my grave. In S, 1738, Dialogue I, occurs this passage:

[*Neverout rises to take up the Chair and Miss sits in his.*]

NEV: You would not be so soon in my Grave, Madam.

Apparently a smart c.p. of (say) 1700–60.

you wouldn't chuckle! is an Armed Forces' c.p., dating since *c.* 1938 and orig. as still, meaning 'You wouldn't think so' and then briskly coming, *c.* 1940, to mean also 'You bet I would!'

P.B.: this is one of the few phrases to which the insertion of the everlasting and monotonous qualifier *fucking* gives a certain assonance.

you wouldn't fool (or **kid**) **me** (or **a fellow**)**, would you?** I don't believe it: US: C20. (Berrey.) 'Sometimes expresses skepticism rather than outright disbelief' (R.C. 1978).

you wouldn't fuck (or **rob**) **it.** And that's no lie! An RAF c.p. dating from the mid 1920s. 'Signifies the complete positive to a question or a statement. "It's cold this morning" – "You wouldn't rob it" (or "fuck it")' (Mr R.M. Davidson, in a letter to me, 1942). Semantically, 'You wouldn't do a violence to the truth' – 'You wouldn't rob, i.e. steal from, i.e. defraud the truth, i.e. lie'.

you wouldn't kick that out of bed. See **I wouldn't kick her ...**

you wouldn't knob it. You wouldn't think so *or* realize it – with the implication that the speaker does know it to be a fact: RAF: since *c.* 1930. Obscurely derivative is the later – since *c.* 1938 – sense, 'You bet I would!' Cf **you wouldn't chuckle!**

you wouldn't read about it. It would amaze you, *or* It beats the band: NZ: since *c.* 1935. Also Aus. (since late 1930s) – as in Mary Durack, *Keep Him My Country* (Australia), 1955, ' "Blimey!" Wilde exclaimed. "You wouldn't read about it." '

John Mortimer, *Marble Arch*, one of the four short plays comprising *Come As You Are*, prod. 1970, pub'd 1971, has:

MAX: Good evening, McNee. 'Morning, everyone.

MISS PARKER [a New Zealand journalist]: Gee whiz. You wouldn't read about it. Is his lordship often to be found among your toilet facilities?

LAURA (*still amazed*): No ...

Not the sort of thing you'd expect to read in the newspapers, some truths being, we are solemnly told, stranger than fiction.

'Expression of mingled incredulity and disgust', notes Wilkes, who gives, as his earliest example, Jon Cleary, *Just Let Me Be*, 1950 – but it existed well before that.

you wouldn't rob it. See **you wouldn't fuck it.**

you wouldn't shit me and **don't shit the troops!** These synon. c.pp., meaning 'I don't believe you', date respectively since the 1920s and, in the Canadian Army, throughout WW2. Here, *shit = shit on, beshit.*

'Current in US [also], since 1920s' (R.C., 1978).

you wouldn't want to know is elliptical for 'You wouldn't want to know about it' – for it was such a tremendous disappointment or failure that it would shock you or you wouldn't believe it: Aus., perhaps orig. underworld: since late 1940s or perhaps a dozen years earlier.

In the Sydney *Bulletin*, 26 Apr. 1975, Neil James – for 30 years a crook – offers, in his fascinating article 'Nodding the nut for a swy and one', this example: 'Here is a brief interchange between two shoplifters ... Jimmy tells the story of a disastrous day at work ... "Well, you wouldn't want to know, we dipped [= failed] on three morals [= virtual certainties]".'

Contrast **I want to know!**

you'd be far better off in a home was an army c.p. of WW1, but it derived from a late C19–20 civilian saying; by *c.* 1955, slightly ob., but not, even by 1975, †. Of its WW1 usage, John Brophy wrote that it 'was sympathetic – in that derisively jocular manner which constituted one of the hall-marks of the soldiers' humour; is fitted almost any occasion on which the man addressed *would* have been far better off in a home' (B & P, 1930).

Rear-Adm. P.W. Brock, 1969, says:

This saying was in regular use [in the navy] in 1920–2 because it went so well to the refrain of a march called *El Albanico* (or *Elalbanico*) much in favour with Royal Marine bands. The music almost sang the words itself –

'You'd be far better off in a home,
You'd be far better off in a home,
You'd be far better off in a home,
You'd be far better,
Far better off,

Far better off in a home.'

To that naval comment, add this by Granville, 1969 'Jocular consolatory c.p. to one who is in a bad way, whether in health or in the matter of fortune, especially ill-fortune.'

An Army var. is *you'd be far better off in the mush* (guard room), which forms the first and last lines of the quatrain, always sung:

You'd be far better off in the mush.
If it weren't for my pay,
I'd be there every day:
You'd be far better off in the mush.

It has very much the same meaning. (Sanders, 1978.) And Mr P.V. Harris recalls, from his WW1 service with the King's Liverpool Regt., that the *mush* version was a marching song, and comments, 'if, you were in the "mush" you wouldn't be sweating on a route-march'.

you'd be (or **get**) **killed in the rush.** Addressed, although not among the *élite*, to a girl who has just said, 'I wouldn't marry you (even) if you were the last man in the world': C20. It derives from, is the c.p. product of, several scabrously entertaining anecdotes.

you'd better believe it! See **you better believe it!**

you'd better have your head examined! See **you need your head examined.**

you'd forget your head if it wasn't screwed on (properly) – often prec. by *forget!* – has, since late C19, been addressed to a very forgetful person. I lack an early written ref.; I do, however, remember it since *c.* 1901 or 1902 onwards.

'In the US, *you'd forget your ass if it weren't screwed (on) tight*; some more delicate people would use "neck" instead of "ass" ' (A.B., 1979). See also **if your head was loose ...**

you'd get killed in the rush. See **you'd be killed ....**

you'd have been taller if they hadn't turned up so much for feet is a Can. c.p., current since the 1920s. (Leechman.)

you'd have died. You would have died of laughing: C20. Cf **you'll die.**

you'd only spend it is the traditional c.p. rejoinder to someone remarking 'I'd like, *or* love, to have a lot of money': late C19–20.

you'd soon find it if there was hair (all) round – or **around – it!** See **don't look down ....**

you'll be a long time dead. Enjoy yourself while you can – and while you may: late C19–20. Cf the † proverbial sayings, *she who will not while she may, may not when she would* and *there will be sleeping enough in the grave* and Marvell's 'The grave is a fine and private place,/Yet none, I think, do there embrace.' It has the var. *you're a long time dead*, which occurs in, e.g., 'Number Two' of John Osborne's *The Entertainer*, 1957.

you'll be in dead trouble is common in barrack rooms and workshops 'and such' and it warns someone against the unwisdom of ignoring Standing Orders or the Rules and Regulations or against the stupid tactlessness of annoying the roomful, especially 'its strong men': since *c.* 1925. (L.A., 1974.)

you'll be lucky! I say, you'll be lucky! was used, sarcastically, in a North Country accent, by comedian Al Read: popular for some years, esp. in the N. Country, where it is extant. The versatile Al Read was perhaps better known for his **right, monkey.**

you'll be saying 'arseholes' to the C.O. next. See **eh? – to me! ....**

you'll be shot at dawn! 'Used as a jesting expression' to 'anyone in a scrape' (F & G): army: WW1; rarely used in WW2. Cf **oh, to be ....**

you'll be smoking next! What a dissipated fellow – *or* girl – you are!: jocularly commenting upon an act far more audacious or improper: since *c.* 1950 or perhaps as much as twenty years earlier. From the story of that father to whom the neighbours have been complaining that his son has been sexually consorting with their daughters and who feels obliged to say *something* to the lad: 'I hear you've been fooling around with the girls. What a young devil you are! Why, dammit, you'll be smoking next!'

you'll be sorry! (Usu. with the first syllable of *sorry* prolonged. [P.B.: rather, almost chanted, with emphasis on both syllables, *sor-ree*.]) That is, you have done something obviously foolish, though the consequences may be delayed. See J. Michener, *Tales of the South Pacific*, 1947.

you'll be telling me, like the girl, that you've fahnd (or **found**) **a shilling**, which alludes to – indeed, derives from – the rather older **come home with your drawers** (later **knickers**) **torn and say you found the money**, q.v. An 'anecdotal c.p. expression of derisive incredulity' (L.A.): Cockney's: C20 – at least until *c.* 1971. P.B.: in these days of decimal currency (a shilling = 5 new pence) and inflation, I suppose it would have to be ... *found a pound*.

you'll be the death of me! Really, you mustn't be so funny – I'll die laughing: C20. Cf and contrast **you'd have died** and **you'll die**.

you'll bust your kefoofle (or **kerfuffle**) **valve.** An Aus. c.p. dating since *c.* 1960 and addressed to someone lifting a heavy weight – i.e., 'You'll bust your appendix.' Prob. related to the RN slang term, *foo-foo valve*, an entirely mythical gadget that is always blamed for any mechanical break-down whatsoever. (B.P., 1975.)

Cf the US *you'll bust your begonias* or *you'll pop your cork!* – which, one or both, may have influenced or even orig. the Aus. version. (A.B., 1979.)

you'll come to the acorns. You will experience adversity: late C19–20. (*D. Am.*) Living no longer 'high on the hog' and reduced to grubbing for acorns. Long since †, according to Ashley, 1984.

you'll die. You'll be vastly amused: *c.* 1670–1740. Elliptical for 'you'll die with laughing', as in Colley Cibber, *The Careless Husband*, 1705, at IV, i:

> LADY B[ETTY]: Well, my lord, have you seen my Lord Morelove?
> LORD F[OPPINGTON]: Seen him! ha, ha, ha, ha! – Oh! I have such things to tell you, Madam – you'll die –.

you'll die after it. 'It is no more harmful than anything else. When this was first used to me when, as a small boy, I asked permission to eat something, I took it literally, and was thoroughly frightened, made worse by all the adults laughing at me' (Keith Sayers, 1984): N. Country: C20.

you'll do yourself out of a job is a jocularity addressed to anyone working very hard: since early C20.

you'll get no change out of me! This 'warning not to expect co-operation' dates from *c.* 1890. (L.A., 1977.) Cf **take your change out of that!**

you'll get something you don't want. Addressed to a male, it warns against venereal disease; to a female, pregnancy: C20.

[**you'll get yourself disliked.** '(*Street, 1878*.) A satirical protest against anyone who is behaving abominably' (Ware, 1909): the grim understatement so weakened that, by *c.* 1930 at latest, it had become a mere cliché.]

you'll hate youself in the morning. 'Orig. (1920s?) a mother-to-daughter or woman-to-woman c.p. [? rather a cliché] recommending chastity: later, as *I'll hate myself in the morning* [and certainly a c.p.], a jocular way of declining a proposition, either sexual or – eventually – of some dubious character, such as betraying a friend' (R.C., 1978). P.B.: I have heard the *I'll* ... version used, with entire justification, by one purchasing that last drink of the evening that is going to produce, inevitably, a horrible hangover.

you'll have no rest in the airship business until you get the ship into the air. 'An old Royal Naval Air Service c.p., as well as a truism' (Granville, 1968).

you'll have your work cut out. You'll find it difficult to cope with the work you're causing yourself: a c.p. only when it is addressed – this is its commonest use in Aus. – to a mother about to have, or having very recently had, her third or fourth baby. (B.P., 1975.) Otherwise it is a cliché.

you'll keep is an Aus. var. of **it's only lent**: since *c.* 1950. (B.P.,

1969.) The *you* is the object lent. But there is a second sense, likewise Aus.: 'I'll deal with you later' (B.P.., 1975).

you'll know me again, won't you? See do you think you'll know me again?

you'll never know! A 'capsule comment on various indescribable, unimaginable or incomprehensible experiences or circumstances. Depending on context or intonation; it may mean anything from "I simply can't describe it" (i.e., "You'll never know what it's like unless you experience it") to "There's no point in trying to explain it to you". The parallel form *I'll never know* is, however, limited to the sense, "I simply can't explain it" – i.e., why I, he or she did thus-and-so. General US, from at least 1950s' (R.C., 1978).

you'll pop your cork! See you'll bust ...

you'll speak one word for him and two for yourself. In the Dialogue I of S, 1738, we read:

> COL[ONEL]: Tom, put on a bold Face for once, and have at the Widow. I'll speak a good Word for you to her.
> LADY ANS[WERALL]: Ay, I warrant you'll speak one Word for him, and two for yourself.

This C18 c.p. clearly means that in doing another a good turn, one intends to do oneself an even better.

you'll wake up one of these fine mornings and find yourself dead. An Anglo-Irish c.p., current since late C19, but not much used since *c.* 1945. Implying a fling at Irish humour and esp. at Irish 'bulls'.

you're a better man than I am, Gunga Din. Half-way between famous quot'n and c.p. When, however, it is used without ref. to, or even consciousness of, its orig. in Kipling's poem, *Gunga Din*, in *Barrack-Room Ballads*, 1891, it has, in C20, been, I think, a genuine c.p., as it certainly seems to be in this quot'n from Gelett Burgess, *Too Good Looking*, 1936: 'And he was looking at her so queerly. "Well," he said. "You're a better man than I am, Gungha [sic] Din!"'

And as, earlier and even more convincingly, in Maurice Lincoln, '*I, Said the Sparrow*', 1925 ' "Well, give the lad my kind regards and tell him that I said 'he's better man that I am, Gunga Din', will you?" '

It was reinvigorated, popularized afresh, esp. among schoolboys, by the film of Kipling's story released in 1939 and starring Cary Grant, Douglas Fairbanks and Joan Fontaine. (P. Daniel, 1978.) The film was titled *Gunga Din*.

you're a big girl now. 'Heard on and off on TV' (Petch, 1974): since the early 1960s. But domestically since very much earlier (prob. since the 1880s or 1890s) and with the covert intimation 'You're too old, or big, to show so much leg *or* to scratch yourself intimately in public or to ...'

R.C., 1978, comments, 'Often rather with the implication "You're old enough to know the facts of life" – with perhaps the hope that the speaker will be allowed to explain or demonstrate them. Current in this sense in Britain from 1930s (see M. Allingham, *The Fashion in Shrouds*, 1937, "I'm getting a big girl now" – meaning "I'm old enough to be exposed to sexual realities") and in US from 1950s or earlier'. The *getting* version is perhaps the more common; cf **you're getting a big boy now**, and **you have grown a big girl.**

you're a big lad for your age is a joc. c.p., addressed to an apprentice or other youthful worker by his older mates, esp. in factories: late C19–20; decreasingly used since *c.* 1945.

you're a dirty stop-out (occ., in the North of England, **stoppy-out**)!; often **all night** is added. This C20 c.p., ob. by *c.* 1970, mostly refers to those who indulge in as many 'nights on the tiles' as they can get. (Petch, 1969.)

P.B.: in our Hong Kong Army Sergeants' mess, mid 1960s, the jibe *dirty old stop-out* was often launched at someone appearing at the breakfast table through the street door rather than down the steps from the sleeping quarters.

you're a Fusilier! was, *c.* 1880–1920, a Regular Army c.p. of contempt, addressed by one rifleman to another. Clearly there's a pun on Fusi*liar*, liar.

you're a gentleman, a scholar; and a judge of whiskey! See gentleman ...

you're a good man, Charlie Brown. W.J.B., 1975, says it is frequently used [in the US] as a compliment, as an acknowledgment of sterling character, based on a Comic Strip character in 'Peanuts' bearing the name Charlie Brown, a modest, good-natured little fellow who is always being picked on by his playmates. There is a popular play based on the character, with the title *You're a Good Man, Charlie Brown* – I believe it is still being revived. The phrase is used frequently to draw a smile from the person so praised, the evocation of the comic strip original being instantly recognized by everyone within hearing distance.... This strip is still going strong in a widely syndicated feature.

See also notes at **good grief!** A.B., 1979, noted that the c.p. was then still current and popular.

you're a good one! is a US c.p., recorded by Berrey, 1942, in a synonymy of phrases that are 'disparaging or sarcastic flings' – here, ironic rather than sarcastic. In 1960, W&F wrote thus about certain phrases coined by comedians as 'joke punch lines or as repetitious jokes':

Thus within the last 15 years such synthetic expressions as *Hey Abbott!*, *Coming, Mother!*, *I dood it!* and *you're a good one* have seen some short-lived generalized use.

Elsewhere they included it in a list of 'synthetic fad 'expressions'.

you're a little bit of something great or **good** or **special** or **swell**. US expressions of admiration: since the latish 1930s or early 1940s. (A.B., 1978.)

'You're a long time coming', said the duchess to the duke, (idly) stirring her tea with the other hand. 'You're a long time getting to the point of your story; you're becoming a bore. 1930s [and after]' (Sanders, 1978). But there is – 'A dirty mind is a constant joy' – there has always, and inevitably, existed the implication that, during the lazy, contented period between the early cup of tea and the postponable need to rise from bed, there ensues the opportunity of, the desire for, a little idle dalliance. P.B.: thus E.P.; a later generation of seekers after the *double entendre* preferred the version '*some day my prince will come*', *as the princess said, idly stirring...*

you're a long time dead. See **you'll be a long time dead.**

you're a poet and don't know it. See **that's a rhyme.**

you're all about: like shit in a field. You're alert and efficient – I *don't* think! Current throughout C20, it is enunciated thus: at first, an apparent compliment, then a significant pause – then the weighty jeer.

you're all heart! is a shatteringly ironic *Thank you!* 'when someone has *not* been particularly generous' (Skehan, 1977): since the late 1960s. The coll. phrase *to be all heart*, extremely kind or generous, whence the c.p., was, by teenagers, imported from US. P.B.: but R.C., 1978, note the phrase's ironic use in US also, 'from 1960s or earlier'.

you're all mouth and trousers and **you're all prick and breeches.** See **all mouth...**

you're all wet! A US c.p., listed by Berrey, 1942, in a synonymy of phrasal 'disparaging and sarcastic flings', but going back to at least the 1920s. Here, *wet* is prob. elliptical for *wet behind the ears.*

'By now this c.p. or its derivatives are fully accepted into British usage. Few phrases are oftener heard on my daughters' lips than "don't be so wet"' (Playfair, 1977). True! And since the very early 1930s. P.B.: *pace* E.P., the Brit. use of *wet* usu. implies that the victim of the insult is just 'soppy', a 'soggy type'. Our ruling politicians saw fit to borrow this childish epithet from the school children's repertoire in the early 1980s – which just about places *them*!

you're another! See **you are another!**

you're as much use as tits on a canary is a 'c.p. hurled at an inefficient player in baseball, or other field sport' (Leechman): since c. 1945. These useless appendages may adorn a Canadian canary, but in US they might also be on a *boar* (A.B., 1979), or in UK, a *bull* (P.B.). Cf **useless...**

you're awful, but I like you. The slovened version of a 'gag' used by British comedian Dick Emery, it has become a well-known, although not a madly famous, c.p. (Fernley O. Pascoe, 1975.) See **you are awful...**

you're blind in one eye and can't see out of the other. 'Jibe at someone (e.g., an umpire) allegedly incapable of perceiving something as plain as the nose on his face: orig., I think, from baseball. US, 1920s or earlier; now ob.' (R.C., 1979).

you're breaking my heart. See **my heart bleeds for you.**

you're breeding a scab... See **watch it!**

you're cooking with gas. See **now you're cooking with gas.**

you're coughing better. See **your cough's....**

you're coughing nicely. An affectionately ironic c.p., dating since c. 1918.

you're damn' (or darn') tooting. See **too damn' tooting.**

you're damned if you do and damned if you don't. 'On the sharp horns of a dilemma: US: C20' (R.C., 1978). P.B.: presumably from the emphatic refusal *I'm* (or *I'll be*) *damned if I do!* or *I'll be damned if I do!*

you're entitled. 'You have a right to say or do what you ask or propose. Orig., Jewish American but some general use' (R.C., 1978): since c. 1970.

you're fond of a job is, in C20, addressed to one doing a job either another's or unnecessary.

you're full of shit! 'Probably still current in company I no longer frequent. Coarser is **your arse is sucking blue mud**' (Priestley, 1975): Can.: perhaps from US (W & F include it, but mention no date): since c. 1930 (?).

Also *you're as full of shit as the Christmas turkey*, 'especially around our Thanksgiving (3rd week in November) and Christmas dates' (A.B., 1979). See also **you're so full...**

you're getting a big boy now. A mild, even if slightly contemptuous, reproof for petulance or bad manners: late C19–20. Contrast **you're a big girl**, and **you're a big lad...**, and see also **getting a big boy now.**

you're getting TV behind has, since the late 1940s, been addressed to a woman very broad in the beam, the implication being that she spends an inordinate time sitting in front of the TV.

you're getting warmer derives from domestic hide-and-seek games and is a c.p. when *otherwise* employed, e.g. in an attempt at logical deduction or in elab. of a mounting suspicion: C20. (Fernley O. Pascoe, 1975.)

you're happy right 'means entire approval of what has been said. An expression that is becoming obsolete' (Sandilands, 1913): Can.: late C19–earlyish 20.

you're holding up production. You are getting in the way; You are wasting (your own or another's or others') time; You're not being very helpful: RAF: 1940 onwards. The c.p. tried to spread to the army, but never got much of a hold. EP, *A Glossary of RAF Slang*, early 1945; PGR.

you're in everybody's way. See **Sister Anna shall carry the banner.**

you're in mourning for the cat. Your finger-nails are filthy: proletarian: C20; by 1970, somewhat outdated. P.B.: in later C20, still occ. applied to someone whose trousers are too short to cover his ankles.

you're in the wrong pew was current among US university students c. 1920 and a few years later. (McKnight.) It is, however, a shortening of *you're in the right church but the wrong pew*, which, c. 1909, turned a song title into a c.p. The song was sung in 1900, by Bert Williams; the words were McPherson's; the music Chris Smith's. Cited by Edward B. Marks, *They All Sang*, 1934, as W.J.B. tells me, 1975.

you're jealous is a joc. insinuatory retort to 'You're drunk!' I've known it since 1921, and suspect that it goes back to the late C19.

you're joking! and **you must (or have to) be joking!** and **you've got to be joking!** (Cf **are you kidding?** and the US **no kidding** and **you're (or have to, or must, be) kidding!**; also the not-quite-a-c.p., yet potential, indeed imminent c.p., **you're joking, of course?** – which expresses a modified, or even a foolish, optimism – and the Aus. **you've got to be kidding.** Meaning: 'You *can't* be serious' or 'I can't, I *don't*, believe you're serious': in the British Commonwealth, fully established only since *c.* 1950; in the US, the native US forms prob. since about the same time and the adopted Brit. forms since *c.* 1960. By the vaguely apprehended yet powerfully operative linguistic processes known as Spontaneous Combustion and Mutual Inter-influencing, it is hardly necessary – come to that, advisable – to separate the Brit. and the US expressions of a universal thought-pattern. Yet it should be noted that, in UK, *you must be joking* seems to have, in the fact, arisen much earlier than is apparent from the evidence. Grose, 1785, records the c.p., *you are Josephus Rex*, you're joking: by progressive punning, *you are Joseph King* (L. *rex*, a king) – *you are Joe King* – *you are joking*. This at first learned c.p. belongs to the very approx. period, 1760–1900.

Clearly the c.p. usage of *you must be joking* comes straight from the lit. use, as in, for instance, Leicester Buckingham's *Faces in the Fire: A Comedy*, performed on 25 Feb. 1865:

GLAN[VIL]: Doubt her! Oh, no! I often think I should be happier if she loved me less.

MRS H[ARGRAVE] (*laughing*): Well, your grievance has, at any rate, the charm of originality. But you must be joking. (*Glanvil shakes his head.*) No! you are really serious? then you make me uneasy ...

The US *you must be*, or *you're, kidding* occurs very neatly in the *New Yorker* of 7 Feb. 1970. It contains a cartoon of the Devil visiting Earth and, to a protesting 'egg-head', exclaiming, '*Persona non grata*? You must be kidding.'

In the same year, the very English W.J. Burley, in his novel, *To Kill a Cat*, writes thus:

'... What's Fehling playing at?'

'I don't know you can blame Fehling.'

'You must be joking.'

A year earlier, a US novelist, Jack D. Hunter wrote in *Spies Inc.*, 1969: 'He gave me one of his long stares. "You must be joking," he said.'

Anne Morice, in *Death of a Gay Dog*, 1971, writes 'What a gorgeous room this is,' I said. ...

'My dear, you must be joking. When did you ever see anything so pretentious? ... I ask you! Just look at the way he's tarted it up!'

And then, 1974, B.P. attests the Aus. form thus: **'you've got to be kidding.** Same meaning as "you must be joking" '. It occurs in, e.g., Alex. Buzo's perturbing play, *Rooted*, performed in 1971.

Here, it's obvious, is a c.p. that, with its variants, merits a little monograph all to itself. 'You must be kidding!' – 'On the contrary, I mean it.'

you're kidding. See prec.

you're kneeling on it. Your hair's too long: Guards' regiments': C20.

'The rest of the Army were as familiar with the inspecting NCO's little ritual:

Am I hurting you?

No, Sergeant.

Well, I bloody well *ought* to be: I'm standing on your hair. Gerrit cut!' (P.B., 1976). Since *c.* 1947; mostly in the days of National Service (–1962).

you're laffin bags. See LIVERPOOL CATCH PHRASES.

you're making the place look untidy. See **you make the place ...**, and cf **don't just stand there ...**

you're not even a proper woman. See MONTY PYTHON.

you're not here! Exclam. when delivered bowls fall short of the target: S. African bowls players': since *c.* 1950 at the very latest. (Prof. A.C. Partridge, 1968.)

you're not just a pretty face. See **I'm not just ...**

you're not kidding! How right you are!: both US, since *c.* 1910 or a little earlier, and Can. since several years before WW1. (W & F; Priestley cites its Can. survival – until at least 1975.) 'Also "you're not joking"' which is probably more British' (Sanders, 1977). This latter complements **you're joking!** A

var. is *you ain't just kidding* (W.J.B., 1977, who notes that it was ob. by mid C20).

you're not made of sugar. See **you won't melt.**

you're not my friend any more! 'Mock rueful; e.g. "It was your idea I ought to go to the dentist and have my teeth checked. Now I've got to have two out. You're not my friend any more." Current for a couple of decades [now], if not longer' (P.B., 1976).

you're not on; or, occ., **you're on next.** I want nothing to do with you or it; You don't convince me; You've failed: Liverpool: since *c.* 1945. From boxing: 'You've been waiting, and expecting to substitute for an absentee – but you're not needed' (Shaw, *c.* 1965).

you're not paid to think. 'Invariable admonition by NCOs and officers to privates excusing themselves by saying "I thought ..." ': (Mr Y. Mindel, MRCVS, 1971): army: late C19–20.

P.B.: cf this, from 'Bill Truck', *The Man-o'-War's Man*, first pub'd in *Blackwood's Magazine*, 1821: ' "I was only just thinking –" "Thinking, be d-d; you've no business to think, but keep silence, and pay attention to your duty," said the [ship's master-]gunner.'

you're not Robinson Crusoe. You're not alone, so don't be so damned selfish (*or* unsociable)! Mostly, and prob. orig., Aus.: since *c.* 1950. B.P., 1969, remarked, 'In general use – not confined to surfers or the younger set'.

Also – still predominantly Aus. – 'You're not alone in *that*': since *c.* 1960. In 1974, B.P. wrote: 'You are not the only one' and exemplified it thus:

'I can't keep up with all these amendments.'

'You're not Robinson Crusoe.'

A.B., 1979, equates it to the US c.p. *you ain't the Lone Ranger*: cf **rides again:**

[**you're not the only pebble on the beach** (C19–20) teeters on the wall that separates clichés from c.pp.; I'd say that it falls on the cliché side. See also **you aren't the only pebble ...** and note that the American song thus titled was sung by Lottie Gibson in 1896, with words by Braisted and music by Carters, as Edward B. Marks mentions in *They All Sang*, 1934. (Thanks to W.J.B., 1975.)]

you're O.K., I'm O.K., everybody's O.K. A US c.p., 'common in the last ten years or so; mockingly summarizing the recent spate of books on "consciousness-raising" and "doing your own thing" ' (J.W.C., 1977, who adds that it has been 'extremely common' during the years 1973–77).

you're off the grass! You don't stand a chance: cricketers': *c.* 1900–14. (Ware.) Outside the field of play.

you're on my hook. You're getting in my way: an Aus. c.p. of *c.* 1946–55. From angling.

you're on next. See **you're not on.**

you're on the pig's back. 'You're living the life of Reilly' (Brit., orig. Anglo-Irish) or 'You have it made' (US). 'The origin of this Anglo-Irish c.p. [dating since latish C19] perhaps lies in the fact that, in early Celtic myth, pigs were sacred' (Shaw, 1968).

you're only making it hard for yourself. 'Jocular doubleentendre classic phrase said by one man to the others at horse-play' (L.A., 1974); but also more widely used, by either sex to its own or the other sex, and in any situation where it makes sense. It must go back at least as far as 1940 and, I suspect, perhaps to *c.* 1910.

you're (or you must be) out of your tiny Chinese mind. You're talking wildly and ludicrously. A Brit. development from the US **you must be out of your tiny mind**, q.v. (Based on a note from Skehan, 1977.)

you're putting me on. Synon. with **you're joking:** US. 'Originally – 1950s, I think – Negro, then jazz-hip; general from 1950s. Semantically, probably related to "leading someone on" through deceitful speech' (R.C., 1978). See also **who're you kidding?**

you're running in and out like a fart in a colander. See **like a fart in a windstorm.**

you're selling tea! A facetious, mercifully short-lived, perversion of **you're telling me!**: *c.* 1945–55.

you're showing an Egyptian medal. You're showing a fly-button: since mid 1880s; ob. by late 1930s and † by mid 1940s. A var. of *c.* 1896–1914 was ...*Abyssinian medal*, from the Abyssinian War of 1893–6. (Ware.) Cf **you're starring in front** and note that all these c.pp. stem from the gen. **you're showing** – or **wearing** – **a medal**, which prob. dates from *c.* 1880 or rather earlier; cf also **flying low** ... Occ. simply *medal showing!*

you're so full of shit your eyes are brown is a Canadian Army c.p. that, in 1939–45, expressed a truly violent dislike. cf **you're full of shit**.

you're so sharp you'll be cutting yourself! A late C19–20 c.p. addressed to a smart-tongued person.

Also, expectably, ... *you'll cut yourself*, the form predominant in Aus. and fairly common elsewhere: Wilkes's examples are all of C20, the earliest being from Joseph Furphy, *Such Is Life*, 1903 (... *you'll be cutting* ...).

B.., 1976, adduces the synon. *you've* (or *who's*) *been at the knife-box today* (or *this morning*), 'a domestic c.p., probably ob.': since early C20 and perhaps since late C19.

you're spotted. See **bob down** ...

you're starring in front is a theatrical var. of the gen.

you're showing a medal or **your medals**, q.v. at **you're showing an Egyptian medal.** To any of these, **today** could be appended. The theatrical version has been vouched for by the late Wilfred Granville, 1968, and also by Mr Michael Warwick.

you're swinging like a rusty gate is an Aus. baseball (players' and watchers') c.p.: since *c.* 1955. (Neil Lovett, 1978, vouches for its oral use in 1947.) Recorded by W&F, 1960, as US.

you're telling me! – emphasis on *me*. 'I'm well aware of that'; 'I agree with you heartily': adopted in UK by 1933 – see an indignant letter in the *Daily Mirror* of that year and cf an advertisement in the 'agony column' of the *Daily Telegraph* on 14 Sep. 1934; in US, it dates since the early 1920s – if not a little earlier – and it duly appears in Berrey, 1942. In 'An Infantry Industry' (*First and Last*, 1934) Ring Lardner cited, as the title of a song, 'You're Telling Me' – apparently being sung in 1932.

In English novels, there are numerous examples; it occurs, for example, several times in Michael Burt's *The Case of the Angel's Trumpets*, 1947. Catherine Aird, *The Complete Steel*, 1969, has:

'It's a bad corner.'

'You're telling me.'

In Tom Lilley, *The 'K' Section*, 1972, a senior British police officer uses it.

Cf **you're selling tea.**

you're the cow's tail. See **all behind, like** ...

you're the doctor – emphasis on *you*. 'Whatever you say – after all, you're the authority on the subject, the expert, the man in charge, and ultimately the responsibility is yours; I'll take your prescription – your word – for it, of course': Can. and Brit.: since, I'd guess, the 1930s (maybe earlier); certainly I've known it since the middle 1930s. By the middle 1940s, also US. I've noted it in E.V. Cunningham's novel, *Phyllis*, 1962: ' "All right, Clancy," he shrugged, "you're the doctor. If that's what she wants, she wants it." ' (Clancy is a detective.)

It's just possible that the phrase was orig. US.

you're the expert has stemmed from the prec., is both US and Brit. (the entire Commonwealth), and seems to have arisen by the middle 1940s. See, e.g., Philip Gleife, *The Pinchbeck Masterpiece*, 1970:

This time Hank was beaten. 'O.K. – you're the expert.'

'No, but I mingle with the experts – in my job I have to know my stuff.'

you're the top! A c.p. of approval, taken from a comedy, *Anything Goes*, 1935, but not, I think, surviving WW2. Cf

the likewise approbatory US *You're* (or *he's*, or *anyone's*) *tops*.

'This is the title of one of the songs written by Cole Porter for the Broadway musical *Anything Goes*' (Eric Townley, 1978).

you're too fresh! A US c.p. of *c.* 1870–90. Here, obviously, *fresh* = cheeky, impudent. See the quot'n at **pull down your vest!** – recorded in *Am*, 1877.

you're way out in left field! You don't get the point; *or* Your guess couldn't be more wrong: US: C20. 'In baseball, left field is at the furthest distance from the batter, to his left; [literally] it means "You're hopelessly far away from where you should be to catch the batted ball and thus put the batter out" ' (J.W.C., 1968). Hence, set for a fall, a beating, a defeat; without a chance of winning; in short, 'You're on a loser'.

It evokes comparison with the almost synon. *you're way off base*, 'very wide of the mark, crazy, conspicuously intrusive'. The latter, however, has become so ingrained in American English as to form part of ordinary coll. speech. Witness, e.g., *D. Am*.

you're wearing your medal today. See **you're showing an Egyptian medal.**

[**you're welcome** is, when used literally, a cliché, but when it's used trivially and humorously or ironically, it verges on being a c.p., Brit. and US, of C20, as, for instance, in Jean Potts, *An Affair of the Heart*, 1970:

' ... How's your head?'

'My what? Oh. Better. Thank you.'

'You're welcome.'

Earlier in Edward Albee, *Tiny Alice*, performed late 1964, pub'd early 1965, at II, ii:

LAWYER [*soft sarcasm*]: Thank you.

BUTLER: You're welcome.]

you've a bad cough (or **that's a bad cough you have**). Addressed to one who has just broken wind: mostly male: C20.

you've been. Your promised trip – e.g., and esp., in an aircraft – has been cancelled: RAF: since the middle 1930s. (H & P.) Cf **you've had it.**

you've been at the knife-box ... See **you're so sharp** ...

you've been doing naughty things. See **you have been doing** ....

you've been reading my letters is an Aus. humorous retort to 'You're a [*figurative*] bastard!' I heard it being used – half a dozen times, at least – while I was serving in the Australian infantry, 1915–19.

The English form is *someone's been looking in my pay-book*, glossed thus, 1975: '(In Services) one man has called another, or referred to him as, a bastard': WW2 and since; prob. also before.

you've been to an Irish wedding. See **you have been to** ....

you've come a long way, baby has, as Col. Moe writes, 1976, 'Been popularized for several years as an advertising slogan for Virginia Slim cigarettes; in this case, "baby" is a non-black usage and is applied to women. It appeared recently in an article, "In Focus: Women Move out in the World and Hit Conflict of Interest", in the *Washington Star*, 5 Sep. 1976, thus: "In every way they were expected to be, well, like Caesar's wife. But, in case you don't know by now, we have, in the weary cliché of the day, come a long way, baby" '. In short, the c.p. is '*you've* come ...'; the free forms indicate and denote a cliché, a conventionalism.

W.J.B. adds, 'It has been much used in the 1960s–70s. Very popular at the moment [Dec. 1978]. We commonly use the phrase to indicate that the modern female is a liberated woman, rather sexy, more daring, more sophisticated. It can be applied to male or female, and may refer to any sudden transformation from the conventional to the recklessly urbane and worldly. See *The Saturday Review*, October 14, 1978'.

you've dropped something! Too late! the flies have got it has the var. **you've dropped something – but it would never have lived, its eyes were too far apart.** Whereas the former implies a sweet and sticky substance, the latter – *à la mode macabre ou surréaliste* – implies an unfortunate babe-in-arms. Current since *c.* 1950. (The former supplied by Cyril Whelan; the latter by P.B.; both, 1975.)

you've fixed it up nicely for me. No you don't!; Do you think I'm green? Lit., You've made this arrangement for me *or* You've schemed this – but I'm not falling for it. Proletarian: *c.* 1880–1914. (B & L.) This, I'd say, provides a good example of ironic Cockney humour.

you've forgotten the piano! is a C20 c.p., addressed sarcastically to one who has a great deal of luggage with him, esp. by bus conductors witheringly to passengers.

'Also "where's the kitchen sink?" Perhaps first asked of the heavily laden soldier of WW1 [I never heard it, but that may have been my good luck] and then of the hiker of the 1930s. Presumably because the sink is the only kitchen fitting that is not removable' (Sanders, 1978). Cf **everything but the kitchen sink.**

you've got a big red conk! Of Ted Ray, who died on 8 Nov. 1977, Michael Billington wrote for the *Guardian* of the very next day an appreciation titled 'Patter Man': 'His show, *Ray's a Laugh*, ran from 1949 to 1961... That was the golden age of radio comedy, when catch phrases like "You've got a big red conk" became part of schoolboy patois'. *Conk* is Brit. slang for nose.

you've got a nerve! See **of all the nerve!** and cf **you've got your nerve!**

you've got a one-track mind – occ. elab. by the addition of **and that's dirt track** – imputes an excessive or, at the least, an absorbed interest in sex; the elab. form sometimes implies what has been called 'martial buggery'. Since *c.* 1920. Moreover, there is a ref. to the dirt track of motorcycle racing.

you've got a smile like a can of worms is a Can. c.p., expressive of a strong dislike and dating since *c.* 1925. Orig., one suspects, among amateur fishermen. (Leechman.)

you've got a swinging brick. You have a heart of stone – no emotion, no sentiment, no pity: North of England: since the (? late) 1950s. (David Wharton, 1966.)

you've got Buckley's. See **Buckley's (chance).**

you've got egg on your face. See **wipe the egg off your face.**

you've got eyes in your head, haven't you? This disparaging c.p. implies in the addressee a slowness of visual understanding and has been current since the 1880s or 1890s.

you've got it all around your neck has, since *c.* 1945, imputed, or even stigmatized, confusion of mind, esp. hesitancy – or outright inability – to complete an explanation. As if it were some impeding garment around the poor fellow's (or girl's) neck. P.B.: but also transferrable, as *I'm afraid I've got it all round my neck.*

you've got it made. See **you have it made.**

you've got me, pal! I can't answer your question; – hence 'I simply don't know': US: since 1920s. (Berrey.) Prob. elliptical for 'You've got me guessing'.

you've got one foot in the grave and the other on a banana skin. In the middle 1920s this c.p. was employed by the youthful and the young-mannish supporters of 'soccer' clubs to decide the opinion, the judgment of their elders. (L.A., 1974.) The phrase is also US (Berrey, 1942).

P.B.: but the phrase *to have one foot in the grave* is at least as old as Swift's *Gulliver's Travels*, 1726, where it is used of the Struldbrugs of Laputa.

you've got sand in the (or your) shoes. You've come to enjoy living in Florida: orig. and still mostly a Floridan c.p., but, by that natural radiation and osmosis which characterize language everywhere, it has a limited spread elsewhere. 'I heard it first in 1940, but it must be much older. Still current' (John T. Fain of Gainesville, Florida, 1977).

you've got something there! You're on to something good; There's much to support what you say: *That's* is a darned good idea: since *c.* 1910. Both Brit. and US (Berrey 1942).

you've got to be in it to win it synonymizes the old proverb,

'Nothing venture, nothing win': Aus. since *c.* 1950. (B.P., 1974.) If you've put no money into a lottery or on the pools, you can't win anything. The c.p. exemplifies the ubiquitous attraction of rhyme.

you've got to be joking! See **you're joking!**

you've got to be kidding is a predominantly Aus. var. of **you're joking**; it shows US influence and dates from *c.* 1945 or a year or two earlier. (B.P., 1974.) It became fairly common in UK during the early 1970s and by late 1977 was widely used there.

you've got to hand it to him. See **I'll hand it to him.**

you've got your nerve! See **of all the nerve!** Also the US **you've got your gall!** – which, even as an Americanism, is less frequent than *you've got your nerve!* Perhaps the commonest of all in UK and the Commonwealth is *you've got a nerve!*

you've had a busy day. See **little man, you've...**

you've had it! You *won't* get it; You're too late; Your chance – e.g., of a transfer, a promotion, a privilege – has gone (*or* is nil): RAF: since 1937 of 1938; hence in army, since late 1940 or early 1941; by 1944, in fairly gen. civilian use. (EP in the *New Statesman*, 30 Aug. 1941; H & P; W-J; and EP, *A Glossary of RAF Slang*, 1945; PGR). Perhaps elliptical for, or allusive to, 'You've *had* your chance (and didn't, or couldn't, take it)'.

In the third person, *he's had it* can also mean, 'He's been killed' (in a raid) or 'He's been so badly wounded, or is so ill, he stands no chance'. This sense, according to Jock Marshall and Russell Drysdale, *Journey among Men* (p. 17), 1962, 'originated in the Gulf Country of Northern Queensland, where one of us heard it as early as 1929.... It was taken to Europe by Queensland troops or airmen': that's as may be; nevertheless it was already current in the RAF in late 1939.

Also, occ., *you've had your time* – 'You're "through"', *or* 'You're too late': RAF only: 1940 onwards, but † by 1950. (Gerald Emanuel, 1945.) See also next entry.

This is perhaps the most famous of all c.pp. orig. by the RAF, although **it's a piece of cake** must run it fairly close.

you've had your time, I'll have mine. In the context of Armed Forces' c.pp., Anthony Burgess writes (*TLS*, 26 Aug. 1977): '...and, sinister enough for *The Waste Land*, you've had your time, I'll have mine'. 'You've had your good times, now I'll have mine', perhaps orig. in the British Regular Army early C20, as from a young soldier beginning his 21 years of service to a much older man just finishing his, with an implication of '*I* shall be fed and housed and clothed for all these years to come – you'll have to live on a pension so pitiable that you'll have to get a job – and what *sort* of job?'

you've made my day! See **made my day...**

you've never had it so good. See **never had it so good.**

you've picked a bad apple – You've made a bad choice – dates from *c.* 1920 but has been little used since *c.* 1960.

you've said it! Yes, indeed!; *or* I agree entirely (with you); *or* You're dead right: adopted, *c.* 1943, by UK from the US, where it had been current since *c.* 1920 – despite the fact that Berrey, 1942, omits it and W & F, 1960, in the very brief entry they accord to it, don't date it; as early as 1931, the witty Oliver Herford, writer of deft and charming light verse, includes in *The Deb's Dictionary* this entry: 'QUITE (or "Oh, Quate": British for "You've said it!")'

A Brit. – or rather, a S. African – example occurs in James McClure, *The Caterpillar Cop*, 1972:

'But that is a strange thing.'
'You've said it.'

R.C., 1978, comments, '*pace* Mr Herford, the "standard" US form is you said it! [q.v.]'

you've saved my life. See **thanks for saving my life.**

you've shot your granny. John Russell Bartlett, the inaugurator and early editor of the rightly famous book of quotations, also edited, hardly less notably, *DAM* 1848. In the latter – *and*, please note, it was in the first, *not* the second (or 1859), edn that he did so – he included this c.p., derived it from the literal sense 'By mistake, you've shot your grandmother instead of the person or animal you aimed at', and glossed the c.p. as meaning 'You're deceived in your expectation', *or* 'You haven't at all achieved what you hoped to achieve', *or* esp., 'You're (badly) mistaken': very approx., *c.* 1830–90.

you've spotted this week's deliberate mistake. See **this week's deliberate…**

you've (or US you) talked me into it. See **you could twist my arm.**

young. See: catch 'em young; good young; it was on; old enough; trap for.

young lad can come to harm that way – a. See **harm can come…**

your arse is sucking blue mud. You're talking nonsense: Can. 'A favourite, *c.* 1920–30. Probably obsolete – I haven't heard for years. Cf **you're full of shit**' (Priestley, 1975). Cf also **your ass hole…**

your ass! 'means the end or destruction' of the person addressed: 'US Negroes': since *c.* 1950. (CM.) Prob. elliptical, as R.C. suggests, 1978, for *up your ass!*

your ass-hole's sucking wind. You don't know what you're talking about: a low C20 Can. c.p., esp. common in the Canadian Army of WW2. The Can. *your ass is sucking blue mud* and *your cock's out a foot* are more precise: 'You're in error': since *c.* 1920.

Prob. of US orig.; and *your cock's out a foot* (obviously a pun) is certainly so – and of anecdotal orig., at that, and dating from the 1920s. (A.B., 1979.)

your ass is grass (and I'm a lawnmower). 'I can and will beat you up, though as much a boast or mock-threat as a genuine statement of intention. Teenage US from 1960s – hence, perhaps, not eligible, since I know of no use beyond this age-group. (Supplied by my son Sam)' (R.C., 1978). P.B.: perhaps, although clearly inspired by the rhyme, a memory of the 1930s visual gag, e.g. in the zany show *Hellzapoppin*', and also used by London's 'Crazy Gang', of a man with a lawnmower rushing across a stage in hot pursuit of a girl who is wearing a South Sea Islands' grass skirt.

your Aunt Mitty! A US exlcam. c.p. of derision or disbelief, or of a combination of both; W & F tell us that it was popular *c.* 1890 but † by 1960; one can, I believe, narrow it down to late 1880s–early 1900s. But who was Aunt Mitty? P.B.: presumably a relation of the Brit. *Aunt Fanny*, often invoked in the same way. And A.B., 1979, adds, 'Cf the roughly equivalent *your Uncle Dudley*. Var., perhaps the orig.: *tell it to your Aunt Mitty!* No longer current'.

your back wheel… See **your wheel's going round.**

your (or yo) bad self! 'Addressed to one who has accomplished a remarkable act or piece of work' (CM, 1970): US negroes': since *c.* 1950. Here, *bad* = 'a simple reversal of the white standard, the very best' (CM).

your best friend won't tell you is euph. for 'you *stink*' – not in the literal sense ('his best friends won't tell him' about his bad breath) but in either the moral or the social sense: since middle 1960s.

The complete slogan was *even your best friends won' tell you*; Nigel Rees, in *Slogans*, 1982, traces it back to an advertisement for Listerine mouthwash, in the US, early 1920s, and compares it with *often a bridesmaid, but never a bride*, which he calls 'one of the best known lines in advertising'.

But the predominant use of the guilt-inducing *your best friend(s)* phrase has, since mid. C20, been associated with advertising campaigns against 'B.O.' (Body odour): both Wedgwood, 1977, and Mrs Ursula Roberts, 1978, mention, independently (and the latter from Hong Kong), a connection with Lifebuoy soap. Did the Brit. attack on *parfum naturel* plagiarize the US one on halitosis?

your bird, I think. See **it's your ball.**

your bitch of a mother. See **or your bitch…**

your blood's worth bottling! See **yer blood's…**

your bosom friends are become your backbiters. In the opening dialogue of S, 1738, we read:

[Neverout *scratches his Neck.*]

MISS: Fye, Mr *Neverout*, an't you ashamed? I beg Pardon for the Expression; but I'm afraid your Bosom Friends are become your Backbiters.

NEV: Well, Miss, I saw a Flea once on your Pinner; and a Louse is a Man's Companion, but a Flea is a Dog's Companion. However, I wish you would scratch my Neck with your pretty white Hand.

This C18–early C19 c.p. puns on one's *bosom* – or intimate – *friends* and on *bosom friends* as a euph. for lice. Cf the contemporaneous proverbial saying, 'No friend like to a bosom friend, as the man said when he pulled out a louse'; (recorded also by Grose, 1785).

your cock's out a foot. See **your ass-hole's sucking wind.**

your cough's getting better; and you're coughing better Addressed, in C20, to anyone who has just broken wind. Cf **you've a bad cough.**

your custom is out. You can no longer follow your usual practice; the even tenor of your life has been broken: very approx. mid C16–early C17. At ll. 222–3 of A. H. Bullen's edition of George Peele's comedy, *The Old Wives' Tale*, 1595, we read that Erastus, telling Lampriseus how he has buried two wives, says:

And now, neighbour, you of this country say, Your custom is out. But on with your tale, neighbour.

your education has been sadly neglected. See **education….**

your eyes are bigger than your stomach (or, since *c.* 1930, **tummy**) is the c.p. form of a very old proverb, *the eye is bigger than the belly*, with pl. eyes soon becoming dominant: witness *ODEP*. And as a c.p., 'it is mostly used by an adult to a child who has helped himself to more than he can eat. Pre-WW1' (Sanders, 1978).

your fadder's mustache! In 1968, my late friend Norris M. Davidson, formerly of Philadelphia, wrote:

It was current some ten or fifteen years ago [i.e., during the middle 1950s]. No one among my limited circle knows its origin, but all agree that it meant much the same thing as '*Sez* your!' or, more agreeably, 'That's what *you* think!' The phrase was always enunciated with a heavy Brooklyn accent and [it] varied between 'Your fadder's muss-tash' – accent on 'muss' and 'me fadder's mustache'. The phrase has lost currency today.

Prof. Priestley, 1975, told me that the Can. version was *your father's moustache* and added that it was short-lived: *c.* 1930. Hence, presumably, the US form; perhaps the Can. version went underground for a decade or more.

It 'is not mid-1950s, because the Woody Herman Orchestra recorded a song of that name in 1945' – as Mr Benny Green informs us in the *Spectator*, 10 Sep. 1977. (I owe much to his review there of the first ed. of this book, and herewith, three days later, record my grateful thanks to Mr Green, a musician – and clearly a musicologist.)

your feet won't touch! and the related but not synon.

your heels won't touch the ground! The former, meaning 'very quickly indeed', 'in no time at all', is an army, hence later also an RAF, c.p. dating since *c.* 1925. 'Any more of that, my lad, and your feet won't touch – you'll soon be up before the CO' (PGR).

The latter is likewise minatory; intended to deter or to intimidate, esp. as a retort upon insult or as a spirited comment on horse-play: since *c.* 1920. (L.A.)

See also **so fast….**

your funeral – it's or that's. The result, the consequence, will be *your* concern, not mine: orig. – *c.* 1850 – US, and in the negative; but, by *c.* 1890, mostly affirmative, anglicized *c.* 1860, mainly in the affirmative – and in C20 almost always so. Cf the quot'n at **believe it or not.**

Gelett Burgess, *Love in a Hurry*, 1913, has: 'Flodie nodded, with a hard look in her eyes. "All right," she said slowly, and gulped something down. "It's *your* funeral."'

your guess is as good as mine. Adopted *c.* 1943 from the US, where current since *c.* 1925, is applied to any obscure situation where neither party knows the facts: 'I know as little as you do.' Hartley Howard, *Million Dollar Snapshot*, 1971, uses it:

'If your visitor wanted to discuss business, why didn't he do it during business hours?'

'Your guess is as good as mine.'

Michael Innes, *Appleby at Allington*, 1968, writes:

'But about that treasure, Allington. Do you really suppose there may be anything of the kind buried within or near the castle?'

'Ah!' For a moment Allington hesitated.... 'Your guess is as good as mine.'

And in *The Malcontents*, 1972, C. P. Snow (Lord Snow), writes:

...Saying that he would be back in time for dinner, he was leaving Stephen, when he suddenly thought to ask whether they could get everything in order by Monday. He had planned to return to Cambridge then.

'Your guess is as good as mine,' said Stephen. 'It might be rather a long weekend.'

your gyros have... See **gyros have...**

your heels won't touch the ground. See **your feet....**

your knees aren't brown is a var. of **get your knees brown.**

your lip's bleeding. What big words you're using! An Aus. juvenile c.p., dating since *c*.1945. (*AS*.) These tongue-twisters are hard to utter clearly.

your mob... the Emden. See **didn't you sink the Emden?**

your mother and father were never married (or, in Anglo-Irish, **your mother an' father was never married**): a circumlocution for 'You're a bastard', whether lit. or fig.: late C19–20. (Shaw, 1968.)

your mother wears army boots is a US exclamatory c.p. – at first, i.e. during WW2, very derisive, then jocularly derisive. An occ. var.: *your sister wears army shoes*, of which Norris M. Davidson, 1969, has written, 'I dimly remember having heard some nineteen or twenty years ago. It must be a catch phrase, as it makes no sense' R.C., 1978, comments, 'like **your fadder's mustache** [q.v.], (to which it was a frequent counter), usually spoken with a heavy Brooklyn accent, approximating **ya mudda weahs ahmy boots!**'; and A.B., 1979, adds the variants *shoes* for *boots*; *your mother drives a tank* or *eats K rations* or *works in a dime store* or *ah, yer mother wears cotton drawers* (the *ah* may precede the other forms also). 'All derisive, of course; there are many other variants'. Cf **your old man...**

your nose is bleeding. Your fly is undone: *c*.1885–1950. By humorous indirection. Contrast **your lip's bleeding**, and cf **you're showing...**

your number isn't dry and **your number's still wet.** See **before you come up.**

your old man has panty lines! is yelled by schoolgirls at boys, as a retort to, esp., **your mother wears army** (or **combat**) **boots!**, q.v.: Minneapolis: 1976–77. (J. W. C. cites a Minneapolis newspaper of early Oct. 1977.) *Panty lines* are the ridged waist and leg elastic of panties; situated over the buttocks, they show under skirts [and jeans, etc.] worn tight.

your pigeon! – it's or **that's.** It's your concern: late C19–20. Hence also, in C20, throughout Commonwealth. This is the *pigeon* that means 'business' in Anglo-Chinese, where it is usu. spelt *pidgin*. P.B.: rather idiom than c.p., for it can *my*, *her*, *their*, etc., pigeon. Cf *that's your chicken*, a brief var. (*c*.1920–35), recorded by Lyell.

your pump is good but your (or **the**) **sucker's dry** was, mid C18–early C20, addressed to one who is trying, not very cleverly, to 'pump' another for information. Grose, 1785.

your saucepan runs (occ. **boils**) **over.** You're very saucy: latish C17–18 BE.

your sister wears army shoes. See **your mother wears army boots.**

your slip's showing. 'You're giving yourself away by saying or doing that' – applied to a venial fault or not very grave *gaffe*: both Brit. and US: dating since the 1920s.

P.B.: prob. influenced by **Charley's dead**, q.v.

your store is open. Your fly is open: Can.: since early 1960s. (D. J. Barr of Almonte, Ontario, 1968.) The implication is that all the goods are now either visible or potentially so. Cf **you're showing...**

your tiny, tiny mind arose in the US during the 1940s and reached UK during the late 1950s (but has never been very gen. there); I associate it particularly with Thurber and the other *New Yorker* wits, who applied it mostly to the supercilious rich male so addressing a luscious, truly dumb, blonde. The insult, orig. upper-class only and applied by male to female, lies in the two 'tinies'; it seeped down to the 'middle' middle classes, to be used almost entirely by married or engaged couples quarrelling. (Shaw, 1969.) 'Always rare in US as well as in UK. Now dead' (R.C., 1978). Cf **you're out of your tiny Chinese mind.**

[**your tongue is well hung**; also **your tongue is made of very loose leather**; **your tongue runs on pattens**; and **your tongue runs on wheels.** Resp. C18 (e.g., S); C18 (Fuller); C16–17; and C15–20 († by *c*.1940); lying midway between proverbial sayings and c.pp., all meaning 'You're very fluent (*or* glib) of speech'. I think that the last is the only one to have been, or to have become, a true c.p.]

your touch. It's your turn to play: Aus.: since *c*.1955. Jim Ramsay, 1977.

your Uncle Dudley! See **your Aunt Mitty!**

your washing is hanging out. Your petticoat or slip is showing: UK and Aus. (and prob. other Commonwealth) schoolchildren's: C20. but ob. by *c*.1945 and † by *c*.1970. P.B.: however, references to 'next week's washing' may still be occ. heard, early 1980s.

your wheel's going round is a late C19–20 street, esp. juvenile street, c.p. shouted – often with *hoy* and a pause, preceding – at a person travelling by bicycle or car.

Also *your back wheel's catching up with your front one*: children's: C20. J. B. Smith, Bath, 1981, recalls this shout from mid C20, and draws attention to E. B. Wright, *Rustic Speech and Folk-Lore*, 1913: 'As fond [i.e. foolish] *as the folks of Token* (Cumberland) is a saying based on the tradition that the first coach that passed through Token was followed by a crowd of the inhabitants who were anxious to see the big wheel catch the little one.'

yours. See: I don't like yours; I wouldn't touch; I'll show.

yours if you want it is, among Suffolk males, the standard reply, late C19–20, to **who's shit?**, who has farted? A pun on *who's* (= *who has*) and *whose*. (A Suffolk correspondent, 1972.)

'Not just Suffolk. A common Services' c.p. for the past 25 years at least' (P.B., 1976) – nevertheless, perhaps of Suffolk origin. Cf:

yours? Or clean ones? Addressed, perhaps orig. by women to a woman, but now by anyone to someone exclaiming *knickers!*: later C20. Cf:

yours or mine? A query addressed to one has just exclaimed **knackers!**, q.v.: male: C20. (*Knackers*, slang for testicles. As exclam., a var. of *balls!*, 'Nonsense!') This and the two entries prec. come from the one Suffolk correspondent: and all three exemplify the earthier sort of public-house wit.

yours to a cinder! is a late C19–20, *non*-upper class c.p. ending to a letter, prob. either orig. in coal-mining areas or prompted by **till hell freezes over.** Clearly, also, the phrases intimate a certain warmth of devotion. By *c*.1945, †.

yourself. See: be y.; chase y.; did you shoot; don't make a Judy; don't strain; enjoy y.; get wise; hello y.; help y.; if not pleased; keep y.; make it easy; make y.; speak for y.; stab y.; take a dagger; that's where you spoil; you must hate; you won't know; you'll do; you'll hate; you're only.

youth. See: sign.

[**yowza! yowza!** A C20 US c.p., 'created by US comedian Ben Bernie. Source: Joe Laurie, Jr, *Vaudeville*, 1953' (W. J. B., 1978). For this kind of c.p., cf **hubba! hubba!** – therefore a borderliner.]

yo-yo. See: up and down.

yunting. See: good yunting.

Z

zack. See: around the world.

Zarathustra. See: Confucius.

Zed is a whoreson letter (a late C17 glossarist of cant): ?mid C17–late C18. Because it signifies the end. Prob. a reminiscence of Shakespeare's 'Thou whoreson Zed! Thou unnecessary letter!' spoken by Kent to Oswald in *King Lear* at II, ii, P68 in W. J. Craig's ed.

zoo. See feeding time at the zoo.